DECCA

DECCA

The Letters of
Jessica Mitford

Edited by PETER Y. SUSSMAN

Alfred A. Knopf   New York   2006

THIS IS A BORZOI BOOK
PUBLISHED BY ALFRED A. KNOPF

Grateful acknowledgment is made to the following for permission to reprint previously
published and unpublished material:

Arkansas Gazette: Excerpt from the essay, "James Dean Walker: The California Connection," by
Doug Smith (*Arkansas Gazette*, March 28, 1981). Reprinted by permission of *Arkansas Gazette.*

The Bouverie Preserve of Audubon Canyon Ranch: Excerpts from June 12, 1973, letter by
David Pleydell-Bouverie. Reprinted by permission of The Bouverie Preserve of Audubon
Canyon Ranch, www.egret.org.

Wendy Cadden: Excerpts from February 17, 1970, letter by Vivian Cadden. Reprinted
by permission of Wendy Cadden, on behalf of the children of Vivian Cadden.

The photographs in this book are reproduced with permission and courtesy of the following:
© Anne Hall: photograph of Robert Gottlieb: page 719
© Katharine Graham Collection: photograph of Katharine Graham: page 719.

Library of Congress Cataloging-in-Publication Data
Mitford, Jessica, 1917–1996.
Decca: the letters of Jessica Mitford / edited by Peter Y. Sussman. — 1st ed.
p.   cm.
ISBN 0-375-41032-5 (alk. paper)
1. Mitford, Jessica, 1917–1996—Correspondence.   2. Women communists—
United States—Correspondence.   3. Women journalists—United States—
Correspondence.   4. Women radicals—United States—Correspondence.
5. Women civil rights workers—United States—Correspondence.   6. British
Americans—Correspondence.   I. Title: Letters of Jessica Mitford.
II. Sussman, Peter Y.   III. Title.
HX84.M55A34   2006
[B]335.43092—dc22   2006041035

Manufactured in the United States of America
Published December 21, 2006
Second Printing, December 2006

TO DECCA

For her inspiration

AND TO PAT

For her love and tolerance

Contents

Introduction

Jessica Mitford, daughter of the second Lord and Lady Redesdale, escaped from the "milk-bland life" of the Cotswolds in prewar England and spent the rest of her illustrious life and career—and her extensive correspondence—in a kind of continuing conversation, or argument, with her privileged upbringing, her unruly family, and the tempestuous political passions of the era in which she was raised.

She once recalled telling an interviewer that *I Led Three Lives* would have made a good title for her first memoir, "only unfortunately it had been used by the FBI and of course I wouldn't have anything to do with them as I despise them." As usual, her arithmetic was wrong, but uncharacteristically she erred on the conservative side. The myriad lives of Jessica Mitford, known to friends—and even at times to the FBI—as Decca Treuhaft, included the three that she probably had in mind in that 1960 interview: rebellious fifth daughter of reactionary and notoriously eccentric English aristocrats; full-time American Communist Party organizer and civil rights activist through much of the 1940s and '50s; and, at the time of her interview, a middle-aged author plugging her first book.

Over the ensuing decades until her death in 1996, Decca was best known in the United States as a distinguished and wickedly irreverent "muckraking" journalist, celebrity wit, and author—most notably of *The American Way of Death*, a runaway best-seller in 1963 that forever changed the country's funeral practices. In England, she may be remembered best as the Honorable Jessica Mitford, one of the Mad Mitfords or the Mitford Girls, the six sisters who entranced and infuriated the British public through much of the twentieth century.

Along the way, she moved easily among the world's Most Important People—aristocrats and meritocrats, politicians, radical intellectuals, artists, writers—as well as the misfits and outcasts whose grievances she championed and whose stories she brought to public attention. Very few people could straddle so effortlessly the many worlds she inhabited, but her ability to do so was a source of many of her most enduring achievements, as a writer, as a social critic and reformer, and as a mother, friend, and mentor.

From the time the teenager first made the front pages as "Peer's Daughter" escaping her largely fascist family and eloping to the Spanish Civil War, Decca was rarely out of the headlines for long. A few years later, after she and her first husband, Esmond Romilly, the brilliant and engaging "naughty boy" nephew of Winston Churchill, emigrated to the United States, their escapades as "Baby Bluebloods in Hobohemia" were serialized prominently in the *Washington Post*—and syndicated to other papers—and her photo was on the *Post's* front page when their daughter Constancia was born. Journalists sought her out every time one of her fascist sisters made headlines of her own. Still later, the press was reporting on Decca's Communist Party activities and confrontations with congressional Red-hunters and her disinheritance by Baron Redesdale. For decades thereafter, with each new book and article, she gained a new measure of renown.

Decca's very public life and her inimitable personality are refracted in her extensive, lifelong private correspondence. Her letters amount to a characteristically uninhibited and revealing form of autobiography, but they are also a kind of social history and commentary. The correspondent list of this self-described "renegade aristo" is an idiosyncratic Who's Who of a century in breathtaking transition, and her always original voice helps to illuminate that century and its quirks.

As newspaper feature writers never tired of reminding their readers, *Time* magazine conferred on Decca the hybrid Anglo-American title Queen of the Muckrakers. "I rather loved it," she told one reporter. "If they were going to mention me at all, I'm glad it was as a queen." But a more appropriate title might be Mother of New Journalism. Decca's work is a reminder that some of the best journalism comes about in the most unconventional ways. She was a brilliant agent provocateur who, through withering humor, offbeat observations, unflinching directness, and sheer force of personality, flayed social injustice and often provoked her adopted country to glimpse itself with unaccustomed clarity. Like many of the New Journalists, her life and her art were at times inseparable, a kind of social and political theater; her writings and her conduct combined to form a critique of the society in which she lived. The two strains merge in her correspondence, along with the biographical and social roots of that distinctive achievement, going back to childhood.

The Mitford daughters and their brother, Tom—insulated from even their peers by the conventions of their class—grew up in what Decca called in her first memoir "a timeproofed corner of the world, foster children, if not exactly of silence, at least of slow time." Their parents, she once said, saw England's socioeconomic classes as "traveling along parallel tracks that could never meet or intersect in any way."

By all accounts, the uninhibited Mitford children lived a self-sufficient life of tradition and frivolity punctuated by their charming but sclerotic father's blustering outbursts. They filled their circumscribed world with a culture of their own invention; one commentator called them "a savage little tribe." They played childhood games that sometimes seemed cruel to outsiders; they communicated in secret, made-up languages, and they patented "the Mitford tease," an unrelenting form of ridicule that Decca later turned outward on the world. She once quoted family friend Robert Kee as saying, "It has always seemed to me that your family regards the rest of the world, and everything that happens in it, as a huge joke put on for their benefit." Foremost promoter of this form of huge joke—at a time when it was still primarily a form of sisterly torture and then, later, in her popular novels—was the eldest daughter, Nancy.

Lord and Lady Redesdale did not believe in school for their daughters. (Throughout Decca's distinguished career as a writer, her résumé included the line "Education: Nil. Autodidact.") Decca's resentment, she wrote, was "absolutely burned into my soul," so that decades later on another continent, "the subject came up and I found myself literally fighting back tears of rage." She told her sister Nancy once that when they were children Decca couldn't confide to Nancy her secret childhood ambition to be a scientist "because whenever one told you one's deepest ambitions it was only to be TEASED UNMERCIFULLY and laughed off face of earth."

When Nancy Mitford delighted her English fans with novels such as *Highland Fling*, *Wigs on the Green*, and *The Pursuit of Love* parodying her family's eccentric ways, their early lives became communal legend, so much so that both the public and the family itself were sometimes hard-pressed to separate childhood legend from childhood fact.

Another family friend, James Lees-Milne, perceived "a vein of callousness" in Nancy Mitford—shared by the rest of the family—"which almost amounts to cruelty." One newspaper critic commented, "I think you could say that again, without the 'almost.' "

Decca found her protected, upper-class childhood insufferably boring: "nothing ever happened." She nursed an "eternal FEAR OF BOREDOM" (often capitalized in her letters). She compensated for the monotony with a braving lifelong passion for controversy and combat. In another letter, she told a friend, "You must remember that English people on the whole are a lot tougher than Americans in terms of verbal torture (had you been raised in the hard school of teasing and being laughed at as a child you'd see why!) and general one-up-manship." Whatever its origins, Decca always took a perverse delight in stirring things up. "Oh dear," she wrote a correspondent in 1988 with mock distress, "I can see I a) caused a flutter in the dove-cote, b) put the cat amongst the pigeons, or c) the shit in the electric fan, depending if you prefer 19th cent English, early 20th Cent English or modern American . . ."

Before she found her voice as an activist, social critic, and writer, Decca's reaction to her stultifying circumstances was to dream of emancipation, beginning at the age of eleven when she sent ten shillings to Drummonds Branch of the Royal Bank of Scotland to establish what she and her "obedient servants" at the family's bank both referred to as her "running away account."

The social and political cyclones that swept through England in the 1920s and '30s ultimately took a heavy toll on the Mitford family. Yet, although big social and geopolitical issues were suddenly of immediate and urgent concern, the time-honored routines of the English aristocracy ground on. Decca responded to her times by becoming what the family called "a ballroom Communist" and nurtured her resentments, always dreaming of escape. Her parents and two of her sisters, Diana and Unity, gravitated with much of their class to fascism, gaining international infamy. Brother Tom appears to have been sympathetic to the Nazis as well, though less openly.

Decca leapt at the chance to elope to Spain with Romilly, who had already made a name for himself as a public school rebel and "underground" journalist, a book author, an emancipated minor, a left-wing functionary in London, and a veteran of the Spanish Civil War—all by the age of eighteen. The two soul mates, with a mix of rebellious hijinks and political high-mindedness, conducted what Decca called "a conspiracy of two against the world" in their four-and-a-half-year marriage before Romilly died on a bombing mission in World War II, leaving his wife well placed in Washington with their daughter, Constancia. The prominent New Dealers among whom she lived and worked were another powerful influence in her personal and political evolution.

In 1943, soon after the start of Decca's second marriage, to radical labor attorney Robert Treuhaft, she realized one of the dreams of her childhood. Now settled with her new husband in San Francisco, she joined the Communist Party. She devoted most of the next fifteen years to the Party, primarily working with the Civil Rights Congress across San Francisco Bay in Oakland, where the family settled in the mid-1940s.

Decca confessed that it was rather uphill work "escaping from the private Mitford cosmic joke, originally fashioned by Nancy, into the real world and eventually into the earnest life of the Communist Party." The organization for which she labored so single-mindedly was indeed earnest; it was also theoretical and ideological—Decca considered herself nominally a Stalinist at the time—but most of her party activities were far from rigid or abstract. She cared deeply for society's victims, as individuals, not concepts, and tirelessly championed their rights. With her husband, for example, she defended a penniless, orphaned black "shoeshine boy" named Jerry Newson who was wrongly accused of murder, continuing to defend him for decades, long after his imprisonment would have ended most advocates' involvement.

Yet, predictably, even during her Communist years, the Mitford in her periodically bubbled to the surface. She was constitutionally incapable of subordinating her humor to any group or ideology. She recalled being hauled before the Party's Security Commission on charges of joking. When she was subpoenaed by the California Senate's Un-American Activities Committee, she had the audience laughing so hard that the committee forgot to demand documents it had ordered her to produce. (She was subpoenaed also by the House Un-

American Activities Committee, which she listed in her résumé under "Honors, Awards & Prizes.") And "Lifeitselfmanship," her first published book—actually, a hand-duplicated and personally distributed booklet—was simultaneously a send-up of bureaucratic Communist Party rhetoric and a takeoff on her sister Nancy's famed essay on U (upper-class) and non-U language. (Acting on the complex rationale of the emotions, Decca emulated her oldest sister and craved her approval as much as she resented her stinging sarcasm.)

Decca finally left the Party, not primarily over some issue of high principle but because it had become dull . . . boring. Rather like London's debutante circuit.

When Decca was hounded by the FBI from a "real," albeit menial, nonpolitical job, she was left with little occupational choice but to become a writer. At the age of forty-three, she published her first memoir, *Daughters and Rebels* (entitled *Hons and Rebels* in the U.K. and in the most recent American edition). As an author, with the public platform that came with it, Decca began to find her life's purpose. She lived out in her new public role the themes that had dominated her earlier lives. That first commercial book was about her unusual upbringing, which had also been the starting point for her sister Nancy's career as a novelist. *Daughters and Rebels* was written with the humor, the fearlessness, the directness, and the elegant writing style that characterized Decca's later work. Her righteous outrage finally found a comfortable home, as did her irrepressible humor.

Decca didn't make highfalutin claims for her writing or her life. She told her friend Sally Belfrage, "I don't think I could ever take myself seriously enough to go grubbing about looking for my soul—that is, I couldn't get interested in it, hence religion, psychiatry, consciousness-raising & the like are all totally beyond my ken." She told another friend and collaborator, "I don't strive for 'substance, depth & scope' as you put it—not that I don't see the importance of these, but merely because I do better—or find it more natural for me—if I stick to specifics, finding out facts & presenting them without underlining for the reader conclusions they should be drawing, or global Moral Messages that I wish them to absorb."

One might argue with her observation that she presented facts without underlining—the choice of facts she chose to present was sufficient underlining—but she certainly never stood back from her writing and pointed grandly to a ponderous significance that it didn't possess. More typically, when she read that Evelyn Waugh had suggested that *The American Way of Death* lacked a "plainly stated attitude to death," Decca wrote to her sister, a mutual friend, ". . . tell him of course I'm <u>against</u> it."

Decca wrote of her life with Esmond Romilly, "We not only egged each other on to ever greater baiting and acts of outrage against the class we had left, but delighted in matching wits with the world generally; in fact, it was our way of life." It was also Decca's way of journalism.

In a sense she was the quintessential journalist, whether in newspapers, magazines, or books. She loved—compulsively—narrative, information, observations, the revealing cultural trivia on which journalism feeds. And she loved newspapers. She once expressed amazement that her beloved old-world cousin Ann Farrer Horne didn't read newspapers: "I could hardly pry my eyes open in the a.m. were it not for the S.F. Chronicle clattering on the porch; although I admit most of it is not only v. boring but v. forgettable. Once ages ago, when I was about 30 & thought I might be dead soon (near-raped in a rather dismal creek . . .) I'm sorry to say that my Last Thoughts (as I thought they might be) were not so much for Bob & children as 'I'll never see tomorrow's paper.' "

The subjects of some of Decca's most outlandish and amusing letters would fly beneath the radar of most serious journalists—a folkloric remedy to discourage dog trespassing with male urine, for example, or the treatment of arthritis with potatoes—but the same eye for life's little absurdities focused the world's attention on funeral purveyors' Fit-a-Fut Oxford with "soft, cushioned soles and warm, luxurious slipper comfort . . . true shoe smartness" for the corpse of a loved one. *Cushioned soles!* Perhaps living in two cultures helped Decca to become so exquisitely attuned to cultural nuances that escaped other commentators.

"I realize," she wrote in a letter to a Communist admirer long after she had left the Party, "that often I get absolutely besotted by <u>trivial</u> subjects which haven't got much to do with the class struggle, but I fear that is a fault of character." Whether a fault of character or not, it was a key ingredient of her professional achievements, every bit as much as her ability—acquired in childhood and refined by the Communist Party—to understand issues of class and race and their relation to such cultural trivia.

In Decca's letters we can also see in stark relief some of the other personal traits that informed and enriched her writing. She was, for example, a verbal clown, an inspired mimic. She dreamed at times of becoming a "character actress in [a] telly sit-com" (to which a friend responded, "But you ARE a character actress in a permanent sit-com"), and she recognized in her grandson Chaka Forman—now a professional actor—a kindred spirit. He is, she wrote, "an Original, a smashing clown & general free-thinker." She delighted in tracing that impish part of her character (and her grandson's) to a branch of her ancestry—"Stanley blood," she called it, telling one correspondent it was "believed by many of the grown-ups to have been thoroughly <u>bad</u> blood & responsible for the aberrant strains that showed up in so many of us."

Decca once said mimicry was one of her favorite talents—"swooping up the essence of people"—and she put it to extraordinarily effective use, sharpening the eye for detail and the ear for dialogue that are so much a part of her writing, in her letters as much as in her previously published works.

The American Way of Death was Decca's best journalism and her break through book. Not only did she authoritatively define a significant yet under-reported social failure, but in retrospect, the book defined her. From childhood, Decca hated sham and hypocrisy and the phoniness of sentimental-ity, and she found the ultimate metaphor for them in the use of chemicals and Potemkin-village clothing to give the appearance of life to those who were, inescapably and irretrievably, dead. As a Communist and social reformer, she hated commercially driven values. Phony pieties and fat profits: put the two together, as they were in the funeral industry, and this Doña Quixote had found a windmill truly worthy of her rapier wit.

That formula—such as it was; it was really only Decca being herself—was replicated in her subsequent books and articles, and it was a unique brew, as many of her flummoxed targets could attest, whether they were funeral direc-tors or Red-hunting legislators, prison administrators or restaurant managers, small-town bigots or international conglomerates, stuffy writers or officious editors. A large cast of self-important characters marches through her pub-lished writings and her letters, sacrificial targets of Decca's caricaturing eye.

The sly Mitford tease—and the fierce honesty that came with it—was bred in aristocratic detachment. In her published works, Decca transformed it into an inimitable combination of social criticism and literary technique, journalism with a twist. She followed in Esmond Romilly's journalistic footsteps, as she had dreamed of doing even during their marriage.

In her correspondence, we see Decca's rare combination of talents unfold in slow motion; we eavesdrop on her life and times as she lived them, and on her work in progress. Because her life was so much a part of her journalism, we can also see the evolution of her craft and the unique mindset that gave rise to it. In the letters, she asked questions that would have occurred to no one else; she recorded her interests, observations, and passions on an often daily basis, and she tested them in narratives, developing her formidable storytelling skills. In her letters, as in her articles and books, speeches and interviews, there was unbounded joy in her stories; she reveled in the pure act of expression. Often, there is no clear line between Decca's published works and the letters, which served variously as a kind of note-taking or thinking out loud, the first-draft observations of a first-rate writer.

Above all, Decca's life and work exhibited courage—the courage to act on her convictions, the courage to speak truth as she saw it, without cosmetic shad-ing, and damn the consequences. If one consequence was shock . . . well, she could enjoy that too; it's part of the Mitford family DNA. Told once by a prison official that he'd let her into his prison if she promised to tell the truth, Decca replied, "I don't promise anything. But I tell the truth by nature, am incapable of doing otherwise." She was as forthright in her letters to friends, however uncomfortable that may have been at times for the recipients.

In some senses, this is a book *about* correspondence as well as a collection *of* correspondence. A surprising number of Decca's letters were about the subject of correspondence, or included references to it.

When Decca was growing up in the 1920s and '30s, the postman came several times a day. Phones were rare and expensive to use, and Lord Redesdale's phone was off-limits to his children. Decca's youngest sister, Deborah, recalls their mother sitting up straight in a high-backed chair at eight thirty every morning in the big drawing room at their London home, attending to her morning correspondence before phoning Harrod's to order food for the day. It was a ritual not unlike that of her American daughter many years later, Decca's husband recalled. An early riser, Decca would be downstairs by seven o'clock. She had some coffee and began her morning of writing, warming up with a few letters to friends. Decca once wrote that Lady Redesdale "absolutely lives for letters." Decca wrote in another context, "Goodness I feel lost and separated without letters."

Decca fussed endlessly about the unreliability of the mails and of her correspondents, even checking postmarks for timely mailing and delivery. (That too was familial. In the midst of the emotional turbulence surrounding Decca's elopement, Lady Redesdale remonstrated with her daughter, "Please date your letters.") A postal strike once set her wailing, "I'm marooned, stranded." Indeed, one of her final requests as she was dying was that checks be made out to a few of the people who were most important in her daily life, including her mail carrier, who had also been a guest at the Treuhafts' fiftieth anniversary party.

It was almost at times as if Decca—English aristocrat, American Communist organizer, acclaimed binational journalist and author—didn't know who she was unless letters to and from her relatives and friends were there to remind her.

The very notion of correspondence is an antiquated one for those living in the computer era, and not simply because of its tempting replacement by e-mail and text-messaging. The centuries-old tradition of letter-writing has devolved into just another consumer commodity with an interesting lineage. "The exciting little pile" from the postman that Decca waited for so eagerly every day would today include mostly computer-personalized commercial pitches. Or as she put it, "Lucky, these days, to get anything remotely resembling a real letter from an actual person." Here, in Decca's letters, written in social circumstances often not far removed from our own, are some of the last, best examples of a nearly extinct art.

■ ■

Compilations of correspondence are necessarily biographies of a kind—biographies of individual consciousness, with less intrusive mediation and interpretation than one finds in a traditional biography. I have viewed my role as editor not as "telling" Decca's life but providing some context and then getting out of the way and letting her words speak for themselves.

In a 1994 letter to her sister Deborah, the Duchess of Devonshire, Decca reported on a meeting with Charlotte Mosley, who had edited a recently published book of Nancy Mitford's letters. In her letter to the duchess, Decca wrote: "After dinner, Cha & I closetted ourselves with her showing me the banned by you bits of Nancy's letters; some v. catty items about me & Bob, many more about the royal family. You shouldn't have done that, Hen. The whole point of letters is to reveal the writer & her various opinions & let the chips fall where they may. Censoring them for fear of offending the subjects is in my view absolutely wrong."

I took that as a kind of directive from Beyond, and yet . . .

With honesty comes, inevitably, hurtfulness. Balancing the two is the editor's high-wire act, and I have made a minimal number of omissions where I felt intrusions into others' private affairs demanded it.

Decca's views were often stated intensely and provocatively. That they were her views, at least provisionally, may be a mitigating circumstance, but no less painful for those offended by their portrayal—indeed, in some cases, possibly more painful for that reason.

In the selection of letters for this book and in the editing of individual letters, I have tried to avoid the private lives of her correspondents, but obviously, a book such as this one is based on many thousands of editorial decisions on how far to follow Decca's comments beyond where they intersected with the lives of people to whom she was writing. I have surely made mistakes in judgment, unintentionally straying into what Decca's correspondents may have considered their personal affairs. I apologize for whatever discomfort these letters cause them. I hope they will understand that the offense results from an attempt to preserve in Decca's published letters the same refreshingly spontaneous, freewheeling honesty that her correspondents doubtless admired in her when she was living. To smooth out all the dangerous edges in this collection would have been a disservice to her memory.

In a few instances, noted in footnotes, I removed the names of individuals for legal or other especially compelling reasons. For example, I have generally omitted the names of people whose Communist Party affiliation was mentioned in Decca's letters if I was not certain that their membership was publicly known or self-acknowledged. It is hard to clarify such issues of decades-old affiliations, and it is especially distressing to have to do so because the organization's nature is still sometimes misconstrued, decades later. Nevertheless, the letters to former and possibly current CP members are often among the most revealing of Decca's own attitudes toward the Party, so I published them but made every attempt not to "out" possibly covert members.

The first task of an editor in assembling a book of letters is selecting those worthy of publication—separating, among other things, the thank-you notes and dinner invitations from the more revealing and important writings. In the process, of course, I was inevitably imposing my notions of importance on my subject's life, which is a tremendous act of hubris but one that I undertook with some background, having known Decca for more than three decades.

Collections of letters have a biographical fascination about them, justly, but built-in distortions of the genre limit their significance. As an editor, I cannot find letters that don't exist, but I can and hereby do warn the reader of the limitations of what they're reading. The letters *do* tell an important story—or many important stories—but they cannot be expected to be the whole story.

Many of the people to whom Decca was closest were usually a local phone call away, so there are fewer letters to them. Additionally, during some periods of her life she simply wrote fewer letters, especially during the 1940s and '50s when she was busiest with family and political organizing. Fortunately, some letters survive from that era, and in letters written years later Decca often reminisced about that important period of her life. She also had fewer national and international connections before her first books were published. Some people with whom she was in active correspondence during those early years—such as Virginia Durr and some family members—didn't save her letters, and it was only in the late '50s or early '60s that Decca began keeping carbon copies of most of her correspondence.

With a very few exceptions, Decca did not polish her letters with an eye to eventual publication. They were often written in a rush, with little regard for the conventions of spelling, grammar, or punctuation. Run-on sentences, sentence fragments, and other such errors abound, as one would expect in this form of communication. Not all the errors were the result of speed. Decca recognized, for example, that the use of commas was "never my strong point." She told a correspondent, "I think commas are often (but NOT always) a matter of personal preference; Nancy hardly ever used them, and E. Waugh used to put them in for her." In general, I refused to play Waugh's role.

Nevertheless, the challenge facing an editor of letters is to ease the contemporary reader's passage through the correspondence while simultaneously remaining true to the text and tone of the original. The result often appears inconsistent. That is, some errors in grammar or idiosyncrasies in spelling have been corrected to assist the reader in following the text or to correct what can be explained by typing haste alone; others have been left untouched because they may reveal something about Decca or her style or because they were possibly satirical in intent or characteristic in some way (such as English or American spellings). My guiding principle was to stick with the oddities of the original, however inconsistent or erroneous, as much as possible, in order to preserve the tone, informality, and accuracy of the letters. Any changes in grammar, spelling, or punctuation were, I felt, inconsequential in meaning.

A few more words about the nature of my approach to editing these letters:

Ellipses generally indicate either the omission of duplicative or ephemeral material that would be of no interest to the contemporary reader or cuts made to reduce long letters to publishable size. Countless times in her hyperactive correspondence, Decca told the same story to different people, sometimes even in the same words. By and large, those duplications have been omitted. The ones that remain are there for what seem important reasons, often because the repetition shows Decca's obsession with a subject or because small variations in a story appear to reveal something important about her relationship with her correspondents. Partial duplications can also show how Decca developed an idea or feeling over time.

Despite the trims, I have tried to maintain some of the original context, even when it was of little significance. My purpose has been to allow the reader the same "feel" for Decca's circumstances as I had in first reading her remarkable letters. I have also wanted to avoid the impression of publishing a book of "Jessica Mitford's Selected Paragraphs," although in places that impression is unavoidable.

Another issue I faced was the identification of correspondents, especially those whose names or titles changed over time, whether because of marital status or for some other reason. In order not to confuse the reader with frequent name changes, in most instances I used the same name for each person throughout, usually the name by which the person was best known to family, friends, and the public. Sometimes I settled on a consistent name after consultation with the recipients. Despite my best efforts, some variations were necessary. Obviously, women's married names were not used for letters before they were married, even if they are best known by those names now. In early letters, I refer to the Duchess of Devonshire as Deborah Mitford, since it would be preposterous to refer to her as "the duchess" before she became one. On the other hand, Robert Treuhaft once told me that his mother, Aranka, was never to his knowledge known by her second married name, Kliot. Throughout her business career, she was known as Madame Aranka. For clarity and consistency, I have settled arbitrarily on Aranka Treuhaft here.

A number of the letters in this book are unsigned. That generally indicates that the available copy was Decca's own carbon. The original, outgoing copies were presumably signed or legible in a way the carbon copies weren't.

Finally, a note on the division of this book. People don't live their lives in chapters, of course; lives are far too sloppy for such easy categorization. Books, however, do come in chapters or sections, as a convenience for the reader. My division of Decca's letters into chronological sections that seem to define periods of her life is entirely arbitrary. I hope it serves more as a convenience to the reader—an easy place to take a breath—than a definitive judgment on stages of life. With Decca, of course, all her life was a stage.

Decca in 1922, at age
four or five.

Decca (right) with Unity,
ca. 1930.

As a teenager, a year or two
before her elopement.

I

BABY BLUEBLOOD AND HOBOHEMIAN

Lord and Lady Redesdale with their children at Swinbrook House in 1934 or 1935. The children (clockwise from upper left) are Nancy, Diana, Tom, Pam, Deborah, Decca, and Unity.

Just enough letters survive from Decca's childhood to give a feel for the peculiar nature of the close-knit, even ingrown, world in which she was raised, mostly in a succession of country mansions and the family's London house. Even without biographical background—available in innumerable memoirs, biographies, and autobiographies of the Mitford sisters and their friends—Decca's earliest surviving letters convey the self-confidence and freedom that come with a pedigree of privilege, as well as the bantering, chattering, brash playfulness and the sometimes stinging wit and candor that characterized this particular family.

As devotees of the family's legend are all too aware, in addition to the secret languages and rituals the children and their parents had numerous nicknames that sometimes showed the daughters' cult of inventive nonsense and sometimes carried political or ironic undertones. In Decca's early letters, Baron Redesdale was "the Old Subhuman" and "the Feudal Remnant," among other names, and both parents were "the Reverends" or the Female (Fem) and Male, although they were most commonly and endearingly simply Muv and Farve.

Decca's parents, she once wrote, were "Edwardian by chronology but Victorian in ideology." Her father, she said, "acquired [an] extra degree of British jingoism, remarkable even for his class and generation," and she noted that her two Nazi sisters used to refer to him, "approvingly and accurately," as "one of Nature's Fascists."

Most of the sisters have published their sometimes contradictory recollections, and it is pointless to rehash all their childhood motivations and influences, much less the long-running disputes over the degree of, say, Lady Redesdale's vague detachment or her husband's fiery temper, unwavering habits, or atavistic views. Decca's letters, as well as her memoirs, convey her own reactions, both at the time and in retrospect. Her perceptions of her childhood changed somewhat over time, and more than most writers, she returned to the subject frequently throughout her life, as if she could never quite make sense of it or, indeed, define herself except in terms of the family she left abruptly at the age of nineteen.

Decca once summed up her sisterly relationships before global and family politics shattered their confined world:

> Boud [Unity] was the one I really adored. Family relationships at that age changed in a kaleidoscope: first one, then

'tother was foremost Loved One amongst the sisters. Nancy was a remote star. Pam, a cypher, a perennial butt of teasing by the rest of us (led by Nancy), & I barely saw her at all; she went off to do farming or something for Diana & [her first husband] Bryan [Guinness] when I was about 12. The Diana relationship (from loving to loathing) . . . Debo & I, closest in age, veered a lot. That is, I think we always had a certain HONNISH* ADORATION of each other, but hardly any common interests, even when v. young.

Although the Mitfords' financial resources were in decline during her childhood, partly because of Baron Redesdale's fascination with buying and building houses, "we were sort of cosseted, lapped in luxury & comfort," Decca has written. There were always household retainers to attend to their needs and whims. The six daughters were tutored by their mother and then placed, in turn, "under the jurisdiction of a series of inept governesses, from whom we learned next to nothing," she said. The sisters tormented the governesses mercilessly. As but one small example of their habitual defiance, Decca recalled how, when forbidden to say the word "damn," they delighted in infuriating the governess by routinely referring to the cities Rotter and Amster.

Decca's parents were Conservatives to the core, comforted by the motto on the Redesdale coat of arms: "God careth for us." Decca dated her earliest awareness of the inequities of the English class system to walks she used to take with her mother near their rural Swinbrook home, bearing small charitable gifts for the "village people." Disturbed by the villagers' poverty, she recalled asking her mother one day why all the English people's money wasn't divided among everyone, so that no one would be so desperately poor. Her mother, she said, replied, "But that's what Socialists want," explaining that "Socialists want everyone to be poor, but we Conservatives want everyone to be rich." Although she never forgot the anecdote, it was years later before she rebelled against the family's politics. At the time of the general strike in England, when she was nearly nine, she recalled being "a confirmed Tory" and harboring fears of being shot by the "Bolshies." She volunteered in the strikebreakers' canteens—a fact that she probably refrained from mentioning when she later joined the Communist Party.

Her early rebellions were apolitical in nature, like the time when she was

---

*"Honnish" was derived from the intricate wordplays that characterized the Mitford sisters' private childhood languages. The two youngest girls, Decca and Deborah, formed the Society of Hens, named for the chickens they raised for eggs that they sold to their mother (who provided free feed). Decca called the hens "the mainspring of our personal economy." The name soon evolved into the Society of Hons (reportedly, like the language itself, based on Oxfordshire country pronunciation); their enemies of the moment were "Counter Hons," and their shared language was Honnish.

forbidden from visiting the estates of shocked neighboring families because she had passed along to her dancing-class friends some information she'd picked up about "conception and [the] birth of babies."

In her early and midteens, Decca followed her oldest sister and role model Nancy to the left, becoming an "avid reader" of, first, pacifist literature. "By age 12, influenced by Nancy," she wrote in one letter, "I was a crashing intellectual snob." Decca then developed a broader interest in Communist and other left-wing periodicals, pamphlets, and books. As she became more earnest and excited about her newfound socialist insights—"suddenly confronted for the first time with a rational explanation of society"—she grew disenchanted with Nancy and her fashionably witty friends, who "didn't take anything very seriously."

Decca once wrote to her grandson James Forman that at about the age of fifteen, "the clarity, the brilliance, the total solution to horrors of war & mass poverty contained in the Communist Manifesto & other writings . . . burst on me like fireworks."

Thus began her growing estrangement from her parents and class, which continued as she sulked through weekend house parties and fulfilled the coming-of-age rituals demanded of her. "You've no idea of the boredom (to me, anyway) of the company," Decca once wrote to the writer Alex Haley. "Try to visualize twittering debutantes and what we (or I, at least) used to call Chinless Wonders, i.e. the deb escorts—goodness they were DULL fellows. What did we talk about? The latest dance, the next ball, who was going." The rituals culminated with her formal presentation at court before "what appear to be two large stuffed figures, nodding and smiling down from their thrones like wound-up toys."

Decca started confronting her parents on their political views, which her mother evidently took as a generalized sign of her unhappiness. She recalled at one point accusing her mother of being "an Enemy of the Working Class." The "genuinely stung" and angry Lady Redesdale is said to have replied, "I'm *not* an enemy of the working class! I think some of them are perfectly sweet!"

Nancy Mitford, thirteen years Decca's elder, was a distant model at best by her teenage years. The only brother, Tom, eight years older, had been sent away to school, as boys were, and was also a less immediate influence. And Pam, born between Nancy and Tom, was so different in temperament and interests, as well as age, that she was hardly an influence at all.

As young women, the two sisters to whom Decca felt most attached—the beautiful and supportive Diana, her elder by seven years, and the ungainly, outrageously quirky Unity, three years older, who was Decca's contemporary in the governesses' schoolroom—followed their parents to the right . . . about as far right as they could go. Diana, after three years of marriage to beer heir Bryan Guinness, scandalized her family and her country by divorcing him and beginning an ill-disguised affair with the then-married Oswald Mosley, founder of the British Union of Fascists, whom she later married at the Berlin home of powerful Nazi propagandist Joseph Goebbels, with Hitler in attendance at the wedding dinner. Still later, during the Second World War, Diana was confined with Mosley in prison. With the exception of their joint appearance at ailing Nancy Mitford's bedside in 1969, Decca was "off speakers" with Diana for the rest of her life.

At the age of eighteen, Unity, Decca's teenage comrade-in-rebellion against their parents, was a debutante in London and frequently visited Diana and her paramour. Decca believed Unity was fascinated by Mosley and his uniform and "fascinated with the idea of belonging to something." At about the time Unity joined Mosley's British Union of Fascists—the Blackshirts—Decca, fifteen, resolved to become a Communist, leading to almost comical competing household displays of posters, swastikas, and hammer and sickles. They threw books and records at each other in their common sitting room "until Nanny would come and stop the noise." Decca sang the "Internationale" with Communist sympathizers she encountered on Sunday walks through London's Hyde Park with her governess, she later reported. Unity gave the stiff-armed Nazi salute to townsfolk and flaunted her BUF membership and increasingly right-wing views on a far larger stage.

In 1933, Unity traveled to Germany with Diana and attended the Nazi Party congress in Nuremberg. It was, Diana later wrote, a trip that "changed Unity's life." While Decca and her cousin Ann Farrer were in Paris for their traditional predebutante "year abroad," Unity took up residence in Munich, which their mother called "her spiritual home." She soon became an obsessed Hitler "groupie," plotting to catch the Führer's eye, and basked in his company by special invitation, in Munich and elsewhere. Published photographs showed Unity visiting with Hitler, attending Nazi events, and giving the "sieg heil" salute. Among her most treasured possessions was the Nazi Party badge given her by Hitler.

Later, Diana and Unity introduced their parents into Hitler's circle, and both were impressed. Lady Redesdale was especially taken with the Führer and fascism and maintained her allegiance long after her husband publicly repudiated his. After a 1937 tea party with Hitler, who incidentally "asked after" Decca, Lady Redesdale gushed in a letter, "He is very 'easy' to be with & no feeling of shyness would be possible, & such very good manners." Decca's reaction: "I was through with the whole lot of them." (Many years later, speaking of her family during this period, Decca commented to a friend, "Do admit they were a rum bunch, & that I'm the only ordinary one of the lot.") Her parents' growing rift on fascism was an important factor in their eventual separation during the war.

At the age of seventeen, as Decca endured the predebutante social rounds and brooded about a way to realize her fervent commitment to leftist causes, the activities of her second cousins, Esmond and Giles Romilly, captured her attention. The pacifist brothers were in open rebellion against the Officers Training Corps at Wellington College, their fashionable military prep school, where they disrupted Armistice Day observances by distributing pacifist leaflets in the prayerbooks. They edited a magazine called *Out of Bounds*, billed as "an exposé of the English public school system." Decca wrote in *Daughters and Rebels** that "Esmond's abrupt conversion to Communist ideas had come about in a way very similar to my own. He wrote: 'I had a violent antipathy to Conservatism, as I saw it in my relations. I hated militarism . . . and I had read a good deal of pacifist literature. Like many people, I mixed up pacifism with Communism.'" And like Decca, he chanced upon the Communists' *Daily Worker* and began subscribing.

Esmond Romilly ran away from the school at the age of fifteen, trailing headlines about "Winston's 'Red' Nephew." He entered London's leftist/bohemian demimonde, editing his magazine and making a living as best he could, for one stretch as a door-to-door salesman. Decca took careful note from afar when Esmond Romilly was detained by police after showing up drunk at his parents' house with another public school runaway, his chum Philip Toynbee. Romilly was declared uncontrollable, sentenced to six weeks in a facility for delinquent boys, and released as a ward of his wealthy elderly cousin Dorothy Allhusen, a widow who was very close to Esmond and whose own son had died in childhood. In her country house Romilly completed the book *Out of Bounds*, coauthored with his brother and chronicling their controversial radical activities. Decca read it with admiration when it was published in 1935.

Decca's world continued to splinter as her beloved sister Unity became an ever more flagrant fascist. Unity thrust herself farther into the limelight in mid-1935 when *Der Stürmer* published her fawning letter of praise for the publication and its virulent anti-Semitism. In a P.S. she wrote, "If you should happen to find room in your paper for this letter, please print my name in full. I do not want my letter initialled U.M. for everyone should know that I am a Jew-hater." And everyone soon did know as the English papers reported on the letter. The headline in the *Daily Mirror* read "Peer's Daughter as Jew-Hater."

Decca, overcoming increasing bitterness and friction over her favorite sister's politics—at one point they nearly came to blows—wrote Unity that she hated what she had written in *Der Stürmer* but loved her nevertheless. Unity returned the sentiment, in a fashion, two years later, after Decca's elopement, by writing her that she hated Communists as much as Esmond Romilly hated Nazis and "My attitude to Esmond is as follows—and I rather expect his to me to be the same. I naturally wouldn't hesitate to shoot him if it was necessary for my cause, and I should expect him to do the same to me. But in the meanwhile,

*Houghton Mifflin, 1960; published as *Hons and Rebels* by Gollancz in Britain, also in 1960. It was reissued under the British title in the United States by New York Review Books in 2004.

as that isn't necessary, I don't see why we shouldn't be friends, do you." She also told Decca that Hitler had asked about her and as a favor had suppressed news of Decca's elopement to Spain in the German press.

While Unity was in Munich in the summer and fall of 1936, often in Diana's company, hobnobbing with Hitler, his inner circle, and his storm troopers, Esmond Romilly headed off to Spain to fight with the Republican forces defending Madrid as part of the International Brigade. He was one of the few English survivors of a bloody battle near the village of Boadilla del Monte and returned to England after six weeks, suffering from dysentery.

Isolated at home with her leftist ideology, yearning to put it to some use, Decca at one point phoned the Communist Party headquarters in London to ask if they needed any women guerrilla volunteers. She also talked with Esmond Romilly's brother, Giles, about the possibility of running away to "where the action was," Spain, which she later said was "a sort of lodestar for people of my generation," in roughly the same way that the black liberation struggle in the South was for her daughter's generation several decades later. She was also trying to find a way to meet Esmond, the cousin she'd never met in childhood because of her mother's dislike for his family. Decca succeeded unexpectedly in January 1937 when she accepted an invitation to spend a weekend at the Marlborough home of Dorothy Allhusen, her own distant relative as well as the cousin and guardian of Esmond Romilly, who Decca subsequently learned was also to be a guest there. (Some accounts imply that Esmond had casually suggested to his guardian that Decca be invited.)

That weekend house party, almost literally on the spur of the moment, began a fairy-tale romance birthed in headlines. Decca said that her "first words" to Romilly were to ask him to take her to Spain with him. He agreed, and over the following days they began plotting secret preparations and inventing a plausible cover story for the escape on which Decca had been intent since the age of eleven. The funds she had accumulated in her "running away account" were critical to the success of the venture. The plot they spun out entailed a series of fictitious letters to Decca's family, beginning with one to Decca herself from her friends and fellow debutantes "the Paget twins," Celia and Mamaine, inviting her to visit them in France. Written with Esmond's help and in Decca's disguised handwriting, that letter was used to secure her mother's permission for the trip. When they reached France, Decca kept her mother informed on her "tour with the Pagets" in a series of chatty letters en route to Spain, where they finally arrived after a number of delays and detours to obtain visas. The plan was for Esmond to report on the war for newspapers and for Decca to serve as his secretary.

The "escape" of the young couple was devastating to her family—"the most frightful nightmare," in Lady Redesdale's words.

Just days into their adventure, Romilly confessed he had fallen in love with Decca, who expressed her delight and, as she said years later, "that was sort of that." The young couple (he was eighteen, she nineteen) were exquisitely matched. "The truth is," their friend Toynbee wrote in a memoir, "that Decca was probably the only member of her class who was suited to be [Esmond's] wife."

Thus did Decca join her sisters in international headlines. Their elopement was also amply chronicled in letters between Decca and her mother, as well as in British government cables after Lord Redesdale, armed with a court order, contacted Scotland Yard and the Foreign Office; Winston Churchill got the latter actively involved. Foreign Minister Anthony Eden cabled the consul in Bilbao, Spain: "FIND JESSICA MITFORD AND PERSUADE HER TO RETURN." Her parents, as Decca put it, "engineered our expulsion," and the British government pressured the teenage escapees to board a destroyer evacuating refugees that was under orders to fetch them. They jumped ship in France, at Saint Jean de Luz, where they were met by a ravenous British press contingent, and continued to report on the Spanish Civil War from a refugee center in Bayonne, dodging English reporters, often with Keystone Kops melodrama, and defying the pleas of emissaries dispatched by Decca's family—sister Nancy and her husband, Peter Rodd. ("Jessica Says 'No' to Sister's Plea" read the *Daily Express* headline.)

Although the couple's marriage and rebellious adventures during their several years together—first on the Continent, where Romilly wrote his second book, *Boadilla*, and then in England and the United States—are recounted in the letters and footnotes that follow and in various memoirs and biographies, a few formative experiences should be highlighted here to cover gaps in the letters that survive.

The longest gap is from the summer of 1937 to March 1939, a period from which only a few mundane notes are available. Virtually unmentioned in the letters from this period are details of the Romillys' return to England late in 1937. They lived a free-spirited existence in Rotherhithe, a working-class neighborhood near the London docks, getting by financially with whatever odd jobs were at hand—and by gambling, ripping off rich acquaintances, and evading bill collectors—while losing no opportunity to do battle with fascists and to bait the social class from which they descended. Decca saw members of her family only occasionally.

Also unmentioned in the available letters from that era was the devastating loss of their first daughter, Julia, who was born in December 1937 and died five months later of measles. The day after Julia's funeral, the Romillys "ran away to Corsica for three months," in Decca's words. Julia's death was apparently one factor in the next stage of their wandering life, the move to the United States early in 1939. An American friend said that Esmond Romilly brought his wife to the United States "to get her out of the terrible sorrow she was in over the loss of the baby."

The emigration was motivated, too, by what Esmond Romilly described in a

1939 article as "the atmosphere of grim depression and resignation" in England that spring. He mistrusted the reactionary "machinations of the Cliveden Set" and was not at all certain what side Britain would be on in the looming war. British Prime Minister Neville Chamberlain had signed the "appeasement" agreement with Hitler in Munich months earlier, and the final defeat of the Spanish Republic was imminent. Romilly vowed to return home to help defeat fascism if Britain entered the war against Germany.

Although it's unclear whether the Romillys were aware of it at the time, or even if the letter was actually mailed, Decca's mother had written a "Dear Prime Minister" letter to Chamberlain on November 11, 1938, saying that Hitler, "whom I know personally," was "above all a person of heart" who was "most deeply hurt by the way the Munich statement on 'No more War' has been . . . generally received here." She suggested overtures of friendship between the two countries, beginning with "a social occasion . . . & a friendly visit" involving Hitler, Prime Minister and Mrs. Chamberlain, and Foreign Secretary Lord Halifax and his wife.

Political factors certainly entered into their decision, but the immediate precipitants for the couple's emigration were a process server pursuing them for unpaid utility bills and Decca's receipt of £100 from a trust fund on her twenty-first birthday—"far and away the biggest sum of money we had ever possessed." As they later wrote in their *Washington Post* chronicles, "Suddenly we hit upon the one obvious thing to do with the money. 'Let's go to America.' That was it. The instant we said it we realized what a wonderful plan it was. It solved everything. America was so vast, so exciting, so far away, that the possibilities in the phrase 'Let's go to America' were endless."

Among the "infinite" possibilities the Romillys imagined for themselves in the New World were striking up a friendship with "an influential businessman" and reaping the financial benefits of the association—or working their way up to the top of the corporate chain starting as secretaries; hitchhiking "starving in the Arizona desert"; working as movie extras in Hollywood; "brawling" with other longshoremen and -women in San Francisco taverns; "bums in New York; lions of society in Boston; newshawks in Washington; cowhands in the wild west." Their plans may not have been fully as fanciful as they portrayed them to the *Post*'s readers, but they were similarly vague, unrealistic, and open-ended.

With friends, including Philip Toynbee, they spun out grandiose joint plans for joining other English "authorities" on the American lecture circuit, expounding on their areas of expertise in dramatized talks with titles such as "How to Meet the King" and "Sedition Spreading at Eton." Their fellow would-be lecturers defected from the adventure, but the Romillys sailed third-class in February 1939, on their way to re-invent themselves. Major American magazines like *Life* and *Time* found them soon after their arrival—perhaps alerted by a passenger manifest—and, once again, the couple "could hardly stir without the press on our heels," Decca said.

They were prepared for all eventualities, with only their wits and twenty-four letters of recommendation from friends of influential Americans, and they spent the next year and a half as well-connected vagabonds on their "Grand Tour" of the country, sampling its regions, stopping here and there to earn a few bucks as retail and door-to-door salespeople, bartender, hostess, ad writer, and the like. They collected new experiences, new insights, new friends, and, always, new contacts. With meticulous documentation that remained in Decca's files at the time of her death more than fifty years later, they amassed fresh letters of introduction and networked, to use a contemporary term, among the rich and well-born, among radicals and New Dealers, artists and intellectuals and anyone else who struck their fancy along the way. It was part adventurous lark, part escape from what they feared was their increasingly fascist homeland. Decca later said they wanted to "make our mark in the U.S. or at least mark time until the war broke out."

Until the news from Europe became urgent and inescapable, the Romillys were, as the *Washington Post* put it, "professionally footloose, unconventional and unpredictable." The *Post*'s headline summed it up: "Two Youthful Escapists Who Fled to America With a Song in Their Hearts." The *Post* prominently displayed the weekly installments they wrote of their exploits for a month and a half in early 1940, even as global events were making their escapism increasingly untenable.

Although trading on the accents and intangible advantages that their nationality and class afforded them, they were, finally, untethered from social or family expectations, or as Decca put it so eloquently in *Daughters and Rebels*:

> We regarded ourselves as "self-made" free agents in every respect, the products of our own actions and decisions. Yet our style of behavior during much of our life together, the strong streak of delinquency which I found so attractive in Esmond and which struck such a responsive chord in me, his carefree intransigence, even his supreme self-confidence—a feeling of being able to walk unscathed through any flame— are not hard to trace to an English upper class ancestry and upbringing.

Throughout, they "stayed glued to the radio," keeping track of the ever grimmer news from across the Atlantic. Sometimes the news came to them in the form of the headlines that shadowed their lives, most notably when the Romillys were living for a time in Miami—running a bar, the Roma, in which they'd acquired a half interest—and it became apparent that Unity Mitford had shot herself in the right temple in Munich's English Garden on the day Britain declared war on Germany. (One headline in the *Miami Herald* read "Sister of Adolf's Perfect Nordic Type Making Own Way as Miami Barmaid.") Hitler arranged for Unity to receive the best of care, visited her in the hospital, paid for storage of her possessions, and ultimately helped transport her to Switzerland, from where she was taken back to England, but Decca's beloved sister was left severely disabled, mentally and physically, for the rest of her brief life, with the bullet still lodged in her brain. In retrospect, Decca said, "I always thought of her as dead when politics first separated us."

The couple was still in Miami when word reached them that Germany had begun its offensive against neutral Norway—an assault in which Esmond's brother, Giles, a journalist, was captured. A month later, in May 1940, when Neville Chamberlain resigned as prime minister and was replaced by Winston Churchill, the Romillys wound up their affairs in Miami and cut short their Grand Tour with a two-week stay in New Orleans, conceiving a child to keep Decca company, and then returned to Washington so that Esmond could enlist in the war against fascism and begin military training.

The letters that track these unique rites of passage begin when Decca was six or seven years old.

■■

To Lady Redesdale   Asthall Manor, Burford, Oxfordshire[1]
                                                ca. September 1923

dear muv

thankyou 4 the hanky. nanny gave me a little purse with 6[d] in it because I have stopped sucking my thumb
            love from Jessica

To Lady Redesdale   mid to late 1920s
Darling Muv,

I hope you had a good crossing?[2] Diana and poor Pam want more than ever to have hair off, and Pam did not injoy her visit at all, because everyone says "oh yes, of course I like short hair best" and "why don't you have your hair off"?[3] please do let them have it <u>please</u>.

1. The Mitford family lived in this large, gabled house from 1919 to 1926, while Lord Redesdale built a new house on nearby property that he had inherited.

2. The letter was written during one of Decca's parents' periodic trips to Canada to work Lord Redesdale's perennially barren gold claim in Swastika, northern Ontario. Lord and Lady Redesdale stayed in a log cabin on the forty-acre claim site.

3. Sister Nancy Mitford had set off a family battle sometime earlier by cutting her hair stylishly short without her parents' permission.

To Nancy Mitford and Diana Mitford Guinness   Pontresina, Switzerland
                                                        ca. January 16, 1930

Dear Nancy & Corbish,

Last night I went to a party & danced with M. Chaliapine. He is so sweet, he jumped about with me and hummed in a sweet voice to the band. I have struck an acquaintance with his two daughters at the Pontresina Hotel. They are good and nyang[4]—aged 8 and 17. It is snowing a blizerd to-day.

Love From Decca

To Lord Redesdale

ca. 1931

Darling Morg,[5]

Thank you FRIGHTFULLY for the delicious cherries they werent a bit too bad. You are an angel. Here's a sample of my writing for you know what* ~~Jessica Mitford Jessica Mitford Jessica Mitford~~ Jessica Mitford.

Well you aren't too bad are you. I don't think theres any news well there wouldn't be likely to be any but still there isnt any. Except could you ask Muv to get (if she possibly could) a present for my Sunbeam,[6] not to cost more than £0 10s 0d, & not much less, not clothes, but some sort of nice present for her birthday—she is aged 14.

Much Love From Decca

* Pen

---

4. A Mitfordism for "very sweet."

5. Morgan (sometimes shortened to Morg) was one of the Mitford girls' many nicknames for their father.

6. Decca said in her memoir *Daughters and Rebels* that her nanny got the Mitford girls involved in an organization called the Sunbeams, which matched rich children with poor children with whom they corresponded and to whom they occasionally sent gifts. Decca recalled in her memoir spending hours packing up old clothes to mail to her Sunbeam, a London girl named Rose, and sending her letters describing "a highly romanticized account of life at Swinbrook." Decca became "obsessed" with getting Rose away from her dismal life in London, but when her mother finally consented to hire Rose as a "Between Maid, or Tweeny," the experiment ended abruptly and uncomfortably for Decca.

To Lord Redesdale   Swinbrook House, Swinbrook, Oxfordshire[7]
                                                        February 9, 1932

You Absolutely Super Jew,[8]

   Well you are a duck I must say dear you do excel in daintiness. Those choco-
lates were <u>the</u> most delicious I've ever tasted, my favourite sort too, logs! My
spaniel has been hinking ever since I got
them the duck but it wasn't any cop atall as
Nancy would say. I hope you are having a
dainty time in London, showing round the
Viters.[9] Do they like the House of Lords?
Was it a good show for Sir Walter? Did
you know the right times to bow and take
off the old bramble, etc? Some of the
wrex[10] have hatched, in fact 7 I think,
they <u>are</u> faithful. I hope you are practising your palsey. (if you don't you be
sorry in the future dear. Fig 1)

   It is fun to tweak up your gorse dear
On coming in from the gorse the Spanner[11]
had a little wireless (He pulled out a few of the wires, but still.)
                    With Thanking Love
                    From Decca

To Lord Redesdale   Swinbrook
                                                        November, 1932

Darling Morgan,

   You really are an angel to send those simply delicious chocs, thank you <u>so</u>
much for them. We did love the films yesterday, Garbo was wonderful, so was

---

7. The spacious country house that Baron Redesdale had built two miles from the village of
Swinbrook and where Decca spent much of her childhood. Most of the family was disappointed
when they moved there from Asthall Manor in 1926. Decca later wrote that it had "the rather
utilitarian look of frankly institutional architecture" and "had aspects of a medieval fortress prison,
from which quite early on I determined to escape." The house was often rented out as the family
fortunes declined (partly because of the extravagant expense of building Swinbrook House.)

8. "The Old Jew" (and its variations) was among the many nicknames the Mitford girls had for
their father. The Duchess of Devonshire recalled that their father had a big nose, which "was
enough to set it off." She says the nickname "was usually accompanied by a drawing with hugely
exaggerated nose and an arrow to the top of the head with BP on it—for Bald Patch."

9. Skating instructors at the Oxford ice rink.

10. Probably a Decca-ism for chickens. According to Decca's sister Deborah, the word "recs"
referred to chickens' breath on a cold morning (derived from "steaming wrecks," as in shipwrecks).

11. Decca's spaniel.

Gwili André, the new star. It was a marvellous programme, with 3 really good films besides the Pathé.[12] Boudle[13] is still alive, not committed suicide yet.[14]

Please tell Muv that Gladys[15] has sent my coat & cape, and they are very nice, and give her my love.

Stubby's[16] new shoes have come, and a lovely red jumper. She is getting ready for hunting.

Love From Decca

To Lord Redesdale   Paris
                                                              late 1933[17]

Dear Old Fellow,

You good creature. The other day the subject of conversation at my cours[18] was "describe the house where you were born." So I described Batsford[19] & what a lot it cost & how ugly & huge it was, & then I said my papa had the same manie de l'architecture as my grandpère & that he also had built a huge house & now we lived in a garage![20] So the mistress said how extraordinary so I said yes you see papa is an être au dessous de l'humanité, un

---

12. A company that produced newsreels and, later, feature, magazine, and other films.

13. Boudle, or Boud, was the nickname Decca and Unity used for each other in their joint code language, Boudledidge. The words of Boudledidge were often formed by an intricate system of substitution of sounds and letters and contraction or expansion of syllables. Thus, Decca told one interviewer, the word "Pal" became Bal, which equaled Baddle, hence Boudle or Boud.

14. References to suicide were part of the Mitfords' childhood "jesting." Decca has said that as a child, when she quarreled with Unity, she would tell her sister to "commit it"—or, in Boudledidge, "gommid id." About seven years after this letter was written, Unity attempted to commit suicide in Munich.

15. The family's live-in sewing maid, whom Decca mentioned in a number of letters as an adult.

16. Another childhood nickname for Decca's sister Deborah.

17. The letter was undated. It appears to be the earliest surviving letter from Decca's year of "finishing school" in Paris before her debutante season.

18. French for "course." Decca appears to have used the word—sometimes with an "s" at the end, sometimes not—to refer to both her classes and the place where they were taught. Her beginners' course in French civilization at the Sorbonne was specially designed for foreigners.

19. The inherited Victorian Gothic mansion where Redesdale and his family lived for the first two years of Decca's life. It had been built by his father, the first Baron Redesdale, who reportedly spent most of his fortune demolishing an earlier house on the site and building the replacement—hence, his "architectural mania."

20. When the family's London house in Rutland Gate, near Hyde Park in Kensington—necessary for entertaining during the girls' debutante seasons—was rented out, the family stayed in the Mews, a tiny flat (formerly the chauffeur's quarters) above the garage behind their house.

pauvre vieux soushumain[21] and they were all frightfully interested dear & LONG to meet you.

Well dear I know this letter isn't very long or interesting but I don't want to tire the murky old brain.

Love From Decca

Dear you can't think how perfectly divine & heavenly this Wilde[22] is (the one who longs for you) & the fem doesn't like her & she's frightfully cold to her & when Miss W. says why is your mother so cold I have to say because it's a cold day. Isn't it a shame.

To Lady Redesdale   Paris
ca. January 1934

Darling Muv,

Thank you so much for your letter, which I got yesterday morning. . . . It is very comfortable here, & I don't have to make my bed, & Annette likes the window open, so altogether it is very oke. I had a <u>tiny</u> little cold the other day, in fact it wasn't really a cold at all, but I sneezed once or twice (that was literally all), and Madame made me breathe in vapour, and she put a horrid mustard thing & masses of cotton wool on my chest, & made me put my feet on a hot water bottle while I was in the house! And yesterday I fell down & gave my knee a really tiny scratch, and she washed her hands in disinfected water, & boiled some water with cotton wool in it to kill any germs that might linger, & washed it for <u>hours</u>, then put on iodine & an <u>enormous</u> bandage with sticking plaster! So you see how well I'm looked after, compared to what I would be at home.[23] . . .

Both the Madames La Directrice are coming to tea tomorrow, the very thought makes me almost faint with terror! but as it's my sightseeing day I shall try to stay out long past tea time.

Well, I think that is all the news I can think of. Give my love to the old Steegson, & to Young Spoon (and to Tray[24]).

Love From Decca

---

21. "The poor old subhuman" ("pauvre vieux soushumain," who was "dessous de l'humanité," or "beneath humanity") was one of Decca's nicknames for her father. She wrote in *Daughters and Rebels* that her mother "confiscated my allowance for calling him 'the Old Subhuman,' but he didn't really mind."

22. Dorothy (Dolly) Wilde, the niece of Oscar Wilde, a family acquaintance and a glittering light in Parisian artistic and social circles. She was a lesbian and a frequent source of suggestive comments among the Mitford girls. In some of Decca's accounts, the sisters' love for Dolly Wilde was part of their jesting, taunting style, with the girls pretending to be in love with Wilde to irritate their mother. In other accounts, Decca portrayed, more seriously, "the tortures of jealousy" she and her sister Unity used to have about her.

23. Decca appears to be twitting Lady Redesdale because she taught her children to let "the Good Body" heal itself.

24. A dog.

To Lady Redesdale   Paris

January or early February 1934

Darling Muv,

Thank you so much for your letter. I don't have much time to write because I have really <u>masses</u> of prep. This week I have 15 pages of history, 6 of history of litterature (mostly dates when books were published, to learn by heart) & <u>30 pages</u> of Bossuet;[25] le sermon sur la mort & Oraison Funèbre d'Henriette d'Angleterre! And one has to almost learn it by heart & anyway <u>all</u> the dates & names etc, as well as learning 6 lines of the Bossuet by heart to recite. I don't know about my rédaction yet but shall hear tomorrow! As the marks are over 20, & they take off 1 for each fault of orthographe & construction, & then take off from what is left for badness of style, or for having put something wrong, I don't expect I shall have a single mark left. Annette read it & said it was quite good but I expect she thought it would be too discouraging to say anything else!

The other English girl is called Dorothy, her head is shaped like an egg . . . & she has got an extraordinary pointed nose & very thin, long mouth. She plays the cello all day & always plays the same note as far as I can make out for hours on end. She is quite nice, though. . . .

I'm going to Comédie Française on Thursday, it is "le Cid." . . . Tomorrow we are going to a play, too, and on Fri. evening we are going to a place which is fort gaie[26] & there is beaucoup de Jeunesse[27] to hear the music. Dorothy is going to play her 'cello, I hope she won't still play the same old note all the time like she does here.

I haven't been to the cinema yet, but I'm going next Monday afternoon with my chaperone.[28] . . .

I am going to the Cours now so goodbye.

Love from Decca

To Lady Redesdale   Paris

early February 1934

Darling Muv,

Thank you very much for your two letters from Gib, I am so glad you enjoyed your voyage in spite of thinking it wouldn't be much fun. My quartier was very

---

25. Jacques-Bénigne Bossuet, seventeenth-century French orator, bishop, theologian, and author.

26. "Very gay."

27. Literally, "lots of Youth."

28. Although Decca reassured her mother about her supervised activities in Paris, she wrote in *Daughters and Rebels* that "it soon became obvious, much to our joy, that Madame had no intention of accompanying us to the theater or indeed of supervising our activities in any respect."

quiet all through the riots[29]—which are finished now, they think—in fact much too quiet, I didn't see a thing except the school boys from the Lycée[30] opposite the Cours who made a slight row in the street, but they were soon chased away by some policemen, & anyway our professeur pulled the curtains at once (because there was a Cour at the time, & we all looked out of the window to see what we could). I saw a manifestation on the screen, taken from above, with crowds of people dashing away from the cavalry charge. We also saw Chiappe, the préfet de police who was sent away, & all the people in the cinema clapped & booed the new préfet. Lots of people think that Chiappe was mixed up in the Stavisky affair[31] & also that he allowed manifestations of the Action Française (the royalist paper) but he seems to have been very popular all the same. The communist paper (l'Humanité) which I bought today says that he furnished Stavisky with a false passport & that he bribed a great many ministers & municipal councellors by helping them with the police. . . .

Yesterday all seemed to go as usual; in our quartier the buses & Metro & shops were all going. The headlines in Humanité say: une grève générale sans précédent. Dans le région Parisienne, ni autobus, ni trams, ni postes (the last is quite true). Usines et chantiers déserts, boutiques fermées. Partout en France, arrêt du travail.[32] The Daily Mail says: French strike ends in fiasco; Metro running; shops & cinemas open.

There is a new girl—the Dutch one—called Pop & I share a room with her instead of with Annette. Her mother & father are being divorced, & today she had a letter saying that her father was going to marry again & although I shouldn't have thought that would matter she seems very miserable about it & cried for a long time & Madame came & comforted her & said that la vie is dure & the best thing for her to do is to find a gentil garçon & marry him & have lots of petits bébés of her own which seemed to me such a funny idea & so typical of Madame that I nearly laughed—although I am very sorry for Pop. Madame literally wallows in misery & adores recounting to strangers. . . . She adores people who have had unhappy childhoods with lots of deathbed scenes, & burdens to bear beyond their years.

I have been to quite a lot of museums lately, this afternoon we went to see a torture museum, it was thrilling, you saw wheels where people were wrenched limb from limb. . . .

Well good bye I must go now.

Love from Decca

---

29. On February 6, 1934, fascist riots followed the firing of Paris's right-wing police chief, Jean Chiappe, by Radical Party Premier Edouard Daladier. Fifteen people were killed in the riots and hundreds injured.

30. High school.

31. Alexandre Stavisky, a financier who had been convicted of fraud in connection with phony municipal bonds, died suspiciously in January 1934.

32. "An unprecedented general strike. In the Paris area neither buses, nor streetcars, nor postal delivery. Factories and docks deserted, shops shut. Everywhere in France, work stoppage."

To Lady Redesdale   Paris
                                                              October 1934

Darling Muv,

Thank you so much for the letter & dough which I got this morning. Now to answer the questions.

1) We certainly haven't had a bath every day as it hasn't been working part of the time, which is not I suppose exactly Madame's fault.

2) There seemed to be enough of fairly good food at first, but it has tailed off considerably, & is now nothing to write home about, so I won't. (Sometimes it's not too bad.)

3) We haven't had clean sheets since Madame came back, and this afternoon I asked her if we could, & she said, well perhaps on Monday, but as a rule I only give them every 3 weeks!! so please write to her & hint for them oftener, as open fights are rather embarrassing when you have to live with the person. Madame is really awfully nice, only rather dirty & probably slightly dishonest, like most French People. Isn't it awful about Peter[33] having his money stolen, Nancy wrote & told us about it the next day. I certainly think they might tell the police, if they haven't already, & I am writing to ask her if she thinks it would be any good.

The exam. results came out this morning, I have got 17 out of 20, and Ann[34] 14. We have got certificates. We are going to the Alliance next month, & have inscribed ourselves this afternoon. We went to a fascinating exhibition of modern pictures, there was one by Tchelitchew of Natalie Paley, it was really lovely. I am longing to see his painting of Diana & the kids, is it finished yet? . . . We are really very comfortable here although I don't suppose it sounds to you as though we were, also we like it very much here. Ann is writing to Aunt J about the sheets, too.

I hope Debo likes her school,[35] I don't expect she does. Goodness how I envy her.

Margaret Kennedy is going to study at London University for 3 years, starting this winter. I suppose you would think that sounded awful too, I must say I think it sounds terrifically lucky.

---

33. Nancy Mitford's husband, Peter Rodd.

34. Decca's cousin Ann Farrer, later Mrs. David Horne. Her nickname was Idden (Id for short), the Boudledidge word for Ann. She accompanied Decca for their year of "finishing school" in Paris. Years later Decca referred to her as "somebody that I once loved more than any other human being." (For Decca's own account of their long relationship, see her letter of August 14, 1980.) Ann Farrer was the sister of Joan (Robin) Farrer, also known as Rudbin, or Rud, and Decca would sometimes describe one and sometimes the other as her "favorite cousin."

35. Deborah had been sent to school briefly after her governess resigned. She had previously attended local school with Decca but left after "three days of hell." Decca was allowed to stay only until the end of her first term.

The other girls here are as nice as can be, & do whatever we tell them, which is fine.

Love from Decca

To Diana Mitford   Swinbrook
                                                                    June 17, ca. 1935

Darling Corduroy,

Many Happy Returns of the Day. I'm sorry this present is so beastly. I got it (as usual) at the Little Shop.

I hope you are well. I had a very nice p.c. from Bryan[36] with a picture of a ship on it. You are lucky to have been out to Germany to see my hated Boudle. Did she write & tell you how she saw the Führer, of whom she writes as "Him" with a capital H, as for Christ or God!! I love my Boude in spite of all.

Love From Decca

To Unity Mitford   Swinbrook
                                                                        ca. 1935

Dee Droudled Boudle,

Well here I am back again. What agony to leave Paris, you can't think what a lovely time we had, but still I am thrilled for my dance[37] which is fairly soon. I do think you might come back for it. I gave Diana a present for you, I am afraid it's beastly & anyhow I hope you will throw it from you with disgust as it was made by the enemies of Germany.

This is the new Boud song, Id came in to my room in Paris one day & found me singing it to myself. I will write it in English as it is easier to understand & takes up less space.

> I went down to St. James' Infirmary
> I saw my Boudle there
> Stretched out on a long white table
> So cold so beastly so fair
> I went up to see the doctor
> "She's very low," he said;
> I went back to see my Boudle
> Good god!!!
> She's lying there <u>DEAD</u>
> Let her go, let her go,
> God bless her;

---

36. Diana's former husband, Bryan Guinness.
37. During her debutante season.

Wherever she may be
She can search the whole world over
And never find a sweet Boud like me.

It has actions, too.

We are going to see Womb[38] today, & stay there a night. Diana has given me a HEAVENLY evening dress.

Give her my love, & hate to Hitler

Lodge
Vrudub
Je Boudle

Wa ha ha
Ee Ubbjellznbided.[39]

To Nancy Mitford   Swinbrook
                                                                        ca. 1935

Darling Susan,[40]

Thanks for curt note written on a little bit of cardboard purporting to be a p.c.

Susan I fully agree with you about how extraorder it was of me not to like (or rather not to read) Dorothy L. Sayers' books. I bought one at the station yesterday called "The Unpleasantness at the Bellona Club"[41] (attracted by that one word unpleasantness, which occurs so often in Holmes) and I simply never stopped reading it for <u>one</u> second; and now that I've finished it I feel I've only had a mere <u>foretaste</u> of that awful feeling one must get when one knows for <u>certain</u> that one has finished the whole series. Susan I shall never, no never, read anything else. When I saw that Ld Peter W's motto was "As my Whimsy takes me" I could have screamed with joy. I note also that the whole book is full of <u>wonderful</u> jokes. Altogether sheer heaven. . . .

Love from Susan

---

38. Apparently Decca's sister Pam, whose nickname in the family was Woman.

39. According to Decca's sister Deborah, the foremost surviving Boudledidge scholar, the signature lines mean "Love Forever, Your Boud." The postscript is more obscure: "Wa ha ha" meant "funny," and the last line, possibly, "I'm Jealous."

40. For reasons that are not clear, Decca and Nancy Mitford often called each other Susan, so that letters between them were often both addressed to Susan and signed by Susan.

41. A mystery novel featuring the witty, eloquent detective Lord Peter Wimsey.

To Diana Mitford   Paris
                                                           November 1935
Darling Cord,

I did mean to write ages ago but somehow time really <u>flew</u>.

It is so lovely being in Paris again, we are all enjoying it terrifically, specially me. Do try & get the Boud not to come as I don't think she'd like it, one doesn't want a really <u>huge</u> wet blanket in such a small flat.

Cordy it was kind of you to lend me that beautiful fur, it's naturally made the whole difference to the coat.

We went to Molyneux dress show, where we saw several lovely things, and we are going to Worth's & Vionnet's if the Fem can get a card for that one. Yesterday we went to tea with Princess F Lucinge,[42] she <u>is</u> a spamp I must say & her house is too fascinating & wonderful for words. . . .

Muv saw in the papers that the filthy old Boud has been putting posters on people's cars, saying "The Jews take everything, even our names" (it didn't actually <u>say</u> Boud, but of course we guessed). Didn't it seem awful & in a way unnatural Lady A.S. & the Duke of[43] having rose petals sprinkled over them. I see it said in the Tatler "<u>part</u> of the h.moon is bound to be delightful as it's being spent in hunting country." Well, Cord, goodbye, I do hope you will soon come.

                    Much Love From Decca

To Jessica Mitford[44]   Garmisch, Germany[45]
Please excuse awful paper   February 3, 1937
Darling Decca,

Twin and I are so anxious to see you before you go off round the world. Now I have a suggestion to make—sorry it's such short notice, but <u>do</u> try and fall in. We have taken a house in Dieppe—that is, Auntie has taken it! We mean to make it the centre of a sort of motor tour to all the amusing places round.[46] We

---

42. Probably Princess Aymone de Faucigny-Lucinge, whose daughter, Anne-Aymone Sauvage de Brantes, later married French politician Valéry Giscard d'Estaing.

43. Possibly a reference to Prince Henry William Frederick Windsor, Duke of Gloucester and third son of King George V (and brother of future kings Edward VIII and George VI), who married Lady Alice Christabel Montagu-Douglas-Scott at Buckingham Palace in November 1935.

44. This is the phony letter Decca and Esmond Romilly composed as a cover for their elopement to Spain. Decca showed the letter to her mother on February 3. She wrote about the circumstances of its composition twenty-three years later in *Daughters and Rebels*, but the wording quoted in her memoir differed from this version, as did the wording in her subsequent letters from this period. In her book, Decca was writing from memory of the letter, which was not in her possession at the time. She didn't see the letter again until 1962, two years after her memoir was published. See letter of July 13, 1962, to Barbara Kahn.

45. The dateline isn't totally legible but appears to be a misspelling of this ski resort on the German-Austrian border, site of the 1936 Winter Olympics.

46. Decca wrote in *Daughters and Rebels* that the motor tour was Esmond's idea, "so that I should be able to write to my mother from various towns in France as we journeyed south without exciting suspicion."

are going there from Austria on Wednesday, and we should so <u>love</u> you to join us next weekend sometime if you could possibly manage it. There won't be much of a party—just two boys from Oxford and us three and Auntie. But if you don't mind that do try and come. Our address there is 22, Rue Gambetta, Dieppe. So perhaps you could send a telegram to me there, if you can come. The boys (Dick and Leslie Cholmley) are coming by Saturday night boats so perhaps you could cross then, or if not on Sunday—anyway, just telegraph. Do you know them, by the way? I think you'll like them. We shall be <u>so</u> disappointed if you can't come; we could have asked you before, only we weren't sure of getting a house. Our house in London is successfully let—I hope yours is.

Much Love, Mamaine

P.S. We hope you will try . . .

To Lady Redesdale[47]   Dieppe, France
                                                                 February 9, 1937
Darling Muv,

I'm writing this in an awfully nice café in Dieppe—it's very amusing. Thanks so much for your letter.[48] I'm writing to Juliet about the invitation. The weather is pretty bad here so we probably shan't be doing much motoring until Thursday or Friday. We have just come back from Rouen; the cathedral is lovely. The Pagets send their love. Dieppe is quite a bright place in spite of this not being the season. I called on cousin Nellie Romilly this morning and was told she was expected here this week. So I'll go & see her then. (Perhaps Giles or Esmond will be there too).

Much Love From Decca

To Lady Redesdale   Bayonne, France
                                                                mid-February 1937
Darling Muv,

I hope you got my telegraph alright to say I was staying a bit longer than I thought. The town has been too lovely, I am simply adoring it, & I don't think

---

47. This entire letter was part of the elaborate ruse to cover Decca's elopement with Esmond Romilly, who is mentioned casually in the letter, along with his mother, Nellie, and brother, Giles. Decca also described this letter, again from memory, in *Daughters and Rebels*.

48. The young couple, delayed in their attempt to get Decca a visa for Spain, went back to England briefly through Dieppe, the city where Decca had told her family she would be staying at the invitation of her old debutante friends the Paget twins. While waiting for the boat back to England, Decca and Romilly found that the fictitious address Decca had given her family actually existed, so they rang the bell and picked up mail from home, allowing her to reply and continue the deception plausibly.

I shall be back till about Saturday (at the latest). We are staying here at Bayonne for a few days in a very nice hotel.[49] Bayonne is a fascinating place, frightfully pretty with a lovely river & old cathedral. We went in the meter to Saint Jean de Luz, which is quite near; it is very attractive but less so than Bayonne, as it is much more of a tourists' resort. We stopped in Paris for two days on the way; I telephoned Mademoiselle and Dolly & one or two people, but unfortunately they were all in the country or abroad. The weather here is too lovely, really springlike, & all the cherry trees are in flower already. The food is delicious & wonderfully cheap; you can get a meal with masses of wine & about 3 courses for about 2/- each. I am looking into the bread question like mad as it is wonderful here, & hope to have lots of interesting lowdown on how it is made by the time I get back. I wonder if you have met the bread & gland doctor yet.

The Twins send their love. Give my best love to Farve & Nanny & Debo. Well I must scram now as we are just going off to see some old Bayonne friend of the Pagets living in the neighbourhood.

Much Love From Decca

To Lady Redesdale   Paris
                                                               late February 1937
My Darling Muv,

I'm afraid this will come as rather a shock to you. I wish I could have explained the whole thing to you before. But after reading this I do hope you will understand, and forgive me for seeming inconsiderate & deceitful.

When I went to Cousin Dorothy's I didn't tell you I had met Esmond Romilly. To put it shortly, by the time you get this we shall be married. I didn't tell you because I thought you would disapprove of him but I'm sure you wouldn't if you knew him. You can't think how happy I am. Peter Nevile[50] (TEM 9301) knows us both & will explain the whole thing. Esmond has got a very good job as a journalist so I expect we will be in Spain and will have a mass of dough. There is no danger at all where we are going but there might be if you tried to do anything to get me back or stop me doing what I want to. I'm sure you won't do this as we are naturally on the Government side and I

---

49. In fact, the couple, still thwarted in their efforts to obtain a visa to Spain, had traveled to Bayonne, near the Spanish border—"posting letters to my mother in towns on the way," as Decca recalled the deception in her memoir—and finally received permission while there to embark for Spain.

50. An acquaintance of Decca, Nevile was Esmond Romilly's good friend and another cousin of Dorothy Allhusen, at whose home the two young men had met. Before Decca met Esmond, Nevile had been her go-between in approaching Giles Romilly to seek help in running away to join the International Brigade in Spain.

don't want all Bobo's[51] associations to be connected with me. Of course you know how strongly I feel about this. Do remember that I <u>won't</u> be in any danger & it will all be terrific fun. You will honestly <u>adore</u> Esmond when you know him & please don't be put off by all the secrecy, the <u>only</u> reason for it was because I wanted to go to Spain with him & I thought you might try & stop me.

I really did feel awful having to invent about the Pagets going to Dieppe, etc. but I couldn't see any other way to going with him. I don't quite know when we shall be getting back, but I am longing for you all to see Esmond. I will try & write to you soon, but don't be surprised if I don't because it may be a bit tricky getting letters through. Give my best love to all the others & tell Robin & Ann & everyone about our marriage; nobody at all knows so far except Peter Nevile.

Love From Decca

To Lady Redesdale   Bilbao, Spain
March 5, 1937

My Darling Muv,

I got your letter this morning,—very luckily as sometimes they take over a fortnight to arrive. We are having an extremely interesting time here & this place is very quiet. I am quite safe here & am not going to the front. It was so nice of you to write, & I <u>am</u> so sorry you were worried. I really <u>do</u> hope you won't want me to return as I am <u>very</u> happy here altogether. Also I can't understand why you are putting off the world tour, I hope it was only a temporary decision & you will change your mind & go.

I will write to you a lot, naturally. It is quite different here from what you might expect; all the churches are open & the government is mainly composed of Catholic Basque nationalists.

Yesterday we visited a prison for political prisoners & prisoners of war; they are frightfully well treated, in fact we thought much better than they deserve when you think how the fascists treat their prisoners.

The people we have met here are very sweet & charming, & we are trying to learn Spanish as quickly as possible. We learn it out of an awful little phrase book of Esmond's with nothing but useless words like "eggplant" which don't mean anything even in English.

---

51. Bobo was one of Unity Mitford's nicknames—the name generally used by all of the family except Decca, who called her Boud. It was derived, Decca told Unity Mitford's biographer David Pryce-Jones, from Baby and her mother's nickname for her, Little Babe, "which became Little Bobe" (*Unity Mitford: A Quest*, Weidenfeld and Nicolson, 1976; also published by Dial Press in 1977 with the title *Unity Mitford: An Enquiry into Her Life and the Frivolity of Evil*).

Do write soon; address the letter to Esmond as before.
Give my best love to all the others.

Love From Decca

PS Naturally I was very glad to get your letter, but not the other message,[52] I do hope you won't go on with this, please.

To Lady Redesdale   Bayonne
late March 1937[53]

I got your later letter yesterday, in which everything sounds very satisfactory. On the question of financial provision, we are quite alright here & seem to be able to live alright for the present, so I don't see why we shouldn't continue like this in future. At the same time, Esmond has of course been keeping me entirely since we left England and I really feel I ought to contribute something to the cost of living here. In view of this, I wonder if you could send me my dress allowance? I can't help feeling it would come in awfully useful.

I'm <u>so</u> glad you managed to arrange everything re the judge etc so well, of course I expect everyone realised that as we had decided what we were going to do it would be of no use in the end to oppose it, & so it was better to give in at once.

Esmond has written a frightfully amusing thing[54] about it all which I am sending you, do show it round to everyone, specially the Rodds. It is really

---

52. An apparent reference to a telegram to Esmond from the family's attorneys that read "MISS JESSICA MITFORD IS A WARD OF COURT STOP IF YOU MARRY HER WITHOUT LEAVE OF JUDGE YOU WILL BE LIABLE TO IMPRISONMENT = HASTIES LONDON =" Hasties was the law firm for Decca's father, who had gone to court to have his daughter declared a ward of the court.

53. This is a fragment of a letter, the beginning of which is missing. Not long before it was written, Lady Redesdale, ignoring entreaties from her daughter, had visited the young couple in Bayonne. This letter was apparently sent in reply to a letter from Lady Redesdale dated March 24, in which she said that she, Lord Redesdale, and Decca's brother, Tom, had gone to court and explained "the whole situation" to the judge, with Lady Redesdale arguing that "you should be married, Farve making no objection." (She indicated that, although "it was not a very easy task," she and Tom Mitford had garnered Lord Redesdale's consent.) The judge then agreed to revoke his order for Decca's immediate return in England, but he withheld backing for his ward's marriage until the families could determine what financial provision the Romilly family would be making for Decca.

54. Esmond Romilly had written an elaborate allegory of "the recent Redesdale-Romilly hostilities" portrayed as a war between the Blues and the Whites. In an apparently earlier and simpler version of the parable, "the Blues . . . all unknown to the Whites, were casting covetous eyes on the treasure of the latter. This treasure was the product of 19 years of loving care on the part of the Whites & was as the apple of their eyes. Little did they dream that in the year 1937 the methods of a past barbarism, combined with lying & deceit would be employed to snatch their treasure from them." Esmond Romilly was cast as the Commander of the Blues and Lord Redesdale as the Emperor of the Whites.

awfully funny & I'm sure will make you all roar. (Don't lose it, will you, as I should like it back.)

Well, I must scram now.

Love From Decca

PS The black mercenaries in Esmond's article refer of course to Hamish[55] & Mr. Whitfield,[56] & the battalion that passed over into our lines is Nancy.

To Deborah Mitford   Bayonne
                                                              March 29, 1937

Dear Old Ho-Hon,[57]

This is to wish you a very happy birthday, and I hope it will reach you in time. I'm enclosing twopence in stamps for you to buy a tuppeny bar with (it's really from Esmond, but the thought was mine and I always say the thought counts most on these occasions). I'm sorry it isn't a diamond bracelet but will make it up to you when we get rich, which I expect won't be long.

We went to lunch with a delicious mad old duchess today in Saint Jean de Luz: it's the first time I've ever been to lunch with a duchess so you see (what with this and the diplomatic society represented by the Spanish and Panama consuls) I have married into very high society!![58]

Yesterday we went to the Bayonne fair, where there is a fascinating fat woman; after seeing her, everyone was made to file past in a row and pinch her legs to show they were genoowine. There was a marvellous shooting range, and your old Hen, who's accounted for so many moors (sez she!) actually hit the target, and Esmond won a bottle of champagne by hitting the pigeon's eye three times.

Muv brought the Tatler with you in it. Who's Mr. Dixon? He looks a bit dried up to me, but perhaps he's far from it.

---

55. Hamish St. Clair Erskine was Nancy Mitford's first love and fiancé. In Esmond Romilly's allegory, the use of black mercenary troops and the tearing-up of treaties "were a specialty of the Whites."

56. Many years later Decca wrote, in answer to a query from Charlotte Mosley, editor of a book of her sister Nancy's letters, "I'm almost sure that Mr. Whitfield was the consul who married Esmond/me. But not totally sure."

57. One of Decca's nicknames for her sister, derived from their Society of Hens, or Hons. Throughout their lives, Decca and Deborah called each other Hen or Henderson. Decca once gave this arcane explanation: "Hon Henderson comes from a Honnish poem based on two sources: John Anderson my Jo John (Burns) hence Hon Henderson my Ho Hon; and the Lars Porsena of Clusium. Hence: Hon Henderson my Ho Hon / By the nine Gods she swore / That the great house of Henderson / Should suffer wrong no more."

58. Decca's mother later mockingly reproved her rebellious daughter in a letter: "I am surprised you fell so low as to go to lunch with a Duchess, I thought your principles would forbid consorting with such."

Write all the family gossip. What do you think of my typewriting. You know I <u>was</u> taken on as a secretary, but I'm still waiting for my first week's wages. Poor old Squalor. . . .

I wanted to send you a delicious French novel called Prelude Charnelle, but they would have torn it at Dover, I expect, as it's awfully improper, so I'll give it to you for your next birthday if the diamond bracelet doesn't mature.

I'm an Old Ho-Hon
from the river Don
best love from squalor

To Lady Redesdale   Bayonne
April 12, 1937

My darling Muv,

I have just got your letter saying all is ok about us being married.[59] I'm so glad everything is so satisfactory now; did you have a tricky time fixing the Judge? I hope not! I'm terribly glad Farve has come round to the idea of it too, that's all very good news.[60]

We got a parcel yesterday of socks for Esmond which I think you must have sent by the writing of the address. Thank you so much for thinking of it; they are awfully useful & it was very kind of you to send them. The postmark is dated ages ago, so I suppose they must have got held up at the customs; I expect you thought we never got them. . . .

What were Esmond's parents like when you saw them?

Well I must scram now; do write again soon.

Love From Decca

To Lady Redesdale   Bayonne
April 20, 1937

Darling Muv,

Thanks for your letter & the lovely Vogues which I was awfully pleased to get.

This morning we got the permission of the judge to marry, so we'll see when it can be arranged. I believe it takes some time on account of the formalities

---

59. Lady Redesdale had written to say that Esmond Romilly's father had also consented to the marriage and the judge had lifted his ban, which she attributed to "my efforts on your behalf." In the days that followed, Lady Redesdale pushed the couple to return her favor and "arrange to get married now in Bayonne," adding that "old as I am I cannot agree with the unconventional idea" of the couple living together unmarried and "I could never in a thousand years get used to such an idea."

60. Although Lord Redesdale had consented to the marriage, subsequent letters made clear that he was far from happy about it.

with the consulate & I'll let you know our plans later, but I don't think we shall be able to marry before the coronation. . . .[61]

St. Jean de Luz is seething with excitement about the English cargo boats (I expect you saw about the "Potato Jones" in the papers).[62] It is full of journalists, & Esmond is acting as "News Chronicle" special correspondent here. He gets a lot of news the others don't as he does all the interpreting between the Basque consul & the captains of the ships. They are simply furious with the Brit navy, naturally. Doesn't everyone in England think it's a bit extraorder of the Admiralty to withhold protection from our own ships? Meanwhile the wretched Basques are starving, & no one is allowed more than one dish of vegetables a day in Bilbao.

By the way, what's this about me taking an action against Tuddemy?[63] In the papers the Judge sent us I am referred to as "plaintiff" & he as "defendant." Do explain what happened.[64] How lovely to be going to Italy & Austria, is Debo excited? Is anyone else going with you?

Esmond has written a lot of his book,[65] & we also have the job here of listening in to the Bilbao & San Sebastian communiques on the radio, all of which brings in dough. I expect the News Chron will pay quite a lot for all the news about the ships, too. . . .

Well I must scram now & will let you know when we shall be married later. Give Blor[66] my love, & show her this letter.

Love From Decca

61. Lady Redesdale had written to ask the couple to plan an early wedding so she could be present, as she planned to go abroad immediately after the May 12 coronation of King George VI, which the family planned to attend.

62. Captain David John Jones was the master of the tramp steamer *Marie Llewellyn*, which attempted to run guns—hidden under a cargo of potatoes—to Bilbao in defiance of a blockade declared by the fascists to prevent outside aid for Republican Spain. The captain, subsequently known as "Potato Jones," was reported at the time, apparently erroneously, to have broken the blockade. He did, however, help to ferry thousands of Spanish refugees to France.

63. Decca's brother Tom Mitford's nickname was Tuddemy (sometimes spelled Tudemy or abbreviated as Tud), which Decca wrote in *Daughters and Rebels* was the Boudledidge translation of Tom.

64. Her mother replied, "I don't a bit understand about you & Tuddemy, plaintiff & defendant? He didn't come into it in any way at all!"

65. Esmond Romilly is in the process of writing *Boadilla*, his account of the battle at the Spanish village of Boadilla del Monte at which most of his fellow British soldiers were killed.

66. The Mitford children's beloved nanny, Laura Dicks, who was also known to Decca as M'Honkert (with and without an apostrophe) or, by some accounts, m'Hinket. In their book *The House of Mitford: Portrait of a Family* (Hutchinson, 1984), Jonathan Guinness, Diana Mitford's son, and his daughter Catherine Guinness said that Deborah Mitford also used the nickname M'Honkert, which they said was derived from the nanny's verbal tic, part sniff, part hiccup, part "little asthmatic gasp."

To Lady Redesdale   Bayonne
"May 7 or 8," 1937

My Darling Muv,

Many happy returns of your birthday. I hope you will get this on the 10th. I'm sorry I haven't written for such a long time, but you know how hopeless I am at writing letters. . . .

The English papers have become such torture about the coronation. I can hardly bear to read them. Thank goodness I shall be out of London for it. Are the others going? I should think unless one was in the abbey it would be skeke[67] worth it.

I <u>do</u> hope the fact we have had to alter the wedding date to the 15th won't prevent you from coming.[68] We weren't able to fix it for earlier. Let me know which day & time to expect you. Is Debo coming too?

You will try & come, won't you. I'm glad no one believed the Rodds' mischief making.[69] I do think they're such a bore really.

Love from Decca

PS Give my best love to Boud. Could you also bring my bathing dress & summer sandals if Blor can find them.

To Nancy Mitford   Bayonne
ca. July 1937

Darling Susan,

Thanks for yr. letter. All <u>is</u> oke now really, but Susan I must just remind you of a few things you seem to have forgotten! Susan <u>how</u> you can say you & Rodd were pro Esmond & me living together when you wrote saying how unrespectable it was & how Society would shun me, & Rodd wrote saying how French workmen would shun me. In fact what you actually wanted us to do was to come home to England, in which case I should have been caught by the Ps[70] & narst old Judge & altogether teased in every way. So what you were really

---

67. "Scarcely" in Mitford-speak.

68. Lady Redesdale was traveling to Bayonne to attend the couple's wedding. They were married in the British consulate in Bayonne, attended by both mothers. Decca said Esmond remarked to her that their mothers "looked more like chief mourners at a funeral than wedding guests."

69. Esmond Romilly had written to Lady Redesdale that he had "heard from two separate sources that thoroughly vile things have been said and believed about me by the Rodds to the effect that I was anxious to get money out of this affair—all the more impertinent because the only reason Rodd could produce for Decca going back to England when we saw him at Saint Jean de Luz was, as he put it, that by doing so D. would get an allowance out of her father!" Lady Redesdale answered that "I pay no attention whatever to what is said & form my opinions from my own observation, which in this case leads me to believe that you have done nothing at all to get money, in fact just the contrary, & I have said this to many people." She added in a letter to Decca that "Actually I admire this independent spirit very much."

70. Parents.

against was <u>both</u> us getting married <u>and</u> us living together not married. Do you admit, Susan. Do you also admit it <u>was</u> a bit disloyal just as I was thinking you were the one I could count on to be on my side through thick and. Anyway it's all such ages ago now I expect you've forgotten a bit what you did do, &, as you say, now we're married there's no point in [illegible]. . . .

I am going to have a baby in January (1st to be exact, oh Susan do you remember poor Lottie's[71] agonies, & I expect it's much worse for humans) yes Susan some of us do our duty to the community unlike others I could name. Shall I call it Nancy, I think skeke as I have a feeling it's going to be a boy, & being called Nancy might prove a handicap to it throughout life. I do hope it will be sweet & pretty & everything. Goodness I have been sick but I'm not any more now.

The bathing here is absolutely heaven, we go to Biarritz nearly every day. Well Soose. End of paper.

Love from Susan

To Nancy Mitford   Dieppe
                                                                     ca. August 1937

Darling Susan,

Thanks v much for your letter, it <u>is</u> kind of you to ask us to stay—is it alright if I let you know later whether we can come? It looks to me as though we shan't be able to but I will write & tell you. I hear you have asked Id too. She seems to be getting awfully famous, did you see her review in the Observer?[72]

I am staying here alone as Esmond has had to go to England for a few days to see about his book.[73] Blor & Debo are coming out here tomorrow which I'm longing for. <u>Susan</u> the people in this hotel. . . . They are all English & mostly cols. & wives, & there is one horrid old lesbian called Miss Austin who follows me hopefully about with the poems of Baudelaire. Cousin Nelly[74] is giving a cocktail party for me today to meet the Dieppe society!!!! I'm sure it will be extraorder.

I went to the dentist here day before yesterday & he pulled out a <u>huge</u> back double tooth without any anaesthetic . . . I felt <u>everything</u>. Susan I never have in all my life of broken arms, appendicitis, typhoid etc. known such agony. I nearly fainted & couldn't stop trembling for about 2 hours. The dent said the reason it hurt so was because it was seriée[75] between 2 other teeth, but I said that was a stupid excuse because all teeth are seriées between two others unless one is a toothless deformity. Altogether I teased him quite a lot & was glad to see I made his hand bleed by digging in my flags[76] while he was pulling. I

---

71. A childhood dog.

72. Ann Farrer was a neophyte actress at the time.

73. In late August, Esmond signed a contract with Hamish Hamilton for publication of *Boadilla*.

74. Esmond Romilly's mother.

75. As she often did in this period, Decca seems to have conjoined two words, one French and the other English: "serried," meaning crowded together, and the French word from which it is descended, "serré."

76. Probably fingernails.

expect he will get blood poisoning now because they are engrained with dirt from the Tour.

When I got back & to bed I was almost delirious & kept thinking I heard Esmond coming up the stairs although I knew he was in London. Cousin Nelly was awfully nice & scrammed about getting aspirins etc.

The Tour[77] is being such <u>absolute</u> heaven, we are <u>simply</u> adoring it. I cook the food, you can't think how good I am at it, it is simply delicious usually I am longing to be off again on it. The scrapage[78] seems to like it quite too, I feel much better than at Bayonne.

Well Susan I must scram now. . . .
Love from Decca

To Lady Redesdale   New York
March 9, 1939

Darling Fem,

We've been here about a week & I must say it really is wonderful, far more so than I expected even. The people are far nicer than I expected & of course very hospitable & kind, for instance one girl we met spent the whole of yesterday taking us round to see apartments for when we leave the hotel. . . .

The hotels are of course wonderful & every room has a private bath & shower. Well I simply must scram now but I'll write again soon.
Love From Decca

PS Please give MHonkert my best love, and Hen.

To Lady Redesdale   New York
August 2 or 3, 1939

Darling Muv,

Thank you so much for your letter. . . .

I did roar at what Winston said to Tud, how typical of him.

We are going away for a bit next week—I have resigned from my job as I have another one at Bloomingdale's, a big shop rather like Selfridges which I'm looking forward to enormously.

. . . [M]y boss at the fair,[79] who I loathe, was <u>simply</u> furious when I said I was leaving. We are hardly on speakers now in fact. We have had a lot of

---

77. The young couple were touring around France for a few months.

78. Although the derivation of the word is unclear, its usage here suggests that Decca may be referring to her fetus.

79. Decca had been hired to work at the New York World's Fair by a woman she described in her memoir *Daughters and Rebels* as "a domineering, fortyish blond." Her job was as a salesgirl at a Scottish tweed "shoppe" that was part of Ye Merrie England Village.

terrific rows, she is an awful woman & a terrible snob so I'm pleased to be leaving.

We have got to know quite a few millionaires which is nice, they have fine wirenetting round their windows to keep out moths & slow flies so I love staying with them.

I was amazed at Woman suddenly turning up here, I had no idea she was coming & in fact the night before she rang up I dreamt that she & Nancy had died of old age. They came out to see me at the fair & last night we all had a wonderful dinner together at their hotel. They are leaving next week, about the same time we are going out of N.Y.

Did Boud by any chance meet a lade called Mrs. Meyer,[80] she is one of the millionaires & she & her husband have gone to Europe & she was very anxious to meet the Boud. So tell Boud to look out for her. She is awfully nice, her husband is a bigshot here & they live in a sort of Winston Churchill-ish atmosphere of other bigshots.

Debo said how you & she might be coming here for the Fair, I <u>do</u> wish you would, if you decide to come I should come in October when it will be cooler, besides New York is rather dull now because it is so hot people can skeke move. Let me know well in advance because it would be much cheaper to take an apartment for a week or two than to stay in a hotel & I could find you one.

Do give my love to the others & get them to write, I never seem to have time to write many letters & anyway they are practically illegible as we've got no ink here.

Best Love From Decca

P.S. Tell M Honkert I'll write soon.

To Lady Redesdale   New York
                                                           September 6, 1939

Darling Muv,

Thanks you so much for your letters. I'm so sorry about your poor Rupert.[81] I heard about it from Woman when she was here. It seems months ago with the terrible news of the war.

I see in the papers that Bobo is in Germany, do tell me if you have any news

---

80. Agnes Meyer, a patron of the arts and education and wife of wealthy investment banker and *Washington Post* owner Eugene Meyer. The couple had met the Meyers through their nephew, John Cook, a friend of Peter Nevile. Through the conservative Republican Meyers, Decca and Esmond Romilly met their liberal Democratic daughter Katharine Meyer, who had recently returned to Washington at her father's request to edit the *Post*'s letters to the editor. They became friendly with Katharine Meyer and her boyfriend and later husband, Philip Graham.

81. Decca's uncle—her father's brother—died on August 7, 1939.

of her[82] & please send her address as soon as you can so I can write to her. Is she going to stay there? Do let me know about her as soon as possible.

We heard the news[83] on our tor,[84] I can't believe it has actually happened. Of course everyone here has been glued to the radio the last 2 weeks, no one thinks of anything else. Do send me news of Tudemy too, if you know any.[85] I don't know if the airmail is still any good, it is supposed to go round by Portugal now.

Poor Henderson, I suppose she is dancing alone in the deserted ballrooms now. Do please write as soon as possible, specially about the Boud.

Best Love From Decca

To Lady Redesdale   New York
                                                     September 27, 1939
Darling Fem,

Thank you so much for your greetings 'gram & letter—I had a wonderful 'gram from Woman too with a person singing "Happy Birthday to you" which you can get here.

I thought perhaps you would like to hear about our holiday, we really had a wonderful time. Csn Dorothy[86] gave us a letter of introduction to a girl called Caroline Dubois, who lives in a typical small-town in Pennsylvania. So we wrote to her, & she immediately asked us to stay. We went, & it was absolutely fascinating: she & her family of 4 brothers & a sister in law all live in the same house though they are all quite old, I should think she must be about 36 or 7, & they own a factory & a tiny little coal mine with only 2 men working in it. The town was exactly as you'd imagine with a ladies' bridge club & a small college. They were wonderful to us & asked us to stay about a week, & then took us on a motor trip to a mountain chalet they have in West Virginia. Caroline is absolutely charming & very unlike the New York Americans.

After that we went to Woodstock, in New England, to stay with some Columbia University professors we met here. In New England people are much more like English people, they talk the same way & one sees village idiots in the country just like England. After that we went to Woods' Hole, a seaside

---

82. Unbeknownst to the family or others outside Germany, Unity had shot and seriously wounded herself three days earlier in the English Garden in Munich, shortly after learning of Britain's declaration of war on Germany. Two days before that, she had written a final letter to her mother asking her to please thank "my Boud"—Decca—"a million times" for birthday gifts she had just received from Decca in New York.

83. Presumably the news of the September 1 German invasion of Poland and the British declaration of war.

84. The Mitfords' word for "tour."

85. Decca's brother, Tom, was in the volunteer Territorial Army, then served in the Rifle Brigade at the beginning of the war.

86. Cousin Dorothy Allhusen, at whose weekend house party Esmond and Decca had met.

place in Massachusetts to stay with an extraorder old millionaire woman called Mrs. Murray Crane who is a sort of patron of the arts & has a jour every Sunday in New York where boring people come & lecture. We were away about a month & drove 2,000 miles in all.

Now we're going to leave New York & travel South, towards New Orleans & San Francisco, but letters will be forwarded & if there is anything important & you write airmail they will follow by airmail in America.

I was very much reassured about everyone by your letter particularly the Boud, I was terribly worried about what would happen to her. . . .

Is there a strict censorship on letters to & from England? I can't make out. None of yours to me seem to have been opened.

Do give old Tud my love when you write to him. . . .

> Best Love From Decca

To Lady Redesdale.   Miami
                                                         November 23, 1939

Darling Muv,

. . . I'm so glad you really think all the stories[87] are untrue, the whole thing seems so dreadful & one just doesn't know what to believe. I wish you could get some real news, but perhaps you will soon. The papers here all had different stories but it did sound as though there might be some truth in it. If so, I feel sure no one would try anything like that twice. . . .

We had a wonderful time driving through the South from Washington. We had letters of introduction to people in a lot of the towns, which of course makes the whole difference. One lot of people in Columbia South Carolina turned out to be part of the old hard-riding Southern gentry, so when we rang them up they asked us to go riding with them that afternoon! Out of complete absent-mindedness I accepted, & of course when we arrived it turned out to be at a very smart Riding Academy & they were all dressed up in special clothes with bowler hats & silver-handled crops, & there was I in a very old pair of baggy corduroy ski-ing trousers & Esmond in a grey flannel suit. However, I assured them I had spent my whole childhood in the saddle & never missed a chance of riding to hounds; but when I got on the horse (I had to be lifted on by coloured grooms) I was <u>simply</u> terrified. Luckily however when the others started to trot or canter I was able to make its head face the other way so I got out of anything really difficult.

We spent a week in Charleston, South Carolina which is a lovely town very like some in the South of France or Spain. . . .

I don't really like Southerners much, they are absolutely different from Northerners (as they never stop pointing out) & are mostly rather snobbish.

---

87. Newspaper reports on Unity Mitford's shooting herself.

Some of the shacks where the poor farmers live are simply incredible, they are wooden & look like old, broken-down chicken houses. We couldn't believe people actually lived in them till we saw them inside.

As soon as we got into Florida everything was completely different. Everything is for tourists here which makes it terrifically rich, & every bit of road is covered with huge signs & advts. We drove through several orange & grapefruit groves which were simply lovely, but you aren't allowed to get out & pick anything. . . .

Tud sent me a cheque for £5 for my birthday, wasn't it divine of him, but the only thing is you can't get any money out of England at all now & I can't cash it; so as you said about poor Rud being so poor I endorsed it & sent it to her. Do you think Tud would think it awful of me? I thought he would have said goodbye to it anyway & wouldn't mind.

If you get any news of my Boud <u>do</u> let me know right away. I think it must be so dreadfully worrying for you & I suppose Blor is miserable about it. Can you learn anything from newspaper people? They might hear something from other correspondents via USA.

Please give Hon Henderson my love & do ask her to write, I wrote to her ages ago from Washington & she's never answered.

Best Love From <u>Decca</u>.

To Tom Mitford   Miami
December 24, 1939

Darling Tud,

I kept meaning to write for Xmas & now it's Xmas eve so this will skeke arrive even by airmail.

We have been having a terrifically busy time here & Miami is a heavenly place boiling hot & with people bathing all through the winter. . . .

[W]e have a terrifically exciting plan on. Esmond got a job here as a bar tender (he took a course in Bartending before we left N.Y.) in a very good Italian restaurant. So now we are going to get a share in the restaurant & both work there. So I have written to Drummonds to tell them to send £300 of my dough for it. If you have some time off from being a Capt. do go & hurry them up about it. I have always longed to have a restaurant & am v. excited about it.

Miami is so extraorder, the first flat we got here was <u>simply</u> filthy & even I noted it; there were 2 cane chairs caked with dirt & if you listened to them you could hear a faint crackling of insects inside the cane. The floor was so dirty that one had to take off one's shoes on the bed so as not to walk on it before getting in. Now we have got a very nice flat which we moved into yesterday. We have got to know some people in Palm Beach; they have a French butler & although he talks perfect English they insist on talking to him in very bad French for the atmosphere.

One hears much less about the war here than in New York, where people talk of nothing else; sometimes one sees a car with a sticker saying "keep neutral." The general attitude in America seems to be a determination to keep out plus an equal determination that the allies should keep at it. Actually since the arms embargo was repealed most of the feverish excitement about the war has died down.

There is a German merchant ship about 10 miles from here which got chased into port by a British destroyer; there are huge notices up saying "50 cents for a round trip to see the Nazi ship."

Do write all news, I haven't heard from the Fem or anyone for ages. . . .

Love From Decca.

To Lady Redesdale   Miami
                                                        December 28, 1939

Darling Muv,

Thank you so much for your Xmas gram—I meant to write for Xmas but have been terrifically hard at work. I got a fascinating job here when we first arrived selling sham jewelry in a drug store, & had to work 10 hours a day (during which one couldn't sit down at all except in the lunch hour) sometimes till 12 at night. In most states girls aren't allowed by law to work more than 8 hours or later than 10 at night. . . . It was amazing to be actually working in the Christmas rush—specially as I only got the job on the strict understanding that I had sold jewelry for 2 years at Selfridges' before coming here. I thought it would be quite easy, but the first morning the head lade snapped at me: "Make the locket displays." In about 2 minutes I had got all the chains of the lockets hopelessly tangled & she said "you obviously don't know how to make displays. It will take me an hour to untangle those." . . . Another depressing thing was that a previous English girl called Miss Rose had worked there & become a store manager in about 6 months, & she was always being cast up at me like previous families are by governesses. However after about a week I became terrifically good at it & really enjoyed it a lot. However I left the day before Christmas as Esmond & I are going to work in a bar here in a very good Italian restaurant. . . . I'm to be the cashier & general helper but I hope to learn a good deal about the kitchen side too.

We've got to know a lot of people on Palm Beach; they are as you may imagine very rich & awful but interesting to see. . . .

Have you had any <u>direct</u> news from Boud yet? Do let me know as <u>soon</u> as you do, & I will too if I hear anything. I do so wish one knew something, it seems such months & I so wonder if she is fairly happy & has enough to live on. I think if you could only get a letter to her it would make a lot of difference.

The papers here have had nothing about her since those awful stories reprinted from England. . . .

I enclose a letter for M'Honkert. Do write soon.

Love From Decca

To Esmond Romilly

Miami

early January 1940

Beloved Bird,

I just got your 2 letters of Thursday & am absolutely bowled over by the news, I never really quite believed it could happen. Do you mean to say you actually have in your possession $1000 of crafty old Meyer's hard-earned savings?[88] I can skeke believe it. As for the news about all the people who are coming down here, I think it's simply WONDERFUL. Let me say once & for all you old creach;[89] 1,000,000 congratulations for being an old miracle working boot.[90] I have written to my slank[91] already. Actually the sight of the old Brown writing was in itself enough to <u>make</u> the Man's day. Also I'm so glad you are having quite an enjoyable time. . . . But please don't stay too long old Bird. There's a <u>love</u>. . . .

Old Bird what did I tell you about how it would be snowing. Do you admit now you would have cut a sorry figure arriving in your pale blue beach suit? I hardly think Meyer would have been impressed.

Do try & stay in someone's house if possible, where you'll be out of the cold. . . .

Very best love from yr

amazed & admiring Man

P.S. I expect by now you've lost the dough at the Bones[92] or on a drunk, but at your present rate it shouldn't take more than 1 1/2 hours to get some more You dear, darling old croat, Goodbye

---

88. Esmond Romilly had flown to Washington to try to borrow $1,000 to pay for a liquor license and become a partner in the Roma bar.

89. Perhaps short for "creature."

90. Decca often called her husband "old Boot," for reasons that are not clear. Her other nicknames for Romilly included old Bird, old Croat, old Thinger, and old Brown.

91. Decca used the word a number of times in letters to Esmond. Since she often referred to herself in letters to Romilly as Slipper, this word appears to mean "Slipper's bank." Among the other unexplained names she used to refer to herself was the Man.

92. Esmond's moneymaking schemes often involved gambling, at which he was notoriously unsuccessful. It was something of a family trait, passed down from his grandmother and his mother,

To Lady Redesdale Miami
January 11, 1940

Darling Muv,

Do please write & tell me all news of Boud, it is of course absolutely impossible to get anything reliable from the newspaper reports, & the last few days have been so terribly worrying, all the papers here have been saying the most dreadful things.[93]

The reporters have been after me like mad tho I can't <u>think</u> how they knew I was here, but they have given me up now. One man offered to arrange a transatlantic phone call to you, everything you said to be recorded & used in a broadcast all over the U.S. Another offered me $1,000 for an article. They've been hanging around with cameras outside the house for days.

Every paper says something different about Boud & how she became so ill, and it is so awful not knowing <u>anything</u>. However I am terrifically glad she is at home now as whatever is the matter with her she must be better off at Wycombe where she can have proper food & Blor & everyone.

Do please write soon & tell all the news.
Love from Decca

P.S. I enclose a letter for Boud.

To Lady Redesdale Miami
February 1, 1940

Darling Muv,

I got your letter today & was so overjoyed to get some news. Yesterday the Miami papers were full of more rumours about Bobo & it has all been so frightfully worrying, until I got your letter dated 9th Jan I didn't know a thing. The

---

who were both drawn to the casino in Dieppe, where they were "reckless" gamblers, in the words of Nellie Romilly's sister, Clementine Hozier, later Mrs. Winston Churchill. Decca is reported to have said that her own mother took an instant dislike to Nellie Romilly when, in her newlywed days, "she was accosted by Nellie in Dieppe, who asked her for a loan of £10 to go to the Casino," a request that Decca's mother spurned—and also reported to Nellie Romilly's mother. Decca has written that Esmond would gamble on anything but seemed especially fond in their London days of dog racing, where he was likely to lose their week's wages, leaving the couple without even bus fare home.

93. This letter was written within days of Unity Mitford's return to England, where her arrival set off a media tempest, with pursuing crowds of reporters besieging the family almost from the moment their ferry docked, as they had in Calais, where the family spent the night before crossing the Channel. Decca's letter was mailed to the family's Old Mill Cottage in High Wycombe (a small house where they had previously stayed when their other homes were rented out but where they lived most of the time after the 1936 sale of Swinbrook House). But after a few days' recuperation from her draining trip home, Unity Mitford had been taken to Radcliffe Infirmary in Oxford, where this letter was forwarded by postal authorities. Doctors at the clinic told the family that no further treatment was possible for their brain-damaged daughter.

papers say her brain is injured but I'm sure that is completely untrue, from your letter it seems that she has just lost her memory like Tud did after his accident.[94] Do you know if it is true that she had a terrible quarrel with Hitler as the papers say.

Do write & tell everything because I have no other way of knowing & I can't think of anything else, it is all so frightful.

I enclose a letter, if she is well enough to read it.

Love From Decca

P.S. I don't know if the English papers published any supposed "interviews" given by me, some of the papers here did & needless to say they were entirely made up. Please write soon or if there are any more untrue rumours you might send a 'gram.

To Unity Mitford
Miami
January–February 1940[95]

Darling Boud,

Your Boud is <u>so</u> sorry you are ill, I've written to you very often but I think the letters may have gone astray. I've been so longing for news of you & am awfully glad you are back home again with Blor & everyone to take care of you.

Esmond & I have got jobs in a Miami bar, you must admit rather fascinating. The other people there are <u>heaven</u> (mostly Italian & Spanish) & we have all our food there which is wonderful, because it's the most delicious food I've e'er noted. We've got to know the most amazing people here; for instance, I have one friend whose only interest in life is birth control, & when I go to tea with her she takes me round in her car for free handouts of contraceptives to nigger[96] families. Miami's rather like the South of France or Venice, all the people here have got something extraorder about them. Well Boud I'll write you again soon . . . & <u>do</u> get well quickly.

Very best love, Yr Boud

---

94. Lady Redesdale had been putting a good face on Unity Mitford's condition. Decca's sister remained profoundly disabled for the rest of her life, incontinent, physically awkward, and childlike in intelligence. She died on May 28, 1948.

95. This undated letter appears to have been the enclosure mentioned in one of the two preceding letters to Lady Redesdale.

96. None of Decca's family members can recall her ever using this word; nor was it used in her childhood home, despite her father's condescendingly ignorant view of both other social classes and foreigners (he had referred, notoriously, to his niece Joan Farrer's Argentinian husband as "a black"). Perhaps Decca, new to the country and to the South, had picked up a term that was in general use around her and was not yet aware of its highly charged connotations in the United States, although it is remotely possible she was trying to connect sympathetically with her severely injured Nazi sister. The word was used one other time in her surviving letters, although the context suggests that use may well have been a sarcastic comment on the values of some very proper acquaintances.

To Lady Redesdale   Miami
                                                          February 26, 1940

Darling Fem,

Thank you so <u>very</u> much for sending a 'gram, also for your letter, it cheered me up like mad. . . .

I wish poor Boud wasn't so depressed, do try & keep people like Rud visiting her as I'm sure that must make her feel better. I would like if possible even more news of how she really is, you see the papers here print such awful lies, for instance last month they had rumours that she was dying. One mag. (Liberty's) offered me 500 dollars for an article about her which naturally I refused; so I see they have an article describing the "fabulous mansion at High Wycombe" & pointing out that Farve is one of Princess Marina's closest friends, & talking of Winston Churchill as Bobo's uncle! . . . We have quite a funny time in the bar because when people come in & ask to see "Unity's sister" I always say "well she's not here just now, but if you come back tomorrow she may be in." One journalist wrote I had said "Unity was always a wild youngster" (I hadn't even seen him!) & next day it was in headlines in every U.S. newspaper. . . .

                              Love From Decca

To Lady Redesdale   Alexandria, Va.[97]
                                                             July 22, 1940

Darling Muv,

Thank you so much for your letter. I really am awfully sorry not to have written for such ages but I hope you got the wire I sent you indicating I was still in the land of the living. We left Miami in the end of May. The last part of our time there was awfully pleasant as there was hardly any work to do & we spent the mornings on the beach & the rest of the time eating up the delicious free Italian food. Then we left & travelled up the West Coast of Florida, which is too lovely for words, much nicer than the Miami part. We stayed in New Orleans for a week or so, it is a lovely place just like a Southern French town or rather like Southern French towns used to be up to this year. Then we drove up through Alabama & Georgia & West Virginia to Washington & N.Y. If you look at the map you'll realise what a colossal distance we've been. I must say it's lovely to be back in the North, I simply loathe the old South & old Southerners, they are completely uncivilised & are too vile about the negroes, in fact they're just like Empire Builders in their attitude & I found them extremely depressing. . . .

Do continue to let me have news of everyone because otherwise I never hear

---

97. Sent from the home of Virginia and Clifford Durr. For more background, see the introduction to the next section of letters.

it. Wasn't it sad about Cousin Bertram,[98] Esmond's mother wrote to him & seemed to be in a terrible state, what with that and Giles being captured.[99] We tried unsuccessfully to get some news of Giles from here. When you next write don't forget to tell all news of Boud. I <u>so</u> hope to hear that she is almost better by now. Robin is always most cheerful & hopeful about her in her letters. Give my love to Henderson. I'll write to her soon, & tell her that if she would like to come over here I could easily arrange a soft berth for the young thing: some millionaire's household where she would be provided for in the manner to which she's accustomed as people here have gone mad on the subject of taking in refugees. Well I must scram now but will write again soon.

Best Love From Decca

---

98. Bertram Romilly, Esmond's father, had died of cancer in May.

99. Giles Romilly, Esmond's brother, was reporting for the *Daily Express* when he was captured in Narvik, Norway, on April 9, at the start of the German invasion. He was sent to Colditz, a maximum-security German prison camp, where he was kept under close watch with other VIP prisoners because he was Winston Churchill's nephew. He remained incarcerated for the rest of the war.

Decca and Esmond Romilly in London, planning their February 1939 "escape" to America.

Late in 1939 or early in 1940, the Romillys, now bartender and cashier-waitress, demonstrated their new professional skills at the Roma bar in Miami.

II

AMERICA,
IN LOVE
AND WAR

At one of her sales jobs in 1939
or 1940, Decca displayed her
wares at a dress shop.

With her daughter,
Constancia, in
October 1941.

Esmond Romilly finally had the signal he was waiting for. Convinced that the turning point had arrived in England and the threat of Nazi appeasement was over, he made inquiries with British and Canadian diplomats in Washington about volunteering in the Royal Canadian Air Force. His other business was to make arrangements for Decca to be well situated during his absence. He turned to his network of friends from previous visits to the capital. The couple felt an attachment to the city. During one earlier visit, Decca had described Washington as "quite a fascinating place, so unlike New York it seems like an eternal Sunday."

The Romillys' hosts in Washington, Michael and Belinda (Binnie) Straight, were among their earliest contacts and closest friends there. Like many of their American friends, they were young, smart, well-connected and well-off; they shared English associations and radical politics. Michael Straight's mother was a Whitney heiress and his father a diplomat and J. P. Morgan and Co. partner who became rich building railroads in China. Michael Straight was educated and met his wife in England, where his mother had settled with her second husband. At a young age, he was a State Department economist and Roosevelt advisor. In 1941 he became editor (and later publisher) of the *New Republic* magazine, which had been founded by his parents.

Through Michael Straight, the Romillys had met Virginia and Clifford Durr, whose grand old farmhouse on Seminary Hill in the Washington suburb of Alexandria, Virginia, was a social center of the New Deal and a hothouse of Southern civil rights activism. The neighborhood was filled with legislators and bureaucrats, journalists, judges, and other Washington insiders. The Durrs, both native Alabamans, were ardent Roosevelt Democrats. Clifford had been a Rhodes Scholar. Virginia was descended from slave-owning Confederate aristocrats. They became passionate civil libertarians during their years in Washington, where they had been enticed in 1933 by Senator (later Supreme Court Justice) Hugo Black, Virginia Durr's brother-in-law. Clifford Durr served as counsel for the Reconstruction Finance Corporation, as a behind-the-scenes administration advisor on Southern poverty and race issues, and, later, as a member of the Federal Communications Commission. Virginia Durr devoted her years in Washington primarily to the welfare of blacks and working-class whites in the South, to the campaign against the poll tax, and to the 1948 presidential campaign of Henry Wallace. (The Durrs returned to Alabama in the early 1950s, where they played a central role in the emerging civil rights movement.)

As Virginia Durr recalled it, Esmond Romilly asked her if Decca could stay with them "over the weekend" while he went north to volunteer. Durr said no because she was going to the Democratic National Convention, but Romilly replied, "Oh do let her go with you." He said that Decca would be very lonely and the convention would be a diverting experience for her. Durr knew Decca at the time only as Romilly's "exquisitely beautiful" wife. When she'd seen them together, Decca "never said anything," Durr recalled. "Esmond did all the talking. He was such a great talker and completely dominated any situation he was in . . . so fascinating and so interesting." The two were "as one," Durr recalled, but "Esmond was the one." She agreed to put up the young woman briefly and take her to the convention. Neither could have guessed it at the time, but Decca remained at the Durrs' for the next two years, becoming a member of the family and a lifelong friend.

Virginia Durr could also not have imagined the inconvenience of taking Decca to the convention in Chicago. Decca was suffering from morning sickness. She "threw up all the way from Washington to Chicago—it seemed to me at every filling station." That was how Durr learned of her pregnancy, which Decca hadn't disclosed previously. They were given access to the convention floor by Durr's Texas New Deal friends, including freshman Representative (and, decades later, President) Lyndon Johnson and Undersecretary of the Interior Alvin Wirtz, who made them members of the Texas delegation. The young Englishwoman and her Alabaman hostess were given delegates' credentials, large straw sombreros, and lariats. "We had the greatest time you can imagine," Durr wrote.

In the sweltering convention hall, they were seated "100 miles from the ladies' room," said Durr, who wrote in her autobiography that she told one of the Texas delegates, "I've got a young English girl with me who throws up all the time. What in the name of God are we going to do?" She said the delegate, wearing a fine felt sombrero, "went over and swept off his hat like Sir Walter Raleigh and said to Decca, 'Madame, use my hat if you need it.' . . . Fortunately, she didn't throw up in his hat, but she kept it in her lap the whole time." The Texans likened Decca's ornery fetus to the Democrats' mascot donkey "kicking up its heels"—a small donkey, or dinky donkey. The nickname stuck, in various permutations, and the Romillys' daughter Constancia is still known to friends as Dinky.

After the convention, Decca had planned to seek work in New York, but she was still suffering when they got back to stifling-hot Washington. Virginia Durr, who had become "very devoted" to her, asked her to stay with them until the expected arrival of an Oxford University librarian's wife seeking refuge with her child from Hitler's threatened air raids. When that guest decided to take her chances in England rather than risk encountering a German submarine en route to the United States, Decca said to Virginia Durr, "Well, if you want a British refugee, you've got one." She stayed on, paying her way with an RCAF dependent's allowance, a portion of her husband's salary, and a succession of jobs. By then she was so well connected that, shortly after her return from Chicago, her job search was reported in the *Washington Post*, courtesy of the Romillys' friend, publisher Eugene Meyer. Decades later, Decca described the two years she remained at the Durr home as "a marvelous introduction to contemporary American history and thought. . . . I was the lucky fly-on-the-wall, afforded a rare opportunity for an unforgettable education, which served me well in my future life."

As Decca became established in Washington as a career woman, student, and mother with a growing circle of influential friends, she was in only sporadic contact with her English family. She was deeply suspicious of their fascism, as, indeed, were the British government and public. The memory was still fresh of Unity Mitford's return on a stretcher early in 1940, when she was said to have told one of the clamoring reporters, "I'm very glad to be in England, even if I'm not on your side." A couple of months later, Lord Redesdale felt compelled to write to *The Times* of London that he wasn't a fascist and had never been one. Lady Redesdale never made any secret of her Nazi sympathies. Diana Mosley was called "extremely dangerous and sinister" by the head of the MI5 intelligence agency, and within days of the time Esmond Romilly headed to Canada to enlist, she was imprisoned for her pro-Nazi activities; her husband had been interned a month earlier.

The Romillys were living apart for the first time in their brief married life. They had periodic phone conversations and visits during Esmond's year of training in Canada, but mostly they communicated in often daily letters, which both of them treasured. (When Decca sold her personal papers to Ohio State University's archive decades later, she had one reservation: she wouldn't relinquish the wartime correspondence with her first husband until photocopies were made for her to keep.)

The couple's separation was more disturbing than either could fully express. As early as mid-July 1940, as Romilly was en route to Canada, he wrote Decca, "I have missed you enormously the last few days—it has been similar to a prolonged dull kind of stomach ache. . . . The car, driving around, having meals, club breakfasts, arriving in new places etc. have all point removed when done without you." He relished receiving Decca's letters "with everything you've been doing down to the tiniest detail."

Among the details she does not seem to have shared is that she began to pick up a few rudiments of housework from Virginia Durr, who was determined to "domesticize her." Durr said Decca arrived at her home without knowing how to wash her stockings and underwear, nor how to make a bed. "She kept saying she saw no reason to make a bed—she thought it was ridiculous to make a bed every day when you got right back into it at night. . . . She absolutely had never done one single domestic task. She either had not done them or had servants to do them."

Another element of Decca's life in Alexandria that isn't adequately reflected in surviving letters was the interest of the FBI and the British Embassy in her background and activities. Virginia Durr recalled that Decca was "watched all the time." Agents' suspicions apparently centered on her sisters' Nazi connections as well as her husband's service in the Spanish Civil War. As Durr summarized it, Decca was "watched both for left and right tendencies. It got so that the FBI would come so often that the children would just call upstairs, 'Mother, the milkman's here,' 'Mother, the grocery man's here,' 'Mother, the FBI's here.' And we just got to accept them as the routine of life." According to Decca's FBI files, the bureau's interest seems to date from 1940, soon after Decca returned from the Democratic convention. At the time, in Decca's words, she was "a staunch fellow-traveller but not a member" of the Communist Party.

Esmond Romilly returned to Alexandria for Christmas 1940. Virginia Durr once described the visit for a documentary film crew: "He was one of the most attentive husbands I've ever seen and one of the most devoted. . . . I've never seen two people more completely in love as they were. I've never seen any two people that seemed to be so completely one, then he went back to Canada." At that point, Durr broke down in tears.

Although the birth of Constancia in February 1941 is described at length in Decca's correspondence, she omitted some details that she has recounted elsewhere. She refused the offer of Eugene Meyer's wife, Agnes, to get her a private room with round-the-clock nursing, opting instead for a public ward. When the nurses weren't responsive enough with bedpans for one of her roommates, Decca—in what she called her "first successful effort at organizing for mass action"—staged a communal "pee-in." According to Virginia Durr, when they brought her home, "the nurses were very glad indeed to get her out of the hospital."

In 1939, while the Romillys, newly arrived in the country, had been visiting with Selden Rodman and his wife on Martha's Vineyard, Germany and the Soviet Union announced their non-aggression pact. Rodman was a poet, essayist, and co-editor of the radical magazine *Common Sense*, for which Romilly wrote. It was during the 1939 Martha's Vineyard visit, Decca wrote in *Daughters and Rebels*, that "[a]fter long discussion, we decided not to go back home until the fighting really started and we knew what side we were going to be on." In the meantime, as the Romillys toured the country and then Esmond Romilly trained to go to war, the American Communist Party was isolationist. At the end of June 1941, in one of those tidy symbolic symmetries of history, the Romillys were back with Selden and Hilda Rodman on Martha's Vineyard for an idyllic four days of swimming, tennis, poker, drinking, and animated laughter and conversation, in the course of which they learned that Germany had just invaded the Soviet Union, reconfiguring wartime alliances for countries and political parties as well as for individuals. The two couples listened on the radio as Winston Churchill addressed the world, declaring common cause with the Soviet Union.

Those two events while the Romillys were on Martha's Vineyard were book-ends for their two years together in the United States. On the morning after the invasion of Russia, Esmond Romilly headed north to Halifax, Nova Scotia, to ship off for England and fight the Germans. Decca never saw him again.

The young couple spent the next few months trying to decide whether, when, and how Decca—and possibly their daughter, Constancia—would join Esmond back in Britain. In mid-November, Romilly lost four of his best friends when their aircraft didn't return from missions. He was devastated. He gave his wife the go-ahead, and Decca inquired at the British Embassy about passage to Britain. She was informed that she would have to go by ship, and she secured passage on a ship sailing from New York on December 5, 1941. On December 2, the day before she was to leave Washington for New York with Constancia, she received a telegram from Ottawa informing her that her husband's plane had not returned from a mission to Bremen on November 30. It was presumed down in the North Sea. Esmond Romilly was twenty-three years old; the wreckage of his plane was never found.

Decca went into a period of deep grief and disbelief, of which there are only hints in her surviving correspondence. In her denial, as in so many other aspects of her early life, Decca reflected her husband's attitude. His good friend Philip Toynbee wrote that, in any circumstances, Esmond Romilly "wore his ability to survive like a halo." According to Romilly's biographer, Kevin Ingram,* Selden Rodman's journal quoted Romilly on the eve of his departure for England as saying, "decisively, but matter-of-factly," that "I have no doubt at all that I will survive this war whether shot down or not." Decca continued to believe it might be so. Virginia Durr once described the desolation and agony that Decca could never bring herself to describe fully in her letters or memoirs:

> It was very hard for her to accept the fact of his death. She kept believing that he wasn't dead and that maybe by some miracle he had escaped. . . . In the night I would hear her saying, "Oh the water was so cold, the water was so cold." . . . She was so brave. I never have seen anyone as brave as she was . . . completely alone in a strange country. . . . The British Embassy was always trying to get her to go home, and she would storm into the house and say she wasn't going back to her "filthy fascist family."

Winston Churchill made inquiries about Esmond Romilly's disappearance at the request of his sister-in-law Nellie Romilly, Esmond's mother, and learned that the young aviator could not have been taken prisoner and had surely died in the crash of his disabled plane. When Churchill, whom Decca knew slightly

---

Rebel: The Short Life of Esmond Romilly (Weidenfeld & Nicolson, 1985).

from childhood family visits, went to Washington in December—leaving London days after Pearl Harbor for his first wartime meeting with President Franklin Roosevelt—he met with Decca at the White House and conveyed the results of his initial inquiries. Decca was inconsolable.

Although reports of the meeting differ in some details, Churchill—perhaps to cover the awkwardness of the moment—at some point changed the subject and assured Decca that he was making sure that her sister Diana was made comfortable in prison and he had recently allowed her husband to join her in a Holloway prison complex. Decca was infuriated. She considered her sister a traitor to her country, unworthy of special favors or prison "servants," and, now, an ally of her husband's killers. On Decca's way out of the meeting, Churchill's aide gave her an envelope that she later found contained $500. She said she considered it "sort of blood money" and "gave most of it to Virginia Durr for the anti-poll tax, and I bought a horse for her daughter Ann, who was crazy about horses and wanted to have her own." Unfounded rumors circulated in London that she had spit in the prime minister's face. Churchill reportedly later told Tom Mitford that Decca was still a fanatical Communist.

After Esmond's death, Decca's family invited her to return home, but Decca considered it "quite pointless to go back. . . . I had nobody to go back to." Although she maintained a minimal correspondence with her faithful mother, she felt that "I was at war with everything they stood for, and vice versa."

She continued on at the Durrs' home through the spring of 1942. During this period, Virginia Durr secretly sent several letters to Lady Redesdale because she was worried about Decca's ability to earn enough to support herself and Constancia. Durr characterized Decca as "a stranger in a strange land" who was "so worn with anxiety and crushed with alternate hope and despair that she cannot look ahead. . . . She has been hurt so much by circumstance and her fierce pride," adding that "I have never seen anyone that so hated to be beholden to anyone." She assured Lady Redesdale that Decca nevertheless retained "in her heart an affection for you and her sisters and for her brother that nothing can erase. . . . [T]here seems to be an intense family feeling still."

In the following months, Decca completed five months of study at the Strayer business school, learning dictation and typing. From March to September, she worked as a secretary in Washington for the Royal Air Force Delegation, where she gained a reputation (the FBI later learned) as a good worker and an outspoken opponent of fascism and the English class system, though she apparently kept her family background to herself. Her boss told FBI investigators the following year that according to office rumor, Decca was "the daughter of some Lord or Earl in England" and the sister of the much-publicized Unity Mitford, "a close friend of Adolph Hitler," but the informant said he did not "place much stock" in the rumor.

Decca resigned from the RAF Delegation in September 1942 to take a position as a clerk-typist in the Office of Price Administration—to "aid the war effort"—and while there pursued various covert strategies, which she recounted years later,* to convey the impression of professional competence. She rose quickly to become an assistant investigator.

In late December 1942, Robert Treuhaft, an attorney at the OPA, wrote his Jewish mother in New York that he had been invited to attend "a dance at one of the most exclusive Virginia homes," where he and his roommate "were the only non-Congressmen or non-Commissioners or non-Directors—and certainly the only non-Aryans, present. . . . All the women were skinny and seven feet tall, and looked down their noses at us." He attributed his "sudden appearance on the Washington social scene" at this and similar events to "my wild, uncontrollable and completely futile infatuation for the most terrific female the world has ever seen," Decca Romilly, whom he had "discovered" in a cafeteria line at the OPA. He told his mother that Decca was "constantly sought after by the local aristocracy and the diplomatic set, and she's constantly throwing them out of her house because she hates stuffed shirts." He praised her beauty and talent, adding, "she shines with a kind of fierce honesty and courage." He assured Aranka Treuhaft that "in spite of my exaggerated claims, the situation is under control." It wasn't.

In February 1943, Decca packed her two-year-old daughter, a tricycle, and thirteen pieces of luggage into a Pullman bunk and moved across the country to San Francisco, where she'd arranged to be transferred by the OPA. As with her emigration to the United States, there were intertwined reasons. San Francisco had always been on the Romillys' dream itinerary, although they'd never made it there together, cutting short their tour in New Orleans so that Esmond could enlist. And, as Decca later revealed to her dear friend Maya Angelou, "I tended to flee the scene if things had gone too wrong there (such as dashing to SF in 1943; I didn't really tell it all in *Conflict*,† but much had to do with Esmond's death & all those associations)."

On another occasion, she wrote that she "was longing to get away from Washington—specifically, from Bob Treuhaft . . . who I thought was courting me but who turned out to be engaged to Ms. Ann Other." Treuhaft had a very different version of the story, saying that soon after he met Decca, while his good friend Mimi Miller was out of town, he and his housemate had recorded a ditty proposing marriage that was sent to Miller and several other young women. "Even more rashly, we played it for Decca," he said, "thinking it would amuse her. Soon afterward, Decca told me that she had decided to accept a transfer to the S.F. OPA office. It was not until later that she admitted to me that she had indeed taken our brilliant effort seriously."

When her train pulled out of Washington, Decca wrote, "To my surprise

* See, for example, letter of January 6, 1964, to Betty Friedan.
† Her memoir *A Fine Old Conflict* (Alfred A. Knopf, 1977).

and pleasure, the faithless Treuhaft came to see us off—he even stayed on the train for several stops until chucked off by the conductor."

The story of Decca's wartime experiences during and immediately after Esmond Romilly's enlistment begins with a letter mailed from the Durrs' house soon after her return from the Democratic National Convention.

■■

To Esmond Romilly   Alexandria
                                                                  ca. July 25, 1940

My Darling Cn,[1]

I'm so terribly sorry you haven't had any of my letters—I sent a long one to the Buffalo but you must have scrammed. I so <u>adore</u> getting your letters. You are sweet to have written such a lot, I absolutely roared about the recruits' yellow liquid & the man asking about the harlots. I'm terribly sorry things are getting so boring—you just have to let me know & I'll come scramming post haste to Canada at once. I <u>do</u> miss you so darling, & please try not to have a boring time, it's so awful to think of an old Boot being bored all by its self in Canada.

I must tell you about the Convention, it was <u>simply</u> wonderful. First of all the convention characters. The Alabama Country boy[2] who drove us turned out to be quite nice once one got past him being an Old Southern Gentleman making coy remarks like "I know why you ladies need so much baggage—it's all that make-up you use!" He turned out quite a staunch old character. . . .

We had no trouble getting seats to the Convention but I found one couldn't see much from the balcony, so the second day I went up to an official looking man & told him I was lost & my friends were in a box & the policeman wouldn't let me in; so he said I could sit in his box, & he turned out to be the Secretary of State for Illinois & I sat right behind Mrs. Woodrow Wilson in the best place of all! Next day found an even more amazing turn of events. Had you been in the gallery just behind the Texas delegation you would have seen, sitting with the delegates & wearing an alternate's badge, 1 small Slipper!!! From then on I was a Texan alternate & so was Virginia (she got the badges, I'll never know how) & I've still got my badge. I've put it in the Interesting Things file!! You must admit it was a <u>terrific</u> triumph.

The whole convention was the most ridiculous & undemocratic thing I've

---

1. None of Decca's family knows or can recall the origins of this nickname for Esmond Romilly.
2. Ervin (Red) James, who worked in Clifford Durr's office at the time. In 1952, after the Durrs returned to Alabama, Clifford Durr started a law practice in Montgomery, sharing offices with James.

ever seen, everything of importance was arranged behind the scenes just as one imagines in smoke filled-ers, & being with Virginia I was able to be in on a good many of those & listen to fascinating conversations about swinging old so-and-so's bunch in such & such a delegation, & putting pressure on the Garner[3] group etc. I longed to know more about all the people & most of all longed for you to be there, you'd have simply adored it. We went to the resolutions committee on the first day (the Man caused quite a furore because Virginia told me to be there early & reserve seats, so I went & sat at the big table in the middle which looked to me a good place but turned out to be only for committee members). More or less anyone can speak before it & there were a number of rather boring ones about insurance companies, & the status of Indians etc & then there was a heated discussion about intervention in the war which was about the only interesting thing we heard between Sen. Wheeler[4] & the rest of the committee. Although the Resolutions Committee is supposed to decide the platform it doesn't really at all, as apparently the platform is written at the White House ages before. There were terrific rumours going around, e.g. that McNutt[5] had packed the gallery with his supporters & that when he made his speech declining the nomination for vice pres. they were tipped off to interrupt him with cheers every time he began "in the first place . . ." & not to let him speak until he started with a different phrase. Certainly there was <u>terrific</u> booing of Wallace's name & everyone said that McNutt was the only man who'd improved himself politically. Also apparently Mayor Kelly (of Chicago)'s boys took a spare microphone into the basement & put on almost the entire so-called spontaneous demonstration for Roosevelt.[6]

Virginia took me to a number of fascinating dinners of high-up politicians, in fact I don't think anyone could have had a better time seeing the convention than I did. Also we were taken round to see the Chicago stockyards & the scene

---

3. John Nance Garner, vice president from 1933, had split with President Roosevelt on a number of policy issues during their second term and strongly disagreed with Roosevelt's decision to seek a third term as president in 1940. Garner put his own name forward as an alternative in order to stop Roosevelt's renomination. Roosevelt easily defeated his challengers and chose Secretary of Agriculture Henry A. Wallace as his running mate.

4. Senator Burton K. Wheeler, a populist Montana Democrat, was a leading isolationist who told the Senate in one debate that the Lend-Lease Bill to send aid to the Allies "will plow under every fourth American boy." Although nominally a candidate for the presidential nomination in 1940, he withdrew after securing passage of a platform plank on the intervention issue that satisfied him.

5. Former Indiana governor Paul V. McNutt was head of the Federal Security Agency. He withdrew from the vice presidential race when Roosevelt announced his preference for Henry Wallace.

6. Mayor Ed Kelly, Roosevelt's friend and supporter, performed his electronic trickery when a message was read from the president coyly informing convention delegates that they were free to nominate whomever they wished for the presidential nomination. According to the Chicago Historical Society, "As this memo was being read, an amplified voice broke in shouting 'No! No! No! We want Roosevelt!' . . . The voice belonged to Thomas D. Garry, Chicago's superintendent of sewers. The convention went into an uproar and Roosevelt won the nomination with 946 votes."

of the Memorial Day Massacre by the local C.I.O.[7] people. Oh and by the way of course we spent the inevitable morning being dragged round a lot of pseudo Gothic chapels & forced to look at the University buildings.

The whole trip cost just $30 each & I've cashed the following checks so far: $25, $15 & $30. I still have $20 left but I bought a black dress with a full skirt for $10 to last till I have to have maternity clothes, the man's tum is beginning to show slightly in some things.

Virginia has very kindly (& entirely due to you, you clever old Bird) asked me to stay as long as I want & so I said I would for a few weeks, but of <u>course</u> if there's any chance of seeing you I could scram North in a second. I'm going to see about my reentry permit tomorrow. It so happens that tomorrow afternoon will find me seated in a plane beside Mr & Mrs Meyer heading for Mt Kisco[8] for the weekend. I'm looking forward to it like mad (tho' Virginia is v. scornful & says I'll be wallowing in the Meyer of reaction) but of course it won't be half as much fun as last time when you were there.

I enclose Meyer's letter, he said if you'd like him to write anything further you only had to say the word.[9] I do hope you'll think it's alright as he already sent it to the RCAF; he explained that he mentioned about the money as proof of your good faith etc as he thought actual proof was very important. Anyway do let me know if you want him to write anything further.

I do so hope darling that you'll soon get settled. I so hate to think of how dull & lonely it must be for you. Yr. Man thinks of you day & night & sometimes when I wake up in the morning I almost think you are there. I so adore getting your letters—by the way night telegrams only cost 58 cents for 50 words so I'll send one tonight as I'm afraid this won't arrive for ages. As you see from this letter my plans are completely flexible & I can use this house as a base as long as I want. However if you should return here don't let's stay here as I think it would be more fun either chez Straight or in the old Westminster. This house is rather cluttered up with children & old mothers etc. Must scram now to catch airmail & do write again soon.

Very Best Love, Yr MAN

---

7. Congress of Industrial Organizations. On May 30, 1937, police had fired on marchers supporting a Republic Steel strike organized by a committee of the CIO. Ten of the marchers were killed.

8. Mount Kisco, in Westchester County north of New York City, was the site of the Meyer family's estate.

9. In a letter sent July 21, Esmond had told Decca that "all I have to do is wait till the school certificate confirmation comes from Wellington, and the character letter from Meyer, and then I'll be told when I'll start training."

To Esmond Romilly   Seven Springs Farm, Mount Kisco, N.Y.
                                               "Friday night in luxurious Meyer bedroom"
                                                                        July 26, 1940

Darlingest Cn,

I got your telegram late last night. You must be awfully pleased everything is settled, yr. Man was <u>so</u> sorry to hear what a dull time you were having—the description of your average day made it all but sob. I'm dying to hear from you about your plans, how long the training will take etc & most of all when I'll be able to see you again, of course I know it won't be for ages. . . . I couldn't help being a bit sad it meant I couldn't come up & see you now, but as everything is fixed I'm going to start looking for a job right away which I'm looking forward to. I've completely stopped being sick by the way, & feel terrifically well. Staying chez Durr has been wonderful, it's such a free & easy household & Virginia has been awfully nice. Of course I'm going back there when the weekend is over.

I've more or less promised Virginia to stay there while she & Cliff go for their hol, which they are going to do next week. The idea is that I should "run the house" (which actually means nothing as it is full of large, competent Blacks running it already) & be company for her old mother. The only drawback is the old mother who is a bit mad & a terrible bore, very querulous & complainy & half ill . . . but the form is to take absolutely no notice of her & just go one's own way.

It so happened that this afternoon at 4 pm the Slipper might have been seen boarding the plane in Washington in the company of an elderly gentleman who proved to be Mr E. Meyer & holding a return plane ticket (paid for of course). At N.Y. (which was reached in 1 1/2 hours) we were met by a chauffeur & Mrs Meyer & drove down to Mt Kisco. Guinea hen in orange sauce for dinner. The Meyers are in very good pro-one form & I can see will be colossally useful. You <u>were</u> a good boot to save them up for me, in fact the usual shrewd farseeing Boot. They both talked about you a lot as everyone does, the old Bird certainly left its mark in Washington society. No one else is here yet, just me & the Meyers which is very pleasant. It seems amazing to scram slap out of the cozy New Dealish atmosphere I've been in into the middle of the Willkyites.[10] I must say Mr Meyer is far more innaresting than most of Virginia's friends, like the Blacks[11] etc. We went out to dinner last night with one of Cliff's relations & the Blacks were there, & everyone was ribbing me about going to stay with the Meyers so I couldn't help saying that I knew which side my bread was buttered, by way of ticking off the Justice about the letter. Everyone roared, they weren't at all offended. . . . You note from all this I'm having a wonderful time in Wash, I think I shall definitely get a job there rather than N.Y. (The Straights are back too, by the way.)

---

10. Wendell Willkie was the Republican candidate for president in 1940, running against Franklin Delano Roosevelt.

11. Virginia Durr's sister, Josephine, was married to Supreme Court Justice Hugo Black.

I'm so longing to hear from you & know where you'll be staying & everything. . . .
I wish the Man[12]

To Esmond Romilly   Seven Springs Farm, Mount Kisco, N.Y.
                                                    July 29, 1940
Darling Cn,
This is my last day of the incredible luxury of Meyerism—I'm taking the
plane back to Wash. this afternoon. I've enjoyed the wknd enormously & must
tell you all about it. Sat morning the Man woke about 9:30 & without bothering to open its eyes reached out & pressed the button M (for Maid). When the
M arrived I directed her to press my dress, clean my white shoes & serve breakfast. Shortly the Man was served with ice-cold California orange juice, 1 strictly
fresh egg, 4 strips young prime bacon, steaming coffee (special brew) with thick
sweet country cream, & jumbo raspberries. It then lay back relaxing among the
pillows while its bath was running. I'm sleeping in Elisabeth's[13] bedroom which
means I'm able to economize by using her Odorono, cleansing tissues etc. The
whole of Saturday till tea time there were just me & the Meyers here. The
Meyers are rather sweet when by themselves, they slop around the house in
bedroom slippers & call each other Pa & Ma, or Ag & Eug.[14] It was considered
a terrific joke about me staying with the Durrs, apparently the Wash. Post conducted the chief press campaign against Mr. Black about him being in the
Klan.[15] Mr. Meyer says he's going to call on me one day at the Durrs to note the
form there, I hope he won't as they would be simply furious. Virulent anti New
Deal talk continued throughout the day. At tea time Dr & Mrs Gallup (poll)
arrived, also Count René de Chambrun, a French man of the greasy type who
is Laval's[16] son-in-law & seems to be here in the capacity of propagandist for
the Pétain[17] régime, and M & Mme André Maurois[18] of the old world courtly
litterateur types. Gallup, who the Meyers told me was the most entirely objective & scientific person they knew, turned out to be a rabid Republican. The

---

12. It's unclear from the available copy of this letter whether this phrase is an obscure signature
line or the beginning of a sentence that ends on a now lost page.

13. The Meyers' daughter, sister of Katharine.

14. For Agnes and Eugene.

15. Virginia Durr's brother-in-law Hugo Black had been appointed by President Roosevelt to
the Supreme Court in 1937. During his confirmation battle it was rumored—and later
confirmed—that for a time the Alabama politician and future liberal justice had been a member of
the Ku Klux Klan.

16. French politician Pierre Laval was a Nazi collaborator who had twice been premier in the
1930s and returned to the top echelons of the government in 1940 under Marshal Pétain, later succeeding him.

17. Henri-Philippe Pétain was the French war hero who became the collaborationist premier in
June 1940 and championed the armistice with Germany.

18. The French writer.

New Dealers say that he's sold out to Willkie for a huge sum & that his polls from now on will show a steady Republican rise, of which fact I didn't bother to inform him. Actually he's extremely nice & interesting. I told him about the J.W.T. mkt rschers[19] & how we used to fill in the forms in cafés half the time, but he claims to have an absolutely water tight method of checking on his investigators. . . .

The talk was all about France & how the defeat was entirely due to the fact that the Front Populaire govt. had given all the army equipment to the Reds in Spain. Even the Meyers seemed to think that a bit far fetched.

Next day (Sunday) the Westbrook Peglers[20] came over to lunch. Pegler talks just like his column, almost spitting with fury about the AFL,[21] New Deal etc. I was sitting next to him, & said I'd been so interested to read his exposé of the Bartenders' Union racket in Miami. He said "Oh were you down there this winter?" So I said "Yes, & my husband was a bartender there." He looked terribly taken aback & everyone simply roared. When I asked him for details, which bars were in the Union etc he couldn't name a single one. After much thought he said he believed the Empire Bar was. So I said we had known the bartender there very well & he'd never even heard of the Union which was rather a tease. The whole thing was v. funny. . . .

Well I must scram now. I'm writing this in my nightie before getting up & it's already 12:30. As soon as I get to Wash. I'm going to investigate the possibilities of a few jobs, Mrs Meyer is being very nice & helpful, & I'm longing to start. . . .

Goodbye you darling old Bird, I <u>am</u> so fond of you.
Very Best Love From Your Slipper

To Esmond Romilly   Alexandria
July 31, 1940

Darlingest Cn,

I was so delighted & pleased to hear all your news, & the news that you would get some leave from time to time made the Man simply hop & skip with pleasure, it really is <u>wonderful</u> & so swell to have something like that to look forward to. The best of all was to hear everything is interesting & the old Boot really seems to be a happy old thinger, your letter from Ottawa describing days in the park spent examining yr. athlete's foot made me feel it was awful for me to be Durring & Meyering in such comfort. I could hardly believe there'd be a

---

19. Decca had worked briefly as a market researcher for the J. Walter Thompson advertising agency before she and Esmond left London for the United States.

20. The pugnacious, right-wing syndicated newspaper columnist was at the peak of his popularity in this period. He won a Pulitzer Prize the following year for exposing labor union corruption.

21. American Federation of Labor.

letter for me today as you'd written so much already, but I scrammed out at crack of dawn in my dressing gown to the mail box (it's across the street & quite a walk but I never wait to dress before going) & sure enough there was a Bird's mess. I'll say I was pleased. . . .

Now to tell my slews or Slipper's news. I spent Monday coming back by plane with Meyer, he showed me the letter you wrote & has really taken the bit about keeping 1/10th eye on me seriously as you will see when I tell you what happened (I mean next day). He had a huge box of flowers the size of a small coffin packed for me to take to Virginia as a sort of joke because of the Durrs being so anti the Meyers. . . .

Virginia quite saw the joke of Meyer's flowers but Cliff attacked me terrifically about staying there & said he thought it most unprincipled of me because they are such vile people & were so awful about Justice Black. Apparently Cliff hates the Meyers worse than anyone he knows.

Virginia told me she'd had lots of phone calls from someone who wanted to give me a job—they'd seen a picture of me in the Post (it appeared Saturday), I've sent you the original under separate cover, with an article saying I was looking for a job (I won't bother to send the article as it's v. boring & I want it for the scrapbook). I was quite excited & called back & made an appointment the next day (yesterday). I also had to go to Garfinkel's store with a note from Mrs. Meyer. Virginia & I went in to lunch with Kathryn Lewis[22] & Alinsky,[23] the man we met in Chi who runs the Back of the Yards Council, which was quite innaresting, & then I scrammed off to see Miss Lilian Rose, the lade who'd phoned. The place turned out to be a v. expensive dress shop called Erlebachers with clothes up to $200 & furs up to $5,000 & I could see the idea was to bring the Man in to give it tone. Miss Rose & Mr Finklebaum (the boss) were too fascinating, she was an awful short lade dressed in black lace with a horrid intimate, pushing sort of smile & he was the getting down to business type who keeps saying "Frankly, Mrs Romilly," & "Now; what d'yer want to do? what's yer experience." However they were quite nice & offered me a job there to start when I liked. When I said what would the salary be he said that Frankly Mrs Romilly a few dollars more or less made no difference in a high class store of that type & that if I liked the place & did well I could be sure they would pay well. So I said I'd tell them in a few days & went to Garfinkels. Things there were much more natural with a terrific form to fill out (colour of hair, mother's maiden name etc) & no results.

---

22. The daughter and assistant of United Mine Workers leader John L. Lewis, cofounder of the Congress of Industrial Organizations (CIO). She was a good friend of Virginia Durr. Like her father, Kathryn Lewis had become a thoroughgoing isolationist. They had split with Roosevelt and endorsed Republican Wendell Willkie for president.

23. Community organizer Saul Alinsky, who helped organize the pioneering multi-ethnic Back of the Yards Neighborhood Council to encourage social and industrial reform in Chicago's depressed stockyards neighborhood.

So then I went to the "Post" offices as I'd told Meyer I'd let him know how I made out. When I told him about Miss Lilian Rose & Mr Finklebaum, Mr Meyer produced your letter to him & said he felt responsible for getting me something really good, & that he would get his advertising manager to check all the stores & find out where I'd be best treated & they wouldn't embarrass me by commercialising on publicity etc; so to cut a long story short he sent for the man, a Mr Barnard,[24] & more or less said "See that Mrs Romilly gets a first rate job in pleasant surroundings & don't fail to do it." Such power almost overwhelms one!! So tomorrow I'm going to lunch with Mr Barnard & the fashion editress & various important heads of stores, & I really think I might get something wonderful. All this, in fact all the pleasant things that are happening, are entirely & solely due to you & your clever old Bird's planning, you really <u>are</u> a marvel & you certainly have done well by your man. . . .

All the New Dealers are very depressed about the election & the others are rubbing their hands & chortling over it, & one definitely has the feeling that Roosevelt's star is setting & Willkie's rising. I'm reading Roosevelt's speeches in 5 vols & have got to where he's governor of N.Y.; in those speeches one can absolutely see he & his ideas were on the way up, just as Willkie seems to be now. Democrats are deserting by the hundreds every day & going over to Willkie.

I must stop now you old Boot tho I could go on writing for ages, I feel almost as though I were chatting to my old Thinger when I write to it. I do wish my letters were funny & interesting like yours.

Goodbye my darling, please have a nice time because that's the one thing I think about.

All my love, Yr Slipper

P.S. <u>Bulletin on Stomach.</u>[25] When I was in Erlebacher's they asked me to walk round as they might want me to model too!! That proves it can't be too bad yet. . . .

To Esmond Romilly   Alexandria
                                                                ca. August 2, 1940

My Darling Bird,

. . . It so happens that yesterday the Man landed a job paying $30 a week, & is to start on the 19th August!!!!! Also that a $5 raise is almost inevitable after a few months, except I probably shan't still be of a size & shape to be working by the time the raise is due. I went to lunch with Mr Bernard, the man I told you about, & there was Mr Weinberger, the head of a terrifically expensive dress

---

24. In later letters he's called Mr. Bernard.
25. A reference to Decca's pregnancy.

shop, who had <u>flown up</u> from Tennessee <u>specially</u> to see the Slipper about the job. The frightful thing was I was exactly 1 hour late for lunch, because I called a taxi to take me to the bus stop & it simply never arrived tho I kept on ringing up but they couldn't find the way for a whole hour. However it evidently didn't matter as the whole pnt was to give the Weinbergers the idea that I didn't specially mind if I took the job or not. First there was some talk of putting in the advts that I was working for them which I absolutely refused to do, so they dropped that & now I'm just going to work there anyway. The shop is fairly small, selling clothes from about $80 to $700 & my salary of $30 is a drawing-account against 5% commission, but I get it anyway for 3 months. I really am terrifically pleased as it won't be at all hard work, I mean not in the sense that Bloomingdale's or any large store would be, & there certainly isn't any snag or disagreeable thing connected with it (like being expected to make one's friends buy) because I explained to Mr Bernard all the things I wanted to avoid in that way, & he arranged the whole job. Of course the whole thing is entirely due to you for Meyering so successfully.

I'm going to stay on here as a P.G.[26] which will be v. agreeable. . . .

We have a very social time here as you note, we go somewhere to lunch or dinner almost every day & people come in here every evening.

I am absolutely established here which is terrifically nice—also entirely due to the Boot. . . .

I'm absolutely living for the time when I can see my darling old Thinger again, I do think about you so much & long for you. . . .

Very Best Love Darling, Yr Small Person

To Esmond Romilly   Alexandria
                                                          ca. August 11, 1940

Dearest Cn,

It was nice ringing you up this morning & chatting. . . .

This morning Katharine Meyer (now Graham) & her husband[27] came over by car to drive me to the Meyer Residence on Crescent Ave for lunch. The Meyer Res is just as sumptuous & wonderful as Mt Kisco, with a drive-in front door like an embassy & pillars & a huge garden at the back. Also at lunch were 2 lawyer New Dealers called Butch & Trench or some such names, they all knew you & said how you were the life and soul of their Xmas party & how extraorder you were to hitchhike there etc. I liked Phil Graham v. much, also Katharine is <u>far</u> nicer than when we met her before & also far prettier. The

---

26. Presumably "paying guest."

27. After going to work for her father's newspaper in 1939, Katharine (Kay) Meyer met lawyer Philip Graham, then a clerk at the U.S. Supreme Court, whom she married in June 1940. Katharine Graham was later to become prominent as the publisher of the *Washington Post*, following the 1963 suicide of her husband, who preceded her as publisher.

lunch was very gay as none of the older Meyers were there & everyone was saying how the Grahams were a wonderful example of love in a cottage etc. . . . Then we came back here & Virginia's boy friend Undersecretary of the Interior Alvin Wirtz was here—he's the one who got us to be delegates at the convention, & Virginia was terribly flattered by him & seemed on the way to be having an affair with him. They are all frightfully depressed about the political situation & say that Roosevelt is ruining his own chances by letting Republicans into the administration & cabinet etc.

Hugo & Josephine (Black) came over after & we had some cold mutton in the kitchen for supper & they said that practically all the rich people in Alabama (where they've just been) are bolting & going to vote for Willkie, a thing never before known in the South. . . .

Well you old Boot it's getting late so I'll go to bed, everyone else went hours ago & I stayed to write to you. Goodbye you Darling & be a Writer & Phoners Bird.

Yr Very Loving Slipper

To Esmond Romilly   Alexandria
                                                   ca. September 1, 1940

Darling Cn,

. . . Well last week things really began to cook up and even whistle slightly. Virginia came in to try on her dress & brought Mrs. A. Wirtz with her. Mrs. Wirtz had refused to come in before as she said she knew we hadn't any dresses under $60. So I brought in all of the cheaper ones—$25 to $35 & she had just about decided to buy a $29.50 dress when the Man streaked out & came back with one for $98.50. Mrs. Wirtz thought it was wonderful & tried it on, & I skillfully removed all the others including the $29.50 one when Virginia in her helpful way said loudly "Well why don't you try on the cheap one again before you decide, honey?" I walked over to Virginia saying "somebody is using it now," & gave her a terrifically hard pinch, so she finally caught on. By this time I had also got in a $25 hat which Mrs. Wirtz said she would buy anyway; & that she would phone about keeping the dress in the morning.

I was on tenterhooks all day, & in the evening she & Alvin came round to see us. Mrs. Wirtz whispered to me "I think I'm going to buy the dress," & I was so excited that as soon as I got a chance I told Virginia. Virginia immediately piped up & said to Alvin "Oh Kitty-Mae has bought the most beautiful dress from Decca, it's a black one you'll adore it!" Alvin looked v. annoyed & said Kitty-Mae didn't need any new dresses & that anyway he hated black & Kitty-Mae said she hadn't bought it & wasn't going to & I felt desperate & this time I burned Virginia with my cigarette stub, you must admit it was maddening of her.

However next day to my great surprise & joy Kitty-Mae did ring up & say she would take the dress and the hat!! I was terribly pleased & Miss Wein-

berger was v. nice & altogether since then I've felt 100% more firmly established there. Another good thing is that Iwa, the black maid, is ill so I do all
the stock work now & don't spend so much time standing indecisively around
wondering if it would be alright to smoke a cigarette or settle down with the
Wash. Post. . . . Miss Wain has turned out to be too awful, a real elderly business lade type, ghastly snob & sucker up etc. Mr. Gilchrist is awfully nice &
likes me much more than Miss Wain on acct. of me giving the place tone; the
other day he told me a customer had said the place had really needed a lady in
it like me. Also Miss Weinberger says she hopes her child will grow up to
speak nicely, & exactly like I do; I refrained from pointing out that that is
extremely unlikely.[28]

On the Social Front: we haven't been out at night for ages but the Man fills
in & keeps contacts going with odd lunches either with Wash Post-ites or with
Brit. Embassyites, my two main entrées into the right Weinberger set. . . .

I can feel the baby skeking[29] around already. It said in the Post the other day
that Ld. Redesdale's magnificent 30-room mansion in the heart of London's
swank Mayfair was among the first requisitioned for refugees from Hitler's
bombs. I haven't had any letters except 1 drear one from Muv saying she
thought I must be in Egypt as my 'gram (requesting marriage license) was
headed "Alexandria." . . .

Tomorrow I'm lunching with Felicity Rumbold,[30] & hope to get her in to
Weinbergers to buy some clothes; will let you know any fascinating Smart Set
talk & developments. . . .

Is there anything I could send up that might gladden an old Boot's heart?
I'll send the Yorker, but I mean extra comforts like cigars, chicken breast in
jelly, etc.

I'm beginning to miss you again like anything[31] & want to see you (not that
I'm depressed or anything because I'm not a bit), of course I know I shan't for a
long time, but remember I think about you such a lot so be a writer's Boot & I'll
write often too.

Goodbye my darling old Thinger. I do so love you.
            Yr. affec Slipper

---

28. In another letter, Decca quoted Weinberger as saying, "Say, since Mrs Romilly has been
around I find I ee-nunciate more co-rectly. After I left school I was always very careful with my
grammar & pro-nunciation & at the end of that time I got to talking correctly almost naturally; but
since going back down home I sort of forgot it."

29. Apparently a Decca-ism for "scooting."

30. Felicity Bailey Rumbold was the wife of Sir Anthony Rumbold, second secretary at the
British Embassy in Washington. She was a first cousin of Decca's first cousins, the Baileys, on her
mother's side of the family.

31. Decca had recently returned from a visit with her husband.

To Esmond Romilly   Alexandria
                                                                                              September 8, 1940

Darling Cn,

I was <u>so</u> pleased to get a letter at last. . . . I can't understand how you never got any of my letters, I've written quite a lot. . . .

I so adored your letter, it was such a scream, specially the part about being checked out like kit bags.[32] Fancy the old Boot at the controls of an aeroplane. I just <u>can't</u> imagine it. People here are so funny. They always say vaguely "it's nice your husband being in the air force, he'll be able to fly down to see you for weekend." I suppose they imagine you get given an aeroplane as a sort of prize for joining. Do continue to write with <u>all</u> details as I adore getting boot news more than anything. This letter is my Bumper Sundayer & will contain complete bulletins from the Slipper front for the entire week.

<u>Tuesday</u>—Arrived at Weinbergers to start the week; Monday was a hol. During the weekend I had been thinking quite seriously how best to improve my position there, which didn't seem to be quite what it should be (& I really think at last I've succeeded in digging in there alright). As a first move I thought I'd better try & get into better, smarter & richer circles, so Tuesday night I went to a party at Miss Wace's, the British Embassyite I told you about. The party was very dull but it bore fruits almost at once.

<u>Wednesday</u>—The next day, Felicity Rumbold rang up & asked me to dinner with a State Dept. friend of hers called Mr Coe. It was the most extraorder evening I've ever spent. First of all I went to Felicity's house which is v. grand & large on Mass. Avenue, the most expensive part of Washington & Felicity was there in white tennis shorts with a French (and English) speaking Polish countess, v. like that horrid Polish lade we met here last year only even worse. Felicity said we were all going to have drinks with a friend. . . . There were some other International Smart Setters there too, all frightful, & the talk was mostly about El Morocco & the Stork Club.

Mr Coe turned out to be a very rich reactionary State Depter, & there was another ditto at dinner, he was telling how sad it was for his sister to have to break up her great friendship with dear Edda Mussolini on account of the war. After dinner Prince & Princess Hohenlohe came round; he is another horrible Pole & really a typical fascist, I mean not just a reactionary but a Jew bater & everything. She is an American glamour girl type & is coming to Weinbergers soon to buy some clothes. At the end of the evening I really felt I'd been

---

32. Esmond Romilly had recently been transferred for several weeks of guard duty to Camp Borden in Ontario, which he described as "all armyish and tenty and hutty and parady," though he was allowed briefly to work the dual controls of a plane during a practice flight. Overall, he said, he spent most of his time in "an endless succession of polishing, sweeping up, parading, waiting around, falling in on marches, right dressing, carrying kit somewhere else, answering roll calls, being assembled in alphabetical groups, waiting to see what's next, being formed in new groups, drilling in the sun, preparing barracks for inspection, and folding sheets and blankets 'Camp Borden style,' as opposed to the 'Manning Depot' style."

dragged through a filthy mire, they were all so awful & it certainly seems depressing that they seem to be the only people here that the British diplomats really like. The Rumbolds were saying how much easier it had been in Berlin to get on with important Germans than it is here to get on with important Americans, so you can imagine what they are like. However by the end of the evening I found that by dint of keeping my mouth shut I had made a very good impression which is lucky as I really do think this is the best way I can make a success of Weinbergers.

Thursday—This was my best day of all. I made my first really big sale—$140 worth of clothes to one customer, a v. drear girl wearing a Woolworth fishnet hat, & Miss Wain kept whispering to me not to waste time on her, then it turned out she was buying her trousseau & she bought her wedding dress & a suit! Clever Man. Miss Weinberger was very pleased & was all congratulaty. She is really awfully nice & I think she quite likes me by now, so Miss Wain has followed suit (she always copies Miss Weinberger) & has suddenly become very smarmy & agreeable.

Friday—Mrs Schoelkopf . . . asked me to dinner so I thought I'd better go, following up my policy of getting into the rich set. They have the most fantastic, enormous house . . . but it was v. dull & I scrammed early. . . .

Virginia came into the shop yesterday & caused a great furore by complaining loudly how expensive everything was; also 2 friends of hers were in the next fitting room & she insisted on discussing them loudly & saying how awful they were. However I sold her a dress, with great difficulty & by pretending it was brown instead of purple (she'll be furious when she sees it in the daylight).

By the end of this week I really felt I'd strengthened myself in Weinbergers 100% which is pleasing, because before I was getting a bit distressed over my obvious uselessness there.

Only bad mark of the week: a new dress came in & Miss Weinb. asked me to put it on & model it for a while, saying "It will be too large on you, it's a size 16." When I got it on it was too large, but fitted PERFECTLY round the waistline & Miss Weinb. said "you've got rather a thick waistline, Mrs. Romilly!!" So you see my chief hope lies in making myself indispensable before they note the facts.

By the way late last night I was in the loo when Ann[33] came battering on the door saying a journalist had come to see me. I was scared absolutely stiff as I immediately thought something had happened to you & they'd come round to get a comment; I was v. relieved when he said "I understand you are Miss Freeman Mitford[34] & have just arrived secretly in America!!!" I convinced him very soon there was absolutely nothing to have an interview about, so they just

---

33. The Durrs' oldest daughter.
34. Although they were generally known as the Mitfords, the family name was formally "Freeman-Mitford."

took a picture & scrammed & I don't suppose they'll even print it. If they do I'll send it so you can see my pompadour.

Have you noted how unpopular Willkie is getting, the form is nowadays that everyone, even the ardent Republican columnists & mags like Time, are saying that his campaign has gone sour just as Landon's[35] did in '36 & that he keeps making ghastly political mistakes & all the old line Republicans are getting fed up with him. Time called him "a fatter, louder Landon" & he hasn't gained in the polls for weeks, in fact he has lost strength in Maine. . . .

You dear old Thinger please write soon & tell your impressions of the Man crashing the Smart Set & everything. Also, admit this letter is simply terrific, the longest e'er written. . . .

All Love from Your Adoring Slipper

To Esmond Romilly   Alexandria
                                                  ca. September 15, 1940

Darlingest Cn,

I <u>did</u> love your birthday gram, it made me roar & I was so pleased to get it. It came over the phone during breakfast. . . .

The other day Mr. Meyer came to see me in Weinbergers, it caused a great sensation & I think upped me a lot in prestige there. The same day I went to lunch at the Post with him & Kay & Mr. Bernard, we had the usual perfectly cooked & served luncheon in the office & the secretary kept being sent for to produce things, like Meyer's letter about you. Incidentally, I noticed that letter is kept in a huge file marked "ROMILLY-ESMOND & DECCA." I suppose it contains masses of stuff about us. Meyer & Mr Bernard were madly planning my advancement at Weinbergers such as giving a cktl pty for me at the Post where there'd be a mass of rich lades. . . .

This afternoon the Wirtzs came to tea & we got into the usual inadvisable argument about the coloured people that always seems to crop up. It amazes me how these supposedly very radical New Dealer types like Alvin Wirtz have whole vast reactionary areas in their minds which one can skeke understand. I see Virginia is really amazingly tolerant for a Southernor tho to me even she seems quite narst about the poor blacks.

The other night we went to dinner at a v. grand country club with some armament manufacturors. They invited the Durrs hoping to get contracts from the RFC[36] & we accepted because I was hoping to get customers for Wein-

---

35. Alfred Landon, the Republican presidential nominee.

36. The Reconstruction Finance Corporation, where Clifford Durr was legal counsel, was initially charged with rescuing banks threatened by the Depression and making emergency loans to faltering railroads and life insurance companies. Under President Franklin Roosevelt, its mandate was broadened considerably, and its loans helped revive many sectors of the economy. It played a major role in financing the World War II military buildup.

bergers. Well as usual with that type thing it was simply ghastly & the people were horrible & one had to dance (but 4 people did promise to come Weinbergering so it was worth it in a way). One couple told me they wanted to adopt an English child for their own, & asked whether I would help them by writing to friends about it; they said "we want one of good blood whose family has been wiped out; we could give it a lovely ho-o-ome, we have tremendous acreage"!!! I said I thought they'd have to wait until a few more familys of good blood had been wiped out.

The whole party was so awful it wasn't even any good baiting them, in fact I saw Virginia giving me a horrified look at one time because I was agreeing with one young man about the wages of labourers being so much too high & that they just spent it on drink & gambling etc. . . .

I do so long for my old Boot & wish I could see it again soon.

Next week I'll try & write oftener, must scram to bed now, so goodbye darling. Your man loves you terrifically so be a writer's boot. . . .

          All Love, Yr. Slipper

To Esmond Romilly   Washington ("in Weinbergers")
                                ca. November 13, 1940

Darling old Fire Piquet R.,[37]

I got your typewritten birdsmess yesterday, faithful old thinger to have written but couldn't you do so a <u>shade</u> more often, even at the risk of missing a few fires (I see that was written at 1:30 a.m., on your beat) as yr letters are so amusing & yr. man appreciates every word of them & in fact lives for the days it gets one. A boot's eye view of the election was <u>wonderful</u>, I simply roared. Goodness I'm longing for Discharge Day. . . .

[T]he Cat is out of the bag (see illustration). On Monday I decided I just couldn't go on squeezing into my tight corset, so I wore a much looser one I found somewhere. Noth-

ing was said, tho I noted several suspicious glances in the direction of my lower abdomen. Next day Miss Weinberger and Mr. Melniker went to NY on a buying trip for the entire week, leaving me & Miss Wain & Mr. Gilchrist. I

---

37. Esmond Romilly had been informed that an ear condition automatically disqualified him for air-crew status, although his hearing apparently wasn't affected. He applied for an immediate discharge, hoping to return to England and enlist in the Royal Air Force (with his uncle Winston Churchill's assistance, if necessary), but getting discharged proved to be a time-consuming bureaucratic process. He performed various menial duties including fire piquet, or fire warden, until his discharge was granted on November 22. Within days of the discharge, he got himself reinstated in an air-observer course with the help of a Canadian member of Parliament who had good connections in the air marshal's office.

noted Miss Wain trying to bring the subject round to babies etc & finally she said "you're not fooling anyone, Mrs Romilly!" Then she pretended to be all nice & helpful but luckily I knew her narst character well enough by now not to pay any attention to her. She promised not to say anything to Miss Weinberger but I certainly don't trust her, & as <u>soon</u> as Miss Weinberger comes back (next Saturday, day after tomorrow) I shall tell her myself. . . . So now it remains to be seen whether Miss Weinberger will keep me on a bit or say I have to leave on acct. of my figure. Neither would surprise me tho I hope she keeps me on a bit as it would be a shame to miss out on all that good dough. Miss Wain really is a brute of the 1st water, I can see she longs for me to be fired. . . .

Last night I made Mrs F. <u>simply</u> furious; the only food was a watery soup with rice in it & I said to Ann "don't bother to say grace tonight, the Lord couldn't possibly make us truly thankful for this even if he made a terrific effort." Mrs F gave a little scream of horror & told Va. again what a bad influence I was.

Well I'll let you know at once about the fate of my job, if I get fired shall I come up & see you for a while? Write again soon.

Your Very Loving Man

To Esmond Romilly   Alexandria
                                                          November 20, 1940
Darling Cn,

I got your letters yesterday & you simply can't imagine how overjoyed yr Man was to hear that an old Boot will shortly be coming down. I had almost begun to fear that the sound of its scrunch on the gravel outside had been heard for the last time & now I'm <u>so</u> happy I skeke know what to do. Also Miss Weinberger said on Monday that after all she didn't think they'd be able to keep me more than about 2 weeks (she has been extraordinarily nice by the way about the whole thing) but that the job would be open for me any time, which is a pleasant thing to know. So I'm not buying a new dress but am conserving all possible cash to be getting fatted calves with when you get back. Do you think you'll be able to locate the motor, by the way?[38] Otherwise we can probably borrow one, I'll start hinting around right away. I do think we should definitely take a trip somewhere & will be trying to think of some good places; & we might scram back Durrwards for Xmas if you think that would be nice. . . .

Monday night I went to dinner with the horrid Fletchers (she's the one we went to the Dem. Convention with), they were all depressing & upper classy & being inoculated for typhoid & smallpox because they're going to spend a week

---

38. Romilly had left the couple's car on a side street somewhere in Montreal, where it had apparently been carted off in the night by trash collectors.

in Mexico City & they are sure all Latins are typhoid & smallpox carriers. However the dinner was delicious & I managed to steal a large size (49¢) tube of toothpaste when I went to the loo. . . .

Today I had lunch with Binny & Kay, Binny was <u>so</u> awful she told Kay about when I stole some of Elisabeth Meyer's silk stockings at Mt. Kisco & it didn't go down at all well as one might have known. However Kay & I are great friends by now so it didn't really matter. . . .

Well old thinger I must scram so goodbye darling & I'm <u>so</u> <u>dying</u> to see you again.

Goodbye you angel
      Love from Decca

To Esmond Romilly   Alexandria
                 early January 1941

Darling Cn,

. . . Yesterday we had a lunch pty of Helen Fuller[39] & one or two other similar f. traveller types & rather a dull girl called Ladybird Johnson,[40] I think you met her once. It was vy. nice as <u>all</u> the children & Mrs Forster were out to lunch & there was a wonderful atmosphere of unadulterated adultness which one seldom gets here. . . . Mike & Bin came over in the evening for Mike to get the whole story of Cliff's defense thing, he's going to put it in the famous New Republic supplement & the whole story is also due to appear in Ernest Lindley's column,[41] so old Cliff may be quite famous 'ere long. Binny tried to sabotage the whole thing by turning the conversation on to hermaphrodite but without success. . . .

Goodbye you <u>dear</u> old Boot, will write a proper letter tomorrow.
      Yr affec. Slipperman

PS I've started making a dress for the baby, I didn't do so while you were here[42] for fear you might throw up at the sight of the Man, its eyes glowing with the gentle light of motherhood, sewing at a Tiny Garment.

---

39. *The New Republic*'s Washington correspondent.

40. The future First Lady of the United States. Lyndon and Lady Bird Johnson often spent time at the Durrs' home. According to Decca, the Durrs called them "Ki-i-ssin' cou-ousins." Once, Decca wrote, when she told her mother that Lyndon and Lady Bird Johnson had come to tea, Lady Redesdale wrote back, "Who is Lady Bird? I looked her up in the Peerage, but could find no trace."

41. In *Newsweek* magazine.

42. Esmond Romilly had spent the Christmas holiday with Decca in Alexandria. Years later, Virginia Durr recalled that interlude in an interview for documentary filmmakers: "I've never seen anybody enjoy Christmas as much as he did." She said Esmond Romilly purchased dozens of tree ornaments and many presents and took them all out to fine restaurants, making "a great event" out of everything. He was very devoted and attentive to his pregnant wife, making her take walks, a couple of miles a day, "which she hated to do," Durr reported.

To Esmond Romilly   Alexandria
                                                                    January 1941

Darling Bird,

The Brown Sermon lunch.[43]

Well it was simply wonderful, the sort of lunch where as soon as you get outside you start whispering to each other "sh sh don't say anything yet, they can still hear." There were 4 other lades besides me & Va, & Mrs B.S. was just like those NY lades we used to meet when we first arrived with husbands called Beaver etc; she was trying to be v. smart settish, saying things like "my dear I get all my horse blankets & stable equipment from Macy's, would you believe it they have the most wonderful sports department," & when telling how she got her mother's beautiful old mahogany sideboard, "but my dear I had to do EVERYTHING short of stealing it—I even threatened her with BOUGHT mahogany for my dining room." Then there was the most awful lade in a huge gray off the face hat & piglike face who Va says is the chief social climber on the hill; she said she thought Beautiful Things had more value now than ever, & that she believed that the average European refugee family would be perfectly happy even with no home & only a crust to eat if they only had one perfect Cellini bowl, which I thought was a curious theory. . . .

The Voorhis Dinner[44]

They had quite a big pty with 2 old Voorhis parents (courtly old world types), Jerry V.'s sister, rather pretty & vivacious & California-y but quite dull, the type that shows round albums of her 2 children; the Livingstons[45] were there, they're going to have a baby in August & were all giggly & being ribbed about it; & Tom Eliot, the new congressman from Boston Mass whose picture was in Life the other day. He is v. nice, rather like Toynbee

---

43. Although it's not clear precisely who the hostess was for Decca's lunch, records show there was a family in Alexandria in those years with the surname Brown-Sermon.

44. Jerry Voorhis was a young, popular liberal Democratic member of Congress from California who would serve five terms before his defeat in 1946 following a now-notorious Red-baiting campaign waged by Richard Nixon. He and his wife, Louise, lived across the street from the Durrs. Virginia Durr recalled in her autobiography that Esmond Romilly and Voorhis, a staunch anti-Communist, had had a "great debate on Spain one night at our house before the war. Jerry had been terribly upset that Spain had let the Communists in." For Decca's accounts of encounters with Voorhis years later, see letter of May 1, 1964, to Ernest Morgan.

45. Bill Livingston was a good friend of Clifford Durr as well as his colleague at the Reconstruction Finance Corporation. Livingston's sister, Louise, was married to Congressman Jerry Voorhis. Livingston's wife, Mary, was a friend of Virginia Durr's. Decca joined the Livingston car pool into Washington, which also included Clifford Durr, economist John Kenneth Galbraith (at the time deputy administrator of the Office of Price Administration, where Decca later worked), and other New Deal insiders.

in a way; his wife[46] is one of Va's best friends & Va has got them a house out here.

Jerry was so like your imitations of him I could skeke keep from roaring, & he made the most typical Voorhisish remark about Kennedy's speech: "What I liked so much about it was it was so <u>honestly confused</u>." He was madly wrinkling his forehead about the Lend-Lease bill[47] & put on his usual act of a tortured soul trying to make up his mind in the best interests of democracy etc. He & Eliot seemed to have the most curious ideas about the war, e.g. they were both horrified by Churchill's statement that he was preparing an expeditionary force to invade Europe as they said that would extend the war & mean the US would eventually have to send an expeditionary force. . . .

Today I took Lucy & Baby Sister[48] for a walk, we went to the Sanitarium & got into conversation with one of the lunatics, she said she had twin boys of 8 & when I asked what their names were she said "I don't know, but I will call them Charles and Richard." She was quite nice tho & helped me push the pram through the mud. . . .

Good-bye you sweet dear old Bootford
Best Love From Decca

To Esmond Romilly   Columbia Hospital, Washington
                                                ca. February 12, 1941

Darlingest Cn,

It was so <u>wonderful</u> to be able to talk to you Sunday night, it absolutely made the whole difference to everything as the Man was so dying to chat to you, & although I was still a bit hazy from the ether which probably made me sound slightly drunk I was quite awake enough to note everything going on. I'm sure no one but the strong-minded old Boot could have got them to let me come to the phone, either. I'm so <u>frightfully</u> sorry I didn't telephone you Friday night when I knew I was coming here Saturday, I'm afraid you must have had an awful time Sunday not knowing what was up; but somehow I didn't want to phone you till the last minute, <u>stupid</u> Man I hope you're not furious with it. Va told me you rang her up again day before yesterday, you are such a sweet Croat to be taking an interest. Now I must tell you about the whole thing from Sat. onwards.

All Saturday I spent packing up my trunk & getting my room straight & arranging for Cliff to come & get me in time etc; from 7 p.m. till it was time to

---

46. Lois Eliot.

47. The bill, passed by Congress on March 11, gave President Franklin Roosevelt the authority to sell, transfer, lend, or lease ships and other war supplies to Great Britain and its allies in the battle against Nazi Germany. The bill, proposed by Roosevelt in response to an appeal from Winston Churchill, allowed the United States to aid the war effort while maintaining ostensible neutrality.

48. Lucy was the middle of the three daughters the Durrs had at that time, and Baby Sister was the nickname of the youngest, Virginia II, also known as Tilla (which Decca said was short for Baby Sister).

scram I was trying to get you on the phone. When it turned out that the address you had left was a ravine (the information lade in Toronto kept saying "but there is no 217 Roxborough Street, the street becomes a ravine after no. 120") I called Mary Foreman[49] to ask her mother's number, thinking you might possibly be there or she might know where you were. So the operator called her to ask (I was still putting through a person-to-person so I didn't talk to the mother, but heard the conversation between her and the operator) & the mother is evidently a dotty old woman because she kept saying "Hullo? Has the baby arrived?" & the poor operator kept saying "This is the Alexandria operator. Do you know where I can get in touch with Mr L.A.C. Romilly?" Finally the old mother caught on & she said "No; I haven't seen Mr Romilly since the Great Blizzard," at which I let out a shriek of laughter which she must have heard. So when it became apparent that the old Boot was probably lost in a ravine in the Great Blizzard I finally gave up. . . . Finally we got to the hossening,[50] which looks from the outside like a huge barrack or factory & from then on things were all nice & narsty. On the ground floor where we came in we walked round & saw all the little black babies in their nursery, they really are carried round in huge hors d'oeuvre trays & look too sweet. Then we came upstairs & were shown my bed in this ward; the others were all getting off to sleep but old Va, true to form, rampaged round the ward organizing things & asking the others questions about their husbands, babies etc till she & Cliff were chased out by the nurse & I went to bed.

Next morning the nurse came in all brisk & civic at 5 a.m. & I was given rather a curious breakfast consisting of a whole tumbler full of castor oil & an enema. I started asking when the eggs & bacon would be served but was soon shut up by the nurse. From then till about 8 a.m. I spent scramming to the loo & then Va came & we sat & had some cigs in the waiting room. I tried to get her to slip me a bit of Hershey Choc. Bar but she wouldn't. Every now & then the nurses came in & absentmindedly felt my stomach, saying "any good contractions yet?" At about 11 they took me upstairs & put me into a horrid white garment which only comes down to my stomach & is open at the back, v. indecent; & without more ado they strapped me onto a sort of medieval torture table where they tie your hands & legs down (I hope you like all these details by the way, if not skip the next bit) & announced they were going to "rupture the membrane." The Dr came in & said I could have a whiff of anaesthetic while he did it, but I said I wouldn't as I didn't want to have much anaesthetic so as not to be all dopey for days; so he stuck a rusty old nail up me (or what looked like

49. Mairi Foreman, whose name Decca usually misspelled. She was a painter and cultural figure and the wife of Clark Foreman, a white civil rights activist from Georgia and old friend and political ally of Virginia Durr. Clark Foreman was an Interior Department official charged with improving the economic status of blacks.

50. The origin of the term is unclear, but Decca uses this word in her letters as a synonym for "hospital."

one) & it didn't hurt much except it was rather humiliating being tied down. After that the nurses wheeled me into the labour room (instead of saying "here comes another patient" or even "here comes Mrs. Romilly" they just shoved me around on the stretcher saying "here comes another ruptured membrane").

Well the labour room was absolutely fascinating. It seems that if you have a private room you also get a private labour room, but being in a ward I was in a labour room with about 6 others. The nurses up there are all v. pretty rather like chorus girls, with a lot of make-up & they stand around chatting about dates etc & two were even playing cards, paying absolutely no attention to the groans & writhing going on all round, except occasionally to say sharply to some screaming woman "Lie down AT ONCE! You're not to sit up. Marie, come over & hold her legs a minute while I fix my hair."

The Dr. came in a few times & kept offering me pills to stop the pain, but I didn't take any for ages as I was longing to keep awake to watch the amazing scene around me, also I was afraid that if I took anything I'd lose control & start screaming like the others were. Actually I was semi-conscious nearly all the time, tho they did give me ether at the end in the delivery room. I'm terribly glad I didn't have much, I'm sure that's why I feel so well now. When I woke up they let me see the baby right away, it is so sweet & has a definite resemblance to the Boot, the same type rather slanting eyes & curiously shaped nose. When I came down Cliff & Va were here (they have been wonderful in the way of coming all the time & Va spent the whole of Sunday here waiting around). By this time I was frightfully hungry & when the nurse came in I ordered up a couple of lamb chops, peas & potatoes; this made her simply furious & she turned on poor Va & said "You're not to give her anything to eat or any cigarettes, we had to take her cigarettes away" (absolutely untrue, I didn't even want to smoke) then she turned on the others in here & told them they weren't to smoke either, & as she left there was a muttered chorus of "sour old bitch," & "who does she think she is," apparently she's well known to be narst but luckily she hardly ever comes in & the other nurses are all terrifically nice.

Here is a chart of the ward to show where the Man is placed. Sunday night there were 3 others here; an oldish one, rather nice & not too chatty about bedpans, enemas, ovaries etc which are apt to be the main topics here; a silent girl who's just had a cesarian, & a very pretty girl of 17 who had just come in but wasn't bad enough to go to the upstairs part yet. Someone asked about her husband & she said she wasn't married & was still at high school, & she wasn't going to see her baby at all but was going to 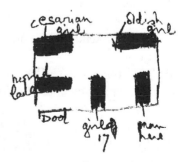 have it adopted right away; the lade from the adoption home came with her, she is <u>too</u> horrid, all mink cape-y & red faced & pretending to be nice, apparently they make masses of dough from getting the babies adopted. The girl didn't have her baby till 4 Tuesday morning, I feel so sorry for her as she is awfully nice . . . & although she had an awful time having the baby & can't see it or anything, she is not at all complainy. . . . Va came in when she was out & I told her about her, & Va immediately started arranging for Marney Abbott[51] to adopt the baby so the horrid adoption lade wouldn't get it; but I managed to stop Va, before she got the whole place upset.

Monday was terribly nice with 'grams & flowers arriving by the minute & I saw the baby twice, she really is so pleasant. I'm so looking forward to you seeing her & hearing a Boot's opinion. Va, Binny & Kay all came on Mon. afternoon. Mon. evening a frightfully scenic thing happened; the room was crowded with people's visitors (none of mine were there) & the nurse came in & said "All visitors out please. Some photographers are here from the Post to take pictures of Mrs. Romilly & her baby," so everyone trooped out & they brought the baby in & took the enclosed. Next morning all the nurses came rushing in with the Post & things reached a peak of scenicness, as when I'd given my maiden name for the form someone had said "are you any relation of Hitler's friend?" & I said "No," & then there it all was. The column under the picture is pretty awful but not as bad as some I've seen.[52]

Yesterday Mrs. Meyer came in (she & Va crossed in the hall & bowed) she brought me a lovely bedjacket, some eau de cologne & a baby blanket & she's going to give me a cheque to get a pram with when I get to Canada, which is simply wonderful as I shan't get the pram but shall conserve the dough for Boot & Man good times.

Do you think you could possibly come for the wknd some time soon? (I mean after I get back home, I could only see you here for 3 hours during the day.) Because I so absolutely long for you to come darling. I think all the time about seeing you again & how wonderful it would be if you'd come down when I get back to the Durrs. Having the baby is terribly nice (I nurse it now so I see it a lot) & the next best thing to the Boot as it looks so like you, but I miss you like mad all the time. . . .

By the way, the picture of me in the Post doesn't necessarily mean I look like that, with a terrific double chin & motherly expression, it's just the angle they took it from. I'll send you the print of it if they send me same so you can see the baby clearly.

Well old thinger I see I've written you practically a novel-length letter & most of it very boring & on the disgusting side. Actually as you will have gath-

---

51. Marney Abbott and her husband, Henry, were friends of the Durrs.

52. Recounting the scene in a letter years later, Decca said that the nurses in her "charity ward" had suddenly become deferential when the photographers arrived. She added, "One of the stupider fellow-mothers was heard by me to say, 'Why are they taking pictures? Was her baby born with teeth?' (To put YOU in the picture, photos of babies born with teeth were a reg. feature in the papers those days.)"

ered the hossening is absolutely fascinating, I mean being in a ward & every-thing, & frightfully efficient, the nurses are v. kind (e.g. I've got one bringing me hot choc last thing at night). . . .

All love my darling Bird.

Yr Man

P.S. This is the first letter they let me write you which is why it's so amazingly long. . . .

To Esmond Romilly   Columbia Hospital, Washington
                                         February 13, 1941

Darling Cn,

2 lovely letters arrived this morning, goodness the Man was pleased to get them. . . .

The flow of visitors, flowers & other fascinating things continues. Yesterday to my amazement the first arrival was Mr Meyer, he was awfully nice & came & sat like an old Dr asking how I felt & whether I had any pain still etc; he kept saying "if there's ever anything you want that we can do for you let me know at once," & when I told him how we couldn't reach you Saturday he said "Why didn't you call me? I'd have found some way to get in touch with him," & I really think he would have. Then he said he'd send some fruit, soup etc which will be wonderful as the food here is rather a particularly long cry from that served at the Meyer table. He saw the Times Herald here with my name on & he said "Hm! What's this?" So I said I'd ordered the Post & they sent the T.H. by mistake & he puffed up like an old turkey & said "So! That's how they get circulation over there! I'll have to look into this!" When he left Elaine (the unmarried girl next to me) said "I was just thinking; wouldn't it be wonderful if President Roosevelt came to see you, do you think he will?" . . .

The baby is getting prettier by leaps & bounds, she really is so sweet & makes the most extraorder faces & gestures. I'm feeding her & she is gaining weight already. I'm dying for you to see her. By the way what shall we call her? Be thinking up some names. . . .

Goodbye angel I'll write again tomorrow.

Yr. affec Man

To Esmond Romilly   Columbia Hospital, Washington
                                         February 16, 1941

Darling Cn,

. . . In the evening rather a scenic thing happened; 2 enormous boxes of food arrived, one from Kay & Phil & one from the Meyers. When the second arrived the nurse said rather reproachfully "Mrs. Romilly, have you been telling people that we don't feed you properly here?" I admitted I had deliberately spread rumours to that effect in the hopes of getting some from outside.[53] . . .

We had chicken for lunch today but only the bony part of the wing & gizzards, all the white meat goes to people in private rooms, so I told the nurse we were treated like the Fr. in occupied France & the private roomers like the Germans, with the nurses acting as a sort of British blockade, she was v. annoyed. . . .[54]

Goodbye old Boot, Yr. Loving Man

To Esmond Romilly   Columbia Hospital, Washington
February 18–19, 1941

Darling Cn,

Thanks for yr letter of the 16th inst., & whatever happens don't think that just because one can now chat on the phone that letter writing can be dropped because this is far from being the case.

Do submit a list of names, I thought Esmé would be rather nice. Unless you hurry I shall put Eugénie Roma on the birth certificate & then will the old Boot rampage & roar. I refer to her by that name to any visiting Meyers, which can't do any harm & may do good.[55] Kay came yesterday, I told her how thrilled you are to have a U.S. citizen in the family to help us out of possible future difficulties & we thought how ridiculous the Smaller Man would look trundling up to the state Dept in her diapers & demanding to see the head of the Visa Bureau. . . .

Your Loving Man

To Esmond Romilly   Alexandria
ca February 20, 1941

Darling Cn,

I just got back to bed after you 'phoned & am writing to you already, which just shows what one can do in the writing way if one wants to, yes you old Boot.

Well the first night back here was a scream (literally so, the baby screamed all night). Josephine came to get me at the hosening & the nurses suddenly

---

53. Years later Decca still marveled as she recalled the "huge hampers" of food arriving from the Meyers. She said she had shared the food with her roommates.

54. Decca later recalled, "On the following Monday, we had chicken soup in which I found a giblet. So I tied a bit of string round it, & called for the nurse. 'Nurse,' said I, 'yesterday we had giblets for lunch & I tied a bit of string round mine. I now see that you SCRAPED OUR PLATES & put it all into this disgusting soup.' Amazingly, she half-way believed it. So you can see a bit of fun was had."

55. Presumably the joke was that the baby was to be named for Eugene Meyer and the Roma, the bar in Miami where the Romillys were able to buy in with the help of a loan from Meyer.

became all nice & not strict any more, they helped me dress & pack & dress the baby (in the hospital they don't let it wear its own things, but special hospital shirts). I gave away Binny's fruit to the others in the ward & they all asked for my address & said they'd write (I rather hope Elaine will, I'm longing to know what becomes of her). When we got back there was a tremendous welcome, Mary & Mrs Daniels[56] hugged me like anything & I felt like an old Southern plantation owner of pre-civil war days. But as the evening drew near & Mary & Mrs Daniels left for the night that impression faded extraordinarily quickly. The baby yelled from the moment I got her settled in bed till her 10 p.m. feed; about 11 she started up again & went on till 2. Old Virginnie was very decent & came in several times but there was naught one could do. (By next morning I felt more like an old Southern plantation owner after the civil war.) Tra la la poor Man. But the really awful thing was that Lucy & Baby Sister & Mrs Forster ALL had diarrhea & the Dr came & said it was contagious! Typical of the Durrs. At this point Va & I decided we'd have to get a nurse for the baby till the others got well on account of the risk of her getting it, so Va phoned my Dr (Dr Willson[57]) & he told her where to get one. Va scrammed to town & came back with a terrifying white uniformed mountain (she is 5 ft 11 ins & looks like a murderess in a play) called Miss Darby, & from then on things have been simply wonderful, all organisy & sterilisy & scheduley & no more fear of the baby getting ill. I have been sleeping nearly all day as the nurse does everything; she is going to sleep in here at nights too & look after the baby which is too wonderful. Also I've got the money to pay her all saved up out of my $20 a week (she costs $20 a week so I shall pay her with my check I didn't spend when I was in the hosening). Miss Darby is quite nice tho terrifyingly efficient & strict; e.g. she came in when I was smoking & made an awful face, she has now cut me down to 3 cigs a day on accnt of the milk. Mrs. Daniels simply hates her already. She came in here in a fury saying Miss Darby had been ordering her about & sterilising everything in sight & telling Mrs D how to look after Lucy & Baby Sister. Of course I pretended to be on Mrs Daniels' side but I can't help noting how someone like Miss Darby has rather a healthy astringent effect on the general Durr sloppiness. . . .

So everything is wonderful now, after the brief horror of last night.

Now old Bird about the baby's name; since you don't seem to like anything I've suggested you must think up one yourself. . . .

Goodbye Bird, write.

　　　　　　　All Love, Yr affec Slip

---

56. Mary was the Durr family cook and Mrs. Daniels their laundress, who often looked after the children and performed other household functions.

57. Decca spelled the name Willson in some letters and Wilson in others.

To Esmond Romilly   Alexandria
                                                              early March 1941

Darling Bird,

. . . How extremely thoughtful of you to decide against Constancia[58] just
after I'd filled in the certificate form & got everything arranged. I don't much
like Carol for a girl & Ann Carol would be a shade arty don't you think? On the
other hand I adore Constancia & don't at all see why it means the Donk will be
called Connie any more than I'm called Jessie. We could call her Stan for short
(after Laurel & Hardy) or Cia, but not Con because it's too like Cn. However
Bird if you really hate it we can always think up something at a later date. Anyway I expect the truth is you have a girl-friend in the ravine called Constancia
& you've just had a quarrel with her which is why you want to change. . . .

I got a letter from Nancy yesterday of congrats—about the baby, & it was <u>so</u>
typical, this is how it started: "I'm <u>terribly</u> pleased about your baby; & only
hope it won't grow up exactly like Joan White,[59] on the other hand let her be
<u>exactly</u> like Mr Wendell Willkie & I shall adore her. . . ."

This morning I got a wire from Debo to say "engaged to Andrew,[60] getting
married next month," so I sent one back saying "Congratulations on excellent
season's duking,"[61] I hope she won't be furious. I think now I should definitely
start claiming that £1000,[62] Debo will hardly need it & we could pay back old

---

58. Decca described in *A Fine Old Conflict* that the name was inspired by her reading "*In Place of Splendour*, the stirring autobiography of Constancia de la Mora, daughter of a Spanish grandee who fled her highborn family to cast her lot with the Republican army during the civil war." She also mentioned the belated arrival of Esmond's letter of disapproval.

59. In 1939, Decca's friend Joan White stayed with Nancy Mitford for a week, after which Decca received a letter from her sister saying that White was the first American she'd ever met and "if they are all like that you must be <u>mad</u> to stay there & like all mad people convinced you are sane." Nancy's impression of White—and all Americans—was to become a recurrent theme in their correspondence.

60. Lord Andrew Cavendish.

61. Decca recalled in her memoir *Daughters and Rebels* how, as a child, "Debo stated confidently that she was going to marry a duke and become a duchess. 'One day he'll come along, The duke I love . . .' she hummed dreamily. . . . [S]eldom have childhood predictions materialized with greater accuracy."

In any case, as the younger son of the Duke of Devonshire, Andrew Cavendish was not expect-ing to become a duke himself. Deborah Mitford had written at the time that she was expecting to be quite poor. Lord Andrew's brother, Billy, the Marquess of Hartington, who was in line for the title and the family fortune, was killed in combat in 1944, four months after marrying Kathleen (Kick) Kennedy, daughter of the former U.S. ambassador to London Joseph Kennedy and his wife, Rose, and sister of future American politicians John, Robert, and Edward Kennedy. With the death of his brother, Andrew Cavendish became the unexpected heir to the dukedom, which he inherited when his father died in 1950.

Years later, in England, Decca came across the telegram she mentioned here; the wording was slightly different than she recalled it. (See letter of September 20, 1955, to Pele de Lappe and Steve Murdock.)

62. Decca was referring to the £1,000 libel judgment her sister Deborah won after the *Daily Express* got its Mitford sisters mixed up, blaring in its front-page scoop on March 1, 1937, that "the

Meyer & still be several thousand dollars to the good. However I don't like to mention it in the first letter I write her but will ease into it gradually. . . .

An angry screaming combined with pungent odour tells me the Donk has shumbled so I'll have to scram.

Goodbye you angelic Boot, Your Slip adores you. If you find you haven't written, a night letter is always welcome & you can send it collect, it only costs 50¢.

Love From Decca

To Esmond Romilly   Alexandria
                                                                March 7, 1941

Darling Cn,

The man really is sorry for its awful lapse in writing, I suppose to the hard old Boot heart no excuse would do, anyway I will try & write more next week, hoping to put the old Boot in a good frame of mind for its Brown visit down here. I got your letter about calling the Donk Carol on the forms, rather unnecessary of you just as everyone has started calling her Constancia & I've got the Birther & everything.

Monday Kay & Phil came to see the donk & we all went off to Sister's[63] At Home. When we arrived there was Sister & the gaunt figure of Lady Halifax.[64] We all sat round very stiffly in a circle & by mistake I found myself ensconced on a love-seat type sofa next to Lady H. Apparently Sister & Va were absolutely terrified I should say something untoward, but of course I didn't, (except to point out (when everyone was saying how brave of Lady H to stay in London through the bombings) that she was probably in very little danger as it was only the badly built East End houses that suffered much damage). When Lady H left everyone except me stood up, & we all drew a deep breath & things became rather pleasant. . . .

Old Bird you don't <u>know</u> how I'm looking forward to next weekend—if you can't get permission to come to the US can I come up there anyway? Let me know in plenty of time which train you're coming on. . . .

Best love, Yr adoring Slipper

Hon. Deborah Vivien Freeman-Mitford . . . is believed to have gone to Spain in an attempt to marry her eighteen-year-old cousin, Esmond Romilly, nephew of Mr. Churchill." Decca wrote years later that Esmond Romilly "never quite got over the unfairness" of the libel award, saying, "You did all the work, and Debo got £1000 out of it!"

63. Virginia Durr's name for her sister, Josephine, wife of Justice Black. Not to be confused with Baby Sister, the nickname of Durr's daughter.

64. Lord Halifax had been foreign secretary under Prime Minister Neville Chamberlain and supported his policy of appeasing Adolf Hitler. He stayed on in that position under Winston Churchill until December 1940, at which point he was appointed ambassador to the United States.

To Lady Redesdale   Toronto
                                                              April 9, 1941

Darling Muv,

I just got your letter of 18th March, so considering Virginnie had to forward it here[65] it arrived amazingly quickly. It says in the papers that no mail arriving this side has been lost, but a good deal is lost going to England, so you probably don't get half my letters.

Do write more news of Henderson's engagement—did you all know she was engaged or did she keep it secret? Why did they have to wait till Andrew was 21? It must have been awful for them. Do write every detail of the wedding[66] etc & tell what Andrew is like apart from speaking indistinctly & being tall & thin! . . .

We came up here about 2 weeks ago, the baby in a basket which she lives in; the journey wasn't at all bad & there was a v. nice (black) Pullman porter who rocked the Donk off to sleep & was wonderful to her. He said he was the eldest of 12 children & knew all about babies. She gets bathed in a large saucepan as I thought I was only coming for the weekend & didn't bring her bath. We are living in a very nice little flat & Esmond comes up 1 day in 4 so it's well worth it.

The Donk is getting awfully fat & pretty. Someone lent me a pram so I take her out every day.

I don't like Canada at <u>all</u>, it seems to me like an awful copy of America, & the people are horrid. They are very anti English & anti American but vastly inferior to both. I expect it was quite different where you were,[67] & Esmond says the West is fairly nice where the people are more of Central European rather than English extraction. . . .

There are several English refugees here & I really feel sorry for them (tho not for those in America as they are very well treated & anyway America is such heaven). . . .

Well I must scram now, give my love to all the others. . . .

                    Best Love From Decca

To Nancy Mitford   Alexandria
                                                              May 20, 1941

Darling Sue,

I just got your letter of 24th April, so it didn't take long. Do write a lot, I long to hear all the inner form & Susan you see letters DON'T get sunk if one WRITES them, admit?

---

65. Decca, with Constancia in tow, had traveled to Canada for a visit and decided to stay for a while in a rented apartment near Esmond's base, the No. 1 Bombing and Gunnery School at RCAF Station Jarvis in Ontario.

66. Deborah Mitford married Lord Andrew Cavendish ten days after this letter was written.

67. On Lord Redesdale's gold claim in northern Ontario.

Yes, I do worry a lot about you all, not so much from the point of view of getting killed as not having enough to eat & having a v. narst time in general. Do say if you'd like things sent, I'll send some anyway next time I go to Washington but say if it's any good & what are the best things.

This is the American form re England: when the war first started there was still a very anti-English sentiment among all but the most reactionary on account of Munich, & the fact Chamberlain was still heading the govt. This feeling gradually swung round as the war intensified & Churchill came in until now everyone here is madly for England except the extreme Right (Lindbergh[68] etc.) and the extreme Left, who still follow the C.P. line. The whole issue is somewhat obscured by the strikes in the war industries as people of liberal thought support the strikers & fear greatly that the whole war program will fall into the hands of reactionaries like Knudsen[69] & Stettinius[70]—& Willkie, Susan—& that America will evolve its own brand of Fascism, thus making the whole war lose its point from their point of view. The Durrs & most of the people I know here think that at the present time in Washington there is great dissatisfaction with Roosevelt for not moving fast enough, & also for putting Republicans & big business people in key positions. Part of the trouble is that here, as in England, people all want to fight for different things; some for the supremacy of the British Empire & America, some for the destruction of Fascism. Very few people follow Lindbergh, who is considered a dangerous defeatist. Americans on the whole talk as though they were already in the war, & all think it will be only a matter of months before they are. . . .

Do tell the Fem & Male's form re the war, of course I never mention it when writing to Muv for fear she will say something which would put one off speakers. Also do tell how Boud is now, Debo was simply beastly about her in some of her letters. I hope marriage will make her nicer. I never met Andrew, he looks rather nice in his pictures, I expect he will get Hon-pecked. . . .

I'll send you some photos of the baby, she is such a marvel & a wonderful friend & companion. Do you think Constancia is a nice name? No one calls her that, she is called the Donk. Were you amazed when she was born, or did you hear I was having one?

Do write again Susan. Give Rodd my love. . . .

Best Love, Susan

---

68. Pioneering aviator and vocal isolationist Charles A. Lindbergh, a leader of the America First Committee and supporter of a U.S. neutrality pact with Hitler.

69. Industrialist William Knudsen held several national defense and production management positions during the early 1940s.

70. Edward Stettinius, also an industrialist and later secretary of state under Roosevelt, in 1941 served as chairman of the Priorities Board and director of the Office of Production Management and Lend-Lease administrator.

To Esmond Romilly   Martha's Vineyard, Mass.
                                                                                    June 26, 1941

Darling Cn,

I was so miserable when you left but now feel as though I was recovering from an illness, better each day—I'm going back tomorrow.[71] A wire came for Selden saying "where in the world is Decca, please advise by Western Union, Virginia Durr" (typical phrasing), so I called her up just now & she read me your wire.[72] She thought I'd been sex-murdered by the Washington Fiend. The Donk is very well, I'm longing to see her.[73]

I've got the most wonderful plan for the summer, I do hope you won't think it [a] complete waste of time & dough: apparently there is a v. good summer school of journalism at the Columbia University starting around July 5th. . . . I know I would enjoy it <u>much</u> more than just hanging around . . . so do be pro it. I know you usually think that sort of thing is useless but I don't think it would be to me. It takes about 7 weeks & sounds fascinating. . . . It seems to me just the thing I was wanting & you know how the Man would love to be all punch packing off in New York, perhaps in some amazing boarding house uptown near the university. Do write at once if you agree & I'll be planning for it. Then I'd feel much more confident about a possible Post job, but even if I didn't do that in the end it would be a marvellous way of spending the summer. . . .

I'm simply longing for a letter telling me about your journey (I'm sure it was beastly) so do write <u>all</u> news. . . .

Goodbye darling old Boot, yr slip adores you.

                              Love from Decca

To Esmond Romilly   Alexandria
                                                                                    August 1, 1941

My Darling Cn,

I was absolutely thrilled to get your letter & cable today, they arrived together & have made the <u>whole</u> difference to Man life and morale, you must admit that a month was quite a long time not to hear but I hope you'll discount any worried or whiney tone in my other letters. The Man won't be like that any more. Your letters were simply swell, specially arriving together as they did so that the better part of the boat trip & officerishness came after the bad part. . . . Oh going to the Savoy eh? So that's your idea of the way to spend your time in War Torn Europe. Is that your permanent address from now on? If not

---

71. Decca had remained for a few days with the Rodmans on Martha's Vineyard after Romilly left for Halifax and then England.

72. Esmond Romilly's telegram of June 25 notified Decca that he had arrived safely in Halifax.

73. Constancia had stayed home with the Durrs during her parents' farewell holiday on Martha's Vineyard.

let me know. . . . The descriptions of the other people & goings on were so fascinating. . . .

My news isn't much as I've been here all the time & looking after the Donk (she gets one string bean for lunch now which I cook for her in greaseproof paper as I refuse to give her canned food) & waiting to hear that you had arrived. . . .

Now old bird, re the Slippery schedule: in case you haven't yet got my letter telling about it, I have a good chance of getting a place on a lend-lease bomber and coming to England. Of course this is what I should adore to do (tho I wouldn't dream of doing so unless you are all for it). If we do decide that I shall come, I think it should be fairly soon on account of the second piker[74] (which doesn't show at all at present, & of course no one knows about it except you; I figure it is due about the 13th March, & so is now under 2 months gone). I mean I think it would be more difficult to get a passage if I was huge. Old Bird I do so want to come so do be pro it, tho if you are not I have packed my punch to no good effect & am tentatively arranging a) to go to NY in August to view the prospects & b) to drive to San Francisco with the Mainwarings. . . .

I do think the war has become much more exciting if not to say worthwhile since June 22nd,[75] so therefore to come to England would be quite as punch packing as any other scheme or more so. So what say, old Boot? And I know you think of the Man as one who relies on good food & lighting up but do admit that is not really its form. However the whole decision is yours & whatever happens don't worry about it, but just say what you really think because I will be terrifically all right & happy whatever we decide. . . .

Well darling the Man sends all its love, & is so happy to know at last where you are.

Do write a mass more—Your adoring Slip

To Esmond Romilly Staunton, Va.
August 16–19, 1941

Darling Bird,

This is going to be the day-to-day Man's trip through the South[76] & I'll post it when I get near some envelopes etc. We're staying tonight in a tourist home at Staunton Va.

First of all it seemed all funny to be off with the Mainwaringmen & not to see the old Browner Bed blowing in the wind at the wheel & cr-r-raning forth

---

74. Years later Decca wrote that she was pregnant with "a much-longed for baby, planned as a friend & companion for Dink, conceived just before Esmond went overseas."

75. The date Germany invaded Russia.

76. Decca was driving with her acquaintances the Mainwarings on a trip "probing the full horror & fascination of the South," as she put it.

to read the Burma Shave ads, however the Man has now realised the Boot is definitely not along & is planning to enjoy itself just the same. I must admit the Ms are amazingly dull tho quite nice. . . . I'm looking forward a lot to getting down to the Highlander School[77] & to Birmingham etc & seeing some other people.

Sunday. We got down into the TVA[78] country today, it is v. beautiful & has a look of quiet prosperity quite unlike the parts of Tenn., Ga, Ala etc that we went through. I can see the Ms are going to be interested in electric turbines etc & insist on long detours to be sure not to miss any TVA dams.

Monday. Rather an amazing day. Before I left I went to see the Dr in Alexandria as I had a sort of suspicion something was up with the 2nd piker. He examined me & said he thought I was pregnant but couldn't be sure, so I told him I thought it might be miscarrying & he said that if so I wouldn't be able to stop it at such an early stage unless I went to bed for months, & that it wouldn't do any harm to go on the trip anyway as it wouldn't make any difference & a miscarriage at this stage is never bad. Then today I definitely did miscarry it.[79] I do hope old Bird you won't be disappointed or think it v. careless of me not to scram to bed. I was awfully annoyed at first specially as it would have been such heaven to have 2 such tiny men nearly the same age; the whole thing is awfully disappointing, but now it has actually happened & the only thing to do is just forget it was ever up & pack one's punch accordingly. Thank goodness Va & everyone didn't know about it. I can't understand why it should have happened & am going to Dr. Willson as soon as I get back, you must say it's very unlike me.

Tuesday lunch time. I feel quite alright again now & not all shaken up as I was yesterday. I do hope you don't mind about it darling because I honestly don't now. We are now cutting & running for the Highlander where I hope there'll be some mail. The Slipper will certainly be cheering the day it gets a letter from you. I know some must be on the way by now, but probably won't arrive till the end of the month.

Tues. night. We just got to the Highlander & I must say it is a fascinating place. There are people here from all over the country (e.g. a girl of 18 from the Mississippi textile mills who organised a union single handed in her mill, where they were only getting $6 a week) & only the best are sent as it costs the union $100. It is rather narst in a way being a visitor as the other visitors are a horrid

---

77. The Highlander Folk School in rural Tennessee—now known as the Highlander Research and Education Center. The center's founding mission was to educate "rural and industrial leaders for a new social order," with a primary emphasis on working with grassroots leaders to build a progressive labor movement.

78. The Tennessee Valley Authority was a showcase New Deal agency to provide flood control, conservation, navigability, electrification, and development in a depressed multistate rural region.

79. Decca wrote years later that "it all happened in a gas station lavatory." She was not fond of the people she was traveling with, "so I never said a word to them about it."

old woman called Dr. Vessel & her scrawny Nevilly son who I kept calling Horst by mistake. She keeps saying "are you really interested in labour dear?" which is v. embarrassing.

Later. I just got your telegram forwarded by Va, old Bird you were sweet to wire so soon about it & of course I absolutely agree with the form of me staying here for the present.[80] The reason I kept on so in all my letters is I had a feeling you might not get some of them & wanted you to be quite clear as to my idea. I do wish now too that I hadn't written so much about the 2nd piker because now you will think I wanted it terrifically, tho actually being only a 2 monther the idea of it was completely shadowy & the Donk would always make up for anything like that. She has changed so much since you saw her & is almost at the stage of being a real person.

I must mail this now old Bird & write again soon.

Your Loving Man

To Nancy Mitford   Alexandria

September 5, 1941

Darling Susan,

. . . I got yr letter, it simply scrammed here. I think the posts are getting much better. I'm so glad the onions arrived, but I was furious because I got lots of other things & then it made the parcel too heavy (you can only send 5 lbs) so they had to be taken out. . . .

Washington is quite depressing in some ways as everywhere you go people talk of nothing but the inefficiency of the Defense Program (that is the war effort, but they still call it the defense program so as not to tease the isolationists too much). Almost every article you read is about the terrific shortages of everything & no one seems to have any plan to solve it. The morale everywhere is simply terrific[81]—the other day all the papers were full of a story about men deliberately getting syph so they would be unfit for the army, & this reached such a pitch that the army has now decided to take people with venereal disease in the primary stages & cure them of it! Rather a tease on those who got it.

Last month I went down to Tennessee & spent some time at a labour school down there where they train union organisers. The staff are all very left wing & so are some of the students, but there is a very noticeable isolationist current & Russia being in the war doesn't seem to have made much difference. The school is of course entirely run for the unions, so there isn't much stress laid on politics except as it affects labour (anti-strike legislation etc.) & whenever the

---

80. Decca had written Esmond Romilly to say that she would like to "scram to England" but was planning "to buckle down" in Washington if he didn't want her to go. On August 17, he replied in a telegram, "Please don't think of coming over for present as my own plans uncertain. Go ahead with other things instead." He later reconsidered that decision.

81. "Terrific" was apparently used here in the original sense: terrible.

war was mentioned the impression seemed to be that it was only the business interests that wanted to get America involved. I spent most of my time there pointing out that in England things had been exactly the other way round & the anti-appeasement forces, before the war anyway, came almost entirely from the Left; but then they couldn't understand how a Tory government could still be in power. I can see the issues would have to be much more clear for American labour to become really interventionist, & anyway most of them, even the very militant ones, don't think much beyond getting better conditions for workers etc. I think the fundamental reason is that there is no political labour party here & no strong socialist party. For instance I was amazed that Russia coming in caused no enthusiasm at all except from a military point of view; people were pleased that the Nazis had another enemy to occupy them but there were no mass meetings or demonstrations.

The various "incidents," like the sinking of the Robin Moor[82] etc tho played up terrifically in the press haven't stirred people up much, I suppose they note what happened when people got so stirred up over the Lusitania.[83]

Do you think people in England note all this about America? I keep seeing articles saying the English are "shocked" & "disappointed" etc at the lack of American interest, & it's quite true there is not much interest except among all-out supporters of the Administration. At least, not much pro-war feeling. All my best friends in Washington are very pro-war but they are all Administration people, & it's only when you get away from here that you realise how the other groups feel. . . .

Do write soon. Give my love to the young Hen, I hear she is broody. . . .

Good boosan—Your afec, Sue

P.S. Do you ever see Cord[84] in the clink or are you still off speakers?

---

82. The American freighter was sunk by a German submarine off Brazil on May 21, 1941—the first American ship sunk by a U-boat. The passengers and crew were rescued. President Roosevelt called it "an act of piracy" and declared a state of "unlimited national emergency."

83. The huge transatlantic British ocean liner was sunk by a torpedo fired from a German U-boat south of Ireland on May 7, 1915, with a loss of nearly 1,200 lives. Despite an international outcry and calls in the United States for war, President Woodrow Wilson responded with a letter of protest, a reassertion of American neutrality, and a call for reparations. Nevertheless, the incident helped pave the way for U.S. entry into World War I two years later.

84. Nickname for their sister Diana Mosley, who had by this time been imprisoned in England for more than a year. Before she was interned, her sister Nancy said she had told a government official that "I regard her as an extremely dangerous person." That comment and the publication in 1935 of *Wigs on the Green*, Nancy's novel satirizing the homegrown fascism of her sister Unity and brother-in-law Oswald Mosley, would certainly help to explain the "off speakers" status that Decca noted here. In fact, Nancy appears to have resumed writing to Diana in January 1941 and later visited her in prison.

To Esmond Romilly   Alexandria
                                                                September 7, 1941

Darlingest Bird,

. . . In the U.S. . . . [t]he only thing one sees, day in & day out in every newspaper & mag is criticism of the defense program & every group accusing the
others of selfishness & lack of patriotism & low morale. Cafe Society taking up
the V campaign (V shaped hats, brooches & chorus girls' spangles etc) is about
the only sign of war enthusiasm! . . .

I've decided that if I'm staying in the U.S. for some time stenography is
essential to get out of the salesgirl-refined type English upper class lending
tone rut, so I know you won't be anti me doing it. Of course it would mean I'll
end up doing 200 words a minute in some dull office, but it will make possible
several fascinating type jobs that you just can't get without it. I shall stay here
till I'm through the stenog course anyway. Daniels now adores the Donk so
much she can hardly bear to take her day off, so she will look after her for me,
much better than going to NY & getting some girl who would probably put the
Donk's head in a gas oven to get her off to sleep, which happened to a baby Va
knew & destroyed its brain cells. (Tra la la silly Man, of course I shall go to NY
if I can't find anything good here, but I do adore being with the Durrs, we get
on so well.) . . .

Do write more about the Toynbee[85] ménage & any other people you see—
does ordinary Mrs. R[86] know you are back? Awful Croat I know she won't find
out for years & will then be simply furious—but yet forgiving, for who could
refuse to forgive one who had chosen the Highest Calling of all, service of his
country? . . .

I hope you are getting the cigs & Hershey bars regularly & do let me know
what other food would be in order. It says in the papers people are not supposed
to ask for things from abroad, so the form is to write "thanks for the soap, razor
blades, canned turkey" etc & then one catches on & sends them.

The Person tips the scales at 17 1/2 lbs now & they are supposed to weigh
20 lbs at one year, everyone says she looks like a year-older. When she wishes
her bottle she says "bo-bo-bo-De-De-De-cca!" Sorry Bird I know these quaint
anecdotes are boring but she really is so sweet. . . .

Best love my darling, do keep writing, your letters are so wonderful & buoy
the Man up like mad.

                    Your affec Slipper

---

85. Romilly was spending time with some of the couple's old friends, including Philip Toynbee.

86. Esmond Romilly's mother, Nellie. For an explanation of Decca's use of this term, see October 13, 1981, letter to Kevin Ingram.

To Esmond Romilly   Alexandria
                                                                           September 11, 1941

Darling Cn,

... The awful thing is you are probably now still getting some rather groany letters tho I'm not being the least groany any more, so do discount any that may arrive. I think what happened was that what with Piker II etc I began to think all avenues to the Boot would soon be closed, plus not feeling very go ahead & tour-spiritish; plus the journalism school turning out to be non-existent (the only one I could find, in NY or Washington, that was a summer course was one for nuns to teach them to run their nunnery mag!). Actually now Piker II is off, tho I guess I was sorry at the time, I feel much better physically as well as much more Donk-&-Man-forging-aheadish. Anyway the point is that all the above reasons made me very pro coming over right away if possible, whereas now I'm completely back to the form we had always decided on. ...

The President's speech tonight was awful, the usual 1 step nearer war, exactly what it was; his speeches have become a regular staircase & one always knows what the next step will be which makes them so dull in spite of all the oratory etc. "Rattlesnake" was rather flat after "gunthirsty buttersnipe" anyway.[87] I'll write again tomorrow darling old Bird & do be pro the Man, it is violently pro you.

                    Your affec Slopman

To Esmond Romilly   Alexandria
                                                                           September 14, 1941

Darlingest Bird,

The Man's plans have been simmering all last week & have now come to a definite head (boil?) at least for the next 2 or 3 months.

Saturday I went to Wash. & scrammed up to see Mr. Bernard at the Post. He said he had been investigating possibilities of various advertising etc. jobs but that nothing very promising had as yet turned up. Tho I know I could get something within a month or so, the prospect of waiting around & finally getting something either all Weinbergery or else all dept. store & 17 bucks a weeky didn't appeal, so I took a snap decision as the Boot would say & immediately went & enrolled at the Strayer Business School, stenography course. This is said to be the best school of that kind here, & it certainly did look rather

---

87. In his "fireside chat" on the day this letter was written, Roosevelt condemned German submarine attacks on American merchant ships and ordered use of American warships to protect them. He justified his orders by saying, "When you see a rattlesnake poised to strike, you do not wait until he has struck to crush him." A few months earlier, in a June broadcast after Hitler violated the nonaggression treaty and invaded Russia, Churchill had called the Nazi leader "this bloodthirsty guttersnipe," a phrase Decca played with here.

fascinating—all bustly & studenty & vigorous & go ahead. You can't think how wonderful it is to have decided on going there & I <u>do</u> hope you won't think it's an extravagant idea. Even while I'm there I can save some of the Dep allowance (the tuition is $28 a month) & I'm convinced it will lead to something fascinating as well as being terrific fun to be at a school.

The hours are from 9 to 3 (rather different from the Boot's schedule I know, but don't despise the little Slippery plans for that reason as I intend to work terrifically hard; I've set myself a time limit of 3 months to become good & quick at it, if possible of course before that). One can also stay and practice till 5 if one wishes. The man in charge explained to me that one can take all that time in simply shorthand & typing but he said he didn't think most people could stand that much concentrated S.&T. & advised me to take Business English, Spelling & a thing called Penmanship. However I was firm in rejecting these 3 as they are to my mind completely beside the point, apart from the fact I expect I know them already (except for the Business part of English, which I don't specially want to know). . . .

Well old Bird I am beginning at the school tomorrow morning & you don't know how glad I am about it. I feel for the first time in ages I am starting at something new, which I wouldn't feel at all if I got a job in a shop here or contacted those beauty specialist lades etc in NY. All this may seem v. exaggerated about something as commonplace as a stenography school but still it will be so new to me to be learning a real trade. What I'm hoping is naturally that something will turn up after I've been there a couple of months. As soon as I've grasped how to type reasonably fast I shall start skeking around after a job. Do write me <u>all</u> your impressions of the usefulness or not etc of me going to the school. Tomorrow I'll write all about the Man's First Day. By the way I am going to be in a class with College Graduates! Tra la la cleva man although I admitted to the man in charge of the school I've never been to college.

I do wish letters didn't take so long, it will probably be at least 6 weeks before I can get an answer to this, & I'm so longing to know what you think of it all. . . .

          Your very Loving Man

To Esmond Romilly   Alexandria
                                          September 15, 1941
Darling Bird,

The Man set off this morning for the first day of its stenography school. I went in with the Bill & Cliff crowd (Bill having got a huge new car there is always a crowd going to work in it) & it was all like the old Weinbergery days only more so, because instead of arriving with scaught to do but read Vogue there was this huge busy school, people making out our schedules, High Schooly & Collegey girls all over the place rushing when the class bell rang etc.

Today there were no classes for the new students, so I just went to a couple of English & Spelling classes, which completely decided me against taking them in my course, they are v. elementary & it would be pointless anyway unless one was planning to stay for months & qualify for some boring job the school would find one, which is not my idea in going there at all. The rest of the school looked exactly as I had hoped—great bare rooms full of people madly typing or taking shorthand dictation. I got my books & have been boning up on the shorthand tonight so everyone will think how clever I am for a beginner. The typing book must have been compiled by some Joycean or at least Freudian mind. This is the first exercise: may any man yes yet you jab big bit try now own book both done down fine walk sign June July wait want back baby! I copied it exactly—rather amazing—

The shorthand book looks just like a Boot's letter. . . .

I'm writing to the bank tonight to ask how much dough there is, I think it's still over $400; so how about paying a bit back to Mike or Meyer?

Naturally I'm still leaving all dough transactions of that type to you. The only thing that worried me a bit was, will you think it extravagant of me to be going to this school? I do hope not, & what you said in one letter about hoping I'd go ahead with the NY journalist school thing made me think it would be OK. I'm convinced it's a really good investment, both for the U.S. where there is a terrific shortage of secretaries & also if I ever come to England, when it would probably mean a much more interesting type job than if one were completely unskilled. . . . Actually things here are terrifically interesting just now, & at last Washington seems to be getting back to its old form of New Dealers in control, more like when we first came here, & I think people will be much more hopeful this autumn.

Goodbye darling. Do write the news on the 2nd war front, one gauges very little really from the papers. What is the Toynbee attitude now & above all the Roughton[88] one, if you see him?

Your Very Loving Slipperman

To Esmond Romilly   Alexandria
                                                              September 23, 1941

Darling Bird,

Thank you so much for your birthday 'gram, & it was wonderful to have the reply paid dough to wire you with, the whole thing was a v. much appreciated birthday present (even tho 10 days late—what's that old Bird?). Fancy the Slip being 24, getting on I should say.

I've been meaning to write for several days to tell all about my school, how-

---

88. Roger Roughton had been a friend of Esmond Romilly since their days of public school rebellion. It was to his large London house on Rotherhithe Street that Decca and Esmond Romilly had moved when they returned to London from France.

ever from now on letters will be sent in a steady stream. Here is a sample Man's day: 7 a.m. angry sounds are heard from the other bed; the Donk is changed & given her rattle, which she waves violently thus giving a pleasant waking up period. Sometimes if I'm not very sleepy she is taken out & played with. 8 a.m. breakfast, now fixed by Va & quite good. 8:30 a mad rush for the car by Ann, Cliff, Viola (Daniels' little girl) & me; nearly always a different car as Bill is away & Va is usually to be heard hopefully phoning all round the neighbourhood so she won't have to take us in. 9 a.m. the Man arrives all efficient & secretarial with case of books & settles to its typewriter. One rather funny thing is up here which is the typewriters have no letters on the keys on account of it being the Touch System. The typing instructress is rather like a horse trainer; she steps around the room saying "SNATCH the keys! ONE two! ONE two!" We type to the tunes of marches which is rather fun. The Man is already typing sentences & has learnt the keyboard except for X, Q & Z, it is about 3 lessons ahead of the others who began the same time (Tra la la I think you know the rest). Then there is a study period for shorthand homework etc, in a classroom, & taken by a v. boring man who keeps talking all the time about how the students shouldn't talk & thus renders study impossible. There are ineffectual little pep messages written on the walls such as "to fail to prepare is to prepare to fail," and "good luck is just hard work" etc. I think you can gauge the fascinating form of the place. The lunch hour is only 40 minutes so I usually spend it in the lade's room where everyone foregathers to chat & the girls hang around asking each other "Say are there any cute boys out your way?" They are mostly like Binny's imitation of a sort of junior tart, all high schooly, but I haven't really got to know any of them yet. After lunch is the shorthand class & then more typing till 5. . . .

We had the first shorthand test today & the Man made 100% Tra la la. . . . The silver cigarette case stage will come later tho, if at all. . . .

Goodbye darling Cn. I'll write very soon.

Best Love from Decca

To Esmond Romilly   Alexandria
                                                            October 14, 1941
Darlingest Cn,

. . . [E]ver since I got your telegram[89] I've had the delicious prospect of being back with you again. I can skeke wait for your letter about it. . . . Dickie

---

89. Romilly had wired his wife to say he now thought it might be a good thing for her to join him in England in the next few months "if you can still come" and wanted to do so, although he wasn't certain yet of the conditions near his base or her access to him. Decca, "terrifically excited," vowed to get the most she could out of stenography school in the next few weeks while exploring transportation opportunities to Britain and child-care arrangements for Constancia in Washington in case it wasn't advisable to bring the baby to the war zone.

Knowles & the Dr came by the other day & Dickie literally begged for the Donk in case I scram. So they are another v. good possibility, probably even better than the Camerons in some ways as Dickie would really adore having her; whereas with the Camerons one couldn't be quite sure whether it was just their War Effort. Do tell what you think about this. She's had masses of other offers, including the Claude Peppers[90] & Thurman Arnolds (trust-busters),[91] & lots of other people.

The other night I went to a huge Fight for Freedom Dinner in the Shoreham hotel, all got up by Mike & Helen Fuller. It really was _so_ extraorder. This was their national convention but of course there were crowds of Washingtonites too, mostly all evening dress, & civic. The out-of-town delegates were just like one imagines delegates to a shoe-salesman's convention or something; several bleary eyed oldish young men looking around restively for a good time & all half saying "We-e-ell, little lady! What state are you from?" etc, & hard faced woman secretary types fraternising with everyone. I was supposed to sit with Mike & Bin, but at the last minute the main speaker . . . arrived dead drunk & had to be supported by 2 men, so Mike scrammed off to rearrange the speakers & ended up at the speakers table, & Bin also got separated; so I was left to sit with a terrific crowd of the most Texanish Texans you ever saw. As I arrived they were all jumping up & yelling "Let's drink to Texas! The finest state etc etc & we could lick that goddam bastard excuse me please, ladies, but I mean that feller Hitler!" There were about 5 half empty bottles of Scotch on the table & everyone was pinning Fight for Freedom emblems & Bundles for Britain posies on each other. A pamphlet on the table had "Calling all Americans" written on it, & one Texan picked it up & said, dead seriously to another "Here's a snappy publicity line, eh Joe?" Sen. Lister Hill[92] made a speech after the dinner in which he pointed out that we were all breathing the pure American air of Freedom where the Heathen Hun could not take our women into captivity & there subject them to base defilements. He's the one who made such a terrible speech at the Dem. nat. convention, but this one was even worse. The really awful thing is that this Fight for Freedom committee is supposed to be about the only dynamic & large pro-war movement here. There are certainly no signs of any kind of popular front[93] being reinstated—outside of big business & these

90. Senator Claude Pepper of Florida was a friend of the Durrs and another Alabama native. Virginia Durr credited him with being "a great champion of the anti-poll tax bill." For more on the Peppers' interest in taking care of Constancia, see letter of March 7, 1984, to Polly Toynbee.

91. Thurmond Arnold at the time was head of the Justice Department's Antitrust Division. He and his wife were part of the Durrs' Seminary Hill set. Arnold later became a partner in a powerful Washington law firm.

92. The Alabama senator was also in the Durrs' circle of New Deal Southerners.

93. The Popular Front, the Communist coalition with antifascist forces around the world, including, in the United States, labor unions and New Dealers, collapsed with the signing of the

ghastly Southerners (who never stop saying proudly how down home any scrap is good enough for a southerner & they certainly want to get in on this one) there seems to be less & less interventionist feeling. Except of course with people like Mike, the Grahams, Retzes etc. Yet all the time the press is dinning into people how united, militant & democratic they are.

Cliff is definitely leaving the RFC to be a Federal Communications Commissioner, which apparently means he'll be regulating the radio, press etc. The Donk crawled for the first time yesterday & has been doing it a lot today—she inches along like a snake after things if you put them out of reach. Chiefly Va's spectacles which makes Va furious as I am always getting them for the Donk to play with. She sits alone all the time now. . . .

Well Bird <u>do</u> keep writing darling, yr. Slip so adores getting your letters. I keep thinking of you so terrifically much & <u>longing</u> to be with you again.

Your very affec. Slipper

To Esmond Romilly   Alexandria
November 9, 1941

Darlingest Cn,

I sent you a cable last night which must have crossed yours[94] asking me to wire, so I expect I'll hear from you tomorrow, but meanwhile I'll write you all the details of my embassying etc. I went to see this same Group Capt. Anderson, the one I asked before about the bomber trip. He was v. nice & helpful (tho slightly the befuddled old Englishman type), & said that while there was no longer any chance of going by air (the regulations have been tightened up a lot & they don't take any women now) I could be sure of getting a sea passage sooner or later, within about 3 weeks to 3 months if I put in an application; they are ordinary passages with about the same accommodations as in peace time, only many fewer available as only a few ships take women. . . . I then filled out a form which I left with the Brit. Consul . . . & then eventually they let one know when one's turn is up. Of course one can't really tell whether it <u>is</u> quite as easy & normal as they made out; but it certainly was awfully encouraging to find I can go that way. (I might even take the Donk if things are looking up a bit, but that can be decided at the last minute; it probably wouldn't be a good idea—Lois Eliot is dying to have her staying with them, which would be swell as she would then be near the Durrs & all the people she knows, so that is more or less what I have planned if you think it's O.K.). So now I'm longing to know

Hitler-Stalin non-aggression pact in 1939 that was subsequently violated by Germany's invasion of the Soviet Union.

94. Esmond Romilly's telegram inquired about whether Decca had made any plans yet for traveling to England.

all about what your form is, whether we could be together at all & what type station you are on, & above all what you really think now about my coming. Because the Man is now completely punch-packy for whatever is decided; for instance it's not all downed & pregnant-y & miscarriag-y as it was a few months ago; & it specially doesn't want to be a constant worry to you, I mean so you'll feel you have to tell me to come over even tho it wasn't really the best thing. . . . I do feel I'm not just waiting aimlessly around; I'm learning a lot at the Stenog. School & then there's the Donk & everything, & if I stay I shall . . . [get] a flat & a job. The Donk is so terrifically nice, she has absolutely made the whole difference to things—when she roars the old Boot sarcastic expression comes into her face, in fact she is exactly like you altogether, rather a scene I should say. . . .

I had a letter from Nancy saying "I heard Esmond had arrived, & there's a strong rumour around that you are here too under an assumed name & heavily disguised." So typical it hardly needs comment. She keeps angling to find out what I'm doing, but I haven't written her for months. . . .

Goodbye darlingest, your Slip thinks about you so much, all the time, & I do so hope things are fairly OK for you.

Best Love, Yr Man

To Esmond Romilly[95]   Alexandria
                                                      December 1, 1941

LEAVING FRIDAY SO TERRIFICALLY EXCITED DARLING STOP DECIDED BRING DONK DO WIRE THAT YOU AGREE HOW SHALL I CONTACT YOU JOURNEY WILL BE VERY COMFORTABLE GREATEST LOVE=ROMILLY[96]

---

95. This letter was in the form of a Western Union Cablegram.

96. The afternoon after sending this wire, Decca received a telegram from the chief of the Air Staff in Ottawa: REGRET TO INFORM YOU THAT ADVICE RECEIVED FROM ROYAL CANADIAN AIR FORCE CASUALTIES OFFICER OVERSEAS YOUR HUSBAND PILOT OFFICER ESMOND MARK DAVID ROMILLY CAN J FIVE SIX SEVEN SEVEN MISSING ON ACTIVE SERVICE NOVEMBER THIRTIETH STOP LETTER FOLLOWS. The news arrived in Alexandria the day before Decca was to leave with Constancia for New York, where she planned to spend two nights with the Durrs—who had gone there for a speech by Clifford Durr— and then sail to Britain on December 5. A neighbor phoned the Durrs in New York, and they rushed home to console Decca.

To Lady Redesdale   Alexandria
                                                                February 22, 1942

Darling Muv,

I'm afraid I haven't written for an awfully long time, tho I've had several letters from you & the Boud, also a birthday 'gram for Constancia.

I'm absolutely <u>certain</u> that Esmond is all right, although the officials (C.O.
etc) take a very unhopeful view;[97] so many different things could have happened, & he might even be in Norway or somewhere. Sometimes it takes as
long as 6 months to hear about prisoners.

Of course the last 2 1/2 months have been simply frightful; at first I kept
expecting every day to hear from him, but now I realise it may be a very long
time, perhaps till the end of the war.

I was actually about to leave for New York, where I'd got a passage on a boat
to England, when I first heard the news. I've now decided to stay here for the
present, at least until Constancia is a bit older. I'm taking a secretarial course
which is nearly finished, & after that I can easily get a job. I've got a part time
job already, which is good practice & happens to be very interesting too, so I'm
really very busy all day. . . .

Please give my love to my old Boud, I'll send her the pictures of Constancia
soon.

                          Best love from Decca

To Lady Redesdale   Washington, D.C.
                                                                October 31, 1942

Darling Muv,

I am so frightfully sorry not to have written for such a long time, and will
write more from now on. . . .

Constancia is very well, specially since the autumn came, the summer here is
much too hot for children, they get very pale and thin, and then spruce up in
the autumn. I've still got the same terribly sweet black Honkert who adores the
Donk. They are called the Two Sweet Things.

---

97. More than two weeks before writing this letter, Decca received a letter from the Washington office of the Royal Air Force Delegation of the British Air Commission describing the circumstances of the disappearance of Esmond Romilly's plane and the fruitless search for survivors. The
letter, based on an investigation requested by Winston Churchill during his December 1941 visit to
Washington—during which he met with Decca—gave no reason for the optimism Decca expressed
here. There was no indication that Esmond Romilly might have been taken prisoner, as Churchill
also informed her in December. The letter reported that his plane had last been heard from over
the North Sea on the evening of November 30, when distress signals were received indicating
"mechanical trouble" and not enemy fire, weather problems, or low fuel. The letter described a
five-hour search by three Air Sea Rescue Service planes, beginning the next morning, with no
sighting of the plane's wreckage or its dinghy. Fog prevented searches the following two days, after
which the search was abandoned.

I left the R.A.F. Delegation about a month ago, and am now working with the Office of Price Administration, an American govt. agency.[98] I like it much better; last week I went out on an investigation which was great fun. I started at $1440 a year, but have been "put in" for a raise to $2,000. Of course I don't know if I'll get it, it has to be approved by Civil Service, but if I do it would be swell—it's about the equivalent of 500 pounds a year. Luckily I don't have much typing to do, mostly things like writing manuals for investigators, etc. . . .

I have 2 boarders here,[99] one sleeping in the drawing-room and the other in Anne's bedroom. Everyone in Washington has arrangements like that now; the room shortage is so terrific, we really are lucky to have a whole apartment. The 2 boarders are extraorder; I call us the three Boards; one is a bawd, the other just an ordinary board, and I am the bored (by them). Actually they only sleep here, and don't have meals with me, thank goodness.

I go out to see the Durrs nearly every Sunday, and they come here to dinner very often. They are amazed by the Bawd and the Board, specially the Bawd, as being very respectable people they haven't seen many before. Virginia is terrifically excited, as she has almost got her Bill through Congress (to abolish the Poll Tax in the Southern states[100]); she has been working on it for 5 years now, and at last it was passed in the House of Representatives, and only has to go through the Senate. Last Saturday all her friends gave a testimonial lunch for her, it was v. exciting, everyone got up and clapped and cheered and Old Virginie nearly burst into tears. She is becoming quite famous in Washington, specially since the Bill went through the House.

Some other boarders may be coming soon, a refugee Italian girl with two children. I invited them without quite realizing that it might be difficult to fit them in; but I suppose the children can sleep in the bathroom or somewhere. I do wish you could come to America; I know it is very difficult to get here now, but on the other hand I'm always meeting people who have just come or who are just going back.

I have definitely decided to stay here, partly because the Donk seems to love it here and I think it's a much better place to bring up a child in, not because of the war, but in general. They seem to have so much fun, and they can go to college almost free, etc. Also, it's so long since I've been in England that I don't

---

98. Decca began at the OPA as a "sub-eligible typist," as she delighted in recalling years later. She recounted some of her adventures and antics at that New Deal agency in *A Fine Old Conflict*. For an account of one of those bureaucratic antics, see her letter of January 6, 1964, to Betty Friedan.

99. Decca had left the Durrs' home and moved into an apartment in Washington with Constancia and another young woman, Anne.

100. The taxes were used especially by Southern states to deter voting by blacks and poor whites. A side effect of the tax was the disenfranchisement of women. As Durr put it in her oral history, *Outside the Magic Circle* (edited by Hollinger F. Barnard, University of Alabama Press, 1985), "As a result, much of the South was run by an oligarchy composed of white, usually middle-aged, gentlemen, or men—some of them were gentlemen and some of them weren't."

feel I know anyone there much now. Of course I shall come back for visits when that is possible again, but I think I'll live here for my permanent home. I do long to see you, and Blor, and my Boud (who hasn't written for even longer than I have, tell her); but if I came back during the war I'd never be able to come back to America.

If you see Cousin Nelly,[101] tell her from me that I think she is the most horrible, vulgar and altogether thoroughly beastly person I know, and I certainly am not going to answer the pages of tripe she writes me.[102] She is the sort of person who traps one into feeling sorry for her and then does something so vile that one just loathes and despises her.

I must scram now, and will try to write again in a few days time.

Give my Boud my love, also Blor. Henderson wrote the other day, I'll write to her soon.

Best love, Decca

To Lady Redesdale   Washington, D.C.
                                                       November 24, 1942
Darling Muv,

Thanks so much for your letters. I do hope by now you've had my letters telling how much the Donk and I adored the dress you sent her. . . .

I hope old Tud will be home soon, I suppose it is awfully worrying to have him out there. Is he a general or anything yet? The goats seem to be a great interest, I always read Virginia the part about them in your letters, she gets absolutely amazed. Never having been to Europe or England she is quite unable to understand life there anyway, and now I think she thinks of English country life as centering around goats, like those Central European countries where the cattle live in the house with the people.

You can't imagine how fascinating my job is, much the best I've ever had. I really am getting along in it, and if it weren't for the fact that I <u>never went to college</u> might get to be a Section Chief. So I'm planning to go next year, to night school, which will be rather strenuous, but they all say I should. However, I may not be able to, as I'm now an Investigator, and may have to travel around the country. If so, the Durrs will look after the Donk while I'm away. . . .

We are going to the Durrs for Christmas, which is always fun, so many chil-

---

101. Esmond Romilly's mother.

102. Although Decca was never close to her mother-in-law, it is not known what specifically prompted her heightened hostility. In one of her wartime letters to Esmond Romilly, she wrote that his mother "can hardly wait to have you awarded a posthumous V.C. [Victoria Cross, Britain's highest military award], which she is probably planning to get away from me so she can be photographed with it for the press."

dren. They now have two sweet little black children there, belonging to their maid. Some of the Donk's friends in the park are black, you can't imagine how sweet they are. Sometimes on Sundays I take some of them to the zoo with the Donk. They are amazingly intelligent, much more advanced for their age than white children, some can talk at 10 months.

Give the Boud my love, I'll write her soon, also M'Honkert. I suppose this will arrive about Christmas. . . .

       Best love, From Decca

To Katharine Graham   Washington, D.C.
                     ca. December 1942

Dear Kay:

Thanks v. much for your letter. I'm sure Sioux Falls[103] isn't nearly as bleak as you make out; do admit it's really rather heaven. I may see you fairly soon, as I'm going to be transferred to the OPA office in San Francisco, which is probably quite near Sioux Falls. I have been made an investigator, and am supposed to get $2,000 a year after 3 months. I am frightfully excited about scramming to San Francisco. . . .

When are you literally coming back? I do hope before I go. Actually the transfer is not absolutely decided yet, but they've written the S.F. office, so when the answer comes I'll know for sure. . . .

I must tell you about being an investigator, it is so extraorder. One gets sent out all over Virginia and Maryland on "field trips," (right now only on rent cases) and you have to get signed statements from people and torture the horrid landlords who have been overcharging. Right now one of the landlords I have been investigating, who masquerades under the pretext of being a sweet old lady of 85, is about to be sent to jail. When I told Mrs. Foster she gave a ghastly shriek; I suppose imagining her turn would come next. It is so wonderful not having to do shorthand and typing any more. Next week I have to go and be a witness in court, so you can see what a fascinating job it is. The Donk insists on helping write this letter, so I suppose I'll have to stop.

I really will write as soon as I get ANOTHER LETTER FROM YOU.

Give my love to old Phil. . . .

       Best love from Decca

---

103. Graham had moved temporarily to Sioux Falls, South Dakota, where her husband, Philip, was stationed at an army radio school.

To Lady Redesdale   San Francisco, Calif.
                                                                        March 3, 1943

Darling Muv,

Thanks so much for your letter of the 8th Feb, which I just got. It didn't take long, considering it had to be forwarded all the way across America. . . .

We are living in a boarding house, there are also 2 marines, 3 boys aged 8, 6 & 3, & one girl about my age with the boy of 3. Mrs. Betts[104] takes care of the Donk all day, & the D. loves it because she is boy-crazy & there are 3 boys here. It is very cheap, so I'm saving a lot of dough with which to buy furniture later on if I decide to stay here for good. So far I haven't seen much of San F as I've been working pretty hard. The office here is very pleasant, but of course I don't know everybody in it like I did at the Washington OPA, which makes it slightly less fun.

We write investigation drives to be used all through the region. I am in the Industrial Machinery Section, & so far am the only one in it! Luckily no one realises I don't know anything about machinery. . . .

However I think it will be pretty nice out here. Of course it is so far one might be in a different country from Washington; but the OPA people come on business quite often. If I don't like it in San F. after a few months I may skeke off to Mexico.

How is Hon Henderson? By this time she will have pigged,[105] I suppose. Be sure & let me know what she gets.

Give the Boud my love, I'll write soon but what with moving etc I haven't had much time. . . .

          Love from Decca

To Lady Redesdale   San Francisco
                                                                       April 11, 1943

Darling Muv,

Thanks so much for your telegram about Debo's baby.[106] I _am_ so glad it was all right this time. I think now she will gradually forget about the other one, which must have made her miserable. . . .

We love San Francisco. The Donk is getting much healthier out here, which is partly why I came, Washington has a horrible climate. The people here are terrifically nice. We do work awfully hard, which is partly why I don't write much.

You asked in one letter whether the Donk has Mitford eyes; no, she hasn't, in

---

104. Decca's landlady. In *A Fine Old Conflict*, Decca called her Mrs. Tibbs, apparently either to safeguard her privacy or to protect her from whatever lingering taint there might have been from Decca's Communist Party membership, which was the book's main subject.

105. Given birth. To be "in pig" was to be pregnant. Decca said the Mitford sisters coined the terms when they had guinea pigs as children.

106. Emma. Deborah Cavendish's only previous child had been stillborn.

fact she doesn't bear the slightest resemblance to any Mitfords either in looks or character, but is exactly like Esmond. . . .

We are definitely going to stay over here. I feel that all my friends are here & those I used to know in England are all scattered around & I don't think I would like it there. Besides America is a much better place to bring up children, people are so much nicer to them here, & the free schools are much better. Also I doubt I could make enough for us to live on there. I know you realise that we couldn't ever come & live with the family. After all I was told once never to come home again, which I know wasn't your fault, but it still means I never shall. Probably now Mrs. Hammersley[107] will die while I am in America, too, so her deathbed reconciliation scene won't come off! Of course I do hope one day I'll see those members of the family I'm still on speakers with; probably after the war.

My job is heaven, tho unfortunately the reactionaries here are trying to prevent a lot of the things we want to do, & it may even result in us all losing our jobs. If so I know I can get another job very easily; but I do love the O.P.A. The FBI (like Scotland Yard) are investigating a lot of people in our division at the moment, including me. This is part of a general Red-baiting program. The Durrs were investigated, too. . . .

Love from Decca

To Lady Redesdale   San Francisco
                                                                         May 30, 1943

Darling Muv,

I just got back from Seattle & found some letters from you at the office. I'm awfully sorry to hear Farve is so ill, you must be worried about his eyes getting so bad. You do seem to be having a very thin time. I wish you could come out here & stay with us; I suppose it would be terrifically difficult to arrange, but do try. I'm sure you must need a change & a rest very badly.

I don't think we shall leave America, or if we did it would be only if I got a job in one of the rehabilitation agencies, & then we would go to Africa, or wherever they are rehabilitating. I sometimes long to be nearer the scene of action, but from what I hear one wouldn't really be nearer in England now than

---

107. Violet Hammersley (née Williams-Freeman) was a Parisian-born and -raised childhood friend of Lady Redesdale who was widowed in her mid-thirties with three young children. Known among the Mitfords as Mrs. Ham, the widow, and the wid, she was a frequent presence in the Mitford sisters' lives and was a source of ridicule, affection, and fascination; the subject of many of their stories, legends, and jokes. An eccentric, persistent, nosy woman who generally wore black and wrapped herself in shawls, she was a perennial hypochondriac and notoriously pessimistic. She was a sometime writer and friend of many well-known writers and artists of the time and was obviously an influential figure for all the sisters. Nancy Mitford maintained an active correspondence with Mrs. Hammersley for many years (and dedicated one book to her), Diana Mosley profiled her in her book *Loved Ones*, and Decca wrote about her often in her letters (see, for example, the July 4, 1962, letter to Virginia Durr).

we are in America. I feel that in my job here I'm working for the cause I always believed in—the destruction of fascism—& that all my friends are working for the same thing, & that I'm really happier than I would be in England. I do long to see you all, & to show you the beautiful Donk, but I think you'll admit that it wouldn't be a good plan for me to come & live at Swinbrook. . . .

Poor Virginia is sick, she is having some kind of nervous breakdown. Her anti poll tax bill almost got through last Autumn, but it was sabotaged by the reactionary Southern senators. I'm afraid this will happen over & over again as they are determined not to pass it.[108] Cliff wrote me that Virginia is slowly getting better, but it will take a long time. . . .

I came out here because I was getting rather restless in Washington, & I asked to be transferred. The work here is far more interesting. I was in Seattle for 2 weeks on a lumber drive, training the Seattle investigators. Just yesterday they asked me (at the office here) if I would go to Seattle permanently on lumber. They offered me a raise up to $2,600 (about $3,000 with the overtime pay—almost £700 a year) so I suppose I shall leave here soon. I'm sorry as this is a really fascinating town, & I like all the people in the office so much. I'm going to try to get a week's vacation about June 12; a friend is coming out from Washington then.[109] It is rather a nuisance about the Seattle job, as I just got moved into my new flat and bought all the furniture. The Govt. will pay for moving the furniture to Seattle, but I'll have to get some arrangement for the Donk there. . . . I don't even know for certain if I'm going yet; so if you write c/o Virginia she will forward it when I give her my address. By the way, please don't put "The Hon"[110] on the envelope, as when I get letters at the office they leave them around on my desk, & of course out here no one knows anything about my family. If they did, it would soon get around to some beastly journalist & all that publicity would start again.

Do consider coming out here if it can possibly be arranged. I know a change would do you so much good, & it doesn't make any difference where we are (here or Seattle) there'd always be somewhere you could stay.

Best love from Decca—A kiss from the Donk

. . . Do give Blor my love & tell her we'll be over to see her as soon as the war is over. She wrote me such a pathetic letter, all about never seeing me or the Donk. Love to Boud, Henderson & Nancy

---

108. The bill failed in the Senate because of a filibuster. The poll tax in federal elections wasn't finally abolished until ratification of the Twenty-fourth Amendment to the Constitution in 1964.

109. The friend was Robert Treuhaft, Decca's colleague at the Office of Price Administration in Washington. See the first letter in the next chapter.

110. "The Honorable," a title that would betray Decca's aristocratic roots.

With Robert Treuhaft
in 1943, at about the time
of their marriage.

A family Christmas in
the early 1950s. The
children, from left, are
Constancia, Nicholas,
and Benjamin.

In the early 1950s,
a visit with sister
Deborah (left) in
California.

III

SUBVERSIVE HOUSEWIFE

A surveillance photo
from Decca's FBI files.

Decca's mother-in-law,
Aranka Treuhaft, in Paris
in 1956.

After her first few months of "tortures" in San Francisco—suffering from loneliness "for the first time in my life," as she wrote her daughter many years later—Decca soon found her place in the city's labor-oriented radical tradition. And she discovered that someone was eager to share it all with her.

In mid-June 1943, Robert Treuhaft flew west to visit Decca during his annual vacation. He wrote his mother an ecstatic letter on the plane heading back to Washington. "I came out here," he wrote, "knowing that Decca loved me, but with little hope of persuading her to marry me. The second day here I asked the question and she said yes before I had a chance to finish—because she had been thinking about this for months, and had already made her decision. When Decca makes up her mind, she <u>never</u> changes it."

The day after he popped the question, they were married by a justice of the peace in Guerneville, California. They took a bus to the quiet river town north of San Francisco, passing Constancia and her suitcase out the window to a family to whom they'd been given a letter of introduction—friends of Katharine Graham—who had agreed to babysit during their absence. Decca wrote in *A Fine Old Conflict* that they chose the remote locale in order to avoid the press attention she abhorred. (The anonymity didn't last long. In December 1943, a *San Francisco Examiner* headline read: "Sister of Hitler's 'Nordic Goddess' in OPA Job Here / Jessica Freeman-Mitford Also Active in Leftist Labor Group.")

After Robert Treuhaft secured a transfer to the OPA in San Francisco, the Treuhafts settled into a crowded rooming house and quickly became involved in left-wing politics. Decca became an officer of the local United Federal Workers union, representing workers in wartime agencies, and nine months after arriving in the city was her union's delegate to the CIO state convention.

She also fulfilled a longtime goal and joined the Communist Party, along with her new husband. Decca wrote in *A Fine Old Conflict* that the German invasion of Russia on the eve of Esmond Romilly's departure for the war had "changed everything overnight. The Western Communist Parties swung straight behind the war effort. . . . And now, we [Decca and Esmond] decided, was the time for us to join the Party, Esmond in England and I in America. . . . Whether Esmond ever did so, I do not know. . . . I remained in America and carried out our resolve." She also became an American citizen to avoid possible deportation as an alien "subversive."

Decca said in a 1992 letter* that the Communist Party, though long past "its glory days" in San Francisco, was "the only game in town in terms of civil rights," and civil rights became her passion. She held a number of party positions during her fifteen years of membership, but she found her political home as the executive secretary of the East Bay Civil Rights Congress, which was listed on the attorney general's list of subversive organizations. "Were we subversive?" she asked in a 1981 lecture. "Absolutely. We spent our waking hours organizing to subvert the racist laws and racist government of the U.S. Were we outside agitators. . . . Yes, absolutely, I'm glad to say—that is, if you consider getting carloads of people to come from outside the neighbourhood to physically protect a black family from racist mobs to be the work of outside agitators."†

Although this defining period of Decca's life is covered in her memoir *A Fine Old Conflict* and is the subject of reflection in letters she wrote many years later, there are only glancing references to her important political activities in the contemporary letters, so it is worth quoting at greater length from her 1981 lecture:

> CRC's twin objectives were defense of the rights of Communists and other political dissidents, and nothing short of full equality for blacks. Meaning, mind you, not just the right to vote (then denied in most Southern American states), not just the right to equal employment and housing, not just the right not to be lynched, but full equality in every sense of the word. In our area (Oakland, California) the membership of CRC was mostly black, so was the leadership. . . . It was the fact of effective black leadership in the fight for black equality that gave our embattled organization its strength, that set it apart from such virtually all-white organizations as the American Civil Liberties Union which concerned itself primarily with the problems of white liberals and generally turned a blind eye to the vicious, rampant discrimination against blacks. . . .
>
> My day-to-day work in Oakland as executive secretary of the CRC consisted in carrying out the directives of the largely black board of directors: local cases, police brutality directed against blacks, police frame-ups of blacks in criminal cases, the physical defense of black homes against threatening white mobs.

---

* See August 21, 1992, letter to Arthur Lubow.

† For details, see footnote 58 on the Rollingwood incident in the letter of October 10, 1975, to Robert Treuhaft.

She was also a leader in the campaign against racially based evictions and discriminatory clauses in home-ownership contracts, and she was an imaginative fund-raiser for the cause, hosting countless benefit parties.

At the time, the NAACP was a prestigious association of largely middle-class blacks trying, with some notable successes, to overturn discriminatory laws in the Supreme Court. As Robert Treuhaft put it, the NAACP was "never involved in day-to-day activities on the street," fighting for the rights of individual blacks, as was the CRC. Decca herself considered the community-oriented CRC a "forerunner" of such organizations as the Congress of Racial Equality and the Student Nonviolent Coordinating Committee. It also had an impact on the children who were to become influential in Oakland's black political resurgence several decades later. Decca was once told by Black Panther Party co-founder Huey Newton that when he was a young boy growing up in Oakland, Robert Treuhaft was "a hero to all the kids" in his neighborhood because of Treuhaft's—and the CRC's—dogged defense of wrongfully accused murder suspect Jerry Newson.

Oakland, the city where the Treuhafts settled in 1947 and did most of their work—Robert Treuhaft as a partner in a radical law firm—had a large black population that was lured from the South during the wartime shipbuilding boom and then left isolated, with inadequate resources, when the boom ended. Police officers often acted like an occupying army in black neighborhoods. At the time, the city was run by a clique of white, right-wing Republicans including the family of powerful Senator William F. Knowland, owners of the *Oakland Tribune*, and county district attorney J. Frank Coakley, a crusading Red-hunter who conducted a personal vendetta against the Treuhafts—and vice versa. As Decca described their new hometown in *A Fine Old Conflict*, "There was nothing abstract about the class struggle in Oakland."

In that hostile environment, Decca frequently marshaled public support for causes her husband and his associates litigated. By all accounts, she was a passionate, disciplined, and effective advocate. And she was, to use the words of her old friend and colleague Marge Frantz, "totally gutsy." Pele de Lappe, another dear friend who knew her in those days, called her "terribly brave." Frantz says that "in most places the CRC was little more than an arm of the CP, but Oakland was the only place in the country where the CRC became a mass movement within the black community. And it was almost all Decca's doing. She was a phenomenal organizer."

Her activities during this era were chronicled in tedious, almost comical detail by the FBI. In voluminous files, numerous informants—their names blacked out—"advise" the government of "the subject's" attendance at meetings of Communist-affiliated groups at specified dates and addresses. Photos taken covertly from nearby observation points show "subject" entering premises.

Not all the surveillance was visual. Bill Turner, a former FBI agent, has recounted how he once overheard a familiar and very distinctive voice at a San Francisco cocktail party in the 1960s but couldn't place the face. He went up to "the lady" and introduced himself. She identified herself as Decca Treuhaft, whereupon Turner realized that the voice was so memorable because, as a twenty-three-year-old FBI agent in the early '50s, he had monitored her family's phone lines for two years. He said he had known the Treuhaft family's daily activities so well he felt almost like a member of the extended family, but he'd never met them in person. He told Decca the story and reported that she "broke out in gales of laughter." In retrospect, Turner said, he didn't learn much about the activities of his "security subject" aside from "things like what kind of toothpaste she used."

As the repression of dissidents gathered steam with the outbreak of the Korean War, Decca also was subpoenaed by legislative committees, state and national, seeking to expose and shame "un-Americans" in their midst. On one celebrated occasion in 1951, she was subpoenaed to appear before California's Senate Fact-Finding Committee on Un-American Activities in San Francisco's City Hall, and ordered to bring with her all the CRC's membership and contributor lists. She didn't bring the records, an act of contempt that could have led to twenty-five years in prison. At one point in the hearing, she refused to answer—on the usual self-incrimination grounds—a question she heard as "Are you a member of the Berkeley Tenants Club?" Only after much laughter from the audience did Decca realize that she had been asked by the committee's counsel—"trying his hand at heavy sarcasm"—whether she was a member of the Berkeley *Tennis* Club, which she described in *A Fine Old Conflict* as "a bastion of posh conservatism." According to a transcript of the hearing, the committee's counsel commented, "I don't think you will find that cited as a subversive group," to which Decca replied, "How do I know what your Committee decided [was subversive]?" The hubbub occasioned by the exchange apparently so flustered the counsel that he forgot to demand her records before adjourning the session, and Decca was spirited into hiding by her attorneys until the committee left town.

Robert Treuhaft made headlines of his own before the House Un-American Activities Committee. On one such occasion in late 1953, described in the *San Francisco Examiner* as "the day's stormiest appearance," he concluded his testimony by telling the committee, "Your Bible is guilt by association," setting off a noisy outburst of support that provoked the chair to clear the hearing room. The committee later bestowed on him what Decca called "the signal honor of a listing among the thirty-nine most dangerously subversive lawyers in the country."

During this era, when newspapers reported on her activities, the shorthand description for Decca was often "Oakland housewife," though she hardly fit the stereotype. She gave birth to two other children: Nicholas, born in 1944, who was killed at the age of ten when he was struck by a bus while delivering newspapers on his bike, and Benjamin, born in 1947. She was devoted to them. Her letters to her mother and mother-in-law are filled with anecdotes about the children. But she later summed up her parenting conduct as "benign neglect," and she gave her daughter full credit for raising Benjamin. Decca was far too busy for many of the day-to-day chores performed by the conventional stay-at-home mothers of that era, and the children often participated in picketing, leafletting, and other political activities.

Treuhaft family lore is replete with stories about Decca's legendary incompetence at housekeeping. One story concerns the time when Decca started to sweep the stairs, only to be corrected by her daughter, who advised that the proper way to do it was to start at the top of the stairs and sweep toward the bottom, not vice versa. (Decca told the same story on herself in *Daughters and Rebels*, placing the incident years earlier and attributing the admonition to a friend of Esmond Romilly.) At one point late in the 1940s, Decca applied to the local probation department for a "Delinquent Youth" as a sitter for the children; she reported that the request was denied because "the probation lade didn't seem to think much of us as guardians."

Through the 1940s, Decca wrote only sporadically to her English family, who continued to make headlines of their own. In 1943, Diana Mosley and her husband encountered a national outcry when they were released from prison. In 1945, the only brother, Tom, was killed in combat in Burma, where according to a friend he was stationed because "[h]e does not wish to go to Germany killing German civilians whom he likes. He prefers to kill Japanese whom he does not like." Sister Unity died in 1948 of complications from her self-inflicted gunshot wound. Sister Nancy published a string of popular novels. And the youngest daughter, Deborah, found herself in line to become the Duchess of Devonshire and chatelaine of the magnificent Chatsworth estate when her husband's older brother, the Marquess of Hartington, was killed in combat in Belgium in 1944; Andrew Cavendish inherited the dukedom upon his father's death in 1950.

In 1944, Decca's mother forwarded to her a letter from Lord Redesdale, written after he learned of the birth of her son Nicholas. ("He did not know your address," she wrote.) The ice-breaking letter was, her father said, "Just to send you my love and every good wish for him and his future. Some day, when things are in a more settled state, I greatly hope to see you all, and judging from all news and the look of things it seems to me there is some prospect that I may last that long—I should much like to." As far as is known, it was his only letter to her after she left home, but if Decca responded, there is no surviving evidence of it, and the day of her elopement was the last she ever saw of him. Still separated from his wife, Lord Redesdale died in his two-room cottage in Northumberland in 1958, more than twenty years after Decca escaped to Spain. Disclosure of his will, in which he apportioned his fortune to his wife and children, "except Jessica," brought a new round of lurid international headlines ("Lord Redesdale Cut Off Daughter Who Wed Leftist," "Peer's Will Snubs E. Bay Leftist Kin," "Redesdale Will Cuts Off Madcap Jessica" . . . and many others).

With her brother Tom's death, Decca, though disinherited by her father, received title to a small portion of Inch Kenneth, the family's island retreat in the Hebrides. She further exacerbated family relations by trying unsuccessfully to donate her share to the British Communist Party.

Despite their only episodic correspondence, Decca did visit with some family members occasionally during this period. In 1948 her mother traveled to Oakland, and a few years later her sister Deborah, "to my surprise and joy, came over for a Honnish reunion."

Lady Redesdale's reunion with her daughter after nearly a decade was both eventful and unexpected. Constancia Romilly was the agent, sending her grandmother a Christmas thank-you letter in which she wrote, "I wish you would come to see us in Oakland one day." The acceptance came soon thereafter in a telegram, with arrival details. Decca was simultaneously moved by the gesture and in "a state of near terror." She later said that in "re-getting to know" her mother she "became immensely fond of her, really rather adored her." Amid her preparations for the unexpected reunion, Decca sought out her local Communist Party chairman because of rules against consorting with "enemies of the working class." She was informed drily that the restriction didn't apply to visiting mothers.

The initial awkwardness of the visit dissolved into laughter, thanks again to Constancia, who asked in the car driving home from the airport, "Granny Muv, when are you going to scold Decca for running away?" Lady Redesdale apparently got into the spirit of the Treuhafts' life, and a few years later when she asked Decca what the CRC was, her daughter replied, "Don't you remember, you made potato salad for them when you were here."

Decca's most extended family visit during this period was in 1955, when she returned to England for the first time in sixteen years, a trip that is well documented in the letters, although—perhaps because of government surveillance—there is no contemporaneous reference in her letters to the Treuhafts' side trip to then-Communist Hungary.* Decca later wrote about the trip for the Communist paper *People's World* ("We Visited Socialism"), and she discussed it at length in *A Fine Old Conflict*. The family's voyage to Europe by ship began with high drama and high spirits when the Treuhafts managed to evade federal agents pursuing them to revoke their passports because of their Communist affiliations.

When they arrived in England, Decca wrote, she felt "out of place, in an odd way," in her old circles. "I sometimes wondered why I had left the satisfying world I had carved out for myself in Oakland to revive often oddly painful

---

* See the letter of November 14, 1956, to Aranka Treuhaft.

memories and relationships from the vanished past." (Some members of her family were equally discomfited by the return of their "Red sheep.")

Decca also corresponded dutifully with her Hungarian Jewish mother-in-law, Aranka Treuhaft. Their relationship was often strained, but Decca managed to maintain an air of cordiality, though not without her usual humorous twist. She once recalled: "Aranka was always trying to get me to make Bob more ambitious, to get ahead in the world, make more money. So one day (during her first visit) I leaned out of the window as he was setting off for work and shouted at the top of my lungs: 'Get to work, you lazy good-for-nothing bum' & other invectives. It was quite effective; pedestrians stopped in their tracks to watch, neighbors up & down the street came to their windows to see what was going on. But she *still* wasn't pleased."

In 1958, Decca and her husband left the Communist Party, long after many of their friends had done so, but they never lost the social passion that brought them to it. She never expressed any sense of hostility to or betrayal by the Party. Although in her correspondence she referred often over the years to her reasons for leaving the Party—and her continuing commitment to its professed values and to those friends who remained Communists—in the letters she omitted some of the political considerations that contributed to her sense that the Party was becoming "drab and useless." (Robert Treuhaft's word for the Party in the '50s was "stodgy.")

The beginning of the end occurred in 1956 when CRC members came under intense pressure from the FBI. Many were harassed at work and fearful for their livelihoods. The national party was also in internal turmoil over Soviet party leader Nikita Khrushchev's revelations of atrocities committed under Josef Stalin. The American party's solution to the two problems was to disband the CRC and other affiliated organizations and work instead to achieve their goals within mainstream American organizations. Decca, whose primary commitments—at least since the defeat of Nazism—had been on the local level, said that the CRC had been "chased out of existence by the FBI," but she accepted the inevitability of its dissolution and "mourned its passing." Her distress, she said, "was compounded by the vacuum it left in my own life."

Decca participated in the continuing self-reassessment by the Communist Party as a delegate to its state and national conventions in 1957. Its coffers empty and its ranks depleted by mass defections after the Hungarian uprising, the Party attempted to regroup. The grass-roots democratic stirrings that gave Decca hope at the national convention soon proved illusory as the orthodox leadership re-established centralized control and maintained its orientation toward the Soviet Union. The Party was no longer productive. "We were going to meetings and wasting a lot of time," Robert Treuhaft said. The next year, the Treuhafts joined the exodus from the Party, convinced that they could pursue their social aims more effectively by working with other radical organizations. In a sense, the Party drifted from Decca as much as she drifted from it.

Decca continued some of her activism without an institutional framework. She maintained her impassioned interest in the civil rights advocacy and the often violent white racist reaction that were convulsing the segregated Deep South in the late 1950s. Virginia and Clifford Durr, by now resettled in Montgomery, Alabama, were in the thick of the battle, and Decca was a sometimes invaluable ally, marshaling money and other resources and funneling them back through the Durrs.

Though hardly a feminist, Decca was acutely aware of a lesson she'd learned from her sister Nancy's prolonged residency at home before she was married: "the obvious fact that one can't be independent of others (whether parents or husbands) unless one can earn one's own living." Left by the CRC's demise without a job, profession, or clear mission, she took a position as a probationary employee in the classified advertising department of the *San Francisco Chronicle*, delighted at last to be a part of the working world—her first non-Party job in thirteen years. Her assignment was to call advertisers in competing newspapers to try to poach their business. Although the job was "as close to rock bottom as any work I had ever done," Decca threw herself into it with her customary dedication, receiving sales prizes and commendations from her superiors. But she couldn't hold on to the job for a familiar reason. Two FBI agents came calling on her employers, informing them that Decca was under surveillance as a suspected Communist. She was told abruptly that her services were no longer needed. (Former FBI agent Turner later confirmed that agents in the early '50s sometimes went to the offices of suspected Party members and sometimes made anonymous calls to employers—"it was done all the time.")

The loss of her menial *Chronicle* job taught Decca that she would have to earn a living on her own. As she summarized her employment dilemma in a letter years later: "a) no marketable skills, b) no education, c) blacklisted for being a Subversive." She stumbled into a new career, "more or less driven into the field of writing because of inability to get other work."

The first result was a mimeographed, hand-stapled booklet written in 1956 while she was still a member of the Communist Party, with profits earmarked for the annual fund drive of the *People's World*. The full title was "Lifeitselfmanship, or How to Become a Precisely-Because Man: An Investigation Into Current L (or Left-Wing) Usage." She spoofed the jargon of Communist functionaries—a service Nancy Mitford had performed in *Noblesse Oblige* for the English upper classes*—and readily acknowledged that her effort was "pat-

---

* *Noblesse Oblige: An enquiry into the identifiable characteristics of the English aristocracy* (published in 1956 by Hamish Hamilton in Britain and Harper Brothers in the United States) was edited by Nancy Mitford and anchored by her 1955 satirical essay "The English Aristocracy." The highly popular book, reprinted often over the years, included essays by other writers, including the scholar whose work on "Upper Class English Usage" Mitford popularized. In it, she highlighted U (upper-class) and non-U behavior and diction. In the process she made "U" and "non-U" an enduring part of the language, as well as a source of endless social analysis and party and pub chitchat.

terned after" her sister's, while strenuously denying suggestions that she had turned to writing out of "sibling rivalry." "Lifeitselfmanship" was an unexpected success, even among many Party members, and Decca wrote that she "basked in the sudden, unexpected fame I had achieved in our circles." The booklet also had the serious, if unarticulated, effect of helping to undermine the dogmatism she was fighting in the Party.

She followed that in 1957 with a story in *The Nation* about the "trial by headline" and subsequent exoneration of a suspect in a sensational rape-torture case in San Francisco. It was her first work in a major national publication and "for me a turning point," she later wrote. She was forty years old and still feeling her way toward a true career.

Coupled with an enthusiastic response from a New York literary agent, publication of the *Nation* article encouraged her to try writing a memoir. The book started out as the nineteen-page draft of a foreword to what she hoped would be a collection of Esmond Romilly's wartime letters, and it grew from there. (It may well have been the experience of rereading those cherished old letters and researching that period of her past that prompted Decca to make carbon copies of most of her contemporary correspondence, which she began doing around the same time, thus making this letters collection possible.)

Slowly at first, then with increasing seriousness, she began to write a full-fledged memoir, with encouragement and editing assistance from a group of longtime friends and political associates she dubbed the Book Committee, or sometimes just the Committee.

Decca also became intrigued by a subject that was initially of interest primarily to her husband but was to evolve into her signature achievement, *The American Way of Death*.* In late 1958, a small, liberal Los Angeles political magazine called *Frontier* published her article on expensive funeral practices and the new low-cost alternatives, funeral co-ops, such as the one with which Robert Treuhaft was working in Berkeley. Decca has said that colleagues of her husband in the cooperative "put me up to writing" the article. Called "St. Peter, Don't You Call Me," it had been rejected by larger publications but was enthusiastically received by the few people exposed to it in *Frontier*, and reprints were distributed among the limited number of people involved in the early cooperative burial societies.

Like her previous two articles, and occasional pieces published earlier in Communist Party newspapers, "St. Peter" was part of Decca's continuing social activism, in a different format. It was a new start, but it was not out of character for the woman who had come with her daughter and a few possessions to make a new life for herself in San Francisco a decade and a half earlier.

■ ■

---

* Simon & Schuster, 1963.

To Lady Redesdale   San Francisco
                                                                        June 28, 1943

Darling Muv,

Thank you so much for your letters, & also for the mags. that come regularly.

You will be v. surprised to hear I am married to Bob Treuhaft. I know I haven't told you about him before, so will do so now: I have known him since about last December (he works for OPA too, & is an attorney in the Enforcement Division). Since coming out here last February I was terrifically lonely without him, & he tried to transfer out here too but they needed him in Washington. 2 weeks ago he came out on annual leave & we decided to get married. I am tremendously happy & all the bitter, horrible past months seem to have vanished.

Bob had to go back to Washington to finish up his job there but we are going to live out here. We will come on trips to Europe after the war, or maybe before if we can get jobs in any of the agencies that send people overseas.

I haven't met Bob's mother & sister as they work in New York, but his mother may come out here. She wrote an awfully nice letter.

I'm still working for OPA, & love it as much as ever. The Donk is fine, she adores Bob.

I do hope you will realise how wonderful everything is. I would have written you about it except it was all so terrifically sudden (I hadn't even thought of such a thing till Bob came out here on his hol.) & then I decided not to cable you as writing is much better.

Tell Blor & everyone about it for me. I will write them when things get more calmed down.

Is Farve any better? I do hope so.

                      Love from Decca

To Lady Redesdale   San Francisco
                                                                        July 21, 1943

Darling Muv,

. . . Letters do take an awfully long time. I suppose that by now you've had my letter about me & Bob getting married. I wish I could tell you more about him except it's almost impossible to explain anyone in a letter. Perhaps one day you'll come over here, or we will go to England on a trip. . . . I'm awfully glad we are going to live in San Francisco; it is such a fascinating town & about the most progressive town in the country; in some ways it seems more like the capital than Washington, anyway as far as the labor movement is concerned.

Bob just called up to say he has been out to see Virginia & she is much better. She has had a sort of nervous breakdown brought on by the defeat of the anti poll tax bill in the Senate last year & by the fact that Cliff is in the middle of constant fights in his agency & is on all the Dies[1] lists etc. Do you read much about America in the English papers? Dies is one of the congressmen over here who is constantly attacking government workers suspected of left-wing tendencies, & is one of the chief Red-baiters. OPA is having the same trouble, but our Union[2] is pretty strong & so far no one has been fired out here. I'm now Organization Director for our local, which means a terrific lot of work after hours. Thank goodness Mrs. Betts really is wonderful with Dinkydonk & takes good care of her all the time. The Donk is so sweet these days, she is my pride & joy. She can dress & undress herself completely, which I think is very good for being only 2, and she can count up to 10 and sing several songs in tune. She is just learning "Ninety & Nine" which reminds me of Blor. . . .

One very lucky thing is that there has been absolutely no publicity about us getting married, which I was quite dreading. I think all danger is now passed since the papers missed it entirely and now it would be too long ago to be news. They would probably have made an awful stink, especially as Bob is Jewish & they would have brought out all the old stuff about our family. Out here no one knows anything about that, & I think the days are over when one couldn't do a thing without it getting in the papers. . . .

I got a letter from Henderson & will write her soon. Love to her & Emma, and to my old Boud.

Best love from Decca

P.S. I really didn't mean to tease when I wrote about being turned out of the family. That's a long time ago anyway. What I really meant was, which I think you'll agree with, that all our ideas & beliefs are so tremendously different & opposed that it would be impossible now to go back to an ordinary family life. I don't think any more, as I once did, that this means one can't be on writers, or even speakers if close enough! . . .

---

1. Democratic Representative Martin Dies Jr. of Texas was the first chairman (1938–45) of the House Committee on Un-American Activities (HUAC), established to investigate disloyalty, propaganda, and subversion. He set the standard for the committee's badgering, contemptuous style of interrogation and its sweeping and unsubstantiated accusations of Communist affiliation. The committee's ideology, tactics, and tone were later adopted by Senator Joseph McCarthy in his notorious Red-hunting investigations.

2. The United Federal Workers union, whose local branch was headed by Doris (Dobby) Brin (later Walker), who became a decades-long friend of the Treuhafts and a law partner of Robert Treuhaft.

To Aranka Treuhaft[3]   San Francisco
                                                          July 30, 1943

Dearest Aranka,

Thank you ever so much for your letter—it didn't take long this time, only 3 days. Bob's letters have been taking nearly a week, even airmail-special.

I'm afraid, in spite of what you say, my letters aren't really much good! So what I'm hoping is that you can come out and visit us very soon and we shall get to know each other. I still don't know for sure what day Bob will be able to leave Washington—he thought he could leave Friday (today) by plane, but now it won't be before Sunday because of the travel budget in OPA. It really is a nightmare; anything done by the administrative section of OPA seems to take an age. I was so hoping he would be here by tomorrow, but now I'm trying not to plan on his coming for another week, so I won't be disappointed again. . . .

Work here is getting very dismal—Bob probably told you about some of the fights that are going on out here. Well the latest thing is that they fired McTernan[4] (head of the Enforcement Division, where I work) and of course everyone is fearfully upset as he has done such a swell job, and firing him is just another dirty manoeuvre of those in OPA who are really against strong enforcement.

Everybody in the office here is so much looking forward to Bob getting out, as I've told them what a wonderful source of ideas etc he will be in getting McTernan reinstated. Of course we are all planning great things for a fight on this issue—everybody is boiling mad about it.

Dinkydonk is fine except she got a fearful black eye last Sunday—she ran full tilt into a stone wall in the park. I'm hoping to get it better before Bob comes out here, he will be horrified if he sees it & think she has been cruelly treated! . . .

Goodbye—I'll write again soon.

Lots of love, Decca

To Lady Redesdale   San Francisco
                                                       November 23, 1943

Darling Muv,

I'm sorry not to have written for so long, but we have been awfully busy, and as soon as we get home at night we have the Donk to look after, which as you

---

3. Robert Treuhaft's mother. Long widowed at the time this letter was written, she was a custom milliner with an eponymous shop, Madame Aranka, on Park Avenue in New York City.

4. John McTernan, who became a good friend of the Treuhafts and later went into private practice in Los Angeles. According to a mutual friend, it was John McTernan who convinced Decca to become a citizen so she wouldn't be deported. McTernan's brother Francis (Frank) was also a lawyer and good friend of the Treuhafts; he later served as Decca's legal counsel when she was subpoenaed to appear before the California Senate Fact-Finding Committee on Un-American Activities.

can imagine makes letter writing impossible, she expects to be played with every minute. . . .

I was simply furious to hear that the Mosleys have been released & am glad to see in the papers that the whole of England is in an uproar about it.[5] I think it is a real act of treachery against everybody who is fighting in this war. I do hope they are not staying with you because if they are I feel I shall have to stop writing to anyone in the same house with them. Please let me know about this. As you know I look upon them as dangerous enemies & the fact I was once related to Diana doesn't make any difference to this feeling.

I'm enclosing pictures of the Donk, taken by Bob. I wish you could see her, she is such a wonderful child. She is going to school in January (nursery school) & I am teaching her to spell already. She can also talk a little French, which is considered quite good for only 2 1/2 by the other mothers I know here.

I'm still working for OPA & got another raise; but I'm planning to leave this job soon & will probably work on a newspaper. Bob is working for the War Labor Board now, it's in the same building as OPA, which is wonderful because it means we can have lunch together every day. We still love San Francisco & have got to know a lot of the trade union people out here. I was a delegate from our union to the CIO State Convention, which lasted 4 days. It was very exciting. Bob came too, as an observer.

Do give my love to Blor, & give her one of these pictures. It is getting almost impossible to get film, but we have one more which will be developed soon & I'll send you the pictures.

We are getting ready for Christmas already, this will be the first year the Donk will really enjoy it. It is terribly hard to find nice things, there is practically no choice & everything is terrifically expensive. We're going out to the country one Sunday to get the tree.

Give Boud my love—Love from Decca

To Winston Churchill   San Francisco
                                                              November 24, 1943

Dear Cousin Winston:

I am writing to you to add my protest to the thousands which I imagine you are receiving against the release of the Mosleys.

---

5. Earlier in November, Decca's sister Diana Mosley and her husband, Oswald, were released from Holloway prison after three and a half years' confinement because of Oswald Mosley's ill health. They were to serve a form of house arrest, under police guard and away from London, with specified travel and other restrictions. The public reaction was intense, with newspapers editorializing against the release, tens of thousands of street demonstrators chanting, "Put Mosley back," and many thousands more writing Churchill in protest. Public opinion polls showed overwhelming public opposition to the release.

Their release is being interpreted in this country, even by the reactionary press, as an indication that there is a real cleavage between the will of the people and the actions of the ruling class in England, and that the Government is not truly dedicated to the cause of exterminating fascism in whatever place and in whatever form it rears its head. Unless the Mosleys are immediately put back in jail where they belong, great harm will be done to the cause of friendship between Britain and America.

My personal feeling is that the release of the Mosleys is a slap in the face to antifascists in every country, and that it is a direct betrayal of those who have died for the cause of anti-fascism. The fact that Diana is my sister doesn't alter my opinion on this subject.

    Yours sincerely,

P.S. If you wish to answer this letter, the above is my permanent address in this country.[6]

---

6. There is no surviving evidence that Churchill ever personally read this letter, much less replied. Although Decca retained an unsigned carbon copy of the letter in her personal files, it is also unclear if this is a draft or the version of the letter that she finally mailed. In *A Fine Old Conflict*, Decca quoted from the letter she sent, using wording that does not appear in this carbon copy. In that version, she told Churchill:

> Like millions of others in the United Nations and the occupied countries, I have all my life been an opponent of the Fascist ideology in whatever form it appears. Because I do not believe that family ties should be allowed to influence a person's convictions I long ago ceased to have any contact with those members of my family who have supported the Fascist cause. Release of Sir Oswald and Lady Mosley is a slap in the face of anti-Fascists in every country and a direct betrayal of those who have died for the cause of anti-Fascism. They should be kept in jail, where they belong.

Decca sent a copy of her letter to the *San Francisco Chronicle*, which published a news story on December 5, based on the wording she later quoted in *A Fine Old Conflict*. (Decca broke her press boycott after being hounded by reporters and photographers looking for a "local angle" on the Mosleys' release. An especially persistent photographer from the Hearst-owned *San Francisco Examiner* had infuriated her, as had the *Examiner*'s headline "Sister of Hitler's 'Nordic Goddess' in OPA Job Here." Decca sought advice from a friendly union editor, who suggested the letter to Churchill clarifying her views; she gave the letter as an exclusive to the *Examiner*'s chief competition, the *Chronicle*.)

In her memoir, Decca also commented on her Churchill letter from her perspective thirty-four years later: "Rereading this letter today, I find it painfully stuffy and self-righteous—and also, as Nancy later pointed out in her understated fashion, 'not very sisterly.' " She went on to clarify her rationale at the time but added that "[i]n my case, no doubt, these views—as comes through strongly in my letter—were admixed with deep bitterness over Esmond's death and a goodly dash of familial spitefulness."

To Lady Redesdale   San Francisco
                                                                        March 27, 1944

Darling Muv,

  . . . The main reason I haven't written for so long is that you never answered my question about the Mosleys. I see in the papers that they are living in Shipton, so I suppose you do see them. I was so disgusted when they were released, & so much in sympathy with the demonstrators against their release that it actually makes me feel like a traitor to write to anyone who has anything to do with them. However I see that it is difficult for you, & not your fault!

  I'm now working for the Joint Anti-Fascist Refugee Committee as their San Francisco director. I left OPA in December because the job involved such a lot of travelling & I hate to leave Bob and the Donk so much. The new work is awfully interesting, and most of my friends are out of OPA too, so I don't think I'd like it much any more. . . . Donk is going to school now, she started going in Jan. & is being what they call "promoted" this month! (It means going into the next class.) She is so independent these days, can dress herself etc. completely & gets furious if you try to help her do anything. She has a new habit now of threatening to run away if we scold her for anything. The other day she got her little suitcase & packed her doll & nightgown & started for the door. We think she has running away blood in her, & is bound to really do it one day. . . .

  I wrote to Tom & sent him a picture of Donk, but he'll probably never get the letter as I just addressed it Middle East. . . .

  The wonderful Mrs. Betts continues to "do" for us & looks after Donk when she gets home from school; I shall miss her terribly if we leave. I get the breakfast at 7:00 a.m. as Donk leaves at 8:00 & Bob soon after; we cook our own dinner too, also out of the American Cook Book, strangely enough. Bob's sister gave us a Mrs. Beeton[7] for a wedding present, very reminiscent of Mrs. Stobie[8] & the kitchen at Swinbrook.

  Give Blor my love. I will write her soon & send some Donk photos. I would love to see a picture of Emma. I wonder if she is at all like the Donk.

                                                  Love from Decca

---

  7. Britain's famed Mrs. Beeton cookbooks were knockoffs of the original 1861 *Mrs. Beeton's Book of Household Management*, which was a favorite of Decca's and figured later in her research and in one of her lawsuits. The book was written by a housewife, Isabella Beeton, married to a publisher who, after her premature death, exploited and later sold his late wife's brand. The original that so captivated Decca was far more than a cookbook. Its breadth can be gauged by its full original title, *The Book of Household Management Comprising Information for the Mistress, Housekeeper, Cook, Kitchen-Maid, Butler, Footman, Coachman, Valet, Upper and Under House-Maids, Lady's-Maid, Maid-of-all-Work, Laundry-Maid, Nurse and Nurse-Maid, Monthly Wet and Sick Nurses, etc. etc.—also Sanitary, Medical, & Legal Memoranda: with a History of the Origin, Properties, and Uses of all Things Connected with Home Life and Comfort.*
  8. The family's cook.

To Aranka Treuhaft   Stanford University Hospital, San Francisco
                                                                    May 1944

Dear Aranka,

I just got your wedding announcement & am sorry to see we spelt your new name wrong every time we wrote.[9] . . .

The beautiful Mong[10] was born with no trouble at all at 12:10 a.m., May 16th. He started to come about 2 in the afternoon (as I was seeing Bob sworn in to the Calif. bar), but the pains weren't bad enough to go to the hospital till after supper, about 7 p.m. Bob & I sat around playing cribbage & chatting till midnight; I felt no pain at all & was completely conscious throughout. At midnight there was a mild explosion, which was the water's breaking, so I scrammed into the delivery room, & ten minutes later the Mong popped out, looking very annoyed about everything, covered with blood & slime but otherwise exactly like old Bob. I didn't even have to have any stitches! After that we played some more cribbage & Bob left around 1 a.m. I had this marvellous new caudal anaesthetic which numbs you from the waist down but you stay awake all through. Ever since he was born I have felt really swell. I know I could easily get up & go out right now, but they keep you here a minimum of 8 days. I've had lots of visitors although there is a rule you can only have your husband & mother for the first 5 days—the trick is, I have them ask for the other girl in the ward who has been here more than 5 days. Also, this room is conveniently located near a fire escape, which means that Bob can get in during non-visiting hours. He has taken pictures of Nick Tito nursing through the window.

The Mong looks just like Bob—he has black hair, with 2 sections of non-hair at the sides, slanting eyes (blue at present, but they'll probably turn brown soon). His nose is broad at the top like mine & wavy in the middle like Bob's. He has huge red cheeks & is very fat & large all over. He is also the hospital champ—the biggest baby in the nursery. The nurse says he cries so loud he wakes up all the patients when she brings him down to nurse! . . .

Dink is [excited]. . . . They say at school that she's been talking about her baby brother constantly. . . .

Love from Decca

---

9. Aranka Treuhaft's new husband was Al Kliot, but Robert Treuhaft has said that she was never known by her married name "except possibly [by] purists like Decca bred to use it as a courtesy title."

10. Decca's early nickname for her first son, Nicholas Tito Treuhaft, born on May 16. Further explanations of his name and nickname can be found in letters of June 15, 1944, to Lady Redesdale, and May 1945 to Nancy Mitford.

To Lady Redesdale   San Francisco
                                                              June 15, 1944

Darling Muv,

Thanks for your letters. I roared at the Honnish rules,[11] so did Bob; the second set was so like the rules for a Union meeting.[12]

Our baby is wonderful, he weighed over 9 lbs at birth & was weighing over 10 lbs at 3 weeks. . . . [W]hen I got home Mrs. Betts looked after Nicholas. I'm starting work next week, and she will go on looking after him in the daytime. . . . I have a new job in Oakland, about an hour away from here by bus & train, so when I start work things will be rather rushed. My new job is financial director for the California Labor School. The school trains union people in organizing, economics etc.,[13] & my job is to raise funds to keep the school going, write publicity etc. I think it will be very interesting.

The Donk adores Nicholas, she rushes in to see him every day after school & helps to give him his bottle. . . . When we get home at night it is like moving an army with all its equipment; Bob carries Nicholas in his cradle, I carry Donk & her clothes for the morning, then we have to get his bottles & her dolls. We have to take them down the fire escape, which is the only entrance to our flat. . . .

We call the new baby the Mong because of his Mongolian eyes (Bob is partly Mongolian). . . .

        Love from Decca

To Lady Redesdale   San Francisco
                                          August 21, 1944, and thereafter

Darling Muv,

Thank you so much for the lovely blanket for Nick, it is so unlike anything one can get here, & reminds me of children's parties in England where they arrive swathed in shetland shawls. I got your letter of July 25 too. I roared about the Union of S. African Republics. I meant <u>trade</u> union meetings.

---

11. Lady Redesdale appears to have unearthed and sent to Decca the rules of the Society of Hons that she and her sister Deborah had conceived as children.

12. Decca's mother later replied to this passage in Decca's letter by saying, "I wish I knew what the 'Union' is, to me it means the Union of S. African Republics. You say the Hons rules remind you of a Union meeting. What funny little objects you & Debo were. . . ."

13. The Communist-affiliated school, formerly the Tom Mooney School, was one of a number of such institutions around the country that flourished during the post–Pearl Harbor industrial expansion, changing its name at about the time Decca went to work there to reflect its expanded role and the infusion of financing from corporations, universities, and other establishment organizations. In addition to teaching labor and Marxist issues, it offered an increasingly broad array of classes in psychology, the arts, and other subjects. One of the school's many celebrated art teachers was Pele de Lappe, Decca's friend and fellow Communist Party member whose first husband, Bert Edises, was to become a law partner of Robert Treuhaft.

We have found a house at last, have bought it and are moving in this week. The only way one can get a place to live here is by buying it, as no landlords will rent to those with children (I mean in San Francisco, which is fearfully overcrowded). The house has 6 rooms—3 bedrooms. I've also found a nurse for the children—she has a husband & 2 children & they are all going to live with us. Her children are school age. So you can see the bedrooms are going to be fairly packed. I'm taking this week off from work to move. Donk is terrifically excited. There's a little garden where she can probably keep rabbits or dogs, if the nurse is agreeable. . . . Nicholas is growing at a terrific rate, he is so fat & healthy & already eating pablum, a kind of sawdust which they mix with water & feed to children here. We shall miss the Dann kids (Donny & Kenny) and Mrs. Betts, but this place is getting awfully overcrowded now there are 4 of us. . . .

I see it is now Sept. 25th & I haven't finished this letter. We are now living in the new house, it is wonderful & convenient compared to the flat. . . . Bob has just got a new job with a labor law firm (TRADE union clients), it is exactly the job he has been wanting, so we are awfully pleased. . . .

Donk has reached the stage of "being" things, the other day she was a frog, & wouldn't answer any questions because she said "frogs don't talk." Sometimes she says my finger is a German, & then if I'm not careful to keep out of her way she gives it a terrible bite. One of her chief amusements is the way I eat (because Americans hold their fork in the right hand & never use a knife). She tells people "Dec eats that way because she used to be in England." She also quite often corrects the way I say words like dance, grass etc. At school her teachers say she is the most independent child they've ever had there, because she won't let them help her dress, or go to the loo.

Nicholas is a rather different type, more serious & thoughtful & with a different sense of humour. I can't tell whether he is going to be independent like Dink, but I think he will be quieter & more studious. He is getting awfully pretty, & has strong eyebrows like Bob.

We are all working hard on the elections, trying to get Roosevelt reelected. Everybody is canvassing in their neighbourhood. Donk & the Ross children are very good at distributing leaflets on the election from house to house, except that if Donk likes the people she usually gives them about 10 leaflets so we run short. She is used to leaflet distribution as she did some last year when the political campaign first started.

Thank Boud for the birthday 'gram, I loved getting it. I must write to Nancy too, she sent me a book called "Little Lottie." What I long for is Edgeworth's Moral Tales, if you ever see a copy for sale do send it. Also, Bob would love to see some pictures of us as children, do see if you can find some.

        Love from Decca

To Aranka Treuhaft   San Francisco
                                                              ca. April 1945

Dear Aranka,

Thanks for your letter, and for the lovely things you sent. . . . [Nicholas] can say "Nicholas" in addition to a lot of other words. Dink is learning to read & write. She can write her name & read several words. I am teaching her as they don't seem to teach them anything like that in her school. . . .

I have enjoyed being home with them very much, & the Dink has been a great help. She knows quite a bit about housework & has been showing me how to do things. For instance, I thought that to clean the stove you just wiped it with a rag, but the Dink showed me how to take the top apart & wash it. She can wash all of the dishes from a whole meal by herself, & dry them. . . .

We are going to a place south of LA called the "overall wearing ranch," it sounds marvelous.[14] It is mainly a Negro resort, but they take white people, & they specialize in children's activities, so Dink should have a wonderful time.

Nicholas & I spent a lot of time at Dink's school. . . . One day Leadbelly, a famous folk singer,[15] was in town & I got him to come over to the school to sing for the children. He entertained them for about 2 hours, & they all sang & even Nicholas was beating time. They had children from 2 or 3 other nursery schools over for the concert. . . .

Nicholas's tonsils, adenoid etc are all in good shape, the Doc says, also he's not getting bowlegged. The only way to prevent him from walking would be to chain him to the floor, which the Doc doesn't recommend. I hope you can come out & see him one day, you would love him. He is exactly like that picture of Bob aged 3.

  Love from Decca

---

14. The Overall-Wearing Dude Ranch in Southern California's Apple Valley, also known as Murray's Ranch, billed itself as "the only Negro dude ranch in the world."

15. Blues singer Huddie Ledbetter stayed at the Treuhafts' home during a visit to San Francisco a couple of years later. Decca wrote in *A Fine Old Conflict* that during that visit "the house would ring with his wonderful music, daily concerts for the children, for whom he improvised special songs." She also wrote of the unease of Aranka Treuhaft, who came to visit while Leadbelly was staying with them: "He and Aranka were ill-assorted houseguests; they would circle one another warily, with little to say. 'Oh Decca'—Aranka sighed wistfully—'I wish I was black like Jerry Newson and Leadbelly. Then you would love me.' " For Decca's later recollections of their association, see April 13, 1990, letter to John Prime.

To Lady Redesdale   San Francisco
                                                                      May 15, 1945

My Darling Muv,

   I have tried to write several times since getting the terrible news about
Tudemy,[16] I felt so awful about it & couldn't think of anything comforting to
say, because to me it seems that anyone who was killed in this war has died for
the most magnificent cause in history—but I didn't know if you would agree.
Since getting your letter, I think that at last you do agree, and that you see that
it would be better for all of us to be wiped out than to live in the same world
with the Nazis. Esmond used to say that long ago, in the days of the Spanish
war, and how true it is.

   I was so pleased with your letter because you sound in good spirits; I do wish
we could come to England & bring the sweet children. Perhaps we can soon.

   The conference is being very exciting.[17] I am working for the Friends of the
Spanish Republic, the object being to keep Franco Spain out of the World
Security Organization. We are making some headway, many of the delegations
are very favourable and the newspapers are writing up the Committee. The
Labor School wants me to go back, but I shall only do it if I can arrange an
8 hour day, otherwise I never see the children. I saw Bob Boothby[18] for a second, he told me about Nancy being a career woman these days (so incredible!)
and we had dinner with Kingsley Martin[19] & got him to contribute $1500 to
the Labor School. He is going to write an article for Colliers (a big circulation
magazine here) & give us the money. It may be $2,000 if we're lucky. He said he
would ring you up when he gets home.

   Dinky is in wonderful shape, she is going to a new school (a much better one
I think) and she was terribly excited over V-E day. There was no celebrating
here at all, not even whistles blowing or anything, I was glad, I don't think anyone felt like celebrating. . . .

   We heard yesterday from Bob's mother in New York who had read that
Giles[20] was rescued by the Russians, I do hope it's true & that we shall soon
hear from him. She read it in a New York paper.

                     Do write soon—Love from Dec

---

   16. Decca's brother, Tom, was leading Indian troops against a contingent of Japanese in Burma
when he was hit by machine-gun fire on March 24. He died on March 30 at the age of thirty-six.

   17. The founding conference for what became the United Nations opened in San Francisco on
April 25, 1945. It has been taken as a sign of the growing mainstream respectability of the California Labor School where Decca had worked that it was chosen by the State Department for the
politically sensitive task of hosting Soviet labor delegates at the conference. Called the United
Nations Conference on International Organization, it lasted two months. The U.N. Charter was
adopted by delegates of the fifty nations in attendance on June 25.

   18. A Conservative Member of Parliament and old friend of Oswald Mosley.

   19. Editor of Britain's *New Statesman*. See letter of July 22, 1964, to Robert Treuhaft.

   20. Esmond Romilly's brother, who had been imprisoned since his capture by the Germans
in 1940.

To Nancy Mitford San Francisco
ca. May 1945

Darling Sooze,

Thanks for your letter. You must have been having a miserable time, I am so terribly sorry and I do wish I were there.[21] It seems like a lifetime since that day in 1939 when Tudemy saw us off at the station—he & Nanny & Aunt Puss—and he was one of the few people in England I really looked forward to seeing again. Are you bringing into your book[22] about church services at Swinbrook, when we used to make Tud blither by nudging him in the parts about not committing adultery? . . .[23]

You would love the amazing Donk, now called Constancia in her new school. Also the beautiful, new improved walking & talking & self-feeding Nicholas Tito (named after Lenin & Marshal Tito to annoy the P's[24]). We would come to England if we could afford it. If we do come, can we stay with you? I've lost track of who else I'm on speakers & stayers with. At the moment I'm not working because my lade who took care of the children has left. So I'm trying to look after them. Luckily Constancia helps a lot by washing up, making beds, etc. She's not at all like we were as children, but in some ways a typical nursery school product. Any chance of you & Rodd coming to America? I know you hate foreigners specially Americans but you would adore Bob & Constancia & Nicholas. Do write again soon, and if you ever see Id or Rud give them my love.

Yr loving Susan

To Aranka Treuhaft San Francisco
September 1945

Dear Aranka,

Thanks for your letter & for the <u>swell</u> package of Hungarian food. . . .

Labor Day we all paraded with the CIO. Dinky was with the section calling for continued child care; a whole lot of kids paraded all the way up Market Street[25] yelling "We want nursery schools." She wore the red outfit you gave her—very appropriate. Nicholas & I were in the Friends of the Spanish Repub-

---

21. A reference to Tom Mitford's death.

22. Nancy at the time was working on *The Pursuit of Love* (Hamish Hamilton, 1947), the caricature of her family that was to become one of her most popular novels and an important contributor to the enduring legend of "the crazy Mitfords."

23. Decca described this game in *Daughters and Rebels*. She wrote that she and sisters Unity and Deborah "were sure [Tom] led a glamorous life of sin abroad and in his London flat, and needed emphasis on this particular commandment." "Blither," she said, was "a Honnish expression for an unwilling or suppressed giggle."

24. Parents, or, as Decca often referred to them, the Sainted P's or the Revered P's.

25. San Francisco's main downtown thoroughfare.

lic truck & old Bob lined the streets. It was a fine parade, we had wonderful weather and a huge crowd turned out.

I am bent on getting some of the new postwar appliances. I don't want a Bendix any more since seeing an ad for a Thor combined washing machine & dishwasher. I spent yesterday hunting for one & enquiring for additional fixtures which will put the children to bed. No luck so far. Ask Al whether he thinks the following suggestions would be marketable: an automatic bed maker & an automatic machine for picking up soiled diapers (illustrated below):

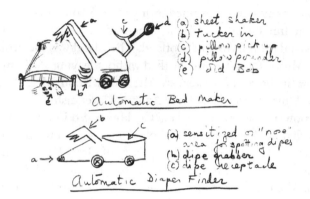

Automatic Bed Maker

(a) sheet shaker
(b) tucker in
(c) pillow pick up
(d) pillow pounder
(e) old Bob

Automatic Diaper Finder

(a) sensitized or "nose" area for spotting dipes
(b) dipe grabber
(c) dipe receptacle

To Lady Redesdale   San Francisco
                                                          January 3, 1946

Darling Muv,

Thank you so much for the books you sent the children, they are really wonderful. I keep them with our books so that they won't get torn up. . . . I got a letter from Hasties, ages ago, saying I had inherited 1/6 of Inch Kenneth.[26] I sent the stuff to Claud Cockburn, of the Daily Worker,[27] as I would like my share to go to the Communist Party. I was expecting to hear from you about it. Did he get in touch with you or with Hasties? . . .

We have a housekeeper again as I'm working full time. I really got to hate

---

26. Although Decca had been disowned by her father, she came into partial ownership of the island on the death of her brother, Tom, the legal owner (see next letter). The other sisters decided to let their mother use the island during her lifetime.

27. The radical British journalist was a former foreign correspondent for *The Times* who founded his own mimeographed antifascist newsletter, *The Week*, and covered the Spanish Civil War for the *Daily Worker* at the request of the general secretary of the British Communist Party. He fought with the Republican forces so he could report on the war from a soldier's perspective. He left the *Daily Worker* and the Communist Party the year after this letter was written. Decca had met with Cockburn when he was in San Francisco covering the founding of the United Nations, soon after her brother's death. According to Cockburn's son, the journalist Alexander Cockburn, Decca and Esmond Romilly had taken refuge in Claud Cockburn's apartment when they eloped. Claud Cockburn later became a good friend of Decca's and her host at his Irish home.

housework while doing it for 3 or 4 months. I am terribly bad at it & much prefer to work. . . .

Love from Decca

To William Gallacher[28]

San Francisco
March 21, 1946

Dear Comrade,

Several months ago I was informed by my father's solicitors, Messrs. Hasties of 65, Lincoln Inn Fields, that I had inherited one-sixth of Inch Kenneth, which is an island off the coast of Scotland. The island was the property of my brother Tom Mitford, and because he died without leaving a will my five sisters and myself are the heirs. The sisters are Mrs. Peter Rodd, Mrs. Derek Jackson, Lady Mosley, Unity Mitford and Lady Andrew Cavendish.

I sent the power of attorney to Claud Cockburn, c/o London Daily Worker, and told him that he should arrange to collect my share of the income from the island and turn it over to the Communist Party of Great Britain. I have written twice to Claud, and have sent him cables, but he has not replied. I find it hard to believe that the Party has no use for the money, or that somebody cannot be found to handle the details of collection.[29] However, if this is so, please let me know, as the San Francisco Party could certainly use it.

We have no way of knowing how much my share is worth, or whether it should be sold in order to realize a lump sum, and were counting on Claud to find out. The island has a large house on it &, I believe, some cottages.

Please send me a cable as soon as you receive this letter to let me know whether or not the Party is interested in handling my share of the estate and receiving the income. Since I have not heard from Claud at all regarding this matter I thought it best to write to you.

comradely, Decca Treuhaft
Financial Director, Communist Party of San Francisco

---

28. Gallacher was one of the founders of the Communist Party of Great Britain and an MP from 1935 to 1950.

29. Cockburn never replied and Decca later revoked his power of attorney, but he did follow up on Decca's mission. He consulted with the Communist Party, where he said he was told, "What the hell does anyone think we can do with a small little bit of a desolate island somewhere off the coast of Scotland?" Cockburn then met with Lord Redesdale and—depending on whose account you believe—was talked out of accepting the island on the Party's behalf (Jonathan Guinness, son of Decca's sister Diana) or "somehow managed to give the island back" (Alexander Cockburn).

To Lady Redesdale   San Francisco
                                                          May 21, 1946

Darling Muv,

Thanks for your airmail letter, and cable. I want to explain how I look on the money to be received from the island. In the first place, I realize that I only got any share of it by a fluke. In the second place, I'm really not a bit interested in getting the money for myself, as we get along perfectly all right on the money we earn by working for it. However, since a share of the island has come my way, I am determined that it shall be put to a good use, and also I feel it's important to make sure that I get the maximum to be realized from my share. One way to look at it is that my share will go to undo some of the harm that our family has done, particularly the Mosleys and Farve when he was in the House of Lords. To me, it seems that money is an important political weapon—and that's the only reason why I'm interested in getting any of it, and also why I'm interested in getting a maximum.

I don't know whether developments in the last ten years have yet proved to you what a criminal thing it was to have supported Hitler and an appeasement policy for England, but you do know what I think about it, so therefore you can see the logic of my trying to do everything possible in the other direction— including using the money from the island in this way.

About the 500 pounds share.[30] It does seem to me to be far too low, and you say yourself that if the island were put on the market much more could be realized. There are two possible ways to settle it. You could make me an offer, which we could discuss by letter. I don't see how a one-sixth share could be worth less than 1500 pounds, judging by advertisements for real estate in the English papers, but of course I'm not on the spot and therefore cannot go into the question. The other way is that a friend of mine will be in England soon, and I could send him the power of attorney, and he could clear the whole thing up for me. . . .

I will write again soon. Hope we can get this matter of the island cleared up quickly.[31]

Love, Decca

---

30. One-sixth of the island's appraised value. Having failed in her attempt to donate her share of the island to the Communist Party, Decca was trying to sell it to her sisters.

31. Decca's sisters were furious at her, and her proposed sale was never completed. Decca kept her share, and Lady Redesdale continued to live on the island with her children's agreement.

To Lady Redesdale   Oakland, Calif.
                                                      August 26, 1947

Darling Muv,

    . . . We moved here about a month ago—it is across the bay from San Francisco, about 15 miles from where we used to live. Bob's work is in Oakland, which is why we moved. Our house here is much nicer than in San Francisco, it's right near a beautiful park called the Rose Garden and there is no traffic on the street, so the Donk & Nicholas play outside all day long. The Donk already has several bosom friends about her own age who live on this street. She gives almost daily lunch parties to which she invites hordes of children. I'm not working at the moment & stay home & do all the housework, which I am phenomenally bad at, except for cooking. Luckily the Donk knows a good deal about housework (things like cleaning the woodwork which I have no idea how to go about) so she advises & helps at every stage. Sometimes she disappears for hours at a time with her gang of friends. Nicholas still stays at home most of the time, he's only 3 & there don't seem to be any children his age nearby.

    I was <u>so</u> sorry to hear that poor Debo lost her baby,[32] I hope she's getting over it alright. It is a very disappointing thing to happen. . . . Is Nancy coming here? Los Angeles is quite near here, a few hours by train, so I hope we'll see her if she comes. All our plans for coming to England seem to have fallen through as it is so expensive and also we are involved in so many things here it would be impossible to get away.

    You would love the children. Nicholas is a terror, he does the most awful things like falling out of the car while it's going, eating quantities of sleeping pills (we had to rush him to the hospital to have his stomach pumped out), almost setting fire to the house with his electric stove, etc. Luckily he doesn't seem to suffer any ill effects from all these things. Dinky is terrifically pretty, even with most of her teeth out. I'll try to get some pictures of them soon to send you. . . .

         Love to all, Decca

To Aranka Treuhaft   Permanente Hospital, Oakland
                                                      October 21, 1947

Dear Aranka,

    At last #3 is here (no name yet—we hope to have one by tomorrow).[33] He sure took a long time coming. I've been in the hospital one week today, most of the time being what they call "induced," consisting of a total of 5 big doses of

---

    32. Decca's sister—by now the mother of two—delivered a stillborn infant eight months into another pregnancy.

    33. Appended to this letter was the following from Robert Treuhaft: "P.S. He's been named—Benjamin."

castor oil, 5 Triple-H enemas (so called by the nurses—it stands for High, Hot & a Hell of a lot) and 45 shots of something or other. Also innumerable pills.

The Dr. says it was a very easy birth—which it probably was for him, I guess it all depends on your point of view.

Anyway, the baby is wonderful, very large & a terrifically strong sucker, I'm trying to nurse him. He is extremely handsome, in his own way, has big eyes like the other children only more slanting than theirs.

The hospital is fine, they give you very good care and they believe in letting you get up right away—you can walk around 24 hours after the baby is born. . . .

Bob . . . comes around twice a day, which is swell, & is planning to smuggle the children in tomorrow evening. If they challenge them, Dinky is all set to say she's a midget & it's not polite to stare at midgets.

Love from Decca

To Aranka Treuhaft   Oakland
                                                                November 7, 1947
Dear Aranka,

Thank you so much for the wonderful present of $100 which arrived last week. I am longing to get a bit thinner so I can go out & acquire the New Look or whatever it's called—at present I'm suffering from The Large & Lumpy Look still.

I would have written you sooner but had another mishap—a breast abscess, which meant going back to the hospital for a few days. I have heard Bob erroneously refer to this as a "slight infection," whereas on the contrary it was far from slight to my way of thinking, very painful & altogether most unpleasant. . . .

Benjamin is really wonderful (by the way his name isn't John Anthony but Benjamin, somehow it really suits him much better as you'll agree when you see him. Dinky thinks he's named after Benjamin Bunny, but I guess it's really after Ben Davis.)[34] He eats huge amounts & is terrifically good, I mean so far as not crying. Also he is a remarkably good looking child for so young, has beautiful long slanting eyes like Bob & a very beautifully shaped head. Dink & Nicholas seem to love him, each in their own way; Dinky, by being terrifically motherly

---

34. Benjamin J. Davis, the pioneering African American Communist leader. A Harvard-educated lawyer from the South, he edited the *Negro Liberator* in New York and later the Communist Party newspaper, the *Daily Worker.* He was the Party's Harlem representative and a tenacious organizer for black rights and economic advancement. In the mid-1940s he became the second African American to be elected to the New York City Council. He later lost the council seat and was imprisoned after being convicted under the anti-Communist Smith Act; after his release, he resumed his advocacy.

to him, & Nick by only having socked him twice so far instead of continually, as I feared. Actually, the day we brought him home I mentioned to Bob that he was hungry & Nicholas trotted into the kitchen & shortly returned with a huge salami on rye bread sandwich, which he proceeded to stuff into Benjamin's mouth.

I'm enclosing a picture of Bert[35] struggling with a cop at our local Un-American Committee hearings (remember we had dinner at his house the evening of our move to Oakland). Hope you are becoming suitably outraged at the Washington committee's actions, & that you see how we weren't so far wrong when we said the U.S. is in danger of going Fascist. . . .

Love from Decca

To Lady Redesdale   Oakland
                                                        January 27, 1948
Darling Muv,

Thank you so much for the lovely things you sent the children; they are really delighted with them. . . .

We spent two evenings with Tim[36] when he was here. The children were awfully funny about him. I told them to try not to behave like spoiled brats, as when we were children we weren't even allowed down when there were visitors; so they spent days practising to be "English children." Dinky taught Nicholas how to bow (she has rather a mixed up idea about English children) and I would hear her telling him patiently "No, Nicholas, you're not supposed to stay down as though Decca was going to wipe you after a poo-poo" (their word for Number 2).

It was very nice seeing Tim after so many years. . . .

Dinky is home from school all day for 2 weeks' Christmas holiday, which is a great help as she looks after Benjamin almost single handed.[37] She brings droves of friends around & they play "house" & use Benjamin for a prop. . . . Nicholas is getting about as independent as the Donk. He has a mysterious friend called Mrs. Coleman who lives in the neighborhood—I have never met her, but he scrams out of the house early every morning & spends most of the day with her. . . .

At last I am becoming fairly good at the housework. I even do all the sheets

---

35. Bert Edises, law partner of Robert Treuhaft and the first husband of the Treuhafts' dear friend Pele de Lappe.

36. Decca's first cousin Tim Bailey, son of her mother's sister, Dorothy Bailey (known as Aunt Weenie).

37. Decca once claimed that her daughter, at the age of six, had been "praying for a baby; so when he was born, I said, 'Here he is, now look after him,' which she did. I think she taught him his first words: 'Dinky's always right, Benjy's always wrong.' "

etc at home, & get on all right without any help. The only trouble is I get ter-rifically bored by it at times, so I expect pretty soon I'll get a job & have a housekeeper again. . . .

Love from Decca

To Aranka Treuhaft   Oakland
                                                                ca February 1948

Dear Aranka,

Thanks for your letter. Possibilities of a trip East are once more fading com-pletely, due to 1) press of work here (I'm working again now), 2) finances. I almost got elected as delegate to the 3rd Party National Convention,[38] in which case I'd have come out East with expenses paid, but lost by 3 votes. So our plan now is to come after the children get married. Benjamin seems the most con-servative & cautious type & probably won't get married till he's at least 21, so count on us in 1969. I hope your trip to Europe is fun. . . .

We have a new housekeeper who I gather doesn't think I'm much of a hand at house work and child care. The other day I got home from work, & she got ready to leave. Benj was in the play pen & she stood looking uncertainly from him to me. Finally she said, "Dinky is out playing, but I think she'll be home soon. Do you mind if I go now & leave the baby with you till she gets back?" . . .

To Lady Redesdale   Oakland
                                                                  March 8, 1948

Darling Muv,

We are terrifically excited about your visit here. When I got your telegram it was all mixed up, so I got the impression you were planning to smuggle some English goods into the country in order to get dollars. This probably wouldn't work and anyhow shouldn't be mentioned in a telegram as telegrams are checked by the authorities. I had no idea one could telephone England but the call went through in no time. . . . Actually, if you can go by plane direct to San Francisco, there won't be any problem about money, as we would meet you there & take you straight to our house. . . .

---

38. The Progressive Party (Independent Progressive Party in California) was not yet formally named. It was formed to support the 1948 presidential campaign of former vice president Henry A. Wallace, who ran against Democrat Harry Truman and Republican Thomas Dewey. The party also supported local candidates (Virginia Durr was its token candidate for the U.S. Senate in Virginia). Wallace received more than a million popular votes but no electoral votes, and the candidate, who had split with President Truman over Cold War issues, ultimately split with the Independent Pro-gressive Party over his increasing anti-Communism and his support for intervention in the Korean War. The party was labeled a Communist front by the House Un-American Activities Committee in 1951 and disbanded soon thereafter.

There is only one thing that concerns me, and that's the possibility of newspaper publicity over your visit. As you know I live in terror of reporters & this is just the kind of thing they might pick up. Most newspapers get a list of incoming plane passengers. Could you look into the possibility of traveling under another name?.... (Be sure to let us know what it is!) Above all, <u>don't</u> talk to any reporters. Simply ignore them, it's the only way.... [D]o bring the Daily Express Song Book, as we have a piano, also family pictures to show Bob & Dink.

We are really awfully excited that you're coming & I hope the trip won't be too awful. Personally I hate flying, it gives me such a frightful headache. But I've only done it with Dink when I've had the problem of convincing the airport people that she is under 2 so we wouldn't have to pay her fare. Last time we did this she was 5, we had to wrap her in a blanket with just her head showing & gave her a bottle. She was hopeless & kept asking technical questions about the plane's engine etc.

I can't wait for you to see the children. . . .

Love, & longin to see you, Decca

To Aranka Treuhaft   Oakland
                                                                       May 3, 1948

Dear Aranka,

Sorry not to have written for so long, but life with my mother here was fairly hectic & tonight is literally the first free evening since she left. . . . Her visit was a great success. I think she really enjoyed it, she thought our house wonderful & very pretty (little houses in England are usually awfully hideous & run to sham Gothic & stained glass, so she thought Oakland was like a musical comedy stage set). She seemed to like the children very much & for the first week, at least, they were quite well behaved. How was your dinner with her? Do write & tell about it. . . .

Bob is becoming famous throughout Oakland, the Bay Area, California, & probably the U.S. for winning impossible cases. . . .

Do write or wire your congressman & senator to vote against the Mundt Subversive Activities Bill.[39] We may all go to jail if you don't. . . .

                                                                       Love from Decca

---

39. The Subversive Activities Control Bill, also known as the Mundt-Nixon bill for its authors, Representatives Karl Mundt of South Dakota and Richard Nixon of California, passed the House by an overwhelming margin several weeks after this letter was written but died in the Senate. The bill would have required that Communist Party members register with the attorney general; it banned Party membership for federal employees and denied passports to Party members. Many of its provisions—along with severe new restrictions such as provision for emergency detention of Communists—were incorporated into the Internal Security Act of 1950 (the McCarran Act), passed over President Truman's veto. Several of the Treuhafts' friends were ultimately arrested as suspected subversives.

To Lady Redesdale   Oakland
                                                         June 11, 1948

Darling Muv,

I was terribly sorry to get your telegram, and waited until the letter came before writing to you. I do so hope you won't be terribly lonely, wouldn't it be best to live in London or Wycombe most of the time? The island sounds so isolated & rather grim if you are there by yourself.

I'm so glad you gave Bobo my love before she died. Of course, I mourned for my Boud years ago when I first realised we couldn't be friends any more.[40]

What are your plans, if any? Why don't you work with your knitting friend & help her to sell the sweaters. Something that gets one out of the house, with a certain amount of routine to it is a very good thing, although I admit selling wouldn't really be your line.

The children are in good shape, they still talk constantly about Grandma Redesdale & how you weren't the mad English type after all. . . .

Yesterday, Dink & Nicholas kept tearing in & out of the house wearing different clothes. After the 2nd change I caught them, & asked why they were dirtying up all their things. It turned out that a new ice cream shop had opened down the street & were giving away free cones "one to a customer," & Dink said "if we sneak in very quietly wearing different clothes they don't recognize us!" . . .

                              Best love from Decca

To Lady Redesdale   Oakland
                                                        August 12, 1949

Darling Muv,

Thanks for your letter. . . . We still talk about coming to England, the only problem being the Depression, which is making it difficult to save up any running away money. Life here is wonderfully transformed since we got our built-in sitter, & in September I am going to be working part time, though unfortunately at no pay. . . .

History has just repeated itself;[41] Leanne's mother rang up in a fury to say that Dinky had told Leanne & several other children about menstruating, & that now Leanne goes up to strange women & asks them "Have you worn your

---

40. For Lady Redesdale's response, see letter of November 19, 1976, to the Duchess of Devonshire.

41. Decca was referring here to an incident in her childhood when she was enrolled in a weekly dancing class. "One fateful afternoon," she related in *Daughters and Rebels*, "the teacher was an hour late, and I took the opportunity to lead the other children up to the roof, there to impart some delightful information that had just come my way concerning the conception and birth of babies," adding that she "couldn't help making up a few embellishments as I went along." One of the girls,

sanitary napkin yet this month?" I explained that it wasn't Dink's fault, runs in the family, etc but I don't think she believed me. . . .

Love from Decca

PS We haven't seen Nancy's book[42] yet as it is too expensive, we're waiting for the 25¢ edition or a complimentary copy.

To Lady Redesdale   Oakland
                                                                   November 2, 1949

Darling Muv,

Thank you so much for the <u>lovely</u> bread board, we were so thrilled with it, it is about the only thing in the house which seems to be absolutely Benjamin-proof. So I imagine it will last forever.

You must be a mind-reader because the bread board arrived a week or two after I started making home-made bread. I admit it is very easy, also practical for me; I get it ready while cooking dinner & let it rise while I'm at a meeting & then bake it. Everyone loves it. I started because Pat[43] said she liked home-made bread, & she only has to breathe a desire for me to rush round to fulfill it because I long for her to stay forever, she is such a wonderful help & terrifically nice.

As you can imagine we are frightfully busy, trying to get the Communist leaders out of jail & hoping to stay out ourselves.[44] I expect you saw in the paper that their lawyers were sentenced to 6 months for criminal contempt of court. One of them is Richie Gladstein[45] from San Francisco, we know him well. He's coming out in 10 days & I am arranging a mass meeting for him in Berkeley. . . .

Love from Decca

---

under pressure from her governess, violated her vow of silence. Decca was summoned by her mother, "her face . . . like thunder." The upshot: "My participation in the dancing class was abruptly terminated; it was clear to everyone, even to me, that I couldn't be considered fit company for nice children after that."

42. *Love in a Cold Climate.* Nancy Mitford's novel, another in her series caricaturing her family, was published by Hamish Hamilton in July 1949.

43. Apparently the "built-in sitter" to whom Decca had referred earlier.

44. The notorious Smith Act trials began in 1949, with eleven Communist leaders convicted weeks before this letter was written, after a nine-month trial. They were sentenced to prison. Two years later the Supreme Court refused to overturn the sentences, clearing the way for more such trials. The Smith Act of 1940, formally the Alien Registration Act, made it a crime "to advocate, abet, or teach the desirability of overthrowing the government." It was purposely resurrected after World War II to go after the Communist Party for teaching the principles of Marxism-Leninism, despite the fact that those charged had never advocated violence.

45. Richard Gladstein was a partner in the first private law firm Robert Treuhaft worked for in San Francisco after the war. All the partners were members of the Communist Party. Their clients included the longshoremen's leader Harry Bridges and his union, the ILWU (International Longshoremen's and Warehousemen's Union), as well as other leftist West Coast unions and the West Coast Communist newspaper *People's World.*

To Lady Redesdale   Oakland
                                                        April 29, 1950

Darling Muv,

Thank you so much for your very helpful work on our voyage to England . . . I really think it's going to come off, we <u>are</u> so excited. Dinky gets all red in the face every time she thinks about it. Do find out if Emma & Boy[46] are on speaking terms with her, she is dying to see them. Also do send us a list of the kind of presents to bring, things you can't get in England. Is Nylon still in that category?

Bob & I have been frightfully busy working on a murder trial, one reason I haven't answered your letters before this. He is defending an 18-year old Negro[47] accused of shooting 2 people. I have been convinced since the beginning that it's a frame-up (oh dear you don't know what a frame-up means. Well, if no-one knows who did a crime, sometimes the police decide to convince people that a certain individual did it although they have no evidence. This is particularly done to Negroes in this country. Very often the police manufacture evidence against the framed-up person, such as paying people to testify against the person, etc.).

So Bob is the defense lawyer & I am chief investigator in the case. The trial started last week, so far it is going rather well for us. The Civil Rights Congress (where I've been working since last September) has taken up the case & we've been getting out thousands of leaflets on it. A leaflet is a bit of paper telling about the case. You give them out on the streets or door to door. I don't remember whether they have them in England.

The children are well. Nicholas is doing wonderfully in school, his teacher told me he is the most intelligent & inquiring child she has ever taught. I know you don't think so but that's because you couldn't understand anything he said except O.K. . . .

Love to Blor.

Love from Decca

---

46. The Devonshires' daughter and their son, Peregrine Cavendish, the Marquess of Hartington (and the current Duke of Devonshire), who was also known at times to family members as Morny and Stoker.

47. Jerry Newson, a "shoeshine boy" charged in October 1949 with murdering a white pharmacist and his assistant in West Oakland. Defending the eighteen-year-old orphan after his arrest and through various trials and appeals was for years a preoccupation of the Treuhafts, the *People's World*, and the Civil Rights Congress. He was convicted in April 1950 despite a supposed eyewitness's admission that he had lied and other exculpatory testimony, and he was sentenced to death. Decca discussed the case and their involvement in numerous letters and in her book *A Fine Old Conflict*.

To Lady Redesdale   Oakland
                                                                    May 11, 1950

Darling Muv,

. . . We have been working literally night & day on the murder case for weeks, it's almost over now. It turned out just as we knew it would; the police had gone around intimidating all the witnesses, they also produced phony (means faked or untrue) ballistics tests of the bullets, tampered with the physical evidence, etc etc. Luckily we have been able to prove most of this in court, so there's some chance of an acquittal. Bob is now a local hero for his work in the case, actually there are thousands such cases here but usually there's no-one to put up the proper kind of defense. The newspapers are full of the trial, I'll send you some of the clippings next week. The police are furious about it & we keep hearing reports of threats they are making about us. Bert Edises (Bob's law partner) is running (standing) for District Attorney (they are elected here, I expect you know). So the District Attorney[48] is furious too. . . .

                                   Love from Decca

To Lady Redesdale   Oakland
                                                                     June 4, 1950

Darling Muv,

I am so sorry not to have written more about our plans. . . . One reason I didn't write was we have been incredibly busy. We lost the murder trial I wrote to you about, that is he was found guilty & sentenced to the gas chamber, but we have great confidence in winning on appeal. The people here are absolutely furious about it, we have held several large mass meetings in protest, & spoken at several unions (not of South Africa, but trade unions), all of which has been taking time. Also right in the middle of it our wonderful built-in sitter left, so as a result things like housework & ironing have reached a completely hopeless impasse. All of which makes the prospect of our Tour all the more wonderful. . . . I wrote to Debo hoping to see her & family. As you know, of course we don't intend to see Diana or have anything to do with <u>them</u>, I'm sure she feels the same way, anyhow.

Give my love to Blor, tell her we long to see her.

                                   Love from Decca

---

48. The family's nemesis, J. Frank Coakley.

To Lady Redesdale   Oakland
                                                                 June 25, 1950
Darling Muv,

... This is mainly about our plans—we don't feel completely settled yet as the passport hasn't come, the State Dept people said we wouldn't get it before July. ...

Could you possibly ring up the Daily Worker next time you're in London & ask them whether they know of any interesting mass meetings or demonstrations in Paris scheduled for late Sept. or early October; if so, we could arrange accordingly about when to go to Paris. Also, ask them if there are any interesting conferences they know of coming off at that time, so we can be sure to get credentials. ...

About who we are on speakers with: actually, everyone except Diana & her family. We should like to see Farve, on condition he doesn't insult Bob or Dinky in my presence. We long to see Id, but perhaps <u>she</u> isn't on speakers with <u>us</u>—I wrote her a long letter about a year or two ago & she never answered. ...

We have been working like mad on the Jerry Newson case. I had a run-in (fight) with the judge. We collected 3,000 signatures on a petition asking him for a new trial. He issued a public blast, in all the newspapers, saying that the 3,000 people & the Civil Rights Congress are in contempt of court, & are a bunch of Reds. So I sent a letter back, which was put out as a leaflet & also was in the papers, saying the judge was trying to intimidate people. But he didn't succeed, we had a mass meeting of about 2,000 people in a park here for Jerry Newson. Bob & I have spoken before dozens of unions, churches etc, & people are furious about what happened. So we think there's a good chance of winning the appeal.

We have a new housekeeper. She is awfully nice but seems to hate housework. I don't blame her, but as a result films of dirt are settling everywhere which makes me long to leave on our Tour.

We are terrifically excited about it, it will seem so amazing to be back in England after all this time. ...

Give Blor my love, we are <u>longing</u> to see her.
                        Love from Decca

To Lady Redesdale   Oakland
                                                                   July 1950
Darling Muv,

Thanks for your letter ... with picture of Debo, which all agreed was like me except for the necklace. The reason I haven't written is, we are now seized with a fearful indecision about our trip. Things are happening very fast here. There are bills pending in the Congress which might make it very difficult for us to go and, as you say, we might not be able to get back. Even if our papers are in order. Of course we are most terribly disappointed at the thought of giving up on our trip. We'll have to decide in the next two weeks or so just what to do about it. Most of our friends advise us not to go. At the very least, we would be taking a risk of not getting back. . . . Oh we are _so_ unhappy about it all. . . .

I do wish we had come last year, because it might be many years before it is possible again.

We'll let you know our plans from day to day.
Love from Decca

P.S. A shocking new case of police brutality came to us this week. A Negro, arrested for being drunk, had both jaws & two ribs broken by the Oakland police. This gives you some idea of the reign of terror here.

To Lady Redesdale Oakland
August 2, 1950

Darling Muv,

Oh dear we are in such agony not knowing whether or not to come. But our latest decision is, we are going to make a try for it, if nothing unforeseen comes up between now & Sept 5th. . . . You can't imagine how hysterical things are getting here. For instance—one _small_ example. Our friend Aubrey Grossman[49] went to Mississippi with some other people to intercede for a Negro frame-up victim[50] sentenced to die for a rape which he didn't commit. The local newspaper ran an editorial advising people to attack this delegation. So Aubrey was ambushed in his hotel room by 8 men and very badly beaten, he had to have 16 stitches in his face & scalp. Someone called me about this shortly after it happened, so I immediately rang up the Governor & told him that we would hold him personally responsible for Aubrey's safety until he was safely out of Mississippi. (I had heard that the hospital where Aubrey was was surrounded by

---

49. Grossman was a well-known labor and civil rights attorney and at times a law partner of Robert Treuhaft. He had also been a colleague of Decca's in Communist Party headquarters when she was financial director of the San Francisco branch. For a time he was a national official of the Civil Rights Congress.

50. Willie McGee, a thirty-six-year-old truck driver, had been convicted by an all-white jury—in under three minutes of deliberation, after a trial lasting less than a day—of the rape of a white woman with whom he had reportedly been trying to break off a four-year-long affair. The CRC and Communist Party organized an international campaign to overturn his conviction, including the so-called White Women's Delegation to Mississippi, in which Decca later participated. She was a tireless worker in McGee's defense and devoted a chapter to the case in her memoir _A Fine Old Conflict._

lynch mobs.) Of course the governor had helped arrange the attack, but hundreds of people rang him up & sent wires & Aubrey did get out alive. Well, I expect you can see from the newspapers what is happening here. However we now feel that if we don't come this year, we never will. So, expect us in September! Dorothy Allhusen wrote, also Esmond's mother. I <u>do</u> hope we won't have to stay with them. I think we should leave our plans quite indefinite till we get to England, specially as we are not <u>completely</u> sure of coming. . . .

Love from Decca

To Lady Redesdale   Oakland
August 20, 1950

Darling Muv,

I just sent you a wire, hoping it would reach you at Inch Kenneth or be forwarded, telling you of the dreadfully sad decision we were forced to come to finally cancelling our trip. You have no idea how horribly disappointed we all were, and also how very sorry to have caused so much inconvenience & planning by the Mother In Laws Coordinating Council, which has now all gone for naught. We were almost on our way, would have left here in 10 days for New York, where Aranka had arranged a school for the Boys. However, the fact is that Congress is about to pass various bills that might result in our passport becoming forfeit.[51] The bills may pass any time—or they may still be held up. In any event we might have been held up at Ellis Island on our way back, perhaps for a long time. I believe there is now a very immediate danger of people being rounded up & jailed here, and of course we wouldn't want to be away if that should happen.[52] It is rather difficult to explain all this in a letter, but I expect you can gather from the newspapers what is happening in America. Our great mistake was not to have stuck by our original decision not to come, which I wrote you about. As a result we may have caused a lot of extra expense. . . . However there is so much more at stake that we had to cancel our plans anyway. . . .

Everyone here is well, Dinky was very brave about the disappointment. Poor child, she had already made an appointment with Bob's partner to draw up her will—mainly for the purpose of cutting Nicholas off without a penny. She wouldn't let Bob make out the will, she said he might "practise her handwriting" and change it! This was all in case the boat went down.

---

51. Decca was referring to what was to become the Internal Security Act of 1950, also known as the McCarran Act. See footnote to letter of May 3, 1948, to Aranka Treuhaft.

52. Decca wrote in *A Fine Old Conflict* that their local Party chairman told the Treuhafts that no lawyers could be granted leaves of absence at the time because they "would be needed to deal with the anticipated wave of arrests, prosecutions and general harassment" under the new McCarran Act.

I quite agree with what you said in your letter about the complete madness of another war. However those who speak for peace here are being imprisoned. There have even been a few local arrests of people circulating the Stockholm Peace Pledge.[53] I'm afraid it's only a taste of what's coming.

I'll write again soon. Give my love to Debo, Nanny, Nancy, etc & tell them how awfully sorry we are not to be coming.

Love from Decca

To Lady Redesdale   San Cristobal Valley Ranch, New Mexico[54]
September 14, 1950

Darling Muv,

We slowly got over our great disappointment, and are now having two weeks vacation at the most wonderful place I've ever been to. This is a beautiful ranch in New Mexico, wonderful weather, everything for the children to do (riding, swimming, long trips to see the Indians, etc). The Durrs have moved to Denver, only 300 miles from here, so Virginia, Anne, Baby Sister and Lulah (the new baby) came down to see us.[55] I was so excited, I haven't seen any of them for 7 years. . . .

Several of our friends are here, we have a campfire and singing and folk dancing in the evening, it is such fun. We will be leaving next week. I have a feeling this will be our last vacation for a long time. Virginia says she will take the Children if anything should happen to us, the only problem is it will probably happen to her, too.

I expect you have read in the papers about the McCarran "anti-subversive" bill, which I fear heralds the advent of Fascism in the United States. However, there is a lot of fight left in people, so possibly it can still be defeated.[56]

Bob and Bert have finished arguing the Jerry Newson case in the State Supreme Court, we have great hopes for him. We are publishing a book on the

---

53. Coinciding with the outbreak of the Korean War in the summer of 1950, a group of peace activists who had met in Stockholm were circulating a statement declaring that "any government which first uses atomic weapons against any other country whatsoever will be committing a crime against humanity."

54. The ranch was an interracial vacation retreat for radicals in the 1940s and '50s.

55. Clifford Durr had started a law practice in Washington after leaving government service. He took on loyalty oath cases, for little or no compensation, and continued opposing government "witch hunts" of purported Communist sympathizers. While Durr was serving as president of the National Lawyers Guild, Congressman Richard Nixon attacked the organization for purported Communist ties, and Durr was put under FBI surveillance. Unable to make an adequate living from his practice, he took a position as general counsel of the National Farmers Union in Denver. He was soon forced to resign that position when the *Denver Post* smeared Virginia Durr for signing what it called a "Red Petition" circulated by Dr. Linus Pauling opposing escalation of the Korean War.

56. As previously noted, the bill passed, with Congress overriding Truman's veto.

case which we hope to sell from door to door throughout Oakland, it is an excellent book and I believe that it will save Jerry's life. . . .

Love from Decca

To Lady Redesdale   Oakland

April 2, 1951

Darling Muv,

Thanks so much for your letter. . . . I haven't written because I've been away for almost a month, working very hard. I went to Mississippi with a delegation of white women from all over the country to intercede for a Negro, Willie McGee, who was charged with rape & sentenced to die. The charge is a frame-up, that is, he is not guilty but they are determined to kill him. It was rather a job. . . . When we arrived, the newspapers ran stories every day trying to incite the people against us. The mayor called a special meeting about us & urged people to call the police if they saw us coming. We spoke to over 150 people, some of whom promised to work for McGee's freedom. We drove a total of 7700 miles, in my new car. It was the most thrilling experience I ever had. Finally there was a stay of execution, so we did some good. I got home last night, it is so wonderful to be back, I missed Bob & the Children terribly. . . .

I'll try to get some copies of the articles I wrote on our trip to Mississippi, they were published in the People's World. Now we are really going to be busy, I have to tour the Pacific Coast to speak at dozens of meetings on our trip— Sunday night is the first one, here, they expect over 1000 people which is a large meeting for Oakland, I'm terrified about my speech. The Negro people here & throughout the country are tremendously enthusiastic over our going. . . .

I must stop now, I have so much work to do.

Much love, Decca

P.S. Fancy the Woman[57] getting divorced. Could it be that I am, after all, the only one who is really settled down, as they say?

---

57. Decca's sister Pam.

To Doris Brin Walker[58]   Oakland
                                                                                   May 7, 1951

Dearest Dobby,

I simply must congratulate you from the bottom of my heart for the brilliant and brave job you guys did in Jackson. Buddy got home last night, we were up till 2:30 hearing the whole thrilling story.[59] He had called me about 9:30 Sunday morning, to say that all were safe, and that "The white women from Calif. and N.Y. were responsible for preventing bloodshed or at least beatings."

You can imagine I sweated all day Saturday. We were having our autocade (incidentally, a smash hit, more than 100 cars were in it) and of course I was frightfully busy, but I listened to every radio broadcast I could get to get some news of you. There was nothing, but Sun. morning I woke at about 6:30 and began to worry again. Then, the Chronicle came and I read that "47 were arrested," etc. It didn't give any details, so I sweated again till Buddy called.

I can tell you, we all think you are the most wonderful heroes, you have made an historic contribution of national significance. It finally hit all the papers, and radio broadcasts, the Negro community is thrilled over it.

I do so wish you were back here[60] so we could stage an appropriate mass meeting of thousands to hear your experiences. We will have one anyway, for Buddy. . . .

This is the eve of the execution date. Somehow, I am very hopeful, because the campaign for McGee has been out of this world. We are waiting to hear the news about the injunction.[61]

---

58. A prominent left-wing attorney and for years one of Robert Treuhaft's law partners, Doris Brin Walker was one of the Treuhafts' closest friends for decades. Decca credited her with inviting her and her husband into the Communist Party.

59. Walker and several dozen other white women from outside the South had driven to Jackson, Mississippi, in a last-minute attempt to appeal for Willie McGee's life. Their San Francisco friend and colleague Walter (Buddy) Green, a black *People's World* reporter who worked with the East Bay Civil Rights Congress, had gone ahead, undercover, to do advance work in the black community. Walker recalls that the white women—dressed in skirts, heels, hose, hats, and white gloves—had gathered on Saturday, May 5, to demonstrate at the Capitol, where the governor's clemency board was hearing McGee's final appeal. They were arrested, as were those blacks who managed to breach police lines and reach the Capitol. When they were taken to the hearing room, the white women encountered a number of the arrested blacks, including Green. The demonstration had surprised McGee's attorneys, including thirty-year-old Bella Abzug (later a member of Congress) and John Coe, who were in town for the appeal. The attorneys rushed to the chambers and negotiated a settlement under which the white women were to be released on condition they got out of town by midnight. The out-of-state white women refused to accept the settlement unless the arrested blacks, who faced severe retribution in the prevailing vigilante atmosphere, were released simultaneously, and the deal was struck. Before driving out of town that night, the white women contributed travel funds for the blacks and escorted Green to the railroad station, waiting until he was safely aboard a train to Memphis.

60. Walker was driving home by way of Dallas.

61. Decca's hope was misplaced. The conviction was upheld, and McGee was executed in the electric chair the day after this letter was written, as a crowd of hundreds of whites celebrated outside.

The autocade was thrilling. When we reached Harbor Homes, hundreds poured out of their houses to cheer us. There were so many cars they about circled the village. On Broadway,[62] people came out of the stores to see what's going on. We honked our horns continuously. A cop shouted at me, "Don't use your horn except for warning purposes!" I yelled back, "O.K., I'm warning YOU!" He went off, scowling. About 300 showed up for the mass meeting at the County Court House, very impressive. The IPP[63] did a wonderful job of getting telegrams sent. . . .

You may be feeling an awful "let down" feeling by now, don't let it throw you. You are terrific, everyone is very proud.

To Lady Redesdale   Oakland
                                                                            September 23, 1951

Darling Muv,

I'm so sorry not to have written for such ages. Thanks very much for your letters, also Nancy's book. I haven't finished reading it yet, which shows you how awfully busy we are. We would love it if Debo comes to visit us, the only thing is we don't have a spare room in our new house, so she would have to stay in a hotel. Do tell her to come, I'll try to get a few days off. The only thing is, I'm not absolutely sure I'll still be at home by that time. I was subpoenaed to appear before the State Legislative Un-American Activities Committee.[64] They told me to bring all the membership lists of Civil Rights Congress and a list of contributors, which I wouldn't do, so then they said they would charge us with contempt (there were 10 others subpoenaed, from different organizations). We haven't been cited yet for contempt, so maybe they will forget about it, but if they can prove it on you it is 6 months for each separate refusal-to-answer, and they must have asked me 50 questions which I wouldn't answer.[65] . . .

---

62. The main thoroughfare of downtown Oakland.

63. Independent Progressive Party.

64. The California secretary of state's office identifies the committee's activities this way: "The Senate Committee focused its attention largely on identifying and exposing communists, and many hearings were held on this subject. In particular, the Committee investigated labor unions, universities and colleges, public employees, liberal churches, and the Hollywood film industry." The office's website notes that "California's attention to un-American activities predates McCarthyism by a decade. . . . However, there was a close and ongoing relationship between state and federal efforts." Decca was subpoenaed for hearings at San Francisco's City Hall on September 11–12, 1951, at which witnesses were questioned about what the state office describes as "alleged Communist front organizations in San Francisco and the East Bay." In *A Fine Old Conflict*, Decca discussed at length her appearance before the committee, but this is the only contemporaneous account in her surviving letters.

65. Decca repeatedly refused to answer the committee's questions "on the grounds that answering might incriminate me." When questioned on whether answering one particular question would truly tend to incriminate her, she replied, "I don't know. With this Committee, you could never tell."

Tim called me up the other day from Miami, he said he was going to be in NY permanently. I told him how glad I was to know that my rich old cousin would be at hand to bail me out if I need it and he said he wouldn't, because he doesn't agree with me, do work on him and get him to do it if the need arises.

The Jerry Newson case is coming up again, we won him a new trial, and now he is in the Oakland jail, so I see him quite often. Did you ever get the book about him which we published? I sent you a copy. We sold over 6,000 of them locally. I'm sure we will win his case. It was a dreadful thing about Willie McGee. I got to know his wife quite well, she is one of the most remarkable women I ever met. She has gone down to that murderous state of Mississippi to live, that's her home, she has four children there. She came out here for a series of mass meetings which we organized, she really is one of the bravest people I ever met.

Fancy Jonathan getting married, I haven't seen him since he was about 4 or 5, I can't imagine him and Desmond[66] now.

I am enclosing a collection speech made by Dinky donk at a party organized by the children for Margaret Lima.[67] She is the daughter of Mickey Lima,[68] Communist organizer here who is jailed under the Smith Act. Dinky's speech really brought down the house. . . .

I will write again very soon, give my best love to Blor.

Love from Decca

ps On re-reading this letter I see it is full of references to jails, sorry, but that is where most of our friends are.

To Lady Redesdale   Oakland
                                                            June 6, 1952

Darling Muv,

Thanks so much for your letter. . . . We loved having Henderson here. She met quite a few of our friends but they couldn't quite make each other out. Tell

---

66. Jonathan and Desmond Guinness, Decca's sister Diana's two sons by Bryan Guinness.

67. The speech, written in a child's beginning script on a series of calendar pages, began like this:

Mad Mister, Chairman and friends as you know there are many people in jail for no good reasons today. And the people who put them in jail are not going to stop with them. Who knows mabe tomorrow you will be one of those people. If you were in jail you would want your friends to help you out as we are doing for the people who are in jail. And in order to help them out we have to get money. Not only to help these people but to help the CRC and other organazations in the constant fight for justice. Many people have been sapenad latly and they are trying to supena others. My mother is one of the people that has been supenad. She has been asked to bring to cort a list of all the people in the C.R.C. I said that she ought to ask them for a list of all the people in the F.B.I. There are a lot of reasons why the C.R.C needs money. In fact to many to list heer so lets see how much mony we can get together.

68. Albert J. Lima.

her I'm sorry not to have written much since she left. One reason is we never have any writing paper except this which you gave Dinky when she was about 4; it has lasted wonderfully I must say.

Poor Nicholas got arrested the other day for selling tickets door to door for a Jerry Newson Defense benefit, I <u>was</u> so furious.[69] Two policemen brought him home & he was crying bitterly. I took all 3 children down to the Chief of Police to protest Nicholas' arrest. The only trouble was Benjamin kept having to go to the loo which rather ruined the delegation.

Paul Robeson[70] was here last night for a concert & we had a huge party for him. It was so exciting but we are tired out from it.

Bob is in the middle of the 3rd trial of Jerry Newson so we don't see much of him while that's going on. I was in Los Angeles for a week with 4 others to go to the Smith Act trial there, you can't think how horrifying it was. Of the 15 on trial about 7 are friends of ours, they face 5 years in jail if convicted. . . .

Do give my love to Blor, & the others with the usual exceptions.

Love from Decca

To Lady Redesdale   Oakland
October 12, 1952

Darling Muv,

. . . Things are really looking up here. We won the Jerry Newson case, after 3 trials the prosecution was unable to get a conviction (the third trial ended in a hung jury) so finally they were forced to drop charges against him. We had a wonderful celebration, it meant a great deal to the people here. . . .

Our friends in L.A. are all out on bail, and there haven't been any more California arrests yet.

The Children are all in good shape. Dinky Donk is now in Junior High School, and you ought to see her. She insists on wearing lipstick, I was a bit shocked because she's only 11, but she says all the others do, and they do. She went on a diet and lost 5 lbs, she is the most strongminded and determined child I ever saw once she makes her mind up, she's just exactly like Esmond. . . .

We still talk about coming to England, one day we will, but can't now because of all the impossible restrictions against us.

I'll write again soon, do give my love to Blor, she wrote such a sweet letter.

Love, Decca

---

69. Nicholas had recently turned eight when this letter was written.

70. Robeson—the internationally acclaimed athlete, actor, singer, writer, and progressive political activist who was hounded, censored, and blacklisted in his native America—was a good friend of the Treuhafts' friends Nebby and Matt Crawford and often stayed at their Berkeley home. Robeson was vice president of the national Civil Rights Congress.

To Lady Redesdale   Oakland
                                                            September 16, 1953

Darling Muv,

. . . Benjamin has at last started 1st grade. He is such a funny boy, he and
Nicholas remind me of Le Bon Toto and Le Mechant Tom[71] (Benj is Le
Mechant Tom). If you can possibly get a copy of that book, do send it, but I'm
afraid it's probably out of print by this time. Last week he committed two
frightful crimes against the blissful French people who live next door to us; he
threw a stone through their car window and threw a heavy piece of lead on their
little girl's head. His excuse for the car window was that he was aiming at some
girls on the other side of the car; and his excuse for the lead was that he just
threw it up and the girl happened to be in the way. The French people were
most forgiving, luckily.

Dinky is becoming a Teenager, and has changed completely. Other mothers
tell me this usually happens. She is fearfully "scornful" of me and Bob. She is
still a wonderful asset in many ways.

I'm sending you some pamphlets about cases we are working on. Do read
them. Also, do write Gov. Earl Warren, State Building, Sacramento, Calif, and
ask him to free Wesley Robert Wells.[72] Send me a copy of the letter if you
write.

Dinky wrote to Winston Churchill about the Rosenbergs[73] before they were
killed, she signed it "your loving niece, Constancia Romilly" but he never
answered. How is Esmond's mother, is she at all interested in Dinky? Perhaps I
ought to write her after all this time. . . .

       Best love, Decca

---

71. Characters in a late-nineteenth-century book of cautionary children's tales by Louis Ratisbonne, a minor French poet and children's writer who used the pseudonym Trim. The book's full
title was *Le Bon Toto et le Méchant Tom, ou la Journée de Deux Petits Garçons* ("Good Toto and
Naughty Tom, or a Day in the Life of Two Little Boys"). Ratisbonne was also the French translator
of German physician-author Heinrich Hoffmann's children's book *Der Struwwelpeter*, a childhood
favorite of Decca's (see April 21, 1992, letter to Emma Tennant), and *Le Bon Toto et le Méchant Tom*
is said to have been written in the *Struwwelpeter* tradition of "black pedagogy."
72. A black prisoner on death row at San Quentin Prison. The Civil Rights Congress championed his case and published a brochure, "My Name Is Wesley Robert Wells," to rally support
for him.
73. Ethel and Julius Rosenberg, executed on June 19, 1953, for sending military secrets to the
Russians.

To President Harry S Truman   Oakland
                                                                    November 1953

Have just learned of your subpoena by Velde Un-American Committee.[74] As Executive Secretary of East Bay Civil Rights Congress I too have been subpoenaed for hearings scheduled to begin in San Francisco December 1. Civil Rights Congress has repeatedly warned that the witch-hunting activities of the Velde Committee will not stop with the persecution of Communists. We have warned that, following the pattern of Hitler Germany, the committee will, if unchecked, go on to destroy organized labor, the church, free universities. Acting as prosecutor, judge and jury the committee destroys innocent people and through this seeks by fear and intimidation to outlaw political dissent. Now the Democratic Party is one of its intended victims. True patriots must challenge the authority of this committee. I pledge to do my part by refusing to cooperate with this committee. You have an opportunity to set an example for loyal Americans by defying this committee and doing all in your power to expose its real aim—fascism in America.

                                                                    Decca Treuhaft[75]

To Aranka Treuhaft   Oakland
                                                                    December 5, 1953

Dear Aranka,

Thanks ever so much for the beautiful hats, they came just in the nick of time & I wore them at the Hearings[76] (one at a time, I mean, of course).

I wasn't called to testify, about 50 others subpoenaed also weren't called.

---

74. The House Committee on Un-American Activities (HUAC) was often known in 1953–54 by the name of its zealous Red-hunting chairman, Republican Representative Harold Velde of Illinois, a former FBI man. Among the committee's victims had been Robert Treuhaft's old friend Abe Glasser, who had introduced him to Decca in their Washington days. Glasser lost his job as a professor of law at Rutgers University for refusing to answer the committee's questions on Fifth Amendment grounds. Velde had also called Decca's friend Agnes Meyer, mother of Katharine Graham, one of the "pinks and others following the Communist Party line." Truman, by this time out of office, was subpoenaed to testify in an investigation the committee was conducting on a former government official who had been accused, vaguely, of subversion. He replied to his subpoena by writing a letter to Velde citing his "personal willingness to cooperate with your committee" but refusing to testify on grounds of the constitutional separation of powers.

75. A handwritten reply from Truman read: "Your message in support of the Constitution of the United States and our free institutions is highly appreciated. Many thanks. Sincerely, Harry S Truman."

76. In *A Fine Old Conflict*, Decca wrote that her husband always supported her in conflicts with her mother-in-law but nevertheless accused her of retaliating against Aranka Treuhaft in letters with sentences like: "Bob and I have been subpoenaed by the House Committee on Un-American Activities on account of being subversives, so could you be an angel and send me a smart hat from your shop to wear at the hearing?"

Must tell you about old Bob. It became obvious early in the proceedings that one of their main targets was Robert L. Condon, Democratic congressman & former law partner of Bob & Bert. A stool pigeon claimed he saw Condon at a meeting, & right after that Bob was called. First he read a 4-page statement about the intimidation of lawyers (I'll send you one). Then he was asked about Condon, & he really ripped into the committee about what their real purpose is etc. Everyone was breathless. He got quite a bit of cooperation from 2 Democrats on the committee. He pointed out that the S.F. Young Democrats, the Episcopal Church, Methodist Church, Truman & others have condemned the committee. When he finally got through there was terrific cheering & applause, so much the chairman cleared the hearing room (only time in the hearing). Afterwards crowds pressed around to congratulate him, ask for his card, etc. You would have been terrifically proud of him. You can be sure he has plenty of support around here. . . .

The children's teachers were all for us, too, & promised to give the kids extra care & attention while the hearings were on. . . .

Best love to you & Margit,[77] Decca

P.S. One thing you'll like to hear: At the committee hearings there were reserved front seats for the people under subpoena & for members of the D.A.R.,[78] Republican women's clubs, etc. Today one of my fellow subpoenees heard 2 of the Republican women talking about me. One said, "SHE doesn't look like one of them! She looks just like us! I wonder what she's doing under subpoena!" I'm sure it was the hat you gave me that did it.

To Lady Redesdale   Oakland
                                          December 10, 1953
Darling Muv,

Such a sad thing happened about our trip again—just before we got your letter, Bob and I were both subpoenaed to appear before the Velde Committee—the Congressional Committee on UnAmerican Activities. This makes it very doubtful if we'll be given a passport, but we have applied. The main thing is, life is so uncertain, that although we are hopeful of coming, you never know when these committees are going to descend on you, and what the repercussions will be.

The UnAmerican hearings were held last week. You can't imagine how revolting they are. They dragged about 100 people into it, plus another 200 who were named by the committee's informers. Many have lost their jobs as a

77. Margit Torok was the sister of Robert Treuhaft's father. She worked in Aranka Treuhaft's millinery shop.
78. Daughters of the American Revolution.

result, including school teachers, university professors, waitresses, electricians, carpenters, just about every kind of person you can imagine. I had to sit through the entire thing, five days, but in the end was never called to testify, thank goodness. . . .

The poor Children were on their own because we were frightfully busy all that week, Benjamin told me he lived on jam and mustard sandwiches all through the hearings. He looks all right though. . . .

We really are still working on the Trip, it may come off yet, we'll hear soon about the passports.

Love from Decca

To Lady Redesdale   On board a Southern Pacific Train to Oakland
June 23, 1954

Darling Muv,

I'm on my way home from a long journey all over the place. First I went to Salt Lake City with a client of Bob's on a case I am investigating for him, too long to tell about. Thence to St. Louis, Missouri, for a 2 day National Conference of CRC leaders. Thence to Montgomery Alabama to see the beloved Durrs, who I haven't seen for years.[79] I stayed with them about a week. They have had the most awful time, the beastly Un-American Committee has been after them—mostly because Virginia is the sister in law of US Supreme Court Justice Hugo Black.[80] During the hearing one of the informers was telling a lot of lies about Virginia, & Cliff completely lost his temper & made a dash for him, saying "I'll kill you for lying about my wife."[81] If you knew Cliff, the

---

79. The Durrs had moved back home to Montgomery after Clifford Durr was hounded out of his job in Denver. He opened a struggling law practice there in 1952, serving largely blacks with meager financial resources, and as a result they were largely isolated from the white community (See Decca's letter of April 7, 1977, to Ring Lardner Jr. and Frances Lardner.) Clifford Durr took on many civil rights cases, sometimes as a behind-the-scenes advisor, as the movement for black rights gained steam in the area.

80. Virginia Durr had been subpoenaed to appear before a special hearing of the Senate Judiciary Subcommittee on Internal Security chaired by Mississippi Senator James Eastland. The subcommittee, which had engaged in various investigations to root out "subversives," was investigating possible Communist ties to the Southern Conference Education Fund, of which Virginia Durr had been a board member years earlier. The SCEF's primary mission was campaigning actively for school desegregation in advance of the Supreme Court's landmark ruling in *Brown v. Board of Education* in May 1954. In her testimony, Virginia Durr gave her name and her husband's name, said she was not a member of or affiliated with the Communist Party, and refused to answer other questions out of contempt for the committee. In answer to questions, she didn't provide constitutional grounds; she simply remained silent—sometimes, her husband later recalled, taking out a compact and powdering her nose while television cameras recorded the drama.

81. Among his other statements, former Communist and paid informer Paul Crouch had testified, in Clifford Durr's words, "how Mrs. Roosevelt would pass cabinet secrets to Virginia and Virginia would pass them on to the Communist spy ring." Clifford Durr, in the audience at the

mildest man on earth, you would realize how unlike him it was, & he had a heart attack immediately & had to go to the hospital. It was all in the papers (last March) & we read about it in Oakland, so I was frightfully worried & wanted to see them. They really have had a dreadful time but seem to be fairly all right now. Of course they are getting quite old. Cliff is about 55 & she is 50, & they are trying to make a go of it in Alabama. She learned typing a few years ago & is Cliff's secretary. . . .

On the train I saw a copy of the Atlantic which is running Nancy's "Mme De Pompadour."[82] They have re-named it "How to Catch a King"!!! So typical, I roared. . . .

I'll write again soon,

Love from Decca

To Nancy Mitford   Oakland
                                                        October 6, 1954
Darling Susan,

Please note my address; your letter took almost a month. . . .

I thought you going to Russia was <u>frightfully</u> unfair. . . . I note you thought they were governessy, I expect you thought they would be Mme De Pompadourish but you know that isn't their form, in fact their main pnt is not being. I expect you would find me a bit governessy too but so would you, if you had 3 children & no governess. By the way are you still leaving the Donk some jewels? I came across some old letters, round the time she was born, where you said you would.

Well Sooze I can't think of anything to write, it's been too long since I've seen you (16 years? or more?) so you'd better come, I can see I won't ever get to Europe now because they won't let us have a passport.

Best love from Susan

P.S. I can't imagine you & Aranka specially liking each other, I was simply amazed when she & Muv liked each other. Do write & tell me what she says about me & Bob, or better still, come & tell.

---

time, later said he "blacked out" during the incident Decca described here and knew details only from reading the newspapers. He was taken to a hospital, where he remained for a week.

82. Nancy Mitford had recently published her biography *Madame de Pompadour* (Hamish Hamilton, 1954).

To Lady Redesdale Oakland
October 25, 1954

Darling Muv,

Thanks so much for your letters . . . I'm sorry not to have written lately, will try to do better. I got a letter from Susan, she tells me that Ordinary Mrs. Romilly is dying. So I wrote the enclosed, thinking to give her a little news of Dinky; but then I thought, perhaps she will construe it as hinting about the will, (if any). Also, perhaps she is dead by now. Anyway, will you use your judgment as to if it should be forwarded, you might even tell her definitely it is NOT hinting about the Will. Oh dear, life is so complicated.

All here are well. So far, the new legislation has not made any particular difference to us; there are enough laws now, both state and federal, under which they are prosecuting people in the most absurd way. For instance, one of my best friends, William L. Patterson, the National head of the Civil Rights Congress, just spent 90 days in prison because he refused to turn over to the Gov't the names of contributors to the CRC. . . .

We are all awaiting the elections with tremendous interest, on their outcome may depend the application of the Anti-Communist legislation. The whole family is campaigning, even Benj.

Best love from Decca

Telegram to Lady Redesdale Oakland
February 16, 1955

DARLING MOTHER NICHOLAS WAS KILLED YESTERDAY BY A BUS WHILE RIDING HIS BICYCLE FUNERAL IS FRIDAY AFTERNOON DINKY AND BENJAMIN TAKING IT WONDERFULLY WILL WRITE SOON GOING TO COUNTRY FOR A FEW DAYS BOB MOTHER COMING PLEASE DON'T WORRY WE ARE ALRIGHT OUR FRIENDS ARE WITH US BEST LOVE DECCA.

To Lady Redesdale Oakland
February 23, 1955

Darling Muv,

We are staying with friends in the country. There isn't much to tell: Nicholas was hit by a bus while riding his bike. He didn't suffer, was killed almost instantly. He was one of the sweetest children I ever knew, kind & generous, everyone loved him. His teacher couldn't go to school the next day, she was so upset. Dinky, Benjy & all our friends are making things bearable.

Don't worry about us, we are all right. . . .

Love to all at home, Decca

To Lady Redesdale   Oakland
                                                   July 19, 1955

Darling Muv,

Sorry not to have written. Terrific news: we got our passport at last![83] It just came today, so we haven't even discussed plans yet. . . . Naturally, if it can be arranged we'll come this year.

In order to plan, could you write by return to let me know if I have any money there still, if so, how much?[84] And could we get the boat tickets with it, if there is any? Too bad about Esmond selling the US Steel shares, he was always a terrific converter into ready cash. (Bob says they would be worth a fortune by now.) Anyway we have started saving up too. We long to see you, & Blor, & Nancy, & Debo, & Rud & Id; also we want to go to Paris & other places, & to the Island.

So do write. Will tell you the rest of our news when we meet. I had a dream last week that I was showing Bob & Dink round Swinbrook & Asthall, rather prophetic.

                        Love from Decca

To Lady Redesdale   Oakland
                                                   August 6, 1955

Darling Muv,

We seem to be burning up the cables & air-mails! I answered your cable yesterday & today got your letters of July 30 & 31st. . . .

About Farve, I agree we should see him, only he will have to agree to be nice to Bob, Dinky & Nebby Lou[85] & not to roar at them. Does he still?[86] . . .

Also, I long to show the others the Widow, do write her. I had a very nice let-

---

83. The receipt of their passports came as a surprise to the Treuhafts and their friends—"hailed by all as a sign and portent—possibly the first tiny indication of a major change to come in State Department policy," as Decca wrote in *A Fine Old Conflict*. As it turned out, the passports were issued by mistake, which they were not to find out until shortly before they were scheduled to sail to England.

84. Decca had been trying to finance her European trip in part with £500 in Drummonds bank in England that had been left to her by her brother, Tom. Her previous attempts to have the money sent to the United States had been foiled by currency restrictions. She wrote in *A Fine Old Conflict* that once, when her mother went to the bank on her behalf, the manager said exceptions could be made and asked if there was a special reason why the money was needed. She quoted her mother as saying "yes, I think there *is* a special reason; I expect my daughter wants to give the money to the Communist Party." Decca wrote that "[t]he manager replied that he thought the Exchequer would take a dim view."

85. Evelyn Louise (Nebby Lou) Crawford, the daughter of the Treuhafts' good friends and political associates Nebby and Matt Crawford, was to accompany the family on their European trip.

86. Lady Redesdale replied that, since Decca would see her father only with conditions, it would be best if she didn't visit with him, and Decca never did see her father again.

ter from her not long ago, all about plans for her Deathbed, perhaps she could arrange to have it while we are there?

Oh, also could you arrange to swim the cows to the mainland while we are there so that we can see?

Best love, Decca

To Aubrey Grossman, Ed Grogan,
Bert Edises,[87] *and their wives*

Aboard the *Liberté*
August 24, 1955

Dear Aub, Ed, Bert & Spouses,

Compared with this ship, our last days in the U.S. were dulles dishwater.[88] As I expect you know, France's night falls earlier than at home, so we decided to leave a little earlier than expected.[89] You should have seen the mad rush at the end—we arrived at Cooks Friday, 9:30 a.m.—the Liberté due to sail at noon that day. Our luggage was scattered between Grand Central Station, Aranka's flat in Manhattan, & Edith's[90] apartment in Queens. By 10:30 we had secured Cabin Class reservations (only $15 more each than the ones we had on the Flandre). We called Dink & Nebby to rush & pack & get a cab; Bob rushed to Grand Central Station; I stayed at Cooks wringing my hands & waiting for everyone to arrive. We embarked 10 minutes before sailing time, to relax at last in the glorious name of our ship. Words can't describe the utter blissfulness of the ship, the food & life generally on board. . . .

The Thurman Arnolds are on board, in 1st Class. I knew them years ago, they were friends of Hugo Black; so we've been seeing them quite a bit & told them all our sad troubles.[91] They were very sympathetic. . . .

Love from Decca

---

87. Robert Treuhaft's law partners.

88. A pun. John Foster Dulles was secretary of state. The State Department had made frantic efforts to confiscate the family's passports, which the government had issued in error. With agents of the State Department sending a telegram and searching for the family at their Oakland home, at Robert Treuhaft's office, and at the New York home and shop of a hysterical Aranka Treuhaft—leaving word that the passports were not to be used under penalty of law—the family went into hiding in New York and managed, within hours of the sailing time, to switch their reservations from the *Flandre* to an earlier departure on the S.S. *Liberté*. They dashed separately to the dock and scrambled aboard just before the departure, keeping out of sight until the ship was safely out of New York harbor.

89. Another playful reference to the reason why they sailed earlier than scheduled. The phrase "France's night" was a pun on the name of Frances Knight, head of the State Department's passport office.

90. Robert Treuhaft's sister.

91. Another intentionally cryptic allusion to the effort to seize their passports.

London
September 11, 1955

Dearest Dobby and Mason,

Thanks for your drunken scrawl. . . . If our house really has burned down, we might as well stay here; we are quite comfortable, and Bob can easily get hold of a wig and start practicing law.

Shall I bore you with an account of our travels? I think I will, just to pay you back for gloating. . . . Of course, I realize that nothing we are doing compares with the glamorous, exciting time you must be having in beautiful S.F. and nearby trails. . . .

We arrived in London August 25, about 1 p.m., and were met by Debo at the station. She rushed us off to lunch in a very fancy French restaurant where we were joined by a rather ghastly friend of hers called Tony Something, he had obviously been invited to view the outlandish American relations. And he wasn't disappointed. In the middle of lunch, he turned to Nebby and Dinky and said, "I say, do I seem <u>fearfully</u> affected to you?" The effect was startling; both girls literally choked into their Lobster Mayonnaise, and had to be revived by waiters with water.

That evening, we left by sleeper for Scotland, accompanied by Debo, Lady Emma Cavendish (aged 12) and Lord Hartington (aged 11 . . .) and their nurse. The children are quite anaemic compared to ours, but <u>much</u> politer, I guess you can't have everything. . . .

The journey took forever, because when you arrive in Oban (8 a.m.) there is a wait till 1:15 for the boat to Mull. . . . We arrived at Mull to be met by my mother and a boatman in separate cars to take us to the other side, 12 miles away, to embark for Inch Kenneth. The drive was a bit terrifying, we went with my mother in her 1930 Morris, she has quite bad palsy but drives like a New York cab driver, honking like mad at anything and everything in sight. She made one truck back up about 2 miles to the intersection! Opposite Inch Kenneth, we clambered over seaweed into a small row boat, for the last lap (about a mile) to the Island. . . .

The island is quite beautiful. About 1 mile long by 1/2 mile, said (by Dr. Johnson who visited it in 1775) to be the greenest in Scotland. It's mostly pasture, a few miniature hayfields, big vegetable gardens, lots of cattle and sheep and poultry which belong to my mother. We soon found that life on the island isn't <u>exactly</u> roughing it by our standards. The house is much bigger than I thought; 10 huge bedrooms, plenty of bathrooms as it was restored about 1930, a drawing room which takes up a whole floor and ditto a dining room. This thing about my mother living alone has also been somewhat exaggerated since she has 6 employees living in nearby cottages. I won't bore you with descriptions of the DELICIOUS food, except to say that it included daily supplies of fresh lobsters, grouse, roast lamb and chicken, home-made bread, in all 4 square meals a day. On the way over, my mother mentioned that Bob and I were to sleep in the tent. Our fears were dispelled when the tent turned out to be a 4-poster bed with hangings. We took a picture to prove it. . . .

We left after about 9 days, to return to London where we are staying in my mother's flat,[92] very comfortable, small but just room for the 4 of us.

We arrived last Sunday, just in time to hear the speakers in Hyde Park. The two who drew the biggest crowds (about 3 to 400 each) were 2 African speakers and the Communist Party speaker. We also happened on a very impressive peace parade organized by an independent women's organization, they came from many nearby towns on foot, bikes, cars, horse-and-buggy, all decorated with flowers and banners, lots of children with them. The cops stopped all traffic, and they paraded round Hyde Park Corner and through the park.

We also were shown round the offices of a newspaper.[93] They have their own huge building, built since the war, an enormous editorial staff, a built-in lawyer who has his office there and does nothing but advise them, several ROTARY presses of the most modern type. Their circulation is about 12 times as large as that of a comparable West Coast paper. Last year they tied with the Times for first place in the official newspaper contest for the best format for a newspaper of their class. . . .

Some lawyers took us to Old Bailey to watch the trials (there weren't any jury trials in progress, mostly sentencing of juveniles in cases already tried). . . .The judges are if possible even more vicious than at home. Also you can hardly tell the difference between the defense and prosecuting attorneys because of all the studied "objectiveness."

Outside of meeting up with various cousins and old friends like Philip Toynbee (and being suitably wined and dined by same) we have met some interesting people here, will tell you all about them on our return.

The Children have been taking Cooks Tours to see the sights (Tower of London etc.). Bob complains that whenever <u>he</u> wants to see anything like that I say "Oh you don't want to see that, besides I've seen it already." . . .

Hope you continue to have a GRAND time in the Bay Area.

Best love from Decca

---

92. In Rutland Mews.

93. The *Daily Worker*, the Communist paper that Decca contrasted in *A Fine Old Conflict* with San Francisco's "poor old ramshackle" *People's World*. The reference to "a newspaper" is intentionally vague because of suspected FBI surveillance.

To Aranka Treuhaft   London
                                                       September 18, 1955

Dear Aranka,

Thanks very much for your letters, and for sending Benjy's letter which I loved.[94] . . .

We just got back from our stay at Debo's, and our tour of England. Debo is at present staying in a lodge at the entrance to Chatsworth;[95] the lodge is enormous and very comfortable, I should say 3x larger than the Kahns'[96] house in Berkeley to give you an idea. They took us round to see Chatsworth; but although we walked for hours and hours we didn't see the whole house. Debo's aunt,[97] Anne Cavendish, came with us, she lived there till 1939, and said they used to have houseparties of 100 (including the servants, about 30) for Xmas etc. . . .

Dinky and Nebby got along quite well with Debo's children, they taught them some American expressions such as "Drop Dead!" and they reciprocated by teaching our kids to say "Bloody Blasted Fool!" So much for the Hands Across the Sea department.

I do long for some detailed news of Benj, is he happy and liking the school? I am beginning to miss him frightfully, as I knew I would. . . .

                    Love from Decca

P.S. Needless to say all my family simply adore Bob, they keep taking me aside one by one to tell me so.

To Pele de Lappe and Steve Murdock[98]   London
                                                       September 20, 1955

Dear Old Neighbors,

. . . So I'll start by copying off Bob's letter to Dobby—at least it gives a fresh approach:

---

94. Benjamin Treuhaft was staying with his New York grandmother while the rest of his family was traveling.

95. The duke had inherited the magnificent ducal estate—including Chatsworth, one of the grandest houses of Europe—from his father in 1950, but he and his wife were not able to occupy it immediately because of the need to arrange finances to pay off the heavy death duties. The house also desperately needed renovation to restore its former splendor and modernize the facilities. It had been used to house schoolgirls during the war and was in general disrepair. The duke and duchess supervised the renovations and finally moved into Chatsworth in 1959.

96. Dr. Ephraim (Eph) and Barbara Kahn and their children were among the Treuhafts' dearest friends for more than four decades. Some of the background of their relationship is related in a letter to Maya Angelou dated August 9, 1980.

97. That is, her husband Andrew's aunt.

98. Pele de Lappe was married to Murdock at the time and using his name, but for the sake of continuity, the editor is using the name she herself used most of her life. De Lappe, in addition to her previously noted role at the California Labor School, was a writer, feature editor, and artist at the *People's World*. Murdock was political editor of the Communist Party paper.

"Following Dec's last report to you we made our tour of the dukeries. Our first stop was with Debo at her little hideaway in Derbyshire, where we spent three ducal days. The main establishment, 'Chatsworth,' is only slightly larger and grander than Versailles, 178 rooms and no baths. Very uncanny, as Grossman . . . would doubtless say. Because of the monstrous death duties the poor dears can no longer afford to live in Chatsworth, so they live in the 'lodge' (which they own) in the village (which they own), and they make do by opening Chatsworth to holiday trippers 6 months of the year. This year they led the league with 250,000 trippers @ 2 1/2 shillings a head. It really is worth seeing, and we will show you pictures of all.

"Having read of the custom of sitting over after dinner port with the men, after the ladies have retired to the drawing room,[99] I have always longed for the experience. It's one of the things I used to day dream about at home while doing the dinner dishes. I was cheated of the experience at the Island, because I was the only man at dinner. All I got to do was carve. So too at Debo's for the first 2 nights. Andrew was away, 'being active'[100] at the races, so Lord Hartington (age 11) and I were the only males in attendance. The last night, however, Andrew turned up, together with Lord Antrim (who I kept calling Lord Sinus by mistake . . . Ed.[101]) who owns half of Ulster. Port was poured after dessert and, as I expected, the ladies began to file out. Then, to my utter dismay, their lordships stood up and headed for the door. I let out an anguished cry. Was I to be cheated again? Reassuringly the Lords called back, 'Hold the port for we are coming—we are just seeing the ladies to the door.' Come back they did, and linger we did for a half hour. Of course it was all disappointing anticlimax. The talk was about prize-fighting (Cockell v. Valdez) and race horses. No sex, no dirty stories—proof to me that I was not socially acceptable. . . .

"We're back in London now, about to take off for 2 or 3 weeks on the Continent. We gave a party here last night for all the nice non-peers who have been so kind to us here in London. Present were barristers galore, an expatriate editor known to you, and an expatriate non editor also known to you."

You must say the above is rather a concise Bob's-eye view of England. The

---

99. Decca wrote in *A Fine Old Conflict* that during their voyage to England her husband had been studying British broadcaster and humorist Stephen Potter's *Lifemanship* (1950) and *One-Upmanship* (1952), "wonderfully funny essays about how to get on in English society chiefly by making others ill at ease." She described how Robert Treuhaft had read aloud to her some of the rules of what was, to him but not her, an unfamiliar game, such as "Snob and Countersnobship." Decca said she replied, "Oh, poor Bob, I shouldn't even try beating the English at their own game. Remember that if one starts with William the Conqueror, they've had almost ten centuries of practice, how can you hope to compare?"

100. When the duchess had visited Decca in California, she was questioned by Decca's politically involved friends eager to know "What are you active in?" On her return to the UK, she sent Decca a photograph of her and the duke, in full ceremonial regalia, with the explanatory note: "Andrew and me being active."

101. The "editor," of course, was Decca.

poor Girls <u>must</u> be getting rather confused by all this parade of mixed-up dukes and expatriate editors and non-editors, but they are bearing up nicely, and really are a panic. Nebby recounted to me a killing conversation they had with Mornington Peregrine Hartington. It seems they were pumping him to find out where his old man got all his money; Ld. H. replied, I am sure truthfully, that he doesn't know. Dinky said "I think he gets it from selling slaves!"

I was going through Debo's scrapbook where she pastes photographs, clippings etc. She had several pages of congratulatory telegrams on her engagement to Andrew, from such as Elizabeth R.,[102] etc. Among them was one from me saying "HONNISH CONGRATULATIONS ON A SUCCESSFUL SEASON'S DUKE-HUNTING."

Sad to say, I can't write to you about some of the more fascinating occurrences and people, will have to wait to tell all when we get home. . . .

Best love, Decca

To Lady Redesdale   London
                                                    September 20, 1955

Darling Muv,

Thanks for your letters, of course I'll write as our plans develop and let you know. . . .

The Tour of Childhood Places was a great success, we got in to both Swinbrook and Asthall, so I was able to show the others various hons cupboards,[103] etc. Swinbrook is quite hideous inside now, I thought.

The most amazing thing was that they still have exactly the same pictures (the Gypsy Maid etc) at the Swinbrook P.O., I remember thinking them so beautiful when a child. . . .

Bob discovered swastikas and hammer-and-sickle cut in the Mews[104] windows in diamonds by Bobo and me when we used to live here, he did roar.

About seeing Farve, don't you think we had better discuss it again when I see you in October? For one thing, I don't see how I could go up there again now as we are just about to leave for Europe. . . .

I'll let you know our plans as soon as we know.

Love from Decca

---

102. George VI's wife, Queen Elizabeth.

103. The linen closet, in which the children huddled for warmth, companionship, and various sisterly conspiracies, served as a sort of clubhouse for their Society of Hons and was known as the Hons' cupboard.

104. The family's London home, in Rutland Gate.

To Aranka and Edith Treuhaft[105]   Paris
                                                                      October 23, 1955

Dear Aranka and Edith,

. . . I can't <u>begin</u> to tell you how much we are loving this trip. . . . We arrived in Paris Oct 21, after driving all day from Bâle (Switzerland) in pouring rain. After finding a hotel we drove to Nancy's flat, got there about 7 pm, only to find she was in England staying at the Devonshires.[106] Her maid Marie was awfully nice to us, let us in, lit the fire etc. So I decided to call Nancy to find out the score. After hours of explaining the address to the operator, I reached her & told her I was calling from her flat. She was simply <u>furious</u> because of the expense & hung up almost at once! To pay her back for being so stingy, we drank up most of her whiskey. (On checking, I found the phone call cost $1.50.)[107] Bob & the girls simply howled with laughter about the whole incident. . . .

It is really heavenly being back in Paris after all these years. I am getting Bob in the frame of mind to spend our old age here (after Benj gets married). Such a pleasure to sit in a bidet once more! Paris hasn't changed, the same rude cops, intolerance of foreigners, beauty & squalor that I remember so well. It's still my home from home. I remember once when I was 9 a furious argument my mother had with a porter, who ended up saying "You are the kind of Englishwoman who murdered Jeanne d'Arc!" . . .

We miss Benj <u>terribly</u>. I do hope he's getting on alright & not giving trouble. I feel guilty about staying so long but at the same time this may be my last chance to come here & there is so much to see & do. When we get to London I shall arrange a study course for Dinky so she won't miss too much school. . . .

            Love from Decca

---

105. Robert Treuhaft's sister's surname changed with her marriage. For easy recognition, the name Treuhaft is used here.

106. According to Mitford sisters' biographer Mary Lovell, Nancy Mitford's absence was based on "reservations at the last minute about Decca's politics," and Lovell quotes Nancy as telling a friend, "I don't die for her as much as I pretend to when I write." Nancy described her reaction to the impending visit this way to her friend Evelyn Waugh: "I'm half delighted & half terrified. Seventeen years—."

107. Decca wrote in *A Fine Old Conflict* that Nancy Mitford, "sounding most relaxed and welcoming," called Decca back after a time—"on Debo's nickel," as Robert Treuhaft observed—and the two spoke at length. Nancy returned to Paris a few days later "in the sunniest of moods." After the sisters and Constancia spent a week together, Nancy wrote to Evelyn Waugh that her sister was "unchanged and so sweet."

To Pele de Lappe, Steve Murdock, and Bob and Dorothy Neville[108]   Paris
October 29, 1955

Dearest Neighbors, and Nevilles,

. . . What to tell you about Paris? . . . The Girls went to the Folies Bergère. Their comment: "very vulgar, no good on the Woman Question!" I did roar. What did you expect, I asked them. . . .

We (Dink & I)[109] are parking at Nancy's (days. Nights still at the foul 2x4, cheapest hotel in Paris, everyone says). She did tell one fairly funny story about her stay in Russia. It seems she was introduced to a wheel in the Culture Dept. for the purpose of getting a line on the Russian writers. She asked how many copies a best seller would sell; was told 1 1/2 million, which made her very jealous. She asked the name of this best seller, was told, " 'Cement,' by the author of 'Glue'!" Far cry from Mme de Pompadour, natch.

Of all relations seen so far she's held up the best, in some ways—at least so far—we've only been here one day. Debo is in an awful rut, I suppose she likes it though she doesn't look specially happy. Rud & Id, my cousins who I used to adore, fell very flat somehow. At least Nancy reads, is still funny . . . & is not a fascist or an idiot. . . .

Goodbye dear Neighbors, I long to see you. . . .

Best love, Decca

To Robert Treuhaft   London
November 2, 1955

Darling old Bob,

I've started several letters to you, but what with all the things to do in Paris and DOING MY OWN PACKING, never finished them. I hope this reaches you before you leave NY. . . .

We had a very good time in Paris. . . . I stayed at Nancy's days, I'm very sorry you missed her but will try to tell all:

I met a few of her friends. The first was a really ghastly American woman (no wonder she hates Americans so if that's the kind she knows). The conversation

---

108. Like the Murdocks, the Nevilles were later divorced, but since Decca throughout the years referred to Dorothy (or Do) Neville by that name in her letters, for the sake of continuity, the editor is conforming with that usage. The Nevilles were longtime friends of Pele de Lappe and among the Treuhafts' earliest friends and political colleagues in San Francisco. Robert Treuhaft credited Bob Neville with being the first African American to make it into the upper ranks of the electricians' union and breaking the union's restriction of its black members to low-paying, unskilled shipyard work (as opposed to more lucrative residential and commercial work, where he himself was then able to work). His wife, Dorothy, who was white and a dental hygienist, Treuhaft said, came from an old California family; her parents were also, in Treuhaft's words, "old-time Reds."

109. Robert Treuhaft and Nebby Lou Crawford had sailed for home two days earlier to return to work and school. Treuhaft picked up his son, Benjamin, in New York en route home.

ran thusly: G.A.W.: My <u>dear</u>, <u>too</u> awful, Clare[110] has simply taken over my apartment . . . and isn't it <u>too</u> awful about Poor <u>Butler</u>,[111] they're giving him such a going over about that budget . . . of course one never does <u>understand</u> about things like that, does one; I must get hold of Spaak,[112] he's really quite a clever little man, and get him to explain it all to me . . .

Nancy: Yes darling but do you think he'd know about <u>English</u> budgets? Etc. etc. . . .

Later conversation developed that the Windsors[113] have a new dog named Peter Townsend,[114] my dear quel mauvais goût.[115] Unfortunately this was all just before the Princess Margaret statement[116] . . . so no special slant on that.

When the GAW left, rather against her will I made her take Dink & me back to the hotel in her enormous Cadillac-&-chauffeur. On the way she said, "My dear this is the most <u>awful</u> nuisance, no good at all in Paris traffic; but Fi-fi (or Icky, or whatever her husband's name is) and I were stuck in the rain in New York and we rushed into the Cadillac place & bought it," so Dink & I were quite nice about it & said we didn't find it a nuisance, specially.

We met the Col,[117] very briefly on 2 occasions. He's about as I expected. . . .

On the Margaret thing, the general consensus seemed to be that she is now one-up on the Windsors. The Fr. papers were full of the incroyable attitude of the Anglais toward l'amour.[118] I'll bring some of the papers for Steve (having failed in my scooping mission). Tell him about the Windsors' dog, that's a scoop.[119] . . .

Giles wrote Muv 2 letters saying he's longing to see me. . . . I suppose I'd better consult with my glorious solicitor[120] before treating with the enemy?[121] . . .

---

110. Decca's own footnote in the letter said, "Boothe Luce." Clare Boothe Luce, the wife of *Time* publishing magnate Henry Luce, was a journalist, editor, author, member of Congress, and diplomat. In 1955 she was American ambassador to Italy.

111. R. A. Butler, British chancellor of the exchequer.

112. Paul Henri Spaak, the Belgian diplomat who served as the first president of the United Nations General Assembly. He had recently been named to head the committee planning a European common market.

113. The Duke and Duchess of Windsor.

114. Townsend was a divorced equerry to the British royal family, a group captain in the Royal Air Force, whom Princess Margaret wished to marry at the time—creating a major furor in the country.

115. "What bad taste."

116. On October 31, the princess called off her plans to marry Townsend.

117. The love of Nancy Mitford's life, Colonel Gaston Palewski, a French diplomat who later married another woman.

118. "The unbelievable attitude of the English toward love."

119. It is unknown whether Steve Murdock published Decca's global scoop in his paper, the *People's World*.

120. Decca characteristically referred to Richard Turner as "my glorious solicitor," sometimes shortened to simply The Glorious or My Glorious or Glorious Richard.

121. The reference to Esmond Romilly's brother evidently involved conflict over the estate of the brothers' father, Colonel Bertram Romilly.

Since Dink's schooling has fallen through, Muv has agreed to teach her spelling (quoi?) & I'm getting her some Shakespeare to read & will send her to see the plays at the Old Vic.

> Best love—do write all, Dec

To Robert Treuhaft   London

November 12, 1955

Darling old Bob,

I just got back from staying with the Widow Hammersley in the Isle of Wight, & to my <u>great</u> joy here was your letter, sent from NY as you were emplaning. I'm so sorry I fretted a bit at you in other letters about non-writing. I know I shouldn't get in a stew but I did—I had the feeling something was wrong, probably re the passport, and sure enough—second sight as Muv would say. I must say I <u>roared</u> over your letter, so did Dinky; the part about you and the passport taking,[122] also Benjy's love life. I'm so awfully relieved that he's in good spirits & fat & happy as I was seriously worried about how he was faring. . . . Shall I tell you all about the Widding? . . . I think you can imagine her from reading the Ballad & the Source,[123] & from my descriptions. She arrived to meet me at the boat (it's about 2 hours train & 1/2 hour boat from London) looking very characteristic, swathed in black scarves, yellow face, jet black hair, somber large eyes. Also, characteristically, she had co-opted a neighbor to drive her to meet me & made her drive us both home. On arrival she arranged everything for a marathon chat by the fire; it consisted of taking everyone in the family, one by one (starting with me, of course) and examining, dissecting & speculating upon their innermost lives. She announced about 6:30 "<u>Child</u>, I always have my <u>big</u> meal in the middle of the day. I <u>trust</u> you are not hungry?" I insisted firmly that I was quite hungry, because all I'd had for lunch was a sausage roll & cup of tea on the boat; so we ended by having quite a decent meal. After dinner the following conversation ensued:

> Widow: <u>Child</u>, at what time are you accustomed to having your <u>bath</u>?
> Me: (wary for a trap) It really doesn't make the least bit of difference to me.
> Wid: Come child, tell me your <u>favorite</u> time for your bath, I <u>must</u> <u>know</u>.
> Me: Oh—well, I usually have it in the morning.
> Wid: (clasping her forehead in gesture of despair) <u>Ohhhhhh</u>!
> Me: Now look here Mrs. H, I <u>honestly</u> don't care a bit what time I have it, just as soon have it tonight.

---

122. Not unexpectedly, given the circumstances of their departure, Robert Treuhaft's passport had been confiscated onboard the ship returning him and Nebby Lou Crawford to the United States.

123. *The Ballad and the Source*, a novel by Rosamond Lehmann (Reynal and Hitchcock, 1945).

Wid: <u>No</u> child, you are <u>accustomed</u> to having it in the <u>morning</u>, and you <u>shall</u> have it in the morning—but you <u>must not</u> take more than <u>this much hot water</u> (indicating 2 inches).

Me: I've decided not to have one at all, & wait till I get home.

(I ended up having it at night, & more than 2 inches at that). All the foregoing was really because the Wid is so stingy she can't bear to think of anyone else using up the hot water, because of the Electricity Bill.

The Wid having carefully organized the agenda to include maximum chatting with minimum eating and/or bathing on my part, she dismissed me in time for me to catch the 9:45 train home, so I arrived at the mews about 1:30. Woman was here to lunch (second sight again. I mean calling her Woman, since she's become a you know what bian). After lunch we tried to teach her Scrabble, but she never scored more than 4 on any one play, & even Muv got a bit restive with her when she said "What does I-C-Y spell?" after I'd put it down for a score of 35.

Sorry to say, I've had one row with Muv, it occurred when I noticed on her engagement pad the words, "Mosleys to lunch" (next Thurs) so I told her that Dink & I would not be present since we do not care to break bread with murderers. She got very cross ("your own sister" & all that sort of thing, plus a good deal more discussion, tell you when I see you). However this all happened several days ago & we both have carefully not provoked any similar discussion since. Hope I can last till the 24th without the usual world-shaking row. Nancy says the reason she never goes to the Island is that Muv always "starts going on" (pro German, etc.) & it ends in a frightful row. I told Nancy (this was before the Diana incident) that Muv appears to me to be a flaming you know what. Nancy replied, that shows <u>she's</u> weakminded & what's more double faced. Now I see there's some truth in that—Of course N. was partly justifying her own weakmindedness & also double facedness, as I pointed out. But she (N) is so irrevocably set in her ways by now that there isn't much use scolding her. . . .

Good night, <u>write soon</u>, love to you & Benj.

Dec

To Lady Redesdale   On the train en route to Oakland
                                              December 10, 1955

Darling Muv,

We're almost at the end of our journey—will be home in 5 hours. I can hardly remember what I wrote to you from NY as I was in a state of utter exhaustion from the seasickness. The last 3 nights sitting up on the train have been blissfully restful in comparison.

Our arrival in NY was almost without incident. You know how Bob kept writing to warn us of the hellish time we'd probably have at Customs?[124] Well we arrived with our innumerable assorted cardboard boxes, the Giant Cracker, suitcases tied together with string—easily the saddest looking luggage on the dock. The customs man looked at this unsightly miscellany in despair, & said "open any 2 boxes." When we did, & the sight was even sadder, like something left over from a jumble sale—he gulped & said "close it up again," just like the song in "New Faces," "Put back the mask," remember?[125] . . .

Give my love to Woman & all.

Best love from Decca

To Lady Redesdale   Oakland
                                              May 13, 1956

Darling Muv,

I am so sorry not to have written lately, I've been getting your letters. . . .

One reason I haven't written is that I got a job about a month ago and have been terrifically busy as a result. You can't think how I love going to work again after all this time. . . . It's a very lowly kind of job, in the advertising department

---

124. Robert Treuhaft on his return had erased a penciled notation on his customs declaration that had read "Hold for Murphy" and cleared customs easily. But he had warned Decca that she might face trouble, based on a conversation with CRC colleague William Patterson, who had told Treuhaft of his treatment by customs agents when he returned to the United States a few years earlier. Patterson said he had been subjected to hours of invasive searches, including a strip search. Decca had vowed, "I am not going to be stripped, for one thing I don't have any decent slips or a good enough garter belt—I'm not going to buy new ones just for them."

125. Although Decca didn't mention it to her mother, her passport, predictably, was seized on her arrival. Following her husband's advice, she handed it over peacefully. She later wrote "a furious letter" to the State Department demanding its return. According to Decca's FBI file, the State Department's passport office replied that her passport had been confiscated because (in the words of the FBI report) "the Department of State had received information which indicated that she was ineligible under Section 51.135 of the Passport Regulations to continue to receive passport facilities. (This Section relates to limitations on issuance of passports to persons supporting the communist movement.)" Again in the FBI's words, "The letter stated that if the Subject were at any time a member of the Communist Party or the Communist Political Association, she should include in [an] affidavit the dates of membership and the description of the offices or other positions that she might have held therein, and if her membership terminated, under what conditions such termination occurred."

of a big San Francisco newspaper,[126] and I only get $52.00 a week, which is supposed to go up to $75 after a year if I stick it out that long. My job is selling classified advts.[127] Such a riotous thing happened after I'd been there a week. It's a closed shop (meaning all Union) and we belong to the Newspaper Guild. So one day the shop steward came round to me with the little monthly union paper, and said, "Your name is in here because you are one of the new employees; I know it's such a thrill to see one's name in print in a newspaper for the first time, so I thought I'd give this to you." I was inwardly roaring, do you remember how I was the first one in the family to be on posters? . . .

Bob's mother is trying to get a divorce from her disgusting husband Al, but it isn't going very well as he is trying to blackmail her into giving him $3,000. Bob told her that for only $100 you can hire people to bump someone off in New York, but I was shocked at this suggestion and offered to go back there with Dinky and throw him out for her, if she'd pay our fare and enough extra for me to visit Virginia in Alabama. So far she hasn't taken me up on it.

Do give my love to the others, if you see them. Tell them I'll write one day, but I really am fantastically busy, I expect it's because I haven't worked at a regular job for so long I don't organize my time properly yet. . . .

Best love, Decca

To Lady Redesdale   Oakland
                                                                                October 8, 1956

Darling Muv,

Thanks so much for your letter. I suppose you are still at the Island. . . .

The extraorder thing about "Lifeitselfmanship" is that the worst offenders love it best (some that is, there have also been a few violent reactions anti it). The other extraorder thing is that I got out 500 copies, thinking we'd never sell more than about 200 at most, but they are selling like mad and we had to put out another 1,000. Over 150 people have written in for them from all over the U.S., and now from Canada because a Canadian paper reviewed it! Also quite a number of bookshops have ordered it. . . .

By the way, did I tell you I got a letter from my glorious solicitor, and it seems that I automatically get 1/3 of Col. Romilly's[128] estate, which he says is "considerable," and consists of docks, ground rents, etc.[129] This has nothing to do with Dinky's possible claim under the marriage settlement! . . . I don't sup-

---

126. The *San Francisco Chronicle.*

127. For a fuller description of her hiring and job duties, see letter of January 6, 1964, to Betty Friedan.

128. Esmond Romilly's father.

129. In a letter to her mother-in-law, Decca wrote that the major impact of the news was that "Bob and the children are being much nicer to me now I'm an heiress."

pose I'll ever actually get it, rather difficult to get the docks out of England; but it does seem to offer hopes of coming back to England again one day, if I can only pry loose my passport. A friend of ours in NY, Leonard Boudin,[130] got his after about 3 years of fighting in the courts about it, so there may be hope. . . .

Love from Decca

To Lady Redesdale   Oakland
                                                           October 21, 1956

Darling Muv,

Thanks for your letter. I've been away for a week (my only hol this year) and returned to find it. We get the New Yorker, and saw the poem when it first came out. In fact almost every issue, for weeks, has had some correspondence about Noblesse Oblige, Nancy must be selling millions here. She told me over 10,000 were sold in the U.S. the first week. Isn't it extraorder? . . .

My Glorious Solicitor wrote (more stuff about the mythical estate, I do wonder if it really exists?) and he said Lifeitselfmanship was reviewed in the Observer (no one sent it to me, do get hold of some and send them, he said it was in the October 14th paper). He also says some publishers who are friends of his, Lawrence & Wishart, want to republish it in England! So of course I wrote back immediately saying I was longing. . . . Orders keep pouring in by mail, I'm terrified we are going to have to mimeograph more, it is such a bother, Nancy is so lucky not to have to.

I had a lovely hol, only too sad that Bob couldn't come, he was afraid there would be an awful pile of work if he did. I went to a place called Laguna Beach with the Krotsers, friends of ours (Henderson met them when she was here). . . . I tried to arrange for Dinky to fly down Friday after school as there was one party where there were a lot of boys and girls of her age. I telephoned Bob to see if she could come; he said he didn't know. . . . By Friday, I was longing to know if she was coming, but didn't want to go to the expense of another phone call. So I put in a person to person call at Bob's office for MRS. S. CONSTANCIA CUMMING.[131] First of all his stupid secretary kept saying there was no one there of that name, but finally I got the operator to talk to Bob and she reported back that the party I was calling was at home and could be reached

130. The radical attorney who represented many celebrated clients over the years, including Dr. Benjamin Spock in a trial that was to be the subject of one of Decca's books.

131. This is the first of many references in Decca's letters to a small-scale scam the Treuhafts—and doubtless many others—played surreptitiously during the days of expensive long-distance phone calls, to avoid charges. Calls were placed through the operator, person to person, for people with elaborately conceived names that included a message, as in this example. The calls were refused on the receiving end with word that the person called was not available. Since the call didn't get through to the fictitious intended person, there were no charges. Decca wrote about the ploy in a 1961 *Life* magazine article.

at home any time over the weekend. So I cancelled the call. Do tell Susan, I know she will be pleased at my frugality, remember how simply furious she was when I rang her up in England from her flat in Paris? By the way that is the favourite story of our trip among our friends here, they think it confirms that our family must be completely mad. . . .

I must rush now as masses of people are coming to lunch,

Best love from Decca

To Aranka Treuhaft Oakland
November 14, 1956

Dear Aranka,

Thanks so much for your letter & lovely blank check. . . .

We have also been terribly upset about the awful happenings in Hungary.[132] I don't think my opinion is worth much, but since you ask I'll give it. Incidentally, I find little agreement among my friends about it. I am pretty sure that the revolt was originated by workers and students with most justified grievances. Why couldn't we see signs of this while we were there?[133] I don't know. We thought there was a high degree of unity around the regime. Sure there were privations and hardships, but it seemed to us that the people were not only better off than before (on Bob's observations, from previous trips) but that above all the youth and children were benefiting enormously and were far better off than those in Austria, France etc. However, the revolt and the continuing general strike would indicate that economic grievances of the people are extremely deep seated. Not to speak of their demands for National independence, symbolized by demands for return to Hungarian flags, uniforms etc and an end to compulsory Russian courses in the schools. However I also gather from the news releases that the rebels were quickly joined by fascists and that a "white terror" was being established. Because of this, I think in the long run the inter-

132. Students and workers had taken to the streets of Budapest on October 23 to protest food shortages and Russian control. After newly appointed Prime Minister Imre Nagy abolished the one-party system and announced that Hungary would withdraw from the Warsaw Pact, infantry units and thousands of Soviet tanks rolled into Budapest on November 4. Soviet MiG fighters bombed the city, and artillery fired on it. There was fierce resistance, but by the date this letter was written, the rebellion was suppressed, with about 30,000 killed in Budapest alone. Hundreds of thousands escaped to the West.

133. In February 1956, Decca had written an article for *People's World* on their travels in Hungary in 1955. Entitled "We Visited Socialism," it was a sunny account of the peaceful, friendly, industrious, and increasingly prosperous country the Treuhafts observed. Decca wrote a long account of their "exhilarating" trip in *A Fine Old Conflict*, where, in retrospect, she characterized her *People's World* article as "rather tedious." In the memoir, she described two encounters in Hungary that might have alerted them to the widespread disaffection in the country. Although she largely dismissed the incidents at the time, she said she included them in her *People's World* manuscript, where they were removed by a copy editor for "reasons of space."

ests of the Hungarian people are best served by entry of Russian troops. The lack of any real news is most frustrating. Except for a few slim releases from the Government (such as the one agreeing to certain demands of the rebellion) it's terribly hard to get a real picture. I worry terribly about the people we met there, specially the Strikers, and wonder if they are still alive. You may have seen in the papers that the National Committee of the U.S. Communist Party issued a resolution condemning the entry of Russian troops. I can't agree with them as I fear that the bloodshed and disruption would have been far worse if they hadn't come in. I think the Russians laid the groundwork for much of the present trouble by establishment of an authoritarian regime and undemocratic practices; but now the damage has been done, I think they had no alternative but to try to restore order and to preserve a socialist system in Hungary against what looks like a fascist coup.

Does this make sense? Probably not, but it's the best I can do at the moment.[134] I know you must worry too about your friends and relations there, and hope you can hear from them soon. We haven't written anyone for fear of somehow causing them trouble. . . .

I enclose the bit on "Lifeitselfmanship" from the Observer, they sent me 15 guineas for it (about $45), which Pele and I will share.[135] . . .

The Children are fine, except that Dinky seems to have hit a streak of boredom and dissatisfaction with life in general. I keep telling her that one is bound to be miserably unhappy at 15, I know I was, but she will soon be grown up and in control of her own destiny. . . .

The Firm[136] is once more on the verge of going broke, but that always happens about this time of year so I've quit worrying. It seems none of the partners has the least idea of business administration, so there are always terrible forecasts of doom when the accountant comes.

Bob is looking into the Television possibilities.[137] Thanks again very much for the lovely present.

Best love, Decca

p.s. What present would you and Edith like from my inheritance, if I really get it? Better put in for it soon, Aubrey is already insisting on a Scotch tweed overcoat, and others are putting in their bids.

---

134. The confusion and ambivalence Decca expressed here was felt by other American Communists, many of whom left the Party after the Hungarian uprising. Decca and her husband remained members for another two years.

135. Decca's artist friend Pele de Lappe had illustrated the booklet.

136. Robert Treuhaft's law firm.

137. That is, the possibilities of purchasing a television.

To Nancy Mitford Oakland
May 2, 1957

Darling Susan,

... You <u>are</u> so typical of the times. We roared at the Art Buchwald clipping.[138] Sometimes his things are in our local paper, the Oakland Tribune, and I've been noting for that one but it hasn't appeared yet. When it does I shall buy extra copies and post them at all the book shops, remember how all your books were withdrawn from the Vienna bookshops when he ran your comments on "Fools and Austrians"?

As I sit drinking my instant coffee from my plastic coffee cup, having just gotten out from under my electric blanket (are you noting gotten?) I long for you to visit my lovely home....

I'm soon off to Alabama to stay with the blissful Durrs, their daughter Lucy is getting married and I'm going for the wedding.[139] I'm awfully excited as I haven't seen them for years. The other daughter, Baby Sister (about 1 year older than the Donk) may be going to England this winter for an "au pair" job. I won't tell her to look you up because remember how awful you were about poor Miss White, years ago? I just found some of your old letters about how you hated her. By the way I shall be furious if you hate Dinky, you must remember that she's far more American than English by now.

Susan the thing is you don't need a weighing machine, just find out how many stamps the Ritz put on and then put on the same amount.[140] Otherwise there's no point in being back on writers.

Well I must go now to make some cookies for the kids.

You really are kind to offer to pay for Dinky, but I'm hoping to be quite rich by then so hope I can afford to. Did Muv tell you about my inheritance? Most extraorder, it seems the Romillies wrote their wills out all wrong and as a result they didn't succeed in cutting me off, and I'm hoping for quite a bit.

Yr. loving Susan

---

138. In a letter to her mother, Decca wrote that Nancy Mitford had "sent me the cutting about the anti-American interview." She added—describing this letter to Nancy—"I wrote back, all in American."

139. Lucy Durr married Sheldon Hackney, who became a historian, author, and educator-administrator, serving five years as president of Tulane University and twelve as president of the University of Pennsylvania. He was also chairman of the National Endowment for the Humanities. Decca's presence at the wedding provoked a crisis in the Durr family; see April 7, 1977, letter to Ring and Frances Lardner.

140. Nancy Mitford's odd and parsimonious mail habits were a frequent refrain in Decca's letters. Nancy had told Decca that she didn't use airmail because she considered it "so middle class," prompting Decca to refer to airmail as "non-U mail." Nancy also told her sister that it was too much trouble and expense to purchase a machine to weigh airmail letters.

To Marge Frantz[141]   Montgomery, Ala.
                                                            June 19, 1957

Dear Marge,

I wouldn't have missed the wedding for anything. Oh dear I'll neaver manage to finish this letter, I'm trying to work Virginie's eleactric typewriter and it's impossible. The a's keep appearing when least expeacted.

Lucy has become a spectacular Beauty, she is slightly prettier than Grace Kelly. The Durr dining room is completely filled with a display of wedding presents, in odd contrast to the very roaachy kitchen (Virginia: "Well I declare, this is the first time I've ever had roaches in my house, I can't understand it." Me: "Virginia, that was the annual slogan on Seminary Hill. Every summer roaches would appear in hordes, and every summer you used to say 'Well I declare this is the first time etc. etc.' " She had to admit a certain truth in this.)

                                    a

The wedding was preceded by innumerable lunches, evening parties with Ladies Home Journal type food (croquettes, creamed asaparagus, ice cream in shape of bridal shoes, jellied salads, etc. etc.) where the conversation tended to run in similar channels: "My, you look lovely." "I deaclare I never did see a prettier bride than Lucy." "Well Tilla will be the next one now,"[142] and similar gems of wisdom and erudition. Lucky I slaved over my clothes, they turned out to be OK thanks to a full week of fretting over them involving Pele, Kathy, Mimi, Do, and everyone else I could lay hands on. . . .

I had an interesting conversation with Lucy's father-in-law. He is a leading light from Birmingham, on the school board etc. We were deploring the state of education all over, lack of provision for bright kids, etc. He asked me what was being done for them in Calif, so I told him about the speacial group at Washington Grammar School for children with IQ of over 150, and let drop the information that in the group are 1 white child, 2 orientals, 1 Negro. He said, in genuine amazement, "It don't seem possible that no Nigra would have no IQ of no 150, do it now?" I answered politely, "Well, I think it do seem possible, I don't think no race has nothing to do with no IQ." . . .

---

141. Marge Frantz is the daughter of Virginia Durr's dear friends and southern political colleagues, Joe and Esther Gelders, and was herself an ally in Durr's early civil rights work. She remained a lifelong friend of Durr's. Frantz initially met Decca at the Durrs' Alexandria home in 1941—a meeting Decca later said she didn't recall—and became one of her closest friends soon after moving to Berkeley, California, from the South in 1950 with her husband, civil rights attorney Laurent Frantz. Marge Frantz and Decca, in their Communist Party days in the early '50s, had adjoining offices, Frantz with the Independent Progressive Party and Decca with the Civil Rights Congress. After leaving the Party, Frantz returned to college and became a professor at the University of California at Santa Cruz.

142. Virginia Durr's namesake, known to Decca when she was living with the family as Baby Sister, was by now called Tilla.

Good bye old Marge, this letter is becoming too much of a struggle to write, and you must say this is a nice long letter. I shall expect an answer. . . .

Love to all, Decca

Write me all about the UnAmerican hearings in S.F.

To Constancia Romilly   Montgomery
                                                              June 20, 1957

Darling Dinky,

Thanks so very much for the telegram, you were a good girl to send it as I got in a perfect stew thinking about you on the bus, & the night before I'd had a bad dream that you had missed a connection & you were crying in the bus station.[143]

I can't wait to get a letter, & hear all about the people there, how you like it all, etc. etc. . . .

Bob arrived yesterday at 5:30, he had had a perfectly gruelling 2 days before leaving because of the Un-American Committee. One man, a research scientist from Monterey, who was a client of Bert's[144] & had been subpoenaed by the committee, committed suicide Sunday night. He left a note saying he couldn't stand the publicity. . . .

Do write a nice juicy letter telling all about the bus ride & all about Mexico City. . . .

Love from Dec

To Pele de Lappe   New York City
                                                          June 27, 1957

Dear Neighbor,

. . . Life here is being heavenly. I just wolfed down a roll, sweet butter & coffee. The air conditioning is humming away unobtrusively in one corner.

Last night we had delicious broiled lobster at the Sea Colony (downstairs) & then went on a Judy-escorted[145] Village pub crawl. Poor old Bob was in an ordinary suit with tie, & drew disapproving stares from the bearded and Bermuda-shorted local yokels. . . .

The New Yorkers are performing as usual—

Scene 1: Bob goes to nearby grocery for orange juice. Asks for <u>frozen</u> juice.

---

143. Constancia Romilly had gone to Mexico to study during the summer.
144. Bert Edises.
145. Judy Glasser, wife at the time of Abe Glasser, who had been Robert Treuhaft's best friend and housemate during his OPA days in Washington. Judy Glasser would become better known as Judy Viorst after she married Milton Viorst.

Grocery man says it hasn't come in yet, why not take a can of juice. Bob says no thanks. Man says, "What's the matter, it's the same thing. Look here, it's hot outside. Why not take the canned juice? You don't want to go on a look on a hot day like this"—Bob escapes.

Scene 2: Next morning he goes to same store, this time for rolls. Man sees him coming. "Juice? We got plenty juice today." Bob: "No thanks, I want some rolls." Man: "That's life for you! Today I got plenty juice, he wants rolls!"

Act II, Scene 1: I see an underclothes sale at Bloomingdale's. Vanity Fair lingerie reduced to 1/2 price. Decide to look for a nightgown to send my mother. I ask the clerk: "Have you got a size 40, long?" Clerk: "No long ones. Why don't you take a shortie?" Me: "Well it's for my mother, I don't think she'd like a shortie." Clerk: "You get her a long one, she is likely to trip on it & break her neck. Shorties are much cooler. They're the thing of the future . . ." Me: "Yes but, don't you see, she's a thing of the PAST"—the argument rages on in a desultory way. Finally I make my escape. . . .[146]

Tomorrow I have an appointment with a book agent,[147] will let you know what happens. . . .

See you soon, Your loving Neighbor

To Constancia Romilly   Oakland
                                                July 23, 1957

Darling Dinkydonk,

. . . I'm just wondering about the social life angle. I'm terrifically pleased that you're having so much fun, also I think you're right about a slight need to "loosen up." But, (as Benj would say) do you really think it's a good idea to make acquaintances so casually in a foreign country? The Nolin business sounds OK, because you met him through the other girls' friends, but how about the 17-year olds you met at the bus stop, and the boy at the fountain who's interested in you?

Although I don't know Mexico, I do know other Catholic countries such as France, where it was possible to get into terrific jams by being more free and forward than the French girls. In other words, English girls (in my young day) had far more freedom than French girls, but if they acted in Paris the way they did at home it was frequently misunderstood, they were considered very "fast," and were treated accordingly by the French boys. So be taking all this into consideration. You seem to have been left very much to sink or swim as far as social

---

146. Decca subsequently wrote her mother that she had bought her a "non-shorty" nightgown, so "be careful not to trip and break your neck, or the sales lady will say I told you so."

147. This is one of the earliest allusions in Decca's letters to her memoir-in-the-making.

life is concerned by the Molinas, but even so I would consult Carmen quite a bit, and take her judgment about who to go out with etc.

I have the greatest confidence in you, but thought a word of advice might be a good thing, it might help avoid embarrassing situations. . . .

Write soon, and let me know what you think about my comments on your social life. . . .

Your loving Dec

By the way your letters are marvellous, terrifically funny and interesting. But NOT ENOUGH OF THEM.

To Lady Redesdale   Oakland
September 9, 1957

Darling Muv,

. . . Nancy wrote me a long account of her chat with Aranka, who she calls Cassandra, very appropriate name. She told Aranka that to Europeans, Russia and America are exactly the same, two enormous countries where you can't get servants and where everything is machine made! I can just <u>see</u> Aranka's reaction. So then Aranka countered by going on about Gracious Living, which she's a great advocate of. It must have been a scream. I'm off writers with Aranka at the moment because all this summer I've had nothing but long wails from her about how awful I am to the children, and how I shouldn't have sent Dink to Mexico or Benj to camp but should have had them Graciously Living here with us. Ghastly thought.

I must be off now, will write again soon,
love from Decca

To Aranka Treuhaft   Oakland
fall 1957

Dear Aranka,

Thanks so much for your letter. . . . [M]ost of my Fortune is still tied up in England and it looks as though it will remain so for some time. I did get $8,000, actually $8,111.74. . . . I've spent almost $2,000 that I put in a special account to be frittered away on things. . . .

The frittering of the $2,000 has been terrific fun. I gave Dinky $500 for her to spend on clothes etc for her Europe trip. . . . I got Bob 2 new suits. . . . I got myself a grey flannel suit, 2 pairs of shoes and a cocktail dress from I. Magnin Designer Salon (you should have seen Bob and me in there choosing it, we <u>did</u> look so out of place. The saleslady said, "If I were you I wouldn't wear any jewelry with it." I told her, "That won't be difficult at all.") It cost $80, the most expensive dress I've ever had. I got Benj some new jeans, that's all he ever seems to wear. Then I got dresses etc. for all my impoverished old friends. . . .

Dinkydonk is fine. . . . Her passport came, she's definitely going to Europe, sailing July 9th on the Liberté with her best friend Katy Hollis. She's considering going to the Alliance Française in Paris to study. I've been corresponding with Nancy and my mother, but I fear they live in Cloud Cuckoo Land and are not much help. For instance, Nancy keeps groaning about some girls she knew who got in the Family Way while in Paris, which after all could just as well happen in America, and doesn't seem too likely.

Sorry about the peaceful coexistence—I HONESTLY didn't mean to sound like that, it's just my poor way of expressing myself, so please don't take it that way. You know Virginia Durr is always saying that whereas most English people have a "stiff upper lip" mine has turned to concrete, she's always accusing me of having a concrete upper lip.

I'm back on the book, finding it very difficult, increasingly so, but I'm determined to finish it. Bob is so wonderfully encouraging about it but at the same time he doesn't get mad when I get stalled for weeks at a time and don't do any writing. When and if it gets finished and I sell it, I'm going to be the sole support of the family, and make Bob save up all his money, it will be an interesting switch making him stick to a certain amount for a weekly allowance, as I do now. . . .

Love from Decca

To Lady Redesdale   Oakland
                                                                 October 16, 1957

Darling Muv,

Sorry not to have written for some time. Life here is much as usual, except for one exciting thing—I've sold an article to THE NATION (sort of U.S. equivalent of the New Statesman). It's about a San Francisco case in which the newspapers went after a suspect in a crime and almost had him executed, then it turned out someone else entirely different was the criminal, anyway of course I'll send you a copy. They're paying $75 which is rather good for an article here.[148]

I'm trying to get a few things arranged about Dink's trip to Europe next year. . . .

---

148. The article about the suspected rape-torturer was reprinted more than twenty years later in Decca's collection *Poison Penmanship: The Gentle Art of Muckraking* (Alfred A. Knopf, 1979). In the anthology, Decca commented, "Looking back, I realize that publication of this slim effort was for me a turning point. It gave me encouragement to continue struggling with my book despite rebuffs—it made me, for the first time, begin to think of myself as a 'writer.'"

Luckily I'll be able to pay for all this out of my Fortune, which ought to be all settled by then. Anyway, Dinky has quite a lot of money saved up for her as I've saved the whole amount of the pension from the Canadian Government[149] for her since she was born. . . .

She is really thrilled over the prospect of the trip, as she is finding school and life here awfully boring. I tell her what you always told us: childhood is a miserable time of life, you have to live through it, next year you'll be grown-up and out of the woods. . . .

Love from Decca

To Lady Redesdale   Oakland
                                                    December 26, 1957
Darling Muv,

. . . Nancy has turned out quite hopeless as far as arranging anything for the Donk in Paris. She now writes to say "what if the Donk should make Communist speeches in Paris, it would make things very awkward." Since I've already told her the Donk is not a Communist and knows no French, she knows perfectly well that would be not only unlikely but impossible. The thing is I think Nancy liked the idea of having the Donk when it was all in the dim future but now it's coming close to reality, the idea appalls her. So I'm sacking her as a helper in making the arrangements, I think my Solicitor will be a far better one and plan to entrust the Donk to him.[150] If only I could go with them! Perhaps in a year or two.

Do write and tell about your Xmas at Henderson's. We went to the Lapins[151] for the day (remember, he was one of the fat healthy Communists you met here but you thought his wife was too pale). . . .

Love from Decca

To Aranka Treuhaft   Oakland
                                                    March 16, 1958
Dear Aranka,

. . . We are having such a time with Dinky's college applications. The latest, to Sarah Lawrence, requires a parent's statement and a great deal about her

---

149. The pension for Esmond Romilly's service in the Royal Canadian Air Force.

150. As it turned out, Constancia's trip was canceled for unrelated reasons.

151. Adam Lapin and his wife, Eva, were close friends of the Treuhafts who moved to San Francisco from New York in the 1950s. Editor of the *Daily Worker*, then of *People's World*, Adam Lapin was underground for years and, following his newspaper days, wrote travel books under a pseudonym. After his death, Eva, a social worker and, later, an expert on Charles Dickens, married Bill Maas. The Lapin children, Nora and Mark, grew up with the Treuhaft children.

forebears, their education, employment etc. Since both Esmond's parents and mine were quite uneducated and unemployed, that part of the form is full of dreary blanks. I thought it necessary to add a note of explanation, as follows:

"The education and occupations of Constancia's forebears unfortunately do not make a very good showing. We were uncertain as to what occupation to list for her maternal grandfather, as he never worked. However, from time to time he was fairly active in the House of Lords; and once he invented and patented a special kind of garage door. The female forebears did not attend school as education was considered unnecessary for girls in those days."

Do you think that will help? I could have put down about my father's gold mine, where he went to mine occasionally, but as there was never any gold in it thought it best not to mention it. . . .

Love from Decca

To Lady Redesdale   Oakland
                                                                                   March 19, 1958

I am so awfully sorry.[152] I know you must be feeling terribly sad & depressed. Now I wish more than ever that Dinky was coming this year because I think she might cheer you up, but I'm sure she'll come in a year or two and we all will if things turn out as we hope.

I have no idea where you are, I hope you are with Debo or someone, I'll send this to the Mews.

Do write soon, & tell me how you are. One other thing: you once mentioned you might be too poor to live on the Island. Please let me know about this because I will gladly share my Fortune with you. I don't seem to be using it up much though I did get some fairly nice clothes.

Best love from Decca

To Lady Redesdale   Oakland
                                                                                    June 4, 1958

Darling Muv,

Thanks for your letters, I'm awfully glad the blouse fit all right. . . .

Re. the island, of course I'm not rushing about it,[153] and hope you'll stay there as long as possible. I just thought it would be a good idea for me to inform

---

152. Decca's father had died two days earlier at the ancestral Redesdale Cottage in Northumberland, where he had retreated years earlier with a housekeeper who had been the assistant parlormaid at the family's London home.

153. In a previous letter, Decca had floated the idea of selling or renting Inch Kenneth with ads in American publications as well as British.

the Glorious that he would have to be prepared to deal with yet another inadvertent inheritance; as I explained to him, I seem to be "inheritance prone" in the way some people are "accident prone."

The Donk's college[154] is in New York, about 30 minutes from Manhattan. . . . She is going absolutely mad with excitement about it, and about the Tor to Mexico which starts June 15th. . . .

All the Good Bodies[155] have been inoculated for everything under the sun, typhoid, small pox, tetanus etc. etc. For some reason Drs. always seem to think one is going to catch millions of diseases as soon as one steps outside one's own door. The car has been readied with new brakes and tyres, and the whole thing has taken up great time. Do you remember the Tors you and Idden and I used to go on, and Idden always complained you used to say, "Mmmm, children, have a choc. bar, it's a meal in itself," and she was half-starved all the time? But now I'm beginning to see the point, feeding all those people is going to be fearfully expensive, and I'm hoping to get them to live on choc. bars most of the time. It turns out we're taking 2 Donk friends along (17-year olds) so there'll be 5 of us going down, then Bob will come later by Aeroplane as he doesn't like long drives.

I must be off now, will write from Mexico,
                    love from Decca

To Pele de Lappe and Steve Murdock   Mazatlán, Mexico
                                                        June 21, 1958

Dearest Neighbors,

Sorry about the relative non-writing. For some reason the driving, seeing to things, & seeing to people seeing to the De Soto, which is being goosed carefully forward every inch of the way, has seemed to take up most of one's time & energy. The Dear Girls[156] are fair on the way to becoming Dear Mechanics, unlike the Dear Mexican Peons who seem to be more like <u>one</u> in that respect. Namely, when anything needs doing with the car, such as it not starting or such as it needing water, the D.M.P's tend to shriek with laughter & sort of throw up their hands. Result: Avril and Dink have learned to fiddle with wires under the ~~bonnet~~ hood to get it going (the starter conked out over 1000 miles ago), & they <u>now</u> know about the tank boiling over & not letting it do so by putting some water in from time to time. As for me, I feel like an inefficient version of

154. Constancia Romilly was to start at Sarah Lawrence College in the fall.

155. The Good Body, which needed little aid from doctors or other modern advances, was one of Lady Redesdale's refrains when Decca was growing up. In adherence to her principles and "in defiance of the law," Decca wrote in *Daughters and Rebels*, Lady Redesdale "refused to allow any of us to be vaccinated ('pumping disgusting dead germs into the Good Body!')."

156. Constancia Romilly and her two friends.

the Swiss father in Swiss Family Robinson, alternately calling on the Almighty for succour & prodding the children to practical measures for the good of all.[157]

Meanwhile, as of today the vacation part is really beginning. Guaymas is a beastly place, American prices combined with the ultimate in Mexican discomfort. No sooner had we arrived than old Eye to the Main Chance Benj took it upon himself to inform 3 youths he met on the beach that he was travelling with 3 beautiful girls. He offered to fix up dates for the 3 youths if t hey would find a girl his age for him. Somehow his whole jolly scheme fell through, just as well, probably. We left Guaymas at 5 a.m. for the 11 hour drive (as the guide book laughingly calls it) to Mazatlan. Arrived here at 9:30 p.m. Mostly desert (maximum temp checked by us was 110°) with occasional pieces of oasis & amazing tropic scenes. The recent opening up of this part of the country to tourist trade has resulted in some rather odd goings-on—such as, yesterday we stopped at a fantastically plush gas station, resembling a palace or my idea of the Moscow subway, a modern architectural gem flooded with neon lighting. We asked for Super Mex, which is the name of the gasoline here. A dozen attendants, all under 20, held deep conference for several minutes; finally they produced a small glass bottle of some sort of lubricant. We countered by pointing out that it would never begin to fill the tank, & might not be too good even if it did. We then pointed to the Super Mex, & showed them how to fill the tank. They had no idea how the water thing worked, so the girls did that part; ditto the air for tyres. Everyone was roaring hilariously throughout, & finally the boys admitted they had just opened for business that day & didn't know how to work any of the equipment.

Neighbors, <u>Mazatlan</u>—it is sheer bliss. This hotel[158] ($5.44 a night for the 5 of us) is a huge, cool, breezy place, we have a large bedroom, a closet the size of a small room, a very comfortable sitting room, & on & on. Also there is an immense swimming pool (if one should tire of the sea, which is right outside) surrounded by tropical plants & a bar. Everything is giant size, which is what makes it so cool in a boiling sort of way—jugs of coffee & hot milk, fresh orange juice & rolls, brought up for breakfast. Have just finished the following lunch: 2 glasses of Tequilla for me, beer for the Girls, a thing called Iron Shrimp in the English translation on the menu (it seemed that the words "to iron" & "to broil" are the same in Spanish) of a quality not often found outside of somewhere like Trader Vic's[159]—under $1 each. There are 2 boa constrictors kept here by the hotel to kill the mice. Benj has just been down to say hello to them. There is a mouse in our room so we are debating whether to ring for a boa constrictor or keep it. There is also a printed notice on

---

157. A playful allusion to earnest Communist Party rhetoric of the type Decca satirized in "Lifeitselfmanship."
158. Hotel Belmar.
159. A San Francisco restaurant with a Polynesian theme.

the wall which reads in part, "IF LIVING PLEASE RETURN KEY TO OFFICE." . . .

Well neighbs, do write. . . . I long for news, such as: . . . Is everyone being decent to old Bob? How was the PW[160] picnic—oh we _were_ sorry to have missed it.

Best love, Decca

To Lady Redesdale   Mexico City
                                                      June 30, 1958

Darling Muv,

. . . The Tor is being simply heavenly. From Mazatlán we drove to a tropical fishing village called San Blas. The hotel there had parrots on bars instead of flowers on the tables. It's the first time I've been in the tropics, oh the fascination of it. The children hated it because of the gnats & mosquitoes & general boilingness, but I loved it. We went for a long boat ride down a jungle river, everything amazingly bright & green & overgrown, with occasional weird screeches from tropical birds, just like in films about Africa.

You can imagine all the packing & unpacking & fitting the suitcases into the car properly each time. . . .

We are all learning Spanish, I find I can speak fairly well & understand the newspapers. . . . Did you know the Supreme Court acted favourably on the passport cases? That means we should be able to get ours back. Shall we come next year for the last Island year? I _would_ so love to. I'd love Benj to see it, too. . . .

Best love, Decca

Isn't it sickening of Nancy to be pro-de Gaulle, I never really thought she was, now I suppose I'll have to go off writers with her again.

To Pele de Lappe and Steve Murdock   Colonia Santa María, Mexico
                                                      July 9, 1958

Dearest Neighbors,

. . . Today has been a fair riot, phone never stopped ringing about the non-legacy.[161] Really you must say the papers are pretty odd in their concept of what

---

160. _People's World._

161. Her father's will, recently probated, as Decca wrote in a later letter, "had 'Except Jessica' after each clause" in his bequests. She told newspaper reporters, who continued calling for days afterward, that "I certainly wasn't expecting to be left anything & couldn't see why it was considered such staggering 'news.' " In 1995, Decca wrote that ". . . once having run [away], [I] never, ever asked for or received any dough from the family. . . . I think everyone has the right to leave his money as he wishes."

constitutes news. Also, their interviewing techniques were stupid, they wasted most of the time (at $20 a minute or whatever it is) asking things they could have found out about at the nearest public library, such as the names of one's sisters, etc. Señora was flabbergasted, she kept hovering round saying "Ai! Ai! Ai!" (Spanish for Ouch, according to the phrase book) "What this must be costing them! Twenty, thirty dollars!" Steve, I was a little hurt that no call came thru for a PW exclusive on the Lord Aneous[162] will, but such is life. I suppose that if the ball had bounced differently (as Pele would say), & I had ended up with Mucking Creek & £10,000 a year,[163] I would have received frantic wires— J.V. QUOTA IN JEOPARDY. MONEY URGENTLY NEEDED.[164]

Anyway, after the 4th call (Bob, Chronicle, Washington Post, Toronto Star) I had to be off to a reception at the Spanish Loyalist Embassy. Cuca wrangled me an invitation. The whole thing was most surprising. . . . I didn't realize they maintained an embassy here, & have not as yet been able to find out what are the duties of the ambassador, who pays his salary & why, etc. . . . It was an all female affair in honor of Señora Cardenas for the work she's done for the Spanish war orphans. As you can see by a bit of ready reckoning, these orphans are by now not getting any younger. In fact they range in age between about 25 and 40. . . . The crowd at the reception was reminiscent of a very fancy PTA sort of thing. Almost all had furs & a lot of jewelry & beautifully dyed hair of various shades of auburn. Cuca explained that most of them have made mints of dough in Mexico in various businesses. . . . The whole thing was completely disorganized, & the phonograph soon broke down—but the poor dancers continued in spite of all with no music! Trays of Spanish sherry & hors d'oeuvres were passed thru the throng, with enormous difficulty. This all went on for hours, 6 to 9:30. All so unlike the sort of thing we used to put on for Spanish causes. . . .

So, neighbs, do write soon. . . .

Your loving Neighbor

---

162. Decca had written a "memo" to her husband and signed it "Miss L. Aneos," so "Lord Aneous" would refer to her father.

163. Decca, like her husband a great Bertolt Brecht fan, quoted elsewhere from *The Threepenny Opera*, saying, "In the words of the 3d Opera, 'Let the prisoner forthwith be freed! And given a castle in Mucking on the Creek, and ten thousand pounds a year till the day of his death.' "

164. Jean Vandever had been chair of the East Bay CRC chapter, which had apparently folded by this date. One of Vandever's functions had been raising funds, which may explain the reference to a "J.V. quota."

To Constancia Romilly   Oakland
                                                                September 25, 1958

Darling Chickadee,

I just got your lovely, mammoth letter, and hasten to answer. You are good to write so promptly.[165] This morning I decided that if I rushed off first thing to the Co-op and got the beastly shopping out of the way before the mail came, I might be rewarded by some interesting letters. So, sure enough. I read the non-Donk letters first to savour fully the one from you! . . .

Believe it or not, Mother has joined Pele and Do's gym class! I've been twice, so far. As I told Bob, the instructor pointed me out and stopped the class to inquire, "Where <u>did</u> you get your physical education training. Never have I seen such exquisite fluidity of movement, such excellent and sustained understanding of the rhythm . . ." (Actually, she only said, "You in the 4th row! You're doing it all wrong, can't you keep time to the music?") Anyway, it's rather fun and probably good for one's poor old muscles. . . .

Do write again soon, you can't think how it cheers me up. I'll buckle Benj down to writing you one of these days.

                                             Your loving Dec

To Constancia Romilly   Oakland
                                                                 October 1, 1958

Darling Dinkydonk,

I can just imagine you having your old wits sharpened by the minute at Slawrence, I do hope you are loving it now that all has really started. It's now 2:30 p.m.—about 5:30 your time. You are probably cloinking about in your little sloping-roofed room, getting ready to be first in the food line before all the meat runs out . . . or isn't it quite like that?

Though longing to hear, I can imagine you are frightfully busy. . . .

I just got a letter from Robin (Fles's assistant)[166] and it looks as though the St. Peter article has been sold to Frontier,[167] not definite yet. She likes the 2 chapters I sent, is holding them for the outline, will present the whole thing to Barbara Kamb (editor at Dodd, Mead) when I send the outline.[168] So, now the

---

165. Constancia Romilly had just arrived to begin her studies at Sarah Lawrence College.

166. Barthold Fles was Decca's first literary agent. She had been introduced to him by Doris Brin Walker's husband, Mason Robeson. Fles's appeal included his continued representation of blacklisted screenwriters whose work was carried by small, leftist publishing houses during the years of anti-Red hysteria.

167. For more detail, see letter of May 1985 to Philip Kerby, the editor of *Frontier.*

168. Decca's first indication of publishing interest was a nibble from Kamb, who asked to see an outline and the two opening chapters.

outline is finished, awaiting a final sprucing by Betty Bacon[169] this evening, should be in the mail tomorrow. . . .

Marge and I are working like mad on the Powell Defense Com.[170] party for Sat. night—the Silent Auction. Bob thought for ages it was the Salad Auction, because that's what it sounds like in Marge's Southern accent. . . .

The Govt. has just asked for an extension in the Powell trial, set for Oct. 13, till January. This looks like a very hopeful sign from the point of view of the defense, as the Govt. seems to be on the run. However, all the principals in the case are crying because they have made the most extensive arrangements for the trial to start in October: Both the Powells' mothers are out here from the East to look after the children during the trial, a house has been rented in the country for the grandmas and children to live in during the trial so they won't suffer in school from the publicity, several people arranged to take their vacations just then so they could give full time to working with the defense staff. . . .

Goodbye darling, do write when you have a minute, I simply long for more news,

Your loving Mother

To Constancia Romilly   Oakland

October 13, 1958

Darling Dinky,

. . . The book went very badly last week. I guess you are in the throes of having to do a lot of writing, and are becoming familiar with the cold, hostile look of the typewriter when you are stuck! It doesn't bother me quite so much as it used to, as I now know from experience that a "break" will come and somehow one will get back on the track. Sometimes, though, writing seems almost more physical than mental—that is, the pages, and the need to fill them and the typewriter and pencils seem like the whole thing—if you follow me. . . .

Your loving Mother

---

169. A Berkeley librarian, writer, and editor who had previously worked at the *Daily Worker* in New York. Bacon was very helpful to Decca in her early days as a would-be author.

170. The plight of John William (Bill) and Sylvia Powell and their colleague Julian Schuman was a concern of Decca's for years. The three were grilled by Red-hunting congressional committees after they returned from China, where Bill Powell had edited and his wife and associate had assisted in producing a Shanghai-based English-language political journal called *China Weekly Review*. Among its purported offenses, the publication had reported on U.S. biological warfare during the Korean War. The three were indicted on sedition charges in San Francisco in 1956. The Treuhafts' good friend Doris Brin Walker was their lead counsel.

To Aranka Treuhaft   Oakland
                                                                October 20, 1958

Dear Aranka,

. . . Benj will be writing soon to thank you for his Birthday present. Guess what the sweet boy did with Margit's $5? Took Bob and me out to dinner at a Chinese restaurant. He telephoned ahead for reservations, did all the ordering etc. He put down all his favorite things and added them up before giving the order, but was sad to find that he had to omit the duck because it would have made the bill come to $1 too much. We underlined this sad lesson, reminding him how often we've said (when we were paying) "Oh you don't want duck, vegetables are so much better for you!"

His birthday party was a fair riot, 20 kids were invited, I provided for 25 just in case, and we ended up with 30! There was one little boy, dressed up to the nines, sitting out on the steps. I asked him, "Who are you?" He answered, "Clarence's brother." I said, "Why aren't you at the party?" "Because I haven't been invited—yet." So now I know the origin of the expression "everybody and his brother." . . .

I am working away on my book, and just learned that the article I sent in this summer has been sold to <u>Frontier</u>, a small West Coast magazine. No great shakes, but I'm glad it will be printed somewhere.[171] . . .

    Love to Edith and all, Decca

To Constancia Romilly   Oakland
                                                                October 31, 1958

Darling Dinkydonk,

. . . The book went very well last week. Funny thing how it hits a log-jam but then things eventually straighten out. Do you find the same thing about writing? Anyway I've got 2 more chapters finished and a pretty good idea of where to go next. . . .

<u>HOORAY</u>! I got back from the hairdresser to find your lovely long letter of Oct. 29th. You really are such a good Donk to write so faithfully, almost as good as chatting. I guess a watched postman never boils; if I am out when he comes it seems to bring better luck.

I'm now over at the Co-op, Bob having volunteered me to spend the afternoon signing people up in his funeral thing.[172] . . .

---

171. Before *Frontier* magazine purchased "St. Peter, Don't You Call Me," the second piece she had published in a mainstream publication, it had been rejected by half a dozen prominent national magazines. The article that Decca here describes as "no great shakes," she later said, "proved to be virtually an outline" for her breakout best-seller *The American Way of Death. Frontier* paid her $40 for the article.

172. The Bay Area Funeral Society.

I think you're right about the stock-taking business. Do remember one month is a terribly short time, really, & it may take ever so much longer to really figure out where you're going with Slawrence. Then, even after it seems you HAVE figured it out, it may all change again—your point of view, I mean, and your perspectives on the various things you're learning. It's rather difficult for me to imagine, never having been to college, however I have an idea one goes thru roughly the same processes as you describe no matter <u>what</u> one is doing—and specially at your age, but at other ages too. Tho I'm not a specially introspective type I can remember the same feeling, on & off, till I was about 30; which gives you roughly 13 years to go. But, at least at college you get an awful lot of direction & help from both faculty & people your age on understanding yourself & the world. I suppose that's the main point of going. Take it easy, Dinkydonk, read a lot, study hard & tell the school psychiatrist I said for him to keep his cotton-picking hands off you. . . .

Dear I was fascinated at the description of the psychology test. I can tell you right now, though, that anger is rough, red & round (see fig. 1) so what do you make of that? Do tell how it works out, how one draws conclusions etc. . . .

Very, very best love to my favorite Donk,

Yr loving Dec

To Constancia Romilly   Oakland
                                                      November 18, 1958

Darling Donk,

Just taking a brief break from the book to "drop you a line," as they say. I'm getting on OK with the writing, have weathered the latest storm (being turned down by Dodd Mead) and am slowly but surely fighting on to a finish. It's getting like scrambled eggs at this point—stiffer and stiffer. No more of this 8 to 10 pages a day, more like 0 or 1 1/2. . . .

Sat. night to Dobby's, a long battle to the end over Dr. Zhivago (Pasternak) with Dobby taking the position the S.U. is completely justified, the rest of us agreeing with Laurent who pointed out that the Nobel Prize people baited a nice juicy trap for the S.U. into which they fell like a ton of bricks.[173] Needless to say, no one had read the book. . . .

---

173. Pasternak's novel about the Russian revolution and its aftermath had been published abroad the previous year—becoming an international sensation—after the Soviet Union denounced the book, banned its publication, and ordered all copies of the manuscript destroyed. The Soviet government made Pasternak decline the Nobel Prize he was awarded in 1958.

Au revoir ma chère, je pense souvent à toi, et ne vie que pour te revoir. (Est-ce bien? J'oublie comment conjuger le verbe "vivre.")[174]

Hasta la vista. Como esta usted? (estas tu?) Trabaja usted en un barco de guerra? O en escuela?[175]

Love and kisses, Mama

PLEASE NOTE ALL THE QUESTIONS IN THIS LETTER—PLACED THERE STRATEGICALLY FOR THE PURPOSE OF TRICKING YOU INTO WRITING BACK.

To Lady Redesdale   Oakland
December 8, 1958

Darling Muv,

. . . Our passports just came! They are good for 2 years. We haven't got any plans for using them so far, as they just this second arrived, but we might come next year.

There really isn't any news. I'll write again soon,
love from Decca

My Glorious Solicitor sent me a very funny cutting about an inquiry in the House of Commons into people selling islands in the Hebrides to the Russians! Remember how I was going to give my 1/6 of Inch Kenneth to the Russians at one point?

To Constancia Romilly   Oakland
January 7, 1959

Darling Dinkdonk,

Thanks so very much for your letter of Jan 4, 1 to 3 a.m., just received and I am hastening to answer. . . .

You seem to be "wigging" (Ray Thompson's[176] expression for thinking) no end, and you may have lost me a little along the way. Remember that poor Mamma was never exposed to ideas as consistently as you are now, and therefore had less chance to develop into a reflective thinker, as you seem to be doing, and rapidly became more of an Action Man. Believe me, I envy you a great deal. . . .

---

174. "Goodbye my dear girl, I think of you often, and live only to see you. (Is that OK? I forget how to conjugate the verb 'to live.')"

175. Translated roughly from fractured Spanish: "Goodbye. How are you? (Or should I use the familiar form of the word you?) Do you work on a warship? Or in school?" The translation was part of a running joke for Decca, who had studied Spanish using records produced by the army.

176. An old friend of the Treuhafts who was also active in the Communist Party and the Berkeley Co-op.

Darling donk ... I am very, very distressed that you are not happy, in all ways, tho I gather you are <u>partially</u> happy. Happiness is such a comparative sort of thing, though, don't you think? ...

As far as I can observe, you do have a better than average chance for happiness: you are generally optimistic and positive about things, I've never seen you really demoralized ... you have an unusually high degree of stability. From my experience I'd say these qualities are the ones that add up to some sort of guarantee of happiness, which after all is a state of mind and not completely dependent on one's outward circumstances.

I hope you are not roaring at poor old Mamma's efforts to philosophize. But one more point: "The Pursuit of Happiness" sounds fine in the ???? whatever document it appears in, but I think it is rather a chimera. The best one can do is to make the practical decisions about life that seem right, and hope for the best. You, of all people I know, have usually done very well in that respect. ...

Your loving Mother

To Constancia Romilly   Oakland
                                                    January 12, 1959
Darling Donk,

... Did I tell you Bob broke a rib up at Clear Lake the weekend we were up there with the Robersons? It's not serious, only a bit painful. The night we got back Eph taped it up,[177] rather inefficiently, with the result the tape all came cloinking off in a couple of days. So by Saturday it was hurting a bit, and Bob went to Dr. Dinaberg to see about it. Dr. D. told him to get me to sew or pin up a dishtowel round his chest, as tightly as possible. I was furious at being given this obviously impossible task; suddenly a brilliant thought occurred. I got an old girdle out, put it over Bob's head and round his chest, and it was just perfect! Snug and tight, stayed put, exactly the thing. So now I'm going to advertise in the Classifieds CASH FOR YOUR OLD GIRDLES, then I'll sell them to Drs. for broken rib patients. A fortune in the offing. Good idea? Only one problem: Bob had to go out to San Quentin yesterday to see Jerry Newson.[178] Well, you know the X-ray machine place where visitors have to be checked in for concealed weapons? So, Bob was in there when a guard roared: "WHAT HAVE WE HERE?" It turned out to be the garters, which were draped about all over the poor boy's chest. Apart from that, the girdle is working perfectly.

---

177. The Treuhafts' good friend Ephraim Kahn was a doctor.

178. Although Treuhaft and his partner Bert Edises had prevailed in court and the murder charges were dropped, Newson remained in prison for thirteen years, ostensibly for an unrelated robbery but actually because he wouldn't accept responsibility before the parole board for the murders for which he was exonerated. The Treuhafts continued to defend him. See letter of January 31, 1960, to Aranka Treuhaft.

Jerry is OK but in gloomy spirits, however there is some hope that with the change of administration (demos) that Terry Francois can do some politicking to get him out.[179] I do hope so. He's been there for so many years now, poor fellow, and has seen others convicted of equal or worse crimes than the robbery come and go out after a couple of years. . . .

Part I of my book is just about finished, thank God, and I do feel I'm ploughing to the end. Oh what a job. Remind me not to start any more books once this one is out of the way. Your turn next, and Benjy's. . . .

See you soon, Mother

To Constancia Romilly   Oakland
                                                                  February 2, 1959

Darling Dinkdonk,

Quite a few things happening. The Powells, now waiting to be indicted for treason, may be imprisoned without bail, after the indictment comes through.[180] No one knows the "time element"—when the trial can be expected to be held, etc. I'm off to a committee meeting tonight, will know more about plans after that. . . .

As a result of the above, I didn't get to go through with the plans to take the Negro woman to see the house.[181] I called the real estate man handling the property to cancel the appt. and said I'd love to see it this week. Just now called, and he said—guess what—they have a "cash buyer" and therefore there is no point in my seeing it. I'm absolutely certain he is lying, for one thing it is grossly overpriced, but for some reason he suspected me. So, now we'll have to figure out a new scheme to get her in. . . .

Well, I must be off to the Powell meeting. I do hope there's a letter from you one day soon.

Yr. loving Mama

---

179. Terry Francois was a San Francisco attorney who had assisted in Newson's case. He was also a civil rights leader and public official who switched parties and endorsed San Francisco Democrat Edmund G. (Pat) Brown for governor of California. Brown was inaugurated a week before this letter was written, which may explain Decca's hope for political influence. Brown had soundly defeated conservative Republican Senator William Knowland, who was an ally of District Attorney J. Frank Coakley, Newson's prosecutor.

180. The Powells' sedition trial ended in a mistrial within days after some of the government's evidence was disallowed. With the sedition indictment still hanging over the Powells' heads, the U.S. attorney then set about trying to gather enough evidence for a new indictment for treason. Although the government requested that the defendants be imprisoned without bail pending the new indictment, the judge disallowed the request and continued the existing bail.

181. Decca worked for years to break restrictive racial covenants and other discriminatory practices in real estate transactions, often fronting for black would-be buyers who would otherwise have been denied the right to purchase homes.

To Constancia Romilly   Oakland
                                                                February 4, 1959

Darling Dinkdonk,

... Did I tell you about S——,[182] the Boy who is Prejudiced Against Fathers? He is a very sweet and intelligent kid who recently moved into our school district, in Benjy's class. . . . Benj confided he didn't much like Bob because he is "prejudiced against fathers." The reason he's prejudiced is that he has had 3 or 4, some for as short as 1 week. He's had his present one for 6 weeks, and doesn't like him either. . . .

2 days ago S—— called up in the morning to ask Benj to tell Mrs. King he wouldn't be in school in the morning because there was "trouble at home." That afternoon, Benj and S—— came over here, and Benj asked, "Dec, if one person attacks another person and a third person sees it, can that third person kill the first person?" I answered vaguely, half-listening, "Oh I should think so, sounds like a good defense . . ." Benj says, "Come on, S——, let's look for a blunt instrument." I wake up, and say sharply: "No blunt instrument leaves this house till you tell me what this is all about." So, it turns out that S——'s current father viciously attacked his mother the night before, S—— called the police, and also threw away all the beer, and was scared to go home, at least without a blunt instrument. So, I gave them a lecture about the inadvisability of blunt-instrumenting people in general, and specially when they are twice as big as you are, and kept S—— for the night here. The story turned out to be true, by the way, I spoke to the mother.

Just thought you might be interested in the squalid doings on 61st Street. I gave the mother a piece of my mind, too, about subjecting S—— to things of this sort; and suggested she tear down to see a marriage counsellor or something of the sort. . . .

Best love, darling Donk, see you soon, Decca

To Constancia Romilly   Oakland
                                                                February 26, 1959

Darling Pink,

Thanks so much for your letter, I was delighted to get it. . . .

Clever of you to prepare us for bad reports[183] when they aren't at all. . . .

I wonder why Mrs. L. added "this is not said as criticism," what's the matter, are they afraid to criticize? I hope not, as how else can one learn? . . .

---

182. Name omitted by editor.

183. Constancia had warned her parents that her semester grades would likely be disappointing, leading her mother to reassure her that that was to be expected in times of indecision such as Constancia went through while considering a transfer. "Only vegetables and flibbertigibbets go through life with no problems or painful doubts about the future," Decca wrote, and "as you are unfortunately neither, I guess you can expect a few ups and downs."

Dink I know exactly what you fear about the loneliness. It reminds me of when we came to S.F., didn't know a living soul here, and you were too young to chat. I really suffered from loneliness for the first time in my life. Although everyone was kind and friendly (on the job, I mean) they were all married and had their own lives, and for about 3 months I really went through tortures. If you do decide to stay in NY, the only thing to do is to plan very affirmatively against loneliness. Such as, lining up a roommate, not even necessarily someone you know. . . . Don't be cross, but I think you are too young to stay quite alone in NY. When I come, I'll do all I can to help you figure things out. . . .

I've taken to greeting Benj (when he comes home from school, etc) with a loud clucking, cross between mother hen and mother parrot (CLU-U-Uck, cluck cluck, sort of thing) so the other day I thought I heard him and started clucking, and it turned out to be Mrs. Gresham,[184] so embeeeeerrassing. . . .

I've got most of my book at the typist. It's terribly on my mind, and on my nerves, I really don't think it's very good after all, so depressing after 2 years of work. Bob has been so good and understanding about it, but now I'm not at all sure it will ever amount to anything. Whole chunks of it are hopeless, I now think, and I'm not sure I can do anything about it. Oh dear. Anyway we'll keep the ms. around as a souvenir for you. . . .

   Yr. loving Mamma

To Constancia Romilly   Oakland
                      March 3, 1959

Darling Donk,

Just writing to keep in touch, aren't I, and because for the moment I'm a touch stuck with the book.

Also to let you know I've started on a tremendous program of self-improvement. It consists of:

1. Getting up at 7 or earlier each day.

2. Doing the stomach and waist exercises (Reduce in Record Time) 15 minutes morn and eve.

3. A diet, 600 to 800 calories INCLUDING LIQUOR.

4. Doing my book first thing till at least lunch time.

5. After lunch buckling down to things I hate, such as sewing up things that need sewing on clothes, taking the car to have its little ailments seen to, etc.

So, I hope to be completely re-molded as the Chinese Reds say by the time I see you. (I only started yesterday, lived on eggs and grapefruit and boiled cabbage, bought 5 things of thread all different colors, etc. But I do intend to keep

---

184. The Treuhafts' housekeeper.

it up, that's why I'm putting it all in writing. I feel thinner already, and have sewn up 3 things.)

Trouble is, 4 dinner parties coming up in succession, so enormous strength of will is going to be needed for the diet bit.

Benj is fine, I'm going to buckle him down to writing you very shortly. Likewise Bob. . . .

Third of March today isn't it. Smack you on the 22nd.

                Yr. loving Mama

. . . Beery I see this letter beats all for utter dulth. It's because of the self-improvement, I think. How much more interesting could I have written, "Dined at Fleur de Lys, got drunk afterwards, held up a department store, etc."

IV

REMEMBRANCE OF
THINGS PAST

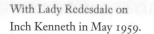

With Lady Redesdale on
Inch Kenneth in May 1959.

Decca with her sister
Nancy during a visit to
Paris in the 1960s.

Still no sale," Decca wrote to a friend in early 1959, speaking of the memoir she'd been writing and reworking for several years. "I'm going to take it to England as I think there would be more of a chance to sell it there." For one thing, she was not "tagged" as a subversive there—a label that she thought made her too hot to handle for the "timorous" American publishing industry in the late 1950s. In addition, much of the book focused on her upbringing in England. Her sister's best-selling novels and the right-wing politics of her parents and two of her sisters had helped to keep the klieg lights on the family there, so it was reasonable to assume that the book might find a more enthusiastic reception in that country. But after numerous rejections from American publishers, Decca was unprepared for the sale of her memoir to *both* American and British publishers within days of her arrival.

It was her second trip back to England from America, and this time she felt more "at home." With this visit and the book she brought back with her, Decca began to put together the parts of her life she had strained to keep separated during her intensely political Communist years: her aristocratic past in England and her radical present in the United States; her English and American friends and her family. Over time, without formal acknowledgment, she seemed slowly to become almost binational and even purchased her family's remote island in the Hebrides where her mother was living—a long, long way from Oakland, Calif.

Decca's search for her public identity as a writer was reflected in her changing byline. On the cover of "Lifeitselfmanship" in 1956, the author was identified as Decca Treuhaft, the name by which most people knew her in Oakland. In her *Nation* article "Trial by Headline" in 1957, "Mitford" crept in as a middle initial: Decca M. Treuhaft. In "St. Peter, Don't You Call Me," in 1958, she was again Decca Treuhaft. The author of *Daughters and Rebels* in 1960 was Jessica Mitford, the name by which she was known in English headlines (after "Peer's Daughter" lost its instant recognition). Still, *Daughters and Rebels* was also the only one of her commercially published books to be copyrighted by Jessica Treuhaft, not Jessica Mitford. Less than a year later, she wrote an article for *The Nation* in which she covered all bases; the byline was Jessica Mitford Treuhaft. But the popularity of her first book soon cemented her public identity. Decca Treuhaft, Communist housewife, became Jessica Mitford, author, in both Britain and the United States.

As Decca's life expanded geographically and professionally, her correspondence assumed a greater importance. When in England or on the authors' public-speaking circuit, she shared every detail of her adventures with family and friends back home; when at home, she kept up with a growing circle of friends and associates in both countries. Her higher profile also put her back in touch with old friends, English and American, such as Katharine and Philip Graham in Washington. Letter-writing was the lifeline that held her many worlds together. She documented more of her thoughts and activities. It was during this period that many of her letters began doing double and triple duty, as chatty updates on her activities, as masterful exercises in storytelling, and as early drafts for her professional writing. She seemed to recognize the changing role of her correspondence as she not only started to carbon-copy most of her letters but took to traveling with a portable typewriter and carbon paper.

Because the story of Decca's emergence and development as an author and public figure were reported in great detail in her letters, with fewer gaps in the narrative than in previous years, there is less need to fill in missing biographical pieces here. Nevertheless, a few broad-brush observations and missing details may help.

It's possible that *Daughters and Rebels,* or *Hons and Rebels* to use its British (and most recent American) title, could only have been written with the perspective of an emigrée, but its publication and her own return to Britain immediately enmeshed Decca once again in the Mitfords' complex family dynamics—the mix of relationships, memories, and legends that she recounted in her book. She followed intensely every nuance of her family's reaction to the writing and publication of the book. They, in turn, had their say both publicly and among themselves. The family's reactions were predominantly negative, reflecting both political differences and the confused response to her re-entry into their lives. According to sister Nancy, Diana, in particular, was "outraged for my mother ... & of course minds being portrayed as a dumb society beauty!!"

The apolitical Deborah, Duchess of Devonshire and first lady of the grand ducal estate, has carried a generous selection of Mitford books in Chatsworth's public gift shop—but none of Decca's. Decca once recounted the story of a friend who visited Chatsworth and mentioned that she knew the duchess's sister; the guide replied, "We don't mention that side of the family." In relaying these apparent slights, which can be traced back to the reaction to her memoirs, Decca said, "I just thought that rather amusing, didn't at all interfere with my friendship with Debo."

Nancy Mitford's response was the one Decca "craved" most. She was the adored oldest sister and childhood model; she was the only sister who had ever held even remotely similar political beliefs; and she was an established, popular writer herself. Nancy's reaction was generally positive in the letter Decca quoted in her own correspondence, and even in one letter to a friend Nancy said that "[m]y sisters I can see mind [the book] more than I do." But in other letters, to which Decca was not privy at the time, Nancy was far more critical, calling the book cold, contradictory, inaccurate, "unperceptive," and even "dishonest."

Most interestingly, Nancy noted that "[i]n some respects [Decca] has seen the family, quite without knowing it herself, through the eyes of my books— that is, if she hadn't read them hers would have been different." More than thirty years later, when a collection of Nancy Mitford's letters was published and Decca read this comment for the first time, she wrote, "Mulling this over, I think she had a point." She said Nancy's early family novel, *The Pursuit of Love*, and Philip Toynbee's memoir *Friends Apart,** about Esmond Romilly and another friend from the 1930s, "eventually propelled me to write my own account of those days. Thinking back, I must have been greatly influenced by both these books and specially by Nancy's."

In short, the first two of her major works, "Lifeitselfmanship" and *Daughters and Rebels*, followed, to one degree or another, in her sister's footsteps. From that point on, however, Decca found her inspiration closer to home—and firmly rooted in her political convictions.

Decca was delighted by an "unforeseen by-product" of her memoir: "the instant respectability its publication in America seemed to have conferred on me." The erstwhile outsider and "subversive" who at first suspected that her manuscript had been blacklisted by publishers in her adopted country now found herself "an Author with a capital A." With her sharp wit, refreshingly frank views, and newfound literary respectability, she was pursued for appearances on radio and television, on the lecture circuit and in various other forums. "I am beginning to grasp the whole thing of mass culture," she wrote. Being a celebrity was "a new and curious sensation and one that I found most enjoyable," and she used every opportunity her new status afforded her—as evidenced in her letters—to further the social-justice causes for which she'd worked so industriously as a Communist. Writing and public speaking were far more effective than picketing.

As Decca mulled over various topics for another book, she wrote a number of magazine articles. Although some were simply targets of opportunity, the sort of offer that comes unexpectedly to any good freelance writer, two in particular were designed to spotlight emerging social-justice movements. Both of the articles may have been inspired in part by the political activities of her daughter, Constancia, who became heavily involved during this period in student politics and civil rights advocacy while a student at Sarah Lawrence College and ultimately left the school to become an organizer for the civil rights movement in New York and the South.

One article, published in *The Nation* in May 1961, explored the evolution of the student protest movement at the University of California at Berkeley. Enti-

---

* MacGibbon & Kee, 1954.

tled "The Indignant Generation," the article cast an early light on the local student movement that grew out of anti-HUAC demonstrations and gained international attention in 1964 with the Free Speech Movement, which in turn spawned the national youth rebellion and antiwar movement of the 1960s and '70s. The city limits of Berkeley, the breeding ground of the New Left, began a block from the Treuhafts' home, and Decca followed the student movement avidly for years, long before it forced its way into the national news arena. She and especially her husband became personally involved at several stages of the Berkeley student movement, serving, in effect, as informal bridges between Old Left and New.

Decca also toured the South. The idea for the trip began tentatively as a possible book project, perhaps a journal or travelogue of the changing South, but ultimately it developed into an article for *Esquire* magazine with the working title of "You-All and Non-You-All: A Southern Potpourri." (It was published in May 1962 under the title "Whut They're Thanking Down There.") Her hope had been to take an "oblique look at people in their natural environment." Although her 1961 trip through the South is well covered in surviving letters, the most significant occurrence—a terrifying night in a black church in Montgomery, Alabama—is mentioned only tangentially. Events apparently happened so fast that Decca reported on them to her family by phone, not letter. An article she wrote describing the incident never ran in its full form, although portions were incorporated into other writings.

Decca had intended to see the South at its most tranquil, long after the biggest wave of sit-ins and the Montgomery bus boycott, but as she wrote once, "violence followed me, and unwittingly I found myself in the middle of it." She chanced to arrive at the Durrs' home in Montgomery at the peak of the violent response to the Freedom Riders, the interracial civil rights activists who were riding buses through the South to test compliance with a Supreme Court decision outlawing segregation in interstate travel—and to test, too, the Kennedy administration's commitment to civil rights.

Accompanied by a college student visiting from the North, Decca borrowed the Durrs' car and drove to a rally at the Rev. Ralph Abernathy's church in support of the Freedom Riders a day after a number of them had been beaten at the Montgomery bus terminal. The Rev. Martin Luther King Jr. had come to town to address the gathering. Seeing menacing whites loitering nearby, Decca and the student ignored her promise to the Durrs and parked near the church "for a quick getaway." While they were inside the packed church—Decca and her young acquaintance were among the few whites there—a full-scale riot developed outside. The 1,500 people in the church were protected at first only by a thin line of federal marshals with tear gas as the white racist mob swelled to a thousand people and threatened to break into the building. In the stifling church, with windows closed to keep out tear-gas fumes, King telephoned U.S. Attorney General Robert Kennedy, who promised help. Local police arrived belatedly, but calm was not restored until a declaration of martial law and the arrival of the National Guard. At 5:30 a.m. the next day, Decca and her companion were escorted out by the National Guard, only to learn that a car overturned and torched earlier by the rioters was the Buick that Decca had borrowed from the Durrs. They were driven back to the Durrs' home by the National Guard general in his Jeep, to the immense relief of the Durrs, who had sat up all night terrified, listening to the news on the radio.

One interest flowed like an undercurrent through these years, as Decca worked on various magazine projects. At times it was barely perceptible in her letters. It was the story that just wouldn't go away, the story of the funeral directors' mercenary excesses that she'd let out of the bag with her low-circulation 1958 article "St. Peter, Don't You Call Me."

At first, Decca described the subject not as her own passion but as "Bob's funeral thing." Robert Treuhaft was a board member of the Consumers Cooperative of Berkeley, a group of local supermarkets governed by the patrons. In late 1957 he was asked to serve on a Co-op committee investigating exorbitant funeral costs. As a union attorney, he was already troubled by the disappearance of workers' contractual death benefits intended to assist their widows. A rapacious and tightly organized funeral industry seemed to tailor funeral costs to the maximum amount available under union contracts to a worker's often-needy survivors. In 1961 Treuhaft sued the California Funeral Directors Association on behalf of an independent director expelled from the association for advertising reduced-cost funerals. At the recommendation of the investigating committee on which he served, the Co-op helped found the Bay Area Funeral Society, a successful cooperative venture that contracted for low-cost funerals for its members. Treuhaft remained active in the new organization. He was "absolutely immersed in this curious project," Decca later wrote.

"Bob's funeral thing" became Decca's funeral thing through a series of chance occurrences that began when a San Francisco public television station broadcast a show about the Bay Area Funeral Society in June 1961. Decca was asked to appear, based on her 1958 article on the subject, and she was fortunate enough to have two undertakers as "wildly comic" foils. A San Francisco television reviewer reported unprecedented reader response, and the broadcast came to the attention of visiting *Saturday Evening Post* writer Roul Tunley. He interviewed both the Treuhafts two months later for an article entitled "Can You Afford to Die?" but his article focused primarily on Decca. Although she later described herself as "sadly inactive" in her husband's Funeral Society activities, Tunley's article in June 1961 portrayed her extravagantly as "an Oakland housewife who is among those leading the shock troops of the rebellion in one of the most bizarre battles in history—a struggle to undermine the funeral directors, or 'bier barons,' and topple the high cost of dying."

The article in the *Saturday Evening Post* was said to have prompted more mail than the magazine had ever received for a single article. The Oakland housewife whom we see striving to become a commercially published author at the beginning of this segment of her letters was, by the end, being propelled by chance toward the epochal book that was to crown her career.

■■

To Pele de Lappe and Steve Murdock

On board the *Liberté*,
en route to England
April 13, 1959

Dear Murdoces,

. . . This is our 4th day at sea, 2 to go. . . .

NY now seems years away; Oakland, centuries. There are some very interesting people in tourist, in contrast to Cabin & 1st Class, which tend to run to American business men. In tourist, most are French. I just heard a typical exchange between a French passenger & waiter. Passenger: Could you direct me to the 1st Class deck? Waiter: "No, Monsieur, it is absolutely forbidden . . ." (then, as afterthought) "however, if you can figure out how to get there, that's your own affair."

Benj, of course, had it figured out the first day on board, & now he lives up there most of the time. . . .

Politics in NY seem slightly less fraught, but only slightly. Ranging from Patterson, who assured me the Yut[1] are rallying to the ranks in droves, to Starobin,[2] who says he's "completely given up" reading the left wing press, even the Guardian. Then there are the solid drifters, as one might term them, like the Selsams,[3] who are still "interested & responsible" but sort of unattached, one gathers. I broached the idea of a book titled "My Life & Red Times" to all factions, met with a sort of shuddering approval from all; but of course they haven't seen the draft yet.[4]

DO WRITE, I long for all news. . . .

Love from Decca

---

1. Decca used the word often. It seems synonymous with "youth" (perhaps spoken with an Eastern European or Russian accent).

2. Joseph R. Starobin, journalist, author, historian, and teacher, had been foreign editor of the *Daily Worker* from 1945 to 1954. In 1951 he went into voluntary exile to escape McCarthyism, but returned to the United States, left the Party in 1956, and got a Ph.D. degree from Columbia University. Among his books was *American Communism in Crisis, 1943–1957* (Harvard University Press, 1972). For a time he was a good friend of Decca's, who sometimes stayed with him and his wife, Norma, when she visited in New York in the 1950s.

3. Millicent (Millie) and Howard Selsam were A-list Treuhaft friends in New York. She was a prolific author of children's science books and he a Marxist philosopher and educator.

4. In mid-1959, Decca began working on a book by this title about the Communist Party. She described it as "sort of an antidote to the Howard Fast I've-Been-Duped school." (Fast was the novelist and former blacklisted Party member who wrote *The Naked God: The Writer and the Communist Party* [1957] in which he broke publicly with the Party.) The book Decca began toying with was the genesis of *A Fine Old Conflict*, published nearly two decades later. She described it in 1959 as "very anecdotal and sort of a series of sketches. I don't know if I will ever actually offer it for publication, too early to tell what it is going to be like, but I'm having an hilarious time doing it."

To Robert Treuhaft   London
                                                           April 14, 1959

<u>Last evening at sea.</u>

Darling Bob,

Benjy's storm has really arrived. Between us and the horizon, the seas like mountains roll. To my immense surprise, I haven't felt the least bit sick for a minute.

Everything on the ship is either fastened down or crashing about. Several elderly ladies have been bowled over and are relaxing, with large gashes in their heads, in the infirmary. One wonders what their right to damages might be under Maritime Law, but it's probably Act of Goddish.

As I write, every glass in the place is rolling madly about on the floor, garcons tearing round picking up the pieces.

Meanwhile, YOUR SON has been—not actively sick, but definitely resting in his bunk all day. He had every intention of what he called "helping" with the packing, but was glad to be excused. . . .

<u>2 days later, at Joan's[5]</u>

The storm got worse and worse. Hardly any sleep was had, because of excessive rolling, it really was a time. We disembarked at Plymouth on time, and the ship was met by thousands of ambulances to take off the injured. (OK, not actual thousands, but one ambulance.) Broken legs, sprained ankles, etc., dominated the scene. Can you believe it, I was perfectly OK throughout, even rather looking forward to evacuating to the lifeboats which I really thought might be the next thing. So different from trouble in planes, where there is no excitement, only sheer terror. I was a little sorry I had carefully missed the lifeboat drill, having been occupied at the bar with a Fine[6] at the time; but Benj was all zeroed in, and ready to rescue everyone.

[W]hen we got to Paddington,[7] there was Joan and the Belfrages,[8] being terrifically welcoming, and full of plans for the evening etc. Just as we were

---

5. Joan Rodker, a fellow leftist and old friend of Decca's from her English years, was Decca and Benjamin's hostess in London.

6. Perhaps the cocktail named a Fine and Dandy.

7. The London train station.

8. Leftist journalist, prolific author, and translator Cedric Belfrage was a longtime friend of the Treuhafts. A native of England, he had been a film critic in Hollywood in the 1920s and '30s. He was a member of the Communist Party, apparently only briefly although he remained a dedicated socialist. He served with British intelligence during World War II and was detailed after the war to de-Nazify the press in France and Germany. In 1948 he co-founded the nonsectarian leftist *National Guardian* (later simply the *Guardian*). In 1953 he was subpoenaed by the House Un-American Activities Committee and was deported in 1955 as an alien subversive. He lived and wrote in exile thereafter, returning to the United States only briefly in 1973. Belfrage and his fourth wife, Mary, settled in 1963 in a resplendent compound in Cuernavaca, Mexico, that doubled as an inn for visiting Old Leftists, including Decca and her family and friends (see full descriptions in letter of December 28, 1968).

getting the luggage, who should totter down the platform, palsieder than ever, but Muv, who had written me several times to say she would be on the Island from April 1st. She told me later that she had arrived at Paddington at 1:30, only to find out that we wouldn't arrive till 3:30. She wondered how to fill the time, and noticed some public baths, so decided to have a bath while waiting. I suppose it was a nice change from the Potterton.[9] So, I sent Benj with her, while I went with Joan to get the luggage established at her place. Went right back to the Mews, where Nancy turned out to be coming to tea. . . . Nancy and I roared without stopping so my face is aching today. Mainly, at Muv, who was being typical of herself about the bath at Paddington Station; and at the Wid (in absentia). . . . I asked Benj afterward what he and Muv talked about while alone together, and he answered mysteriously, "various bathrooms and things." Couldn't get a clearer picture from him. After tea, I told Benj to take a walk round the square garden, so Nancy started a long thing about how he was sure to be murdered if he did, as children here are always getting murdered. It's Jolly Murdering Weather in London, sullen and dark as a Hitchcock movie, but fairly warm. Benj said afterwards he thinks Nancy is very beautiful; which I told her, today, and she was very set up, saying she should have thought that to him she would seem like a very old lady. She really does look marvellous, not much changed, tho greying slightly. Muv does seem a lot older, the palsy considerably worse. She looked sadly at some pills she is supposed to take for it; so far, hasn't been able to bring herself to have any of them. . . .

Arrived back at Joan's just in time for dinner. To it came Doris Lessing (you know who she is, a best-selling English writer of the Angry Young school), her boyfriend, a fairly nice American called Clancy something,[10] he's from LA, and knows a lot of friends of ours, esp. in the ILWU; and, joy of joys, 12-year old Peter Lessing, who had learned about Benjy's arrival and has planned his whole Easter vacation around showing Benj London! Peter is a super-nice boy, and he and Benj became bosom friends immediately. He called for Benj early this morning, they got back at 6 p.m., having seen all the science museums, walked for miles all over London, ridden on tops of innumerable buses, etc. Peter phoned here at one point to say he had decided Benj should "see the West End," so we thought they were probably having cocktails at the Savoy. . . .

I went to the Mews to lunch, and of course when I came in without Benj Nancy immediately started on, "See! Murdered already, what did I tell you." We were just sitting down . . . when Aunt Weenie[11] came in, looking more

---

9. The water heater at the family's London home, which figured in *Daughters and Rebels*. In the manuscript for that book, Decca wrote, "Even having one's bath was an adventure at the Mews. The bathroom . . . was dominated by a big, round, evil-smelling water heater called the Potterton. Lighting it was an action fraught with danger."

10. Clancy Sigal, the Anglo-American screenwriter, novelist, and journalist.

11. Dorothy Bailey.

dead than alive (she's Tim's mother, Muv's younger sister), took one look at us, said, "Oh, YOU'RE here; then I shall leave." Nancy and I offered to leave, but finally everyone stayed, and a delicious lunch was had by all. No offense meant by Aunt Weenie, she was just tired and not in a mood to face us. We are having lunch with her in her club on Sunday. Mabel[12] came to lunch too (not so much to it as to help Christine[13] serve it). She asked fondly after you, and we had a long chat after lunch. . . . She went on a good bit about His Lordship,[14] and how he loved to find fault, and how disappointed he always was if everything was just right. She and Nancy were reminiscing about some things that happened after I left. It seems that Farve had a favorite taxi driver called Bates, and wouldn't be driven by anyone else when he was in London. He had an arrangement with Bates to phone him at frequent intervals during the day. Once when Nancy was there, Farve answered the phone: "That you, Bates? Where are you? Oh, at the India Docks? Well, will you drive to the Army and Navy Stores, present my compliments to Mr. Barker there, and tell him I want a ball of string?" Hours later Bates arrived with the string, 3 pounds on his meter. Mabel loved the whole conversation, kept punctuating it with "oh he was a rum one, His Lordship was; but we miss him now he's gone, don't we?" . . .

There was a slight flurry this morning. Christine phoned me to say a newspaper reporter had been round asking where I was staying, when expected there, etc. He got short shrift from her and Muv, but stayed outside for some time, parked in his car—of which Christine had carefully noted down the number! However, he had left by the time I arrived. . . .

Getting back here, the greatest was getting your letter. But old Bob do tell the Ladies[15] about the postal rates, it's 15¢ a half ounce, and I note it was sent back to you for insufficient postage. Natherless, it arrived amazingly quickly, and I can't complain. I was so glad to get it, as I feel so out of touch—do keep writing, and do keep going out to dinner every night. . . .

Goodbye darling angel. . . . I so long for you to arrive.

        Yr. loving Dec

p.s. . . . Benj is being loved by everyone, they all think he is terrifically good-looking, and very polite. Joan was fractured when she passed his room; and overheard him saying to Peter Lessing, "How blithering!"

Good night darling, see you soon. Do remind me not to plan these long trips without you any more, as I miss you fearfully. . . .

---

12. The Mitford family's longtime head parlormaid.
13. Lady Redesdale's cook.
14. Lord Redesdale.
15. An apparent reference to Robert Treuhaft's secretarial staff.

To Robert Treuhaft   London

April 19, 1959

Darling old Bob,

Thanks for the lovely Funeral Home postcard. Do keep them coming. It makes all the difference to old Dec's day to hear from you—even non-letters, or postcards, but do write lots of letters, too. . . .

Yesterday Peter didn't show up so I took Benj to lunch with Muv at the Mews, and a hot game of Scrabble. Benj said to me, "I love Muv, she's exactly like you, always roaring and awfully vague." Vague she is. . . .

Monday is Agent-and-Fortune day. I called James MacGibbon of Curtis Brown,[16] he sounded v. enthusiastic at the idea of the book, and I have an appt. with him Monday. In the afternoon, to the Glorious Solicitor's for a discussion of the Fortune and prospects; dinner with him and wife that night. . . . So we're not doing badly—specially Benj, who is being feted all over. . . .

The journalist (from Evening Standard) is still pursuing. He called Richard Turner to ask where I was staying (how did he find out about Richard? Via Randolph Churchill via Giles, do you suppose?) and yesterday he called the Mews while I was there. I answered the phone, told him I didn't know where Mrs. Treuhaft could be reached, thought she had gone abroad, Lady R. was not expecting her that I knew of etc. . . .

Nancy said that during the great Will (disinheritance) story, she was called to the phone in Venice, where she was staying, for a "very urgent phone call." It turned out to be a reporter inquiring for the whereabouts of her sister in America. Nancy just said, "Why don't you look her up in the Peerage?" and hung up. So typical of her.

Goodbye Darling, I'll write again tomorrow or so. . . .

Best love, Decca

Typical Muv story: Background: Nancy had been very ill this winter . . . laid up for quite some time; remember, she wrote us about it. So anyway, we were commenting on how marvellous she looks now. Muv said vaguely, "Yes, I really think it was very good for her, being ill all that time, she looks _so_ much stronger and better now." Even Benj fell off his chair, roaring. . . .

To Robert Treuhaft   London

April 22, 1959

Darling Bob,

. . . The other day I was mentioning to Muv how sad the education is at home, we'd like to send Benj to school here, but can't because it is too far. She said, "Yes, it _is_ too far; unless you decided to come and live over here." I said,

---

16. The literary agency.

"We couldn't, because of Bob's work." She said, "Oh yes that's true, he probably <u>would</u> find it a little dull, not working after all this time, he's used to it and might get bored if he had to give it up." Hopeless to try to get across the concept that other, and crasser, considerations, such as eating regularly, might be involved. . . .

I met Muv and Mabel at 11 a.m. to do the packing; Muv's winter things in a trunk, the Good China in locked places where the tenants won't find it. The packing was a fair riot. A black silk brocade evening dress; I say, "this looks awfully familiar." Muv: "Yes, I should think it does; I got it in 1926 for Pam's coming-out dance." Mabel, pottering around among things done up in tissue paper, hands me a paratrooper-type knife: "I should think this belonged to His Lordship, no use keeping it, is there?" I examine it, find it to be stamped all over with official looking swastikas. "Miss Unity's, do you suppose?" So it turns out to be. I find an unfamiliar looking tweed suit, say to Muv, "this is new, isn't it?" she answers, "Yes, I didn't have that when you were little; got it just before the war, after you went Abroad." . . .

Back to Joany's to connect up with Benj (who arrived windblown, exhausted and filthy from riding and Zoo at about 6 p.m.), to get him quickly ready to go out to dinner with Woman. . . . Woman was as ever, going on about the problem of Irish servants (DON'T TELL HAZEL),[17] and still complaining about her car accident (2 years ago) when her skull was slightly cracked, she still has occasional headaches . . . She is very sad that she has never met Barb (you, they all pronounce you Barb because they think I do; everywhere I go, they say, "When is Barb coming? . . . How is Barb? . . . We hear from Muv and Debo that Barb is an utter charmer"). We are invited to Tullamaine Castle (Woman's house, in Tipperary Co) any time we can come, but don't let's go. . . .

Rud's ghastly husband wasn't in sight except briefly, thank God. Benj may go to stay with them for a few days just before the Island, to learn to ride.[18] Rud longs for him. She said he looks just like Ali[19] Mosley; Muv immediately agreed. I was simply furious and said he doesn't look a bit like Ali, but since I've never seen Ali, my opinion didn't count for too much. . . .

Muv seems fairly all right, once you get used to her. But, the fact is, she is failing a bit. Deafness and palsy considerably worse, also vagueness. . . . I had a heart-to-heart talk with her about the Hearing Aid. The thing she hates about it is the wire thing that hangs down. However, you can buy ones that don't have the wire thing. . . . I said we would get her one of those, if she would promise

---

17. Hazel Grossman, wife of Robert Treuhaft's law partner Aubrey Grossman, is of Irish descent.

18. Decca's cousin Rud—Joan (Robin) Farrer—and her husband, a White Russian horseman named Paul Rodzianko, were living in Brayfield, Buckinghamshire, where they operated a school for horsemanship.

19. Nickname for Alexander, the son of Decca's sister Diana Mitford Mosley and her husband, Sir Oswald Mosley.

to practice with it and use it. She said, "No, little D., these are just Nature's warnings that it is time to step off the stage." Before she actually steps, she should see Dinky, who she asks after constantly. Possibly next year, or the following? . . .

Get that plane, old Bob. If you miss it, the fury of me will be unbounded. . . .
Longing and hoping, Yr. loving Dec.

To Robert Treuhaft   London
                                                             April 26, 1959

Darling old Bob,

At last I have time to write and tell you all about the Red Letter Day[20] and circumstances that led up to it. This part is addressed to you in your capacity as Chairman of the Old Dec Writing Committee, the other members being Marge, Murdoces, and Betty Bacon.[21] Not to forget Kathedises,[22] whose constructive advice to dump the book was so helpful.

Friday, I was out with Benjy all day. . . . As we approached Joan's house, I heard a scream of "DECCA!" 'Twas Joan, calling out from the liquor store next door. She dragged me in, pointing to a bottle of whiskey she was buying, and all incoherent from excitement, finally managed to convey that a message had come from James MacGibbon while I was out, book sold, $1500 advance, bottle was being bought to celebrate.

Here's what happened. I saw James (as I now call him) on Monday at his office. He said he would read the manuscript on the weekend (this weekend) and let me know if it was at all publishable.[23] Then he called me the very next day (Tuesday) to say he liked it very much, would immediately send it to Gollancz. I asked him how soon we might expect a decision, he said about 3 weeks. This sounded very quick to me, as Fles's publishers always seemed to take 6 to 8 weeks;[24] so I was pleased at the speed. So James did send it to Gollancz, but meanwhile he spoke to a representative of Houghton Mifflin[25] about it. Apparently gave it such a good build-up that the Houghton-Miffliner wanted to see it right away. So, James got it back from Gollancz. The H-M-er read it, phoned

---

20. Decca had received official word that her book had finally found a publisher.
21. The membership of the informal, ad hoc "committee" that vetted Decca's memoir varied with each telling. It included a few of Decca's longtime local friends and associates, notably Bacon, Frantz, Pele de Lappe and Steve Murdock, Barbara Kahn, Dorothy Neville—and, of course, Robert Treuhaft. See further description of the roles of committee members in subsequent letters, especially the August 8, 1959, letter to Marge Frantz.
22. Kathy Edises was married to Robert Treuhaft's partner Bert Edises after Pele de Lappe.
23. For another oft-told aspect of Decca's first meeting with MacGibbon, see May 1, 1964, letter to Ernest Morgan.
24. Decca's American agent, Barthold Fles, had circulated Decca's manuscript to numerous American publishers, all of whom had rejected it.
25. Lovell Thompson, vice president of the publishing house.

his office in Boston (what would Nancy say) and got the OK—so it all happened within the space of a week. Don't you think $1500 is a huge advance? Doesn't Betty Bacon think so? I was hoping for $500. Now, I have to gently fire Fles, James helped me work out a weasel-worded telegram saying "have decided to try the book in England, please send me the ms," then a little later we'll break the news. I feel bad about it in a way, as Fles was rather faithful and he did show it round etc. but I'd much rather deal with James, a different and better ilk altogether. James assures me there is nothing unethical or illegal in dumping Fles at this point, so I do hope he is right. . . .

Back to Friday evening. I could hardly stagger upstairs, I was so excited, amazed, bewildered—my knees were weak, and whiskey had to be forced down my throat. To my sorrow, Joan had to go out almost immediately as she had an appointment. Benj was a very satisfactory co-celebrant, he really was decent, rushed out then and there to the corner flower stand to buy me a dear little fivepenny orchid! The awful thing was I had a date with Woman for dinner, so had to bottle all during dinner as of course I don't want any of <u>them</u> knowing about it till 'tis actually out.

Saturday, I went to James' house at 12 for a long business chat. I asked him about the possibility they might renege (the contract won't be made up for about 3 weeks, he said) but he assured me this was not in the cards, that the sale is absolutely definite. . . . And he said that as soon as an English publisher is lined up I would have an editor to help a bit with the revisions. He wants me to get on it and finish it right away. I didn't follow through with the trip to the USSR, because I had a feeling that the time should be used to work on the book; now, I feel it is essential, and possibly Benj and I could stay in a pension somewhere in Brittany, from the time you leave till I have to go home, and I could work on the book while he gambols on the shore, and in the casinos. I will also do some work next week, after Benj goes to the Rudbins . . . and at the Island, if I can hide the ms. from Muv. Shouldn't be too hard. . . .

I have missed you <u>so much</u> through all this (including the old Bob astringent taking one down a peg or two) it is really too bad it couldn't have happened after you got here. . . .

Here's my opinion about your trip: COME TO THE ISLAND AS SOON AS POSSIBLE, AND BY QUICKEST ROUTE. . . .

My feeling about the book is now, it's a bit like the situation where one is trying to get someone to propose. One lays all one's plans to that end, works and frets inwardly for it—then, when the person <u>has</u> proposed and all's in the bag . . . one is immediately confronted with the practical consequences of this action—arranging for the Wedding, where to live, how to get on with the in-laws etc. Thus, in the case of the Book, how to finish it expeditiously and how it will look actually in print. . . .

Yr. loving Dec

p.s. Today's conversation with Muv, by telephone:

Muv: Hullo, Little D, that you?

Me: YES, HULLO, MUV

Muv: Little D? I think you said that was you, didn't you?

Me: YES, SPEAKING

Muv: Ohhhhrn, well, Alec[26] just telephoned, wants you and Benj to go to lunch with him tomorrow, very sweet of him really poor old thing. Can you go?

Me: YES, LOVE TO, OF COURSE. WHERE IS THE LUNCH? (This is repeated several times, with Muv saying, "What?" in between. Finally she gets the question.)

Muv: 3 Lexham Gardens, I think—either 3 or 5—or is it 7? How mad of me not to know . . .

Me: WHICH ONE SHOULD I GO TO? 3 OR 5 OR 7?

Muv: (when she finally gets the drift of this question) Oh yes I quite see, which one . . . let's see . . . well, little D, why don't you just go to Lexham Gardens and ask for the man with one leg? I think that'd be best. I can't hear a word you're saying, darling, so goodbye . . .

(Cloink, she hangs up.)

To Robert Treuhaft   London
                                                               April 30, 1959

Darling old Bob,

Resuming the Adventures of Dec. I think I've discovered the secret of Eternal Youth. It is, keep on the move, and time seems to stand still. Just came back from a very enjoyable one-night visit at the Toynbees, yet it seems ages since we were in London.

Wednesday was Army & Navy Stores day, Uncle Alec day, and going to Toynbees in the evening day. . . .

Thence to lunch with the one-legged man at ???Gardens. He was looking fine, and I really did think it a good thing he had it off.[27] . . .

He told me some fascinating gossip about Uncle Jack (Farve's next-to-youngest brother, now seventyish). Seems Uncle Jack was made Secretary of the Marlborough Club, a paying position, and within 18 months he had run the club into bankruptcy. Furious meetings of the members ensued, Uncle J. really in hot water. There was a happy ending because an American firm bought the building for 150,000 pounds, and each member was given 400 pounds from this sale. "It really was rather too bad of Jack," said Uncle Alec,

---

26. Decca's uncle Alec Kearsey, husband of her father's sister Frances.

27. Decca told the full story of her uncle Alec's amputation—and her own possible role in it—in a letter to Dr. Arlan Cohn, on May 5, 1987.

"because you know your Grandfather and the Prince of Wales really started that club, and now it's all finished." I had to think twice to remember that the Prince of Wales was King Edward VII. Uncle Alec went on to say that Uncle Jack has become very queer, lethargic you might say, and often doesn't get up till after 10 o'clock; Benj piped up at this point to say, "Just like my father."

We met Philip at the 4:30 train to Colchester, in Essex. He is in fine shape and we got on much better than last time—which I find true of most of the people here, incidentally, none of the awkwardness and strain which rather dogged me on the last visit. His wife Sally, from Ohio, is very nice but completely unlike the sort of wife one would imagine for Philip; she's a real home-town girl type, nice looking but not pretty, interested in books etc. but not intellectual, a really ordinary one. I liked her very much and teamed up with her against Philip in a long-drawn-out argument Wednesday night. Sally is constantly being brought up short by the class thing in England. She has become very close friends with a farm laborer's wife (a neighbor) but Philip won't let her have this friend to dinner with _his_ friends on the grounds that she "wouldn't fit in." Philip was furiously maintaining this has nothing to do with class as such, only with lack of common interests—he is the _least_ snobbish man alive, etc. The fact he has no friends outside his class is pure coincidence. Reminds you of the unprejudiced-against-Negro people at home. Anyway, Sally and I nailed him to the wall before long.

Much time was taken up in reading and discussing my ms. which by the merest chance turned up in my suitcase. Philip read most of it. He thinks it is _jolly_ good, which delighted me. Marge's Roarometer should have been registering 'cross the Atlantic; Philip was a very satisfactory audience. He loved the bits about him, his only complaint is there is not enough about him in it. I begged him to finish it for me, he said he will, but in that case the last 3 chapters will be pure Toynbee biography.

They live in a very nice, comfortable, roomy thatched cottage. There are many American touches—washing machine, dryer etc—and a real Hands Across the Sea bit in the john; a choice between English and American toilet paper! . . .

The Toynbees haven't seen the Romillys for ages; no estrangement, but paths haven't crossed. However, they confirmed the battiness of Giles. Seems Mary[28] confided in them that Giles went for her with a knife a few times, also he left home one night without a word and didn't show up for 6 weeks; just went off to France by himself. He has been to a Psychiatrist who told him not to worry about the knife thing as it is a way of getting rid of one's aggressions; which may be true, but a bit depressing for poor Mary. . . .

---

28. Giles Romilly's wife.

Goodbye old Bob, only a few more days now till you come, <u>thank goodness</u>, I do so long for you to be here. . . .

                Your loving Dec

To Marge Frantz   London
                                          May 2, 1959

Dearest Marge,

Thanks so much for your letter. My cable address, should you need it, is ELKSHATRACK; Pele wrote me saying, "you need news from home like an elk needs a hat-rack." Typical formulation?

I'm still scarce believing the news about the book; and must say, from utter bottom of heart, I could never have done it without your help. 'Tis the honest truth, when I think of the <u>hours</u> you spent on it, and your poor boss languishing at the office probably <u>longing</u> for you, you really were a marvel about it all. . . .

Dear James (as I now call Mr. MacGibbon, me new agent) . . . says there's practically no editorial correction needed, but he will write me a letter to the Island giving his own criticisms; he says they are extremely minor, etc. Now this worries me a bit, as <u>I</u> think it needs a hell of a lot of changing, and was counting on cosily working with an expert editor to that end. So I'm on my own, no old Marge, no Betty, and I feel a bit scared that it won't be a very good book in consequence. . . .

I'm trying to think of a way to break the news to the Revered,[29] as if I don't, she'll think it tricky of me; besides, if I'm writing it at the Island, even she is bound to notice. So I think I'll write and tell her I'm doing a book on the contrasts between English and American life. How would that be?

Old Marge do write, keep writing, and I'll answer pronto. How I wish you were here. What gift from Europe do you crave? Out of me royalties. <u>Anything you desire.</u> . . .

                Your loving Decca

To Pele de Lappe   On train to Didcot, Oxfordshire
                                        May 2, 1959

Dearest Neighbor,

Thanks so much for the most welcome Elk's Hatrack. I can't say you've been too loyal about writing up to now, but then neither have I—mainly because after I finish writing to old Bob, it's usually bedtime.

I'm still in a haze of unbelieving excitement about the Book. . . . Now I've

---

29. Her mother, a short form of "the Revered P" (parent).

got to finish it completely before I leave as Gollancz wants to publish it in January. What bliss not to have to staple it oneself.[30] . . . <u>Now</u>, neighbor, is the time for you to submit sketches for the cover. I have no idea if they would accept them, or if they always have their own artists do it, but I would very much love one by you & will ask Mr. Gollancz[31] when I meet him. . . . I loved your idea of ONE[32] under glass, & you could surround that with a border of Red Indians, French Apaches, marching workers etc—the things one was trying to escape <u>TO</u>.[33] So, do get on it, and send it to the island. . . .

We had a glorious party last night—all my newfound friends plus some old ones; Dear James, Cedric Belfrage, Doris Lessing (a very nice writer), various lawyers I've met through the Turners. There was a Negro (American) woman there who told a long thing about a man she met called William Mitford, who claimed to be a cousin of ours & on the strength of it bummed thousands of free meals; was finally imprisoned for bad checks; & Nancy issued a news release on behalf of the family saying he was an imposter & no relation. The Negro woman said Wm Mitford is awfully nice in spite of being a bit of a burglar, so I plan to look him up & claim him as my long lost cousin. That'd throw a spanner in the machinery, as the English say, wouldn't it? . . .

Neighb, I do so miss all of you. At least old Bob will be here quite soon now. . . .

Best love to you, Steven, Pele & Nina[34] when you write,
Neighb

To Barbara Kahn   London
                                                                   May 4, 1959

Dearest Barb(ara),

. . . I miss you all fearfully, specially now, because if one mentions to an English person that one's book has been accepted, the answer is most likely: "Oh, really." Because most of the ones one's met have had masses of their own published. Such is life; as I have remarked to Benj more than once, one has to learn to take the bitter with the sweet.

I was also v. interested about the Berkeley election. Believe it or not, the English are way behind us in some respects. For example, there is a strong rumor current that Certain People[35] are planning to put up a colored candidate

---

30. As Decca had done with her self-published "Lifeitselfmanship."
31. Victor Gollancz, the founder of the publishing house.
32. Decca often referred to herself as "one," as in "oneself."
33. In coming to America.
34. Pele's daughter from her first marriage, to Robert Treuhaft's early law partner, Bert Edises.
35. The capitalized initials are, of course, CP, as in Communist Party.

against Mosley (running in the dist. where I'm living),[36] an almost fatal move, in my opinion, much like the housing proposition in Berkeley as far as the probable effect. Am hoping to see some of the C.P. in question to try to talk them out of it. My idea is to make a few huge posters of Mosley, with photos of him hobnobbing with Hitler and Mussolini, and circulate those—just to remind people. This idea has been accepted with A. Lacrity. The only trouble is, all news photo agencies have been canvassed, and there aren't any such photos. So, I guess that leaves it up to us to steam some out of Muv's scrapbooks at the Island; I do hope she won't notice. . . .

Bob wrote that Eph is being sticky about Muv's health problems, is refusing to diagnose and insists that "she see a doctor." Bob said that he accused Eph of "setting impossible conditions," and stormed out. I agree. . . . She won't go to a doctor; she is still annoyed with me about the Hearing Aid, which lies unused on the shelf; she says the proof they're no good is she keeps seeing them advertised in the Lady,[37] the ads. saying "practically unused." I suggested the users may have gone to meet their maker, and the survivors may have thought the phrase, "practically unused," an encouraging one for the potential market. As she can't hear a word at this point, these words of wisdom are wasted by and large. Perhaps this whole problem depends on one's will to survive, and perhaps at 80 it is not so strong as it once was. . . .

Fondest love, Decca

I MISS YOU! WRITE SOON.

To Robert Treuhaft and Constancia Romilly   London

May 4, 1959

Darling Bobndonk,

'Tis now 12:30 on the first day I was to really work all day on the book. As you can see, in spite of the good news I'm as bad as ever—ANYTHING to keep from it. Except, this is the last thing to keep me from it, I promise and swear. Was awake half the night stewing over the problems of a Socko (or socko-er) beginning and ending for it. . . .

I finally mustered energy to write to Muv, Debo and Nancy about the book. Here's how I phrased it: "I just had some terrifically exciting news. A book, which I've been slaving over for literal ages, has been accepted by publishers in England and the U.S. It is sort of memoirs of my life with Esmond[38] . . ." That's

---

36. In 1959, Decca's brother-in-law Oswald Mosley was an unsuccessful parliamentary candidate in the Kensington district, campaigning for restrictions on black immigration. He received 8 percent of the vote.

37. *The Lady*, England's oldest women's magazine, was a Mitford family venture, on Decca's mother's side.

38. It is, in fact, more of a memoir of Decca's upbringing.

a good ice-breaker, don't you think? You see, if I <u>didn't</u> tell them, they'd think it tricky of me when they finally find out. . . .

The great treat of the weekend was to go to Stratford on Saturday to see Robeson in Othello.[39] Beautiful drive, past Swinbrook and Burford and Chipping Norton, Stow-on-the-Wold etc. Robeson was really magnificent, robed in white and gold cloak, and really heart-rending; not so, Desdemona and Iago, they were crummy unfortunately. The place packed, it's an enormous theatre and every inch taken by standees. Seats for the whole run were sold out ages ago so I was very lucky to be invited. Afterwards, we went to see Paul backstage; it was like a dream to see him in the so-familiar surroundings of the Stratford theatre. He longs to see us in London, after you get here. . . .

I can see I'm not going to get one ounce of editorial help around here, they just don't work that way in England, but cruelly leave one on one's own. It does make me a bit sad as I really thrive on suggestions and help. . . .

This letter is really to thank both of you for 1) reacting so utterly satisfactorily to the Book news . . . and 2) for all you did to get me to write it, as I am such a hopeless weakling I honestly wouldn't ever have got it done without all the cheering on. (Don't be like that, Donk; now is the time to resolve not to be.)

Now, forward to work. I have no excuses left; have had lunch, bought some typing paper, arranged my ms . . . wish me luck.

Greatest love and kisses to you both, Decca

To Barbara Kahn   Inch Kenneth, Gribun, Isle of Mull
                                                         May 11, 1959

Dear Kahns,

I'm sure I probably sent you this same postcard[40] before, but the thing is there isn't much range. Naught changes around here, including the postcards. We arrived to find Christine not here (she had to rush off to see about her brother, who just had his appendix out) so WE (that is, ONE, actually) are doing the cooking. I have already streamlined things to cut out one of the 4 square meals a day—we are subsisting on breakfast, lunch, and high tea, instead of tea and dinner. My next move will be to gradually introduce brunch, and finally brupper. . . . I am working, too, tho. Every morning, afternoon and evening—between the getting of, clearing of, and washing up after, aforementioned meals. The horror of actually finishing the book is now weighing heavily on me. Muv . . . asks leading questions (as to when it begins, etc) and makes oblique suggestions, such as "there should be no bitterness in it." I merely look

---

39. After years of legal action and international protest, Robeson had had his own passport restored by the U.S. State Department the year before and was on a triumphal trip abroad. Illness soon sidelined him, and this was his last performance of *Othello*.

40. A "6 view Lettercard of Isle of Mull."

blank at all this. Anyway, <u>there's</u> at least one copy sold, to look on the bright side. . . .

The mail here is the MAIN thing, the great brightener of the day, so please note. . . . We've only been here 2 days, yet it seems like months or even years. The MacGillivrays (boatman and wife) are awfully nice, and provide an incongruous note of sanity in this fairly nutty place. . . .

Fondest love, and DO write, Decca

To Pele de Lappe   Inch Kenneth
                                                            ca. May 15, 1959
Dearest Neighbor,

. . . Life here is now utterly peaceful & routinised. . . . Muv hinted broadly for several days to read the book. With great trepidation I gave her the first several chapters (childhood bit). She simply loved it—to my surprise & relief! Also says it's all true & she had forgotten some of the bits. . . . Well Neighb, back to work I go. Love to all the loved ones at home.

Decca

To Marge Frantz   Inch Kenneth
                                                            mid-May 1959
Dearest old Marge,

You haven't been very faithful about writing, I must say. ONE letter, so far. I shall hope for improvement immediately. . . .

Old Bob arrived. . . . Now, we have the following division of labor: Benj brings in the morning lobster catch from the pots, eggs, cream, butter and milk from the dairy; Bob supervises the cooking and the going bad of the meat (throws it out when it does, which is constantly on acct. of the unseasonably hot weather); I double as scullery maid and parlor maid. The latter two offices actually are quite distinct, because the house is set up that way. There is a pantry, the parlor-maid's domain, in which one washes up the table china and silver, and a scullery, miles away [on] the other side of the kitchen, in which one washes up the kitchen things, pots and pans etc. Bob and I had the mad idea of introducing American efficiency methods, sort of streamlining the dishwashing operation to all take place in one center, but needless to say, it hasn't worked, as Muv simply refuses to understand it, and insists in putting the "dirties" in their respective, and proper, places.

I do love it here as it really does combine comfort with beauty. I have several complaints, natch, such as: not a single even half sharp knife in the house; a perfectly good refrigerator that hasn't been working for years, simply because no one has bothered to get it going apparently, so consequently everything goes bad at a frightening rate; fresh vegs. of any kind, even cabbage, quite unobtainable because they haven't come up yet, and no canned or frozen ones to substitute for same because they are "so disgusting"; no egg-beater (new-fangled, I suppose); etc. etc. . . .

Philip wrote a very nice letter. . . . He said one rather amusing thing when I was there which I'm going to try to work in. He was talking about the visit to the Marxist Heaven (described in his book) and the hat-stealing episode,[41] going into details about it all, saying "don't you remember so-and-so happening" etc. I said, "well, vaguely, but I don't seem to remember it all nearly as clearly as you do." Philip responded sadly, "Well it all made an enormous impression on me; but I suppose that to you and Esmond, it was just another day's work!"

Next week we are going to have a tea party on the Isle, all sorts of oddballs, Lady Congleton of the I. of Ulva, various MacThings from Mull, etc. The etiquette of Island entertaining is that one sends one's boat to round up the guests, then to distribute them back to their various islands. . . .

I do so wish you were here to give a hand with the Book. Awfully disloyal of you not to have come, I'm quite sure your mother-in-law would have gladly taken care of the darling Children for you. Gollancz had 3 main criticisms: 1) beginning too diffuse and skippy and rambling; 2) middle part tends to be "bald narrative"; 3) not enough about Unity. So far, I agree with 2 and 3. The bald narrative bit comes, I think, from the fact that part is just as I first wrote it, hasn't been carefully worked over, and I wasn't as used to writing at that time as I am now. . . .

Do write, old Marge, and get the others to, also. Enough of this blithering, back to the salt mines.

Fondest love to you, Laurent and Kids, Decca

To Constancia Romilly   Inch Kenneth
                                                            May 1959

Darling Dinkydonk,

I know I've been a lousy, awful correspondent lately. The reason is I am desperately worried about ending the book. . . .

Now Dinkydonk, here is some exciting news (if it comes off, that is). Bob

---

41. In an impromptu romp, the Romillys and Toynbee and his brother had driven off to Eton in search of a friend who was there for a family visit. As Philip described the escapade in his memoir *Friends Apart,* they were in line to join a gathering of visitors in the exclusive academy's chapel when it was announced that "only Old Etonians could now be admitted." Decca somehow gained entry—presumably based on her aristocratic manner—but the three young men were left to their own devices, which tended toward the anarchic. They began taking top hats from pegs in the chapel anteroom and then went on to other local gathering points to add to their haul, about thirty hats in all, which they stowed in the car. The four of them then drove back to London in high spirits, singing and wearing top hats. Esmond was so taken with the success of the rebellious prank that he toyed with the idea of putting a notice in the personal column of *The Times:* "Look out for your boaters! We strike at Harrow next." The next morning he sold the hats to a used clothes dealer.

and I have decided to try to buy the Island from the others—buy out their shares. . . . Muv has been fussing to get real estate people here etc. to look into auctioning it. She thinks the others would be pleased if I were to buy it; that way, it would be kept in the family, and Muv, of course, would live here rent free for the rest of her life or as long as she wants to. A great consideration in making this decision is your feelings in the matter, I know you always wanted to keep it if we could. The thing that would make it possible is that the Romilly estate is at last being settled, so we could buy it out of that money as an investment.

We have already spoken to the MacGillivrays to see if they would want to stay; it turns out that is their dearest wish, they would like nothing better. . . . We'd work out a profit-sharing deal with them about the farm. . . .

I'm going to get my solicitor to write to my sisters to ask if they want to sell to me. Seems quite likely that by the time I see you again I'll be the Chatelaine of Inch Kenneth!

I'd very much like to have your views on all this, Dinkydonk. For instance, might you be interested (a few years from now) in taking a real hand here, either the farming end or possibly running a summer guest house? With Benj as (un)handy-man? Muv is very much for it, for our buying it, I mean, which is why I think the others may agree without giving trouble or trying to charge an outrageous price. But, a big point in buying it would be for you children. . . .

Fondest love, Mother

To Marge Frantz   Inch Kenneth
                                                 May 23rd ("I think"), 1959

Dearest old Marge,

Hooray! Tonight's post brought your glorious long letter. . . . Do continue to send all news (if any) on the Powell case. I've come to the conclusion that it will be pretty hard even to get a meeting together in London to discuss it in the present limboish state.[42] For one thing, talk about the Left being all fraught and disunited! Boy, you haven't seen anything. The result is inaction on all fronts.

Well, you're not the only one who has been slaving away on sandwiches etc. WE, too, have been active. Yesterday was the great Tea Party. . . . The guests were rounded up by boat, and were seen struggling over the seaweed in good time for me to put the kettle on. They turned out to be virtually indistinguishable from the rocks and crags that abound in these parts; it took a good 20 minutes to divest them of their gumboots, mackintoshes and shawls. We sat them

---

42. The Powells and their co-defendant and attorneys were in limbo because, with sedition charges pending, the U.S. attorney was still seeking a treason indictment. Despite determined efforts, including travel to China, government attorneys were never able to gather enough evidence to secure the indictment. The three were kept in legal suspense until 1961, when Robert Kennedy, the new attorney general, ordered the case dropped.

all around the u-shaped dining-room table in the bow window. Whether or not we would ever get 11 people round it was a question, up to the end. Benj and I kept asking Muv, "Are they fat?" "Reasonably fat, I should say," was all we could get out of her. Reasonably fat most of them turned out to be, with the result that Benj had to take his tea out into the kitchen. I must say I felt <u>awfully</u> young at the party, as the late 60's was the predominant age. The guests, in turn, apparently felt extremely youthful in comparison to my mother; they came up one by one to comment to me, "your mother really is <u>wonderful</u> for her age." All in all, we all felt positively like kindergarteners before the tea was o'er. There was Lady Congleton from I. of Ulva, with another woman; they were the only ones to come in their own boat, which gave them a certain edge, I felt. Col. Yeaman and his wife from I. of Mull across the way. The Col, who looked even craggier and rockier than the others, started telling me: "Extraordinary how far one can see with ordin'ry opera glasses from my hill over there. For years and years I've watched your sister the Duchess when she comes up here . . ." but he stopped in mid-sentence, possibly realizing that his bird-watching habits made rather odd telling, so I never did find out if he could see her having her bath.

Then there were a Mr. and Mrs. Leicester from I. of Iona. They have a parrot which escaped out to sea the other day, and was seen by the Leicesters perched precariously on a bit of drift wood. Mrs. L. stripped to the underpinnings and swam out, about 200 yards, to rescue it. Mr. L's sole contribution was to stand on shore, yelling out "Keep her eyes out of the water!" Better on the parrot question than on the woman question, wouldn't you say? There's a return tea party by Lady C. on I. of Ulva next Sunday, at which WE shall probably be the only ones to come in our own boat. . . .

If I should succeed [in buying the island], we will expect you to refer to Bob as The Young Laird in the future. I do hope we get it, as I can't wait to get you all over here. Terrific trees and all the things you like. Also, we should put in a few American touches, such as a proper egg-beater, a rubber dish drainer, and a knife sharpener. Possibly, even, a garbage can with a lid. Curious how one misses these handy aids to normal living when doing all the cooking and dish washing.

Bob took some pictures of the tea-party, I do hope they come out so we can bore you with them. One of the ladies—Mrs. Yeaman, I think—kept saying nervously, "oh dear! Photos! I always come out looking just like a chicken," and as she said it, she did indeed begin to take on the appearance of a white leghorn just before it is slaughtered. . . .

Muv has offered some criticisms of the book. These boil down to mainly two: 1) that she paid the governess 120 pounds a year, not 100 as I said; 2) that she really does think I should not quote her as saying that our Conservative Member from Oxfordshire was "such a dull little man," mainly because he is still alive, and probably never realized that he is dull. . . .

To Marge Frantz   London
                                                                May 31, 1959

Dearest old Marge,

   You have completely ruined my day. I had all sorts of plans, such as working
hard on me revisions of the book, then possibly going to Hyde Park to hear the
debates, or to a movie. Instead of which, I am paralyzed and miserable at home,
and all because of you. The thing is, in an excess of caution I gave everyone this
address with "C/o Mrs. O'Casey." Now it turns out that all such mail goes into
Mrs. O'Casey's post-box, to which only she has the key. Today being Sunday,
she is off in the country. Earlyish this morning, about 9 a.m., Bob went down in
his dressing-gown to get the papers, and reported that IN Mrs. O'Casey's
locked mailbox there glimmers and shines a letter for us, on which he barely
made out the return address of Frantz. He had already looked in obvious hiding-
places in case she had hidden the key in some convenient spot, but no soap. I
rushed into my dressing-gown and started out of the door, armed with a
kitchen knife; Bob said I would terrify the DuBois's[43] (who are in the downstairs flat) if I appeared near their door with blood in eye and knife in hand, but
I went anyway. Very gently, praying for guidance the while, I tried to ease the
letter out, but only succeeded in making it fall down in a position where one
can't possibly get it out. We considered several obvious things like wire and
chewing gum, but of course there isn't any such equipment around. Bob suggested telephoning the Queen, since the mail here is called the Royal Mail, to
see if she has a duplicate key. The whole thing is most depressing, as I was longing for a letter, so how can one settle to anything till Branson (Mrs. O'C) comes

back? The letter is now in a position (see fig. 1) where only
a pair of high forceps, the kind used in extremely difficult
childbirth, could get it out (see fig. 2) so I am just sending
Bob down to Harley St, quite near here, to borrow some.

Fig. 1. Showing
mailbox, & position
of slot (a) &
letter (b).

   The letter had BETTER be interesting and up to or
above your usual standard after all this trouble.

   Later. Bob just read this over me shoulder, said "Oh, do
you really want the letter?" descended with an elaborate
rig-up of safety pin, knife and fork. Just came back up, tri-
umphant, having succeeded. The safety pin fell in, but the
knife-and-forkmanship won the day. Anyway, you are good
to have written, and send the next letter to Nancy's, we
leave here 1 week from today for Paris. . . .

Fig. 2. showing
kind of forceps
needed.

   We've been having a very contrasty time in London. So far, lunch with Debo

---

43. W. E. B. DuBois, the leftist scholar, writer, editor, and civil rights activist, and his wife.
DuBois, author of *The Souls of Black Folks* (1903) and other influential books, was a co-founder of
the National Association for the Advancement of Colored People and the longtime editor of *The
Crisis* magazine. A pioneering Pan Africanist, DuBois lived in exile in his last years.

at Prunier's (there is no equivalent of Prunier's in S.F., so I won't try to think up one); a left-wing lawyer's party in honor of Bob; dinner with Peter Hesketh, an old beau of Nancy's and general friend of family; a party last night at Cedric's, composition of which rather similar to your description of the Pete Seeger concert. . . .

The left-wing lawyers party was at Glorious Richard's. . . . They are eagerly taking up some of our suggestions about an effective anti-Mosley campaign, by the way—since the murder,[44] they are less prone to look on it as a local diversion. . . .

Oh by the way, a Marge-like episode at the Isle.[45] And, please don't comment on it if you write me c/o Nancy, human nature being, as you see, what it is. Well, I happened to see my name on a letter to my mother and couldn't help reading the letter. The letter was buried at the bottom of one of her desk drawers, and I happened to see my name on it when I happened to know she was taking a nap. Anyway, it was from Diana and said: "I hope Decca's book won't be too embarrassing, I understand from Nancy that it is only about her life with Esmond," and all about how Mosley got his sister-in-law (Lady Ravensdale)'s book completely stopped on grounds of libel, and that Gollancz doesn't seem like a very good publisher, but Lady Ravensdale's publisher was also a Jew publisher!![46] So, I wrote at once to Glorious James to urge they have a lawyer familiar with ins and outs of English libel law comb it thru carefully. Luckily, there really is hardly anything about Diana in it. I already crossed out the part about her living in sin.

Sorry to be so preoccupied with the ruddy book, but I am, and won't really rest easy till it's finished. Somehow, the thought of it really and truly getting out is now rather terrifying, and as a result it is fearfully on my mind. I was very glad Muv liked it so much. She made several quite batty suggestions for revision, all of which I've done, such as . . . my appendix scar was only 8 inches, not 12; I shouldn't mention the Potterton (water heater) by their real name and say it was foul smelling, as they might sue for libel.[47] She was awfully upset about

---

44. In 1958 Notting Hill, in the London district where Oswald Mosley was running his parliamentary campaign, had been the site of rampages by white racist mobs inspired by Mosley's racial exclusion policies. Less than a year after the Notting Hill riots, and a few weeks before this letter was written, the neighborhood was the site of the notorious murder of a West Indian pedestrian, Kelso Cochran, by a gang of white thugs who were never apprehended.

45. Decca frequently kidded about Marge Frantz's love of gossip and snooping, which resulted in a practical joke that Decca retold often over the years. See letter of November 10, 1982, to Ann Farrer Horne.

46. Twenty years later, in what may have been a reference to a different letter or may have been a faulty recollection of this one, Decca wrote, "After my mother died, I came across a letter to her from Diana written a few months before Hons & Rebs was published saying 'I wonder what Decca's book will be like? You realize the publisher is a yid.' Charming."

47. After her mother wrote "libellous" in the margin, Decca later said, "I dutifully changed [the Potterton] to the Amberley."

being quoted on our M.P. from Oxfordshire, that he was "such a dull little man," but just as I had agreed to strike that she got a letter from an aunt telling that she had just attended his funeral! Benj now refers to the M.P. as "the man Dec killed."

We had lunch with Celia, the surviving Paget Twin. To my horror, I learned that the other one died of asthma five years ago (she was married to Arthur Koestler.)[48] Celia was awfully nice, just as I remember her in 193??? and she is still mad because I never wrote to tell her that she was the unwitting key to the running away, says she could have arranged a far better cover-up for us had she only known.

We went to see Idden in a play.[49] It just opened in London, and has had the most ghastly reviews I've seen in years—fairly well deserved, I'm sorry to say, tho Id was awfully good in it. Robin told me she has had a Nervous Break-down, a couple of years ago. I'm finding out that lots of English people are going mad these days, just like at home. Muv thinks it is because of the white bread. Anyway, I'm to see Idden tomorrow. She sounds all right over the phone.

Oh dear I must close now, tho one is allowed 5 pages of this paper for 1/3 postage. We are off to dinner with the DuBois's. Probably too L. for you, so I won't bother to write you an account.[50] Haven't met up with any Unitarians, or even (like you) Ex-Unitarians, in this uncivilized town. . . .

Your loving Decca

To Aranka Treuhaft   London
                                                                  June 1, 1959

Dear Aranka,

. . . We are having a terrific lot of fun in London—specially Bob, as I have to work all day and can't go with him to Old Bailey trials, House of Lords and Commons etc.; but everything has been lined up for him. . . . I'm slaving each morning; meeting up with Bob for social life afternoons and evenings . . . [including] dinner with various shades-of-pastish people I used to know when I was a debutante. . . .

We went to dinner the other night with the Heskeths. Peter Hesketh is an

---

48. Mamaine Paget was the writer's second wife, from 1950 to 1952.

49. Decca's cousin Ann Farrer was an actress who had married well-known character actor David Horne.

50. "Probably too L. for you" means "too left." Frantz explains, "I left the [Communist] Party about six months before Dec, very shortly after the Khrushchev revelations. . . . Of course, I didn't cease to admire DuBois at that point, but she was needling (her view!) or being defensive (my view!). Anyway, it didn't significantly affect our friendship."

old beau of Nancy's, and he used to take me out occasionally too when I was a girl. The dinner party was a riot. There were about 8 rather dullish people there, including Peter's rather dullish wife, and his daughter who popped in and out between dances, she's in the middle of her first season. We were invited for 7, and between then and 9 there wasn't a sign of any food, just <u>enormous</u> drinks of whiskey. At 9, Peter set a table for 8, groaning and complaining bitterly as he did so about what a lot of trouble it was; on it he set a small platter of bought cold meats, legs of chicken and the like, and a <u>tiny</u> salad. As I was served first, I took almost all of everything. And that was all, except for some strawberries and cream (strawberries are currently selling for about 2s each). No coffee, bread, vegs., almost no nothing. Masses of wine, tho, with dinner, and brandy after. We reeled home at midnight. This is just what Cedric was telling us about that sort of English person; if they don't have servants, or if the servants are out, they simply give up, and would rather starve than cook. From now on I don't think I'll accept any invitations unless they are in restaurants. . . .

Gollancz has accepted a sketch by Pele for the cover of my book! I'm <u>so</u> pleased. First they said they never take covers by outside artists, but they liked hers very much, and said OK. . . . The title is settled, <u>Red Sheep</u>. It comes from a headline in a Canadian paper last year: Red Sheep Disinherited. . . .

Bob showed Muv the latest Un-American Committee report on red lawyers, in which he rates a couple of pages as "one of the 38 most dangerous Communist lawyers in the country."[51] Among other things, he is accused of having been counsel for the Berkeley chapter of Minute Women for Peace. "Minute Women!" said Muv, pronouncing it to rhyme with Canute. "<u>How</u> sweet!" My solicitor, Richard Turner, wasn't much better. Bob showed it to him; he said, "a midget troupe, I presume?" So, you see, I'm not the only English person who's never heard of the American Revolution.[52] . . .

Nancy wrote to my solicitor saying that if the others are willing to sell the Island, she will give me her share for a present! Isn't that amazing of her, I am bowled over, and wrote to say it is much too expensive a present as the shares are worth at least 1,500 pounds each. She wrote back to say it is because she thought I got a raw deal about Farve's will;[53] so, as they say, "It's an ill will that

---

51. Other accounts put the figure at thirty-nine. They were cited in a report entitled "Communist Legal Subversion," which concentrated on the Lawyers Guild, characterized as "an alleged nationwide organization for 'liberal' lawyers concerned with human rights in general and civil liberties in particular." Decca later wrote that unlisted guild members were jealous, in much the same ways as, years later, Nixon-haters were upset not to find their names on that president's secret "enemies list."

52. Decades later, when Decca retold this story, she conflated the two quotations, attributing the "midget" remark to her mother as well.

53. Nancy Mitford couldn't resist adding, in a letter to her mother, "What does [Decca] want [the island] for? She doesn't say. Atom base I suppose—you'll probably see Khrushchev arriving any day, to be greeted with jugs of cream by the simple islanders."

brings nobody any good." I haven't heard from the other sisters yet. Imagine Diana will be sticky.[54] . . .

Love to Edith, Children, and all at shop, and fondest to Dinky, do make her write even if just a note.

Decca

To Pele de Lappe   London
                                                                              June 5, 1959

Dear Neighbor,

Yesterday we went round to Gollancz's, to talk with Miss Livia Gollancz who is in charge of covers, and Mr. Rubinstein, in charge of editorial department. There has been an agonizing going around on the question of a title, which has now become urgent as, if you are doing the cover, you must know the title in ample time. The cover comes first. . . . Anyway, the title is now settled. It is:

                              HONS AND REBELS
                                       by
                               Jessica Mitford

Thousands of others were considered and discarded. The one I liked best was <u>Revolting Daughters</u> but the Gollancz people put their feet down on that one. James thought it up. I do hope you all like Hons and Rebels? I don't think it's at all bad, and only rather fear Nancy will think it's cashing in on her stuff. Anyway, no need for any of them to know what the title is till I'm safely back home. . . .

The family are being a riot about the book. Tremendous speculation as to what it will be like (I'm not letting any of them read it, natch, except Muv, who read the first few chapters and swore not to discuss it with the sisters). Debo keeps saying "Oh Hen, I <u>do</u> hope it's not going to be frank," and the other day we were in Heywood Hill's bookshop (right around the corner from Debo's house in Mayfair, and Nancy worked there for years during the war, Heywood is sort of an old friend and associate of all the family). Heywood told us that a Gollancz salesman had been in and told him they were publishing my book, and that a day or so later Debo, Nancy and Diana were all in his shop twittering and wringing their hands about it.

I've got it all in shape except for the knotty last chapter. . . .

We have bought the Island. Are you amazed? It really does seem an awfully good investment. . . . It does seem a bit extraorder that after all that's happened, ONE ends up with the whole estate or what's left of it. . . .

---

54. Within the next two days, Decca's sisters Deborah and Diana said they were willing to sell, provided that she give their mother a lifetime lease, which had been Decca's intention from the outset. The other sister, Pam, who was out of the country at the time, also consented readily.

We've seen a bit of the Old Dutch,[55] but not the children, who are at school. Emma is being crammed for Oxford, it seems odd (but encouraging) that one of Debo's children should want to go there. . . .

Write soon, by return of post if possible, to Paris, as a) we probably won't be there very long, and b) I absolutely long to hear from you. . . .

Your loving Neighbor.

To Marge Frantz   Paris

June 10, 1959

Dear old Marge,

. . . The houseparties won't start [at the island] for a while because all will be left exactly as is as long as Muv wants to live there, twill be her place, run by her, for as long as she wants. I think she would fade away if she had to leave the Isle, she so adores it, and seems relieved by the present arrangement. Also, she takes daily walks looking over the status of things ("mmm, Little D., I think it's time we had the hay cut. Ohhn, the poor calf is lying down, I hope she isn't ill . . .") which I could never do because I wouldn't have the brains to know the hay needed cutting etc. All we now have to fork over is about $12,000 cash, and it will be ours. We're going to pay out of the Romilly ill will money, so that's all right. A good investment, I think. . . .

Re. the book. . . . No contract so far from Houghton-Mifflin, and I must tell you about that bit. H-M doesn't even have a copy of it! The H-M representative . . . didn't have time to read it, so he gave it to his wife to read. She read it, was all for it, the H-M man agreed, sight unseen, and that's that. . . .

You can't conceive of the intense curiosity on the part of the family about it. . . . Debo found out by a chance remark of mine that our Cruise saying to Ld. Rathcredon, "Rathcredon, Red, Come to Bed" was in.[56] No sooner do I arrive in Paris than Nancy confronts me with this. Every tidbit about the book is flashed from Ireland to England to Paris in less time than it takes to tell. Should be good for 4 sales, at least, don't you think. . . .

Pam is here, staying with the Mosleys. She just arrived, and Nancy is trying to arrange for us to see her; tho Nancy claims this is rendered near-impossible because of the non-speakers of us and the Mosleys. . . . We envisage scenes as in corny French bedroom farces, the Mosleys popping out of one room, down an oubliette, us hiding in the stove, etc. As I pointed out to Nancy, just their cho-

---

55. Duchess.

56. That is, the sisters' old saying was in Decca's book. Deborah and Decca, on a family cruise at the ages of sixteen and eighteen respectively, used to chant those words to a young man on board named Lord Rathcreedan. Decca told various versions of this story over the years. In one letter years later, she gave the words of the chant (or song) as "On the good ship Lollipop / It's a night trip, into bed you hop / With Lord Rathcreedan / All aboard for the Garden of Eden."

sen place for us anyway, too bad it isn't lit in summertime, from their point of view. . . .

Dear old Marge, so sorry I haven't described Paris. It is really beyond description. Do keep writing, I <u>so long</u> for letters. . . .

your loving Dec.

Fondest love to Laurent and Children, do get them to write.
ps. I'm trying to think of a Socko Beginning for the book. . . . Possibly the clue is in some of the voluminous scrapbooks [at the island]. Muv has kept every clipping about any or all of us, gathered and pasted in huge bound tomes. She said reflectively the other day, "whenever I see a headline in the papers beginning 'Peer's Daughter . . .' I know it's going to be about one of you children."

How would it be to gather a few of the more interesting, and representative, headlines and somehow work them into a brief prologue?

Or, alt. idea, a brief prologue about coming back for the 1st time in 1955, at age of 38, and noting various reminiscent things—this would give more range. The things would be in the form of what Steve calls "teasers," hinting at their future significance. This sort of thing:

Walking down Rutland Gate, seeing the White Slavers house, the hammer and sickles followed by swastikas carved by diamonds in the mews windows, my coming out photo and the chocs, talking to Mabel (our old parlormaid) and her telling how Farve would never have hired her had he known she was going to get married (30 years after she came to us) and going to Debo's and seeing in her wedding scrapbook, next to Elizabeth R.'s t.gram of congrats., my own saying "honnish congratulations on a successful season's duke hunting";[57] and meeting Philip in the Mews for the first time in 16 years and how he was literally like a dog returning to his vomit, as the last time he was there was for our farewell party when we left for the U.S. and he threw up all over the floor . . .

You get the idea, sort of a medley of memories, which get explained later on in the book itself. Do let me know if you have any ideas on this.

Bob did love the Farewell Party you gave for him, but the hopeless old thing is awful about reporting. He said SOMEONE there said "Decca is the Clare Booth Luce of the Left Wing," and now he can't remember who said it. Do tell me, so I can strike them off my list.

---

57. Lighthearted references in the memoir to her sister Deborah's "duke hunt" were a source of worry and, evidently, family friction as the memoir was being edited and after it was published. After talking with her mother about Deborah's reaction, Decca apparently cut some of the initial material and wrote her sister offering to remove the section.

To Marge Frantz   "Somewhere in La Belle France"
                                      June ("20th, I think"), 1959

Dear old Marge,

Thanks so much for yr letter—the one with critique of draft plus loads of news, received just as we were taking off from Paris. Offhand I don't agree with the starting point of your criticisms (that one can't generalize about classes of people—I've always thought one could; the Dutch, for instance, are as depressingly clean as one is always told they are; the Southern French, as warmly filthy; Southern U.S., faintly squalid etc. etc. and the Petit Bourgeoisie, as Lenin so truly said, vacillating). However, I am going to comb it over & over to make it make more sense, if you see what I mean, in view of your comments.

The Last Time I Saw Paris (2 days ago) Dobby & Mason were there [and various other friends]. . . . Those who had been treated by the Govts. behind the Iron Curtain were complaining loudly about the accommodations in Paris they could afford—a big come-down. Some even came down to our Hotel de Suède—characterized optimistically and accurately, by Nancy (who found it for us) as "above the bug level." . . .

Mason avers there is no housing shortage in the Soviet Union, after hearing which I stopped listening. (In spite of the fact I, unlike you, wish nothing but the best for the Soviets.) . . .

                                      Love from Decca

To Marge Frantz   Hotel Paradis, Mont des Roses,
                                      Bormes-les-Mimosas, Var, France
                                      June 26, 1959

Dearest old Marge,

I'm not showing off, that really is our address. We are now settled, and by great good luck (and by assiduously avoiding following Nancy's advice) in a very good place. The Cote d'Azur is, on the whole, one Frenchified Coney Island after another. . . . However, the name of this place, which we found listed in the faithful Guide Michelin, was not misleading. It is a lovely old-fashioned hotel with flowered terrace (for eating on) and we have a cottage to ourselves in the garden, with all the conforts modernes as they say in these parts (I think it means a john one can sit on as contrasted to hole in floor), delicious food so far, all for about $3.50 a day each, including breakfast and dinner. . . . [I]t is much cheaper not to live at home.

Nearby is Le Lavandou, a honky-tonk beach for Benj, with bikini'd beauties and boats for hire; also nearby is a terribly pretty little town (in the hills) called Bormes. . . .

The schedule here is going to be for me to get down to work—starting tomorrow morning. And to really stay at it till all is finished. So do write, otherwise I won't have the classic excuse (got to answer letters) for quitting from time to time. . . .

Tonight before dinner, we got in a conversation with a middle aged Fr. couple in a nearby café. Monsieur turned out to be an executive of a major Fr. newspaper (in Lyons); he proudly told us several times that he is in charge of all the journalists on his paper, and is the boss of 1,000 workers. We tried to get them into an argument about the Algerian war, but every time things began to get interesting they would say, "but Madame" (that's me) "has the peaceful face of an angel, she wouldn't understand these mournful things . . ." Bob kept asking me, "what's French for 'misleading'? I want to tell them your face is misleading," but natch I wouldn't tell him, specially since I couldn't think of it right off. Then we tried to get them about the De Gaullist censorship of the <u>Express</u>, etc., but they turned that off by saying "one would take Madame for Belgian, her French is so academique!" Which made me feel good. The other day someone asked me if I were Swiss, but I thought that was probably just a polite way of asking if one was German.

Germans abound here, I'm sorry to say. The Fr. say they got a taste for French cooking during the Occupation; whatever the cause, there are too many for my liking. There was a large group of them, guzzling champagne, at the 3-star place in Baux, middle-aged fatsoes, made one shudder to look at them. Benj gave the usual trouble, just as Dink and Nebby Lou did last time: "But how do you <u>know</u> they're bad?" Trying not to get into a long argument, I said, "by the backs of their necks" (which were classic: huge, red and beefy). "Just like the guys down South," Benj complained. "You shouldn't be against someone just because of the color of his neck." Hopeless child, I should never have let you inveigle him to that Unitarian Sunday School. . . .

Love to all, kiss the Children, and do teach them French before they come here, as poor Benj is severely handicapped by not knowing any.

Dec

To Barbara and Ephraim Kahn   Bonnes-les-Mimosas, Var

July 3, 1959

Dearest Kahns,

Sorry about this address. . . . In mitigation, Bob claims I chose it because it was the most pollinated-sounding place I could find, and calls it (with his accustomed grouchiness) Hotel Allergie. . . .

Life here is even-keelish to say the least. It's the sort of hotel where Fr. bourgeois gentility reigns supreme. Dinner, eaten out of doors on the terrace in full view of bougainvillea-shrouded sunset, is a near-silent meal, the only greetings exchanged between one and fellow-guests being a polite, grave bow and "bon soir." It is served by a sloe-eyed (and fast-footed) young waiter of courteous-verging-on-grim demeanor. The courses are many and absolutely delicious.

The only people we've fraternized with during the past week (since arriving here) are a One's ageish Jewish couple, English, also. . . .

They are fairly nice yet fairly awful, if you know what I mean. On the other hand, they are extremely easy to one-up. They are the sort of Jewish snobs who look down most contemptuously on the "loud, nouveau-riche" (to quote them) Jews. So the other day they were raving about Benj, who they adore, and saying that when "races and cultures are mixed, often a really superior child is produced as a result—providing there is <u>good stock</u> on both sides to begin with." I inquired about the good stock, turns out that from the Jewish side it means in general a non-garment worker and non-nouveau riche. After leading them on quite a while on this theme, and getting them thoroughly committed, I described Aranka to them (I must admit I laid it on a bit thick), immigrant factory worker at 13 in New York, made her name and pile in the Garment Industry. (I suppose hats <u>are</u> garments, in a way, wouldn't you say so?) . . .

Best love to all, Decca

To Robert Treuhaft and Constancia Romilly   Bormes-les-Mimosas, Var
July 10, 1959

Darling Bob and Donk,

Decided to make use of my carbon paper so kindly procured by Bob to write you a joint letter. . . .

THE BOOK IS FINISHED! I could scream with joy. Isn't it amazing, I was so terrified it wouldn't be done before time to go—or ever, for that matter—then suddenly everything fell into place and the last chapter is DONE. I'm just getting to work on the prologue thing, which will a) be a breeze, and b) if it proves hard, I don't have to do it. Oh how hard I wish you were both here to celebrate. A few days of typing lie ahead, as I've got to make a clean copy for the Ed., then I'll be free as air. Debo in her letter offered to BE the editor, ha ha. It really is a scream how <u>fearfully</u> curious they all are about it. . . .

Late bulletin: the prologue is now finished, I think it quite good and adds a lot. Won't affect Chapter 1, which stands as is. The pleasure of having it done is indescribable.

WRITE WRITE WRITE

To Robert Treuhaft and Constancia Romilly   Bormes-les-Mimosas, Var
July 13, 1959

Darling Bobandonk (still using handy carbon),

I just put the completed, final, corrected, nicely typed bit of ms. in the mail to me Editress. Oh the enormous feeling of relief, and I'm quite pleased with the end after all. I do so wish I could have shown it to you. . . . Dinky I put in a page with my ms. saying <u>Dedicated to Constancia Romilly</u>. Benj is furious at being left out, so now I'll have to write another one to dedicate to him. The book is about 85,000 words, as far as I can tell, not a bad length, do you think? . . . I have worked out a series of teases on Benj to occupy me now the book's done. Tease #1 is to go down to the beach and say a few words in rapid French to Martine, the beautiful 13-year old. Then, when he anxiously asks me afterwards what I said to her, I answer: "oh, nothing much, I was just telling her all about Marian and Rebecca and Gail . . ." Tease #2 is to say to him, "Benj I know you don't have much time for writing letters, so I just wrote a long letter to Marian telling her all about Martine." One can work the dear boy into a near-frenzy in no time by these simple methods. To get even, he tries (and usually succeeds) to muddle me when driving, make me take wrong turns etc. All in all a gay time is being had. Note I am trying to beat the Bormes post office people by no paragraphs thus getting all on one page, they are fearful about stamps, always make me put on two. I think it is from a misguided sense of patriotism, getting foreign money for the Govt. Do write. I shall take a cab directly to Richard's office to see what mail there is, so if there isn't any 'twill be waste of a cab fare. . . .

Your loving, and letter-longing, Decca.

To Robert Treuhaft   London

July 29, 1959

Darling old Bob,

Thanks so much for yrs. of the 26th, with fascinating enclosures. . . .

After break.[58] Muv was having a rest in her room, the phone rang, and a voice just like Debo's said "Is Muv there?" I said, "Yes, she's resting . . . Debo?" "No, it's me," said the voice—obviously Diana. So Muv called her back when she came down, and said "do come right over, darling"; so I went and sulked in Muv's bedroom for an hour or so while Diana was there. The complications of life! . . .

Benj and I are going up to stay with Debo for the Bank Holiday weekend, which should be much fun. I think I'll leave the ms. with Philip, as I don't dare leave it around here, the Mews, or Debo's country house, not trusting human nature that far.

Muv was on at me again about making her out to be a snob in the book, this really rankles, it seems. Her arguments to prove she wasn't one were: 1) that it wasn't only middle class people we weren't allowed to stay with as Diana wasn't allowed to stay with the Astors once when she was 16 as she was considered too young. 2) it is dangerous to allow young girls to go to tea with strangers, even if the strangers are other young girls of the same age, as their parents might turn out to be criminals. I was just going to remind her of Diana's stretch in Hol-

---

58. Breakfast.

loway, but thought better of it. . . . She is really glad about the book, though, I think. By the way she adores you, said "I do so wish Bob was here, what a shame he had to go back." . . .

Your loving, and longing to be home, Keezar.

To Barbara Kahn   London

August 4, 1959

Dearest Barb,

Thanks v. much for your lovely long letter. . . .

Re. the Sheilah Graham[59] book, I didn't save Philip's review. The main point he made was that although it is quite a bad book, there is something rather well done about the whole way she crashed "society" and also something very interesting about her relationship with Scott Fitzgerald. I haven't read it, just the part about the Mitfords (which I looked up in the index while standing in a bookshop) which made me roar, specially the crumby old International Sportsmen's Club, where to this day one sees naught but aging Mitfords creeping about in various stages of decomposition—Uncle Jack, Aunt Helen etc. etc. . . .

We had a lovely time at Debo's. . . . Last night she and I had a long, cosy chat, and she told me all sorts of fascinating news and gossip. Mainly I am sorry now that I missed Farve's funeral, it does sound a riot, apparently they were all in fits of giggles from start to finish. Not that they weren't sad, they were. It started when they all met for dinner in some ghastly hotel in Northumberland (he died in Redesdale Cottage, a tiny 2 room cottage) and as the disgusting meat course was served, naught but canned vegs, Nancy put on her mourning face and said "I wonder if we will be invited to dinner at the Great House tomorrow?" and kept saying "Helas" all though the horrid pudding. Doesn't sound very funny told, I see, but I can just visualize the scene. Muv kept roaring too but saying, "Children, stop it, what will everyone think." . . .

Fondest love to all of you. Tell old Bob I'm not writing today as he is now about 8 letters behind.

Your best friend, Decca

To Marge Frantz   London

August 8, 1959

Dearest Marge (Butfor) Frantz,

Your middle name is now Butfor, as in But for your help & encouragement. I am writing this in the train on my way back from a day with me Editress.

---

59. The Hollywood gossip columnist and lover of novelist F. Scott Fitzgerald who early in life tried to obliterate her origins as a working-class orphan in London and live as an aristocrat, with the aid of Decca's uncle Jack. She had also been a friend of Tom Mitford. After Graham's death, her daughter, Wendy Fairey, learned that her father was philosopher A. J. Ayer, Philip Toynbee's friend.

Unlike old Fles, she loves the idea of the Committee & wished me to convey to all of the members her warmest congratulations. I described all of you to her in detail, & the different roles . . . & she longs for you all. . . .

Mabel says I haven't changed a bit in all these years (meaning since I was 2), that I'm just as untidy & hopeless as ever & that she'll have to go to bed for a fortnight after I leave. But she's coming to sleep over at the Mews the night before we leave to do the packing. She also showed up with a Man & some string to tie up the cartons (overflow from suitcases) so that's all very constructive. . . .

Life here is so extraorder, Marge, you'd be amazed & I do wish you were here. We are up at crack of dawn & then Muv rushes out immediately after breakfast saying she must "be in time for the opening!" "Opening of what?" "Of Harrods, they open at 9."

One rather noticeable thing is the solid anti-Americanism of all sections of the population, rich & poor, right & left. I've yet to meet one person who has the least desire to go to America, or one who has been there & liked it. It is a queer mixture of ordinary English chauvinism, snobbishness, intellectual snobbishness, & disapproval of American policies. Rather well worth analyzing & cataloguing, it might make a good article. . . . Madeau Stewart,[60] 35 year old executive at BBC, no doubt solid conservative: "Aren't Americans awfully ignorant on the whole? Don't you find it depressing not having anyone to talk to?" . . . Well I could go on & on with this, from Nancy to Glorious Richard, from Mabel to the people at Cooks. . . .

To Robert Treuhaft   London
                                                                            August 11, 1959

Darling old Bob,

I was so pleased to get your letter despite yr. horrid threat to go on living at the Kahns' after we get home. . . .

Pam wrote to say she was leaving Ireland Saturday by car, driving to London. We have been expecting to hear from her momentarily but so far no call. Last night at Scrabble, Muv began laughing the inner laugh of one who has thought of something frightfully funny. I said what's the joke, she said "I was just wondering if Woman has been kidnapped for ransom on her way to London." I suggested we should start making pledges in that case, and offered 10 pounds for a start; Muv said "I'll double that." "We should make Debo cough up, don't you think?" I suggested. Midst gales of laughter, Muv said, "Debo will have to plunge." We agreed Nancy should have the Film Rights to the story . . . but the awful thing is it may be true as we still haven't heard from the old Woman.

---

60. A cousin of Decca's.

Later: We got a letter from Woman, she wasn't kidnapped at all, but is in the country, coming up to London tomorrow.

It is now 5:30 and we are sitting around waiting with bated breath for the Specialist, known alternatively by Muv as the Expert and the Adept. Poor thing, I don't envy him his task. Short medical note (I am counting on you to read all this to Eph): I found a potato in my bed. Was just putting it back with the others, remarking to Muv how odd to find one in one's bed, when she explained it is against cramps in the feet; I had mentioned that sometimes I get them, and Eph was cold comfort about suggesting a cure, and she says that potatoes in the bed are sure-fire. So glad to hear of it. I have kept it there since, and no cramps at all. I suppose you will seize on this as another reason for staying permanently at the Kahns, if you've got to look forward to potatoes in our bed in future. But do mention it to Eph in case he has other patients with this trouble.

Had lunch with Philip today, my last social engagement of the trip; all my buddies are out of town on their holidays. We met over at the Observer. . . . David Astor was there, we went to the restaurant in his car-and-chauffeur. I goofed by asking him if he worked at the Observer too; it turns out he is the editor and owner of it. . . . David Astor lives part of the time in the Hebrides, says he has just come back from there and all the Old Residents are on their ear about us buying Inch Kenneth, gossip is flying at a frightening rate about what is going to happen there. I told him confidentially that all will remain the same, we just bought it as a good investment, but on no account should he let on to the gossipers about this, 'twould ruin their time. I told him Khrushchev may go up to measure, as Nancy says.[61] . . .

Later still. The Adept has come and left, and a most successful time it was. Dr. Bell ("Hmmm, such a nice little woman") came too, as she had promised.

The whole thing got off to a crashing social start. The Adept asked Muv, "How old are you?" "Almost eighty," she replied. Dr. Bell gushed, "but one would never take you for more than sixty-five." "Are you really, one would never think so, you are certainly remarkable," Muv answered to this. Dr. Bell, who is about 10 years younger than I, gave a really remarkable look at this, and I had to dash out for a few minutes to re-straighten my face. Later I pointed out to Muv what had actually been said, and I must say she simply roared, though a bit sad because as she pointed out, there is no way now of recovering the situation with Dr. Bell. . . .

From time to time, when he asked her "have you ever fainted" or "can you do up buttons" etc., things to which the answer was positive, I noted her groping for the table leg—touching wood. Thank goodness I have a

---

61. See reference to Nancy Mitford's letter in footnote 53 to June 1, 1959, letter to Aranka Treuhaft.

rational approach to Drs. and their works, and do not rely in the least on superstition. . . .

I do so wish you were here. . . . I am v. lonely and longing for you.

Your loving Decca

To Robert Treuhaft

London

August 12, 1959

Darling old Bob,

. . . Well today there was a fascinating row, I guess it is about time I was getting home. Aunt Weenie has been acting a bit strange for some time. She lives in Rutland Gate & has been studiously avoiding me, only comes round if she knows in advance I'll be out. This, while OK with me, I found puzzling, as she had me to lunch at her club when I first arrived & was fairly polite. So this afternoon she came to tea (Woman is in town & was coming with one of her Foreign friends). Muv & I were sitting in the drawing room waiting for them all to come. Aunt Weenie arrived first. I rose to greet her, put out a hand to shake, was ignored. She sat with back to me, conversing with Muv. One could see she was working herself into an absolute rage. Soon she jumped up & said she was going, wouldn't wait for Woman. She said goodbye to Muv, then turned to me & said "I want a word with you." I followed her downstairs to the entrance hall (feeling about ten & back at Mangersbury, her horrid house at Stow-on-the-Wold where I spent many a miserable week as a child). She turned on me & delivered the following speech (the delivery was <u>excellent</u> by the way, no tremor of voice or hesitancy, more like a person on the stage in a way): "I, for one, can never forget the savage cruelty with which you treated your mother & father. And now, you filthy little cad, you come back & write a lot of horrible things about your mother & then come here & sponge on her." Rather conscious that Woman & her Foreigner might at any minute pop along the Mews, & that Mabel was hovering at top of stairs etc, I simply said "I'm not interested in listening to all that drivel" & went back up.

Muv was anxiously waiting to see what had occurred, so I told her, & she said, "Mmm, Weenie always did love a good row." . . . The puzzler, of course, is: is she referring to the book? If so, where did she hear anything about it? Muv didn't tell her, so all remains a mystery. Benj was astounded at the whole thing, is threatening to phone Aunt Weenie & give her hell. . . .

I am longing, panting, sighing, fainting, dying for Calif & you.

Fondest love & XXXX, Decca

To Constancia Romilly   Oakland
                                                        November 21, 1959

Darling Dinkydonk,

Only less than a month to D-Day!! I'm so excited. What plane, what time, what day?

I must tell you a frightfully funny story about Koko.[62] He has been in rather bad shape lately—has an unexplained limp (I took him to the Humane Society about it but they could find nothing wrong), wormy and throw-upy, also long-haired and filthy. So I decided to put him at the Berkeley Woggin[63] and Cat hospital for a couple of days for thorough overhauling, clipping, bathing, worming etc. etc.

Yesterday Bob went to get him out. Koko looked absolutely marvellous, they had done a spectacularly good job of sprucing him up, and Bob was deciding to give Benjy hell about keeping him looking like that until you arrive. Koko acted very strangely about getting in the car, had to be forced in, tried to jump out etc. When Bob got him home, he ran away down the street and had to be caught and locked in a room. You've probably guessed it: a few minutes later, the vet. called up and said "you've got the wrong dog." Sure enough, Bob had taken a pure-bred cocker by mistake! If Benjy ever has to go to hospital I'm not going to send Bob to fetch him home. . . .

I'm working up a tease on my cousin Idden. Remember I took her daughter Clare to an X movy while in London?[64] Well so now "Lolita" (Banned in England) has come out in pocket book. I bought one, put an "Aesop's Fables" jacket on it, marked the outside of the package CHILD'S BOOK, and sent it off to Clare. Thereby striking a blow for freedom from censorship, and at the same time living up to my reputation with Clare. (Have you read Lolita? Extraordinarily good book, it really is, do read it.) . . .

Fondest love, we are all longing and longing for D-Day,
Mother

To Victor Gollancz   Oakland
                                                        December 9, 1959

Dear Mr. Gollancz,

I just got a letter from my Mother saying she has written to you about the book title, so thought I had better hasten to write.

She wrote to me a couple of weeks ago (probably after the Daily Express

---

62. Koko was Constancia's dog, a mini-variety Hungarian puli sheepdog whose full name, the editor is informed, was Kokomo Ruggamole Fleasome Humdinger Treuhaft Romilly Treuhaft.

63. "Dog" in Decca-speak.

64. For details, see letter of April 30, 1994, to Clare Samson.

story) to say she violently objects to the title, Hons and Rebels. I answered to
say that I also did not care for it, and had preferred Red Sheep, but that it was
too late to do anything about it, since I had accepted the judgment of James
MacGibbon and the editorial people at Gollancz.[65]

Please don't be worried about all this. It was my fault for not coming up with
a title I was really sure of, and I don't suppose the title matters too much. There
are many opinions on Hons and Rebels: my husband likes it, most of my friends
here don't, but of course it doesn't mean anything much in America.

If my mother expresses herself in strong terms, and attributes equally strong
feelings on the matter to me, please remember she is <u>very</u> old and apparently
this has been on her mind. I was frankly most surprised that she took so much
interest in it. She is the only one of the family who has read parts of the book,
and said she liked the parts she read.

I realize it is much too late to change the title. I did tell her, when I answered
her first letter, that I was writing to you to convey her opinion—which was a lie,
but done to mollify her.

I would so appreciate it if you would write her a nice letter sort of to set her
mind at rest, perhaps giving some positive reactions to the present title. Forgive
me for bothering you with all this.

Warm regards, Decca

To Constancia Romilly   Oakland
January 29, 1960

Darling Dinkydonk,

I was so glad to chat (though I'm hopeless at long-distance chatting) on the
phone. Never, never feel you shouldn't tell worrying things etc, really dear
that's naughty, and I was longing to hear your dear old voice anyway.

Pink, I wish I could have some words of wisdom re. your letter. I'd do
absolutely anything to help you get over feeling so depressed, but of course it's
not that easy. I do think I know what you are going through, though.

Part of it seems to me to be along the following lines: One is only really
inwardly comfortable, so to speak, after one's life has assumed some sort of
shape. Not just a routine, like studying or a job or being a housewife, but something more complete than all those, which would include goals set by oneself
and a circle of life-time type friends. I think this is one of the hardest things to
achieve, in fact often just trying doesn't achieve it but rather it seems to develop
almost by accident. (Clear as mud, dear, sorry, but I'm not very good at explaining all this. I do feel there's some truth to it however.) Usually I don't think one

---

65. Many years later, recalling the title switch, Decca wrote that the editors had objected to *Red
Sheep* because they thought it "could be taken in the sense of sheep being a docile follower." She
added, "I still think Red Sheep would have been a far better title."

comes by all this at a very young age. Even after one has, all may be knocked out of shape, so one has to start over again to some extent—which happened to a lot of us when the Party and CRC etc. folded, and some of us . . . went through a lot of suffering perhaps a bit like what you are going through now. . . .

Darling donk, I can't think of anything more to write. I know I haven't cheered you up, though I'd give anything to do so, and can only tell you what you already know: how much we all love and adore you and wish you well. Please be a good Donk and write, by return post if possible, as I'm so concerned about you, and don't feel you have to write a phonily "cheery" letter as that isn't the point, I just long to keep in touch and to know your real feelings. You were always the one that kept me going in the darkest days (like when Esmond was killed) and I'd give anything to be able to do the same for you. See you at Easter, one way or other.

Fondest love, masses of kisses, Mother

To Aranka Treuhaft   Oakland
                                                                        January 31, 1960

Dear Aranka,

Thanks so much for your letter, I am longing for the hat to come. . . .

We did love having you to stay, and the mad social whirl that resulted; and things were just beginning to simmer down to normal when the most extraordinary development took place in the Jerry Newson case. Bob and Bert had filed for a writ of habeas corpus, to compel the Adult Authority[66] to set his time. They charged that Newson was in effect being held in prison for the murders, of which he was never convicted, since the average first offender in robbery cases serves only 3 years and he has been in for ten years already with no end in sight. Each time he comes up for questioning (re. parole) to the Adult Authority they ask him, "now, are you ready to tell us about the murders?" Well anyway there was a good flurry of publicity about the writ, and an editorial in the Chronicle; then, as a result of this, an honest-to-God mystery witness got hold of Bob. He is an auto salesman, 32nd degree Mason, pillar of society type. He was at the drugstore the night of the murders, a few minutes after closing time, trying to buy a newspaper; he saw three people in the drugstore, the druggist, his assistant, and a "short, light-skinned Negro" (evidently the murderer). He was waved away and left. Subsequently he saw Jerry's picture in the papers as the accused person, and he went to the D.A.[67] to tell him they had the wrong man, as his picture was nothing like the person he saw. The D.A. took him to City Hall where he saw Newson, and again said he was not the man. So, for all

---

66. The official name of the parole board.
67. The district attorney, J. Frank Coakley, had campaigned for years to keep Newson in prison, citing the murders of which he had been exonerated.

these years the D.A. has concealed this information. You can imagine our excitement. . . . Tomorrow there is to be a court hearing in San Rafael at which the witness will be present. . . . Don't you think this is a terrific break, after ten long years. We are trying to figure out a way to put the D.A. in jail for malfeasance in public office or some such.

Benj is fine, he got an A plus on the famous social studies paper. Mrs. Samon was sick all week to his joy. Finally she came back on Friday, and announced no one was getting higher than a B on the English. She said, "None of you understood the point of the character sketches, except for Benjy Treuhaft—if he did them himself." We are simply furious, and Bob and I are going to have it out with her this week. Bob thinks I could sue her for libel, as an author, for suggesting that I wrote the corny stuff Benj turned in! . . .

          Love from Decca

To Constancia Romilly   Oakland
                                                  February 10, 1960
Darling Chickadee,
    . . . The Newson hearing was a terrific shambles. Never, in my born days, have I seen such a prejudiced judge. Completely buddy-wuddy with Coakley, needless to say; we heard him say "see you later, Frank" during the recess. As for Coakley, he was like a caricature of McCarthy. Bob was absolutely splendid in his questioning of Coakley, like baiting a bull. So was Bert; he shouted at the judge at one point to admonish the witness to keep a civil tongue in his head (I thought he was going to say a civil rights tongue, as much of what Coakley had to say was about CRC. A welter of red-baiting, you never heard the like of it.)[68] Benj and David[69] were astonished, we had brought them along to see how the Constitution (which they are studying in Social Studies) works out in real life to protect the rights of citizens like Jerry Newson. They saw. . . .

    [T]he Chronicle had an excellent story, and oddly enough so did the next day's Tribune.[70] . . . The next stage is the District Court of Appeal. . . .

          Fondest love old Donk, see you shortly I hope. Mother

---

68. In *A Fine Old Conflict*, Decca cited an unspecified habeas corpus hearing in the Newson case—probably this one—at which Coakley was subpoenaed to testify. She wrote that "he spotted me in the courtroom audience. Pointing at me from the witness stand, he shouted, 'That woman's a Communist! She's been spending the last five years thinking of ways to torment me!' "

69. A friend and classmate of Benjamin Treuhaft.

70. The *Oakland Tribune* at the time was owned by District Attorney Coakley's political allies, the conservative Knowland family.

To Constancia Romilly   Oakland
                                                        February 15, 1960

Darling Dinkydonk,

 . . . <u>Don't</u> be worrying that another birthday and no plan of life in offing. . . .

Somehow in crises I have had I've always found hard work the very best cure (in contrast, for instance, to too much self-examination, or even to getting frightfully involved with other people's problems). These are just suggestions as I know everyone must work out these things for himself.

Dear I think that next summer (1961) we should give some thought to going to England to look after the Island a bit. . . . I don't want to go back until the book has died down, as I am rather terrified about reactions. I have asked Philip to be a spy for me and relay all what's being said. . . .

The enclosed marvellous story was in This World on Sunday.[71] Not a word about all the red baiting and lies told about B and B at the hearing. Seems the Chronicle is ready to campaign for Newson's freedom. Our new found friends the Demorests (Bob's funeral lady, and Dick Demorest is Editor of This World) have had a hand in it. Quelle tease on Coakley! . . .

Typical conversation with Benj. I was telling him the sad news that the Kahns' lovely black cat, Hector, was killed by a dog. Benj: "Better than being run over by a car; at least he died in battle." Me: "For me, I'd rather be run over any day than be killed by a dog." Benj (patiently): "Yes Dec, but you're not a cat. To him, it was like being killed in a fight with Coakley would be to you; at least he had the satisfaction of inflicting some injuries before he died." Rather true, in a way, don't you think? . . .

                                        Your very loving Mamma

To Virginia Durr   Oakland
                                                        March 10, 1960

Dearest Va,

You'll never know how absolutely delighted I was with your letter, and how very, very much it meant to me. Frankly, I've been in a terrific sweat for the last few days: not because I actually thought you would object to the parts about you, but because your opinion of the book as a whole was so important to me. You see, not a soul of all the people out here who gave encouragement etc. knew Esmond, or knew me in those days. So the people whose opinions really counted most for me were yours and Philip Toynbee's.

The thing that mixed me up in writing about Muv is that she has changed <u>so completely</u> in the past 20 years. Nancy and I were talking about that in Paris last

---

71. A summary of the habeas corpus hearing for Jerry Newson had appeared in the *San Francisco Chronicle*'s Sunday section *This World*. Robert Treuhaft and his partner Bert Edises (B and B, in this letter) represented Newson throughout the years of conviction and appeals.

summer. Actually, Nancy still rather dislikes her I think, but then she had an awfully big dose of her—up to age 30, when she married P. Rodd—in Muv's militantly horrid days. Also Muv once gave Nancy a dressing-down for being an old maid (shortly before she married Rodd) which I think absolutely soured Nancy on her for good.[72] The change is that now she is a really staunch and devoted mother to us. I don't think she will live much longer, at least that seemed to be the opinion of the Dr. I talked to in London, and it seemed fairer to portray her as she is now, improved, since improving at any time of life is such a struggle, don't you think? Besides having mellowed a bit myself, as you point out.

You must be having a time of it in Montgomery, we are following events there with terrific interest. How I would love to come and see you some time this year. . . .

I'm still in somewhat of a stew, as publication in England is so soon—March 21st—and I'm living in terror of the reviews. Awful how self-centered one can become at times like these. Do remember to order it at your library, that's the greatest help of all according to my librarian friends—then, since you've read it, you won't have to bother taking it out, but they'll have to get it. . . .

Fondest love, and many, many thanks for your letter, Decca

To Nancy Mitford   Oakland
                                                        March 28, 1960

Susan,

For some reason I longed for, but feared, your reaction more than anyone's, even the reviewers. So I was most <u>awfully</u> glad to get your letter, although you <u>might</u> have sent it non-U mail for once. I am enclosing some slightly worn postal coupons which can be exchanged for airmail stamps of any country, so do use them in future.

Sorry about the cold wind to the heart, I didn't really mean it to come out like that.[73] . . .

The reviews have been sent on v. promptly, and I have been v. pleased. Did you note the Graph?[74] March 25th, best so far I thought.

---

72. Reports of this highly charged incident made a great impression on Decca, who discussed its provenance with her sister more than a decade later. See letter to Nancy Mitford of October 13, 1971, along with the associated footnotes.

73. In her letter, Nancy Mitford said the book was "<u>awfully good</u>—easy to read & very funny in parts," but she also mentioned "a slightly cold wind to the heart perhaps," in that Decca didn't seem in her book to be "very fond of anybody," which she attributed to a need to make her family life "seem horrible, to explain why you ran away from it."

74. As Decca explained many years later, she and her sister Nancy "were traveling somewhere—Channel steamer? and I picked up the D. Telegraph & said 'I must just note the graph.' For some reason N. thought that v. funny so it was used forever—as, for example, 'I long to note your graph' meant 'I long to see you.' " In this case, of course, the reference is literal: the *Daily Telegraph*.

Benjy as usual is being a hopeless tease, and when called on to read the reviews insists on reading the cooking hints and Letters to Editor etc. on the other side.

No Susan, Esmond was not a pioneer Teddy Boy.[75]

If you should chance to note any other reviews of me book, such as the Widow or any of the Relations, do not fail to let me know, using the Postal Coupons. Do you realize your letter was posted on 12th March and only just arrived today? But you have to take the Coupons to the P.O., they won't work if just stuck on. . . .

> Lots of love, and do write sometimes, Susan

To Lady Redesdale   Oakland
                                                                April 2, 1960

Darling Muv,

. . . I'm so glad you thought the book funny. I do wonder what Debo thought of it? I sent her a copy, but expect she has been much too busy to write.[76]

Sorry about the bit about H's car.[77] It really was a misunderstanding: you had written in the margin, "not H's car," so I took out that <u>he</u> had lent it; but somehow it had stuck in my mind that someone had lent a car (the gov't, or tourist bureau, or something). Probably it was in some newspaper story and that's how I got hold of it. But I did try to make all the other corrections you suggested. . . .

I heard from Nancy that she thought it good. However, she couldn't let it go without the usual "barb"—"Esmond was the original Teddy Boy, wasn't he?" Just as you always say about her, a small knife concealed somewhere in each letter. But I was very pleased with the rest of her letter.[78] Do let me know any other reactions you run into, the Wid, any Relations, etc. . . .

> Lots of love, Decca

---

75. The Teddy Boys were young English hoods—juvenile delinquents, as Nancy Mitford wrote in another letter—who got the nickname because they affected Edwardian (Teddy) attire.

76. In an earlier letter to her daughter, Decca explained the fact that neither her mother nor her sister Deborah had written since the publication date by saying, "I'm afraid they are cross about the Duking although I cut out most of it." See also the letter of June 10, 1959, to Marge Frantz and associated footnote 57.

77. The reference is to a visit to Nazi Germany by Lord and Lady Redesdale. Decca wrote in her book that "they were lent a chauffeur-driven Mercedes-Benz and shown all the gaudy trappings of the new regime, and they returned full of praise for what they had seen."

78. Nancy Mitford's own letter to their mother about *Hons and Rebels* was far more critical than the letter she sent to Decca. Although complimentary about some aspects, she told Lady Redesdale that it was not an "honest book" and was often contradictory, and she suggested that Decca was incapable of feeling affection for anyone except her husband and children.

To Lady Redesdale   Oakland
                                                    April 21, 1960

Darling Muv,

I just got your letter of April 13, it did take a long time, must be the storm.
All sounds blissful at the Isle, in spite of cold! . . .

I've been getting absolutely swamped with masses of reviews, forwarded by
my agent. . . . Most seem to say that you emerge from the book "charming and
eccentric," a far cry from "dull and arrogant"! I'm not sure how many to an edition. As to the royalties, they are 10% for the first 2,500, then 12 1/2%, then
15% and so on. As I am hopeless at working out percents, specially in L.S.D.,[79]
I have no idea what it will amount to. . . .

Once more, Bob roared about your comments on the typewriter.[80] He
thinks I am just like you about these things. Once my car door began giving
trouble (opening and shutting of) and I suggested giving it a complete rest for a
few weeks to see if it wouldn't get all right. Sure enough, it did.
                                    Much love, Decca

To Constancia Romilly   Oakland
                                                    April 21, 1960

Darling Dinkydonk,

. . . Any news fit for our ears about your academic standing? . . .

Don't worry too much about the expense of summer plans as I feel I shall be
quite rich soon—not a penny yet though have I received from Gollancz. . . .

Dear you should <u>see</u> the reviews. They arrive by the barrel load by every
post, and with about 2 exceptions are amazingly favorable. Also, 4th on the best
seller list! Bob got me a lovely scrapbook which I shall prepare and bring to NY,
and make you sit down and study all the reviews. That silly Diana wrote to the
Times Lit. Sup. attacking the book,[81] Bob thinks 'twill up the sales by 500 to
1,000. . . . Nancy liked it v. much, which was a great relief. No word from Debo
or Pam so I guess they loathe. . . .
                                    Fondest love, Mother

ps. Here's an idea for me to do next fall: Go to Alabama and other points South
for a month or two or three. Via Virginia and other liberals meet the Negro

---

79. Pounds, shillings, and pence.

80. When Lady Redesdale's palsy worsened, the Treuhafts bought her a portable typewriter.
Decca later wrote that "to my amazement, she was quite good at typing, remembering it from age
14 when Grandfather caused her to type all his speeches for H. of Commons. So then hers went on
blink. Eventually she wrote from Inch K. to say 'In the lovely clean air of Scotland, my dear little
typewriter is working perfectly.' Which gave me the idea of turning Inch K. into a rest home for
broken-down typewriters."

81. In a letter to the publication, Diana Mosley called Decca's portraits of their parents
"grotesque."

leaders and white progressives. Via me publisher, meet the white women's club elements and old south aristocracy. Do a book, loosely woven character sketches, no great emphasis on The Struggle as that's been done so much before by much more able and equipped writers. Make it mostly funny, the moral to emerge by inference. What think you? Lucy's wedding[82] and all could be in, too. Also, meeting Faulkner during the Willie McGee case. Don't you think it might be fairly blithering, as Benj would say?

To Lady Redesdale   Oakland
                                                              April 27, 1960

Darling Muv,

I just got your letter of 21 April, and note that you probably are not getting mine—must be the storms, but they'll probably be delivered eventually. . . .

The Times Lit Sup is the absolute exception in thinking the life depicted "dull and arid" etc. . . . It seems to depend entirely on the individual reader, as I have noted before with reviews of other books. I just got a letter from Abe Glasser, one of our very best friends (he and Bob had digs together in Washington) and he says, "I did not know you had so much warmth for your English family." . . .

Of course now it's all in print I can see masses of places where it could have been much improved, but you have no idea how difficult it is writing a book, and in a way, how muddling. When I first started I did about 20 pages a day, hoping to finish all in 6 or 8 weeks; then I threw away all that part and did it all over again about 3 times, it took two years or more. By the end, it got slower and slower going. I wonder if Nancy finds the same thing, probably not by now as she has done so many.

Two or three of the reviews think as you do that the beginning is the most interesting; on the other hand, Ld. Birkenhead and a few others liked the American part. Hard to tell. . . .

Love from Decca

To Katharine Graham   Oakland
                                                              May 13, 1960

Dear Kay,

Thanks so much for your letter. I am so glad you liked the book. As you can imagine there's something a bit unnerving about writing about living people, and then wondering what their reaction will be.[83] . . .

---

82. See letters of May 2, 1957, to Nancy Mitford and June 19, 1957, to Marge Frantz.

83. Decca had mailed her memoir to friends and relatives mentioned in it. This exchange with Katharine Graham appears to have marked the active resumption of their friendship after almost

I long to know just when you are coming to Calif? And why for only 2 days? Such a long way, do plan to stay a bit longer. . . . I would so love to see you, and all your millions of children whose pictures I saw in Time, ages ago.[84]

Thanks again, ever so much, for writing and for liking the book and for all you said about it.

Love from Decca

To Constancia Romilly   Oakland
                                                                    September 17, 1960

Darling Chickadee,

Marvellous dividend this morning. Mail came, naught of interest; 2 hours later, there mysteriously was yr. lovely and v. interesting letter! Goodness I was pleased, hasten to answer. . . .

I have been having a screamingly funny time with book doings (no word from Harper's yet, incidentally).[85] First, a week or so ago I was on a 1/2 hour program (TV). It was easily the most intelligently handled, I think the interviewer could actually read, and he seemed to have read D. and R., more than I can say for most. So he asked things like "what have you been doing with your life in Oakland," and I told all about the Jerry Newson case and how he was framed by the District Atty. and Oakland police; also got in a crack about the FBI. I said "I led three lives" would have been a good title for my book, only unfortunately it had been used by the FBI and of course I wouldn't have anything to do with them as I despise them, or words to that effect. . . .

Well anyway, next morn, at crack of dawn, I was due at the Amer. Assn. of University Women (lined up ages ago by Pauline Miller).[86] When I tell you that Pauline and I were easily the youngest people there, by a good 15 years, you'll get a picture of the set-up. So a lady came up saying "I am Mrs. Pflaum, chairman of the Current Books Committee, and I'm the one responsible for this program. My dear! Our whole family heard you on TV last night; you can imagine the effect it had. Of course, you know my background." Fascinated, I asked: "No—what is it? Do tell." "Law enforcement, my dear," she answered. I asked what branch of law enforcement—it turns out she is the wife of the Chief of Police of Piedmont![87] So this time I decided to really let them have it, talked a lot about the Newson case, named Coakley by name as framer-upper etc.

---

eighteen years, since Decca moved to San Francisco from Washington. In the ensuing decades, they corresponded and visited frequently.

84. Decca caught up with the Grahams a month later in New York. She commented that their seventeen-year-old daughter was "an exact replica of Kay at that age, a bit eerie, like seeing a movie where the same actress does mother & daughter."

85. Decca had been commissioned by *Harper's* magazine to write an article on the student movement.

86. A friend of the Treuhafts.

87. A rich, tree-shaded residential city perched on the hillside above its larger and poorer neighbor, Oakland.

Such is the magic effect of the written word, or being an Author with capital A, it went over extremely well. Masses of the Ladies came round afterwards to say what a marvelous and instructive talk it had been, and they bought loads of books, which I autographed.

Then was lunch. Luckily I was sitting next to Mrs. Pflaum. She said she and her husband know the Coakleys well, are old friends; I answered that we also know them well, and are old enemies. I said, "do ask them about us when you see them—you'll get an earful!" Mrs. Pflaum really seemed v. nice, in spite of Law Enforcement; so I told her all about how we sold a house on Coakley's block to Negroes and how Coakley moved out the next week.[88] Pressing home my advantage, I added, "Doesn't it seem extraordinary to you that the District Atty. of a huge county, who is sworn to uphold the rights of all the people, is so prejudiced that he can't bear to live in the same block with a Negro?" She said, "But my dear, don't you think it's more Kitty's side of the family than Frank's?" I explained that we are hardly on Kitty and Frank terms with them. Anyway, it all went over beautifully. This morning I got a rave letter from Mrs. Pflaum, how much they loved the speech etc. (Actually it was lots more than I've told— a regular book talk sort of thing, problems of writing etc.—the Newson part just chunked in for good measure.) . . .

Dearest old Donk, you are so nice to be a good writer. Do write again soon. . . . Lots and lots of love from all of us,

Dec

To Virginia Durr   Oakland
                                                                                    October 6, 1960

Dearest Va,

. . . We're moving. For some time we've been realizing that now the children are growing up, we need more space. After the termite thing, we found another, terrifically nice and much larger house, close to this neighborhood. The real estate person is a friend of Bob's, and has been scouting possible houses for us; found out that the seller, a certain Mr. Barros, was planning to move eventually. The house wasn't on the market, so we were the only prospects. We went around, liked the house very much, and Mr. B. was there— said significantly (I thought) "What's the name? Treuhaft? How do you spell it?" I mentioned to the real estate lady that I betted he was thinking we were

88. Decca had unwittingly tweaked the Treuhafts' nemesis when she fronted for a black couple trying to purchase a home in an exclusive, all-white Oakland neighborhood, an activity in which she engaged fairly frequently in those days of homeowner-enforced residential segregation. During the interview with the seller, she was informed, to her (suppressed) glee, that District Attorney Coakley lived across the street. When the sale was consummated, Coakley put his own house on the market at an abnormally low price, confiding to an acquaintance of the Treuhafts—as Decca reported in *A Fine Old Conflict*—"That pinko Treuhaft outsmarted me this time."

fronting for Negro buyers; she pooh-poohed the idea, said I was reading things into his questions. Since she is married to a Negro, I assumed for the moment that she would be normally more sensitive about such things than I. How wrong I (and she) were.

Next thing, wanting to avoid another hopeless termite situation, we went back, this time accompanied by an architect to tell us what condition the house was in. He did, said exceptionally good, so we put down an offer. The offer was accepted, with a number of annoying provisos: one, that we couldn't get occupancy till next June (because the seller, Mr. Barros, figured it would take him that long to find the lot of his choice and build), two, that he wouldn't sign the accepted offer until Oct. 15—for the same reason as #1. Are you with me? Because all these boring preliminaries are necessary in order to understand subsequent developments.

Forgot to say, Mr. Barros also asked significantly for the name of the architect. I at this point mentioned to the Real Estate lady that I was sure he feared we were fronting for Negro buyers; and that perhaps we should line up some exceptionally white people to front for us. Again, she pooh-poohed.

So, the legal status is now that described above. No real contract, all depends on what HE decides (Mr. Barros) as of Oct. 15.

Then the architect calls us. Says Mr. Barros has called him, to ask whether in his opinion we are really planning to occupy the house, or to turn around and sell to Negroes. Bob and I flipped—over-reacted, possibly, we were damned annoyed at the whole way this thing had been developing. So we called the Real Estate lady, and told her the whole deal was off. Almost 5 minutes later, Barros called the real estate lady to say he wanted now to close the deal, as he had found the lot he wanted, was counting on the cash from sale of his house to buy it. So he was told the sad news; that his behaviour had made it impossible for us to buy the house at all. Next thing, he called Bob (with the explanation that he didn't want to cause a "situation" in the neighborhood). Bob gave him a terrific tongue lashing, said he couldn't do business with such as Barros, couldn't let him occupy OUR house until June as he would contaminate it, by his presence. Barros called back, asked "under what conditions WOULD you complete the purchase of the house?" Bob answered, only if you get out right away. So Barros is getting out right away, and we are getting the house. There was quite a bit more to it; but the main (corny) point that we drove home to Barros, is that Crime Does Not Pay. Because now he's going to have to rent a house for his family, fearful expense, between now and June.

Eventually, after the whole thing was legally a water-tight contract, we went round to give Barros hell. Turned out to be one of those rather awful, seemingly innocuous types, who "only wants not to cause troubles and rows." Catholic. Five small daughters who he wouldn't want to marry a etc. etc. So we told him he is a bad Catholic, and a few other things; he almost seemed to agree. So we are moving in, shortly.

It's a lovely house, much nicer than any heretofore. Special little room for my writing things, so they won't overflow the living room, and v. nice living room, dining room, kitchen etc. Also, masses of rooms, and a huge attic. . . .

Dreading the move, that is all the packing etc. But longing to be in the new house.[89]

Fondest love, Decca

To Constancia Romilly   Oakland
                                                                 December 1, 1960

Darling Dinkdonk.

I can't understand why you never write. Are you OK? Please, please let us know. . . .

Here, we are very much occupied with the new house. Various crises: the sale of this house fell through (because the buyer was laid off from her civil service job) and fell back non-through again (because she got the job back) thank goodness. . . . I am heard these days saying quite naturally things like "water-soluble paint" and "vinyl is more durable than linoleum." . . .

I was at the PTA board meeting today, oh dear. To liven things up a bit, I suggested—or rather, made a motion—that we should send a letter of support and encouragement to the 2 white people in New Orleans sending their kids to the Frantz school.[90] I brought the front page of Chronicle with picture of screaming mobs etc. So, usual thing; absolutely no soap because "the district" would have to approve. I changed my motion to direct the suggestion to the district; failed for lack of second. Enough to feed one up, don't you think? . . .

Your loving Mother

---

89. The Treuhafts were to remain in their new house for the rest of their lives. The house was in Oakland, near the Berkeley border, on Regent Street, provoking Nancy Mitford to ask Decca, "Who was the Regent of Oakland?"

90. In mid-November, a six-year-old black girl named Ruby Bridges was ushered by her mother and federal marshals through a jeering white mob into previously all-white William Frantz School. A few white parents braved personal threats and a White Citizens' Council boycott to send their children to this and another newly integrated New Orleans school, but Ruby was the only child in her "class" during that first year. Mobs of whites attacked city and school offices. Ruby Bridges's story was later recounted in a number of books, including her own, *Through My Eyes* (Scholastic, 1999), Robert Coles's *The Story of Ruby Bridges* (Scholastic, 1995), and John Steinbeck's *Travels with Charley* (William Heinemann, 1962). It was also the subject of a famous Norman Rockwell painting and a TV movie.

To Constancia Romilly   Oakland
                                                                February 1, 1961

My Darling Dinkdonk,

I've been terribly remiss about writing, and am awfully sorry. . . . I <u>think</u> I dimly see the light on the direction of the bloody article; but never have I had such trouble with anything. . . .

I was on a TV program the other day, called What Kind of Funeral For You? On Profile Bay Area.[91] It was great fun. There were two gloomy ghouls from the Funeral industry, a great mound of blubber called Mr. Brown who is a funeral director and (get this) the dean of the local embalming college! On our side, Rev. Bartlett (Unitarian type)[92] and me. I think we won. Pele came along to put on me eyes (eyebrow pencil, eye shadow etc) and Benj came. I asked him which was prettiest, me or Mr. Brown, and he gave the right answer for a change. I flashed pix from Mortuary Management, and read bits from same on some of the gorier practices. There was a full-scale write-up in O'Flaherty's column.[93] . . .

                                Fondest love and lots of kisses, Decca

To Constancia Romilly   Oakland
                                                                February 4, 1961

Darling Dinkdonk,

More mental telepathy—yr. letter and postcard crossed mine. Your letter was simply marvellous, v. interesting. . . . My impression in these parts is that the students are about now coming up with a bang against forces they hardly knew existed, let alone knew the strength of—FBI etc.[94] How they'll react is an interesting question. The thing that's now under hot discussion is, should they issue a non-Communist disclaimer? Arguments for: they <u>are</u> non-Communist,

---

91. The moderator of the weekly public TV program was lawyer and Republican politician Caspar Weinberger, who later did stints as chairman of the Federal Trade Commission, secretary of Health, Education and Welfare, and secretary of defense.

92. Dr. Josiah Bartlett, one of the founders of the Bay Area Funeral Society, was an ally of Decca's in the campaign against what he called "the Pagan atmosphere of the modern funeral . . . the morbid sentimentality of dwelling on the physical remains."

93. Terrence O'Flaherty was the *San Francisco Chronicle*'s television columnist.

94. A University of California student organization called SLATE was active at the time on issues such as free speech (fighting the university's so-called "speaker ban"), racial restrictions in fraternities and sororities, and compulsory ROTC, as well as such off-campus issues as nuclear disarmament, affordable housing, and the death penalty. In May of the previous year, hundreds of students organized by SLATE and others had been washed down the steps of San Francisco's City Hall with fire hoses during a protest against hearings of the House Un-American Activities Committee, which had subpoenaed a UC student, among others. Much of the student radical movement of the '60s can be traced to SLATE. It spawned organizations across the country, including Berkeley's celebrated Free Speech Movement in 1964. Decca had met with SLATE leaders and attended some of their protest meetings.

they disagree with CP tactics and the way it is organized etc. Arguments against: it will weaken the free-speech fight by unnecessarily capitulating to pressure. (Needless to say, I'm for the latter position.) . . .

Goodbye dear. Must get back to my morne[95] work. I shall be giving you a hit with the telephone as the Fr. say on yr. birthday, so be there; I'll keep trying till I reach you. Be thinking of something to say, and so will I. ("How are you dear?" "Fine." "How's the weather?" "Freezing." That sort of thing.)

Your loving Decca

To Constancia Romilly   Oakland
                                                February 10, 1961

Darling Dinkdonk,

It was lovely chatting with you. Didn't you think I did a bit better this time? I was most delighted to hear of the good work you're doing, and you did sound all cheerful and Donklike. I'm a bit more cheerful, too, as me article is ploughing out of the doldrums. . . .

Dear I got a letter from my mother enclosing a huge bill for repairs to the Isle (jetty etc). It says in part, "Laying concrete floor. Forming steps to laundry. Picking and pointing at Piggery." Are you roaring? I think I'll write back and say I'm not sure I want my piggery picked and pointed at. . . .

A Satevepost man[96] is in town, he's going to do an article on Bob's funeral thing—based on my TV program! Sort of odd Mitford pursuits or some such. We've had a couple of meetings with him, and he got an OK from the Post to go ahead. As a result of the program, and O'Flaherty's columns (he did two, the one I sent you and another) the funeral co-op is simply booming, they got 93 letters in one day, are averaging about 80 a day, and masses of new memberships. Bob's delighted. I'm longing to see if Mortuary Management comes out with some blasts—oh dear do you think we've driven them underground? . . .

Well dear I must dash along. Do write dear. Are you a little bit older?[97]

Your loving Mother

To Robert Treuhaft   New York
                                                April 25, 1961

Darling old Bob,

. . . Yesterday, went with Edith to get a pair of comfortable Beck shoes. Cab driver, on being asked to go to a shoe shop, immediately volunteered fact that his wife wears size 9 1/2A, and his 14-year old daughter size 9. His wife is 5'8",   .

95. French word for "dreary."
96. *Saturday Evening Post* reporter Roul Tunley.
97. This letter was written a day after Constancia Romilly's birthday.

and the 14-year old is 5'6". Since it was only a few blocks drive, that's about all he had time for—but you must admit, not everywhere would one be able to get such information thrown in with 45¢ cab fare. I think they see me coming.

Aranka seems fine. Had break. with her Sunday, am checking into the shop daily between appointments. Told them all the ash-scattering bit, Mr. R——'s ashes and the odd procession to Sacramento, and they all absolutely split sides. I mean absolute gales of laughter rang. Aranka says if we put her through the coffee grinder she will haunt us through eternity.[98] . . .

One would have to practically dictate into a tape recorder to keep up with pace of things, letters hardly do it. . . .

Had lunch with Candida[99] and Harold Hayes, feature ed. of Esquire. Status is now as follows: Lovell Thompson[100] wrote a charming, amusing, flattering letter to Candida, the actual upshot of which is that he does not think much of the idea of the book, just as he told me. According to C., she has spoken to some other publishers who think it is a dandy idea. This doesn't worry me anyway, as I don't blame Lovell, one will only be able to tell whether or not [his judgment is] valid after the trip and after some writing has been done. However, Mr. Hays (young, 3 years out of Harvard, a North Carolinian) is mad for the idea, thanks mainly to YOU—the thing that hooked him was your phrase, U-All and Non-U-All. So, he wants about a 20 page article, to be done as soon as I get home!! He's getting some intros. together for me. Spoke to Dave Scherman[101] today, trying to arrange dinner with them tonight . . . and HE was mad about the book idea—and wants to do a pic. story in Life based on it. If either one of these possibilities come off, 'twill pay for the trip at least. NY is so extraorder. . . .

Today's cab driver had a nail clear into his foot, was laid up quite a while and is just back to work. You can't be too careful about these things as they are apt to turn very, very nasty, and if it weren't for the new drugs, where might he be today? . . .

<hr/>

98. This is an allusion to an incident Decca mentioned in *The American Way of Death*. California law at the time effectively outlawed the scattering or private burial of ashes after cremation, and Robert Treuhaft was lobbying for a bill to overturn the restrictions. In her book, Decca described the cemeteries' campaign, based on fear and misinformation, which ultimately led to the bill's defeat. In the course of the campaign, proponents of the "scattering" bill brought a box of cremated remains and a coffee grinder to a legislative hearing to grind up body parts that the bill's opponents maintained were still present after remains had been cremated. The box was opened to reveal that there were no body parts left for the coffee grinder. (As Decca did in her book, the editor has removed the name of the deceased to protect his identity.)

99. Candida Donadio was Decca's American literary agent at the time.

100. Thompson was the Houghton Mifflin vice president who happened to be in London when *Hons and Rebels* was being peddled there and bought it immediately. (See April 26, 1959, letter to Robert Treuhaft.)

101. A friend of Decca's from her earliest days in the United States. He was a writer and photographer for *Life* magazine who had been assigned to do a story on the newly arrived Decca and Esmond Romilly.

Wednesday: Having lunch later with the Lifeslady re. the $500 article.[102] I'm really scared about that article, have very few ideas for it; but obviously must have a crack at it. They tell me contract is in mail. Ask Marge if she can think of any bright and jolly incidents for it. Also if she can think of any jokes about Yellowstone Park and/or the Grand Canyon as they are going to make me do those, too, and of course I've never even been to either place. . . .

Goodbye darling, keep writing. Fondest love to you and Benj,

Dec

To Robert Treuhaft   New York
                                                                April 28, 1961

Darling old Bob,

Just taking out a few minutes from writing my article for Overseas Life Mag. to send you the following article about writing an article for Overseas Life Mag.[103]

I never did give you all details on how it came about. Pat McManus[104] arranged a dinner with "our little gang" at H-M. Met said little gang. . . . With them, downing martinis at a great rate, was somebody called Iola Haverstick— just tagging along for a drink, about to take off. Everyone said do stay for dinner, so she did. Due to martinis, and perhaps personality, she gave me a good deal of gratuitous advice about me South book; it mainly consisted of repeating at regular intervals, "Have <u>fun</u> with it. I mean, have <u>great fun</u> with it." Pat at one point happened to mention our last year's drive across country, dinner at Detroit, etc., which convulsed Iola. That was about all for that, because after dinner we dispersed; till next day, the call about the article, which you know about.

Day before yesterday, had lunch with Iola to discuss article. She wasn't too specific, but did say I should have fun with it. This, I rather unhappily agreed to try to do. Her job is Research Lade[105] for the whole U.S. Tourismo issue they are doing, so she promised to send me some interesting stuff that might be useful: I suggested ads. about motels, specific info. about the Howard Johnson chain, possibly, if she could get it, a glossary of English/U.S. automobile language (which I once saw, issued by an auto club). . . .

This morning, very early (six-ish) was awakened by special del. letter. Proved to be me research material from Iola, consisting of 1 (one) Esso road

---

102. Decca had been commissioned by *Life* for a "quickie" article on a four-day drive the previous year across the United States. (She vowed to shorten the road trip the next time by starting three hours earlier . . . to beat the time change.) For details, see next letter.

103. In a previous letter to her husband about her *Life* travel article, Decca wrote, "I could do a much funnier article about writing an article for LIFE."

104. Houghton Mifflin's "long-suffering . . . publicity lady," as Decca described her.

105. At *Life* magazine.

map of the U.S., and a letter which said in part: "Be sure and let go and have as much fun with it as you can."

Decided to do a bit of research on me own. Called Howard Johnson's NY office (feeling rather grand) and said, "I'm doing an article for LIFE Overseas Edition" (by the way, I still don't know if that's the right name for it, or if it's Foreign Edition or Continental Edition—I had asked Iola, but she wasn't sure either) "and would so much like to bring in the Howard Johnson restaurants." I then outlined certain things I'd like: Menu, how many H-J's there are, when built, a list of all the facilities they offer, etc. etc. Memory refreshers, so I won't say "Jumbo New Orleans Shrimps" when it should be "Extra Sweet Double Fried Jumbo New Orleans Shrimps." The lady there said they don't give out any such information from the New York office and that I should contact their publicity director in Boston. His name is Mr. Robert Parks. I was pretty amazed, but called Mr. P anyway, as all on me new-found LIFE account. He wasn't there, but Miss Solomon was. Outlined to her the same request, giving same credentials. She rather unresponsively responded, "When will this story appear?" I said I had no idea; why did she want to know? She answered (honestly, I am not kidding) "For reasons that cannot be disclosed." Trying to get back on even keel, I reiterated that all I was asking for was a menu and a couple of things I could easily get by just getting them, but I didn't have time to be dashing off on freeways to out-of-town Howard Johnson's. She said she would call me back after consulting Mr. Robert Parks, but that meanwhile, I should find out date the story would appear.

I settled down to other aspects of the article, and a few hours later Miss Solomon called back. Her first words: "Did you find out what date the article will appear?" I said coldly, "No. It will probably never appear. How about my menu?" She softened up a bit at that point and said, "Well the real fact is, we can't give out any publicity material whatsoever for any article that might appear before June 1st, because Howard Johnson's is going on the stock market on that date." Utter confusion. I said, "But—I thought I was talking to the Howard Johnson's that's a chain of restaurants. What could that have to do with the stock market?" She said something about stock now privately owned, some shares about to be released—I didn't really get it. I asked if the restaurants were being auctioned, but apparently not. So, since I hadn't found out the date the article would appear, by mutual consent we rang off. . . .

Later, Iola called me back. I didn't want her to think I was having too much fun, for fear they'd cut my wages, so merely told her I had been unable to secure Howard Johnson menu. She said, "Oh there's a Howard Johnson's right across the street. I'll send one of our messengers for it, and he'll bring it right up to you." At dinner time, messenger arrived—with menu from Howard Johnson's, but the wrong one. Not a word about the clam rolls etc—different set-up entirely. Iola sent covering note saying, "This isn't much help, I know. It comes from the store across the street. However, I have been in touch with a man in Wollaston, Mass., and hope that I can get some or all of the things you want sent to you. Will call Monday. Best, Iola. ps. I think they are the supidest bunch I have ever dealt with." Supidest spelt as I gave it. I have all the originals of these, old Bob, and am filing them for yr. edification. Only wish I had transcript of phone calls.

Have fun, Decca

To Robert Treuhaft   New York
                                                                 May 1, 1961

Darling Bob,

I worked hard, and miserably, all weekend, since last in touch. . . . The rudiments of an East Coast committee formed by magic. By Monday morning, it did look much better. Took me hours to type it all neatly, then, by 12:30 I was down at Life, and tremblingly gave it to Miss Saint. She said they would call me back by 3. Went over and had lunch with Aranka, got home a little before 3. By 3:05 I could almost hear them (the Life editors) talking over how to break the news that it was n.g.[106] They didn't actually call till 3:10; then 'twas glorious Mr. Whipple, saying they loved it. Would I have any objections to very minor word changes here and there? And if they left out the bit about long-distance telephoning? (I knew they would but Dave S.[107] made me put it in, including Checkbookunderseat.) Mr. W. loved the telephoning bit and kept asking just how it's done, but for policy reasons. . . .[108]

May 2nd. So the situation is as follows: $500 from Life, $200 from Esquire against a $600 fee if they accept the You-All and Non-You-All. NY trip thoroughly worth it, don't you agree? I'll send you me copy of the Life article (me

---

106. No good.

107. Dave Scherman, Decca's friend at *Life*, whose family had joined Decca in New York and helped edit the manuscript of her article.

108. Decca's paragraph about using their ploy while traveling to evade person-to-person telephone charges was included in the published version, both in *Life International* and in the domestic edition when the article was republished in August. But there were repercussions, which Decca described years later in her anthology *Poison Penmanship*. She wrote that she never expected *Life*, in her first article for a major commercial magazine, to run the paragraph about tricking the telephone company because "surely these giant corporations stick together against the slingshots of us little Davids." She wrote that after publication of the article, her friend Dave Scherman described the predictable reaction at *Life* when the phone company, "fit to be tied . . . called all the brass at Life on the carpet and ordered them to show cause why the phone company should pour millions of dollars into advertising in Life only to be knifed in the back like this." According to Decca, Scherman reported that the phone company was told "we fired Murphy" (the "fictitious editor who is always fired whenever some high-up in politics or business complains of being maligned in an article"). In addition, Scherman told her, *Life* smoothed the company's ruffled feathers by arranging to produce "a special eight-page color spread on the company's contribution to the space program."

only copy, so don't throw away) and you can see it's all pretty obvious stuff, rather amazing that it should be worth almost $100 a page. Such is Life. An undetermined amount from beastly old Harper's.[109]

Tonight having dinner at the Selsams. They seem to be about the only married people I know here. Honestly the amount of divorce in NY is phenomenal. . . . You're not to ditch me, old Bob, ever, even if I do go off on occasional trips. I do wish I was coming right home and hadn't set myself this lengthy task; the only good thing to be said for it is that the time will pass, and in 6 weeks or so I'll be home; and that I do think something good will come of it, writing-wise. Just my experience with the Life thing has shown me how important it is to be doing something with a view to writing, keeping pertinent notes of all etc. I kept thinking I'd have given anything to have some sort of trip diary of last year's motor tour. I shall be working really hard in the South keeping up daily writing while all is fresh in mind. It may even be that this will prove the best form for the book; a journal, like Boswell and Johnson's. . . .

I miss you terrifically, goodness I did wish you were there while I was slaving over the Life piece, I know you would have improved it no end.

Very, very much love, Decca

To Robert Treuhaft   Washington
                                                          May 5, 1961

Darling old Bob,

. . . [Today I went] to Kay's. She's got TB, and is laid up resting. Phil was there for a short time (looked a lot iller than Kay, but I gathered mainly from hangover) and he said someone had sent him me Chron. article on book censorship. He was rather amazed that the Chron. would publish it—I gathered he wouldn't have. There's more than a little feeling of fraternizing with the enemy, going chez Graham, as great bitterness against them in the ranks of the reporters (some of whom I've met   ) Seems old Phil has got extremely exploitative in his old age. Even Kay admits he's going in madly for Tycoonsmanship, now says he must have a private plane etc.

Last evening, was summoned for dinner to Mrs. Meyer's.[110] All there unchanged, same startlingly huge house, even the cigar box from which Esmond stole in plain sight in its usual place. It was just the 2 of us. Mrs. M. was having scotch . . . and I asked for bourbon. Was brought an immense tumbler full of it. Believe it or not, even I couldn't finish it, it was so sad, I was longing to ask that it be wrapped up for me to take home to the dog. Sorry old Bob but I must just tell you what we had for dinner: crown roast of lamb, my absolutely

---

109. Evidently a "kill fee" for her article on the student movement, which had been rejected by the magazine.

110. Katharine Graham's mother.

favorite thing for just the 2 of us! And the familiar thing, ringing down thru the years, of "you must have some more asparagus darling, it's from our farm you know." Used to make Kay and me roar because they always said it, every meal— "from the farm, you know." Other sample bits of Mrs. Meyer conversation: "I love travel, and generally take a yacht for the summer. This year I'm going to do the Norwegian fjords." . . . "This place is getting to be a regular slum, all the embassies have moved out and there's nothing but Puerto Ricans and Negroes here now." "I'm so glad you are going to write about the South, we of course are doing what we can to bring about integration." "Kay's children couldn't possibly go to the public schools here, my dear do you realize they are 90% Negro now?" . . .

Am awaiting Satevepost photog. who tracked me down here.

Goodbye darling, <u>do write</u>.

Love from Decca

To Robert Treuhaft   Louisville
                                                                   May 13, 1961

Darling old Bob,

Leaving here tomorrow. I've had a relatively successful time, and have met various ones; the Testing Committee[111] people, some sit-in students, some country clubbers.[112] Had two goes at the latter, because when it developed (late in the evening) that I was going to the testing the following day, they insisted on taking me out to lunch to hear all.

The country clubbers were Mr. and Mrs. Jack Doyle (advt. agency) and Mr. and Mrs. Byron ? Needless to say, I neglected to note their last name. All middle-aged folks, business people with fairly wide connections. . . .

The conversation turned, as they say, to books, in honor of me I think. Mr. Byron said he hadn't read my book because he is a slow reader, and consequently does not read any book unless it has been condensed for the Readers Digest. Mrs. Byron, on the other hand, jerst lerves to read, will go through as many as 3 or 4 books a week. Later, of course, the conversation turned to integration. Mr. B. is against it (although thinks it inevitable) because it will lead to the mongrelization of both races. Like most people in these parts, he knows a great deal about horse racing and breeding, and he drew rather at

---

111. People organized to go out in groups to assure integration compliance at lunch counters and restaurants—that is, to make certain they really were serving blacks.

112. In her published article on the Southern trip, Decca wrote that being invited to country clubs "was, for me, a little like being shown around a steel factory behind the Iron Curtain; never having seen the inside of one at home, I had no basis for comparison. Nevertheless, a certain amount of Southern life revolves around these country clubs, and I thought it would be a good thing to have a look."

length on the parallel about breeding race horses and cart horses and the sad results of same. I asked him whether, in that case, he didn't think it a bit inadvisable to breed slow readers with fast readers, a point that hadn't occurred to him.

We went on to other matters, notably the Bradens.[113] I learned[114] that Carl Braden is a convicted Communist, that he and Anne Braden separated shortly after the Wade house episode, that Mr. Doyle has "access to documents" proving the B's are spies and traitors. None of them had read Anne's book, but all promised to—except Mr. Byron, who is presumably waiting for it to be condensed by Readers Digest. I didn't let on that I knew the Bradens, said I intended to go and see Anne later.

Next day, at lunch, (Pendennis Club this time, v. fancy place in town) all was much soberer. Of the party were Mr. Doyle, Mrs. Byron and me, the others being unable to make it. They questioned me at length about the Testing (from which I had just come) with the sort of gentle care one might use in discussing a schizophrenic's illusions with him: "so you saw the little men coming out of the flying saucer. What did they look like? What did they say to you?" . . .

Everyone keeps saying this is a border city and not typical of the South, which one can readily see is true. For instance, this hotel has been desegregated for years, both as to rooms and dining room, and there is no staring or scowling at Negroes who eat here. Also, no problems about driving with them, or having them over socially. The Country Clubbers' attitudes could, I'm sure, be found as easily in similar circles in Calif. Likewise, complaints of the students who attend integrated high schools that there is in fact complete separation of the races, remind one of Tech[115] and Berkeley High. . . .

More later, Decca

---

113. Decca's friend Anne Braden and her husband, Carl, both journalists, were active in civil rights and labor advocacy in Louisville, Kentucky, in the 1940s and '50s. In the '60s and early '70s, they directed the Southern Conference Educational Fund (SCEF). The couple achieved national prominence in 1954 when they purchased a ranch-style house in an all-white Louisville neighborhood on behalf of black friends, Charlotte and Andrew Wade. Neighbors objected, a cross was burned, shots were fired into the home, and finally it was bombed. The Bradens were called as witnesses before a grand jury, where they were quizzed on their political affiliations and beliefs, including what books they owned. Prosecutors suggested that the bombing may have been a Communist plot to stir up racial animosities and overthrow state and national governments. The Bradens were indicted for sedition, and Carl Braden was tried, convicted, and sent to prison on the charge. Two years later, all charges were dropped after the Supreme Court invalidated local sedition laws. Anne Braden's memoir describing the episode, *The Wall Between* (Monthly Review Press, 1958) was a National Book Award finalist and one of Decca's favorite books.

114. Decca is being facetious here.

115. Oakland Technical High School.

To Robert Treuhaft "Nyaaashveal, Tenn."
May 15, 1961

Darling old Bob,

Life proceeds at such a pace, not much time for writing. . . .

[Kay Jones is] one's age, a social worker, and has that indefinable thing one can recognize as more than a brush with the L. movement at some time or other. She's now full-time Exec Director of Nashville Community Relations Conference. We sat on her porch and chatted for ages. This is the town where the "better class" of white people organized as "observers" to aid the sit-ins. About 100 whites were involved, mostly women. Their job was to go, in shifts, to the newly integrated lunch counters and movies and observe what happened when Negro students came to be served. There was no communication with the students, but it seems that by some sort of telepathy it was obvious to the students who the observers were. A couple of amusing things Kay related: white-gloved, hatted matron (not the sort who usually patronizes a Woolworth lunch counter) expressing surprise that they "serve coffee in such places." . . . Another, arriving for her shift, spots a friend and says angrily "What are you doing here? This place is reserved by the Unitarians." When the movies were first opened up, agreement was reached by the demonstrators and the movie management that there'd be no hanging round in the lobby, going to the rest-rooms etc. by Negroes at first; they should simply go and sit in the theatre, watch the movie, and depart, until it was determined how things were going. A white lady "observer," seeing a Negro patron in front of her move as though to rise from his seat, reached forward and grabbed him, saying loudly "You're not supposed to go to the rest-room!" . . .

I'm heading at once for Montgomery, because I know from past experience that there's really more copy there for the sort of thing I had in mind.

So, farewell to the Athens of the South (as we call Nashville) and on to Roachville.

Lots of love to you and Benjy, Decca

To Benjamin Treuhaft Montgomery, Ala.
May 16, 1961

Darling Benjy,

I'm getting good reports about you from Bob, which pleases me muchly.

Just as I started this letter, the phone rang and a weirdo, half-baked southern (female) voice asked for Mrs. Durr. I said she was at the office; could I take a message? The voice said, "This is Mrs. Wingard. Tell her the Ku Klux Klan is after her husband and they're going to get him." I asked what time they'd be here (as I didn't want to be in the tub when they come) but she hung up. I guess this was just to make me feel I'd really arrived in the South. Cliff is representing a young Negro who was framed by a psychotic white woman (usual charge, that he made advances to her) and there's been a lot in the paper about it here, so I guess that accounts for the call.[116]

Have you been reading about the Freedom Riders? I just missed all that, it happened the day before I arrived in Ala.[117] Surprisingly, the Ala. business men's club issued a pretty good statement against the police for failing to protect the Freedom Riders. . . .

Keep up the good work, and if you find time to write to your aging Mamma she will be most delighted.

> Lots of love, Decca

To Robert Treuhaft   Montgomery
                                                                                    May 17, 1961

Darling old Bob,

. . . Your most welcome package of letter and clippings etc. just arrived. I'm terribly pleased that you really liked the Life article. . . .

By the same post arrived a huge packet, addressed to Mrs. Jessica Metford c/o Fried, re-directed c/o Anne Braden, re-directed here, from guess who? Howard Johnson's. . . . It's a gem of a haul, with an illustrated pamphlet called "Howard Johnson's Means People Serving People." A glance at the myriad photographs reveals that it really means, white gentiles serving white gentiles. Some ghastly pix of horrible Howard Johnson Sr. and Jr. pinning awards on various people— both with a clear-eyed, sincere look that's enough to make one vomit. So, good copy for me Article on Writing an Article for Life International.

Just came from my first bona fide Montgomery luncheon. . . . About 6 ladies there, one's age to Va's age; they are W.I.L.[118] types, milder Montgomery liberals than the last night's crowd, but good kind people. A blessing was said before eating. The talk went much thus: "So Jim Ward, you know who he is, married that cute little Nancy Dell who was such a beauty and all the boys were just crazy about her—she's kin to Sonny Dell, the boy who caused such an awful

---

116. In retelling the story of the threatening Klan call some years later, Decca said that "this sort of thing happens constantly" at the Durrs' Montgomery flat. She said in other letters that Clifford Durr's client—a married, twenty-two-year-old janitor and father with a perfect job record, a good reputation, and an alibi—had been arrested at his home, viciously beaten, and charged with disturbing the peace, but Durr ultimately prevailed in court after learning that the white accuser had previously been put on probation for making obscene phone calls. Even after the initial verdict, the accuser was said to have called police to complain about a Negro prowler outside her house, but police found nobody.

117. Several days before this letter was written, busloads of Freedom Riders were assaulted by mobs in Anniston and Birmingham, Alabama. Under federal pressure, state authorities agreed to protect a new attempt by Freedom Riders to reach Montgomery, but the civil rights workers were beaten nevertheless on arrival at Montgomery's Greyhound bus station three days after Decca wrote this letter. By chance, she and Virginia Durr were at the bus station on the day of the violence, and Decca got caught up in the turmoil of the following days.

118. Women's International League for Peace and Freedom.

scandal that time in the Methodist College and he finally became an alcoholic—so anyway Jim, well you know they had a little boy who wasn't quite right in the head, and Jim was just crazy about that little boy, and his aunt, not Miss Maudie but the other aunt, she never did get married but she was going with Dr. Kingston's brother, the one who had that big drugstore in Birmingham, you know that drugstore, it's right on the corner there by the First Baptist Church, and Miss Sissy, that's the other aunt, (she never did get married) she took the little boy to stay with her, and of course by that time Nancy well you know she simply lost her head over that handsome Buck Taylor and she had simply run off and <u>they</u> ended up in Knoxville and no one ever did quite get the right of what finally became of them—well so while the little boy was staying at Miss Sissy's somehow he just went off completely, and Jim poor fellow was so distraught, I mean he wasn't himself because when he <u>was</u> himself he was just the nicest fellow you'd want to meet, and Nancy did treat him bad because you know he was just crazy about her, always was, poor boy; so anyway he just up and took a shotgun and blew his brains out. Blew his brains clear out. And of course you know Miss Sissy, I mean she took on so—she was really such a sweet woman, and it was such a shame she never did get married but you see the thing of it was was that she was always sort of overshadowed by Miss Maudie, Miss Maudie was really such a great beauty, they say it was for love of Miss Maudie that that poor fellow Sappy Fogarty took to the bottle so, and you know his father simply cut him off without a penny and it all went to the other son, Moulty, the one who married Fran's youngest girl, and so poor Miss Sissy just carried on so after all that happened to that little boy, Jim's little boy you know, and she just went into sort of a decline, wasn't anything nobody could do for her it seemed like, she'd just sit in her winder all day just wringing her hands and the tears streaming down her face, and of course by this time, you see this was a good ten years after Miss Maudie had <u>her</u> trouble, so by this time even her own sister Miss Maudie wasn't really in any position to see after poor Miss Sissy, so it really wasn't any wonder, I mean it wasn't any surprise to anybody, because we all saw it coming but you know we were sort of helpless because what could anyone <u>do</u>? So poor Miss Sissy was found in the river one day and it really was a perfectly dreadful thing but there wasn't a thing in the world any of us could have <u>done</u>, unless it could have been Miss Maudie but you see this must have been lets see, a good ten years I'd say after Miss Maudie had had <u>her</u> trouble, so there really wasn't anything she could have done either . . ."

Well maybe <u>all</u> the conversation didn't go quite like that, but that's my best recollection of the general drift of a good bit of it. The part that did go like that was a good deal more long-drawn out, I'm just giving you a condensed, brief version.

One lady there, Anne something, has promised to take me to the Operation Alert meeting, it's about saving Montgomery from Communism and you have to have an invitation. . . .

love . . . Dec

To Robert Treuhaft   Montgomery
                                                                  May 23, 1961

Darling old Bob,

... I won't go any further into details of the Sunday night business[119] as I'm working like absolute mad, against frantic deadline of Thursday, to finish my Life article. ...

Other Montgomery notes of interest (aside from what's in the paper, I'm sure you are getting that): After Cliff got in touch with the fire dept. re his car (which is totally destroyed, so is Va's pocket book and little transistor radio, which were in trunk), 2 fire marshal chaps came over to see me. They took down routine information; name, address, time I left the car, and they left. This morning, they returned with the fire chief. He repeated the routine questions, then added some: who was with me? Had I asked the Durrs to come to the meeting, and had they refused? Did I meet my companion at the Durrs' house, or elsewhere? Had I come directly to Montgomery from Calif., or had I made other southern stops? To all I answered that they were not germane (substituted "relevant" when I noted his puzzled expression) to his main job, which was to find and arrest the people who set fire to the car. He asked whether I thought I was recognized by anyone in the crowd outside the church? I said I doubted it, they didn't look much like book readers or review followers. He said crossly, "that's their business, whether they are book readers, I'm not saying they are and I'm not saying they aint." He asked whether the Durrs had given me the car of their own free will? I said I had not stolen it, if that's what they thought. He asked why I went to the meeting? I answered, to hear Rev. King speak. He asked whether the Durrs and I had attended regular church that morning? Not relevant, I replied. Honestly, he was such a riot, trying to be all efficient like a committee investigator, but it didn't come off at all, I was roaring throughout most of it.

Lots of anon. phone calls ("dirty nigger lover, get out of the state, communist russian" etc)

Cliff had no insurance to cover burning of his car, so I'm afraid we are stuck with getting him another. Doesn't have to be an expensive one, this one was about a 54 Buick. He is being sticky (gentlemanly) about it, so if you have time, write him to insist that he buy a car at once and bill you for it.

You and Benj seem so awfully far away, you've no idea how homesick I am, whenever I have time to be. I'm cutting out Birmingham and Jackson, going to Atlanta for a bit, thence HOME.

                    XXXXX Fondest love to all, XXXXX, Decca

---

119. Decca was referring to the terrifying night she spent at a civil rights rally in a church besieged by a white mob. See introduction to this chapter for details.

Montgomery
                                                                    May 24, 1961

Darling old Bob,

Quelle extraorder evening. Va. had invited an assorted group to dinner. Jim Dombrowski,[120] Ray Jenkins and wife (he's a reporter on local paper, and trusted friend of the Durrs), various ones to drop in after dinner such as . . . Peter, the Antioch student who accompanied me to the meeting.

As we were sitting down to dinner (cooked by me) Va casually mentioned, "the F.B.Ah are coming at 9, so we'd best put on mo coffee." Honestly, can you beat it? They'd been round to her office, she told them Peter and I had been at the meeting, they expressed an interest in talking to us, so she told them to come over this evening. Suddenly, Jim had to catch a plane and the Jenkins remembered some other commitments.

Promptly at 9, they arrived. Said they would like to interrogate Peter and myself separately and alone. I coldly replied that, since Va. had invited them, I would speak to them, but only in the presence of the assemblage. They confined themselves to routine questions about the car. I must say they had a bit of a time keeping to the point, what with Va saying don't you think Montgomery is a mighty pretty town and where are you from? Georgia? Well I declare. Peter agreed to be interrogated separately and alone, so they retired with him to the dining room where they stayed for a couple of hours. Seems (from Peter's account) they really were asking mostly about the violence at the bus station, which he had witnessed. Only extraneous question he could remember, was "what are you majoring in at college?"

Earlier, Mr. Ralph Graves (Life editor) called up. Now, let's see if this sounds to you as sinister as it did to me: He was v. friendly (how are you, did you get any sleep, etc). So I told him about the Chief Fire Hydrant coming round and his line of questioning (same thing I told you). Said Mr. Graves, "well isn't that fantastic. . . . By the way, what <u>did</u> bring you to Montgomery just at that time? Had you been there for any length of time <u>before</u> all the incidents?" etc. In other words, the same line of questioning as the fire hydrant. Interspersed, of course, with aren't we lucky you happened to be in Montgomery just when all this was happening, and not in some other town. He then casually added they were about to close my other story today, but pulled it out, because it wouldn't do to have a funny, light piece by me just at the same time as this other, grim piece; they'd use the tourist thing later. Suddenly, I can see all going down the drain. Oh, I'm so unhappy, and homesick, and longing to get out of this Claude Cuckoo Land as Va. would probably call it. The article is going v. badly. No committee in this town, worst luck. If <u>only</u> you were here.

                              Your loving Decca

---

120. A co-founder of Highlander Folk School. See letter of August 16–19, 1941, to Esmond Romilly, and associated footnote 77.

To Constancia Romilly   Montgomery
                                                        May 25, 1961

Darling Dinkdonk,

. . . So sorry not to have written, but life here is positively kaleidoscopic. . . .

I spoke to Bob last night, after you called. The poor boy is vastly over-worked, which is why he never writes, but I made him <u>promise</u> to write to you. You must feel you haven't got any parents left, what with me not having time to write and Bob being one of Nature's non-writers. . . .

The most interesting development of this whole thing concerns a couple called Frederick and Anna Gach. Don't know if NY papers have carried their story. She is a typical Alabamian, 39 years old, graduate of Ala. university (and law school, but doesn't practice law), works (or rather, worked) as typesetter for Montgomery Advertiser. These two were by utterest chance at the Greyhound station Saturday. They saw a Negro being horribly beaten, just a few feet from them. They shouted to the crowd to stop it, tried to intervene. They shouted to a nearby cop, who was standing with back to incident, to do something. The cop did; he arrested the Gaches. They have been found guilty of disturbing the peace and failing to obey an officer, fined $300. She was immediately fired from her job. He will most likely be expelled from nearby Auburn College, where he is a student. Cliff is taking their case on appeal. I'm trying to raise a lot of $$$ for their defence. If you possibly have time, do call a few people and ask them to send some money down. No organizations . . . as that would do more harm than good to their cause, just individual contribs. are needed. I'm going to try to get some big nat'l medium to publicize the case. . . .

Bob is trying to raise some in Calif, too. Their bail has been raised to $600 and the local bail bondsman refuses bond. Then, there's the matter of Cliff's fee. I should say a good $1,000 will be needed before all this is over. . . . In my opinion, this case of Mr. and Mrs. Gach is the most important of all, as it points up the utter living horror down here—but also goes to show there are some who will try to do the right thing. As Cliff says, they were fined for being the only ones in that crowd to show any decency. They have absolutely no liberal connexions here, just ordinary folks. So do try to do something about it. Eleanor Fried[121] might call some people too, don't you think? Get them to send nice large sums if possible.

There's masses more to tell, but no time to write more.

I love you dearly, good little Donk.

I'm so homesick, you can't imagine. All I long for is for us all to be together at home in Calif. again one of these days. . . .

Your very fond Mamma

---

121. Decca's good friend, frequent host in New York, and occasional traveling companion.

LATE NEWS FLASH: MY ARTICLE TAKEN BY LIFE, WILL BE IN NEXT WEEK'S ISSUE, FULL ACCOUNT OF LAST SUNDAY'S MASS MEETING!!![122]

To Robert Treuhaft   Atlanta
                                                                  May 29, 1961

Darling Bob,

The absolute bliss of hotels. I really was a bit done in over the weekend; for one thing, the natural wear and tear of life with the Durrs at any season, let alone riot-and-subpoena season. . . .

[M]iscellaneous tidbits I forgot to tell you. . . .

There is a magnificent system of public parks in Montgomery, tennis courts, pools, and a zoo. A few years ago Negroes brought suit to gain admittance, and won in the appeals court. Consequently the parks are now padlocked, grass and weeds growing up on the tennis courts etc; the zoo has been totally disbanded. People who want to take their kids to the zoo now have to go all the way to Birmingham—<u>where the zoo is integrated!</u> . . .

On to the country-clubbery:

After poor Ruth Waller's debacle, and rumoured linkage with me,[123] she told me she "didn't day-are tra" to see me any more—<u>but</u>, it seems several of her friends were rather longing to get a glimpse of the Oddity (me), and had complained bitterly to her at being deprived. So she told one of them to call me, by name of G——.[124] G—— called, asked me to come to her house for a drink

---

122. Within days, *Life* reconsidered and decided not to publish Decca's first-person account of her "nightmare" night inside the besieged church. She was paid a $500 "kill fee" for the article, entitled "The Longest Meeting," which was subsequently rejected by *Look* magazine and others. A truncated version ran in her *Esquire* article "Whut They're Thanking Down There" (changed from Decca's "You-All and Non-You-All: A Southern Potpourri," under which title it was later reprinted in *Poison Penmanship*). According to a later, and not necessarily definitive, recollection by Virginia Durr, "The Longest Meeting" was never published because another of the trapped attendees published his account first. At least one of the magazines said it was dated by the time it reached them.

123. Through Ruth Waller, "a society type lady, young and charmin'," Decca tried to get an invitation to a party of the English Speaking Union, or as she called it "the Only Fairly English Speaking Union . . . purely a snob group, society people." The invitation was not forthcoming because Decca was said, wrongly, to be staying at the Durrs with a young English student who had been scheduled to be guest of honor at the party. The student, Anne Pike, was "disinvited" after being quoted in a newspaper "man-in-the-street" interview as saying, "Negroes should be allowed to go any place they wish. I am for integration of the races 100 percent." Pike was also the cause of disapproving gossip in the Union because of what was considered her scandalous relationship with a boyfriend. Decca was told that the party that neither attended featured mostly chatter about Pike and Decca and that Ruth Waller herself "is being accused of being an old friend of mine in NY, probably a member of the same Communist cell." The Anne Pike affair became "the main topic [of conversation] in certain circles thru arson, assault, attempted murder and all," Decca told her husband.

124. Names omitted by editor.

Sunday at noon. So I forewent the trip to Pee Level[125] with the Durrs, and went to G——'s. She lives in quite a fancy house, suburban, is about 35 I judge, one of the Smart Young Marrieds. The sort of person who gaily insists, "all my friends think I'm quite mad!" Such as asking me over. When I arrived, she called someone to get a message to a neighbor to say I was there. In other words, to call direct wouldn't have been the right thing. Soon, the neighbor and husband arrived, Mr. and Mrs. L——. G——'s husband, who is a surgeon, was safely off operating—I gathered the plan was not to tell him much about the day. The L——s are also Smart Young Marrieds. . . . Evidently, the plan was to look me over—and then, if all seemed well, to take the bravest step yet—lunch at the country club. Albeit a late, late lunch, after most people would have left. So that's what was done. There were still a few lunchers at the club, and much jockeying to prevent having to introduce me. I'd have given <u>anything</u> for you to have been there.

First of all, there was a warning note. G—— said she knows I am a writer and all, but it could bring very grave embarrassment to her and her friends if I were to write about them, specially if identifying things were said—such as "madcap young wife of prominent surgeon"!! Not wishing, at this point, to break up the day, I forebore suggesting a disguise: "deadly dull young wife of prominent surgeon."

The piece de resistance, from their point of view, was to have me tell about the Rev. King mass meeting. Which I did, in all gory details, while they sat goggle-eyed. I told them I simply couldn't imagine, no matter what their point of view, how they could have foreborne to go—even just out of ordinary curiosity. They squealed with horror at the very thought. Then, I carefully led them around to a vantage point from which they could, so to speak, see themselves as others see them: allowing themselves to be governed by thugs, getting themselves into a position where they are simply terrified even to meet people like me, for fear of being associated with "outside agitators," etc. . . .

G——'s attitude throughout was one of producing an absolutely rare sort of freak, goodness she was sad when we had to part. . . .

Lots of love, Decca

To Robert Treuhaft Atlanta

May 31, 1961

Darling old Bob,

. . . I don't think I'll have to cash that $500 you sent me. I tried to press it on Cliff to pay for a new car, but he wouldn't accept. We really will have to fight

---

125. The Durrs' rustic retreat in Wetumpka, Alabama, twenty miles from Montgomery, was named Pea Level because peas once grew there. Decca repeatedly misspelled the name, intentionally.

him down on that and insist on ponying up for a car. If only Life would keep on not taking a few more of my articles at $500 a crack, we'd be able to get him a Cadillac.[126] . . .

Huge difference in atmosphere between Atlanta and Montgomery. For instance, here's a typical Montgomery thing that couldn't happen here: One day while Jim Dombrowski was in town he called Va. to ask whether he could invite a Negro lawyer over to the house for a few minutes, as he had to see him on business. Va. got v. cross and said absolutely not. As she tends to be a bit weather-vanish about this whole thing, I was interested to hear what Cliff would say. He agreed completely with her, said Jim was a dope to have suggested it. I asked <u>why</u>. It seems that on 2 or 3 occasions, white liberals (some of those I met, with large fancy houses) have had Negroes drop in for tea or something, by chance a neighbor or postman or errand boy has seen them sitting together having tea, called police, and the whole lot carted off to jail. The charge is "inciting to riot"! Same charge as in the MacMurray case that Cliff defended (white prof. and students eating in Negro restaurant).

Maggie[127] tells me that sort of thing wouldn't ever happen here. . . .

Maggie is a real charmer. So's Sissie, called by Maggie "my little ole jail-bird daughter." Sissie is . . . about 20, goes to college in New Orleans, has been in the sit-in movement from the start. . . .

Like all the integrationists in these parts, it seems to be their whole life and preoccupation. Which results, from a Northerner's point of view, in a sort of slight distortion of them as personalities, if you see what I mean. They see everything in terms of The Problem. Maggie only came to her present position about 10 years ago.

Last night, Maggie took me to dinner at the home of Mr. Sinclair Jacobs. He's old, rich, retired, art-connoisseur type, magnificent house, about 20 people to dinner. The opposite of Va's mammoth dinner parties, because seated, served by about 5 servants, all very beautiful and comfortable. I sat next to Eugene Patterson (no relation to Gov. P) who is the editor of the Atlanta Constitution, a "moderate-liberal" according to Maggie. There were various other VIP's. . . .

Eugene Patterson is a soul in agony because he has that love-of-soil-and-home-folks thing, like Cliff—but the home folks he loves are precisely the sort that formed the mob, as he admits. He kept saying he wishes he could take me out to some of the surrounding country towns to see how blissful the home-folks actually are. I wish he could too, but no time.

The civilized thing about the dinner party (compared to Montgomery) was that just about everybody there favors compliance with the law on integration,

126. Decca later wrote that she convinced her own insurance company, with what she considered "rather specious reasoning," to reimburse the blue-book value of the car. Her husband, she said, "told me I didn't have a chance on the claim."

127. A local newspaper writer.

and said so (this is terribly dangerous talk in Montgomery). There was great disagreement about the Freedom Riders—that is, whether they had incited the violence by coming etc. People about equally divided on that. There again, in Montgomery (country club circles) they simply try to avoid talking about it, won't take a position etc. . . .

Do give old Benj my fondest love and kisses. I'd love to bring him down this way one day. Imagine Benj and Lulah Belle[128] together, I don't think they'd even half-way understand each other, she can't understand a word I say.

Goodbye darling, see you very shortly.

Best love, Decca

To Benjamin Treuhaft   Atlanta
                                                            June 1, 1961

Darling Benj,

I was delighted with your letter, have been roaring on and off ever since it came this morning. . . .

The school desegregation here is being handled in an utterly insane way. Here's what they are doing: 300 Negro high-school students applied for transfer to all white schools. These were immediately whittled down, for geographic reasons, to 153. The 153 were given an immense battery of tests—personality, IQ, achievement, etc. About 10 hours straight of testing, according to one report I heard. Of the 153, 50 ended up above the 50th percentile of kids in the schools they had applied to enter. This was, it seems, too many, so there was more whittling down for geographic reasons (they lived "too far from school" etc). Leaving, 16 kids. The 16 still have to face personal interviews before they will become eligible for transfer. In other words, only Negroes above average are even considered (whereas all whites attend automatically, don't have to take the test first). But being above average does not do the trick either. Seems as though the "separate but equal" theory is being replaced by "together but unequal." People are guessing that only 7 or 8 will end up with transfers. Meanwhile, the network of meetings and organizations in the community designed to head off violence and educate the whites to be decent to the Negro transfers is most impressive. . . .

See you next week, looking forward to it greatly and all that sort of rot,

Lots of love, Dec

---

128. Lulah Durr, Clifford and Virginia's youngest daughter, was born well after Decca lived with the family.

To Constancia Romilly   Oakland
June 26, 1961

Darling Dinkydonk,

I'd much rather write to you than work, any day. Papa came home at noon to show me your letter, I was so glad to hear you'd arrived[129] and all. We had the usual argument, or rather a continuation of the argument about whether you should have gone in the first place; ending with Bob accusing me of being soft with you children and just like Aranka, and me accusing him of being an old ogre and just like my father. He still thinks the Mexico trip was an undisciplined move on your part, probably with little relation to your school work. I still think as I did when we discussed it. In case Bob is now expecting me to write, "enjoy life while you're still young!" (as Aranka always does, in each letter) I shall now say, "for god's sake study hard and get good marks, and send us your final Slawrence reports, and buckle to in general."

Talk about buckling to. Here's what happened to me the other day. It was a non-Mrs. Gresham day, and the house was a horrible mess from head to foot (head to foot? Attic to basement) with cesspools of things to be tidied, straightened, picked up, washed etc. all over the place and in every room. I gave Benj his mammoth break., consisting these days of 8 pieces of bacon, 4 eggs, 6 slices of toast and marmalade and 1 bottle of milk. This merely caused more things to need washing and putting. Benj went off to his tennis. I looked helplessly around, decided things were too awful for words—and slunk back to bed with a good novel. Hadn't even had my bath or washed my face; real slut-work. Besides, I'm supposed to be writing at least 3 hours a day. About 12:30, or even 1 p.m., the phone rang. 'Twas a stranger who had read the Satevepost article about the funeral thing (lots about me in it, June 14 issue, do get hold of it). She said, "I was amused that they described you as an 'Oakland housewife.' I've read your book and several of your articles, and I don't regard you as an Oakland housewife at all. How I should love to be a writer! But I don't have the self-discipline. I suppose one <u>does</u> need a great deal of discipline to be a writer?" "<u>Does</u> one!" I said, snuggling further under the covers. "I am at my desk by 8:30 every morning, work for a definite number of hours, get all my housework out of the way . . ." Anyway, I think I ruined <u>her</u> day for her. The only moral to that sad tale that I can think of is don't be like Mother whatever you do. . . .

I'm still getting nowhere fast with me work. For one thing, I've received over 70 letters from all over the country about the funeral thing, so I had to answer them (many asking how to go about organizing a funeral society etc) and I hired Kathy Kahn[130] to help me for a couple of days. The funeral society itself is getting letters at the rate of 70 a day, over 1400 at last count. Bob is

129. Constancia Romilly was traveling in Mexico.
130. The older daughter of Barbara and Ephraim Kahn.

delighted. Looks as though a national organization may come out of it all. . . . I told Fred Sweet to come to our national organization meeting, where we may serve dry mort-inis and die-queries. (ha-de-ha) . . .

WRITE WRITE WRITE WRITE

love, love, love, Decca

In front of the Duke and Duchess of
Devonshire's estate, Chatsworth, in 1962.

The Treuhafts on Inch Kenneth with
James MacGillivray, the boatman
and caretaker, in the 1960s.

V

DEATH
AND THE
AFTERLIFE

The scourge of the funeral industry posed at a Berkeley, California, mortuary chapel in the 1960s.

Decca and Robert Treuhaft with their children, Benjamin and Constancia, on the porch of the family's Regent Street home in Oakland in the early 1960s.

In the American funeral industry, Jessica Mitford finally found an institution truly worthy of the merciless Mitford Tease. The funeral directors' self-serving piety and mercenary psychobabble—as well as their use of deceptive sales tactics, frivolous ostentation, technological gizmos, and artful cosmetology to disguise the biological finality of death—all left the industry open to the kind of ridicule that only Decca could dispense. The industry was equally vulnerable on social grounds, taking commercial advantage of families in mourning and maximizing profits through monopolistic legal stratagems.

Despite her acute sense of injustice, what seems to have enthralled Decca most, initially, were the funeral trade journals her husband kept around the house, publications like *Mortuary Management*, *Casket & Sunnyside*, and—Decca's favorite title—*Concept: The Journal of Creative Ideas for Cemeteries*. Robert Treuhaft said she showed little interest in his cause until he began bringing the journals home. She loved the manufacturers' ads touting an array of backless garments, embalming gadgets, and other expensive products designed to prettify corpses (or the portions that showed when they were laid out in coffins) and to create meretricious "memory pictures" for the distraught and financially drained next of kin. She mounted a number of those ads on the walls of the family's downstairs bathroom. It wasn't just the ads. She told one correspondent with glee that she had just received the latest issue of *Mortuary Management*: "There's [an] editorial headed 'CHILDREN'S FUNERALS: A GOLDEN OPPORTUNITY TO BUILD GOOD WILL.' Do admit they are a lark." And then there were the trade catalogues. One firm, Decca was delighted to discover, "has added to its line of burial negligees a line of burial *brunch coats*. Honestly . . . The Last Brunch."

It was rollicking good fun, but it was much more than that. This was a subject whose time had come. In that era, the anguish of death and many of the arrangements that followed were handled privately and secretly. Death and funerals were treated as proprietary information by black-suited salesmen who pushed their costly services in muted voices and passed themselves off as experts in "grief therapy." Dr. Elisabeth Kübler-Ross didn't publish her influential book *On Death and Dying* until six years after publication of *The American Way of Death*; it was another five years before the first American hospice was founded. Decca almost single-handedly moved the subject of death, embalming, and burial out of hushed, windowless, flower-filled rooms and into the public domain. Perhaps only her brand of brash humor could have yanked aside the shrouds of this deeply ingrained American taboo.

One of Decca's dearest friends, Pele de Lappe, finds an unacknowledged motivation for the Treuhafts' passionate interest in funerals. Their son Nicholas's sudden death in a traffic accident in 1955, three years before Decca published her "St. Peter" article, was rarely discussed in the household, nor could Decca bring herself to write about it in her memoir, but she adored the boy and mourned him, in her own subterranean way, for the rest of her life. De Lappe recalls Nicholas's funeral at the Chapel of the Chimes in Oakland; it was the sort of funeral Decca later lampooned, replete with "all the trappings of that kind of thing," white roses on a white coffin "and the whole gloomy horror of . . . the conventional commercial funeral system." One can only speculate whether Nicholas's death was also the reason why it took so long for Decca—an author in search of a subject for her second book, inundated with supportive letters—to come to the obvious decision to write a book about funeral abuses.

Within weeks after publication of Roul Tunley's "Can You Afford to Die?" in the *Saturday Evening Post*, Decca gained more nationwide exposure with an appearance on a television show called *P.M. West* on the high cost of dying, but she still thought of it as her husband's project. She told her daughter, "That subject has suddenly become a sort of number-one issue, all over the place, mostly due to old Bob's unremitting work."

As the number of letters mounted into the thousands, the *Post*'s editor remarked with evident understatement that the article "seemed to have touched a sensitive nerve." Decca suggested to Tunley, the author, that he follow up with a book on the subject, and she offered research material and other assistance. Tunley replied, "Why don't you write it?"

So she tested the idea on her literary agents. Her American agent, Candida Donadio, responded, "It's a superb idea, so kookie that it is definitely possible." From there the project took shape rapidly, and the chronology is well-established in her letters.

As originally conceived, the Treuhafts were to write the book together, and Robert Treuhaft did a substantial amount of the research and preliminary writing. Library research was exclusively Robert Treuhaft's domain; Decca detested that kind of plodding paperwork. She explained another division of responsibility to her mother-in-law, reporting that her husband "is the cemetery man around here (I am the funeral parlor man)." But agents and publishers balked at a joint byline, and her husband deferred to them. In the book itself, Decca's acknowledgments begin, "Large portions of this book could well be labeled, 'By Robert Treuhaft, as told to Jessica Mitford.' "

In some senses, the entire funeral industry also served as reluctant co-authors, responding to the Treuhafts' requests for information or commenting publicly on their early writings with self-inflating comments that Decca recycled in her book. She recalled that "Howard C. Raether, Executive Secretary of the National Funeral Directors Association . . . unwittingly supplied some of the best lines to *The American Way of Death*, including the epigraph: 'Funerals are becoming more and more a part of the American way of life.' " Decca told one correspondent she had offered Raether a two-thousand-word chapter in her book, "anything he wanted . . . which threw them all into a terrible state trying to decide; they decided not, which I regret but I do think wise from their point of view."

Decca's letters chronicle the greatest obstacle she encountered in trying to write the book in her own inimitable way: the resistance from her squeamish publishers to what they saw as the inappropriateness of her chapter on embalming. The subject matter was deemed too revolting and the tone too playful. Decca persevered, although many years later she told her sister Deborah that, rather than remove the chapter, the Treuhafts had been prepared simply "to mimeograph the book for those who wanted it, & pack it up." Fortunately, a change of publishers saved the project. Decca's longtime business assistant Catherine (Katie) Edwards reports that more requests have been received to reprint that controversial embalming chapter than any of her other works; she says the requests continue to come in, more than forty years after the initial publication. Decca herself was quick to observe that the reprint rights, often in college textbooks, had brought her far more money than the original advance for the book.

Decca never envisioned more than a small and specialized audience for the book—"too dismal a subject." She showed an uncompleted manuscript to her sister Nancy while in Europe and reported that "she shrieked for a bit, but then stopped reading saying it is too revolting. Rather a bad omen for me, I thought; suppose the Great American Public agrees with her? Not too good for sales, if they do." But some people did foresee a bigger impact and told Decca so. One magazine editor who read an early version of the manuscript told her, "This book is going to break them (the morticians). It's going to smash an entire industry." Decca laughed it off, telling a correspondent that the reaction "made me feel very good, never having had the pleasure of smashing an industry before."

The American Way of Death was an instantaneous and overwhelming hit. The response is well documented in her letters, but a few more details might flesh out the picture. Just ten days after publication in August 1963, Simon & Schuster sales manager Mac S. Albert wrote to his salesmen that "[w]e wanted to let you know, in case you haven't felt it as yet, that we are sitting on a bombshell of a book . . . which is going to explode any minute now. . . . We're being bombarded with wires and phone calls . . . screaming for additional copies." Stores were reordering in ever larger quantities, sometimes placing several reorders a day, and the publisher was simultaneously reprinting and ordering paper for tens of thousands of additional copies. Within weeks of publication, *The American Way of Death* was on the *New York Times* best-seller list, where it remained through the fall and winter, until the following March.

As Decca knew they would—and as the book publicists hoped they would—funeral directors and others responded to the book's success by falling back on Red smears, but this time the attacks didn't stick (as they might have just a few years earlier). When the book was released, *Tocsin*, a gossipy, far-right-wing newsletter in Berkeley that billed itself as "The West's Leading Anti-Communist Weekly," featured an "exposé" of Decca's Communist associations under the headline "Writer Jessica Mitford Equals Communist Decca Treuhaft." The article called *The American Way of Death* "a clever attempt to bury capitalist America's funeral customs." The head of the National Selected Morticians also picked up the theme, suggesting that Decca was trying to replace the American funeral service "with that practiced in Communistic countries such as the Soviet Union." The National Funeral Directors Association's official press release advised those who "wish further data as to" the authors to check the transcripts of hearings of state and federal un-American activities committees, and they helpfully provided the dates.

On October 15, two months after the book's publication, the *Congressional Record* reported that Congressman James B. Utt of California announced to Congress that "Jessica Mitford, also known as Jessica Mitford Romilly Treuhaft, author of a recent book entitled 'The American Way of Death,' " was "the wife of Robert Treuhaft, twice identified as a Communist in the Seventh Report of the Un-American Activities Committee of the California State Senate for 1953" and that she too had taken the Fifth Amendment before the committee "to avoid incriminating herself when her associations were documented." He went on to detail some of her "associations" and suggested that Central Intelligence Agency director Allen Dulles and United Nations ambassador Adlai Stevenson, who were to appear at a luncheon with Decca, "have been made dupes to attract a large audience for Jessica Mitford to plug her new book. While hiding behind the commercial aspects of the mortician and the cemeteries and mausoleums where our dear departed friends and relatives are commemorated, she is really striking another blow at the Christian religion. . . . [Her] tirade against morticians is simply the vehicle to carry out her anti-Christ attack."

Speaking personally, Utt said, "I would rather place my mortal remains, alive or dead, in the hands of any American mortician than to set foot on the soil of any Communist nation," a statement that Decca footnoted thus in *A Fine Old Conflict*: "In 1970 Mr. Utt exercised that option. His obituary in *The New York Times* . . . records that during his ten years in Congress, 'his most newsworthy action came when he called Jessica Mitford a "pro-Communist anti-American." ' "

Decca parried all the attacks, often with humor—in one Associated Press story, she is quoted as calling the Communism charges "a red herring"—but sometimes the menace was palpable. There was a bomb threat in Boston, and Decca wrote her friend Barbara Kahn from Dallas, "So far, no bombs in these parts; only the feeling one is just a step ahead of them, accomplished by scramming out of town as soon as one has had one's say." It is chilling to note that that letter was dated nine days before President John F. Kennedy was assassinated in the same city.

Nevertheless, Americans in general, with strong press support, shrugged off the Communist charges and innuendo, laughed along with Decca . . . and kept buying the book. If anything, the controversy boosted sales. Within a couple of years, more than 100,000 copies had been sold in hardback and half a million in paperback.

Decca had become respectable. "Ironically," she observed later, "to my extreme pleasure after the book was published, the same editors who had rejected [her article] 'St. Peter' were after me to write follow-up articles on the very subject they had found so distasteful" five years earlier, when only *Frontier* magazine would publish it. Among those who solicited stories, she wrote, were "such Middle America magazines as Good Housekeeping and Saturday Evening Post—an enemy invasion of the undertakers' own turf, so to speak."

With all the publicity on their misguided rhetoric, "One might have thought," Decca wrote, that "the funeral industry spokesmen would have learned to keep their mouths shut, or at least to moderate their rhetoric; not a bit of it, their counterattack provided colorful material for any number of follow-up articles."

She also received widespread support from the clergy, prompting her to observe in her book *Poison Penmanship*, "[I]t seemed that for once in my life I was literally on the side of the angels, or at least their temporal representatives. I think that only those who have been, as I was, a target of the Truman-McCarthy-era assault on radicals can appreciate the feeling of decompression on having one's work accepted at its face value, no longer subject to the ad hominem (or should it be feminem?) attack that was such a depressing feature of those years."

Decca was not reluctant to wield the influence that popular acceptance placed at her disposal. She told one reporter that her new national prominence "enabled me to at last give full rein to my subversive nature in a way that would not have been possible (before) . . . reaching millions instead of dozens with a frontal attack on one of the seamier manifestations of American capitalism."

More than two years after publication, *The American Way of Death* was still a subject for attention in the news media. Funeral societies were proliferating, and Americans' burial arrangements were changing. A writer for *The Times* of London was prompted to gush, "From the extent of the brouhaha it is clear that Miss Mitford's impact on the transatlantic scene is only slightly less than the Beatles', and may be a good deal more lasting."

The life-changing drama of those hectic years begins here with the letter Decca wrote to her agent, pitching the idea for her new book.

■ ■

To Candida Donadio   Oakland
                                                                   July 7, 1961

Dear Candida,

Did you see the enclosed article in the Satevepost?[1] Believe it or not, on a very <u>lively</u> subject. Well, life here has been a madhouse since it appeared. I have personally received over 100 letters (addressed only, "Jessica Treuhaft, Oakland"; the post office phoned us about it and made special arrangements to deliver the letters) and the Bay Area Funeral Society has received over 2,000. Most of the letters are long, interesting and very intelligent.

As a result of the really astonishing response to the article, Bob and I have conceived the idea of collaborating on a short, or medium length, book—a practical guide and handbook about how to beat the funeral racket.

Bob, as you know, was one of the founders of the Bay Area Funeral Society (has been their lawyer for a number of years) and I have made excursions into that territory—I wrote the enclosed piece for Frontier several years ago, since reprinted and used for promotion by several of the societies. Through the Bay Area Funeral Society, we have access to material that would otherwise require considerable research. In fact we supplied the Post writer with most of the material he used. So, we would be in a good position to write such a book.

Our idea is that it should be a cheap paper book, possibly Ballantines or one of those. I realize that my contract with Houghton Mifflin requires offering it to them first, but I doubt if they would be interested.

We have prepared an outline indicating the subjects to be covered and the general scope of the book. If necessary, we could prepare a chapter, but would much prefer not to until you have sounded out the possibilities for acceptance. I was hoping the Frontier piece could serve as an example of writing on the subject.

Bob's vacation is coming up soon, and if we had a definite agreement with a publisher he would devote a few weeks to working on the book. Thereafter, I would do the bulk of the writing with his help on weekends, etc. The whole thing shouldn't take very long to write.

There is only one book we know of bearing on this subject—a scholarly tome called <u>The American Funeral</u>, by LeRoy Bowman, published by American Affairs Press in 1959. It's rather extraordinary that, in view of the tremendous interest in the subject, there's no popular book on the market which deals with it.

Hope to hear from you soon. I am working on my other stuff.

             Love from Decca

---

1. The Roul Tunley funeral article.

To Lady Redesdale   Oakland
                                          October 19, 1961

Darling Muv,

Thanks for the cutting.[2] Every time I see the words, "Hon's Mother" in a headline, I know it's going to be something about you.[3] I loved the photo of you striding, also the one of the house was good.

To my delight I just this minute got a t.gram saying that my article for Esquire is accepted. . . .

Meanwhile, Bob and I are engaged in the most extraorder thing—a book on The American Way of Death. Describing the funeral industry, trade mags. etc., and consumer movements for cheap ordinary funerals. Bob is going to take off time from his law practice to help. We wrote a sample chapter and outline, sent it to me publisher (Houghton Mifflin) and they sent a contract with lovely huge advance.[4] The only rather sad thing is I don't suppose we will be able to get it taken in England, as it would hardly be of interest there. It's supposed to be finished in a little less than a year, although I am hoping it won't take anything like that long. We may have to do it a bit up at the Isle if not completed by next summer. In a way, I am rather loving doing it, it's sort of like having a job again rather than the usual writing I've done. . . .

Do give my love to my old Hen and Nancy when you write to them. I've rather lost touch, my fault because I can never think of anything to write to them about from so far away.

                         Lots of love, Decca

To Kathleen Kahn[5]   Oakland
                                          November 24, 1961

My Dear Madame de Stael (as I now think of you, having been permitted to read some of the letters to sainted P's, and I can see you are <u>actually</u> planning to be a great lettriste (although you haven't written one to me for ages, which makes me triste), a noble career in these uncertain days I must say. Yes I know there are supposed to be 2 dots over the e (or is it the a?) but you know how these modren

---

2. The *Scottish Daily Express* had published a profile that Decca characterized as a "sort of 'Mitfords' Mother' story."

3. Decca was playing off the comment by her mother that she recounted in her letter of June 10, 1959, to Marge Frantz: "Whenever I see a headline in the papers beginning 'Peer's Daughter . . .' I know it's going to be about one of you children."

4. Houghton Mifflin ultimately didn't exercise its option to publish the book, for reasons explained in subsequent letters.

5. Kathleen Kahn was a student at Vassar College at the time this letter was written, and not too happy about it. Decca took it upon herself to cheer up her young friend and goddaughter. (Kathleen's mother, Barbara Kahn, was quick to point out that " 'goddaughter' was Decca's nomenclature, i.e., she never appeared before the font and promised to bring Kathy up in the faith. But a happy relationship.")

typewriters don't hardly have any accents or things to them. How's this, by the way, for a fair parody of the ineffable style of Lettriste K. Kahn?) Paren. a bit off, maybe, but there's many an honored precedent for that in Lit, as you know—

How are you. We are fine. Or, as me dear old Nanny would have said, "we can't complain." Unlike you, judging by aforementioned lettres.

What can I think of to cheer you up. Last week I was in L.A. for a week, most of the time digging Forest Lawn (as you teen-agers say), making pre-need arrangements etc.[6] The pre-needery was rather bliss. I was accompanied by a Forest Lawn aficionado, head of the English Dept of the Immaculate Heart (Catholic girls) College. Our story: his mother, my sister (for I was his aunt for the nonce) was dying of the usual. Cancer. We had to go through all this because I was dying to see the Slumber Rooms, Casket Display Room and all. So, through them we went. After much consideration, we turned from the $145 casket (honestly it was a bit frightful looking) and our choice was between one at $675 and another at $995. We decided on the $675 one—I suggesting that it would suit Mother's complexion better (it was a dull beige). After we finally got out, my companion, a bit green about the gills, made a dive for the nearest phone booth, muttering to me: "Excuse me, I just want to call Mother to make sure she's feeling OK." That's what I like to see, someone who can really identify in a dramatic role. I did wish you were there. You'd have loved the slumber rooms, especially. I almost took a nap there myself. . . .

Oh yes another nice thing about F. Lawn. Among the multiplicity of final resting places (all named things like Brotherly Love, Garden of Memories, etc) is one called Patriots' Hall. I asked the man if one had to be a citizen to finally rest there, he said oh no, not a bit necessary. (I mean the Final Resting Place salesman said all this.) So I said, Well, I should think you'd at least ask for some sort of loyalty oath, after all it's supposed to be for Patriots? He said absolutely not, as long as you've got the money to pay for the site, all would be OK. Don't you think that's really pretty crumby? Who should we protest to?

I brought your parents back a very nice present. It is a tin ashtray in the shape of twin hearts, joined by a vermillion arrow. One side (heart) has a bright bronze and blue raised pic of the Great Gates to Forest Lawn. The other has a bronze, scarlet and green pic of the Great Mausoleum. It cost 49¢. The lady in the F.L. gift shop where I bought it said it would make a lovely wall plaque in any home (when not in use as ashtray) so this being the pre-Xmas season I got several for gifts. On top of the twin hearts are various scrolls and leaves, and crowning all, the words JAMAIS ARRIERE. We think that means, translated, NEVER IN ARREARS. Please ask your Fr. teacher.

---

6. Forest Lawn Memorial Park is a cemetery empire in Glendale, California, that Decca lampooned in *The American Way of Death*. It had previously been the subject of a bitingly satirical novel, *The Loved One*, by Evelyn Waugh, a good friend of Nancy Mitford.

Your sainted P's are moping because you sound so miserable. I, being a reader between the lines, have suggested to them that a) you are rather loving being miserable, and that it certainly suits your literary style—although I do not approve of letters without a salutation at the beginning because it makes one feel that you have carelessly flushed the first page down the john, or that b) you really are miserable, but then who isn't at your age? or even that c) why shouldn't anyone be miserable with the very drear prospect of the non-future in case of war. Which has rather understandably been bugging everyone lately, even the Sainteds and us. Specially us, because it is so very tiresome to be spending hours writing a book advocating speedy cremation and simple disposal of the remains, only to find one's complete idea being cribbed by the K.[7] administration. I mean think what it will do to <u>sales</u>.

Do write. Shall you be there next Spring, when we come? We'll hopefully telephone to see when we get back East.

Lots of love, Your Fond Godmother

To Constancia Romilly   Oakland

January 10, 1962

Darling Dinkdonk,

. . . I got a screamingly funny Va. letter about your time together. She adores you. She raved on about how well you look, slimmed down and beautiful etc etc; then, she said "I suppose by now you know about my terrible goof in speaking to her about her father." Then she went into that old story (made up by Virginia in the first place) about how probably Esmond was Winston's illegit. son all along. And oh dear she did hope you weren't really upset by hearing it, she tried to tell you it was just an unproved rumour etc . . . So I couldn't help writing back to remind her that she is the main source of this unproved rumour![8] . . .

Life at home: Up at 6, or 6:30, or even once or twice at 5, as I am just about as stuck as you are, my old problem of <u>organization</u>. As for Bob, he finally got down to some actual writing (after spending several days at the embalming school).[9] Gave it to me to type, and it turned out to be 3/4 page of typing. I teased him about it a bit; now he's doing a whole chapter on embalming. Yester-

---

7. Kennedy.

8. Decca had various takes over the years on what she called here "this unproved rumour" about Winston Churchill and Esmond Romilly. Most often, she attributed the rumor to her sister Nancy Mitford, not to Virginia Durr, although Durr clearly enjoyed spreading it. Decca herself gave the rumor various degrees of credence over the years—in a 1978 letter, she wrote that "E. was most likely the natural son of Winston Churchill"—but finally came to believe that it couldn't be true. For further details, see letter of January 12, 1983, to Kevin Ingram.

9. Robert Treuhaft had been doing research at what Decca dismissively called "that fine old academic institution," the San Francisco College of Mortuary Science.

day, he hopefully suggested going to play tennis with Mimmy;[10] I said, "You're <u>not</u> to go out and play before you finish your chapter. First things first." Shades of Bob telling Benj the same! . . .

I must be at my book. Goodbye dear. Do write by return, it is such a joy to hear from you. . . .

Your loving Dec

Dear it made me cry when you said, "I know I am not meant to succumb to moods." You <u>are</u> supposed to. I can see now we've been beastly to you (specially wicked Papa), not letting you be moody or daydream.

To Constancia Romilly   Oakland
                                                                              January 16, 1962
Darling Dinkydonk,

. . . I'm in the stage where I worry about the book night and day, and it is going all too slowly. We've done a little over 100 pages (about 9 chapters) which I hope is about 1/3 of all. Somehow, this week we've hardly got anything done. The days slip away, and we are always behind. Some of it is because of interviews (like yesterday, we spent all morning with a mortician, most of the afternoon with some economists who are helping) and the pile of papers doesn't seem to grow anything like fast enough. Sometimes I measure them, dear; 1 inch if just left plain, or 1/2 inch if pressed down (thick, you know). I guess you know the behindhand feeling all too well.

Dear shall we do as Muv suggested and give up all this slaving? But the trouble with me is I don't like not doing anything, either. For instance I should loathe the life of Barbara Kahn, nothing but a lot of boring community work like PTA and Planned Parenthood.

Well, Beer,[11] back to work.

Your loving Ma

---

10. Apparently a playful nickname for Miriam (Mimi) Miller, the woman whom Decca had wrongly presumed to be her rival for Robert Treuhaft's affections in their Washington days. Miller had since moved to the San Francisco area and become a close family friend.

11. Apparently a variation on "Dear."

To Kathleen Kahn   Oakland
                                                              February 2, 1962

Dearest Goddity,[12]

    . . . Thanks v. much for your letter, the more appreciated because I can imagine how busy you must be and bored of thought of writing poor old God-mothers.

    Did you know one can get a thing called "new Bra-Form, Post Mortem Form Restoration, Accomplishes so Much for So Little?" They only cost $11 for a package of 50. Shall I send some? Barb is longing to try them.

    One foot in the grave hereabouts, as you can see. We are working like mad and I think are almost at the half-way mark. . . .

    We are going to Chicago for a bit at the end of Feb, on the blissful train. . . . I bet you didn't know that Chi. is a main funeral center in this country, National Headquarters of Selected Morticians of America, and site of the famous Foundation of Funeral Service?[13] See, they never teach the important things in our schools these days. Anyway, that's why we are going.

    We've finished our Embalming chapter. It's rather blissful in spots. For instance, I ran across an ad. for Tru-Lanol Arterial Fluid, in the form of a testi-monial letter from a satisfied customer. He describes a very difficult case (69-year-old woman, was 40 hours in heated apartment before being discovered) and how after 4 days of Tru-Lanol treatment, all was OK. He adds wistfully, "I wish I could have kept her for four more days." Don't you think that's rather a poignant thought? They do so love their work, and so understandably hate to part with it. . . .

            Lots of love, Decca.

To the Duchess of Devonshire   Oakland
                                                             February 15, 1962

Dearest Henny,

    Glad you liked the Prac. Bur. Foot.[14] Yes, there are some other fascinators: such as . . . The Final Touch That Means So Much, it's mood-setting casket hardware. . . .

    Hen do you prefer a gentle Tissue-Tint in yr. arterial? It helps regain the Natural Undertones. It's made specially for those who prefer a fast Firming Action of medium-to-rigid degree. . . .

---

    12. Goddaughter.

    13. National Selected Morticians, a trade association of independent funeral homes, was among a number of such organizations that Decca took on in *The American Way of Death*. The Foundation of Funeral Service, a funeral management school, taught many of the tricks of the trade that Decca mocked in the book.

    14. Practical Burial Footwear. See next letter.

Hen I bet you don't even know what is the best time to start embalming, so I'll tell you: Before life is quite extinct, according to the best textbook we've found on it. They have at you with a thing called a Trocar, it's a long pointed needle with a pump attached, it goes in thru the stomach and all liquids etc. are pumped out. Thence to the Arterial. I do wish the book was finished, it seemed to be going along well for a bit but now it's all being totally reorganized.

One thing you could do which would be a terrific help: write and describe an English funeral. That is, if you've been to any lately. Who goes to them—just the family, or what you call inties too? Here, everyone goes (such as people who work in the same office etc). Anyway do try to go to one soon and write and tell all. Because I've never been to one in England. . . .

Much love, Yr. Hen

To Candida Donadio   Oakland

March 2, 1962

Dear Candida,

Thanks very much for calling, the conversation did me much good. And thanks also for steering us through these difficult waters. Now, on to some comments on the book:

1. To leave out the gruesome parts would, I think, be wrong.[15] For one thing, as we say in the book, this is a subject on which literally nothing is known outside the funeral profession itself; yet, it is the ultimate fate of almost 100 percent of all Americans. I am not in favor, generally, of writing in horrors for the sake of horrors—for example, sob-sister stuff about the suffering of condemned men in a book which is an argument against capital punishment. This is something different. In the first place, one is speaking of what is done to an inanimate thing—but done under such a phony guise. In the second place, it is so almost universal; people have a right to know what they are paying for.

2. So far (without further clarification as to what is meant) I am not in favor of cutting out what Lovell referred to as the "foolishness," as I think that only by making it slightly funny in spots is the gruesomeness alleviated.[16]

3. Naturally, one of the reasons that editors (of magazines) have shied away so from this subject is its gruesomeness—and, no doubt they feel, its

---

15. Based on a sample of the manuscript sent to Gollancz, Decca's English publisher, which had previously sent her a contract for the book, rejected it because—as James MacGibbon put it, in relaying Gollancz's rejection and stepping down himself as her English agent—"I don't like these chapters, and Victor Gollancz doesn't like them either. The joke, such as it is, surely is going on far too long—it already has. I cannot imagine any publisher here wanting it."

16. The letter from Houghton Mifflin's Lovell Thompson reacting to Decca's sample chapters advised her to "cut out the foolishness." Describing her original American publisher's reactions in *A Fine Old Conflict*, Decca wrote that Thompson objected to the length and the "too gooey detail" of her descriptions of embalming.

painfulness to people who have recently had a death in the family; they don't want casual readers to be subjected to such articles. A book is different; it is offered only to those who <u>want</u> to read it, not as part of a "family" newspaper etc. Therefore the reader has a right to expect that it will include all information on the subject, and especially information that has been deliberately withheld.

4. The chapters we are doing now deal with more familiar territory, and will, I hope, find more favor and less opposition. The following chapters are almost finished: 1) The funeral transaction, just how the selling is done, the psychological factors on both sides. 2) Funerals and the clergy; violent reaction to criticisms from all the major denominations; how the clergy view the funeral. 3) Public relations (the funeral director's self-image, and how he tries to put it across). 4) History of protest (beginning with a lovely quote from St. Anthony, 3rd century, anti-embalming, and on through some English critics, to present day). After these are finished we shall proceed with the outline, pretty much.

5. I'm more and more beginning to see the subject matter of the book in this way: it illuminates in weird, gruesome and distorted fashion many of the crazy things about our society. For example, it is true that advertising has become madder and more outlandish over the years, and the Practical Burial Footwear people are only doing for their product what other advertisers do for theirs. But the fact this practical footwear is destined for the dead is what exposes something rather terrifying about their whole outlook. The point of all this is that the book will try to be one of protest, not just against high costs, but against something more sinister: destruction of standards, taste etc. (This is what one hopes will <u>emerge</u> from the book, rather than being explicitly stated.)

6. The chapters on the funeral society movement will now be delayed until after the national meeting of funeral societies in Chicago on April 16th. We think the discussion of funeral societies will be improved by handling it from a reportage point of view—who was at the meeting, what they said, what problems they brought up etc. There will be a lot of Unitarian types, university people, egg-heads of all descriptions at the meeting, and most likely an account of it—of what got these people interested, etc—would be the best point of departure.

7. On to the subject of publishers. As I said on the phone, I think the book will need quite a bit of special handling to get it going, and that an enthusiastic (rather than luke-warm) publisher would be of greatest help. . . . A stuffy approach, on the other hand (such as might very likely be Lovell's) could be bad both from the point of view of editing and from the point of view of publicity when the book is published.

If you get the feeling that H. Mifflin only want to go ahead because they feel committed, I do think you should consider making a change in light of the above considerations. I shall be most interested in your advice on this.

Thanks again for all,
love from Decca

To *Constancia Romilly*   Oakland
March 3, 1962

Darling Dinkydonk,

. . . I'm longing to know about your reports. Please send along as soon as possible—or else copy out the appropriate words, the ones I always read aloud to Bob ("intelligent, high potential" etc) while omitting certain other words ("failed to turn in a major report, doesn't study hard enough"). . . .

Well, our news: Very bad in some respects. We got an F (as Benj would say) from English agent and publisher on the chapters of the book we sent. James thinks . . . it is unpublishable. So does Victor Gollancz. I am terribly depressed by this as I have the greatest respect for both James and Victor. I am also afraid that Lovell Thompson may have the same reaction.[17] Can you imagine the horror, after the months and months of work we've put in, and Bob leaving his practice to work on it? I can't tell you how upset I am about it. Bob is less so, for some reason; perhaps because less of the actual writing was his. It is a severe body-blow.

However, Candida writes: "I am very pleased, and impressed, with the chapters; they are sprightly and sharp and skillful—I see this as a very good book indeed." Yea, Candida.

In any case, we are ploughing ahead—have about 3 more chapters just about ready to be typed. This is the only thing one can do, don't you agree? Because we have confidence in the material. . . .

Best of luck with your work—hope it turns out better than ours,
Decca

To *Constancia Romilly*   Oakland
March 10, 1962

Darling Doncaster,

. . . Our own fortunes have been veering wildly: no word to this day from the Crummy Bastards (H. Mifflin) about the ms. we sent. So yesterday Candida called. She has a firm offer from Simon & Schuster ("I am sorry, but Henry does

---

17. Thompson clearly had the same reaction to the portion of the manuscript he'd seen (see the letter of the previous day to Candida Donadio), but he had not rejected the manuscript as unpublishable and apparently was still committed to their contract to publish the book.

not like the book," remember? Dau. and Rebs), for a much larger advance[18] and all sorts of nice things. So the fate is not decided, but now <u>we</u> are trying to cut loose from the Crumbs. All this <u>confidential</u>, natch.

Lots of love, write soon, Decca

To Constancia Romilly   Oakland
                                                                    March 28, 1962

Darling Pleasant Young Person with Noble Mind,

You can't think how pleased I was to see, <u>at last</u>, your letter. I must say when you do write, your letters are terrific. . . .

The book news is most varied, plots thickening all over the place. All the following also confidential, in the sense that it would be disastrous should it get over to the publishers etc. concerned. OK to tell Aranka, though, or other interested parties, as long as <u>they</u> realize 'tis secret.

Houghton Mifflin, after weeks of careful thought, have decided they love the book, they want it, they intend to go ahead. So I wrote to them last weekend begging them not to, asking to be released from the contract (so we can go ahead with Simon and Schuster, of which H. Mifflin knows naught). Isn't that all a hilarious mess?[19]

The other thing is, Candida just called up to say Hutchinson (an English publisher) is willing to offer 500 pounds for the book. So all depends how it strikes a person, apparently. . . .

Lots of love, Decca.

To Kathleen Kahn   Oakland[20]
                                                                     April 4, 1962

Dearest K, How are you? Cooking on all four burners, I hope? That's just an expression, but much on my mind just now. Sorry not to have written much, but there has been a dearth of news. Now, there's a hot bit of news, so I thought I'd write about same.

Your sainted P's have bought a new stove. Oh you should see the stir it's been

---

18. The offer was for $5,000, which Decca wrote in another letter "seems to me enormous."

19. Houghton Mifflin acceded to her wishes after refusing to publish the embalming chapter. Within weeks of this letter, Decca wrote that "the publisher question is at last settled" and Simon & Schuster was to publish the book. She said that "fortunately, we parted from Lovell Thompson . . . on excellent terms, no quarrel or anything involved."

20. The return address on the preprinted envelope had the Treuhafts' street address. Above that was typed in "Reasonable Burials, Inc."

causing.[21] First crack out of the box, they had the fearful decision as to whether to buy a brand new one or a 2nd hand one. The 2nd hander available was said, in the ad, to have belonged to "a bachelor." (Lie the first; he was a divorcé, it subsequently turned out—and <u>already remarried</u>. Well, you know your mother's attitude to such things; but I'm getting ahead of my story, as the drearier writers say.)

So anyway. Our opinion was asked, and foolishly we gave it. The point at issue was: the new one would be $500, but free installation. The bachelor's one (I mean the person posing as a bachelor's one) would be $150—<u>but</u>, $10 for the installation. So as your father said, all we'd be saving is $200 (which I privately thought there was something wrong about the addition not to say the subtraction of, but you know how frightfully positive and intimidating Eph can be, and not wanting to cross him I said nothing). Bob said, why don't you get the $150 one, since it is cheaper? Rather brave of him, but he said it; and after a good deal of agonizing (this took several days alone, I mean the agonizing) they did.

Today was the Delivery. That is, the stove was delivered, which cost (as you will see by re-reading para #3) $10. Your mother is close to a nervous decline, because of the following considerations: 1) The broiler is towards the floor, you know the sort, you have to stoop. She specially keeps saying <u>YOU</u> (you, of all people) will disapprove. I keep saying you've never been known to cook so far, besides you don't live here any more. This has not comforted her, because of 2) The oven door only fairly closes, not tight shut. There are 2 ovens; the other oven which's door does close OK is warm to the touch . . . oh, the horror of it. The actual reason for the warmness to touch is a thing called the Pilot Light (look it up in the dictionary, it's a little gas thing that keeps going day and night for some reason) but Barb fears it will make the gas bill higher. Such are the fears that assail us in this far Western community. Also, 3) there is a frightfully nice thing called a timer (look it up in dictionary, too. It so to speak <u>speaks</u> when things are done). The Timer on this stove merely gives one <u>very</u> brief grunt, instead of ringing loudly. Barb says, and I do see, one could never hear it in the living room. I have made two very practical suggestions: a) (not to confuse you by repeating lettering 1 and 2) that a) (oh I already said a)) but anyway, a) she should look at the little needle from time to time to see if it is or isn't almost done, that is the thing in the oven; and b) she should purchase a very long ear trumpet, the sort that will reach into the kitchen, and listen in when she has company to see if the timer is actually grunting. She did not like either of these suggestions.

I think I have listed the main things wrong with the stove, although there

---

21. Decca considered Kathleen's mother, Barbara Kahn, the quintessential housewife and often ribbed her about her domesticity. Decca's letters to Barbara Kahn frequently included anecdotes about notable stoves and other household appliances she encountered in her global travels.

was some mention I think of <u>grease</u> on it. Which I said, as softly as I could, there usually is on stoves. By the time we saw the grease we already knew the marital status of that two-timing non-bachelor, which explained all, including the non-working of the (one) timer, according to Barb.

Anyway, all this has taken up a good deal of all of our time. I did also mention the starving Chinese, and how pleased he/she would be to have any sort of stove. This did not go over, like telling children to eat their beastly vegs because of the starving children in Europe. Anyway, because of the stooping broilers, they have (the Sainted P's) bought a Hibachi. I rather rudely asked if it was a high Hibachi. They did not reply. So I gathered it actually isn't.

By 5 o'clock today, both Eph and Barb were near collapse. We brought them over here, soothed their respective brows with martinis and lamb chops, tried sort of to get their minds off the stove. Not too successful. They are now, covertly but natherless pretty obviously, blaming us for the whole thing.

Not much other news. This has been about as much excitement as one can manage for one week, or rather two weeks—the stove bit has been going on for at least that long. . . .

Lots of love, Yr. Godmother

ps. They left here just a little while ago; ostensibly to pick up Ray,[22] but we fear actually to put their heads in the respective 2 ovens to commit Hibachi.* By the way, in all the Human Interest excitement I see I have forgotten to describe the actual stove. Well, it is colored white and silver (you know those things in kitchens, with little black things one cooks on?) and it is honorably named after a well-known brand of English china, Wedgwood. In fact, it is actually a perfectly OK and ordinary stove. It has 4 of the little black things one cooks on, and thousands of marvellous lights that are supposed to go on and off, in case of emergency. I am hoping your mother will recover soon from the experience of getting it. But do write to her very soon, as this has been a <u>most</u> upsetting week for her.

*If so, it will be interesting to see which one picks the oven door that doesn't actually close.[23]

---

22. Ephraim Kahn's mother, Ray Kahn.

23. This letter prompted a reply from Kathleen Kahn on the letterhead of the Boyerton Burial Casket Company, New York. Here is part of that reply:

Dear Godmamma,

I have sold the movie rights of your last letter to work my way thru college. I hope your professional pride will not be hurt but you see a Vassar education really is the most important thing of all especially for one as eager and deserving as myself. I am afraid a few changes will have to be made for the public, you understand, we feel a stove is a bit too homey and dull (it will never sell) and so we would like to substitute a casket and end it with a military funeral and possibly a bomb or two in the background to give it Significance For Our Times. . . .

I have just got a letter from the sainted papa who says that he wants your letter himself to correct the arithmetic in it. <u>He</u> won't make any movie for you. Or for anyone. I think you will have to keep an eye on him.

To Barbara Kahn   Aboard the *California Zephyr*
                                                            April 14, 1962

Dear Barb,

Bob keeps looking at his watch & making unfavourable comparisons about when we should have arrived in Chi. had we come by aeroplane. I'm afraid I'll never get the old thing on a train again. But I am adoring it & already regretting that we shall arrive in a few hours now.

Bob is a great one for reading out loud from the guide brochure, things like: "At 5:28 you will notice the great 6.2 mile bore . . ."

There are several of these to be noted at all times in & around the dining car & lounge. Conversation with them consists of trying to top them (as with our milkman):

Fellow Traveler: "As my husband always says, you see so much _more_ from a train."

Me: "Well yes. As _my_ husband always says, 'What's your rush?' "

F.T.: "Of course the planes are convenient if you're in a hurry."

Me: "Yes that's what I always say. You really do save time . . ." and so it goes. . . .

                          See you shortly, Decca

To Barbara Kahn and other friends and relatives   On train to NY
                                                            April 20, 1962

Dearest Barb, Eph, Benj, Mimi,[24] et Al,

We just had an idea for title of chapter on cremation: THE JOY OF COOKING. As you can see, travel has not broadened our interests. The three of us (Bob, me & a bottle of whiskey) are sitting happily in our lovely roomette before Dinner.

Shall I tell you about Evanston? Well rwas fascinating The Foundation is housed in a sham Williamsburg building, columns & red brick & discreet all-green large reception rooms when one gets inside. (By the way I am speaking, of course, of the National Foundation of Funeral Service. To my astonishment, the Goldbergs,[25] who have lived in Chi. for years, have _never heard of it_. Neither have the Turners[26] or any other of the dozens we met in Chi.) So, well, we were met with Courtesy Plus, the Little Things that Mean so Much. Secretaries fell all over each other with the friendly, human touch. The only fly in

---

24. Miriam Miller.

25. The Treuhafts' well-connected Chicago friends, architect Bertrand (Bud) Goldberg (one of Robert Treuhaft's roommates during his freshman year at Harvard) and his wife, Nancy Florsheim Goldberg.

26. Joyce Turner had been a friend of the Treuhafts since their early years in San Francisco, when they knew the "dimpled 21-year-old ingenue" as "Dear Joyce." By this time she had moved to Chicago.

this fearfully thick ointment was that we were left cooling our heels from 9 a.m. till 1 p.m. in an office; the library, we were told, was tied up because "Dr. Nichols (2nd in command) is in conference there." We had driven out to the Foundation with Mrs. Stone, the young, intellectual secretary of the Chi Memorial Society. By 1, we were pretty cross; had gone out for brief lunch & returned. We were then informed that Mr. Krieger[27] (head of all) was on the phone for us from Canada. Well we got the distinct impression that hell was given by Mr. K to his staff. Result of phone call: we got an appt. with Krieger (who was on his way home) for the following day, and the conference in the library mysteriously came to an abrupt end so we could start our work.

Pressing the advantage, I cornered Dr. Nichols & said I should like to interview him extensively. Barb it may be one's overwrought imagination but he absolutely does look like a Beautiful Memory Pic;[28] the same taut, faintly powdered skin & carefully fixed smile. About 40, I should judge. He's a Dr. because he has a PhD in Education. In spite of me being impressed with this fact, I got him on the run in no time flat. . . . The number of times he said "I don't know" or "I couldn't say" was rather astronomical. Such as (on public health aspects of embalming) Q: Could you give me an example, either of your own knowledge or from any written source, where a person has become ill because of the presence of an unembalmed dead body?" A: "To tell you the truth I've never heard of a dead body not being embalmed." Bob & Mrs. Stone, working in the library, noted he mopped his brow & loosened his tie a few times in the course of the interview.

Krieger, the next day, proved a much craftier old fox, also quite a Memory Pic in his own, older way. I'll tell all when we get home—or rather, I promise not to, because I have just noted that I haven't told you anything about the Goldbergs' stove & other points of interest in Chi.

All was well up to par. We arrived at the Turners, took a taxi. The driver kept saying "You must have the wrong address, that's a colored neighborhood," & Bob kept answering, "We don't know what color our friends are, forgot to look" etc. So we got there, & masses of fur-coated chic looking people were in & around the house; turned out to be a Bar Mitzvah for the Turner son (one of 4 kids). So champagne for ages, & all sorts of types both friend & enemy. Joyce's stove, not much. Rather as 'twere your old one.

---

27. Wilber M. Krieger, managing director of National Selected Morticians and director of the National Foundation of Funeral Service, whose mercenary funeral merchandising tactics and folkloric, pseudomedical defense of embalming Decca was to skewer in her book. She wrote later that "[h]is pronouncements were always absolutely sure-fire, marvellous copy," so, she said, when he died—or, as she put it, went on "to a balanced-line casket"—she mourned the death of her valued enemy.

28. In *The American Way of Death*, Decca described the "half-digested psychiatric theories" behind the mythology of American funeral rites. Included was the funeral industry's stress on the importance of the "memory picture," which she defined as "the last glimpse of the deceased in open casket, done up with the latest in embalming techniques and finished off with a dusting of makeup."

On to the Goldbergs, in a day or two. Typical quiet night at home: 15 for dinner and (<u>so</u> like the really rich) we all troop through & past the lovely dining room into the kitchen . . . the very latest thing with several refrigerators—and a <u>hibachi instead of a stove</u>. . . . There was, we found out at breakfast one day, actually another ordinary stove with gas and electricity; but they are all immured (as one might say) sort of in the place where your hall closet might be, had you one. . . .

    [L]ots of love to all,

        Bob & Decca

To Roul Tunley   Oakland

                                              May 6, 1962

Dear Roul,

    . . . The florists say (this is from the Florists Review): "FLOWERS OMIT-TED FROM POST BLAST AT COST OF DYING: It is a rare occurrence when florists can be grateful that funeral flowers are omitted. But such was the case when [Tunley's] article titled 'Can You Afford to Die?' appeared in the June 17 issue of the Saturday Evening Post. . . . The important point here is that this omission of funeral flowers did not just happen. Derogatory references to flowers did not appear in the article because of intensive behind-the-scenes efforts of the florists' information committee of the Society of American Florists. By working closely with the magazine's advertising department, the FIC committee successfully headed off statements which would have been extremely damaging to the industry."

    The article goes on to say that Howard C. Raether[29] tried some of the behind the scenesery too, but it didn't work in his case. . . .

        Best Regards, Decca

To Philip and Katharine Graham   Oakland

                                           May 16, 1962

Dear Phil and Kay,

    I am deeply engaged in writing my dismal book about funerals, to be published (if ever finished) by Simon and Schuster, next spring. Fortunately, it actually is <u>almost</u> finished, but the quite finishing always seems impossible.

    At the moment, I'm doing a chapter on the Menace of P.O.[30] You probably

---

29. The longtime executive secretary of the National Funeral Directors Association became Decca's leading and indefatigable antagonist in the industry. In July, Decca described with delight the lead editorial in *Mortuary Management* magazine: "Howard C. Raether Meets the Treuhafts."

30. A play on the old advertising slogans for deodorant that decried the menace of body odor (B.O.), which, so the ads said, even your best friends wouldn't tell you about.

don't know what P.O. is (your best friends won't tell you because they won't know) but it stands for Please Omit—flowers, in funeral notices. The reason it is such a menace is that between 65% and 70% of the annual revenue of the flower industry comes from funeral flowers; over $400 million a year. P.O. is also a threat to the American way of life because it imperils sentiment, one of the foundations upon which we have built our country, and history shows what happens when countries abandon it. I know all this from reading florists' journals and funeral trade mags.

Several years ago, the Florist Telegraph Delivery Assn. set up an organization to combat the Menace of P.O. with an annual budget of over $2 million. They canvassed hundreds of newspapers. Their plan of attack was to take a series of 85-line ads. on the obit. (as I now call it) pages of leading newspapers, then to threaten to withdraw the ads if the papers continued to carry P.O. requests in death notices. . . . Over 200 major newspapers have complied (as we florists and near-florists say: complied! Reminds you of laws and such) and the papers do not carry P.O. notices.

In 1960, when Pres. Eisenhower's mother-in-law died, the Eisenhower family requested no flowers but gifts to charity instead. The Florists Review (a little-known paper, you will say, but now well known to me) was of course awfully upset, and referred to the announcement as "Ike's Bombshell" against the flower industry.* The Florists Telegraph Delivery Assn. tried unsuccessfully to get a retraction from the White House. The Washington Post reported Pres. Eisenhower's request (issue of September 30, 1960) but the New York Times did not, although they presumably must have had access to the same information as the Washington Post. I wonder why? (Incidentally, we note that both the Washington Post and the NY Times continue to carry Please Omit notices. No San Francisco papers do.) . . .

What I should love to know is some of the inside negotiations that go on between the flower folks and the advertising departments of newspapers. I am hopeful that perhaps somebody in your far-flung news empire could give me some dope on this. Such as letters from florists, or accounts of meetings with them? And possibly a statement of policy (of the Wash. Post) on the question of P.O., if such a thing exists. . . .

Lots of love to your many and fascinating children, Decca

* called by them the Florist Industry, but it sounds a bit ungram.

To Barbara Kahn   Chatsworth, Bakewell, Derbyshire
                                                      June 30, 1962

Dearest Barb,

...I'm sitting in me bedroom, by lovely fire...in the Chintz Room, so called because the walls are covered with white chintz. All else is green and gold brocade. There are about 12 full-sized paintings (by whom? I haven't found out) and another 12 or so drawings and miniatures of various 18th and 19th cent. Devonshires. Bob's room, adjoining, is the Chintz Dressing room, also far from chintzy, and also with huge 4 poster and hangings going up to a crown neath which one sleeps....

Modernity mingles with authentic palace life here. There's a house telephone in every bedroom, and a card, printed, giving the code number of every other telephone in the house—28 in all. Bob studied the card a bit when we first arrived, and said in puzzled tones, "it doesn't say anything about breakfast."

Conversation is rather like the old sort of lawn tennis . . . in that it goes at a very leisurely and trivial pace for ages, naught but generalities and how to get best results with lighting pix and so on—but suddenly, wham! And if you're not looking, right in the eye you get it.

Bob had the pleasure of hearing the following bit. . . . Sir Julian Huxley[31] was explaining about pollinating. He said that bees can't see red things too well, so therefore in parts of the world where bees are the main pollinators of flowers the flowers don't grow a true red; on the other hand, birds do see red things, so in the tropics etc. where the birds are main pollinators very bright red flowers grow. Upon which Lady Huxley (who's rather a little silly, with mincing manner) interjected, "Oh dear, do you know that last week I was almost pollinated in the bird house!" Naturally everybody roared (Debo said, "really!") and Sir J. got a bit cross and shut Lady H. up, saying "dear," in silencing tones. . . .

Mrs Ham had her dream morning this morning; she was put on a chintz sofa to pose for Cecil Beaton[32] and Duncan Grant (who turns out to be a painter).[33] So she's in a frightfully good mood for the moment. . . .

This evening: Barb, slides. I begged to not have to go, and explained all about our Calif. slide insurance; to no avail. Sir Julian had specially brought them, the slide thing had been fetched, there was no way out. They were as

---

31. The biologist and humanist, grandson of zoologist Thomas Huxley and brother of writer Aldous Huxley, who lectured and wrote prolifically on the philosophy of science and helped to popularize evolution and other central scientific concepts.

32. The British portrait photographer who specialized in elaborately staged, opulent photos of glamorous people.

33. One of the most prominent British painters and designers of the early twentieth century, he was favored by some of the royal family. Among his better-known works are portraits of members of the Bloomsbury Group, of which he was a central figure.

usual. Hours and hours of Ghana and other parts in Africa, being squeezed in and out of focus by Lady Huxley. . . . People murmuring "marvellous color," "marvellous costume," "I say what character," "oh jolly good," "oh jolly funny, look at the face," "oh I say the market, you were there too weren't you Debo?" and so on. Mrs. Ham slept throughout, and said at the end "best, most interesting and fascinating evening I can remember," and then dashed to bed. Slides, Barb, must be terrific fun to take and develop and be in charge of showing and all, but dross to have to watch. People never seem to think that the world is so full of such wonderful things, like Life Mag etc where one could see many even better pix of same scenes if one subscribed, and wouldn't have to wait for Lady H. to click the thing and then go through the agonizing (to one's eyes) process of focussing. Idea for a terrific new book by Julian Huxley: Slideless in Ghana.[34]

The sad, disappointing but natherless true thing is that people like J. Huxley are much better at writing than at being about. Bob and I have the distinct impression that he is the usual sucker up to dukes in real life, so unlike his terrifically good, clever and reasoned essays. . . .

So you can see, Barb, life here is a bit thick. We miss you all v. much. Sorry to blither on so, but it does help pass the post-slide part of the evening.

Lots of love, look up the Children (in fact, you might relay this letter, if they are interested), and send an account of them and you,

Dec.

To Virginia Durr   London
                                                                                     July 4, 1962

Dearest Va,

No time to catch breath, much less write letters. This is a rare 1/2 hour between the mad rush. I know you're longing to hear [about] the Ducal Weekend, so will start with that: Staying at Chatsworth is sort of unbelievable. As Bob wrote to the children, "If we were invited to stay with Jack and Jackie at the White House, for instance, at least I'd know which century I was in and would have a vague idea of how to behave." It's authentic palace life here. . . .

Mrs. Hammersley was the sort of pivotal one of the weekend, it was more or less organized around her. I know I must have told you about Mrs. Ham. She is a contemporary of my mother's, a bit older in fact, and was an exotic influence in our childhood—completely unlike most of my parents' friends, she's 1/2 French and a very literary sort, she translates Fr. books (letters of Mme de Scvigny, that sort of thing). She was fascinating to us, because she knew all the

---

34. Aldous Huxley, Julian's brother, was the author of a novel entitled *Eyeless in Gaza*.

writers and painters and non-Swinbrook types (still does). We found out how the owners of great houses spend their spare time; they visit other great houses, as trippers. An expedition was organized to Haddon Hall. Mrs. Ham, Bob and I went in one car with the chauffeur, Debo and the others in the station wagon. When we were almost there, Mrs. Ham started whispering to me in French; the burden of her conversation was that she has a heart condition for which she is taking some medicine. The medicine is supposed to draw water off the legs to relieve pressure on the heart; but in doing this, the water gets deposited in the bladder. Apparently some had just been deposited. I'm sure she's got it all wrong, but anyhow she wanted to go to the john. So to my sorrow I had to go back with her to Chatsworth (missing the Haddon Hall trip), leaving Bob off at Haddon Hall. I knew I should be bitterly blamed if I let her return alone. . . .

Giles Romilly has gone off his head and he has fled the country with the two oldest children (Lizzie and Eddie, aged 12 and 10) and is believed to be headed for California to see the Dinkydonk. So I've written to her, with instructions to cable us if he shows up, and to detain him if possible until Mary Romilly[35] can get there to recover the children.

Yesterday morning I spent hours with a <u>charming</u> undertaker in Clapham.[36] So different from ours. I asked him if there is much "pre-need" in England (the great and growing thing in U.S.; did you know that <u>three times</u> as many graves are sold annually as there are deaths?). He said, "very little. Occasionally an old woman may come in, to say I want you to take care of my funeral; then we put her name in our N.Y.D. file." "What's N.Y.D.?" "Not Yet Dead." He showed me all the coffins, and I was murmuring "lovely, lovely" because it seemed the thing to do; but he said "I think they're awful things. Look at all that dreadful silk and lace!" I did love him. . . .

Do write. Write to the Isle, I shall be so longing for letters.

Fondest love to all, Decca

To Aranka Treuhaft and Margaret Lourie[37]

Inch Kenneth
July 11, 1962

Dearest Aranka and Midge,

I arrived in this haven of peace yesterday. The pace in London and other parts was killing, as you can imagine, and I'm awfully glad to be here in this timeless, beautiful part of the world, hoping to get on with some work at last. . . .

Last weekend, I went to the Toynbees, Bob to Moscow to the Peace Confer-

---

35. Giles Romilly's estranged wife.
36. L. C. Ashton, whom Decca featured in a chapter on English funerals in *The American Way of Death*.
37. The daughter of Robert Treuhaft's sister, Edith.

ence. The Toynbees have a very nice, ramshackle old house in Monmouthshire, where they live with their 3 kids. They took me to two dinner parties, which seemed to exemplify the two main trends among the English country dwellers since the war. The first was in a very well-appointed house, iced cocktails, excellent dinner cooked and served by the hostess. The second, in a huge house which was falling apart in every direction. Every chair and couch had holes in it; most of the windows were broken; carpets in shreds; the linoleum in the hall so far worn down that all that was left were sort of pools of linoleum surrounded by the wood of the floor. Dinner in huge dining room on rickety deal table with half-dirty cloth which only partly covered the table. Drinks (un-iced) were martinis made with Italian vermouth, dinner was cold cuts and salad. The 8 children of the family came down briefly in their (torn) dressing gowns to say how do you do, and then went up to bed. How they get enough to eat beats me—I didn't. These are the sort of English people who have completely given up the struggle.

I arrived at Inch K. yesterday at teatime. My mother seems in much better shape than I had thought. Her palsy doesn't seem any worse; she is <u>fearfully</u> vague, but then she always was. She asked me, "what are your plans for this place when I leave?" I said "where are you going?" She went into gales and shrieks of laughter, and answered, "departing to the next world soon, I expect." But she doesn't seem to be departing at the moment, thank goodness. On the contrary. She walks all over the farm and still chases the goats with her umbrella. . . .

The Isle is looking lovely, lots of wild flowers and all the animals looking well. My mother has redecorated a lot of the rooms, so all is clean and beautiful. They have a washing machine now, which is a great improvement (clothes, not dishes); next thing you know they'll get a refrigerator. She still sends the sheets to London to be washed, though. . . .

Lots of love, Decca

To Barbara Kahn   Inch Kenneth
                                                                         July 13, 1962

Dearest Barb,

He who writes to old Dec at the Isle gets a gold star (or perhaps a present from Oban, which luckily I've already sent, do hope it arrives). Because there's naught sadder than watching for the boat for hours and finding one has drawn a blank. I was <u>most pleased</u> to get yours of the 9th. I got another letter, too; at least it was addressed to Bob, but in his absence I opened it. It starts, "Dear Mr. Treuhaft, This is just to tell you that I found not a trace of fungus in the specimens of nail that I removed from your right thumbnail." . . . Anyway, it was a nice letter, all about Bob's thumbnail and "distorted little toenail," it does make me miss him. . . .

There are 2 maids here, Mrs. Campbell the cook, and Betty. . . . The MacGillivrays are v. frank about my position on the Isle. Mrs. MacG. told me the Campbells (Mr. C. is the gardener here) loathed my book and were v. annoyed when they heard Bob and I were coming. She said opinions on Mull were divided about the book; I sent her a copy and she lent it around all over the Hebrides. She said some hated it, others thought it was wonderful. Anyway I'm setting out to neutralize the Campbells; haven't done well so far. . . . [T]he Scotch are not easily won over once they decide to loathe you.

Barb I found the most extraordinary haul of old letters here, saved for me over the years. Masses of them; somebody must have found them at Rotherhithe St. after we left and turned them over to my mother. They are all the letters I got from the others at the time of running away and while E. and I were in Bayonne. I so wish I'd had them when I was writing D. and R. I spent all yesterday after-noon reading them. It seems that after I ran, the others settled to ordinary life; they went to Germany, to Venice, and other parts. Also there was the Corona-tion, taking up a lot of the letters. The ones from Germany give 3 separate accounts (Muv, Unity and Debo) of their time there. Muv: "Had tea with Hitler. He is very agreeable and has surprisingly good manners."[38] Debo: "We all went to tea with Hitler today. Delicious cakes. Bobo gets quite different when she's with him, all trembly and can't take her eyes off him." Bobo: "Tea with the Fuhrer. Muv kept talking about home-made bread and asked if they couldn't pass a law in Germany making it illegal to take out the wheat germ." Then there are lots from Nanny, saying do come home, you only packed two pair of knickers and both are too small for you; the grey trousers you asked for are full of moth holes, should I alter Bobo's white ones and send them to you? If so, measure from waist to ankle and advise. Gosh they're a lark. And one from Nancy, very stuffy, "society (and I don't mean duchesses) has certain rules and can be pretty beastly to those who break them," and one from Rodd, pointing out the prosecu-tion possibilities if we continued to "live in sin," his expression, the old fraud.

All this very destructive to work on the book. . . .

While [at Philip Toynbee's house], I witnessed the birth of an article for the Observer. Sat. morning, Philip announced "David (Astor) just rang up to say Faulkner has croaked, and I've got to do an emergency obit. for tomorrow's paper." Turned out Philip loathes Faulkner and has only read 2 of his books. I wasn't much help; told him the Willie McGee bit and F. saying "they should both be destroyed."[39] Neither of us could remember the name of that county in his books that begins with a Y. So with this slim info, he got to work. I enclose

---

38. This may be a paraphrase. A letter from Lady Redesdale to Decca on June 12, 1937, covered the same subject in slightly different words. (For the wording, see introduction to first section, "Baby Blueblood and Hobohemian.") Lady Redesdale's letter also included the news that Hitler had "asked after little D."

39. The reference was to a 1951 meeting between Faulkner and Decca's Women's Delegation to Mississippi on behalf of Willie McGee, in which Faulkner had made seemingly contradictory com-ments on the black man and the white woman he had been convicted of raping. (Decca wrote a full account of the meeting in *A Fine Old Conflict*.)

the result, not bad considering the handicaps. In para 5 ("it has also been said by critics . . .") I am the said critics.[40] What I esp. like is para 6: "In all except the marvellous and inimitable The Sound and the Fury . . . ," realizing that's about the only one Philip has read. To our sorrow, the Times obit. was full of specifics like the Snopes family and Yoknapatawpha County, v. one-up. . . .

Barb do keep writing, and so will I. Please send constant news of the kids as I miss them like mad. . . . All the journeying so exhausts, and London was really madsville, so I'm loving being here in absolute quiet. Old age, Barb, I fear. . . . It's now almost 7 a.m. and I must get to work. One thing you wouldn't like here; it's a bit dry. That is, Old Buall[41] and sherry and a little wine with dinner, but no real booze. I've got 2 bottles stashed away for when Bob comes, but don't quite dare have nips, even in my room, as I think my mother, with the observingness of the very old, would note. Eph would probably say it's good for me, but I don't think so; I know I'd get more done on the book if I could have a good stiff drink in the p.m. Lots of love to all of you. Please show this to the children, and get them to write. One day, you MUST all come here.

Dec

To Barbara Kahn et al.   Inch Kenneth
                                                                 July 15, 1962

Dearest Barb and All, including Mimi and Children,

'Tis Sunday. I've been up since my usual 5:30, it's now 1, and I'm waiting for the others to get back from church. Unfortunately I was unable to go as I did not have a hat. But I took advantage of the general exodus to get meself a nip of whiskey, 1st to cross my lips in 6 days. The usual note here is, "Have a drop of sherry, little D, it'll warm you up." (You say it will, but will it?)

Yesterday, Lady Congleton of Ulva and her brother-in-law [came] to tea. They are so reminiscent of the same sort of neighbors at Swinbrook. Their major characteristic is freedom from fear of being boring, so unlike us Americans. Also, freedom from fear of offending. Thus Lady C. went on for ages about a certain by-election which "our side" won handily; a by-election, I might add, of several years ago, "our side" meaning the tories. The bro-in-law explained to me in the most detailed way exactly how to import ponies from Iceland to Scotland and train them to carry dead stags. In fact, should I ever be faced with this exact problem at some future time I really do think I'll know just how to do it, one should be grateful to learn something new. Sorry to assign

---

40. In his "appreciation," Toynbee had written, "It has also been said by critics who judge writers mainly by their social and political attitudes that Faulkner was ambiguous in his whole treatment of race in the Southern States. . . . But I believe that this too is a mistaken criticism. . . ."

41. An apparent reference to the Madeira wine known as Bual.

motives, but I honestly think they came hoping for the famous almond cake, a specialty of my mother's famed for miles around in these parts. Unfortunately, there wasn't any, as it turned out; only scones and pancakes and 2 sorts of sandwiches, and what I call "cookies." . . .

Later: They didn't get back till 2. It seems the car wouldn't start, Muv says because of the Heatwave (temp. up to 68 yesterday). I said I should be v. cross with my car if it didn't start at 68 degrees, since it's usually 70 or more at home; she said vaguely it's all about what they are accustomed to, and it must have been the heat wave because somebody else's car wouldn't start either. Ideas of hot and cold round here are anyway rather strange. For instance, the MacGillivrays are campaigning for a refrigerator, in fact I think their ultimate aim is a deep-freezer. I broached the refrig. idea to Muv but she said it always seems to make the food so <u>cold</u>. To which what can one answer? Because it really does, in a way. She hates cold cream on the puddings, so I suppose best not to have one. . . .

Anyway all in all I was lucky not to have brought a hat. . . .

What will tomorrow's installment of this thrilling serial bring? Will the Campbells succeed in ousting MacTrueheart and his bonnie son Benj? Will the young Laird bring peace between Ulva and Inch Kenneth (or just the far-off steppes of Moscow)? Will the Toynbees be warmed up by a drop of sherry? Will the temperature rise to 69 or drop to 67? For another exciting episode, tune in to this same station . . .

Fondest love to all of you, Dec.

To Virginia Durr   Inch Kenneth
                                                                 July 24, 1962

Dearest Va,

I've finished the whole chapter on English funerals, 24 pages, and it has been read and approved by all here   the Toynbees, Bob and even my mother. So I feel justified in taking a moment off to write to you. . . .

We find Philip awfully good company. He loves the Island life, is mad about fishing, goes swimming on the coldest days, and has done a lot of things to help around here, like helping Bob to cut down some of the dead trees that were done in during the stormy weather. . . .

Philip isn't really cynical, in fact he has from time to time really plunged into the peace movement—not for long chunks of time because it isn't his nature (organizing, I mean); he's a born writer and intellectual and you know how that sort never sticks to all the putting out mailings and making up lists and contacting people for their signature etc that the likes of you and me are so good at. He is though most deeply concerned about the nuclear war threat—and typically, his concern is very emotional as well as practical. All this is in preface to a Toynbee tale for your amusement.

Last night Philip and Bob went out fishing with MacGillivray, and Sally and I had a long chat. . . . Anyway . . . one of Philip's main waking nightmares is what to do about the children (whom he adores) should the bomb fall. Sally explained that he had decided that, in order to prevent them from dying a hideous and lingering death from radiation burns, he would kill them. So he bought masses of sleeping pills against the day, and also won Sally over to the scheme. As she is not the reflective type, she is rather easily won over to things, I think. So last summer they were on holiday—up here on the I. of Mull as a matter of fact, staying at Tobermory. They suddenly realized they'd forgotten to bring up the sleeping pills—and to make matters worse, that was the time when the Russians resumed testing. Philip got in an awful stew, and went to the tiny chemist shop in Tobermory to get some; but natch, they didn't have any, you have to have a Dr's prescription. So instead he settled for several bottles of <u>aspirin</u>! I simply roared, and pointed out to Sally that it's difficult enough to get a child of Lucy's age (6, then) to take even a couple of aspirin, let alone 50 or 100 or whatever is considered a killing dose. I asked her at what point were they prepared to do the deed? She said, "Well if the earth began to shake, one would know . . ." I begged her not to come to Calif. and start on our children, because the earth is always shaking there just from ordinary earthquakes every once in a while. Sally, who has no sense of humor, was rather cross with me for getting the giggles over the whole scheme. When Philip came back I confronted him with the aspirin, and I must say he's got a great ability to laugh at himself, and he did roar a bit about it. . . .

Do write soon, and give best love to Cliff and the Children.

Lots of love, Decca

To Barbara Kahn   Inch Kenneth
                                                                July 31, 1962

Dearest Barb,

Honestly I don't know what I should do without you. I don't think you really believe about my thirst for keeping in touch with the old homeland, but it is true, and you've been simply wonderful about writing. . . . The kids simply don't write at all. Were it not for you I should have been cabling, which would cause a frightful scene at Gribun, not to mention gossip and speculation. Then, imagine if the Postmistress squealed and told the local population that the contents of the cable was simply "do write, long for news," for which was paid the equivalent of a day's wages in these parts. . . .

I will now give some notes on Rural England. I should suggest reading them to yourself to see if they are fit for Eph, before transmitting. The main thing is, Barb, that once one has got used to not doing a single stroke of cooking or any other housework[42] (which one does <u>amazingly</u> fast; the positively pleasurable aspects, in which one luxuriates etc., last about 4 days) one notes that an awful amount of time is natherless consumed in—for lack of a better phrase—<u>consuming</u> the results of housework. I should say that a total of an average of 8 hours each day here is spent getting ready for, and eating, meals. You should be downstairs and ready 15 mins. before the meal, to have a bit of the warming sherry. Then there are all the courses. Then there's coffee. I really think one saves time by the routine at home: no breakfast, lunch and shopping at Khruschon's and the Co-op a total of 2 hours, no tea, cooking and eating dinner 2 hours. 1/2 the time, see?

Further notes on Rural England (I should be saying, Scotland; picked up your phrase there). Things on the Isle are anyway in a period of transition. That is to say, me mother is losing touch, in a way; she no longer does accounts; in fact says she has become inaccurate with them. Since I, at my prime of adding (probably aged 9 or so) never mastered the adding, subtraction and long division of pounds, shillings and pence, there's no point in me taking them on. Besides, to what effect? I still wouldn't know how and where to order the grain or the lumber and so on needed from time to time here. So the future of the Isle is rather miserably hanging fire. . . .

As for the old opus, it occupies our waking thoughts, at least until tea-time each day. . . . I did love the stuff Mr. Raether sent along. Here's a quote from it (R. is in turn quoting Habenstein, the same one who the NFDA[43] paid to write 2 books for them), and it is in response to my question on the therapeutic benefits of viewing the remains: "Bereavement needs best be understood not only in terms of genetic development of self vs. cross sectional pressures, but with reference to socio-cultural conditions. Other relevant variables are role configurations of bereaved persons (sociological), the import of religious beliefs (psychological), the functions and dysfunctions of funeral practices (social psychological-anthropological), the part played by empathic responses (psychiatric), and matters relating to community support of bereaved families (sociological)." There's lots more like that. Rather blissful, don't you think? . . .

We miss you all v. much. Lots of love,

Decca

---

42. As Decca told one friend, describing the deference given to the kitchen staff, "Household management is rather different here from at home. Such as, one can't go into the kitchen because 'they wouldn't like it,' and conversely one cannot ask for anything not on the table because that would be 'giving them trouble.' "

43. The National Funeral Directors Association.

To Barbara Kahn   Paris
                                                           August 17, 1962

Dearest Barb,

I was v. delighted to get your letter. But <u>awfully</u> sorry to hear that Ray is so badly off.[44] As a matter of fact, you might tell Eph (or better not tell him, it will only annoy) that I have seen and heard enough of the miseries of old age to have decided on a short life and merry one. I mean what's the actual point of foregoing various simple pleasures, like smoking and drinking, if all it does is to keep you going, only to be attacked from some unforeseen direction like palsy or not being able to breathe? It really is most extremely rough about Ray, and I do sympathize terrifically, both for her and for all of you. Old age is a sorry condition, alright. Even Muv, who is on the whole a very optimistic and down to earth sort, is I think rendered more than half miserable by her various maladies. In a way, had she died 10 years earlier of lung cancer or liver disease, as you and I probably will, she wouldn't have missed an awful lot. . . .

Lots of love to all, Mrs. Bobby Treuhaft

To Miriam Miller   Paris
                                                           August 24, 1962

Dear Mimi,

Thanks so much for your All Is Serene telegram, and also letter (just received) of 22nd August. All <u>what</u> is serene, I do wonder? . . .

Nancy has really put herself out, she's in a marvellous mood, I do hope it lasts until Tuesday. Yesterday, she had a cocktail party for us. Mostly (in fact entirely) rugged old American lesbians and ditto queers. The Queen of the Lesbians is one called Miss Arthur, whose great-grandf. was Pres. of the U.S. Must say I've never actually heard of him, but Bob thinks he did exist.[45] Miss Arthur and her crop-haired, beige-suited entourage are a v. odd lot. They talk 1/2 American and 1/2 English. Miss A. is a terrific name-dropper; sort of drags in "last time I saw Franklin, at the White House, you know" (she still pronounces it <u>White</u> House, tho, the English all say White <u>House</u>) and then tells some rather trivial and unimportant thing Franklin said. I do think it's a bit unfair of Nancy to loathe Americans so, based on this lot. . . .

My sister Pam arrived with her German wife, a ghastly one called Jedita, to whom I cottoned not. Pam was her usual vague, 1/2-mad self; told Nancy that the Concierge thought her voice was Nancy's, which did not please N. I'll have to do Debo's imitation of Pam's voice, so you'll see why. . . .

---

44. Ephraim Kahn's mother, Ray Kahn, was suffering from chronic asthma and died the following January.

45. An apparent reference to Chester A. Arthur, who did exist and was president from 1881 to 1885.

Paris is <u>so</u> empty, compared with '59, when nary a room could be had. Perhaps people are afraid of the bombings.[46] One does hear an occasional shot, but could be back-firing; Nancy, the least nervous of all people, goes outside to check if somebody comes into her courtyard unannounced, because she says they do sometimes leave a bomb. More likely, people are afraid of the prices, which are <u>steep</u>. . . .

Lots of love, all, and <u>so longing</u> to see you, Decca

To Peter Nevile   Oakland
                                            September 25, 1962

Dearest Peter,

I was <u>most</u> <u>delighted</u> to get your letter. The more so, because for a long time now I had the unhappy feeling that possibly you actively loathed Hons and Rebels (you know, because you <u>didn't</u> write).[47]

Actually, we've been to England 3 times in all; in 55, 59 and this year, 62. I did try to find you once or twice, specially the first time, but no luck. Because of various things (mainly having a bit more money, on acct. of me working) we probably will come back again in a few years; so don't move, or if you do, let us know where.

Giles. He did show up here, with the children. I fear he is quite a bit mad. It was v. hard to make any sense of him, or his plans. Philip Toynbee (who I've seen each time I've gone to England) is on Mary's side, and I must say so am I; mostly, because of the wretched life for the children. Wretched? Actually, they are loving it, fleeing from the law and all; but you know what I mean, now I've grown old and stuffy it seems to me they ought to have a more regulated existence. . . . I'm afraid I gave Giles a bit of a lecture, so did my husband, so did the Donk when she saw him; so he has vanished out of our lives. I think he is still living very near here, though.

Our life. Too long to tell. But the Donk is grown-up, and has gone to live in NY where she has a job (of sorts) but mostly seems to have gone off with a Freedom Rider, who sounds heavenly. They speak not of marriage, but this seems to be the note these days.[48]

We've also got a frightfully nice child called Benjamin, aged 15, who is being a comfort to me in my old age. . . .

Much love, and thanks again for writing, Decca

---

46. Paris had been in spiraling turmoil during Algeria's war of independence.

47. Decca and Nevile had apparently been out of touch since she and Esmond Romilly left Britain for the United States. He had been their closest friend and ally during their 1937 elopement. See letter of late February 1937 to Lady Redesdale. Decca wrote of Nevile in her 1960 memoir, discussing his role in the elopement.

48. Constancia Romilly had been traveling with Charles McDew, then chairman of the Student Nonviolent Coordinating Committee, to meetings of organizations like the National Student Association, on behalf of the civil rights movement. While in New York, she spent all her free time volunteering for the SNCC office in New York. She broke up with McDew the following summer.

To Virginia Durr   Oakland
                                                          September 30, 1962

Dearest Va,

Believe it or not, I have written the word FINIS at the end of Chapter 20 of
The American Way of Death. But don't get too excited; that doesn't necessarily
mean it is finished, because revision ahead and two of the chapters have got to be
entirely rewritten. However it is a complete manuscript now, you've no idea the
relief. Betty Bacon, my dear friend and guide in lit. matters, came over this
morning and spent hours reading it. She thinks it's 1st rate! Which pleases me
greatly. I am longing for it to be at the stage where I can send you a copy. . . .

[I]t has been such a job; not really my sort of thing, either, can't think how I
got talked into it. So uphill work it was. . . .

Bob goes back to work tomorrow. Sad to say, his firm lost a lot of money
while he was away, so tiresome just as we were getting nice and rich. Perhaps
they'll do better this year. Perhaps the book will sell well, although I don't
really think it will, too dismal a subject. My absolute terror is that I'll be sued
for libel all over the place. Bob is not an expert on libel law; we did get a book
on the subject, but it wasn't much of a help. . . .

I'm sending you Nancy's article[49] (which will be the first one in a new book
of essays coming out in October in England) to make up for not writing and
for generally being hopeless and not sending those books I promised or
anything. . . .

The Blor article is being the cause of much fury in the family, my mother
loathes it,[50] she wrote a very cross letter to Nancy saying "I wish you would not
do any more portraits of me until I am dead." The day the letter came, Bob and
I were at the Louvre where we saw among other things the Whistler's Mother
painting. I told Nancy she probably said the same thing to Whistler. Debo has
also joined the fray on Muv's side. I am on Nancy's side, as I think it is a very
good and true account of all.

Much love & to Cliff, Decca

To Virginia Durr   Oakland
                                                          December 13, 1962

Dearest Va,

. . . Dinky sounds fine, really taking hold of life and job. . . . She is a terrible
correspondent. I just got a letter from her saying, "Dear Dec, this is a business
letter" and asking for a loan of $200, to be repaid after Xmas on weekly install-

---

49. A portrait of the Mitford girls' beloved nanny Blor. It was reprinted in Nancy Mitford's *The
Water Beetle*, published in 1962 by Hamish Hamilton in the U.K. and by Harper & Row in New York.

50. Decca once wrote that in describing their mother in the essay, Nancy was "more or less
making Muv out a bit of an idiot."

ments. So I wrote back, "Dear Madam, am in receipt of your business letter of 9th instant" and told her that her request for a loan was now in the hands of our Loan Department, and was she prepared to meet our usual terms—a letter with each payment? I did add, "thank you for the opportunity to serve you," so I hope this brings a letter on account.

I just got the Author's Form from S. and S. (Simon's Shoe Store, the New Yorkers call them). Have got to describe book in 200 words, I suppose for the blurb. Galleys are due in mid-Feb, publication about May or June. Seems like ages, but they did say 6 or 7 months after I turned in the ms. They sent the rest of the advance, though, which is why our loan dept. is considering Dinky's application. The author's form also asks for a list of opinion makers who should receive an advance copy on the basis of interest expressed; so far, have thought of John F. Kennedy (who told Debo he thought the book was a smashing idea)[51] and Harry Bridges[52] (who told me the same). . . .

Goodbye, dear Va, lots of love to you and Cliff, Decca

To Robert and Benjamin Treuhaft   New York
                                                                  ca April 1963

Darling B & B,

Twas a lovely plane ride (smile). I think I should have liked it even better had the pilot not announced over the intercom, "We are flying through an impene trable cloud belt, trying for higher altitude . . ." then in a few minutes, "Because of unusually heavy traffic we can't reach the higher altitude." Why couldn't the silly idiot just do all that & shut up about it, I wondered?

A blissful ride in the limousine on the dear old solid earth. At the terminal sat a fattish young girl with long sloppy hair & specs; I rushed forward to hug her, stopped just in time. Soon the Donk herself appeared, in chic dark green silk shirtwaist & Alexandre piled on top of head hairdo. She is looking really smashing. . . . The flat isn't at all bad, she's decorated it in a tasteful combination of greens & blues, has got curtains, carpet etc & it looks fine. . . .

She is much grown up. Lives an odd life, to my way of thinking, but it seems to suit her. She has lots of friends, works several nights a week at various meuve-ment offices helping out. I gather she still hasn't figured out what you might call a basic plan of life, but I think she's getting there.

This neighborhood is like a stage set for West End Story, Dead End Kids, Love on the Dole or any other such. Drunks on the sidewalk in various stages from red-eyed slobberers to out cold; sinister groups of slouching teen-agers,

---

51. The duchess, whose late brother-in-law had been married to Kennedy sister Kathleen, had remained a close friend of John F. Kennedy.

52. San Francisco longshoremen's union leader Harry Bridges was a friend of the Treuhafts and sometime client of Robert Treuhaft. There had been repeated unsuccessful legislative and judicial attempts to deport him on the grounds that he was a covert Communist.

millions of kids, old folks, prostitutes etc etc. I should be terrified of coming home alone late at night but Dinky doesn't seem to mind a bit, of which I am v. glad. It's called Little Italy, the district, I mean. . . .

Lots of love, Decca

To Robert Treuhaft   New York

ca April 26, 1963

Darling Bob,

Note the belle enclosure. I had a time prying it loose because they wanted to make us wait to see the proofs which are due next week (jacket proofs) and which will be in color; the wreath[53] will be in what Bob Gottlieb[54] calls nauseous reds and greens.

Yesterday I got back from New Haven and went over to S. and S. for me appointment. I do wish you had been there. It exceeded my fondest hopes; the shoe store swinging into action. Present were Nina[55] and two fellows whose names I didn't get (but will today) and whose roles are, respectively, promotion and publicity directors. . . .

For the annual booksellers convention in Washington (May) they really are going to try to get a casket; I suggested that W.W. Chambers might lend one; do you think he might? In any case they are ordering a giant wreath to be made exactly like the jacket design. Also, getting some Builders Creeds,[56] F.L. Ashtrays, nutshells etc for door prizes for the salesmen.

This was, in a way, the least of it. Discussion turned on how to create national news stories around the book, how to make it the cover story for Newsweek or Time etc etc. How to get legislation introduced, how to get somebody to sue us ("Once they're in court, it's bound to be news!"), how to get the morticians to apply for an injunction to stop the book so they (S and S) can counter with another injunction. How to get the book attacked as subversive and me attacked as a red (surprising how little trouble they are going to have in this regard, I was thinking to myself), how to stir up the John Birch Society[57] to go for us. Goodness you'd have roared.

---

53. The cover drawing for *The American Way of Death* was a funeral wreath in the shape of a dollar sign.

54. Robert Gottlieb was the young editor at Simon & Schuster who was instrumental in acquiring *The American Way of Death*. He remained Decca's editor and became a lifelong friend and trusted professional consultant. (He is also the editor for this book.)

55. Nina Bourne, Robert Gottlieb's colleague, who was the head of advertising at Simon & Schuster and later at Knopf.

56. The "Builder's Creed" (or "Builders Dream") was the visionary document written by Hubert Eaton, the man who transformed a scruffy cemetery in Glendale into the extravagant Forest Lawn Memorial Park (or F.L. as Decca calls it here).

57. The ultra-right-wing organization formed to combat Communism in America. Its targets included such "dedicated, conscious agents of the Communist conspiracy" as President Dwight D. Eisenhower.

They are making up a brochure of all the attacks in the funeral press, and they are longing for more; also, a special clergy letter with quotes from the Nosy Clergy chapter,[58] possibly a trade union letter, and a letter to the Memorial Societies. They are ordering a special printing of paperbound ones, not for sale but stamped "Advance Copy" to be sent round to Key People. All these special letters and special approaches did so remind me of CRC. They are trying to get David Susskind[59] to have a Raether/Treuhaft debate on his telly program. They have various ideas for television. They are talking of hiring outside P.R. agencies to stir up the legislation etc. They really are a riot, and if 1/2 their plans come off or 1/10 of them all will be rather marvellous.

Next week there'll be various appointments with book page types, interviews to be written now and saved for publication time. . . . After all this is over I'll come home; but you can see these plots are worthwhile. Wed, I'm having some new pics taken by their good photographer.

They say that 6,000 copies have already been ordered by the book shops, that their goal is to sell more advance copies than D. and Rebels sold altogether. . . .

If you've got any promotion ideas not covered in the above, do write (or ring up, I'm beginning to feel rich), as they are being most receptive. . . .

[T]onight, a party at Dinky's. She really is marvellous, came home yesterday from work and before going to the ballet to clean up all. She is a 1st rate and effortless housekeeper. There goes the ribbon.[60] Goodbye.

Lo, Decca

To the Duchess of Devonshire   Oakland
                                                              May 25, 1963

Dearest Hen,

That must have been a terrible, terrible fortnight.[61] I did so agonize for you all; and it was extremely good of you to find time to write and send the t.grams as I was so longing for news, could think of naught else.

I know that you, specially, will miss Muv so dreadfully; I always thought you were easily her favourite child, she relied so much on you and when letters came from you (while we were staying there) she'd absolutely light up.

I'm so glad that we did go to stay with her last year. We rather thought at the time that it would be to say good-bye. . . .

Various mothers of friends have died in the last year or so but all in beastly hospitals, sometimes in what's known as the "intensive care" ward (the horror

---

58. The chapter in which Decca discussed funeral directors' resentment of religious leaders who help defend their parishioners against commercial exploitation in funeral arrangements.

59. Stage and television producer David Susskind hosted *The David Susskind Show*, a long-running and highly regarded TV interview-and-debate program on NBC.

60. Typewriter ribbon.

61. The illness of their mother, concluding with her death that morning.

of it) where all they do is concentrate on prolonging life a few weeks or months—while knowing perfectly well the person can't ever really recover. Thank goodness Muv didn't have to go through that sort of thing but was at Inch K which she loved so much and with all of you there and the nice nurses instead of the Intensive Carers.

> Hen, this is just to send masses of love,
> and from Bob and Benj.
> Decca

Dinky is terribly sad; the only time she really knew Muv was when she was 14 that time, and we stayed at the Mews one autumn. They hit it off amazingly well (considering their difference in background as school teachers here say).

To Aranka Treuhaft   Oakland

May 27, 1963

Dearest Aranka,

Thanks so much for telephoning. The past two weeks must have been such a nightmare for Debo and the others. She wrote or cabled to me almost every day, so did Nancy. First news of Muv's illness was about May 10 (her 83rd birthday), and all the sisters assembled at Inch Kenneth. They had 2 nurses, and the sisters also took turns to sit up with her at night. The weather was simply ghastly, in fact the whole lot of them were storm bound for 3 days, the Dr. unable to cross; but the Dr. could anyway do no good in this situation, for one thing because Muv always refused to take any medicine. She had had a small stroke, which triggered this illness. For the last week she was unconscious most of the time, they said. So in a way her death was a great relief to all.

I felt like a terrible shirker not to go. I cabled Debo immediately to say I would come if she thought advisable; but in view of the changing situation and imminence of Muv's death, which could be any minute, she urged me not to come; for which I was most grateful.

Nancy always manages to crack a joke or two in any situation; she wrote to say all her clothes were getting so dirty, so she asked Pam to teach her to wash them. "She did the washing while I stood and looked. Now I'm going to get her to teach me to iron them." . . .

I was working hard on the index for the book; all finished last week. To my horror, I found I had forgotten to send the W's! They were lost in the confusion on the table. I rushed them by airmail special, so hope they got in. I am not cut out for indexing I fear.[62]

> Much love, and to Edith, Decca

---

62. Decca had taken on the task because she insisted the book have an index. "Simon & Schuster tried to sabotage it," she claimed, "as the editor there hates indexes, said they remind him of his

To the Duchess of Devonshire   Oakland
                                                          June 2, 1963

Dearest Hen,

You are an angel to keep on writing. If it hadn't been for your letters (and
Nancy's) I should have felt so v. lonely. Your description of the funeral in the
letter that just came—talk about floods. It was absolutely as though I'd been
there and tested the pews etc. Also thanks <u>so</u> much for thinking of sending
flowers from me. (By the way my new book is all about the ridiculous waste of
money on funeral flowers & an attack on the Florist Industry for inducing people to send flowers! But I can see not, in this case.)

Nancy wrote all about the last journey in Puffin,[63] piper, flag 1/2 mast. Oh
Hen I do wish in a way I had come, but from what you all said it could never
have been in time because of the coma of last few days. I shall keep all yr. letters forever, with Muv's last one to me. It was all about the new foal etc in
extraordinarily firm typing—until one came to the end and she said Madeau[64]
was typing it for her. She told about the rough journey and said "So I went to
bed and stayed there until now—which is lunch time the next day." When I
read that I had a bitter premonition, because it's so unlike her to stay in bed all
day. . . .

          Much love, and from Bob and Benj, Yr. Hen

To Nancy Mitford   Oakland
                                                          June 12, 1963

Darling Sooze,

. . . I honestly didn't mean to annoy about the flowers. Just noting how odd
life is; that I'd just been writing about the very thing. Everybody who wrote to
me (such as Rud, Debo, Woman etc) said how utterly smashing the flowers
were and how much they added. The realness you noted was probably the
point. Here, the flowers are a complete racket, not the least of which is the fact
the florists deliberately send old dead done-for ones, because they count on the
fact the mourners are not likely to come round and complain. The other point
is the fearful standardization imposed, not by custom or the desire for burial
with formality, but by the <u>undertakers</u>, who rule the roost as far as all plans for
funerals. Consequently the sort of thing you described (piper, crofters, any-

---

chemistry book as a child." As she related the history, the publisher "knuckled under all right, but
still kept saying it takes 3 weeks to make an index. I said I bet I could make one in 2 days, working
round the clock (but privately thinking it would only take about 2 hours). So they gave me another
set of galleys. After 2 hours, I realized it would take me about 2 months." She was granted a few
more weeks.
    63. The main boat on Inch Kenneth.
    64. Madeau Stewart, Decca's cousin.

thing the least out of the ordinary) would be nigh impossible here. Wait till you note the book, esp. the part about Roosevelt's funeral and how all his express wishes were flouted. Sorry to go on about it. I agree about Rule A, not dying in hospitals; but also easier said than done, at least in the U.S. . . .

Much love, Susan

To Virginia Durr   Oakland
                                                         June 18, 1963

Dearest Va,

. . . Thanks v. much for sending on the Dink letter. I had not realized she planned to go and work in Atlanta.[65] . . .

Yes, I do think that "feeling personally let down" is a sin. Actually I think this is the root of Marge's sinfulness (the wicked old creature), too; only <u>she</u> feels that she has been let down by the CP, which (she says) put blinders on her, and prevented her from getting out in the wide world. <u>You</u> feel let down by Marge, because you defended her in other days; and by the Rude Young People who don't realize how much you have done for them. I could probably also feel let down, on these counts and others, if I put my mind to it. Why bother? It's all so pointless. What it boils down to is putting one's own feelings on a special plane; most unwise, if you come to think of it. Because the bitter but true fact is that the only person who cares about one's own feelings is ONE. Oneself. That's the trouble in this country, Americans are always going on about their mothers and fathers, their friends and siblings or whatever it's called, and the letting-down of them by one and all. I must say I never felt "let down" by, for instance, anybody in my family; I expected nothing and got nothing. Or by friends, some of whom I've fallen out with from time to time; some once very close, now irrevocably far. So, Marge now says she thinks red baiters are often wise to bar reds from meetings. For one reason or another, this is anyway not a terribly important issue right now. Personally, I regret that it is not, because I <u>am</u> a red myself, consider myself one and am considered one; only left the Party because it got rather drab and useless, not on any principled issue. So I disagree with old Marge. But shouldn't think of making it a cause for enmity with Marge. I argue with her constantly about this sort of thing, and she argues back. I always win, I think; she perhaps thinks she wins. (She can't, her position is all off, no matter what she thinks.)

---

65. Constancia Romilly was leaving New York and going to work for the Student Nonviolent Coordinating Committee in Atlanta—or, as Decca put, "SNCCing her job and going to work for Chuck." Constancia's friend Charles (Chuck) McDew had stepped down as chair of SNCC and been replaced by John Lewis.

To Maytor H. McKinley[66]   Oakland
                                                                    ca June–July 1963

Dear Mr. McKinley,

Thank you so much for your letters, copies of letters to the President, resolutions, speech etc. I found it all most interesting.

You ask me to comment on your address to the Preferred Funeral Directors of America. I shall be glad to do so. I thought it showed great imaginative talent—particularly in the part where you speak of the funeral director who "with his professional skill prevented spread of disease, possible plagues and epidemics and RENDERED AN UNSELFISH and most fruitful service to the living." I like your use of the word "fruitful" in this context. On Page 2 you suggest that American funeral directors make a contribution to the community, help to perpetuate civilization etc., much as the Egyptian Pharaohs did. This struck me as a most original thought.

There is one part of the talk that puzzles me a little (and I am hoping you may be able to clear this up for me), that is the quotation from Gladstone. I have seen variations of this quotation many times, in the funeral trade press, in funeral association convention speeches and so on—although never quite the version you have used. I should be most grateful if you could furnish me with the source for it. I made an effort on my own some time ago to ascertain the source; I wrote to a History Fellow at Oxford University who is an expert on Gladstone. He was unable to track it down for me. Do let me know where in Gladstone's writings you found this observation which you attribute to him.

I was interested, too, in the version you used. You quote Gladstone as follows: "Show me the manner in which a peoples care for their dead, and I shall measure, with mathematical exactness the degree of civilization attained by these peoples." I wonder a little about this use of the word "peoples," which strikes me as not altogether Gladstonian. Should it not rather be "in which a people cares for its dead . . . attained by this people"? A small point of English grammar and usage; but Gladstone was rather a stickler in such matters.

Thank you again for corresponding with me. I would, of course, very much appreciate your comments on my piece,[67] which you say is full of holes.

                    Hoping to hear from you again,
                    Yours sincerely, JM

---

66. The president of Utter McKinley Mortuaries in Los Angeles.

67. "Have the Undertakers Reformed?," an article in the *Atlantic Monthly*. It had prompted a flood of reader responses. As Decca commented after reading some of the mostly complimentary responses, "Extraordinary how this gloomy subject interests people."

To the Duchess of Devonshire   Oakland
                                                          August 1, 1963

Dearest Hen,

Glad the book arrived and I'm so longing to hear yr. frank and true reaction to it, so keep pointing yr. way though it. Also glad you loathed the pic . . . as I was thinking The Camera Cannot Lie. Linden[68] seemed to have focussed on the bags under me eyes and just taken them. It was on a freezing day in NY, I had near-pneumonia anyway and I had had my hair done but done-for, unfortunately, by my mother-in-law's h.dresser. I was hoping the pic could be taken in a nice warm office but I think the photog. mistook me for the outdoorsy type (on acct. of the awful hair-do, no doubt) so he dragged me out into the wind, oh it was horrid. Bob showed the book to the judge in one of his cases and the judge said, "Your wife has a very strong face." We don't like that, Hen, do we. Anyway I'd say pudgy rather than strong is more like it. The English cover is going to have a nicer one.

Yes the book club is like the Book Society, it means all the members have got to buy it. Also another book club has now taken it for their Oct. selection, so all their members will have to have it too. Just as well as I can't imagine anyone voluntarily plunking down $5 for it. Did I tell you about the telly show? . . . [I]t's called CBS Reports, a 1-hour show, and it is viewed by the 23,000,000 most intelligent people in the United States according to the man who does them.[69] Anyway he's coming out here in a few weeks to do the filming of us. He has already been to England, to interview Mr. L.C. Ashton (see chapter called Funerals in England) and to Switzerland to case the joint re. state funerals (see chapter called New Hope for the Dead) and they are spending $100,000 on all this. He also went to the convention of the National Casket Company Assn., the lucky. The whole point, of course, is to get the 23 million to rush out and buy copies.

As you can see, I'm v. preoccupied with it all. There are several other telly shows too (local ones) coming off, plus various interviews and articles in such as the Wall St. Journal. Also somebody telephoned from the NY office of the Daily Sketch and he turned out to be Romy Drury-Lowe's son![70] He [said] . . . "It's going to be a bombshell! Aren't you afraid the undertakers will sue for libel" etc. Me publisher is longing to get them to sue because of the stir it would create. NY publishers are v. quaint, not a bit like English ones.

Well I must be off because thousands are coming to dinner, chicken paprika this time Hen, another peasant dish. . . .

                          Love, Yr. Hen

---

68. Seymour Linden, who took the book jacket photo for the first edition of *The American Way of Death*.

69. *CBS Reports* was a highly regarded television documentary program that had obtained exclusive rights to an interview with Decca. It was written, directed, and produced by David Lowe.

70. Rosemary Drury-Lowe was a friend of Nancy Mitford.

To the Duchess of Devonshire   Oakland
                                                        September 4, 1963

Dearest Hen,

I just got a smashing and side-splitting letter from Dinky, goodness I was surprised as she is noted for non-writing. Anyway, she said you were the Hero of the Day for utter kindness, o'erwhelmed she was. Found Nancy simply terrifying, which I could have easily told her but you know how they never listen at that age.[71] I do so wonder how it all came out—and where she is. Perhaps another letter will come.

Hen, the book. Lord it's a scream, what's happening. Reviews pouring in, but all rather alike, and I've sent you the main ones (<u>or</u> meant to; sent some to Dink to show you). The enclosed thing is the all-time smasher, because of the clergy-adoring-it aspect. It came out this morning in the NY Times. Now, I learn that the publisher has been getting notes of congratulation (t.grams) from all over for publishing it! The point is, partly, the Simon & Schuster history. They mostly publish ordinary books (that is, ones they are for), but about a year ago they published one called Calories Don't Count. The point of it was to advise people to eat anything they want to, but with their meal to have something called Safflower Oil Pills, and then (no matter how much they'd eaten) they would lose weight. The book sold millions of copies; and some of the Simon & Schuster-ers had cleverly bought stock in a safflower pill company, and had arranged for the pills to be sold <u>with the books</u>. So the Fed. Govt. got livid, and prosecuted them for doing this, as the whole thing is a fearful fraud. This whole thing came to light during the last stages of our book, before it was really ready even. I wrote to me editor suggesting changing the name to Coffins Don't Count, and furnishing a knock-up cardboard do-it-yourself coffin, which we could all buy stock in. This was the only letter he never answered.

Anyhow, now they are being praised like mad for doing a public service, are actually re-becoming respectable, via <u>our book</u>. You must admit life is queer.

It's all building up amazingly; the undertakers are complaining bitterly that it's atheistic, and the clergymen are being all for it. So extraorder.

Do write, and do tell all, the wedding and so on,
                                        Yr. loving Hen

To Aranka Treuhaft   Oakland
                                                      September 17, 1963

Dearest Aranka,

. . . Book news. I'll have to do this staccato style, as there's so much, it would take pages: 60,000 copies now in print . . . will be No. 4 best-seller in

---

71. Decca's daughter had visited with her aunts at the wedding of the Devonshires' daughter, Emma.

next Sunday's Times (up from No. 10) . . . has been No. 1 in Chronicle for past 2 weeks . . . a religious book club has ordered 34,000 paper-backs (exclusive for clergymen) to retail at $1.95, 10% commission split between us and the publisher . . . huge spread in both Life and Time this week . . . Good Housekeeping is taking 15,000 words (of the book) in their Feb. issue, will pay $5,000 to $10,000, price to be negotiated, to be split bet. us and S & S . . . Saturday Evening Post wants an article from me of 1,500 words, will pay $2,000 . . . Benj is angling for a $2 weekly increase in his allowance . . . at least two local high schools have it on their recommended reading list, and a junior hi. called to ask me to speak to the biology class on "Life, death and sanitation"(!!!) . . . reviews are pouring in from all over, not a bad one in the lot so far (except Krieger, head of National Selected Morticians, who said it is "atheistic, and tries to bring Russian communist style funerals into America"), our dining room table covered with them . . . I have hired Judy Bernal[72] to come and do a scrap book of them, she's starting tomorrow . . . smashing review in Wall St. Journal of yesterday (16 Sept) and on p. 14 of same issue, story about the Govt. prosecuting Simon & Schuster for the Calories Don't Count book . . . English clippings beginning to arrive, just got a 1-page story in Mirror (similar in format and awfulness to NY Mirror, but excellent review) . . . S. & S. are threatening to send me on a national speaking tour, to wind up in NY, but no details as yet. . . .

There must be more, but can't think of it all. Mostly, masses and masses of letters, and all good. That's the really peculiar thing, to me. Not one person (except undertakers) has approved modern funerals, either in letters or in those radio and TV things where the public can telephone in questions and comments. Everyone is saying it's a revolution in burial customs. Can't wait to get back to THE revolution (in living customs). . . .

I've already done a couple of daring things, such as to buy a salad bowl (to replace the beat-up old wooden mixing bowl we've been using) at cost of $12, without consulting Bob. I shouldn't have; he doesn't like it, so am returning it tomorrow. Oh yes and Bob Gottlieb said: "Do you want some money? You've only to say the word, you know, you don't have to wait for the royalty report with the way things are going." So I said what a smashing idea, do send loads. Hope he will.

Much love, Decca

---

72. The wife of Martin Bernal, son of Decca's friend Professor J. D. Bernal, the English scientist (physicist, crystallographer, and molecular biologist) and Marxist writer. Martin Bernal was at the University of California at Berkeley at the time, and the couple became good friends of the Treuhafts.

To the Duchess of Devonshire   Oakland
                                                                October 7, 1963

Dearest Hen,

. . . They've now gone into a 5th printing, meaning 100,000 books printed, so I expect they are longing to unload them, and hope all this TV and radio stuff will help. . . .

I had to hire an English girl[73] to come and help answer all the letters. She is a riot, wife of one of the Commonwealth grant students at University of Calif, sort of a deb type actually. As I don't know how to dictate letters, I asked her to make up the answers herself. So she did this sort of thing: some serious old soul in North Dakota wrote to say having thought it all over she decided to bequeath her bod. to med. school. So my sec'y writes back: "What a perfectly smashing idea. I'm sure the medical school people will be <u>so delighted</u> to get it." Anyway it's marvellous having her, as so much to do.

Did you note the E. Waugh review in Sunday Times? I was amazed to note that it was quite pro, actually, at least said the book was funny etc. But he said I don't have a "plainly stated attitude to death." So if you see him, tell him of course I'm <u>against</u> it, but hardly thought it worth saying so, I mean what's the use. . . .

                    Much love, Henderson

To Robert Treuhaft   20th Century Limited, en route to New York
                                                                October 21, 1963

Darling Bob,

. . . This sort of thing has been happening: me and Dear Joyce in a taxi. I say, "do send clippings because the publisher is so inefficient and I rely upon friends to send letters to editor and so on." The cab driver says, "have you seen this one?" and passes back a copy of the Observer with review of book. In lobby of Ambassador Hotel, a woman comes up and says "saw you on television last night, it was marvellous." I've barely finished saying oh thanks, when <u>another</u> comes up, same general message, and (of course) going on about her father's funeral. I fear that I may become swell-headed over it all, so hurry up and get to NY to sober me up. But you must admit, the cultured cab driver was pretty impressive. I asked him if he likes the Observer, and he answered guardedly: "I dunno. It's something to pass the time with."

Dan G.[74] is a fair scream. He alternates with being impressed by me and being sort of terrified at what he's getting into. He is fearfully polite in the door-opening and cigarette-lighting sense. . . . Also, he realizes that his present

---

73. Auriol Stevens, who later became a prominent English authority on education and editor of *The Times Higher Education Supplement* (1992–2002).

74. Dan Green, who was at the time a young Simon & Schuster public relations employee sometimes assigned to accompany Decca on her book tours.

job is my Image, which I keep ruining for him in one or another way. Don't
remember if I told you, that during a press interview the reporter asked about
the English reviews. I said that one of them started, "Miss Mitford is one of the
minor curiosities of our time." Later, Dan chided me for having said this. "We
are trying to soft-pedal that," he said earnestly. "Do remember, you've written
a best seller, you're _not_ a curiosity, you're a best selling writer." . . .

Dear old Bob, hurry along to NY, and be good to Benj and give him my
fondest love. . . .

> Yr. loving Dec

. . . Am now in diner. Hot conversation about funerals in progress at next table.
But I'm incognito! The bliss!

P.S. Am now in club car. No longer incognito. Chap shouted out: "Loved you
on TV last night . . ."

HELP!!!

To Barbara Kahn   En route to Detroit
                                                          October 22, 1963

Dear Barb,

I see you have decided not to correspond. However, I shall make 1 more try.
(Please note hurt _undertone_, I mean a bit beastly not to write to poor old belea-
guered one, far from home & Utt-ridden[75] . . .)

I'm on a beastly jet, bound for Detroit, brought to airport in hired ~~hearse~~
limousine by one of the S. & S. Maybe men—as I've learned to think of them.
They are the new-look in Yes-men, & their current job seems to be to refur-
bish me poor old Image. They keep getting the whole Image mislaid, or else
the _real_ Image starts popping annoyingly into their focus. Anyhow, interesting
to me e'en tho boring to them. They _are_ a lot. Wish you were here to note
them. . . .

In air now. Am calming nerves by writing to you. The Maybe men had glorious cops & robbers morning. Two of them (pretty girl and pleasant youth,
both v. fresh out of college) were assigned by Bob Gottlieb to Protect me from
the Press. _Rather_ an hilarious idea you must admit; me the old expert at that.
The usual thing of various journalists calling every hour on the hour for whereabouts of one ("what plane? where staying?" etc). S & S & the Maybe boys &
girls near-panicked. Natch all was OK, a murmured "no comment on that" or

---

75. This letter was written a week after the _Congressional Record_ reported Congressman James B.
Utt's attack on Decca's Communist associations, her "anti-Americanism," and her "anti-Christ
attack."

"sorry, have to be dashing" saved all. This mostly took place at Trib. lunch, under protection by now of Mr. Schuster, Mr. Jack Astor & other ilks—not to mention Mr. Allen Dulles.[76] . . .

Yr. loving <u>Image</u>

To Marge Frantz   New York
October 27, 1963

Dearest old Marge,

Oh dear I shouldn't be writing this because this is Free Day, and many a task awaits me. But I did love getting yr. letter and clippings. . . .

As things are popping along like crazy, I'll have to pick a few to tell. Such as, meeting set up next week with Tony Richardson who wants me to do the screen play for The Loved One. I explained to Candida that I wouldn't know where to put in the things like "fade in" and "fade out," but for $50 to $100,000 I could learn. . . . By the way I shouldn't spread around the Loved One bit, as it is only a twinkle in eye at this point; but rather a smashing idea, don't you think. . . .

Wednesday is the S & S party for us. It's a cocktail party given by the Schusters. Dan let me in on some of the behind-the-scenes-ery of it. He was detailed to meet with Mrs. Schuster (who sounds like a fairly difficult one) to plan the invitations. He suggested a printed card, to be ordered at nearby stationers. Mrs. S. vetoed that because she said "we don't want it to look like a Bar Mitzvah." So Tiffany's said it would take 3 weeks (besides costing $500, but that was the least of the worries). So Mrs. S. said the cards would have to be handwritten in that case; and all the execs. of S. and S. were tied up for 2 days handwriting about 200 invitations. This was being done all the time the Utt crisis was brewing. I sometimes feel sorry for the other authors of S. and S. in these trying days.

Dan is a Love. He is always putting his foot in it and letting on about things he shouldn't. Such as when I explained about the suite[77] and the extravagance, explained they got it at a terrific cut rate via the p.r. person at this hotel! which I'm sure he wasn't supposed to tell. . . .

Much love to all. I'm rather longing to get back, but it won't be for ages, so what's the use.

Dec

---

76. The path of Allen Dulles, the former Central Intelligence Agency director and younger brother of Eisenhower's secretary of state, John Foster Dulles, may have crossed Decca's because he was also a recently published author (*The Craft of Intelligence*, Harper & Row, 1963).

77. In the Savoy Hilton Hotel.

To Barbara Kahn   Washington, D.C.
                                                                October 31, 1963

Dearest Barb,

You and Marge being my only firm correspondents, I'm sort of juggling my bits of news between the 2 of you. The bits of news pile up at such a frantic rate, though.

Please note the enclosed H. Tribune story.[78] Came out this morning, since when naught but phone calls from reporters: "how do you feel" etc. Another show canceled this morning; but we went to the Arlene Francis show,[79] which was one of the best interviews yet. She said that despite the non-ness of the Todayery and Tonightery, they talk of nothing but our book on these shows; such as Groucho Marx devoting lots of time to it etc.

Because of the canceling of the morning show, we were able to spend a bit of time at the shoe store with Bob Gottlieb, Candida etc discussing a bit of strategy. Dan Green is all upset because bomb threats in Boston—the station there where I'm supposed to be interviewed was threatened. I said as long as it's a <u>clean</u> bomb, I don't mind so much. Police protection promised, plus a bomb-proof Unitarian minister to escort me, so that's all right.

However, Bob was thinking this is getting to be diminishing returns; why face the Birchers in Dallas etc. etc., in view of what's happening? So we had a conf. on that; but poor old Dan and others were v. sad about all their plans being brought to naught if I don't go, so after much discussion I am going through with it all. The S. and S.ers are hard to get to see the point of anything, I think <u>they</u> think I'm afraid of being beaten up and so on (although I kept explaining that isn't the point; the point is, will this all really do the book any good, or will it only result in extraneous issues muddling sale of the book). So, it was decided by them to send Dan along as protection from Houston to Dallas to Tulsa. He doesn't mind coming along but wailed bitterly that he doesn't want to have to integrate Texas—because of Ye Old Peachtree Hotel[80] where Dinky has got us reservations in Atlanta. He's terrified I may make him wear a CORE[81] button. . . .

---

78. The *New York Herald Tribune* reported that NBC had canceled Decca's previously scheduled interviews on the *Today* show and on Johnny Carson's *Tonight* show. The *Herald Tribune* quoted its sources as saying that producers of the two shows were told to cancel Decca's appearances for unspecified "moral" reasons. The paper said NBC maintained that Decca was "never booked" on the two programs.

79. The actress of stage, screen, and radio dramas became a popular radio and television panelist and host. Her daily radio interview program, *The Arlene Francis Show*, ran for twenty-three years on WOR in New York.

80. The Peachtree Manor Hotel. According to Constancia Romilly, "it was the only hotel in downtown Atlanta that was actually integrated after Mayor [Ivan] Allen [Jr.] declared that Atlanta was the 'city too busy to hate.' The entire downtown, hotels, restaurants, etc., resegregated after the early sit-ins and desegregation agreements were made and broken, except the Peachtree Manor. So, visiting black people and progressive whites stayed there."

81. The Congress of Racial Equality.

Oh well. How will I ever adjust to life at home? Actually, rather longing for it; us sallying forth to Yales and the Co-op,[82] and Benj drifting back from school each day, and me whipping up a bit of beef and yorkshire. By the way, I wonder how Benj is? Shall call him and find out soon.

Much love to all, Decca

To Barbara Kahn   Dallas
                                                                    November 13, 1963

Dearest Barb,

. . . Tonight there's a cktl party and dinner in honor of ONE, various book reviewers etc I gather, so that should be blithering. . . .

So far, no bombs in these parts; only the feeling one is just a step ahead of them, accomplished by scramming out of town as soon as one has had one's say. . . . Since arriving here there have been various things (short TV interviews, and interviews with all Dallas papers) but the best part was a 2-hour radio discussion this afternoon. The station people said they had received 200 protests against my appearance on this (which they had publicized in advance) but the voices all sounded like the same person. Like everybody else they had Tocsin and Utt and they [asked] "what do you say about this?" The roughest part is avoiding saying "I am not a member of the Communist Party," which is what they all want to hear (the good guys want to, I mean). It's not any good explaining the principled reasons for <u>not</u> saying that. For one thing I'm not too sure what the principled reasons are (although Anne Braden explained this to me at length and is v. good on the subject in public appearances) and for another I don't want the word getting round to people like Nancy and the FBI that I have quit. For a third, any explanation begins to sound stuffy and also to sound just <u>like</u> a Communist talking. So my strategy is to make thousands of jokes in succession (plays on the word Underground, all the best embalmers are Communists vide Lenin, etc)[83] and quickly change the subject. This has worked so far. When I got back here, there was a phone call from the L.A. Times (a syndicated part of it). V. sympathetic reporter. He tells me that today 20 undertakers had a Summit Meeting there re. my book. It was v. secret but they did tell him that they are now planning some real blasts, based on latest Utt-erance which is in turn based on Tocsin article. So I said I'd love to discuss the book with all 20, any time any medium, weapons of their choice so to speak; made my usual jokes, and he seemed satisfied. . . .

---

82. Both were stores in Berkeley.

83. A November 6 *Washington Post* story said that a news release from the funeral industry "charges that her book is an effort to 'substitute the funeral service, as we know it in this country, with that practiced in communist countries such as the Soviet Union.' " The *Post* quoted Decca as responding, "The best embalmers in the world are Communist. Lenin is the best example of long term viewing in history. I can turn around and say all the embalmers are Communist."

14th November

The party was a gasser—Dallas version of the Great S & S cocktail party, but nicer because dinner. Sat next to Mr. Greene, book editor of one of the papers.[84] He told me the following amusing thing: His review of my book appeared during the NFDA convention here.[85] The next day Howard C. Raether appeared with a NFDA p.r. man. They demanded a meeting with Greene and the mging editor of the paper for the purpose of calling Greene on the carpet for his review. Greene was slightly upset as the managing ed. is sort of unpredictable; and in view of the Utt charges etc, outcome of this meeting seemed uncertain.[86] The managing ed. is also a card, it turned out. The discussion went like this:

p.r. man: Of course you know that both she and her husband are Communists.

mging. ed (says nothing; writes on a pad.)

Raether: What are you writing down?

mging ed (reads): Mr. ****, p.r. man for NFDA, stated: "Of course you know that both she and her husband are Communists."

Raether: Well I don't think we ought to put that in. I mean we don't really know that for a fact.

mging ed. (writes in silence)

Raether: What are you writing now?

mging. ed: reads: "Howard C. Raether stated that it is not known whether she and her husband are Communists."

Raether: I didn't mean that.

mging ed. (writes again)

Raether: Now what are you putting?

mging ed. reads: "Howard C. Raether today denied that she or her husband is a Communist."

Exit Raether.

Rather good work, wouldn't you say.

Please call up old Marge and thank for sp. delivery letter which arrived this morning mit clippings. Perhaps I'll write to her from Tulsa, if I don't die a Martyr's Death there.

Longing to be home, back on the old schedule, lunch-and-Co-op, with occasional pieces of gin.[87] . . .

Your loving Decca

---

84. A. C. Greene was the book editor of the *Dallas Times Herald*.

85. In another, unpublished letter, Decca described it as a "rave" review.

86. In her other account, Decca said she had been told that the managing editor was "a pretty conservative chap." The *Times Herald*'s managing editor at the time this letter was written was Hal S. Lewis Jr.

87. A pun on "occasional pieces of skin," from the ghoulish Tom Lehrer song "The Irish Ballad"—a Treuhaft favorite.

To the Duchess of Devonshire   Oakland
                                                  November 24, 1963

Dearest Hen,

I can't describe the feeling of utter horror at what has happened.[88] I was at home when the news came (had just got back from my long trip a few days before), and Bob telephoned from his office to say a client of his had rung up, there was an "unconfirmed rumour" that the President had been shot at. Then I went outside and several neighbours were crying, as by that time it was known he might be dying. It was the same everywhere. . . .

Hen thanks so much for writing while I was on the tour, and sorry I didn't answer but was <u>incredibly</u> swamped. Now of course I don't feel like writing any jolly letter.

So, this is just to send lots of love,
                                                  Yr Hen

To Betty Friedan[89]   Oakland
                                                  January 6, 1964

Dear Betty,

I know I owe you a memo by tomorrow; will hopefully send this special-delivery. A few things came up which prevented me from really getting down to it;[90] but the real problem is that I'm still in the stage of not knowing how to organize my piece. So, the best I can do for now is just to jot down some ideas of what will be included; and should very much appreciate hearing from you soon, so I'll know if this is the sort of thing you had in mind.

If the whole section is to be called THE FOURTH DIMENSIONAL WOMAN, the enclosed might serve as introduction to my piece.

I could then go into detail describing some of the more gloomy jobs I've had (picking one or two of them) and emphasizing the fact that there's no such thing (in my experience) as an "easy" job.

For example, in order to escape from the ranks of the completely unskilled—sales help, etc—I took a typing course during the war. This was the period in which it was said that there was such a shortage of typists that applicants for government jobs were put in a room with a washing machine and a typewriter; if the applicant could identify the typewriter, she was hired. Nevertheless the best I could qualify for was the cruel category of SUB-ELIGIBLE

---

88. The duchess's good friend President Kennedy had been assassinated two days earlier in Dallas.

89. Friedan was a founding mother of the modern women's movement, largely on the strength of her pioneering book *The Feminine Mystique* (W. W. Norton, 1963), which became a best-seller in 1964. In 1966 she co-founded the National Organization for Women.

90. The "it" was an article for a special issue of the *Ladies' Home Journal* to be edited by Friedan.

TYPIST. Mocking me from above was the bright, efficient world of the properly qualified secretaries (this was in the Office of Price Administration). Even in those days of extreme personnel shortage I was only able to hang on to my job by a series of subterfuges (such as taking my copy to a typing pool in some other agency and pretending to be a boss: "I want twelve copies of this by noon, please," and then lurking in the ladies room until noon). My boss was a woman lawyer in the enforcement division of OPA. We worked in a huge noisy barn-like room, our tiny desks squeezed in with hundreds of others. One day I was mooning around the hall as usual waiting for the typing pool to have finished my work, and I noticed a snug little private office, deserted and unused. I typed up a number of tags reading WHOLESALE-RETAIL COORDINATING COM. and stuck these on desk, chair, typewriter of the little private office; later I moved all our stuff in. Other workers stopped by to chat: "You're new here, aren't you? What do you do?" "Oh . . ." (pointing to the tags) "we just coordinate wholesalers and retailers . . ."

The rock-bottom job of all I have had was working in the classified advertising department of a local newspaper. I think a fairly amusing account could be told on how the job was presented in the help wanted ads ("DO YOU WANT TO BE PART OF AN ENERGETIC, STIMULATING TEAM IN THE CHRONICLE'S ADVERTISING DEPARTMENT? APPLY TO ROOM XXX . . ."), how the interviews of applicants were conducted (there was no mention of what the job consisted of, what the pay and hours, until after the third interview, in which I was hired; the interviews were entirely automated, consisting of written personality tests, IQ tests etc.). The job itself turned out to be telephoning for 8 hours a day to advertisers in the classified pages of rival newspapers, and trying to persuade them to switch to our paper. The pay was $50 a week. There was a 10-day training period for new employees; the training itself, and what the job was actually like, would I think make interesting telling; and the sorts of women who worked at it etc. I was 38 years old at the time.

I think that somewhere in the piece I should explain why I was driven to apply for jobs like this; mainly, because I had no education. At one point I thought of enrolling in the University of California as an undergraduate—only to find out that you had to have a high school diploma or equivalent to get in. I sent for one of those things on match book covers telling how to get a high school diploma in your spare time through a correspondence course; but it seemed so excessively long and difficult that I never did it. (My parents wouldn't let any of us go to school, which was thought to be unnecessary for girls. My mother taught us to read when we were little, and after that we were more or less on our own.)

After the Chronicle job came to an end I started writing a book. Some of the ups and downs of that could be told briefly; and then the sudden change when it was finally published. This is the part where my husband's support (in fact, flogging on: "How many pages did you write today?") could be told. Then, our joint work on the funeral book (he took 10 months off from work to do the research).

The above, then, would be the narrative bits of the piece. What, exactly, would be the point I'm trying to make of it all isn't exactly clear to me yet—perhaps because my own experiences (and how I got more or less driven into the field of writing because of inability to get other work) don't fit into any particular pattern or category that would apply to other women. However I think the point would emerge in the course of the writing and further thinking-through.

I'm very sorry that this so-called "memo" is a bit of a muddle. But I thought I'd better get something to you right away, even if very rough.

        Yours sincerely,

To Ernest Morgan[91]   Oakland
        February 29, 1964

Dear Ernest,

Thanks so much for your fascinating, and hilarious, account of the Great Debate.[92] We think it has the Clay-Liston fight all beat for sheer round-by-round suspense. It sounds as though you did extremely well.

As we are working together on so many things, I thought I should comment on the part in your letter where you point out that you don't know anything about my background.[93]

First of all, I've taken the position publicly all through this most unexpected flurry of publicity that my political ideas are completely irrelevant to the subject at hand. This is not just to duck the question, but for the reason that if once you get into this area it becomes the whole topic of discussion, also it is near-impossible to explain one's philosophy in the course of short interviews. So, because I have taken this position, I should appreciate it if you would consider this letter confidential.

I was a Communist, for a number of years. When I left the party, it was not in any Howard Fast-mea-culpa-I've-been-duped spirit, but rather for the pragmatic reason (is that the right word?) that I thought the CP was no longer doing anything of any significance. Also because I did find the so-called "discipline" a bit confining and tiresome, and like your friend Rockwell Kent I'm

---

91. Morgan, author of a guide to simple, low-cost burials, provided Decca with guidance and practical help in the preparation of *The American Way of Death*.

92. Morgan had sent Decca a detailed, five-page letter reporting on his late-night televised debate, as a stand-in for Decca, with Lawrence Doyle, sales manager of Forest Lawn Memorial Park.

93. Morgan had reported that halfway through the program, Doyle "trotted out the Red herring" with a "harangue" about Decca taking the Fifth Amendment and refusing to deny she was a Communist.

afraid I never was terribly "disciplined." It is interesting to think, however, that had you and I met in those years I would probably have put you down as a Social Democrat or some such hideous title. Oh dear we <u>were</u> so rigid! Anyway, to continue: For years I was exec. secretary of the local chapter of Civil Rights Congress, on the Atty General's list as a subversive organization. Consequently I was subpoenaed rather often by the State and National un-American Activities Committees. However I must say I look back with considerable pride on the CRC work. Much of it was local in nature, we conducted a really successful campaign against police brutality in Oakland, got into innumerable free-speech fights etc. etc. I should mention, I did not part from the CP with any bitterness, in fact some of my best friends are Communists (to coin a cliché), such as the editor of the People's World etc, and I still think they are some of the <u>best</u> people I've ever met. I should also mention that I am very much against the suppression of civil liberties in communist countries, and follow the developments in better directions in Hungary, Poland etc with much interest.

Now, I've never made any secret of any of this, but how and when to discuss it does raise some problems. For instance, take my relationship with Simon & Schuster. The people I deal with there are all brilliant youngsters under 30, with absolutely no background of those days in the 1940's. So at what stage (speaking of the early negotiations about the book) should I have sprung on them this information about myself, which they no doubt would find completely shocking and incomprehensible? At the same time, it is (I think) tremendously important to level with people, and not to lead them unknowing into some trap—in this case, the trap of publishing a book by somebody who turns out to be a Red. So what I did was to deliberately bring up the subpoenaing by HUAC, the fact I was labeled "subversive" etc without actually telling them I had ever been a member. They did not ask, incidentally. Same problem with David Lowe of CBS Reports except that he is a lot older and wiser so he twigged right away. But I did not want him to go through all the business of hanging that TV program on my book without knowing just exactly what might later confront him. It's all complicated, and often one simply has to play these things by ear depending on one's estimate of the intelligence, sophistication etc of the person one is dealing with.

I've been extremely interested, and heartened, by the general response of the mass-media people to the whole red-baiting attack on me. I must give you a couple of examples, which seem to me to indicate that the old label business is losing its magic.

In Chicago I was on the Kup television programme,[94] debating with that

---

94. Irv (Kup) Kupcinet, the *Chicago Sun-Times* columnist also known as "Mr. Chicago," was the award-winning host of a series of variety and informal late-night talk shows over the years, one of which was a precursor of *The Tonight Show*. He was friends with and interviewed many of the most prominent people in the country in every field, from sports to politics to entertainment.

wicked old fraud Dr. Edgar Jackson.[95] This was after Krieger had said I was trying to substitute communist, Russian-style funerals for our fine American ones,
etc. etc. So half way through the debate (also one of those informal round the
coffee table affairs, like yours), who should wander in late, because his plane
was delayed, but Harrison Salisbury.[96] Kup said, "Now Harrison, we're talking
about funerals. You've been in Russia a lot, tell us something about Russian
funerals." So Salisbury (not knowing anything of what had gone on before)
launched into a most touching, lyrical, interesting description of Russian funerals he has attended; the gathering of the family, the support of the community,
the strong religious strain (!) and ended by saying, "and of course there's no
financial exploitation." Before the program started, Kup asked if he could bring
up the Congressman Utt charge against me. I said, if you do I shall simply
refuse to discuss it—and I shall say on the air that I told you this before the program. But he did bring it up anyway, and I said just that. So Stanley Kramer (the
film producer) who had been part of the panel from the beginning, but who had
been pretty bored and silent, suddenly sprang to life. He said: "I must say I
think Miss Mitford is perfectly right to refuse to answer! What's that got to do
with it? I'm getting damn tired of the fact that whenever anybody produces a
film, writes a book, does a play, that says anything, the opposition immediately
brings up the communist bit . . ." etc. etc.

In Denver I debated with Mr. VanDerbur, head of largest mortuary in
town.[97] For several weeks thereafter, he ran huge ads in the Denver Post giving
the entire Utt statement to the Congressional Record. Then things began to
happen: About 30 ministers signed a letter to the Post protesting the ad and
supporting me (there were masses of other letters on the same lines, but this
was the most important). The Governor of Colorado appointed Van Derbur to
the morticians' board and this was blocked by a coalition of Republican and
Democratic state senators on the sole issue of the anti-Mitford ads! . . . It's still
going on, and now the state leg. is launching an investigation of the whole
funeral industry. . . .

So now back to the question, why not discuss frankly with Digger Doyle[98] or
whoever else brings it up the fact that I was a Communist and am still not an
anti-Communist? Two reasons, it seems to me. The first (and least important)
is the practical impossibility of making any sense out of it all in the context in
which the question is asked. So I say yes I was one. They say, why did you leave

---

95. A Methodist minister and psychologist, Jackson wrote and lectured extensively on grief,
bereavement, and the healing power of funerals. He was allied with the morticians, and the funeral
industry countered Decca's book by heavily promoting Dr. Jackson's views and his book *For the
Living*.

96. The *New York Times* reporter and editor, who won a Pulitzer Prize in 1955 for his coverage
of Russia.

97. Francis S. VanDerbur of Olinger Mortuaries, Inc.

98. Decca's name for Forest Lawn's Lawrence Doyle.

the party? And round and round we go, leaving the listening audience completely confused.

The other, more important reason is a principled one. You said in your letter that if you, an anti-communist, were asked you'd probably be sore enough to refuse to deny it. I think there is a strong civil-liberties principle underlying that statement. As long as people's liberties are still being abrogated because they <u>are</u> communists, and because the 5th amendment is under attack by the reactionaries on grounds it is just a shelter for communists, I think everyone should refuse to answer.

So sorry to be so very longwinded; and of course, even at that, this is a mere outline. Perhaps some day we shall meet and be able to discuss it all. Or perhaps I'll write a book called MY LIFE AND RED TIMES, a sequel to my first book, DAUGHTERS AND REBELS, and try to tell people what the party was <u>really</u> like. . . .

With best regards, Jessica

To Ernest Morgan   Oakland
May 1, 1964

Dear Ernest,

I'd much rather correspond with you about politics than get on with my silly article. . . .

On to your letter. The going to Spain is all described in my 1st book (or 2nd, if you count Lifeitselfmanship) called Daughters and Rebels, pub. by Houghton Mifflin in 1960. . . .

As for helpful Nancy, she said (in her vague way) years ago to some reporter, "oh, I think my sister Decca is married to a Hungarian communist." These deathless words have occurred over and over again—but, I must say, through no fault of Nancy's; it just doesn't occur to English people that this sort of thing could have dire emotional overtones, or could be in any way harmful. For instance: In 1959, I was in England, my ms. of Daughters and Rebels almost (but not quite) finished. It had been turned down by about 8 of the top U.S. publishers, and I was very doubtful if it could ever be published. I had an introduction to a London literary agent; a slim intro, but nevertheless I went to see him.[99] We chatted across his desk, and he said, "Tell me, Mrs. Treuhaft, are you a member of the Communist Party in California?" I gave him the narrow and searching look (in America, this would be the question of an enemy—unthinkable from a friend!) and seeing his candid stare, simply answered: "Well, no, not at the moment. I was for years; but the whole thing seems to have folded up." He answered, "Oh, <u>so</u> was I, and I quit for the same reason."

---

99. The agent, of course, was James MacGibbon.

Can you imagine a similar interchange here? P.S., he sold the book within the week to an English and also a U.S. publisher.

Your suggestion as to how to handle the Communist charge is easily the best I've seen so far.[100] I have been accused of being stubborn in refusing to comment, and your idea of how to meet it seems, in some ways, to satisfy most of one's objections. But, actually, not all of them. Sorry to go on about this, but even your formulation still amounts to admitting their right to pester people— and to demand some sort of informal loyalty oath. Loyalty oaths are anyway repugnant to me, and particularly when demanded of one by disreputable elements in our society like TOCSIN, Cong. Utt, and (as we say in Lifeitselfmanship) their Ilk. As long as people of various shades of opinion—ranging from communist to mild liberals—are subjected to this sort of harassment I feel that as a matter of ordinary conscience one should be rather definite about saying, "None of your business."

As for Jerry Voorhis, this came as no surprise to me.[101] Actually I once knew him very well; in 1941–43, when I lived in Washington. He came out here a couple of years ago to speak at a dinner for the Palo Alto funeral society, and made it very clear at that time that he wanted to have nothing to do with us, he barely greeted us; and his speech was simply awful, all about how the funeral society movement is part of the battle against international communism!

I find it interesting that people like Jerry are 10 times more easily scared (and consequently very bad on civil liberties) than many avowed conservatives. For example, since all the Utt hoop-la I've been asked to do articles for Sat. Evening Post, Ladies Home Journal, and Good Housekeeping. While I don't personally know the editors of these magazines, I do know the outlook of the magazines is pretty much tory. I regard the fact they've asked me to write for them as a good omen, not so much for me but for the general cause of free speech.

Supposing I wasn't having all this good fortune, and that because of the red smear I was barred from writing for these mags (as indeed I think I should have been, 10 years ago, when the atmosphere was pretty thick). I don't think that would change my position any.

Laile Bartlett[102] tells me that my possible political views were a matter of

---

100. In his letter, Morgan had suggested that Decca "counter-attack" with a statement that she is neither a Communist nor an anti-Communist and that the question is irrelevant to American funeral customs. He sent two paragraphs of suggested wording for such a statement.

101. Morgan had reported confidentially that the former liberal Democratic member of Congress—and neighbor of the Durrs when Decca was living with them in the early 1940s—had "expressed concern over your unwillingness to refute the red smear." After his 1946 re-election defeat by Richard Nixon, Voorhis spent years as a national leader in the cooperative movement, in which Robert Treuhaft was involved locally. He was, in Treuhaft's words, "a rather virulent anti-Communist" who "was afraid of any red taint."

102. A sociologist active in the Unitarian Universalist church along with her husband, Unitarian minister and educator Dr. Josiah Bartlett.

much discussion and concern at the Continental Assn. meeting.[103] Well, I think that's silly. In the first place it's none of <u>their</u> business, in the second place it's so typical of these wishy-washy types who, when you come right down to it, are simply afraid for themselves, terrified of being "linked" in some way with a person who has been accused. . . .

Once I get rid of funerals (presumably with the Post-Mortem article[104]) I think I'll try to buckle down to some writing of an autobiog. nature, including some of the more hilarious aspects of these attacks and so on. . . .

Best regards, Decca

To Charles McCabe[105]   Oakland
                                                                                            May 1964

Dear Charlie,

Here's my idea for your penultimate (or please omit flowers) column. Anything rather than get along with my own work:

As you know, the Chron. was the major source for the chapter in AWOD[106] called The Menace of P.O. It was <u>your</u> Miss Black (the generic name for the lady who takes down paid death notices) who refused to accept a P.O. notice we called in, and it was <u>your</u> Mr. Pickett, then head of Classified, who said, "Why, if we accepted an ad like that the florists would be right on our necks."

So, natch, while preparing my current article (Post-Mortem) I got back to the Chronicle to see what was doing on the P.O. front. I was anyway intrigued to see that Miss Black's name had been changed to Miss Blake (see obit. page: "for further information and rates call Miss Blake" etc.).

First I called yr. editorial chaps, and got on to Mr. Mellinkoff.[107] He professed to know naught of any anti-P.O. policy and said that if there was one, it

---

103. Decca apparently was referring to the annual General Assembly of the Unitarian Universalist Association.

104. Elsewhere, Decca described the article this way: "It's a final tease on the funeral furor. (Their sales are down like mad; but Practical Burial Footwear announced that *their* sales have increased greatly since 10 million viewers saw burial footwear on television! Aren't they marvels.)"

105. Although the full name is not noted on this letter, the "Charlie" to whom the letter is addressed appears to be *San Francisco Chronicle* columnist Charles McCabe. Around this time, McCabe married an old English friend of Decca's, Mary St. Clair Erskine, and moved to her Wiltshire farm, where Benjamin Treuhaft was to spend some of the summer as a farmhand. Decca once wrote that the tempestuous, hard-drinking McCabe was "known in British circles as Macabre." He took to his new role as country squire with relish. He left sports writing and became a general-interest *Chronicle* columnist, posing for a new newspaper logo photo wearing a bowler. The marriage proved to be relatively brief, and McCabe later returned to San Francisco. Over the years, Decca referred to Mary St. Clair Erskine using various of her married names, including McCabe and, later, Dunn. She was the sister of Nancy Mitford's first fiancé.

106. Decca's usual shorthand for *The American Way of Death*.

107. *Chronicle* City Editor Abe Mellinkoff.

certainly does not extend to the reporters who take down the news obits. He asked some of the reporters while I was still on the phone and they verified this.

So then I got on to Mr. George Putz, replacement of Mr. Pickett as boss of Classified. He sounded a bit nervous, sort of short-spoken, the way one is when reporters beard one about something. . . . I asked him about P.O.; he said the policy is "under review." I asked who is reviewing the policy, he said "I am." I asked why, and he said "We've got to keep abreast of the times." Or maybe he meant, "We've got to keep abreast of The Times," as the NY Times is one of the few papers in the country that does accept P.O. ads. . . . So I said, "Are you contemplating changing your policy so that you will in the future accept P.O. ads? He said, "I didn't say that, I simply said I am reviewing the policy. I'm reviewing a lot of things." . . .

Then I asked about the policies of other papers in the area; does he know if they are also reviewing P.O.? He said he didn't know but was going to attend a meeting on Sat. of all the classified people in Northern Calif, and would ask them about it.

So the following week I called him again to find out about the Saturday meeting. I think he was ducking me because his sec'y kept saying he had just stepped out; finally one day he answered his own phone. So I asked him about the meeting, what he had found out. He said he asked for a show of hands as to which papers did accept P.O. ads, and only a couple of tiny out-of-town papers said they did. This appears to have changed his mind a bit about the review, for he then said he didn't see any cause to accept "negative" advertising. This made me rather cross, because these chaps equate Please Omit Flowers with No Negroes or Christians Only, which is idiotic. So I said that obit. notices are not "advertising" in the ordinary sense of the word, people are not "advertising" something when they send in a death notice, it's just by accident that this happens to be handled by Classified.

The other maddening thing is that he obviously hadn't read my book, as I had to explain to him in the first case what P.O. is. I mean it is rather sad when even the people who are featured and starred in one's book (in this case Chron. classified) don't bother to read it. . . .

I note in Florists Review that all of the St. Paul, Minn. newspapers have reversed themselves since AWOD was published and that they now do accept P.O. death notices.

What about civil liberties for the dead? 1st amendment and all that jive? And what about the Calif. law that specifies a person's final disposition shall be in the manner that the decedent has requested, provided that such requests are legal? So if somebody requests P.O. in their death notice, shouldn't it be in? Makes my boils bleed to think of the liberal old Chron. being so sticky in this department.

Much love, Decca

ps. One other thing: both Mellinkoff and Mr. Putz pointed out that the Chron. carries practically no florist advertising, that therefore this policy can't be put down to "florist pressure." Maybe. In that case it can be put down to a sort of blah Babbitt-ism of "we don't want to knock another fellow's business," that sort of mentality.

To Robert Treuhaft   London
                                                                June 11, 1964
Darling Bustler,

All is forgiven—yr. Sunday letter just arrived. . . .

A couple of English slices of life:

1. I was in Woollands Cotton Dress dept. looking for suitable country garb. (Easier said than done, by the way; all the shops here are full of nylon cocktail horrors.). Heard very lah-di-dah voice of County-type lade behind me, addressing the salesgirl. You know, that mixture of bullying, confidential-trying-to-be-democratic-with-lower-orders tone. I don't know if you would detect it, but to me it's red rag to bull, reminds me of countless aunts. Anyway, the lah-di-dah was saying: "I've been asked to do an <u>extraordinary</u> commission for a friend; her daughter's going to Inja, and she wants <u>me</u> to find a suitable dress for her." Salesgirl: "How old is the lady, Modom?" Lah-di-dah: "Same age as the Queen." As for me, never too steady on my pins, I actually fell into the rack of dresses I was casing, I was roaring so.

2. The salesgirl class strikes back: I was next in Liberty's, also seeking same cotton dress, but now slightly exhausted; so asked the lift-girl what floor the tea-room's on. "There is no tea-room in Liberty's, Modom." Greatly disappointed, I said "But I thought I remembered there being one here? I was longing for a cup of tea." Lift-girl: "You can get tea, Modom, in the restaurant on the 4th floor." If I hadn't persisted, I should have never known tea was possible there. . . .

Fondest love, and keep writing. Decca

To Robert Treuhaft   London
                                                                June 11, 1964
Darling Bob,

Sorry to be writing hourly again; this is a brief mo. back at the hotel and I've got a lot of letters I must write, that I've put off, so this is a warm-up for those.

Spent a marvellous day with Debo. She's looking smashing as always; is going very grey, but it really is silver threads among the gold, not that depressing beige that attacks most blondes. . . . [W]e had a mammoth chat lasting most of the day except for lunch.

She told more of the <u>dreadful</u> details of Muv's death, the 11 days they were there before a Coma set in, which lasted for 6 more days. She said Muv had long spells of real misery, nobody could tell actually whether of a mental or physical nature, when she actually groaned out loud. (I forbore to mention that your mother often does this when in perfect health.) . . . Poor Hen I think it has made a fearfully deep impression on her, as of course it would, and lasting so long.

Stoker[108] was there, now aged 20, seems sweet and amusing but naught in his head except society gossip, like a ne'er-do-well out of a Victorian novel; in fact there is something so pre-20th Cent about all of them, it's extraordinary. . . .

So, that's that for now. I wish you were here to fight the good fight . . . with the management of the Cumberland.[109] I just had a bit of a chat with him to point out that while Trentham is a fine old English name, and Trefeuille is a fine old French name, and Trefka a fine old central European name probably, none of them is my name. That I wish they'd stop giving me those letters, and hand over a few of my own. That I wish letters postmarked from London 8th June arrived for me before 11th June.

> Yr. loving Decca

To Robert Treuhaft   London

June 23, 1964

Darling Bob,

Talking of . . . Debo, must tell you a couple of things learned in our private chat just before I left, after the others had scrammed.

1) Bobby Kennedy sent me a message[110] to say that he was the one in charge of getting coffin,[111] and was offered a choice bet. one that cost $900 and one that was $2,000. Said he had read my book, and for that reason alone chose $900 one; otherwise, he would have felt he must get the most expensive, last gesture he could make for his brother, etc. Don't ask me to explain all this—I mean, why were they only offered 2 choices, and why so cheap etc., because I asked Debo all and of course she didn't know. Also she didn't know about switch to mahogany. My guess is that the mahogany one was what Bobby was talking about, don't you suppose? I mean you couldn't get much in the way of bronze for $2,000, let alone $900.

2) All those phone calls she used to make to me from Washington were from JFK's private phone, put through by him: "Get me Mrs. Treuhaft . . . Regent St," etc.

3) Last time she was in Wash. before the Assassination she had dinner with

---

108. The Marquess of Hartington, the duke and duchess's son.
109. The hotel where Decca was staying.
110. Through the duchess.
111. For his brother, President John Kennedy.

him 5 times in a row. She went to Palm Beach with him; does a v. good imitation of him saying, "I go Presidential, you go Commercial." (Plane.) I asked her if she knew Jackie, she said hardly at all. So much for transcontinental gossip. . . .

Oh how I long for a letter.

Much love to all, Decca

To Aranka Treuhaft   Inch Kenneth
                                                                             July 8, 1964

Dearest Aranka,

I'm so looking forward to your arrival next week. . . .

Our gurrrls arrived night-before-last. They didn't get here until 9 p.m., as they took a late boat, so we made a huge stew, lucky as they arrived starving. They are dears, but not country girls at all. They came in high-heeled shoes, and had to be decanted out of those for the boat. The MacGillivrays went to meet them. Mrs. MacG. is a card. The girls asked how we get provisions at Inch K? Mrs. MacG said "it's been too rough to cross for provisions, but luckily an old sheep died, of course it was full of maggots, but Mrs. Treuhaft got those out and made it into a stew for your dinner." Then they heard a cow mooing in the dark, and one asked fearfully, "What's that?" Mrs. MacG. said, "That'll be Mrs. Treuhaft, calling for you."

I lay awake the night they arrived wondering how to instruct them in their duties. The expression "air the beds" kept recurring, but I'm not sure exactly what it means.

They made us a good breakfast of kippers etc, and then (inevitably) came trouping in to ask what we'd like for lunch. I said, "Cheese souffle and grilled tomatoes, please." Babby[112] thought this was going too far, and that I should have said scrambled eggs or something easy. The girls exchanged a Look, so I pointed to a recipe book; and the souffle was absolutely delicious. They admitted later that it was the first they had made, but you see I was right, now they know how to make souffle. So I hope to have them well trained before you get here. Today they're going to do chicken with hollandaise sauce and rice pilaff. Think of the favor I'm doing their future husbands!

I've heard from Bob quite a bit, he sounds fine, is staying at the Kahns, his home-from-home. I miss him terribly, wish he could come a trifle sooner. Haven't heard from Benjy, but I expect he's too busy with his farm duties to write.[113] . . .

much love, and to Edith, Decca

---

112. Helen (Babby) Dreyfus was accompanying Decca on the trip. She was the wife of civil rights attorney Benjamin (Barney) Dreyfus. The two, whom the Treuhafts met in about 1943, were among their dearest friends. Benjamin Dreyfus was the founder of the National Lawyers Guild.

113. Benjamin Treuhaft was working at Mary St. Clair Erskine McCabe's Wiltshire farm.

To Robert Treuhaft   Inch Kenneth
                                                         July 11, 1964

Darling Bob,

Remember "Three Sisters" (Chekhov)? And how they hang around moaning, "Moscow! If we could only get to Moscow." Well Babby and I are hanging around moaning, "Glasgow!" which we are going to, next week. . . . The excitement of it! I mean, the very thought of getting into one's good suit and going to a town for a day or two; seeing all the streets and cars; buying things like a cheese grater, unobtainable in Tobermory. . . .

Having little else to do, I've been pondering about Human Nature. Take Barb, for instance. You know how she tends to think Berkeley is boring? And how she would have loved to come to Inch K. if only she'd had the price of the fare, and so on. Well honestly, I dread to think how she would make out at Inch K; there isn't even the excitement of the dryer-repairman either coming or not coming, as no dryer. The poor gurrls just did a lot of washing, and down came the rain again. 'Tis Man against Nature in these parts, all right. "Glasgow, Glasgow!" would be Barb's cry of anguish. . . .

　　　　　Much love, Decca

To Robert Treuhaft   Inch Kenneth
                                                         July 22, 1964

Darling Bob,

Sorry to say I am really in despair over the non-letter situation. I <u>do</u> <u>hope</u> nothing awful has happened, such as you falling in love with somebody else, or going off with someone; if so, do say, so I can at least rush home and fight for my rights. . . .

The past encloses me here. It really is a bit odd without Muv in the first place (but I knew it would be, was thoroughly braced). I'm very glad that Babby came, she was a life saver as I dread being alone here. . . .

Which leads me to the fascinator of all time. There was a medium-sized hamper done up in Burlap and marked For London in one of the cupboards. Curiosity getting the better, I got it down and opened it. It contains <u>thousands</u> of letters, neatly filed by writer, of my mother's. Really it's worth coming for, so <u>do come</u>.

Here's a glimpse of what's there:

1. Muv's letters to her Father, between ages about 7 to 18. Most of them are when she was 12–14. At that time, she was the administratrix of all; he was abroad a lot, one gathers; she was living with the other children either on a moored yacht or with somebody she couldn't stand called Lady Malet, in Wilts. They are mostly long accounts of bills, servant problems, animals to be bought or sold, prices of things she had to buy for the household; interspersed with lessons with Miss Shell (Tello! Grandfather's mistress) and turkish baths, pre-

scribed by Grandfather. Easy to see why and how she got so bossy in middle-age, when I was growing up, early training—or perhaps actually character, in her case. An account of her presentation at court at 18. So <u>extraordinary</u> of her not to have noted about her Father & Tello. We would have at that age, I bet.

2. Nancy's letters to Bobo just before the publication of Wigs on the Green.[114] Bobo was Bonehead at that time, so the letters are full of "Head of bone! Heart of Stone!" Terribly funny (to me, at least).

3. Nancy's letters to Muv about 1939–48. The wartime ones, in partic., are fascinators.

4. Piles and piles of letters from Tom, these are the bulk of it; everything he ever wrote, I imagine. . . .

5. My letters to Muv, about 1940–48, INCL. ONE IN WHICH I SAY, "You may be a bit surprised to hear I have just married Bob Treuhaft. Sorry not to have told about him before, but I hadn't realized I was going to marry him." And masses that bring back the Labor School days, CIO etc.[115]

None from Debo, they must have been separately kept; a batch from Woman, which I can't plough through; ditto, Diana. All sorts of miscellaneous fascinators, like Muv's campaign to get Diana out of prison; goodness she was a good organizer, all sorts of corresp. with the Foreign Min. etc. Also, some P. Rodd scullduggery directed at me, re. the Island, when it was first known we had a share in it: "Let's plan a sale by auction on a rainy day in Oban. Nobody comes. We bid £6,000, give Decca her share, she'll never know the difference." That sort of thing.[116] Also, a rivetting account by Nancy of Kingsley Martin's account of you (U.N. conference, 1945; remember he promised to give $2,000 to the Labor school, and never did? Now we know why). It's all full of "very reassuring account of Mr. Truehaft (their sp). Decca is said to look pretty, so I suppose that means she's happy." . . .

Shall we sell the lot to Boston University to keep in their archival what-not?[117] Or, make photostats of the more titillating ones, and hint to the others that there are many more where those came from, and sell to the highest bidder in the family? Or (most likely) say naught, and lug the whole thing back on the plane . . . ? Come, and help decide all.

Aranka seems utterly OK here. Don't tell Eph, but her arthritis is almost

114. In Nancy Mitford's savagely satirical 1935 novel, a homegrown English fascist named Eugenia Malmains—a transparent caricature of Unity Mitford—goose-steps around town, haranguing villagers and her fellow "Union Jackshirts" under the leadership of Captain Jack, modeled after Diana Mitford's then-lover and future husband, Oswald Mosley.

115. Many letters from this part of the cache are published for the first time in this book.

116. For more on this example of Peter Rodd's "scullduggery," see letter of May 14, 1993, to the Duchess of Devonshire.

117. Decca had received a letter from Boston University Libraries saying that they wanted to have her manuscripts as, she later wrote, "a nucleus" for their collections. She then discovered that her sister Nancy and Philip Toynbee had been sent identical letters "saying they wanted them to be the nucleus."

over, as Babby can cure it with raw potatoes. You put one in yr. bra, and the arthritis simply vanishes. Which it is doing. I know Eph loathes anything like that, but in a way it is rather smashing? Esp. for America, what with the cost of doctors there. I may bring back a few raw potatoes (or even get them at the Co-op at home) and practice quietly on a few people. It is startling, how it's working. It seems the arthritis simply seeps away into the potato, according to Babby; and the potato hardly minds at all, one hopes. . . .[118]

Fondest love, Decca

To Barbara Kahn   Inch Kenneth
                                                                                       July 24, 1964

Dearest Barb,

Oh dear I do so miss you. I was getting livid because you never wrote; but now I see it's probably the strike. . . .

Aranka has got 3 kinds of itis: arthr, col, and fleb (or phleb? no dictionary to hand), but she seems utterly OK, all are vanishing in the salubrious mists of Inch K. She's getting a bit restless, how she does, and just said, "Can't we go somewhere?" Pouring rain outside, mind you; so I said sure we can, and then outlined the <u>how</u> of it; to Iona, 2 hours each way in open boat; to Tobermory, a day's outing any way you look at it, and then what? As the official guide book says, outlining the joys of that town, "If fishing does not appeal to you, you can always row in the bay, or bathe. Landwards, there are several good walks." That says it, man.

My article is going v. badly.[119] I can't get it to be a sprightly account of a hol. in the Hebs, somehow. All the amusing and interesting things about Inch K. flow from my mother's life here, and the way of life she imparted to the Isle, so I'm afraid it's turning into sort of a memoir of that, I do hope they won't mind.

Apart from the article, the other thing I've been trying to do is think. Which I am also slow and bad at. But Inch K. rather lends itself to this occupation, because a) there's nothing else much to do, and b) it's all so redolent of the past, esp. finding all those old letters I wrote to Bob about; so that here, one is on a sort of peak of middle-age, if you know what I mean, with one's cheery youth behind one and old age in front. So, what to do? The last year or two have been too much of a mad rush, with naught really much accomplished (except I must say it was all rather terrific fun, I mean all the silly book hoop-la and so on). Next year looks like more of same, because the Lecture Tour now looms; got a letter from the agency, saying they've got 10 bookings in the months of Jan,

---

118. For more on the amazing potato cure, see Decca's letter to her doctor, Arlan Cohn, on March 6, 1986.

119. Decca had contracted to write an article for *Venture* magazine on the Hebrides, to be entitled "It's a Pairrfect Day for the Games."

Feb, March 1965. They are now pressing for an agreement about 1966, which I'm v. loath to do. I'm not at all sure it's my line, also (except for the money) it's rather a waste of time. I only agreed in the 1st place because of the enormous amount of dough it seemed to promise, and it seemed almost wicked to turn it down, flying in face of Fortune like; and, I thought, I might as well strike while the iron is still warmish, as such opportunities may not come again. . . .

But anyway, that's only 3 months; and what to do after it's over? Do be having some ideas. I suppose you also feel more than a little jolted by all the Goldwater bit,[120] and also the Mississippi bit,[121] and one really should be figuring out a way of doing something useful about it all. But, what, is the trouble. . . .

Thank god Bob's coming early, I pine for him. Shall never leave again, once I get home. Benj might pop in, I hope, any day now; I keep scanning the sea to see if there's anyone swimming this way with a guitar in their mouth and a trombone on their back, which is rather how he arrived off the plane in London, and you know he never writes his plans. He did sound so marvellous when I telephoned to him from Glasgow. Do you suppose he's taken a turn for the better? I've just been reading Tom's letters from his trip Abroad, when he was 18 or so (he went for a year to learn German and Hungarian etc). I must say, in spite of the fact he was always held up to us as the perfect paragon of brilliance and studiousness, the letters are full of directions to send his white tie and tails to Vienna or whatnot, and accounts of various girls.

Sorry to be driveling on so, Barb, but the fact is I'm avoiding getting on with me work and also missing you like anything. . . .

Fondest love, Decca

To Barbara Kahn   Inch Kenneth
                                                         August 12, 1964

Dearest Barb,

All having now nicely simmered down since my last . . . letter to you, the Young Laird [has arrived and] has decided on the wheres and whens of last stage of trip. . . .

You know, Barb, I'm just beginning to see that a smashing article could be written (by you) about the relative difficulty and/or easiness of our domestic lives. By domestic, I mean things to do with household and children. For example, remember how in one letter to me your vacuum cleaner had broken down in some way. . . . Well how would you like to hear (as I did, today, having turned

---

120. The conservative senator from Arizona had won his party's nomination for president at a contentious Republican convention held a week earlier in San Francisco. He was soundly defeated in November by President Lyndon Johnson.

121. Probably a reference to the disappearance of three young civil rights workers a month earlier. They were murdered near Philadelphia, Mississippi; their bodies were found a week and a half after this letter was written.

a deaf ear yesterday and even the day before) that the <u>boat</u> has broken down? The main one, I mean, the Puffin. Leaving only 2 rather drab things called dinghies. Oh well I'm not one to complain. The MacG's are saying that a new engine will cost £400, to which I reply, "Goodness, how awful." Inaction, Barb, is what's called for in such circumstances. I have a very strong feeling that if I keep inacting, ere winter the Puffin will have been fixed up to go again (as the children's schooling depends) and it will not have cost no £400. Sink or swim should be the motto, and it could apply in a way equally to vac. cleaners. . . .

Benj getaway yesterday. Visualize the scene. First, to backtrack: I guess you know that the dear old bad penny showed up here on 31 July, which was ages ago. . . . Benj, who (the funny old thing) really is taking seriously the Year of Constructive Achievement suggested by St. John's College, did not wish to tarry at Inch K. He wanted either to finish out his time at McCabes[122] till end of summer, or else to enroll at the Cevenol summer language course for people who don't know proper French. So I said to him, well write to . . . the College C. to find out when, where and if the summer course exists. Spelling it out, Barb, I was. But Benj, also, is an inacter. Day after day drifted by, and he kept saying, "oh, the boat's left for the post? Damn, I had a couple of important letters to write." I rather stopped thinking about all that, on acct. of other things impinging. . . . About last Sat, Aug. 8th, day before banquet, Benj urgently said he hadn't meant to linger beyond the banquet and must get out of here soon. (I <u>do</u> see what he means.) Easier said than, said I. Idiot! Now you'll have to telegraph the College C. So laboriously we composed the telegramme. He went off in the boat to send it. No answer for several days. I said, "Did you give your address for the answer?" You've guessed: he hadn't. Partly my fault, for not including the address in the 'gram in the 1st place. I had just done the French bit, him not knowing it, assuming he'd add on the address.

So ha, ha, ha! says I. You'll never get an answer, now. You're stuck here, dear, for life. We're off next Saturday; but as for you, here you are, no plans, no nothing. (We mutually concealed all of this from Bob, because you know how cross and anti-Benj and doubly anti-me he gets when this sort of thing occurs. Bob was his usual blissful non-observant self, not actually noting that Benj had no plans, just being off on fishing trips with Toynbees etc.) . . .

Days passed. No answer from the College. Finally came the day when Polly Toynbee,[123] having accomplished all of her Inch K. objectives . . . had decided to get back to London. . . . She was to leave by the 1:15 ferry, which means she was to leave Inch K. at 11:30 a.m. About 9, the flag went up on the garage. Boat crosses; t.gram arrives. It is from the College Cevenol, forwarded from Oakland (clevers! Having no local address they sent it to Benjy's last known address, and it arrived one day later). The t.gram tersely said that the summer course

---

122. His stint on the McCabe farm.
123. Philip Toynbee's teenage daughter by his first wife, Anne.

starts on 17th August. It is by now (by the time it arrived and we read it) 10 a.m. Inch Kenneth time. Benj announced he is leaving at once, for the College, will in fact leave with Polly on the 1:15 boat.

Barb. To be done are the following:

Get the list of things he'll need, all in French, like draps (sheets), couverts (non-sheets, blankets in fact), 6 paires de chaussées (Bob thought it meant bedroom slippers; I thought it might more mean socks) and masses more. We read the list. It is now 11, and Benj hasn't even packed; let alone think of how to get his student visa needed from Fr. consulate, etc. And, if he leaves Inch K. for other places, what then? Where to stay in London, for instance, while he unravels the chaussures and draps and consuls? And even arranges to get a lettre de cachet or whatever it's called for changing money abroad? Luckily, I know about Travellers cheques, and immediately write to Drummonds to give him some. Joan Rodker volunteers the key to her house, so he can stay there until he has consuled and draped. Benj dashes, and so-called packs. He's got too much stuff to get in his meager luggage; so he packs most of it in his enormous gumboots, just acquired while here and also on the list under "bottes de caoutchoux" or some such Frog phrase. What else? He's off down the rocks . . . gumboots dangling over his shoulder. What else, indeed. Joan R. shouts, "Benj! You've got my key, but do you know my address?" He embarrassedly admits, "No, actually, what is it?" (He also doesn't know her name, I think.) It is now getting v. close to 11:30. If they don't dash, they'll miss the boat. I've left out a few things like Benj's socks and tennis shoes, being missing, and Bob saying don't give him more than 10 pounds and me pointing out that 10 pounds, these days, would barely get him to London; and me reminding Benj that his so-called suit is in a London cleaners, and his so-called luggage at the Left Luggage place at Paddington. Ah me. And where are his tickets for them all? Got them, got them he yells from the rocks. Good luck, Benj! Achieve constructively, dear boy! I yell back. All in all, a v. unsatisfactory way of getting somebody off for a year abroad; but such seems to be the custom, in these remote parts.

I've no idea if he'll actually find his way to the College Cevenol, or if he does if anything will accompany him (like luggage, draps, guitar, trombone, typewriter, good suit, all scattered from hither to yon around the U.K.). If he does, it will be terrifically Constructive Achievement, don't you think.

So the moral is, either live dangerously at Inch Kenneth, or don't complain about having to get the vacuum cleaner mended and Kathy's bus ticket. You have no idea how the other 1/2 lives! Don't forget, Barb, that all this had to be unobtrusively dealt with (for fear of boring the guests) and in the middle of discussing with the gurrls the menu for the day, and discussing with MacG. the boats to be bought and so on.

Much love, Decca

To the Duchess of Devonshire   Paris
                                                      August 24, 1964

Dearest Henderson,

 . . . Nancy is in finest fettle. . . .

I told her about the marvellous find of letters at Inch K, and that I had sent
them to you for curating under maximum archival conditions;[124] she thought
that a splendid scheme, and that we should eventually collect all such extant
(Muv's letters to various ones, etc) and send them to you to curate. Also, we
both thought that Woman should be made to curate the scrapbooks[125] chez
vous. Otherwise something stupid will happen to them, like getting left behind
in a Move. . . .

> Much love, and many thanks for all,
> and I do hope you'll come to Calif ere long.
> Yr Hen

To Barbara Kahn   Paris
                                                      August 24, 1964

Dearest Barb,

 . . . Barb, in the lobby of this hotel there is a framed thing with Historical
Notes about the hotel, and an English translation of same. The English trans
lation says in part, "The famous writer Chateaubriand was leaving here from
1810 to 1816." I was reading this last night and burst into absolute shrieks
(because you know how long it always does take to leave a hotel) and the
Concierge came rushing up to see what the joke was. I explained as best I could
(not easy), and he finally got it, and ambled off muttering "Une grave erreur.
Faut corriger."[126] Which makes me sad, as I fear they will now change it. . . .

We tried to call Benj on Sunday; no answer at the College. Tried again this
morning, and were told the chill news that students are not allowed to receive
telephone calls. I mentioned this to Nancy, who said "Well, I do see. It would
be rather tiresome if they were all telephoning constantly, all 400 of them."
Rather governessy of her, I thought. Reminds me of the rule in the one school
I ever went to (in High Wycombe) against whistling in the corridors, and the
justification for same: "Imagine if 300 girls were all whistling in the corri-

---

124. The reason for sending the letters to Chatsworth—the duchess's assurance that they could
be kept there in "maximum archival conditions"—later became a source of amusement for the
Treuhafts, who often referred to it by such shorthand terms as "max. arch. cond." It also became a
source of resentment during Decca's periods of conflict with her sister. See, for example, the letter
of October 26, 1976, to the Duchess of Devonshire.

125. The scrapbooks to which Decca refers here were later to become a source of bitter bicker-
ing among the sisters.

126. "Terrible mistake. Must be corrected."

dors." <u>Not likely</u>. Even the concierge here said it must be an école très sévère.[127] So we sent him a telegram, <u>ordering</u> him to telephone <u>us</u>. Surely a parent's command still counts for something, in this modern age? And hoping he will.

Anyway, we still don't know if he is actually there, and about the draps and couverts. I sent him a diagram (ages ago, in a letter) of him sleeping in his guitar case; but in winter months it might get chilly. I expect he's alright, otherwise we'd have had a wail. Gumboots for bedsocks can get a bit sweaty, I should think.

Shopping with Nancy is a fair lark. I just got back from it, shuddering the while for thinking what old Barb (Bob) wld. say when he heard the worst. Thinking it over now, I realize that the 1st mistake was going to Dior in the first place. N. had told me a tale of somebody called Baroness Thyssen, an English person married to a Foreigner. N. says that English girls in such circs. often assume a phony foreign accent; and this Baroness said to Debo (about the Thyssen baby daughter), "Pooooor leeeetle Cissie, she is so riche, I feel sorry for her." So no sooner had we entered the hallowed precincts of Dior than Nancy began saying (just almost in earshot of the vendeuses)[128] "My pooor leeetle Seester! She's so riche" and so on. Barb, never go shopping with Nancy, if you can avoid it.

Suffice it to say, she immediately plucked out a thing and said, "This would look smashing on you, couldn't be nicer. Lucky you, you've found it," etc. It was rather marvellous (is, I should say, as I got it), black silk cloqué skirt with pink blouse. N. kept saying it would be just the thing for having dinner with the movy stars in L.A. in;[129] I kept saying, I bet they'll all be wearing cotton drip-drys. However, it was rather marvellous, so I suddenly saw that I had bought it. Then the vendeuse came on with a matching coat (v. conservative, also black cloqué, and a terrific fit). N. came to life immediately: "What coat were you planning to wear with it—<u>in fact</u>, what coat did you wear with the dress you got last time?" I confessed to the camelhair, and now the blue check tweed. "Pooor leetle Sissie, she's so riche," N. moaned; so I got the coat. Now comes the horror or all. The pink top thing was beautiful as a thing, but <u>only fair</u> on me. It being size 10 didn't help, of course, but hovering characters were offering to remake it in my size. Then, one of the vendeuses brought in another top which was a lot better: white crepe, with high embroidered collar. Alternate top, so to speak. So N. said, "Terribly becoming. I'd have that, if I were you." In terror, by now, I murmured "how much?" Nancy, predictably, starts again with

---

127. "Very strict school."
128. Salesladies.
129. Decca had been commissioned by *Show* magazine to do an article on the filming of *The Loved One* and was to travel to Los Angeles to observe the shooting and meet with screenwriter Christopher Isherwood and some of the actors.

"Pooor leetle Sissie. . . ." Well, Barb, it was $70 <u>more</u> than the pink top. I staggered out.

And then, N. kept saying, "So much cheaper in the Boutique, don't you think. Debo spends 3 times that much at the real Dior."[130]

I was a bit scared of Bob's reaction (although I did buy him a frightfully nice Burberry jacket for 16 gns).[131] He was, as always, utterly pro the whole thing. Which came, to my absolute horror, to much more than the fare on the France. And I'm still not at all sure it'll be the sort of rig to wear in H.wood. Oh well. . . .

Much love, write back, loads of time for letters, Decca

To Aranka and Edith Treuhaft Oakland
September 26, 1964

Dearest Aranka and Edith,

The deadline for my article was murderously short so I've been living and breathing it ever since returning from L.A.; <u>finally</u> got it done. I'm actually pleased with it; hope the ed. will be. . . .

Liberace is a casket salesman in the film! Isn't that perfect. I called him up (in Las Vegas, he wasn't due for his part yet) and he sounded very sincere like a casket salesman should.

On the way back here, I stopped in Monterey to see Martin Ransohoff who is producing The Loved One and also The Sandpiper, with Taylor and Burton.[132] I was promised to meet Taylor and Burton, so of course I thought I'd just say how de do to them and that would be that. But I ended up closeted in their company for the whole day, they took me out to lunch (just the 3 of us) which lasted 4 hours. I must say they are fascinators, he is, specially. . . .

Much love, Decca

To Edith Treuhaft Oakland
December 9, 1964

Dear Edith,

Actually I <u>was</u> asleep when you called, sorry if I sounded dopey.

---

130. Elsewhere, Decca summed it up as "the most expensive day's shopping of not only my life, but my wildest dreams; equiv. of 2 years' ordinary shopping, I'd say."

131. Guineas. The name for an old English gold coin with a value eventually fixed at twenty-one shillings. After the coin was replaced by the sovereign (value twenty shillings), the term continued in commercial use indicating twenty-one shillings.

132. Elizabeth Taylor and Richard Burton, then at the height of their popularity, costarred in the film.

This is the story: Bob has been lawyer for the Free Speech Movement[133] right along. On Thurs. night, the night of the big sit-in at Sproul Hall, he got a call from his clients asking to confer. So he went over after dinner. Police were not admitting anybody, so he showed his lawyer card and explained he had come to see clients. Police at once admitted him (so he was there officially, at permission of police). Actually the main thing he was doing was to screen juveniles (people under 18, and high school students who had come along to see the fun) and get them to leave the building. After a while he went into the press room and was chatting with reporters when a deputy district atty. came up and said "You're not part of the press." Bob answered, "Neither are you."[134] So the D.A. had him arrested forthwith. He was booked in the basement of Sproul Hall (where they had set up a full-scale booking procedure, fingerprints, photos, the works) and eventually was taken to Santa Rita Prison farm along with the other 860 arrested. There he was given a v. bad time, put in a solitary cell with stone floor and nowhere to sit, so he stood for about 3 hours. Meanwhile I was going quietly bonkers as our British cousins say. I had been called at 4 a.m. to say he was arrested, but natch I thought he'd be out at once. He wasn't released till 11:30 Friday. He is livid, as you might think, planning massive false arrest suits against all concerned.

However the dear boy rather thrives on this sort of thing. The whole free-speech fight has been simply thrilling, I guess you've followed it in the NY papers. It's a new and marvellous development, much like the sit-ins of 1960. Bob is very much the hero of students and faculty members, it's all been terrific.

This wknd. we are going to L.A. for 2 days, at the invitation of our new-found friend Julie Andrews. She said she would show us Disneyland if we would show her Forest Lawn, so that's the deal. . . .

Much love, and thanks again for calling, Decca

ps. At one point the cops in Sproul Hall started locking up the johns, presumably to discourage students with weak blads. So some of the men students took

---

133. The Free Speech Movement (FSM) began as a broad-based student protest against restrictive free-speech policies at the University of California at Berkeley and became a landmark in the development of the New Left and the national antiwar movement. Robert Treuhaft, invited by FSM leader Mario Savio to serve as the students' volunteer counsel, sat in on negotiations with faculty and unyielding administrators. On December 2 and 3, after the breakdown of negotiations and with disciplinary charges pending against some of the student leaders, about eight hundred students were arrested during an all-night FSM sit-in at the campus administration building, Sproul Hall. Among the students sitting in were many young friends of the Treuhafts. Robert Treuhaft himself was the first of those arrested—to the indignation of much of the legal profession—at the behest of District Attorney Coakley's deputy, Edwin Meese, later attorney general of the United States. His trespassing charge was finally dropped a few years later in exchange for his dropping his own suit against Meese for false arrest.

134. As Robert Treuhaft later recalled the episode, Deputy D.A. Meese said, "Sheriff, there's somebody here who is not a member of the press," at which point, Treuhaft said, "I turned around and said, " 'Well, that makes three of us.' "

the doors off by the hinges, and they had what you might call a shit-in. Bob said he met Joan Baez[135] in one of the johns!

Also, the other night Bob addressed the 860 defendants at a mass meeting, starting off with "Fellow Jailbirds." He got a standing ovation. They simply adore him.

To Barbara Kahn   On train to New York
                                                    March 5, 1965

Dearest Barb,

Once more, I've telephoned to Bob so am writing to you, sharesville. That way I know you'll be forced to invite the dear thing to dinner. . . .

The whole Albion[136] day was so marvellous, I'm now v. sad the lecture tour is over as I'm beginning to adore it. It seems there was the usual fuss over me coming, Albion being a Methodist college, and Dr. Meredith, the nice young man in charge of the theological bit was besieged with complaints about me being a red and an atheist etc. So to calm people, he promised to arrange for an official representative of NFDA to be on hand for rebuttal. I was to speak in the morning, and in the p.m. the NFDA-er was to rebut, with me on hand to debate-like. My morning talk went off comme ci comme ca, well received but nothing exciting. The bliss was the afternoon. After the morning talk (10 a.m. to 11) was a series of scheduled informal chats, I mean no free time at all, till 1 p.m. Then, Dr. Oman arrived for rebuttal. He at once explained that he is <u>not</u> an official spokesman for NFDA, he is a leading Methodist. His credentials were read off to the meeting by Dr. Meredith, sounding v. impressive, for instance he is among many other things a psycho-dramatist which I don't even know though what it means. He spoke for about 45 mins, all the usual stuff about high American standards in all things, people are satisfied with the funeral dir. and his work, tradition, "who seeks to meddle with these deep seated desires of the American people in the care of their dead had better go slowly as force of public opinion is so powerful it will sweep him into oblivion." He also had some screaming psychological points, like one who is cheap about a funeral is an anal-regressive etc. Then came my turn. I said v. little (having had my say in the morning) but did mention that I had actually been swept <u>out</u> of oblivion by meddling; I made a couple of other jokes then sat down. So Oman again, trying to recover the situation: "When I was chaplain at the State Prison there was one convict who was very tough, and very funny, kept us all in stitches, but he wasn't very <u>honest</u>." Forest of hands go up. The first speaker, a most eloquent chap, rips in about an ad hominem attack on this lady, says he is an anal-regressive as when his father died he got the cheapest funeral possible

---

135. The folk singer and peace activist.
136. Albion College in Albion, Michigan.

and it was <u>still</u> far too expensive in his opinion. Oman tries to put him down by calling him a loud-mouth or something of that sort. I guess Oman thought he was an older student (I did) but it developed later that he is a professor, head of the Polit. Science Dept there. Then there was a free-for-all, I never saw anybody ripped up and down as Oman was. The discussion went on for 1 1/2 hours. Two Methodist ministers rose to disassociate themselves from Oman's views, to say he does not represent Meth. min. thinking on this. The students were <u>smashing</u>. Oman turned all colors of the rainbow. I sat saying nothing, just looking proud like Molly in the crowd.

Oman made an utter ass of himself; couldn't fail, I guess, as he was proceeding from a hopeless position. The students were shrieking with laughter throughout. Finally Dr. Meredith, who was also shrieking, said (trying to be fair) "doesn't anyone have a criticism of Miss Mitford?" The anal-regressive said, "I do. I read her book and couldn't help thinking she had exaggerated a lot. Now, I feel she didn't go nearly far enough."

A student asked towards the end, "If you really think 'the American public' approves of all you say, what about this audience? Are we something special and different, how do you account for the views expressed here?" No answer, literally. It was a shambles. Oman departed flanked by six or eight undertakers and their wives who had come along, all looking utter daggers at me. . . .

These little colleges are fascinating. I mean imagine Albion, Mich; it couldn't have very high standards, is miles from anywhere and even when you go somewhere it turns out to be Detroit; yet there's a terrific lot of spirit among students and profs, a v. bright lot on the whole. . . .

Much love to all, Dec

To Barbara Kahn   Le Chambon-sur-Lignon, France
                                                             March 30, 1965

Dearest Barb,

Thanks ever so for your wail of the 27th, which arrived in record time and was doubly welcome because I was beginning to think Bob (or you) hadn't got my address here. As the faithless old creature hasn't written for days. Do tell him. . . .

You're right about articles being a lot of work, <u>specially</u> when they are not accepted, like the Reagan one, finally turned down by Esq. after all this time.[137] Now here's a funny thing: Time was when if I got an article accepted, I was astonished and delighted. Now, if one is rejected I am astonished and <u>simply livid</u>. The worst of it, you know, is the damper it puts on future work—the

137. *Esquire* had asked Decca to do an article on (as she put it at the time) "Ronald Reagan, an aging film actor being touted for Governor by the Birchers in Southern Calif." See letter of June 19, 1978, to Katharine Graham.

horrid uncertainty, I mean, which dogs you at every stage while you are working. Do you think the reason is that articles are in general pretty tailored things, cut to a measure and arranged to suit what one thinks will be the taste of a certain mag? At this point, I've got masses of things 1/2 cooking . . . So I'm wailing too, a bit, because after the awful debacle of the Esqu. piece there isn't much pleasure in the actual doing of them, more the lurking fear they won't be right. . . .

I do love being here. The hotel is the best sort of cheap Fr. hotel, clean, huge airy room, bath that works and ditto john just down the hall, freshest rolls and strongest cafe au lait, lovely meals, in a little cafe-bar part as the dining room is closed. Benj and school chums come for most meals. . . .

You know how extraordinary it is when one's baby first says a real, intelligible sentence? Like hearing a horse talk. Well it's a bit the same to me, hearing Benj rattling away in French with his pals. Obviously he would; by now, as he's the only foreigner in his pension (7 French kids), it was sink or swim and he's been there for ages; but it is still a source of pride and pleasure. . . .

Today I went to see Mme. la Directrice, to square away about Benj leaving early. God what an intimidating experience. . . . I had my speech all set: Benjy's papa had communicated to me his decision that Benj must at once be sent to Italy to learn Italian, which every educated person must (in the opinion of Benjy's papa) be adept in. Madame countered that we don't even teach Italian here as so few people speak it, it is not an important language. I said that may be true, but I can't very well go against my husband's express wishes. Much sniffing by her. She opened Benjy's file, and poured over it (as Va. would write it). More sniffing. His marks in mathematics had not been very good. He had missed a devoir in philo. I said, but don't you think he has made a lot of progress in French? She answered, we have four levels. The fourth means a perfect grasp of French, written and spoken. He has only reached the third. Which, she said reluctantly, was all the same quite good. Does the fourth mean bilingual? Yes. The point of all this interview was that he should leave with permission all around, rather than sliding himself furtively out, just in case of repercussions with St. Johns[138] if he left here without proper formalities. I think it's OK. Goodness she's a formidable old bag. This is a rum place all right.. . . . Lots of love to all of you. WRITE.

      LOVE, <u>DEC.</u>

---

138. Benjamin Treuhaft was studying at College Cevenol preparatory to attending St. John's College in Annapolis, Maryland.

To the Duchess of Devonshire   Oakland
July 1, 1965

Dearest Hen,

The ball. It must have been a marvel. I got a terrific letter from Nancy about it. . . .

As for Benjy, I do long to hear if he turns up. He must be in absolute rags by now, he was when last seen by me, but refuses to buy any clothes in England on the ground the trousers aren't made right! So don't let him into the house if he's too filthy, he can easily sleep in the car. But of course what I <u>really yearn for</u> is your Hen's-eye view of him, an account, Hen, so if he comes do give a <u>minute</u> one.

Here's a story (true) about the President, told by somebody who was there. A salary increase had been granted to the White House advisors, or staff, or whatever they're called. So one of them said to L. Johnson, "Thanks awfully for the increase. We were wondering if it could be made retroactive to January?" Johnson answered (but you've got to imagine his voice, Hen, which you can, because you've met him, haven't you?) "Ah am the President of the United States. Ah am the leader of the Free World. And you ask me a chicken-shit question like that."

There is an Eliz. Arden slimming and beauty resort here where Mamie Eisenhower goes, costs $700 a week. One of the mags wants to send me there for a couple of weeks so I can do a tease on it (article) for them, so I think I shall, prob. in the autumn. Isn't there a place called Tring or something in England, along the same lines? Do you know anything about it, anyone who has been there, or could you inquire? Do, Hen, it would be a help. I promise to sing All Things Bright And at yr. funeral, if you do. . . .

Yr. loving Hen

To the Duchess of Devonshire   Oakland
September 11, 1965 ("48 today, Hen, pushing 50")

Dearest Hen,

How I wonder where you are. From yr. last letter I note you were off to Venice, Athens and to see Emma & Toby.[139] So you may be e'en now in this hemisphere, I <u>do wish</u> you'd come this way, it's on the way home anyway. <u>Do try</u>.

Benj got back and scrammed again, off to his college (here in America, this time). Thank goodness you warned me of the beard, I should have fallen out roaring otherwise. He told lots more about his time with you which he adored, and he was fascinated by Sophy.[140] Him telling reminded me of a toy I'm get-

---

139. The duchess's daughter and son-in-law, Emma and Toby Tennant, then living in Argentina.
140. The duchess's younger daughter, Sophia, who would have been about eight years old at the time.

ting her any day. People are always asking me to join committees against the wicked toys they've got here (like model H-bombs, etc) but I can't bear to join because I know I should have rather longed for a model H-bomb if they had been about when we were little. Anyway, the wickedest toy of all, and the one that has been written up and condemned bitterly all over the U.S., is a real guillotine (real model of, anyway) and a toy person with toy head that comes off when the knife drops, and a colouring set with red for blood etc. So be expecting it, but don't tell Sophy for fear the campaign has been successful and they've stopped selling them. . . .

Do write,

Yr. loving Hen

To Virginia Durr

Oakland

October 9, 1965

Dearest Va,

Sorry about crossing letters. . . .

About the young—your discussion in (I think) your penultimate letter.[141] I still think you are a bit hard on them. I've got a feeling I've said all this before, but here's a go at what I think about them:

First, none of them can even remotely remember WW II, therefore it is as unreal and far off to them as old Bogey (Napoleon) was to us as children. Or, more like it, it's like WW I was to me—an old, bad joke. No use to get irritated, because it is a fact of life that the heroes and causes of the past generations almost never excite the present one. Anyway, what they do know about is things like the dropping of the H bomb in Japan, which they find almost as revolting as Hitler's concentration camps—and a good deal more current in terms of a threat to them.

Second, I think we should only applaud the efforts of the kids—even rich kids, like the Harvard ones you describe—to investigate, learn about, and write about the Negro revolt, or rather the situation of the Negroes. You say it's their

---

141. Decca appears to be replying simultaneously to several letters from Durr, written over a period of a few months, about "rich Harvard boys" (staff members of the *Harvard Crimson* who went to Alabama to start a newspaper for blacks without "a Negro on the Staff as far as I can discover") and other well-intentioned Northerners who went to the South, often for short periods, to write about and help the blacks because it was a "fashionable cause." Durr at once praised the dedicated young idealists and bemoaned their lack of economic "sophistication," their dismissal of the civil rights achievements that preceded them, and their lack of a permanent commitment. In one of the letters, she wrote, "I think the worst thing about them is that they always leave, they never stay. . . . They seem to think all of History started with the Movement in 1960 and their involvement in it. . . ." Decca had previously written to Durr, "Isn't it an extraordinary advance from a few short years ago—when nobody would lift a finger except us reds?" (Quotes from Durr's letters during this period are from *Freedom Writer: Virginia Foster Durr, Letters from the Civil Rights Years*, edited by Patricia Sullivan [Routledge, 2003].)

fathers who caused the trouble in the first place by exploiting the south. I can't see how this in any way detracts from what the kids are trying to do? You say they don't work with the southern whites. Well, neither do you, really, and mainly because it's impossible just now. I shouldn't think it always will be, and I expect that when there does develop some sort of receptiveness to decent ideas among southern whites, these same kids will be the best equipped to jump in and seize advantage of it.

Third, I think you are too easily hurt and annoyed when people (I mean, young people) don't pay proper attention to your ideas. I agree they <u>are</u> annoying, sometimes, in that way; yet the one really new and hopeful thing about the youngest generation, as distinct from the 30-ish, is their refusal to listen to their elders and their insistence on discovering things and ideas for themselves. They really don't want to be told. In some ways this is tiresome of them, and also leads to silly mistakes they could avoid. I happen to think the disadvantages are outweighed by the advantages of them taking what amounts to real, total responsibility.

End of lecture. Also, apologies for presuming to give lecture. . . .

Aren't the newspapers being revolting about LBJ's gall bladder,[142] if there's one thing I could do without at breakfast it is a clinical description of gall bladders, on the front page. Dave Scherman wrote to say that when the Pope came, LBJ was heard to say to the chief of protocol: "You mean now all I have to do is kiss his <u>ring</u>?" Oh dear he is frightful. I always thought so, in the days when he and Ladybird used to slop around your garden with their outlandish manners and accents.[143]

Nothing much doing here, except lots of work. . . .

Much love, Decca

To Bettina Aptheker[144]   Oakland
November 12, 1965

Dear Bettina,

Well. We were going to phone you (but didn't, figured your phone would be busy all night with the Old Hate Peddlers[145]). So then we were going to send you a telegram, but we didn't, because we couldn't think of what to put in it.

---

142. The president had recently had gall bladder surgery and had, infamously, lifted his shirt to show his scar to reporters.

143. Decca, who had met Johnson through the Durrs when he was a young New Dealer, once told Virginia Durr that "[when] I first met him . . . the uncouthness of him and his way of talking was quite striking to me; the idea of him being a Congressman a bit odd, let alone President."

144. Bettina Aptheker, a family friend of the Treuhafts, had been a leader of the University of California Free Speech Movement of 1964–65. Her father was Communist historian Herbert Aptheker.

145. Probably a glancing allusion to Tom Lehrer's satirical song "The Old Dope Peddler."

Anyway, we were impressed and delighted with what you did.[146] I love the way the press adores you, like the Chron. saying "smiling, curly-haired student," am longing to see the national mag. coverage. (Will Time say "scowling, straight-haired"?)

What I think is, you nailed this stupid, provincial American thing about the Communists as nobody else could. As this is the whole propaganda for the cold war, it did rather need doing. Everyone says (it's the new style, in the past ten years) "he (or she) was unfairly smeared as a Red," and then all the guys come to the defense of the smeared non-Red; but you said, I am! It was a pleasure.

Of course, "refuse to state" is good enough for us ex-reds—or has been, until you broke the barrier. If pressed, I have gone so far as to say to a reporter, "I would still be in the Party, but it's so inactive." Or, "I'll tell you off the record, if you absolutely swear not to tell the FBI, Coakley, or Tocsin: I'm not."

This will no longer do. I should much love to chat with you about the whole thing. If you've got time, please ring me up. . . .

Admiringly, from both of us, and much love, Decca

---

146. Aptheker explains that "on November 9, 1965, I published an open letter in the UC-Berkeley student newspaper, the *Daily Californian*, in which I affirmed that I was a member of the U.S. Communist Party. At the time the McCarran Act was still in force and the Party was still in a semilegal status. Acknowledged members of the Communist Party were required to register with the government under the act, which meant affirming that we were members of an organization that sought to overthrow the government by force and violence and that we were foreign agents. Of course, no one registered. The whole thing was a sham. If we had registered we could have been prosecuted under the Smith Act, which made it a crime to be a member of such an organization. In any event, I proclaimed public membership in the Party because I was running for . . . Rules Committee on campus. . . . I didn't want to run for an office and not have students know that I was a member of the Party. I was elected by a landslide vote. . . . Of course, I was never prosecuted, and a few months later the Supreme Court knocked out most of the McCarran Act in a 5–4 decision declaring portions of its provisions unconstitutional."

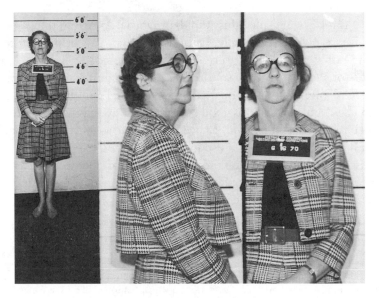

Decca's 1970 booking photo, taken before her twenty-
four-hour "imprisonment" at the Women's Detention
Center in Washington as part of a conference on prisons.

On the lecture and interview circuit after publication
of *The American Way of Death*.

VI

A CAT AMONG
THE PIGEONS

Virginia Durr, Decca, and Constancia Romilly
at the 1980 wedding of Constancia and Terry
Weber.

What does one do for an encore after changing a nation's funeral practices with a breakaway best-seller? Decca's legions of readers and fans had plenty of suggestions. She told one friend, a doctor, about "all the people who write to me saying Why don't you expose Bar Mitzvahs, why don't you write about the high cost of weddings, hearing aids, Christmas—but 9 out of 10 say 'DOC-TORS NEXT!!!'" She remembered the rankings differently about fifteen years later, when she wrote, in *Poison Penmanship*, that after publication of *The American Way of Death* "I got hundreds of letters suggesting other infamous rackets that should be investigated and exposed. . . . Surprisingly, complaints about hearing aids led the field. . . . [B]ut somehow, although there may well be need for such an exposé, I could not warm up to hearing aids as a subject."

In the years covered in this next section of her letters, after *The American Way of Death* and its many spinoff articles and appearances, Decca pointed her lance at a number of quintessentially American institutions, including a "fat farm" for rich and pampered women and a predatory correspondence school for would-be writers that made big bucks for some of the most powerful figures in the publishing world. The article on the Famous Writers School elicited more mail than anything Decca had written since *The American Way of Death*. "Do you suppose that there is a connection?" she asked in one letter. "Both undertakers & Famous Writers promise a measure of immortality, then not only overcharge for it, but fail to come through." Both of those exposés set off investigations by the Federal Trade Commission.

Interspersed with her periodical journalism during this period, Decca also wrote two books on pressing social issues, the politically motivated conspiracy prosecution of prominent Vietnam draft protesters, including pediatrician-author Dr. Benjamin Spock, and the shocking state of the country's prisons, even those that prided themselves on their enlightened intentions. In each case, she painstakingly agonized over the intricate implications of social dilemmas and legal remedies. Yet even in these weightier books, Decca generally cut her subject matter into revealing, shorter segments, more journalistic than analytical. As she observed many times in different words, not always accurately, "I realize I'm not much of a theory person."

Years later Decca characterized her subject matter, in her self-deprecating fashion, as "odd pockets of American enterprise that happened to strike my fancy (or, as the OED would say, appealed to my 'depraved interest in what is morally unsavoury or scandalous')." She went on to say that she wished she could "point to some overriding social purpose in these articles; the sad truth is that the best I can say for them is that I got pleasure from mocking these enterprises and the individuals who profit from them."

After *The American Way of Death*, Decca honed the techniques that led *Time* magazine to call her, also during these years, "Queen of the Muckrakers." She wrote journalism with an attitude—her own inimitable attitude. Explaining her style of journalism in response to suggestions that she was less than "objective," she wrote, "If to be objective means having no point of view, or giving equal weight to all information that comes one's way, I plead guilty—although *accuracy* is essential. . . . But I do try to cultivate the *appearance* of objectivity, mainly through the technique of understatement, avoidance where possible of editorial comment, above all letting the undertakers, or the Spock prosecutors, or the prison administrators pillory themselves through their own pronouncements."

Her targets often pilloried themselves because Decca reused a technique that she had stumbled onto, and used with stunning success, when exploring the funeral industry. For her prison book, *Kind and Usual Punishment,** she pored over old issues of *The Grapevine*, a publication of the American Association of Wardens and Superintendents, just as she had once devoured *Casket & Sunnyside* and *Mortuary Management*. Once again, she eavesdropped on her subjects discussing their innermost professional secrets. Prisoners, she said, "don't make a particularly interesting subject of study. . . . Of far more interest is the mentality of the keeper." She also gained the confidence of those, however ignoble, who were uniquely qualified to understand them—the prisoners themselves. As one prison official commented when she visited the mainline with him, "The tomtoms started beating, as soon as they heard you were coming."

She was also dogged. If prison wardens didn't give her admittance to their institutions, she sued—again and again, "more or less touring the country and strewing the landscape with lawsuits," as she put it.

Robert Byrne, who had done some preliminary writing on the Famous Writers School before Decca laid siege to the institution, says her article was "something I couldn't have written because I didn't have her access . . . and I didn't have her nerve." When novelist William Styron pressed Decca's target Bennett Cerf on whether he would resign from the embattled Famous Writers School, Cerf reportedly replied that he planned to resign, but "not until it all blows over." As Robert Treuhaft remarked, "Blows over, with Dec doing the blowing? Not likely."

To each article and book after *The American Way of Death*, Decca brought other effective, self-taught muckraking skills that had proved so helpful in that book. (She later explained some of those tactics for wannabe muckrakers in *Poison Penmanship*.) She pulverized her deserving victims with meticulous research as well as understated humor; with precise character sketches and com-

---

* *Kind and Usual Punishment: The Prison Business*, Alfred A. Knopf, 1973.

pelling anecdotes; with artfully designed interviews and disarming personal confrontations.

The biggest difference in her writing, post–*American Way*, was not in her techniques but in the response. She was working now—and living—on a larger stage. Her articles appeared in a wide spectrum of publications, from *McCall's*, the large-circulation women's magazine, to *Esquire* and the *Atlantic Monthly*. She was "at home" in New York and London as well as Oakland. When Decca published an exposé in magazine or book form, people—from book critics to members of Congress to the general readership—were likely to pay attention. She was in demand on the lecture circuit, at colleges and universities, and in the electronic media, as well as in print.

It was an eventful period personally, as well. Decca's mother had died shortly before the publication of *The American Way of Death*. Now her oldest sister, Nancy, was failing, and Decca shuttled several times to her bedside in France. Her social circle grew to include such prominent figures as Julie Andrews, Tony Richardson, Vanessa Redgrave, and the woman who was to become one of her dearest friends—her "sister"—Maya Angelou.

Despite Decca's international travel and renown, she and her husband remained in their comfortable home, modest by her new standards, in an unpretentious upper-middle-class neighborhood in even more unpretentious Oakland. When time permitted, she kept up her political activism, organizing picket lines against President Lyndon Johnson and the Vietnam War, for example. ("Doesn't it remind you of '39?" she asked Virginia Durr. "But with us being the Germans.") Decca also remained deeply attached to her circle of longtime friends in the San Francisco Bay Area, sending back frequent dispatches with all the news of her travels and her wondrous new career. Those letters, lovingly saved by their recipients in shoeboxes and cartons, represent a good share of the material in this book, helping to chronicle the arc of Decca's career as a celebrity author.

In those letters we again see a key ingredient of Decca's vivid professional writing: her laser-sharp eye for the overlooked but telling detail.

In *Poison Penmanship*, Decca was explicit about the value of her correspondence in helping shape her published works: "One technique I have found useful in the early stages of an inquiry is to write letters to friends about what I am doing. In that way I perforce start editing the material for fear my correspondent's eyes will glaze over with boredom if I put in everything I have learned. Also, one's style is bound to be more relaxed than it will be at the dread moment when one writes 'page 1' on a manuscript for an editor."

Nowhere did Decca make more effective use of this form of epistolary "note-taking" than when she visited Elizabeth Arden's Maine Chance beauty spa in Phoenix, Arizona, researching an article called "Maine Chance Diary." The story was published in March 1966 in *McCall's* magazine and later reprinted in *Poison Penmanship*.

■■

To Robert Treuhaft
Arizona Maine Chance, Phoenix
November 15, 1965, 9:30 a.m.

Darling Bob,

I arrived more dead than alive, the plane being 2 hours late in the end. Shall draw a veil over that. Was met by a gliding lady (they all glide here, rather than walk) and driver. The latter drove me here, the glider having to leave and fetch another arriving flower. As you can imagine, I was pretty well sloshed by the time the plane finally downed.

My room is on a balcony overlooking pool. My maid met me, and eventually brought a sandwich & coffee (having missed dinner easily). She said she used to live in Oakland, worked at Permanente.[1] I must get her to enlarge on the difference between the 2 joints. Anyway she said she lived on Grove Street, BUT (as I knew what was coming, I chanted the rest in unison with her) there's an awful lot of colored moved in there now.

The room: like a fairly good motel room, Aubusson carpet my eye,[2] it's an ordinary white wall-to-wall-er. Cotton sateen pink curtains. As for the $150 bath tub,[3] it's just a perfectly ordinary bath tub. As for the bowers of flowers, 5 small roses. In the bathroom are 1/2 dozen jars of E. Arden face cream, hand lotion, deodorant etc., prices on the bottom, total retail value about $11. . . .

I'm sitting in my "little blue exercise suit" (see brochure) waiting for the torture of the day to start. . . .

Oh yes, the maid said last night (when seeing what to bring for breakfast) "do you want to lose or gain?" To which I answered dreamily, "Like either way, man, as long as it thwings." Do you think I'll survive the week? Where's that lawyer you were mentioning, just in case? . . . One had to give a urine specimen for the Dr.; why? Do ask Eph. Rather embarrassing as I expect mine was pure gin, what with the send-off and plane drinks.

Later—4:30 p.m.

Immediately after writing the above, I repaired to the pool area. . . .

---

1. Kaiser Permanente hospital.

2. Decca's article on the experience for *McCall's* quoted a Maine Chance brochure as promising "The flowers in every room are breathlessly fresh. The carpet beneath your feet will be an Aubusson, the floor beneath the carpet, marble."

3. As her ensuing article made clear, Decca derived the $150 figure from information given by an Elizabeth Arden phone reservation person who told her that a few rooms with showers only were available for $600 and that rooms with bathtubs started at $750. In the commentary published with her article when it was reprinted in *Poison Penmanship*, she noted *McCall's* generosity with her expenses for the Maine Chance article. She wrote that she "really loathe[s] not having a proper bath" and had asked editor Vivian Cadden specifically whether the magazine would underwrite the extra expense of "the $150 bathtub." Decca reported that Cadden's reply came by telegram: MCCALL'S WOULD NOT WANT YOU TO BE WITHOUT A BATHTUB.

So, sitting round the pool all in the blue exercise suits and terrycloth dressing gowns was about a ton of human flesh in various stages of disintegration. Average age about 55, I should guess. . . .

Some of the pool sitters were already having things done to them. One having her hair brushed, one having her legs creamed and massaged, another having a manicure. Others were already at different ploys. . . . If unoccupied for a few minutes you are expected to submit to one of the many machines in the pool area—sort of electric rolling pins up against which you put your behind to be rolled.

My first thing was massage, interminable and very vigorous. Then came the exercise, conducted by an elongated lady whom one is, I guess, supposed to try to get to look like. The class has about 5 people. . . . Oh, I forgot: the masseuse weighs one (I weighed in at 140-3/4 lbs) and the exercise lady measures one. "Half an inch needs coming off here," she murmured as she did my upper arm. At exercise, you lie on the floor and do various things to the cry of "tuck in! tuck in!" from the exercise lade. . . . Then, 20 mins. of water exercise (it is in the water, as I feared) kicking one's legs and arms etc, under water.

Then lunch, by far the most interesting part of the day so far. We repaired to a patio for it (by the way, paper napkins which I did think squalid) and I sat with some of the older crowd, 60 and up I should guess. One of them, who had misheard my name, introduced me as "Mrs. Fruehauf" and murmured "husband in trucking,"[4] so I let that stand. Some tid-bits of lunch talk: One of those at my table, from Florida, has a lot of darling dogs at home. She couldn't bear to leave all of them, so she brought her favourite one, and a maid, and took an apartment for them in town. She visits them twice daily, and again after dinner. . . . Another is having her husband come for her in his private plane. This one also complained about a queer thing that always happens at her parties: guests bring along bowser bags, and behind her back get the servants to fill it—she knows it isn't really for dogs, they just take it home to eat. I was startled into saying that I must say nothing like that has ever happened to me when I give a party; she said "my dear, check with your butler, I'm sure he'll admit to you that it goes on all the time."

So you do see I'm a fish out of water here. . . .

After lunch, mask. This is done in the nurse's office; I saw the person before me, looking like the victim of a mad doctor, face completely covered with a pinkish bit of plastic. You lie down, they cream your forehead and chin, attach the mask, turn on some electric things, and it gradually gets warm. That's literally all there is to it; she said it is good for sinuses. Next, face. Endless (a good 45 mins) of massaging with cream, applications of iced lotion etc. etc. No makeup; they only do that when you leave for good. Also they do your eye-

---

4. The Fruehauf Trailer Company pioneered the manufacture of truck trailers.

brows (pluck them), dye your eyebrows and eyelashes if any, and wax off the hair on your legs all at the end, so it'll last longer in the Outside World.

Next, hair. All they do is brush it, put a lot of muck on it (greasy kid stuff),[5] massage yr. scalp and neck. Meanwhile, somebody else is going after your feet and digging things into your toenails. Most uncomfortable; it's hands tomorrow.

Last of all, a thing called "shake-away"; you are strapped into a thing very much like an electric chair (hoping for the best while fearing the worst), they turn on the electricity, and the thing vibrates for about 10 minutes. Must be fake? I mean, how could it do any good? I see the point of the exercise and possibly the massage, but these other things do not look to me likely to do much good.

So 1/7 of my time is up—if I really stick it out. . . . I'm hoping to circulate a bit more and case the people more—to try to plumb their characters and find out what on earth could induce anyone to come here as a serious project. . . .

          Fondest love, Decca

To Barbara Kahn   Arizona Maine Chance, Phoenix
                                          November 16, 1965, 4:30 p.m.

Dear Barb,

. . . More Notes from Maine Chance—and please consider them that as they are much too boring to be proper letters, as I'm terrified of forgetting bits of the goings-on, also don't dare keep notes around here for fear of Discovery.

I'm trying to think what the people round the pool remind one of. This is where we all live all day, from 9:20 to 4:30 p.m. with one hour for lunch on a semi-enclosed terrace (patio-like). Between activities, which are scheduled to the minute, there may be 10 or 20 mins. free time—never more. . . . Anyway, the people: once I went to visit a friend in a private S.F. loony bin (a terribly expensive place, like this). The quarters (living room etc) were pretty nice; but the women (all ages but mostly oldish) were ineffably sad-looking, draggled hair, vacant faces. Soon, one noted that a lot of them were doing things to themselves, such as endlessly brushing or twisting their hair, or making little pleats in their clothes. All were in housecoats. The similarity is in the utter concentration on themselves, and the terrible drabness of the faces compared to the surroundings. Here, leg-creaming and hair-brushing go on all round you. While the faces aren't sad, they are all completely in the raw—and everyone's hair (this is like the bin) is dank, straggly, greasy. Mostly because each day one gets a 40 min. scalp treatment, consisting of application of something called 8-hour cream and masses of brushing and scalp massage. No shampoos till the end of the stay. Then there are the electric rolling machines round the pool,

---

5. A men's hair cream ad at the time contrasted the product with the competition's "greasy kid stuff."

about 4 of them, always occupied. There is one sort that you sit on, for inner thighs. One can see the upper thigh flesh whipping merrily like sails in a stiff breeze. There are also aspects of shipboard life, mainly the bouillon at 11 a.m. and juice at 4, and the utter isolation from the Outside World. (How I long for it; but I've done 2/7 of my stay.)

Back to the characters. Of course once you get to know them they become individuals but Barb not <u>terribly</u> individual; it's more a sort of democracy (or diversity) of the very rich. There is a range of accents. A lot of deep-south complacent whines (complaisant is in contrast to the deep-south shrill whine, there <u>is</u> a difference I'm sure, based on money), a lot of the Ohio sort of nasal tone, and a fair amount of what I can only describe [as] the New York-Westchester County upper-class snort and flounce. A few anglicized—not quite English but almost, brought up here probably. The help mostly have foreeen ac-cents, either Swedish or French.

One thing I can't help wondering, as I note the faces round the pool, is this: Won't the lady with the cross face and bedraggled neck look <u>exactly</u> the same, at least to everyone but herself? And as for the real tubs of butter (a minority, I mean the ones 50 to 75 lbs overweight) won't they soon revert? I fear it's a bit like taking Koko to the vet for his bath & clip, only lasts till the next bath and clip. And the nice bovine freckled girl (35-ish, one of the youngies) will ever be nice, bovine and freckled, I <u>think</u>. . . .

At meals, I try to change company each time to case them the better. Had lunch today with the cultured, symphony-supporting set; they were exchanging notes about committee work, activities of Junior League etc. in their various home towns. They all agreed about the ridiculous, absurd amount of money spent on hospitals, mental care and the like when it could go for subsidizing opera. Especially mental care, one of them pointed out; if only more people could get to the opera and to concerts, there wouldn't <u>be</u> all this mental illness, so much of which comes from sheer idleness and just hanging round the house. But not often does the talk get on this high level; it's mostly a) about the regime here, b) about boring trips they all seem to be on constantly when not here— boring, because this tends to be a recital of foreign towns and hotels, comparison of various airlines, and what they got abroad. One lady had been to Russia and picked up a perfectly darling rug made of squares of reindeer skin—looks perfect in her NY apartment. That sort of chatter. . . .

Ardena bath and massage . . . pure torture-chamber. The attendant pours some boiling hot wax into a bed sheet and makes you get in (ignoring cries of ouch and too hot), then pours more hot wax all over you (more than a gallon, I learned) until you are completely coated, then wraps you to the neck in sheets and warm blankets; arms and legs immobilized, like swaddling clothes. . . . She said it draws all the poisons out of the body. "All <u>what</u> poisons?" But she was vague on that point. (Do ask Eph.)

Massage: tremendous kneading, slapping, picking up of handfuls of flesh and throwing it around. I found out various things from the masseuse, such as the help's food is foul, mostly starch and grease, masses of mashed potatoes and spaghetti; for meat, frankfurters. I asked her what sort of cream she was using (she covers you with cream in course of massage). She said "Orange skin-food, but don't tell anyone, we're not supposed to as it is very expensive." I asked how much; $4.00 a jar. (Retail, natch; I happen to know that you can get it made up for a fraction, as Idden and I used to do as children.) I asked how many massages she could do to a jar, she said about 6! Barb, it's not right; that means less than 50¢ a jar retail per person,[6] about 1¢ wholesale, no doubt, and here I am paying $800 a week. Oh yes, and the wax bath: the attendant there said it was "the most expensive bath ever dreamed of," because of all the wax used. But . . . one of the gliders, a higher-up, told me when pressed that it is ordinary paraffin wax. Can't wait to find out how much that costs, at wholesale.

After massage, weighing. I've gone down (in one day's treatment) from 140-3/4 lbs to 138 1/2—loss of 2 1/4, right? Of course, most of it is probably sweat, from the bath thing.

It's a bit early to tell what one will possibly be able to make of all this, article-wise. One problem, obviously, is the intense blandness of the conversation around one; a bit of upset would help, I think. I think either tomorrow or Thursday, I'll simply tell them I'm doing an article on the joint. Or, perhaps start off by saying I'm a writer and hinting I might do a story? Or saying I'm a spy for McCall's Magazine? I can't decide on the best approach, I guess time will tell. I might start with the NY upper-class-ers, less likely to lynch one than the Nashville-Florida crowd. Then, gradually work up to formally interviewing the gliders (duennas, people in charge) for a more general view? . . .

Love to all, Decca

To Robert Treuhaft   Arizona Maine Chance, Phoenix
                                              November 17, 1965

Darling Bob,

About the unveiling. Not only is the talk here too, too bland, but now that Mrs. Barry G.[7] has arrived I feel I must come clean. (By the way: she is revoltingly well-preserved, easily the best-looking person at lunch today).

There are two International Set types, friends who came together, called Mrs. Frelinghuysen, sister-in-law of a New Jersey congressman Frelinghuysen (who he? Ask Barb, she always knows things)[8] and Mrs. Griscom. . . . Mrs. F., having been brought up in England, is at least human to talk to. She and

---

6. Math, as Decca would have been the first to admit, was not her forte.

7. The wife of Barry Goldwater, thirty-year conservative Arizona senator and—a year before this letter was written—the Republican standard-bearer who was crushed in the presidential campaign by President Lyndon Johnson.

8. Twenty-two-year Republican Representative Peter Frelinghuysen, father of Representative Rodney Frelinghuysen.

Mrs. G. do things like dash out and buy look-alike dresses for dinner in the nearby town of Phoenix. But they seem to like me (unlike most of the ones here), always save a seat for me at meals etc. They are about my age, namely the young crowd. . . .

I have accomplished Part I of the unveiling, which was to ask Mrs. F. to get the current Life Mag "because I've got a review in it, just wanted to see how much they mucked it up." . . . If they get it, and if the review is in, curiosity will impel them to read it and politeness will impel them to say something to me about it. Right? What's more, as there is absolutely naught to talk about here, chances are they'll say something about it to some of the others. Mrs. F. is reading the Life of Dylan Thomas, so there's a hopeful sign (only other books I've seen in people's actual hands were James Bond and a couple of mysteries). . . . So, we'll see what happens at dinner tonight, will write more of that later. The point of the carefulness of the unveiling is that I don't want to be completely boycotted by all of them, as that would rather defeat part of my purpose here (casing the ladies). So, if I do it in easy stages starting with one who might be an ally, that's better, don't you think?

Part II, I'm hoping to keep off till Friday evening, when Eliz. Arden's New York public-relations people will all have gone away for the weekend. That's when I shall go cozying up to Mrs. Simple (that's the duenna's name, but all the Southerners pronounce it either Sample or Semple) and say that I do do occasional freelance writing (giving name if asked) and would love to do one on Maine Chance. Then I'd regularly interview her on a million and one things I'm curious about. I fear that if I ask her too early on, she'll first check with NY and it won't be such a satisfactory interview from my viewpoint. Then, when we go back East, perhaps various other cats can be put among the pigeons by seeing the official P.R. people—just to round things off.

Now, back to a few other notes.

The staff of masseuses, hairdressers, facial-givers etc. are pretty run-of-the-mill in looks, technicians, what you'd find in any good beauty shop. Most of them have been here for years. Like most people whose working lives are devoted to serving the very rich, they have completely taken on their coloration and are devoted to their interests. One does not put on one's own shoes after a foot treatment (which is every other day, hands are alternate), one does not pour one's own bouillon at 11 a.m., one does not fetch one's own towel after swimming. Willing hands do all.

The gym teachers are a different breed, smashing looking. Their job is to impart enthusiasm ("Feel that in the abdomen, class? Goooood."). . . .

Mrs. Simple is iron hand in velvet glove. . . . [She speaks in] soothing, dulcet tones, which is the form around here among the top staff; could drive you faintly nuts in time. On the other hand, she had some relatively brisk words to say to Mrs. Frelinghuysen and Mrs. Griscom, who had been caught sneaking an apple (100 calories) into their room. . . .

The faces here run to two extremes, as I've often noted in very rich Americans: <u>fearfully</u> discontented and complainy-looking, and unfailingly bland. Sorry to keep saying bland—but it's not quite smug, not quite cheerful. . . .

I have cased the visitors book, which runs back quite a few years—<u>wish</u> I knew more about the names and who they are. Part of it reads like a list of products advertised in the daily press (Heinz, Ford, Fleishmann etc), part like a roster of leading Republicans (Dulles, Eisenhower, Goldwater). Very few movy people: Greer Garson, Ava Gardner are regulars.

<u>Thursday morning</u>:[9] . . . The unveiling went as planned, so far: Mrs. Griscom and Mrs. Frelinghuysen brought <u>two</u> copies of Life, one for them. There's a lot of do-you-know-so-and-so here at meals, for instance the New Yorkers and Nashvillians all turn out to have friends in common, which so far I've been out of, natch. So at dinner, Mrs. F. said, "I know your sister who lives in Paris!" So I was pleased, until she added, "Charming Lady Mosley." Wouldn't you know it.

Now, about the end result of all the beautifying. In the first place, they are rather clever about not guaranteeing anything; merely say, "Well you'll feel better and look better, if you follow the regime." Personally, I feel and look <u>exactly</u> the same as at home, and I bet the others do too. As for the 3 1/4 lbs I'm supposed to have lost, my dress felt slightly tighter than usual when I got ready for dinner last night. So it will be the same old Dec. Sorry, but there it is. Except I'm getting a sort of sleek look on the skin that I don't specially care for, which I guess will wear off in a day or two of not having the facials & being doused in skin cream all day long. The tip-off, I suppose, is at dinner-time, when the aging raw flesh of the day is transformed by girdles, bras, powder & lipstick and good clothes and jewels. While they all look human for a change (except for hair which stays greasy and lank) basically it's the same old faces, same old wrinkles—or, with the minority, same handsome young faces. . . . The spirit of Miss Arden (as we call her here) hovers over all, and her name is often invoked. "What kind of cream is that?" "A special formula that Miss Arden learned from a doctor in Rome, many years ago." "How do you work out the diet?" "Miss Arden personally decides." . . .

Wish you were here to see if there are any Jews, you know how I can never tell. There is one, I think. . . . Not a dark face in the place; all the maids are either southern-white or foreign.

Much love, Decca

---

9. The next morning, November 18.

To Marion Conrad[10]   Arizona Maine Chance, Phoenix
                                                      November 18, 1965

Dearest Marion,

OK, I am writing. . . .

Finances: Mrs. A. is 2nd in command around here after Mrs. Simple, our chief duenna. . . . Mrs. A. is a nice English person, so I thought best to start with her, by saying "I think I may do an article about this place." She said, "Oh well you would have to check that with Miss Arden, there is to be no publicity unless it has been cleared with New York." I didn't bother to pursue this curious thought further except to say that luckily I'm going to New York soon, and certainly will check personally with Miss Arden (not a bad idea). So anyhow tonight I asked Mrs. A. why they were against publicity. She explained that it is because they run this place only as an accommodation to clients and not as a commercial proposition. "You mean it is run at a loss?" "Well, it might break even, but I doubt it when you consider the overhead." Now Marion. Maine Chance is open 6 months of the year (the whole staff then goes to Maine Chance in Maine for next 6 months). A. says there is a staff of about 50, including all—gardeners, maids, masseuses and all. My guess is that the average price per week for staying here is $800. The staff gets paid prevailing wages (I asked A. that question and she said yes). What would the median wage be, I mean obviously the masseuses get quite a lot and the maids quite little—would $125 a week be about right?

So, multiply 50 by $150, and 40 (number of guests) by $800, for a start. Then, take food. Top quality food, marvellously cooked, served as at an English houseparty. But another way of putting it (and one that, I understand, means a terrific saving in terms of restaurant business) is that it's served family style, all at once in one serving, absolutely no choice of menu—and tiny portions, no seconds. Also: no butter, no wine, no masses of fattening and expensive things we could think of. Safflower oil in the salad dressing, much cheaper than olive. . . . OK: so, service and food (I should think usually the most costly items in running a resort or hotel). I know there are masses of other items (linens, supplies of all sorts; but you get the picture). Boutique: At any hour of the day you may see some old fattie in there, fingering the Arden Xmas Stocking (a white satin stocking filled with teenzy samples of Arden preparations, price $27.50) and saying, "How cute! I think I'll take twenty of those, solve my Christmas present problem." In fact, "I'll take that, and that, and that, and two of those" seems to be the constant cry of all these ladies when they are in the boutique. . . . That boutique must be a goldmine. . . .

---

10. One of Decca's good friends, Marion Conrad ran a small public relations agency and was married to wealthy outdoorsman, socialite, and corporate lobbyist William Hunt Conrad (brother of author-artist Barnaby Conrad). She was a noted hostess and introduced the Treuhafts to many luminaries of San Francisco social and intellectual society.

You know how in hospital the entire talk is of oneself—but the others are also interested in <u>your</u> plight? Like, "I get my stitches out today!" "Oh <u>wonderful</u>. And nurse told me I could start on solids tomorrow" (that sort of thing). It's like that here, too. "I lost another 3/4 lb today." "Miss Pierce told me I'm ready for four sessions of exercise." . . . We get the newspaper with breakfast. The headlines are full of bitter battles in Viet-Nam, the Governor of Rhodesia deposed, Supreme Court reverses C.P. case. Not once, in 4 very concentrated days here, have I heard the word "Viet-Nam," "Rhodesia" or "Supreme Ct." But one woman did explain to me, whilst showing me her all-blue room, that she had requested all blue this time as it is so relaxing, and that last time she was here she had a pink room which she found far too stimulating. . . .

Yesterday, Mrs. Griscom and another lady and I went to see the brand-new art center here.[11] Some books about the collection ($7.50) were being sold at the entrance. Before even glancing at the collection, Mrs. G. said "I'll take two of those." I think it's a sort of reflex with them, when anything is being sold. The collection turned out to be really excellent (some awfully nice Renoirs and Corots, Paul Klees etc). The woman who guided us said, "To give you some idea of the cost of these pictures, recently in New York a Renoir was sold for $350,000." Ooooh, aaaah, we said. A novel way to introduce an art collection, I thought. . . .

On the way back, the other lady asked me "Where do you generally winter?" At home, I answered, although I occasionally Spring in New York or Fall in London.

So far, the most kindred spirit is Mrs. Harvey[12] (although she also voted for Goldwater, how I long for a Rockefeller supporter![13] I asked my nice Swedish masseuse if any Democrats ever come. "Ach, yes," she said in her gutteral accent, "Ve have Mrs. Dwight Eisenhower, Mrs. Dulles, all of dem come." "Any Kennedys or Stevensons?" "No, I don't remember any of them."). Mrs. H. is also planning to write about Maine Chance (she does occasional funny pieces for Chi. papers) but said she can't see anything funny in it; she loathes it, finds it intensely boring. . . .

I've got to dash to face.

Much love, and longing to see you, Decca

---

11. Probably the Phoenix Art Museum, which opened in 1959 but was greatly expanded in 1965.

12. In another letter, Decca said Mrs. Harvey and her husband owned a chain of resorts and hotels. She was also a friend of the Treuhafts' Chicago friends the Goldbergs.

13. New York Governor Nelson Rockefeller had been defeated by the more conservative Barry Goldwater for the Republican presidential nomination in 1964.

To Aranka Treuhaft Arizona Maine Chance, Phoenix
November 20, 1965

Dearest Aranka (and Dinky; please show her this, as I haven't time to write two),

. . . Guess who I kicked in exercise class today? Mrs. Barry Goldwater! (The way you do it is not to change legs when the exercise teacher say "and now, the left leg.")

Oh dear this has been a weird experience. Thank God today is the last day. On vital statistics: I have lost 4 3/4 lbs, 2 inches in waist, 1/2 inch upper arm, 1 inch each thigh. Also: hair off legs (with wax), hair on head tinted, eyelashes and eyebrows dyed, nails varnished pink. In the words of Poor Jud is Dead, my fingernails had never been so clean.[14] But (and this is the disappointing part) I actually look <u>exactly</u> the same, as I knew I would all along. Everybody says, "But you feel so <u>well</u> after a week here." As I always feel perfectly OK anyhow, I haven't noted the difference. . . .

Aranka, <u>you</u> should have come instead. They are all bridge players, and not a Scrabble player in the place.

Much love, Decca

To Julie Andrews Oakland
December 2, 1965

Dearest J.,

. . . I've just got back from one of the rummest experiences of my long and rum life: a week at Maine Chance (where rich fatties like Mamie Eisenhower go to be dried out and slimmed down), did it for McCall's Magazine, am now racing to finish the piece for them. It cost roughly $1,000 (with tips and transportation) and I lost 5 lbs; so that's $200 a lb. Wish I knew how it compares with the 3,000 ducats in Shylock's Venice; considering the international rate of exchange, I mean. Must ask a Shakespearian expert. . . .

I shall be seeing the Redbook folks in NY (re. the profile of you) and should much love to talk to you ere going, as I'm having extreme trouble over it. Hard for me to sort out what the trouble is, but I think it is this (in a nutshell): It is fearfully hard for me to write about somebody I really like. I'm much better at what you might call combative writing—that is, sticking in the old knife, like with the undertakers. I should have known this ahead of time, and never agreed to do it; everything I put down just sounds sappy. Writing about the making of <u>Hawaii</u>, which was the original idea, would have been quite different, as that's a

---

14. A reference to a song from the Rodgers and Hammerstein musical *Oklahoma!*, in which Jud Fry is laid out in his coffin as mourners gather round. In the words of the song: "He's all laid out to rest / With his hands acrost his chest / His fingernails have never been so clean."

reporting sort of job which I like and can do; but, as you recall, nobody seemed to want that story.[15] Alas. . . .

Please give my love to all the loved ones in Los Angeles. . . .
much love, and from Bob, Decca

To Barbara Kahn   New York
                                                            December 21, 1965

Dearest Barb,

. . . A SNCC party on Sunday . . . was given by a shirt-mfr. called Van Heusen, and all the guys were there: the Bloomingdales, who own a store hard by at 58th and Lex, Peter Tishman[16] . . . it was just like Maine Chance. The speeches were pretty bad, esp. when my commonlawsoninlaw[17] passed up a note to the host, who said, "And among our honored guests is Mrs. . . . Mrs. . . . Jessie Midriff, the famous writer." Benj did not help the situation by saying loudly, "We call her Bulge at home." Mrs. Belafonte made a speech, mostly about Viet Nam, upon which a lot of people got up and left; consequently, only $2500 was raised. Well that's life, I say. . . .

That clever Dink's idea of living seems to be to starve you until about 5 p.m., then take you to a series of parties where you are stuffed. . . .

McCall's adored my article, so that's OK. Shall be at the shops at crack of dawn, spending the loot from same.

The kiddies are smashing, at least to me! Just to see the dears is a <u>treat</u>. To whit: Benj <u>loathes</u> St. Johns, mostly I gather because of the geometry. Dear (I say ineffectually), it's either the geometry or a rifle on yr. shoulder.[18] Bob, of course, being a gentleman & scholar, is giving deeper and better-reasoned reasons for staying in college. Time will tell.

The Dink is a pleasure, esp. her eyelashes, always smashing; I tried to pull them off today (thinking they must be false, because of their extreme luxuriance and length) but they stuck. She is the essence of sloppy hospitality, I <u>do love her</u>. . . .

Fondest love to all the loved ones, Decca

---

15. In a letter a few months earlier, Decca wrote, "I'm supposed to do a 'profile' of [Julie Andrews] for Redbook Mag. I dread this for several reasons. Redbook said they want an in-depth sort of thing, not just a string of anecdotes, said they would send me some samples of articles about filmfolk to show the sort of thing. So they did, and . . . they are purest fan-mag style, too awful for words."

16. Presumably the New York real estate tycoon.

17. Civil rights leader James Forman—Freedom Rider, militant voting-rights campaigner, and masterful organizer—who was executive secretary of the Student Nonviolent Coordinating Committee. Constancia Romilly worked for him in SNCC's Atlanta office, and they were partners for about a decade, beginning in the winter of 1963–64. They moved to New York in 1965. Forman was the father of Constancia Romilly's two children, James and Chaka.

18. The military draft was then in effect for young men without student deferments.

To Barbara Kahn   New York
                                                    December 29, 1965

Dearest Barb,

Thanks v. much for yr. wail, <u>faithful</u> of you to write. . . .

Life is so kaleidoscopic (sp?) that I scarce know where to begin . . .

The nourishing Pleydell-Bouverie[19] is in NY, staying with a Russian lady; he had a dinner pty. for us, v. grand with the Swedish ambassador and several White Russian fascists—"because, my dear, incongruity is the <u>salt</u> of life." He called up to tell us his seating plans. "Tell Benjy that I prefer to seat the youngest of the party next to the oldest. On his right will be a beautiful young woman, but on his left will be Marianne Moore.[20] Now he may think she is just a homespun old lady, quiet and mild, but tell him that underneath it all she will be <u>probing, probing, probing</u>."

Had lunch with Bob Gottlieb, a soul-searching session; result, I've really and truly and definitely decided to cut out all the crappy articles (the Vogue horror is the last) and get to work, Red Times-wise. . . .

Today I went to see the ed. of McCall's (Bob Stein). Maine Chance will be in their March issue. . . . They tried to get Arden's to send them some pix of the joint (just saying McCall's wants them, not mentioning me) but they wouldn't because of the Herb Caen[21] item, I mean they were on to the whole ploy. That silly Marion's fault, I shall speak to her. . . .

On Xmas eve, we were invited to a party at Dinky's boss's house. I got rather dressed up for it, and we went at 9. To my extreme surprise, it was a 4th floor walk-up in the Village. To my extremer surprise, the boss[22] looks about 15 (is actually 23), and <u>sweet</u>. So is his common-law wife (they are all common-law in these parts. I call J. Forman my common-law-son-in-law, and just introduce him as "Common," for short). This kid was a SNCC worker, and got the job of running the enterprise from a multi-multi type SNCC contributor. He and Dink are the chief execs. of the outfit;[23] she just dashed out to buy $8,000 worth

19. David Pleydell-Bouverie was a friend of the Treuhafts, who were often among a glittering parade of luminaries invited to stay at his showplace ranch near Glen Ellen, California, which featured a huge outdoor chandelier, Old Masters in the kitchen, and other grand eccentricities. He was a retired architect who had once been married to heiress Alice Astor. Decca met Pleydell-Bouverie, whom she described as another English "renegade aristo," through "Mary St. Clair Erskine/ Dunn/Campbell etc," when she was married to local journalist Charles McCabe. In other letters Decca called Pleydell-Bouverie "a rare soul" and an "English nabob, awfully good value, on board of all local art museums etc., mostly had tycoons to his place—Bob & me possibly for comic relief." He was apparently "nourishing" because Decca's old friend Dave Scherman, fascinated with his name, used to joke, "I'll have a nice, hot Pleydell-Bouverie."

20. The poet.

21. The longtime franchise columnist of the *San Francisco Chronicle*, who was universally called "Mr. San Francisco." Known mostly for his insider gossip, his razor wit, and his dripping-with-nostalgia portraits of San Francisco life, he was a friend of Decca for several decades.

22. Mark Suckle.

23. Constancia Romilly, who had worked for John Marqusee, a SNCC benefactor, since moving from Atlanta, had recently taken a position as an office manager at Marqusee's new venture, the

of office furniture, and next week has to hire 15 office workers. Can you beat it? The enterprise is selling pix on a Book-of-the-Month Club type deal, originals, prints, etc. Quelle drôle whole thing.

Back to Jim: I'm getting to adore him. His beard has vanished without leaving a trace, by the way. He has a merry quality, and above all (as Aranka would say) he makes my daughter ha-ppee. No indication of Intentions; the wife still hasn't buggered along to Mexico for the divorce, I gather. The other main thing is that Bob likes him very much. In fact old Scrooge knocked himself out to buy him a chess set for Xmas, j. decent. . . .

> I note the ribbon is giving out just in time, and Benj isn't here to phix it, so will close with fondest love to all loved ones, Decca

To Pele de Lappe   New York
                                                   December 30, 1965
Dear Neighbour,

. . . Today turns out to be New Year's Eve Eve; in this wild city, where pleasure reigns, everything clams down shut at 12:00 noon today. Some offices are not planning to reopen till middle of next week. . . . I expect you are e'en now slaving.

I just floated back to the hotel after lunch with Candida (me agent). It was an extraorder session. I told her I had decided to cut out the articles and like crap, to do me a book on Life & Red Times. She said, would you like a contract? I said, not specially because then I'll have to submit a 1st chapter and outline. Don't be daft (she said), you don't have to do anything, just say if you want the contract, and I'll negotiate it. She went on to say that she and Bob Gottlieb had talked me over and decided that psychologically, I'm the sort that would work much harder if I had a contract. (They are all in deep analysis so approach everyone and everything from this viewpoint.) So I said well that's very nice, but I warn you this book won't sell, as it will be a sympathetic account of life in the CP. She said you said the same thing about AWOD, and look at what happened. Anyway, on we chatted, and she explained there is a formula for working out advances, based on what the last book sold. She took out her trusty pencil and paper, did some figuring, said "somewhere between 50,000 and 125,000." Of course, I thought she meant books, and that I would get 10% of that; turns out she meant <u>bucks</u>! Bob was sitting there roaring, having noted how I had misunderstood the whole transaction up to then. So, there you are. I told Bob that the next time that chap who keeps coming round to our house saying

---

Collector's Guild, which sold limited-edition lithographs. She worked there for about a year and a half. She subsequently returned to college, receiving an associate degree in nursing and, years later, a master's in adult health. In 1975 she began a career in nursing.

"That your Chevy? I do body work, could take out the dents and fix the chrome," I've a good mind to say "<u>Do</u>." It'll be like a brand-new car.

I'm quite curious to find out if they decide on $50,000 or $125,000; my guess is, they'll discuss me from a Froodian viewpoint, possible Oedipus complex, penis envy and the like, and decide on this basis. Wish I knew their analysts, who will prob. end up by deciding all. Anyway, so now I'll have to write it. Will you do the jacket, as usual? . . .

Decca

In honor of New Year's, postal difficulties, potential blackouts etc and my new contract, plus the fact that Bob gave me some stamps for Xmas, I'm sending this Sp. Delivery. Can <u>just see your face</u> as the Sp. del. man knocks you up at crack of dawn! Of such small pleasures is life made up.

To Aranka Treuhaft   Oakland
March 17, 1966

Dearest Aranka,

. . . [O]n the electoral front: YOUR SON is planning to run against Coakley, our old arch-enemy, for District Attorney. I shall be his campaign manager. The only hope of winning is that there are no other contenders, and Coakley might easily conk out from sheer apoplexy in the course of running against Bob. So, if Bob wins, I can see the national headlines: UNPARALLELED CRIME WAVE IN OAKLAND, as I'm sure he would never actually bother to prosecute anyone. This is serious, I mean he is actually seeking the endorsement of the Calif. Democratic Clubs. Next weekend will tell the tale. It ought to be rather fascinating, if he really does run. Why don't you come out, and help run his campaign? You could at least mobilize the Hungarian vote.

We got a memo from Bob's financial advisor, it does all sound weird. All I can say is, it looks to me as though 3 alternatives face us: 1) getting rich, 2) jail, 3) spending our last days in the poor house. Looked at objectively, either one of those three would be quite interesting; so let's go along, say I.

Late Flash: Bob just got home, says that the D.A. (Coakley) is already having fits, because he has learned that B. might be running against him. So be looking forward to a really wild campaign.

Much love, & to Edith when you write, Decca

To Cedric Belfrage (and various other friends)   Oakland
                                                                April 9, 1966

Dear Cedric,

Loathing form letters as I do, I am nevertheless impelled to write an urgent letter to old friends in other parts, to tell you that Bob is running for District Attorney of Alameda County in the upcoming June elections.

It came about this way: The incumbent, J. Frank Coakley, has held the office for 16 years without opposition, mainly because the lawyers here are (for obvious reasons) scared to run against him. Coakley's administration has been marked by the most vile sort of racial bigotry. As prosecutor of the 800 defendants in the Free Speech Movement trial, he was unspeakably vicious and vindictive. In fact he is an utter brute in all ways, as anybody who lives here would tell you.

As the filing deadline drew near, and no other lawyers had come forward to enter the race, Bob began to think about running. Last Saturday we went to the county convention of the California Democratic Clubs—more or less to sound people out about what they would think of Bob's candidacy. The outcome was really astonishing. Bob was nominated, there was a standing ovation, he was overwhelmingly endorsed by the 900 delegates. (A spontaneous grass-roots movement to nominate me for Coroner, with the campaign slogan "drop dead," fizzled, however.)

He took a deep breath and filed, just before the deadline. It is a 2-way race (Bob and Coakley). It could have tremendous repercussions, not only in this state, but nationally—because of Coakley's links with the Knowland[24] machine, which runs Oakland and influences national policies.

The campaign shows terrific promise in terms of people offering to help, enthusiasm etc. There are a number of very important campaigns going on hereabouts (Congress, state legislature etc), which in one way is awfully good—because voter registration will be high, and precinct workers for other candidates will carry Bob's literature.[25]

In another way it is not so good, because the trouble is, money is scarce as hen's teeth in these parts (much of it has been siphoned off by the other candidates), and there are half a million voters to be reached in the next two months.

If you are thinking to yourself, "What a hell of a nerve to ask me for a contribution with all the demands on me for local causes etc. etc.," I can only agree. But if you can find it in your heart to help, we shall be most extremely grateful.

> Yours for Treuhaft for D.A., Decca

---

24. The Republican senator and *Oakland Tribune* publisher.

25. The Treuhaft campaign was closely allied with the congressional candidacy of journalist Robert Scheer, who was running on a New Left Vietnam peace platform against incumbent Democrat Jeffrey Cohelan.

To Leonard Boudin   Oakland
                                                          June 24, 1966

Dear Leonard,

. . . The election campaign was tremendous fun and tremendously tiring; I
went into an absolute decline after it was over. All you lovely New Yorkers <u>were</u>
dears to contribute. Bob got 28.5% of the vote county-wide, which was amazingly good considering that 1/2 of the county is a vast wasteland of transplanted
white southerners. He carried a majority of the Berkeley precincts, and won
overwhelmingly in West Oakland.[26] It was all worth it, and stirred many a
lovely stink in these parts. The greatest was having Dinky come out, she was
marvellous, a true diplomat and so efficient.

   Give my love to all the NY chums and chumesses. . . .

                         Love from Decca

To Aranka Treuhaft   London
                                                     September 29, 1966

Dearest Aranka,

. . . We hired a car and drove to Wales to stay with the Toynbees last weekend. On the way (or rather, about 100 miles out of the way) we stopped to see
Mabel, used to be our parlormaid at Swinbrook, now aged 85 and living in
Yeovil. We just drove up and rang her bell, she was <u>astonished</u> as you can imagine. We had an intensive chat over tea. She reminisced about the sad event of
Debo's birth—the whole family went into mourning, because a boy was
wanted. "I could tell the minute I looked at his lordship's face, like thunder it
was, oh he was put out," said Mabel. "I don't think anyone looked at her for several weeks. But she turned up trumps, didn't she." . . .

                         Much love, Decca

To Robert Gottlieb   Oakland
                                                      December 14, 1966

Dear Bob,

   Are you there? I heard you had been cavorting in London amidst the mini-
skirts, which is partly why I haven't written to you since <u>we</u> returned from those
parts at end of October. But the other reason for non-writing was extreme dis-
couragement with my so-called book that I had started. All of a sudden, just
now, a <u>bit</u> of light is looming, so I must tell:

   As you had so brilliantly foreseen when we discussed that possible book a

---

26. A largely black district.

year ago, the question of tone proved rough indeed (you may have forgotten, but you said "What will be the tone of it?" And tone-wise, it has been foundering badly). Not only tone, but shape of, has been giving extreme trouble—as it isn't going to be a narrative, the way Hons & Rebs was. So I've been having a perfectly beastly time not getting on with it.

I had actually done about 4 chapters ages ago, before starting on AWOD— about 5 years ago, I suppose. On re-reading those chapters, I thought they were rather good. But going on from there was beastly, and everything I wrote was dross and had to be thrown away the next day.

So I was just starting to wonder what to do next in life, such as have a restaurant which I've always wanted to or Learning a Skill, when an idea struck. Mary Russell Mitford wrote a book called Sketches of English Life and Character (c. 1810, I think) so why not Sketches of American Life and Character? . . . [O]rganized into sections of which me 4 chapters could be a part. That way, one wouldn't be stuck with narrative or sequence—or even with just one subject, which had been going to be the CP and life in same.

Anyway, I shall be striving in this direction. I'm coming to NY . . . so that will be Goal #1, to have bits of it done to bring for you to see. Can I sit and watch you read it to see if you think it's funny? . . . Do be for this plan. . . .

Love from Decca

To Barbara Kahn   New York
                                                            February 6, 1967
Dearest Barb,
     Faithful of you to write. . . .
     Last night . . . I went to dinner at the Dink's, cooked by Jim, delicious broiled chicken. I gather from my conversation with him (and from what I've heard from others) that he is mainly trying to act as a brake on the SNCCers who want to exclude all whites etc. He gave me some chapters of his book to read (he's doing an autobiog. and hist. of the Move-ment). Alas, it isn't very good; yet I think it could be if he would really struggle with it a bit. Barb, it is too predictable, somehow. I mean guess when he first learned he was a Negro (aged 7). When he wasn't allowed to sit at the counter and have his Coke in a glass, but was caused to buy one out of the machine, and he ran home crying all the way. Which I bet happened; yet I think I've read this before. In other words one wonders if people are not enormously influenced by what they've read before in relating the (perfectly true) things about themselves. Because all autobiog. is by its nature fearfully selective, I mean one has to pry out a few telling points from the huge morass of recollected things. Also what I care not for in his writing is the constant use of words like shit (not going to take any, from no cracker). Pity, because what he has to tell is fascinating; but he will have to

buckle down to it more than he has so far. (I shld. talk! At the moment, being the prize goofer-off of all time.) . . .

Much love, Decca

To Nancy Mitford   Oakland
                                                                    April 6, 1967

Darling Susan,

. . . Muv's diaries: the thing I loved was her engagement books, of which the 1937 vol. had entries like: "Heifer born today. Mabel 2 weeks hol. Decca married. Tea with Fuhrer."

News from here: Susan you won't like what I'm about to tell you, except I expect you know it already (because Sonia Orwell[27] was here for ages, entering into our lives): Dinky's going to have a Baby in June. Beige power is my slogan, as I expect that will be its color. I don't quite fathom why she doesn't get married (as the babe's father, Jim Forman, and her have been living together for ages); but she seems happy with her rum lot, so that's a comfort. . . .

Much love, Susan

To Nancy Mitford   Oakland
                                                                     May 4, 1967

Darling Soo,

. . . The Isle is sold![28] Finally, after all this time. . . .

Loved yr. review in Life of B. Russell, and him being a tease like Voltaire.[29] I thought him more teased than teasing (in the book, I mean). I'm sending along mine.[30]

The other day Prof. Arnold Toynbee[31] came to dinner, he is lurking nearby as visiting prof. at Stanford University. He is a <u>dear</u> old soul. I had never actually met him, over all these years; but looked him up on the grounds of Philip. . . . Prof. T. made some remark at dinner about Esmond; I said I didn't

---

27. Sonia Orwell, a much younger woman who married the terminally ill George Orwell three months before he died, was a habituée of arts circles, an editor, and the much-maligned custodian of her husband's legacy. Known as a drinker and a difficult woman, she was a loyal friend and sometime hostess of Decca's at her London home until her death in 1980.

28. Following the death of her mother, Decca received a "gloomy" report from her attorney on Inch Kenneth's financial prospects—either as a working farm with an absentee owner or as a rental property—and had decided reluctantly to accept his strong advice to sell it, since, as she put it, "neither child seems inclined to be a farmer."

29. Nancy Mitford had previously written a Voltaire biography, *Voltaire in Love* (Hamish Hamilton, 1957).

30. Decca had also written a review of the first volume of *The Autobiography of Bertrand Russell* (Little, Brown, 1967). Hers appeared in *Ramparts* magazine.

31. Philip's father, the historian Arnold J. Toynbee, who was the nephew of the economic historian also named Arnold Toynbee.

realize you knew him? "Indeed I did! And he gave me a great deal of trouble!" said T., indignantly. He proceeded to tell the trouble as though it was yesterday; actually, it was in 1933, when Philip ran away from Rugby, and Esmond sheltered him. . . .

Yes I do agree about the drugging being awful. It is spreading like mad here (LSD, which is the dangerous sort; what Muv used to call Marriage Uana is apparently not specially dangerous). And apart from the danger, the annoying thing is the people of one's age who try it. Goodness they are boring about it. They at once become pitying of one for not having some. Asked what it is like, they can only say, "Indescribable!" Also it makes one love everyone, they say. For instance, a locally well-known poet called Ginsberg[32] said it made him feel very sympathetic to Lyndon Johnson. I wish they would invent a Loather's Drug.

Mrs. O.[33] slightly mis-reported me about minding no marriage. I only said that now, if someone says "Would you want yr. daughter to marry a Negro?" I could answer, "Rather." New York friends say she is v. happy, and the word radiant recurs. . . .

Bob is in the midst of re-torturing the CIA, this time about the CIA financing of the Co-op movement.[34] He adores that sort of thing. . . .

Much love, Susan

To Barbara and Ephraim Kahn and other friends   Chatsworth
                                                                   May 31, 1967

Dear Barb, Eph, Mimi et al, incl. Pele,

Well I must say extreme disloyalty your end—not a bloody word from any of you so far. I feel v. cut off. (Bob doesn't; but then he never writes letters, either.)

We are in the throes of arranging a Theatre Party in Bristol (2 hrs train journey from London) next Tuesday, to see the musical of Pursuit of Love,[35] now playing there. Bob & me are taking a select group of cousins & so on & people like Joany, booking overnight rooms in a Bristol hotel, my idea of heaven. But easier said than. In 1st place we just thought of it today & it at once became clear that one was very discouraged from telephoning before 6 p.m. when the cheap night rates go into effect. ("Let's telephone Rudbin," says I. "Yes let's, this evening—she's probably out in the daytime," says Debo.) So after 6, of

---

32. Allen Ginsberg, the famed Beat poet.

33. Probably Sonia Orwell.

34. It had been revealed that the Central Intelligence Agency had been secretly funneling large sums of money to various civilian organizations such as student and labor groups and the Co-op League. The Berkeley Co-op was intensely politicized and contentious at the time, and Decca wrote her mother-in-law that Robert Treuhaft, a board member, was "in the thick of [the] infighting, esp. demanding to know just how witting they all are about CIA (the international co-op movement)."

35. Nancy Mitford's novel.

course, most people are out to cocktail ptys or something. The way you phone from Chatsworth is to pick up the instrument (it's called here) & a Chatsworth operator takes your order. You hang up while he gets the party on the line; then he rings you back. So after about 5 no answers, the operator chap said "Seems that everyone has gone off to the Riviera!" After 55 mins. of trying (I started at 6:05) it was clearly time to change for dinner; so I rang back the operator & said "Don't call me, I'll call you. Time out for a coffee break as we say in America." All awfully irregular. The operator lives downstairs with a complex of burglar alarms, which Debo showed us today. If you so much as nudge one of the Van Dykes or Rembrandts, an alarm rings in his office & all hell breaks loose; police arrive in 2 minutes, he says. So far there haven't been any burglaries, so his life is a bit dull, & I for one hardly can blame him for cutting loose about the Riviera.

Anyway Joany & Rudbin are both coming to the Bristol Follies, which I'm more looking forward to than anything on this trip. Debo, who saw it on opening night, said it starts out in the Hons' cupboard, with all the linens & hot water pipes just like the actual one at Swinbrook. (It got rather bad notices, not surprising, since I can't actually imagine anyone except us noting the point of it.) . . .

As always I'm rather longing to get back to London. There was a bit of conversation about Idden today (you know, me cousin who wrote If Hopes Were Dupes, the nervously-breaking down one),[36] and Emma[37] & Debo were saying the whole thing cld. have been avoided had she only lived in the country! Honestly. So pointed out I'd be bonkers in no time in the country & that was not the cause, as Idden wanted to be an Actress which by nature live in towns. . . .

Fondest love, Brutes though you are for not writing, Decca

To Pele de Lappe and Steve Murdock   London
                                                      June 3, 1967

Dear Brutes,

Not one word from any of you. Who knows how Koko is, or if Dinky's had her Baby, let alone Mimi's exams, Georgia's[38] London trip, Eph's beefs, what you think of the Mid. E. crisis, etc. etc.

So here goes with some London notes. . . .

Steeple Bumstead 267 has been long since discontinued to the worst sort of numbers game ever.[39] You have to dial about 16 numbers, now, to get a country

---

36. The subject of Ann Farrer Horne's book was her nervous breakdown.
37. The duchess's daughter.
38. Barbara and Ephraim Kahn's younger daughter.
39. One of Decca's favorite stories was about the time her flustered husband couldn't understand the English telephone operator from whom he was seeking a friend's number. Treuhaft finally put Decca on the phone. She was told, "Well, I told him in pline English, Steeple Bumstead 267."

number; as in all things, once the English discover the American Way, they go utterly overboard. Same with packaging. You know those horrid bits of transparent plastic over our meat at home? Well, here, <u>apples</u> are in boxes of 4, with thick, obscene looking cellophane tightly wrapped over. . . .

All who have been interested in the Dink babe have at once asked, "oh, is she going to have it at home?" Which necessitates the boring explanation that it's almost against the law in America. "No, in hospital." "<u>Oh</u>," they say. "What a good idea, on the whole, because if something should go wrong they've got all that equipment." (I adore equipment, because nobody actually knows what it means. Help, Eph! What <u>does</u> it mean? Except for iron lungs and so on, which one is on to?) . . .

Bob is going home on 10 June, that is, he's leaving here for NY on that day; arr. S.F. on 11 June. Time difference being all in our favour, going home; he'll have masses of time in NY.

This is awfully good, because as I was trying to explain to Martin, when I get the t.gram that Dink's babe is being born, what with the 6 hours time difference to my advantage, I shall get there in masses of time, even if it is born quickly. He simply couldn't see the point. Neither could several others to whom I explained this theory; on the other hand, they also could not refute it satisfactorily. Yet it is so obvious, don't you agree?

I do hope all of you are all right; loathe being so out of touch.

End of paper, much love, Decca

To Miriam Miller   New York
                                                              June 26, 1967

Dearest Mimi,

I'm sitting waiting for the Grandbabe to be brought home; have bought a drip-dry black & white dress (sort of a uniform, it's meant to be) for me duties as Grandmother. Oh dear I do hope I last in this job. . . .

Love from Decca

To Virginia Durr   Oakland
                                                              August 9, 1967

Dearest Va,

Sorry about inadequate letters. Now I'm supposed to be doing another article—more up my alley, it's for Good Housekeeping (of all things) on subject of cremation. A dotty woman wrote them a long wail about her mother's cremation, and I'm supposed to answer it. I shouldn't bother, but they pay such huge amounts that I can't bear to turn it down.

Anyway, I'm not doing it (you'll be glad to hear, as that means I can write to you instead!) because just too many upsetting things have happened all at once.

Such as our adored dog Koko has got to be destroyed (we just found out) because he keeps chewing up the kids on the block. It's become a police matter, as he has bitten two just recently; and the neighbors are getting a bit fed up about it.

But worse than that, Giles Romilly committed suicide in a hotel room here last week. I got a phone call from a Dr. asking if I am related to Giles, I said yes, in a way; so the Dr. said he was dead and that his bride of a few months, Coral, was in his office. Bob and I dashed over there. It turns out the Romillys had been here for 5 weeks (they never got in touch with us, so we had no idea they were even here). Last Monday, they entered into a suicide pact; he died, she recovered. He was evidently dead since Tuesday, but she only woke up on Saturday enough to stagger to the Dr.'s office. The whole thing is such a ghastly horror story, you've no idea. We took Coral home with us and of course as you can imagine she's a hopeless sort of girl, would have to be to marry him in the 1st place. She hadn't eaten anything from Mon. to Saturday except one apple; so I plied her with food. She's a 30-year-old former teacher. Bob was <u>heroic</u>, went to the stinking hotel room and packed up all their things & generally coped. I made fast plans to ship her back to her mother in London; we put her on a plane on Sun. night. Those 2 days with her seemed like a month. (Also the Dr. told her we were pinko-commies, which I found v. annoying.) . . . Virginnie the horror, the squalor, the dreadfulness of it all. Unfortunately Coral is the Frank Type, and she regaled us with the gruesome details of their deviant sex life. I do so fear for his 3 children. . . .

Otherwise, all is fine. (Ha.) . . .

Much love, Decca

To Virginia Durr   Oakland
                                                                                    August 18, 1967

Dearest Va,

Thanks awfully for yr. letter. . . .

The thing about Giles and Esmond was that they were the two most entirely different characters you can possibly imagine.[40] Giles was 18 months older than E., yet Esmond was always completely the leader of the two—as boys at Wellington, he did all the planning of their joint rebellion.[41] Giles was far more

---

40. Although it is not fully reflected in this letter, Decca was very close to Giles Romilly and spent a lot of time with him when she and Esmond were living in London before coming to the United States. She told Giles Romilly's son that she adored Giles, whom she considered very sensitive and very brave ("running away to the front" during the Spanish Civil War when the International Brigades tried to keep him behind the lines on non-combat duty, apparently because he was Winston Churchill's nephew).

41. Wellington was the private school—"public school" in English parlance—from which Esmond had run away as a politically radical fifteen-year-old, in open revolt against the Officers Training Corps and other traditional and stodgy aspects of "public school" life.

scholarly, and if truth must be told was really in some ways a better writer. I was just re-reading his piece in Out of Bounds (the book), and it is simply first-rate, esp. when you consider he was only 15 when he wrote it. Giles was a complete & thorough-going homo in the days when we knew him best, always had some drear boyfriend in tow. He was also terribly mother-bound, and under the influence of Ordinary Mrs. Romilly, in contrast to Esmond.

When I saw him in 1955, he was absolutely changed—I shouldn't even have recognized him. He is exactly my age; looked 60 then, and 70 when last seen by me. It turns out that when he got back to England from prison camp[42] some stupid Dr. put him on the drugs to which he finally became hopelessly addicted (barbiturates; he wasn't on LSD or marijuana). In 1962, when he was here with the kidnapped children, he showed me a partial ms. of a novel he was writing. It was utterly weird yet fascinating—written in the disjointed style he by then was talking in. I sent it to Bob Gottlieb (Simon & Schuster). Bob told me he lay awake all night after reading it, wondering if it was a work of genius or the work of a madman; decided the latter, so did not take it.

He showed up in Berkeley last February (this is before he married Coral). He sort of kept popping into our lives, then popping out again; but we saw quite a lot of him. A great friend of mine (English, called David Pleydell-Bouverie) met him here with us, and took me aside to warn that Giles is insane, might harm us if he stayed around. Then Giles left, as suddenly as he had come. Next thing, I got a clipping sent by a friend from D. Express, telling of his marriage to Coral. I went to tea with them at Pimlico Rd. (Ordinary Mrs. R's house, from where Esmond and I planned our running-away); they both seemed utterly nutty.

Why Berkeley? I'm fairly sure, because I live here. No other explanation made any sense; he was supposedly doing research for a book on a group of Chicago novelists (and had taken about 20 of these novels out of the Cal. library here, Bob found them in the hotel room). Yet it made no sense at all to come here for that. . . .

Did you ever read this book called The Privileged Nightmare,[43] all about his war experiences? Awfully good. . . .

The English papers were full of it; but luckily no mention of suicide (the coroner is simply saying overdose).

     Much love to all, Decca

I forgot to say, Giles absolutely <u>adored</u> Esmond. And I think E's death was almost equally as responsible as the prison experience in driving him off balance.

---

42. Colditz, the Nazi prison where he had been incarcerated during World War II.
43. Co-authored with Michael Alexander and published in 1954 (Weidenfeld & Nicolson), the joint memoir was reissued later under the title *Hostages of Colditz.*

To Nancy Mitford   Oakland
                                                                    August 22, 1967

Darling Soo,

Yr. letter (which crossed my wail about the Giles histoire) made me shriek, as usual; esp. Kay Graham being wowrm.[44] She is actually noted for being a <u>freezing terrifier</u> by the people who work for her; although not by me, because I knew her best when she was young and v. nice. Sorry you loathed her.

The Babe's[45] name is James Robert, called Lumumba by some and Jamie by others. P. Toynbee said "I bet it will look exactly like your mother only pitch black." But on 2nd thoughts he said "Won't you be disappointed if it's pure white?" Actually it is jolly fair; but those in the know say they are often born light and get pitch as life staggers on.

The piano tuner[46] turned up here the other day in the middle of the night, as is his wont, having earned enough money in NY to fly out. He stayed for a bit, has now disappeared into the sub-culture I think it's called. . . . He looks smashing, shaved and cleaned up. He was in the country with Dink & Baby for a bit; says the Babe's first words will be Uncle Ben/Has done it again, as that's all Dink says to it. (By the way, she adores it, and is a 1st rate mother, as I thought she would be.)

Well there was no Mitford (10/—),[47] cremation. Now they[48] want the ashes sent back, but the crematorium people are making a fuss because Susan it's against the law in Calif. to send ashes to a private individual, they must be sent to a cemetery or churchyard—a law passed by the niche-and-urn lobby, yes Susan. I pointed out to Bob that we've got lots of perfectly serviceable ashes about the house we could send; he's always rescuing them from the niche-and-urners for clients, then the clients forget to come & fetch them, so they pile up in my cupboard.[49]

---

44. In her letter, Nancy Mitford had described a chance meeting with Graham, whom she described as "one of those *wowrm* Americans I can't care for," adding that she only really liked the "tough brute" type. Nancy told Decca that Graham "loves you, but she's so wowrm I guess she kinda loves the whole human race." The word *wowrm* was Nancy's exaggeratedly American pronunciation of *warm*.

45. Constancia Romilly's newborn.

46. Benjamin Treuhaft had become a piano and harpsichord tuner.

47. Nancy had asked Decca whether she had "hurried [Giles Romilly] into a Mitford (10/—)." After publication of *The American Way of Death*, "a Mitford" became the lingo in some quarters of the funeral industry for a cheap funeral or cremation. Nancy was teasingly suggesting that Decca would arrange a quick 10-shilling cremation for Romilly. For another such reference, see letter of July 10, 1973, to the Duchess of Devonshire.

48. Presumably members of Giles Romilly's family in England.

49. Included in the "associated materials" in Decca's papers at the Harry Ransom Humanities Research Center at the University of Texas in Austin are, in the words of the archivists, "Neva Perkins' cremated remains." When asked once what they were doing in the collection, Robert Treuhaft said that Decca was always annoyed by the unclaimed urns of ashes that were stored in the house and must have thrown one in a box when she sold her papers to the university—possibly to "pad" the boxes because she was compensated according to the bulk of the material sold.

Oh dear those poor Romilly children, I do wish I knew some nice motherly person to give a hand with them. No, Susan, I'm not suggesting ye. . . .

Much love, Susan

To Vivian Hallinan[50]   Oakland
                                                                                August 30, 1967

Dearest Vivian,

I've been thinking and thinking over our meeting of yesterday and wanted to jot down my thoughts. Some of them will be repetitive of what was said there. Yet, I thought perhaps you might want to present these views to some of the people you will be consulting with in Chicago, including Rev. Martin Luther King.

First, I must say how very sorry I am to be in disagreement with you. I have the greatest admiration for you and your family & for all that you stand for. But I feel it would be wrong to let friendship stand in the way of what is really a very profound difference of opinion in such an important matter.

Basically, I suppose, I see the Jeannette Rankin brigade[51] as a golden opportunity to "escalate" (to use a horrid word) the peace movement in a brand new and totally different way—as Marion Conrad put it, to provide an umbrella under which those women can gather who hate the war, but who would not come near the existing peace movement. There must be literally millions of them. So, how to provide an avenue of expression for these hitherto silent voices?

Not, in my opinion, by projecting a plan that is by its nature super-militant: the plan to get 10,000 women willing to be arrested to go to Washington. Perhaps super-militant is not even the right word here. I think many will view it as a theatrical gesture, rather than a serious and urgent demand for an end to the war. I don't think we could hope to top the magnificent Spring mobilization marches in San Francisco and New York; also, I don't think that getting arrested per se is necessarily a proper goal, unless one thinks through terribly carefully just what it will achieve. The press is almost certain to sneer at it or else ignore it.

In contrast, if we could gather a sponsoring group of outstanding women who oppose the war, who would in turn mobilize other women for more traditional forms of political protest, it might be almost realistic to hope we could turn the tide.

---

50. Vivian Hallinan, longtime friend and ally of the Treuhafts, was a legendary San Francisco civil rights and peace activist and an astute businesswoman. She was married to fiery radical attorney Vincent Hallinan, who ran for president in 1952 on Henry Wallace's Progressive Party ticket.

51. On January 15, 1968, the day Congress convened, about 5,000 women of the Jeannette Rankin Brigade, a coalition of women's antiwar groups joined together for this purpose, demonstrated against the Vietnam War outside the Capitol. The demonstration was led by Rankin, then 87, the Montana suffragist and pacifist who was the first woman elected to Congress and the only member of Congress to vote against U.S. involvement in both world wars.

I agree with Marion's proposal that the plan of action should culminate in a delegation of 100 women to Washington—who, instead of picketing, would give a Washington Tea Party. This, I believe, would get a good press. Don't forget that there are newspapers across the country that oppose the war—and that in generally hawkish publications like Newsweek there are editors at all levels who oppose the war, and who would welcome the chance to give good coverage to this sort of protest.

Vivian, those of us who, like you and me, have for years been identified with the left-wing militant movements are (paradoxically) curiously sheltered. That is, I don't think we can know of our own knowledge much about how huge numbers of our fellow-citizens think & react. (For instance I don't personally know a single person who voted for Reagan;[52] do you? Yet quite a lot must have, judging by the election results.) Therefore I think we must take counsel from people in touch with wider circles. . . . I was brought up short when I learned that Helen Meiklejohn, one of my oldest friends,[53] didn't want to sign a Lawyers Guild appeal if I were to be a co-signer. I was brought up even shorter in an incident that happened a few years ago with Women for Peace. It was the time that the WFPs were lobbying all city councils and other public officials in the area. The Mayor of Oakland refused to meet with them because I was scheduled to speak at the evening meeting! Now it's true that the Chron. chastised him for this silly bigotry; yet, how many of the Oakland Women for Peace faded away because of this incident? I don't know, but I bet a lot did. Obviously sophisticated people like some that we listed for the Rankin Brigade (Eliz. Taylor, Bel Kaufman, Marianne Moore etc) would hoot at the Mayor of Oakland. Yet, oddly enough, they still might refuse to join the Brigade if 1) the objective is getting arrested, and 2) people like you and me are listed on it. And Marion's (excellent) idea was to start off by trying to enlist far more conservative women than those I had suggested.

One more personal example that I think has some bearing. About 20 years ago, the Civil Rights Congress was fighting to save from execution Wesley R. Wells, a Negro prison inmate convicted of attacking a guard. CRC, which was on the Atty. General's subversive list, had picket lines, delegations to the Governor, all the usual forms of militant protest. Then a Dr.'s wife (not a CRC member) suggested writing to all the doctors in the Alameda County Medical Assn., asking them to mount a defense of Wells based on a single element in the case—the medical proof that he was "stir crazy" at the time of the attack. The letter to the doctors was signed by a few doctor-sponsors. To everybody's com-

---

52. Future president Ronald Reagan, who was elected California governor in 1966.

53. Dr. Helen Meiklejohn and her husband, philosopher Alexander Meiklejohn, were experimental educators who founded the San Francisco School of Social Studies in the 1930s, dedicated to adult education through often confrontational dialogues of diverse labor leaders and leftists of all social classes, in the hope of furthering democratic values. She also helped found the Pacific Coast Labor School.

plete astonishment, 175 doctors responded including the head of the Calif. Medical Assn. This is, everyone agrees, what turned the tide in the Wells case; CRC, with best intentions, simply couldn't do it alone. I was exec. sec'y of Oakland CRC at the time; and was almost expelled for devoting all my time to the Doctors' effort, instead of organizing CRC street demonstrations and the like.

This is pretty long-winded; sorry. I said on the phone that I would help anyway, no matter what is decided. However, thinking it over, I shall not be keen to help if the objective is simply to rally those who are already active and on record, which I fear will be the case if the 10,000 arrests are pushed rather than the broader effort. So I shall wait anxiously to hear from you.

Much love, Decca

To Virginia Durr   Oakland
                                                        September 20, 1967
Dearest Va,

I went away to the country for a few days to stay with my great friend David Pleydell-Bouverie. . . . He has a huge & beautiful ranch in the Jack London country. I had a whole house to myself (it's a complex of lovely houses), break. in bed, lapping up the luxury as Benj wld. say. Bob came up to fetch me, bringing the European Post, letters from Nancy, Debo, Toynbees, Sonia Orwell etc. They were all saying how awful about Giles, but all of them started their letters by commiserating about our dog Koko, who we feared had to be destroyed because of munching the neighbours' children. Nancy said, "There must be so many American children, surely some of them could be spared?" Anyway we've decided to try fencing in our back garden, so he is reprieved for the mo. . . .

The latest absolutely beastly bit of news is that Evy Frieden[54] is dying of leukemia. I learned of this last Sunday; a friend rang up and told me. Evy only just learned of it, via a multiphasic or whatever it's called, physical exam. The friend said the Dr. does not expect her to live more than a year at the outside. Isn't that vile. . . . Dorothy Neville and I are driving down to L.A. tomorrow to see her. . . .

Va, I'm 50. Bob and a friend called Sally Gossage put on the most spectacu-

---

54. Evy (or Evie) Frieden was an old comrade and friend of Decca's and one of the women she recruited for the "White Women's Delegation" that went to Mississippi in 1951 to try to save the life of condemned "rapist" Willie McGee. In *A Fine Old Conflict*, Decca called her "a rollicking, jolly warehouse worker" who often volunteered to help out at the CRC office. Decca extolled her "buoyant *joie de vivre*," her "moral toughness," and the absence of the "mawkishness" she found in other Party members. Frieden and her husband, Mike, had given up their educational ambitions to take factory jobs at the request of the Communist Party, and their decision in 1958 to leave the Party helped convince the Treuhafts to do likewise.

lar 1/2 century party for me and Howard G.,[55] Sally's husband also turning 50. It was on a ferry boat[56] in the S.F. harbour, a live band, a whole roast pig, a Chinese dragon dance. Never saw the like in all my born days. I can hardly wait to be 60. It really did take the edge off the dreaded entry into Old Age.

I'm trying like mad to get back to The Fine Old Conflict; but as you can see . . . am not really into it properly. I do hope for a bit of inspiration from Evy, in a way; she is such an example of the absolutely best sort of Communist. . . .

Much, much love to all of you, do write soon, Decca

To Virginia Durr   Oakland
                                                                          November 20, 1967

Dearest Va,

. . . Was riveted by account of Toynbee dinner. I think you've got him slightly wrong in the sense that I don't recognize the cruelty bit. You must remember that English people on the whole are a lot tougher than Americans in terms of verbal torture (had you been raised in the hard school of teasing and being laughed at as a child you'd see why!) and general one-up-manship.

I like old Sally and agree she has a hard row to plough. There's a marvellous story about when they were first married. Finding herself in the utterly unfamiliar and rarefied atmosphere of the English intelligentsia, she was in tears much of the time. Philip's friends gave a big wedding party for them in a fancy restaurant. Robert Kee (writer, editor, TV commentator) said to Sally, early in the evening, "At midnight I shall make you cry." In the course of all the eating and boozing she forgot about this. At midnight, Kee took her aside and said "We thought you ought to know that Philip is a queer"; upon which Sally burst into loud boo-hoos! An English girl would probably have said "Is he? Oh well, I'll soon take care of that." But poor Sally, brought up in the mid-west, took it as major tragedy. (Of course he isn't one, it was just a ploy to tease Sal.) . . .

---

55. Visionary and unconventional San Francisco ad man and intellectual-provocateur-at-large Howard Gossage, who is often credited with "discovering" Marshall McLuhan. In the spirit of the honorees, the invitations to the one-of-a-kind party specified "Black tie or red shirt." Decca first met Gossage after he wrote a fan letter when *The American Way of Death* was published. Gossage was what Decca called "a sort of senior advisor, or guru" for *Ramparts* magazine and, to spur advertising, cooked up the idea of selling Inch Kenneth with a back-cover ad on the condition Decca agreed to be listed on the masthead as "Contributing Editor from Oakland." Gossage's last words to his brother-in-law before his untimely death in 1969 were said to have been, "I think I'm going soon. When I do, call Decca; she knows how to ferret out the cheapest funeral in this whole town." Decca told a friend proudly that she "got a funeral for $150!!!! As Howard was *extremely* rich, that really was a coup & well worth the effort."

56. The docked ferryboat had been permanently converted into offices to serve as the headquarters of the design firm of Walter Landor.

You'd love old Arnold T.[57] They came to Stanford last year and we met for the first time. He's far to the left of Philip, and far more of a dove; as Bob says, you can't trust anyone under 70 these days. . . .

Much love . . . Decca

To Aranka Treuhaft   Oakland
                                                              November 27, 1967

Dearest Aranka,

Many apologies for not writing before now. The fact is I <u>did</u> write a letter, & gave it to YOUR SON to add on to; but you know how he is about writing.

I went to Los Angeles for Evy Frieden's funeral. She died last Friday, and Mike (her husband) rang up, because he wanted me to say a few words about her at the funeral. . . . There were about 500 people at the funeral—including Jerry Newson and his wife![58] He went to L.A. after being released from prison, and Evy was really pretty marvellous about looking after him—got him a job in the garment industry, he's now a foreman, makes blue-jeans and the like; and she gave him a car when he first arrived. Lots of old friends from those parts. . . .

Evy's brother-in-law, Seymour, was sort of in charge of arrangements. He told me afterwards that he had noted that there was only one chair by the rostrum; so he went up to the funeral director, and said "We shall need three chairs; one for the minister, one for the rabbi, and one for Jessica Mitford." Upon which the funeral director fainted, and had to be revived with water. . . .

I shall miss Evy for ever. She was such a bright spot in one's life, I can hardly believe she is actually dead. . . .

Sorry to write such a dreary letter.

Lots of love, Decca

To Cedric and Mary Belfrage   Oakland
                                                                March 18, 1968

Dear Cedric and Mary,

I'm so terribly desolated about cancelling the trip—had been absolutely slavering for it, and for seeing you. I sent a cable the second I knew, in hopes of minimizing any inconvenience to you.

Here's what's up: I've been asked to do a book about the trial of Dr. Spock[59]

---

57. Toynbee.

58. Newson, whose cause the Treuhafts had championed from arrest through his imprisonment, had been paroled in 1962 at the age of thirty-two. He was eighteen when he entered prison.

59. Pediatrician, author, and social activist Dr. Benjamin Spock and four other prominent opponents of the Vietnam War and the military draft—collectively known as the Boston Five—had been indicted on January 5 for "conspiracy to aid, abet, and counsel violations of the Selective

(Knopf is the publisher; my editor, Bob Gottlieb, left Simon's Shoe Store in a big shake-up, and is now at Knopf). It is the first really exciting thing that's come my way for a long, long time—even beats undertakers for sheer thrill. . . .

I spent last Saturday with Leonard Boudin, who is Spock's lawyer. I learned that the conspirators, Spock and the other 4 defendants, had never met each other until they assembled in Leonard's living room for a conference with the lawyers! Can you beat it.

Seems to me that this is the political trial of the decade, as the Hiss trial was in that decade (although there the similarity ends).

I do so hope I can see Gen. Hershey[60] and others of that ilk. Time will tell.

Meanwhile, Bob is swamped with local Spock-type cases (see enclosed rather bad leaflet; a proper pamphlet will be forthcoming shortly).[61] So, although he too is awfully sad we're not coming, in one way finds it convenient. . . .

Love from Decca

To Pele de Lappe   "En route New Haven-Washington"
                                      April 4, 1968

Dearest Neighb,

Well I never did write from the plane; & since then life has been <u>one rush</u>. Seems like a month since that hangoverish drive to airport (for which, again, THANKS).

Isn't it all weird & wonderful—I mean what's happening. Or seeming to happen. I was at Dinky's (by Dinky, as Aranka wld say) when LBJ spoke last Sunday.[62] We were just drowsing off when—"I say, <u>what</u> did he say? Did you hear what I heard?"

The peaceniks are all vying for credit, & quite rightly. Spock thinks <u>he</u> did it, Coffin thinks <u>he</u> did it, the kids think <u>they</u> did it, the Doves-on-Mass-Mags

Service law." The other defendants were the Rev. William Sloane Coffin Jr., Michael Ferber, Mitchell Goodman, and Marcus Raskin. "Overt acts" to further the conspiracy included holding a press conference, distributing "A Call to Resist Illegitimate Authority," and accepting draft cards and delivering them to the Justice Department.

60. General Lewis B. Hershey was director of the Selective Service System (the military draft) for twenty-nine years.

61. A reference to the Oakland Seven conspiracy indictments. (For more details, see letter of March 28, 1969, to Aranka Treuhaft.) Decca was troubled by the use of vague, all-purpose conspiracy laws to stifle dissent by charging peace demonstrators with felonies based on their "conspiring" to commit misdemeanors such as trespass and public nuisance. She had commissioned a pamphlet to explain in layman's terms this political use of conspiracy law in the Oakland Seven case. She once described the conspiracy law as "*so* complicated, it's like the Theory of Relativity; when somebody is explaining it to you, you can dimly understand it, but 10 mins. later it flees the brain."

62. Decca was referring to the president's surprise announcement that he would not seek re-election, which he coupled with several initiatives to seek peace in Vietnam.

(like D. Scherman of Life and Viv Cadden of McCall's) think <u>they</u> did it. Not far wrong, all of them; although personally I think the V.C.[63] did it. (Do send the PW saying the C.P. did it, which I predict it <u>will</u> say.) . . .

Tomorrow, Dept. of J.[64] They do not seem too anxious to discuss the case, for some reason. So far I've got an appt. with one Cliff Sessions, chief of P.R. for Dept of J. Shall try to do better.

Have not seen many Loved Ones in NY—too busy, so far. Took Aranka to Spock press conf, & she loved that. Dink is being smashing & helping in all ways.

Much love, Decca

To Pele de Lappe   "En route N.Y.-Boston"
                                                   April 14, 1968
Neighbour,

Thanks v. much for most welcome letter. I'm back on the train, about 1 other passenger (this being Easter Sunday, 3 p.m.). So have settled in diner, with typewriter. . . . The diner is manned by <u>two women</u>, most unusual (usually they are womenned by several men). . . .

Taxi notes: Getting back from Washington, told the cab to go to 12 1/2 St. Lukes Place. <u>Nobody</u> knows where that is, but he of course claimed to know. "You are a writer, I presume?" he starts off. "Yes, how do you know?" (I know how he knows, actually, because he has noted me typewriter.) "I pride myself on a certain perspecuity and indeed a sort of extra-sensory perception when it comes to characterizing the possible career propensities of my customers," he said, and added: "I too am a writer, that is I won several prizes in high school and my English teacher commended me more than once on my literary talents." (He was about one's age). He went on quite a lot about his non-writing career, and meanwhile I noted we were hopelessly losing the way. I pointed this out. He said: "Yes, I admit we are taking something of a circuitous route. But how many taxi drivers will you find that even know the meaning of the word circuitous?" So of course I had to give him a circuitous tip for all this high-flownery.

Washington was rather extraorder, and beastly; what with the curfew,[65] and rather dense smoke, one couldn't get out much, and most of the people I

---

63. Viet Cong, the South Vietnamese and American governments' name for the guerrilla forces allied with North Vietnam during the Vietnam War.

64. Department of Justice.

65. Washington had been the scene of three days of devastating riots in African American neighborhoods after the assassination of Martin Luther King Jr. on April 4.

wanted to see (like Andrew Kopkind[66] and Izzy Stone[67]) were too busy. . . . However, I did have some surprisingly full & complete discussions with Justice Dept. and Gen. Hershey.[68] By now, my suitcases are crammed with Govt. and defense briefs in the Spock case, and Xerox'd research stuff on the defendants, and notes of interviews. I do wonder if a book will emerge from all this sea of papers, one day? Hope so. . . .

See you v. soon. . . .

Much love, Dec.

To Barbara Kahn   Boston
                                                                    May 23, 1968

Dearest Barb,

This is just a glorious (and 1st) moment of sheer recreation—I mean, writing an ordinary letter to you. . . . Do you realize I've been turning down all dinner invitations (and you know how unlike ONE that is) because I literally haven't got time to go.

Here's the approx. schedule each day: Up at 7, read the papers & do a bit of writing. . . . Court is 9 a.m. to 1, and 2 p.m. to 4, with 10-min. recess morning & afternoon. But (this is the part you'd hate) I haven't even bothered to find out where the ladies' room is—there is none on our floor—as even if I knew, I shouldn't have time to go.

I rush back here (and go), and then start my Bobletter which takes until at least 8, at which pnt. I nip down & get something at one of the vile restaurants in this block, back to clip the newspapers, & so to bed. . . .

The feeling of pressure is enormous. 1. Having to take down what amounts to a daily transcript in longhand. Now I know that in one way this is silly (because Leonard[69] has promised access to the real transcript), yet it comes from being inexperienced in covering trials. The one thing I have learned is that the moment one's attention wanders—or one stops taking careful notes— is always the moment when a violent storm blows up in Court over something

---

66. The self-described "radical journalist" who started out at conventional publications such as the *Washington Post* and *Time* but moved later to magazines on the left, including the *New Republic*, the *New Statesman*, *Ramparts*, and, years later, *The Nation*. He wrote about most of the major social upheavals of the second half of the twentieth century.

67. I. F. Stone, radical editor-publisher for nearly twenty years of the influential and fiercely independent investigative newsletter *I. F. Stone's Weekly*, which specialized in exposing government lies that other publications didn't know how to uncover or feared to touch. During World War II, when Stone was working for magazines in Washington, Virginia Durr once helped Decca get a job with him as what Decca called "sort of Girl Friday (now perhaps called Person Friday?)." The job didn't last. "Alas," she later wrote, "I couldn't understand a word he said and HE couldn't hear a word I said, being v. deaf. So v. sadly we called it quits after 2 weeks."

68. For Decca's later recollection of her "*very* curious conversation" with the longtime director of the military draft, see letter of March 24, 1972, to John O'Sullivan.

69. Boudin, Benjamin Spock's attorney.

or other—and then it all goes zip zip zip and one has lost the trend of the whole thing. So, I think I'll stick to my inefficient method of simply writing down everything that's said. Then, at a later stage (say one wants the whole Xcript of the lovely part about FBI agent Miller . . .) one can write to Dinky to rush over to Leonard's office and Xerox that bit. 2. Same about the daily Bobletter, takes 3 to 4 hours—not because it's so long, but because it is a prelim. sorting-out and distilling of my terribly huge notes. And a sort of evaluation along with. 3. The feeling one isn't following up on a whole mass of things that should be done: having many more intensive discussions with the defendants (not to mention completing the Raskin interview begun in Washington), interviewing some of the bit-players, such as the Clerk (a Negro with impressive delivery) and the Crier (who is straight out of Daumier; his only role in life is to reel off the opening of court in the morning. Today he worked overtime, because at one point he had to admonish the spectators not to talk whilst bench conferences are going on; I should rather like to be a Crier, in my old age). 4. Going over to the Boston Globe and mucking through their files. 5. Spending some time at the Arlington St. Church[70]—I even missed the riot yesterday, which was so sloppy of me.

I can see I shan't stir from Boston for the duration. . . .

But I am rather adoring it. And am v. glad to be staying in this hotel, expensive and crummy though it is. Various ones have asked me to stay, but I think I won't, because then one wld. have to be a guest along with everything else. . . .

They are now saying the trial may go into July. So be expecting me to have lost 10 lbs, if so. This is far more thinning than any known diet, as there isn't time to eat.

Barb <u>do write</u>. And make the God[71] do so, and Mimi if there, and anyone else you can think of. . . .

      Much love to all, Dec

To Pele de Lappe   Boston
                       June 8, 1968

Dearest Neighb,

. . . Had a long interview with Barshak this morning. Edw. Barshak of the CLUM (awful initials! Means Civil Liberties Union of Mass), who is counsel for Mitch Goodman.

Barshak is the only straight-man amongst the lawyers. The others are all Characters with a capital C. In Court, they turn before your very eyes into Daumier or Spy cartoons, as follows: Wm. Homans, counsel for Mike Ferber,

---

70. Scene of continuing demonstrations after the Unitarian Universalist church gave sanctuary to two Vietnam War resisters. The previous year, the church had held a Draft Card Turn-In and Burn-In service to protest the war.

71. Kathleen Kahn, Decca's goddaughter.

is a large, rugged man, shock of black hair, face like a bit of New England gran-
ite, Mayflowerish heritage (some people called Adams, it seems: Steve, Help!
Who are they? Any relation of Adam of Adam & Eve?). Homans is not particularly effective—a woolly thinker & examiner—but his very looks rescue him
each time. Next, James St. Clair, portly, humorous, divine smile—looks about
60, is actually 47! Next, Leonard Boudin, unruly grey hair (why doesn't he
comb his hair, say the symp. presspeople?), a marvellous special sort of NY Jewish (but rich Jewish, someone said) accent . . . a special way of rounding out
words like (say) "road," almost "rew-d," an English undertow to it. Leonard has
a <u>great</u> courtroom walk, almost a waltz—he's got rhythm, anyway. Guaranteed
that all eyes are on him (no short snoozes when <u>he</u> gets up), & also has mastered
the seraphic smile just as he's nimbly sticking in the knife. Calvin Bartlett, the
enigma. He is the most extraordinary looking of all of them. Visualize a human
goldfish. He's quite old, going on 70 I should think, with rather florid complexion, very slow of motion (<u>unlike</u> aforementioned waltzer, whose Dr. told him
it's good for the heart to spring about constantly). Calvin B's mouth is simply
riveting; I've had many a success saying to the corridor crowd (press etc) "Who
am I?" And do extremely pursed lips, stoop over, walk slowly as a tortoise with
hands behind back, and in funereal tones, very slowly, say: "Object, Your
Honor, for defendant Marcus Raskin." Or (his only other contrib. to the trial,
said to every Govt. witness): "Have you ever testified before a Grand Jury
in this case? No further questions." (Forgot to say: St. Clair is counsel for
Coffin.) . . .

To Barbara Kahn   Boston
                                                                June 9, 1968
Dearest Barb,
    Disloyal of you not to write. But Aranka said you wrote to her, so you get a
star for that. Poor old thing, I'm afraid she is quite unable to sort out her feelings about Al's death.[72] In fact Mimi was exactly right when she said that even
the months of non-speakers etc. was better for A. than being quite alone without all the tension of having someone <u>not</u> to speak to. . . .
    You should see how the Judge treats [Spock's] character witnesses. When a
character witness comes on he is first examined as to his own background—the
ones for Spock are, as you can imagine, eminent folks, heads of medical
schools, Sen. Young[73] of Ohio etc. That established, the next question is "Do
you know the defendant Dr. Benj Spock? In what circumstances have you
known him?" Then, "Do you know whether or not he has a reputation for
integrity, veracity in the community? Answer yes or no." And lastly, "What is
that reputation?" This is the prescribed form of interrogating character wit-

---

72. Al Kliot, Aranka Treuhaft's estranged husband, had died several days earlier.
73. Democratic Senator Stephen M. Young.

nesses, from which there can be no deviation; and to the last question, a one-word answer is sought. If the witness starts to say "Well, Dr. Spock is . . ." old gravel-voice[74] cuts him right off. No no none of that. What is his reputation? Good, bad, or whatnot?" One witness, riled, said "It's certainly not what-not, it's excellent." Then, the Judge, "Step down, please." In the cold transcript, we shall just see the words, "Step down, please" (or sometimes he doesn't say please); but if you could see how he does it, the contemptuous way he barks it out the very second the witness has got out the word "excellent." Obviously doing his best to reduce these luminaries of medicine & education in the eyes of the jury. . . .

The closing arguments should be thrilling. This is where I hope the conspiracy law will become clear (so one won't have to plough through innumerable law review articles to get a proper grasp of it). . . .

We assume that Spock . . . being the last defendant to testify will bring the trial back out of the bog into which it's been sinking. . . .

I've got a beastly task ahead, so better get on with it: an immense pile of unclipped newspapers to be gone through, and then the move to a glorious double room for me & Bob, you can't think how thrilled I am that he's coming today. And specially, of course, that now he'll be at the trial, to help me sort it all out. I'm longing to introduce him to all me newfound friends—in that way, this has been an extraorder experience because it seems as though I've lived here with the defendants, their families, the press chums and lawyers for most of my life! Because the trial does have a sort of life of its own, and we also are sequestered in a way, thrown as we are into each other's company every day and all day. . . .

PLEASE WRITE, BARB.

Much love to all, Decca

To Pele de Lappe and Steve Murdock   Boston
June 13, 1968

Dearest Neighbs,

. . . [A]ll closing arguments to jury are now in, and tomorrow old gravel-voice gives his charge (instructions), expected to last 2 hours. . . .

This morning, Leonard started his closing arguments. . . . He was just getting well into stride. This morning's Globe had reported the napping-off of two or three jurors while Calvin Bartlett was meandering on in his argument; but all were alert and apparently alive this a.m. Leonard has this fantastic mixture of charm, informality, erudition—and the whole courtroom was reacting, encouraging smiles from all sides. So, suddenly, as he's in full flow, Judge Ford: "No demonstrations will be tolerated in this courtroom, including by facial expres-

---

74. Federal Judge Francis J. W. Ford, who was presiding at the trial.

sion." Dead silence; we all look at each other to see <u>whose</u> facial expression was demonstrating. (Van de Kamp, Govt. atty,[75] told me later he thought it was me!) Uneasy moment ensues. Then, Judge Ford: "I'm speaking of your partner, Mr. Rabinowitz."[76] Leonard shuffles a few papers and resumes speaking. Act II of this small drama occurred out of our presence, in chambers; we were told of it later by several witnesses. The lawyers were all in there on some other matter. But Vic Rabinowitz, stung, said in passing to the Judge, "Why did you call me down?" (or words to that effect). So Ford: "You were smiling at your partner." Vic: "Well, I wasn't, but even if I was it was not a reason to interrupt Mr. Boudin . . ." Judge, furiously barking: "GET OUT OF HERE!" And you would have to hear that ominous bark to get the full import. How we have all come to loathe that Judge! Even the formerly open-minded press folks, now firmly defense-minded—mainly because of Judge Ford, I think. . . .

I'm giving up after the jury verdict, for the moment; shall return for the sentencing. . . .

[M]uch love to all, Dec

Late flash: Verdict's in,[77] so we scram to Woods Hole[78] tomorrow. WRITE!

To Marge Frantz   Woods Hole, Mass.
                                                                      June 17, 1968
Dearest old Marge,

. . . I am now trying to sort out this here trial, at least in a prelim. sort of way. I mean, what <u>are</u> the issues in it? I have a feeling that the defendants still don't know what hit them. . . .

Leaving Raskin aside (his motives were always slightly different from those of the others), Spock and Coffin particularly were demanding (and I think expecting) a confrontation with the Govt. on the legality of the war, and hence of the Selective Service Act. In Spock's case, because he had Leonard Boudin for a lawyer, his lawyer was fully responsive to this—filed all those motions to bring in some 50 war crimes by U.S. forces and also would have testified as to the origins of U.S. involvement. Is this what's meant by "going through the motions"? Because, let us follow this through: it wouldn't even have

---

75. Decca wrote in *The Trial of Dr. Spock* (Alfred A. Knopf, 1969) that John Van de Kamp had been placed in charge of a special unit in the Criminal Division of the Justice Department "to speed up investigations and prosecutions of violations of the Selective Service Act and 'related statutes' . . . with special attention to violations of the 'counsel, aid, or abet provisions and the 'obstruction of recruiting' provisions."

76. Civil rights attorney Victor Rabinowitz, Boudin's longtime law partner, was a good friend of the Treuhafts and of their daughter, Constancia Romilly.

77. Spock and three of his co-defendants were found guilty; Marcus Raskin was acquitted.

78. Constancia Romilly was staying with friends in Woods Hole, Massachusetts.

meant that a Federal Judge would have to decide this issue, but that the 12-man jury would have to vote up or down the question of whether the war is in violation of international law and of the U.S. Constitution. Consequently it is clear that such a thing could never be adjudicated in a trial Court; so the defs. were laboring under a misapprehension all along in wanting such a "confrontation." . . .

Ergo, these defendants haven't really had their day in Court after all—because the issues they sought to bring out were not issues in the case at all. Furthermore they were trapped in the unreal and unfamiliar world of legal procedure. . . . (By the way, the Judge had instructed defense counsel early on in the trial to address their clients as "defendant Spock" or "defendant Coffin," obviously a crude attempt to diminish them! But Leonard coldly disregarded this all along, referred only to "Dr. Spock"; eventually the other lawyers followed suit ("Rev. Coffin" etc) and no more was said about that.) . . .

[The entire closing argument] of William Homans, counsel for Michael Ferber . . . consisted of a recitation of where Ferber wasn't, if you see what I mean—he wasn't at the Oct. 2 press conference, he wasn't at the Whitehall Induction Center demonstration, he wasn't inside the Andretta Room at the Dept. of Justice; furthermore he didn't know Dr. Spock, he didn't know Marcus Raskin, he didn't know Mitchell Goodman, he barely knew Rev. Coffin . . . So here is poor Mike Ferber, one of the real heroes of the Resistance[79] (and real leader of same) turning into a sort of grin on the Cheshire Cat at his crowning moment in Court. Yet, what could Homans do? After all, the charge was <u>conspiracy</u>, not opposing the war; so his job was to point out that his client was not a part of the conspiracy—if indeed (etc; you know the rest, such a conspiracy existed). . . .

[I]t all seemed perfunctory, because what counsel were really bent on doing was picking legalistic holes in a legal case. So it was two worlds: the world of the defendants, conscience-driven, haunted by the nightmare of the Good, Obedient Germans, determined to do absolutely anything in their power to stop the war; and the fettered world of the Court, with its rules of evidence, rules of procedure, everyone with half an eye on the appeals court to come. Coffin summed it up when he said ruefully, "If only we could have had a seminar with the jury!" . . .

BUT—what was their alternative? As we know, some of the Resistance people think they should not have defended, should have entered a guilty plea and gone off to jail. . . . [I]n the <u>extremely</u> irritating course of the trial itself, and seeing the defendants struggling within the bonds of legal procedure, I often rather wished they <u>had</u> decided to forgo the trial. Do you remember how in the first Smith Act case we rather welcomed the trial, as a public platform where

---

79. The first national organization formed to resist the Vietnam War and the draft. The organization was sometimes called simply Resist.

the Party's full position could be put forward in the spotlight of national publicity, etc? And how it never turned out that way? Another thing about the Spock trial: There were no demonstrations of any kind around the trial itself. This was because the Boston lawyers had put their feet down on this subject. So, in a sense, the defendants were also prisoners of their <u>own</u> counsel—actually, of the legal process, I suppose. . . .

The appeal is going to be as drab, or drabber, than the trial. Because then we'll really <u>see</u> the obscuring of the issues. Of course I suppose Leonard will press the legality or not of the war, & that will be chucked right out. . . . I do wish the appeal could be won on the issue that defendant Raskin was not allowed to go to the bathroom when he wanted to in the middle of his testimony—that sort of thing would be so appropriate to the way these things are decided. But he <u>never asked</u>, so that's moot, I fear. . . .

So the Jury find . . . all not-guilty of <u>counselling</u>. Aren't they lucky to know the difference between counselling, aiding, and abetting? I was asking Van de Kamp the diff. between aiding and abetting the other day in court. He said, "Well, aiding is physical—no, wait a minute, I mean abetting is physical—oh, I'm not sure. I'll get the exact wording to you if you'll give me your address." Which I gladly gave him.

> End of paper, end of letter, please write back by
> return of post, much love to all,
> Decca

To Virginia Durr   Woods Hole, Mass.
                                                                    June 19, 1968

Dearest Va,

. . . Here we are in Woods Hole, and a rather perfect set-up: Bob and I are in a delightful motel, at quite some distance from the Dinky mob, so we can escape from the assorted shriekers at will. The regime is that I stay here and work all morning, then late afternoon go along and cook their dinner. . . .

As you can imagine, the main thing is to start coming to grips with this weird trial. As you predicted, of course, the whole thing ended up in a ghastly sort of fizzle—built-in fizzle, from the moment that Judge Ford excluded the issue of legality of the war & Nuremberg defense.[80] . . . <u>How</u> we came to hate that prosecutor, John Wall! He's young, about 36, pallid, mouse-blond hair, just the traces of beginnings of bags under eyes and saggy jowl-to-come. Of course, the

---

80. In another letter, Decca wondered whether her publisher would have contracted for her book if they had known "what a fizzle that trial was going to be, both from the viewpoint of drama and general interest and (above all) from the viewpoint of advancing and clarifying the issues—war crimes, legality of war etc."

great speculation was how he appeared to the Jury. Was he Mr. Clean, wrapped in the American flag, Young America defending Our Boys overseas? . . . [D]oes the Jury see him as a Boy Scout? Or a Torquemada? If they think he's a repressive sort, they might just go the other way." We still don't know . . . yet in Wall's closing argument the one he really <u>went</u> for, and ripped up and down, was Raskin. The only one they let off. And why did they find the defendants not guilty of the "counselling" charge? It's all a mystery. . . .

The jury went out about noon on Friday, and we all hung around the courtroom, then eventually were released by the Judge to go to dinner. After dinner, a strange sort of euphoria set in. Mrs. Lindsay, Rev. Coffin's upper-class-rich-sister, brought along two bottles of Chateau Something or other; "It's only 1966 vintage," she kept saying, "but that was quite a good year." Coffin asked the Clerk of the Court if there was a ping-pong table anywhere around; he said there was one, but we couldn't use it because it was marked as an exhibit in evidence in another case! So we were just getting ready to play a game of Charades in the corridors when the jury came back with the verdict. The defendants were told to stand. The foreman gave the verdict, and then each juror was separately polled by the Clerk as to his vote on each defendant. A sort of litany: "Juror Number Two, what say you? Is the defendant Coffin guilty or not guilty?" "Guilty." "Is the defendant Ferber guilty or not guilty?" "Guilty." And so on down to Raskin: "Not guilty."

The only one who was really upset by the verdict was Raskin, near tears. (As Bob said, "Well, he could always demand a new trial.") But he cheered up after a bit. After the verdict we all went over to the Parker House cocktail lounge—masses of us, all defendants and wives and the symp. press and some of what Bob calls the U.C.C.—Unindicted Co-Conspirators, like Arthur Waskow. They have music there, so after a bit the Spocks got up and started to dance—everyone applauded, not just our table but the Parker House Bar regulars as well.

I did get to love them all. It's really an odd experience, like a lifetime—like being on a cruise, apart from the rest of the world. Mrs. Coffin Sr., Bill Coffin's mother, is marvellous. Tremendously patrician grande dame type. The day Coffin testified, lots of teen-age nephews and deb-type girls (relatives) showed up, and Mrs. Coffin was going round greeting them, and saying "Isn't this <u>nice</u>." One could almost hear the Spode teacups rattling in the background; it was like some rite of passage—a wedding reception? . . .

Much love, Decca

To Barbara and Ephraim Kahn   Oakland
                                                                July 14, 1968

Dear Kahns,

Home at last. . . .

I guess you know about the sentences by now. All got 2 years, and all but Ferber got $5,000 fine; he got $1,000; the special student rate? There was a fairly large—yet somehow tame—demonstration outside the Courthouse, the first one of the whole trial, and a press conference at which Spock in particular was magnificent. . . .

Man-on-the-street reaction in Boston seemed disastrous—poor Mrs. Coffin Snr. took a daily poll of taxi-drivers as she taxied from her club to the court-house and back, and out of some 40, only one found the least symp. for the defendants—the others all thought hanging would be too good for them. And after such a discussion with a cab driver, Judge Wyzanski[81] had said to me "There's your reason for the Boston venue!" . . .

[The jurors] got tied up in fantastic knots trying to explain why they found the defs. guilty of conspiracy, and of course they got the indictment all muddled in their heads—as who wouldn't. . . .

Here's a bit of q. and a. with [Wall, the prosecutor]:

Q. Why did you chuck off the 2 women and one Negro from the jury?[82]

A. I can't remember why we challenged the first woman, but the second—it was for practical considerations. The marshals would go through hell, having to figure out entertainment and so on for one woman with all those men.

Q. I should think that would be rather an entertaining situation for her, in some ways?

A. Ha, ha, ha.

Q. Further on the women: why did you challenge the first one?

A. For one thing, she was a U.S. attorney's daughter, that would be sufficient reason to challenge her.

Q. How did you know she was?

A. I found out afterwards.

Q. Then that <u>wasn't</u> the reason you challenged her?

A. I guess not. I don't recall.

Q. Why did you challenge the one Negro?

---

81. *Boston Globe* editor Tom Winship, whom Decca had met at a dinner party in Boston, introduced her to Federal Judge Charles Wyzanski, from whom she hoped to learn "all the gossip" about Judge Ford. Wyzanski regaled her with background information.

82. Decca had previously been told by Noam Chomsky, peace activist and Massachusetts Institute of Technology professor, that a Harvard math student had found that "there was a .00000000001 chance that, had there been a truly random selection of jurors, there'd have been 5 women and 100 men" in the pool from which the jury was selected. As she put it in *The Trial of Dr. Spock*, "the hand that rocks the cradle and turns the pages of [Spock's book] *Baby and Child Care* was notably absent."

A. We challenged a lot of people who <u>weren't</u> Negroes!

So there you have it. All wrapped up, and now to the dread task of writing—or rather the even dreader task of figuring out an approach. Wish you were here to help.

Kay Boyle[83] is staying with us, she is covering the Huey Newton[84] trial for Liberation Magazine, so decided to stay here for it. Yesterday, me 1st day home, we went to D. Bouverie's for his annual poetry reading. Sorry to say Bob recited The Cremation of Sam McGee. But the lunch was <u>heavenly</u>.

Much love to all, Decca

To Aranka Treuhaft   Oakland
July 26, 1968

Dearest Aranka,

Thanks awfully for letter and Spock clippings. . . .

There's no news to tell from here, either, as I'm work-bound at the moment: up at dawn, at it until I flag. Bob and all are fine. So I'll tell you a funny story. Or I guess it's a play. I won't tell the title (as that would give the plot away) until the end.

<u>Act I</u> When I got back, I said to Bob "Anything new happening around here?" He said no, nothing special. Knowing <u>your son</u>, this doesn't mean too much, because if one says "What happened today at the office?" he usually answers "nothing much," then it turns out 2 days later he forgot to mention there was a 4-alarm fire, our best friends have come to see him about a divorce, his secretary had quintuplets etc.

---

83. The writer and ardent leftist, best known for her short stories and novels, had been a literary hero of Decca's since publication of Boyle's early works as part of the literary avant-garde in Paris in the late 1920s and early '30s. Decca first encountered her idol in person when Boyle moved to San Francisco in the 1960s to teach at San Francisco State College. They met at parties and political meetings but became better acquainted when Boyle became a client of Robert Treuhaft's law firm after being arrested with scores of others in a Vietnam War protest. Decca and Boyle often participated together in protest demonstrations, petition campaigns, and political fund-raising activities, sometimes getting in the middle of contentious factions—"but that's life with Kay Boyle," Decca observed; "it's a bit like living in one of her stories." Decca quoted her husband as saying Boyle was "marvelous, incredibly brave and incredibly difficult," to which Decca added: "All my favorite characteristics, rolled into one."

84. Co-founder of the Black Panther Party, Newton grew up in Oakland and served as the revolutionary group's minister of defense. He was wounded in a 1967 shootout with police and arrested for the murder of an Oakland police officer. Defended by many nationally prominent New Leftists, united under the slogan "Free Huey," Newton was found guilty of voluntary manslaughter in 1968, but the conviction was subsequently overturned and the charges dropped. In 1974 he was charged with assault and accused of murdering a teenage prostitute. He fled to Cuba. Returning in 1977, he was tried twice, each trial ending with a hung jury. He earned a doctorate in social consciousness in 1980 from the University of California at Santa Cruz. In 1989 he was convicted of embezzling funds from a Panther social program. He was killed by a drug dealer on a West Oakland street in August 1989.

Act II A couple of days after I got home, Bob says: "Oh, I forgot to tell you—Georgia Kahn is 4 months pregnant." "Is she?" I say. "Well, I bet Barbara won't be best pleased when she gets back from Europe to find that out. How do you know?" Bob says he had dinner with Dorothy Neville just before I got back, and Dorothy said that Mimi told her. Mimi is staying at the Kahns', looking after Georgia while they are in Europe.

Act III I call up Mimi, but she is out of town for a few days. I call up Georgia—just to say hello, I'm back, but hoping she will confide. Georgia says "I'm feeling crummy," which of course confirms all. I wonder if it's really four months along? Our friendly neighborhood abortionist (when contacted by phone) always says "If they've had the merchandise more than three months, it can't be returned." I'm wondering if Dorothy got the message straight—it's usually in the first three months one feels crummy? Perhaps we can still return the merchandise before the Kahns get home?

Act IV I call up Kathy Kahn (hoping for sisterly advice to Georgia) but she also is out of town for a few days. No help there; and the Kahns are expected back on 24 July! What will they say? And the merchandise can't be getting any newer, or more returnable, as days go by.

Act V Mimi calls up—she's back! I immediately ask her, "What's this about Georgia Kahn being pregnant?" "Is she?" says Mimi. "How do you know?" I explain to Mimi that she told Dorothy Neville, who told Bob. Total mystification follows; Mimi doesn't know what I am talking about. Gradually, light breaks. Mimi has a young friend called George Bland, who got married a couple of years ago. Mimi is talking to Do Neville on the telephone, and says "George is going to have a baby." "Oh, really?" says Do. "How far along is it?" "About four months . . ."

End of play. The title is, The Quick and Easy Pregnancy of Georgia Kahn. It would be easy to perform as there is only one stage prop: a telephone.

But don't you think that's a scream? The Kahns got back a few days ago, and I quickly told them all, so they can ward off the sympathetic and commiserating glances of friends—because Dorothy had spread it far and wide. . . .

Much love, Decca

To Virginia Durr   Oakland
                                                                 August 16, 1968

Dearest Va,

. . . We are in the midst of a drama: Remember the Painter case, Calif. father judged "too Bohemian" by Iowa's Sup. Ct., who awarded the Painter son to the Iowa grandparents?[85] The son, Mark, is visiting his father, under visiting rights allowed by the court decision. So Bob's reopened the case under a new theory:

---

85. The Iowa Supreme Court had ruled that the boy could continue to stay with his maternal grandparents, where his California father, Hal Painter, had sent him temporarily after his wife was

that Iowa never did have jurisdiction of Mark, who is a Calif. boy, and there's to
be a hearing later this month. Meanwhile Bob's got a temporary order appoint-
ing Painter as Mark's guardian. So a day or two ago, the grandmother said she
might give over altogether if she was satisfied that Mark really wants to stay;
and that she was sending an emissary, Rev. Clay Lumpkins who is the family
minister and also school busdriver, to come out & talk to Mark. Don't you
adore the name Clay Lumpkins? I mean imagine being called Lumpkins and
then naming one's son Clay. I've started an Ode to Clay Lumpkins:

> Lump of clay and kin of clod,
> School busdriver, man of God,

but can't think of any more lines. Anyway, the press got hold of the fact that the
Lump is coming, so the phone's been ringing constantly—AP, UP, NY Times,
all the local press—to try & get in on the meeting of Lump and Mark. Bob is
livid with Lumpkins and the grandmother for giving the story to the press in
the 1st place. The unspeakable Ladies Home Journal rang up to offer $2500 for
"Mark's Own Story." Ugh. The Painters, and Mark, are in hiding from the
press. The meeting will be in an "undisclosed residence" (here) this afternoon.
I'm supposed to be on hand to make tea—also, I guess, to hit on the head with
a large iron frying pan any reporters who may show up.*

Mark does want to stay with his father except for ONE THING—his dog is
in Iowa. I'm trying to make Bob get a writ of habeas doggus.[86]

Lots of love, and to Cliff, Decca

* Brutal Mitford Style

To Nancy Mitford   Oakland
                                                                    November 30, 1968

Darling Susan,

. . . The Sir O. hoop-la[87] has made nary a ripple out here, but someone sent
me C. Cockburn's review of his book[88]—not exactly what you'd call a selling
review. Do tell about the book.

Tud was a pure Cuddum[89] when he used to come to see us at Rotherhithe

---

killed in a car accident in 1962. The court held that the father, a writer-photographer, was "either
an agnostic or an atheist and has no concern for formal religious training" and the boy's life with
him would be "unstable, unconventional, arty, bohemian." Hal Painter had written a book about
the case entitled *Mark, I Love You* (Simon & Schuster, 1967).

86. The minister dispatched by Mark Painter's grandparents was satisfied that the boy was
indeed happy living with his father, and the California judge ruled that the ten-year-old could continue to do so.

87. Nancy Mitford had ridiculed Oswald Mosley for saying he was never anti-Semitic.

88. *My Life*, by Sir Oswald Mosley (Thomas Nelson, 1968).

89. Cuddum (or Cuddem) was Boudledidge for "Communist."

St.[90] Esmond adored him. (The only one of our family he did.) And don't you remember how he used to say Diana was silly and so on? But of course he adored the Boud, in some ways I always thought she was his Favourite Sister. . . .

Well Susan a lot of people are coming to dinner so I'd better start cooking it. Goodbye for the present,

Much love, Susan

To Candida Donadio   Oakland
                                   November 30, 1968

Dear Candida,

. . . Vanessa Redgrave wrote the other day (we have become penpals over things like Spock), and she said, "Would you be interested in preparing a film about yourself and your sister Unity—thinking of Lynn as you and myself as Unity? I've had the idea on my mind for ages."[91] I haven't answered yet. I wonder if she had the idea that the film would be based on Hons & Rebels? I should be rather for that, but only if it ended with the outbreak of the war and did not go into the terrible end of Unity. What do you think I should answer? I'm not at all sure I should want to work on it, it would be a matter of finding some other person (English, it would have to be, because I don't think an American would be too good at the actual language), and perhaps I cld. sort of help? All, of course, after Spock is wrapped up. Please advise. . . .

Love from Decca

To Doris Brin Walker and Mal Burnstein[92]   Puerto Vallarta
                                          December 28, 1968

Dear Dobby and Mal,

. . . Life here is marvellous and quite unreal.[93] That is, the Belfrages seem to know no Mexicans whatsoever, so absolutely naught but Old Lefts as far as the

<hr>

90. Nancy Mitford had said she was upset with Mosley for saying Tom (Tud) Mitford was a fascist, which she called untrue, although she acknowledged that he was "a fearful old twister" and could have suggested to Diana that he was fascist. The sisters' dispute on whether Tom was a fascist or not continued for years. See, for example, the letters of January 9, 1980, to Robert Gottlieb and February 23, 1980, to Ann Farrer Horne (in which Decca entertained the idea that Nancy might have been putting her on).

91. Redgrave told Decca in the letter that she loved "the idea of a film in which the heroines are communist & fascist! And I have always loved Decca and Unity."

92. This letter was addressed to Robert Treuhaft's law partners, at least partly to keep them abreast of the Treuhafts' whereabouts since, as Decca put it, "you know how one loathes losing touch altogether in case of emergency."

93. Decca was staying at the lush guesthouse and home-in-exile of Cedric and Mary Belfrage. In other letters, she described it as "a pasturing ground for the Old Left" and "very much a Marxist heaven." She commented that in talking with other guests, "there's a certain family atmosphere of entendu background."

eye can see (for instance, Frances Herring and Alice Richards just showed up here). I guess one reason is that he is tired of getting chucked out of places; and he says that if you intermeddle to the slightest degree in Mex. politics you are <u>out</u> the next day. So, safer not to even know any like-minded locals. Cedric is more stuck in the past than anyone I can think of. The other day someone was telling about that Guardian meeting that Rap Brown walked out of—familiar stuff to us, the audience shouting imprecations at the speakers & all in high confusion. So Cedric: "But we used to have those meetings <u>perfectly timed</u>, down to the last minute!" We got the feeling that the thing that distressed him most of all was the loss of that perfect timing. I do think that the book he is writing is perhaps the only thing he could succeed with at this point (history of American repression from Palmer Raids to 1960) as it is history, wouldn't require much in the way of noting what's going on Black-power-wise or student-wise today.[94] Oh, and the morning after the Guardian meeting discussion he told us he had a bad dream that he was chairing a Guardian mtg. and everyone in the audience was shouting "Motherfucker" at him. (The <u>awful</u> thing is, they prob. would.)

We've got the most divine room with 2 balconies from which I watch the sunrise over Popocatapetl[95] (Bob snoring soundly the while), utter perfection for working. Xmas was a lovely orgy of food, drink, swimming, community singing; they've got as far as "There once was a Union Maid" & "Solidarity Forever." Oh it <u>did</u> bring me back.

>Wish you were all here. H. New Year to all, Much love,
>Decca

To Virginia Durr   New York
                                                February 22, 1969

Dearest Va,

I can't remember if I had heard from Bob Gottlieb (editor) at the time I last wrote. Anyway, I have now. He called up last Saturday, and (<u>fortunately</u>) seems well pleased with the ms. I sent in. You've no idea what a relief this is, as he is the first independent reader (that is, contrasted with Marge, Bob and other local loved ones). So I'm really <u>fearfully</u> relieved. . . .

I've seen all the briefs.[96] They are wonderfully in character. Goldberg[97]

---

94. As Decca told other friends, "Revolution at their doorsteps, but no way to participate, so on with history." She specifically mentioned discussions about the McCarthy era, with "not one word about the [contemporary] student revolt in Mexico City."

95. A nearby volcanic mountain.

96. The draft conspiracy appeal briefs.

97. Arthur J. Goldberg, who among his other positions had served as justice of the Supreme Court and U.S. ambassador to the United Nations.

dwells on the uprightness of that man of God Coffin (presumably, if he were some scruffy kid with a beard instead of Chaplain of Yale he wouldn't have the same 1st am.[98] rights?) and the thing that <u>really frosted</u> me, says Coffin would never do a "<u>violent act</u>" like burning a draft card. Really!!! . . . The Govt. brief says that Chomsky and Dwight MacD.[99] etc. are all conspirators too, just as I thought.

Of course the maddening thing is that the whole book is becoming increasingly irrelevant, because: 1) I'm sure the circuit court will reverse, Jack McKenzie of Wash. Post, who covered the trial, thinks so too. He called me up the other day from New Orleans. . . . (Virginnie, not that I shan't be pleased if they reverse, but you do see the problem, bookwise?). 2) I see from the newspapers that Nixon is ending the draft, or at least changing the rules of it. 3) The war will be over, long before it's published. Oh well. It's a good wind that blows somebody some ill. . . .

I shall be in NY for a couple of weeks working like mad. After the work (can't tell just how long), should so adore to see you. . . .

Much love, Decca

RSVP. I <u>long</u> for letters when away from home.

To Marge Frantz and other friends New York
February 28, 1969

Dearest Marge, and Barb. Kahn . . . and Mimi,
as I haven't got any carbon paper. . . .

I've written most of what's to follow to Bob, but he says he has no social life (please correct, immediately!) so I assume it won't have reached you. . . .

Boudin came to dinner here the night after I arrived. . . . L. read the book while I sat riveted. It was hard at times to tell if he was nodding agreement with the text, or just nodding off. However, he made a lot of notes & suggestions (on the legal side . . .). Then he said he liked it very much, but as he only has 6 months to live according to the Drs., had to dash home. I <u>begged</u> him to get the Drs. to reconsider, as the book prob. won't be out for 8 months; but he is a fearful hypochondriac, according to Dinky.

So then of course I tossed & turned all night wondering if he just <u>said</u> that, like Marge always does, to be encouraging, and actually loathed it. But! A couple of days later Eleanor Furman[100] called. She had wormed out an independent

---

98. First Amendment.

99. Linguistics professor Noam Chomsky and writer Dwight Macdonald were among the many signers of "A Call to Resist Illegitimate Authority" that served as one of the "overt acts" in the conspiracy charge.

100. Decca's old friend and hostess Eleanor Fried, now married to Sylvan Furman.

(that is, not in my presence) opinion from L., who said "it is the best thing of its kind I've ever read." So now: what does _of its kind_ mean? That is, possibly this is the only thing of its kind he's ever read? As you can see, life is a struggle. . . .

The day after Leonard came to dinner, Aranka was on the blower to the Sooper,[101] Mr. Meyer: "Oh Mr. Meyer, my daughter in law from California is here, she is a very famous writer, and last night she had a very great lawyer to dinner, he came only to consult with her about her work busy as he is. But Mr. Meyer, the windows! The floors! The stove!" So Mr. Meyer came bustling up. (I, of course, was in me dressing gown with no shoes on, looking fairly filthy.) Mr. Meyer: "Madame Aranka, I assure you, believe me, persons of a literary or artistic bent don't notice de doit." However, Aranka won, alas; yesterday, the place was awash with floor men, window cleaners etc.

Also, Aranka is heard occasionally by me on the phone talking to various friends from the Club (Hungarian card players): "Yes, she had Leonard Boudin to dinner . . . What, you've never heard of him? Well, he's a very big lawyer. He's associated with Arthur Goldberg, of the Supreme Court and the United Nations. . . . Arthur Goldberg? Yes, of course she knows him. I think she said he is coming tomorrow night for cocktails . . . I'm not sure which night, but she knows him very well. In fact he consulted her about the appeal for the Rev. Coffin . . ." So it's a lovely atmosphere for working in. . . .

Well, that's about it. Do ring up Bob once in a while; after what all of you said about how he always shows up if one stays anywhere long enough, I think I'll wait it out. At least another week of gruellingness bookwise. After that, I shall dance all night & take me grandchild to Bloomingdales for some new togs.

Much love, Decca

To Marge Frantz   New York
                                                            March 11, 1969

Dearest old Marge,

Am finally surfacing. . . . [D]elivered ms. to BG. And now the whole thing's over at Candida's being Xeroxed, so it's not even here to be fiddled with (which I do eternally, when it is here) so utter decompression has set in. Talk about being sequestered! Ugh. . . .

Aranka liked all except the references to the Rosenbergs and Smith Act victims etc:[102] "Why do you have to bring in so left-wing people? Ai, ai, ai, everybody except you thinks they are guilty." L. Boudin liked all except him being untidy with unruly wisps of hair; he clutched his head or rather patted it down, muttering "must get a comb" as he read that. . . .

---

101. The building superintendent.

102. In her postscript, Decca discussed the commonalities of a number of "the more celebrated political trials of this century," including those mentioned here.

By the way, watch out for Aranka on a jury. After reading all, and the juror-interviews, she said "But they <u>were</u> guilty, weren't they?" "Of conspiracy, Aranka?" "Well they were guilty of something, don't misunderstand me, I love Dr. Spock, and I think his wife is <u>wonderful</u>, so beautifully dressed, such a lady . . ." . . .

Marge. Thanks SO MUCH again,

> Much love, and to Laurent & kiddies,
> DO WRITE
> Decca R.S.V.P.

To Doris Brin Walker   New York
                                                                    March 12, 1969

Dearest Dob,

This is a description of your ward (as I think of her—Dinkydonk), her flat, her life & times. . . .

Today is the first time I've been there, to her house. . . .

Luckily, it was a typical day in a landlady's life. That is, she was renting the basement apt., ($185.95 a month, I think she said—she prices them like coffins, not a direct figure, but lots of confusing little things to make the buyer think that somehow it is less than $200, or even $186).

I can't say I ever saw the apt., because as soon as I got by Dinky's (Aranka-ese for chez Dinky), the phone never stopped ringing, and the doorbell, and somebody, namely Grandec (as he calls me loudly, insistently) had to look after Jamie, while Dinky was dashing from phone to door, dealing with the putative tenants.

It was a rattling experience. Dink had decided to get black or Puerto Ricans. She had asked Jim what <u>he</u> thought: he had answered, "Get the most needy, and the most responsible." Having mulled this over, the Dink decided it was a contradiction in terms; nevertheless, that's what she was (still is!) actually trying to do.

Visualize the scene. Doorbell rings. She flees. Jamie: "Mamaya! Mamaya!" (which he calls her, short for My Mother, I suppose). Me, trying desperately to comfort J., and then the phone rings. I can't tell, by their conversation, whether these prospective tenants are either needy or responsible, and I don't like to ask; so I simply say the landlady isn't here at the moment (Jamie is being livid, so I have to have a word with him, too). Oh dear, it <u>was</u> a day. All she did was to advertise one time in the Village Voice, and that was the result. At least 85 applicants, I should say.

Among applicants was a pretzel-salesman and his wife or girl-friend! A Benj-type. Dink was fascinated with him being a pretzel-salesman, said "My brother is a Yoghurt salesman," which the pretz. salesman (a Benj-ager and type) loved. But I don't think she rented to him; he was neither needy enough nor resp. enough. Poor him.

Another one was Mrs. Scott, she called at <u>least</u> 5 times while I was there, absolutely longing. "Sorry, the landlady is not here at the moment, shut up Jamie, she'll be back in a sec," I said to Mrs. Scott and Jamie.

Dobby, it's a very sad scene. The ones she seems to be choosing are a white Puerto Rican couple (her description), he works in a super-market. She is worried about whether he will make enough in the super-m. to pay the rent? What do you think? I said, well he probably does, otherwise why would he be renting it in the 1st place? (As you can see, I'm not too good at this.) So, time will tell. She turned down several applicants with jobs as teachers etc. as not needy enough. Quite right, says I. What we should do, Dob, is to gradually buy up all the blocks around there and turn them over to Dink to look after. . . .

Jamie, adorable. He can say all words, everything, but no sentences yet. Next week, perhaps? She reads to him, and he reads along, he really <u>is</u> sweet. During one of the moments when a) I had just come home with groceries for dinner, b) Mrs. Scott was calling in her hopeful way, c) Dink was fleeing downstairs to show another tenant, I said to Jamie, Could you put the salad in the refrigerator? So he gladly did so. Put it all into some gravy, actually, that she had in a bowl there; but he is v. responsive & clever about doing anything. I did not mention to the Dink about the salad being put in the gravy, as she had enough on her mind at the moment. She'll find out, soon enough! Don't you agree. . . .

> Much love, Decca

P.S. Do send Bob here, we pine for him. Just for a few days? PLEASE, Dobby.

To Pele de Lappe and Steve Murdock   New York
                                                        March 22, 1969

Dearest Neighbs,

Sorry to have been a rotten (or rather completely non) correspondent. This has been a truly curious visit: You know how books are never really finished until they are in print? Well, I've been working my head off (one terrible day, 5:30 a.m. until 2:30 next a.m.) getting it all done. I think it's finished at last; at any rate, on Mon. it's supposed to go to the Production Dept. . . .

The greatest was the last-minute editing. On Mon., I had an appt. with B. Gottlieb for his editorial suggestions. I took Dinky along as a body-guard, but the brute defected and agreed with all B. Gottlieb's suggestions. So, he said "Dink I see you understand what needs doing, so give your mother a hand with it." Which she did. She brought Jamie along to also give a hand. She was sitting reading, Jamie wakes up from his nap wailing, so Dink: "Oh I think the next four pages slow down the narrative," and she chucks them in the waste basket and dashes to change Jamie's diaper. I told Bob Gottlieb this (and explained that the book is now entirely different and a good bit shorter than the one he thought he bought, because of the Dink system of editing). We agreed the

Dink/Jamie system is prob. no better and no worse than any other system; he's going to borrow Jamie for the Knopf editors from time to time.

The best thing that came out of the whole book was the Knopf lawyer letter. They gave him the ms. to read for libel. Pele, he sent a six-page legal-sized letter of libelous bits, of which the first para tells the tale. Here it is:

"Chapter 1, page 1. It is alleged that Mitchell Goodman, Michael Ferber and Marcus Raskin were co-defendants with Dr. Spock and Rev. Coffin, which would be libelous if untrue."

Here's another gem:

"Chapter 11 page 28: "The statement that Bertrand Russell was prosecuted is libelous and should be deleted unless it can be proven true from court records."

Don't think I didn't order 10 Xerox copies of this lovely document. Goodness we howled. Bob says he prob. charged at least $300 for this garbage! . . .

much love, Decca

To Aranka Treuhaft   Oakland
                                                                March 28, 1969

Dearest Aranka,

I can never thank you enough for all NY hospitality. . . .

Even with all the pleasures of NY, it's a joy to be home. Benj met me at the airport, and came to dinner last night. Also, I met him in court yesterday, under the following circumstances: I had gone down with Marge Frantz to watch the end of the Oakland Seven trial.[103] . . . The jury is out deliberating, but they have asked for a lot of testimony to be repeated, so we heard the tape-recordings etc. of meetings at which the defendants spoke.[104] It couldn't be a more different atmosphere than the Boston trial. In the recess, Judge Phillips (the trial judge) signalled to a policeman to call me over behind the barrier; the Judge was v. cordial, said how much he admires my books, looks forward to the Spock book. I said, "Well, the main point of the Spock book is to say that the conspiracy law is the very devil." (The case he's trying is a conspiracy case.) He answered, "I couldn't agree with you more, the conspiracy law has got to go." The defendants had brought a football along, and a merry game was in progress in the corridors. Suddenly, Benj showed up, was greeted "Hullo, Benj!" by the marshals, who know him because he's attended the trial quite a lot. He happened to be in the courthouse on another matter: a speeding ticket.

---

103. In January 1968, seven young men, who became known as the Oakland Seven, were indicted on felony conspiracy charges for their roles in a large Stop the Draft Week demonstration at the Army Induction Center in Oakland the previous October.

104. The Oakland Seven were acquitted. See letter of October 4, 1995, to Benjamin Treuhaft.

He said that he watched the other speeders and listened to their spiel. One boy explained that he was rushing to his mother's side in hospital, and that in the rear-view mirror saw a gorgeous chick in a sportscar, which made him forget that the left-hand turn was illegal. The judge, a Negro: "Yeah, Man! Tell it like it is." When Benjy's case was called, he explained that he was speeding to an emergency harpsichord tuning, and the judge reduced the fine accordingly. . . .

Again, a million thanks for everything,

Much love, Decca

To Virginia Durr   Oakland

April 17, 1969

Dearest Va,

. . . Curiously, for the last several months I thought there would be nothing more heavenly than to have finished Spock and do absolutely naught but relax around. Yet already <u>fierce</u> boredom is setting in. Lucky old Bob sets forth each day for the marts of trade & commerce, and each night comes home & asks "what did you do today?" "Cleaned out my closets. Spoke to the gardener." "Oh, I see, you're getting just like Barbara Kahn." (B. Kahn, while a best friend, is also epitome of bourgeois housewife.) I think he's hinting that I should get back to work? But what? Montgomery Revisited—or better yet, collaborate on yr. autobiog? Except that way lies madness, or the rupture of a lifelong friendship. . . .

The book: All done, waiting now for the galleys, which should be ready early in May, I think. I shall be terrifically anxious to know what you think of it. It still occupies a lot of my thoughts (although it really is done, so no point in worrying further about it). . . . I'm not at all sure I'm satisfied with it. Also, I think it is destined to be a flop, I doubt it will do more than earn the advance (which was a very mingy amount, or so I thought, & I've spent it all on traveling etc. whilst writing the book); but as long as Dr. Spock and some of the trial followers like it, I shall be pleased. To my sorrow, I don't think Bob much likes it. That is, he said it was "a workmanlike job but not up to your best standards." Benj said it was a "solid piece of writing," which made me furious. In other words, the reception of nearest & dearest has been tepid—except for Dink, who <u>adored</u> it, but then I do think she is the partisan sort, don't you?

Nancy is very ill. I wrote to her from NY, saying "I just wrote the blessed words THE END on my book," and she wrote back saying she is flat on her back with what the Fr. doctors call "une colonne vertébrale dégradée" (a degraded spinal column, presumably) and "une grosse masse" in her stomach. (Huge lump.) And then she said "I think it is THE END, like your book." Well, so that sounded worrying, esp. the grosse masse, so I wrote to Debo, fount of all family knowledge, for fuller details. The grosse masse is on a kidney (the other thing is a slipped disc), so the fear is it might be cancer. Nancy now insists it is her twin—the lump; pictures it as grey-haired, with a beret, and a <u>very</u> good cook, calls it Lord Redesdale. She told all this to the lump man (cancer expert) who must have wondered about her sanity? But anyway, I can see she's making her usual huge joke of the whole thing, so that's a mercy. . . .

Much love, Decca

To the Duchess of Devonshire   Oakland
May 13, 1969

Dearest Hen,

Oh dear things are getting <u>madly</u> out of hand, plan-wise. Got yours of 9 May today . . . and <u>three</u> from Nancy which more or less go as follows: 9 May, she says do come any time before end of June. 10 May, she fears it will be so dull for me because she simply must get back to work. 11 May, she says <u>don't</u> come, because Marie[105] is too tired & there's no point in offering to help as she won't allow, and she says "I'm so sorry but it's out of my control, I feel too tired to sort of struggle, I must simply exist until my life is re-organized . . ." etc.

These crossed mine to her, saying I'm arriving on 20 May & should like to put up in a hotel in Versailles.[106] <u>Alas</u>, Hen, so by now she'll have got that and I'll have fussed her up no end.

Behind it all, she prob. thinks that what a bore having to work out the oubliettes for me & Honks,[107] or some such. On the other hand if Honks & I turned up at same time & all was OK, & normal, it would seem like Mrs. Ham's dreamed-of death-bed scene, don't you agree? But if I cld. stay in a hotel (& scram there quite a lot) this cld. be avoided. . . .

I rang up Bob at work, & read out all the letters, to see what he thought shld. be done. Apart from saying with some acerbity "your family is v. difficult to fathom," he thought I shld. go anyway. So, am. The pt. being that . . . mainly, I do awfully want to see Nancy. . . .

<u>Later:</u> HEN! You just rang up, so this is an ongoing conversation.

I couldn't quite make out all you said re. the medical facts except that it's obviously very bad; yet somehow, in back of mind, I always thought it would be in spite of all the seeming improvement that you and she told of in letters. So all I want to do is a) come, b) do anything possible to help, c) not be in any way a bother—and I can see from N's letters that this will be the most difficult of all. And in this regard, Hen, I do implore you to make clear to Honks how I long to avoid all friction etc. etc., as I think I did say in another letter.

105. Nancy Mitford's longtime housekeeper.
106. Decca's plan, she told Nancy Mitford, was to spend days at her home as "a helper," doing typing or light housework, "or even heavy housework, which is as far as I can tell the only sort."
107. One of sister Diana's childhood nicknames.

One thing has puzzled me a good deal: why have you so firmly decided <u>not</u> to tell her anything at all about what's wrong with her? That is, I can quite see one would have to exercise a good deal of judgment about that (no point in giving gloomy reports right after the operation when a person is at lowest ebb, etc) but I must say I think I should far <u>prefer</u> to know, for masses of reasons. Which would range all the way from the thing you said about her book (wanting to get all done possible on it) to the horrid disappointment of getting iller & iller without knowing why.

Oh Hen. It's all so very sad & bad and unbelievable, such a nightmare & those Drs. sound so awful, never getting in touch with you for all that time.

Am so longing to see you, Yr Hen

To Aranka Treuhaft   Versailles
                                                        May 22, 1969

Dearest Aranka,

. . . I'm really awfully glad I came, as Nancy still can't get about, is <u>very</u> weak from lying in bed so long, still has pain. However she's in v. good spirits. . . .

Well, I must tell you about my life here—might be on the moon, so far does it seem from home in Calif. or lately in NY. Marie, whom you remember, now aged 75, is sort of my boss, that is, she explains what to buy and where. My main job is the shopping; but now I'm being trained as a gardener, too. It goes like this: There's an excellent street of lovely little shops a block from here. I'm allowed to get <u>some</u> things there, but not <u>all</u>. The butter? The kind in the little shops is no good for the table, because it is pasteurized and comes packaged, so can only be used for cooking. The table butter comes from the market, only 1 1/2 miles away, Marie explains, a nice walk. So I trudge to the market. I am told to get the butter at the stall of Mme. Gentlet, so I do that. I ask Mme. G. which is the best butcher in the market. She answers expressively "they are all terrible and all excellent, it depends on the shopper." She sees I am about to burst into tears (I know they'll all be terrible for me, an obvious foreigner and hopeless shopper) so she relents, directs me to a butcher and says I can say Mme. Gentlet sent me. I cheer up and do that. Then I see some dear little new potatoes, and buy those; but when I get home Marie throws them at my head, because they've been scraped at the market (all the mud taken off, I suppose) and will therefore be tasteless. No use to point out that they were quite heavy even without the mud . . . It's all like that, takes me a good morning to get it all done, and this is shopping for <u>three</u> people, Nancy, Marie and me. Then Marie says there's enough bread for lunch but not for dinner. Shall I get the dinner bread? No, best to go again in the afternoon for that, so it will be quite fresh. Needless to say the meals that come from all this care are indescribably delicious. Also, I begin to feel indispensable—clearly one of us has to be here while

Nancy is ill. . . . I feel that I'm getting on well with Marie, I offer to do all errands she requires, and we work together in that way. Of course, no use to point out that things could perhaps be delivered etc., as neither M. nor N. is about to change the habits of a lifetime. This afternoon, having finished my Morning Work, I was put to clearing spaces around the peonies (cutting weeds), and was told I had done quite well for a beginner. . . .

This house is the prettiest ever seen, and the <u>garden</u>! Wonderful poppies, roses, peonies and dozens of flowers that I don't know the names of. Nancy's out there quite a lot when she is feeling all right, as she is today. (Of course she never says anything about the pain, you know how they are; one can only tell if her face goes grey and she rushes off to her room.) . . .

I crave letters, so do write some more; I'll be here until 4 June, it seems. Pam will come back then and be the helper. . . .

Much love, Decca

To Marge Frantz   Versailles
                                                                    May 22, 1969

Dearest old Marge,

It seems like many a year since there you were, pouring (as Va. would spell it) over me galleys at home, and I never have thanked you properly. Truth is, I was <u>so nervous</u> about Nancy at the time that I simply couldn't have done it without you. Am far less nervous now I'm here on the scene, which is so often true? Don't you agree. Anyway, that whole book also seems like a far-off memory. . . .

I suppose what you really want to know is how Diana and I are getting on. . . . Rather well, actually. That is, whilst cutting the grass round the irises I forebore to say I was giving the irises <u>lebensraum</u>,[108] although it came into my mind. In other words, all efforts are bent to Nancy's welfare, & that's all we talk about if we're alone together. . . .

Marie and I are running the medical scene (gave prunes today, for constipation, and it worked!!) but I've written to Eph <u>begging</u> for advice. Debo is, as Bob says, the only really intelligent one of the family, but she can't talk French, so is useless with the Drs. and Marie etc. . . .

Marge, I LONG FOR LETTERS. PLEASE, PLEASE WRITE. . . . I do long for proper news. Much love to Laurent, nippers and you,

Decca

---

108. Literally "living space," the term was used, beginning in the nineteenth century, to justify the movement for the unification and imperial ambitions of the Germans. The notion became a cornerstone of Hitler's program as a justification for the invasion and colonization of Eastern Europe and Russia.

To Virginia Durr   Versailles
                                                              ca. May 26, 1969

Dearest Va,

So sorry not to have written sooner—I came away in <u>such</u> a rush, & have been occupied here at Versailles with so many tasks. When I first got here, Nancy was very ill, had a ghastly pain in back & legs. But miraculously, she seems to have taken a terrific turn for the better—the pain has gone, for the moment at least, and she's back at work on her book. Pam was here with her for ages. Diana lives about 12 miles away, and Debo was staying with her. To describe the daily life here is as difficult as for someone trying to describe an L.S.D. trip to somebody who has never even smoked pot (equiv. of pot being an ordinary weekend at Swinbrook or Chatsworth). . . .

I am the shopper. . . . In between times, the sisters swoop down for an hour or so, and shrieks of laughter ensue, the neighbours must wonder. Even when N. was in the worst pain she still managed to shriek, it is her way of life. . . .

The medical situation is so hopelessly confused that I've given up on it. There are <u>five</u> doctors in the picture: the Paris G.P., the Versailles G.P., the surgeon, the stomach expert, the back expert. None of them have been near her since the operation. The only person who comes is a terribly nice pharmacist called M. Suchard who lives next door here and whose shop is in our shopping street. All v. unlike being ill in America, or even England I should think. . . .

So, so sorry all this happened and we couldn't come to you, as planned. I feel fearfully out of touch; do drop a line to me. . . .

Much love, and to Cliff, Decca

The butcher in our shopping street knows me now. "Ah! Enough for three ladies who don't eat very much," he shouts when he sees me coming, as that's what I asked for the 1st time, not being able to cope with kilos. It's a French Cranford here, small-town all over, not a bit like Paris, you'd love it. In the evenings we all (Marie, N. and I) watch the presidential candidates on telly. Marie's comments being worth the price of admission. On Sundays, she goes to church (as Nancy says): "to confess her saintly sins."

To Pele de Lappe and Steve Murdock   Paris
                                                                  May 26, 1969

Dearest Neighbs,

I've written masses to Bob about the utter dottiness of the medical scene here, & how difficult to form any sort of view of what N's real condition is. . . .

Longing for news of Berkeley.[109] Bob sent some clippings of 19–20 May;

---

109. Berkeley at the time was wracked by protests and rioting during conflict between student and community activists and the University of California over a plot of land dubbed People's Park,

needless to say, there's no pnt. to discussing it with Nancy as she's completely against the students. So I do feel v. cut off.

The most curious thing of all, of course, is seeing Diana after all these years—34 years, in fact. She looks like a beautiful, aging bit of sculpture (is 59), they don't have this thing of wanting to look young here, her hair is almost white, no make-up, marvellous figure, same large, perfect face and huge eyes. We don't, of course, talk about anything but the parsley-weeding and Nancy's illness. God it's odd. I thought it must have given her a nasty turn to see me, aged 18 when last seen by her. But she told Nancy she thought I hadn't aged except for my voice. I explained to N. that if one talked in America in one's childhood voice, people would think it so affected they wouldn't talk back, which would make for a lonely life there. . . .

Much love, Decca

To Aranka Treuhaft
Versailles
June 1, 1969

Dearest Aranka,

Thanks so much for writing. Yes, this is like the last century, I shall be making the Great Leap Forward into the 20th cent. on 9 June, arrive NY 1:25 p.m. I'll come straight to your house, if I may; if you're out, please leave keys with the local burglar & ask him to watch for my arrival. At least, that is my plan. But I rather stupidly let my U.S. passport expire; so if I don't show up on the 9th, please check at Ellis Island. . . .

I'm terribly glad I came. . . . The first day I arrived, our sister Pam, who had been here, picked me up at Orly airport. On the way home, I said "please fill me in—what sort of useful things can I do at Nancy's?" Pam thought for a while (she's not too good at thinking) and answered, "Well, I always make my own bed on the day Mme. Guinon doesn't come." Mme. G. is the daily domestic who helps Marie. "What day doesn't she come?" "Sunday." Well, it seemed rather curious to me to have come all the way from Calif. simply to make my bed on the day Mme. G. doesn't come. Luckily, I arrived on Tuesday, so the dread bed-making was some time off. . . .

[Nancy and Marie] are madly for Pompidou,[110] wouldn't you know. Marie signed something for Pompidou, so the other day she got a notice to a meeting, 9 p.m. Friday night. She was quite fussed over this: "I do hope he won't be disappointed if I don't come. But after all, I put my age, 75, on the paper I signed,

where the university had bulldozed housing with the intent of building athletic fields and later fenced off the block when activists responded to the demolition by occupying the land and planting a community park. Governor Ronald Reagan dispatched 2,500 National Guard troops to the city.

110. In 1969 former Gaullist prime minister Georges Pompidou won election to succeed Charles de Gaulle as president of France. He served until his death in 1974.

so perhaps he won't be upset if I don't come? He'll think, she's 75, it's a late hour for her, do you think he will understand?" . . .

I shall miss being here; you should see the parsley beds, lettuce beds, roses & lavender, all of which I've weeded daily. In the afternoon, we generally have company (one or two friends of Nancy's) & sit and shriek with laughter in her bedroom. But actually she's not getting much better, alas. . . .

> Much love, see you soon, write c/o
> Sonia and give me news of Dinky,
> Decca

To the Duchess of Devonshire   Oakland
July 17, 1969

Dearest Hen,

Thanks awfully for yr. v. informative letter of 13 July from Versailles. . . .

Now, the point you said about telling Newlington.[111] As the medical scene is so thoroughly dotty (Nancy wrote to say she had sacked the Versailles G.P. and also the Masseuse), I can't see what difference it will make, to tell or not to tell. As no local Dr. will now appear to instruct her what to do. As long as she eases the pain, that's the main point, don't you agree?

However, I do feel most terrifically strongly, and must stress this point Hen very much, that it is now verging on wicked not to tell Nancy, in view of Dr. Evans' report. Because don't you see, it's awful enough to get such news when one is feeling fairly OK & strong; but if it is delivered very late in the thing, when one was completely weak anyway and in much pain, so much harder to bear, I should think. Now might be the time. Bob suggested that it be put in terms of new information from Dr. Evans, newly discovered, or some such. In fact, I think Dr. E. should be imported to impart this, as those Fr. Drs. have turned out so drab & uninterested. To me, it seems a sort of awful betrayal not to tell the truth, & I must say it caused me many a horrid moment when there. . . .

Life here is chugging—did you read that Dr. Spock was freed by the appeals Ct?[112] He was. Am writing an article for N.Y. Times Mag. about all that. Shall send me drab stuff (the book, and article in Atlantic Monthly) although you may find it rather boring, but just to show, Hen, that I've actually done it all. . . .

---

111. Nancy Mitford's housekeeper.

112. On July 11, the First Circuit Court of Appeals overturned Spock and Ferber's conspiracy convictions and sent back the cases of the remaining two defendants, Coffin and Goodman, for retrial. Eight months later, the government dropped the charges.

To Clifford Durr   Oakland
                                                      September 6, 1969

Dearest Cliff,

Well I was <u>elated</u> by your letter, thanks so, so much. . . .

As you can imagine, I was particularly pleased you thought it might be useful as an attack on conspiracy doctrine. The Old Trial Hand[113] was v. helpful
about all the that. . . .

The Old Trial Hand's role was a curious one in some ways. He thought from
the beginning that the book should take the form of an essay on the nature of
political prosecution. Well you know how hopeless I am at essays, or anything
that requires much thought. So I started writing up the trial itself. I'd read out
bits to Bob when he got home from work, & he'd say "that's boring, irrelevant,
who wants to read about an old trial that will be way out of date by the time the
book's published?" Which made me cry, because I value his judgment. So I
stopped showing him bits. Then came the deadline for submitting the ms. Two
days before the deadline, Bob had the day off (somebody's Birthday), and he
sprang into action, doing last-minute proofreading, collating etc. By now it was
so late, we had to take it to the airport & send it airfreight (not trusting the post
office). On the way to the airport, Bob said, "I wish you had put in more about
the trial, all that was fascinating." I kicked him so hard he almost skidded across
the freeway.

Yet in some ways he was invaluable: the chapter on conspiracy law, the last
chapter, the appendix about role of ACLU. So he was soon forgiven. . . .

Other news & views: My Son the Harpsichord Tuner is in great shape, at the
moment. As he is the apple of my eye (or one of them, Dink's the apple of the
other), this pleases me. Do your children smoke pot, take LSD etc? Dink
doesn't, she's too elderly; but Benj did (LSD), worries me to death. Now, he
says LSD is passé! Vive that passé. He's utterly self-sufficient, makes his own
living (is now building a harpsichord with a partner . . . [who] was a juvenile-
delinquent friend of Benjy's since junior high school days, is now the solid
influence! To me, they seem like a comedy team, Laurel & Hardy. My day
brightens when they drift round here). . . .

                    Much love and again, dearest
                    Cliff, THANKS for all you said.
                    Decca.

---

113. *The Trial of Dr. Spock* is dedicated to Robert Treuhaft, "who counseled, aided, and abetted
the writing of this book, and who appears in its pages as the Old Trial Hand."

To Pele de Lappe   London
                                                    October 24, 1969

Dearest Neighbour,

London is an autumn festival—more like autumn in a film than the usual London reality: the right amounts of mist & <u>hot</u> sun, crunchy gold leaves underfoot. WISH YOU WERE HERE. I've been to the country quite a lot, too. Am doing the cousins (Rudbin etc) while Bob's away as I fear they bore him stiff. Last wknd was at Rud's tiny country cot, having a brief whiff of that milk-bland life that seems utterly unchanged since childhood (except there are fewer grooms, gamekeepers, cooks). I've come to the conclusion Bob only really likes the statelier, Chatsworth-style English country life. We did have one such weekend before he left for Japan, at Ld & Lady Head's (my newfound revolutionary friend Dot Head). Lord Head is dyed-in-wool Tory. Dot not only went to Ho Chi Minh's funeral service in London, but wore full mourning for a week thereafter. (She's about 60; her conversion is rather like Dr. Spock's, came about as result of Vietnam war.)[114]

Debo was at the Head weekend, and a marvellous old codger called Lord Hardwick. A sample Hardwick story: "There was this fellow I know in the Foreign Office. A memorandum came across his desk—it was full of utter bosh, don't you know, so he was going to write BALLS on it. But he thought that was a bit steep, so instead he wrote ROUND OBJECTS. Memo comes back from Tony Eden[115] with a note: 'Who the devil is this fellow Round, & what <u>does</u> he object to?' " . . .

I've seen quite a lot of the Martin Bernals. Old J.D.[116] is, alas, dying of a series of strokes. It seems that <u>all</u> of his ex-wives & ex-mistresses are coping. They take turns in shifts to look after him. So there <u>are</u> compensations to his sort of lewd & lascivious life? These ladies, now aging themselves, were on non-speakers with each other but have buried all hatchets for the nonce. Rather touching, & marvellous, don't you think?

The Moratorium[117] sounded from newspaper accounts nothing short of extraordinary. We picketed the U.S. embassy a bit that day, & were hailed by all sorts of Berkeley types who've shown up here. . . .

---

114. A month and a half earlier, the Treuhafts had met Dorothea Head in California through her son Simon, who was in the United States as a Commonwealth Fellow. Decca had been leery of meeting Lady Head, whom she assumed to be "a typical English countryside Tory . . . a friend of Debo's" and told a friend she hadn't been certain how to dress for their dinner together. Her fears were allayed when "the Mum appeared in psychedelic Capri pants!" Decca "adored" her new friend, a "terrific peacenik" who was married to Churchill's former secretary of state for war, Viscount Head, and she reciprocated by inviting mother and son to join her in a visit to a mortuary to observe "pre-need planning"—an experience that reportedly thrilled Lady Head.

115. Foreign Secretary Anthony Eden.

116. Martin Bernal's father.

117. The massive Vietnam Moratorium peace demonstrations of October 15, involving millions of protesters in Washington and other locations throughout the United States. Sympathetic demonstrations also took place at American embassies in Europe.

Pele <u>do</u> let's come here together one day. Bob & I had a smashing few days touring Normandy—you would have adored it.

Longing for a letter,

Much love, Decca

To Marge Frantz London

October 25, 1969

Dear old Marge,

. . . <u>Thanks awfully</u> for the reviews. The tone of the New Yorker one ("adoration of each man is cloying") is also present in a number of others sent from Knopf. The WORST SO FAR is in Nov. 6 issue of NY Review, long & panning. The awful thing is there are some good points in it: he takes me to task for not interviewing Ramsey Clark,[118] not pursuing more vigorously the genesis of the prosecution. Which was extremely remiss of me. I shall long to discuss all this with you when I get home. The point is, the 1st huge batch of reviews were marvellous, & the 2nd turning v. sour indeed. (Shall I give up writing & take Laurent's massage class, instead?) . . .

Here goes with some slices [of life] from the Wales safari. Both of Philip's wives & most of his children rendezvous-ed at a marvellous country restaurant nearby. I drove down with Anne (now Wollheim),[119] Josephine Toynbee aged about 25, & Rupert Wollheim aged about 17. Also of the party was Ben Nicolson, a Philip best-friend who is an artist & lives in London.[120] He & Philip told their recent experiences with the M-I (English equivalent of the FBI). To visualize it, though, you've got to imagine it all in a <u>super</u> public school accent. Ben (who, unlike Philip, has never been a Communist, although most of his friends were in the thirties): "They said they wanted to ask me some questions, so I made an appointment for them to call round at my office. A Mr. Right appeared. He really seemed <u>very</u> civil, said he <u>hated</u> to trouble me & so forth but that's part of his job, don't you know. He asked me whether, in 1936, I had lunched in Paris with Guy Burgess[121] and two others. I said that I did remember the luncheon, & that as I kept a very full diary in those days, could supply him with the details. He was pleased to know about the diary—but now I'm

---

118. Attorney general of the United States from 1967 to 1969.

119. Philip Toynbee's first wife, Anne, had remarried in 1950, to philosopher Richard Wollheim. They were divorced in 1967.

120. Ben (Benedict) Nicolson was a critic and historian. Decca used to enjoy his company during visits with Philip Toynbee, describing him as "a smasher" and "a delightful ally in my sometimes losing, often winning, tussles with Philip about God and Mammon; Ben was clearly on Mammon's side, if a trifle out of touch with the latter's modern ways." After Nicolson died in a London subway in 1978, Decca wrote, "So silly as he must have been v. rich, cld easily have afforded a taxi; but that's the English for you."

121. BBC broadcaster, British intelligence agent, and diplomat who was later unmasked as one of the four members of the 1930s Cambridge-educated Communist spy ring. He defected to Russia in 1951.

wondering if I did the right thing to tell him about it?" (And so on. Philip invited his chap to lunch in Wales—he was also on the Guy Burgess track. Looking for the Fourth Man, I guess.[122] Who will it be—Ben or Philip? Watch your daily newspaper for further details.) . . .

Gottlieb wrote: said the book's doing OK (but no details), but thinks it has been "over-reviewed," & that people have read so much about it they don't bother to buy it. Bother.

Much love, Decca

To Barbara Kahn   Oakland
                                                                    December 3, 1969
Dearest Barb,

. . . I'm supposed to be working on a revised foreword for Trial of Spock, for Vintage paperback coming out in April. But I'd far rather write to you. Anyway, part of this letter is going to be work, as I want you to show it to Viv[123] and get her views. Here goes (you know part of this, but Viv doesn't, so I'll have to repeat):

Act I On way back from airport after my trip, Bob was telling me about a case involving a 72-year old woman who applied to Famous Writers School, was visited by a salesman, and signed up for a $780 course, $200 down. She soon regretted this (is on Social Security, an old wid), and tried to get out of the contract; but no, she had signed on the dotted line. Bob wrote a furious letter to the school about how the salesman had conned her and demanding refund of $200. Got furious letter back, including one from the salesman who said Bob's letter was a "deflamation" (his sp.) of character etc. Bob then caused his client to write out in her own words what had happened; she did so, producing a semi-literate account with German words interspersed!! Bob sent a Xerox of this to the school, and covering letter saying: "This is by the lady you found to be 'very qualified' to take your writing course. I wonder if Mr. Bennett Cerf[124] is aware of the cruel deceptions to which he lends his name?" And, carbon copy to Bennett Cerf. Bang by return of post comes the $200. End of act I.

---

122. The identity of the so-called "Fourth Man" in the spy ring was a source of official investigation and public speculation for years. When his identity was finally publicly revealed years later—it was royal art historian Anthony Blunt—the informant turned out to be an old friend of Decca's. See letters of August 21, 1982, to Virginia Durr and February 25, 1983, to Michael Straight. It was not disclosed until 2002, six years after Decca's death, that among the people wrongly suspected of involvement by British intelligence agents years earlier had been Esmond and Giles Romilly.

123. Mutual friend Vivian Cadden, whom Barbara Kahn was visiting in New York.

124. Bennett Cerf, the chief promoter of the Famous Writers School, was a distinguished literary figure: publisher (co-founder and chairman of Random House), lecturer, popular television quiz show personality, humorist, and editor of numerous books of jokes and puns. He was featured in the school's advertisements and had a financial interest in the company as well.

Act II Waiting for me here, amid the myriad things, was a book called <u>Writing Rackets</u>, by Robert Byrne, all about Vanity Press and phony writing schools.[125] The best part of the book is where his wife assumes the name and personality of one Louella Mae Burns, a 62-year old housewife whose favourite authors are Kathleen Norris, Margaret Mitchell and Wm. Shakespeare; she applies for the course, takes the test, supplies the required essay (going as far as she dares, fearing to make it too atrocious) and is accepted.

Act III I was having lunch with Billy Abrahams,[126] W. Coast editor of Atlantic Monthly, & happened to mention all this to him. He said why not do a piece (part review of the book, but mainly an essay) on the whole thing for Atlantic? I said I'd love to, so he rang up Bob Manning (ed. of Atlantic) who said OK. I make an appointment to meet Mr. and Mrs. Byrne, who live in Mill Valley, to find out a bit more—what prompted him to write the book, what sort of response if any he's had from Famous Writers' victims, whether his book is being reviewed in media that accept FW ads etc.

Act IV (This is the best act so far, so keep reading): Just as I'm leaving for the appointment, B. Abrahams calls back. He says that Bob Manning has had second thoughts about the piece. Manning has decided, with approval of publisher, to stop accepting these ads of Famous Writers, because they are unethical. However, since they've accepted many a $1000 over the years from the school, it would be equally unethical to publish a piece blasting them!!! I am <u>furious</u>. Oho, so if a mag. accepts from tobacco industry, it's unethical to run articles about lung cancer, I suppose? Billy saw the point right off (especially when I told him I was going ahead with the article anyway, and should feel ethically bound to relate our conversation in it, if forced to submit it elsewhere than Atlantic).

Act V Met the Byrnes, they are charmers. The most interesting thing he told was this: His first plan had been to do an article about Famous Writers. He wrote the article; and having noted from his research that the <u>only</u> public voice raised against FW had been that of Granville Hicks, sent it to him, at Sat. Review. Hicks wrote back with high praise for the piece, but said that he had no say in accepting articles for SR and was forwarding it to the appropriate editor. Next thing, Byrne gets a letter FROM FAMOUS WRITERS SCHOOL!!! saying, "We heard you have submitted an article about us to SR, we wish to see a copy of it, if you feel your application to our school was badly handled we will take steps to correct this," or words to that effect. Byrne wrote an outraged let-

---

125. The book was the first by the self-described unknown writer who has since published more than twenty other books. After Decca went to work on the story and carried it further, Byrne's early spadework—despite Decca's best efforts—was ignored by the media that lionized her and her subsequent exposé. Byrne says that Decca remained "incredibly helpful and generous" in supporting his career.

126. William (Billy) Abrahams, the former poet and novelist who became a literary editor and a dear friend of Decca's, as well as her editor.

ter to Sat. Review; all this produced was a routine note from Tobin, an editor who had formerly worked for Famous Writers, rejecting the article.

I asked Byrne why he had not related all this in his book, why he had not got in touch with some of the FW's directly for interviews. The answer is, he's half-scared himself: "I'm afraid of the power of people like Bennett Cerf," he said. "They could blackball you in the entire writing industry." (Like ducks they could.)

Byrne first submitted his book to Luther Nichols, W. Coast ed. of Doubleday. Nichols liked it, recommended it to the NY office—who rejected it on the ground that "it's too negative. People want to keep their dreams, they don't mind paying for them." Don't you love that?

It was eventually published by Lyle Stuart, a small crusading publisher . . . Byrne showed me his reviews; needless to say, none of the big mags. have reviewed it, only papers from the styx, or sticks or however it's spelled, Kansas City Star & the like. Plus a fairly good one by Hogan.[127] But no NY Times, Bookweek, or other soi-disant lit. magazines. All of these are heavily implicated with huge amounts of FW ads.

Now, here's the situation (and here's what I want Viv's advice on): Billy A. is trying to get Bob Manning to reconsider. But if they still turn it down, I'm still going ahead. However, who would take it? Might McCall's? The point of the article would be not only to tell about the victims (great parallels, here, with undertakers' victims—both lots are too unhappy and ashamed to broadcast what happened to them), but also to blast away at the power of these Famous Writers to intimidate people. Byrne just mentions in passing in his book that it's a funny thing that whereas there have been lots of articles in pop. mags. exposing vanity publishers, almost nothing has appeared about the writers' schools. He fails to make the connexion with his own finding that the schools in 1967 spent $18,055,382 on advertising.

Well, as you can see, one is into yet another conspiracy. Byrne is terrified of being sued—I told him that's ridiculous, the last thing these people want is that sort of publicity, what they hope is that his book will quietly die a natural death (which it will, I think, for lack of reviews).

Does Viv have any inside dope on the schools—for instance, do "students" submit stuff to McCall's? . . .

Love to all NY loved ones. . . . Do write.

Forward to the foreword, Decca

---

127. William Hogan, book editor of the *San Francisco Chronicle*.

To Vivian Cadden   Oakland
                                                              January 1, 1970

Dear Viv,

This is sort of a progress report on Famous Writers (may be a trifle disjointed, because we're having a huge party in a little while).

I. By an enormous stroke of luck, I've found someone here locally who took the WHOLE COURSE!! One of the (I now estimate) 10% who finish. She's quite a bright lady, middle-aged, no doubt the upper level of those who take the course. She has lent me the entire thing: textbooks, her corrected lessons etc. etc. The textbooks are really pretty trashy, rather to my surprise. Her reaction? "Mixed feelings . . . grateful to the school in a way for getting me started . . . think the whole thing vastly overblown and overpriced."

II. That wretched school never sent all the things they promised; Bob says he's sure they never will, why should they, etc. To many of my questions, the director answered "don't know, Mr. Miller (or somebody) would have that information." So I made up a list of the info. he promised to provide, called the school, & dictated the list to his sec'y. Here it is:

1. The number of lessons received and corrected for the past 12 months. (They are in a bind over this. If the figure is high, it means the instructors don't spend much time on each lesson; if low, it means, as I suspect, that close to 90% of the suckers who take the course never finish, although they are held to paying— the stockholders' report indicates amt. of tuition $$$ received annually.)

2. A file of the form letters sent to a) successful applicants, b) dunning letters for delinquents.

3. A copy of the current contract, and a copy of the contract before the FTC[128] got after them for not stating the terms correctly.

4. The number of students who pay for the course but never send in any lessons (they indicated there are quite a few of these).

5. List of contents of salesmen's kit, and any written instructions, sales manual, sales course material.

6. The names of the "more than 100 publications" that their publicity says students publish in.

7. Written job description for instructors and for graders of the aptitude test.

8. Amounts refunded to students (they said "it runs into 6 figures").

9. Name and address of Northern Calif. sales manager, so I can interview him.

The secretary took all that down, on Friday, 19 December. She said it might take a while to get all the info. together because the following week (Christmas) would be only a 2-day week. I said fine, but please send me the stuff as you get it—any that's easy to come by, send it straight away, and the rest as you turn it up. Goose-egg, so far.

---

128. Federal Trade Commission.

Question: Assuming I hear nothing from them by, say, next Wednesday or so, what do you think I should do? Ring them up and ask what happened, I suppose. I expect they've been wigging over it like mad things, & have decided NO FURTHER COOPERATION in constructing a noose to hang themselves with.

I also asked for a number of things from the FAS[129] office on Madison Ave (the one in charge of advertising etc), such as: sample ads. over the years, especially the personalized ones (Bennett Cerf talking in 1st person, ditto Faith Baldwin[130]), and a list of the 1500 articles that the stockholders' report says the school planted in newspapers and magazines. Needless to say, goose-egg from that department, too.

Virginia Knauer[131] called up, couldn't have been more friendly. Turns out she's a terrific fan of Amer. Way of D. She promised to a) turn her own office upside down for complaints and info. on the school, b) to try & pry loose from FTC some 25 complaints they told me they have on file, but which they say are confidential. I said that if she sort of guarantees that I shall use the info. discreetly, not mention names etc., they might relent. Some smashing quotes from Knauer, who flings around words like "reprehensible, totally misleading advts." etc with gay abandon. She loved hearing about Bob's widow. Said "no wonder they never sue on the contract, a law suit would expose them—somebody ought to take them to court!" My only fear is that she'll move in on them prematurely, before the piece is out.

That's about all. I've got a fair start on the writing, about 11 pages done, and on that score can only say I'm dashing ahead as fast as I can, hope to finish fairly soon. Oh, and a neighbor has applied, hoping to lure a salesman so I can come & hear the pitch. . . .

Much love to all, Decca

To Aranka Treuhaft   Oakland
                                                 January 3, 1970
Dearest Aranka,
    . . . I'm working on an article for McCall's, about the Famous Writers School—that thing that's advertised everywhere, with Bennett Cerf promising to make you a Famous Writer if you take the correspondence course. Of course, the whole thing is a terrific fraud. I went to see Bennett Cerf when I was in New York last time. I said, "How can you lend your name to a fraudulent

---

129. FAS International (named for the affiliated Famous Artists Schools) was the parent company, which was listed on the New York Stock Exchange.
    130. The prolific and popular author of light fiction was one of the big names listed as "Guiding Faculty" of the Famous Writers School. She was also featured in the school's advertising.
    131. President Richard Nixon's special assistant for consumer affairs.

thing like this?" He answered, "The fact is I'm a terrific ham, and I love to see my picture in the papers." I don't think he's going to like the article. As he is president of Random House, which in turn owns Alfred Knopf, my publisher, I rather think I shall have to turn elsewhere if I ever write another book????

Bob and all are fine. Do write soon.

Much love, Dec

To the Duchess of Devonshire　　　　　　　　　　Aboard a plane, en route
from London to New York
February 17, 1970

Dearest Hen,

Oh dear I <u>didn't</u> go to Nancy's after all. Was to go today for 2 nights, but she <u>rang up</u> (fancy!) this morning at Sonia's to say that Woman's got a v. bad stiff neck, can really hardly move; & also they are snowed in, so not to come. I'm so sad about it Hen, but what could I do? So changed all plans, & left for America instead. Diana rang up yesterday & we had a long chat about Nancy, but it was all about what I was to look out for etc., so all has come to naught. I am in near floods about it all.

Meanwhile Dinky's baby was born last week, a bouncing 8 lb 8 oz boy. I was <u>so nervous</u> until I heard, isn't it stupid because <u>she</u> wasn't, but you know how it is. Bad dreams about her falling down stairs etc. His name: You'll shriek, a string of names like a royal baby: Chaka (I think, couldn't quite make out, after a Zulu hero of last century) Esmond (after you know who) Fanon (Wretched of the Earth & other works). P. Toynbee calls him Bongo Esmond, refusing to remember Chaka. So I'm on my way back to that scene—longing to see all of them, yet bitterly sad not to have seen Nancy. You know: wondering if ever shall again? Diana said she's <u>so</u> thin in spite of eating heartily. . . .

Hen, this letter is naught but a wail, so sorry.

Yr loving Hen

To Barbara Kahn　　　　　　　　　　　　　　　Aboard a plane, en route
from London to New York
February 17, 1970

Dearest Barb,

. . . [W]as [the London trip] all worth it? Prob. not. I should have been in NY with Dinky, & slaughtering B. Cerf (who has got my article stopped in McCall's[132]). One or two good things did come of it, though. James

---

132. About a week earlier, Vivian Cadden had written a furious letter to Decca on her magazine's rejection of the Famous Writers School exposé. Her letter began, "I was going to wait to

MacG.[133] is going to re-issue BOADILLA with foreword by Hugh Thomas[134]—proceeds, to Bongo Esmond, or rather his mother. So I'm really frightfully pleased about the that.

Also I did rather love all the varied life—but the trouble is it was too short, not worth all this flying & missing Dink's double birthday.[135] . . .

[A] lot of sad things, not the least of which is not seeing Nancy. Bloody-minded though she can be, I was fully prepared to risk all that as always (door-mat that I am) but the horror-thought, implanted slightly by the sisters—Debo under dryer, only time we cld meet & Diana amazingly rang up—is that she is actually quite a lot worse.

So, forward to B. Cerf: Viv says Esqu. better than Atlantic, for him? Village Voice, says I, if all else fails. Also I shall revise the parts about him no end (all that stuff about "May I call you Jessica?" that I left out out of pure niceness) & hope to destroy the brute. . . .

Decca

To Virginia Durr   Oakland
                                                                              March 10, 1970

Dearest Va,

I feel terrible not having got back in touch whilst in NY. The reason was, I did a v. stupid thing: caught my thumb in a cab door, with very drab results. . . .

There was one rather good bit of comic relief connected with it, though. It happened about midnight, and some nice kind people took me to the emergency hosp. to get it seen to; they finally took me back to Aranka's around 3 a.m. Aranka was in near-hysterics, had been working herself into a fine terror over me being so late coming home. I soon got her calmed down, and she told me she had called the police to report me missing. "Ai, ai, ai, my daughter-in-law hasn't come home, it's three in the morning!" "How old is your daughter-

---

write you until after the official letters went out but dammit, I'm not going to." Acknowledging that she was getting the information secondhand, she blamed the rejection on editor Shana Alexander, who she said didn't "want to take on Bennett Cerf as an enemy." According to Cadden, other editors were similarly infuriated by the rejection. Cadden advised that Alexander was composing a letter to Decca and said, "Hope she is squirming. And also hope it's the kind of letter that would [be] nice to quote in the article," wherever it was ultimately published. She concluded that "the gossip columnists will all love the story and it will sell a billion copies of whatever magazine it comes out in."

133. MacGibbon, Decca's former agent, who had become editorial director at Victor Gollancz.

134. Thomas, for years a history professor at the University of Reading in England, is a wide-ranging scholar and author, one of whose specialties has been the history of Spain. He wrote the definitive *The Spanish Civil War*, first published by Eyre and Spottiswoode and Harper & Row in 1961 and reissued decades later in a Modern Library edition.

135. Constancia Romilly's birthday is February 9. Her son Chaka was born on the same date in 1970, eight days before this letter was written.

in-law, Ma'am?" "Fifty-two." Do admit that's pretty funny. So then Aranka said, "She's never done this before," and the cop, "Well lady there's always a first time." . . .

I really will work on coming to Alabama. But the first thing I've got to do is straighten out in my own mind an approach to this prisons thing.[136] The problem, in a nutshell: They want a five to seven thou. word piece. Quite obviously, the only way one can do that is to hope to illuminate some tiny corner of the thing—as reams have been written on the subject and we all know about the chain gangs, mass graves in Arkansas etc. from films and the newspapers. Therefore, I was thinking of concentrating on the so-called model prisons, run on reform lines, & show up the difference between the talk ("human potential," "human resources" etc.) and the reality. Kind and Usual Punishment—what is it? . . .

This is the first letter I've typed with my wretched thumb. So shall close with love,

Decca

To Deborah Rogers[137] 　　　　　　　　　　　　　　　　Oakland
April 1, 1970

Dear Deborah,

I seem to choose unfortunate days to answer yr. letters—Friday the Thirteenth, and here we are at April Fools Day. Natherless, here goes:

. . . Famous Writers: The piece is now taken by Atlantic Monthly, which will publish it in either July or August.[138] They have cancelled all adverts. for Famous Schools (two full page ones were scheduled for July!!)[139] and Bob Manning, the editor, is speculating that Harpers may well follow suit. Of course what I long for now is to topple their whole house of cards. Shana Alexander,[140]

---

136. An article commissioned by the American Civil Liberties Union on the civil liberties of prisoners. Decca quoted one criminologist as telling her, "That's easy! Just turn in some blank sheets of paper—they *haven't* any civil liberties!"

137. Decca's British agent at the time—Candida Donadio's UK representative.

138. *Atlantic Monthly* took the piece only after a long migration through the magazine world. *McCall's* turned it down but gave Decca a "kill fee." Then *Life* "took it," she said, but "just as all was set and it was cleared by main editor, said ed. happened by the advertising mgrs. office and discovered they'd got 1/2 million dollars of ads. from the schools scheduled in upcoming issues." The article finally appeared in July's *Atlantic* under the title "Let Us Now Appraise Famous Writers." Decca said that editor Robert Manning took the piece against the advice of counsel, who feared a libel suit.

139. Pulling the ads cost the magazine $6,000 in July alone.

140. Alexander, *McCall's* editor, had met Decca through their mutual friend David Pleydell-Bouverie. Alexander was at different times a columnist for *Life* and *Newsweek*, a liberal commentator for the television show *60 Minutes* and the author of numerous books. After a temporary estrangement following rejection of the Famous Writers School article, Alexander became a longtime chum of Decca's.

while chickening out on the article, tells me she has also recommended discontinuing their adverts. So, financial hint: sell short their wretched stock (listed as FAS on NY stock exchange). I don't know how this works, but what it means is you gamble on the stock going <u>down</u>. All sorts of people are now longing to get in on the act, such as Wall St. Journal wants the galleys of the piece when available so they can do a story on it, also several TV shows in NY wanted me to come on and tell all about those Famous brutes. As you can see, it's all rather enjoyable, mainly because they're such super-respectable right wing asses.

Thanks for all,

Best, Decca

To Aranka Treuhaft   Oakland
                                                                April 20, 1970

Dearest Aranka,

. . . Life here is chugging along quite quietly on the whole. We did have one dinner party (can't remember if I told you about it?) of Lillian Hellman,[141] who was out here briefly, and an Irish authoress called Edna O'Brien (wrote Girl with Green Eyes, which was made into a film).[142]

My advice: don't ever invite two lady authoresses to the same dinner party. Miss Hellman is smashing-looking, in her late 60's I think, with a marvellously ravaged, wrinkled face, all her life shows on it, one feels. Miss O'Brien is a v. sexy Irish lady (Benj was a bit in love with her once, I think), and she arrived in full fig with silver stockings & shoes and diaphanous long skirt. There were quite a lot of other people here, such as the Kahns, Eleanor Furman who was out visiting, and some men for all these ladies, one of them my friend Billy Abrahams who is West Coast ed. of Atlantic. Well! We got a letter next day from Edna O'Brien. She had liked everyone except Lillian Hellman. She wrote, "It's sad to see somebody who has completely lost all interest in everyone except herself." Later, I heard from Billy that Miss Hellman had said, "That Miss O'Brien is the most completely self-centered woman I've ever met, takes absolutely no interest in any conversation that's not about her." . . .

Much love, Decca

---

141. The leftist playwright, screenwriter, journalist, memoirist, and contentious literary figure.
142. Novelist and short-story writer who also has written plays and screenplays.

To Robert Manning   Oakland
                                                                    July 8, 1970

Dear Bob,

My inclination would be not to answer that silly letter from the Pres. of Famous Schools.[143] I think he hangs himself in it, don't you? Saying there were 23 errors "at last count" (I wonder how many counts they plan on having?) and then not mentioning any of them.[144] Anyone who has read the article can see it is not based upon a 1965 *Fact* mag. piece, nor does it center round two former students.

I think space that would be taken by my answer is far better used to publish other people's letters. . . .

Perhaps you could say something in the letters column about the very large number of letters received and then give the percentage for-and-against, like Nixon does on his Cambodian policy? (Only more truthful.)

Thanks so much for forwarding everything. To all those people who write saying "I long to stop payments but don't dare," I am answering: "Stop paying! Tell the school I advised you to! If they sue, I'll come and testify as a witness." Hoping, actually, to sting the school into suing me, which would be most diverting. . . .

        Best, Decca

To Barbara Kahn   London
                                                                 August 30, 1970

Dearest Barb,

Chatsworth has come & gone—that is, we've been & went. . . .

Next thing in the offing is D. Pryce-Jones's interview with Nancy, due to appear on Thursday 3rd Sept in the *Telegraph*.[145] The story is going around that Nancy told him Hitler wanted to marry Bobo, & only didn't because she was so fearfully promiscuous, slept with all the S.S. men. So the question is,

---

143. The company's president, John J. Frey, had written a long letter to *Atlantic* editor Manning charging "gross misrepresentation" in Decca's article on the school. He said the article was "riddled with error and innuendo, and is composed of half-truths, statements taken out of context and similar material." Frey asked that the school's statement in response be printed in the magazine's July issue.

144. Frey had included "misrepresentation" as well as "errors in fact" in his list, and his letter did include some instances of what he characterized as misrepresentation.

145. Decca was staying at the home of David Pryce-Jones, the British editor, critic, novelist, and nonfiction writer, whom she met through his father, also a writer. The Treuhafts came to know him when he was teaching in California, and they decided to do a summer house swap. Through books he read from the Treuhafts' home library, Pryce-Jones became interested in Unity Mitford and subsequently wrote *Unity Mitford: A Quest* (Weidenfeld and Nicolson, 1976), a book that was to cause much dissension among the surviving Mitford sisters.

will this be in the article? Terror in the family (or at least Debo's section of it).[146]. . .

What news from home? Have only had one letter from you so far, sounding rather sad. . . .

Much love, Decca

To [recipient unknown][147]   Oakland
                                                                October 15, 1970

Dear Barbara,

Here's the plot, in outline:

Last summer, I attended an extraordinary 8-day conference sponsored by the National College of State Trial Judges, an org. devoted to continuing education of judges (and boy do they need it). Conferees were all D.C. Corrections people: judges, prosecutors, policemen, prison administrators, defense lawyers, criminologists etc. 18 convicts attended for the full time: 6 men from the rough-tough men's prison (Lorton . . . for long term offenders), 6 juveniles, 6 women. We called them the con-sultants. As part of the conference, all free-world people were required to spend 24 hours in a penal institution: the judges all went to Lorton (and emerged <u>shaken</u>), the younger men to Juvy, 9 women to Women's Detention in Washington.

We were handcuffed, booked, mugged, stripped, the works. All play acting, of course, as the guards and our fellow-prisoners all knew we were visitors. The prison is about 90% black, including personnel, director is a black woman. We were assigned cells (I was in with a frightfully nice murderess), had our 4:30 dinner with the others. Our corridor reminded me of a mix between a college dorm (a certain amount of jokes, chatter) and a lunatic asylum (underlying sense of ineffable sadness & futility).

The director had arranged for our group to sample all aspects of prison life: two women were sent to the sick-bay for the night, others went to "recreation" etc. I was called down for a disciplinary hearing and there accused of homosexual acts with another prisoner (the girl from the Washington Post). I fought back: demanded to see the statute under which this was a crime, to call my lawyer, to confront and cross-examine my accuser. "Remember, you're an inmate now," I was told. And given 10 days in the hole (which luckily was up in 1 1/2 hours, as my cell was needed for another trouble-maker). That's where I

---

146. Decca told others that "Debo wrote a furious letter to Nancy, saying how could you tell a reporter things like that. N. wrote back saying she's sure David is a gentleman, & wouldn't print anything of the kind. Since when he's known as Gentleman Jones."

147. This letter was sent to an editor to whom Decca was pitching an article, but the surviving copy of the letter includes only the recipient's first name. Although Decca wrote to Kay Boyle in January 1971 that her article was originally intended for *Redbook*, it ultimately appeared in *McCall's*, entitled "Women in Cages," in September 1972.

heard the screaming: 17-year old, shouting to be let out, and another woman, ditto. That's when it all became real instead of jolly fun.

The advantage of being a VIP was that I was able to quiz the director at length about a number of things.

1) the 17-year old. She was in there because of a mistake made by a juvenile court judge. Considered incorrigible in the children's lock-up, he remanded her to the Women's Detention. But by law, she can't mix with the adult population (crazy—the reason, of course, is she might get "corrupted." She was in for prostitution). So they chuck her in solitary. "When will she get out?" "When she turns 18, in 3 months from now." "Aren't you afraid she'll go completely mad by then?" "That's a risk we have to take." The other screamer: Viola, the guards said she was in "for her nerves." I remarked to the director it didn't seem to be doing her nerves much good; the director then admitted Viola is a diagnosed schizophrenic; but because of recent court rulings, she can't be sent to a mental institution without a sanity hearing, and the courts are too clogged at the moment. "When will she get out?" "I don't know." Note: Both these measures (not letting youngsters mix with older offenders and requiring a sanity hearing) are for the <u>benefit</u> of the inmates. Such are the contradictions that constantly bop you in the face in the arcane world of prisons.[148]

2) I asked what sorts of crimes they are mostly in for. Answer: prostitution and drug addiction. "Do you consider drug addiction a crime?" "Not really, in the circumstances these women are in." Contradiction: the heads of institutions don't really believe in what they are doing.

3) What about rehabilitation? "It doesn't exist" (much more on that would be in the article). Same contradiction as above.

There's quite a bit more to it, but that's the general idea.

Prisons are fast becoming Topic A in the media. One reason: Black militancy and New Left ideas are seeping into the prisons. Another: a new type of offender: civil-disobedients, Panthers,[149] collegiate narc. users etc. are coming into the prisons. Hence, new and more sophisticated demands by prisoners. . . .

---

148. Elsewhere, Decca wrote: "No doubt 100 years ago Viola and the juvenile delinquent would have been soundly flogged, and the others compelled to sew mail bags or whatever it was female prisoners were always sewing. But there's no point telling them all that, because as one woman prisoner said in a moment of frustration at the conf., 'You're always saying how much better things are than they were—but <u>we</u> have to live with things as they <u>are</u>' (couldn't care less, was the idea, about hist. of penology etc)."

149. The militaristic and militantly leftist Black Panther Party was founded in Oakland in October 1966 by Huey Newton and fellow Merritt College student Bobby Seale. Dedicated to black self-defense, party members established police patrols and often posed provocatively with rifles and bandoliers in their "uniforms" of black leather jackets and berets, but they also worked politically and socially both through collaboration with other blacks and New Left whites and— especially later in their history—through their community service projects such as medical clinics, a free food distribution program, and a school. They campaigned for black freedom and self-determination and release of black prisoners as well as such basic social rights as jobs, decent hous-

Back to my terrible task—I've never had so much difficulty with a piece as I'm having with this ACLU thing.

      Best regards, Decca

To Robert Gottlieb and Maria Tucci   Oakland

                   October 23, 1970

Dear Bob, Maria, and Unknown,[150]

Here's this monster.[151] Do write soon as poss. and say what you think. . . . The detente of finishing it is <u>unbelievable</u>, so here are a couple of cheery tales:

A friend of my sisters', young and beautiful, committed suicide the other day because of an unhappy love affair. She fetched up in Harrods Funeral Parlour, made up to the nines, head showing out of the coffin for the Viewing! So I got letters from Nancy & Debo relating this odd circumstance, in which the character of each can be noted. Debo: "In spite of all you did, it <u>is</u> coming to England." Nancy: "All your fault. Harrods would never have known about all that if it wasn't for you. What <u>would</u> Muv have said?" (Harrods[152] was my mother's home-from-home, she used to go there every day.) Last time I was in Harrods, I noted on the board where they list departments: Funeral Arrangements, 4th Floor. So I scrammed up to the 4th fl, but Funeral Arrangements was locked; there was a note on the door saying, "If shut, please apply to Adjustments Dept." So their friend was Adjusted. Am amending my will to be shipped to Harrods for final adjustments, & have told the sisters they'll jolly well have to come & view. . . .

Just now somebody rang up from NY to say the State of Iowa has enjoined the Famous Writers School from circulating mail in that state, on ground that it's a fraudulent use of the mails!!! It wasn't in our paper—she heard about it on the radio. Also, yesterday, a v. diverting phone call: from the admin. assistant to Congressman Weicker,[153] Republican, Connecticut, who's running for Senate . . . Background: the other day the NY Times ran a story about the Internal Security Comm. announcing that 65 subversives are lecturing at colleges all over the country including <u>moi</u>. So Mr. Frey, pres. of FWS, had sent this clipping to Cong. Weicker asking him to read my horrid record into the Cong. Record. Because, what I hadn't known before, another Cong, Lawrence Burton

---

ing, food, and education. They fought police brutality and police/FBI harassment and disruption, and on occasion they literally fought the police (about twenty-five Panthers died in gun battles with police or prison guards). At its peak, the party had more than two thousand members and branches in cities around the country.

 150. Tucci, Gottlieb's wife, was pregnant at the time. Their daughter, Lizzie, was born on January 5, 1971.

 151. The prison article Decca wrote for the ACLU, which was subsequently published in *The Atlantic*.

 152. That is, the department store, not its funeral department.

 153. Lowell Weicker.

of Utah, had read out my whole Famous Writers article in the Record. Frey's letter said he wanted to discuss "the nature and depths of the damage done to our reputation," and "the matter has reached urgent proportions." Don't you think that's all terribly jolly stuff? In the course of me quizzing him about Frey's letter, the admin. asst. almost forgot what he had called about—but then he remembered. "Are you a member of the CPUSA?" "Aha," said I. "That's a long story, if you ever come to Oakland I'll tell all. But meanwhile, loathing loyalty oaths as I do, I'm not about to take one at the request of mobsters like Bennett Cerf and his gang." Also, I said if I've ruined their reputation why don't they sue? They wouldn't even have to send a subpoena, I'd meet them any time, any place . . . So you see there have been some rather decent things happening, despite general gloom at the news here. Do write by return of post.

Much love, Decca

To Bill Outsi[154]   Oakland
                                                              November 30, 1970

Dear Bill,

Thanks very much for your letter. This, too, will be rambling—because I found yours immensely interesting, and if I don't answer at once, off the cuff (I'm no good at drafts) I risk losing the train of thought. Shall try to have a stab at least at some of the thoughts yours provoked. Will preface it by explaining that (as you already know) I knew nothing whatsoever about this gloomy subject until last February. Have been more or less immersed in it ever since in an amateurish sort of way. So, advance apologies for obvious gaps in knowledge & understanding. Here goes . . .

"Corr. system now is responsible for some very, very dangerous people." I'm sure that is true. You say the tendency of those on the outside is to underestimate dangerosity of said people. I should have said the opposite—that is, it depends who on the outside we're talking about. Does not the average law-abiding citizen, as he drives by San Quentin or Sing-Sing etc. experience a frisson of self-congratulation that all these violent wretches who would harm himself & family are safely locked away? Yet, is he right? Statistics in the thing I quoted from the Calif. legislative committee say: 1) most criminals are at large, in the street. 2) 97% of prisoners are eventually released on parole. . . . [D]oesn't that mean that lots of very very dangerous ones are released, as a matter of policy? Also, the committee says that longer confinement makes them more dangerous, not less so. (You indicate the same, in parenthesis . . . [in] your letter.) . . .

---

154. Outsi was with the National Parole Board in Ottawa and had written and taught on the criminal justice system.

What are these dangerous people? To the ordinary newspaper reader (me) they would be people like Kaplanjy or whatever his name was, that Hungarian freedom-fighter who tortured his wife to death with acid. Where does he belong? Most would agree he should be locked up (and no conjugal visits in his case, please), forever. But where? San Quentin? A lunatic asylum? From his viewpoint, both might be equally unpleasant. Likewise, the chap who killed all those nurses, the one who shot a lot of people in a Texas college etc. etc. Nobody knows what to do with the likes of these, except to keep them away from the rest of society for the rest of their lives. And to further befuddle the brain, one is told by authorities up and down the line (from progressive criminologist to conservative prison warden) that murderers, as a class, are the best risk of all—least likely to repeat, most likely to repent, 80% of murders are committed in homes, victims are lovers, family members, friends. What are the other 20%? I should surmise they are 1) psychotics, 2) people who kill in course of a robbery or other crime. The former don't really belong in prison. The latter? Who knows?

So we are back full circle: somebody has to decide who is very very dangerous. I asked Bernard Diamond[155] about this. He's at war with the Behaviourists, in fact I think he thinks they are very very dangerous. He said that if given the task of identifying the 100 most dangerously inclined (potentially dangerous, I think was his expression) of, say, the 28,000 students at UC, Berkeley, he would have to choose 1,000 to net 100, or overpredict by 10 to 1. I said, but even then how could he be sure? Suppose he had that job somewhere in the mid-west a few years ago, could he have picked from the fresh-faced young gasoline station attendants etc. the young men who would commit the My Lai massacre?[156] Isn't it the circumstance that usually makes one commit a crime? Well, that was different . . . and so it goes. You can't really get a straight answer, mainly because (as you pointed out in the publications you sent me) there isn't any straight answer. . . .

I'm not . . . too stuck on "due process," having seen results of same over the years. That is, I do not believe that the presumption of innocence and other aspects of due process are working for the poor and black, & I don't think they get justice in the courts. Nevertheless due process is now a slogan of the prisoners themselves. Without it, they are totally at the mercy of the individual warden (in prison), parole officer (when released). As you say in your letter, "many humane people get broken, embittered" in the system. . . . I read an interesting

---

155. Bernard Diamond, a forensic psychiatrist, held joint appointments as a professor in the School of Law and the School of Criminology at the University of California in Berkeley. In addition, he was clinical professor of psychiatry at the University of California medical school in San Francisco. In 1969–70 he was acting dean of the School of Criminology.

156. The slaughter of hundreds of civilians by U.S. soldiers at a Vietnamese village on March 16, 1968.

study about parole by Christopher Nuttall, an Englishman. He found an immense range in Calif. parole officers, all the way from splendid types who really try to help the parolee to one who kept a 6 foot whip and picture of Q.[157] gas chamber in his office. That's why I think a spot of due process is needed, as a curb on the latter type.

Have you read <u>Soledad Brother</u>, by George Jackson?[158] . . . It's quite an extraordinary book. Is George Jackson one of the dangerous? I should think so, by most people's standards. So what should be done with him? Do read the book, & tell me what you think. . . .

I guess it's really the common-sense-defying irrationality of the prison system that gets me more than anything. The incredible paradoxes. . . .

Again, many thanks for the extremely interesting correspondence. . . .

With best regards, Jessica

To George Jackson   Oakland
January–February, 1971

From: Jessica Mitford

The New York Times Book Review has asked me to prepare an interview with you to be entitled "The Literary Life of George Jackson." If you are agreeable to this, it appears the only way we can do it is through a list of written questions—an awkward way to conduct an interview, but the only one open to us, as the prison authorities have refused to let me come and see you.[159] After I get your replies, I will prepare the final article, editing as I should if taking notes. Thus you should be as discursive as you want. But if there is anything you particularly don't want edited out, please so indicate. . . .

I am hopeful that if it comes off well it will stimulate a lot of interest in <u>Soledad Brother</u>, on the part of readers of the NYT Book Review as well as librarians, bookshops etc.

---

157. San Quentin Prison.

158. *Soledad Brother: The Prison Letters of George Jackson* (Coward-McCann, 1970). Jackson, an incarcerated felon continuously from the age of 19, was a field commander of the Black Panther Party. He and two other prisoners were charged in 1970 with the retaliatory murder of a white prison guard and sent to the maximum-security cellblock in California's Soledad Prison after three black prisoners were killed by a white guard. Jackson and his codefendants were known as the Soledad Brothers. From extensive reading during long periods of solitary confinement, Jackson had become an articulate radical theorist who was highly regarded by many free-world radicals, black and white, and his book received national attention. Nine months after this letter was written, before he turned thirty, Jackson, brandishing a smuggled pistol, was killed by guards' gunfire at San Quentin Prison in what was said to have been an escape attempt.

159. Decca did finally get into the prison to interview Jackson in late March after his lawyers obtained a court order permitting it, although a guard tried various ploys to monitor their conversation, supposedly for her protection. She rejected all the guard's offers of assistance and later wrote, "Thus my interlocutor unwittingly acted out for my benefit the most pervasive cliché in all prisondom: 'They treat convicts like caged animals.' "

The fee for the finished article is $350. At first I thought I should contribute this to the Soledad Brothers Defense Committee; but then I wondered if (in view of the thrust of the interview) a more dramatic use of it might be to order from publishers books that you think should be in prison libraries, and have these books sent to San Quentin and Soledad. What do you think of this idea?[160]

The main difficulty, of course, is the lack of the ordinary give-and-take one usually has in an interview, where the answer to one question may suggest another that has not previously occurred to the interviewer. Therefore, it would be very good if you could yourself expand (that is, anticipate any unasked question that you feel should be asked), and write in anything you think is pertinent to the inquiry. Conversely, if you feel any of the questions I have submitted are dull or irrelevant etc., please so indicate, and in this way we'll drop it, just as we would in a real interview.

Before you decide whether to go for this whole idea, I should mention that there are conflicting views as to whether we should even attempt an interview in these circumstances. For example, Alex Haley (author of Autobiography of Malcolm X) thought not. His words were something like this: "It's difficult enough to get political, revolutionary people to talk about themselves and their individual development without this additional handicap—you could only get something worthwhile by sitting down with George Jackson for many hours." Conversely Maya Angelou[161] (author of I Know Why the Caged Bird Sings) thought it would be well worth a try—there's nothing to lose, and it may deepen people's understanding of yourself and your struggles, thereby having a special sort of usefulness to some readers; and it may do the book some good, which is the main purpose anyhow.

In his preface Jean Genet[162] says your letters "perfectly articulate the road traveled by their author—first the rather clumsy letters to his mother and his brother, then letters to his lawyer which become something extraordinary, half poem, half essay . . ." An ex-convict put the same point to me in slightly differ-

---

160. Jackson opted for payment to the legal defense committee. Decca had been upset that the warden of San Quentin wouldn't allow Soledad Brother into the prison library and was considering establishment of a committee of librarians, writers, book review editors, and others to visit prison libraries and "make a fuss about" the censored books. She also talked of asking dozens of publishers to donate books to prison libraries.

161. Angelou, the singer, civil rights activist, actress, and writer, met Decca in the late 1960s at the London home of mutual friend Sonia Orwell.

162. Like George Jackson, radical French writer Jean Genet had taken up writing while a prisoner. After he became an established writer, he supported a number of radical political causes, including the Black Panthers, and early in 1970 he entered the United States illegally to tour the country in support of the Panthers. He was hunted down by immigration authorities and left the country. In July he wrote the preface for Soledad Brother. It was apparently during his illegal 1970 U.S. tour that he was guest of honor at a tempestuous gathering at the Treuhafts' home. For details, see letter of February 1, 1993, to various friends.

ent fashion: "He's much more intact intellectually now than when he entered the prison system. In the first letters, there's no hint of the cohesive, coherent thinking at the end of the book."

The objective of the interview is to trace this road, not just in political terms (which you have already done in the autobiographical letter to Greg Armstrong[163]) but in terms of intellectual development. Or, to put it another way, how did you become such an astonishingly good writer and what are the lessons in this for others?

Another objective is to answer questions about which other writers are curious—were you able to correct your own galleys and to see the book in all stages of production as "free-world" authors do? Are you permitted to receive letters from readers of your book, how many have you had, what do they say? These questions will be posed in the following pages.[164]

To Virginia Durr   Oakland
                                                          March 7, 1971

Dearest Va,

... PRISONS. I know, it is a drear enough subject—funerals were <u>so</u> much jollier. But mine wouldn't be another "ain't it awful" book, that is, I hope it wouldn't. I don't really want to do a book on prisons but the awful thing is I think I'll have to. It's like quicksand, and I'm getting sucked down under.

For example: Early in Jan. I got a letter from a prisoner in McNeil Island Federal Pen, a long & smashing letter . . . asking me to come up and investigate convict complaints, and to be their "spokesman." Well I couldn't do that (as there's no point in spoking about things one is not informed on) so I wrote back (via his wife, he can't get letters from the likes of me) a generally gung-ho letter about how similar their grievances are to those of the Cal. prisoners etc., and to keep in touch.

Next thing you know there's a full-fledged strike in McNeil, started on 22 Feb, the whole place shut down tight, all cons. refusing to go to work. Curiously, there's a total news blackout all over the country about this, although (according to Tom Murton,[165] former warden of Arkansas prisons, the one who told about mass graves etc) this is the first strike in a federal pen. since the 40's.

---

163. Armstrong was at that time the editor of Bantam Books, publisher of the paperback edition of *Soledad Brother.*

164. The rest of the letter—pages of detailed questions about Jackson's literary and other influences, techniques, and goals—has been omitted here.

165. Murton was one of Decca's key informants and the person who had most effectively publicized the prison conditions that led a judge to rule that the state of Arkansas was violating the "cruel and unusual punishment" standard of the U.S. Constitution.

A prof. from U. of Washington came & told us about it, & asked me to go up to Seattle, so I did, this past week.

Va., it was a circus. I got a total runaround from the Warden (he said he would be too busy to see me), so I started at 6 a.m. Seattle time, 9 Washington time, to call the U.S. Bureau of Prisons, various congressmen, senators (six of them), to insist on being allowed on the Island. I got several local newsmen to go along with me: CBS television crew, UPI man, Seattle Times man. I said let's just go, and insist on being allowed on the island. So we did. I didn't even bother to call back the Warden, just went along to the dock, which is 1 1/2 hrs. driving time from Seattle. We arrived. We got to the heavily guarded dock. The heavy guards sprang forward: "Are you Miss Mitford?" "Yes." "You can be admitted. Stand back, all of the rest of you, you are not admitted." Fury on part of local newsmen, we waved a sad goodby to each other, they took pix of me waving from the boat. Pure surrealism.

Well it's far too long & boring to go into the whole thing, and not a smidgeon of marital strife & all those things that you find so fascinating to recount, because I forgot to ask the warden if he was even married, let alone divorced. DUE PROCESS, Va, I swear it's far more interesting. Ask Cliff.

The point is the Bureau of Prisons had told me there is a long-standing rule that reporters cannot interview inmates. Why, said I? Because to allow such interviews would be an infringement on the inmates' right of privacy. You must be kidding, said I. Not so, said they. Then I said you are not only kidding, but lying. I have a letter from a prisoner asking me to come & see him, so I shall do that, as he has waived the right to privacy you so kindly conferred on him against his will.

So I got to the prison—it's a very pretty island, reminded me of Inch K. in some ways. Was received by the warden. "So, you made it here?" he said, in his charming and disarming way. We had a good giggle over that. All his important meetings had vanished like summer snow. Two hours we spent (seemed like 5) on the interview. VIP treatment all the way. E.g.: I asked, "How big are the solitary confinement cells?" Instead of saying oh about as big as from here to there, warden snaps fingers, tells a flunkey, "Get the precise dimensions of those cells for Miss Mitford, please." After a bit, said flunkey returns with some square foot statistics. This was not what I was after, actually. I did make the warden go through all possible paces (went through the strike demands one by one with him, got a profile of prison composition, etc). Then asked to see Charles Armsbury, the con. who had written to me. "I haven't the authority to let you see him." "Who has?" "The Bureau of Prisons." Back to square one, the B. of P. having told me that only the warden could grant that right . . . Lots more transpired. Eventually I said to the warden, "I have a message for Charles Armsbury. Will you give it to him?" "Yes." "The message is: I came over to see you, was denied the right to do so, but shall be back shortly to visit you after a few things get straightened out."

Then I left, VIP all the way, because the asst. warden took me back to the dock in his private speedboat!

Following morning, press conf. called by ACLU, which is filing suit on behalf of numerous plaintiffs (Newspaper Guild, various reporters, me, etc) to force authorities to let us interview prisoners. Smashing turnout: all four TV channels, all Seattle newspapers. A Washington Post stringer showed up later, saying the Wash. Post wanted an interview. So possibly the amazing press blackout is ended? Not too likely, I don't know if the Post carried anything. The strike demands, I forgot to tell about. They are EXTREMELY MILD, minimal, and the strikers don't even use the word Demand, they call them <u>Proposals</u>. Thirteen proposals. Most of them are merely proposals that the fed. regulations be carried out!

I was only in Seattle 2 nights, but it seemed like 2 months. Va, I'm actually v. lazy, by nature, and getting more so. So it was quite a switch to be going to bed at 2 a.m, getting up at 6, no nap, pure work all the way—and actually survived. Adrenaline, I think. It seeps up & rescues one in places like Seattle, don't you agree?

The newspaper people couldn't have been more smashing. They really sprang to life, helped in all ways. . . .

ACLU is quite uncertain if its suit will prevail; probably not, they fear. So I shall have to plough on, via all those friendly legislators (the ones I called, beginning 6 a.m.) who swore they were in favor of freedom of the press & due process. I can see that now, for my sins, I shall have to muddle around in the federal prison system. I should very much like to find out how they arrived at their quaint way of protecting inmates' right of privacy and a few other things. . . .

Sorry for such a terribly long letter with no juicy bits, merely facts of MY life for the moment,

> Lots of love,
> RSVP, Decca

To Vivian Cadden   Oakland
                                                                   April 9, 1971

Dear Viv,

How are you? Where are you? And when are you? Coming this way, I mean. . . .

Guess who I had lunch with today? You will never, so I'll have to start at the beginning (comedy in a few acts):

<u>Act I.</u> A couple of weeks ago Shana Alexander called up Bob, but got me by mistake, to find out how to reach Margaret Burnham[166]—she wants to see

---

166. One of Angela Davis's attorneys (see next footnote).

Angela Davis,[167] and has been told M. Burnham is key to that. So I rather coldly gave her the phone number of Al Brotsky (old friend of ours, in the Davis case, works with Burnham). But I did then take the precaution of calling Al to explain that I was not particularly sponsoring, or introducing, Shana into this scene, had merely given her his number.

Act II. We get carbon from Shana of her letter outlining her desire to become the "official biographer" of Angela Davis. She had sent it also to Bettina Aptheker and the lawyers in the case. Bettina, whom I see a great deal & adore, she's a smashing girl, mentioned this letter to me and said "Who is she? Is she Black?" Aren't these party stalwarts marvellous; B. is in charge of P.R. for the Davis case! But I believe that her total innocence of that scene is some protection, in a weird way.

Act III. I'd arranged to meet Bob downtown for lunch today. He arrives, announces a mystery guest is coming—she soon does, Shana herself, with a v. drab Black lawyer in tow. They are more or less killing time waiting for their appointment with Margaret Burnham; Shana had called Bob, saying let's have lunch, so he said do let's. In passing, please note that she's been after Bob all this time, not so much me. Oh dear she is a rum one. But, to proceed: I deftly changed the subject to Famous Writers, and told Shana that poor Bennett is now a bit under the gun, as a lawyer from FTC was here the other day—he tells me they've taken depositions from B. Cerf, Rod Serling,[168] the execs. of the school etc. etc. and are really pursuing their investigation. So the drab Black lawyer starts asking about it, & Shana explains how I'd written this article which she turned down. "Why did you?" asks the Black lawyer. Shana pouts, doesn't answer. I said, Well, you didn't think it was very good, don't you remember? Shana: "Decca, you've got to see my position—I was trying to get McCall's to be better than the usual women's magazines, have better fiction etc., and to antagonize all those people would have been, I thought, a very bad move. But I tried to get them to stop taking ads from the school, I tried to get Bennett to resign. . . ."

So this time she changes the subject—back to the Angela Davis case, the dif-

---

167. Davis, a philosopher and former graduate student of radical political philosopher Herbert Marcuse at the University of California at San Diego, was a member of the Student Nonviolent Coordinating Committee and the Black Panther Party. In 1970, she was fired as a philosophy lecturer at the University of California at Los Angeles after the FBI told the university's Board of Regents she was a Communist. She was active in prison reform and was a defender of the Soledad Brothers and a friend of George Jackson. After Jackson's brother Jonathan, a judge, and two prisoners were killed in a shootout during a failed escape-kidnap plot at the Marin County Courthouse, Davis was charged with providing the weapons and went underground. She was placed on the FBI's "Ten Most Wanted" list and apprehended two months later, in August 1970, in New York. A defense committee marshaled international support on her behalf. She was acquitted of all charges at her trial in 1972 and went on to a career as a writer and professor.

168. The television and movie writer and producer best known as the creator and host of *The Twilight Zone* on television.

ficulty of getting in to see her etc. I said there's no difficulty at all, all you have to do is to get Angela's permission, permission of her co-deft. Ruchell Magee,[169] and both sets of lawyers. Which is true. (I forebore to rub it in by saying that I'd had a long chat with Angela and Bettina the other day.)

Shana asks me what I'm doing, and I tell about PRISONS. She asks if I've any sort of outline, or plan, for the book? No, alas, say I; I'm still mucking about on the fringes, very unsure of what tack I'm taking or what to cover or how. So Shana, very sympathetically, writer-to-writer like, "That must be so hard—such a vast subject—and not having found any approach." I know (I said), I'm afraid it won't be very good, just like the Famous Writers article. OH DECCA, she said. I think I got to her, at last!

But honestly don't you think this is all really very extraordinary, the way she's pursuing us, of all people, for entrée? I'm trying to figure out her whole character. In a way, she's awfully like B. Cerf (the sophisticated us-folks-up-here bit, we all understand it, no hard feelings etc). I wonder if I could somehow be the official biographer of Shana Alexander? I must ask Bettina for permission next time I see her. . . .

Much love . . . Decca

To Raymond Benedict[170]   Oakland
                                                               July 12, 1971

Dear Mr. Benedict,

Thanks very much for your extremely interesting letter of 7 June, and apologies for not answering sooner. . . .

Actually I was quite aware that the last para. of my Atlantic article was a cop-out.[171] I'm now writing a book on prisons, in which I hope to do better. But shall need a lot of help, and I now proceed to solicit your help:

In the book the first thing to do (it seems to me) is to describe. Some of the points in the Atlantic article will be much expanded, and the picture will be one of total failure of prison "reform," and will point out the shallowness,

---

169. Magee, who had written Decca to comment on her prison article in the *Atlantic Monthly*, was the sole survivor of the three prisoners involved in Jonathan Jackson's deadly courthouse escape attempt.

170. Benedict, a state prisoner at the time his correspondence with Decca began, had written to praise Decca's *Atlantic* prison article and thank her for her efforts to expose prison conditions. He also said that her remedies, although correct in principle, would prove inadequate for meaningful prison reform, and that they were also politically unrealistic. He argued that thoroughgoing social reform was a prerequisite for prison reform.

171. In the last paragraph of the article, Decca wrote: "I believe the first essential step is to penetrate the closed doors behind which the authorities, from prison administrator to parole board, operate. The new access roads should be broad enough to accommodate the courts, legislators, the media, political activists who are spearheading demands for fundamental change—and that amorphous entity, the public, which bears ultimate responsibility."

superficiality—perhaps even dishonesty?—of aforementioned prison buffs, who are all good kind people with the best interests of convicts at heart. At least that's how they think of themselves.

Proposals. That's going to be a lot tougher. . . . Because supposing the Calif. prisoners win their major demands (end to indeterm. sentence,[172] abolish Adult Authority, due process at all stages from prison disciplinary proceedings to parole hearing and parole revocation etc.), then what?

Oddly enough the "vast and radical reform" that you speak of is an implicit recommendation of even people like Ramsey Clark and the Pres. Crime Commission Report. They all talk blandly of abolishing the slums, providing full job opportunities, education etc. etc. for all—without, perhaps, realizing that this means redistribution of wealth. Which in turn means a long & bloody fight, because when and where has any ruling class gladly surrendered its wealth?

I think my book should certainly press for all the immediate demands, some of which are already before the Calif. legislature (e.g. the bill to abolish solitary confinement) and some of which are pending in court cases. If it could help to bring some of those about, it's still worthwhile. However, the whole history of prison reform is the co-option by prison administrators of well-meaning reforms.

In August, I'm going to a five-day conference—the 101st annual Congress of the American Correctional Association. In preparation for that, I'm scanning through the published volumes of proceedings, from 1870 on. There is much to be learned from these about the underlying punitive purpose of the indeterminate sentence and other reforms instituted over the years. Here is a revealing bit from Prisons and Beyond by Sanford Bates,[173] a book written in the thirties: "One of the practical reasons why more privileges are given in the prisons of today is the possibility of depriving prisoners of these same privileges, as part of the imposition of punishment. If all inmates are at a dead level of misery and deprivation all the time, how can we differentiate between those who conform and those who do not?" . . .

So, as you can see, exploding the reformers is relatively plain sailing. Fundamental proposals are far harder to come by, and here is where I should much like your views, and those of others:

1. Almost everyone, including wardens if they are leveling with you, will say "75% or 50% or 95% of the inmates don't belong here, could just as easily be on the streets." But then of course somebody has to decide which those are, which puts us right back where we were, in the grip of behaviourists, people-changers, guards etc. who make these determinations about prisoners.

---

172. The indeterminate sentence—with the prisoner's release conditioned on his or her progress in completing often contradictory or questionable programs or meeting vague standards to achieve release—was one of Decca's main prison reform targets.

173. Macmillan, 1936.

2. Even official govt. reports say prisons are meeting none of their stated functions (reform, deterrence etc).

3. What are your deepest thoughts about the future of prisons—should there be prisons? If so, who should be in them?

In my view, just as do-gooding suggestions of whites about improving the lot of Blacks are pretty much doomed to failure—because only the Blacks themselves have the real insight to formulate their own program—so do-gooding suggestions of people like me about prisons won't do much good, unless they express the views of the prisoners.

I hope you'll write back soon. . . .

Yours sincerely, Jessica Mitford

To Marge Frantz   Miami Beach
                                                                    August 17, 1971

Dearest old Marge,

In spite of extreme infidelity of you not writing me here, here is an account of the ACA[174] convention to date (highlights of).

The exhibits are smashing, vast halls full of them.

In a way, they exemplify the Correctional contradictions: here a booth of learning materials, simplified high school courses etc., and next to it one that looks like a medieval torture chamber: huge thick chains, restraining belts and handcuffs of all kinds, and the latest kind of mace etc: "The Advanced 'Han-Ball' Tear Gas Grenade" is the one I liked. The leaflet says "It instantly pours out a dense and continuous cloud of CN or CS tear gas right at the place where it will do the most good." The leaflet describing the chains for "maximum security in transporting prisoners" tells how to tie him up, and adds "Other uses will readily suggest themselves to officers who become familiar with this equipment."

The first night there was a memorial service for those who had passed on (wardens etc., natch, not prisoners who had passed or been caused to pass). . . .

Lots of frenemies[175] here: good old Joe Spangler[176] came nuzzling up in the bar yesterday. Actually, snarling with rage he was. "There's been a lot of discus-

---

174. American Correctional Association.

175. One of Decca's favorite words. In a 1977 essay in the London *Daily Mail* (reprinted in the *New York Times* and later in *Poison Penmanship*), she wrote that "frenemy" (which she sometimes spelled "frienemy") was "an incredibly useful word that should be in every dictionary, coined by one of my sisters when she was a small child to describe a rather dull little girl who lived near us." Her sister and the neighbor girl, she said, were "inseparable companions, all the time disliking each other heartily."

176. Joseph Spangler was at the time the administrative officer of the California Adult Authority, a nine-member board overseeing sentencing and parole.

sion of that article of yours." Oh, good! I do hope you liked it?" "Liked it! It's the most diabolically clever hatchet job I've seen yet." Marge, that pleased me no end as you can guess. "We spent hours with you and your friend (you[177]) explaining everything, how we have the most dangerous prison pop. in the country, and you put in none of that." I said sorry but space limitations . . . but that in my book I'd put it in, and also put in how Robin Lamson[178] says it isn't true.

Dr. E. Preston Sharp (exec. secretary of ACA, who invited me) seems a bit nervous now that he did. He asked me up to his room and begged me to tell the truth about Corrections. So I said of course I will, I always do. He said the trouble is so many writers only print the inmate's side, never tell what the corr. people are doing. I said I'd put in everything the corr. people say, that's why I am here. . . .

There are innumerable meetings one could attend (about 1500 to 2000 people here), so I've decided to stick with the wardens as far as possible—they're the best copy, but only meet in the mornings. . . . As one warden put it, "Corrections has moved forward in the past 100 years, at least in our thinking, if not in reality." (That's a direct quote.)

The marvellous thing about the wardens is their looks, straight out of an old Cagney movy, grizzled, stone-faced old brutes they are for the most part. They also tell smashing jokes (to keep each other awake?) such as one [who] started his talk, "Now, I was explaining the other day how you can spot a homosexual: they wriggle in their seats, look over their shoulder at the other fellow, get up and walk around a lot—yes, fellows, I'm watching you-all while I make my remarks." Ha ha ha. . . .

A warden admonished another man who had declared he was "tough": "Words like tough are not good. Say, rather, 'control.' Also, say 'therapeutic segregation'—it's still segregation, but it doesn't sound so bad." (Marge: one really has to be attuned to the speaker at this conference to know what's being driven at. The Aesopian language works both ways. For instance, Al Schuman, Supt. of the D.C. juvenile detention center and one of the best people I've met in this racket, told me he's become adept at camouflaging words. He has let out most of his charges into a community place which he calls for safety's sake "Youth Crime Control Center." He said the congressmen who control funds etc. never look beyond those words! They assume it's just another prison.)

Well I'm afraid this is getting rather long (and I am expected at a cocktail party to which Spangler injudiciously invited me after about 8 martinis), so I shall try to close on a positive note.

This p.m., I went to a panel called American Assn. of Correctional Psychol-

---

177. That is, Marge Frantz.
178. At the time Robin Lamson was chief researcher for the California State Assembly Office of Research.

ogists Committee on Personnel Standards and Training. They were young and sweet-looking, utter lambs compared with those old wolves of wardens.

One of them is at a highly funded research project at Draper in Alabama (Draper is famous as an innovative, experimental corr. place for young men—I've read masses about it, and its phenomenal success in producing scientific analyses of problems etc.). He produced an extremely grand and huge chart, and proceeded to explain it.

It seems that in the clothing shop, inmates had a terrible record of "tardiness" (they use that awful word, natch, instead of lateness, but so do the schools, or Benjy's school used to as I recall—rather vividly, in fact, as he was much like those clothing shop inmates in this regard). . . . Although it took about 1/2 hour for him to explain this brill. experiment, it boils down to this: the corr. officer told the men that anybody who was tardy would have to spend 2 hours in the evening on overtime work. And then the most amazing thing happened; part 2 of the vast chart shows that TARDINESS DROPPED TO ALMOST ZERO!! Then they went back to the old system (no penalties for tardiness) and—you'll hardly believe this—the 3rd part of the chart shows that after that the TARDINESS WENT BACK UP! As the psychologist pointed out, "Findings such as these show the Correctional Officer he can become an agent of change." Too true.

Tom Murton is here, and I seem to be the only person who talks to him. We are two sad pariahs, not included in the Rotary Club jokes—I must try to change this. Perhaps Spangler will prove to be the Agent of Change at tonight's cocktail pty? Time will tell.

I think I've got the perfect thing to go in front of my book: Mort Sahl, in the record The Future Lies Ahead. He is describing in his restless way an interview with the warden of San Quentin. When asked why he chose that particular career, the warden answered, "Because I love people." They are such ducks, just like undertakers who say exactly the same. Serving people in grief/serving misfits of society . . . some, in both groups, really believe it—or most do? Have to, in order to live with themselves. . . .

Your loving Dec.

To Marge Frantz   Oakland
                                                                               August 28, 1971
Old Thing,

Once again I'm writing despite fearful infidelity of you not doing so, because I want to jot down a few more things re. that conference before I forget & it's so much easier in a letter.

Mostly about Procunier,[179] with a few other characters thrown in for good

---

179. Raymond Procunier, director of the California Department of Corrections from 1967 to 1974.

measure. E.g., after the non-stop all-night cocktail party (5 p.m. to midnight, at the end of which Spangler slobbered over to ask whether I'd go for a skinny dip with him—<u>honestly</u>, I noted that none of these characters would ever be able to abide by parole conditions for a minute) Pro. came round the next day seeking yet another meeting. . . . I took him through a few things of interest, i.e., why all that stupid stuff about <u>Soledad Brother</u>? When the publisher brought Jackson a hot-off-the-press copy of it, it was confiscated by a guard. Why? Because, said Pro wearily, it's contraband unless <u>mailed</u> by the publisher. I tried to explain that obviously an ordinary person . . . wouldn't understand their weird rules. Also, if it wasn't considered contraband, why did a guard take John Thorne's copy[180] that he happened to have in his briefcase? Because a book is always contrab. unless mailed from publisher. Why, because drugs etc. might be concealed in it? Yes. In that case couldn't drugs be concealed in a lawyer's legal papers, briefs etc? Well, perhaps it isn't very logical but it's a rule, and the guards have to abide by it and enforce it.[181] But, he said, the general censorship rules have now been relaxed to the point where <u>anything</u> is allowed in except actual instructions how to make bombs etc. (Of course, that was before last Saturday.)[182] In other words, they are (or were) running scared from all the lawsuits, I guess. Other Pro. news & views: he said he was v. put out with me because New Jersey & Maryland were about to institute the indeterm.[183] sentence, but didn't because of me article. Of course I don't believe a word of that. . . .

To cheer you up, here's another thing that happened. I got a long distance call last evening, and made Bob play 20 Questions (which he is usually madly good at) to find out who it was. . . . He never did guess. It was Sargent Shriver,[184] asking if I'd come to participate in a symposium organized by or in honor of the Kennedy family about the moral and ethical consequences of new discoveries in genetics! I said you must be joking, I don't know a bloody thing about genetics, let alone the moral consequences of them. So then he said Robert Lowell is coming, Wm. Styron, all the guys—they want to have creative people. So I explained that I'm not a bit creative, besides too busy on me prison book.

Thus does life chug on in its mysterious way . . .

                 Lots of love,
                 GET IN TOUCH SOON, Dec

---

180. Thorne was George Jackson's attorney.

181. In another discussion on a related issue, Decca said she asked Procunier "why, in view of [a state law] requiring authorities to allow inmates to subscribe to all mags. etc that go through the posts except obscene & inciting-to-violence stuff, San Quentin allows Playboy and not Ramparts? He answered, 'I guess the warden doesn't like Ramparts.' "

182. The day George Jackson was killed in the prison yard at San Quentin in what authorities said was an attempted escape. He was armed with an automatic pistol that was said to have been smuggled in to him.

183. Indeterminate.

184. Politician and diplomat Sargent Shriver Jr. is married to Eunice Kennedy, sister of John, Robert, and Edward Kennedy.

To Nancy Mitford   Oakland
                                                      September 21, 1971

Darling Susan,

The incredible things you've been through. And that unspeakable faith healer—I got a letter from the Hen about her, in which the Hen said she thought the f.h. would just hum a few faithful hymns like All Things Bright & Beautiful. Had no idea she'd go for the ill nerve.

But the main thing is how v. much better you are—oh I <u>do hope</u> it's still keeping up. . . .

Susan, wasn't it sad about Bennett Cerf croaking.[185] I felt v. put out about that, as it takes almost as long in my experience to make satisfactory enemies as satisfactory friends, and there he's not. By the way: those Famous Writers have gone bankrupt.[186] I wish one cld. sink the prisons as easily. . . .

OH I'm so hoping the improvement is still holding up by the time this reaches you. Actually, you know, even yr. handwriting looked so much healthier, or rather more robust.

Lots of love, & to Woman, Susan

In B. Cerf's obituary, it said he thought of the title <u>Love in a Cold Climate</u>. Did he?[187] If not, say the word & I'll waylay the obit. writer in a dark alley along with the faith healer & do them both in with one blow.

To Nancy Mitford   Oakland
                                                      October 13, 1971

Darling Soo,

The few things you said about Muv in yr. letter opened up a perfect <u>flood</u> of thoughts in that direction, so I must just impart them.

The fact is that unlike you I actively loathed her when I was a child.[188] (esp. an older child, after age 15), and did not respect her, on the contrary thought she was extremely schoopid and narrow-minded—that is, sort of limited-

---

185. Cerf had died August 27 at the age of seventy-three.

186. Decca had pronounced herself "<u>quite proud</u>" when the Famous Writers School was suspended from trading on the stock exchange, which an article in the *Wall Street Journal* attributed to her article. Although the school filed for bankruptcy, Decca reported in *Poison Penmanship* "a sad addendum: the Famous Writers School is creeping back," with some of the same features as the organization she had done so much to torpedo.

187. In her reply, Nancy Mitford confirmed that Cerf had indeed suggested the title of her novel.

188. Nancy Mitford had written that she had a great respect for their mother and enjoyed her company, "but I never loved her, for the evident reason that she never loved me." The reminiscences in this and subsequent letters were occasioned by Nancy Mitford's intention to write her memoirs. Decca later wrote that her great regret during Nancy Mitford's terminal illness was that she didn't have the strength to write the memoir.

minded with hard & fast bounds on her mind. But then, after re-getting to know her after 1955, I became immensely fond of her, really rather adored her. Therefore in my memory she turns into 2 people; I'm sure she didn't change much because people don't except for a certain mellowing with onset of old age.

The thing that absolutely burned into my soul was the business of not being allowed to go to school. So much so that when she came here when Dinky was 7, the subject came up and I found myself literally fighting back tears of rage. Do admit it was maddening. One thing I specially remember: when I was about 11, I wanted to be a scientist (natch I didn't tell you about it, Susan, because whenever one told you one's deepest ambitions it was only to be TEASED UNMERCIFULLY and laughed off face of earth), because I had just read The Stars in Their Courses by Sir James Jeans. So, noting I should have to go to college in that case, I biked to Burford and rather shudderingly went to see the headmaster of the Grammar School. He said I could be admitted to the grammar school (which had a scientific laboratory, that's why I wanted to go) if I could pass a fairly easy exam., which I cld. learn to do by reading a list of books he gave me. I was v. excited over this, rushed home to ask Muv if I could get the books, take the exam., and bike to school each day. A cold NO was the only answer, no reason given. After that lessons with the [governess] seemed totally pointless, although I admit I could have learned far more than I did.

She must have been fairly horrid when young, too. For instance when she was about 30, living in Dieppe, Nelly Romilly (not yet married) aged 20 came to her in deep despair to say she had lost 10 pnds. in gambling, owed it as a debt, and could Muv lend it to her? Muv went straight to Aunt Natty[189] and told all, I expect poor Nelly was bitterly punished. Muv herself told me this, but simply couldn't see what a vile thing it was to have done. I guess it's that awful disapproving quality that I always hated about her.

Another thing I remember—but perhaps you've forgotten, or perhaps I dreamed it: when you were about 29, we were going for one of those long, wet Swinbrook walks when the rain seemed like one's inner tears of bitterness because of boredom & general futility of that life. You told how Muv had given you a terrific dressing down for not being married, having just turned down yet another proposal of marriage, & that you would be an old maid if you pursued this hopeless route. Something like that. Did it happen?[190]

I know it must have, I can almost hear squelch of one's gumboots as you imparted this odd bit of information. And the certain conviction, in my mind, that one had to get away from that dread place at all costs.

As for the Hen, I don't think she was much of a noter of anything until much

189. Lady Blanche Hozier, mother of Nellie Romilly.
190. Nancy Mitford replied, "I think I was telling lies if I said Muv wanted to marry me off. . . . I think I was probably in a blind temper about something else & talked wildly."

older—and by then, was fairly free of the Reverends. I mean she never specially wanted to <u>do</u> anything except what was there to be done, rather adored the daily life at Swinbrook. When things came up such as fainting dead away on the flagstones on acct. of Woman's engagement to Derek, that was more or less from outside causes (such as being in love with D) rather than from inner, don't you think?

After the Reverends became Nazis, Swinbrook life became even more intolerable; but by then, you had more or less left. Again, no effect on the Hen; don't you remember Mrs. Phelps[191] saying she was perfectly happy picking fleas off Jacob? Or ticks out of? Which is quite an oversimplification of that complex Hen's character, but nevertheless a telling observation, in its way.

When one thinks of all the things Muv told about <u>her</u> extraorder childhood, being in charge of Grandfather's household & political campaigns etc., one can dimly see how her naturally bossy nature got more so, given that unnaturally free rein from age 14. . . .

Oh dear I <u>still</u> haven't read M. McCarthy's novel,[192] in spite of the fact it's the only new book I crave to read. The fact is I don't read anything anymore except PRISON stuff, on acct. of me being a CRUSADER.[193] Yes, Susan.

I am <u>cheering</u> for your continued recovery,

Much love, Susan

To Merle Miller[194]

Oakland
November 3, 1971

Dear Mr. Miller,

This is a fan letter to say first, how HUGELY I enjoyed <u>Dick Daring</u> when it first came out, I thought it immensely funny and good; and second, I've just read <u>On Being Different</u> and think it is a very smashing piece of work. . . .

Perhaps you would be interested in a few thoughts about the contrast between attitudes of English and Americans as I have observed them. Almost every English boy I knew had had a terrific lot of exposure to homosexuality, because they all went to public schools. Talk about 37%! More like 99%. Some stuck to it, some didn't, but nobody paid too much attention either way, as I recall—and I'm talking about EONS ago, late twenties-early thirties. Now of

---

191. An American who had rented the family's Swinbrook cottage before the war.

192. Probably Mary McCarthy's *Birds of America*, published in 1971 by Harcourt, Brace and Jovanovich.

193. The characterization of Decca was their sister Diana Mosley's, as reported by Nancy Mitford.

194. Editor, novelist, screenwriter, and biographer Merle Miller came out of the closet with a 1971 *New York Times Magazine* article entitled "What It Means to Be a Homosexual." His was one of the earliest public declarations of homosexuality by a prominent American. The article was expanded and published as a book, *On Being Different* (Random House), later that year.

course the Grown-Ups (as we called those of our parents' generation) were implacable, tight-lipped on the subject. I remember once asking my mother, "But what did Oscar Wilde <u>do</u>?" "Something dreadful," she answered. "And please don't mention his name in front of your father." Of course I was snickering up my sleeve as I knew all about it (aged 10), was just trying to be annoying.

My first husband, Esmond Romilly, ran away from school at 15 and lived amongst the disreputables and exciting revolutionaries in London. One day he met WH Auden at a party; Auden invited him to his flat to read his poetry. Esmond, very flattered, went. Alas! Auden made a pass at him and E., furious, chucked all his clothes etc. out of the window. The point of this story is the contemporary attitude of Londoners who heard about it: with one accord, they rounded on Esmond as a barbarian, possibly prejudiced against homosexuals. Of course the real reason for E's fury was hurt pride: he thought he'd been asked up because of his intellect, discovered to his chagrin it was for other motives. How many girls have gone through the same? I always thought it was a fairly funny story.

My brother-in-law, Giles Romilly, was a homosexual from the time I knew him (he was about 21 when we first met). He had some pretty horrible experiences in the war. Came back, got married, had 3 children. Divorced, remarried, went totally bonkers, committed suicide. I can't help wondering if he wouldn't have been far better off sticking to his original metier, so to speak? . . .

OK, I'll do what I can to straighten out the straights. How does one begin? (And by the way, for God's sake don't publish any of this letter, it's purely personal to you, in appreciation for your book.) I'm really quite horrified by said straights. What about that word deviant, which recurs in all the sociology crap to explain everything from crime to sex to wanting a bit of privacy? Please advise. I'm writing a book about PRISONS, and somehow your book has a lot of relevance to that subject: not the sex angle, but the DEVIANT angle. End of paper so end of letter,

To Nancy Mitford   Oakland
                                                                November 16, 1971

Darling Susan,

Well I shrieked about the counter-senility pills, & wish I cld. lay hands on a few, just what I need about now. Otherwise the <u>medical</u> news sounds so incomparably better, with 2 trusted Drs. in the act, and pain receding.

I agree bossy isn't the word:[195] more, implacably <u>disapproving</u> and thus arbitrarily disallowing anything one craved to do. (I mean she didn't make one do things, which was too often the fate of other wretched children in those days—being forced to eat food one loathed, or Susan in the case of one I know having

---

195. A word Decca had used to describe Lady Redesdale in her letter of October 13.

one's BOWEL MOVEMENTS EXAMINED by the [governess] each morn.)
While the Hen may not have noted this, I bet Diana did, having been on
receiving end of said disapprovingness from at least age 14 to 18 & then again
when The Divorce Courts were Nigh! said Annie to Pam.

Also, I agree with Diana that she prob. didn't change, as people don't, much,
esp. after middle age; more likely we did. Or at least—and in my view this is
more like it—the balance of power changed once one had fled the coop. So one
met on totally different terms. I was much struck by this when she came to
Oakland that time, about 1947 or 48 after what then seemed like eons of time
since I'd seen her. I was in a state of near terror about her visit. And then she
tottered forth from the aeroplane (it was a v. rough trip, she was quite done for
by it) and at once it became apparent she had come to make friends at all costs.
Same thing when we went to Inch K. in 1955 et seq. And I could see what an
incredibly thin time she had had, on the whole, in life.

Do you remember the letter that Jim Lees-Milne wrote to the Times after
she died?[196] I thought it was marvellous, (although it took me to task for falsify-
ing),[197] and if you haven't got it I'll send, if of any use, as I have kept it somewhere & cld. easily find it. All about how she had the soul of a mariner. All very
well for J. Lees-Milne, thought I, but who wants to be brought up by a
mariner? And, at that, a fairly ancient mariner by the time I came along. I think
one trouble is that people sometimes get militantly nasty in middle age (oh
dear, my age) and that's the time of her life when I was growing up. . . .

Much love, Susan

To Nancy Mitford   Oakland
                                                                March 7, 1972

Darling Sukie,

Thanks awfully for yours of 24 Feb—I've been away, so only just got it. . . .

The Obs[198]—well I've never seen it, although the brute of a lade who rang
up promised to send. But I think you said that sisters are a shield against cruel

---

196. James Lees-Milne, architectural preservationist, socialite, and author especially noted for
his voluminous diaries, was a longtime Mitford family intimate who had been a passionate friend of
Tom Mitford's at Eton. He was lifelong friends with most of the sisters and an admirer of Lady
Redesdale. His tribute in *The Times* of May 28, 1963, portrayed Lady Redesdale as "a woman very
much out of the common," as the author said would be expected by her unconventional upbringing, "spent mostly at sea on her father's yacht."

197. The letter described Lady Redesdale's "patrician reserve" as well as her perceptiveness—
"surprised by nothing and amused by practically everything"—adding, "Nothing however is further from the truth than the popular conception of her, gleaned from *Hons and Rebels*, as a philistine
mother with hidebound social standards."

198. Nancy Mitford had heard from someone who liked what Decca and she had written in the
Observer, but Nancy could not recall writing anything for the paper and asked Decca for details.

adversity, and I said I thought you were the cruel adversity, or something like that.[199] Oh how beastly of me, but do admit you were, a bit?

I didn't see the Mosleys on telly, how maddening, never even knew they were on telly until someone told me they'd seen Sir O. on the Today Show. Fancy that, I suppose it was Cord's first time in the U.S.?

I've just come back from NY, hadn't seen the children for absolute ages so was v. pleased to clasp the dear things. The following intelligence about the Piano Tuner: He was working at a place called the Somer Piano Co . . . & making a fairly decent wage for a change. Then about a month ago he got a t.gram from the Steinway Piano Co, asking him to come to them and tune naught but concert grand pianos—he has to go to all the great concert places and be on hand for the whole thing—and Susan he gets $100 a night (divide by 2.4 for pnds, so about 40 pnds) for doing this! Don't you think that's too extraorder. The main thing is he's simply adoring it—he's got so frightfully nice lately, seems to be off the dread drugs altogether. . . .

I'm so sorry that horrible pain keeps up. . . .

Much love, Susan

To Nancy Mitford   Oakland
                                                                              March 19, 1972

Susan, now don't be like that; after all it is but the Teaser Teased, wouldn't you say? But you sounded BITTER, saying I don't know why you bother to keep up relations etc. Anyway I still don't know what the Observer said, as nobody sent it & I haven't seen it. Do send, if you've got it. And also do stop being cross; it makes me v. sad as I thought you'd be AMUSED. (That is, assuming they did not misquote.)

Thanks for the info. about the Fr. businessmen's club prisons. Mine's going to be about how the supposed to be kind prisons are far crueller than the known to be vile ones—my dear Susan how would you like to be forced to go to GROUP THERAPY as a condition of being let out on parole? . . .

We are vaguely hoping to come to England etc. in Sept, hoping the book will be finished by then. Can I still come & see you, in spite of all?

Much love, Susan

---

199. This story has been retold in many ways. In her most complete account, Decca wrote in *A Fine Old Conflict* that a writer from the *Observer* phoned her for an article on the subject of sisters. As Decca told the story there, ". . . she had already spoken to Nancy in Versailles, who had said, 'Sisters stand between one and life's cruel circumstances.' I was startled into saying that to me, sisters—and especially Nancy—*were* life's cruel circumstances, a remark that did not find favor with her when it appeared in print."

To John O'Sullivan[200]   Oakland
                                                                   March 24, 1972

Dear Mr. O'Sullivan,

That business about the Spock indictment being a sop to Gen. Hershey was sort of dropped (perhaps inadvertently?) by John Van de Kamp when I went to have a chat with him at the Justice Dept. It might be worth while asking Ramsey Clark about it? Although he'd probably deny all. I haven't any additional info. about it.

I did have a very curious conversation with Gen. H. which for some reason I couldn't fit into the book. I went to see him in his huge, flag-draped office at Selective Service hq. He was making the point that a lot of people made at the time: that Dr. Spock may be a very fine baby doctor, but he doesn't know anything about foreign policy and the draft, he should leave these technical matters up to the experts. To press this home (the role of expertise), Gen. H. suddenly said, "Have you ever ironed contour sheets?" No, never. "My daughter-in-law just puts them straight on the bed without ironing them," he said, "but we do things differently in the Hershey home." "Do you iron contour sheets?" I asked. "Yes, Mrs. Hershey hasn't been too well lately, so I iron them. You start with a large rectangle. Then you fold that over and you've got a smaller rectangle. Then you fold that once more . . ." I was getting quite muddled with all these rectangles, so I asked when he has time to iron contour sheets?" "On weekends." "Surely you don't iron on Sundays?" I asked, quite shocked. No, Saturday afternoons . . .

From all of which I inferred he was a touch over the hill.

                                           Yours sincerely, Jessica Mitford

To David Scherman   Oakland
                                                                  ca spring 1972

Dear D.,

I'm writing to ask a favor, but only if it's not too much trouble. Somebody told me that a year or two ago Life had an article about highway death traps, places condemned by engineers and safety types, warnings disregarded by city fathers, resultant carnage of motorists. Needed for me chapter on Types of Crime (more or less showing how the average random murderer catches it while other murderers aren't even prosecuted). If you could possibly find & send, shld. be most grateful. . . .

I got the Guggenheim. Are you amazed? Bob said I'm prob. the least qualified person ever to get one. Noting the studies of my fellow Fellows, I can but

---

200. O'Sullivan, at the time assistant professor in the Department of History at Florida Atlantic University, had written Decca to say he was doing research for a biography of General Lewis B. Hershey. He was inquiring, he wrote, about "the statement [in *The Trial of Dr. Spock*] that the trial was designed in part to appease Hershey" and requested further information.

agree; I don't even know the meaning of 1/2 the words they use to describe what they are doing. Such as: "Studies in the chemistry of macromolecules." "Studies in the genetics of cultured rust fungi." Ugh! How cultured can you get, not to mention "Afro-Bahian cult music." Anyway I feel in v. exalted company and as you can see have started my research, which consists of writing to you for that copy of Life. . . .

Much love, & to R, Decca

To Marge Frantz   Oakland
                                                                        ca summer 1972

Dear old Marge,

Since I can see you're never going to come round I'm writing one of my pathetic efforts. . . .

The main thing I'm writing about is a conversation we had the other night with John Irwin[201] and Fay Stender.[202] . . .

John Irwin . . . made these points: The world is full of odd types who might/might not turn dangerous. But if you arrest them because they <u>might</u>, and before they <u>have</u>, it's a great injustice. There are some problems, he said, to which there <u>is</u> no solution, and [a menacing client of Robert Treuhaft] is an example. Perhaps he'll calm down and start to fly right on his own accord, his cure effected by some random circumstance to do with his own life? Perhaps although he <u>seems</u> threatening he never would actually do anything? Nobody knows, and no known procedures can predict. Conversely, if you lock him up you <u>know</u> he'll get worse—and one doesn't exactly put someone away for life for that sort of erratic behavior—so he'll be <u>more</u> threatening when he comes out. But oh dear (said I), what to do if he comes back again? <u>Poor</u> old Bob. John thought in that case he shld. be told fair and square, If you don't leave at once, we'll run you in for trespass. . . . John also thought there shld. be Crisis Centers; if he comes back, call up one of those radical black ministers, Angela Davis's doctor, etc. instead of police? But I pointed out that black ministers hardly ever show up even when invited miles in advance, <u>a fortiori</u> doctors, so this didn't seem an efficient solution. . . .

Fay told the following thing that happened to her dau. Fifi a few years ago, when F. was about 8 years old. Fifi and another little girl were playing in a nearby park. They got in conversation with a man who eventually took their pants down & started feeling them about; he also offered his private parts for

---

201. A San Francisco criminologist and professor, author of *The Felon* (Prentice-Hall, 1970) and, a number of years earlier, a prisoner himself.

202. A friend and colleague of Decca's, Fay Stender was chief counsel for the Prison Law Project in Oakland and a passionately committed and controversial advocate for prisoners. She was closely involved with the Black Panther Party and for a time represented Huey Newton and George Jackson, whose book, *Soledad Brother*, she helped to edit and bring to publication.

them to feel. Fifi told all this to Fay, who called police. Police came not once, but three times, to interview Fifi and make her go over the same story. They showed her photos of sex offenders, but she couldn't identify the one. All rather reminiscent of Dinky's lily-waver.[203] . . . Fay's reason for calling cops, she said, was <u>not</u> to avenge her daughter but to apprehend a possibly dangerous fellow who next might murder some child. Both John & I pointed out that types who do what that man did almost never turn violent (this fact is in all the Annals of Crime). John said, & I agree, the whole thing was made far worse for Fifi by all the police fuss, that in general it's the parents who get kids all upset & traumatized by things like this which would be soon forgotten if just casually treated. Also if the chap had been caught he'd get 1 to 15 years, or even Atascadero.[204] But (said Fay) shouldn't my kids have a right to play in the park without being molested? Again, said J., some problems simply haven't got a solution. He thinks that the punishment for this should be 5 days in jail, and if he does it again, 10 days. . . .

I think all this sort of thing shld. be discussed in the book, don't you?

I am beginning to note that Fay has if anything less of a theoretical grasp of this dire subject than I have.

Love, Dec

John also pointed out that children are in far more danger from dangerous drivers etc. but this wouldn't stop one from letting them go out to play. He also said that as part of the Convict Class he couldn't call police under any circs., although he might recommend such a course to a non-con. I guess that sort of burns into one's psychology, like us and trotskyites?

To Doris Brin Walker   Oakland
                                                                    April 6, 1973

Dearest Dob,

Your splendid letter just came. . . . [R]eading it brought all my old affection for you flooding back—I'm afraid we haven't got on well the last 2 times (France, and back here). I'm sure a lot of that was my fault, being as I was in a high state of nerves over my book; but perhaps I should, to quote yr. letter, lay it "out on the table"; because I do cherish our friendship v. much. . . . [T]he discussion we had about secretaries. My point is this: I agree all that "legal worker" stuff,[205] or much of it, is pretty silly such as those offices where the lawyers have to take it in turns answering the phone etc. so as to show they are not "elitist." <u>However</u>, I gathered from what you said that you do literally, and

---

203. See November 24, 1989, letter to Laura Shaine Cunningham.

204. A state mental hospital.

205. The discussion had been going on since at least a year and a half earlier, when the National Lawyers Guild—of which Walker was then chair—voted to admit legal workers to membership, following a heated controversy.

genuinely, think that lawyers are in some way superior to sec'ys, that the latter are incapable of understanding or contributing to policy. Which may be v. true of your secretaries, as one of the shortcomings of the firm (in my view) is that you've made no effort to hire movement types, also no effort to develop intellectually and politically the sec'ys you have. All I can say is that when I was a subeligible typist at OPA I was madly interested in policy, and also lawyers, such as Bob, did take me to lunch—not just me, but there were loads of clerical types who were v. keen on fathoming the purpose of OPA and frustrating the higher-up business-oriented administrators. Wasn't that partly what the Union[206] was all about? So, to cut this short, I think it is snobbish and unbecoming to a Marxist to think of one's self as automatically superior because one happens to have a better job; and to say there's no point in having lunch with the sec'ys as they are too boring.

Other news & views: I went to Washington to testify before Sen. Kennedy's committee on prisoner/drug experiments.[207] . . . That was a v. rum experience. The hearing was more or less structured by moi (French for me, check with Emily[208]), I fed them names of experts, Bernard Diamond came all the way from Calif., ditto a young law prof. from UCLA that I'd suggested. They also had FDA and HEW[209] types (villains in my piece) and a marvellous chappie from the drug industry, PR man, whose role apparently was to say "I don't know . . . I can't answer . . . I'll furnish the information . . ."

Anyway the thing lasted from 9:30 a.m. to 1 p.m., so you can imagine how hungry & tired one was, dying for a drink. Bernard D. and I wandered in search of same, and on the way out the HEW man came up and offered to join us. There had been two prisoners, ex-cons from Philadelphia, who had given rather dazzling testimony; they had actually been in the drug programs, and unlike the Calif. Prisoners Union (which has been pussyfooting about the issue, for fear of losing their Vacaville[210] constituency, who love the drug programs on acct. of the $30 a month) came out foursquare for abolishing all testing in prisons. So, on the way to lunch the HEW chap said to me, "Wasn't it surprising how intelligent those two coloured men were? They really do surprise you,

---

206. The United Federal Workers union in which both Walker and Decca had been active in the 1940s.

207. Midway through her book, Decca learned of abusive medical and pharmacological experiments on California prisoners. In a progress report to editor Robert Gottlieb, she said the information was "rather hot stuff, and nobody—including all my prison knowledgeables in the Dept. of Criminology and the state legislature, and the [Ralph] Nader drug busters—seems to know beans about it." Decca developed her newfound information into an article for the *Atlantic Monthly* and a chapter of her book entitled "Cheaper than Chimpanzees." She hoped to use the *Atlantic* article to elicit new tips on other instances of medical experimentation on prisoners.

208. The daughter of Doris Brin Walker and Mason Roberson.

209. The U.S. government department that, at the time, was named Health, Education and Welfare.

210. The California Medical Facility at Vacaville, a state prison.

sometimes." Which, as you can imagine, put me in a raring bad mood. At lunch, HEW came over all smarmy: "Your article, and your testimony, are very valuable to us—I'm sure Sen. K. will advocate larger appropriations for HEW so we can really do the job." Me: "Why was all that valuable to you? Didn't you know it already? I just found it out by sitting at a telephone in Oakland." HEW: "No, we weren't aware of most of it." Me: "What do you do in the morning when you get to work?" HEW: "You've no idea the amount of paperwork in an agency like ours." Me: "Did you know about the syphilis experiments in Tuskegee, where 100 blacks died hideous deaths [even] after the penicillin cure was discovered?" HEW: "Well, yes, we did know something about that, as the experiment was written up from time to time in medical journals. But nobody seemed to care, until some journalist blew the whistle." Me (now in a tearing rage): "I shall write to Sen. Kennedy tomorrow, proposing that your staff be cut to two people: one, to read the medical journals, the other, to act on what has been read. All you'll need is a desk, a telephone, and a cheap car to spring about in." Bernard was roaring! So, do admit, it was all clean fun, even if nothing comes of it. . . .

Lots of love to Mason & Emily, do write, Decca

Galleys of my book are due v. shortly, mid-April. . . . The title seems to be: <u>KIND AND USUAL PUNISHMENT: The Prison Business</u>.[211] I'm not mad keen on it, but nobody seems to be able to think of a better one. If it's taken in England, how about <u>Cons and Rebels</u>?

The publisher says they are having a first printing of 25,000, <u>amazing</u>, as I actually don't think it will sell; it has sort of missed the boat, in a way, as much of the concern and interest aroused by Attica[212] etc. seems to have died down. . . .

Dob, please don't be cross at the beginning of this letter, as I'm quite sure and prepared to admit that I contributed to any coldness between us. Do let's be friends from now on.

To Doris Brin Walker   Oakland
                                                                      May 6, 1973
Dearest Dob,

I was v. glad to get your letter, as not hearing from you I feared mine had offended bitterly. Anyway I think you're right; there have been trivial things (disagreements over trip etc), possibly masking weightier things (political). . . .

---

211. The book was published by Alfred A. Knopf with that title. Decca once wrote that "titles should, in my view, be dead clear & recognizable to any fool . . . totally DESCRIPTIVE" and that *Kind and Usual Punishment* was in her view "hopeless, far too murky—title in England was changed to *The American Prison Business* which it shld have been called here, too."

212. The four-day uprising in September 1971 at the Attica Correctional Facility in New York, which resulted in more than forty killed, including eleven hostages, focused unprecedented national attention on prison conditions.

My friendships with some people, rejection of others, class/political implications: Some of our friendships <u>have</u> worn out over the years . . . [such as] some of the more plodding erstwhile comrades. Of the old friends, I'd say the following have all held up: Marge, Al Richmond[213] (never very close with them, but always like & admire), Pele, the Kahns, Matt Crawford, the Dreyfi, Kurzweils,[214] etc. (I cld. think of lots more, but those are the main ones.). . . . I admit some of [our newer friends] are a bit odd to say the least from a class/polit. angle, but you know how one loves variety and dipping into other sets & circles.

To sum up the political thing, I guess I think you are a bit rigid and sectarian, and you think I'm a bit sloppy and opportunistic. Possibly, a lot of truth in both?

The main thing, though, is where you say "I never lost my affection for you"—well, neither did I for you. <u>But</u>, affection and friendships don't exist in a vacuum, and they can be dissipated by unspoken disagreements—which is why I'm so glad we are having this out by letter. Don't you agree? . . .

We're having a mammoth benefit for the new national Wesley Robert Wells[215] committee—he's been sent to Vacaville for "stress assessment," can you beat it. The effort is to force a pardon. . . .

Much love, dearest Dob, and to Mason & Emily,
Decca

. . . Have you heard about the Great Rape Flap at the office? Seems that David[216] has a black client accused of raping a Chinese student while she was taking a shower at the UC gym. (Bob, musing over possible defenses, said how about diminished capacity? He sees this pretty nude girl and can't help himself. I said <u>that</u> wouldn't do, because how about if somebody saw masses of money in a bank behind the teller's window and got so overexcited he decided to pinch it all?) Anyway, led by Drucie[217] the 3 younglings all took the position a progressive firm shouldn't defend an accused rapist since the defense wld. necessitate dragging victim's reputation thru mud etc. Jerry[218] has a madly confused article in Conspiracy making same point, all about the sexist prosecutors not really prosecuting etc. All of which I think is ridic; am working on a counter-article for Conspiracy, saying rape charge is historically a racist weapon etc. and telling abt. the Willie McGee case. Too long to explain it all here, if I do the thing I'll send it, along with Jerry's article. . . .

---

213. The West Coast Communist was a longtime editor of *People's World* who left the Party in 1969, although he was disaffected with many of its policies long before that.

214. Bettina Aptheker and her then husband, Jack Kurzweil.

215. The black prisoner whose cause Decca had championed back in the '50s (see September 16, 1953, letter to Lady Redesdale).

216. Walker and Treuhaft's partner David Nawi.

217. Drucilla Ramey, another attorney in the office.

218. Probably a reference to Jerry Garchik, at the time an attorney in the office.

As she delighted in doing at her lectures, Decca
explained the embalmer's use of a Natural Expression
Former to give a corpse a more lifelike facial expression
"after rigmo sets in, as we call it in the trade."

VII

FINE CONFLICTS

Constancia Romilly in 1980 with her family, husband Terry Weber and (from left) son James Forman, stepson Ben Weber, and son Chaka Forman.

Decca with son Benjamin in 1980.

In 1964, not long after publication of *The American Way of Death*, when Decca was back on her family's island in the Hebrides for the first time since her mother's death, she had written to a friend that "Inch K. is redolent of death (don't tell the prospective buyers, if any!). It's so queer to be here without Muv." She described the trove of old letters she had discovered there—"lots of mine about the birth of Nicky and so on, and various yellowing telegrams from various wars announcing the deaths of various ones. I do long to be back in un-ghost-ridden Calif. Except that the whole of America sounds pretty ghost-ridden, with potential ghosts, that is, what with Goldwater and the dear old South and Harlem." And she added:

> I'm trying to think a bit, while here.... One thing I've thought of is ... to settle seriously to My Life and Red Times, or, It's A Fine Old Conflict.... I would like a few years ... to do something that might be a tiny bit useful before croaking time rolls round. As I said, Inch K. is redolent of croaking.

Beginning even before publication of her first memoir and continuing through the 1960s and much of the 1970s, *A Fine Old Conflict* was always on Decca's writing agenda. She wanted to "set down some personal reminiscences of the Party, and in doing so to try to exorcise a destructive poltergeist that kept knocking about in the furniture of American politics: the Communist conspiracy, or Red Menace . . ."

Memoirs can be elegiac. Not Decca's. Hers were as high-spirited and sometimes combative as her life itself. The title of her second memoir—conceived in 1960 and finally published in 1977—was based on a childhood mishearing of "The Internationale," the Communist anthem: "'Tis the final conflict." It does not seem surprising, at any stage of her life, that Decca would hear "fine old conflict" when "final conflict" was intended. She reveled in the *joie de combat*, and when conflict didn't find her, which it often did, she found it, as if by instinct. She meant the title *A Fine Old Conflict* as a literal description of her Communist years, saying, "to me it was, and ever shall be."

While her second memoir was "cooking," Decca periodically found herself enmeshed in fine new conflicts. Some she litigated—a favorite pastime; almost, at times, a sport—and others she transformed, like a literary alchemist, into brilliant magazine vignettes of petty bureaucracy and shabby commercial arrogance. Not infrequently, she took, or at least explored, both routes simultaneously. Not all of the conflicts she wrote about were worthy of the effort she put into them—or the national attention they generally received after her reputation was firmly established—but most of them seemed to illuminate, in personalized, anecdotal fashion, characteristic vagaries of American (or sometimes British) life.

Through much of the mid and late 1970s, however, Decca was simultaneously drawn back into her contentious, "ghost-ridden" family in England. Although she did not intentionally seek out conflict with her sisters, her presence and prominence were often the catalysts that turned mundane slights into epic battles. The famed English sisters' fragile but decorous façade papered over the family's notorious political history, but the façade seemed to crumble whenever the blunt, leftist American sister barged back onto the scene. Decca became embroiled in a number of prolonged spats with her sisters during this period. Although the issues in contention were as trivial as a supposedly lost (or stolen) scrapbook, their roots often stretched deep into the past—the Nazi past.

The oldest Mitford sister, Nancy, died in 1973. Within a few years, the British fascination with the family she had done so much to publicize in her satirical novels became almost a national craze, spurred on by a series of books, documentaries, articles, and appearances—even, in 1981, a musical—by and about the six sisters. In the mid-1970s, the *Evening Standard* described the various phenomena as "the Mitford Industry." It was a term Decca adopted with relish, beginning with a 1976 letter to sister Deborah, the Duchess of Devonshire, in which she said she was looking forward to "the next episode in the Mitford Industry" on an upcoming visit to England. She repeated the term often over the years, with a number of abbreviations and variations, such as "the Mit. Ind," and once wrote the duchess: "I wonder if there will be Mitford T-shirts & comic books soon? If so, how do we split the profits?"

Two years after Nancy's death, Harold Acton published his *Memoir of Nancy Mitford,* written with assistance from Nancy's sisters—but not Decca, who felt she had been "excluded" by Deborah and Pamela.

The next year, 1976, saw the publication of *Unity Mitford: A Quest,* by David Pryce-Jones, who drew inspiration and some minor assistance from Decca, much to the resentment of the other surviving sisters, who had no wish to remind the British public of Unity Mitford's Nazi fanaticism and flagrant anti-Semitism. "There is another factor at work here in this recent fracas," Decca wrote at the time; "what they really loathe today is not so much newspaper attention per se as the rattling of unfortunate skeletons such as the Mosleys' role in the thirties, and my parents' Nazi leanings."

Also in 1976, sisterly hostilities broke out over the duchess's missing scrapbook, with accusations that Decca had taken it. What she called "the great Scrapbook Fracas" preoccupied Decca for years, as is amply reflected in her letters. After she and the duchess re-established cordial relations, Decca still refused to "set foot in her territory," the scene of the supposed scrapbook theft. "So we are on speakers (and meeters) but NOT at her house."

In 1977 both Decca and Diana published memoirs. Although Decca's *A Fine Old Conflict* dealt primarily with her years as an American Communist, her English sisters took offense at several sections, including a recapitulation of her earlier life that set the stage for her account of the Communist years. Decca was despairing at the unexpected reaction. "Perhaps," she wrote to one friend, "it's pointless to even hope to one day make it up with Debo as she clearly hates my book, takes everything in it amiss (whilst adoring the D. Mosley product!). Nevertheless I am fully, <u>chronically</u> sad about it all."

Diana's unrepentant memoir, *A Life of Contrasts*, like Decca's, received widespread press and public attention. Further roiling the waters was a BBC documentary on Decca, *The Honourable Rebel*, timed to coincide with release of her memoir. The documentary contained references to a 1955 episode that deeply offended the Duchess of Devonshire, though the sisters had clearly read the episode differently: Decca as a comment on Robert Treuhaft's gauche response to upper-class manners at the Devonshires' house; Deborah as ridicule of those manners. Preparation of a subsequent documentary, a profile of sister Nancy in 1980 for which the surviving sisters were interviewed, only intensified the distrust as they wrestled for "artistic control"—in effect, control over references to Nazi-era memories.

The sisters' boisterous relationships led Decca to remark, after the film on Nancy was aired, "Fancy her believing in Heaven! I wish I did, imagine the amusement of all of us meeting up there; although I shouldn't think St. Peter would welcome this thought, poor him, all of us clattering through the Pearly Gates & generally mucking up the terrain." She also noted that her sister Deborah "was the only one [in the film] with her feet on ground, [bringing a] welcome breath of sanity into general welter of eccentricity."

Summing up the disputes with her sisters, Decca wrote in one letter, "there is something so non-twentieth-century about all that; I can far more visualize aging ladies in 1820 falling out over such things."

With the sisters engaged in an often public, albeit unintended, "competition" of memoirs and memories, Decca exclaimed in another letter at the time, "Poor old British reading public—Nancy by Harold Acton, Unity by D. Pryce-Jones, Diana Mosley last month, now mine."

The satirical publication *Private Eye* got some measure of revenge on behalf of the public with a 1977 feature headlined:

At last—the Unknown
Mitford Sister tells it
like it really was
I, DOREEN!

The article announced, "Despite the fact that this book was never written, and never will be, for the simple reason that the author does not exist, it has already sold over 2 million copies, and the film rights have been purchased for an undisclosed figure." The book was said to feature such characters as Lord Readersdigest, known as Parg, and Hitler, known as Ducks—"plus a cast of thousands of other Mitford sisters."

Despite the pull of England and her family's larger-than-life past, Decca continued to pursue her periodical articles and popular lectures in the United States and sometimes in Britain as well. She turned out a drumbeat of articles and writing proposals, remarking once, "OH I DO so loathe working—but I loathe not working even more, which is so odd." Many of her articles were collected in *Poison Penmanship*, published in 1979. Among the essays included in that volume was "My Short and Happy Life as a Distinguished Professor," first published in the *Atlantic Monthly*, which recounted the characteristically high-profile imbroglio that begins this section of Decca's letters. It started with an invitation that was especially gratifying for a writer with no formal education: to teach a course on muckraking at San Jose State University.

■■

To Robert Gottlieb   Oakland
                                                                   May 25, 1973
Dear Bob,

Suzi says that Martha says[1] that you say you do not care for homicide—I can't think why. Please enlarge on this curious bias of yours.

Anyway that's not what I'm writing about. Read the back of this letter (done on Bob's inefficient Xerox—a close second to Knopf's—oh damn, just when I was trying to be non-abrasive, that slipped out). Are you shrieking? Distinguished Professor,[2] and what's more I'm going to do it. Snell Putney, Ph.D., hero, patron, the <u>best</u> of Acting Chairmen, as you can well imagine I adore him, sight unseen. At first, I rather loathed him (have spoken to him plenty on the blower) as he said I was only one of many under consideration; and then at one point he said, What is yr. academic background? A jolly unkind question, you must admit.

The others under consid. have apparently faded, so Bob (who was vastly for the whole thing) has changed his sabbat. plan to next February, & since San Jose is only 1 hour's drive from here, I shall be Distinguishedly Professing various things from home. It's all a trifle terrifying, as I've never actually even <u>taken</u> a course, except in typewriting when I was 23 and did v. badly in, let

---

1. Suzi Arensberg and Martha Kaplan, both Knopf employees.
2. On the other side of this letter was a photocopied letter inviting Decca to take an appointment as a distinguished professor in the Department of Sociology at San Jose State University for the fall semester of 1973. The invitation from Snell Putney, acting department chair, cited her ability "to present an intellectual challenge to our students," a passage that Decca underlined in some of her copies of the letter, with the annotation: "Help!"

alone <u>given</u> one. Shall be expecting masses of SUPPORTIVE ADVICE from the likes of you, Martha, Suzi, and anyone else you can think of who is educated. . . .

PLANS (ours) are now all changed around. We'll prob. take a holiday in August to early Sept., then if you & blissful Bill Loverd[3] so desire, cld. come to NY for all the smashing parties you are probably planning to arrange,[4] thence to the arms of Snell Putney, Ph.D., Acting Chairman. So do be settling on a publication date for KAUP, as I now call it.

The Index of KAUP is coming along like gangbusters, I shall be v. sad when it's finished as it cheers my lonely days. I may in fact found a Famous Indexers' School shortly.

Your loving Professor Mitford

To Robert Treuhaft   Versailles
                                                                                      June 13, 1973

Darling Bob,

Here I am, back in my Impasse.[5] . . .

[A] robber disguised as a taxi driver dumped me off here, more dead than. So the nice people at the Impasse drew me a fool-proof map how to get to R. d'Artois, a 10-minute walk. As I got to said rue, what should I hear but shrieks of HENDERSON! It was Debo, just arriving from other end. You can imagine I was pleased by the that. So we had the invaluable briefing session. No point in going into it all, as the letters rather told the picture. N. is quite changed, her face all grey, can't get up—in fact, can't be moved without truly awful agony. No jokes, no gossip, nothing but—well, here's how it is: She seemed really pleased I'd come, vast welcome smile (Debo said N. had offered to pay for my fare if I'd come! Which D. rightly saw as rather amazing.) Nancy takes lots of things in, had loved the Snell Putney, Ph.D. letter which I sent her & all those 1,000 majors.[6] Mostly, she's fearfully sleepy, which is all to the good don't you agree? Dozes off. The awful thing is the well-known stoicism has faded & she cries a lot, oh Bob you can't <u>think</u> how awful that part is. So vile to think of Nancy helpless & crying out of sheer weakness, pain etc.

The drill is to simply sit in her room all day, read, write, do as you please, but be there, so that when she does come to she sees you are there. So that will be

---

3. The head of public relations at Alfred A. Knopf.

4. Celebrating publication of *Kind and Usual Punishment*.

5. Decca was staying at the Hotel Clagny, Impasse Clagny, in Versailles. (*Impasse* is the French word for a dead-end street.)

6. A few weeks earlier, Decca had been informed of her teaching load in a phone conversation with the acting department chair. Among her classes in the sociology department was to be a lecture course for 1,000 majors. As she told another correspondent, "I said to him, on the phone, perhaps that could be about the Pentagon Papers or other matters of interest to the military? But it turns out they are not that kind of major."

my odd & unaccustomed tempo, for a bit. Debo says it is the most debilitating life in the world (being a Sis. in residence), and if it is for her, what will it be for me? So I said, I'll stay for at least a week, more if wanted, but must return from London 26 June. (I say: don't forget to meet me in LA, Bob.) . . .

Lots of times I've had a dream in which Nancy is a huge daddylonglegs, those terrifying large flying things with immense thin legs, in agony. Do think of me, Bob, in these foreign parts and do write as often as poss.

It's now midnight Versailles time, lord knows what your time.

Much love, Decca

To Robert Treuhaft   Versailles
                                                          June 14, 1973
Darling Bob,

This a.m. I had a mysterious errand to perform: seems Nancy was awarded a Croix of something-or-other (medal for Arts et Lettres) to be fetched at the Sureté (police station). So I slogged over there—to find that one bureaucrat is much like another; the brute said she'd have to come in person so I explained she is mourante[7]—I had brought her passport along. He demanded to know every detail such as maiden name of mother, Xian name of father etc etc—so after all this I still didn't get the bloody thing, he said it might take months.

I'm not sure how long I'll last here—I mean I'm willing, but am I pleasing? Not at all certain of that. When she's dozing, or semi-unconscious, which she is quite a lot, she seems glad enough to have one nigh. When alert, she can be jolly nasty, as just now. . . . Awkwardness is the word, but of her making. As you know we've always been slightly arms-length in contrast to Nancy/Debo, Nancy/Diana or even Nancy/Woman. So it's one of those things where most likely one can't do anything right. Also I think she's taken a distinct turn for the worse just since yesterday—Ann[8] reports she had a rotten night & rang the bell every 1/2 hour. There's no conversation or virtually none. It is all deeply depressing—I rather hope to be fired, in fact.

Yr loving Dec

To the Duchess of Devonshire   "Mon Impasse," Versailles
                                                          June 14, 1973
Dearest Hen,

Sorry to be peppering you with letters (as I realize I wrote to you this a.m.), but you know how it is back at the Impasse, one rather longs to have a word with somebody & this is the only way. So here goes . . .

---

7. "Dying."
8. Nancy Mitford's nurse.

I'm not at all sure how well I am doing as Sis-in-residence. I feel always either too-little-and-too-late, or too-much-too-early. Two examples (& remember this is my first day on the job, always fraught with awkwardness in my experience): Hassan[9] brought in massive vases of roses soon after I came, whisking away the old ones. Suddenly, her eyes filled with tears & she said, "everyone says there are masses of roses in the garden, why doesn't anyone bring them up here?" So I said I'll dash & get some, which I did. As you may have noted, it does take a few minutes to get them (as most of the prettiest fall to bits in one's hand, they are getting a bit done for actually), & I raced back with 3 more vases. So N., in cuttingest tones: "I see your life does not contain much art and grace." Too true, perhaps, but Hen! So I got lots more & put 'em round. Nancy: "I can't think why you didn't get them earlier, you haven't got anything else to do." In other words, I think she's rather taken against me. Except that later I found some smashing other flowers at back of gdn. and brought same in huge vase, I believe that found favour. Yet I can't make out whether me sitting in her room & reading or writing letters as distinct from you, Woman or Diana doing ditto pleases or annoys. The other example is La Visite de Mme. La Baronne de Rothschild, and please bear with me Hen as I'm quite sure this sort of thing is old hat to you, but I must just tell: Said Baronne was due to come at 5, the only visitor N. wanted. At about noon N., who had had a perfectly rotten night and day what with the roses etc., said she couldn't face it & would I telephone to put the Baronne off. So I did, but the B's sec'y pointed out she wasn't expected home until the evening, and no way of reaching her, but she'd try. Two hours later, N. said she felt far better & would like to reinstate La Visite, so I re-telephoned the sec'y to that effect (as N. said the Baronne being the correct sort would have been sure to telephone her house to see if there were any messages); so the secretary, who had been making massive efforts to reach the B., and had left messages all over the place telling her not to render herself chez Rodd, got straight to work putting all that in reverse.

At 5, Nancy got one of those total disaster pains & took 2 Palfrey (?) and 1 English pill, and told me to tell the B. she couldn't see her after all, I should chat with her in drawing room instead. So I did all that, & the B. turned out to be an extremely cozy type, aunt of D. Pryce-Jones (house-swapper with us) (which of course I hadn't fathomed), also had many an amusing tale of how we all went to lunch there when I was abt. 15 and so on. Soon, Ann came down to say Nancy was longing to see the B., so we went up; Nancy so bright & herself, even looking pink instead of grey (which to me was the huge change in looks first time I saw her yesterday—the greyness of face), and it all seemed to go terribly well. The B. had asked me to give a sign when she should leave; being uncertain (this is the too-much-too-early part) I did, after 1/2 hour, give a sharp pinch to the leg, only place I cld. impart the sign without N. noting. So she rose

9. Nancy Mitford's cook.

to leave; N: "Oh <u>do</u> stay another five minutes." So she stayed a good half hour more, me in terror it was too much etc. I left and went downstairs—which is another thing; <u>should</u> one stay or <u>not</u>, when there are visitors? Again, I think it depends—she might have wanted you to stay but not me. You know. Oh dear. Perhaps tomorrow will go a lot better?

Diana rang up & I told her all the part about the roses, saying I long for advice & instructions; turns out one was automatically <u>supposed</u> to do the roses each day, so now I shall, but one can't exactly guess these things. Of course Diana pointed out, which I absolutely do see, she's not herself etc., so one must just get on with it—which I'm totally willing and longing to do, Hen. Isn't it extraorder how utterly preoccupied one is with this horror scene, everything else fades such as Watergate (my favourite reading & telly-viewing),[10] hubby and kids, all one's usual interests. . . .

> Goodnight, Henny. Think of me sometimes in
> these foreign parts, Yr loving Hen

To the Duchess of Devonshire   Versailles
                                                                        June 19, 1973

Dearest Hen,

Just a word to say I do think the events of yesterday, Dr. visit & ordering 4 double morphine injections daily, have made a huge <u>difference</u>. . . .

She lies there smiling instead of crying. . . .

At times (although infrequently) seems far more actually alert, the sense of chatting & reading, far less what Ann calls "confused," meaning sort of halluci-nations like thinking her bed's leaking. . . .

The whiskey: Diana brought some & to everyone's amazement she took quite a swig (for her, I mean) & got fairly tiddly & happy last evening. So this a.m., about 11 o'clock, I said something like "Oh good, look at that lovely whiskey, shall we have a Cocktail Hour before dinner?" To which the answer was, "Why not before lunch—now?" So I poured a bit & she downed it. I said "Oh Soo the whiskey's made you look so pink & pretty." She said "it makes me <u>feel</u> pretty." Are you amazed? Not that I think the whiskey kick is likely to last, you know how changeable she is, prob. will say she loathes it next time offered. The <u>whole</u> thing, in my view, is the injections that's caused the real change. I honestly don't think she is in much pain at this point, except for when she's got to be moved, washed etc. So I <u>am glad</u> & only hope this keeps up—realizing, of course, that sudden changes are much the mark of this illness.

All this makes me not so much mind abt. leaving tomorrow (and feeling that when I do I'll probably never see her again). I'm afraid I haven't been much help. . . .

---

10. The congressional hearings on the Nixon administration's Watergate scandal. Decca enjoyed the live hearings so much, she wrote, that she would be "sad when it's over."

I think Ann is really splendid, v. quick to catch on to the form—I told her she must think of herself as working for dotty people out of another century & behave accordingly, so she is. She did say that in every other job she's had, all medical procedures (pills to be taken, injections etc) are strictly between nurse & Dr, & relations of the patient never interfere like here, all depends on which sister happens to be on hand—as said sisters countermand the Dr's instructions & generally run the medical scene! I think she's rather got a point there.

I do hope you had a jolly horse show. Sorry this writing's so illegible, I was doing it under the dryer at the local h.dresser.

　　　　　　　　　　Much love, Yr Hen

Late Flash: Another cktl hour, this time at the more usual hour of 6 p.m! She only takes a thimbleful but it seems to turn the trick. The really smashing thing is the beatific smile—I haven't seen the dread look of total agony, or even tears, since yesterday morning. Also I've got the hang of the roses thank God, that's all found favour in the last several days. . . .

Hen sorry abt. this non-stop letter but there isn't much else to do at the Impasse except try to wipe out the flea population, like all guerrilla wars a losing proposition for those who believe themselves to be powerful.

I'd written all the aforesaid before returning here. So must just say a word abt. the saying goodbye which was pretty ghastly. After supper I got my things together (such as they are, you know, bag, basket, coat but dawdled over) & then went to have a word with Hassan. I said that in every single letter my sister has written ever since you came here she has spoken of you & can't say enough abt. how good you are to her (etc etc) & he responded, "I look on her as a mother" (!!!) so I said I am your aunt, in that case, & we both fell to sobbing, Hen. So I mounted to N's room, full of resolve to say briskly "well goodbye for the present" but sensing I was losing control just said "goodbye Soo" & fled in floods. Ann said [Nancy] gazed at my retreating back & noted the floods & started crying like mad but long before I actually left was sound [asleep], so all that part's OK. As you've perhaps noted in life, she's a) a hurler of slings & arrows as in last few days re roses etc (yet starting when I was 5, in my recollection) & b) stellar attraction, sort of alternating between these. And now she won't be there to alternate.

Hen sorry for this dreary wail, any blood on this paper is pure flea blood, the brutes.

　　　　　　　　　　Yr loving Hen

To Marge Frantz　　　　　　　　　　　　　　　　　　　　London
　　　　　　　　　　　　　　　　　　　　　　　　　　　June 21, 1973

Dearest old Marge,

Sorry not to have written, I guess I was too miserable to write to anyone except Bob, which I did every hour on the hour—poor creature he must have been inundated with boring letters. I stayed in Versailles for 7 days. Deathbeds are v. tiring work as there's nothing whatsoever to <u>do</u>—one can't settle to reading etc. I feel like getting out of prison.

There's something so totally depressing abt. seeing someone turn into a corpse before one's very eyes—and a jolly <u>cross</u> corpse at that, the old cutting edge still much in evidence. . . .

For the 1st 5 days she lay there dozing or crying. On Monday the dread fluid, with which her legs are filled, took over in one arm. On Tues, she said it had started in the throat & she couldn't swallow.

I called the Dr., who came pronto. [Nancy] said (in French, he speaks no English) "I wish you would dispatch me from this world. I know you're Catholic & don't believe in such, but I'm <u>not</u>, and I long to depart this world." The Dr. replied he couldn't do that but wld. do all to alleviate the pain. So later, in the drawing-room conference with me & Ann, the nice Aussie nurse, the Dr. said "I don't believe in euthanasia, yet the morphine is a kind, gentle form of euthanasia." He then told Ann to give 4 injections a day, stepped up from 2—and said she cld give 2 <u>double</u> injections <u>twice</u> a day. As Ann can't speak French, I translate; & told her he said to give 4 double injections a day.[11] So she did & I [can only] hope . . . that all this morphine will send her into coma soon. I do hope the Dr. won't be livid when he finds out (as he's bound to, when Ann says she's running out of the stuff & needs new prescription). I'll write a jollier letter soon. . . .

Much love & to the family, Decca

To Barbara and Ephraim Kahn and Miriam Miller   London

June 22, 1973

Dear Loved Ones

. . . [I]t's <u>marvellous</u> being in London after all that. Dobby rang up one night at the Impasse & I was so pleased & surprised to hear a familiar voice that I burst into tears (& after all the horrors of the day at R. d'Artois). I didn't go to Paris at all. . . .

Had dinner last night with the Pryce-Jones's & their <u>marvellous</u> little girls aged 9 & 11. David wants to do a biog. of Unity[12] but all her papers were left by Muv to Jonathan Guinness so I doubt if D. will be able to pry them loose. I told him if he <u>does</u> do it I'll send all her letters to me, which I've still got after 40 yrs. Every year or so somebody writes to say they've been commissioned by a publisher to do her biog., but I've always said NO to requests for info etc. But I think David would do really well? Judging by his interview with Nancy in the D. Telegraph. End of paper and of letter. Much love to all,

Decca

---

11. Although the precise dosage details are confusing in this and other letters, Decca clearly doubled the dosage the doctor prescribed. See also letter of July 20 to Eleanor Fried Furman.

12. This is the first reference to a book that was to disrupt the Mitford sisters' relations for years.

To David Pleydell-Bouverie   Oakland
                                                                      July 1, 1973

Dearest David,

Thanks so much for yr. letter. I loved the part about my beautiful skin (although all I see in the mirror, alas, is wrinkled leather)[13] and loathed the part about me being boring[14]—and that white Mercedes[15] is jolly unfair as I was against having a Kraut car from the beginning & you shld. see the Decmobile, a 1963 Valiant. That Merc. is strictly Christ-like Bob's car. Next time we'll drive up in mine, so you can see for yrself. However I showed your letter to a friend of mine (Marge Frantz—I don't think you know her) & she said it serves me right as it is no more cruel & cutting than things I routinely say & get away with, or something along those lines. So perhaps she has a point?

As you can imagine I'm terribly glad I went to Versailles, although it was a total nightmare. . . . [I]n some ways she had a remarkably beastly life—deserted by that awful Prodd (Peter Rodd) whom she adored, and then the Col.[16] getting married etc. If you could only have seen her, you'd realize one can't mourn her death,[17] but only regret it couldn't have happened sooner. For instance had she died on the operating table 4 years ago, how miserable we should all have been—how deluded to be miserable. The only one good thing was that she finished her book on Fred the Great[18] after that, which she really longed to do.

Will you come and see us soon, dear David? Name the day and I'll put on some of those consumer goods which I affect to despise while I enjoy them[19] (namely, roast beef & Yorkshire).

Lots of love, Decca

---

13. Pleydell-Bouverie had written of all Decca's attributes that he admired "in spite of your naughtiness."

14. Pleydell-Bouverie said in his barbed but jocular letter: "Apart from your occasional unkindness to me (and this is usually because you never knew me when I was poorer and more hardworking than you ever were) I have nothing but affection and praise for you excepting your absurd and boring indictment of America and Americans as though it and they were solely responsible for the ills of this world."

15. In another comment in his florid letter, Pleydell-Bouverie had written: "To have survived these years insulting the innocent rich and maligning poor patriots . . . while you ride around in a white Mercedes, while your Christ-like husband protects the innocent poor, to have survived these years without getting yourself exterminated should prove to you that you live in a freer and more democratic country than the two you idolize. (Bob, on the other hand, is big enough to admit that he differentiates between the great Lenin's dream and the ruthless tyranny of the Soviet government.)"

16. Colonel Gaston Palewski, Nancy Mitford's longtime love.

17. Nancy Mitford died the day before this letter was written.

18. The biography *Frederick the Great*, published in 1970 by Hamish Hamilton.

19. Another allusion to a remark in Pleydell-Bouverie's letter.

To the Duchess of Devonshire   Oakland
July 10, 1973

Dearest Hen,

Thanks awfully for yours of 8 July (which came in incredibly short order, 2 days) & enclosures. . . . All made me feel I'd almost been there.[20] Yes isn't it extraorder how, whenever thinking of her (which I do, a lot) how v. pleased one is that all that incredibly beastly suffering is over. Also, you know, how she'd have shrieked at aspects of the funeral. She's the one who said once, re an American friend's father who had passed on, "The on dit[21] is he's to be buried in a Mitford and you get 10% of the cost in royalties." Several people sent the Times obit, one cld see it was written by a friend of hers—I had thought possibly C. Connolly? But note it was R. Mortimer,[22] anyway terrifically good. I still think E. Longford's[23] thing in The Queen last year the best, as far as capturing that odd spirit, & so good it came out when she was still alive.

Tell Sto[24] I absolutely share his views re Ld. Redesdale,[25] whom I met only once since he was grown up & loathed beyond words. Do you remember how he came to Swinbrook aged 3 mths. & Farve took a tremendous hatred to him because of his mingy face & bad manners (cried all the time)? When I next saw him, in 1955, I must say I did rather see Farve's point, a sycophantish creature. Did the New Wave of Mitford Sisters[26] go to the funeral? I suppose they're almost grown up, poor things. . . .

My drear PRISONS book is about to be launched on an unreceptive public; I've asked them to send you one, not to read, Hen, I hardly expect you to choke it down, but just to place around in strategic spots if you have any criminals to stay at Chatsworth. . . .

                     Much love, Yr Hen

Thanks for sending a wreath from me.

---

20. At her sister Nancy's funeral.

21. Scuttlebutt.

22. Both Cyril Connolly and Raymond Mortimer were prominent writers, editors, and reviewers and friends of Nancy Mitford.

23. Apparently Elizabeth, Lady Longford, the biographer.

24. Stoker (the Marquess of Hartington).

25. The title had changed hands several times since the death of Decca's father.

26. The six daughters of Decca's cousin Clement Redesdale, who succeeded Decca's father and two of her uncles as Baron Redesdale. Decca once wrote that her father not only took a great dislike to him when his future successor was three months old but he "cut him out of all wills."

To Eleanor Fried Furman   Oakland
                                                        July 20, 1973

Dearest E.,

A brilliant postman delivered yours of 17th inst., but do get a new address bk. & enter [return address] above in same. . . .

Nancy: . . . The only useful thing I did, on looking back, was to . . . double the dose of morphine. After that, N. lay there smiling whereas before she'd lain there crying which was so horrible to see. The Dr. found out on his next visit (because most of the prescription had been used up) but by that time I was well away.[27] . . .

I'm sort of in a state of suspension; the finished books are due late this month . . . longing to hear what recipients of same say about it, including you. Mainly, I'm wigging on my Dist. Profdom, making outlines & preparing exam questions. <u>DO come out for it</u>. . . . I'm rounding up everyone I can think of to be guest lecturers—the head of the SF FBI is coming!!![28] As well as masses of reds etc. Bob's doing one called The American Way of Debt, or How To Be A Successful Deadbeat.

                        Much love, Decca

Nancy, you know, was so many different things to me. . . . Anyway I adored her, even though she betrayed me by siding with the grown-ups when I ran away. And I think she rather liked me, in a way: "dear little Suzie," she called me. The last to call me dear little anything, I fear; as when Mrs. Hammersley, a contemp. of my mother, died, Nancy & I agreed that was the last person who would always address one as "Child." Isn't death <u>beastly</u>?

I don't mind old age so much, at least so far. But here is one lesson of N's illness, 4 1/2 years of more or less continuous pain: All medics agreed that but for her iron constitution she'd have died long ago, but she never smoked nor drank spirits, walked for miles each day, gardened etc., hence was immensely strong. Thus self-indulgent lazy types like me, who smoke & drink like mad & never walk if there's a taxi to be had, won't suffer as our lights & livers will give out in no time, don't you agree?

To Barbara Kahn   Truro, Mass.
                                                      August 31, 1973

Dearest Barb,

. . . This place is bliss though vastly overpriced—the main thing is the heaven of not staying with people for a change, which we did for the whole rest of the hol. . . .

---

27. Years later Decca said that her sister Deborah "said I cld be had up for murder, but I wasn't; by now the statute of limitations wld have run out."

28. Decca wrote her sister the Duchess of Devonshire that the "whole point" of the invitation to the head of the FBI in San Francisco was "it will be fixed up to be a terrific tease on him when he does [appear]," and she added, "Isn't it odd how people fall straight into one's plan."

Caddens: a most <u>idyllic</u> stay. Dink & Co. were hard by, so we saw them daily whilst not having to actually cope with grandchildren. Said grands are <u>far</u> nicer, or at least getting there; Jamie/Lumumba can read like a dream, he's just 6, & the other one is a comical creature. We lived off the land, Bob went clamming every day. . . .

I get lots of letters thanking for the book, mostly saying I shall start reading it shortly or something to that effect. . . . [N]o feedback as yet except for one letter. There's a chappie called F. Lovell Bixby (Marge thinks I make up 1/2 these names, like Snell Putney) who was a bigshot in corrections, now aged 75. I had corresponded with him quite a lot—never met him . . . [b]ut from his letters I cld. tell he was a right nice person & much in my line of thinking abt. prisons. So I sent him an advance copy & got a letter back which I found really moving. He said he'd settled down to read the book, read it for 3 days—and, while he agreed with much/most of what I'd put, found himself unaccountably annoyed. So he said to his wife, "She hasn't said anything about what I, and many others, tried to do to improve things." Wife answered, "I guess she hasn't set out to write about what you tried to do." After he finished it (he said), he realized that he'd spent forty years campaigning from within the system for improvements, such as classification of prisoners, indet. sentence, treatment, prison industries—and now realized he'd been wrong all along.[29] Barb. Don't you call that pretty touching? I mean, I expected the prisoners to like it, but somehow this is special. This codger was almost elected pres. of the Amer. Correctional Assn; he also said, he now regards his defeat for that job as a victory! . . .

I'll send you the Op-Ed thing when/if it appears; title is "Of Caskets, Corrections, Corpses and Convicts." The theme: similarities of 2 industries, costs, lingo, Red Menace (threatens both), secrecy of operation, etc. Socko ending along the lines that despite these similarities, there are differences, mainly, that we (undertakers) treat corpses like living people, lavishing best on them & prisoners like dead people (civil death, legal definition of prisoner's status). . . .

Fondest love, Decca

To Barbara and Ephraim Kahn   Oakland
                                                          September 23, 1973

Dear Loved Ones,

. . . The Tour was a gas, v. exhausting. Just to tell one amusing episode: I was on a thing called Kennedy & Company in Chicago, their version of Today Show, early morning news & talk. I learned that Warden Russell Lash (Indiana pen., the one who spoke at the warden's mtg. in Miami) was to be my fellow-guest; so the night before, I got hold of one of the authors of Eye for an Eye (all

---

29. Decca herself, who once noted that ending the indeterminate sentence was "the theme of my book on that subject," later lamented that "They've done it, and replaced [it] with far more punitive determinate sentences."

about that penitentiary)[30] who's now out on parole, he & his girlfriend came over to the hotel for lavish room-service dinner & we plotted what to do about Lash. L. is a v. suave, sophisticated type, & we feared he might run circles round me. However, I think it went off OK and that I nicked him a bit. It got off to a bad start from his pt. of view in 2 ways: 1) he and his beehive hairdo wife showed up about 6:45 in the green room where we were all to gather, we said howdy do etc—and suddenly who should walk in but Ed, the ex-con! Lash looked most disconcerted, mumbled something about how are you doing etc. 2) When it was our turn to be on, Kennedy (host of the show) said, "On my right is a naive revolutionary nincompoop, Jessica Mitford—I believe that's how you described her, Warden Lash?" So poor Lash, glug glug, couldn't think of much of a rejoinder. Having been well briefed by Ed, I was able to nail lots of outright lies, so that was rather fun. But then, as we walked out, Kennedy said to me in an aside, "What's that Tocsin publication? Warden Lash gave it to me when he came in & said to be sure to read it (etc)." Can you beat it? Tocsin went out of business at least 8 years ago, so apparently they are reviving that whole issue about me that was put out in 1963 and circulated to all media by the undertakers. Thus in subsequent TV & radio interviews I was able to make great hay of the that. Indiana state pen. is only about 40 miles from Chi, so TV etc. in Chi is heard there. . . .

I avoid thinking about my terrifying lectures, now at my throat, starting [this] next week. I move down there[31] tomorrow with all my gear, such as books, whiskey, coffee, cigarettes, files, vodka and I don't know what-all. Oh dear, be praying. Novelle Johnson, my adored student-assistant, came up last eve for the pty & stayed the night here, she's taken down all sorts of things such as an armchair, rug, card table for my v. monk-like room. . . . [I]t is all a terror. That's why I'm writing to you, instead of wigging about what to do. . . .

Much love, do write, Decca

To Barbara and Ephraim Kahn   San Jose, Calif.
                                                       September 25, 1973

Dearest Kahns—Eph, Barb, and Eleanor if you see her,[32]

This is going to be a Day in the Life of a Distinguished Professor—the first, in fact, and as you shall see, perhaps the last. Alas. I just put a call in to Bob's office saying I need a lawyer, but there weren't any; so instead, I write to you. It will have to be in a few acts—the exciting part will be at the end, so don't stop reading the boring parts.

---

30. *An Eye for an Eye: Four Inmates on the Crime of American Prisons Today* (Holt, Rinehart and Winston, 1970) was co-authored by four Indiana State Prison prisoners, H. Jack Griswold, Mike Misenheimer, Art Powers, and Ed Tromanhauser. Decca read it as part of her background research for *Kind and Usual Punishment.*

31. To San Jose, where Decca was to stay three days a week during her visiting professorship.

32. The Kahns generally saw Eleanor Furman during their annual trips to New York.

Act I (24 Sept.) DP rises at 5 a.m.—WHY? Because, like Barb, she's uncertain what to pack. It's only one hour to San Jose, though, she keeps saying. Packs a bit like the Owl & Pussycat, to wit: 1. Practical Burial Footwear, the actual samples she's kept intact all these years, as the University bulletin said visual things or something wld. be good; these are not only vis. but tact.[33] 2. Books & files—but which? Anyway, the poor old creature looked about the house for anything pertaining to Sociology (which is, in fact, her Department), found little—but found masses of old Tocsins about the place, so packed those. 3. Liquor, masses of, arranged by Bob. 4. Coffee, clothes etc. Left in a cloud of turtle turds, as Pele wld. say.

Act II (24 Sept) DP arrives in San Jose! Which is marvellous, in a way. She surveys her home-from-home in the Faculty Club; one rather sad note is struck in the bathroom, notice on wall saying please clean ring after each use. Clean ring, thinks D.P.? She looks, & notes a huge amt. of general filth all over said bath, so rings for ring-cleaner. Said ring-c. says DP will have to do that herself! Oh well, she shuts her poor old eyes and has a bath, flees, non-ring-noting.

Act III Sorry, this is actually pre-bath, rotten sequence. Bettina[34] & colleagues came over & took me out to a smashing lunch, various deans and near-deans as far as I cld. gather, anyway all good folks, or rather folk-esses, all women. I got smashing Novelle (me stu. asst, without whom I couldn't stir) to come, so a good time was being had by all—when—

Act IV (24 Sept) Who shld come up to say hello but the Dean (I think he was the Dean—there seem to be thousands of deans for some reason, must ask Novelle abt. that) and a rather beastly looking chap, the Watergate type, young, spruce etc. So b.l.c. greets Bettina—says, "We were classmates at U.C. Berkeley." D.P.: "Oh, then you must have been in the free-speech movement?" B.l.c. (coldly) "no, never." But he did say he's a lawyer for the Trustees here, so I said how v. fortunate, as I need a lawyer—had, in fact, just got a note from the secretary of our dept. saying I'd got to be fingerprinted!!! So I asked b.l.c. all abt. the that, & he said yes indeed you do have to be fingerprinted. I said it wasn't in me contract, and in fact I've never been fingerprinted, having discovered eons ago that you don't have to, for driving license in Calif., & have never been arrested. He said, what's your objection? I said, Suppose one was wanted for a felony conviction—it would make things so much easier for cops/FBI etc. The brute said I'd have to be fingerprinted to get my paycheck; I said, please furnish legal citations—and anyway (holding up one finger with a Band-Aid on acct. I'd broken a nail) I've got one Band-Aid, have 9 more in case of fingerprints. Bettina, Novelle & the others were all shrieking.

---

33. Decca later wrote that her students "adored" her exhibition of Fit-a-Fut Oxfords from Practical Burial Footwear.

34. Decca's young friend Bettina Aptheker was teaching once a week in the university's speech department that semester.

Interval Between Acts

All the foregoing in Act IV was, I'd assumed, mere banter, nothing substantial—that is, I was <u>scared stiff</u> of me 1st lecture, mainly, & just trying to make ordinary triv. conversation with that lawyer. I did, however, ask him for his card, and when he hadn't got one asked him to write his name & address in my diary; which Bettina & the others thought he was v. reluctant to do. But you know how unobservant I am, I just says thanks awfully, see you in court etc.

<u>Act V (25 Sept 11 a.m.)</u> DP on stage!! This morning, 11 a.m. Suffice it to say in the end I adored it, and them (students), and Marge's roarometer would have been going out of its mind. So that was all v. smashing, plus now I see exactly how to do all the others (nerves have subsided, thanks to Novelle & students, & Bettina & Ms. Mary Timothy, foreperson of A.[35] Davis jury, who came to the class). Bettina, Mary, Novelle & me all came back to lunch at the Faculty Club—where the lunches aren't actually too marvellous, yet one can have a drink in my room, liked by all—when . . .

<u>Act VI (3 p.m.)</u> A message from the head of my dept., Mr. Rudoff is his name, saying to come & see him!!! I was v. excited over that (had I already been promoted on acct. of smashing morning performance?) No. He'd had all sorts of flak re the fingerprints, plus the loyalty oath I was supposed to sign—none of this in me contract, as I ptd. out to him. He's jolly nice. Said he'd gone to get me a temporary faculty card, entitling me to library privs (fat chance!) etc., but that the Vice Pres. has said that if I don't sign the loyalty oath, they'll just cancel my classes. So I said, pity, but I shan't sign, so I'll merely swoop up my wages & run. Prof. Rudoff's idea is to just shut up about it, so is mine; teach on, and see what happens. Apparently the Deans, already noting this situation, wish to avoid what they inelegantly call a "confrontation," so do I.

<u>Act VII (6 p.m.)</u> Late news flash! Bob just called, he'd consulted ACLU, I haven't got a leg to stand on! The oath thing was fought out, & all that stuff abt. overthrow etc. dumped out by courts. . . . I'd told Novelle I shan't sign, so better not, don't you agree? Also it says "I take this obligation freely, without any mental reservation"—big deal! Was is das freely, when one's wages depend on it?[36]

> Much love from a former Dist. Professor,
> Do write—not a word from you thus far,
> Decca (R.S.V.P.)

---

35. Angela.

36. The dispute over the loyalty oath and fingerprinting ballooned into a major confrontation at the campus and in the press, which played out in part in front of Decca's lecture class, which was titled "The American Way." In the course of the dispute, Decca was fired—or, as administrators later put it, "dehired"—by a dean, who read a statement to that effect in front of her raucously supportive class. Faculty, students, and the student newspaper surprised Decca with their overwhelming support.

San Jose
October 3, 1973

I am informed by university officials that I must sign an "oath of allegiance" as a condition of my employment at San Jose State University. I have done so under protest—for although I think the requirement of any test oath is a breach of academic freedom, the language of this one is so contradictory that it seems to me to be meaningless. Faculty members with whom I have discussed it agree the oath is obnoxious, silly and demeaning.

I am asked to swear that I will "support and defend" the Constitutions of the United States and California "against all enemies foreign and domestic." I have defended to the best of my ability several provisions of these Constitutions (such as those guaranteeing racial equality, freedom of religion, speech and press) against enemies, especially domestic, and intend to do so in the future. But the annotated Constitution of the State of California runs to three hefty volumes and covers all manner of subjects. Do I support and defend, for example, Article 4 Section 25 3/4, limiting boxing and wrestling matches to 15 rounds? I don't know. Perhaps it should be 14 or 16 rounds? I do know that I could not support and defend the amendment reinstating the death penalty, which I believe conflicts with the 8th Amendment to the U.S. Constitution prohibiting cruel and unusual punishment.

The oath contains this language, added in 1952 at the height of the McCarthy era: "I take this obligation freely, without any mental reservation." Since this is hardly accurate in my case, I offered to strike these words and substitute "under duress," but was told this wouldn't be acceptable.

So where does this leave us? There is a section of the Penal Code attached to the oath, which warns that "Every person who, while taking the oath . . . states as true any material matter which he knows to be false, is guilty of perjury, and is punishable by imprisonment in the state prison [for] not less than one nor more than 14 years." Presumably, this would apply to anybody who swears he/she has taken the oath "freely, without mental reservation" when in fact he/she has taken it under duress and threat of loss of employment.

However, the same penal code would seem to contain an equally stiff caveat for university officials who require employees to swear they have signed the oath "freely" etc., when in fact signing is a condition of employment: "Subornation of perjury: Every person who willfully procures another person to commit perjury is punishable in the same manner as he would be if personally guilty of the perjury so procured."

It is all highly confusing.

Jessica Mitford

---

37. The surviving copy of this letter has no salutation. It was most likely written either as an open letter to friends, with names possibly plugged in later, or for the press or campus community.

To David Pryce-Jones   Oakland
                                                        January 16, 1974

Dearest D.,

Thanks for yours from Welsh mud—I assume you got mine, written some weeks ago re the Bobo book?[38] Anyway, I do think you could do a rather fascinating job with it. How interesting that Diana seems semi-willing to be interviewed. . . .

Of course I'd love to read the book. Not sure abt. the dedication—so much depends on thus-far imponderables, such as stance of sisters etc. . . .

One interesting sidelight (which of course for God's sake don't repeat to anyone): Nancy, in one of our few confidential chats, said she thought Diana had always been intensely jealous of Bobo on acct. of Bobo being the Fuhrer's favourite. To understand this, visualize them growing up together: Diana 4 yrs. older, a staggering beauty from childhood; Bobo, technically thought plain because of being so huge (although later she got marvellous looking, more like a monument than a pretty girl, however). They never liked each other as children, I was Diana's prime favourite—which usually happens in families, I think, the fast friends are the ones a child apart in age. Then, they appeared to be absolutely thick as thieves after both became fascists. But if N. is right, perhaps this was false front on Diana's part? . . .

Longing to see you all. . . .

Much love, Decca

To Aranka Treuhaft   Oakland
                                                        January 17, 1974

Dearest Aranka,

I've won my fingerprint case!! We just got the judge's decision,[39] since when I go around singing "Some day my prints will come . . ." As you recall, they are in a sealed envelope (the prints) in custody of the court. It was all on television last night, so I said I was going to cremate them, put them in an urn, donate them to the University and take a tax deduction for their value.

Last weekend was non-stop things to do. The party for my students was

---

38. Pryce-Jones had decided to go ahead with his biography of Unity Mitford. See letter of June 22, 1973, to Decca's friends the Kahns and Miriam Miller.

39. The resolution of the legal case came after the class had concluded. Judge William Ingram ruled, in Decca's words, "that the university's fingerprint requirement was unsupported by any 'validly adopted statute, rule or regulation'" and was therefore legally unenforceable. That decision followed a ruling in a related dispute over Decca's withheld paycheck, a controversy that had previously ended with the judge asking the university's lawyers if Decca had "performed the duties for which she was hired." Told that she had, the judge "roared," "Then pay the lady her money!"— words that she said were "immortalized in headlines in the next day's Spartan Daily."

smashing,[40] about 300 or more came (each brought a spouse or loved one), and the faculty presented me with a lovely hand-lettered plaque. Then on Monday I was on Firing Line![41] (taped, supposed to show this Sunday so do watch). Bob, Benj, Benj's Louise, loads of students & other friends came to be the "live audience," plus ex-convicts from the prisoners' union, so I felt well supported. Do say what you think of it, if you remember to watch.[42] . . .

Bob thought the Firing Line was OK and that I won against horrible Buckley, so as his opinion is the only one I care about I was pleased.

Much love from all, Dec

To the Duchess of Devonshire   Oakland
                                                 January 25, 1974

Dearest Hen,

We are <u>practically</u> on our way, it does seem so unbelievable & exciting—that is, we actually get to London on 2nd March,[43] but I'm off on various lecture things between now & then. Shall be back here in between some of them, though, so do drop a line.

You may/may not know about D. Pryce-Jones' plan to do a biography of the Boud. Anyway, a publisher just rang up to say David told him he's doing it "with your cooperation" (meaning <u>my</u> coop). As it's not quite like that, I'll put you in the picture re my position.

David got after me re this some time ago, last time we were in England for a longish while. He said somebody is bound to do such a book eventually, so why not him? I tended to agree with this as innumerable writers have written to me saying they've been commissioned by a publisher for a book on Boud & would I supply any letters etc., to which I've always replied non, non, non. In my view, if anybody does do it D. would be the best person as a) I think he's a v. good writer (I've read some of his books, & liked the interview with Nancy—did you? I can't remember), b) he seems to have a strange sort of sympathy, or affin-

---

40. Early in the semester, Decca began musing about the idea of a variety show at the end of the class "instead of exams," because it would be more fun for the students. Included in the fantasy was a conga line of her guest speakers, including "2 smashing undertakers who came to tell how we care for our dead, various Cuddums," the San Francisco bureau chief of the FBI, the local ACLU counsel, Maya Angelou, several prisoner attorneys and ex-convicts, a judge, and San Jose State dean Dan Sawrey, "who, alas, made a <u>very</u> brief appearance [in the lecture hall], as I recall . . . [he's] the one who announced to me students that I was 'dehired' (not in dictionary)."

41. A television interview show hosted for more than thirty years by acerbic conservative political commentator William F. Buckley Jr., prolific author, syndicated columnist, and founder of the *National Review* magazine.

42. Decca's claque also included her son's huge dog Jeckyll. She later said, "I had studied Buckley's technique—mostly, 'When did you stop beating your wife?'—and thanks to spirited and inspiring audience response, didn't get too badly dented."

43. The Treuhafts were renting Polly Toynbee's house in London for most of the year while Robert Treuhaft was on sabbatical from his law firm.

ity, with the actual Boud, c) I don't think he'd do the sort of sensational horror-tale that others might.

So I told him that while I am not averse to his having a go at it, the other sisters might be;[44] and that I thought it would be hopeless to try to do it in the face of family opposition, because he would need to get the things Muv left to Jonathan, interview cousins and so on; and that these would most likely refuse unless you & Diana were pro. In which case he'd be left with a bunch of yellowing cuttings from the Yellow Press, & might as well drop the idea. After that I forgot about it until now, when it seems to be hotting up again.

So that's it, Hen. I like David v. much, & think he could write a good & fascinating book. (For one thing he is evidently stuck on the idea, having been on about it for all this time, which is a prerequisite for writing anything worthwhile as any practitioner of that drear trade will affirm.) . . .

To Marge Frantz   London
                                                                                   August 29, 1974

Old Thing,

Not one word from you for ages—are you livid with me about something? Have I done some awful thing to make you cross? Well I've searched my mind, soul & conscience (which according to you wouldn't have taken long, as I know you don't think I've got much in way of above attributes), and haven't come up with <u>anything</u>, exiled as we are in this green, unpleasant land, as Wm. Blake and/or Nancy would have said. I mean, I'm far too far away to have done anything deeply annoying, aren't I?

I thought you might be coming over in the autumn, but I can see you're not, as it almost is the autumn. Do come anyway; but better check with the Kahns & Mimi, all of whom are in the planning stage but seem to be suffering from indecisitivity as Benj wld. prob. say. Room here is however limited (B. ——— ,[45] re importance of Party work on, e.g., Mexican problem: "We must mount a campaign, however limited." Do you remember?) Which brings me to this point: I'm actually at Fine Old Conflict. B. Gottlieb loved the idea. I'd sent him a draft of Dist. Prof. article & he loved that, hence that will be a late (possibly last?) chapter. B. Gottlieb claims I see all life as a conflict, with me in adversary position against all comers (such as him), so he loves the title. Somehow that wretched book, which I note from my notes has started/stopped many a time beginning literally in 1960, is starting to work. Be praying, though. Wish you were here to help, or at least in touch via letters. . . .

---

44. Within a short period, Decca was apprised of the sisters' position. As she told a friend in early March, the Pryce-Jones book "seems fair to start a medium-to-large-sized family row. . . . Debo is v. ANTI." At the time, Decca was living in London and said she had "seen lots of the Pryce-Joneses."

45. Surname omitted by editor.

[O]ur trip to America in July . . . was smashing in all ways, esp. the Dinky mob—I'm even getting to be a passably good granny now that they're a bit older. The oldest, aged 7, can do the most amazing mathematical things in his head, such as you say what's 4 times 68 and soon he comes up with the answer (grown-ups, meanwhile, busy at work with pencil & paper). Then you ask how he does it & he comes up with the most astonishing rigmarole, I never did get the hang of it. The little one, aged 4, is a face-maker like me so we spent lots of time being fish-in-tanks together. . . .

After the dread lecture in Athens, Ohio (the meal ticket for trip) I went to stay at Kay Graham's. So I was wandering about her embassy-sized house in Washington, lapping up the luxury as Benj wld. say, until she came back from work at the Post. Kay, in her incredibly nervous fashion: "Dec, how do you feel about being in the same room with Kissinger?"[46] Me, on guard: "Well, Kay, would you mind explaining the precise import of that question?" Kissinger had got theatre tix for me & Kay the following night, it transpired. So I explained that while being in same room (say he'd come for tea or something) was one thing, & as fellow-guest I shouldn't spit in his face, a theatre was another; a public place, possible gossip columnists . . . how should I ever explain it to my friends, if it got out? So I didn't go. . . .

Well there's masses more, but why should I tell as you never write or COME here which you said you might.

> Lots of love, RSVP, Dec

To the Duchess of Devonshire   London
                                        September 19, 1974

Dearest Hen,

I did adore staying with you & thanks so very much for everything. . . .

Re Diana: it's not exactly politics now (except for the feeling one must draw the line somewhere & you know all that part), it's more that having really adored her all through childhood, it makes it 10 times more difficult to have just casual meetings. That's why even our meetings over N's illness (in which Diana was marvellous) were rather agony. Do you dimly note the form of that? . . .

> Again, Hen, Millions of thanks, much love to Sophy and all,
> Yr Hen

---

46. Henry Kissinger, the powerful assistant to the president for national security affairs since 1969, had been appointed secretary of state the previous year. He had also been named co-winner of the Nobel Peace Prize in 1973 for his work on a Vietnam War peace accord but was universally despised in leftist circles for his vigorous pursuit of that war and his apparently cavalier attitude to human rights and legal process in Vietnam, Chile, and elsewhere.

To Marge Frantz   London
                                                          October 1, 1974

Old Thing:

I've just about given you up, but will have one more try. I can see the only
thing you ever really liked about me was my car registration, as that's all you've
written about in past 6 months or so. Oh well. . . .

Forward to merrier subjects, to wit, these enclosures which . . . are, in fact,
for yr. Commune.

Background: Ben Nicolson (son of Harold N,[47] I'm sure I've told about him)
and I went down [to Philip Toynbee's home/commune] for a few days. Commune is now established; the idea is to live completely off the land as Philip's
convinced civilization is on last legs & soon shall all be starving except far-
sighted folks like him. One must live on vegs. because no cows or sheep have as
yet loomed. Discomfort is, or should be, the watchword. However, when Ben
& I went, all was fairly much as usual; sherry hour starts about 11 a.m., thence
to stronger & better things, off to lunch at a blissful inn called the Crown
where Philip ordered quail—and so it went. Of course, the wretched young
couple who are the Communards weren't let in on any of the this. They actually are having windmills; also P. & I were saying how we loathe the with-it
expressions like "I'm into windmills." . . .

It's bliss having Dink and Oys here[48] (Rudbin insists Oy is a Scrabble word
for grandson), esp. since the Oys are in school all day, & Luisa[49] looks after
them when/as wanted. Also they are getting v. nice, esp. the oldest aged 7 who
can read anything, such as read all of Emil & the Detectives which has lots of
grown-up words & is quite long. . . .

There's masses more to tell, but what's the point if you never answer,

                    Lots of love anyway, Decca

To Philip Toynbee   London
                                                         November 8, 1974

Dearest Philip,

Of course you're absolutely right. Yr. letter, blinding flash of TRUTH (but
also, I thought, v. friendly in the circs).

I mean had you decided to squander your energies, emotional input or what-

---

47. Diplomat, author, and politician Harold Nicolson was married to novelist and poet Vita
Sackville-West, Ben Nicolson's mother. Ben Nicolson's brother, Nigel, co-founded the publishing
house Weidenfeld and Nicolson.

48. Constancia Romilly and her children were staying with the Treuhafts in England during a
personally difficult time for her partner, James Forman. The couple subsequently split up.

49. Luisa McCubbin was the Treuhafts' household helper during their stay in London. "Luisa's
not only a super cleaner," Decca wrote, "but at drop of hat does all marketing & cooking for dinner
parties, lunches, cocktail parties. So I'm constantly dropping hats all over the place."

ever vile phrase is now used to describe whole-hearted devotion, income, "expectations" . . . to further any one of the following causes, I should of course have been <u>totally</u> on yr. side & have turned the deafest of ears to cries, pleas, complaints & blandishments of Sally, Clara, & Lucy & Jason[50] if they had dared to object:

1) Co-operative burial society, with Barn House as central mortuary, crematory to be installed in present barn by necrophilist architect, extensive grounds for free graveyard, scattering etc.

2) Centre for prison escapers. Barn House to provide rooms for same, present barn to be re-designed to accommodate safe-cracking courses, classes in smuggling & the like, by a criminal architect chosen by the escapers.

3) Home for semi-retired piano tuners, their sisters & nephews. Quite OK as it is, actually; no architect needed, just a very slight adjustment in living arrangements, to wit: Semi-retired piano tuner's sister & nephews to occupy present Master Suite & bath, present owners to present barn, Tuner to live mostly in London with occasional amusing excursions to his semi-retired dwelling.

So do be choosing one of these. Give lots of love to God when you see him[51] & do ask him to stop being so damn jealous; I mean, what's the point? <u>We</u>'re all jealous of <u>Him</u>, speaking for myself. Also, quite cross with him, what he'd call wrathful in his boring old-fashioned way.

Yr loving Decca

To Aranka and Edith Treuhaft   Oakland
February 15, 1975

Dearest Aranka & Edith,

. . . Naughty of Dink not to thank for the fruit. My last day in London, I had lunch with my sister Pam who had sent the oys each a pound and a book for Xmas. So the entire lunch she was complaining about Debo's grandchildren: "I sent presents up to Chatsworth in plenty of time for Christmas Eve, and here it is the <u>third of January</u> and none of those children has written!" I pointed out that some of them are only about 3 so not much writers yet. But I took the hint, & as soon as we got home I wrote two childish scrawls with lots of misspellings & crossings-out: "Dere ant ~~Pm~~ pam," that sort of thing, & sent them to Debo to forward (explaining they were forgeries, & telling her to tell Pam they got sent to Chatsworth by mistake). I got a letter from Pam yesterday, saying she'd had <u>such</u> sweet letters from the boys, and she said "I fear it must have been a great effort." Little does she know . . . But I can't do the same for Dink. She's

---

50. Clara, Lucy, and Jason were Philip Toynbee's children by Sally.
51. Toynbee had had a religious conversion, which Decca teased him about continually.

just got back to NY, phoned right after you did; sounds fine, says oys are in prime shape. I sent them all birthday cards; proper ones for Dink & Chaka, and a Deepest Sympathy one for James (as it's not his birthday).

Much love, Decca

To the Duchess of Devonshire   Oakland

June 21, 1975

Dearest Hen,

. . . It's been naught but funerals from coast to coast the last 2 weeks. To wit: Cliff Durr died,[52] aged 74, actually he's been said to be dying ever since I first met him in 1940. . . .

Anyway, so this morning Bob's sis Edith rang up to say Aranka died in the middle of the night. By a terrific stroke of luck (or perhaps from E's viewpoint bad luck) Edith was staying there; despite all efforts on our part, Aranka wouldn't budge from her flat & usually nobody there at night. So Bob has scrammed to NY to see to things. Actually, an absolutely Blessed Relief as I saw Aranka a lot just a week ago . . . & she was pretty chipper. In fact I got such a touching letter from her just today. Poor old soul, when I think how I <u>loathed</u> her & vice versa when Bob & I were 1st married; but we did get to be pals as life staggered on. Do admit it's a bit of a mercy she died so swiftly, c/f some we can think of. Oh Hen. It still leaves one with a blank & drab feeling—although v. glad in lots of ways, I mean suppose she'd had to go to hospital for ages, or—horrors!—come here to live.

The Cliff memorial service was amazing, about 700 people I should think. . . . Abe Fortas, a former US Supreme Court Justice who was fired for the usual sort of thing[53] . . . went on for at least 35 minutes—trying to rehabilitate himself, I suppose.[54] So it was all of interest, to me at least.

Well Hen, that's all the news so far. . . .

Yr loving Henderson

---

52. Clifford Durr had died unexpectedly on May 12.

53. Decca had known Fortas during her years with the Durrs. At the time he was a prominent New Deal official. He was a powerful Washington attorney before his Supreme Court appointment. In 1969, Fortas resigned from the Court under pressure after a series of disclosures of alleged ethical improprieties, the most sensational of which was acceptance of a lifetime income from a foundation set up by millionaire Louis Wolfson, who had been convicted for his own, financial improprieties.

54. Decca noted in other letters that "almost nobody kept to their time limit. Also, nobody except me said anything about Virginnie, which I thought was the whole point of the exercise." Several of the long-winded talks, she said, were "all I-I-I- and me-me-me." When Decca spoke— "absolutely my least favourite thing, but Va asked me"—she kept to the five-minute time limit, as she proudly told friends. Indeed, she said, she called her daughter, Constancia, at various stops en route—because, as a nurse, she had a watch with a second hand—to time her remarks until they were well below the limit.

To Robert Treuhaft   London

October 10, 1975

Darling Bob,

Oh dear I've only been here 2 days but there's so much to tell already . . . you know how it is. So thought I must write ere it all flees my head. . . .

Mainly, you are TERRIBLY missed by one & all, but esp. by one. Goodness I'm looking forward to 17th Oct, so do be sure to turn up. . . .

Dinner last night at Pryce-Jones. . . . David is almost finished with his book, promises to send a typescript perhaps at the end of the year; so far it's all in handwriting. I do so hope it's good, even if only to squelch the sisters who continue to give vast trouble. He went to see Diana (at her invitation) & she gave him a terrific tongue lashing. I really think they are being the absolute limit about the whole thing. He showed some v. good pix of Bobo, dug up from God knows where.[55] He still thinks D.[56] (as lit. executrix) would be able to sue him if he uses Bowd's letters to me, although I can't see how, can you?

Which brings me to Harold's book about Nancy,[57] which I got 1st thing on arrival. I've been reading it on & off every spare minute, still haven't quite finished it, am longing for you to read it. It's given me a few ideas for my chapter about the family.

First off, two things about it: 1. I can't imagine it being of much interest except to people who knew her or really devoted fans who've read all her books. Much too slight, not a patch on Xopher Sykes' Waugh book. Mostly based on letters, & at that not the best letters, I feel. Silly of him not to have asked me for mine. 2. Makes her out much too "good, sweet, kind" . . . the acerbic side hardly comes through. Well I shall correct that, never fear, in mine. In fact I've about decided to concentrate on that chapter (Happy Families, or alt. title, but about seeing them all in 1955 plus other bits about them) whilst in Italy. I guess he wanted mainly to please Debo & Diana. I wonder if it's selling? . . .

He has quoted a lot of Hons & Rebs—sometimes straight, sometimes to contradict what I'd put. But he does say it's "required reading for all Mitford fans"! So maybe that'll ginger up the sales of said book. In one part he says Nancy liked H & R but the rest of the family won't speak of it.

As he wrote to please, he's omitted some frantically catty letters that I saw at Chatsworth (some, to the others, about me) which makes it v. unbalanced in my view. The uniqueness of her, & her style, doesn't come through—she seems just an amusing, rather trivial, girlish person. I'm going to start my account of her, "My mother often said 'Nancy is a very curious character,' " & then try to pin her down better than Harold has!

---

55. The source of the photographs was to become yet another bitter bone of contention among the Mitford sisters.

56. Deborah, the Duchess of Devonshire.

57. Harold Acton's *Nancy Mitford: A Memoir* was published in 1975 by Harper & Row.

Anyway, the whole thing has made me think deeply about my book. . . .

Viv was saying (re the Oakland chapter) that the family (ours) disappears altogether, except for birth of Benj—"when you wrote 'at times like this one hardly slept' (re Rollingwood)[58] what was happening to the children etc?" I know she's right, I mean Gottlieb said same re Mississippi chapter, & I think you felt the same way. So I really want to work on correcting the that. . . . As you have probably fathomed, I'm in some distress about the whole thing of Nicholas—I really can't bear to face the agony of his death in this book. So I thought I almost might just say that? Even in the foreword (which I know you say I'm always talking about but never do, but I will, I will)—something like "our adored son Nicky was born in 1944, killed in an accident at age 10, I am still too sad to write about him so have left him out."

Trouble is the whole book is changing character as it goes. If you remember, when I started it in 1960 (which is when I wrote the Financial Dir. part) it was going to be a sort of light-hearted thing a bit on the order of Lifeitselfman-ship.[59] Well it isn't, any more, and nor do I want it to be.

I think I've learned some lessons from Harold's book about how not to approach it.

Am looking forward to digging in to the Families chapter—it'll be a bit more about us, Dink, Jean St—maybe the Lily Waver[60]—and your mother, my mother . . . Muv's visit, Aranka's visits (contrast of), Europe, all that. Oh dear it sounds like a book of itself, but I'm going to really try. . . .

> Fondest love, darling Boooooby,
> do be sure to come to Italy
> if you remember,
> Dec

---

58. In 1952, Decca summoned hundreds of her political allies—Communist Party members, burly union longshoremen, and others—to come to the rescue of a black family who had moved into the previously all-white Rollingwood development in San Pablo, California, and were besieged by a raucous, rock-throwing racist mob. Until Decca arrived and braved the mob with her black friend Walter (Buddy) Green, contractor Wilbur Gary and his family were trapped without assistance in their house while a lone sheriff's car cruised the area but made no attempt to come to their aid. The rescuers Decca rounded up stayed for days, often sleeping in the house or in their cars out front, to protect the family. Decca described the confrontation in detail in *A Fine Old Conflict*. Green's first-person account is available at the *Albion Monitor* website, http://www.albionmonitor.com/decca/gary.html. See also letter of May 1, 1980, to Maya Angelou.

59. Decca's early self-published satirical booklet was published for the mass market for the first time as an appendix to *A Fine Old Conflict*.

60. See November 24, 1989, letter to Laura Shaine Cunningham for an account of the "lily-waver," a man who was exposing himself to children when the Treuhaft family was living on Jean Street in Oakland.

To Doris Brin Walker and other friends   Bellagio, Italy
                                                          October 18, 1975

Dear Comrades,

It would be too cruel to describe the beauty of this place,[61] the <u>total</u> comfort of it, to you Fraughtway[62] toilers, so I shan't. Suffice it to say it's like Chatsworth without the Devonshires, which is such a mercy, + one doesn't have to fraternize with fellow-guests except at mealtimes. (No ampersand on this typewriter, which has Italian keys, so + is it.)

Whilst in London I got a friend of mine to promise to Xerox the application, plus a memo of how to do it successfully (the applying), and gave her a list of loved ones to send it to; you are on this list, so I expect you'll all fetch up here one day. The memo includes information about how to get here if traveling with far too much hand luggage as I always seem to. As this is useful for <u>any</u> travel, I shall repeat it here: Get a young friend (in my case, Polly Toynbee in London) to ring the airline + say that a pathetic old relation who has sprained her wrist is going on Flight So + so, and could they help her with the luggage. That way, a spry young man will spring about the airport with all your stuff; or rent an iron lung at any hospital supply shop, might be even better. I've saved my bandage for the homeward trek.

The other Scholars are a pretty fraudulent lot. One is furnished with a list of the cast of characters + their projects. E.g.: Prof. Goldsmith, "a study of the national balance sheets of several major countries for ten selected years between 1850 + 1972." Well I happen to know he isn't doing any such thing, I drove in from Milan with the codger & he admitted he won't be able to get on with it because his electric computer doesn't work on the current here. Prof. Denis Sinor of the Dept. of Uralic + Altaic Studies (??? well that's what it says on the list) of Indiana U. is doing the first vol of the Cambridge History of Inner Asia. So I asked what inner Asia is + he replied that if you lop off India, the Arab countries + a few more it's what's left. Honestly.[63]

As in any other mode of existence in this vale of tears there are disabilities. As Bob has so truly said there's no such thing as a free dinner, well he might have added or a free villa. Thus the other evening Mrs. Sinor was prevailed upon to play the piano, which she did interminably + with many a false note;

---

61. Decca had been awarded a resident scholarship at the Rockefeller Foundation's Bellagio Study and Conference Center in northern Italy. The center, to use its own words, "provides a contemplative environment for convenings and residencies in which scholars, scientists, artists, writers, policymakers and practitioners from all over the world may pursue their creative and scholarly work."

62. Decca's joking term for her husband's law firm, located on Broadway in Oakland.

63. As Decca put it in another letter, "Fancy lopping off India + the Arab countries!"

unfortunately, she's a teacher of the history of music so she gave the history of each piece she played, oh dear I practically faded away from the boredom. . . .

Key to this place are Prof. + Mrs. Olson, the directors. Unfortunately they are not much my type, esp. her, she reminds me of many a governess we used to have as children. I made the great mistake of beating her twice at Scrabble, damn. Henceforth I shall try to worm my way into their hearts.

The high point of all was Bob's arrival, <u>oh</u> I was pleased to see him. . . .

Do write, you know how one longs for letters when abroad. . . .

RSVP, love to all, Dec

To Constancia Romilly   Bellagio
                                                        Nov. 9, 1975

Darling Chicky,

. . . A row of huge proportions has blown up in this serene dovecote. Background: Besides the resident scholars like us + Maya Angelou + Paul du Feu,[64] they have conferences here of abt. 20 people, in which they open up the huge staterooms that abound, we (scholars) and conferees all have dinner together. So this weekend there's one on "parliamentarian studies," whatever that may be.

<u>Act I</u> Bob and I and Maya are playing Scrab after dinner, leaving Paul to roam amongst the conferees. One had a sort of feeling this might be a mistake, as by after dinner he'd have had lots to drink + he's a bit of a barroom brawler. So sure enough all of a sudden we hear an explosion from the next room. A Scottish Labor MP called Mackintosh has just remarked about a Nigerian politician that he's a "failed wog." Paul has offered to kick Mackintosh's teeth in. Maya eventually leads Paul off to bed; Bob + I have a go at Mackintosh and other English conferees who have gathered round, trying to get through their thick heads that wog is an insulting + unacceptable word. We get nowhere with them; typical Mackintosh response, "I didn't realize Paul was married to that black girl." We don't even bother to protest "girl," feeling what's the use? I tell Mack he should send them a note of apology; he agrees to do so. And so to bed.

<u>Act II</u> No note of apology is forthcoming. About 9 a.m. the next day, which was yesterday, Paul + Maya come round to our room for a strategy conference. Their first idea had been to send a note to the Olsons (directors of this dump) saying they want to leave + find a room in the village. On 2nd thoughts, they decided to tell the Olsons they would like their meals sent to their room for the

---

64. Angelou and her husband, du Feu, had arrived for Angelou's own scholarship six days earlier and were met by Decca in Milan. On the drive back to Bellagio, Decca, as she put it, "briefed them thoroughly on all the cast of characters here—they said they knew that by the time they arrived battle lines would have been drawn and they'd find a ready-made (by me) set of friends /enemies."

duration of the conference. This turns out to be a brill. stroke of strategy—for a while, at least. Needless to say, it's a sort of demonstration of the 1st order to have made this request, so the wog remark becomes the talk of the Villa + Maya + Paul have loads of support, esp. from the non-English who get the point of what an insulting word it was etc. So they stay imprisoned in their tower room; Bob + I go visit the Little Princes in the Tower, as I call them, bring them drinks etc. Soon there's a stream of visitors, all on their side.

Act III One of the brighter English, Sir Leon Radzinowicz (Polish extraction, which makes him brighter I guess) has a long word with Mackintosh, who now realizes all are turned against him, + persuades him to go up to the Princes in the Tower for purpose of apologizing and making up. Mack. does so. Here stories of what transpired conflict somewhat. Anyway, Mack extends hand to Paul, who shakes (but he doesn't apologize, just says let's shake hands), then Maya extends hand, Mack kisses Maya's hand and either does or does not, depending on who's telling it, slap her behind! Upon which Maya smacks him in the face. Mack denies the behind slap; Maya insists he did it.

Intermission, that is, we don't yet know what Act IV will be as it hasn't happened. Bob + I are holed up in our room speculating on next steps: will Paul throw Mack over the battlements? Will Maya + Paul throw Mack over the battlements? Will Maya + Paul pull out + go home to Calif? Sir Leon, up to now strongest element of our United Front vs. wog-talk, now thinks Maya should apologize for the Mack smack; Paul thinks Mack should be forthwith evicted from the premises because of the back slap. An impasse has been reached—pity, because the demonstration (absence from meals) really was v. educational to all concerned.

The main new elements in the situation are that 1) Maya has decided to unleash Paul, up to now held in check by her, as she feels the slap was personally insulting vs. the wog talk being more abstractly insulting. 2) We think they should quit while they're ahead on points. But doubt they'll do so.

Later: Act IV. Paul came to our room about 9 a.m. with the astounding information that the Olsons have acceded to his demand to evict Mackintosh. The more amazing, because as the one and only MP here, also a full professor (means far more in England than U.S.) he's easily the Most Important Person in the Room—or was, rather, until Paul elevated Maya to that status. So, a v. clearcut victory. Mack will be put on first plane out from Milan, the du Feus will resume lunching with the crowd. But I'm afraid that does mean there'll have to be an Act V—after lunch, where we shall fathom everyone's reactions to this surprising development. Bob rather takes credit as he'd spread the word that Paul is a v. dangerous bloke to tangle with, perfectly capable of mayhem or murder, which doubtless had its effects on the Olsons whose one desire is to have everything on blandest even keel. I wonder if those Limeys have learned anything from all this? . . . I suppose I come off rather badly as I was trying to dissuade Paul from his rash determination to evict Mack; I expect now I'm almost 60 I've become a mellow old soul, not all that militant on these matters. But of course, as you can rather see, reading between the lines, I did adore the whole drama; it livened things up no end. Before it all broke loose, I had to content myself with teasing Gerda Lerner, grim feminist who talks sociologese (sample tease: Gerda: "I'm trying to structure my book . . ." Me: "Really? How very quaint, I'm trying to <u>write</u> mine."). I've got her so she doesn't know which end is up because sometimes I have a Be Nice to Gerda campaign which gets her thoroughly muddled. You know that 50's-ish song, Please Send me Somebody to Love? Mine is Please Send me Somebody to Tease. Gerda's made to order for the purpose, esp. if one gets Sir Leon and nice Mr. Graham Storey in on the tease, which they rather love. It's almost lunch time (pre-lunch aperitifs in 10 minutes) so will be back in a flash with Act V. (I expect you're wondering when I get my book written? Well I am getting on a little bit, but as you can see there are certain distractions.) Bob, of course, twinkles away at it all and only comes in on serious matters of principle such as wog talk. By the way, are you on to "wog"? It's sort of an English equiv. of nigger, fuzzy-wuzzy etc. Every English child of my day had a gollywog, as essential a toy as a teddy-bear, which was a hideous black cloth doll with fuzzy hair, huge red lips etc. Oooh it's going to be interesting to see what they all say at lunch . . .

<u>After lunch: Act V.</u> It was a subdued lot that gathered for aperitifs this noon. I was down first (to savour the action as it developed), and got there just as Mackintosh was being hustled off into a waiting car to take him to airport. Bill Olson now claims God or somebody similar came to his rescue. Bland Bill, you understand, was fairly terror-struck by the whole episode, so counter to his whole nature—hail-fellow-well-met, a greeter by predilection and avocation. Here is his odd version: The other day a dead body, someone who had apparently been murdered, was found in Mackintosh's garden in Scotland. (Actually, I know this part because Mack. had told me of this odd occurrence <u>before</u> the crisis, when we were great chums on acct. of him being a Labor M.P. Rather odd, isn't it? I see Scotland is getting just like NY.) So, said Bill, Mackintosh has to give evidence at the inquest, hence the police called and urged his return. Like ducks, as Benj wld. say, because a) nobody gives evidence on Sunday esp. in Scotland, it would be unheard of, and b) Bill let drop that the inquest is several days off. So, it's well-known face-save on all sides. The du Feus appeared, and I forebore a standing ovation which would have been a typically hopeless + disruptive Dec move, although I did long to stand + clap.

That's about all, and <u>about enough</u> you'll be saying at this monstrous long letter. Sorry, but it was of interest to us while it lasted.

What will Paul do next?

How will they survive after we've left?

Will Bill spill the <u>real</u> beans (how he engineered the Mack sack)?

Time will tell, but I shan't as I must be getting on with my book. . . . Also forgot to say I was murmuring to various conferees last night how I was going to write it all up, + did they think it would go best in Sunday Times, or Observer? Just a tiny stimulant, on my part, as I've no intention whatsoever of writing it up except in a letter to toi; but they fair panicked at the thought, which was nice.

Fondest love . . . Mama

To Robert Treuhaft

Calhoun College, Yale University,
New Haven, Conn.[65]
January 16, 1976

Darling Bob (also Dobby & Co if interested):
. . . Went to lunch (by the way, meals here are as 'twere in a prison or hospital: lunch 11 to 1, dinner 5 to 6:45) and was waylaid by several students who had applied & not been admitted to my pathetic class.[66] What to say to them? You can imagine the quandary. . . .

Anyway this afternoon has been <u>torture</u>, approx. six of the unadmitted either telephoned or came over to plead their cause; they were all absolutely smashing, I explained most sadly how frightful it had been choosing & how I longed for them, but couldn't have more than 18, & how it wouldn't be fair to chuck over the ones already accepted. So here I was, in mourning for the unadmitted, when a note arrived from one Dean John Palmer, the dean of one of the other colleges. He pleads for his student ——,[67] an extremely qualified young man etc. etc. who is floored by not getting in the class. So I consult <u>my</u> dean, blissful Mark Ryan (blissful so far, that is; I suppose one shouldn't judge these deans & things too early on), and he said it was quite a bit out of line for Dean P. to have sent this message; I said I'd call Dean P., & point out the difficulties.

WELL! Here's what Dean P said when I called (prefaced by all the pish tosh about how he knows the difficulties I am facing etc.): ——, the student in question, is devastated by not getting in. He was really counting on it, he's bright, brilliant, dedicated. So I said oh dear what a pity but so are lots of others & it would muck up the class no end to have all these smashing types, as I was hoping for a splash of concentrated work with a few. Well (said Dean P) ——'s only interest in life is journalism. So (said I) why doesn't he go to Columbia or some-

---

65. A month after the *Atlantic Monthly* published "My Short and Happy Life as a Distinguished Professor," Decca received an invitation from the dean of Calhoun College, who had read the article, inviting her to teach a semester-long seminar there on "Muckraking and Investigative Journalism." He assured her there were no fingerprint or loyalty-oath requirements.

66. Decca's first "dread task" upon arriving for her guest lectureship was to select eighteen students for her class from almost two hundred worthy applicants. Her selection criteria were doubtless unorthodox for Yale. For example, she said she couldn't pass up the student who wrote on his application, "I think I would make a good journalist as I am tall enough to look over walls and thin enough to hide behind trees."

67. Name omitted by editor.

where which has a reg. journalism department? No, said Dean P, more in sorrow than in anger; when he leaves here he will take his place in charge of a huge newspaper empire as heir. . . . Heavily implying that I had been extremely thick-headed not to have admitted this scion of the newspaper industry. Damn, there goes any chance of good reviews of me book in [that paper]. Can you beat it, aren't they <u>awful</u>? Shall sick my students on Brute Palmer.

Comes the clincher: Palmer then said, "Forgive me for asking a personal question but are you a member of the English Mitford family?" Yes, said I. "I used to date Unity a lot," said Palmer—he was a Rhodes scholar before the war. So I said I should adore to meet him . . . and do let's get together soon. . . .

To Robert Treuhaft   New Haven
                                                  January 20, 1976

Darling Bob,

It's 8 a.m., day of first class, you can imagine how over-excited I am.

Well! Last evening about 9 there was a knock on my door and it was ——, [newspaper] scion . . . in person. . . . Goodness I'm glad he's not in the class. As I think I told you, his card was in the "favoured" pile for a bit until I noted he'd put "I might possibly learn something useful in this seminar"; the "possibly" did him in. . . . He said he had come because he wanted to know what criteria I had used in selecting students? I told him it had been v. difficult, faced with all these excellent-sounding people, some of whom had attached articles they'd written. He said he didn't see how any of them would have had superior experience to his own, since he has worked for many summers on newspapers. I explained that didn't count for everything—some applicants who I accepted explicitly said on their cards that they don't intend to be journalists but want the experience of gathering info. for other reasons. He then said that many students flatly lie on their applications, and gave examples. I said I shouldn't wonder, as when I was their age I used to flatly lie on job applications; anyway, I had no way of knowing. He told me he'd looked me up in Who's Who and discovered I'm not a journalist at all, in the sense he means it, just the author of some books. He also asked if students would be required to turn in weekly stories? No, said I, that's not the idea at all. They will more likely be working on subjects that will take up the full 3 months; some may not even produce a finished article in that time. Had I any newspaper experience, he demanded to know? No. In that case, the seminar wouldn't have done him any good—he's <u>glad</u> he's not in it. He was misled by the course description. (Balls. I looked up said course description after he left, it's not at all misleading.) . . .

Gottlieb called. Used words like "absolutely blissful" re the Happy Families chapter. . . . But now, of course, he wants much <u>more</u> on the families. . . . I said in that case I should be requiring a larger advance, as it will take so much longer to do. We shall see . . . Anyway, I'm v. glad he likes it, although I'd rather forgotten about it in all the excitement of preparing me class, you know how one-track my mind is. . . .

I told him I'd love to do a text book—the point is, that just the planning for today's class sort of shows what it could be like: the story-behind-the-story of various articles, how one chooses a subject, all the technique bit from interviewing to picking other people's brains (such as getting Alex Frantz[68] to do all the ratios, percents etc.). He was not thrilled at the idea; but I think I will do it anyway, after Fine Old is finished.[69] What say you? . . .

> Fondest love . . . Decca

To Barbara Kahn   New Haven
                                                                January 28, 1976

Dearest Barb,

. . . Tuesday was me second class, none of the alternates showed up thank God (the 1st class was jammed with people waiting to see if some of those admitted didn't show), and all the original 18 did. . . . Anyway they are smashing beyond all hopes. The crucial thing is, will they be Dears & choose interesting yet manageable subjects to investigate, as I keep begging, or will they put down grandiose things like Mental Health & get totally lost? But I think they are quickly getting the point. They come up here quite a lot to discuss these matters (by appointment—I said they could call any time, rather rash as they do, they do—yet I so long to get them quickly on some definite track) & I must say I find them v. good value. Some are a trifle mercurial & seem to have picked about 6 topics, which I should have thought quite impossible with all the rest they've got to do here, so I try to get them more pinned down. Here's one idea that I thought awfully interesting: One boy (my tall, thin lad . . .) when he was in high school got a letter from an outfit called Who's Who in High School, saying that he had been chosen as one of 4% of the nation's high school graduates to be included in their volume, which he could have for $25, plus another $5 if he wanted his photo printed in the book. Have you ever heard of this racquet? Naturally tall/thin was terribly proud, would have plunged at once with his $25 had not his canny parents intervened. But visualize boy/girl in midwest, south, getting this letter; parents overjoyed, buy copies for all the folks, don't you agree they might? Anyway, it sounded like a good thing to look into. Have you ever heard of it? . . .

Dink & James came for the night last Sat., <u>oh</u> what a super-treat for me. Actually it's not a bad oy-hangout, as in the nick of time I discovered there's a colour TV set right downstairs plus a games room with pinball machines & other pleasures such as ping pong & billiards. . . . One rather embarrassing

---

68. The youngest son of Marge and Laurent Frantz.
69. Decca did indeed publish a book much along these lines three years later: *Poison Penmanship.*

thing happened: there was an old copy of Psychology Today lying around, & it had in it IQ tests that college undergraduates with an IQ of 100 or less had found difficult. I had tried them, but couldn't work out most of them. James seemed to do them quite quickly. Then the Master (Master Davis) dropped round for a drink, & James unfortunately gave him the tests, which he failed miserably. . . .

Much love to all, Dec

To David Pryce-Jones   New Haven
                                                  February 26, 1976

Dear David,

Your manuscript[70] arrived yesterday, needless to say I've been at it every possible minute. I found it incredibly upsetting, but then what else could it be? I mean stirring up, from my point of view. In fact to calm my nerves I made a list of a few things that might be inaccurate (although totally unimportant) which I attach. . . .

It's an extraordinary book, totally absorbing (well obviously it would be to me) and a tour de force of research the likes of which I've never seen. Simply amazing, all you found out, the people you saw—as you know, I didn't know the half of it even for the years we were all together, let alone the German/Hungarian bits.

On to the substance. (I shan't even try to comment on your view, which I think is all wrong, that Fascism/Communism were 2 sides of coin; that would take a year's debate; I can only say that if you'd been around in those days you would never have made this equation.)[71] But about Bobo's actual character. You've got it terribly well <u>up to a point</u>. What you said when I telephoned to you in Wales abt. her making the Jews blub while she was measuring the flat for curtains[72]—the total vileness of that side of her, which as your book shows became the dominant side—well there's no forgiveness possible (nor would it have been sought by that feckless, unregenerate soul).

---

70. The draft of the book *Unity Mitford: A Quest*, which was published later in 1976 by Weidenfeld and Nicolson.

71. The view Decca expressed here was one of her strongest and most consistent convictions, as it had been of her first husband, Esmond Romilly. Biographer Kevin Ingram quoted the Romillys' friend Selden Rodman as reporting in his journal, just before Romilly shipped out to England, "He did not agree that in practice Nazism and communism are opposite sides of the same coin."

72. In his biography of Unity Mitford, Pryce-Jones described her hunt for a new apartment in Munich: "On Hitler's orders, his private office offered her a short-list of four apartments in Munich requisitioned from Jews in the aftermath of the *Kristallnacht*. . . . She inspected the four apartments. Some of the Jewish owners, on the eve of their forcible dispossession, were still in their homes, actually looking at her and listening to her in the very rooms which Unity was absorbed in measuring up, imagining colour schemes and decorations and improvements. She was oblivious to the cruelty of the scene."

Bob's view, which he said after reading quite a lot of yr. book but before my copy arrived here at Yale, was what I told you: "stupid, sadistic, physically ugly—sausage fingers—childish" etc. etc. Having now read it, I can see that all that <u>is</u> attested to by your various interlocutors. And quite rightly, I mean that's all clear from all records, esp. fondness for darling Streicher,[73] plus everything else you've discovered, plus my own recollections (which I never did put in Hons & Rebs as too revolting) of her gloating over a battered behind of elderly Jewess in <u>Brown Book of Hitler Terror</u>, oh dear well it's all so awful, anyway you've found it all out so why go on.

So what was lovable about her? That was what I meant to write to you about, yet now I've got to that point I can't think quite what to say. I see that M. Ormsby-Gore[74] is v. cold to her in yr. book, yet all I remember of them is that they were utter bosom friends, adored each other, shrieked without stopping—but about what? And why did I adore her, which I really did—Bob says oh you probably had a romantic view of her, but that's not quite right either. There is a dimension, or facet, of her character missing in your book; but what is it, exactly? Trying, trying to think back. Well she was so 'uge & obdgegjoinable, such a joke, after Wigs on the Green partly a Nancy-created joke—and she (Bobo) saw the joke of herself. I see you quote a few people as saying she was "amusing" yet they don't give examples, perhaps because her sui generis form of amusingness is really untranscribable. I can't think of any examples, either. Rudi Simolin[75] comes closest, of all the people you quote, to showing that side of her. Note also Betjeman:[76] "UV[77] <u>was</u> funny, she had a lot of humor which doesn't come out in the accounts of her." There; if you can make any sense at all of this ramble, please add it to where you quoted me. (<u>Not</u> the part abt. Brown Book of H. Terror, please.)

---

73. Julius Streicher was a rabid, sadistic anti-Semite and an early friend and backer of Hitler (he carried Nazi Party membership card no. 2; Hitler's was 7). Publisher of the virulently racist publication *Der Stürmer*, Streicher has been called "the spiritual organizer" of the Nazi campaign against the Jews, and he boasted of personally inflicting cruelties against Jews, including a notorious incident in which he ordered some Jews to tear out the grass in a meadow with their teeth. Pryce-Jones's book quotes Unity Mitford as calling him "darling Streicher." Unity reportedly told a friend that Streicher was her favorite Nazi, and she praised him publicly and appeared at his hate rallies. Streicher was found guilty of war crimes at the Nuremberg trial and was executed in 1946.

74. Mary Ormsby-Gore was a good friend of Unity Mitford from their days as debutantes together. She saw a lot of Unity in Germany when Ormsby-Gore was married to Robin Campbell, a Reuters correspondent in Berlin.

75. A friend of Unity's in Germany, now Baroness von St. Paul. Although it's impossible to know what precisely it was that Decca found accurate in her portrayal of Unity, Simolin did speak of her freedom, her practical jokes. She was also quoted by Pryce-Jones as saying that Unity's "only hope was to shock people and make them shut up with outrage, and she excelled at that. How much sense and responsibility do you feel at twenty-four? She was a romantic. She would act the heroine, and war would be avoided, like in a simple fairy tale."

76. Poet and critic John Betjeman, a member of Diana Mitford's circle when she was married to Bryan Guinness, was friendly with all the Mitford sisters.

77. Unity Valkyrie Mitford.

Another thing you might do (since I have such trouble sorting all this out in my own mind) is to quote from Hons & Rebs . . . ("I pondered over the unsolvable riddle" etc), because that is where I really did try to come to grips with my own feelings for Boud. I think this would help a lot, esp. as you've quoted me about how sullen & rude she was in Sweden. At least from my viewpoint, it would give a far more rounded picture of how I saw her. In fact I really urge you to do this, if it is still possible in the context of printing deadlines etc. . . .

I'm v. glad you stuck it to Sir O. Mosley about that cable ("power of Jewish corruption"), ditto to Skidelsky[78] whose book struck me as a total puff-piece for Sir O. Nancy used to call Mosley "the quiet European" which I thought pretty funny.

Your point that it was now or never to do this book (people dying off) was certainly borne out. I do think you've done a marvellous job. And THANKS for leaving me out of acknowledgments—as it is, I expect Debo will be on non-speakers for the next forseeable bit of time, although my part in it turned out to be v. minimal. (Needless to say, <u>no</u> dedication, please!) . . .

> Much love to all, Decca

To Maya Angelou   Oakland
                                                                   September 16, 1976

Dear Miss Absolutely Amazing Thing,

Here goes with a comment or two abt. your <u>really smashing</u> book.[79] I should start by saying I think it's the best you've done yet—although this may displease you, because you'll be thinking well what about the other ones? (Reminds me of a Philip Toynbee story about a young writer he knew whose first novel was reviewed in the Times as "one of the best first novels I have read in more than a decade." The writer was thrilled until he started examining that sentence, then exclaimed furiously "<u>ONE</u> of the best? More than a <u>DECADE</u>?")

The actual writing, use of language, is terrific; I presume that the intense discipline of poetry, where the precise choice of each word, the cadence of each line, is so important has stood you in good stead. There are some <u>superb passages</u> all through the book—I meant to mark them, but there were too many. Shall do so on a re-reading. (One <u>wee</u> criticism on this score, & the only one: p. 183 "a party she planned to host." I happen to dislike this usage, straight out of P.R.)

---

78. Pryce-Jones wrote in his book that Robert Skidelsky, author of *Oswald Mosley* (Macmillan, 1975), failed to explore the relationship of Mosley and his movement to the virulently anti-Semitic Streicher. In what he called "a most extraordinary omission," Pryce-Jones said that Skidelsky nowhere mentioned a telegram that Oswald Mosley sent to Streicher—publicized in the Nazi press—saying, "The power of Jewish corruption must be destroyed in all countries before peace and justice can be successfully achieved in Europe."

79. Angelou's third autobiographical book, *Singin' and Swingin' and Gettin' Merry Like Christmas* (Random House, 1976).

Of the themes that run through, the ones I found totally fascinating from the pt. of view of yr. treatment of them were 1) the formation of black/white friendships, 2) the whole Guy[80] bit.

The first is of special interest to me as I see it all from the other side of the fence, so to speak, & it evokes so vividly <u>my</u> terror of inadvertently putting a foot wrong (and stepping on black toes) in the early CRC days. Had it not been for the guidance—and often FURIOUS CRITICISM—of Hursel, Buddy, Matt C.[81] et al, I should never have been able to steer myself through those dangerous shoals. . . .

The Guy bits are lovely & will also have a universal fascination for all us rotten mummies who because of our drive to do something neglected our wretched (but beloved) brats.

What else. I could write a book about your book because I found it so intensely moving, spirited throughout, survival sense that I find so attractive. . . .

The other thing is, it happened to arrive on my birthday. For some unknown reason, turning 59 was rather beastly. I mean, as you know I don't a bit mind getting old & ugly, as it is the fate of all humans (except a few like Kay Boyle, but then they work like mad at being old & beautiful, which I have neither the time nor inclination to do). The usual traumatic birthdays—30 and 40—had no effect on me. Perhaps it was the advent of Dink & Oys; James born 9 years ago, seems like yesterday, ditto Dink born 35 years ago—anyway, the musty & disagreeable wings of the Angel of Death seemed to be fluttering about in the kitchen.

So when yr. book came in the post, it was the most tremendous lift, & recoloured the whole day, because I sat straight down to read it, & there was a lovely breath of life. . . .

Idea: How about one day, when/if both of us has the time, expanding a trifle via a conversation between the two of us about the black/white friendship thing? We could talk it out, or exchange letters about it (possibly the best way, as I hate those tape-recorded things), and eventually work it up into an article, or book, or something. I think it might be rather a good thing, as I know that for my part there's masses of those nuances . . . that I never put into mine. E.g., your book page 104, "There was a saying . . . what ails you?"[82] So interesting to me, because in the 50's . . . stalwart Marge, working her head off in all the defense activities for Blacks, was brought up on charges by a Black worker in CRC for looking sloppy on the picket line, & for never having her hair properly done. She was disgracing the picket line etc. There is a subtle & interesting point here. I mean, Marge never would, never could, be well-dressed or well-

---

80. Guy Johnson is Angelou's son.

81. Hursel Alexander, Walter (Buddy) Green, and Matt Crawford.

82. Angelou had described her family's reaction to Phyllis Diller, with whom she shared a billing: "Black people rarely forgave whites for being ragged, unkempt and uncaring. There was a saying which explained the disapproval: 'You have been white all your life. Ain't got no further along than this? What ails you?' "

turned out, it isn't her style. Yet one did see the point of the black comrade who felt demeaned by said sloppiness of Marge. Some of these sensitive & complicated points, developed via the 2 sides of fence, might be of interest?

Sorry to be so long-winded, I just wanted to say how much I adore yr. book, Fondest love, Dec

To Pamela Jackson   New York
                                                                                    October 4, 1976

Woman:

I was absolutely enraged by your foul letter, implying that I've stolen one of Debo's scrapbooks & given P-J photos from one of Muv's scrapbooks. As you well know, Muv left all hers to Jonathan Guinness so why don't you get after him. I have practically no photos of Bobo, & have given none to P-J. There are, obviously, huge amounts to be had in newspaper offices & I suppose that is how he got them.

Once & for all, the sequence of the P-J book:

1) As I told Debo at the time, I advised him not to go ahead without access to Bobo's papers, left to J. Guinness by Muv.

2) He went & saw Diana, who apparently whetted his appetite & told him all sorts of things that I for one didn't know about Bobo.

3) Ditto his interview with Nancy published a few years ago in D. Telegraph.

4) Seeing he was determined to proceed, & had in fact gone to Germany to see various decaying old Nazis such as Putzi Hanfstengel[83] or however he spells his hideous name, I thought best to put P-J in touch with people who could give a more sympathetic view of Boud than he would otherwise get from her—so to speak—public life: Rud, Timmo, Clementine etc.

5) You say he'd never have gone ahead if I hadn't helped; totally untrue. Mine was v. minimal, as you'll see if you ever read the book. I knew naught about the St. Margarets Bushey Herts[84] part, naught about the German part. In fact I never saw Boud again after early 1937. My thoughts about that strange character were set down in Hons & Rebs, which you probably haven't read; anyway, I asked P-J to quote what I'd said & he did. He would have done the same for all of you.

---

83. Dr. Ernst (Putzi) Hanfstaengl was a Munich heir and an old friend and early supporter of Hitler, who later placed him in charge of the Nazis' foreign press relations. Diana and Unity Mitford met him in London. Hanfstaengl facilitated their access to Nazi rallies and the party hierarchy in Germany. He later fled Germany after he suspected he was marked for murder by Hitler—as a result of indiscreet comments he made to Unity Mitford that he presumed she had relayed to Hitler.

84. St. Margaret's in Bushey, Hertfordshire, was a boarding school attended by a number of Mitford cousins. Unity Mitford was expelled from the school for rebelling against the rules.

6) Am sending a carbon of this to Debo, with assurances that I did not pinch her scrapbook.

Decca

To Sonia Orwell   New York

October 14, 1976

Dear Sonia,

I <u>was</u> pleased to hear from you—Bob read your letter out, as I am in NY doing the final-final sprucing of my book (which, amazingly, is finished; I never believed it would be, after all these years). . . .

Well, the P-J book flap.[85] <u>Oh</u>. By now you'll have seen the piece in Sunday Times, & 2 stories in Ev. Standard, & will prob. have talked to David who can fill you in on the sisterly efforts to suppress the book. The Mosleys are leading this, we suppose because things in the book will undercut Sir O's attempts to rehabilitate himself via his own autobiog.[86] & Skidelsky's more or less official, or authorized, biog in which Sir O. never really was all that anti-semitic etc.

As for the family side, I got a letter from Woman virtually accusing me of <u>stealing one of Debo's scrapbooks</u> from her drawing-room & giving the photos to David. This put me in a blind rage so I wrote an absolutely livid letter, with a carbon copy to Debo; I fear it's curtains with me & the sisters.

Ld. Weidenfeld[87] is in NY, & I had a long chat with him. David will know all the details (Andrew Devonshire's surprisingly conciliatory role etc) so will skip that. The main pt is that W. wants me to review it for the Eve. Standard. My first inclination was non, non, non; but thinking it over, I just might do it. Diana's done a scorcher for Books & Bookmen, & I think I'd want to see hers first. I had been thinking of writing my own letter to the papers blasting the efforts to suppress; possibly I should do this in a review? What do <u>you</u> think? . . .

[I]f I review it, I think I'll concentrate more on my own (minimal) role in it, & on the dismal business of the sisters getting a powerful crowd to try & stop it.

Now, here's the thing: don't tell anyone but I think I'll be coming to London in December for a short spell. Do you remember how Michael Barnes of BBC was keen to do a 60-min programme about my life in Calif? Maybe I never told you, as a) it seemed a slightly embarrassing idea—60 mins on one's poor old life. But now it seems to be firmed up, & the plan is that I should come to England for bits of filming with P. Toynbee (if he agrees), Claud Cockburn and the

---

85. Sonia Orwell had said in her letter that there seemed to be a "fair fuss" on David Pryce-Jones's biography of Unity Mitford.

86. *My Life* (Thomas Nelson, 1968).

87. The chairman of Weidenfeld and Nicolson, publishers of David Pryce-Jones's book on Unity Mitford.

ilk, people from one's dim past; then Michael & crew come to Calif to do bits on ex-convicts, morticians, students at San Jose etc. The Deb. Rogers folks wrote to say it's all set, so perhaps it is. I don't care either way, should be just as pleased if it falls through because this seems an awful time to come to England with all the fuss about the Unity book. . . .

Decca

To the Duchess of Devonshire   Oakland
                                                 October 26, 1976

Hen:

I don't know where we stand, having no word from you since I sent you a carbon copy of my letter to Woman. I was in a blind rage when I wrote it, & I bet you'd have been, too, had you been the target of those snidely-phrased accusations. Here's exactly what she said, copied from her letter:

"Some of the photographs were in Muv's album so I suppose you gave them to him. You could have asked us first if we wished them to be published. The album full of newspaper cuttings & photographs that Debo always had in her drawing room is missing & can't be found anywhere. Did you borrow it perhaps, as I believe you are writing your own life. If so we would all like to have it back."

All incredibly infuriating & I can't help thinking you and/or Diana may have put her up to it. . . .

I shan't say any more about my part in it as I've said it all a thousand times before. I do think that the sisterly efforts to suppress it (led by Sir O. Mosley, as I gather from the newspapers) were most ill-advised, a rotten thing to do & from your point of view disastrous as it gave the book enormous pre-publication publicity.

I'm mainly <u>terrifically sad</u> to think that perhaps this all means it's curtains for us, that we shan't be seeing each other any more or writing. If so, that's absolutely up to you, I mean if you don't answer this obviously I shan't have another try. So as this is prob. my last letter, it may be rather long (sorry Hen, I know how you loathe reading long things but here goes).

There were obviously deep things to be said, dating from more or less child-hood, that I was really unaware of until <u>1974</u>, 37 years after the event, when you said that my running-away without telling was the worst thing in your life. I was v. astounded, and I honestly think you've revised all that, somehow, in yr. mind; as I remember us in those days, we weren't all that adoring. That is, we weren't interested in the same things and I was probably v. jealous of you for being so much prettier; it was far more Boud & me, strangely enough. Then you also admitted (in 1974, when we went over all this) that if I had told about running you'd have told Muv & Farve, so do admit my instinct <u>not</u> to tell was right.

That whole year in England (1974) was a bit strained, as far as you & I were concerned. I suppose the P-J book was already a cloud, no bigger than a man's hand. But also, I noted that you excluded me completely from anything to do with H. Acton's book.[88] I asked you if you'd like to have any letters from Nancy to me, & you said no you'd got tons of letters, mine were not wanted. Then H. Acton asked if he could quote from Hons & Rebs & I said of course, & he did, extensively, but only to contradict everything I'd said. You & Woman were closeted with him about the book, but not me.

I admit that at that point a certain stubbornness set in; I mean, why should you be the final arbiter of everything about the family? It was a bit maddening, so when you issued the Directive to the cousins etc. not to talk to P-J I did not feel bound by this, on the contrary. In fact, they were the only ones who brought out a bit of the true Boud we know.

To chuck in a reminder about a couple of other things: Not only didn't I steal your photo album, I sent you all the Muv letters from the Isle for max. arch. conditioning.[89] Ditto, I sent anything else any of you asked for from the Isle, such as Nancy's bookcases she wanted, yr. writing table, Woman's table. As Bob remarked at the time, "your sisters know the price of everything and the value of everything." (A paraphrase, Hen, in case you hadn't noted. See Oscar Wilde.)

Needless to say I've been asked to review the P-J book by mags & newspapers from hither to yon; so far I've said non, non, non. But I may yet do it, haven't seen the finished vol. If I do, though, it will prob. be more about the drear efforts to squash the book than a review of the actual book. Haven't decided, but thought I should say this so as not to be accused (once more) of duplicity.

Well Hen I'll be coming to England in December. . . .

I don't know if Abyssinia, am anyway in floods of tears re-reading this last letter, so will close with love,

              Henderson

To Sonia Orwell   Oakland

              November 5, 1976 ("Gunpowder, Treason & Plot")[90]

Dearest S.,

Advice in yours of Oct. 29[91] absolutely spot on, so am taking it to the letter, viz: buttoning the old lip. No word from Debo so far, so who knows. Am bring-

---

88. The Nancy Mitford memoir.

89. See discussion of "maximum archival conditions" in letter of August 24, 1964, to the Duchess of Devonshire and related footnote.

90. Decca's reference in the dateline of her letter is to the origins of Britain's Guy Fawkes Day, November 5.

91. Sonia Orwell had sent Decca a long analysis of David Pryce-Jones's book. She explained to Decca why her sisters might have despised the book and how they could have come to the conclusion that Decca played more of a role than she did in its preparation. Orwell advised Decca not to comment on the book in broadcasts or book reviews unless she was prepared to discuss in depth personal questions, including reported attempts by members of her family to "suppress" the book.

ing all correspondence when I come, so you'll see what's what. As I can't live forever in the slough of despond I'm sort of getting over it (the sadness re sisterly estrangement), & am <u>much</u> looking forward to staying with you.

Your letter <u>was</u> fascinating, to be answered in person when we actually settle down to chat. The "painful moment of some sort of truth with the sisters"[92] is <u>so</u> accurate. Actually it's all been skating on the surface (sometimes over v. thin ice) with said sisters over the years, including of course Nancy; or perhaps specially with Nancy.

Involvement of my family with Nazis: the only real surprise, to me, was Tom—I'd actually no idea of how for them he was. Never breathed as much to me & Esmond, he was the only one who liked E & vice versa. Pam, too Woman-like if you see what I mean (dim-brained), Debo too young to have been very much in it. Also, both completely bored by politics.

Oh well this is just a telegraphic message to say am longing to see you. . . .

Much love, Decca

To the Duchess of Devonshire   Oakland
                                                     November 19, 1976
Hen of course I want to be friends, that was the whole point of writing as I did. I can't begin to say how pleased I was to note yr. envelope, having been passionately looking through my post for it day after day. I absolutely agree that we'd mind terribly if we cut it off—I know I would, in fact I've been incredibly upset because when you didn't answer for such a long time I thought you'd decided on this dread course. Bob & everybody here noted I was deeply miserable & v. shaken; but you know how difficult it is to explain to anyone outside the family so it was SUFFERING IN SILENCE.

To answer: As for being deeply divided in thoughts about many things, that is v. true. I sometimes have felt a trifle hurt that you are totally uninterested in things I write etc., but on the other hand I admit I'm not much of a hand at farming or horse shows! So I suppose we're about even on that score. But I also agree about the ancient ties being far stronger than the fact we happen to have completely different interests & viewpoints.

I don't think the P-J book itself should divide us, but I do fear your attitude to me re it might. You seem to think I'm in some way responsible for it, although I've told you dozens of times exactly what I did & why—and I was glad, at least, that you thought the quotation from Hons & Rebels was good. I

---

92. Orwell's letter discussed Decca's isolation from the political and personal troubles that had beset her family since her departure for the United States. She felt that some of the issues with family members had to be settled directly with them and in any case could not be resolved or explained adequately in brief public comments.

agree with much you say about the book.[93] . . . However I also thought the efforts to suppress it very wrong,[94] so to me the shortcomings of the book faded before that.

The way it came across to us here, from the newspaper accounts, was that Sir O. Mosley was leading the pack for suppression. . . . Of course I realize your motives (suppression-wise) are v. different, as you said in yr. letter. Anyway, that is why I came to the defence of the book when the Sunday Times man rang up. In fact if I had reviewed it (which I'm not going to) that is what I shld. have stressed, the Mosley effort to suppress not the book qua book.

In your letter, you go very lightly over the main divider, viz. Woman's really vile accusation of scrapbook thievery, & that I gave P-J photos out of Muv's albums (which as you very well know I haven't got, & never did). You say you "didn't try to stop her" writing, so I assume she did discuss it with you? Also you say "we must all be allowed a point of view," well I don't call implying I'd stolen your scrapbook a "point of view."

Woman's written too, saying let's forget it all but she also says not one word about her letter re the scrapbooks. So while I'd love to forget it, I can't bring myself to write to her pretending all is OK when it isn't at all, with me. In fact I think she bloody well ought to apologize and you might tell her this.

There's another thing, this BBC film. Essentially it's about Calif (Civil Rights Congress in the 1950's, funerals, prisons, other aspects of Calif life). But also there'll be some brief background out of Hons & Rebels, & of course Boud will come into that. What I intend to do is to say all you said (I might even crib your very words—"huge bold truthfulness, funniness, generosity, courage"[95]) and particularly to say how much we all adored that amazing character. After she died, which was just after Muv came to stay here, I wrote to Muv saying that in a way I had mourned her as dead when politics first parted us. Muv wrote back, "Yes, I suppose Bobo also mourned you in that sense, she knew you would probably never meet again, but her love for you was quite unchanged. When I gave her your love when I came back she knew it was with one part of you, I could see by her face. I think you both understood each other. I remember saying to you, I am so glad you sent a message, after all we shall all be dead soon. But how little did I think she would so soon go away, I thought I would be the first." Hen I wrote all this out from Muv's letter because that is the sort of idea

93. In her letter to Decca, the duchess had been scathing in her denunciation of the Pryce-Jones book, calling it "hateful on every page" and "insulting in an insufferably condescending way re Muv & Farve." She said the book missed Unity's personality entirely, "wildly misquoted" various people, and put words into the mouths of the dead.

94. The duchess never specifically acknowledged trying to suppress the book, though she did admit to a family role in having various sections removed that she described as libelous and "incredible."

95. The duchess's letter had cited these as qualities of Unity that Pryce-Jones had never mentioned.

I should like to get across in the film (although v. briefly as the film isn't about that).

Now I hear from the producer, Michael Barnes, that he'd written to Mrs. McKinnon[96] for permission to film some background bits at Swinbrook. She wrote back (saying it would be OK but not in the house) and said "the family are horrified at the idea." I should like to know what that is all about? I note that you were on an hour-long BBC programme about Chatsworth, so why not me at Swinbrook? Again, it's the irksome feeling that you set out to be Arbiter of everything to do with the family—if it <u>was</u> you who was horrified, but perhaps it was Woman.

I'm putting all this down (afraid the letter's getting monstrous long—are you still reading, Henny?) in aid of, for once, trying to set forth some inner feelings about us and specially what I think are the <u>dividing</u> things. Because otherwise although I, for one, am v. much in favour of The Reconciliation on <u>any</u> terms, I also think it would mean v. much more if some of these murkier areas of our relationship could somehow be cleared up, & at least a mutual respect for each other's opinion be arrived at. Viz., you thought it was RIGHT to try & suppress that book & I thought it was WRONG, but I can sympathize with your reasons (although <u>not</u> with those of Sir O).

There are also suspicions between us.... I'd still like to know if you'd <u>actually</u> suspected me of lifting the scrapbook, or if that was just Woman's work.

Reading this letter over, there really are heaps of things to discuss from childhood on, & I should love to try, although I suppose neither of us is specially good at introspection. But we might be getting better at it now we're getting OLD? (<u>60</u> next year for me.) . . .

[D]o drop a line c/o Sonia.

      Yr. long-winded Hen

To Ring Lardner Jr. and Frances Lardner   Oakland
                      April 7, 1977

Dear Ring & Frances,

I <u>did</u> enjoy that evening with you, thanks so very much. But it also made me rather sad, as I should SO love to see more of you, & for you to get to know Bob—I know that if we lived closer we'd be best friends, but there you are, 3,000 miles away, dammit.

I'm afraid I wasn't a very good interview,[97] so thought I'd jot some Durrish observations:

I suppose the crux of it is that they fell between two (or rather several) stools, which is what makes their story so interesting and poignant. To take the more

---

96. The owner of Swinbrook House at the time Barnes's documentary was filmed.

97. According to Virginia Durr scholar Patricia Sullivan, Ring Lardner Jr. "was planning to do a film on the Durrs (both of them, I think), but it didn't get very far." He apparently interviewed Decca as part of his research for that project.

obvious stools first: They were never in the CP (although they, esp. Va, had many close friends who were), hence were deprived of that sort of safe-harbor feeling (even in dangerous days) that I, and perhaps you, enjoyed: the sense of history-is-on-our-side, plus the instant comradeship the very minute you met another Communist—for the first time, say, in some distant town. Shared viewpoint, shared dangers, made one feel extremely safe in some way! The Durrs, on the other hand, were totally isolated. This isolation, I think, you'll find v. important to convey in the film because it is also the key to their special brand of bravery. I mean, we were all brave, or thought we were—but how much easier to be brave along with a lot of other brave ones!

Another stool (sorry, I seem to have stuck myself with this absurd metaphor): their generation. Va is 15 years older than I, for example; Cliff about 20 years older, hence in an avuncular position vis à vis people of my age, and yours, who during the 40's and 50's were sort of the backbone of the Movement. So while lots of us loved them, revered them (and in my case, I'm afraid, laughed at them because that is my rotten nature), we perhaps weren't satisfactory close friends the way people of [the] same age group can become.

Stool #3: the whole black-white thing, crucially important when you get to the Southern part of the story. In the 2 1/2 years I lived with them, they never had a black person to dinner; wouldn't have dreamed of it. Of course in those days, as you well remember, nobody did except Communists. So the Durrs are forced to go back to Montgomery where they live on the charity of his (vile) old mother (Va, by the way, has softened her approach totally re her ma-in-law, but don't believe a word of it: they loathed each other deeply). There Cliff, all his instincts for justice aroused, starts defending blacks in his law practice: not just the bus boycott case, but loads of minor frame-up victims etc. . . . The consequence is the total isolation from white community—whites will no longer employ his services—but the black community doesn't, either. Blacks with substantial personal injury cases, for example, go to eminent establishment white lawyers in Montgomery, blacks with criminal cases (who can afford a fee), ditto, as the main point is to plea-bargain & make a deal with the judge, which Cliff in his isolated position might not succeed in.

Socially, Durrs & blacks are not at ease. I don't think you can survive their sort of childhood in the deep South & come out of it untainted by a sort of visceral racism. They tried, but did not succeed; I've seen them trying & not succeeding, specially Va. Example: I went to stay with them in (date? 1950's, I suppose, or maybe later—anyway, when Gomillion of Tuskegee was challenging the gerrymandered voting boundaries).[98] On the way, Va was cautioning me

---

98. Tuskegee University sociology professor and dean Charles G. Gomillion led the fight against 1957 legislation excluding most blacks from the voting rolls in Tuskegee, Alabama. As the founder of the Tuskegee Civic Association, he became the lead plaintiff in a legal case, *Gomillion v. Lightfoot*, that resulted in a landmark Supreme Court ruling and the enfranchisement of the city's black majority. Phillip Lightfoot was the city's mayor.

"Now Honey, don't be talking about race problems, them folks don't like that, just act natural" etc. etc. So we get to Tuskegee, absolute heart of black bourgeoisie (or was then): elegant light-skinned black women talking about my daughter at Vassar, my son at MIT etc. (So it must have been the sixties? Not sure.) Virginnie, totally disregarding her good advice to me, starts straight in with "What do you-all think of—" some discrimination thing. Blacks got v. frosted, were being jolly polite but obviously resentful. Very much like that tape you played me of Va & Tuskegee students ("white lady go home" etc), only in a different historical period, or year rather. Another example: Va and I are in a taxi in Washington, where we are staying for Cliff's memorial service. Va starts straight in on the black cab driver: "I hear you-all are about to vote for Wallace,[99] now what sort of foolishness is that, don't you know he's one of the most poisonous snakes that ever crawled the earth, you-all think he's goin' to do you good"—etc. Black driver non-committal; I start fainting with embarrassment.

I went to stay with the Durrs at Pea Level (Wetumpka) shortly before his death. We all went to a party in Montgomery, or suburbs thereof, to which Va had to wangle an invitation—they hadn't been invited, but we went anyway. Turned out to be a celebration of the election of Fred Gray (black lawyer . . .) to public office. It was most amazing, to me, as I hadn't dipped back down into the South for some years: visualize an ante-bellum mansion the likes of which one has only seen in the movies, vast terraces, wonderful reception halls, tons of exquisite food/drinks laid out—and the guests, 1/3 to 1/2 black. Goodness how extraordinary, I thought, it was like a dream & I supposed Va would be extremely pleased. Not at all; she was livid. Newfangled uppity Northern millionaires! (the party givers). Bitterness had set in. She & Cliff had, after all, ploughed this ground; crops were gathered by these nouveau-riche newcomers. As you can see, the complexities are v. great—which, if you can capture them, is what will make a great & enduring story.

I told you, didn't I, the whole story of Lucy's wedding to the right nice boy?[100] Anyway, I'll recapitulate it because here's where all possible stools are fallen between.

Virginia was in state of collapse on wedding day—I assume it's because of the loss of her favourite daughter, or general party nerves. Turns out to be a lot more serious, to wit: Hugo Black had forbidden his daughter Jo-jo to be a bridesmaid if I was going. Durrs hold family council (all this I learned later), Cliff led the fight for my admittance, on ground of 1st Amendment I gath-

99. George Wallace, the former segregationist governor of Alabama who ran several times for president of the United States.

100. Decca once explained in a letter that when Lucy Durr got engaged to Sheldon Hackney, Decca wrote to Virginia Durr to ask about the young man. The reply didn't name him, Decca wrote; it simply said, "Why Lucy is engaged to a right nice boy from Birming-ham." And "the right nice boy" became Decca's name for him thereafter.

ered—Right of Association etc. Jo-jo, obedient daughter, does not come. Meanwhile, Lucy wanted to be married in her own (Methodist? can't remember) church. Fred Gray was amongst those invited. Durrs had in fact been to his wedding shortly before, and had been ushered up to sit in special family pews as honoured guests. Deacons of Lucy's church inform Va. that Fred Gray can come but only if he sits in balcony with black servants. Durrs capitulate (not wishing to disturb Lucy's wedding). Gray does not come to wedding. Do you see how awful it all was? That wedding in itself would make a whole short story, I know it isn't exactly part of your film but to me it was so telling about the Durr plight in those days. . . .

Ring, you have to realize you are working at the edge of sanity when you venture South. . . .

Re-reading the above, I can see it's far more about Virginia than Cliff—who was, to me, a kindly but on the whole boring person, which I suppose shows how stupid I was at age 23–25; yet even when I met him often, went to stay with them ever so much later (50's & 60's) found him awfully long-winded. I wonder why? Perhaps your film will end up being more about them as a couple— fire-brand Virginia, stubborn upholder of Bill of Rights Cliff—than just about Cliff.

I do hope you'll do it, & do keep in closest touch with all developments. . . .

Much love, Decca

To Clare Douglas and Michael Barnes   Oakland
                                                         April 12, 1977
Dearest Clare, & Mike,

. . . I was fascinated by yr. letter & description of Diana's interview. . . . I too was most struck by the fact that D's comments on fellow-prisoners were pretty much confined to the female convicts sent to clean up their apt.[101] One of my favourite bits of her book was when Goering had an unobtrusive* hock for dinner (not a grand wine). Shall we have a bit of unobt. hock when we come over? Oh dear. . . .

NY was marvellous (I nipped there from Montgomery for a week of intensive Oy-work, seeing chums etc.) The best part started as the worst part, to wit: I invited a friend, Mimi, who works in the fashion industry, to have dinner with me in restaurant of her choice, on 1st April. "Let's be adventurous," she said gaily (meaning don't let's go to one of the old tried & true), & suggested The Sign of the Dove; thither we repaired. It turned out to be one of those incredibly fancy over-decorated places, looking like a pink wedding decor. Menus arrived; to my sorrow, the entrees were in the range of $18.50. We ordered fru-

---

101. The prison complex Diana and Oswald Mosley shared for the time they were incarcerated together during World War II.

gally: one drink apiece, 1/2 bot. chablis, she had lamb chops ($18.50), I had plat du jour not on menu, shad roe. Shad roe overcooked with charred bit of bacon on top; her potatoes cold. I asked for proper bacon, & string beans to replace cold pots. She has coffee, I none. No starters or desserts. Bill arrives: it is for $76.10. Fuming inwardly (but not wishing to embarrass Mim, whose idea TSOTD had been), I add a measly tip of $9, cheque for $85. Waiter says can't accept personal cheque. Manager looms, calls us into the lobby. Have you no credit card? No, say I. A cheque is just a piece of paper, he says. So is a dollar bill, say I. At this point, Mimi & I are surrounded by MENACING waiters transformed into TRAINED GUARDS. He now says he is GOING TO CALL THE POLICE!!! I sternly order him to do just that, we'll wait until they come. He has 2nd thoughts about police, but seizes our coat checks, says we won't get our coats until we pay cash. Mimi & I storm out into the night, freezing & coatless—but not before I have snatched my $85 cheque from manager. We go back to the apt. where I am staying, & start telephoning. 1st, to Bob who to my amazement is at home (usually he never is, 7 p.m. his time). Bob says <u>we</u> should get police & go back & arrest the lot of them at Sign of Dove for falsely arresting <u>us</u>.[102] But then he says better phone a local lawyer, so I do: Vic Rabinowitz, old friend & left-wing defender of underdog. He is v. cross at being disturbed, says there's nothing he can do—don't I know there's no law compelling business-man to take personal cheque? I call Craig Claiborne of NY Times (food critic); he says I should have known better than to go there, it's notorious for its absurd prices & vile food. I begin to feel like the rape victim who is told she asked for it.

Next day (my last in NY) I've promised to take the Oys out to lunch & play, so Mimi goes back with cash to ransom our hostage coats. She demands a breakdown of the $76.10 bill—turns out they'd added tons of things we never ordered, so they reduce it to $63. This time, she offers not the mingiest tip so my net saving is approx. $21. A windfall! But now me dander is up, & I get Nora Ephron (whom you would <u>adore</u>, by the way—wife of Carl Bernstein,[103] & a v. talented journalist) on the phone. She says, don't budge—I bet New York Mag. would love this story, I'll ring the ed. & ring you right back. She does. It works. I'm getting $500 for 2 1/2 pages** (Title: April Fool at the Sign of the Vulture), all in & accepted![104] As it is customary for mags. to reimburse one for

---

102. In another, unpublished letter written at the time, Decca said she told her husband, "That's all very well for <u>you</u> to say, but actually doing it is another matter—here we are in high-crime-area NY, what will police think of being called to help 2 old ladies get their frigging coats back?"

103. The *Washington Post* reporter who helped uncover the Watergate scandal. He was the son of Decca's old friends and colleagues Al and Sylvia Bernstein.

104. Decca, who was heading out of town the next day, wrote the article in a matter of hours, as she described in her collection *Poison Penmanship*. The article was approved by the magazine's lawyers except for the title, which was changed from "April Fool at the Sign of the Vulture" to "Checks and Balances at the Sign of the Dove," in order not to invite a lawsuit.

out-of-pocket expenses in doing assignments, I am now thinking of billing
New York Mag. for the $63, plus Mimi's cab fares, don't you agree? . . .

Fondest love, see you soon, send ALL CUTTINGS, Dec
* Sorry, it was <u>unpretentious</u> hock, a phrase I'd thought only used as a joke vs.
wine snobs.
** $200 a page!! Most I've ever got.

To Chaka Forman   Oakland
                                                                June 17, 1977

Darling Chaka,
    Dink told me about your discussion of grannily/gransonily relationships, &
how you said that if you live to be 96, James will be 98, two years older, hence I
shall always like James best. Well this melted my cruel old heart, because I do
see there's a bit of truth to it & it is v. unfair. So here goes with an effort to sort
things out between us:
    Thinking over your general nature and disposition, I suppose you & I are a
lot alike in some ways. You are a TERRIBLE TEASE, I have been accused of
same. You have AN ODD AND PECULIAR outlook on life, so do I, in some
ways. In other words, we both have a screw loose in our make-up—which isn't
<u>too</u> bad, as long as we don't let it get <u>too</u> loose. Being older than you, I've learned
to control mine to some extent; I expect you will, too, as you approach age 96.
    To get on with this: I adore the comic side of you, shall never forget
how great you were in the Passover play as a slave-owner, whipping James all
round the room! Also, the brilliant side of you—the way you can read so well,
understand things, you always have some amusing comment about whatever's
going on.
    The negative bit, I mean the things I <u>don't</u> like, probably arise as much out
of my <u>own</u> failings as of any of <u>your</u> faults. There are some things that
absolutely drive me up the wall—but might be completely overlooked by other
grown-ups, depending on the person. You'll find out—perhaps you already
have—that people have various levels of tolerance of various things. For example, one person might really loathe untidiness, get terribly upset with it;
another is quite oblivious to his or her surroundings, I mean doesn't notice
clutter and messes. I gave this example because I'm more or less in the latter lot,
and it is an example <u>not</u> to do with us. An example <u>to</u> do with us is that I can't
stand a) whining, b) random fighting, such as you & James used to do in London. Luckily, I think you've outgrown most of that; but that time in Macy's,
when I left you & J. to choose shoes & you were being a <u>touch</u> provoking—do
admit? When I got back to the shoe dept? Yet James rather stood up for you,
said "Grandec, he's only 7," when I roughly shunted you to another seat. You
might have forgotten all this, & I don't bring it up at all in a censorious spirit,
rather as a small example of what seems to have come between us.

Shall we be the firmest of friends from now on? I'd love to, if you would. And I promise to support you in your old age, after age 96, if you'll do the same for me.

Your rotten old but loving, Grandec

To Philip Toynbee Oakland
June 17, 1977

Dearest Philip,

I WAS PLEASED to get yr letter, esp. the holes in black cloud. Actually, I'm in a bit of a black cloud myself as it looks like total warfare with the remaining Sisters (mainly Debo, also Pam) who simply loathed both book & BBC film, & now claim to have actual proof (based on pix in book/film) that I pinched their maudit scrapbook. While possibly this all has its comic side, I actually <u>mind bitterly</u>, and have become chronically gloomy over it. Yet, shall opt not for shock-treatment; I doubt if it would bring back their friendship. (Perhaps <u>they</u> should have a splash of s.t.? Can one arrange this without the person knowing it's happening?) . . .

Bob & I went all over England doing telly interviews etc. re Fine Old Conflict, & a v. rum experience it was; a purely American concept (these promotion tours) but with a distinctly English accent. A high-light was the Yorkshire Post Lit. Luncheon, held at the Doncaster Racetrack Restaurant, about 600 people in the <u>most</u> fantastic get-ups, loads of hatted ladies etc. I was (natch) at head table, between Lord Glumsville (actually, Ld. Grimthorpe but amounts to same thing) and another landed gentleman. They talked across me for all the lunch: "How are your partridges doing this year, old boy?" "Not so well, my gamekeeper says there are a lot of infertile eggs due to the drought." "Oh, <u>my</u> gamekeeper says <u>we've</u> got a lot of infertile eggs, due to the <u>floods</u>." And so it went. . . .

This is just to send lots of love to you, Sally, Clara, the Communards, God, and other chums of yours,

Decca

To Charles Rembar[105] Oakland
July 2, 1977

Dear Cy,

Incredible development re Sign of Dove (wildest dreams come true), viz., I got a letter from U.S. Post Office in NY saying:

---

105. Charles (Cy) Rembar, New York attorney and an expert in publishing and obscenity law, had been an old friend of the Treuhafts since their days in the OPA, where he, like Robert Treuhaft, had been an attorney in the Enforcement Division.

Kindly be advised that the holder of Postage Meter #1147184
is Med-Den Inc., 1110 3rd Ave, NY 10021[106]

Kinder advise has seldom been received as 1110 - 3rd Ave is address of Sign
of the Dove: Med-Den Inc. is doubtless Dr. E. Santos,[107] the owner. Dr. E.
Santos is listed in NY telephone book. . . . [S]o far my spies haven't been able to
reach him there. . . .

Meanwhile . . . It seems that Eliz. Crow (ed of NY Mag) had jumped the
gun slightly—no suit in sight, just that the PR people for Dove were hinting
they might sue. PR tried to get the managing ed. of NY Mag to have lunch with
Dr. Santos, but NY Mag said they were not interested. Also, the PR person
repeated the LIBEL in those letters to the ed. of NY Mag—and said that my
friend (Mimi Miller) now totally denies my version of the story! I immediately
called Mimi, needless to say no Dove-related people have been in touch with
her. Don't you think the whole thing is getting libellouser & libellouser? I
mean after all, I make my pathetic living such as it is out of writing, & here they
are peppering EDITORS of mags where I publish with cruel & unusual lies.

So, the question is, would you be happy & interested in representing me in
this case on a contingent fee basis? Do think this through as I detected a slight
sigh of boredom, & would need an enthusiast because I think it's such a smashing case. Also, do admit I've got a small start on the investigation, just by getting the postal meter inf., & addresses of the Libellers. . . .

Much love, Decca

To Emma (the Good) Tennant[108]   Oakland
                                                                July 20, 1977
Dear Emma,

I've started to write to you many times (in fact have written & torn up various letters), but I think I absolutely must, as you are the only person left in the

---

106. Decca was tracking down the writers of two letters sent to *New York* magazine in response
to her "Sign of the Dove" article. Both letters were from women claiming to have been present at
the restaurant when Decca was there and noting that she had been drunk and rude during the
episode she described in her article. As Decca related in a follow-up story several months later for
New York magazine and again in *Poison Penmanship*, a secretary noted that the letters ostensibly
from women in Westport, Connecticut, and Kew Gardens, New York, bore the same postal meter
number. Decca subsequently tracked down the actual senders of the letters and spoke with them in
tape-recorded phone calls, eliciting tearful confessions that they were agents of the restaurant—all
of which was described in the follow-up article, using pseudonyms to protect "those of the guilty
who have already suffered enough."

107. Decca sometimes spelled the name Santo and sometimes Santos.

108. Decca knew two Emma Tennants after her niece Emma Cavendish, daughter of the Duke
and Duchess of Devonshire, married Toby Tennant (nephew of Anne Wollheim). Thereafter, she
referred to her niece as Emma the Good. The other Emma Tennant, dubbed Emma the Bad, was
the novelist once married to Alexander Cockburn. The name was not meant as derogatory, and
indeed Decca once referred in a letter to "Emma the Bad, who we like v. much." Both were aware
of their nicknames.

family that I feel on any sort of terms with. I fear this will be monstrous long, but here goes:

As you probably know, things ended up v. badly with me & Debo in London. Above all, I don't want you to construe this as some sort of message to her as a) I should never put you in awkward position of go-between, b) there's no between to be gone, at this point. I can only ask you to deep-six (as the Watergaters used to say) this letter & enclosures, or put it all in a Time Capsule to be opened after all of my generation are dead, which shouldn't be too precious long now.

Our disagreement was actually two-pronged: 1) she obviously loathed the book,[109] took everything in it amiss; e.g., the Bob/lordly dinner story[110] . . . a story told by Bob on himself, but she construed it as an attack on her & Andrew, trying to make Bob look small when in fact they'd done all to welcome us. That's only one example, she took the whole book as an attack on the family. There is clearly naught one can ever do about that, even if one wanted to try, which I don't. She skipped 9/10 of the book (all of the Calif. etc bits) because she thought them boring, so there you are. To her, it was Mit. Industry all the way. (Only Sophy has mentioned the Chatsworth Industry, which she did to me in her salty way: "I told my mother she's being v. two-faced, accusing you of exploiting the Mit. Ind. when she does it all the time with Chatsworth Industry!")

Prong #2 is the main point. In London, she absolutely went for me. Bob & I had gone to dinner at Chest. St.,[111] first words were "Here's Lord Antrim, to make you feel uncomfortable again." So there we were, with Ld. A., not feeling terribly comfortable in view of this intro. In the course of dinner, it became clear that the whole point of inviting us was to produce absolute proof that I had indeed stolen the wretched scrapbook. Proof was based on some photos she said could only have come out of it, viz., one of her, Andrew & A's brother taken in 1941 at the time of her wedding, & one of Muv at Inch K. taken by Madeau[112] of which only one print was made. Cross-examination of me getting

---

109. The recently published *A Fine Old Conflict*.

110. In Decca's memoir, and in the Michael Barnes documentary *The Honourable Rebel*, Robert Treuhaft described his first visit to Chatsworth, in 1955, for which he had prepped by reading Stephen Potter's humorous "etiquette" books and then found himself "feeling like an oaf" for his social ineptitude during dinner with the Devonshires and Lord Antrim. See Robert Treuhaft's contemporary account of the incident in the letter of September 20, 1955, to Pele de Lappe and Steve Murdock, which differs in some details from the later accounts. In *The Honourable Rebel*, Treuhaft was less harsh than in his contemporary letter, suggesting he had had a pleasant conversation over port and cigars despite his awkward social blooper, but the retelling of the episode in *A Fine Old Conflict* and in the documentary soon caused great family dissension. When she watched the documentary with friends, Decca said all had agreed that "Bob stole the show with his Chatsworth bit & his discussion of FBI intimidation etc.," but she said the duchess "was livid about Bob's guying-up of the ducal dinner."

111. The Duke and Duchess of Devonshire's London house, on Chesterfield Street.

112. Their cousin Madeau Stewart.

arduous, I fled in tears, prompted by Bob who said, "let's get out of here before they start counting the silver."

Scrapbook facts for deep-sixing, so far as I can reconstruct them:

Enclosed are Xeroxes of letters from Muv re wedding pix (rather brill of me to have kept them all this time, but such is my wont). As for the Muv on Isle pic, searching my memory I'm pretty sure Debo herself gave it to me once ages ago when I was at Chatsworth. I know she gave me a photo of Muv on Isle. . . .

The pix of Bobo in the P-J book (cause of original scrapbook accusation): I went over these with P-J, & he told me where he got the ones not listed in photo credits in the book. He asked me not to tell the name of the person who gave them to him as he says she has already been badly victimized by the sisterly barrage; although a close reading of the text would make the source pretty obvious.

I'm so sorry to burden you with all the above dull information, but I absolutely have to give it to somebody, & you are that unlucky somebody—there's nobody else I can write to. Woman wrote (visualize the voice) all about how exhausted she was by the Jubilee celebration & birth of baby chicks etc., & do let's be friends but I am not inclined to write back. Anyway, I shan't be coming to England, no point now.

You know those absurd expressions, "Wounded," "Pained." "Hurt"? Well I must say they can be pretty accurate: a sort of physical feeling when you wake up each morning of actual pain. It is debilitating; yet, as with actual wounds, pains, hurts, fades with time. Eventually I shall forget Debo, & that awful dinner in London.

Fondest love to all, Decca

To Miriam Miller   Oakland
                                                                July 21, 1977
Dearest Mim,

. . . Do ring up the <u>minute</u> you return. As you can see from enclosure, Dovetale escalates! Our legal advisors (Cy & Bob) didn't think we had much of a cause of action, costs of depositions etc. would amount to thousands of dollars; so instead, in my modest fashion, I've done another article for NY Mag, sent off to them by this post. Bob now thinks they prob. won't take it, as if the Dove has indeed gone bankrupt it's all a bit mootish. Who knows. Anyway, Eliz. Crow (one of the editors at NY Mag) sounded v. enthusiastic & upped the ante to $600 for this one (last one, $500) so we shall see.

Well! Talk about me needing a Project to keep me alive. I've been <u>consumed</u> by this article, & the long-winded mailing ladies whose every word was taped by a smashing little gadget lent me by Bob's investigator (don't tell anyone, as I gather from Watergate & other sources that taping without telling may be only fairly legal). . . . [E]ven my cruel old heart melted as [one of the women] sobbed on and on.[113] . . . I've got all transcribed (at <u>massive</u> cost, $55 to be precise, I <u>do</u> hope the mag will pay up but doubt it). So one day, when you come out here, I'll play it for you. Or send you Xcript. . . .

Do admit it's all fairly jolly? . . . Boiling it all down to 7 pages was a job & a half, I can tell you. . . .

> Longing to hear from you,
> Much love, Decca

To William L. Patterson   Oakland

August 9, 1977

Dearest Pat,

I WAS pleased to get your letter; I was going frantic because you & Louise[114] were the people I wanted to get the book first. When it hadn't arrived last week, I told the publisher to send another. . . .

I'm fairly sure you'll have a lot of criticisms along the lines of what you said re the title (not a serious enough approach). But the awful thing is I can't help seeing the funny side of things—I even tried to explain that, & rather blamed Nancy for it, in the introduction. . . .

Actually, thinking it all over there are farcical chapters (such as Every Body a Contact, about being financial dir. of the SF CP) and non-farcical. Of course, the ones I long for your comments on are those dealing with CRC. . . . I only used real names with written consent of the person—except for public figures like you & Bill Schneiderman.[115]. . .

Aub.[116] says he hasn't made his mind up, but he finds the family bits extremely boring. Also says I never did explain properly why I left the Party. I guess he's right about that; it's not too clear in my own mind. I know if I was French or Italian I'd be a Communist today; it was mainly what I saw as the ineffectiveness of the CP that made me leave. In other words, I realize I'm not much of a theory person, more of a pragmatist—wanting to get things done. . . . Bill Schneiderman said it read like an affectionate account of an old and valued friend (the CP) who somewhere along the line took a wrong turning. But he really liked it (unlike Aub). Bettina Aptheker, who read it at many stages in ms., is very much for it, so is her hubby Jack Kurzweil. I was pleased about that. Those in the Old Left (Leftovers? People who quit the CP about the time I did but still are in general sympathy with its aims) seem to be the main fans. . . .

---

113. The women were confessing to their roles in sending their false and pseudonymous letters to *New York* magazine.

114. William Patterson's wife.

115. In her book, Decca called Schneiderman the "revered [California] state chairman" of the Communist Party.

116. Aubrey Grossman.

[W]ho does one write for if not for one's friends? I can never imagine that amorphous entity "the public," can only visualize Bob, my children, and a circle of people like Buddy Green, Dobby, you, etc. etc. that I really wrote it for.

Oh yes, one other criticism from a Jewish friend: he said the bits about Aranka were deeply anti-Semitic, I'd obviously never read Jewish history to discover why a person like A. would be so dead keen on making money! Can you beat it, that's one criticism I reject, I thought I was jolly nice about her considering how vile she was to me when Bob & I were first married.

One extremely annoying thing is the numbers of people in the book who have died, as I should so have loved their views. . . . Actually I think Aranka would have liked it, despite my friend's criticism. Isn't death too tiresome for words? My mother, who kept chickens, used to call it "the dropping off of the perches" when her contemporaries died—old hens do just that, flop off dead. So now there I am, experiencing the same boring business.

Sorry for this long-winded letter! Do write, & get Louise to; I absolutely crave your comments, good, bad or indifferent: things you liked, things you hated, anything you feel inclined to say. . . .

Much love, Decca

To William L. and Louise Patterson   Oakland
                                                                September 13, 1977

Dear Pat, and Louise,

I <u>do</u> thank you for setting forth your views, even though I was saddened by your letter.[117]

To answer a few points: The main thing I do agree with is that the book does not suggest "through what organized forms" socialism could be achieved. I've been asked the same question in interviews, and by students; and the fact is I

---

117. William Patterson called his letter—written in the first person but, he said, a joint effort with his wife—"one of the most difficult letters I have ever written." He wrote that the reason for their displeasure with *A Fine Old Conflict* should be obvious: "you write that the CPUSA, and even more, the world-wide movement led by the CPSU has failed. I, an avowed representative of the CPUSA, feel the future of mankind lies in socialism. . . . You mention the 'abysmal mistakes' of the CPUSA. What were they? You speak of the CPUSA's blindly following the CPUSSR. But give no specifics. This does not help to clarify issues on which there may be honest differences of opinion. In the context of your book, was the Party wrong in its defense of victims of racist and economic oppression. Did the Party err in fighting for Social Security or in its support of strike struggles and the drive to organize the unorganized. Was the Party the cause or the target of the McCarthy period, and more significant, that that dark period could not and did not obliterate the Marxist-Leninist movement in our country." Calling Decca a "dear friend," Patterson expressed his great respect for her many talents, fearlessness, and love for oppressed humanity but questioned why she did not vet with him in advance the sections in which she directly quoted him. He said he feared that "they" wouldn't quote Decca's portrayal of the human side of Communists, "but rather that the CPUSA is ineffective, often ludicrous and therefore unable to effect social change." He concluded that they and Decca do have "many things to agree upon and work around. . . . And what are friends for if not to frankly exchange opinions?"

haven't any answers. What I tried to do in the book was to give a purely personal account of what it was like (from my point of view) being in the Party during those years.

You say I don't enumerate "abysmal mistakes." I could, of course, have given examples of Party positions with which I totally disagree—an outstanding one would be the expulsion of Al Richmond & Dorothy Healey.[118]. . . I could also have written about the more dislikable side of Rudy Lambert (called Moody Bramlett in the book) as head of the State Security Commission—I recall that when Stalin was quoted as saying "I'll shorten you by a head" some of us shuddered at the thought of our heads if Rudy had had the power.

But this was not my intention. My effort was to show the positive side of the CP, and (since it was a personal memoir, not a history of the movement) particularly of our work in CRC—which is why I don't say much about the CP role in unions etc., since I hadn't any direct experience of that. Your rhetorical questions in para 4 of your letter ("Did the Party err in fighting for social security" etc) are surely answered in my book? . . .

At the risk of seeming self-serving, I enclose a review & interview from the English Communist paper, Morning Star. Needless to say, I was v. gratified by these.

You will have noted that the "Cap. Press" reviews (NY Times etc) although on the whole friendly say I'm myopic, naive—but they do also say the book demystifies the CP & its role in those days.

Thanks, particularly, for your last para (many things to agree upon & work around). . . .

Much love, Decca

To William L. and Louise Patterson   Oakland
                                                              September 15, 1977

Dear Pat & Louise,

This is an addendum to mine of 13 September, as I realize I failed to respond to one important thing: failure to send you the bits of your conversation as quoted in the book, failure to consult you about the whole CRC operation.

On the quotation, I think there is only one direct quote that is so vivid in my mind to this day that I can still hear you saying it: "you may have to fight all the way to expulsion" (p. 127).[119] Don't you remember that? It made the most pro-

118. Dorothy Healey, a Los Angeles Communist Party member and official in the 1930s and '40s, had been jailed under the Smith Act until the law was declared unconstitutional. Years later, she was active in progressive Democratic Party affairs. She had a weekly radio show, *Marxist Commentary*, on Pacifica station KPFK in Los Angeles.

119. The quotation involved a discussion of Decca's inattention to national party directives and issues (like the Smith Act prosecutions) in favor of local issues (like police brutality), as directed by her own board, especially the black members representing their local constituency. In her book, Decca portrayed William Patterson as an ally in such conflicts.

found impression on me at the time. No tapes needed for that. Do think back, it was your view, vividly expressed.

On the CRC: Both Buddy & I asked you what <u>we</u> should answer about the genesis of that organization—as our members were always asking us. This was in 1950's. But, Pat, you were jolly evasive; the person who told me about CRC's formation was Marge Frantz, who was present at the meeting. Now it's all ancient history (CRC having been dissolved in 1956) isn't it a good idea to try & explain <u>what</u> it was, <u>why</u> it was, & how it came about? Also, I got lots from your own book <u>The Man Who Cried Genocide</u>[120] which was v. useful.

I did, also, whilst writing the book ask both you & Aubrey about the McGee case (when did CRC get involved, how did Bella Abzug get into it etc) but both of you said you'd forgotten those details & referred me back to each other. . . .

Sorry to bother you with another letter so soon; I suppose the reason is that I feel somewhat wounded that you didn't like anything about the book, esp. the CRC bits, & the whole chapter about Mississippi.

Let each stand in his place, much love, Decca[121]

To Maria Temechko[122]   Oakland
                                                    September 15, 1977
Dear Maria,

Many thanks for that marvellous schedule. In case I don't actually survive it, I thought I should set forth my funeral plans in the certain belief that Knopf will be fully capable of carrying them out. However, I do think (and am sure Bob Gottlieb will agree) that the expense, which will be considerable, should be shared with Simon & Schuster? As the <u>Amer. Way of Death</u> is still selling quite briskly. . . . I feel this matter should be decided in some sort of joint meeting, with my agent Scott Meredith being the final arbiter; as of course I do not intend that one red cent (so to speak) of royalties from <u>A Fine Old Conflict</u> shall be deflected from my children's inheritance. (I mention the children in this context, rather than Bob, because you know how these things go: in no time he'll have married some scheming young chick who'll try to cut out my children, such is la bloodie old vie . . .) So here goes:

1. "Pick up at the hotel" (see your notation for Sept. 21, Pittsburgh), or "Friday, Sept. 23: Anne Schwartz will pick you up at your hotel." <u>Poor</u> Anne! But perhaps the porter will give her a hand, I mean I know I've gained weight over

---

120. William L. Patterson's autobiography was published by International Publishers in 1971.

121. Mary Louise Patterson, William and Louise's daughter, says Decca and her parents had little if any contact after this exchange of letters. She added that she has the "impression that there was some sort of softening before William Patterson died" in 1980, although she doesn't know if it was actually a rapprochement.

122. Temechko, of the publicity department of Alfred A. Knopf, had just sent Decca a schedule for her publicity tour for <i>A Fine Old Conflict</i>. She had previously accompanied Decca on her author's tour for <i>Kind and Usual Punishment</i>.

the years. However, pick up at hotel is fine <u>except</u> for such appointments as (see your list for Sept. 29, Boston) "Good Day, WCVB/TV—<u>live</u> [your italics]. Until 10:00." I mean I don't suppose WCVB/TV will actually notice the difference? As long as Anne, or Caroline or somebody, has picked up at the hotel and swiftly complied with Instruction #2, which follows:

2. Contact Howard C. Raether & get him to spring over with finest trocar plus a Natural Expression Former; Benj and also Bob Gottlieb know the expression needed, a sort of huge wink. Actually, Howard C. Raether could do all this on the Good Day show, WCVB/TV? I bet they'd love it; also, he can do the brief autographings following talks—actually he's a terrific chatter, so he can do the talks, too.

3. I do hope you will give considerable thought to the casket which, as I'm sure you realize, should reflect one's station in life. The question is, what <u>is</u> my station in life? If Gottlieb thinks he can get away with one of those cheap pine boxes, tell him he's got another think coming. Anyway, do be looking out some nice samples for the liner; not yellow (jaundice) or red (scarlet fever), more likely a soft grey-mauve, for FATIGUE.

4. I'm sure your nice travel agent, "Sun & Fun Tours, Inc" will cheerfully issue tickets (billed, of course, to Gottlieb) to the 70-odd people who came to my 60th birthday party—Bob's got the list, plus everybody in my address book from London to Wetumpka, Alabama.

Again, thanks SO much for everything—I can hardly wait,
Much love, Decca

To the Duchess of Devonshire   Oakland
November 23, 1977

Hen, <u>your telegram</u>.[123] I was amazed, as had expected it to be found 100 years hence mouldering in a trunk like the Bride at Minster Lovell.[124]

Obviously I'm incredibly pleased. Yet there is, it seems to me, a certain amt. of Unfinished Business (an expression from agendas, Hen—but I expect you know that from the Royal Bantam Club etc.). I suppose what I really want to know now is whether, from your point of view, true friendship is still possible— as perhaps in your mind the scrapbook thing was only a small part, the major

---

123. The telegram had said, "EUREKA PHOTOGRAPH BOOK HAS TURNED UP LOVE HENDERSON."

124. A reference to a legendary tragedy in the Oxfordshire village of Minster Lovell. According to the legend and a Victorian ballad based on it, the bride of a young lord in the Lovell family disappeared in the manor house while playing a game of hide and seek during their Christmas-season wedding festivities. The bride went to hide and was never found. For days the distraught groom and the rest of the wedding party searched every nook and cranny of the large hall in vain. Years later, a skeleton in a wedding dress was found in an old oak chest in the attic, where the young bride was presumed to have been trapped when the trunk's heavy lid snapped shut.

point being that you loathed my book & the BBC film? I've no way of knowing if this is so, so please say.

As for me, 18 May (date of that horrible evening [on] Chesterfield St.), marked the beginning of what seemed like an interminable & incurable illness, or a sort of non-stop condition of mourning. At least, with the scrapbook find, convalescence is now setting in.

I'm going on a dig, in Egypt! Next March, a place called the Temple of Mut (Luxor-Thebes, I'd no idea where these were until I looked them up on a v. inefficient map). I do hope that Mut doesn't turn out to be an early version of Mitford, hence yet more Mit-industry. No, Hen, I don't think so judging by pix of Mut, a goddess with v. slanting eyes.

But the major archeological find of recent years was, to me, the one at the Temple of Henderson.

Not much news otherwise. . . .

Yr loving Hen

ps. I should love to have details of the Find, if possible set forth in proper Archeological fashion including use of such up-to-date data as X-ray technology used by the diggers. In any event, The Great House of Henderson Shall Suffer Wrong No More, don't you agree?

But actually, Hen, I can't say how delighted I was to get the 'gram. And to think it might be the prelude to Peace Talks.

To Michael Barnes and Clare Douglas   Oakland
                                                   November 30, 1977

Dear Mike & Clare,

. . . Another odd bit of family news: whilst I was in NY I was interviewed by Catherine Guinness, Diana's grandchild. . . . She seemed like a nice, moony sort of kid, is working for a mag called Interview got out by Andy Warhol. She just sent mag with the interview in it (the interview is unexceptional) prefaced with this:

". . . I received a letter from my father, Jonathan Guinness from which the following is an extract: 'I await your interview with Decca, literally, with bated breath. She's a very tough cookie, a hardened and intelligent Marxist agitator who knows very subtly how to play on her upper-class background so as to enlist residual snobbery (on both sides of the Atlantic) in establishing Marxism. But this leads to problems of identity; to an ambiguity as to what is real and what is an act. All this was very evident in her TV appearances here. Bob Treuhaft came over better; at least he is what he is, he is in one piece, so to speak, the bright Jewish boy with his ready-made 'red diaper' principles, seeing (e.g.) Chatsworth from the outside with the healthy irony of the social historian. Of course you had fun with her on the Island [C. came to Inch K. when she was 7 with nanny & sister to stay with my mother] when you were little, didn't you? And there's no doubt that she has all the talent and funniness, rather as Milton's Satan still had a lot of the charisma of the angel.' "

I bet Jonathan won't be best pleased that she quoted this letter? . . .

Toughly yet angelically yours, Decca

Bright Jewish boy sends love.

To the Duchess of Devonshire   Oakland
                                                          December 8, 1977

Dearest Hen,

Thanks for yours of 29 Nov, which crossed my p.c.—sent in usual fit of paranoia, thinking mine was lost in the post as does actually happen sometimes.

I must say the account of the Find is very strange indeed. In other words it was there all along?[125] I suppose just after you had convinced yourself that I'd pinched it, you just stopped looking. What about the photo of Muv with sheepdog on Isle, subject of 3rd Degree in London—was it there? If so, had Madeau made two copies, not one as she told you? If not, was the copy I've got given to me by you, ages ago? Because while I agree that the Find is, in itself, a great lifting of weight as you say, the above points were jolly weighty from my pt. of view, having been cast into considerable gloom over it all.

Egypt: Well might you ask, because it's absolutely not my speed. It came about as follows: We met a fascinator called James Manning, foremost Egyptologist (not that I'd have known that, knowing absolutely naught abt. Egypt, but he is) who was here with the Tutankhamen exhibit now being trotted round America. He was telling about his excavations at Temple of Mutford & did make it sound pretty riveting; he kept saying do come on the dig & I said no not at all my sort of thing. Got home to find a letter from a Kraut mag. called GEO offering to send me anywhere, all exp. paid plus fat fee—so greedy as I am I said how about Egypt & they said done. However the more I think of actually going the colder the feet—or rather the hotter, temps. are 100 & up & I loathe hot climes. Oh dear. Dink gave me a book she'd bought for Chaka called "An Alphabet of Ancient Egypt," it's incredibly good (recommended for ages 7 to 10) & I already know how to write Tutankhamen in hieroglyphics. So far, my only research tool. So I think I will go. . . . J. Manning is sending the unpublished memoirs of 2 doughty Victorian Lades who went to Egypt in the last century, dug about without a clue as to what they were looking for & thus mucked things up for fair; I think I'll cast my article for Geo in vein of those Vict. ladies. What sort of shoes does one get? I was thinking of sandals (sandals, naught but sand there) but people say that's hopeless, boots are the note.

---

125. The duchess's explanation had been that the "the bloody thing was suddenly there, in its place." She said some young friends of her daughter Sophy had been looking at albums when the duchess's eye "suddenly lit on it."

Woman's birthday[126] bash sounds amazing, fancy her & Derek walking into the sunset in the Golden Years; or Diamond more likely, I suppose, knowing him.

Much love, Yr Hen

To Pamela Jackson   Oakland

December 8, 1977

Darling Woman,

Yes Debo told me about the photograph book being found; apparently it was there all along. <u>Very</u> strange.

Of course now that that obstacle has been removed (or rather found!) I'd love to see you again. But you must realize that it is pretty impossible to rub out of one's mind your original accusation, and all that followed from it. All that business about borrowing—once & for all, to borrow something means to take it with permission of the owner with promise to return. Doesn't at all apply to swiping a huge scrapbook, size of a table as I remember it, smuggling it past everybody at Chatsworth, and using photos out of it, which I was accused of doing. . . .

I'll be coming to London in March for a couple of nights. Perhaps we could meet on neutral ground? . . .

Much love, Steake[127]

[also Geriatric—60 last Sept. 11!]

To Ann Farrer Horne   Oakland

December 12, 1977

Darling Cystling,[128]

Thanks awfully for yours of 4 December, just rec'd   not too bad, considering Xmas is at our throats with consequent total disruption of the posts? . . .

P. Toynbee: It would take a book to describe that odd character & luckily for you there are, several, written by him. Get: <u>Pantaloon</u>, a v. long novel in verse that describes his childhood & which I thought totally riveting although novs. in v. are not usually my speed; and <u>Friends Apart</u>, which while purporting to be about Esmond & another friend of P's, both killed in the war, is actually v. revealing about PT. . . .

---

126. The duchess's letter had told of their sister Pamela's seventieth birthday party, for which Pamela's former husband, Derek Jackson, came from Paris for the night, bearing red roses. The Jackson visit occasioned some speculation, to which Decca alluded here.

127. Pamela's nickname for Decca.

128. Ann Farrer Horne, in a book she co-edited, described her and Decca's nicknames for each other this way: "They shared the enormous excitement of filmgoing together when they were about twelve, hence their use of the American 1930s term Sister (and Cyst)."

Other PT data: He is one of 3 sons of Arnold T. I never set eyes on the other two. The one Philip really loved committed it after Esmond & I had come to America, P. wrote to us about that & it was a perfectly beastly moment in his life. The other brother is a painter; he & P. loathe each other & have an incredibly squalid nonstop row going about inheriting old Arnold's dough; I can't remember all the details as you must admit other people's rows about dough are a bit tedious? Although since Philip got born-again Xian I fear I have a sneaking sympathy with his rotten brother, who doubtless thinks (& perhaps rightly) that P. will squander all on his mad Xian schemes.

. . . He's actually frightfully funny when in a good mood; as you said in yr. letter, affectionate, opinionated, ruthless—all v. good qualities, don't you agree? . . .

Your question ("what's Philip really like")[129] reminds me of same posed to Philip by Michael Barnes. According to Philip, MB rang up & said "Could you tell me in a nutshell what Decca is really like?" PT roared, said NO. Nutshells don't work when describing old chums. . . .

Fondest love . . .

Yr Sister

Yes isn't Orphan Island[130] marvellous? I just re-read it 'tother day. After I'd chosen it as the book I'd take in "Desert Island Discs"[131] I got quite a lot of letters (out-of-blue fan letters re the programme) from people who said they'd found it in a library & loved it. It was one of the first full-length grown-up books I'd read as a child, so it made a huge impression.

To the Duchess of Devonshire   Oakland
                                                                February 25, 1978

Dearest Hen,

Just got back after 2 weeks away to find yr letter. . . .

About the things you minded in book/television programme: no, don't write them down if you'd rather not. Anyway, you said some of them when we met in Manchester. . . .

But I might as well say some of the things I minded. Principally, I suppose, that you took everything amiss & the opposite of the way it was intended; e.g.,

---

129. Ann Farrer Horne subsequently got into direct touch with Toynbee, conducting what Decca described as "a long correspondence . . . abt. going mad, God, & other joint interests."

130. A 1924 novel by Rose Macaulay about a group of Victorian orphans shipwrecked with their governesses on a South Pacific reef for decades; they reinvent society before being discovered by the outside world.

131. A popular, long-running BBC radio program on which celebrities are asked to name the eight recordings they'd most like to have with them if trapped on a desert island. They are also interviewed on other topics, including the book they'd take with them, in addition to the Bible and Shakespeare. See letter of June 27, 1991, to Herb Gold.

Bob and the lordly dinner. You said I'd made out that Bob felt he was made to feel small when you'd done all to welcome us. In fact any ordinary reader would note that it was a joke Bob had told <u>on himself</u>—not at all the construction you put on it. Perhaps all dates back to Hons & Rebels? I had sent advance copies to all of you, but the only ones who wrote back were Nancy & Muv, both v. complimentary, so there you are. In fact Muv read bits of it at Inch K, in manuscript, & made corrections which I incorporated. . . . Otherwise, in her letters to me she was v. pro the book; I can hardly believe she was dissembling, not like her. I mean, did she complain about it to you? I know she loathed Nancy's essay on Blor, which I must say was a bit of a killer & <u>not</u> very daughterly. In Fine Old Conflict I did try to explain Muv a bit more, but I suppose you loathed that part too. When she was dying at Inch K, I got a t.gram from you saying MUV SAILING ALL SISTERS HERE—one of the better typographical mistakes for FAILING. Now we are all pretty much sailing to same destination, I was v. glad that Muv & I did make up, & I tried to put that in the book. Also (in both books) tried to explain the Boud a bit; a near impossibility to get her down as she really was, so no doubt I failed. To this day sometimes I dream about her, arriving fresh from Germany in full gaiety, all her amusingness, etc.—but Hen don't you see <u>how awful</u> it all was?

One last thing: you say you didn't wrongfully accuse me. In that case, I don't know what the horror-evening in May was all about, when you were being more like a cross-examining prosecutor than a Hen.

Anyway, I'm longing for 8th March. . . .

Much love, Henderson

To the Duchess of Devonshire   Luxor, Egypt
                                                                    March 14, 1978
Dearest Hen,

If this arrives (a bit like throwing bottle with message in sea) do note arrival date; everyone says you can't post letters out but oi doiter.[132] It's just a line to say how v glad I was to see you in London, & to tell a bit of Luxor news & views. To wit: Turns out that my original friend here, J. Manning, is at <u>daggers drawn</u> with all his colleagues (professional jealousy sort of thing, you know how that can go) & the awful thing is I'm getting more & more pro the colleagues. Intrigue abounds. The real life saver is E Lessing,[133] the Viennese photog. who's doing the picture part of GAY-O[134] article. He's <u>so</u> nice, one's age I shld judge but far spryer (well it wouldn't take much, you'll say), v. civilized, knows Egypt & speaks a bit of Arabic, so that's all OK.

Hen the digs. I have to drag myself away from the intrigue, which is far more

---

132. "I doubt it" in Mitford-speak.
133. Erich Lessing.
134. Decca's phonetic version of the name of the German magazine *Geo*.

interesting, to Digsville as that's my job here. E.g. yesterday I went to see a charming middle-aged couple, both Egyptologists officially assigned. They were herding pots when I arrived, piecing things together like a jigsaw puzzle into some not very pretty, in fact rather ordinary roundish jars. I had a long interview with them. For 8 years they've been working on their major find: The "Treasury," unique, they said. So they told at great length all about it, how they stumbled on it etc. At end of interview I said I'd love to see the Treasury. They were simply amazed: "But you passed directly by it coming here!" Which I had, so we went to have another look. Hen it's a field, size of a large paddock, of drear flagstones with a few round things in the middle. EIGHT YEARS. Oh well. I've long since concluded that Egyptologists are a special breed of mad-men like Paranoics or Schizophrenics; yet they are v. agreeable despite all.

I think I'll call the article The Diggers & the Dug, with me concentrating on the souls of Egyptologists & E Lessing taking lovely photos of the Dug (Pharaohs, etc).

The Temple of Mut (supposed to be my main concentration as that is where J. Manning & Co. are working) is a sea of sand & rubble with a few scattered headless sphynxes about the place.

However the hotel (Winter Palace) is bliss, Swiss-Victorian in looks, huge marvellous gardens. . . .

We didn't get down to very substantive talk in London; but perhaps you'd rather not? For me, there's still a rather deep shadow cast. Ditto, Bob, who says that evening last Spring is only about the 2nd time he's ever seen me cry. . . .

Much love, Henderson

To Comrade E——135   Oakland
                                                      May 18, 1978

Dear A——

Thanks so much for your interesting letter. . . .

Just some general answers. . . . I think the Party in NY is a lot more rigid than out here. In Calif, lots of comrades still in CP remain close & much-loved friends of ours—I don't think that would be true in NY. . . . I think the NY CP is far more factional & prone to see enemies under the bed than the Calif. CP; I always used to think those bitter factional fights were due to the awful weather

---

135. Name omitted by editor. Decca had a brief exchange of letters with this Communist Party member, who had apparently first written her a fan letter after reading *A Fine Old Conflict*. In her initial response, Decca used his last name, prefaced by "Comrade"; in this follow-up letter, she addressed him by his first name. Her correspondent had argued that "the CP is the only game in town," to which Decca replied in her first letter that he "may well be right . . . [but nevertheless] I couldn't rejoin at the moment (even if they'd have me!) because I know in my bones there are certain things I couldn't really stomach. . . . I can't imagine that these harsh, rigid, circumscribed viewpoints will find much favor amongst the young folks" (as her correspondent had hoped).

in NY, so freezing in winter & hot in summer that it made everyone bad-tempered; but I fear Marx would not agree, as he said geography has little to do with politics. . . .

Re failure of Party press to review my book . . . [It] was tossed around like a hottish potato. Eventually Mickey Lima after long pondering did write a review, but the National Leadership squashed it. . . . Now, I do think it's a bit ridiculous, in fact one might say cowardly, to duck reviewing these books—for my part, I should welcome a critical review or even a total blast more than this deep silence. . . .

I guess what I try to do, mostly, is write things that I hope will be useful in the struggle—e.g. the prison book, which I could never have done had it not been for some understanding of the class nature of crim. justice system acquired in the CP.[136] Before that, I did one on the Trial of Dr. Spock (enclosed herewith). I realize that often I get absolutely besotted by <u>trivial</u> subjects which haven't got much to do with the class struggle, but I fear that is a fault of character. See enclosed pieces in New York, re the Sign of the Dove! But I can't help <u>loving</u> that sort of thing, the joy of the chase.

In any event, I hope I'm not a good German. My only reason for not being in the CP is that it seems to me to be in a sort of doldrums at the moment, hence a waste of time from my point of view. . . .

Best regards,

To Katharine Graham   Oakland
                                                                June 19, 1978
Dear Kay,

. . . Dread Lynn[137] called this a.m. Bob had advised me <u>not</u> to tell her that I had talked with you as then she'd find some way of putting this fact in her book. So I thought that was jolly good advice; merely told her that I was unable to reach you as you were out of Washington, but I'd thought the whole thing over & decided that since you didn't want the book written, I should prefer not to be interviewed. So she sighed & cried & damn near died. (Not really, but she was cooing away about how disappointed she was & wouldn't I reconsider.) Then I got all cozy & writer-to-writer with her. I said she had an awfully uphill task,

---

136. When *Kind and Usual Punishment* was later published in Russia, Decca was "a wee bit disappointed and confused" by the preface written by a Russian scholar. As translated by one of her acquaintances, the preface faulted Decca for her essentially political and moral judgments of prisons, which were "not social in the Marxist understanding of that word."

137. An apparent reference to Lynn Rosellini, who wrote a five-part profile of Katharine Graham that appeared in the *Washington Star* in November 1978. In her memoir, *Personal History* (Alfred A. Knopf, New York, 1997), Graham wrote that the series had earlier been killed by the *Star* as too negative but then resurrected—and heavily promoted—when Time Inc. purchased the newspaper. Although *Washingtonian* magazine reported in August 1978 that Rosellini had received a $35,000 advance from Simon & Schuster for a biography of Graham, no such book was published.

and that if I were her I'd chuck it & look to some other subject to write about. I told her the sad (and true, for once) story about an assignment I had to interview Ronald Reagan many years ago, when he was but a twinkle in the eye of Republican far-right, for Esquire. RR refused an appointment with me; I told this to Esq., but they said to go ahead anyway. I labored mightily, went down to Hollywood & saw everyone who had ever known him—did my absolute best. But the thing was a total fizzle; Esq. rejected it, so I had to peddle it to some obscure mag that nobody reads. I said I feared the same thing might happen to her book, & that the smart thing to do would be to pull out now without all that investment of time & work.

I much doubt this will have any effect, but anyway I tried. . . .

Love, Decca

Back to Bob Gottlieb:[138] I'd suggest seeing him in some private place such as his house, as his office is, like most, a hotbed of flapping ears (sorry for mixed metaphor but you know what I mean). Also I wouldn't bother about an agent as yr. lawyer could read the contract. I don't know why I have an agent as my output is v. small; just a security blanket I guess. I don't think they do that much for you unless you want to auction a book to highest bidder in which case you might get stuck with some idiot of an editor. . . .

To Philip Toynbee   Oakland
                                                                                    September 30, 1978

Dearest Philip,

I <u>did</u> love "innocent but wily" (Ben),[139] perfect. I wonder what they'll say about you? and me? Am rather hoping you are not assigned to write <u>mine</u>—which may be coming up sooner than you think as I've been stricken with PHLEBITIS (Nixon's disease, which makes it even more boring). Joke, actually, as it was a light attack & better now. One thing you'd have liked: We were staying at a super-plush seaside house in E. Hampton when it happened, & went to see a Dr. there. In the course of examination the Dr. said in a tentative sort of way, "Do you like an occasional glass of wine?" "DO I!" said I, "absolutely, whenever available"—thinking he was going to say well you'll have to cut that out. Instead, he said that's v. good as alcohol acts as a blood-thinner, so the more the better—as 'twere turpentine for paint-thinner, I suppose?

So, the only treatment was lying about with legs up (Bob says I always do

---

138. This is an early instance of Decca's continuing discussions with Graham through the years about the possibility of Graham writing her autobiography. The book, finally published in 1997, won the Pulitzer Prize and was a runaway best-seller. It was edited by Robert Gottlieb.

139. Decca apparently was commenting on an obituary—perhaps written by Toynbee—on his friend Ben Nicolson, who died in 1978.

anyway, so no great sacrifice) whilst incessant troops of interesting folks who live nearby plied me with lovely doses of Thinner.[140] . . .

Fancy the community folding—glad Mammon is back on his (or her) feet, though. What became of Blissful Bim?[141] . . .

Have just finished a collection of me articles published over the years, to be called The Making of a Muckraker.[142] . . . It's got a longish introduction—how to make people talk, how to gather info etc—plus a Comment on each article, story-behind-story, spurious research all the way and even more spurious intent: to sell it to journalism students who will think it is useful. Mammon, mammon all the way. Will be published here in the spring, I'll shoot a copy along. Actually it was rather fun doing it. . . .

Fondest love to all, Decca

To Mildred Hamilton[143]   Oakland
                                                    December 10, 1978

Dear Mildred,

That story was REALLY EXCELLENT, but yours always are. . . . So marvelous the way you managed to re-kindle those old flames (Amer Way of Death) & make them burn as brightly as ever!

I've just returned from Darkest Tennessee, Murfreesboro (I am not kidding, that's the name of the town), Mid-Tennessee University, where I gave a lecture on prisons. There was only one amusing moment: a total troglydyte (sp?) of a

---

140. In another letter, Decca credited the ministrations of her daughter, Constancia, who had become a nurse. Decca said Constancia visited from New York City on her day off and "glared at the Dr., just like Farve."

141. Bim Mason was a young member of Philip Toynbee's agricultural commune and the subject of one of his Decca "teases." Toynbee described this exchange in a 1977 Radio Times article, reprinted in Decca's book Faces of Philip: A Memoir of Philip Toynbee (Alfred A. Knopf, 1984).

> "But Bim is bliss!" said Decca.
> Bim, a bearded young man in sweater and jeans, went even redder in the face; but did his best to keep his end up.
> "What did you say your next book is about?"
> "Unrequited love!" moaned Decca, looking at him with languishing, beautiful but shortsighted eyes behind her specs.
> Bim gave a rough guffaw of defeat; and the party had begun. On Decca's terms, of course.

142. The American title was changed subsequently to Poison Penmanship: The Gentle Art of Muckraking after Decca's friend Nora Ephron said the original title made Decca sound, misleadingly, like "a reincarnation of Lincoln Steffens." When the book was published in Britain, the title reverted to The Making of a Muckraker because, Decca wrote, editors at her English publishing house, Michael Joseph, "thought connotation of poison-pen is vile old maid writing anon. letters re vicar's sex life."

143. A reporter for the San Francisco Examiner who had written an article on Decca.

sociology teacher had brought <u>two</u> of her classes, thus packing lecture hall to my pleasure—she hadn't a clue as to what my point was going to be. So in the question period she mentioned studies she had read which prove that criminal genes can be transmitted from parent to child so wouldn't it be a good idea to pass a law requiring sterilization of all criminals? Well, said I, possibly; but one would have to start with the Nixon family, & I'm not sure the public would go for that poor Tricia & Julie & their offspring being seized by the sterilizers. Upon which the soc. teacher stormed out—but the STUDENTS STAYED! So it was all worth it. . . . TONS OF THANKS for your superb article,

Love, Decca

To Lorin Wertheimer[144]   Oakland
                                                                January 8, 1979

Dearest Lorin,

I have read your manuscript with the greatest interest and pleasure. There were many fascinating moments: the idea of mouse & canary nipping off into the blue! The suspense-filled pictures of a bear's paw and a snake's tail—leading to the next page!

In my view, it is not, however, publishable in its present form. Of course I may be quite wrong and you should consult other writers and editors about this.

I have a few suggestions for your consideration, some purely technical, others of more substance:

1). There should be a cover page, giving your name & address and the date of completion of the ms.

2). Write on one side of the page only. Number all pages (the copy you sent me had some pages numbered but not all, which makes for easy mixing-up by reader).

3). Get some plain writing paper—or, if the only paper you have is that of the Columbia Gas System Service Corporation, cut the top off before getting to work. HORRID THOUGHT: Suppose your book were published as is, and all your fan letters went to 120 East 41st Street, which is the address given for Columbia Gas System? If you haven't got any writing paper, please tell me & I will send some.

4). I thought the story started off very well, creating an atmosphere of high suspense. However, later I detected a certain repetitiveness; "finly they made friends" occurs more than once. (Incidentally, another spelling for that word is "finally," preferred in most up-to-date dictionaries.) I believe that your diffi-

---

144. The Romilly-Formans' young housemate was eight years old when this letter was written.

culty in constructing a good ending is one suffered by <u>every</u> writer. Think it over very carefully next time; perhaps write the ending first? I mean, a draft of possible ending, so the whole story doesn't taper off?

Again, very many thanks for letting me read your ms., which will be returned under separate cover.

Much love to all, Grandec

To Katharine Graham   Oakland

February 1, 1979

Dear Kay,

... Did I tell you that Carl[145] has done the most smashing "Afterword," for me muckrake book? Oh I'm so pleased, he's such a hero to the young (& for good reason).

Am not sure just where I'll be for that extra week ... might nip down to see Va Durr in Wetumpka, Ala., for the weekend. But one way or another, do let's give it a try (the reunion).

Yes do forget that super-forgettable Rosellini creature—in fact what you should be doing is getting on with your own memoirs.

Much love, Decca

To Katharine Graham   Oakland

April 30, 1979

Dear Kay,

... Have just finished reading Halberstam[146]—not <u>quite</u> correct as I skipped over Luce & Co. & actually only read the Washington Post bits, a book in itself.

I must say that (although it was an enormously fascinating rag-bag of gossip) I did not recognize you at all. What's all this business (repeated 84 times) about you being dowdy, insecure, middle-aged etc etc? Absolutely ridiculous as when we knew you (Esmond & I) we noted that you were very pretty, amusing, & well-educated & informed about all that was going on—I admit I mainly remember shrieks of laughter with you & Phil, but couldn't for the life of me repeat the actual jokes; that's only because of old-age forgetfulness. Obviously your life stopped being a joke fairly soon thereafter, but I still resent & <u>really hate</u> the Halberstam portrait of you. Am keen to know what you thought of his book. I shall contrive to choke down the rest of it (CBS, Time Inc, NY Times etc) one day. Was also surprised to note whilst leafing through the Index that

---

145. Bernstein.
146. Journalist David Halberstam's *The Powers That Be* (Alfred A. Knopf, 1979).

Ramparts magazine[147] isn't in it. I mean, they should be if only because NY Times used so much of their stuff in front-page stories, the first ever to actually document CIA malfeasance. In a word, I feel that Halberstam must be a bit of a light-weight, a facile (and v. fascinating) writer but bemused by POWER as he sees it & not terribly depthy (if there is such a word, I hope there isn't).

Much love, Decca

To Maya Angelou and Paul du Feu   Oakland
                                                                March 30, 1979

Dear Souls,

I was trained from a v. early age to send a prompt bread-&-butter letter if one had gone to stay somewhere. E.g., at age 9 one would be writing to some dismal aunt (having frozen and been ill-fed at her house): Dear Aunt Joan, Thank you very much indeed for having me to stay, I enjoyed it enormously. Age 17, Dear Lady Astor, Thank you so much for including me in your delightful house party, it was all such fun. Yours (in)sincerely (etc).

Well! I'm at a loss for words re yr. incredible hospitality. . . . The way you both nip around those ghastly freeways looking after this old creature. . . . I thought a lot about that on the plane. I mean, why didn't you chuck me out at Gate 6 or whatever? But no, you came all the way—I can't say how smashing it was of you. I was thinking of you going back in ghastly rush-hour traffic; oh dear.

Mainly, of course, it's the incredible feeling of enclosing & enfolding kindness & huge jokes & marvelous chats that you both engender. Oh I did love it all. We really shouldn't live all this far apart, come home, all is forgiven, & live in the Bay Area.

On to other subjects: . . . I thought a lot abt. [a political discussion we had] & I think, Paul, that you & I were being pretty elitist if that's the right expression re said folks. We should start thinking through our mocking attitude, beginning now in my case—because you WERE awfully amusing about that whole campaign. Unfortunately there we are . . . it's so far easier (speaking for myself) to laugh at things rather than weep or be constructive. Pity. I shall contrive to reform in me old age. . . .

So: a ton of total thanks for all, Decca

---

147. Founded in 1962 as a magazine for "moderately hip Catholic lay people," *Ramparts* became more political, radical, and brash when San Francisco journalist and character-about-town Warren Hinckle took over as editor two years later. The upstart magazine featured nationally prominent writers and regularly scooped major established publications. Its circulation rose as high as 400,000. Decca served for a time as a contributing editor and even tried to help the magazine survive by selling ads part-time. After years of fearless anti-establishment journalism, the magazine went through a period of internal upheaval and decline, finally closing in 1975.

To Philip and Sally Toynbee   Oakland
                                                                July 22, 1979

Dear Toyns,

We'd love to come and stay. . . .

It will be such fun meeting God after all we've heard about him over the years. But I do hope he's not the sort to monopolize the conversation? Or deliver pontifical Judgments in the middle of a joke?[148] . . .

Am getting quite over-excited at the thought of it all. Clara trouble: we also are having Benj trouble. I mentioned this fact to B. Gottlieb—& how worrisome one's children are, to which he replied, "Yes, of course you never gave your parents a moment's worry."

                              Fondest love to all,

To the Duchess of Devonshire   Oakland
                                                              November 9, 1979

Dearest Hen,

Welcome to Texas. I've put on the envelope "From her sister in Calif," as sometimes self-appointed protectors of those on tour don't give over letters for fear they are from mad people. So I tore up the first env. which said "From her old Hen in Calif" as then they'd have known it was from a mad person. . . .

Now Hen you've got to get on with yr. book.[149] Are you doing it at all? Am still shocked by lack of cash advance. Point of advance is to provide FOOD and SHELTER to author whilst he produces ms. I can only suppose that your rotten publisher thinks you have adequate food & shelter without a penny from him. . . .

The only other thing of interest (supreme interest to me, anyway) was an incredibly SANE and AMUSING letter from Benj, who is now living in Illinois. First time I've heard from him for such ages . . . his old self. I do wish I could get him to take the treatment (a thing called Lithium) for his malady.[150] Trouble is, when I get that sort of letter—or see him in his ordinary Benj-like

---

148. In a letter a month later planning their upcoming visit, Decca was still mercilessly teasing Toynbee about his religious conversion: "Will God be coming, & if so does he mind sharing? I only ask because from what I've read about him in the Old Testament and other Public Relations handouts he doesn't sound much like the sharing type. In fact if he isn't given the best room he might get a bit jealous (see, e.g., Exodus XX 4)."

149. The duchess was writing a book about her resplendent home. It was published in London in 1982 as *The House: A Portrait of Chatsworth* (Macmillan) and in New York the same year as *The House: Living at Chatsworth* (Holt, Rinehart & Winston).

150. Benjamin Treuhaft suffered periodically from bipolar disorder, or, as it was commonly called then, manic depression.

mood—I am so delighted that I can't bear to say anything adverse, that might result in yet another non-speaking many months, so I shut my mouth (Old Texan Expression, Hen, means shut up as you have already divined). . . .

Yr loving Hen

ps . . . Do send all impressions of Miami, a place I hated like none other on this earth. I was there for 6 mths or so in 1939 (bar, written up in a book I don't think you've read called Hons & Rebels), then again in 1971 (written up in yet another book, on prisons). Oh what a horrid town . . .

To Robert Gottlieb   Oakland
                                                                            January 9, 1980

Dearest Bites,[151]
      . . . BBC have been here non-stop. A dear soul called Julian Jebb is doing a film of Nancy's life, based mainly on interviews with N's sisters. He says he was warned by any number of people <u>not</u> to do it, that he'd be stepping into a hornet's nest; so here he is, in midst of said nest. To wit: He let drop the fact that my sisters Debo & Diana had extracted an agreement with BBC to see the rough cut of the film, & to excise any portions they thought objectionable. Well! Don't you agree that was terrifically nervy of them? Goodness I was cross on hearing this news. So I drew up my own memo, & caused J. Jebb to sign receipt of same, saying that unless they included a passage of one of N's letters to me I should withdraw all permission to use any part of my interview or any reference to any of my books. The passage in question, dated November 1968 (the year that Sir O. Mosley's erroneous autobiog. appeared) is as follows: "Have you noted all the carry on about Sir Os? He says he was never anti-Semitic. Good Gracious! I quite love the old soul now, but really—.! Also I'm very cross with him for saying Tud (Tom) was a fascist which is untrue though of course Tud was a fearful old twister & probably was a fascist when with

---

151. This nickname for editor Robert Gottlieb—and its variations—originated while they were working on Decca's prison book. A number of years later, Decca explained, "Gottlieb is called BITES, BITER or JAWS because in my prison book I described an experiment on convicts in which fleas 'in specially prepared biting cages' were applied to the fellow's arm. In a moment of exasperation, B. Gottlieb shouted out: 'I sometimes feel that I live in a specially prepared biting cage!'" Although Gottlieb was often called Biter when it suited Decca's mood, the editor maintains now that that was "a calumny, since I was usually too busy laughing with her to bite. My view, of course, was that *she* was the biter." And indeed, the first use of the term in Decca's letters was to Gottlieb as "Bitee."

Diana.[152] When with me he used to mock to any extent & he hated Sir Os no doubt about that. If Randolph (Churchill) had been alive he would have sprung to his defence. I miss Randolph."

So there was terrible flapping throughout BBC. I presented my memo to J. Jebb who started back-pedaling like mad, said he never had told me the sis's had final say. In that case, said I, you can sign receipt with no qualms. Next thing, Jebb's boss at BBC rang up from London (this was all before the filming started) to say there was no such agreement—although apparently the Peters agency had in fact sent a letter saying that Debo must have final say-so as to what went in film. There was a short, sharp tussle of wills (mine & Bill Morton, the boss) which I won; after all, by now J. Jebb was out here, had got a TV crew together at vast expense, so what could they do?

The whole point is that obviously they take tons of footage of which only a wee fraction will be in the finished product—and so easy for them to say that an aeroplane was going overhead at the time I read out that letter, or a thing called "a hair in the gate," tele shorthand for something in the way of the photo. I've written all this to D. Rogers, & asked her to incorporate my memo into any contract with BBC, or release, etc. . . .

The other feature of the program: it consisted of a) an interview by J. Jebb re one's recollections of Nancy, b) reading out bits of her letters, c) reading from one of her books. I, natch, chose Wigs on the Green—send-up of Sir O. Mosley's Brit. Union of Fascists, called the Union Jackshirts in Nancy's book; and of Bobo, called Eugenia. Have you ever read it? Not likely as it surfaced but briefly in England in 1936 or thereabouts, never published in USA.[153] . . .

RE-reading N's letters (from circa 1935 on) was fair torture, oh it did so make me miss her all over again—and miss not writing to her at least once a

---

152. Tom Mitford, the only sibling who had frequented Esmond and Decca's Rotherhithe Street home in London, had studied in Germany, had met Hitler through his sister Unity, had been photographed at German Nazi and British Fascist rallies, and, though by all accounts not an anti-Semite, had told friends before the war that he was sympathetic to the Nazis' role in Germany. But he obviously gave Decca and her husband a very different impression. Late in the war, Tom Mitford reportedly volunteered to go to Burma rather than participate in the invasion of Germany. Diana and Oswald Mosley maintained that he had been a paid member of the British Union of Fascists, a fact that Diana insisted on revealing in her interview for Julian Jebb's documentary after learning of Decca's condition for participating in the project.

153. Although difficult to obtain in the United States, there was, in fact, an inexpensive American paperback edition of the book, published by Popular Library of New York in April 1976. The volume also included Nancy Mitford's novel *Highland Fling*. In a 1974 letter, Decca also made reference to a forthcoming American edition, adding that Nancy Mitford didn't want the novels re-issued in England at that time.

week. Then, the ones about her illness—words fail. God that was all too ghastly, 4 & 1/2 years of it.

Much love, dearest Bites, & to all at Knopf, Decca

ps All that stuff about my memo to BBC is absolute EYES ONLY, because it is only to be sprung IF the sisters want that bit cut out. The last thing I want is another mammoth family row. That is, I know you think I thrive on rows but I don't, I don't. I long to be friends with Debo until death do us part which shouldn't be long now.

To Ann Farrer Horne   Oakland
                                                                                February 23, 1980

Darling Cyst,

. . . Latest news this end: I went into near-decline over the Nancy film & poss. non-speakers forever with Debo. . . . I <u>dread</u> losing Debo forever. On the other hand, I bloody well don't see why she is self-appointed arbiter of all that goes on re the family (e.g. Pryce-Jones row), esp as I am 3 years older than she is. Anyway: I believe all is OK. Got a calming t.phone call from Julian Jebb (making the Nancy film) re the screening of rough cut for sisters. He said they loved it, much shrieking etc, & that Diana is to have right of rebuttal of my reading of N's letter re Sir Os. Mosley—which is perfectly OK with me, because what can she <u>say</u>? But she did make one rather good point to J. Jebb: N's letter had said that Tom was a fearful old twister, may have pretended to be a fascist when with Diana. Diana said that Nancy was also a fearful old twister. Rather true?

Also I've had various v. cordial letters from Debo (since my condition of being in the film was bruited). Did you know that SHE is writing a book? History of Chatsworth. Well, Nancy & I always used to think that if she ever put pen to paper (or even sharpened pencil) she would outshine all—one can tell from her letters that she's one of Nature's Writers. She keeps saying it's v. boring, but I don't believe a word of it.

No other news darling Id. . . .

Yr. loving Sister

To Maya Angelou   Oakland
                                                                                   April 23, 1980

Dearest M,

A few observations on that incredibly interesting lunch with you & Louise[154] (for which, by the way, a trillion thanks):

1. In a curious way I have the feeling that since Pat's death Louise is really

---

154. Louise Patterson, widow of William Patterson.

coming into her own at last as a full-fledged PERSON. Did you get that impression at all? Because while she was always a revered Black Woman Leader with caps (also often FEARED—not by me, but others thought her intimidating) her essential role was that of helpmate to the Great Man. Hence when one saw them together, for obvious reasons it was Pat who was in the limelight, the doer of deeds, the perceptive & brilliant head of CRC etc.

2. As I started to say on the telephone, I was most fascinated by all the interlocking points & people that you two, generations apart in age and entirely different in politics, were able to discover. I don't think this would happen with white ex-CPers. We were far too much painted into a corner, isolated by a) outside repression, FBI etc and b) our own sectarianism. For instance when I was aged 22 to 25 or so, living in Washington, I knew (mainly through the Durrs) all sorts of people such as the Galbraiths (long before he was famous),[155] Kay Graham etc. And while I've re-made friends with these two now, late in life, when I joined the CP I dropped them as much as they dropped me. Apparently this didn't happen with black CPers. Or at least not to the same extent.

I wonder why that was? Perhaps for one thing Blacks not in the Party were always far less susceptible to redbaiting than whites, hence less averse to maintaining ties with friends in the CP even when said friends were on headon collision with FBI etc., as the Pattersons were. And the CP blacks far less sectarian, more flexible, than their white counterparts. . . .

                    Decca

To Virginia Durr   Oakland
                                                  April 25, 1980
Dearest Va,
    . . . Will you be coming to Dinky's wedding on 7 June?[156] Now here's something to KEEP UNDER YOUR HAT, if you can—just a wee slice of life—actually it's partly to whet yr. appetite for the wedding. You know how it's human nature to want to find out all about one's child's intended. . . . Bob & I were avid for info. re Terry's past life, his parents, his brothers etc. So Dink & Terry told all that. But when they went to Montserrat, where Dink met her future in-laws for the first time, the in-laws didn't ask one word about us. The nearest the subject ever came to being broached was one night when friends of the Webers came to dinner. They were lower-class English who had made millions in real

---

155. Decca described economist John Kenneth Galbraith and his wife, Catherine (Kitty) Galbraith, as "Seminary Hill pals." The economist, then a top official at the Office of Price Administration, where Decca also worked, drove into Washington in a carpool with her and others. He was a Harvard professor for fifty years and has written more than thirty-five influential books, including *The Affluent Society* (Houghton Mifflin, 1958). He also served as an advisor to several presidents and held other top-level positions in public service, including U.S. ambassador to India.
156. Constancia Romilly was marrying Terry Weber. For details, see following letters.

estate, old folks now retired, very agreeable Dink thought. Somehow the fact she has dual citizenship came up, so the English wife asked where her mother had lived in England. Dink, telling this to me: "I <u>knew</u> that if I said Swinbrook she'd twig immediately to who you are, so I just looked blank & said I don't know where my mother lived." The Oys were quite astonished at this lapse of memory. But the thing is, Va, do you think the reason the Webers don't inquire is because they KNOW—not only know, but disapprove? Anyway I wrote them an incredibly proper sort of letter, literally about 6 lines, merely saying how very much we had enjoyed meeting delightful Terry & his son Benjamin[157] & were much looking forward to seeing them (Webers) at the wedding. . . .

As I was writing the above news came of the Carter unspeakable.[158] Words fail me. Ring up when you get back,

Much love, Decca

To Maya Angelou   Oakland
                                                                      May 1, 1980

Dearest M,

. . . Your letter: There's so much to it I doubt I'll get far answering . . . but here goes.

Louise as dutiful member of church: spot on. Also Comms. as religious zealots[159]—there's a lot to that. It was indeed a sustaining faith, the more so because of the history-is-on-our-side aspects; I mean it seemed so ODD that more didn't rally to our banner. Actually white ex-Reds have some of that churchish quality—I can always tell an Ex (if one is working, say, in a political campaign or on some special issue) by the sense of super-dedication plus unusually well developed organizational ability.

Black CPer & non-CPer: Again spot on. For one thing, Blacks in deep South active in anything, such as NAACP, were branded Communist by such as Jackson Daily News. This all came back to me so forcefully when in Jackson last autumn. Esp. the common oppressor,[160] in which blacks (having been

---

157. Benjamin Weber lived with the Romilly-Webers. Decca sometimes called him her "step-oy."

158. This letter was written on the day of President Jimmy Carter's aborted attempt to rescue fifty-two American hostages held in Iran. In a televised address that morning, Carter said of the operation, in which eight servicemen were killed, "It was my decision to attempt the rescue operation; it was my decision to cancel it when problems developed in the placement of our rescue team for a future rescue operation." The hostages were moved to a secret new location.

159. In the letter to which Decca was replying, Angelou had said that Louise Patterson "reminded me more of a dutiful member of a large successful Baptist church than a lifelong CPer." She noted in passing what she said Decca already knew, that she thought of Communists as religious zealots.

160. Angelou had written that black members of the Communist Party and other blacks shared a common oppressor. Decca appears to be modifying that, saying that blacks generally and Communists, white and black, shared a common oppressor.

called every name under the sun) often tended to identify with persecuted whites in McCarthy time. Here's an example: When making Mit. Spectacular (BBC, Mike Barnes) we went out to see Mr. & Mrs. Gary[161] in Rollingwood. They were very conservative—or perhaps non-political is more accurate; middle class, he was head of (Jim-Crow) American Legion post etc. Anyway during the recent interview, Buddy[162] asked straight out if they realized that the leadership of the defense group was CPers. Reaction: "Is that so? Well, we were called Communists anyway for moving into Rollingwood." Mrs. Gary said "I always wondered where those huge longshoremen came from!"

Comms./white oppressors/house niggers:[163] See Richard Wright's essay in "The God that Failed"[164] (a symposium of essays by former reds,[165] incl. Stephen Spender[166] & I can't remember who else; I read it ages ago, hence Wright's points are dim in my mind. But that was one of them).

But consider also "The Struggle against White Chauvinism" as it was called. This would be in the early 50's (long after R. Wright had quit the Party). Matt Crawford lent me massive files, lots of carbon copies of letters back & forth between Negro comrades, articles—it was a huge endeavor. We've talked about this before. I told you about Libby Mines (white woman in her 30's) being brought up on charges by 18-year-old Florida Washington, black secretary in CRC office, because Libby had asked her to undo a parcel & said "I have weak hands, please do it for me." This was considered at the time one of those silly excesses of the S. against W.C. But Paul[167] pointed out (when we discussed it) that Florida was reacting as being treated as a strong field-hand type v. Libby, white lady. I think he's right (never could quite make up my mind about that long-ago incident).

Amongst Matt's treasures is a faded copy of a sort of transcript, or notes, of a white c. trial in St. Louis. Facts: Jewish couple, staunch CPers of many years' standing, give wedding for their daughter who is ditto staunch member of YCL,[168] or Labor Youth League (whatever youth branch was then called).

---

161. The Wilbur Garys were the black homeowners whom Decca helped protect from racist mobs in 1952.

162. Walter Green.

163. Angelou, speculating with Decca about various nuances of black-white relations, had written that "some blacks were afraid to be connected to some black CPer[s] (note the lack of support for Robeson and Du Bois)." She said they were afraid to "compound their already vulnerable, tenuous security." In addition, she wrote, "Communists were white, as white as the oppressors and therefore couldn't be trusted." Blacks in the party, she said, "were under the aegis of powerful whites . . . as much as 'house niggers' were under the protection of the slave owners, and therefore did not need or even really want support from the common garden-variety black field hand."

164. Edited by Richard Crossman, the influential book was published in 1949 by Harper and subsequently reprinted several times by others.

165. Among the six essays in the volume were four by former Party members and two by former Party sympathizers.

166. The poet, who was a friend of Decca in the 1960s.

167. Presumably Angelou's husband, Paul du Feu.

168. Young Communist League.

Invited hundreds to the wedding but no blacks. Their defense: had they invited blacks, their business wld. be in jeopardy as it would prove they are CP. At the trial—they were fair fit for expulsion—after they had absolutely agreed to the rottenness of their actions, it was (curiously) the black comrades on the trial committee who voted not to expel. One said something along the lines of "Oh for God's sake, this is all so trivial, let's get on with the job" (i.e., basic defense of civil rights etc).

Excesses in Struggle vs. W.C. did indeed exist; e.g., one was asked not to say "black coffee, please." At one memorable meeting here in Oakland, Bill Schneiderman said "There are dark days ahead, Comrades" upon which Ray Thompson (still going strong—a leading Black comrade of the day) got up & made v. strong objection.

There's a book called The Decline of American Communism (sponsored & paid for, incidentally, by the Ford Foundation) in which the author, whose name I've forgotten, attributes the shrinkage of CP during 1950's largely to the struggle vs. W.C.—all those expulsions of whites.

I can only say that for myself I learned a huge lot from said Strug. I also think that it laid a certain foundation for the children. At least the dear things were brought up (or dragged up, some might say) in the very midst of the Strug.

What we should really do one day, everyone's sched. permitting, is to get Matt, Buddy, Libby Mines etc. & have a go-around on this topic. I meant to include a lot about it in <u>Fine Old Conflict</u> but failed to do so. By the way: Florida was eventually expelled as a possible FBI agent. This again was TOTAL paranoia; Bob sees her (client in his office) & thinks v. highly of her. You do have to think yourself into the situation of the 50's to get the drift of these odd occurrences. Buddy thought she was a spy, so that was enough in those dread days. (Nothing to do with the weak hands episode; in fact I've rather forgotten <u>why</u> F. was considered a spy.) Expulsions on the flimsiest of evidence were rife.

Example: Ray Thompson (op. cit) was then head of dread County Security Commission. He came round to my house to say he had ev.[169] against a white man—not a CP member, but a dedicated CRC member & contributor—that he was a spy. Ev. consisted of fact this bloke (who was young, attractive, on the make for girls etc) went to ALL social events in the Bay Area, & always carried a petition for some cause—gathering the names of people there, was the implication. Also, he had been seen entering the Oakland main post office on numerous occasions—where the FBI headquarters were then located.

Ray's other case was against someone who NEVER went to any social occasions. I said well you can't have it both ways—but he did. Both were expelled,

169. Evidence.

put on "non-association," meaning that if you talked to them you, too, would be expelled.

Bloke #1, it later turned out, frequented the P.O. because he had a box number there & was collecting his mail. Can't remember Bloke #2 at this point.

Oh dear it's now almost 10 a.m. & here I am drivelling on . . .

Fondest love, Decca

To Hillary Rodham[170]

Oakland
May 10, 1980

Dear Hillary,

Thanks so much for your very interesting letter re changes in the Arkansas prison system, from which (as you put it) the "stigma of unconstitutionality" should be removed by March, 1981. Which, of course, might seem rather a long time to those confined in the prisons.

Obviously I applaud many of the changes you enumerate. If I am skeptical of such concepts as "American Correctional Association standards" (page 2, para 1 of your letter) you must forgive me; I had my fill of those alleged standards when researching Kind & Usual Punishment.

Some disturbing questions remain. I had been told that numerous Arkansas citizens, knowledgeable about the prison system of that state, were prepared to testify that James Dean Walker's life would be in danger if he were returned to the Ark. penitentiary, & so stated in my telegram to you. My copy is long since lost in the maw of my (non) filing system; but as I recall, those willing to testify included a former judge & a former prison advisor. I expect my copy will turn up one day—doubtless just after I've mailed this letter!—but I wonder if you, or anybody in the Governor's office, ever got in touch with these people re their proposed testimony?

A suggestion: Since Tom Murton first put the Ark. prisons on the map, so to speak, why not invite him for a first-hand look at the changes being made by the new administration? I realize he is a thorny, irascible, difficult character—but so often it is just such types who have what it takes to stir up HUGE and (in his case) EFFECTIVE rows.

Again, very many thanks for writing,

---

170. Wife of the then Arkansas governor and later president Bill Clinton—and still later a United States senator in her own right—Hillary Rodham had been a summer clerk at Robert Treuhaft's firm while at law school (see letter of July 4, 1992, to Virginia Durr). Decca had wired her to advocate on behalf of James Dean Walker, who was facing extradition from California to Arkansas, where he had escaped from prison. The extradition—as well as Walker's guilt or innocence of the murder charges of which he was convicted—was to engage Decca's political passion and professional attention for years. For more background on the case, see July 16, 1980, letter to Miriam Miller.

To Shana Alexander   Oakland
                                                                  May 12, 1980

Dearest Shana,

. . . News of the Century (for us) is that Dinky is to be married! Fancy me
having a Married Daughter—about time, you'll say, since the grandchildren are
now aged 13 & 10.

So Bob & I are nipping to the nuptials in Atlanta; & having nipped that far
will proceed to NY, 8 to 16 June. WILL YOU BE THERE? Do give a shout &
indicate yr. movements.[171]

We've met Dink's intended & like him no end, name of Terry Weber. Much
the same background as hers (SNCC, Freedom riders, Vista[172] etc), & is now a
telephone lineman—in keeping with "Movement" theory of being in touch
with the masses, I guess. Which provoked Bob's classic comment, "I'm glad
she's found a nice Jewish boy but what's he doing climbing up telephone poles
when he should be going to medical school?"

Anyway we are v. pleased over it all. I looked up & Xeroxed for them the C.
of E.[173] Solemnization of Matrimony which reads in part ". . . It is ordained
for a remedy against sin, and to avoid fornication; that such persons as have
not the gift of continency might marry, and keep themselves undefiled members of Christ's body." Have a nice day. Also looked up Duties of Bride's
Parents in E. Post's Etiquette, 1922 edition—they are V. ONEROUS and
COSTLY. . . .

                    Much hoping to see you,
                    Love from Decca

To Hillary Rodham   Oakland
                                                                  June 20, 1980

Dear Hillary,

I've meant to write to you for some time to ask if you got my letter of 10 May
re the James Dean Walker case. But Bob and I have been away—principally to
the wedding of my daughter Constancia Romilly (known as Dinky) in
Atlanta. . . .

On our return, I found a most interesting letter from James D. Walker. He
says in part: "The case has broadened in scope considerably since it first
began—there are now 28 other states that are looking at our case—16 states
that are presently under Federal Court ruling because of 'unconstitutional'

---

171. The Treuhafts did spend a few days with Alexander in East Hampton, a stay that Decca
later described to Virginia Durr as "non-stop soap opera conducted by the Rich & Famous, mostly
slanging their agents/publishers/each other; good spectator sport for a few days."

172. Volunteers in Service to America, now part of the federal government's AmeriCorps program, provides full-time assistance to local community agencies.

173. Church of England.

conditions,[174] plus 12 more that are being sued because of inadequate and brutal conditions.

"This means that any rulings in my case could affect extradition of inmates being returned to 'unconstitutional' prison systems. However, the question involved may take considerable time to resolve, as we are currently awaiting a ruling by the U.S. Supreme Court as to just who should have jurisdiction to hear the questions raised in our writ. Personally, I feel that it is time for the courts of our land to protect, as well as prosecute. I believe there is a sociolegal issue involved, and if it can help to correct any aspect of our totally inadequate criminal justice system, then the effort will have been worthwhile."

I concur with the above sentiments. But what I really want is an answer to my letter to you of 10 May, plus any additional material and/or thoughts that you may have about this whole issue.

Do write back.[175] I'd love more news of Chelsea Victoria—what a marvelous name! How did you come by it? Was she conceived in Victoria Station, or Chelsea?

Best regards, Decca

ps I should add that James Walker's letter was (as you can see from above quotations from it) extremely lucid, non-self-pitying, intelligent. Does Arkansas really want him back in the prison system? WHY? R.S.V.P. re all this.

I enclose a copy of relevant passages in my May 10 letter in case you have lost it.

To the Duchess of Devonshire   Oakland
                                                                  June 30, 1980
Dearest Hen,

The wedding was a smasher, now faded into Golden Memory because after that we scrammed to NY & environs. . . .

It was out of doors in a sort of small farm belonging to a friend of hers who raises cows, chickens etc. Approx. 175 people came, 30 from out of town . . . of which masses were children of all ages & colours—SNCC Revisited 20 years later. (When Jamie was born Nancy wrote hoping his name was Watt Hugh, well there were many hues at the wedding.) Dink—pushing 40, remember how Bob was pushing 40 when you 1st met him—looking marvellous despite her

---

174. In their prisons.

175. Rodham replied with a long, handwritten, and personal letter acknowledging the deficiencies of the Arkansas prison system but citing improvements in recent years and crediting her husband, whom she put in the "reformer" camp, for negotiating a consent decree in a key Arkansas lawsuit challenging prison conditions, despite opposition from "many people in and out of state government who hoped to avoid responsibility" for state prison conditions. She also said she had researched the Walker case and did not believe it had any merit.

ancient age, in a white wedding dress of alt. pleated panels & a sort of coarse Mexican lace with appliqued pink roses. Sounds hideous but was v. pretty. It all went off like clockwork. Brill. Bob found champagne for $3 a bottle . . . we were told that if you get it COLD enough people won't note the three-dollarishness of it, so I hope they didn't. Two bands: a folk-singing group, and one of those vile loud dance bands for later on. . . .

Va. Durr was there from Montgomery, & she had all scrunched up in her bag the J. Jebb article in the Sunday Times that somebody in England had sent her. So she came up to Mrs. W (Evelyn, I call her)[176] shouting out in her high Southern scream, "Whaaa, Mrs. Weber, I know you'll be dying to read all about Decca & her family." I tried to fend this off saying "Oh no Virginia, Mrs. Weber is not remotely interested in that sort of thing," but Va. thrust it at her. Next day was the Brunch with the Webers. . . . Mrs. W. said not one word abt. the Jebb effort.

The main thing is that Terry is incredibly nice, & what a terrific fluke that they met at all. Hen she seems SO delighted & happy, which as you can imagine pleases MY old heart no end, esp. after the thin time she's had over the years. . . .

Id wrote to say what would Dink like? I said, a pretty dish cloth, easy to pack; so Id sent same, to Dink's great pleasure. . . .

The Oys were a great pleasure this time. We went to Atlanta in time for Oy 1's graduation from Junior High School, where he copped all the top honours for essays etc. & made a speech from the platform, oh I was proud. Oy 2 (Chaka) is a marvellous clown type, like a v. young Marx Brother. They've absolutely stopped fighting & screaming, such a mercy. I do so wonder what will become of them in later life? But fear I shall be beneath the sod before finding it out.

To Philip Toynbee   Oakland
                                                                July 4, 1980

Dearest P.,

Myriad (almost) copies of <u>Friends Apart</u>[177] came clattering into my postbox, one now on its way to good Billy Abrahams with strong recommendation to publish it here. Anyway I re-read it, & must agree with what you said some years ago when <u>you</u> re-read it: it's a damn good book. Also a damn good new intro. Except—imagine Esmond in the "transcendent realm of Heaven"! It would jolly well have to be an "inconceivably altered state of being & consciousness," as you say. I can't imagine him getting on with all those angels.

---

176. Mrs. Weber, groom Terry Weber's mother.
177. Toynbee's 1954 memoir of Esmond Romilly and Jasper Ridley in the 1930s had just been reissued by Sidgwick & Jackson.

Teaching Gabriel to play Carmagnole on his horn? Getting after St. Peter re his restrictive admissions policy? Starting up a new edition of Out of Bounds? That would get him nowhere but DOWN, don't you agree?

Natch I am <u>livid</u> about yr. obit of me.[178] Why couldn't they have got someone sensible to do it, such as Blissful Bim? I can only say, WATCH OUT. If you are too mean, you may find a HUGE and HORRIBLE incubus astride yr. shoulders for the rest of your natural life. (Am not actually sure what incubuses, or incubi? are, but you'll find out soon enough. I am fairly sure they do get astride backs or shoulders.) . . .

The very least you can do is send me a carbon of the obit. for perusal & correction.[179]

Fondest love, & to Sally, Decca

To Sally Belfrage[180]   Oakland

July 14, 1980

Dearest Sally,

I think the Finale is a great improvement, but must confess that I still can't make it all out.[181] That is, your comments on dread Bagman or rather Bhag wan[182] . . . seem v. much to the point—but why play his wretched cassettes? Felicitations to yr children for making you turn 'em off.

---

178. As Decca discussed in her book *Faces of Philip*, Toynbee had written her in June to say: "Believe it or not, I've just been asked to write your Times obituary. In some ways I see that this is tremendously one up on you—unless, of course, you've also been asked to write mine. On the other hand, it does give me a good deal of freedom, doesn't it: I mean either you'll never read it, or you'll read it From Beyond where all is forgiven in every conceivable direction." He later asked her for "a potted autobiography with dates of all books etc." Decca replied with a list of her books, including "Fair Game: Genuine Sportsmen's Clubs or Cover for Vigilante Operation? Publisher: Weidenfeld." She said in a letter that she wondered "if he will twig before it's TOO LATE that I made that up, never wrote any such book? . . . [D]on't you think the title is rather good, exactly the sort of plunking book I <u>might</u> have written, if I had. Can't wait for the Obit to appear with this glaring error in it—except again, the annoying thing is not being here to enjoy it."

179. Although Decca dismissed her exchange with Toynbee about the obituary as a "tease," well over a decade later she was still thinking of her late friend's obituary sitting unseen in the *Times*'s files (see letter of November 25, 1993, to Sally Belfrage, and associated footnote 109).

180. Daughter of Cedric Belfrage, and a friend and near contemporary of Constancia Romilly, Sally Belfrage became Decca's good friend, confidante, and loyal correspondent. They met in 1955 in London when Sally Belfrage was a teenager, not long after Cedric Belfrage was deported from the United States as a subversive alien after refusing to testify before the House Un-American Activities Committee. Sally Belfrage later became a world traveler, independent journalist, human rights activist, and author, publishing the first of her five books, *A Room in Moscow*, when she was in her early twenties.

181. Belfrage had evidently sent Decca all or part of the manuscript of what was to become her book *Flowers of Emptiness: Reflections on an Ashram*, published the following year by Dial Press of New York.

182. The Indian guru Bhagwan Shree Rajneesh, at whose Poona ashram Belfrage had stayed.

But you still seem to be in a muddle over it all, which natch leaves the reader in a state of puzzlement. This may be compounded in my case because a) I don't think I could ever take myself seriously enough to go grubbing about looking for my soul—that is, I couldn't get interested in it, hence religion, psychiatry, consciousness-raising & the like are all totally beyond my ken, although of course I know (and love) many people who go in for that sort of thing & seem to get some satisfaction out of it; and b) all you say in the Finale about pseudo-religious cults . . . appears to contradict all the positive stuff about gurus, & Bhagwan in particular, that you've said in other places. . . .

Also what's with "permission from Poona, quite worrying" in your letter? Since when does one need permission from Poona to quote something in an English book? Please enlarge on that. . . .

Thanks SO much for sending review of Diana's ghastly book.[183] Be an angel & send any & all others that you see. The book is TOO extraordinary with chapter headings like "A Young Lady from Baltimore," "The Prince In Love," "Storm Clouds" & the like. The review you sent absolutely summed it up. It made me turn quite pink to think that one of us could write such total trash & so badly—it's Woman's Day all the way. Am LONGING for more reviews, so PLEASE, PLEASE be looking out for them. . . .

> Lots of love . . . Decca

To Miriam Miller   Oakland
                                                   July 16, 1980

Dearest Mim,

. . . Life here has changed slightly, to wit: the Mediterranean cruise is definitely off, so we shan't be going abroad after all. Reasons: Bob's incredibly important police brutality trial is scheduled to start July 28 . . . plus I've finally found something to do with my trivial life, a v. interesting extradition case which has absolutely got me by the throat as it involves not only a v. important prison issue (now pending before U.S. Sup. Court) but a particularly promising cast of characters. At risk of boring you, here it is in a nutshell: Fellow by name of James Dean Walker convicted of killing an Arkansas policeman in 1963, sentenced to cruel & unusual Ark. prison. In 1975, Walker walked away from work furlough & took a plane to Calif. Has worked thereafter in Tahoe area[184] in his own leather goods shop—until December 1979, arrested in connection with minor drug offense, was discovered to be escaper from Ark. prisons. Do keep

---

183. *The Duchess of Windsor* (Sidgwick & Jackson, 1980).
184. Lake Tahoe, on the California-Nevada border.

reading because here comes the interesting bit: Tom Murton, former Warden of Ark. prisons & real-life figure of "Brubaker," Robert Redford movie, got in touch with us last Feb. to send t.gram to Gov. Brown[185] saying he (Murton) plus numerous Ark. luminaries including an Ark. supreme court judge were prepared to testify that Walker would face certain death if returned to Ark. prison. So we did that; and sent a copy to Hillary Rodham, former law clerk in Bob's office when she was 2nd yr. law student at Yale—now 1st Lady of Ark, married to Gov. Wm. Clinton of that state. So Hillary wrote back a long letter, mostly abt. reforms her hubby is effecting in the prisons—a form letter, but hedged round with personal messages to Bob including fact she's got a baby called Chelsea Victoria! . . .

Anyway Brown denied extradition hearing (most unusual) & signed extradition warrant—apparently not wishing to embarrass his good friend Wm. Clinton, Gov. of Ark, another self-styled super-liberal. Walker's lawyer got the case before the U.S. Supreme Court where it will be decided next term (October, maybe). Next steps for me:

Shall be going to Tahoe, where Walker is in jail, to see him, his lawyer, & his girlfriend who sounds smashing—she's a shill or barmaid in local casino, & super-bright from our correspondence. Shall be staying with C.K. McClatchy who has a house in Tahoe (he's publisher of Sacto. Bee)[186] & has promised to help with research etc.

Thence to Sacto, to torture Gov. Brown & associates about this poltroonly act of returning Walker to Ark.

Thence to Ark—where Tom Murton says he'll come with me! A terrific bonanza, as he knows (both literally & figuratively) where all the bones are buried in Ark. prison system. (Alas, he doesn't look anything like Robert Redford, but you can't win 'em all.) Also in Ark, shall look up Hillary & hubby.

Sorry to burden you with above boring stuff but it's terrifically on my mind, & I'm v. excited about it.

Other news & views: PELE IS HAVING HER FACE LIFTED! Is probably even now under the knife. . . . Don't you call that amazing? . . . Actually I adore her ordinary face, & said so to Bob who replied "Well it is getting a bit craggy," which made me shriek. She's got some sort of special deal . . . I do trust it isn't a Learner, like those places where you can get a haircut for $2 from student practitioners. . . .

My sisters, discussing face lifts: Debo: "I'm afraid I'm not vain enough to have mine done." Diana: "I'm afraid I'm too vain to have mine done"—

185. Edmund G. Brown Jr., known as Jerry, whose father, Edmund G. (Pat) Brown Sr., had previously served as governor.

186. McClatchy was president of the McClatchy newspaper chain as well as publisher of the *Sacramento Bee.*

meaning she's eternally beautiful enough already. Rather true, I guess, from her Snowdon[187] photo in London Times? . . .

Much love,

To Ann Farrer Horne   Oakland
                                                                                July 24, 1980

Darling Sister,

. . . Yr. poem: "Where meanwhile <u>is</u> God?" Good question. You may know the following story of WWII: Peter Rodd, Evelyn Waugh & Randolph Churchill were all billetted together somewhere in Italy. (I think it was, in fact, in Prod's parents' house which led to yet another story—he cut up all their antique chairs for firewood, the weather being slightly chilly at the time.) Anyway, Prod & E. Waugh got thoroughly fed up with Randolph, non-stop talker, so to shut him up bet him 10 quid he couldn't read the Bible in 3 days. Randolph did, & was heard loudly declaiming as he read, "Isn't God a SHIT!" I must say I agree after reading yr. poem. If I was God I'd be FAR nicer, not just in the comfort of a perfect understated phrase etc. But perhaps he does his best in the circs? I mean, what with wretched Satan in partial control? Sister do you believe in Satan? How do he & G. divide up the territory, so to speak? . . .

Yr loving Decca

To Maya Angelou   Oakland
                                                                                August 9, 1980

Dearest M,

You were on the warpath last night—well, I don't blame you. The high point (or low point, depending on how one looks at it) was when Barb Kahn said— "But what can we DO about racism?" & you said, "YOU are asking ME?"

The last time this almost identical conversation took place was at the Panther-sponsored Jean Genet meeting here. I know I've told you all about this. . . .[188]

Back to Barb Kahn: I know you don't like her, & I often feel I wouldn't like her, specially, if I met her now for the first time. The fact is, though, that she's

---

187. Lord Snowdon (Antony Armstrong-Jones), the photographer who was married to Princess Margaret.

188. Some details of that meeting are omitted here because they duplicate a more detailed account that Decca sent to a number of the participants in a letter written many years later. See February 1, 1993, letter to "various friends."

one of those oldest & dearly cherished friends with whom one has been through everything together (death of Nicky, dread business about her brain-damaged kid etc). . . .

We first got to know the Kahns when they lived in Vallejo, he was working for Kaiser Hosp (Permanente) there. They were the total sparkplugs of CRC in that horrid navy-ridden little town. They did pioneering work re frame-ups of Blacks (saved at least one from the chair); it was really Eph who led all this, Barb tagging along loyally. I used to go up there quite often, in the Dec-mobile of the day, in my capacity as chapter secretary of CRC. . . . You rather have to visualize the totally embattled position of <u>everyone</u>: the Blacks, mainly gov't workers, risking their jobs as CRC members; the Kahns, also at risk with annoyance of constant death threats by telephone. I think Barb was genuinely upset by these threats, feared being boiled in oil by the Fascists or some such.

So she is a complex character, like most characters. But when she said what she did ("What can we DO?") I think she was being v. honest. Perhaps she is more honest than I am in this respect? You say that Buddy is the token Negro. Could be true; that is, we've known & loved him for eons. Have lost track of many others (Blacks), such as the stalwart church sisters of CRC days. All we really had in common was CRC work, so when that went by the board so did our friendship, genuine though it was at the time. Matt said something of the sort last evening; it was the common struggle that held us together, except for the few who will always be close loved ones. . . .

Such is la bloody old vie. RSVP,

ps . . . Matt & I have much the same—Basic Training, you might call it—hence I thought he made more sense last night than anyone else. But we have had grave disagreements over the years. . . .

Years ago, 1950's, when the CP was underground, Matt was assigned to take me to task for a terrible infringement of security. What had happened was that I said something in the CRC office (presumed to be bugged) about a comrade which would indicate his whereabouts. I immediately realized what I'd done & told the leadership. It meant reassigning the comrade to somewhere else—immense dislocation, all my fault. So Matt absolutely took me to the carpet or whatever the expression is: said as a non-member of the Working Class, & a non-Black, I would never be able to overcome my dread background, hence would continue to make stupid mistakes like that one. I was in near tears. Matt now says he has completely forgotten this conversation! But it made a terrific, never to be forgotten, impression on me.

So: now you have a brief run-down of cast of characters, as seen through my jaundiced eyes, of last night's warpathery.

To Ann Farrer Horne   Oakland
                                                                    August 14, 1980

Darling Sister,

I wrote a few days ago trying to make amends for my STUPID & insensitive letter, which clearly irked you no end.[189] But the whole thing is to me so awful—that is, that I could have triggered your response—that I must have another go. None of what follows is an effort to MITIGATE my hopelessness, merely trying to recapitulate the (to me) ever-valued past.

We first met at a fairly oldish age (considering we are 1st cousins), 13 or 15. I adored you on sight, & felt that at last I had a Best Friend. We used to go walking all the way to—Chipping Norton?—anyway, 10 miles there & 10 miles back to get the <u>most</u> heavenly sausage rolls & fizzy lemonade (both banned at Swinbrook), chatting like mad all the way there & back. Then there were moments like Uncle Geoff saying "I like your hair, so nice & smooth" (when all the others were screaming away about waves & curls). . . .

Crowning glory was going to Paris with you, & falling in love with Emile.[190] As I remember it, we were going to be more or less a menage a quatre, as neither you or I had prior claim to Emile & we'd be needing Georgette to do the actual cooking, besides she was married to Emile. As for Maurice, menage a trois (although I harbored a fearful fear that you & he might chuck me out after a few days), as again neither of us had much of a lien on him. In the event he never seemed to notice us much, merely signed his autograph. Silly of him, in a way; think how his future might have changed!

After that you became an actress & I married Esmond, & we didn't see each other much; after I went to America, correspondence dried up as it usually does when you haven't seen somebody for ages & no common friends to write about. But I still have the lovely photo of Clare, aged about 5, with wreath in hair. (Or maybe aged 2?)

When I came back to England for the first time in 1955, I sensed that things had changed. You did ask us to tea & so on but all seemed constrained & different. I only realized why ages later, when I read "If Hopes Were Dupes."[191] Again, my stupid insensitivity—but Sister, do see how difficult it would have been to fathom what you were going through.

Then, the last many times I've been in England, all seemed to be getting back to normal, or ordinary. . . .

---

189. The offending letter was apparently the one Decca sent her cousin on July 24, teasing her about her poem "Where meanwhile is God?"

190. Decca wrote in *Daughters and Rebels* about her and her cousin's "brief bouts of flirtation" with unnamed French students during their year abroad—as well as some of her misadventures on Paris's seamier side, which were deliberately excluded from her sunny letters home to her mother—but none of the details in her memoir seem to match the particular liaisons she discussed in this letter.

191. Horne's memoir of her mental breakdown.

As you know, I cherish our correspondence, & seeing yr. poems and/or [other writings].

So PLEASE darling Id don't be angry any more. . . .

Sister—AM I FORGIVEN?

This brings all my love. And PLEASE not goodnight yet, Sister, do wait a year or two until I come back to England.

Yr <u>Sister</u>

To the Duchess of Devonshire   Aboard an airliner
                                                                                December 7, 1980

Dearest Hen,

En route from Los Angeles to Arkansas I read in L.A. paper that Sir O. Mosley died. Diana must be so incredibly sad & lonely. For obvious reasons I shan't be writing, but if inclined do transmit message of sympathy.

Much love, Henderson

Oh dear what a v. odd & awkward letter. But you know how it is, Hen.

To Robert Gottlieb   Oakland
                                                                                January 5, 1981

Dear Bites,

We just got back from Mexico. I won't bore you with the beauty of the scenery, the beaches etc (esp. as I never went near any of that), or how horrid Mexico is in some ways. Forward to my topic:

You know how you wrote, ages ago, re a possible book about that extradition case? Well I wasn't at all for it at the time, but now I'm slightly warming up to the idea. However, I should like you to bend your large brain to the subject so don't simply skim this letter & then dash off a one-liner back. Also not appreciated will be your usual sarcastic rejoinder, as when I eagerly asked you if you liked the intro to Poison Pen you said "My dear, I've never been so moved since I first read Madame Bovary." You've prob. forgotten saying that but I haven't, the sort of thing that seres the soul. So do try to pay attention for once & send a sensible answer.

1. I still haven't got any sort of focus on the thing—how to make it of any interest to anyone but me & a few close chums.[192] I did write to James Walker (the prisoner) as you suggested, saying you thought his story might make an interesting book etc. Well he was AVID at the idea (who wouldn't be, in his unfortunate position?) and urged me to go ahead, with his full cooperation. . . .

---

192. As Decca was preparing an article on the case for *New West* magazine, she wrote to a friend, "I don't think anyone but me is remotely interested in this arcane issue, so it'll probably be another loser."

2. Since the article came out (3 November, in *New West*) there have been several developments, to wit: To the amazement (and shock) of people in Ark such as Philip Kaplan (inmate counsel, see article) Gov. Clinton was defeated in the election by a relatively unknown Republican, Frank White (said by some to be a card-carrying member of KKK). Hence Gov. Clinton's assurances of safety for Walker are clearly down the drain. Letters to this effect, urging Brown's reconsideration of the extrad. warrant, have been sent by various ones including the Human Rights Committee of the SF Bar Assn., under the prompting of You Know Who. Paul Halvonik, a really brill. constitutional lawyer, has agreed to represent the prisoner without fee under same prompting.[193] . . .

I seem to be thoroughly up to the neck in it all. Yet I still can't see how to make it into a book. To try to recapitulate our conversation of some months ago: You thought one might retrace the original crime, 1963 cop murder; get that all straight; follow the career of J. Walker in Ark prisons; his eventual escape; and la-di-dah. I was saying that the total arbitrariness of extradition proceedings was of interest? And you said extradition is boring. Perhaps it is, but not to me. . . .

Please send an outline ("Must be able to follow simple instructions" as my job description for subeligible typist said); also money for a stout winter coat, motel room, etc.[194] . . .

Agréez, cher Monsieur, mes compliments les plus sincères,[195]
G. Flaubert

To Benjamin Dreyfus   Oakland
                                                   March 28, 1981
Dear Barney,

[The] enclosed [is] from Ark. Gazette.[196] . . .

Actually, it's rather a clever job. I mean the writer (as Bob pointed out) has absolutely got me dead to rights: see bit about Oscar Fendler in para starting

---

193. Despite Decca's best efforts, Walker was subsequently extradited back to Arkansas, leaving her "spitting with rage."

194. Despite her long preoccupation with the Walker case, Decca never did write the book she contemplated here.

195. "Dear sir, accept my most sincere greetings."

196. An op-ed essay by reporter Doug Smith entitled "James Dean Walker: The California Connection." Smith wrote that "most Arkansans probably don't fully appreciate that on the West Coast, James Dean Walker has acquired the status of Joe Hill, Sacco and Vanzetti and the Scottsboro Boys." He said that "Miss Mitford is artful and—in one sense—thorough. She interviews and quotes everyone who, intentionally or unintentionally, reinforces the position she is espousing. Those who make a strong case for the other side get shorter shrift, and are always placed on the defensive, leading the careless reader to conclude that there is no other side, or none that is morally defensible. But that is in the nature of muckraking. Miss Mitford herself probably makes no claim of 'objectivity,' her journalism is personal and passionate."

"An Arkansan reading the accounts . . ." Well, I did fairly well know what I was doing by calling O. Fendler "former Justice" etc, but little dreamed that anyone would take me up on it.[197] Ditto, in penultimate para, my reasons for concealing the born-again aspect of JDW—the writer is absolutely spot on, that WAS why I never mentioned this, so off-putting to one's readers, I thought.[198]

So in one way I can't help admiring Doug Smith of the Gazette Staff, because he did the one thing nobody else has ever done to me, i.e., gone behind what Philip Toynbee has cruelly called my "spurious research,"[199] & carved it up. I must just tell an example, when I was cringing lest some clever reviewer (or lawyer) would nail me: When preparing Kind & Usual I ran across a quotation from Hugo Black in another prison book. It was an absolutely perfect, & beautifully written, comment on parole boards (see heading, Chapter 12, Parole). It was followed by a string of numbers & letters (citation), so I asked Bob's office to check it out; they did, & said it didn't exist, citation all wrong etc. I threw myself on the mercy of Laurent Frantz (super-legal-researcher) who confirmed the Bob lot. So I just put it in anyway, as a quotation from Black (no citation). Needless to say, it went unchallenged. . . .

Much love, Decca[200]

To Robert Gottlieb
Oakland
May 26, 1981

Dear Bites,

. . . When in England we heard all about Sonia Orwell's funeral a few months ago.[201] It seems that people gathered in twos & threes saying things like "Well of course I adored Sonia — BUT — ." As my temp. soared, I got to thinking about MY funeral. Perhaps the best plan is to arrange for a large

197. Smith had described Oscar Fendler as "a colorful and contentious lawyer who is a former member of the state Pardons and Paroles Board and who served as a special justice on the Arkansas Supreme Court when Walker's first conviction was reversed by the Court."

198. Smith had written that the "big nit of the 'Free Walker' reportage . . . is its failure to note the one thing about Walker the prisoner that truly distinguished him. He was the greatest jailhouse evangelist this state, and probably any other state, has ever seen . . ." He asked, ". . . do his champions feel they must conceal this aspect of his character, lest they alienate Californians more offended by Bible-thumping than by drug-dealing or cop-shooting?"

199. Philip Toynbee's characterization of her research, which Decca delighted in citing repeatedly over the years, began with his reaction to the manuscript of *The American Way of Death*. Decca told a friend at the time that Toynbee didn't like her history of embalming "because of what he calls its 'spurious scholarship.' " She added, "I can't get it through his head that Bob did all the scholarly bits (and therefore they're not spurious), he thinks I just made it all up."

200. Decca sent a copy of this letter also to Marge Frantz with the marginal comment: "Please return this one day. Or give it to Doug Foster for dissection by his journalism class!!" (Foster was a journalist and, later, journalism educator who met Decca when he was a student at San Jose State University during her distinguished professorship and remained a good friend.)

201. Orwell had died of cancer, penniless, in November 1980.

group of doting former students (who don't really know me very well) to be on hand, their sole function to circulate amongst the mourners & circumvent the BUTs.

This end, more weddings than funerals: 1) Dink's, last June (photo enclosed), 2) Benjy's this March.[202] . . . Re Benj: You know how desperately worrying he was (manic depression-wise). Well he's been absolutely OK for more than 2 years, despite adamant refusal to go the lithium route. He is so smashing when he is his dear self, so you can imagine how v. delighted we are. But it is a bit puzzling—how that dread disease came & went; he was approx. 28 when it all started, is now 33. There is a v. excellent book called MOODSWING by Dr. Fieve,[203] who was a lithium pioneer; and he does say somewhere in the book that in some cases the sufferer recovers sans treatment. . . .

Sorry for such a VERY MELLOW LETTER, you'll think I've gone all sugary in me old age. . . .

[L]ots of love, . . . Decca

To Kay Boyle   Oakland
                                                                              May 29, 1981
Dearest Kay,

. . . Maya told me that Ernie Gaines[204] called her to say he'd had a call from the T. Olsen Committee to discuss his remarks at the ceremonies.[205] As nobody had thus far ever asked him to speak he was highly annoyed. But accdg. to Eva's account, he got even: devoted his entire remarks to what a saintly character Jack Olsen[206] is—& pointed out that Jack, instead of being on the platform with the dignitaries, was stuck in the general audience.

We went to a lunch party at Billy Abrahams' on the Great Day (T. Olsen Day). You know how Billy sort of dances & glides about?[207] So we got talking

---

202. Benjamin Treuhaft had married violinist Sue Ann Draheim in Berkeley.

203. *Moodswing: Dr. Fieve on Depression*, by Dr. Ronald R. Fieve, now available in its revised version but apparently known to Decca in its 1975 edition, *Moodswing: The Third Revolution in Psychiatry.*

204. Ernest Gaines, the author of *The Autobiography of Miss Jane Pittman* (Dial Press, 1971) and other novels.

205. The city of San Francisco had declared May 17, 1981, "Tillie Olsen Day" to honor the former manual worker, activist, and author of the book of short stories *Tell Me a Riddle* (Lippincott, 1961), which was revered in some feminist circles. Decca had known Olsen through Communist Party activities since the mid-1940s and considered her "an old frenemy . . . One of Ours [who] had made it" with publication of *Tell Me a Riddle*, which she called "a marvellous book." Decca once wrote that Olsen was known in Party circles as "the 2nd worst housekeeper anywhere (1st worst being me). So that story 'I Stand Here Ironing,' in *Tell Me a Riddle*, is certainly fiction, I never noted any signs of same in her children's dresses and this was before drip-dry, you must realize."

206. Tillie Olsen's husband.

207. For this reason, Decca's nickname for William (Billy) Abrahams was "the Glider," and she referred to Holt, Rinehart & Winston, where Abrahams was then a senior editor, as "the Gliders."

about T & he danced & glided like mad, telling his own tales of woe, to wit: Her publisher, who is a friend of his, asked him to do the favor of going to see her & trying to talk her into writing one or two pages of explanation of genesis of <u>Yoniminda</u> or whatever that dread book was called, begins with a Y any-way.[208] As he (the Tillie editor) had no luck whatsoever in persuading her to furnish a brief explanation of why the book was unfinished. He'd sunk a huge lot of money in the advance, expecting a proper book. So Billy went, anticipating 20 mins max. discussion; it went on for TWO HOURS, Tillie in tears etc. etc. because she was asked to ACTUALLY WRITE two whole pages. Next story: Billy & P. Stansky[209] went to a Virginia Woolf symposium for only purpose of hearing a paper written by one of Stansky's students. They got there "and we heard a horribly familiar voice," said B. So they dashed to get some lunch. The voice went on & on, & by the time she had finished everyone at the meeting was famished & made a dash for the lunch room. It soon became clear that Tillie had pre-empted the student's time and she wouldn't get on until hours later, so P & B regretfully told her (the stu.) that they couldn't wait. Turned out that Tillie wasn't even on the program, had just been asked to make a few extemporaneous remarks. . . . The above, dear Kay, is for your forthcoming Appreciation (or is it depreciation?) of Tillie Olsen.

Other news & views: I'm rather giving up on [an article about] the Evangelists . . . I have a better idea, & one that would dovetail with England trip: Brixton Riots,[210] which happened when we were there in April. Point being that I've noted ever since 1955 when I first went back to England how extraordinarily smug & thickheaded the English are about anything to do with race problems. Huge riots in Bristol a couple of years ago, but they haven't learned a thing. . . .

     Fondest love . . .

---

208. *Yonnondio: From the Thirties*, a novel that Olsen had begun at the age of nineteen and finally published decades later, in 1974 (Delacorte Press), still unfinished. Olsen's book *Silences*, published in 1978 (also by Delacorte Press), discussed the circumstances that inhibit literary production, including her own.

209. William Abrahams's partner, Peter Stansky, professor of history at Stanford University

210. Several days of riots in the severely depressed, largely black area of south London were occasioned by continuing friction with police, including a "stop-and-search" campaign targeting young local residents.

At home in the 1980s, Decca played her favorite game,
Boggle, with her husband and Maya Angelou.

Facing page, top: Launching *Grace Had an English Heart* in
September 1988 at the Longstone Lighthouse on an island in
the North Sea, near the scene of Grace Darling's fabled rescue.

Below: Posing for publicity shots during her book tour in
England in September 1988, as Robert Treuhaft stood by.

VIII

AN
ENGLISH
HEART

In a note to her husband in March 1986, Decca discussed an upcoming public-television documentary on her life and career. "I must say," she wrote, "I was cheered *no end* by seeing that film. Of course it was the ego trip of all time hence v. DANGEROUS." She mentioned a friend of theirs who was at the peak of her career and had "developed an adulatory following that she's fully earned . . . but seldom gets off the subject of me-me-me." And then she asked her husband, "Bob, am I, toddling towards the end of MY career, like that? Do say I'm not, or if I am (as at this moment, flushed with pride over the [documentary]), give a swift kick. I do long for you to see the film—the theme song is GRACE DARLING! In other words, I've turned into Grace Darling with her English heart, just as Sally [Belfrage] said."

Whether Decca had been seduced by her reputation or not, her comments are nonetheless revealing of her state of mind during the 1980s. With pride, perseverance, and gusto, she had battled her way through numerous fine old conflicts—political, familial, and literary; some self-instigated, some not—and, like the Treuhafts' friend, she had reached the peak of her well-deserved reputation. Through all the distractions of her literary career, she maintained her political fervor, fighting as tenaciously against what she considered the injustice of an escaped prisoner's extradition back to Arkansas's notorious prison system as she had in an earlier era against the wrongful conviction of accused murderer Jerry Newson. She traveled to Central America to observe and write about the revolutionary movements in Nicaragua and El Salvador; she was arrested in an anti-apartheid protest at the University of California at Berkeley; she wrote about the terror gripping Atlanta during a killing spree directed against black children; she participated with her family in a civil rights March Against Fear and Intimidation in Georgia.

And yet . . . Decca's "attack instinct" against injustice of every stripe sometimes found targets more personal and occasionally less worthy of the relentless dedication with which she pursued them, including a highly publicized suit against a novelist for plagiarism of small sections of *Daughters and Rebels*. In general, she reveled in the drama of litigation and righteous indignation. (She once asked an attorney, only half in jest, "Whom shall we sue next??? Do be giving this some thought.") Such no-holds-barred crusades seemed at times little more than an atavistic reflex, almost a caricature of her noble confrontations with, for example, the smarmy potentates of the funeral industry. (The funeral directors were indeed a formidable target and did not capitulate easily. As late as 1976, thirteen years after the publication of her exposé, Decca testified before the Federal Trade Commission, convulsing the hearing with laughter as she skewered her old adversary, industry spokesman Howard C. Raether. Yet it was not until eight years later, in 1984, that the regulatory agency finally adopted some of the funeral reforms that Decca had recommended in 1963. The so-called Funeral Rule was subsequently weakened and, in any case, rarely enforced.)

Simultaneously, as she'd suggested to her husband, Decca seemed drawn back increasingly to her "English heart," albeit sometimes not with the bravado of the folk heroine Grace Darling. Following the death of Philip Toynbee in 1981, Decca tried to interest others in writing about her old friend or, at least, publishing his latest memoir in the United States. Failing that, she wrote a memoir herself, *Faces of Philip*. She seemed to have no great illusions about the book; it was a matter of the heart. Well before the book's publication, she wrote to a friend and critic, "I suppose I was the wrong person to take on a memoir of Philip. But nobody else was keen to do it. My effort was (as per the title) to show the complexity of him via interviews, letters etc. from his friends & family; but I can see from what you wrote that I haven't succeeded in conveying this."

Her next book, four years later, was also an English book with a limited market: *Grace Had an English Heart*,* in which she explored the fame of the legendary country heroine, subject of a rousing folk song that Decca sang with her family as a child and loved to warble at parties with California friends, often after a few drinks. There is no need to explore the origins of that book here, as Decca explains them fully in her letters, but it does seem noteworthy that the longtime emigrée and combative "muckraker" chose to write two successive low-key meditations, albeit different from each other, arising out of English nostalgia.

Her English past loomed large in other ways during the '80s. *Daughters and Rebels* was reissued, and the *Mitford Girls* musical fed on the family's legends. She revisited the subject of her childhood in print yet again in 1982 for *TV Guide*, in conjunction with the broadcast of an eight-part television version of Nancy Mitford's novels *Love in a Cold Climate* and *The Pursuit of Love*; her sister Deborah, meanwhile, published her "diametrically opposed views of [their] Swinbrook childhood" in *Dial*. A few months later, Decca wrote an article on "the Mitford Country" for *Diversion*, which she characterized a "huge boring glossy trav. mag." sent free to doctors' offices. She wrote frequent articles for the British press, often at the request of editors in search of an American perspective. One such article was entitled "Mrs. Thatcher's Britain: An Exile Returns";† another was on the four black Members of Parliament.

---

* Published in 1988 by Viking Penguin in Britain and in 1989 by E. P. Dutton in the United States.

† Margaret Thatcher, longtime Conservative member of Parliament and government minister, had become prime minister in 1979 and remained in the position until 1990.

During the 1980s, Decca brought her two biracial grandsons to England to introduce them to "their roots"—their white roots. (While planning her grandson James's visit, she noted, "Won't he be surprised? Also the ROOTS.") She visited often herself, staying at the homes of her growing coterie of English woman friends and confidantes, many of them closer in age to her daughter than to Decca. Some of her younger chums lived in the friendly, downscale Kentish Town area of London. It was far from the England of her childhood, but Decca clearly felt at home there.

Also pulling her attention back to the world of her childhood were still more family biographies, including one on her first husband, Esmond Romilly, and another on her sister Nancy. Yet another book, *The House of Mitford: Portrait of a Family*, written by Diana Mosley's son Jonathan Guinness and his daughter Catherine Guinness, reflected the extreme right-wing views of Diana and rationalized the Mosleys' anti-Semitic history. Decca detested the book and toyed with the idea of filing another lawsuit.

As far as is known, Decca never seriously contemplated moving back to Britain permanently, although several of her English intimates thought she might. Her center of gravity was in the United States. Indeed, she wrote to one correspondent after a trip in the mid-'70s, "I, for one, realized I would never want to live in England again." But that she even addressed the question seems to confirm the increasing emotional attraction of her native country in this period.

This section of letters begins with the impending opening of the *Mitford Girls* musical and with Philip Toynbee's precipitous decline and death.

■■

To Shana Alexander   Oakland
                                                                                    June 2, 1981

Dearest Shana,

I haven't dared write to you (let alone telephone) as you must be in midbook. But I do long for news of you & it. . . .

Don't you think it's amazing that my aging children have both found Married Bliss within a year? I must say Bob & I are incredibly pleased at this unexpected development—removes whole vast areas of nagging worry, if you see what I mean. When they were little I always thought oh well once they turn 16 they'll be grown up & no longer any concern of mine. How wrong I was. . . .

Bob & I are going to England July 6 to Aug. 6, partly to see a musical at the Chichester Festival called <u>The Mitford Girls</u>, can you beat it. . . . The amazing thing is that the Sisters are FOR it. We've got a tape . . . of a sort of run-through of the words & music, the latter mostly songs of 30's with one or two new ones. So B. & I are going to lead a safari of various cousins & London chums to see it—NOT the opening night which will be crawling with my more unpleasant relations such as Diana & Jonathan Guinness (not Sir O. Mosley, he croaked last year), but in the following week.

I think Debo, who pretty much controls the other two (Diana & Pam) must have fallen for Ned Sherrin,[1] or else why did she agree to the musical? Last time I was in NY I had lunch with him at a v. posh restaurant called 1 Fifth Ave (at least I thought it was posh), & couldn't refrain from a few refrains, much to amazement of other lunchers, such as a song we used to sing on the Mediterranean cruise my mother took us on when we were 15 & 17. . . . Debo had also sung a few for N. Sherrin, & she said in her letter he complained she hadn't got Perfect Pitch. I repeated this to NS, who replied, "My dear, compared to Debo, YOU arc CALLAS." Which of course I told Debo in my letter. . . .

Much love, & to Hampton loved ones, Decca

To Ann Farrer Horne   Oakland
                                                                              June 17, 1981

Darling Sister,

You were wonderful to ring up yesterday.[2] It was so extremely comforting to have that glorious long chat with ye. As I said the marvellous thing was having someone to talk to with same outlook—I mean people this end have, natch, been v. sympathetic but except for Bob none of them knew him except via his books. . . .

Yesterday, Terry Kilmartin[3] rang to say they are having brief bits by various friends (Robert Kee, Paddy Leigh Fermor,[4] Freddie Ayer,[5] Steve Spender) instead of a reg. obit. So he wanted one from me, to be ready at 7:30 a.m. our time. Oh Sister. I did it, but it's not very good—a really awful job to have to do, 300 words limit (although I fear it's longer) within a few hours. As usual, started various beginnings; one was that P. once told me an Oxford don said he looked like a washed-out version of Gary Cooper. There was indeed a certain facial resemblance—but I thought it wld. be truer to say that G. Cooper looked like a washed-out version of P. Toynbee. So I fiddled round with that hopeless start whilst precious hours flew by. Also bits about what he was like in Rotherhithe

---

1. The co-producer and writer.

2. Horne had called to discuss Philip Toynbee's death the day before. Decca had been preparing to rush to his bedside when she was informed that his death was imminent.

3. Literary editor of the *Observer*.

4. Travel writer and longtime Mitford family friend Patrick Leigh Fermor.

5. A. J. (Alfred Jules) Ayer was a widely published critic and philosopher who popularized logical positivism in England. He had been a young don at Oxford when Philip Toynbee was an undergraduate, and they became good friends. In later years, Decca had no recollection of meeting him at the time, but as Ayer recounted when the two were introduced at a publisher's cocktail party in 1986, Toynbee once showed Ayer a letter Decca had written him saying, "Esmond & I loathed Freddie Ayer." Decca commented to a correspondent, "Goodness I was livid; but now Philip's dead, no way of getting back at him."

days vs. now—none of that got in. I finally settled on the letters [from Philip Toynbee] approach. But I don't know if it really comes off because one had to clean it up so considerably. E.g., in last quote occurred this: "Booze & God take up most of our time: we are both on both, which makes for a rather up & down journey through late middle-age." So I XXXed that out, fearing it might offend Sally. Such are the agonies of composition. . . .

Sist, as you may perhaps imagine, Life Itself had to chug along despite inner gloom & misery. . . . Actually, of course, all this is vastly to the good in one way as one HAS to do it willy nilly so it takes one's mind off. . . .

Yr loving old Sister

To Doris Brin Walker   London
July 27, 1981

Dearest Dob,

. . . Aside from usual full-up social life here, main events were Philip Toynbee's memorial service & going to see The Mit. Girls in Chichester. The memorial was v. good: started off in a Fleet St. pub, where we all gathered—one could almost see the dear soul (PT) shrieking with laughter in the rafters. The service itself was largely drowned out by a continuous high whistle. Various church flunkeys went around with geiger counters, or possibly divining rods? trying to locate the source of the noise. Turned out to be PT's least favorite aunt's malfunctioning hearing aid. Again, I think the Guest of Honor would have enjoyed that hugely. . . . Afterwards, we all went to Terry Kilmartin's . . . house for delicious kedgeree.[6] SO much better than funeral baked meats. If Hamlet's ma had served kedgeree, whole outcome might have been different.

Mit. Girls: I wrote it up for the Sunday Times (which paid the deliciously huge sum of £750, paid for much of our trip). . . . The play is a sell-out, Ned Sherrin tells me up to 200 queue every day hoping for seats. It's also a sell-out in another way as you'll see from my review.[7] We are having lunch with Debo tomorrow, so shall get her reaction to my reaction; am hoping it won't all lead to another huge family row.[8] . . .

Much love, Decca

---

6. A mélange of flaked salmon, eggs, and boiled rice.

7. Decca wrote in the review, "But wasn't I, too, something of a sell-out, having raised no objection to the text when it was first sent to me?" and she went on to quote at length a friend who, at a postmortem, "put her finger on the central flaw of this thin and pretty musical." The friend, identified only as young journalist PT (perhaps Polly Toynbee), is quoted at length on the musical's trivialization of the Mitford sisters, "their lives just a series of crazy larks," with no reference to "the deeply-held beliefs that took Esmond and Decca to Spain; no explanation of the violent political differences amongst the sisters." PT objected to the finale, in which the sisters embrace and sing "Thanks for the Memory" without regard for the fact that "Decca never spoke to her two fascist sisters after she ran away at the age of 19."

8. Decca later quoted her sister Deborah as calling the musical "La Triviata."

To various friends   London
                                                                                                July 27, 1981

Dear Assorted Friends,

    . . . Bob & I went to France for a week, got back to London yesterday, day of publication of the Sunday Times piece. There has, by the way, been a huge amount of publicity re the musical. You know how the current U.S. bestseller is "The I Hate Cats Book"? Bob thinks that the "I Hate Mitfords Book" might go well here—followed as in the U.S. by "100 Ways to Kill a Mitford."

    Be that as it may, the whole thing was much on my mind. I rang up Caryl Brahms & Ned Sherrin (co-authors of the show), & they are cutting out the Hitler scene![9] They liked my article which I thought rather amazing. Caryl Brahms, an amazing old babe of 80, said she had 6 brandies to brace herself for reading it. She said: "I was glad you wrote it, I felt exonerated, I'm going to have the Hitler figure removed. Because I'm a Jewess, and don't know about politics, I hoped you & your husband—who I like enormously—wouldn't have been hurt by the musical, but the joke's on me." . . . Can't wait for the royalties to start rolling in. All expect it to go to the West End.[10] I also reached Ned Sherrin. . . . He said mine was "a good spirited piece." . . .

    We took a huge safari—9 people—to Chichester to see the show & put them up in a hotel. . . . Sally Belfrage brought her 11-year-old Moby. I asked what he thought of the show; answer: "there were too many songs." But later he told Sally, "I didn't want to offend Decca, but actually I thought it was the worst thing I'd ever seen." . . .

                                   Much love, Decca

To Kevin Ingram[11]   Oakland
                                                                                            October 13, 1981

Dear Kevin,

    I am deeply abashed not to have written to thank you for Ordinary Mrs. Romilly's ghastly pages (I used to address her envelopes that way to distinguish

---

    9. Decca's *Sunday Times* review took note of the musical's lighthearted approach to Diana Mitford's "charming wedding scene in Goebbels's house." She described the scene this way: "A male dancer, identified as Hitler by a swastika on his armband, sagely comments that Diana would enjoy 'Parsifal' more and more as she grew older; stage-Diana agrees that this proved to be the case." Decca quoted co-writer–producer Ned Sherrin, in the postmortem discussion, as saying he had expected a gasp of horror from the audience at the end of this scene but didn't get it from the "youngish crowd" in Chichester. In the review, Decca questioned whether, if the play went to London, "the jolly Fuehrer sequences [would] be amputated? If so, will Diana sue for Malpractice? If not, will there be a gnashing of socialist teeth?"
    10. London theater district.
    11. Ingram was working on a biography of Esmond Romilly that was published in 1985 by Weidenfeld & Nicolson in the United Kingdom and E. P. Dutton in the United States, entitled *Rebel: The Short Life of Esmond Romilly.* For background on Ingram and his interest in Romilly, see letter of February 24, 1985, to Edward Pattillo.

her from me, Hon. Mrs. Romilly). Well—no, Esmond never mentioned her dread book to me. By the time E. & I met he had an implacable loathing of her. Even cold-hearted me had twinges of pity for her. Legend had it that she would sally forth to Trafalgar Square—merely hoping to get a glimpse of Esmond, who might—just might—be selling the Daily Worker on a street corner. . . .

By the way—did I ever tell you about Ordinary Mrs. Romilly's classic remark to Lady Astor? Told to me by Esmond; may be apocryphal . . . but may not. Nellie to Nancy, whom she was meeting for first time: "I so admire you Americans, you're so energetic, so lively—it must be all that Negro blood in your veins." Collapse of Lady A.

Much love, Decca

ps . . . That vivid picture of Esmond aged—12? 13?—arriving at Wellington with treasured possessions including Nelly's book may well be true.

That's where YOUR skill as biographer will come in.

I've never written a biography (only autobiogs, alas!).

But if I was doing one, I think I would chuck in all such reminiscences for what they are worth—whilst being extremely careful NOT to indulge in pop-psychologizing, so boring & often patently untrue, as to why (in this example) E. never again mentioned his Ma's book.

I.e.: Give bald facts (E. arriving at Wellington; me saying he never mentioned said book), & let reader draw own conclusion.

To Maya Angelou   Oakland
                                                           October 23, 1981

Dearest Maya,

It WAS lovely to see you for a hot mo. when you came this way. I've now lost track of yr. movements, so have sent this To Await Arrival. . . .

The appalling business of Kathy Boudin.[12] As I'm sure you realize, her papa Leonard & ma Jean are old, old friends of ours. K. was one of Dink's best friends—when they were aged 17 (Dink) & 14 (Kathy). I can hardly express the total horror of it all. Both WICKED and STUPID, is all I can say. Kathy has managed in one deft moment to rehabilitate the discredited FBI, possibly ensure passage of the "terrorist" bill which would re-establish HUAC in a new & more palatable form, plus senselessly murdering the three people. Appar-

---

12. Boudin had been arrested three days before this letter was written in a rented getaway truck after a bloody $1.6 million Brink's truck robbery in Nanuet, New York, by members of the Black Liberation Army (also known as the Family). A Brink's guard and two policemen were killed in the course of the robbery and escape attempt. At the time, Boudin, a member of the Weatherman movement (or the Weather Underground, a violent faction of the New Left Students for a Democratic Society), had been underground for eleven years after escaping from the rubble of an explosion in a New York town house—a so-called "bomb factory"—where three young radicals died. Boudin remained in prison until September 2003.

ently one of the cops was a well-liked black policeman, only one in Rockland County. . . . Oh Maya I can't say how gloomy I am about it all. Leonard, by the way, just got out of hospital (heart trouble) from a very long illness. Kathy & co. have evidently completely lost touch with reality as any of us know it. On top of all she's got a one-year-old babe that nobody (her parents etc) knew about. Madness reigns.

At the risk of boring you I must just tell one thing about Kathy—this was ages ago, she'd have been about 16. We got an appeal letter. Not the usual scruffy mimeo job of those days—no, it was hand-typed on Leonard's office stationery, obviously by one of his secretaries, starting "Dear Bob & Decca." The appeal, which was for an organization called "The Second American Revolution," asked for contributions for a fund needing $200,000. Bob said "I bet the first American revolution didn't cost anything like that."

Well—that's OK, maybe, at age 16—but THIRTY-EIGHT??? which she now is. What happened to her noggin in the meantime? Next time I heard of her was in the Spock trial. Kathy (we are now in 1968, she's out of college, graduated with highest honors) was living in Cleveland where she became great friends with the Spocks. When Dr. S. was indicted, K. said "There's only one lawyer worth having & that's my father." So Spock, who didn't know many lawyers, got Leonard. However, I didn't put this in my book—at Leonard's request I deleted it from the ms, because he thought it would annoy Kathy who by then had got to the position that her father was a hopeless revisionist. . . .

Sorry to inflict all this on you but I must say I've been in a state of semi-shock over it all. . . .

Here's something on a slightly jollier note. Last week I got a call from Catherine Guinness, my great-niece, Diana's grandchild by her oldest son Jonathan Guinness. Jonathan, born when I was 12, hence now approx. 52, is head of the Monday Club, English equivalent of John Birch Society. So Catherine rang to say she is travelling with the Rolling Stones, doing a book about their concerts etc., & would I like to come to the concert?? Non, non, non, I answered; but invited her to lunch.[13] Background: In 1959, when Catherine was about 7, she & her younger sister & tiny brother called Weenie all came with their Nanny to stay at Inch Kenneth with my mother. Bob & I were there. In the English custom we all gathered at 6 p.m. to listen to BBC news, which happened at the moment to be all about the Notting Hill Riots in which the Mosley boys (Diana's), then teenagers, were [present when some in the crowd were] beating up blacks. Usually when one listens to the news the form is to comment. I.e., if there's been a murder: "Goodness me!" or "Good show!!" Or "What a pity," etc, depending on murderee. But we all listened in deepest silence, because of

13. Decca told another correspondent, "I think she was a bit disappointed that I didn't spring for the concert, as she said people told her 'Your great-aunt Decca would do anything.' . . . But the Stones would be a bit much for this old soul at her time o' life."

presence of Catherine & co., & only started comments when the news announcer said: "Weather: Bright intervals . . ." when we all breathed a sigh of relief & said "Bright intervals, <u>how</u> nice."

When C. came to lunch the other day (which she did, & I got the Tuner & Sue to come too) the only thing SHE remembered about that long-ago visit was that we had mushrooms for dinner & I wouldn't let her have any, saying that "mushrooms are bad for children," which she has apparently held against me ever since. I was able to explain that, FINALLY, to her satisfaction. We had spent hours gathering said mushrooms all over the Island. We put them through all the tests in my mother's cookery books to see if they were edible, or poisonous toadstools; they failed all the tests. But having gone to the trouble, we ate them anyway. However I decided <u>not</u> to give any to Diana's grandchildren, as if they had died of poisoning she might think I did it deliberately to tease.

It was rather fun noting these disparate relations—Catherine & Benj & Sue—noting each other. I did ask about the other Diana grandchildren. Weenie, now called Valentine, is a rock band-leader in London. Marina Guinness (dau. of Desmond, Diana's other Guinness son) lives in L.A., has a baby of unknown parentage . . . & sells USED CARS for a living. How the mighty have fallen!! Needless to say, I crave to meet Marina & bastard. . . .

Fondest love—ring up one day,

To Katharine Graham Oakland
January 7, 1982

Dear Kay,

A couple of enclosures:

1) a jolly good recipe for duck, in case you are in need of it[14]

2) dread Cobden Trust lecture.

I fear the latter is monstrous long—it absolutely got me by the throat, I worked at it all the autumn.[15] . . .

---

14. Enclosed was a recipe by Decca from the *San Francisco Chronicle*, with the headline "Mrs. Treuhaft's Duck." The essence of the recipe is: "Well, you get a duck, put it in the oven and roast until done." Accompanying the duck was to be a green salad ("You get some lettuce and put dressing on"). The recipe had originated as answers to questions posed by Benjamin Treuhaft to his mother when he was 7 or 8. Benjamin brought Decca's brusque replies to school, where all the mothers' favorite recipes were collected and published in a PTA cookbook, to Decca's surprise.

15. Decca had been invited to give the prestigious Cobden Trust Lecture in December to raise funds for Britain's National Council for Civil Liberties (later renamed Liberty). She reported to another correspondent that after all her work on "the wretched thing . . . the worst part was that all I did was to blast the host organization . . . for their genteel English brand of racism. But anyway they loved it; perhaps people like being blasted???"

One rather funny thing happened: when I got to the part saying "My husband and I were in England last summer . . ." (page 1, last para) there was a roar of laughter from the audience. I was slightly rattled; what was the joke? I was clued in later: it seems that the Queen starts all her public speeches with "My husband and I . . ." & people thought I was doing a take-off of her. . . .

Love from Decca

To the Duchess of Devonshire   Oakland
                                                                                January 7, 1982

Dearest Hen,

. . . How is S.[16] Hastings's biog of Nancy coming along? She asked me to send copies of N's letters. I'm not too inclined to stir my stumps on this, means a huge sorting job & getting somebody to nip to the Xerox place. Anyway, she never sent things that she has written, promised last spring. Hen I <u>do</u> regret your choice of her as Official Biographer. Think what a smashing job could have been done by the likes of Sybille Bedford, Xopher Sykes (if they are still alive) or 1/2 dozen writers one could think of. Selina is so incredibly vague; has little grasp of the Cast of Characters, the dates of when things happened, the skeleton of the whole thing. I'm sure she's well-intentioned—not a trace of artifice in her conversation which may turn out to be a DREAD PITY, as it would be needed for a sharp & interesting book ferreting out the truth re Nancy. Even if S. Hastings is a good, plodding workhorse of a writer she would have read all the memoirs in which N. appears & have arranged her interviews with live ones with those in mind. But no. Uphill work all the way (mine with her in December), having to explain all sorts of things she should have choked down early on. . . .

End of complaint, end of paper, end of letter.

To Famous People's Eye Glasses Museum[17]   Oakland
                                                                                February 9, 1982

Dear Friends,

As eye glass experts, you should be able to date the enclosed pair of spectacles, as they were called in my young days.

---

16. Selina.

17. Billed this way on its letterhead, the Henderson, Nevada, museum consisted in fact of display cases in an alcove of Dr. M. J. Bagley's small optometry office. He had written Decca, as he did other celebrities, requesting a pair of her old glasses, in any condition—along with "a letter attesting to their authenticity"—to add to the collection in the "museum."

In case you are not up to carbon dating as practiced by antiquarians study-ing Egyptian tombs and Greek temples, the hideous frames might supply a clue—in which year or years did we wear those dreadful spangles in the cor-ner? Over to you on that. I've long since lost the doubtless huge bill from the optometrist; perhaps today I should welcome his fee as quite reasonable, given inflation.

In your letter you solicit anecdotes re eye glasses, so here goes: After many years of estrangement, my mother came to visit us in Oakland when I was about 30 years old. Her first words were, "Little D," (as she called me), "why are you wearing those horrid spectacles? Most unbecoming." I answered that I couldn't see without them, to which she responded, "Oh, that's right, you never could see as a child." A firm believer in the Good Body righting itself, she had never taken me to an eye doctor.

The first time I realized the advantage of glasses had been a few years before, when I was staying with a friend who suggested going to the movies. We went, and I headed for the front row as usual. She demurred, and lent me a pair of her glasses—which she eventually gave me. I had never before realized that one could see the individual leaves on trees, for example, or the faces of people a block away. So I became an addict.

Please put the enclosed eye glasses as far as possible from those of Ronald Reagan, for fear of an explosion.

Yours truly, Jessica Mitford

To Katharine Graham   Oakland
                                                    February 19, 1982

Dear Kay,

. . . Mit. Girls folded in London, so that's ONE chore you can avoid. (Is said to be possibly opening in GERMANY, serves those wretched Krauts right if so.)

But here's a thought: DO ring Debo. I can't remember if you know her? I bet she'd love to see you. . . .

I think you'd find her to be good value. Despite absolutely horrendous dif-ferences & quarrels over the years, I rather adore her. . . .

Re her forthcoming book—I can't remember if I've told you this, if so skip & put it down to Nominal Aphasia (which I will explain in a P.S. in case it is not in your vocabulary): She sent me the ms of it. Large chunks are the notebooks of the "Bachelor Duke," early part of last century. One of the B. Duke's notes con-cerned some native artifacts given to him by one Williams, not otherwise iden-tified. "The fate of poor Williams is, of course, well-known," writes the Duke. So I said to Debo the fate of poor Williams may be well-known but not to me; needs a footnote. She wrote back that she, too, had no clue as to fate of

Williams. So (spurious researcher that I am) I looked up Williams in the Encyclopedia Britannica (1914 edition) and there he was: a missionary, & his fate, as you will have guessed, eaten by cannibals. Serves him jolly well right for having stolen their artifacts to give to the Duke of Dev??? Don't you agree. . . .

    Love from Decca

ps <u>Nominal Aphasia</u>: I only learned this useful phrase recently, from a dear duck called Henry Nash Smith, former head of English Dept at UC, long retired.

 Here's how it works: First, you forget proper names (people, places). Next, common nouns (butter, coat etc). Next the VERBS go. Followed swiftly by ADVERBS & ADJECTIVES. You are then left with "the," "and," "but" . . .

 I am getting there . . .

To the Duchess of Devonshire   Oakland
                February 22, 1982

Dearest Hen,

 I DID love yr Country Life article, & so did Bob—in fact he bore it off to his office saying he was going to write to you about it. (That'll be the day; he seldom writes letters.) So I haven't got it in front of me for a cozy discussion. . . .

 This is mainly to say that me old friend Katharine Graham is going to London to give a lecture, & I urged her to ring you up; so if she does, be noting the form of her. (March, I think she said.)

 In fact you may have met her? Can't remember. She is <u>the</u> most incongruous friend for me to have—all pretty much based on Old Lang Syne, when she & Phil Graham & me & Esmond were close buddies, circa 1939. Oh they were so amusing in those days—instant friends, the way people were in youth.

 Time staggered by, Phil committed it, many years ago, mad & alcoholic. Kay became publisher (owner) of Washington Post, Newsweek etc, known in the press as Miss Power, which she is.

 Despite the Miss Powerishness of her, whenever I see her I fall back into the bad old habit of rather adoring her. I can also visualize you & Kay (if you do happen to meet) disloyally discussing the hopelessness of me.

 She prob. won't get in touch, because of propensity of the Powerful to dash from point to point; the above is only in case she does. I've told her all abt. yr. book, including Fate of Poor Williams, hoping thereby to get advance booking in Wash. Post, Newsweek etc. . . . but she is far above the writers/editorialists etc. of said publications, grand Chairman of Board, meaning money manipulation. . . .

    Yr loving Hen

To Ann Farrer Horne   Oakland
                                                      March 6, 1982

Darling Sister:

. . . I'm all alone by the telephone (to quote a Famous song). It rings; a checker from a mag called Dial, which I've never heard of. To explain checkers: they are something fairly new in mag. world. . . . Well—the name says it, they check the facts. Sometimes actually rather useful? Although not often. So anyway the Dial checker said "Did your father call people he didn't like 'a meaningless piece of meat'?" I started shrieking with laughter—"absolutely," said I. Checker continues: "And did he do all his shopping at the Army & Navy Stores, getting there when they opened at 9 a.m. because later he was 'impeded by inconveniently shaped women'?" "Too true," said I, "but why do you want to know?" Answer: Not at liberty to tell.

. . . Turns out the Hen had written an article for said Dial, to coincide with the Nancy films on U.S. telly!!

To Robert Gottlieb   Oakland
                                                      April 2, 1982

Dear Bites,

I've been thinking quite a lot about our conversation in NY. . . .

The more I think (difficult for me, at my time of life) the more I incline to just a memoir of Philip Toynbee, rather than a collection of essays about various ones.

I realize that P. Toynbee is not exactly a household word in America, so it might be more for English publication? . . .

It would be a memoir, not a biog. For one thing, I lost track of him completely between 1939 & 1955; and we only gradually & intermittently got reacquainted. Yet he became an indispensable part of life; letters, safaris to his dread commune, and I can't <u>say</u> how I mourned his passing. He was such an odd, really peculiar, & amusing person. He didn't a bit mind being teased about God; well, he expected that from me, & responded in kind. . . .

So (to cut this short), I've got many letters, many memories; and <u>all</u> the obits, v. variable. What I'd do is to interview various ones when I'm in England (month of June—might extend that, if necessary) as refresher stuff. I do long to see some sort of commemoration of PT; all those obits. will soon become fading & thrown-out old newspaper clippings. All this would be (to me) of far more interest than a mix of Characters I Have Known.[18]

Incidentally, I've been turning handsprings ever since he died to get SOME-

---

18. Gottlieb had previously suggested such a book, which Decca characterized as "a Dec version of *Some People* or whatever it was called by Harold Nicolson. In my view, easily the best book

BODY to make a collection of the obits (some of which are quite marvellous), plus letters to Sally etc., plus the unheard remarks at above-mentioned funeral service, to compile these into a booklet for family & friends. My idea was a privately-printed book, to the expenses of which we would all contribute, so it doesn't all get lost to posterity. I asked Robert Kee (one of the unheard at service), Terry Kilmartin (ditto, main speaker & Philip's boss at Observer), Polly Toynbee & many others about this idea; they were all for it in principle, but none sprang forward to do it. So my Memoir would be in lieu of . . .

Do let me know what you think abt. all this as actually the idea was inspired by <u>toi</u>.

Have a look at <u>Friends Apart</u>, Philip's memoir of Esmond & another boy killed in the war (I sent you a copy of the reprint, I think? Sidgwick & Jackson, 1980).

In his introduction he says: "There is at least one simple distinction between writing about the dead & writing about the living. Not only have the dead that completeness which makes them more amenable subjects for a book, but also they are incapable of reacting to what is written about them . . ."

Same to you with nobs on, Philip, says I. This will be the epigraph to my book.

Now Bites if you <u>don't</u> like this idea because of aforementioned non-household-wordishness of PT, I think I'll do it anyway & mimeograph it for PT's children & grandchildren. Or even Xerox it, 2 cents a page at Kopy Kat in Berkeley.

Or—how much would YOU charge me for publishing it?

> RSVP, Much love to all at Knopf & at home,
> Chewed Up (or expecting to be)

To Patricia Dooley, Children's Literature Association   Oakland
                                                                   April 9, 1982

Dear Ms. Dooley,

Thanks SO much for your marvelous letter of 23 March to Jackie Cantor at Holt, Rinehart & Winston.[19] For a long & cherished moment, it seemed fair to bring DRAMA and perhaps RICHES into my normally humdrum life.

---

by that extremely trivial character whose diaries I read with fury—imagine him having a say-so over our destinies!" (Nicolson had been a member of the British diplomatic corps.)

19. Dooley had written the publishers to alert them to passages in a new novel, *A Woman of Her Times*, by G. J. Scrimgeour, that Dooley believed were "borrowed" from Decca's book *Daughters and Rebels*, recently reissued by a division of Holt, Rinehart & Winston. Included with Dooley's letter, meticulously copied and underlined, were passages from the two books containing the similarities, which she found "too faithful, I'm afraid, to be coincidental or even inadvertent." She wrote,

Here's what happened: Jackie Cantor sent your letter to Billy Abrahams, her colleague & a longtime friend & neighbor of ours. Billy rang up in HIGH EXCITEMENT, & read out your letter & enclosure, plus review in Publisher's Weekly saying that <u>A Woman of Her Times</u> is clearly slated for bestsellerdom: 75,000 advance printing, 75,000 dollars promo, 1st choice of Lit. Guild etc.

PLAGIARISM, HERE I COME! thought I, & my husband dashed out & bought the book. Oh dear, this sort of thing: ". . . her throat rose white and vulnerable . . . Her stomach moved restlessly against the hardness of his swiftly risen member . . ." Not, alas, cribbed from <u>my</u> book, more's the pity. Made me wish <u>I</u> could write a bestseller, but I fear I haven't the stomach (restlessly moving) for it.

So the next act was to send a Xerox of your letter & pertinent passages[20] to Charles Rembar in NY—by now, in my dreams I am RICH & prepared to share equally my vast damages with Patricia Dooley, without whom . . . as authors say in dedications.

By the way—did you twig to G. J. Scrimgeour's dedication? It reads: "For Norman Collins, who first gave me London, and for all the other writers who made their worlds belong to me." (Including MOI???)

Final act: Dies, dies, dies, as W. Shakespeare would say—our hopes for a comfortable lifetime income for J. Mitford & P. Dooley. Charles Rembar says that the passage is TOO BRIEF to be actionable. Pity, isn't it? I did circumspectly suggest a spot of blackmail, but he wouldn't go for it. (Rembar, by the way, is one of our oldest & best friends, a copyright lawyer in NY, author of a v. good book called "The End of Obscenity."[21])

So what shall we do next? Possibly fling it to the <u>New Yorker</u> for their "Funny Coincidence" column? Or, as Billy Abrahams suggests, should I try for a piece in, say, <u>New York</u> magazine about the whole lovely mess? If you've got any ideas, please phone <u>COLLECT</u>. . . .

This is mainly to thank you VERY MUCH INDEED for your kindness in writing,

    Jessica Mitford

"I'm a little sorry to have noticed this, but as an editor and reviewer I could not ignore it," and she added that the offense was compounded in her eyes because the material was used not only wrongly but "gracelessly."

20. Among the "pertinent passages" was a quotation from *Mrs. Beeton's Book of Household Management*, which Decca maintained was identical—but wrong—in both *Daughters and Rebels* and Scrimgeour's novel. In what she elsewhere called "a guilty secret that I have harbored since circa 1958 when I was writing Daughters and Rebels," Decca wanted to "dramatize the plight of a 'Between-Maid,' or 'Tweeny,'" whose job "was lowest in the hierarchy: as her title implies, she worked between head housemaid and cook, at the beck and call of each." Not finding a listing for "between-maid" in Beeton's book, "I mendaciously copied her section on the *General Servant*. . . . Mr. Scrimgeour swallowed it whole."

21. *The End of Obscenity: The Trials of Lady Chatterley, Tropic of Cancer & Fanny Hill by the Lawyer Who Defended Them* (Random House, 1968).

To Robert Gottlieb   Oakland
                                                                                April 10, 1982

Dear Clever Old Person,

Many thanks for yours of 5 Inst., which I thought encouraging. (Reading between the lines—I know you are far too fine to mention money—I see you are offering $250 thousand for brief memoir, thanks SO much.)

So I shall be gradually ploughing on. Trouble about Aranka is that I rather milked all to be had from that strange & unique character in Fine Old Conflict. (Have you read it? A jolly good book if I do say so myself.[22]) Anyway, what I honestly am going to do is get on with a bit of P. Toynbee—also, when I go to England in June, settle down for a long winter's chat with people like Anne Wollheim, Polly T, many others. So I think I'd better be doing that sort of thing for the moment, not plotting a multi-character book—although, as you so wisely say, you might bully me into something of the sort. But I really am pleased about your encouragement; shall be on to Deb. Rogers also, re any interest in the jolly olde lande. Did you see Mrs. Thatcher on telly? Peter Sellers in drag, I thought, oh she was true to form. The whole Falkland Isles[23] was such pleasure in the beginning, all out of Gilbert & Sullivan; but may end up being such pain. Those poor shepherds! Yet I suppose it is in a way a diversion for them? Or at least for their children; imagine being a teenage Falklander, & for the 1st time in life a wee bit of excitement. I know I'd have welcomed it, at their age. By the way—which side are you on? Perfidious Albion, or rotten fascist Argentina. I can't seem to make up my mind. . . .

   Your loving Silly Old Person. Decca

To Herb Caen   Oakland
                                                                                 May 10, 1982

Dear Herb,

Your note absolutely made my day—thanks SO much. It came at a particularly gloomy moment, to wit: Nina King, the v. nice book editor at Newsday (for which the Lady D. Cooper review was written) rang up to say that the Paul Robeson/niggy-wiggs passage was not in the finished book,[24] had been deleted

---

22. Gottlieb had indeed read it; he'd been the book's editor.

23. The Argentinian navy had seized the islands from the British colonial government in early April, precipitating a brief war with Britain. At the time this letter was written, the major British counterattack had not yet occurred.

24. Decca had reviewed *Diana Cooper: The Biography of Lady Diana Cooper*, by Philip Ziegler (Hamish Hamilton, 1981). She told another correspondent of an anecdote from the book in which Lady Diana was quoted as describing a party given by Noël Coward: "They had a huge and fero-

from the American (Knopf!! my publisher) edition—the bound galleys were copied from the English edition, Hamish Hamilton.

So I said well that's all right, just put a footnote saying all that. Nina said fine, she'd do that.

Later that day Nina rang back to say that the Managing Ed. of Newsday had overheard our conversation & said that the Robeson passage must be deleted. WHY?—wait for it—NOT because of the caveat on bound galley not to quote without comparison with finished book. No, because Newsday's policy is not to print racial slurs.

Imagine my fury. So—(said I)—I suppose that if the KKK marches through Long Island shouting Death to the Niggers, Newsday would be too fine to print that???

So I told Nina I was going to withdraw the review in that case, & try to place it elsewhere (not bloody likely, because who would want it at this late date?).

Then came . . . word from Nina that the managing ed. had had a change of heart, would run review as is with the note about changes in U.S. edition. . . .

Love from Decca

To Ann Farrer Horne London
June 29, 1982

Darling Sister,

Thanks SO much for the lav. paper comment—of course you are right abt "toilet paper"; 'tis my long sojourn in America that gets me into these bad habits. . . . I'll work it out. You ARE a good editor. . . .

Frighteningness of Philip as father. . . .

Walking with [him and his daughter] in London, he'd pretend to be a gibbering idiot. Rather reminds me, however, of a time when Dink was approx 17 & we had to travel for about 2 hours on the NY subway (underground, Sister). So to pass the time, I pretended to be an old mad woman, mumbling & making faces. Whenever Dink objected, I gave her a tickling poke under the arms which made her jump & squeak like mad. Then I'd shout out "Stop that—be quiet, everyone's looking at you"—which, of course, they were. As soon as she calmed down I started being the Old Mad Lady again. She was a fair wreck by the time we arrived at end of journey. . . . So I suppose P. & I did have certain similar characteristics? I'd never known, until now, about his idiot act. . . .

Yr loving Sister

---

cious negro called Paul Robeson to sing. His voice is amazingly beautiful and soft but niggy-wiggs have no accent or bone or grit and it doesn't stir one."

To Virginia Durr   Oakland
                                                                August 21, 1982

Dearest Va,

How VERY fascinating about Mike Straight.[25] . . .

[H]e made no bones about his Communist affiliations in Cambridge days; yet at the time Esmond & I knew him, from 1939 to when Esmond left & after that, when I saw him a lot before scramming to Calif., his politics seemed about like ours, i.e. staunch fellow-traveller but not a member.[26] Then he wrote a virtually unreadable book called <u>Make This the Last War</u>[27]—which I've still got, somewhere, & shall contrive to find it & choke it down for CLUES. . . .

I can't quite see why Binnie is upset about the book; surely she isn't implicated in any way? Va—won't it be DISAPPOINTING if we're not in it. Shall spring for the index first thing, natch, to see if you & I are listed.

Is it your impression that he was mainly a spy in Cambridge, or did it extend to Washington days? I wonder if he knew McLean[28]—must have. McClean was a great friend of P. Toynbee, is all through his early diaries (1938). He & PT had many a drunken brawl in the Middle East; and Philip kept up correspondence long after McC. went to Russia, although by then Philip had long forsaken the CP. Can't remember if Philip & Mike were ever acquainted; probably not, one being in Cambridge & the other at Oxford. Philip was an ardent CP member in those days, first Communist to be elected president of the Oxford Union etc.

I'd love to know more about the Anthony Blunt business. Will that be in the book, I wonder? How <u>very</u> naughty—in fact HORRID of Mike to do that to poor Sir A, don't you agree?

Do keep in touch re everything. . . .

---

25. Previously unbeknownst to Decca or Virginia Durr, their old Washington friend Michael Straight, former State Department employee and *New Republic* editor and publisher, had been a peripheral figure in the Cambridge University Communist spy ring of the 1930s that included such well-known names as Kim Philby and Guy Burgess. In 1964, when he was being considered for a position as chairman of the National Endowment for the Arts, Straight informed secretly on the so-called "Fourth Man" in the ring: prominent English art historian Anthony Blunt, whom Straight described to intelligence agents as the one who had recruited him to spy for the Soviets. Straight revealed his role publicly in his 1983 memoir *After Long Silence* (published by Collins in the U.K. and by W. W. Norton in the U.S.). See letter of February 25, 1983, to Michael Straight.

26. Although Decca appears not to have recalled it, even at the time she had some concerns about Michael Straight's politics. In a 1941 letter to Esmond Romilly about their good friend, then editor of the *New Republic*, Decca mentioned "Red-baiters like Mike (he really has almost become one, & in unsigned [*New Republic*] editorials refers scathingly to 'the comrades' & 'democrats of June 22nd' etc. which seems a pity)." When she wrote to Straight after reading his memoir (see letter of February 25, 1983), she reiterated the view she expressed in this letter that their politics at the time had seemed compatible.

27. *Make This the Last War: The Future of the United Nations* (G. P. Putnam's Sons, 1945).

28. Donald Maclean, another member of the Cambridge spy ring. Decca varied the spelling of his name throughout this letter; it's not clear if she did so inadvertently, so it has been left in its original form.

To Michael Tigar[29]   Oakland
                                                          August 31, 1982

Dear Mike,

I'm loving our lawsuit, thanks so much for sending it along. . . .

Page 5 of draft complaint, para (d): How very smashing, damages trebled. Trebled from what, though?[30] In my young days, before you were born, I was working in the Office of Price Administration. The law required that if you were overcharged for anything (price, rent etc) you should be paid TREBLE DAMAGES OR $50, whichever was more. So Bob & I went to a horrid bar called the Pig & Whistle (known by us as Piss & Wiggle) in SF. I ordered a Dubonnet, Bob ordered sherry. Bob's sherry was 35 cents, my Dubonnet 50 cents. Having worked in a bar, I knew the Dubonnet was overcharged by 15 cents. Bartender said it was imported; I asked to see the bottle, which said "Made and Bottled in the United States." I got a receipt, & took Pig & Whistle into Small Claims Court the next day. My testimony was (I thought) impeccable, irrefutable. FIFTY DOLLARS, HERE I COME!!! In those days, $50 was a HUGE amount. But no; the rotten judge, in absolute violation of the law, ruled in favor of Piss & Wiggle. "I shall appeal this to the highest court in the land," said I righteously. But no . . . can't appeal from Small Claims Ct, it turned out.

That soul-searing experience (I'd already decided what to get with the $50 due me) shattered my faith in the legal process.

It is now renewed by you, dear Mike.

I am longing for the next Act in this Drama.

                    Be in touch, Decca

Enclosed: An amusing article in The Observer re the Scrimgeour scrimmage.[31] . . .

---

29. Tigar, an old friend of Decca's, had agreed to serve as attorney for a lawsuit against G. J. Scrimgeour, for a third of the amount of any settlement. He had also told Decca that she would be listed on the complaint as an additional, *pro se* attorney so that she would be able, as she said she wished, to take Scrimgeour's deposition, an arrangement that Tigar surmised in advance would be "effective and enlightening." He suggested that the deposition be videotaped.

30. Commenting to Tigar on a recent prominent plagiarism case, which reportedly had been settled confidentially for "an undisclosed sum" of money, Decca said, "I long for an undisclosed sum."

31. The article, published in June, took note of Decca's "anarchistic impulses," and "skillful uses of the law . . . greatly assisted by her husband . . . who enjoys spreading discomfiture in a good cause as much as she does." The author, Michael Davie, noted "Ms Mitford's indignation, tempered with glee, when she discovered that the Scrimgeour book was prominently on sale in Britain! And not only on sale, but published by her own British publishers, Michael Joseph!" Stories appeared in many other papers as well, including a prominent feature in the *Los Angeles Times* while the American Book Association was meeting in town—which, as Decca put it, "much to the discomforture of [the book's publisher] Putnam's . . . meant that every publisher in the US (and every bookseller) would have read it." She said that Putnam's "begged" the *Times* literary editor "to hold off until after ABA left town, but he wouldn't comply."

I say! How interesting that we are also suing Simon & Schuster,[32] another of my publishers. Bob said I'm always biting hands that feed me. But—why not?

To Ann Farrer Horne   Oakland
                                                       November 10, 1982

Sistling—yours of 3 Nov. to hand. Thanks SO much. . . .

Clearing your table before Xmas: I wish I had worthy goals like that. Aeons ago (when Amer. Way of D. hit) we had a special study built on, point being that NEVER AGAIN wld dining rm table have papers on it. Wish you could see it today: whole house awash with papers, unanswered letters, the works. In my Will, I've left all my papers to Marge Frantz as she adores reading other people's letters. Am posting a sign: IF I SHOULD DIE BEFORE I WAKE, I PRAY MARGE FRANTZ THESE THINGS TO TAKE. That way, she'll feel bound to, don't you agree?

I must just quickly digress to a Marge story. . . . Anything to take me mind off me work. Here goes:

Background: Marge is a great friend of Virginia Durr, ditto me. So for years, M., herself a Southerner with the great Southern failing—or virtue—of adoring cozy gossip, used to come round here & seeing a letter from Va. Durr on table immediately glom on & start reading it. I chastised her from time to time for reading my letters without permission; no results as she is born that way.

One day about 20 years ago, Marge rang up to ask if she could come over to our house to do some typing, so I said absolutely. Thinking this over, I rolled some paper into me typewriter & wrote Page 2 on top. Went on with: "and for God's sake, Dec, don't breathe a word to Marge about all this. When I think of her, and Laurent, and their four little children—I can't say how distressed I am for all of them. What in the world is going to become of them?" And I signed off, Devotedly, Va. Which is how Virginia Durr always signs. I left this by the typewriter.

So after a bit, Marge arrived. I was in the kitchen, & said oh good, you're here; do type as long as you like . . .

A—well, silence you could cut with a knife. Marge appears absolutely white as any sheet in kitchen door. "WHAT'S THIS LETTER FROM VIRGINIA ABOUT???" I said oh dear I AM sorry, actually it was written to me, not to you. But as I cld see she was near fainting, I did admit all. Being her, she SHRIEKED, luckily, at explanation. But I did think it was lucky that I was here; otherwise she'd have torn up the floors looking for Page 1. But Page 2 WAS rather cleverly contrived, because at the time Laurent (M's hubby) was a) under dire attack by the McCarthyites, b) thought to be unfaithful. Hence the Va. comments could have applied to either situation. . . .

---

32. Pocket Books, a division of Simon & Schuster, had purchased reprint rights to *A Woman of Her Times*.

To Monique Mendelson[33]
Oakland
ca November 1982

Dear Monique,

I can't say how grateful we are for your advice[34] re stopping dear dogs from using our driveway as their normal toilet facility—IT'S WORKING, beyond wildest dreams.

Incidentally, if you should glimpse an indistinct figure exposing himself in our drive, PLEASE don't call the fuzz—it's merely Bob, following yr excellent advice. Pity to waste any, says I. . . .

[S]ince it's MALE URINE ONLY, we (rather Bob) only have just enough for our own driveway.

What's needed, evidently, is a WHOLESALE OPERATION.

Be thinking . . .

Decca

To Michael Tigar
Oakland
December 1, 1982

Dear Mike,

You ARE a wunderkind—thanks SO much for your excellent & fruitful efforts. And here I was, lusting after the $2,000 offer in your letter of Oct. 20.[35] You must be the world's best poker player.

What shall we do next? Are you also an expert in PATENT LAW? If so, please study the enclosed.[36] It's an excerpt from a letter to my agent in which I was bemoaning sad state of publishing, Bob's law practice in the doldrums etc., & suggesting a way to make our living in the Sunset Years. (Actually, the agent is trying to peddle it as a short-short for New York, or Playboy.)

POOR old Scrim—& I bet his book didn't sell all that well in the end. Actually, if it hadn't been such a thoroughly DREADFUL book (soft porn of the worst kind) perhaps I wouldn't have pursued him.

I wonder what the apology will say? One word—SORRY—will suffice as far as I am concerned.[37]

Much love, & again a million thanks, Decca

---

33. The Treuhafts' next-door neighbor.

34. For a full description of Mendelson's advice, as Decca subsequently developed it, see the following letter to Michael Tigar.

35. The negotiated settlement with Scrimgeour was for a written apology and $15,000 in cash.

36. See below.

37. In Scrimgeour's "official" apology, he expressed his "regrets for the similarities between pieces of thirteen sentences in my 408-page novel . . . and fourteen sentences of your autobiography . . ." He blamed an accidental confusion in his notes. More than a year later, Scrimgeour wrote another letter, in which he cited the costs of the settlement and legal fees, which he said deprived him of most of the profits from four years of work on his novel. He said he had heard in New York and London of Decca's rotten reputation and was collecting Mitford stories for an article to be published after her death.

(Extract from letter to my agent bemoaning state of publishing, Bob's law practice in the doldrums—how shall we make our living in the Sunset Years?)

I've got one good idea—IF you can think of a way to market it.

Background: There are lots of HUGE dogs in our street, who routinely use our driveway for a dog's lavatory, with resultant HUGE TURDS every morning. Our next-door neighbour Monique, who is a psychiatrist's wife hence well-informed on such matters, told Bob that MALE URINE is a certain deterrent to dogs. So Bob's been doing it. . . . The amazing thing is that it actually works. Not a single pile of dogshit has been seen since Bob started this routine.

Future plans: How best to market this unique and useful commodity?[38] First off—we shall have to neutralize (???) the Women's Lib Movement, since it is MALE urine only that produces this amazing result—at least that's what Monique says. But mainly—have you thought of problems of packaging? If it's bottled, people might mistake it for a delicious salad dressing. If frozen, for delightful fruit juices. Either way, could be disastrous for the unsuspecting housewife. There is also the danger that the market could be flooded (so to speak) should word get out before we are ready to organize and promote our nationwide sales campaign.

Should we apply immediately to the Food & Drug Administration for their OK? To the U.S. Patent Office for a patent to protect our invention? Will we have to cut Monique in on the profits? No, come to think of it, because ideas can't be copyrighted, right?

I shall expect a well-thought-out answer to these important though difficult questions. Meanwhile, my advice: START SAVING FOR A RAINY DAY. (Point of that being that one day it did rain, wiping out Bob's invaluable contribution; huge dog turds in drive the next morning. He's trying to double his output; not always easy.)[39]

---

38. One promotional idea, suggested by James Dean Walker, was to affiliate with Prison Industries. Decca explained: "I'd . . . sent the dogshit extract to wretched James Dean Walker in Ark. prison. For ONCE I got a cheerful letter back (poor soul—he'll prob. never get out despite all efforts) as he loved the idea for Prison Industries. He proposes marketing the product under name PPP, for Prisoners' Pee Project, in black & white striped bottles."

39. In a formal reply on his law firm's stationery, attorney Tigar laid out some of the problems associated with Decca's contemplated business venture, including the need for "a reliable and continuous supply of the product." He speculated on various ways to harvest the substance from men's rooms of large office buildings but cautioned on the "serious question whether the donor retains the property interest in the product." He also proposed various alternative strategies, one of which was "a so-called 'output' contract relating to a single Sigma Chi beer party" that would "guarantee quantities of the product, although the question of quality would remain open." Finally, he floated the idea of forming a sect whose members would go "lawn to lawn and driveway to driveway" making voluntary contributions.

Decca later wrote up this business proposal, along with much of Michael Tigar's response, in a short essay that was published in September 1983 in the *Village Voice*, entitled "An Immodest Proposal." It had been commissioned initially by the London *Sunday Times*, but that paper "got cold feet," Decca said.

To Kevin Ingram   Oakland
                                                               January 12, 1983

Dear Kevin,

Your letter & the 5 chapters arrived today. . . .

First off, I thought most of it extremely well-written; & I was v. impressed at the amt of research into backgrounds etc. (I never learned a huge lot abt Esmond's forebears—I suppose I was never interested enough to find out some of this for myself.) . . .

Re. Esmond being Churchill's natural son: Actually, that rumour was ever slightly afloat, but I don't remember E. paying much attention to it. The only time I got what seemed like some sort of solid info was from Nancy, in the 1960's. Giles had gone mad (or fairly mad), & I was in Paris seeing Nancy. I said oh dear I do hope it's not hereditary (thinking of Dinky). Nancy said that anyway the madness would have been inherited from Col. Romilly, who was not Esmond's father: "Everyone knows he's Winston's son," she said. I pressed her for details and SHE was the one who told about the cruise, non-existent as you found out.[40] Well—Nancy was a great one for semi-inventing things. Anyway, as she was born in 1904 she'd hardly have been in a position to know these interesting details about 1917, when she was 13. Slight credit was added by the extraordinary resemblance of Churchill & Esmond as teenagers (see photo books of Churchill, & photo of E. in Friends Apart).[41] Main point is, E. never made anything—to me, at least—of alleged WC parenthood; may have mentioned it as a rumour/joke. To sum up: I think you make too much of this.

To Michael Straight   Oakland
                                                               February 25, 1983

Dear Michael,

News of your book was first bruited to me last summer from super-heated Martha's Vineyard—mainly by Va Durr, who for some reason feared what you might conceivably say about her & Cliff (by the way: she won't be best pleased at yr comment that "food was never a high priority at the Durrs'." Too true! but let that pass).[42]

Before I could get a copy (ordered from England) I read all about it & can

---

40. According to the discredited rumor, Esmond's mother and Winston Churchill had gone on a cruise together without her sister, Clementine Churchill, nine months before Esmond was born.

41. On another occasion, Decca wrote that the rumor "DID seem rather likely, given the quite startling resemblance between them" and that photos show Churchill at fifteen was "an absolute ringer for Esmond at that age."

42. In an earlier letter to Virginia Durr about Straight's forthcoming book, Decca wrote that "I still can't imagine what he might say about you—or me—that would be particularly nasty? As MY life is an open book—two of 'em, in fact. Don't know about you & the Polish ambassador; and you say you don't, either. Perhaps we'll make our fortunes out of libel suits?"

see that you've been fairly thoroughly trampled into the dust by commentators from far-right to far-left. But—what did you <u>expect</u>???

I've now read, riveted, <u>After Long Silence</u>. To me, the incomprehensible thing (and to many reviewers) is—why did you keep stringing along? You could have got out any minute—esp. when Michael Green had lost the other bit of the torn-up picture;[43] or at any time. Just say "bugger off," or words to that effect.

I, of course, should have loved to be a spy; but nobody asked me. In fact I always thought you might be one, & must have dropped many a hint when we knew each other in those days.

Back to the book: I was v. glad to see that the English edition starts with a page of ERRATA. When I was a small child all the best & grandest lovely books started with ERRATA; so at age 9 I wrote a book starting ERRATA. Not a bad idea; but reading yours, I detect other ERRATA throughout the time we knew each other.

First off, one small ERRATUM (if that is the correct singular), page 48 of English edition re contrib. of twenty pounds to refugee fund. My recollection is a hilarious story that you told me & Esmond, as follows: You had decided to join the CP & give a contrib. to the Daily Worker. You went to London, & up to the DW desk. "Comrade, I'd like to make a contribution." Comrade behind the desk says, without looking up, "Yes, Comrade, what'll it be? Ten bob?[44] Fifteen bob?" You: "I was thinking of a thousand pounds." Fellow behind desk does a double-take. "A thousand pounds, comrade? Perhaps you would like to see Comrade Pollitt."[45]

Second off, we always thought (Esmond & I) that you were pretty much in our stream, viz a supporter though not a present member of CP. <u>Weren't you?</u> I don't mean the spying stuff, I mean being thoroughly in favour of CP policy both foreign & domestic. In yr book you are constantly pulled, and/or pulling—not when we knew you. Pragmatically, the CP program was (to quote a vile U.S. expression) the only ball game in town, & you were for it—or so we thought at the time.[46]

In Washington, you/me/Binnie were all best friends, with many a sortie to

---

43. Michael Green was the name given by Straight's Soviet "handler" at their first meeting in a Washington restaurant. The stranger who identified himself as Green said he had "mislaid" the other half of the drawing that Anthony Blunt of the Cambridge spy ring had torn in two; Blunt had told Straight that the missing part would be returned to him by his new Kremlin contact. Until then, Straight wrote, he had "persuaded" himself that after moving to Washington his "underground life in Cambridge . . . would never catch up with me."

44. Ten shillings.

45. In his friendly return letter, Straight said that he had been talking about a different incident and had forgotten the one Decca mentioned until he received her letter.

46. Straight replied that the major issue at the time was foreign policy and that he broke with the Communists over the Nazi-Soviet Pact, at about the time they knew each other in Washington. He said he remained friendly with leaders of the Youth Congress.

the Durrs'. I do remember one smashing evening chez Durrs (food never a priority) when Cliff's backwoods cousins from Deepest Alabama were there. We tried to teach them The Game; you did "You can't go wrong on a Simmons Mattress," to the total horror of the Durr clan. (You on floor, going wrong.) Later, the backwoodsmen said to Virginia: "Decca is a lady. But AS FOR THE STRAIGHTS!!!"

So there you are.

Came the 1940's, in 47 or 48 (can't remember which) you were in SF on some sort of junket—with Henry Wallace, I suppose. I turned handsprings to reach you, & finally you rang back—VERY COLD INDEED. I couldn't think why, in view of former rather solid friendship. Was it because I was now a card-carrying Commie?[47]

I've written a book about my CP experience called A FINE OLD CONFLICT. A bit different from yours. If you would like a copy, send a postcard & I will forward same. . . .

I should add—just to make this quite explicit—that I deeply disapprove of what you did re "clearance," Blunt[48] etc. . . . In fact—while I did think the narrative bits re Washington politics etc. were v. good, your whole life seems to have been a muddle. Oh well—perhaps you think the same of mine? But I don't. In fact I am sinking contentedly into Old Age with few regrets. Smug, you'll say? Not totally, I hope. Too long to tell; anyway, it's all in A Fine Old Conflict.

To William Abrahams   Oakland
                                                          July 20, 1983

Dearest Billy,

. . . Toynbee memoir proceeds at snail's pace, what a bore. Sometimes I wish that a) he'd never been born, b) never died, c) never left all those diaries for me to extrapolate from, d) never had all those wives & children for me to not step on the toes of.

Oh well—such is life. Ages ago Mary Clemmey, lit. agent,[49] to whom I was moaning about unfinished prison book, helpfully said that a client of hers who suffered from Writer's Block committed suicide. Wasn't that HORRID of Mary? But (I keep thinking) I have finished some books, & no point in com-

47. Although Decca didn't mention it in her letter, she had also seen Michael Straight in 1971, noting then too his "v. peculiar" response to her.

48. At the time Straight revealed his role in the student spy ring, Anthony Blunt was the curator of Queen Elizabeth II's art collection. In his reply, Straight told Decca that Blunt was relieved at the time he informed on him and that the two had been in touch subsequently, without apparent ill will.

49. Decca once described Mary Clemmey, sometime carpenter as well as literary agent, as "a terrific chum of ours." The Treuhafts frequently stayed at her house in Kentish Town, London.

mitting suicide at the moment. Anyhow I haven't got time (or inclination) to do it before Dink & family arrive on Aug. 3—treat of all time. Do come & have a squint at those amazing OYS. . . .

Much love, & to Peter, Decca

To William Abrahams   Oakland
                                                                August 27, 1983

Dearest Billy,

. . . Bob's off in the High Sierra, hiking/camping.[50] My farewell pres. was a notebook in which to record—not so much Nature Notes as Interpersonal Relationships (there are 9 people on this ill-begotten trek). I did say that the last thing I want to see are scattered pages saying "18 days without food or water . . . this is the end . . . saw a plane circling but he didn't hear my shouts . . ." as one can read this drab stuff in the Chron. any day. Ditto "How I survived on diet of ants." Disgusting AND depressing, don't you think? He thinks to come home on Sept. 1, if he survives . . .

Much love, Decca

To Jonathan Guinness   London
                                                                October 10, 1983

Dear Jonathan,

Yours of 28 September to hand, as they say in business letters—and come to think of it, this IS a business letter.[51]

To answer:

First off, I can't think why you want to interview me, or to quote things out of my books, since you told Catherine in a letter printed some years ago in Interview Magazine that I am a liar, not to be trusted, or words to that effect.

Second off, I've said everything I wanted to say in my own books, and do not want to be quoted by you in any context.[52] Please leave me out of yours; you'll have plenty of copy from the rest of the family.

So that's about it. Catherine rang up here the other day, but she didn't leave her number. Hence no way of ringing back.

---

50. Decca was emphatically *not* a camping enthusiast. On one occasion in the 1950s or '60s, when she was "conned" by her husband into going on a ten-day hike in the Sierra, she "went round muttering 'Nature, nature, how I hate yer,' " she later recalled.

51. The letter was written in strict business format, topped by the address of the recipient and his name: "The Hon. Jonathan Guinness." The letter to which Decca is replying was more personal in tone and was signed "love, Jonathan." Guinness had asked to spend an afternoon with Decca, show her portions about her in his and his daughter Catherine's nearly completed book, *The House of Mitford*, and obtain permission to use quotations from her.

52. See letter of November 3, 1984, to Robert Gottlieb.

I gave Polly your kind message. But she says she has never met you and did not go to Padworth.[53] So much for research—isn't it a DRAG?

        Your etc., Decca

cc Deborah Rogers, Literary Agent

To Robert Gottlieb   Oakland

                                            November 4, 1983

Dearest Bites,

Lovely to hear yr snappish tones on telephone this a.m., esp as you liked ye foreword. . . .

Anyway, just to show I haven't gone totally sugary round the knees here's some correspondence with my nephew Jonathan Guinness. I was in a fairly venomous mood in London what with bad news this end etc, so was glad to take it out on him.

To clue you in: Jonathan is my sis. Diana's eldest son, born when I was 12, hence now in mid-fifties. I last set eyes on him when he was five & I was seventeen; but have followed him in the press. He's a [former chairman] of the Monday Club (far-right Tory society like John Birch Soc. here).

According to Debo, they got a 40,000 POUNDS advance from Hamish Hamilton.

Do you happen to know—or could you find out—if their ill-begotten book is taken by an American publisher?

Also, from a legal point of view does my refusal to be quoted (in my letter to him) hold water? Note that I put "cc Deb. Rogers, Lit Agent" hoping to throw fear of God into him. Accd'g to Polly Toynbee the fair use rules of copyright material are FAR stricter in England than here.

Note also that I signed off "Yours etc.," used by U English to persons of the middle or lower classes (bank managers, doctors & the like) instead of "Love from," usual in families.

        So—this is just to say LOVE FROM Decca

To Edward Pattillo[54]   Oakland

                                         November 10, 1983

Dearest Eddie:

. . . [W]hen I was in London . . . I did go down to Brayfield for the day. . . . Robin was in tearing good sprits, had made the MOST magnificent lunch of many courses although she's crippled & a bit blind still. So we spent the day

---

53. Guinness had asked that Decca give his love to "Polly"—apparently Polly Toynbee. He said he had been "on the board of a mad school she was at called Padworth, she'll tell you of it if you ask."

54. Edward Pattillo, a Montgomery, Alabama, antiques and fine arts consultant, became a correspondent of Decca's after meeting her at Virginia Durr's home. Pattillo expressed a lively interest in Decca's family and had once worked with the stepson of Decca's cousin Joan (Robin) Farrer. At

shrieking with laughter. Can't remember if I told you about this, but here goes anyway. It was just family: my stupid sister Pam (called Woman in family circles) & 1st cous. Rosemary Mitford (now Bailey) & Michael. We got talking about nursing homes (for Ann). Woman said she knows a v. good one in Cirencester, where she visits an ancient dame in late nineties. "You know who I mean, Steake" (she calls me Steake), "sister of that famous woman writer." So I said I couldn't place her right off as there've been several famous woman writers down the ages . . . "Steake, the one who wrote very bad short stories." Further questioning developed that it was KATHERINE MANSFIELD!!! One of my favorite writers. Next Womanism: conversation turned to Polly Toynbee, with whom I was staying, & her mother Anne Wollheim. Woman: "Oh, she died." Me: "Really? It must have been in the middle of the night, as I had dinner with her last evening." Woman: "She's the widow of that famous <u>man</u> writer." Me: "Well—there've been quite a few of those . . ." and I named some, such as Shakespeare, Milton & so on. Woman: "Oh I've got it all muddled again." Turns out she meant Sonia Orwell, widow of George O. . . .

Ann's letters re Nursing Home-search are SO good & often SO funny. One of those she saw informed her that inmates should "not attempt to buck the system." I wrote back to Ann to say THAT'S the one I want to check into—except that I'd end up in the loony ward, tied hand & foot, for bucking the system. . . .

Much love Decca

To Virginia Durr   Oakland
                                                      November 30, 1983

Dearest Va,

I DID so love having a word with you this morning. But somehow I always feel v. inept as a comforter—& will try to explain:

First off, I do absolutely know about DEPRESSION, as so many people I love have suffered from it. The way I visualize it is something like the blues accompanying menstrual periods (such ages ago! But I dimly remember) multiplied by a thousand times. Hence, only dimly perceived by somebody who <u>hasn't</u> ever had a real DEPRESSION. Once years & years ago, when I was having Change of Life (Menopause) I did get v. edgy, felt nervous etc.—but still, nothing like clinical depression.[55]

Decca's encouragement, Pattillo entered into what became an extensive correspondence and friendship first with Robin and then with Ann Farrer.

55. At the time, Decca had been worried enough about her lack of productivity to write about menopausal symptoms to her sister Nancy. Decca recalled their exchange vividly decades later, calling it "a v. odd corresp. . . . because it was so unlike her to answer seriously—and unlike me to consult her of all people." She said her sister, who "NEVER usually talked about anything [in letters] but purely surface things," said that "the only answer to that state of mind is to plunge into really hard work. I think she was dead right . . . it did work for me."

Second off, I know far more about grief & unhappiness, having experienced both many times in my long life. But that's different because it is caused by actual things happening (in my case, death of E's & my Baby, death of E, death of Nicholas) and so one goes through v. great agony, but it is of a different kind, somehow, from what the psychiatrists & doctors call <u>depression</u>. Hence, easier to overcome with time—I don't mean to say the beastly sorrow ever goes away (it doesn't), but it does fade, or recede, & one lives on and plunges into causes & other interesting things.

Well—as you can imagine, life with Bob has been (is) v. rewarding & fascinating; the whole Dink scene, a constant source of life-giving interest; ditto, Benj—now he's totally recovered from HIS dread malady called manic depression, lasted from approx. age 28 to 34 in his case. Now vanished thank goodness. . . .

Philip Toynbee had assaulting depressions in his last years. I haven't put much about that in my book—enough to clue the reader, though. . . . [H]is family all say that he was hooked on innumerable kinds of pills & drugs. That wasn't his undoing, though. Cancer was.

Va—sorry for this EXTREMELY un-cheering letter. I did want to somehow confide a few thoughts. I'm sure that far wiser people such as Dinky (to me, fount of all medical/psychiatric wisdom) & yr daughters will have far more intelligent thoughts re all the above. I just wanted to set down my own ideas, worthless though they may be.

To Constancia Romilly   Oakland
                                                          December 21, 1983

Chickie—OH you were interesting about that whole Va scene. Am practising the look of intense interest concealing actual fading away from boredom. . . .

You said crisis of old age. Well we know about crisis of adolescence, ditto of middle life. One would have hoped that by OLD age one might sink into a pleasant fog—or bog—& turn into a Gay Old Stick or a Kind Old Thing. (Nancy & I used to ponder these alternatives. She, of course, plumped for Gay Old Stick. I am rapidly becoming a Kind Old Thing—OR AM I??? Time will tell.) . . .

What seems (from this distance) to have happened in Va's case is a huge intensification of all the least desirable characteristics like her general Queen-Bee-ishness—amusing & charming in the past, now getting v. out of hand. This is merely a composite impression. . . .

Much love to all, Decca

To Virginia (Tilla) Durr   Oakland
                                                                March 6, 1984

Darling Tilla,

. . . [O]f course you are right in thinking that my account of life in Seminary Hill was but the tip of the iceberg of my actual thoughts about it.[56] . . .

I thought Va was fascinating, & I totally applauded her involvement in politics; she seemed to have masses of servants to look after the house & children, so that was OK as far as I could see. I loved Cliff, but still to me Va was the real fascinator in the family.

But now, even after 44 years, all of you are still something of a mystery to me. Dipping in to yr family (as I did, for example, last New Years . . .) is still a bit like walking through a mined field, never knowing what deep explosives may be concealed beneath the surface.[57] Perhaps I'm just unusually thick-headed, obtuse, insensitive to nuances. Who knows.

One thing I cld never fathom is the attitude towards MONEY, which may be the root—or one of the roots—of all evil. Having myself fluctuated from time to time from VERY POOR to quite well-off, I never gave it much of a thought; when poor, I reduced my standard of living accordingly (didn't buy things, or have a car); when better off, spent all I had—taxis, once a great luxury; presents etc. Can't you more or less accommodate to fluctuating income? . . .

I can see that I'm being horribly censorious—sorry. . . .

I'm afraid I was a rather rotten mother to Dink & Benj, as I was totally preoccupied with CP politics when they were growing up; so while I was v. fond of them, I didn't pay too much attention to them when they were little.

But they seem to have turned out quite well?

Much love darling Tilla. Keep writing; one day your book will all come together, I'm sure, as you have real talent. . . .

Decca

---

56. This letter is part of a lengthy correspondence between Tilla Durr and Decca that started after Durr began sending Decca long letters accompanying portions of a book-in-progress about her family. Decca served as Durr's mentor and confessor. She told another correspondent that she hoped that "Virginia won't come out [in her daughter's book] as Mommie Dearest," adding, "but I did say to Tilla that if writing autobiog., no point in thinking ahead to accommodate the family sensitivities—as I above all should know!!"

57. On another occasion Decca wrote that it was "a bit like living in the middle of a Tennessee Williams play."

To Polly Toynbee   Oakland
                                                              March 7, 1984

Dearest Poll,

A letter from you! How amazing, almost worth having a stroke[58] (but not quite). Also thanks SO much for ringing up. I guess the main beneficiary of the whole episode was the phone company; even Debo rang, unheard of.

I'm far better—& beginning to feel an awful fool (& fraud) for causing all that uproar. It was rather creepy for a bit: hand not working, ditto foot. I couldn't type for a wickertoo, which was v. frustrating, absolutely OK now as you can see. . . . J. Steele[59] was a total lifesaver, <u>never</u> saw such saintly kindness; he changed his plans to take me through dread Miami airport. . . .

Adopted children: After Esmond was killed some friends of Va Durr's (Senator & Mrs. Claude Pepper of Florida) went to see Va & said that obviously I shouldn't be able to bring up Dinky (as I was too poor), so they offered to pay $5,000 to adopt her. I was rather cross, & told Va that English people are on the whole unaccustomed to selling their children—forbearing to mention that I thought the price a bit low. Now, if they'd offered ten thou. . . . Am looking to hear about yr book so do enlarge.

FACES OF PHILIP: proofs have loomed. . . . As for its likely reception—I suppose that despite all efforts it will end up by displeasing everyone. But do tell yr Mum that it's a bit late in the day to have 2nd thoughts abt loopy aunts' poss. reaction. Oh well never mind, at least it's off me back. I suppose it was a silly idea from the beginning, & I sort of got hooked into it.[60]

Much love to all of you. Large hugs to nippers, who if misbehaved will NEVER BE REPROVED by their loving old friend

Decca

---

58. Decca had had a minor stroke while she was in Central America. She went to El Salvador and Nicaragua as part of a women's delegation that she described as a "sort of Counter-Kissinger Commission." Former secretary of state Henry Kissinger chaired President Ronald Reagan's National Bipartisan Commission on Central America, known informally as the Kissinger Commission. It was charged with helping to "lay the foundation for a long-term unified national approach to the freedom and independence of the countries of Central America" and issued its report on January 11, 1984. It generally endorsed the hard-line policies of the Reagan administration.

59. Jonathan Steele, the *Guardian* reporter, had met Decca during her Central American trip.

60. Decca's self-doubts had been fed by at least one of Toynbee's good friends, who had discouraged her from writing the book. She said he favored "a good, long, probing book (vs a short snappy memoir à la Dec). . . . The unspoken thought that I detected was that I'm not the right person to do it, at least not within the framework of my present plan. This jolted me—mainly, because as he developed his ideas I couldn't help thinking that he's largely right. . . . I did point out that this

To Constancia Romilly and family   Oakland
                                                                  April 3, 1984
Dearest Atlanta Loved Ones:

First off—TERRY, thanks SO much for a) informative letter & b) smashing photo of Dinky. Should like to have that blown up for a wall-sized poster. How about that—for my next Birthday present?

Second off, oh Jamie how I FEEL for you, waiting for dread April 18. I say—won't it be amusing if you're not accepted ANYWHERE for college after all this sturm & drang? No, not really. . . .

Now, James, how about coming to London with us when we go—roots-wise?[61] We'd pay for yr passage & all expenses whilst there. Might be rather fun, also a lovely moment of total pleasure? Please let me know PRONTO, I've already written to London folks (principally Sally Belfrage) to see if a house or flat can be arranged to accommodate you, Grandbob and & me. So do let me know v. soon if you would like that arrangement. Here's the way I see it: a) you'd be totally on yr own as far as what you want to do/see/ explore. b) We'd take you everywhere with us—IF of interest to you, but not if not. E.g.: our London chums . . . and selected relations of mine. . . .

If I believed in God, I'd be praying for you to get into the college of yr choice. Last time I prayed was when I was about five, & it went like this: "God bless mother & father, brother & sisters & Nannie, and make Decca a good girl, amen." Well??!! He didn't do ANY of that, so I soon gave up.

Chaka: I hear wondrous things . . . about YOU; how v. amusing you are (well, you always were) so as soon as you get through high school, will YOU come to England with old Grandec/Grandbob, as per above suggestion to James?

                              Much love to all. . . . Decca

To Claudia Williams[62]   Oakland
                                                                  April 13, 1984
Dearest Claudia, You suggested keeping a nonsmoker's journal[63]—but I'd rather do it in form of a letter to you.

---

would be just an initial effort to preserve P's life & times, in hopes it might generate a 'proper' biog."

61. Decca wrote Maya Angelou in another letter on the same subject, after James Forman accepted the invitation, "I'm FEARFULLY pleased he's coming. As Dink says, finding his ROOTS, or at least bits of them. He <u>will</u> think those roots a bit ODD, but there you are. Up to [his father] Jim Forman to re-root, or re-route, him in the other direction, don't you agree?"

62. An old friend and hypnotist. See the following letter for more biographical background.

63. Decca had acceded to appeals from her doctor, husband, and daughter that she give up smoking—"stroke-inducing, they say."

To be precise, it is now 9 a.m. (I get up approx. 6 a.m.) & I am deeply unhappy. I did play our tape 1st thing this a.m.; also took a BANTRON pill.[64]

As today is—or should be—one of the least distressful moments I ever yet have seen (paraphrase of WEARING OF GREEN), I thought all would be v. simple: just don't smoke, period. You've got absolutely nothing to do (I told myself) except mosey along to the hairdresser at 4 p.m.

So, what have I done since 6 a.m.?

1) tape, Bantron pill, coffee, read paper.

2) Jitter about the house. Write a few letters.

4)[65] Think over our session. The point is that I did that, replayed our tape. While I do think yr general approach is excellent, I'm not sure it fits all types. It presupposes an overriding interest in being healthy—never, alas, much of a preoccupation of mine. A secret fear is, in fact, going through all the trouble of giving up smoking—and going down in a FLAMING AIRCRASH!! My last thoughts: "Oh hell, I could have been smoking all this time . . ."

Think back, then, to the bit on our tape when you suggest that I should visualize a lovely country or woodsy scene, from childhood, invented, what you will. A very good idea, I'll warrant, for most people. Somehow doesn't quite work for me; I loathe the country. Pleasurable times, for me, are usually doing things with people. Never mind.

Noon, April 13: I got out my Income Tax records, planning to do it. Haven't, so far. Lay down instead for a wee nap.

However, it's now 24 hours since the last cig. Claudia says physical need disappears in 72 hours. What's 72 minus 24? Hopeless.

1 p.m., April 13: No progress on Income Tax (records still spread out on table). Luckily some friends came round (avoid loneliness & boredom, you said on the tape). . . . Chatted about last night's program. . . . Subject came round to non-smokers; all deeply supportive—"How brave! How good"—all that sort of thing. Was longing for a puff after they left. But no. Something rather awful about that "brave-good" business. . . .[66]

To various friends   Oakland
                                                                  April 20, 1984

Hypnosis Report: 15 April, 1984 (three days after the event, hypnosis being on 12 April).

Background: Claudia Williams, a great friend of ours since circa 1943 when we first came to Calif, has become a Hypnotist. She has cured many of smoking,

---

64. An over-the-counter smoking cessation aid also known as lobeline that the Food and Drug Administration has classified as safe but with no proven effectiveness.

65. The misnumbering was Decca's and perhaps indicative of her state of mind at the time.

66. Decca later updated her hypnosis diary for friends. See the following letter.

drinking etc—even of failing to pass Calif. bar exam due to fear of exams. So when I decided I simply MUST give up, I enlisted her services. She said that in order for it to work, one must be "highly motivated" (U.S. expression meaning that you very much want to do something).

Method: Claudia came over, we had a delightful chat & lunch, then started hypnosis. Her method is to make a tape of the hypnosis session which the subject (me) is to play twice a day, as 'twere self-hypnosis. I've been doing the that. She also suggested that I should keep a journal of giving up smoking; I'm doing that, too.

Hypnosis session: I know a bit about hypnosis from Bob; seeing it done as an act on QE II; Michael Barnes's research etc. So the actual session was v. predictable. Started with Claudia telling me to get comfortable . . . relax . . . lots of that, muscle by muscle. Then concentration on your body, yr inner self. Imagine you are in some lovely country or woodsy place—could be a real place from childhood or even an imaginary place. (etc.). Then of course comes the crunch: "Smoking is a poison in my body . . . I owe my body respect . . ." etc, which one is to repeat. And all very true.

I'm sure Claudia's technique is absolutely right for 99.9 percent of people. . . .

I am wondering if a different series of suggestions by hypnosis might work better for some people (like me). Example: Instead of imagining a lovely country scene, imagine the Salvador Death Squads are after you!! They've already captured Bob, Dink, Benj etc & are torturing them. Now they've got you surrounded. Want a cig? Don't be silly, at a time like this. That way it would be the opposite of relaxing, thinking about one's health, respect for one's body etc—no, it would be TENSION all the way.

Later: 20 April, 1984. (EIGHT days after stopping cigs). Am still a soul in agony—unable to settle to anything, no respite in sight. I'm only really happy when I'm asleep (which is lots of the time). Otherwise, more like a mortally wounded animal seeking its lair. Have done NO work—haven't even answered many letters . . . I am told that this condition lasts from 2 weeks to 6 years. . . . Oh for the Death Squads, to put one out of one's misery . . .

To Chaka Forman   Oakland
                                                             April 21, 1984

Darling Chaklington,

Somehow I feel v. out of touch with you—although Dink has told various bits of news, such as you in the ORATOR'S CONTEST—sounds v. excellent, & how you are choking down ALGEBRA.

(OK, so what does this mean? Asquared minus Bsquared equals A squared minus 2 AB plus B squared. Ask yr TUTOR. It's the only bit of algebra I know; but nobody explained WHY.)

Dink says you got SUPER GRADES this time, <u>clever</u> fellow.

All the whizzing back-&-forth excitement has been re James (or Jams, as I now call him)—college-bound, coming with us to England etc.

So you seem to be a bit left out—of current PLANS, that is, but not from Grandec's HEART (if she has one, which some doubt).

I thought I'd send you the enclosed TOKEN OF MY ESTEEM, which is to be used purely for pleasure & NOT for any Worthy Purpose. So don't let Dink get her hands on it for some future college fund, or sturdy clothing. . . .

When do YOU plan to graduate from high school, approx? Shall we spin away to England? And/or France, Spain etc? Can you speak Spanish? If so, you can be the interpreter. But do hurry up—Grandec can't last forever. Having given up smoking I DREAM of a flaming airplane wreck—or being done in by Salvadoran Death Squads—<u>anything</u> to put me out of my misery.

Fondest love, dearest Oy #2. Grandec

To Nell Painter[67]   Oakland
                                                                    May 12, 1984

Dear Nell,

. . . A Jesse Jackson[68] anecdote: A few weeks ago Bob & I were up at the amazing pad of a fellow English emigre (David Pleydell-Bouverie) who manages to assemble all sorts of unlikely people. So amongst the company was one of those dread SOCIALITES, name of Nan Kempner—one sees her name in society column all the time. Conversation turned to politics, & I happened to mention that I was endorser of Jesse Jackson's Calif. campaign. <u>Nan:</u> Well I suppose he's thrilled to have <u>any</u> white support. <u>Me:</u> I don't know what you mean by that. <u>Nan:</u> The way those people breed, they'll rule the country anyway by the turn of the century. <u>Me:</u> (in my MOST lah-di-dah English accent): I don't know what you know about breeding, perhaps not much. I, however, know a lot about it as my father was one of 9 children, and I was one of seven. <u>Nan:</u> But these black families are all illegitimate, single mothers who don't even know the names of their children's fathers. <u>Me:</u> Ah! It's a wise child that knows his own father in the best of societies. Illegitimacy was RIFE in our background. Descended from a mistress of Charles II, and so it goes . . .

Luckily, about now dinner was served. End of me & Nan. . . .

---

67. Painter, a teacher and historian, was an old classmate of Constancia Romilly. After a long correspondence, Decca and Painter finally met in person in North Carolina a few years before this letter was written.

68. The civil rights leader was an unsuccessful candidate in 1984 for Democratic presidential nomination.

To Patricia M. King[69]   Oakland
                                                                        July 31, 1984

Dear Ms. King,

. . . My great friend Kay Boyle, known mainly for her short stories written between the wars, clued me into the idea of SELLING one's old letters. She said that if she had a huge dentist's bill she'd simply sell off a letter from Hemingway, or G. Stein etc of her Parisian youth. I thought this was a smashing idea. Kay came & stayed with us in the late 1960s; she'd leave a note saying "I shan't be in for dinner," or "Please save today's Chronicle" etc., all of which I squirrelled away for my children's inheritance.

Came the time when our house was bursting at the seams with files, boxes of this & that—would have cost a lot to have somebody to haul it all away to the dump, so I sold it to the Univ. of Texas for $10,000. This was just research material, letters etc. re three books: <u>American Way of Death</u>, <u>Trial of Dr. Spock</u>, <u>Kind & Usual Punishment</u>. I was very glad of the money, which I used to finance a year in England (1974). But I didn't include ANY personal letters. A few years ago my sister Deborah Devonshire was staying with Lady Bird Johnson (with whom she has for some reason become friends) & they went to the U. of Tex. library. A librarian said to Debo, "Would you like to see your sister's archives?" Yes, said Debo, so the librarian opened a box. Debo picked up the first paper which simply said: "Bob, call Sarah Jones before 7 a.m." "POOR Sarah Jones," Debo wrote to me . . .

Next act was effort (unsuccessful) to sell PERSONAL letters to U. of Texas. So I sold these letters via same intermediary, Brick Row Bookshop, to the U. of Ohio.[70] Again—vast boxes, this time letters from my family & other assorted people, including loads from Va Durr. Huge amounts from childhood/Esmond R. days/etc.

I hope that this explains present position. I'm sure that if you want copies of Va's to me, those could be arranged. . . .

                                            Yours sincerely, Jessica Mitford

---

69. Former director of Radcliffe's Schlesinger Library on the History of Women in America, which houses the papers of Virginia Durr.

70. Ohio State University. Decca once called the sales to university archives "a sweet racquet, or rather racket. . . . [O]ne gets far more from selling worthless junk to said Univ. than from writing said junk." The papers Decca frequently dismissed as "the junk" include most of the letters that make up this book—and without which the book would not have been possible—as well as various manuscripts, tape recordings, clippings, and everything else Decca could think of to fill boxes, since she was paid by volume. Included in the collection at the University of Texas, for instance, are the following, as itemized in the archive's inventory: "one pair of black funeral shoes," "ashtray from Forest Lawn Memorial Park," "cardboard casket with plastic figurine," and—with no further explanation—the previously mentioned "Neva Perkins' cremated remains."

To Ann Farrer Horne   Oakland
                                                                August 25, 1984

Sistling the SPEED of Twinks—yrs of 21 Aug arr. today. . . .

So rushing to answer. . . . J. Guinness: I'm afraid I'd be hopeless at answering, as I don't want to encourage that lot. E.g.: When I was in London with Benj, aged 11, Diana sent a message through the sisters that she'd love to see us. I sent a message back saying I thought better not, as I didn't want Benj turned into a lampshade.[71] End of messages. But—come to think of it, Jonathan isn't Diana, although from all I hear of the lad (now aged 55, I reckon) he's not far different. If I did answer, what shld I say? . . .

                          Yr loving SISTER

To Robert Gottlieb   Oakland
                                                              November 3, 1984

Dearest Bites,

. . . Jonathan's book[72] is approx. 600 pages long, v. small type, so I haven't read it yet (it arrived yesterday by special delivery, sent by good Polly Toynbee— an advance copy that she got at the Guardian). Publication date in England is Nov. 19 or 23.

Needless to say the book is a total justification of Diana (J's mother) & downput of me/Esmond. Despite my injunctions against any quotation—reinforced by an official letter from Deb. Rogers—he seems to have drawn quite freely from Hons/Rebels, ditto other books like Fine Old Conflict.

I long to sue; but where? and whom???

Is Kay following through on autobiog. discussed years ago with you? I DO wish she would. Quelle fascination THAT would be.

Naught else new this end. Benj seems to be slightly coming down from the worst of manic phase; but then what? He's thrown everything away: his wife, his piano tuning practice, his friends. I <u>can't bear</u> it. Oh Bites . . .

My oldest grandchild James Forman is loving Brown University. And— bonanza of all time for his poor old granny—he FLUNKED CALCULUS!! After winning huge prizes for expertise in maths in far-off Georgia. So he's decided to chuck maths in favour of hist. & lit., from my point of view far easier to discuss than, say, calculus. (By the way what <u>is</u> calculus, if you know, which I bet you don't? I thought it meant a slide rule . . .)

                          Much love, Decca

---

71. Decca was alluding to reports that the Nazis during the Holocaust had made lampshades out of the skin of murdered Jews.

72. *The House of Mitford.* For background on Decca's refusal to participate in the preparation of the book, see letters of October 10, 1983, to Jonathan Guinness and November 4, 1983, to Robert Gottlieb.

To James Forman Jr.   Oakland
                                                        November 7, 1984

Darling Jamie,

Many thanks for yrs of 4 November re yr visit to Harvard, the football game etc. I note you said that Brown lost by 24 to 10—which isn't <u>too</u> bad, is it? Considering Harvard prob. had more time to practice? Being an older university etc.

How VILE for you about having to go to the dentist, wisdom-tooth-wise. By the time you get this letter, it will be long over I guess. I do hope it's not TOTAL TORTURE. . . .

Fortunately your letter came too late for me to suggest possible way out of going to maniacal dentist—not that it would be likely to work for you, as I assume you are a non-believer? Here goes with a DENTIST STORY that has ever stuck in my mind:

It concerns Mrs. Hammersley, an old family friend, contemporary of my mother's, hence born approx. 1880. So when Mrs. Ham (as we called her) was about 8 yrs old, her Mamma told her that she had an appointment with the dentist in two weeks. Mrs. Ham—a devout Roman Catholic—prayed every night that the dentist would die. Came the day of the appointment, & her mother called her in. "My dear child, I am sorry to say that you will not be going to the dentist today after all. He died in the night." Don't you call that rather effective, prayer-wise? CAUTION: Don't try it on YOUR dentist as who knows what DIABOLICAL tricks he's got up his sleeve. He might send you to sizzle in Hell if he finds out what you are up to. . . .

We called Dinky yesterday—Election Day. She said you were deeply depressed as the returns came in.[73] I suppose everyone was; except that it was so absolutely expected. It's all very well, you know, to blame "lack of leadership" (us having to choke down voting for bores like Mondale—which has been MY experience almost ever since I came to America, with possible exception of FDR)—and of course the electoral process does seem to throw up mediocrities. After XX years these dull presidents become enhanced with a sort of rosy glow—that excellent old Father Figure Ike! Good, down-to-earth Harry Truman!—etc, you can write the others. I can't say how AWFUL they seemed to us at the time.

But I do see that FOUR MORE YEARS is—from yr. point of view—a possible death warrant. At my age, it doesn't really matter because like Pres. Reagan I've lived my life, so bang-bang out you go wouldn't be too awful. But it might be extremely annoying for you. I expect you will muddle through, however.

Fondest love, & to yr unknown room-mate & other chums,

---

73. Ronald Reagan was re-elected president by a lopsided margin over Democrat Walter Mondale.

To Benjamin Treuhaft   Oakland
                                                                  January 24, 1985

Benj—to state the obvious, our meeting last week was a disaster. I realize that both you AND Bob thought it was awful of me to lash out at you. Having thought it over a great deal, I can't apologize as that is very much the way I feel. However, all along I'd had the idea that I might do better to write you a letter than to meet; so here goes. In your letter to Bob, you said you had made lots of notes—well so have I, mainly mental notes whenever I think of you, which is, I'm sorry to say, <u>extremely</u> often.

Perhaps I should start with a flash-back, sort of a Dec's-eye-view of how things were before we went to England last summer. From my observation, for several years (before & during your marriage to Sue[74]) you were absolutely one's favorite sort of person: intelligent, quick, amusing, in all ways terrific good company—that can all be summed up under a sort of blanket designation of CHARMING. But after you married Sue, something far deeper & better than just CHARM seemed to develop, viz. a huge amount of kindness & compassion. You seemed to cherish Sue in the most delightful, sweet way—looked after her when she wasn't feeling well, egged her on to cultivate her musical talents, planned lovely treats for her birthday—or was it your wedding anniversary? When we came over to your house, or you & Sue would come here, I absolutely basked in the pleasure of your company as a couple. All this led me to believe that those dreadful, absurd, disgusting manic episodes were in the past & perhaps you had somehow outgrown them.

After we got back in July . . . you were clearly going mad again. . . .

I'm not sure just how you are—or where, in terms of the progression of yr disease—at the moment; when you came over last week, your voice was more normal (not that DREAD horrid squeak that it turns into); but nothing else, it seemed to me, boded well. All that tiresome concentration on YOURSELF— <u>oh</u> the boredom. The total transformation of you into a totally selfish creature, wanting money-money-money. . . .

What's happening this end is that Kevin Ingram, an English lad who is writing a biography of Esmond Romilly, is staying here. We've had various people over to meet him . . . and ordinarily, of course, the first person we'd have thought of to invite would be you. But that would have been hopeless in the circs., as you wouldn't be remotely interested in anybody but YOU. That's what is so incredibly disheartening & depressing. That is where your whole character has totally changed, so that you have become a rather dull stranger, the sort one doesn't want to see much of for fear of being dunned for money and/or bored by lots of empty talk about how awful this society is (which I know already . . .) how unfair the law courts & police are. Not terribly original, you must admit.

---

74. Benjamin Treuhaft and his wife had divorced the previous year. In 1990 he married Jungmin (Min) Kim, from whom he was divorced in 1995.

It's interesting that you rejected that article called "Playing the Manic Game" on the ground that the people described were all in loony bin at the time hence under unknown—or unfathomable—pressures from awful psychiatrists. Not totally true. See, for example, page 257: "Alienating Family Members." Actually the whole article seemed to me amazingly descriptive of what I have seen of you in these nightmarish times.

You started to describe the onset of manic phase: a feeling of extreme energy, getting up earlier in the morning, able to do more, to have satisfactory conversations with people with whom you are normally shy such as blacks. All that, of course, sounds marvelous: just what one wishes one cld feel every morning!

So when does the nightmare start? That is—the nightmare for everyone else except for YOU? We didn't get that far. And as your condition seems to shut off any insight on your part, perhaps you don't really know. As for me, I can't help linking—or relating—things happening in my life to you—in the sense of constantly thinking "Oh I must call Benj about thus-and-so . . ." only to realize there's no point, you wouldn't be at all interested. It's a bit like wishing one could talk to somebody who is dead. Example: On the day of SUPER BOWL, I organized a COUNTER-BOWL consisting of a theatre party to see matinee of the movie PASSAGE TO INDIA, followed by dinner here. Exactly the sort of thing I should have longed to ask you to! Obviously a hopeless idea.

If the latter example makes it all sound trivial, it isn't, let me assure you. For me, it's more like a hateful heavy cloud that makes everything horrid & difficult, takes pleasure out of life.

I'm afraid this letter may strike you as simply an extension of what I've already said when you came round last Thursday. The point is, though, that I've just tried to set forth in writing my reflections on what's happened to you.

But still (you may be wondering) why bother? And re-reading what I have written, I am rather wondering myself. Perhaps it is that, as you are hardly ever out of my thoughts, I was slightly hoping to exorcise, as it were, the ghastliness by writing it down.

Also, it goes without saying that if you should ever tire of the manic condition & wish to get back to ordinary life, which wld. doubtless require some sort of therapy, we would absolutely stand behind you & do all possible to help.

To Edward Pattillo   Oakland
                                                             February 24, 1985
Dearest Eddie,

Many thanks for yours of 8 Feb from Auckland. I'd written to you to Colombo, so here goes trying Bombay! A bit like flinging a message in a bottle into the sea. . . .

Quitting smoking: No useful advice from me. I gave up on 11 April, 1984, & still CRAVE a cig. Someone told me the first 6 years are the worst. . . . I have gained approx. 16 lbs & am absolutely disgusting looking and very unhappy over all that . . . My advice: don't do it. You've given up drinking which is enough for one lifetime. My next advice: don't pay any attention to ME. . . .

Now, for a cheerier note: . . . Kevin Ingram is staying here. . . . His biog. of Esmond Romilly now all spruced up for publication, due in November in England & next spring in America. I must say I think it is SURPRISINGLY good. To clue you in: Kevin is a working-class lad, his dad a Ford motorcar assembly line worker, his mum a cook who has worked in such institutions as hospitals, the Army etc. Kevin is an only child. He's now 28, has been working on his book for SIX years, i.e. almost all his adult life. He got on to it as a result of being assigned to write a paper on the Spanish civil war when in college (he went to Sussex, a redbrick (means workingclass) university) & he came across Esmond's BOADILLA. This got him fascinated; then he came out here to see me, hitch-hiking with a girlfriend. I was impressed by his enthusiasm & intelligence, so gave him intros. to various people here & in England who knew Esmond: Va, Kay Graham, Selden Rodman & others, plus Philip Toynbee, Peter Nevile et al in England. So he did go to see them all. He started writing the book—at first it wasn't too good. He asked me for E's wartime letters; I said firmly that I would send him copies WHEN AND IF he had a contract to publish. Which did happen, approx. a year ago (Feb. 1984).

Suddenly he really hit a stride. I'm extremely pleased with his book—which doesn't mean much, but more important Billy Abrahams & the English publisher (Weidenfeld) think very highly of it. . . .

Much love, Decca

To the Duchess of Devonshire   Oakland
                                                                 March 1, 1985

Dearest Hen,

. . . I'm off to Florida of all horrid places in a few minutes so this is just a line to tell of Topic A[75] developments:

COULDN'T be better. He's not only totally down from dread manic high, & his usual smashing self, but he has NOTED AND AGREED that he was simply awful & destroying himself etc. when manic and he's gone [to see] a therapist. Point is that this is the first time ever that he wld admit there was anything wrong.

He even said rather gloomily that he spends his time going round to apologize to people for his awful behaviour—you see, it's not just us obviously who suffer from it but all his friends and his piano clients—everyone in his life. So this is all a HUGE STEP forward. Best of all, the therapist is giving Lithium & Benj is agreeing to have it. It requires lots of careful watching by the Dr—i.e.

---

75. Benjamin Treuhaft. The term "Topic A" later became shorthand for other crises in Decca's family life.

blood tests etc. to make sure the dose is right for the particular bod—and Benj is doing all that, means going to hosp. v. often for said tests. Well you can see how extremely pleasing it all is. . . .

To Dr. Arlan Cohn[76]   Oakland
                                                                               April 11, 1985

Dear Arlan,

I've got the most awful thing to tell—and for God's sake don't forget your OATH of doctor/patient confidentiality. Not a word must be breathed to a soul of what follows.

As you have probably already guessed, it concerns s——g, a dirty word, no doubt, in your vocabulary, hence I fear to spell it out.

I'd done so well; it had been close to a year, during which I weathered every sort of circumstance . . . [a]nd trips to London, L.A. & many more—always in the non-s——g section.

As you so wisely warned, one puff can start one on the Road to Perdition. At first, it was just O.P.'s (Other People's) cigs. at parties etc. Then, realizing the bliss of it I <u>bought</u> some—called Sherman's Queen size Cigarettellos, which are nice because you can put them out if you hear somebody coming & then relight them.

Now—I've GOT to quit again. As you may realize I'm hopeless at the psychological route. Hypnotism etc. does me scant good, ditto Aversion Therapy; Bob collected a ton of disgusting butts & ashes, & all I did was to breathe in deeply & say "HOW divine."

Should I re-start on that chewing gum?[77] Somebody gave me the MOST revolting thing called "Skoal Bandits,"[78] same principle I guess—some sort of nicotine substitute. Also, what about Acupuncture?

HELP!!! Please ring up when you have a moment, & advise. I do of course realize that I shall have to set a DAY to start stopping, & all that.

Otherwise I'm in good health—still fat as an elephant, but planning to do better. . . .

                        Regards, Decca

Please call after 9 a.m., weekdays. <u>If a man answers, hang up.</u> Bob hasn't a clue—so far.

---

76. Decca's family doctor, a published writer himself under the pseudonym Oscar London.

77. Decca was referring to Nicorettes, a nicotine-laced gum on which she became "hopelessly hooked." She joked about an announcement on an airliner: "In preparation for our landing the captain has turned on the No Nicorette sign. There will be no more chewing until you are well within the airport."

78. A brand of snuff.

To Virginia (Tilla) Durr   Oakland
                                                                      April 19, 1985

Darling Tilla,

Thanks for yrs of April 10th, which just fetched up here (postmarked, however, April 15th! As I have noted in the course of a long life, letters seldom arrive until after they've been mailed).

I was v. interested in all you had to say and really should v. much like a splash of elucidation—esp. of OUR relationship, which I had thought of as just that of a devoted (and sometimes bossy) old friend, & a talented (but sometimes sloppy) young writer.

I'm afraid I'm too thick-skinned, or dumb, to have fathomed the nuances—i.e. the "incredibly strong complicated but positive feelings for you" of which you write . . .

Can't you, by this late age, adjust to the Lucy-ness of Lucy[79] and the Tilla-ness of you? . . .

As one of 7 children, 6 sisters, I noted many who were far something-or-other than I was: Debo, super horsewoman, ice skater, beauty—<u>incredibly pretty</u>, admired by all the chaps. Nancy, brill. writer & marvellously funny company. Diana, once adored by me—the undisputed BEAUTY of not only our family but of her generation.

What I swear I don't remember is being <u>jealous</u> of any of the others. My sights were set in a totally different direction. . . .

Incidentally, interviewers often ask me if it was "sibling rivalry" with Nancy that made me turn to writing? Absolutely <u>not</u>, is the answer. . . .

To Dr. Arlan Cohn   Oakland
                                                                      April 20, 1985

Dear Arlan,

I believe you said that I should ring you on Friday? Instead, I'm writing on Saturday. Somehow I rather hate to telephone doctors for fear they are in the midst of curing somebody from a DIRE DISEASE, or setting broken legs etc., hence might find it a dull distraction to hear from a self-indulgent old soul who hasn't the brains or the will-power to give up smoking. . . .

In a way, just writing to you the other day with FULL CONFESSION may have been Step #1, i.e. a splash of determination.

On Wednesday, 17 April, I went & fetched the disgusting chewing gum & pills from Chimes.[80]

On Thurs, 18th April I started doing all that, ditto Fri. 19th & today, Sat. 20. Now here's the amazing thing: I was fully expecting to be a quivering mass

---

79. Virginia (Tilla) Durr's sister.
80. A neighborhood pharmacy.

of misery (like last time, only perhaps worse), unable to work, concentrate etc. So it came as a delightful surprise that it wasn't a BIT like that; in fact it's now Day 3, and actually I'm feeling perfectly OK, quite ordinary & not in any agony.

A couple of observations: The fall from grace was rather gradual, not precipitate. Started with the odd puff from somebody's cig. at a party. Then—oh dear—Bob had brought home from Mexico a little package of cigars, which I smoked up. Wishing to replace them (as I hadn't asked him for them) I bought a few more—and, alas, smoked those. Next I found these really heavenly things called Sherman's Cigarettellos which I hid (I am sorry to say) behind a shelf of Bibles & prayer-books, thinking that's the LAST place anyone would look. I was having approx. 10 of these delicious treats a day—vs. about 30 a day in the dear, dead old days of Chesterfields.

Needless to say, the incredible kindness of Bob and Dinky over the original horrors of quitting—not to mention other friends, & even the nice lady at the liquor store who was my source for CHESTERFIELDS & who said "Good for you!" when I told her I'd quit—were a bit of a knife in the heart, when I became a CLOSET SMOKER.

I do think that the lifesaver for the hopeless, abject addict may be that absolutely horrible chewing gum.

I've had about six a day—the literature says "Do not take more than 30 a day"—not bloody likely!

I've also had about 2 a day of those pills you ordered; but those seem to have no effect whatsoever.

End of MEDICAL REPORT.

Thanks VERY much for bothering about all this, Decca

To the Duchess of Devonshire   Oakland
                                                                  April 26, 1985

Dearest Hen,

S. Hastings's manuscript[81] arrived & I read it non-stop, so here goes with a few words about same. (If you haven't read it I shall be livid, as you were the one who chose her for the job—also, you're the only one who I can discuss it with.)

I thought the first half of the book was pretty atrocious, a) a rehash, or patchwork, of all the other Industry books, b) not well written—that is, a sort of Women's Own[82] lowest-common-denominator style. I feared as much after she sent me some examples of her journalism a few years ago; drear & trite they were. H. Acton's memoir—which I thought at the time all too superficial &

---

81. The manuscript of Selina Hastings's biography published later in the year under the title *Nancy Mitford* (Hamish Hamilton).

82. A women's magazine.

one-sided, failing to get into the complexity of N's character—seems, in comparison, a marvel of good writing & good use of material, e.g. N's letters to Muv from Italy (aged 16) & her correspondence with Brains O. Grant. In fairness, this must have posed difficulties for S. Hastings as I suppose that H. Acton had copped all the best stuff. But mainly—oh the difference of quality of the writing!

The second half does pick up a lot, partly because the whole horror of the Col. love affair has not been told in myriad other books but mostly because there is a lot more quotation of Nancy's own letters; as you will note (if/when you read it) these are the real nuggets midst a ton of dross. All through, there's an annoying assumption that readers will know the cast of characters & all too little identification of people N. speaks of in letters. . . .

There are many unexplained things . . . even how/why you & she became terrific friends after her scorn of you when you were first married. One would have thought that S. Hastings could have ferreted some of this out via letters & interviews. But no; if she did ask you about all that, she didn't include it.

The bits about Nancy's books, how she happened to write them, how they were reviewed, how received by friends are incredibly thin—esp. considering that her books are what she will be remembered by. Hen DO have a look-see at Xopher Sykes's brill. biog. of E. Waugh & for God's sake don't say you haven't got time to read it. He devotes pages to each of E. Waugh's books—reviews of them, letters about them—all of the deepest fascination. . . .

She did describe N's illness very well. When I got to the end, I caved in & sobbed.

So now, Hen, what to do? I'll have to write to her, as she sent me a v. cordial letter—"most anxious to know what you think, I do so very much hope that you will like it" etc. etc.

Knowing the awfulness of writing books, & realizing that I really do think hers is a fairly pathetic effort, am in a quandary.[83] . . .

I think I'll send a letter saying "JM is out of town at the moment, for several months in fact, and will be very pleased to read your book at the earliest opportunity. She gives full & free permission to quote her recipe for max. enjoyment of sausages. Jane Freeman, secretary." I do LONG for Jane Freeman, who n'existe pas except in my imagination.

HEN: Please write back, in detail, by return of post.

---

83. Decca wrote Hastings a diplomatic letter a few weeks later, emphasizing the portions of the book she liked. She mentioned but soft-pedaled her criticisms and offered to meet Hastings to discuss her reactions in greater detail when she was next in London.

To Philip Kerby[84]
Oakland
May 1985

Dear Phil,

First off—a thousand congrats. on retiring, although I fear you'll be sneaking about actually working long after retirement. (And I HOPE you will, as do all your myriad fans.)

Second off—Here is my opportunity to acknowledge, once and for all, my indebtedness to you for giving me the confidence to take up writing as a trade. For a flash-back:

A middle-aged lady aged 41 sent you, through her agent, an article about the funeral business entitled ST. PETER DON'T YOU CALL ME. The agent had, in fact, sent this piece around to all the mags, who had coldly turned it down. But YOU, dear Phil, accepted it for FRONTIER—and to my extreme surprise & pleasure, sent a FEE of $40. Oh the <u>deep</u> pleasure of that; one can write and even get MONEY for it? Euphoria this end. The year was 1958. (I had, of course, done lots of writing before, mostly leaflets with headlines: "RALLY ON TUESDAY TO PROTEST OAKLAND POLICE BRUTALITY," or "SUPPORT THE HOLLYWOOD TEN! Dinner, $2. Students and unemployed, free." What the critics (or at least some of them) might call "spare, pared-down prose.")

I can't, at this late date, remember just what I did with the $40 except to flash it around to all my friends saying "LOOK AT THIS! Forty dollars, more than you make in a week I bet." Which might have been true, in those far-off days.

The first words of "St. Peter, Don't You Call Me" were: "The American Way of Death, though not extolled in song, story, and news articles to the same extent as its more popular counterpart, the American Way of Life. . . ." etc.

So that was the seductive title, all thanks to YOU, Phil. . . .

[A] ton of thanks for giving me my belated start in life, and many congrats. on YOUR new start in life as a Retired Person. . . .

Much love, Decca

To James Forman Jr.
Oakland
May 23, 1985

Darling Oy #1,

. . . [H]ere is the conundrum for you & Chaka to sort out (my generation failed, and so on the whole did Dink's, so over to you):

. . . If one wished to change the world, substitute a decent system for an indecent (see, for example, the Communist Manifesto by K. Marx), how does one get this done?

---

84. The founding editor of *Frontier* magazine. In 1976, while at the *Los Angeles Times*, he won a Pulitzer Prize for editorial writing.

Be thinking about this. Be pondering theories of the United Front vs. a more militant stand. When I was your age—or actually perhaps more Chaka's age, <u>circa</u> 15—the clarity, the brilliance, the total solution to horrors of war & mass poverty contained in the Communist Manifesto & other writings (Dink must have them? <u>Wage Labour & Capital</u>,[85] <u>What Is To Be Done</u> by Lenin etc) burst on me like fireworks. The marvellous thing was (I thought) that if only everyone could read these astonishing books, all would AT ONCE turn to communism, there'd be no more war, all people would be equal & free.

When Dink was born, I was quite certain that the Comm. revolution would happen long before she grew up. Silly of me, but there you are—total optimism reigned.

I was quite surprised when none of this occurred. WHY? That is the question for you/Chaka to ponder.

Oh—sorry, it's NOT the end. . . .

Montg'y bus boycott, 1956, widely thought of as the opening shot in CR[86] struggles of the 60's—the second shot being student sit-ins that began early 1960.

If you were a Man from Mars, or (like me) a Woman from California & England who had dipped into Montgy. from time to time, as I did, to visit Va & Cliff Durr, you might be fairly amazed that this issue took hold & lit the fuse, so to speak (or to coin a cliche, yr. English prof. wld say).

Staying with the Durrs, being driven round the countryside by Va—. . . in days when there were still near-starving black sharecroppers—and observing through the Durr daily life the total lack of rights, civil or otherwise, of blacks—well, I'd have thought that where they cld SIT ON A BUS would have been the least of their worries.

Clever old Grandec; wrong again.

Apartheid: All those horrors have been known for years & years. What suddenly set the students afire? Was it the example set by congressmen etc., being arrested at the Embassy?

Do ponder these matters, when you have time.

My dear Oy, don't forget yr birthday present. What will it be???

To Emma (the Good) Tennant   London
July 15, 1985

Dearest Emma,

I'm SO sad we shan't be meeting this time round. Hoping for next year.

We had a super day at Robin's yesterday, Debo came all the way from Chatsworth & there was naught but Farrer relations there, family only.

Here goes with a splash of confidential info—I'm only burdening you with

---

85. By Karl Marx.
86. Civil rights.

this because you are the only one who knows all the background to it, & in case you can possibly shed some light.

At the end of the (blissful) day, a v. strange conversation, as follows: Rud & I were walking up the drive, & Bob was walking with Debo back to her car. Debo asked Bob "How is Decca?" (meaning post-stroke-wise) so Bob said fine, doing v. well etc. Then Bob on an impulse said "Now, may I ask you a question?" & he went over the scrapbook thing, how v. miserable I'd been over the accusation, & how all Debo had said was "Eureka! it's turned up" with nary an apology for all the super unpleasantness that ensued; & the upsettingness of her never apologizing for orig. confrontation re same. He asked whether the reason was that she reckoned I really might have pinched the scrapbook—hence the fact I hadn't was in her mind immaterial. Debo said NOT ONE WORD. She got in her car. Bob said, "Were you going to say something?" Answer: "Goodbye, Bob," & she drove off.

Now don't you call that v. ODD? I know you once said—& I agree—that Debo automatically skates away from anything that might conceivably become turgid; yet one wld think that Bob having sort of bared his breast re scrapbookery she might have given some sort of response, even if it didn't involve saying she was sorry.

It's such a puzzle. Because of the DETAILS she advanced at that long-ago frightful evening at Chesterfield St. with Ld Antrim. . . . I keep wondering if she still thinks I did somehow get hold of the scrapbook? And then what—had it surreptitiously replaced at Chatsworth? The logistics of such would boggle the most devious mind.

So what does she REALLY think? I know you said ages ago that you didn't want to bring it up with her. But if you cld supply any sort of hint as to her frame of mind re the subject, it wld help her far-off American Hen no end. I hasten to add I don't mean to ask you to probe the subject if you don't want to. Am really just writing to keep you in the picture in case something occurs to you.

Do ring me here. . . . Not just about that; I long to chat further about dread Lady Selina[87] as I call her & her atrocious book. . . .

Much love, & to Toby & nippers, Decca

To the Duchess of Devonshire   London
                                                                    July 25, 1985
Dearest Hen,

That was really most good of you.[88] It's put a FINAL end to that perennially nagging business—or such it was to me. Thanks, Hen.

---

87. Decca referred to Selina Hastings derisively as "Lady Selina" after, she said, Hastings solicited recollections about Nancy Mitford in a letter in *The New York Times Book Review* and signed the solicitation "Lady Selina Hastings."

88. The duchess had sent Decca a note apologizing "unreservedly" about their scrapbook row.

S. of France was v. blissful.[89] One huge bonus was Grizelda Grimond,[90] turns out to be a great friend of Emma's. We couldn't quite fathom the Grizelda-Tony Richardson relationship; she lives in London with their dau. aged 12, he lives in L.A. except for summer months when they meet up in S. of France. It was a bit like coming into a play during the 2nd act, not knowing what went before. But I think all is told in (awful) John Osborne's autobiog so shall scram to get that. . . .

Ken Tynan[91] & Kathleen's children were there, a sultry-eyed 18-yr old Roxanna & a clever 14-yr old Matthew. He wrote a play for us to act in, full of matri-patricide. Bob had a non-speaking part of corpse of murdered father, I was the mother & Matthew & Grizelda's dau were the murderous children. It was rather good, but I wouldn't be in Kathleen Tynan's shoes after hearing their plans. She's due to arrive there this week. Poor her.

Grizelda's mum is Laura Bonham Carter, P. Toynbee's first love at age 17. G. came across a hatbox full of his love letters—HOW I wish I'd had those for me memoir! . . .

We scram to Calif on 30 July; rather sad, yet longing to get home.

Much love, Yr Hen

To Sally Belfrage   Oakland
                                                    August 8, 1985

Darling Sall,

I loved our early morning chat, e'en though not totally satisfactory from my pt of view—had been craving a splash more gossip, but I do appreciate yr situation so will drop it.

Now, re point of me coming to England. I know you'll think this is pretty WEIRD but will do my best to explain.

Background: Emma the Bad[92] & a colleague, Tony Lacey of Penguin, are organizing publication of short (35,000 words) books about Famous Women. They've been after me from time to time about this with suggestions, such as Mrs. Roosevelt, which wld bore me stiff so it's been Non, non, non, out you go (Benjy's successful words, aged 11, to a would-be rapist in French swimming pool).

---

89. Decca stayed at the French compound of film director Tony Richardson.

90. Grizelda Grimond, whom Decca called "my newfound friend," was the daughter of former U.K. Liberal Party leader Jo Grimond and Laura Bonham-Carter.

91. The English theater critic, whom Decca had met twenty-five years earlier in San Francisco.

92. Adding to the confusion at this time between the two Emma Tennants was that both of them had a role in publication of the book Decca begins to describe here. Emma the Good, Decca's niece, lived near the Grace Darling Museum and assisted in preparation of Decca's new book, which was dedicated to her.

The other day Bob & I had lunch with E. in her garden & Bob came up with the brill. idea of Grace Darling. In 1838 she rescued a shipwrecked crew: "Grace had an English heart, and the raging storm she braved/She sailed away o'er the dashing spray and the crew she saved." I expect you've heard Dink & me belting out this song in our tuneful voices?

We used to sing this round my mother's piano as children—according to Debo, when [she was] 16 or more [and they] sang it at Inch Kenneth, shouting out the stirring words "HELP! HELP! she could hear the cry of the ship-wrecked crew," boats would put out from neighboring Hebridean islands to see what the matter was.

In the early 1960s I sang it to Lou Gottlieb of the Limelighters, & he put it into his nightclub act, also made a record. (The first time it was done in a night-club the copy had been read over the phone, & song came out in the program as Grey Starling.[93]) He threatened to change the words to "Grace had a Jewish heart," I was appalled as there are masses of Jewish, Black etc. heroines & only one English heroine, Grace Darling; so he gave over.

In 1962 I was staying with my mother at Inch K. & we read in the paper about a lawsuit brought by the Grace Darling Museum against somebody who had pinched a bit of the prow or something of the wrecked ship. So I wrote off post haste to the Hon. Curator, whose name was given in the story, telling him all about how we used to sing the song etc. He wrote back the most informative let-ter, saying in part that the museum hadn't got the song. My mother immediately wrote a codicil in her will leaving the sheet music to the museum. Next year she died. There ensued a minor flap, solicitor for museum writing to solicitor for her estate saying where's our song. Debo (as usual in charge) wrote to me saying these letters cost her a pound a page—she was living in a dream world, I bet ten pounds is more like it—& that I should tell MacGillivray, my ma's boatman, that the sheet music is on right side of piano & to send it to the Museum. Which he did.

Are you getting bored? Now to the point:

Ever since my corresp. with the Hon. Curator, who sent lots of brochures etc., I've been nosing around the idea of writing about Grace Darling. But the story is too long to do in the 8,000 or so words allowed by mags. such as Atlantic or Harpers; too slight to merit a whole book. Hence 35,000 wld be about OK.

I've got three biogs of GD published in the last century, wonderfully SAC-CHARINE, might be v. good copy. She was the first ever MEDIA STAR—I know that's wrong as there was only one MEDIUM in those days—her fame spread by the most fantastic newspaper coverage. I'd always rather assumed that this kind of personality hoop-la & build-up had started in this century, principally after WW I with emergence of Yellow Press, Daily Express, News of the World, Time, Hearst Press etc.

---

93. A coinage Decca later adopted in much of her correspondence.

Not a bit of it. GD & her family were BESIEGED by newspapers, promoters, fans as 'twere the Beatles in our era. There were so many requests for a lock of GD's hair that she went bald. . . .

So the whole thrust of my book would be an exploration of this early Victorian press phenomenon.

Bob's trying to spread the rumour that Grace CAUSED the wreck by sunbathing naked on the rocks & luring the sailors; but that won't get far, judging by descriptions of the rocks & the WEATHER in those parts.

Just before we left London I rang up Emma the Good who lives not far from the GD museum, & has often visited it. She offers to take me for a tour of GD territory if I come back to England. By the way—she's adorable, in no way a Chatsworth production, the opposite in fact. VERY bright, terrific sense of humour, all the things we like. She's already sent me a copy of the song, of which I'd forgotten some of the verses, which I would print in front of the book.

Do you think this is all a ridic. waste of time & energy? I was hoping it cld be quite amusing, what with the heroine press build-up, quotes from the biogs etc—and, of course, interviews with such as the Hon. Curator. Possibly a final chapter about GD detractors, such as Mary Clemmey who was APPALLED at the whole idea, she loathes GD from childhood—and Bob's luring crew theory . . .

Possible title:

GRACE HAD AN ENGLISH HEART[94]

. . . Back to Topic A[95] for a moment: Things are, indeed, ever so much better, although the SQUALOR of it all & all the lies etc tend to come back on me in waves at unexpected moments, causing me to lash out at B. perhaps unfairly. Also, in London I couldn't refrain from the occasional slight needle such as when something went agley with our trav. reservations: "Oh I DO wish you'd brought Joanne along, she's SO good at making all the arrangements." (Which he had said she did, with the one exception of disastrous Mother's Day plan, organized by him!)

I X-examined[96] the poor soul about his week in East Hampton, & final encounter with J. They'd all been somewhere at a dinner pty, later he & J. went to a bar to talk. He said it was all over. "What did SHE say?" "She didn't agree, said we should leave options open." "What did YOU say?" He slid off, finally said "I suppose options are always open," which I found disheartening.

---

94. This did, in fact, become the title of Decca's book when it was published in 1988 by Viking Penguin in Britain and in 1989 by Penguin's E. P. Dutton in the United States.

95. A term Decca applied during this period to her husband's affair with Joanne Grant Rabinowitz, wife of civil rights attorney Victor Rabinowitz, both of them longtime Treuhaft family friends. When Decca learned of the affair, as she mentioned in this letter, she shared her anguish with only a very few female friends, including Sally Belfrage.

96. Cross-examined.

So who knows. I did say that if in future he takes up with her again, for God's sake let me know. Answer: "I won't, and if I do I'll let you know." Which I thought a wee bit equivocal. . . . He gets v. annoyed when I bring up the subject so I've rather stopped doing it. By the way, I asked him if Joanne liked my post-card: "Yes, she laughed." A bit different from YOUR version. I DO wish you'd enlarge on what she actually said.

We did have a v. good time in London, ditto in S. of France, the week with Tony Richardson. . . . Bob said repeatedly that he enjoyed all that, not yearning after that young, vibrant, 56-yr-old (accdg to you & Dink) lover. So I hope that's true; hard to tell.

I'm hoping that my trip to England in early Sept. for a few weeks will supply a welcome breathing space for both of us, although Bob did say—rather to my annoyance, not once but thrice—that he hadn't suggested the Grace Darling topic in order to get me out of the country. Actually that hadn't crossed my befuddled mind, but now it has.

I was telling Maya, that wise soul, about GD trav. plans. Well, said she, absence makes the heart grow fonder—but on the other hand, out of sight out of mind! Too true, but I'm going anyway, as I told Maya which made her giggle.

Sorry for this inordinately long letter. As I told you, you are the only one besides Dink/Maya privy to Topic A, so I had to inflict a few inner thoughts. By the way, Dink reported in an unsatisfactory phone call (as what phone call isn't?) that somebody had told her that Victor is displeased with J's constant absences from home—incidentally, Bob in one of my X-exams, said the same. J.'s explanation: she couldn't care less what Victor thinks. She'll do as she pleases. . . . THE AFORESAID, EYES ONLY, SALLY. Dinky would not like this, told to me in confidence, to be bruited about.

I, too, regret that you/Bob had no chance for private chat when we were in London. I did tell him about the Loved One's unsatisfactoriness as a guest—stayed with you for 2 weeks on & off (the off being Bob's Hungarian tryst), never bought a slice of bread or a leaf of lettuce, let alone a meal, was only inter-ested in meeting people she conceived of as important whereas you, like most ordinary people, had yr own chums & were not interested in the IMPORTANT whoever they might be. I also told about yr conception—alerted for the first time by me to this alliance—of least likely, such as a circus freak-show in which the Tallest Man in the World is married to the Smallest Midget in the World.

Must dash to get a few things ready for the Bob Birthday party,
     Much love, Decca

To Virginia Durr   Oakland
                                               August 9, 1985

Dearest Va,

. . . We had a big party for Bob last night, & the cream on the cake was appearance of James Dean Walker (Ark. convict who I've been writing about forever), now out on bail, the 8th Circuit having ruled in his favor—Ark. must either give a new trial promptly, or free him.[97] The vindictive prosecutors are appealing to U.S. Sup. Ct. so the Dear knows when he'll be finally & totally free; but he was admitted to bail, & is staying here for a couple of nights with his stunning girlfriend Leeta.

It was the long-awaited "'tater water" party. The point of that: some years ago when I was writing about his case, I went to Ark. & was given a tour round the prisons, including the solitary cells which were the nether region of hell. I asked the warden what they were in for. "Various infractions such as fighting & making 'tater water." What's that, I asked? Alcohol made from fermented potato peelings. We then went to the commissary for lunch, & I was asked what beverage I'd like. Half faint from the sights, sounds & smells of the solitary cells I answered, "A double 'tater water on the rocks." Which was not forthcoming; but ever since then, Walker & I have pledged to have a 'tater water party when he was released. (Luckily it turns out that vodka is made of potatoes, so we had some of that.) . . .

> Fondest love, & to the Gang of
> Four[98] & their unknown (to me) progeny,
> Decca

To Sally Belfrage   Oakland
                                                                August 22, 1985

Sally—oh <u>poor</u> you, I've been absolutely peppering you with letters, some of which X'd yours of 18 Aug. But at least one of those was NAUGHT TO DO WITH TOPIC A. . . .

Anyway I loved getting yrs of 18 Aug. Vive la "deep depression!" Serves her bloody well right: might be as salutary, if not more so, than Maya's knee-cap job?

This end, things have lightened up unbelievably; that is, I really do think that all will turn out OK with us. See my letter to you of 15 Aug., Bob saying he hadn't been in touch with her. Which, by the way, in spite of all his previous lying I do rather believe—mainly because he's not one to GET in touch all that much! (With him, it's very much out of sight out of mind, as I have often noted to my sorrow when away from home.)

J's letter (the bits you quoted) very odd indeed. E.g.: ". . . all this would have amounted to was to make their relationship better, or so I choose to believe." What on earth does THAT mean? Do write to her for clarification. Needless

---

97. Investigative reporters had turned up previously suppressed evidence that brought into serious question Walker's guilt on his initial murder charges, and a court hearing had been scheduled for the beginning of October. He ultimately went free.

98. Durr's daughters.

to say, I find it slightly tiresome of J. to pride herself on "shaking her marriage to its foundation." A bit of a moulting feather in her cap? Anyway, it hasn't worked, tell her.

Needless to say there are still masses of things to be sorted out bet. me/Bob—but we really are at it, should work given persistence & good will (no snappishness on my part; a modicum of lying on his). By the way, re yr last para about Bob/my long-lasting marriage: yes, you're spot-on in yr description of how it was. But—"important to a lot of people"? Role models—or in my case (fat as butter) ROLL model? Never. Ghastly thought, misleading Louts & their ilk about the pursuit of happiness—an absurd idea, never should have been written into the U.S. Constitution.

. . . Do an IMMENSE FAVOR & ring up when you get this—just ring here collect for Wanda Spikdec, who will then get the number to ring back immediately . . . prime time is after 8 a.m. in Calif, for private chat. I really long to have a word with you.

Again—tons of apologies for taking up so much of yr time & energy; awfully important to me, as you are super-confidant.

Much love, Decca

To Virginia Durr   London
September 27, 1985

Dearest Va,

. . . Your letter of 10 September . . . was a puzzler. You kept saying "Don't read the J. Guinness book, too painful" etc. Well of course I read it, ages ago when it came out in England, partly with a view to bringing suit for plagiarism (unauthorized paraphrasing of my books). I thought I'd written to you about all that? I was also successful in getting the book thoroughly trashed by reviewers in S.F. Chronicle, Boston Globe, & NYT Book Review, having pointed out to reviewers—all friends of mine—some of the stupider passages. My favorite was the one about Kay Graham, that notorious Jewish left-winger who was responsible for hounding Nixon out of office & turning over South East Asia to the dire rule of communism.[99] . . .

Much love, Decca

99. The Guinnesses wrote in their book that Katharine Graham had "played a vital part in preparing the American public for the abandonment of Indochina to Communism as well as in exploiting the Watergate burglary to hound President Nixon out of office."

To Sally Belfrage   Oakland
                                                              November 22, 1985

Dearest Sall,

I was overjoyed to get yr MARVELLOUS letter—esp. since it was unexpected since we'd talked by phone. . . .

Topic A: Your advice, & yr analysis re Bob's silence, is spot-on—I think you are absolutely right on both. I've re-read that para a dozen times & it's full of WISDOM & insight. Isn't it odd how it sometimes takes another person (but only an exceptional person like TOI) to show you what should be obvious, & right under yr nose? Anyway, you've done it & I'm not only v. thankful but it's made me feel far more at peace. I was sort of getting there, but yours was decisive. All this end does point to the fact he's sincerely dropped J. (SODDEN THOUGHT: I wonder if it was easier & less painful for him to give up J. than for me to give up smoking?). That is, all the old feelings of pleasantness & fun between us have come back & we are (I believe) really enjoying life together. . . .

Her letter to me: I rather took the "generous" as an effort at heavy irony. How v. odd of her to think of the exchange as a "dialogue," & to be (as you put it) "overjoyed." . . .

On to other topics . . .

Grace Darling: I'm getting on with it but in my own way—bits & pieces, which I hope will one day clatter together & turn into a book. (Mary[100] said she had told you that's NOT the way to write a book; sorry, but it's my way—and yours, I gather). How I wish I was in London so we cld have a splash of show-&-tell of each other's. . . .

One of the bits & pieces Grace Darling-wise is to find out how news was gathered & disseminated in 1838—pre-telegraph & virtually pre-trains, just a few then running but only in South of England, none to Darling territory in Northumberland or Scotland. Who were the journalists, how compensated, how regarded by the public? . . . All I know so far is the following extract from the Dic. of National Biography re a collateral ancestor.

John Mitford, 1782–1831

. . . Mitford was discharged from the navy as insane, and he took to journalism and strong drink . . . The publisher who employed him found that the only way to make him work was to keep him without money. He therefore limited him to a shilling a day, which Mitford expended on two pennyworth of bread and cheese and an onion, and the balance on gin. With this, and his day's supply of paper and ink, he repaired to an old gravel-pit in Battersea Fields, and there wrote and slept till it was time to take in his work and get his next shilling . . .

---

100. Mutual friend Mary Clemmey.

(Needless to say I sent this to Bob Gottlieb saying that's EXACTLY how he
treats me, no wonder I live in an old gravel-pit.) . . .
Much love & EXTREME gratitude for
yr brilliant analysis/advice, Decca

To Robert Gottlieb   Oakland

January 10, 1986

Dearly Beloved Bites,

. . . So sad that I never see you any more—but we hardly ever come to NY,
Atlanta being the strong magnet. We were there for New Year's. The Oys are
all grown up (thank God). . . .

In Atlanta, some Dink friends had us all to dinner—Benj was there. . . . Anyway, pre-dinner they'd asked a classmate of Bob's from Harvard & his wife
(needless to say B. & c-mate didn't recognize each other but let that pass). The
wife was blithering on abt. her grandchildren the way we dull old folks are
prone to do. "Clarissa is at Vassar, Johnnie's at Harvard . . ." & James appeared
in doorway. "He's Brown, isn't he?" said the wife. I, unthinkingly, said "No,
actually he's black." Tremendous kick in shin by Benj who fled with Jamie into
the kitchen whence their loud & raucous laughter cld be heard for miles
around. Naughty things.

Dink's in absolutely prime fettle. She's got a new job teaching nurses & others how to revive dead—or rather, deadish people,[101] so that's a good thing. She
& hubby (Terry Weber) v. devoted. . . .

Much love, dear Bites, & to yr family—I'd SO love to see you all again one
day. . . .

Decca

To Maya Angelou   Oakland

February 1, 1986

Maya—some random thoughts about THE COLOR PURPLE,[102] pursuant
to our discussion this evening.

1. If criticisms by other Black writers are, as you seemed to imply at one
point, motivated by envy of A. Walker's fame & wealth, that is indeed shabby to
say the least—in fact, downright sinful because isn't ENVY one of the Seven
Deadly Sins? (I'm not sure, as I haven't a list of the 7 D.S.'s to hand.)

---

101. Constancia Romilly's new job was staff development instructor for the Emergency and
Ambulatory Care Nursing Department at Grady Memorial Hospital in Atlanta.

102. Alice Walker's Pulitzer Prize–winning novel (Harcourt, 1982) had been made into a successful 1986 movie directed by Steven Spielberg.

2. Be that as it may, I gather there have been some real and deeply-felt criticisms of the content of the film, that just because it is so brilliantly acted, hence a sure OSCAR winner, to be seen by audiences in the multi-millions, this is a destructive message for whites & Blacks & is not representative of Black culture, Black family life etc.

3. Alice said to you that "the work is a gift," true. But that doesn't hold it exempt from criticism of its message. C/f down the ages, Shakespeare criticized for portrayal of Jews in Merch. of Venice—and, come to think of it, what malign effect did this in fact have for English playgoers for 3 centuries? The word Shylock has virtually passed into the language (you might challenge in Boggle as capitalized, but let that pass). Anti-Semitism is alive & well in England, has been forever. (So, of course, doubly has racism in spite of Shakespeare's casting of OTHELLO as a heroic, brave, tragic character. This is a diversion. Sorry.)

4. Voltaire once said "Qui plume a, guerre a."[103] Too true, as you & I & other scribblers have found out. So those who have a pen should be prepared for the ensuing war! Meaning, should be prepared to defend what they have written, its potential impact on readers in the given moment of its appearance. . . .

End of paper, end of random drivel.[104] RSVP,

Decca

To Dr. Arlan Cohn   Oakland
                                                                  March 6, 1986

Dear Arlan,

I have a terrible, nay horrible, confession to make—but you've already guessed it: I did start smoking again. . . .

As of today, I'm off it again & on that vile chewing gum—which, I must admit, is a huge help. But here's the question: Did you see Delaplane's[105] column about ACUPUNCTURE & smoking cures? Do you know any good acupuncturist around here? What are yr views about that whole thing? DO send a line, or ring up, if you have an opinion. Any medical journals on subject? . . .

Now, here is something of interest. This is about ARTHRITIS, actual case histories compiled by me, hence their accuracy is of course impeccable (ha ha). But honestly—these are True Stories.

---

103. "Whoever has a pen [in their hand] has a war [on their hands]." The quotation was brought to Decca's attention by her sister Nancy, who had been asked by their mother not to write about her anymore.

104. In other letters, Decca and Angelou continued, without resolution, their dialogue on the issue of whether negative characterizations of young black men in the *Color Purple* film would encourage already prevalent racist attitudes or whether the film was important to furthering black openness in confronting painful truths.

105. Stanton Delaplane of the *San Francisco Chronicle*.

I. Aranka Treuhaft my mother-in-law, who died in 1975, (but not of arthritis) hence unable to give evidence. In late 1960's she suffered terribly from arthritis—fingers wouldn't work, legs were agony etc. So I sent her one of those special bronze bracelets from Wales: no good. Then, someone told me that raw potatoes can do the trick. Aranka tried these, cut them up & plunked them in her ample bra, & found MUCH RELIEF.

II. Babby Dreyfus. Calendar leaves now flip forward to 1986. I'd quite forgotten my successful suggestion to Aranka, until I ran into Babby (widow of Barney Dreyfus, super-illustrious SF lawyer & v. great friend) at lunch a few weeks ago. She had suffered tortures from arthritis, near-immobilized by it. Somebody (not me) had told her about the potatoes. She put an unpeeled small red potato in her bra. After some days (and possibly replacements of the potatoes?) all was OK. No more pain.

III. Rita Wiggins, my housekeeper (I think you've met her?) a Black aged 75 from New Orleans originally. She had awful unexplained pains in calf & thigh; went to a doctor who advised aspirin, but she loathes aspirin as she is allergic to them.

Rita Wiggins is the non-complainer of all time. Hence her even mentioning pains in leg was v. unusual. I told her about Babby Dreyfus & the potatoes. Mrs. Wiggins did all that, in two days, legs ABSOLUTELY CURED.

IV. Miriam Miller, the editor of Stanford Alumni Press, Stanford University. For years she's had awful, inexplicable pains in her feet. She's been to every imaginable kind of doctor; but as they can't find out what's wrong, they can't prescribe a cure.

So—after Mrs. Wiggins' rave review of the potato cure—I rang up M. Miller to suggest she could cut up a few slices & put 'em inside her socks, stockings, or feet.

Mimi Miller did all that, & rang up to say that indeed pain in the feet had somewhat subsided, for the moment but she feared it was only psychological.

I thought that reaction slightly tiresome: Isn't everything physical also partly psych?

To come: report from Maya, who's got this awful thing with her knees. I told her about the potatoes (she's on the road, so this was by phone) & she's going to try them.[106]

One interesting thing is, as you can see from the Case Hists., the total disparity in personality, upbringing, philosophy etc etc. of the four Success Stories. There must be something to it, not just a form of faith-healing? Have you ever run across this phenomenon of the potatoes? Should we have a potato analyzed by a chemist to find out the magic component, then market same & make our fortunes?

---

106. Decca later reported that Angelou tried the cure, putting the potatoes in her stockings, "but the potatoes kept falling down to ankles so she stopped doing it."

In the Good Old Days, one cld have anything analyzed by the ordinary sort of chemist who had a shop. When we were teenagers, we took some Eliz. Arden face cream to Burford chemist—it cost 4/6 a jar, 4 shillings sixpence, a huge chunk out of one's allowance. So he did it (turned out it was mostly pig's lard! How disgusting) and then made it up for us at about sixpence a jar. Perhaps I'll try when we go to England in spring. . . .

Best regards, Decca

To Virginia Durr   Oakland

April 3, 1986

Dearest Va,

After we talked yesterday, I re-read the <u>Nation</u> review,[107] & have the following comments:

On the whole, it's what many writers would like—what's known as a "selling review." The first 3 paragraphs are, I think, extremely good in setting the scene. Ditto, the last sentence: "Her triumph is that despite the ambivalence, she made the commitment and chose to pay the price."

The trouble with reviews—in general—is that they seldom fully satisfy the author. (Philip Toynbee once said that there is only ONE review worth having, the one that says "This is the <u>best book I ever read</u>.")

In this case, the reviewer picked up on the alleged "aristocratic past" which I agree is annoying. But that's how reviewers are, as I have discovered through a long life—they tend to fasten on just what you might rather they'd ignore. But the point is—the writer is ultimately responsible for feeding them these lines, or for making these ideas available to them.

The reviewer then puts his own interpretation on the author's work—in your case, your account of your life & development from "longing for aristocratic past" to "genteel poverty" to Washington/New Deal scene, rejection of racism etc.

The emphasis of the review is, I agree, most tiresome. Yet the overall tone of it is positive and friendly. The reviewer is obviously without a sense of humor or irony—as when she quotes you, deadpan, as saying that in the South you're nobody unless you can be "placed"—which I'm sure you meant to be taken as an ironic comment.

If I were you, I'd rejoice in the good things she said, & ignore the annoying ones. As I told you, I think it's a mistake to reply to reviews unless you've been deliberately misquoted; in which case one should, of course, fire off a furious letter!

---

107. On March 29, 1986, *The Nation* had published a review by writer and critic Wendy Gimbel of Virginia Durr's *Outside the Magic Circle: The Autobiography of Virginia Foster Durr,* edited by Hollinger F. Barnard (University of Alabama Press, 1985).

I'd love to know what further thoughts you have about the <u>Nation</u> review, & to have yr comments on the above thoughts of mine. So do write back.[108] I'm away for a few days next week . . . in dread Texas—lecture, which is how I make my drab living! But long for a letter re above. RSVP,

Much love, Decca

ps . . . If you don't want to be quoted as saying "common as pig tracks," you shouldn't have put it in yr book.[109] I do rather remember you saying that about—Alma? Was that her name? Anyway, a sis-in-law, who I thought was rather jolly. I used to chat with her in the kitchen when you & Cliff were out to dinner. Can't remember, though, why she was COMMON.[110] Do remind.

To Ann Simonton   *Oakland*

May 21, 1986

Dear Ann,

Thanks so much for bringing round the copies of HUSTLER & other material.[111] I didn't look at the slides, because a) I couldn't work them—too small, and b) they didn't seem to carry identification as to what/where they were, so I gave up on those.

<u>Hustler</u> was much as I expected: incredibly boring, bad and in all ways rotten. Those centerfolds are so repetitive—at least in the two copies you lent to me; one after another stroking her genitals, followed by several all doing same at once. Dullsville, I thought. As for the joke columns! And the rest of the editorial material! ghastly. The only editorial bit that I found semi-enlightening was the one in the issue of last April that quoted various newspapers/magazines saying that yes, Flynt[112] is indeed a disgusting specimen and so is Hustler, but you don't ban them 1st Amendment-wise. Which is, I gather, also your position.

Far more interesting, to me, was the article in San Jose Merc. News of June 24, 1985, about your own background, & your development from fashion

---

108. Decca noted, in a letter to another friend several weeks later, that Durr did not respond to this letter, "possibly annoyed by my PS." Decca nevertheless wrote a letter to the editor of *The Nation* praising both the Durrs and Virginia Durr's book and taking issue with the reviewer's "perception of Mrs. Durr's 'inherited desire to be a Southern aristocrat.' "

109. The phrase was used in Virginia Durr's description of Senator James Eastland.

110. Elsewhere, Decca recalled the sister-in-law as "the only interesting, bright person" among the relatives on Virginia Durr's side of the family, a number of whom she characterized generally as "loutish." The sister-in-law, she recalled, "was common as pig-tracks because she'd been a millhand, or daughter of a mill-hand," who married into a family where "there was, indeed, a good bit of harking back to alleged aristo origins."

111. Simonton and a colleague were said to have persuaded twenty-five Santa Cruz County stores to stop the sale of *Hustler* magazine, which specializes in photos of naked women in provocative poses.

112. *Hustler* publisher Larry Flynt.

model to counter-model, demonstrating against those obscene Miss America pageants & the like.[113] I thought that was a very good idea & well worth doing for the publicity it generated about the awfulness of said pageants.

According to the <u>Merc. News</u> story you forsook the glamorous and well-paid life of model after 13 years of it, and became a political activist. So that was a terrific, important decision & step forward.

But reading further in the <u>Merc. News</u> article, I came across all sorts of really peculiar things. (I should quickly add that I know the newspapers often get things wrong, they misquote you or garble the meaning of what you said—it happens to me constantly, & perhaps to you, too). Just one example. The article quotes you as saying: "For every woman who shaves her legs and denies her maturity, and for every man who responds to that—the immature childlike innocent qualities—they are collaborating with child molesters."

Is that really your view? I find it quite extraordinary—almost over the brink in terms of any sort of logic.

Another point: at the meeting, you said that over 80% — 83%? 89%? I can't remember the exact figure—of rapists/murderers had been readers of pornography. Could you furnish me with the source for this information? It sounds awfully like the sort of thing that Ed Meese's[114] Commission is putting out; but perhaps you have a more authoritative source.

Again—many thanks for lending me all that interesting material,

Best regards, Decca

To Marge Frantz   Oakland
                                                               May 25, 1986

Old Thing:

I'm in a blissful lull at the moment—3 chapters of GD to typist, Bob & Dobby gone to see the tide-pools, naught to do except to think about next ch. of GD, & write to you. . . .

---

113. Simonton told the *Mercury News* that after one suggestive modeling photo appeared in a full-page linens ad, "I saw that I was an object. I saw myself encouraging rape." She turned from modeling to political protest and began working at a feminist magazine. Her dramatic protests, according to the *Mercury News,* included taking off her top in public to protest anti-nudity laws, walking in front of the screen at a movie theater and temporarily halting a showing of *Texas Chain Saw Massacre,* and pouring her own blood at the entrance to the San Jose Center for the Performing Arts, site of the Miss Nude contest, while telling all who would listen: "Every man who enters this auditorium walks on the blood of raped women."

114. Attorney General Meese, at President Ronald Reagan's direction, had formed a commission in 1985 to study pornography, apparently to obtain results more to their liking than those of a previous President's Commission on Obscenity and Pornography. A key focus of the commission was the asserted linkage between pornography and violence. A majority of Meese's appointees were antipornography crusaders. The National Coalition Against Censorship and a number of prominent national figures denounced the commission even before it issued its contentious findings.

Dobby came to dinner & spent the night here, as they had to leave at 5 a.m. for thrilling tide pools. So she told how you'd said "Dec hasn't a feminist bone in her body"; perhaps true, but I do have splashes of—cartilege? But forward to the interesting part:

I told about Ann,[115] near-hysteric, & showed my letter (copy enclosed) re leg-shaving leads to child molestation.

This led to a v. interesting discussion about a) leg-shavers, b) purpose of same.

To my amazement, Dobby ended up rather on Ann's side—and so, to my further amazement, did that MCP[116] (as you think him) Bob. Dobby thought back to her teenage days, and how her mother made her shave legs—to attract men. So I thought back to my teenage days when we were forbidden to shave legs (we did it anyway)—why? Fads of the moment? We weren't allowed to use lipstick—then all the rage with girls our age. Why? I suppose that my parents, Edwardian by chronology but Victorian in ideology, disliked the idea of trying to attract men by these artificial means. Needless to say we shaved legs like mad, & got all sorts of lipsticks, thus attracting the wrong sort of men, such as Hamish St. Clair Erskine in Nancy's case & Esmond in mine. Although—thinking back, I doubt if E. noted shaven-ness of legs, and I lost my one lipstick in Bilbao in flurry of packing. Perhaps he just liked my personality? Who knows? Too long ago to recapitulate. Anyway I'm sure I got another lipstick in Bayonne.

Bob & Dobby got quite deep about women's subservient role, necessity of a man to support them—not just financially, of course the prime reason histori-cally, but also in all other ways leading to things like leg-shaves & lipsticks. . . .

All very consciousness-raising, you'll be glad to know. Although I took it all with large bits of salt. . . . I must be off to shave my legs, a forest of horrid hair at the moment—although I've nobody to ATTRACT in London. Pity.

Much love, Decca

ps Have you thought about peacocks, magnificent tails & display, whereas pea-hens are drab old creatures? There must be a MORAL somewhere. Over to you to elucidate same. . . . Oh DO write to me in London—you've no idea how one craves letters when in foreign parts.

To Constancia Romilly and family   Oakland
                                                        November 15, 1986

Darling Dink & Co.,

In our a.m. chat, I forgot to go into something of interest about which I'd love yr opinion: CHILD ABUSE. I don't mean beating the poor things to

---

115. Ann Simonton (see preceding letter).
116. Male chauvinist pig.

death (understandable, but v. regrettable speaking as a Mother & Granny of two naughty boys), but <u>sexual molestation</u>.

<u>Item</u>: We tuned in to <u>60 Minutes</u> the other day—didn't catch the whole program, but got the gist of it. Subject was a nigh-incredible case in L.A. in which the entire staff of a nursery-school, for children 2 to 6, were indicted for said awful crime. Head & founder of the school was herself a grandmother; her son, plus staff members hired by them, all accused of raping—or fiddling with—these children. Eventually charges were dropped against all but two. Strong implication in <u>60 Mins</u>. program was that there'd been a huge frame-up, overzealous DA and coaching of the child witnesses by prosecution-minded social workers etc. Implication was that children turned into little witches, as 'twere the Salem case.

<u>Item</u>: This got me thinking back to when Bob came out, 1943, & we were all living in Mrs. Betts's downstairs apt. Bob, who had had no experience with children, one day came to me in a sort of Bob-like twinkling embarrassment, & said "When I go to the bathroom, Dinky often comes in with me and she likes to hold my penis and direct the flow, spraying the walls etc. Is that OK?" Of course I roared & said absolutely OK. <u>NOW</u>, as Bob & I were saying after the <u>60 Mins</u>. show, if that had happened today—Bob the stepfather of a 2-yr-old—and I'd told it as a joke to the neighbours, he'd be hauled off for his own protection as convicts don't like chaps who bugger little children. . . .

<u>Item</u>: You & the lily-waver,[117] when you were 7. You know all that, so no need to repeat.

<u>Item</u>: I was discussing this with Renée Golden[118] when we stayed with her in LA. She told the following, about a friend of hers who is a young, happily married free-lance writer with 2 children, girl 4, boy 2. He took pix of the kids, cavorting about naked, to send to their grandparents, & brought the films to the local Thrifty Developers or whatever. Imagine his surprise when the following morning two squads of police came with flashing sirens & a warrant to search his house—which they did, tore the place apart looking for further evidence of his involvement in child porn. He talked his way out of it—after being brought in & booked. Oh dear.

So, to come to the point: what's <u>your</u> view of all this? Is sexual child-abuse just a new fashion in crime (like drugs, for example) or is it really a huge & horrid problem? Nurses may have some sort of fix on this, prevalence, etc. Mulling

---

117. See November 24, 1989, letter to Laura Shaine Cunningham.

118. Decca's Hollywood lawyer and agent, whom she met in Arkansas in connection with the James Dean Walker case. Golden became a good friend and sometime houseguest of the Treuhafts, and Decca was very grateful to her for several top-dollar deals she negotiated on Decca's behalf. But in the early '90s, their relationship began to deteriorate after Decca became upset about what she considered Golden's confusion of her lawyer and agent roles in representing her and writer friends she'd referred to Golden. Their relationship descended into bitter recriminations, and Golden formally resigned as Decca's representative early in 1995.

it over, I've discussed the subject with Katie Edwards, my smashing assistant & former social worker, & Marge Frantz.

Both thought it really is a true & awful fact. Katie says that literally hundreds of cases of the sort came to her attention when she was working as social wkr. Marge says that MANY students at UC Santa Cruz have confided hideous tales of incest/rape etc. that blighted their lives. . . .

Dink—Terry—Oys—I must say, I find this subject of horrible fascination & wld v. much like yr views. How on earth cld anyone, male or female, get enjoyment out of raping 2-yr olds? (Making love with 11-yr olds, yes, but quite different. See Lolita, a marvelous book.) Is it a sort of spreading hysteria, analogous to the politician-engineered drug hysteria—that is, with some foundation in fact, but built out of all proportion?

As you can see, I'd far rather spin out a letter to you than get on with WORK. But do admit it's rather an interesting thing. . . .

Much love, Decca

Specifically, do emergency ward nurses see much evidence of above horror-tales?

To James Forman Jr.   Oakland
                                                                February 9, 1987

Dearest Oy #1,

Dink rang & had just had a long winter's chat with you, so she told some of yr main news—VERY pleasing. However she says that letters take 15 days so by the time this reaches you[119] all will be totally out of date from her phone call. I mean—what cld happen in 15 days. Lots. You could be married. Or in jail. Or run over by a slow-moving vehicle such as a mule or camel—do they have those in Brazil? My ignorance of said country is vast. Anyway, as of her phone call all was VERY serene—non-stop social life, great beaches & so on. (She didn't mention any actual studying, so perhaps that will come later if at all???)

News this end: we went to Atlanta for the March,[120] my account enclosed. The funniest thing cannot, for obvious reasons, be told in an article, so here goes for Oy's Eyes Only: Having failed to find the Calif. delegation in that huge milling crowd, we began to fear that we'd never get on a bus. All the buses were filling up fast. Dinky spotted one marked VIP'S ONLY, so she barged up to it and said in tones of positively MAJESTIC authority, "This is Jessica Mitford from California," and shoved me forward. The driver (who certainly had nary a clue as to who JM was) let me on, upon which Dink, Terry, Benjamin,

---

119. James Forman was in Brazil from January to June of his junior year of college.

120. A march in Forsyth County, Georgia, organized by national civil rights figures after about fifty participants in an earlier March Against Fear and Intimidation had been violently attacked by hundreds of whites.

Chelsea[121] and Bob all piled in. I said to Dink later, "how on earth did you pull that off—nobody here has ever heard of me." "It's not <u>what</u> you say, but <u>how</u> you say it," she answered in her firm fashion. Can't you visualize the scene? So that's how we came to be on the same bus with Rev. Lowery[122] & assorted city & county bigwigs. Isn't yr mum a marvel; but you know that already.

We did have a lovely time with the Dink mob, too short, we were jet-setting for the march, so only spent 2 nights.

You know how Chaka is to come & stay with us in London in June? Dink said that she'd suddenly realized that his manners are atrocious (actually I cld have told her that, but mothers don't like hearing that sort of news from GRANDMOTHERS) and that she plans a crash course, as follows: <u>Weeks 1 and 2</u>: No elbows on dining table, no shoveling food as 'twere a horse with feeding bag. <u>Weeks 3 & 4</u>: "Proper manipulation of utensils" (her words), i.e. what to do with one's knife, fork, spoon. <u>Weeks 5 & 6</u>: Conversational English. Oh POOR Chaklington! Perhaps he'll decide not to come. But if he does come, we'll have to shape up to his new manners & not embarrass him with our bad ones. Isn't life difficult. Anyway I've already done a certain amount of advance work (you know what that means, from political campaigns—arranging contacts in far-off places) and have spotted out people who can lead him to soccer games & other dubious activities suited to his age & interests. My main idea is not to bore him with things like museums etc. but to let him roam free. Agree? Any thoughts you have on the care & treatment of Chaka v. welcome, so jot some things when you've got time between now & June.

Your loving Grandec

To James Forman Jr.   Oakland
                                                          February 28, 1987

Dearest OY #1,

Dink sent me your MARVELOUS & fascinating letter all about the family where you are living, social life—films, to neck or not to neck??? etc.[123]

But she also said you've gone off by train into the interior, & she'd read about a dread TRAIN WRECK in Brazil, 40 killed, so you are probably dead by now. If so, what a drag, & waste of all these stamps which cost the earth. If, by chance, you have survived, do drop a line.

---

121. A friend of Chaka Forman.

122. Civil rights leader the Rev. Joseph Lowery, co-founder and longtime president of the Southern Christian Leadership Conference.

123. Decca wrote to another correspondent that her grandson had "written killing letters re his love life" in Brazil and that when his mother, who was planning to visit him there, asked what she should bring along, according to Decca, "the answer was several doz. condoms!!! Aren't children these days ODD. I was trying to imagine anyone asking Muv to do this errand."

Anything needed your end? Just say the word . . .

Dink said she's going to have a peek in March, lucky her. Wish I cld go.

Fondest love, & from Grandbob, Grandec

To Dr. Arlan Cohn   Oakland

May 5, 1987

Dear Oscar/Arlan,[124]

Thanks SO much for KILL AS FEW PATIENTS, just arrived. I've been browsing through it, & it's delightful—as I expected it would be. Full of WIT & WISDOM, & a great treat to read.

Did I ever tell you about Uncle Alec's leg? If so, please forgive repeat of same.

Uncle Alec was <u>such</u> a sweet person—NOT a Mitford, an uncle by marriage. One of one's childhood favourites. In 1955, my first visit back to London after 16 years, I inquired about him & my mother said he was in the Seamen's Hospital, so thither I repaired—a good 2 hours by bus from West End, and a regular horror scene straight out of Dickens. There was Uncle A. with his foot up in a filthy bandage. So we chatted, & he said he thought it was GANGRENOUS—awfully painful AND smelly. Oh dear. So I said if I were you I'd have it off.

I told my mother about the visit, & poor Uncle Alec's beastly leg. After I got home, some months later, she wrote & said "You will be glad to hear that Uncle Alec had his leg off as you suggested." People like Eph Kahn (who was our Dr. at that time) near fainted at the thought of ignorant nieces DARING to make such a suggestion. . . . But on the other hand, it was a good thing, I think. Except that the next time I saw him, a few yrs later, long out of hospital & getting round v. spryly on his peg leg, he did complain that "I told them to take it off at the knee, but they went & took it off at the thigh. People are so unreliable these days." Oh well, can't win 'em all. But I think he had a jolly nice old age, living in a decent old gents' home in Gloucester Place. . . .

Thanks very much for curing my stupid ankle; at least I think it's almost cured, & I'm taking all the pills you suggested. (Any other ideas? If so, do give a ring.) . . .

Decca

---

124. Cohn, who has written extensively under the pseudonym Oscar London, had recently published *Kill as Few Patients as Possible, and 56 Other Essays on How to Be the World's Best Doctor* (Ten Speed Press, 1987).

To Carrie Longton[125]   London
                                                                                        July 1, 1987

Dear Ms. Longton,

Re SERVANTS programme. . . .

Here are a few thoughts about my own relationship to servants. . . .

When I was 15 I decided to become a Communist. My mother's annoying reaction: "Well, Little D" (which is what she called me) "If you're a Communist, I should think you'd be much tidier and try not to make work for the servants." Being tidy wasn't my idea of being a good Communist. Anyway I soon left home for good and there weren't any servants. My first husband, Esmond Romilly, and I lived mainly in bed-sitters where the landlady did what tidying was done (not much, actually).

More to the point would be mid-war & post-war years, approx. 1943 on. I was married to Bob Treuhaft, a lawyer, & we lived in San Francisco. We had 2 children; & worked things out on a sort of barter system, being quite poor (not enough money to pay decent wages to somebody to look after house & children) & were jolly hardworking, so didn't have time to be all that tidy. Let alone mind the kids.

We had a 3-bedroom house in San Francisco. Housing was v. scarce. The system was that we'd find a couple with their own children. All children in one bedroom, the couple & us in the other 2 bedrooms. We supplied room & board, the others minded their children & ours. (I described this in <u>A Fine Old Conflict</u>.)

Books about servants: Mrs. Beeton's Bk of Household Management, 1880 edition, has a huge amount about duties of butler, menus for Servants Hall Dinner for 12 etc., plus How to Choose a Wetnurse—must have firm breasts & erect nipples etc. When I was pregnant Bob kept saying he was off choosing, clearly the husband's duty he thought. . . .

Am looking forward to info. re others on programme. Many thanks,
                              Jessica Mitford

To Mary Clemmey   Oakland
                                                                                    August 26, 1987

Dearest Mary,

Yr account of the Maya farewell was simply marvellous—far better than actually being there, in a way, as one didn't have to sit on the ugly leather/brocade chairs or listen to Adelaide Tambo's[126] thing about her ancestors (JOKE— she sounds smashing, I long to meet her). Ancestors: Grandfather Redesdale

---

125. A British television producer.
126. The wife of Oliver Tambo, former president in exile of South Africa's African National Congress.

went to some trouble to "prove" that we are descended from Charlemagne, and he said in his insufferably boring book MEMORIES, BY LORD REDES-DALE that he hoped his grandchildren wld take comfort from the thought that the blood of Charlemagne was coursing through their veins. Well I tried that a few times, such as on witness stand before the Un-American Activities Comm., but it didn't seem to work so I relied on the Fifth Amendment, far more efficacious. . . .

The main thing is—I shall never, ever forget yr immense kindness in coming over to help in the getaway. I did write on the plane, so that letter should fetch up. If it doesn't, I can only say that you saved my worthless life. . . .

This is . . . to send TONS OF LOVE, & thanks. . . .
Decca

To Marge Frantz   Oakland
                                                      September 10, 1987

Old Thing:

A couple of enclosures, to wit:

1. A Memorial Urn Capacity Study, which I thought you'd rather love for the light it sheds on uses of Research, esp. when conducted by high-up academics like a prof. of Harvard Business School. But to get the flavor you have to read it word for word, preferably aloud. Don't you rather adore those charts? The whole thing gets better as you go on. See, for example, last para page 67 in which we learn that "on average, men produce cremains 40 cubic inches larger than women." I wonder if that's true. What would Andrea Dworkin say?[127]

2. Correspondence with Dobby. . . . I did think it's food for thought & of interest for light shed on the Dobbyish pt of view. Note, e.g., her comment . . . nastiest, most vicious attacks come from women. Later, we did discuss such things as what it's like to have a woman boss. I said that easily the nicest boss I ever had was Marie Berger, who hired me in 1942 to work for her in OPA; and that I loved working for what amounted to "bosses" in terms of their power in CP such as Oleta Yates, & Celeste Strack. So actually I never really noted any particular difference bet. working for men bosses & women. What differences there were arose from faults of character & intellect . . . & not them being boys or girls. Then we got on the subject of JEALOUSY. Dobby thinks the young women lawyers are jealous of her because of her superior knowledge of the law, her self-confidence etc. Bob & I rather doubted the jealousy factor: Bob said that younger women don't get jealous of old ones, it's vice versa. I said that I'd worked with

---

127. The author, theorist, and self-described "feminist militant" was a frequent target of Decca, who described her once as someone "who seems to think that all men are rapists at heart." Dworkin had written about prostituting herself, as well as being sexually abused as a child, being raped, and being beaten by a former husband. Decca noted that her decision to become a prostitute was a "*most* unsuitable" career choice for her—"like someone who doesn't like food becoming a cook."

people like Marge—when we were both in sort of the same stream, you in IPP & me in CRC—who were obviously better educated, cleverer, better at their job which in this case was organizer. And while I admired all that, and v. much enjoyed working together—and possibly did feel more than a trifle INFE-RIOR—I don't a bit remember being JEALOUS of you. So then Dobby said that's because of my upper-class English upbringing, which I said was nonsense, so the discussion began to deteriorate. Your views, please?

Much love, Decca

To Peter Stansky   Oakland
                                                                                  January 31, 1988
Dearest Peter,

As you are my only link with the English Speaking Union in Northern Calif (and, as you may remember, [I] have at yr bidding come to meetings etc. to honor high school children's essays) I do implore you to read this letter & enclosures—with a view to expelling the Montgomery, Alabama chapter of ESU in a public statement, to be written by you, dear Peter, and if you wish countersigned by ME—but not needed. Here goes with the whole story:

Act I Year is 1961. I was in Montg'y staying with Cliff/Virginia Durr. Went to mass mtg for FREEDOM RIDERS, locked in church all night, howling mobs out of control, tear gas etc. V. uncomfortable. Released 5 a.m. but Durrs' car burnt to a crisp by howling mobs. Same weekend, an English girl, Anne Pike, student at posh girls' college was interviewed by a Man-on-the-Street journalist—he stopped the first 8 people & asked his question which was "What do you think of the Freedom Riders?" The first seven all said they should be boiled in oil, hanging's too good for them etc—but unlucky Miss Anne Pike answered that she thought they were doing the right thing and should be commended. So that was in all the Montg'y papers, together with me & the burned-up car. Anne Pike & I had been guests of honor at an ESU meeting and were SWIFTLY disinvited, which I thought a bit unfair as A. Pike & I were the only actual English speakers in Montgomery.

Act II Year is 1988. Dinky & I drove to Montgomery from Atlanta, spent 2 nights with Va. Durr; non-stop parties, as is usual in that amazing town. At one of these, I met Mr. Rinehart, present president of Montgy ESU (the disinviter long dead and gone) & we has a wee contretemps abt ESU. Mr. Rinehart said the Freedom Riders weren't nothin' but outside agitators (a LONG time since I've heard that ancient phrase), but that Nigras could join the ESU if they want to; none have applied, he said. (I wonder why?) Incidentally ESU hold its meetings in the Montg'y Country Club which does not permit Jews as members although they are allowed to come as guests of members.

Act III A young lad calls up from Montg'y newspaper for an interview. He starts off with things like "How are you enjoying your stay, Mizzz Mitford?"

So, thinking it might be a bit boring, I clued him in on ESU. Hence enclosed front page story, which caused a) flurry in the dove-cote, b) put the cat amongst the pigeons, or c) shit in the electric fan, depending on whether you prefer 19th Cent. English, early 20th Cent. English, or modern American. Anyway—you should SEE the letters re all this! In which I've learned that ESU is fully behind the move to retain Confederate Flag over Stars & Stripes. . . .

Please advise ESU to expel their Montgomery branch.

Much love, living in hopes, Decca

ps The letters from Montgomery chums are SUPER. One, Kate Elmore, niece of Virginia Durr, wrote that she'd been to an ESU mtg to listen to gossip about JM. She overheard one group. Discussing the issue, one said "Who is Jessica Mitford?" Another: "She must be a black woman. She was involved with Martin Luther King."

To William Abrahams   Oakland
                                                February 4, 1988

Dearest Billy,

Various things, life's vicissitudes (sp?)—to wit:

. . . [N]ews Penguin-wise: They'll postpone publication a few days to make it come nearer to THE DEED.[128] . . . But the thrilling news is that sometime around date of DEED, there'll be a church service in the Farne Isles—at which the Duke of York will be main speaker!!! Can you beat it. Tony[129] got this info through corresp. with the Royal Lifeboat Institution. So I said to Tony "Duke of YORK? Meaning the Andy & Fergie mob?" Oddly, T. hadn't made the connexion but cld see I was on target.[130] I suggested that I cld come up to the service & lead a community sing-song of the Grace Darling Song, if the publisher wld supply sufficient mimeographed copies of the words for the audience. So— won't you & Peter come? You MUST, 'twill be the Event of the Year if not the century. I've alerted Clare Harington, Penguin's v. nice & able publicity adept, to book rooms up that way for me & Bob—so advise you to do likewise. But hurry, or the Royal Entourage will have bagged all the best ones. . . .

Much love, Decca

---

128. The anniversary of the rescue by Grace Darling and her father.

129. Tony Lacey, of Penguin Books.

130. "Andy & Fergie" were the nicknames of Queen Elizabeth II's son Prince Andrew and his then wife, Sarah Ferguson. The lively and popular couple had been married less than two years when this letter was written. Decca later told another correspondent that Lacey's reply had been "oh yes, I suppose so," but that "a less vague character at Penguins says it's actually the Duke of KENT, not York."

To Sally Belfrage   Oakland
                                                          March 24, 1988

Dearest Sall,

Thanks awfully for letters & enclosures. . . .

Fancy you not realizing that pop. songs—actually, from c. 1900 on—are my favourite thing, in fact the only sort of music I like—which is why I tend to slide away if people suggest going to the opera, or concerts, or like M. Clem to a programme of ethnic African music etc. I think that "Just My Bill" is more 1930's than 1950's. . . .

Chicken soup: Yes, there was lots of that after Bob got home from hosp.[131]

He really is absolutely OK, or anyway FAR better—can dress himself! What a mercy. Soon after he got back from hosp. he was spending hours in the office & in court, driving about etc., what's known as OVERDOING IT. As my favourite thing is UNDERDOING it, i.e. slopping about the house, I did get a tad worried; so conspiring with Jeannie, his adored sec'y, we sent him off for a week to Palm Springs, Calif. All sun & rest, and it really worked. That's where he learned to dress himself—it's a bit like having a baby, Sall. When he first came out of anaesthetic, totally done in & weak, he was awfully sweet, & quiet like newborn babes. Next, aged 2 (the next day) cross as 2 sticks.[132] At home, aged 3, still rather up-&-down in moods—easily annoyed, yet pleased when the chick. soup loomed. Kindergarten in Palm Springs—"I can dress myself!" And getting better by the day. By the time we get to NY (25 March) he'll be a spry teenager, and so it goes.

Meanwhile, down on the ranch—literally, viz. I went to stay with Alex Haley in his amazing spread near Knoxville, Tennessee. Occasion was his first house-party there, Maya the guest of honour, and other guests all invited by her. About 20 in all; I was the only white person. It was too fascinating . . . The Haley ranch is a dream/nightmare of marvellous comfort & incredibly hideous décor. I shared a cottage with Dolly McPherson (gt. friend of Maya's—a black prof. at M's university, & most agreeable[133]) furnished with fake Louis XVI things & false flowers & false ferns.

There were many a fascinator amongst the other guests. The only flaw in the ointment (a Va. Durr expression) was that we were constantly herded into cars for dismal treats like brunch in a nearby artsy brunchery etc. Anyway, I was v. glad to have gone. (I must say the plane to Knoxville isn't much fun; one changes in Atlanta into a teeny-weeny plane, prop (meaning not jet), seating 20

---

131. Treuhaft had had a shoulder operation.

132. Decca later wrote to her daughter about this period, saying Treuhaft seemed to be "in a permanent rage with me because of my utter hopelessness as a part-time nurse. (DINK: Where on earth did you get yr nursing genes? Certainly not from my side, nor from the Romilly side. . . .)."

133. Dolly McPherson taught in the English department at Wake Forest University. Her Ph.D. thesis had been based on a study of Angelou's autobiographical work.

people—I couldn't help noting that the pilot was studying a map throughout the flight.) . . .

Much love, Decca

To Sally Belfrage   Oakland
                                                                                        May 16, 1988

Dearest Sall,

. . . Life this end: nonstop hot-beds, viz. M. Bernal here for 3 nights followed day of his departure by Marina, Johnny & Conrad.[134] . . .

Marina/Johnny/Conrad. For this, I had really planned ahead, my objective—cleverly achieved if I do say so myself—to minimize the presence of dear little Conrad now aged 11 whom I remember so well aged 8 as incredibly spoilt & tiresome. As he's now 11, normally the Golden Age, he's much nicer but oh—the pitfalls of adoring mumhood & step-p.hood. Goodness they are annoying with him. If he's out of sight for one moment it's "Oh dear where did Conrad go?" And they chase around the house & neighbourhood looking for him, poor fellow. At dinner it's "Conrad, do eat your peas, good for you." "Conrad, I know you're not used to beets but try some." "Conrad, here's a nice slice of just the sort of chicken you like . . ." This was just the five of us, me Bob & them, but in view of total concentration on what Conrad was or wasn't eating, little gen. conversation until I did speak up & say couldn't Conrad just eat or not eat whatever he wants to, & us talk of more trivial matters such as Marina's novel just accepted by Simon & Schuster? Johnny's art show in LA? U.S. politics?? Chances of Jesse Jackson[135] vs. Conrad liking or disliking his peas???? Well Marina, never slow on the uptake, got the pt straight off. We had subsequent discussions in which she said things like "I can see you think I'm an overprotective mother," & I said absolutely, dead right you are. I guess that Johnny is, perforce, an overprotective stepfather, so poor Conrad—who seems to be a potentially rather nice little chap—is surrounded by huge bales of cotton wool from which he'll have to fight his way out eventually.

The plan worked beautifully. <u>Day 2</u>, as Cruise brochures say, we chased the lot of 'em—Marina/J/Conrad—to SF in the Bobmobile for a lovely family outing whilst we prepared the dinner for 40 Sat. evening. Saturday was a day of total peace consisting of Bob's baked beans, my ham, my roast chicks, Mrs. Wiggins' jambalaya, Katie helping etc. . . . AND, my brill. move, amongst the company were Leah/Jerry Garchik[136] and sons Sam aged 14, Jacob 11. I had

---

134. Marina Warner, her husband, and her son. Warner, an author, a prolific historian, and a novelist, was a neighbor when Decca stayed in Kentish Town and became a good friend of hers, as did her second husband, artist John Dewe Mathews.

135. Jackson was running again for the Democratic nomination for president.

136. The Garchiks were both good friends of the Treuhafts. Jerry Garchik is an attorney who once worked in Robert Treuhaft's office. His wife, Leah, is a longtime editor and columnist at the *San Francisco Chronicle*.

prearranged all the that, Sam to be tour leader, to make the plans, give me a budget and TAKE CONRAD HOME after the Sat. party. All went like total clockwork. Day 3: Sunday. Us & Marina/J to David Bouverie's incredible pad for the day & lunch. D. Bouverie loathes children unless they are accompanied by a nanny who whisks them off out of sight. So all went v. well, great time had. Then we went to collect Conrad at Garchiks'—he'd ADORED the whole thing, night away from Marina & all on his own with other children. Marina was extremely solicitous—"Darling, were you really happy" "Did you like the day?" etc. Me saying "Conrad, take the Fifth Amendment," but I'm not sure if he knows what that is being a) 11, b) English. Later that eve we watched telly & it was "Conrad, are you sleepy? Would you like some food?" etc. until I crossly put a stop to all the that. Day 4: They've left! I really loved having 'em here, a v. interesting peek into The Life Of. Shall be watching the progress of Conrad through the years to see how he turns out. Children are such a toss-up—and so interesting to glimpse 'em at various stages, don't you agree? . . .

To Miriam Miller   London
                                July 29–30, 1988, "eve of departure for S.U."[137]

Dearest Mim,

I WAS so pleased to get yr letter—thanks awfully & sorry for long time answering, am swamped this end.

Yr Russian trip does sound interesting but ARDUOUS—a shame you got ill. I long for more details abt the Russian publishing scene.[138] Are there huge Glasnost-ish changes, as one gathers from snippets in the papers here?[139] . . .

The brightest spot in forthcoming Russian trip is that Eve Arnold is the photog. being sent by the mag.[140] She's so smashing and FUNNY, shld be great good company. Also incredibly efficient; she's just got our tix upgraded to 1st class, and has got a car to pick us up on Thursday. So if the visa looms, all shld be v. prime.

Another bright spot . . . is the trav. cruise brochure, or rather mimeo'd sheets about How to Behave. It's beamed to Yanks, hoping they'll be nice to the Russians. Examples:

"If you find poor service from a guide or in a restaurant or in your hotel, RELAX and take it in stride."

---

137. Decca was leaving the next day for a cruise on the Volga River, an assignment for *Traveler* magazine.

138. Miller had been there to lecture to Russian publishers.

139. Mikhail Gorbachev, Soviet leader from 1985 to 1991, campaigned for liberalization in the country and Party with the slogans "glasnost" (greater openness and public participation) and "perestroika" (greater local economic autonomy).

140. For more on Arnold and Decca's history with her, see next letter.

"If a customs official seems to be taking longer than necessary in examining your baggage or your papers, RELAX; do not let it annoy you."

"Touring in the Soviet Union: A RELAXED attitude will go a long way in helping you enjoy your visit."

I'm thinking of calling my article "RELAXNOST." Do you think that's a good title? E. Arnold is all for it.

Another injunction, all in caps, is "DO NOT SELL YOUR BLUE JEANS!" Eve & I agreed that there is not much danger of us transgressing that rule. . . .

Anyway it's now Wednesday 30 July, eve of departure—visa still not arrived so how can one RELAX? I'd far rather write to you, & contemplate my packing—cruise info. sheet says to bring toilet paper, soap and pepper. I think I'll skip the pepper, awkward to pack. So far, I've packed my BOGGLE set (hoping to induce E. Arnold to play, or some of the cruise passengers if they are Boggle-minded types), paperclips, stapler, Scotch tape, notebooks. Tomorrow I'll pack my so-called clothes (for 6:30 a.m. departure) & hope for the best.

I'd so love to have some information about the cozier, or sleazier, details of YOUR trip so do write back if you've got time.

Mim—you're the ONLY faithful corresp. in Calif. Not one line from Barb, but if you think she'd be interested do send on this letter.

       Much love, Decca

To Barbara Kahn   London
                                       August 5, 1988

Dearest Barb,

I WAS so pleased to get yr letter of 11 July, found here yesterday on arrival from Soviet Union midst a huge clatter of mail. . . .

Russian cruise: sorry to say, it was a total bust. In a nutshell: we were 80 tourists, most of the others middle-Americans in all senses. grizzled old heads, closed old minds—what Eve Arnold described as "a floating Rotary club." So, scant inspiration there. We had two bilingual American tour guides of unbelievable ineptitude so half one's time was being herded, all 80 of us, & interminable waits. The only bright spot was Eve Arnold who is v. good company. As I've now got to write it up for TRAVELER, I'd better get on with the that & send you a copy than try to tell it in a letter. How to write it? I fear that if I tell it like it was, the mag. might turn it down as they presumably make their revenue from ads such as ads for this here cruise. However I spoke to Marina Warner, who's just done one for the same mag re her trip to Oregon . . . and she says that TRAVELER prides itself on being truthful & not just a commercial vehicle for ads. So I think I'll just go ahead & speak me mind. By the way . . . during one of the interminable waits a fellow-passenger remarked "I could have more fun changing kitty-litter at home."

Eve Arnold: she's American, lives in London. We met her glancingly aeons ago in Bob Gottlieb's office, he was her publisher. He gave us one of her many picture books, & suggested that she & I cld collaborate on a book, her to do the photos & me the text. But I read her text which I thought excellent, no need of intervention esp. by one like me who doesn't know anything abt photography, so that came to naught. Turns out she's a gt. friend of S. Belfrage so Bob & I saw a lot of her in the few days after we met before the cruise. She's so amazing—been everywhere, literally all over the globe, plying her trade. . . . Amongst other virtues, she a) upgraded our plane tix to Club class, b) insisted on separate cabins on ship—sharing wld have been torture, cabins miniscule— c) insisted on separate rooms in Leningrad hotel—in short, a terrific organizer of comfort. . . .

Much love . . . Decca

To Barbara Kahn   London
                                                     August 20, 1988

Dearest Barb,

. . . [T]he publisher's mad plan [for the Grace Darling book launch] is that on 6 Sept (Deed was 7 Sept, 1838, 150 yrs ago) we all go on a specially hired boat to the Lighthouse in the morning—telly, journalists etc, so they claim— then return for lunch at the Lord Crewe Arms, a pub in Bamburgh. Accdg to my niece Emma, who lives in those parts, it's the season of the Equinoctial storms—well natch, that's what caused wreck of Forfarshire.[141] So don't you think that if our boat is wrecked & all are drowned it wld be smashing publicity for my book? Be praying for bad weather, Barb. Not that you'll need to at this time of year. . . .

Much love, Decca

To Carl Bernstein   Oakland
                                                   September 17, 1988

Dear Carl,

Knowing too well the horror-scene that confronts one after returning from 3–4 months away from home, I'd resolutely decided to put off reading yr book[142] until most of the detritus had been cleared away. But once started, I couldn't stop—I thought it compulsive reading and DAZZLINGLY GOOD.

To dispose of a few v. minor points: . . . I don't think Nixon was ever in the

---

141. The luxury steamer, several of whose passengers and crew members Grace Darling had helped to rescue.

142. Decca was reading the manuscript of Bernstein's book that was published soon thereafter as *Loyalties: A Son's Memoir* (Simon & Schuster).

SF Regional office of OPA, [as you] implied. . . . When writing A Fine Old Conflict I tried to ascertain just where he was—no one seemed to know, incl. the then personnel mgr in Washington, Billie Rembar—Cy's wife (he was at lunch 'tother day). . . . I—and Bob—may find a few more such trivial things on a re-read, but thought I shld jot these whilst fresh in mind.

Here is my major and really DEEPLY FELT suggestion for a change. It's right at the beginning, hence amongst the pages stupidly left on the aeroplane, and too early for new lot to arrive by Fed Express—but I must just dash it off, may write again re this after re-reading the first pages:

Your description of Al's appearance, how offensive it was to you as a child— the spindly legs & arms, cigar ashes, how you were semi-ashamed of him for all that. I imagine that this may have been painful for you to write, in a way. I'm certain it will be extraordinarily painful for him to read. From yr p.o.v. (Holly-woodese for Point of View) perhaps it seems important to set this forth as a sort of catharsis, a let-it-all-hang-outishness to put the reader in the picture as to early father/son relationship.

Now for a flashback. When Al left SF OPA, we had a huge farewell party for him & Sylvia,[143] & Bob & I wrote a song for him, as was our wont on such occasions. His sloppiness, his cigar ashes, his general disregard of conventional manners was, of course, familiar to all of us at the party—I think his desk had to be fumigated after he left OPA? Anyway, it was full of old socks. So we wrote this stupid poem, including the lines "No more shall the halls of the Furniture Mart/Resound to the sound of the Bernstein fart" (Fur. Mart was h.q. of OPA) which I rather liked because of its brilliant inner-rhyme. The point is that the Al sloppiness was to us extremely ENDEARING, I adored him;[144] to me, he was much as described by you, i.e. he wasn't handsome but he was extremely attractive—well, like father like son. (Once somebody asked me what's Carl Bernstein like? I answered, "just like his papa, ugly as sin and fatally attractive.")

After the party, & after yr parents had left for good, Dobby seriously took me to task for this awful poem. I can still remember her massive lecture about my total insensitivity, that Al would have been terribly hurt, that it ruined all the conviviality of the occasion—well, I'm afraid she was right on at least one score: Al v. hurt. (Of course, he never said so. He'll never confess to being wounded by your description of him as recalled by you as a small boy. His criticisms of yr book will be otherly.)

To this day, I regret that poem.

I much fear that his opinion of all the rest of yr book—[his] brilliantly

---

143. Carl Bernstein's mother.

144. Elsewhere, Decca has written that Al Bernstein was one of her favorite OPA co-workers: "I loved him for many reasons, not the least of which was that his desk was even messier than mine and drew fire from the Supervisors who would otherwise have been gunning for me."

described . . . obdurate sliding off the subject of CP and yr eventual under-standing of the reason, via the actual things that befell him & Sylvia—will be irrevocably colored by those first few pages.

I wish I cld think of some good parallel to impress on you the dire unpleas-antness of that sort of adverse physical description, & the effect on the persons so described. But DO try to absorb the point.[145]

Otherwise, I think the book is a triumph. I love the way Woodward pops in & out. . . . Portrayal of Sylvia, ditto. She's such a smashing person, & that comes through. . . .

I don't at all mind what Al said re FOC—lots of truth in it, I'm afraid.[146] But you know how one is, quite incapable of taking everything as seriously as one should even at the time, when things did indeed look pretty dismal.

To Tony Lacey   Oakland
                                                   October 5, 1988

Dear Tony,

I'm still all a-glow over that absolutely memorable GD caper. It was a mar-vellously eccentric idea, beautifully executed—a high point of my life. I mean—honestly, think of the trad. London publishing party in which one is herded into a serried mass of humanity with a glass of warmish white wine. <u>What</u> a switch.

There were so many unexpected people. . . . The whole thing was a tri-umph—we loved the account in Daily Tel. & me having a voice like a croaking crow. . . .

The ducal lunch. Here's what happened: E. Tennant (the Good) & Bob & I were wandering about the churchyard after you all had left for London. The churchwarden recognized Emma, & came up to say hello. Emma asked if he'd show us round the church & he said he'd rather not, as he wanted to finish his cigar—which I thought was quite right & v. unchurchwardenly of him. She said "my aunt's just written a bk abt Grace Darling," and introduced us. He mut-tered about coming to lunch on 7th Sept for Duke of Kent, so I said we'd love to; the enclosed letter[147] showed up at the Ld Crewe Arms. Do read it with

---

145. It's unclear if Bernstein softened his draft in response to Decca's appeal, but his book does mention his father's "short arms and spindly legs that I allowed to embarrass me when we went to the beach," and he paints a picture of his absentminded father "dressed in a robe haphazardly tied, a cigar stuck in the corner of his mouth, head cocked to one side, ashes tumbling onto the burgundy robe as he paced the room."

146. In *Loyalties*, Carl Bernstein wrote, "In the final analysis, my father pointed out, Decca's book is really about why she *left* the Party. In fact, the book trivializes the whole experience of hav-ing been in the Party, reducing it to almost farcical anecdote."

147. The letter from Barbara Cresswell invited the Treuhafts to "a small informal private lunch party" at Bamburgh Hall for the Duke of Kent. The form letter, which said that "we cannot ask any

care; a bit of a classic, don't you think? Incl. misprint in 2nd para "High Royal Highness," but mainly the all-male character of the lunch and the WIVES TOLD TO WAIT IN THE CAR!!! Which is exactly how it was, only females the hostess & me. The D. of Kent has one of those faceless faces that seem to go in the Royal family—no features to speak of, watery blue eyes, & no conversation. The duchess might be better value but I suppose she was waiting in the car eating her soggy sandwich.

This is mainly a ton of thanks to you for dreaming it all up—AND to Annabel for arduous attention to detail, which made the dream come true. . . .
Much love to all Penguins, Decca

To Joan Mellen[148]   Oakland
                                                                              October 18, 1988
Dear Ms. Mellen,

Sorry to be so long answering. I've been pondering yr letter, so here's what I think:

First off, Kay, who has been a close friend for ages—that is since at least the 1960's when Bob represented her in an anti-Vietnam war demo—is undoubtedly terrifically CAPRICIOUS, as in her curious & ambivalent treatment of you. Obviously, you are one amongst many who she's taken up, and then inexplicably dropped. . . .

Second off, I don't think I'd be a good respondent about Kay's lit. work—stories, novels etc.—and I don't much admire her excursions into political/journalistic writing, articles she did about, for example, the Huey Newton case and other pieces in the 1960's which are far too turgidly partisan for my liking. Just not the right vehicle for her particular talent. As for the stories/novels, while I LOVE reading them—and have, ever since she wrote for New Yorker before the war—fiction is not my field, hence I shouldn't be of much help to you on that score.

Anyway, suggestion: why don't you ring me when you get to Calif. after 12 December. I'd love to meet you, even though I don't honestly think I'd be useful for yr book. Mum's the word, of course; if Kay thought we were to meet,

of the wives," was amended in handwriting to say "with the exception of you!" The reason given for the exclusion of wives was that the lunch would be "a seriously male party" and "there simply is not room" in the "small farm house." The letter advised, "If anyone is coming with you, they can stay with the car if they want to, while you have lunch."

148. Mellen was working on a biography of Kay Boyle that was subsequently published as *Kay Boyle: Author of Herself* (Farrar, Straus and Giroux, 1994). She had written Decca asking for an interview and relating that Kay Boyle had "inexplicably decided not to cooperate [on her book], after having spent days with me in Oakland and agreeing to the project." This letter marked the start of what turned into a hurtful feud between Decca and her old friend Boyle.

she'd be livid & consider it an act of disloyalty on my part, although I may well tell her about it, in due course. . . .

     Yours sincerely, Jessica Mitford

To Doris Brin Walker   Oakland
                         December 7, 1988

Dearest Dob,

 Thanks for the Hungary article. I'm afraid lots of it was over my head—the economic scene and the altercations with Rumania, about which I don't know enough to have an opinion. . . .

 I'm all for a further discussion re CPUSA, so be proposing a venue. You now say you never accused us of redbaiting but actually yr view was that <u>any</u> crit. of the SU for putting poets, Jews, dissidents in prison or loony bins was redbaiting. In fact, all the things that Gorby is now going on about incl. perestroika & glasnost are things that <u>we</u> were on about 30 years ago—ever since the 1957 convention.[149] But that's all ancient history.

 The CPUSA today is what I'd like to discuss. You say you haven't any vote? Can't you vote for leaders, at least on local level? How amazing. You say that in spite of not having a vote you make yr position known. How, and to whom? Have you any disagreements with the Line—if so, how do you express them? I do remember v. distinctly the discussion period post-Krushev (sp?) report & pre-1957 convention. <u>THAT</u> was a splash of glasnost, all those position papers etc—to me, intensely interesting at the time. So was the convention itself. Somewhere around the house I must have the thick vol. issued post convention with a list of the non-Party observers & their v. positive comments at the end of the convention. . . . But as I tried to say in <u>A Fine Old Conflict</u> all that, & the resolutions, were swiftly swept into the DUSTBIN OF HISTORY by Wm. Z. Foster[150] & other powerful old-guard leaders with an assist from gutless wonders like Mickey Lima who <u>agreed</u> with all the Calif delegation proposals at the time but never <u>fought</u> for implementation of them. Then, the brainier & more dedicated people . . . cut out, made abortive efforts to organize afresh; and everything seemed a wee bit pointless, so we cut out, too.

 Today, if for example one was in the CP and thought the DPW[151] a hopeless

---

149. The national Communist Party convention that Decca attended as part of the California delegation, which was committed to liberalization within the Party, greater autonomy for the Party's U.S. branch, and, in general, opposition to the national party's "hidebound, orthodox leadership," in Decca's words.

150. William Z. Foster, veteran general secretary of the Communist Party USA and a three-time candidate for U.S. president in the late 1920s and early '30s. Foster, who became the Party's chairman emeritus in 1957, was a Stalinist and a strong supporter of Soviet party leadership and policies.

151. *Daily People's World.*

travesty of what a socialist or Communist paper shld be, how cld one influence its management? . . .

What about recruiting, Comrade? I know that many years ago during the Angela Davis trial, it was claimed that young people & many blacks were flocking into the CP. Are they still members? In this new Gorby-ish period, are you trying to get people to join? What about all the people round the country fervently supporting Sandinistas—has the CP made any official approach to them? I don't mean random attendance at their meetings, but an organization approach. Has the CP any discernable leadership role in this or any other current struggle—South Africa? Domestic issues such as homeless, trade unions, disgraceful & disgusting public health failures—you name it?

The other evening, when we asked for an example of how being a CP member has enabled you to operate more effectively, you gave the example (white Guild member refusing to be co-chair with a black); I still don't see how being currently in the CP was decisive. I do v. much agree that all we learned aeons ago about many things—in this case, alertness to white chauvinism—lasts through life.

It's my impression, gleaned mainly I admit from the DPW, that the CP is jolly stagnant & hasn't much of a clue as to how to catch hold of new people, new ideas.

The DPW account of the anti-Comm. conference was v. nostalgic—to me, that is, couched in pure Lifeitselfmanship lingo. Perhaps it shld be reassuring to find that some things never change?

Actually I don't see DPW any more; it was with a heavy heart that I finally cancelled our Lifetime Sub . . . and wrote a v. nice letter explaining that as we are away lots of the time, it's a waste of their valuable paper to keep sending it.

Over to you,

Much love, Decca

Decca in 1993
with her sisters
Deborah (center)
and Pam (right).
In the background
are Charlotte
Mosley, who had
just edited a book
of Nancy Mitford's
letters, and
Nancy's friend
Alastair Forbes.

The Treuhafts
at the celebration
of their fiftieth
wedding anniversary
in 1993.

Constancia
Romilly and her
sons, James and
Chaka Forman, at
James's graduation
from Yale Law
School in 1992.

IX

A FEISTY OLD DAME

Decca and the Dectones at a 1996 gig. Kathi Kamen
Goldmark, who dreamed up the gimmick, held a sign
to prompt the audience to sing along on the refrain of
"Maxwell's Silver Hammer."

Decca was not one to rage against the dying of the light, but neither was she constitutionally capable of submitting meekly to the demands of advancing age—or any other presumed inevitability. Yet it is hard now to think of her at this stage of her life without being aware of age. She celebrated a number of milestones in the early 1990s—her seventy-fifth birthday and her husband's eightieth, as well as their fiftieth wedding anniversary—and many of her dearest friends and colleagues were dying.

In late 1989, Leonard Boudin died; Cedric Belfrage in 1990; Tony Richardson in 1991. The two beloved cousins Decca knew as Rudbin and Idden died in 1993 and 1995. Polly Toynbee's husband, journalist Peter Jenkins, died in 1992. Two close younger English friends died prematurely: Jill Tweedie in 1993 and Sally Belfrage in 1994. Also, Decca's longtime New York friend, writer Penelope Gilliatt, died. Decca's sister Pam and good friend David Pleydell-Bouverie died in 1994, and her dear old friend and colleague Vivian Cadden in 1995. "People are dying these days who never died before," Decca said frequently, quoting a friend, as the drumbeat of deaths became an inescapable preoccupation.

Simultaneously, Decca was slowed by a number of injuries and infirmities and resorted to a walking companion to accompany her around her neighborhood. She continued to grapple with her smoking habit and finally confronted her alcoholism.

With each old friend's death, Decca's thoughts turned increasingly to her own mortality, although without the depressing ruminations that often accompany such reflections. As she wrote to a friend in the early 1980s, "In the last few weeks I've been to THREE memorial services—friends of my age are being Called to their Maker at a frightening rate. So am now planning mine (based on deficiencies of the ones I've just been to). Slogan will be BREVITY FOLLOWED BY LEVITY, i.e. none of those 30-min. Appreciations; 2 minutes per speaker, followed by lashings of booze & grub. Am sending these directions to Dinky & Benjy. Will YOU both come? Do. Should be the Bash of the Year."

Still, she took on new and ambitious writing projects, and she never throttled her spunky ways. "I love being a feisty old dame," she told one friend, apparently quoting a characterization in Britain's *Daily Express*. When she spoke at a benefit, less than a year before her death, on the subject "Coming of Age," it was with another irrepressibly spirited old radical, Studs Terkel, before a packed house of guffawing fans. She also took to the stage with indiscreet enthusiasm as the featured singer of Decca and the Dectones, a fund-raising gimmick dreamed up by a young acquaintance, Kathi Kamen Goldmark, a musician and professional author escort who had previously started the Rock Bottom Remainders, a band composed of celebrity authors acting out their rock 'n' roll fantasies, mostly at booksellers' conventions. Decca called Goldmark the Dr. Frankenstein—"I'm the Monster"—of "my new Persona as popsinger." She sang, in her inimitable warble, at a number of benefits and on radio and television broadcasts, and her performances and recordings were reviewed in major publications including Britain's *Daily Express* and *The Independent*.

As forthright as ever, however imprudently, Decca engaged during these years in several painful personal conflicts with two old friends, authors Kay Boyle and Maya Angelou. The spat with Angelou was especially troubling because, as Decca wrote to one acquaintance, "she's the most incredible friend one cld hope for ever, in life."

The combative septuagenarian was an immensely proud mama when Benjamin Treuhaft—sometimes described in childhood as "Dec's Bad Boy"—followed in her footsteps as a prankster and gadfly, making headlines of his own. He enlisted the help of his fellow piano tuners and others, including his parents, in a personal crusade to defy the American trade embargo on Cuba by replacing some of that country's aging, deteriorating stock of pianos with donated instruments he arranged to have shipped there. His project, Send a Piana to Havana, received worldwide attention and was the subject of a British documentary called *Tuning with the Enemy*. He jousted publicly with the State Department, which considered his venture a violation of the law but appeared reluctant to make too big a federal case of trafficking in music.

Decca loved it all. During one period of heightened tensions with Cuba, Benjamin Treuhaft briefly lost contact with his family while traveling there. Decca wrote his wife, Jungmin Kim, "I see in the papers that Benjy's gone & started a war between Cuba & U.S., naughty boy. Do let us know if you hear anything from him!"

Decca asked another correspondent, "Don't you find it rather comic when the whole progressive world is scurrying to provide dried milk, essential life-saving medicines etc to the embattled Cubans, the Benj effort is for PIANO PARTS? Which he feels is just as essential for the life of the musical Cubans. Give me bread, but give me roses as the old saying has it." She made it her cause too. For several years, on her new fax machine—a device she took to as enthusiastically as if she had discovered the printing press—she sent every update, fund appeal, and press clipping on her son's exploits to friends throughout the U.S. and abroad. "Brings me back to the CRC days," she said, "all these mass mailings, volunteers, getting coffee for them etc."

Professionally, Decca continued writing—almost, it seemed at times, out of habit as much as passion. During the period covered by these letters, she wrote *The American Way of Birth*.* Partway through the writing, she wrote to a friend who was also in the middle of a book: "As I see it, the whole subject of yours is

---

*Dutton, 1992.

inherently interesting; not so with birth, damn it." Writing about medical matters seemed an odd choice. Decca disliked doctors "as a tribe," although acknowledging "there are a few good apples in that rotten barrel, and I've met lots of those." She avoided visits to her own doctor except for an annual flu shot, and "Then he says 'while you're here, I'll just take your blood pressure.' 'OH no, I'm far too busy, I've got to dash,' I say, suiting the action to the word."

So Decca understood full well the irony of becoming an expert on medical practices, and she was frank about why she had agreed to do so. As she told her good friend Dr. Ephraim Kahn, "I'm sure you deeply disapprove of the idea of hopeless me writing a book abt childbirth which is chockablock with technical matters esp. in the field of medicine. Well I don't blame you; I often wonder as I plough ahead with said bk WHY am I doing it? I'm afraid the answer is filthy lucre. It all started as just a possible article idea . . . and only burgeoned into a bk after [her agent negotiated] a shower of gold the likes of which I've never seen."

That book generated yet another entertaining British documentary, and it was followed, two years later, by another reprise on *The American Way of Death*. Channel 4 in Britain produced, with Decca's active participation, *Over My Dead Body*, about the spread of American-style funerals to Britain. The producers interviewed Robert Waltrip, the head of Service Corporation International, an American funeral-home conglomerate. It was a red meat for Decca, who interested editor Robert Gottlieb in a reissue of *The American Way of Death*,* by then out of print. She contemplated writing an "Afterword," but in time it became apparent that a more comprehensive revision was needed. The multinational SCI was her last villain and victim.

Decca was working on that revision when she got a diagnosis of rampant cancer, and the updated classic was ultimately completed by her husband, after her death.

Despite the rapid progress of her cancer, Decca characteristically faced her impending death head-on, on her own terms. She told the hospital that since she was dying anyhow she would thenceforth be eating nothing but chocolate mousse. She returned to her home (and a refrigerator stocked with chocolate mousse), slipping in and out of consciousness in a hospital bed set up in the center of her living room as family and friends came by to chat, say goodbye, and, of course, laugh. Angelou flew into town and sat at her bedside, singing the raucous songs they loved, with Decca rousing herself occasionally to sing along.

The final chapter of Decca's life and letters begins with the germination of her last full book.

■■

The American Way of Death Revisited, published posthumously by Alfred A. Knopf, 1998.

To Renée Golden   Oakland
                                                              December 14, 1988

Dear Renée,

Here's what I've sent to the Kalmen père et fille.[1]

I realize that it does not as yet reflect your view that the bk should be broader than just midwives—shld comprise many ways of birth.

I do hope I don't have to watch an ACTUAL delivery when in Chico—after all, I got through The American Way of Death without going near an actual embalming. Bob did all that, thank goodness.

Mdwves don't use any anaesthetic which sounds so drab; they caution the patient that it's going to hurt a lot!!! You can say that again. My mother once said it feels like an orange being forced up your nostril. Fancy doing that seven times, poor her.

Benjy's birth: he was literally one month late, weighed approx. 10 lbs. Waters broke so off to hospital; Drs. gave labor-inducing shots of something v. potent; labor wld start, then fade away. This happened over 3–4 days, as they cld only give 15 shots a day (huge long needle in one's behind—so 45 of those in all. Me a pincushion). FINALLY it was the real thing; but the anaesthetist & Dr. had gone out to dinner. In labor room next mine, somebody was screaming her head off so all nurses & aides rushed to her. As I was trained not to shout in public places, I didn't. Eventually somebody did come & pulled the dear thing out. Later, I heard Bob and the Dr. saying it had been an easy birth, which made me quite cross.

Back to your idea that bk shld be wider in scope: this may come clearer after I read Dr. Horowitz[2] (see point #1 of my letter to Kalmen) & interview him. No pt in going into this with Kalmen as they are only interested in midwife aspect. . . .

      Decca

To Ted Kalman   Oakland
                                                              December 21, 1988

Dear Ted,

Thanks v. much for yr letter—I thought the typing PERFECTLY BEAUTI-FUL. Don't expect ME to master one of those dread machines.[3] . . . Many of my

---

1. Ted Kalman was a longtime political friend of the Treuhafts in Oakland. His daughter, Janice, twenty-seven, a skilled lay midwife from Chico, California, was chair of the California Association of Midwives Certification Board and was being investigated by the Chico district attorney's office for practicing medicine without a license. Her treatment at the hands of the state medical board fascinated Decca and ultimately led to the writing of *The American Way of Birth*, for which Ted Kalman served as Decca's chief researcher. The book was dedicated to Kalman and his daughter and wife, Peewee, "for their inestimable help through a long and difficult labor."

2. *Taking Charge of Your Medical Fate*, by Dr. Lawrence Horowitz (Random House, 1988).

3. Kalman had said in his letter that he was trying to write it on an unfamiliar Macintosh word processor without assistance from his mentors, his daughter and son-in-law.

writer friends now have word-processors and swear by them, so good for them. Some even have home Xerox machines—and FAX machines!!! Never, says I. . . .

Book comments . . .

I think it would be a mistake to approach this or ANY piece of writing with the concept that it's going to change people's thinking. At least, that would not be my perspective IF I actually plunge into it . . . I don't strive for "substance, depth & scope" as you put it—not that I don't see the importance of these, but merely because I do better—or find it more natural for me—if I stick to specifics, finding out facts & presenting them without underlining for the reader conclusions they should be drawing, or global Moral Messages that I wish them to absorb.

Perhaps I can clarify the approach that works best for me via the example of The American Way of Death. . . . The whole point of AWOD was that it wasn't about DEATH at all, but about the death INDUSTRIES. Hence the book is v. short on anecdotal tales of poor widows, their suffering, & how the wicked undertakers took advantage of them—many other bks on same subject went on interminably about that sort of thing.

Likewise, when I was writing Kind & Usual Punishment (re U.S. Prisons) I steered away from prisoners' hard luck stories—and my God one cld fill volumes with those, & extremely interesting many of them are—and concentrated on all the veneer that goes into the prison business, the "rehabilitation" scam, the vast profitability of prisons to a range of beneficiaries from architects to psychiatrists to bureaucrats in general. . . .

IF after all the prelims. outlined in my previous letters to you I do decide to take it on—which means, Ted, a couple of yrs of v. concentrated work—I'm fairly sure that my interest, & emphasis, wld be far more on chicaneries of medical profession, greed of same, politics of same, than on the admittedly v. important aspect of loving/caring sisterhood aspect—which of course comes into it, but not a major emphasis. . . .

Merry Xmas—love to Peewee & Janice, Decca

To Joan Mellen   Oakland
                                                                                      January 24, 1989

Dear Joan,

. . . Sorry I put you "on trial,"[4] but as you know Kay is an old friend & at that point I was seeing you sort of counter to her instructions and I was longing to

---

4. After Kay Boyle adamantly opposed Decca's cooperation with her would-be biographer, Decca asked Mellen for documentation of Boyle's previous support of the biography, including copies of letters Boyle had written endorsing the biography, providing names of interviewees and otherwise assisting in the project. Although confessing to feeling "a bit on trial" at an otherwise enjoyable luncheon meeting with Decca, Mellen sent her the letters, including one in which Boyle acknowledged her previous "commitment" to the biography. Mellen says Boyle's refusal to cooperate occurred well into the project and followed an unsuccessful demand by Boyle that she have control over whom Mellen interviewed.

get to the bottom (if any) of the you/Kay drama. Jerry Garchik sent me a copy of the letter AUTHORIZING people to talk to you[5]—a smashingly well-crafted bit of work, I thought. As for me, I don't specially like being ordered to talk/not talk to whom I may choose, so I did disregard Kay's instruction in your case. And I admitted as much to her, when she phoned to ask if I had seen you so I said yes I had. Since when, total <u>froideur</u> on her part. I didn't tell her anything about our discussion, just that I had in fact met you—that's about all that was said.

I must say the letters are REALLY EYE-OPENING—couldn't be warmer, more affectionate. Her sudden dumping of you is too extraordinary. Aside from the extremely friendly tone of letter of Aug. 22, 1987—and list of people to see—in the next one, April 13, 1988, says "You are a very talented young woman. You write with vigor & grace . . ." In conversations about you with me (and I'm sure others) she said you'd never written anything plus many other uncomplimentary comments.[6]

It's awfully sad in a way, as it's put a total damper on our longstanding friendship with Kay, mainly because I can't bear the two-facedness of her in dealings with you. As I think I told you, we knew she's jolly capricious . . . but this business of on-again-off-again re you & yr work beats all. Another maddening thing: she's been bad-mouthing Jerry Garchik, who has been incredibly good to her over many years—tons of free legal work, plus the Garchiks put her up time & again for days/weeks & were v. hospitable.

Oh well. It's all a bit mystifying. Do you think that a) this sort of behaviour is part of the creative personality, or b) she's been driven slightly dotty by all her physical problems, pain etc? . . .

Best regards, Decca

To Sally Belfrage   Oakland
                                                                         February 22, 1989

Dearest Sally,

Security was tight at Heathrow. Brit. Air official asked sternly "Did you do your own packing?" Yes, said I, mendaciously—fearing to admit it was actually done by an Irish domestic worker. . . .

I can't believe the rudeness of me not writing before now to thank for yr massive hospitality & kindness. . . .

---

5. Mellen says the authorization letter referred to here was a result of still another reversal by Boyle. She says Boyle changed her mind again because she didn't want it said in the book that she'd refused to give friends permission to talk about her with Mellen.

6. Decca said Boyle was "livid" when she learned that Decca had read her private letters "to another person" (Mellen). Thereafter, Boyle refused a dinner invitation from Decca: "Deep-freeze. The answer was NO." As Decca summed it up, ". . . friendship with Kay must be strictly on her terms which are a) NO criticism of anything she does, b) NO jokes as she's got, alas, absolutely zilch sense of humour."

This end, shuddering amounts of things to do [including] . . . lots on S. Rushdie[7] such as READINGS by local (Bay Area) writers at the SF Library, all of us deeply hoping we won't be assassinated on the spot by those dire Muslims. Time will tell; if we are, sure to make the London papers? Don't forget you are my lit. executrix.

Now, fast-backward to NY. What follows is pretty much EYES ONLY, yours, so don't be spreading it . . . well, bits of it, but not the BOTTOM LINE—DOLLAR SIGN.

I'd been rather longing to get home—breaking the journey for 1 or two nights in NY—but Renee[8] absolutely insisted that I shld stay until 18 Feb as she'd arranged numerous meetings with publishers at Viv Cadden's flat for 17th. I couldn't quite see the point of these meetings, as in my (admittedly limited) experience with publishers ALL they care about is the written word, a proposal or outline, NOT meeting the author. Others such as Shana Alexander and Viv agreed. I showed Renee's list to Shana & Viv & they both said "that's the cream of the publishing industry!" and were impressed that Renee had managed to fetch them up.

I'm up about 4 a.m. on morning of 17th, madly trying to scribble down what I'm going to TELL those publishers about plans for the book. Renee bustles in at 7:30, having taken all-night "redeye" flight from L.A. She says it's quite unnecessary for me to bother with an outline of things to discuss (bookwise) as she's told them what it's about, and that it's for ME to audition THEM & decide who I'll have for editor/publisher, not the other way round! I am astonished. Renee also explains that she's told everyone that she's only considering offers over $100,000. As the highest advance I've ever had on any book was about $30,000 I'm simply amazed.

There are 6 appointments of one hour each, and 1/2 hour between for relaxing. The day proceeds like a French farce as part of the Renee scheme was not to tell each publisher who the others invited are. So, it's 9 a.m. Delacourt-Bantam. 11 a.m., Simon & Schuster. 12:30, Crown. 2:30 p.m. Susan Kamil & Joni Evans, Random House. 4 p.m., Jane Isay, Addison/Wesley. 5 p.m., Harper & Row.

I still can't imagine why these bigshots of publishing should stir forth from their midtown offices to come up all the way to Viv's on 85th Street; but they do. Everything goes off pleasantly enough—general chitchat, some questions abt the book; then off they go, clearing deck for next lot.

Halfway through the day, phone starts ringing. Renee answers & reports:

---

7. About a week before this letter was written, Iranian spiritual leader Ayatollah Ruhollah Khomeini had issued a fatwa, a religious edict, calling on Muslims to execute novelist Salman Rushdie because of his book *The Satanic Verses* (Viking Penguin, 1988). Rushdie went into hiding, and many writers around the world came to his defense.

8. Renée Golden.

"Simon & Schuster offers $175,000." "Crown offer $200,000." She doesn't tell 'em yea or nay, nor does she reveal amt of offer of other publishers. My head's reeling.

At 2:30 Susan Kamil & Joni Evans of Random House loom. They seem v. splendid—ask a few sharp questions, seem to be in a hurry. Then Joni (head of Random House): "Well I don't see the point of hanging around any longer. Here's our offer: $500,000 for hardcover rights only...." I faint (almost). Sally—it's a FORTUNE. Can you believe it? Bob didn't at first, when Renee & I rang him at the office, but I think he's coming around to it.

Renee said that by the time paperback etc. are settled, it should come up closer to $1 million. Goodness I'm excited—would be more so except that now I've got to write the bloody book.[9] ...

Point of not telling about the FORTUNE is that I don't want to be squandering it quite yet—at least not until I've got it actually in hand—and shall still be looking for a cheap let in June or so. Bob & I to discuss London dates when we have TIME TO THINK, which hasn't happened yet.

> Yr loving Decca

To Constancia Romilly   Oakland
                                                 March 21, 1989

Dink—

... I'm in the midst of writing my BOOK PROPOSAL (for publisher). Severe LABOR PAINS (sorry—contractions; no pain to speak of accdg to midwives though I rather doubt that), now coming about once every five minutes. Am trying to induce labor with massive input of telephone calls & letters to Loved Ones (like you). It may have to be a C-section birth, editors with their bloodied knives (red pencils, in the context); or at the very least, a painful forceps delivery in which the wretched book is dragged from the screaming author with huge hooks

Oh well, such is life. ...

> Fondest love, & to Terry, children etc., Decca

To William Abrahams   Oakland
                                                  May 7, 1989

Dearest Billy,

In preparation for our mtg on May 9, a few comments on various book things.[10] ... Here goes:

---

9. It was some time later that the euphoria was punctured by the realization that Decca's contract with Dutton for *Grace Had an English Heart* gave that publishing house the right of first refusal to her next book. A deal was subsequently negotiated with Dutton, which paid a $525,000 advance for the hardcover rights.

10. Abrahams at the time was a senior editor at Dutton and Decca's editor for her birth book.

1. <u>Vocabulary, medical</u>. Needless to say I am abysmally ignorant of all the scientific medical words. For example, do you know what episiotomy means? I bet you don't, and better you shouldn't as it's TOO revolting: means cutting through the vagina to let the baby's head through. (I rather remember that, from one of mine, & the doctor saying after the babe was born, "I'm just putting in a few stitches," and me saying rather stupidly in view of location of said stitches "Oh—I <u>do</u> hope they won't show.") My mother was even far more hopeless abt medical terms. Told that a young friend had had both her ovaries removed, Muv gave a little scream: "But I thought there were thousands of those!" I shall need a glossary for such as Muv & me.

2. <u>Vocabulary</u>—modern vogue words which recur depressingly (to me) throughout the midwifery lit. Obviously the whole thrust of my book will be <u>for</u> the embattled midwives vs. medical establishment—but here are a few examples of their lingo that cause discomfort, malaise, wincing.

<u>Bonding</u>. Importance of client bonding a) with midwife, whom she has got to know over many months, b) bonding with newborn who is put straight on her breast as soon as it emerges. I'm all for being friends with midwife, and of clasping newborn babe to one's bosom but why must it be called BONDING? (Incidentally, do these bonding mums become overbearing, tyrannical disliked mothers, overprotective—all the motherly faults? Who knows.)

<u>Parenting</u>. We all know what "mothering" means—giving motherly atten-tion & love. <u>Parenting</u> is presumably meant to include a father's role, since the word fathering has specific connotation (as in "He fathered a child out of wed-lock"). Parenting is yet another of those nouns-made-into-verbs like network-ing, concretize etc.

<u>Birthing</u>. Why not giving birth?

There are tons more examples—"primary care-giver"—of new hifallutin' sisterly gush, but why go on? Above wld be at most a para or so in a preface— or might not get in at all. . . .

To John Kenneth and Catherine (Kitty) Galbraith   Oakland
                                                                    August 5, 1989

Dear K&K,

KITTY: Thanks for kind words about poor old Grey Starling. . . .

KEN: Yr comments re title for my new book—spot on. In fact, I got the contract changed to say "Amer. Way of Birth—working title, may be changed" etc. What about "Childbirth in America," which preserves the idea without as you say "hitchhiking on an early success"? You're the great wordsmanship expert. Be thinking. Book not due until June 1991, if one shld live so long!

What I really loved was yr comment ". . . it is a subject to which I had not previously given more than three minutes' thought." Conjures up picture of Kitty suffering the torture of travail whilst busy Ken is occupied with Affairs of

State. I'm thinking of a chapter called Father's Day with that as a lead-off. These days, as you may or may not know, the wretched Dad is not only required to be on hand for the whole messy business but is often expected to CUT THE UMBILICAL CORD. Ugh. Also, up-to-date hospitals for the rich have a Mom & Pop champagne dinner on her last night in hospital. All too odd for words.[11] . . .

> Much love to you both, and to products of less than
> 3 minutes' thought if they are there, Decca

To Annie Fursland[12]

Oakland
August 23, 1989

Dear Annie,

. . . The only bone to pick in yr letter is the part about tremendous privilege . . . respect—more in awe. . . . Am I that much of a dragon??? DO say not.

To me, the "tremendous privilege" is all on the other foot, the fact <u>you</u> chose <u>me</u> as subject for yr Ph.D. thesis. Am reminded of time when Nancy told me (and, I may add, spread the news far & wide) that a French Ph.D. candidate chose HER for subject. We all thought that was an extremely grand & high honor.

Now, forward to the 62 pages. . . .

Knowing naught of the exigencies of Ph.D. writing, I do rather wish that yours could have more of the TONE and WRY OBSERVATION of your letter to me of 17 Aug—but perhaps that's not the form? I mean, it wld make for far jollier reading. . . .

I thought that on the whole you got my relationships with sisters down right—the exception is Debo; I thought you were a bit rough on her, and didn't completely fathom the me/Debo ins & outs. Or rather, ups & downs.

We adored each other as children (even though when she was small I used to be rather horrid to her). Ditto as teenagers. As she was completely apolitical, there were none of the complications as in the Boud/Diana situation; just enjoyment, jokes, non-stop Honnish poems & songs.

---

11. Decca did use Galbraith's comment in her book, adding, "If the scene could be reenacted today, we might visualize Galbraith being dragged by a giant hook, like those used in French theaters to remove unpopular performers, off the world stage and into his wife's delivery chamber. There his attention would be concentrated for a lot more than three minutes, as he breathes and strains . . . in unison with Kitty until the great moment when he is called upon to himself cut the umbilical cord." When her book was published, Decca sent a copy to the Galbraiths. Not having heard from them in response, she wrote them expressing concern that Kenneth Galbraith might have been offended by her use of the quotation, although "that wee bit was rather fun to write as typical of Papas throughout the world."

12. Fursland, writing from Columbus, Ohio—where she had been reading Decca's papers in the Ohio State University archives for her doctoral thesis in psychology on Decca—had told her subject in a letter "what a tremendous privilege it is to be researching your life."

Turns out she was <u>incredibly bitter</u> about me running away and not telling her—so amazing, and I never knew this until the 1970's. However, all was fairly well patched up—I saw her whenever in London, & loved seeing her—until the great Scrap-Book Row. Actually quite comic in a way—ancient ladies squabbling over a lost scrap-book!—but not to me. Perhaps you gathered this from the letters. Next act: scrapbook found, all patched over. Next: she liked <u>Faces of Philip</u> (loathed all my things about the family) and absolutely loved Grace Darling. (As Bob said, she must have been v. relieved that it wasn't another about us.) Since then, she's been a super booster. It's all rather complicated, too much to go into in a letter; and I don't know to what extent it's of any use to your project.

Love, Decca

To Laura Shaine Cunningham[13]   Oakland
                                                        November 24, 1989

Dear Laura,

Thanks so much for your ABSOLUTELY DELIGHTFUL book. I did so love it: the uncles, the grandmother, mother—the whole thing was a terrific treat. . . .

Re exhibitionists (one of the absolutely memorable passages in <u>Sleeping Arrangements</u>), here goes with another experience—nowhere near as interesting as yours, but on the same order.

When Dink was about 7, we were living in a rather beastly sort of petty-bourgeois neighborhood in Oakland, Jean Street, up the hill from the municipal rose garden. (Petty-minded, our neighbors were.) Dink & other small girls used to run down to play in the rose garden after school. Rumours that a man was seen "exposing himself" to said children. Lynch spirit in our block; irate fathers saying if they caught him they'd cut his balls off etc. I discovered to my pleasure that the police term for exposers is "lily-waver." A committee of mothers, furious, called on me to complain that Dinky had been seen <u>speaking to him</u>—the other little girls, obedient to the mums' instructions, had <u>never</u> spoken to him. So I asked Dinky, "did you speak to the lily-waver?" "Yes!" she answered in her stout fashion. "So what was said?" "Well, he asked me 'Have you ever seen one of these before, little girl?' And I said 'Of course, loads of times.' " Upon which, I suppose, the lily must have wilted.

The lily-waver was caught & held in a police car at the bottom of the hill. Dinky's sweet little chums came running to fetch her: "Say he's the one! Then we all get the day off to testify in court." Bob had a strong word with Dinky. If he's innocent, he'll go to prison on your word. Only say he's the one if you are

---

13. Author of the memoir *Sleeping Arrangements* (Alfred A. Knopf, New York, 1989).

<u>absolutely certain</u>. I think he also explained that lily-wavers are on the whole harmless bores, don't go on to rape or harm. Anyway, she went down the hill & scrutinized the suspect. "No, I can't be sure he's the one." The waver (for I suppose it was indeed he) said "Thank you, dear." However, thereafter the other dear small witches wouldn't play with Dink any more, so stupid of her they said. . . . That's one of many reasons we left Jean Street for an integrated neighborhood in West Oakland.

Again, a million thanks for superb book. Perhaps we'll meet one day? . . .

Best regards, Decca

To Kay Boyle   Oakland
                                                    December 6, 1989
Kay:

Bob told me about your phone conversation. For my part, I've been terribly sad at loss of our friendship, I miss you a great deal and should much love to make up.

However, to me it seems that friendship should be a two-way street and shouldn't prohibit disagreements, shouldn't depend on total uncritical mutual admiration. . . .

You wrote to Bob that "Many times in the past I have realized that Decca has very much sought and hoped to find a justifiable reason for rebuking me. She finally found that reason on a very unworthy issue." I must say I was completely floored by this news; I reviewed every scrap of our quite massive correspondence over many years and simply can't imagine how you could have dreamed any such thing. Ditto, searching my memory for our myriad conversations— nothing to begin to justify that sort of comment.

The very idea of me trying to find a reason for rebuking you is so ridiculous. Have I ever said anything critical of you? Quite likely (though I can't recall any specific occasion), but isn't that part of the give-and-take of ordinary FRIENDSHIP?

Anyway, that's why I thought it rather hopeless to make an uphill effort to get back on anything like old terms.

As to the Joan Mellen episode, I thought you behaved capriciously (first encouraging her, then casting her out and telling people not to talk to her), and I said so at that disastrous dinner last spring. I also said I dislike, as I'm sure you would, being told whom I may/may not talk to, and couldn't feel bound by your stricture not to see Joan Mellen. It would never occur to me to order my friends not to talk to XYZ, no matter who XYZ is—friendly or hostile. Who cares? In a long life, there must be plenty of both, don't you agree?

About the 20th Century Lit. journal. It was mostly unalloyed hagiography which, of course, we all rather adore—but I did note that Malcolm Cowley struck a familiar note (page 271) when he said "Also I questioned Kay's accounts of events in which we had both played a part. I thought she fabulated . . ."

Nothing wrong with fabulating, if one is essentially a novelist. But did you brace him about his comments? I thought your letter to D. Bryant[14] (who fabulated, but according to her, at your suggestion) rather mean-spirited, as hers was the only adverse note in a torrent of praise.[15] Poor her. Oh well.

I should much love a resumption of friendship on equal terms, if you are ever willing to try. I am. . . .

To Kay Boyle   Oakland
March 3, 1990

Dearest Kay,

Thanks for yrs of Feb. 25. Bob & I also enjoyed enormously our evening with you,[16] & hearing all about the Redwoodians.[17] I must say they sound a bit drab—and unlikely converts to more enlightened (or less fascistic, take yr choice) views of the world. . . .

Professional men: I can't really agree. Well obviously there are some dedicated & v. smashing lawyers/doctors, but in my view the HUGE majority of those professions are supremely venal, money-grubbing, self-aggrandizing bores/monsters. To my interest, I've noted that in occasional polls in which the public are asked to rate "professions," lawyers rank just under Undertakers (sorry—Funeral Directors) for unpopularity amongst the masses.

As for doctors, I'm immersed in the subject (my bk Amer. Way of Birth) and I must say they are a pretty boring & often wicked lot.

That's not to say that you (and I, for that matter) haven't been lucky—or rather, skillful—in choice of lawyers/doctors. There are many heroes in both trades, all through history in fact, but these are a distinct minority. In fact—an infinitesimal minority, if you come to think of it.

You say that the lit. critic & biographer manipulate the written word. Again, I'm not sure quite what you are driving at. You say they "deal with personal prejudices & fantasia" & in contrast the doctor or lawyer has acquired a broad framework in which to commit himself to all mankind.

---

14. Dorothy Bryant, a novelist and former teacher, is a Berkeleyan who was a member of the Treuhafts' social circle.

15. Boyle had asked Bryant to contribute to a book of essays paying tribute to Boyle. Bryant says she demurred at first because she didn't have enough to add but Boyle told her to "make something up." The resulting essay contained actual incidents intended to show Boyle's integrity and political contributions, but details were disguised to protect others mentioned. The essay infuriated Boyle. When Bryant wrote an abject apology, Boyle circulated it widely and explored a lawsuit, which Robert Treuhaft evidently advised against.

16. Decca and Boyle evidently had a short-lived rapprochement, but their friendship turned out to be irretrievable. As Decca put it in a letter to her son when Boyle died almost three years later, "I didn't give an inch, Kay didn't give an inch, so there you have it. An irreconcilable end to a very long & much cherished (by me) friendship."   •

17. Boyle had begun living at The Redwoods retirement center in Mill Valley, Calif.

I would that 'twere true! Not in my experience of these professionals in general.

Much love, Decca

To Mary Clemmey   Oakland
March 20, 1990

Dearest Mary,

Thanks SO much for yr letter, what a pleasure to get it. PUBLISHING: Too ghastly here, too, as I'm sure you know. . . .

All the papers this end are blaming the disruption partly on the ridic. huge advances given to some writers—sums that can't possibly ever be earned. So in one way, I'm a Guilty Party in all this. Reading the press on the subject, I may have been the very last to get one of those outsize absurd advances, thanks to the curious genius of Renee Golden; now, it seems, that bubble has burst & publishers are no longer forking out that sort of money for books that obviously won't sell all that well. So I feel v. fortunate   secure in old age, & lots to leave my children & Oys. The only problem is having to write the actual book. I'm chugging slowly along, have just about finished Chapter 3. . . .

To Katharine Graham   Washington
April 9, 1990

Dear Kay,

I did so enjoy having lunch with you—thanks awfully. But as always after leaving I thought of myriad things I was longing to discuss—too late.

However, a few comments re yr book. It seemed to me to strike very much the right tone—the fragments I read—& as I said, some of the fascinators such as Cissy Patterson[18] & Alice Longworth[19] could stand quite a bit of elaboration: not just to put the uninformed reader in the picture as to who they were, but mainly yr own impressions of them from a) meeting them when you were a teenager & b) things you remember yr Pa & Ma & other grown-ups saying about them. Done in yr extremely lively & readable style, this cld be both painless to write & v. enjoyable to read.

Which brings me to the painful subject of PAIN.

What follows is just an account of my own (admittedly cowardly) ducking of some of the unutterably beastly experiences. For example, in Hons & Rebels I simply couldn't bear to write about getting the telegram that Esmond was missing & the gradual dawning of the fact he was actually dead—Winston

---

18. Eleanor Medill Patterson, newspaper editor and publisher and member of one of the country's great publishing families. She had been a friend of Katharine Graham's parents.

19. Alice Roosevelt Longworth, oldest child of President Theodore Roosevelt and a good friend of Graham's father.

Churchill got the classified info—so all I did was put a footnote: "Killed in action, November 1941." <u>Very</u> weird, I reckon, but that was all I cld bring myself to do.

Another example: Bob's & my first child Nicholas . . . born in 1944, absolute apple of eye, an enchanting & v. amusing boy—killed in an accident, 1955. Absolutely wrecked all happiness for a v.v. long time. When I wrote <u>A Fine Old Conflict</u> (about life with Bob, Oakland, CRC etc) I simply airbrushed Nicky out. His birth, his short & delightful life, never mentioned. Very odd indeed; but again, I simply couldn't bear to go into all that in a book.[20]

I'm not at all suggesting that you could—or should—try to do anything of the sort in <u>your</u> book. The foregoing prob. has little or <u>no</u> relevance to what you are writing. Obviously you can't duck—for example—Phil's suicide in a footnote. But you can, & should, remember that it's <u>YOUR</u> book & deal with events according to your own taste. Write it for yourself & friends & <u>not</u> for some faceless public.[21] Well—I'm sure you will. . . .

Kay—sorry for longwinded, unsolicited comments. Do get back in touch. . . .

Love, Decca

To John Prime[22]   Oakland
                                                                           April 13, 1990

Dear Mr. Prime,

A biog. of Leadbelly sounds like a really good idea; I'm so glad you are doing it. Actually, I don't remember the Life mag. article of 1977, so what follows is a bit of stream-of-consciousness. See, also, my autobiog. <u>A Fine Old Conflict</u>, which has a photo of the children's concert,[23] also a few paragraphs (page 119) about his visit at our house. Page 143 in American edition.

---

20. Although Decca apparently had forgotten the incident, more than a decade earlier she had discussed the same subject with Graham. Soon thereafter, she apologized that "I damn near blubbed at lunch when explaining why I hadn't included Nicholas in my memoirs—most odd of me, as he died in 1955 at age 10 & I should have supposed I had totally recovered; not to mention that we were brought up <u>never</u> to cry in front of other people. So please forgive this strange & totally unaccustomed lapse on my part."

21. In another of her encouraging letters to Katharine Graham, Decca noted that "the wretched public will be expecting lots of tell-all. I think the idea is to write at length & avidly about the things that interest you; that's what interests any reader."

22. Prime had written to Decca saying he was working with fellow Shrevesport, Louisiana, writer Monty Brown on a biography of Leadbelly, Huddie Ledbetter. He was interested in Decca's correspondence with the singer, her reflections on his life and work and futher recollections of the several weeks that Ledbetter had spent with the Treuhafts in the 1940s, which he said were recounted in her 1977 article in *Life* magazine.

23. The photo shows the singer performing in a living room for Constancia Romilly and her friends.

<u>Recollections:</u> I think we met him through Alan Lomax.[24] . . . Can't be sure at this late date how he came to us. At that time, he wasn't well-known except to a few <u>very</u> devoted fans. The children's party would have been circa 1947; my daughter would have been 6 yrs old. . . .

As I said in my book, Leadbelly would come down to breakfast in a stark white nightshirt.[25] One morning the doorbell rang; a neighbor asking to borrow a cup of sugar or some such. Leadbelly went to the door—the neighbor let out a wild shriek & fell back down the steps, one hopes breaking a leg or two. You must remember that these were days of total discrimination. Thereafter nobody ever came to call in our neighborhood (we were living in Clayton Street at the time, all-white needless to say).

Here is the <u>really sad</u> thing. Bob & I were extremely busy—dashed out in the morning, masses of evening meetings, so we didn't see all that much of Leadbelly who himself had tons of appointments & things to do. However, one evening we took him to dinner in our favorite SF Chinese restaurant, a lovely interlude. After he left, he sent us a record—a super-cherished memento of his visit—called "Bob and Decca in Chinatown." Again, I sadly can't remember the lyrics but they were super-Leadbellyish; we adored the record, a prized possession. Alas, it disappeared in one of our many moves to Oakland and other places. I mourn its loss. I wonder if, by chance, he'd made another copy? Do let me know, if so.

That's all I can remember. Lots of luck with the book; should be a winner.

To Terry Weber   Oakland
                                                                                                 May 15, 1990

Dearest Terbaby,[26]

I have carefully conned over your touching appeal, & decided on 10 cents a mile. I do hope you won't find that appallingly cheap of me? I can see that those monitors etc. will be a barrel of fun for the lucky chaps & chapesses who have the delightful experience of being subjected to them. But as I didn't understand a blithering word of all that, I thought that $35 wld be about what I cld contribute.

I must impart one thing: I was actually <u>very deeply hurt</u> at not being invited to participate in the bicycling project. I realize that you & Dink may (wrongly)

---

24. The left-wing folklorist who preserved folk music and stories around the world and went into exile during the heyday of McCarthyism.

25. Decca noted in her memoir the "spectacular" visual effect of the "very large and very black" Leadbelly in his long white nightshirt.

26. Decca once described her son-in-law's nickname this way: "Terry Southern was in movie *Loved One* by Tony Richardson—so he was known, H.wood style, as Terbaby. When we took Dink & Terry to stay with Tony . . . needless to say Terry Weber was immediately known as Terbaby, which has stuck" (at least with Decca).

think that I have no feelings to speak of, no inner soul to be damaged by the sort of neglect that you have subjected me to. Don't you realize, though, that in a mere 365 days I could have surpassed your goal of 350 miles by 15 miles? Doing one mile a day on my stationary bike, which is about my speed? After all, what's the great rush—a year, more or less, for the CAUSE?

I don't ask for an apology. Just for a bit of human understanding of my incredibly injured psyche at lack of invitation as a well-known cyclist to contribute to the event.

Yours—more in sorrow than in anger, Decca

To Robert Gottlieb Oakland
May 26, 1990

Dear Bites,

. . . I absolutely gobbled up Caro.[27] Va Durr was livid about it & said he misquoted her; pressed for details, she couldn't supply any.

Although I knew LBJ & his dull wife Ladybird only casually (1940–43, approx) via the Durrs, to know him was to loathe him. But some of the bit-players in Caro came SO vividly back to mind—people I hadn't thought about for ages, but adored in those distant days such as Tex & Wicky Goldschmidt.[28] Once they invited me to quite a grand dinner party—people like the Abe Fortases etc—the purpose of which was to inspect & view in operation the most extraordinary acquisition. It was a Bendix washing machine. Unforgettable, a miracle, clothes going round & round in soapy water—the most amazing sight. None of us had ever seen the likes of that before.

Much love & to Maria, Decca

To Sally Belfrage Oakland
June 12, 1990

Darling Sall,

Are you there? If not, why not and where are you? . . .

News of Brits Abroad. M. Warner[29] arr. yesterday more dead than a, plane hours late—on acct of her, Bob & I were bid to a V. GRAND dinner pty, over 100 I reckon, part of huge writers conference—lasts several days. . . .

---

27. Robert A. Caro's *Means of Ascent: The Years of Lyndon Johnson* (Alfred A. Knopf, 1990), the second volume of a projected four-volume biography. Decca had first read excerpts months earlier in *The New Yorker*, of which Gottlieb was the editor.

28. Arthur (Tex) and Wicky Goldschmidt were friends of the Durrs. Tex Goldschmidt worked in the water conservation division of the Interior Department, and his wife was in the Works Progress Administration. It was through the Goldschmidts that the Durrs met their fellow Texans Lyndon and Lady Bird Johnson.

29. Marina Warner.

Bob & I were at Table #1 with Marina, assorted others, & Ld. Weidenfeld, me next him. . . .

Ld. W. & I had a brief alliance (not to be confused with dalliance) many yrs ago over D. Pryce-Jones's biog. of Unity which my rotten anti-semitic sisters tried to get stopped, me on side of P-J obviously. Ld. W. tells me that these days whenever some routine request is sent to Chatsworth for, e.g., some flower prints, or historical document etc. depending on the book in hand, the answer is NYET—Chatsworth staff have been ordered to refuse any request from that quarter. He gets on quite well with Andrew Devonshire; they both joined the SDP[30] and both quit at the same time, a sort of bond. He told a story which he says is apocryphal although it sounds right. Phone rings, Debo answers. "Mrs. Levy, for you, Andrew." Andrew: "Oh Mrs. Levy of course I'd LOVE to come to your son's bar mitzvah. No, I'm afraid my wife can't make it . . ."

. . . Much love and DO ring up when you get this, Decca

To the Duchess of Devonshire   Oakland
                                                                  July 7, 1990
Dearest Hen,

Thanks for GID.[31] Sometimes I feel I may be coming down with a touch of it—could it be lying dormant from Miranda's day?[32] I do remember lying down beside the dear thing when she was chewing the cud & scooping out bits from her mouth to see what it tastes like. Actually rather horrid, like v. sour spinach coarsely chopped; an acquired taste no doubt as she seemed to love it.

Speaking of words unknown—you've no idea the amt. I have to learn the meanings of, e.g. CRANIOCLAST, an instrument to break open skull of unborn babe & dismember it & pull it out bit by bit to save life of the mum. All the rage until invention of forceps in 1588 to save both mother/child. . . . Luckily there was also a "syringe for baptism in utero" filled with holy water to be brought into play just before the cranioclast.

As you can see from the above, I'm mired in history at the moment—some of it jolly fun, esp. discovery of chloroform & its use by Queen Victoria in 1853 for her EIGHTH child (she was 33 at the time). The first baby delivered with chloroform, 1847, was christened Anaesthesia—rather a pretty name for a girl? First Russian child to be vaccinated was a boy called Vaccinoff.

I've got lots of biogs. of Q. Victoria but none totally satisfactory re the in-

---

30. Social Democratic Party.

31. The duchess had sent Decca an article of reflections she had written for the *Telegraph Weekend Magazine*. Among the issues she discussed in the article was a pamphlet sent in response to her request for a simple technical guide to the native breeds of sheep. She said the pamphlet—a "gripping read"—included the many regional names for gid, with which she tantalized her readers. Gid is a disease of herbivores, especially sheep, caused by tapeworm larvae in the brain and characterized by vertigo.

32. Miranda was Decca's beloved pet sheep in her childhood.

teresting CHLOROFORM experience. So I wrote off to the Archivist at Windsor Castle & I must say he was incredibly obliging; sent amongst other things some letters from Q. Vict. to the Duch. of Sutherland re chloroform— all in her hopeless handwriting, learned no doubt from that rotten Baroness Lehzen, what a fool for a governess. However I got some hist. students to transcribe them. Such is la bloody old vie trying to write a book while suffering from GID.

Do send every word about yr dance[33] . . . avid for a letter from you.

               Much love, Henderson

Did you succeed in fending off the press? In my experience, the more one fends 'em off the more avid they get & make up tons of bosh. Or they subvert guests to spy for them. Actually I think that on the whole the Brit. press are even worse than Yanks for this sort of thing. . . .

To David Pleydell-Bouverie   Oakland
                                         July 31, 1990

Dearest David,

Last wknd surpassed everything so far <u>chez vous</u>: perfect company, smashing food, adorable newcomers such as various Johns (John biologist & v. amusing John butler—I wish you cld have seen his killing act of trip-near-fall with precious leap-frogs)—everything just about PERFECT. And TOI—in a sunny mood, <u>for the most part</u>, always the high point of every visit.

Having said all that—every word from the heart—don't be X if I take you to task . . .

Dec-baiting—which I am, of course, used to from you but seemed to take on a rather virulent tone at Sunday lunch. I'd love to explain to you a) reason for joining CP, b) what we did in said org. in Oakland, 1947–56, c) reasons for leaving in 1958. However, why should I, as I wrote it all down to best of ability in <u>A Fine Old Conflict</u>, which I sent to you when first published—if you've lost it, will gladly send another with relevant pages marked so you don't have to plough through the whole boring book. But I should much love to get through to you on this perennially knotty thorn in side, to hopelessly mix metaphors. (Oh dear! Split infinitive, to top all.) . . .

A final word about censorship Mapplethorpe-wise[34] & feelings of majority taxpayers: Your point was that of course you have no quarrel with pornography

---

33. See August 24 letter to the duchess.

34. On April 7, 1990, police raided the opening of an exhibit of 175 Robert Mapplethorpe photographs—some of them with sadomasochistic, child nudity, and homosexual themes—at the Contemporary Arts Center in Cincinnati, temporarily closing the museum. The arts center and its director, Dennis Barrie, were charged with pandering obscenity; they were acquitted later in the year. The National Endowment for the Arts, among the Mapplethorpe exhibit's funders, became the focus of a long and vitriolic dispute about the role of the government in arts funding.

per se, it's had a huge & important role down the centuries in art & lit. However, gov't supported projects involving TAXPAYERS' MONEY is another matter, if majority of said taxpayers are bound to hate the product, as per Mapplethorpe.

Are you aware that the self-same argument is used by Southern library trustees to ban the works of the likes of Maya Angelou, A. Walker,[35] almost all blacks and a huge number of blk. female writers? "Our taxpayers—who pay for the public libraries—hate & loathe these books." Do you want Mr. & Mrs. Average Taxpayer to decide—state by state, region by region, even city by city—what books shall be in public libraries, supported by tax money? A huge row in our home town—Oakland, Calif.—a few yrs ago when THE COLOR PURPLE was banned from school libraries on exactly your reasoning. Reinstated thank goodness by huge protest by local citizens including MOI.

David dearest—the Lecturer Lectured. Sorry, I couldn't resist.[36] . . .

Fondest love, Decca

To the Duchess of Devonshire   Oakland
                                                                      August 24, 1990

Hen—thanks awfully for scholarly report of yr ball.[37] Here's one for you, spotted by a sharp-eyed London chum. Fancy lobster & lamb en croute! I thought you'd be having a kedgeree, as Muv always did for her dances.

I do wish I knew who Miss Jerry Hall, tall Texan, is.[38] Supreme ignorance this end re the London scene let alone the Mick Jagger scene.

Obviously what one really craves is a splash of info. on the inner logistics of the enterprise which must have been akin to moving a small army from place to place. But I suppose that wld take a book (are you writing one?). . . .

No news this end, but one crse[39] note: We had a day in Stockholm where Muv had taken me & Bobo when I was eleven, reason being that it was last time I cld go 1/2 fare. The one thing I remembered was the City Hall, a sort of 7th Wonder of the Modern World. So it was amazing re-visiting it—entrancing. Tour guide told crse group it took 12 years to build. Red-faced chap with

---

35. Alice Walker.

36. Several weeks later Decca wrote to a mutual friend about Pleydell-Bouverie: "Actually the dear old soul has a long history of chucking over—banishing supposed fond friends. . . . I see from his latest that I am not totally banished."

37. The "scholarly report" was an account in the Mandrake column of the *Sunday Telegraph* that began, "Some scholars of these matters have been assuring me all week that the Duke of Devonshire's ball last Saturday night and Sunday morning was the grandest the country has seen since before the Second World War. Others held out for it having been the grandest of the whole century. But all agreed that the only one definitely to beat it was the last to be given by the same family"—in 1897.

38. Hall, a model and—as of a few months later—wife of rock icon Mick Jagger, had been one of those in attendance at the ball.

39. Decca was working at the time on an article about her recent Scandinavian cruise.

matching red trousers: "Twelve years! Didn't they put it out for competitive bids? I'd have gone broke if it took 12 years." He's a building contractor, natch, from Dallas. . . .

Much love, Yr Hen

To James Forman Jr.   Oakland
                                                                October 1, 1990

Dearest Oy #1,

Thanks awfully for that AMAZING diary—obeying yr instructions I dashed it straight off to Dinky so haven't got it to refer to in a letter. I was fascinated (so was Bob) by the glam. threesome—Sarah, Cindy, Kathy—what a cliffhanger. As Dear Abby wld prob. say "I don't think you are quite ready to settle down, dear." Anyway keep us abreast of that soap opera. In a way, a bit reminiscent of Bob's early life—accd'g to what I've been able to gather, he was proposing marriage to Mimi whilst sleeping with her room-mate. And was never married until ripe age of 30 when he married yr Grandec. Re boy/father relationship: not much point in worrying about that unless it occurs (you having children). I must admit that in my case although I was v.v. FOND of my children, I successfully managed not to have to look after them all that much (company of teeny kids can be quite boring)—see A Fine Old Conflict for details. Or ask Dink; I bet she remembers lots of benign neglect. . . .

As for yr African trip—we couldn't make out much about what you were actually doing and/or thinking.[40] . . . Longing for more details re the that. Am hoping they will surface in the final report—also hoping, perhaps too optimistically, that said report will NOT be one of those ghastly consensus academic things written in the boring lingo of sociology. Do contrive to inject a splash of originality & individual style!

This end—naught much new, just plodding on in our various trades. Marvellous news that Dink/Terry are moving to NY! One will see far more of 'em that way. Your views of the move, please? . . .

Much love—write when you've got time, Grandec

To Shana Alexander   Oakland
                                                              November 15, 1990

Dearest Shana,

We had THE most smashing time chez vous from start to finish—superb dinner party with all those fascinators, and cherished chatting time with you.

---

40. James Forman had traveled to Namibia and Zimbabwe for five weeks with five other first-year Yale law students and two faculty advisors. The purpose of the trip, sponsored by the Schell Center for Human Rights at Yale, was to study the transition from military rule to democracy in those countries.

NY was also good value, lovely & <u>warm</u>. (I was in London one February which is usually enough to terrify because of the freezing cold but it was balmy weather. All the papers were nattering on about the Greenhouse Effect; but there was one letter-to-ed which said merely, "Sir: I like the greenhouse effect. Yrs truly . . ." My sentiments, I fear.) . . .

The Bouv dinner was a bit of a bust. His relations . . . were there—fairly OK but not exactly rivetting—and the most dread lady called Dr. Ruth Anshen or something of the kind. "She's brilliant, a philosopher, has a very keen mind," David said. She teaches at Manchester University. Trying to fathom the brilliance, I asked about her students—very interesting young people, they ask such intelligent questions. "Such as??" I pursued. "One asked, What is the meaning of the universe?" Jolly good, said I, and what is the answer? She didn't seem to know, too precisely. Later, she came up & sat by me & fixed me with her glittering eye & said: "You've been such an inspiration to me. I find your writing so profound . . ." etc. I was totally nonplussed & explained that I don't write profound or inspirational things, just journalism. I kept edging away on the sofa, she kept edging nearer if you get the picture. Later, I gathered that she had me mixed up with an awful writer on death called Kubla Ross[41] who specializes in the Afterlife etc.

Lit. lions:[42] pretty exhausting, 6:15 arrival, nonstop things going on, 9 p.m. dinner. They raised A MILLION DOLLARS for the library; means, I reckon, each paying person gave over $1,000 for the privilege. I asked . . . Jean Stein[43] (at whose table we were) how on earth this can be, & she said, "People love parties." A memorable quote. . . .

Bob was next Joan Kennedy, who kept taking notes all through dinner. When he asked why, she explained that when she was married to Ted she met so many interesting people; now she's no longer married, thinks she shld make notes for her children on people she meets.

As the Lit. Lions assembled, long before the paying crowd, one cld see they were dressed in their unaccustomed best (in my case, a top loaned by Maya). When the paying crowd came in, an hour or so later—my dear Shana, one was in the midst of every Vogue or equiv. advert you've ever seen. Cascades of diamonds/rubies/emeralds flowed up & down their necks/ears; one woman in a pure white satin dress—how will she keep it clean, one wonders? Only worn once, is the answer given by one who knows.

That's about all I can remember, aside from a few (VERY few) chums such as Ken Galbraith, awfully deaf so not much getting through to him. . . . [He] &

41. Dr. Elisabeth Kübler-Ross, the psychiatrist who pioneered the study of death, dying, and grieving and came to have a consuming belief in an afterlife.
42. The annual New York Public Library Literary Lions fund-raising dinner has honored notable literary figures, including Decca.
43. Editor of the literary and art journal *Grand Street*.

others passed by like ships in the night. Wave of the hand was all, no time to chat. In all, a weird & forgettable moment in the Sands of Time. . . .

Much love & a ton of thanks
for a marvelous time with you, Decca

To Polly Toynbee   Oakland
                                                                      January 11, 1991

Darling Poll,

What a smashing letter—worth (almost, as Philip always qualified every-thing) waiting X years for. I did love the Thatcher exit description.[44] And your coverage of Major Grey. . . . Never heard of anyone called Major before except for Major Major in Catch 22. . . .

Is Jon Snow[45] a chum of yours? I love him dearly. Once when Bob had gone home leaving me with the task of packing & fetching home a tombstone for Benjy's adored dog Jeckyll plus six souvenir Andy/Fergie mugs, Jon came over & did the whole thing with special bubbly paper & boxes etc. So Debo was on a telly programme flogging her book <u>The Estate</u> (all about the faithful old retainers at Chatsworth) . . . one of the other guests being Tariq Ali.[46] So Debo said "All our family are very right-wing conservative." T. Ali: "Not Jessica, surely?" Debo: "Well yes she says she's leftwing but she can't do a thing for her-self, gets Jon Snow to come over & do her packing." Stunned silence; E. Stan-dard said "All England was mystified." Doesn't take much to mystify all England, I guess. . . .

Fondest love to you, Peter, Nippers etc. Decca

To Marge Frantz   Oakland
                                                                      January 19, 1991

Old Thing:

. . . Tell Eleanor[47] that I'm v. keen to hear all details re tooth implants. I decided against, after hearing the HUGE PRICE and boring long visits to get 'em done. I know I'm v. rich, but wld far rather spend my dough on other things; and live on scrambled eggs & mashed potatoes with plenty of cream & butter. The periodontist (why are they all called dontists these days instead of dentists?) said "You don't want to look like a toothless old woman." I said, why not, as I am in fact a toothless old woman?

Much love, Decca

---

44. Margaret Thatcher formally resigned as British prime minister on November 28, 1990, and was succeeded by John Major.

45. British television journalist and a good friend of Decca's. She called him "The Packer," for reasons explained in this letter.

46. Left-wing British author, broadcaster, playwright, political activist, and polemicist.

47. Eleanor Engstrand, Marge Frantz's partner of many years.

To Sally Belfrage   Oakland
                                                          January 25, 1991

Dearest Sally,

I WAS pleased to get yrs of 19 Jan, amazingly fetched up here on 24 Jan.
How absolutely vile about yr burglary. I wish I knew what a plastic strip is, &
how to defend against them. This erstwhile tranquil block of Regent St. has
become something of a high crime area, viz: a 74-yr-old friend of ours who lives
a few houses down burgled & raped. 3 a.m., can you beat it; an old chap [who]
lives on the corner mugged about noon, wallet stolen & he was a bit roughed
up, nothing too bad but TERRIFYING nonetheless. After the rape, neighbors
were summoned to a block meeting where everyone exchanged addresses &
phone numbers but WHY? I mean if I was being raped (don't laugh, I'm a year
younger than the one who was) I shouldn't be ringing neighbours for fear
they'd be in the middle of a dinner pty or some such. I think I'd try police.
Therapy? Why don't they take up a collection to replace stolen goods? Do suggest it. How odd, come to think of it, that your London "support group" is
therapizing and our Yank ditto not. Quel switch of stereotyped roles of 2 countries. I'd love to know more about YOURS, I mean what do they DO? Stiffen
yr upper lip, or hold hands? . . .

To William Buchan[48]   Oakland
                                                         February 28, 1991

Dear Billy,

I've just finished reading Rags of Time which I enjoyed enormously. To
comment on a couple of things: your horrid Old Nanny had the exact same
phrases as our adored Nanny (see Nancy's essay about her, "Blor," in The
Water Beetle). "Come on Nanny, do run!" "I can't, darling, I've got a bone in
my leg." And, "as old as my tongue & a little older than my teeth," if one was
cheeky enough to ask her age. . . .

I'm deeply envious of your ability to describe places, houses, woods, etc in
such smashing & often lyrical detail. I can never remember anything about how
things looked, a great disability. People & conversations—yes, but the landscape? The house or room etc? Hopeless.

Needless to say, I was v.v. gratified at all you said about me, & that memorable tea at Swinbrook. You were a bit of a star in my life; I wonder if you
remember sending me a record of L'apres-midi d'un faune—it was sort of an
eye-opener as I was (and am) atrociously un-musical, but I played it endlessly.
Also, did you send a recording of E. Sitwell mournfully reciting her poems?

48. William Buchan was an early friend and apparently a onetime suitor of Decca's. The son of
John Buchan, the first Baron Tweedsmuir, he wrote a number of historical novels and other works.
His book *The Rags of Time: A Fragment of Autobiography* (Ashford) was published in 1990.

I think we were both fearful little intellectual snobs, going for the latest . . .
which made correspondence v. compatible compared to anyone else I knew in
those days. That had its good & bad aspects: at least it opened up a world of
modern lit. & thought. The bad part as far as I'm concerned: I never read any
Priestley, Galsworthy etc. as being too "middle-brow." How ridic. . . .

Love from Decca

To William Abrahams   Oakland
                                                    April 24, 1991

Dearest Billy,
    . . . I've been thinking a lot about yr memo & notes re the Certified Nurse
Midws chapter. Interestingly, Renee (who is usually all Hollywoodish glowing
praise for anything I send—the form in H.wood is that everything is FANtastic
etc) rang up re that chapter to say she found it disappointing, not the "Mitford
voice." Hence quite a bit along the lines of your criticisms. Ted Kalman
thought it should be "lightened up." In a word—BORING, the last thing one
wants.
    On l'autre hand as my friend Pele says, Dinky, Bob T, & Marge Frantz all
thought it was OK. Trying to sort it all out, I guess that my idea was to get away
from the Mit. voice which doesn't suit in all cases (fear of cuteness, overdoing
said "voice"), & the actual material in the chapter, covering such un-amusing
subjects as the Frontier Nursing Service, has to be put in for a proper overview
of role of mids. . . .

Much love—be in touch. Decca

To Constancia Romilly and family   Oakland
                                                    May 4, 1991

Dearest Dink, Terbaby, Ben:[49]
    All the interesting news is your end. . . .
    The NY move—must be v. time-consuming for Dink—or rather Constancia
as I hear she's now to be called. . . .
    Medical News. Bob's got an appt. with the walk-on-water Dr. next week, so
naught to report yet.
    And—you'll be amazed—I'm going for a check-up! Every autumn, when I
go for flu shot, long-suffering Dr. Cohn says it's time for a check-up, to which I
say "Absolutely. How about April—the cruellest month?" That's gone on for
several Aprils, so I finally gave in. Before going, one has to have various chari-
ous tests such as blood test & exrays & a thing called a MAMMOGRAM. Have

49. Ben Weber, Constancia Romilly's stepson.

you ever had one, Dink? Katie Edwards has one every yr & thinks they shld be reported to Amnesty International, as what happens is exactly like the tortures one hears described to compel a prisoner to confess or name names. I thought of screaming "STOP!!! Stop, and I'll tell you all the names of my subversive confederates . . ." but I was afraid the X-ray lady wouldn't get the joke. Anyway, I've a shrewd idea what the doc. will say: a) no breast cancer, so the whole thing was a waste of time/energy, b) you should give up drinking (fat chance), c) do more exercising (even fatter chance).

End of paper, end of letter, do ring up when things your end are more settled.

Love, Decca

To Herb Gold[50]

Oakland
June 27, 1991

Dear Herb,

Thanks v. much for the Mosley cutting. . . .

The Mosleys: a couple of anecdotes. When David Pryce-Jones published his book about Unity, he & Sir Oswald were on a TV debate, BBC . . . feigned politeness all round. Program over, BBC flunkies called a taxi & in the usual subservient way told the driver, "Please take Sir Oswald Mosley to the Ritz." Driver: "Not in my bleeding cab," and speeded off like a bat out of hell.

My sis Diana was a guest on an English radio program called Desert Island Discs, a program listened to by all England. It was set for a date that turned out to be Yom Kippur. Furious response from Jews, so it was re-set by BBC for an equally inappropriate date—commemoration of the dead in Buchenwald? I've got a huge file on it all. Anyway, here's how Desert Island Discs works (I was on once, aeons ago): You meet with the director, and discuss what records really meant a lot to you & you'd like to have on a desert island. (In my case, the choices ranged from The Red Flag to I'm Sex Appeal Sarah to Dancing Cheek to Cheek—the brill. researchers fetched them all up.) Then the interviewer asks you about bits of yr life, why you chose those, etc.

Accdg. to massive clippings sent to me from London, Diana was too ghastly for words. Repeated, predictably, the total lie that Mosley was never antisemitic. And prodded by the interviewer, said how v. intelligent & interesting A. Hitler was—he had such soft hands, and hypnotic blue eyes. One of the better clippings was from the Daily Mail, a cartoon showing devils burning in Hell with the boiling cauldrons; one devil is fetching up a body & saying "Come up, Adolph—Mosley's wife says you've got hypnotic blue eyes, so let's have a look."

Keep in touch, Love from Decca

---

50. San Francisco novelist.

To Sally Belfrage   Oakland
                                                                July 7, 1991

Sall—

. . . When in Oxfordshire, do go & have a look at Asthall church & manor,
where I lived until I was nine. Our night-nursery window looked out on the
churchyard. Once an uncle asked me if I wasn't afraid of seeing all those tomb-
stones at night? Not a bit (I am alleged to have replied), when there's a full
moon I enjoy watching Farve dig up the corpses to feed the chickens. What a
DEAR little girl I must have been.

My book's coming along at the usual (snail's) pace. I've finished Electronic
Fetal Monitors & Forceps Delivery, am about to start on Caesareans. My
smashing assistant Katie gets a bit uptight at the disgusting photos of forceps
delivery in my huge textbook of obstetrics, so I have to quick shut the book
when she comes. . . .

                                                                Love, Decca

To Dolly McPherson   Oakland
                                                            September 4, 1991

Dearest Dolly,

. . . Yours of Aug. 27, with copy of Maya's article,[51] just arrived. Maya rang
up a day or two ago to say she was sending the article plus numerous comments,
so far hasn't arrived.

Anyway, what follows is <u>Eyes Only</u> as I'll be writing to Maya when/if the
promised package with comments arrives. At that point, I'll tell her my opinion. <u>This is just for you.</u>

I was first puzzled, then appalled, and finally alarmed at the article. <u>Disorder
out of chaos</u> would be my characterization.[52]

There seems to be a Fatal Flaw in her logic (or rather lack of) as she
approaches her peroration of endorsement of C. Thomas. Starting off in
pseudo-scholarly fashion (OK, omit the pseudo—just that I objected to that
sort of TONE but it's unimportant) with "The Prince," whence as she points

---

51. Angelou had written an Op-Ed essay that was published by the *New York Times* on August
25, 1991, entitled "I Dare to Hope," in which she had endorsed the controversial appointment of
conservative African American judge Clarence Thomas to the U.S. Supreme Court. In the essay,
Angelou said, ". . . we know as well that if efforts to scuttle his appointment are successful, another
conservative possibly more harmful, and one who has neither our history nor culture in common
with us, will be seated firmly on the bench till death or decision rules otherwise." She argued, "The
black youngsters of today must ask black leaders: If you can't make an effort to reach, reconstruct
and save a black man who has graduated from Yale, how can you reach down here in this drug-
filled, hate-filled cesspool where I live and save me?" Angelou summed up: "Because Clarence
Thomas has been poor, has been nearly suffocated by the acrid odor of racial discrimination, is
intelligent, well trained, black and young enough to be won over again, I support him."

52. McPherson was the author of *Order Out of Chaos: The Autobiographical Works of Maya
Angelou* (Peter Lang Publishing, 1990).

out the adj. Machiavellian. . . . Maya seems to have lost her way hopelessly—esp. when saying "I am neither naive enough nor hopeful enough to imagine that in publicly supporting him I will give the younger generation a pretty picture of unity . . ." To me, that sounds quite presumptuous as the younger generation of readers of the Op-Ed page must be well aware that there is no pretty picture of unity with Maya in the forefront, as all the major black organizations from NAACP to Black Caucus are unanimously opposed to Judge Thomas. . . .

And who is going to "find answers that will help us to avoid falling into the merciless maw of history?" (Oh dear—what a dreadful super-grand style—but let that pass). Not by supporting Judge Thomas, I reckon. I'm afraid that Maya is falling into that merciless maw by her support of him.

What a disgraceful effort, & v. uncharacteristic of Maya. I'm appalled. What's happened? RSVP,

Much love, Decca

To Maya Angelou   Oakland
September 9, 1991

Dearest Maya,

Many thanks for sending yr Op-Ed article (which arrived, by the way, by Fed. Express last Thursday, 5 Sept). By that time Dink & others had already sent the piece. The enclosures were both from right wing supporters of Judge Thomas; didn't you get any letters from the opposition? If so, they weren't in the package you sent. I'd have thought that lots of pro-&-consville wld have clattered into yr mailbox. If you've got any more, please send Xeroxes of same as I'm v.v. interested in these responses, and in the variety of viewpoints about the nomination.

As you will have no doubt have guessed, I disagree strongly with your conclusion. Having pondered the article at length, it seemed uncharacteristic of you. There seemed to be a few lapses of logic that I found disturbing.

For example, as you point out, the word Machiavellian means manipulating the powerless for benefit of rich/powerful. I always thought that Pres. Bush was the Machiavellian one, when he appointed Judge Thomas? Not, as you seem to say, "the recent vocal opposition to the nomination of Judge T. to the Sup. Ct."

When you say that "we need to haunt the halls of history, listen anew to the ancestors' wisdom," what ancestors did you have in mind? Can't you visualize Frederick Douglass, W.E.B Dubois, Sojourner Truth (to name a few) if they were around to contribute to the debate in the Op-Ed page? And what about M.L.K. Jr.? I know that second-guessing the opinions of dead people on today's issues is a rather fruitless endeavor. But you did urge people to listen to the ancestors, without specifying which ones. . . .

Back to the "recent vocal opposition," that was mainly from the Black Caucus, NAACP national office, pro-choice (abortions) groups. Are THEY trying to manipulate the powerless for benefit of rich/powerful? Not as I see it.

End of paper, end of letter—longing to hear from you. PLEASE GET IN TOUCH,

> Much love, Decca

To Peter Nevile   Oakland
                                                    November 20, 1991

Dearest Peter,

Many thanks for SUPER batch of cuttings Thomas-wise; do keep it up, sending things from Blighty newspapers. . . .

Debo wrote to say that if we hadn't been sexually harassed as girls, we'd have been livid. A good point; the whole thing about Judge Thomas is that he was a hopeless choice (totally political, as all have pointed out) and shld have been rejected as an incompetent & a liar by those disgraceful senators.

Aunt Weenie: my mother's youngest sister. Her family consisted of two boys, George & Geoffrey, my mother, then Aunt Weenie. When Uncle George died I wrote to ask Muv what he'd died of. "He died of a nasty pain," she answered. Which I suppose we'll all do, eventually.

Uncle Geoff was the author of a self-published book called Writings of a Rebel, consisting of all his letters both published & unpublished to the Times.

He became a total recluse, lived alone in a London flat—nobody in the family heard from him or saw him for decades. After my mother died, Aunt Weenie rang him up. "Geoff," she said: "George is dead, and now Sydney's gone. Don't you think we should meet?" A long pause, and then: "But we <u>have</u> met," said Uncle Geoff. End of conversation.

Back to work on my bk, The American Way of Birth (from the Grave to the Cradle, so to speak).

> Much love, Decca

To Maya Angelou   Oakland
                                                    December 12, 1991

Dearest, dearly beloved Maya:

I can't tell you how vastly relieved & pleased I was to get yr letter.[53] I've been in ghastly shape ever since yr shitty/pity note in my mailbox. Talk about losing

---

53. This letter followed a period during which Decca and Angelou had, in Decca's words, "a terrible falling-out." Angelou had been enraged by a letter Decca wrote her, but Decca was never certain which one it was. In the course of their estrangement, Angelou had left a vulgar doggerel note in Decca's mailbox. At one point, Decca wrote Angelou to say that she "craves" to hear from her, and she cited a song she had heard at Tony Richardson's French home, a 1954 hit for a British group called the Beverley Sisters: "It went something like: 'God save the mister/Who comes between me and my sister, and God save the sister who comes between me and my man.' Ref. in this case is obviously Justice Thomas. So let's drop him as a topic; we've both had our say, and we each knows where the other stands. No point in pursuing the subject—unless YOU want to, obviously!"

arm or foot—to me, it was approaching the misery of <u>death of a friendship</u>. I was longing to ring you up but feared to do so, thinking you might just hang up on me. Well—ask Dinky, or ask Dolly, as I confided in both those stalwart souls about the terror that you would forever be on non-speakers/non-writers. Their advice was "just pick up the phone . . ." which I didn't, for aforementioned reason.

Another problem was—I wasn't at all sure WHICH letter was the shitty one. . . .

As to the Bouv factor, I expect that I did tell him that you/I had a disagreement Clarence Thomas-wise, & I very likely did say that I'd written to you re the that. I hadn't realized that the letter was bruising—I thought it was just a dissent from yr view. Hence, no intention of causing you anguish by mentioning it to the Bouv in some glancing phone chat, no doubt. The very idea that such a discussion would be thought of by you as somehow an act of disloyalty on my part is most distressing.

Where I come from (and I don't just mean England, although that's perhaps the origin of what I'd thought of as ordinary behavior), one does discuss both in letters & conversations all sorts of disagreements on myriad subjects—without endangering friendship. In fact, perhaps enhancing friendship? A wee bit of hammer-&-tongsville, all cards on table etc. can be a splash of salt, just makes life more interesting, & friendships more enduring.

So this is just to say your letter was an absolute high spot, & thank you VERY MUCH INDEED for everything you said.

Yr loving (not unnecessarily mean) Decca

To the New York Times Book Review[54]   Oakland
                                                                          April 8, 1992

To the Editor:

John Irving's article (March 29, 1992) on pornography was a brilliant effort. I especially enjoyed his comments about cause and effect—whether there are fewer incidents of women being force-fed eels in Canada as a consequence of "The Tin Drum" being banned in that country?

Consider Amsterdam, acknowledged porn capital of the Western World, where you can't walk downtown without being assaulted on every side by filthy, absolutely revolting, movie marquees offering everything the most rotten heart could desire in the way of dirty films; sex shops, with God knows what for sale; porn bookshops and so on.

Yet Amsterdam claims to be freer of crimes of assault against women than any Western city. Why? One theory is that would-be rapists act out their fantasies by watching the dirty movies, reading the dirty books. (I don't pretend to

---

54. This is the letter as Decca submitted it. See April 23 letter to Sally Belfrage for the *Book Review* editor's comments.

know if this is true—it has a sort of spurious sounding logic, possibly dreamed up by the Amsterdam Chamber of Commerce. But let that pass.)

Further on cause and effect, I do remember being fascinated by the Kinsey Report on the sexual habits of the American male, in which we learned that one out of every eight American men has had intercourse with animals. At any large party, I couldn't help glancing around to try and guess which of the men had done it—and with whom? Man's best friend? A sheep? A horse? The report was disappointingly reticent on this score. Have the Animal Rights advocates been heard from on this subject? For is it not possible that a reader of the Kinsey Report might become so titillated as to have a go with a pig, just to see what it's like?

Yours truly, Jessica Mitford

To Emma (the Good) Tennant   Oakland
                                                                   April 21, 1992

Darling Em,

. . . Am writing in a terrific rush as am still mired in book galleys—by the way, feminists may rather loathe it as it takes a few digs, though on the whole pro their pt of view.

Children's bks.

From earliest days, Struwwelpeter.[55] A marvellous book, now of course banned by the pseudo-psychs on ground of the AWFULNESS to the infant psyche of the messages therein. One of the crueller lines, in Conrad & Long-Legged Scissor-man,[56] is when Mamma comes back & sees his bleeding stumps. "Aha! said Mamma. I knew he'd come to naughty little suck-a-thumb."[57] Which I admit was rather cold of her—I mean she might have thought of a bandage or something.

Next, about 5 or 6 yrs old: The Little Duke by Charlotte M. Yonge. . . . A thrilling book, only marred for me by the memory of Muv reading it to us, & there was a phrase in there about the little Duke & co. having their dinner at a "rude table." I exclaimed about that—"fancy a table being rude!" Cruel sisters shouted with laughter at my ignorance.

---

55. Heinrich Hoffmann's popular nineteenth century children's book *Der Struwwelpeter* (usually translated as *Shock-Headed Peter* or *Slovenly Peter*). Hoffmann believed in scaring children into obeying their parents, a form of teaching that came to be called "black pedagogy." Decca said the book "was a great favorite of all of us—my sisters and myself" when they were very young. When she subsequently gave a copy to Julian Quick, the three-year-old son of her friends Barbara and John Quick, Decca wrote in the cover letter, ". . . a word of warning. It's exactly the sort of book that modern parents LOATHE," and indeed the recipient's mother withheld the book from her son until he was nearly ten.

56. "The Story of Little Suck-a-Thumb."

57. The "he" is "the great tall tailor," also called "the great, long, red-legged scissorman," who "always comes to little boys that suck their thumbs" and "cuts their thumbs clean off."

Next, 9 or 10—maybe younger? Can't remember. Mrs. Edgeworth's[58] <u>Moral Tales</u>, and another by her called <u>The Parents' Assistant</u>. Wonderful stories with enduring morals & very long words such as one titled "Rosamund and the Prodigious Jar." If one didn't know what prodigious means, one learned p.d.q.

After or about age 11—discovery of blissful trash, in shape of Angela Brazil's school stories, absolute heaven as one became the heroine—the adored Head Girl—as one read. Also, perhaps a bit earlier? all of E. Nesbitt.

By age 12, influenced by Nancy, I was a crashing intellectual snob. . . . I did love all the first real grown-up books I read, & shall ever remember them: Rose Macaulay & Rosamond Lehmann for example. I soon graduated to all of Aldous Huxley & D.H. Lawrence. . . .

Much love. . . .

To Sally Belfrage   Oakland
                                                          April 23, 1992

Dearest Sall,

I feel awfully out of touch   mainly, all the ANNOYING requirements of last-minutery re book. . . .

Was election outcome a horrible shock?[59] Must have been. . . . Ours[60] shaping up to be about the same. A rather good joke in Herb Caen's column. Newspapers full of that absurd creature Clinton who admitted smoking marijuana aged 25 but didn't inhale. Someone said that Jerry Brown[61] also smoked at same age but he never <u>exhaled</u>. We are supporting Brown but with heavy heart. . . .

[Enclosure] on pornography—read from back, starting with John Irving's v. good article in NY Times Bk Review. <u>Amusing moment</u>: the editor of NYT Book Rev. just rang up. He said they are going to publish my letter, but he had checked with the Kinsey Institute who told him it wasn't one in eight U.S. males but 8 percent, which in his view is one in 12. I said nonsense, one in 8 & 8 percent is about the same in my opinion. However, Bob agrees with him. He also said it wasn't sexual intercourse, just sexual contact. So Lord knows what will actually be printed of my effort.[62] . . .

> Fondest love dearest Sall—longing to hear from
> you & above all longing to SEE YOU in London.
> Decca

---

58. Maria Edgeworth.

59. In the April 9 general election in Britain, despite polls that had pointed to a narrow Labour Party victory, the Conservatives, led by Prime Minister John Major, won their fourth consecutive national victory.

60. The U.S. presidential election campaign.

61. The former California governor was running a quixotic, low-budget grassroots campaign for the Democratic presidential nomination. He surprised political insiders with his electoral strength in the primaries but lost the nomination decisively to Bill Clinton.

62. The *New York Times* published Decca's letter on May 3 with only minor changes. Decca's "one out of every eight" was changed to "8 percent," and "intercourse" was changed to "some kind of sex."

To Sally Belfrage   Oakland
                                                                  April 29, 1992

Darling Sall,

Our letters X'd. I was SO pleased to get yours. I ought to be packing[63] but
shld far rather write to you. To answer:

. . . Yr book.[64] Cedric's father is worth the earth for quotes. I have memo-
rized "It is no exaggeration to say that constipation may well bring the downfall
of civilization in its train." Be sure to put all that in. I've noted over the years
that most people's favourite bit in Hons/Rebs is quotes from Uncle Geoff along
the lines that "It is an actual fact that character is largely a product of the soil.
Many years of murdered food from deadened soil has made us too tame.
Chemicals have had their poisonous day . . ." etc. People love these rare old
eccentrics, esp. those with medical views. Also from Cedric's pop: concept of
allowing "free and fair play to the colon." . . .

Maya. I must have told you about our great falling-out—in fact, v. close to a
total end of friendship—re her Op-Ed piece in NYT endorsing Clarence
Thomas? . . . Anyway, we just got a letter from her saying how gracious
Princess Margaret is, oh dear. And yr cutting from Independent about her
White House visit & making Pres. Bush weep because she was so moving. Of
course she'd rung us up re that when it happened; her platitudinous words to
Bush along the lines "Our history is full of tears, full of laughter . . ." you get
the picture. Accdg. to Dolly McPherson, Maya has completely cast her lot with
right-wing Republican blacks, all Bush toadies. I'll tell all at more length one
day. No time at the moment as . . . I've got to scram packing-wards. I do wish
that Jon Snow was here to do it.

So—be in touch,

                                            Much love, Decca

To Maya Angelou   Oakland
                                                                  April 30, 1992

Dearest Maya,

Thanks v.v. much for yr London newsletter, rec'd eve of departure. . . .

Anyway, your London time was clearly a triumphal moment—Sally sent a
smashing article from Independent re same. . . .

Princess Margaret, & smallness of her: Nancy used to call her the Royal
Dwarf. I rather loathe the Royals, esp. Princess M. Many yrs ago, Bob & I
were at a dinner party at Edna O'Brien's house—all sorts of actors etc. at din-

---

63. Decca was flying to New York the next day. `
64. A possible reference to the book Belfrage later published, *Un-American Activities: A Memoir
of the Fifties* (HarperCollins, 1994).

ner. After dinner, a new crowd came, Gore Vidal[65] & followers, plus Princess M. The latter plunked herself next me on a small love-seat in the drawing room. "How's Debo?" she asked in her silly little voice . . . So I muttered "I suppose she's all right," edging away. Bob comes over, so I say, "This is my husband Bob Treuhaft." Bob: "Typical English introduction! What's your name?" Princess M. comes over all royal & says "Decca, please present your husband to me." "I can't think why you can't simply SAY your name," says I. So she calls over a sort of Gold Stick character to do it right. "May I present Mr. Treuhaft?" Such bosh, when she shows up with the Gore Vidal heavy drinking, heavy drugging set. When the princesses were little, I tried to spread a rumor in London that they'd been born with webbed feet which was why nobody had ever seen them with their shoes off; also, that Princess Lillibet (as Elizabeth was known by an adoring Brit. public) was actually the Monster of Glamis. . . .

Much love—Call us at Dink's! And come to NY.
Decca

To Dolly McPherson and Maya Angelou Oakland
June 29, 1992

Dearest Dolly & Maya,

I suppose you've seen the many obits. of Mary Frances?[66] If ever a death was what Victorians called a blessed release, that was one. I'll never forget the good days, my favorite memory of that smashing person was the gossips we used to have. Bob & I would stop down the hill from a Bouv weekend & sort of sneak into Mary Frances's house to chat about the whole thing. It was all Upstairs/Downstairs, MFK filling us in about the inner rhythms of the Bouv household, all those semi-lunatic servants etc. Oh she was so amusing. I can see her now, twinkling away as she told all that. And, of course, her incredibly good company at innumerable lunches/dinners in the Bouv quarters. Wonderful creature—and what a perfectly beastly few years she had at the end. (Dink wld never let that happen to me—she knows all the ways to put one out of one's misery. Also, come to think of it, she's my principal beneficiary, so it wouldn't pay her not to, if you get the drift.) . . .

Much love, Decca

---

65. The novelist, screenwriter, playwright, politician, and sharp-tongued, sardonic social critic and polemicist.

66. Famed author and food writer M. F. K. Fisher died a week before this letter was written. Mary Frances Kennedy Fisher, long in declining health, had lived in a home that Pleydell-Bouverie built for her on his ranch, where she moved in 1971.

To Arthur Lubow[67]   Oakland
                                                                                  June 29, 1992

Dear Arthur,

A few items:

. . . I forgot to make a list of the people that I suggested—both sides Atlantic—whom you might talk to. . . . It occurs to me that it wld be v. important to include ENEMIES—often far more interesting than friends, who are bound to give bland endorsements: E.g., American Med. Assn. types. Best of all, Kenneth Wagstaff of the Calif. Medical Board who wrote a furious letter to the SF Chronicle (not published, as it arrived too late) about my Chron. article. He'd be prime copy. He was featured on 60 Minutes the other day—marvellously evasive & self-serving. There must be others. I'll be pondering. Prime enemies were various spokesmen for the Funeral Directors but I fear their ranks have been sadly decimated by the Grim Reaper. Let me know if you are interested in this angle. . . .

Jokes for which I was brought up on charges by the CP Security Commission: The main one was when I was Literature Director (one has to assemble the lit, & make a pitch for the various items) when one of the pamphlets I had to sell was "Mastering Bolshevism" by Stalin. I introduced it as "Bolstering Menshivism"—hoping, no doubt, for a cheap laugh. Oh well, Such were the joys . . .

            Best regards, Decca

To Virginia Durr   Oakland
                                                                                  July 4, 1992

Dearest Va,

I DID love yr letter, do keep it up. Dink was so delighted that you came. . . . I v. much agree about Terry, a splendid chap. Sheet & pillow-wise—must be OK? As they've been married for ages, 12 or 13 yrs, & seem v.v. happy. He's a super son-in-law which makes our visits with them v. pleasant. . . .

Yes I do think [Marge Frantz] was put out because of yr attitude to the Eleanor liaison, although being herself a Southerner she must be v. aware of the weird prejudice against Lesbianism or any sort of homosexuality. That's something I could never really understand. In England, in my young day, it was an absolute given—nobody paid much attention, just took people as they were. Most men & boys one knew had been homo at some point. . . . Later in life, they either did or didn't switch to hetero. As you love reading about the Bloomsbury crowd, you'll see what I mean. . . . Of course male homosexuality was v. illegal until the 1960's—not so lesbianism, as Queen Victoria said she didn't know what it was, so they escaped the law! . . .

---

67. A *Vanity Fair* writer assigned to do a long article on Decca.

POLITICS[68] . . .

The background is that in 1980 I had a furious falling-out with the Clintons and Jerry Brown. It concerned the extradition to Arkansas of an escaped convict who had lived for 4 1/2 blameless years in California. . . .

When I was researching the articles [on Walker], I went to Little Rock & had lunch with Gov. Clinton & Hillary via an intro. from Bob. All to no avail. The interesting thing is the Bob/Hillary connection.

Hillary Rodham, as she then was, came to work for Bob as a student intern when she was a Yale law student, in the 1960's. Top students like Hillary were much sought after by huge prestigious Wall Street type law firms—some, like Hillary, were far more interested in left-wing firms like Charles Garry's[69] in SF & Bob's.

Fast-forward to 1992, & the election campaign. There was a v. long article in Vanity Fair by Gail Sheehy, an interview with Hillary in which every detail of her life from childhood on was explored—no mention of the internship in Bob's law office. Quite right, I thought, as obviously if that came out it wld be prime meat for the Bush[70] campaign.

Last act in this mini-drama: Bob & I were having dinner with Diane Johnson (a v. good writer, neighbor of ours) & she said, "I hear that Hillary Clinton once worked for you when she was a Yale law student." How did you know that, we asked? Turns out her son-in-law works in the White House dirty-tricks division . . . whose job is to dig up dirt on all the Bush opposition. So the son-in-law mentioned to Diane that "your friend Treuhaft" once employed Hillary. Presumably, the Bush campaign is hoarding this bit of non-news for later springing on the public.

From all I know about her, Hillary seems to be an excellent person—president of Children's Defense Fund etc. . . . Viv. Cadden spent some days with Hillary (can't remember the context) and thought she was smashing, which is also our impression.

Much love, Decca

To Maya Angelou   Oakland
                                                                                                     July 8, 1992
Dearest Maya,

Thanks a trill. for yr adorable letter of 27 June (rec'd yesterday—postmarked 1 July). I can't say how v.v. delighted I am to have it.

As to our one real row: It did arise out of a real disagreement on a v. impor-

---

68. This letter was written about a month after Bill Clinton sewed up his primary battle for the Democratic Party's nomination for president and less than two weeks before the Democratic National Convention at which he was formally nominated.

69. A radical attorney best known for representing Black Panther Huey Newton. He was a friend of the Treuhafts and legal partner of their old friends Benjamin Dreyfus and Allan Brodsky.

70. President George H. W. Bush, who was then running for re-election.

tant subject. I'm sure that my failure was to write letters that were abrasive, and what my children used to pronounce as "sour-castic." That was pretty stupid of me, & I v. much regret an offensive tone that may have crept in. However, for me, true friendship <u>does</u> include being able to discuss differences of opinion on substantive matters. That is, I don't relish the idea of taboo subjects on which one may deeply disagree, but which have to be swept under the rug as too sensitive for airing—or slugging out. Your views? Maybe one day we can have a rational discussion—which, no doubt, will not actually change the views of you or me but at least get this knotty question out of the way. . . .

Your comment about loved ones dropping off like flies. . . . [N]owadays much YOUNGER people keep dropping, such as J. Baldwin,[71] Peter Jenkins,[72] Tony Richardson. That stupid Grim Reaper has no concept of suitable times to be reaping. What a drag.

Longing to C U as soon as poss. Do give a shout when you get home. . . .

Your DEVOTED & ever-loving Decca

To James Forman Jr.   Oakland
                                                                July 20, 1992

Dearest Oy #1,

What a smashing account of yr adventures! After reading yr description, I yearn to see the Montg'y memorial and the Memphis museum.

A couple of comments:

Montgomery state capitol has been under construction for <u>years</u>, I'm amazed it still is. My favorite recollection of said capitol is circa 1961, when I was there. Within the cupola is a huge mural titled "The Happy Years," depicting jolly slaves grinning with pleasure as they tote bales of things. I've always wanted a photo of the mural—or a series of photos, as it goes all round the inside of the cupola; but there aren't any. No picture postcards, and by the time I got round to asking friends to go & take photos, the bloody thing was off-limits to the public as undergoing repairs.

Money, Mississippi: I can still see in memory a <u>Life</u> mag. spread showing laughing murderers of Emmett Till[73] & their companions after they were freed by an all-white jury. . . . There was a <u>most</u> ghastly book called "Against Our Will" by a then super-Feminist, Susan Brownmiller.[74] It's more or less a his-

---

71. Novelist and essayist James Baldwin, whom Decca had met through friends.

72. Polly Toynbee's journalist husband.

73. In 1955, while visiting relatives in Money, Mississippi, fourteen-year-old Emmett Till of Chicago was abducted from his bed and killed. His offense, apparently, was whistling at a white woman in a local grocery store.

74. *Against Our Will: Men, Women and Rape* (Simon & Schuster, 1975). Decca commented frequently over the years about her dislike of Brownmiller's "atrociously boring and erroneous book about rape." She told one friend, "[W]hat is feminist writing, if you know? I mean, how does it differ from just plain writing? If Brownmiller is an example, it means an incredibly plonking, heavy style with a revolting underlay of sisterly sentimentality. Ugh."

tory of the world told in terms of rape. S. Brownmiller wrote that when she first heard about the Till murder she was horrified; but on second thoughts, she decided that a wolf-whistle is after all a form of <u>verbal</u> rape, so perhaps he had it coming to him. I've always hoped to meet her one day to give her a piece of my mind—or better yet, now I've got my stout walking stick, a bit of a clobbering. . . .

Porn: well—you caught me out, <u>in a way</u>. After I've advanced my cogent 1st Am. arguments against censoring porn, people always say "so what about censoring racist, inflammatory remarks?" To which I answer, "That's <u>totally</u> different. Sorry, I've got to leave—see you later. . . ." Or if the argument is on the phone: "Sorry, somebody's at the door, I've got to hang up." By the way—the porn/great lit. debate is a bit abstract. To be absolutely truthful, when I was about 12 I read Lady Chatterley's Lover (having smuggled a copy in from Paris) but, I regret to say, purely for its prurient aspects as I was longing to know WHAT HAPPENS. (Smuggling was easy for a neatly dressed, polite little girl as Grandec once was.)

Yr. Loving Grandec

To Arthur Lubow   Oakland
                                                                        August 21, 1992

Arthur—a few thoughts for today's meeting. . . .

Debo's notion of me as a sort of dinosaur of the Left—hanging on as an old unreconstructed Stalinist—is, it seems to me, contradicted by my actual life over at least the last 30 yrs. But you'd be a better judge of that, having been obliged in Line of Duty to read all my wretched books!

The point about Debo (aside from the fact I doubt if she's read any of my bks except for Grace Darling & possibly Faces of Philip) is that while she's a Tory by nature, she's essentially a-political, takes no interest in either side as far as noting what's happening in the world outside Chatsworth. Anyway, by mutual consent we NEVER discuss politics—it wld be quite fruitless by any measure. She did once vouchsafe that she greatly admires Mrs. Thatcher's hairdo; she was sitting behind her one day & thought it was extremely well done. I think that's the only political discussion we've had for many years—or ever.

When Bob & I joined the CP in 1943, its glory days (CIO organizing, 1934 SF General Strike etc) were long over. However, for us it was the only game in town in terms of civil rights—the liberals, ACLU & NAACP, all fled from onslaught of McCarthyism.[75] Enough of that bosh as it's pretty much all in A Fine Old Conflict.

---

75. Once, in the late 1970s, Decca served as emcee at an ACLU event and, of course, approved of most of its policies in support of civil liberties. But she wrote to a friend at the time, "I more & more realize that I loathe everything ACLU stood for from 1940 to about 1970; but one can't very well get up & blast them at their own meeting."

But that's what I meant the other day when I said that one's political outlook is mostly a product of the situation in the country where one is living.

Decca

To Shana Alexander   Oakland
                                                December 4, 1992

Shana—it WORKED, at least I think it did.[76] The bit of paper disappeared into a sort of pit like place—the encouraging word SENDING on the screen. Enough of this blather. To explain how I got this amazing thing:

To my extreme delight, BBC are making a documentary of me bk as a part of their BIRTHNIGHT theme program. . . . So BBC requires FAX for them to be sending bits of script from hither to yon.

(later—Friday a.m., 4 December) YOUR ANSWER arrived! Oh it's a miracle. . . .

The Maya or rather Dr. Angelou news[77] . . . I've been in touch with her (she's one of my FAX pals) but a day or two before the news. . . . Catty thoughts: mine dwell on our erstwhile really serious row over the Clarence Thomas business (I'm sure I inflicted all that on you at the time???)—we patched it up, thank goodness as I do cherish her friendship. However, then she went to the Bush Black History event at White House. . . . However, I never discussed the White House thing with Maya—fearing another onset of non-speakers.[78] . . .

[E]nd of FAX, much love . . . Decca

To Mary Clemmey   Oakland
                                                December 22, 1992

Dearest Mary,

You are a wicked old soul, & so is Michael Davie,[79] for leaving that tantalizing message on my machine about Diana Mosley's review and NOT SENDING me the review. PLEASE DO SO PRONTO, or tell Michael . . .

---

76. Days earlier, despite her firm resolve (see December 21, 1988, letter to Ted Kalman), Decca had acquired her first—and at this point still alien—fax machine, for reasons explained in this and other letters. No one was more surprised by this development than she, but her astonishment soon turned to delight and she canvassed friends for their fax numbers, writing to one friend after another: "I've got FAX! Are you amazed?" Weeks later, she said she had become "addicted" to the machine and "besotted" with it, though still "terrified" because of uncertainty as to whether her faxes had arrived at their destination.

77. President-elect Bill Clinton had just tapped Angelou to write a poem for his inauguration, the first time a poet would address an inauguration since Robert Frost had done so at John F. Kennedy's.

78. The Clarence Thomas row was never far from Decca's mind. In one letter to a friend, talking of an upcoming visit with Angelou, she wrote: "Reminder to me: keep off politics."

79. The author and longtime *Observer* writer and editor.

I was away when you (or Michael) phoned here, in thrall to the BBC who are doing a documentary of me birth bk—to my extreme pleasure, needless to say. The two who came out here are Liesel Evans, researcher, and Steve Ruggi, director. I love them, they are incredibly young, dashing, enthusiastic & clever. . . .

Needless to say they are entranced by things like the Empathy Belly & the Uterine University[80]—I kept having to rein them in to get to the real point of the book. With some success, I hope & believe: they interviewed midwives, Good & Bad doctors etc. But they did make me go all the way to Seattle just for the Emp. Belly which was much fun. Also, you shld SEE the way they got into hospitals. Visualize me in a tiny hosp. room, other occupants being a woman 1/2 way through pregnancy & her doctor, who was doing Ultrasound. Plus, however, three TV technicians (camera/sound man/& the bloke who does CUT) and Steve, Director. Why did the doc. & the preg. lady agree? Because people love being on telly, I guess. Worse yet, the others (sans me) filmed a Caesarian, can you beat it. I wasn't there, so missed the director saying "Cut!" or if it was twins, "Take Two!" at appropriate moments during the operation. And, I wondered, what if something went wrong (as it always did, when I was on film) such as helicopter overhead, or camera man ran out of film? Did they insist on the Dr. putting the baby back for a re-take? I didn't dare ask. . . .

Merry Xmas, tons of love, Decca

PLEASE FAX BACK as soon as possible.

To Maya Angelou   Oakland
                                                                      December 31, 1992

Dearest Maya,

I was incredibly pleased to have a word with you the other day. . . .

[T]he agonizing over the poem.[81] I knew that wld be the case, I mean how cld it be otherwise? . . .

At one point, you bemoaned the fact that sayings like "Beauty is truth, truth beauty" keep creeping into your mind as you toss & turn—or Langston Hughes-isms, so that all sounds trite or semi-plagiarized. <u>Idea</u>: Spend some solid time re-reading every single one of your <u>own</u> poems. Simply read over

---

80. In her book, Decca described the thirty-five-pound Empathy Belly as "a huge womb-like structure with large breasts, priced at $595, [that] is designed to be worn by the male partner so that he can appreciate the discomfort of the later stages of pregnancy." (She also wrote that it would be the perfect Father's Day gift for the likes of John Kenneth Galbraith.) The Uterine University was Decca's term for a range of devices for "the *in utero* education of the fetus" through lessons or music communicated through speakers on maternal body belts. One such device was called the Pregaphone.

81. Decca appears to be referring to Angelou's upcoming poem for the Clinton inauguration.

each poem as though you were someone who was reading them for the first time—not as the author. Perhaps, if you did this, the unique Maya rhythm—or rather I shld say series of rhythms, as you vary everything depending on subject, and many of yr phrases within the poems may seem v. apt. Not, obviously, that you'll repeat them, but just be inspired by YOUR work not somebody else's.

Enough of that blather. That suggestion comes from my own experience as a lowly scribbler of journalism. Often, when I'm totally bogged down & can't think of how to write the next para, I get a certain solace from re-reading something in a long-ago bk—makes me think Oh! So I can write, after all?

KIT (short for Keep In Touch) dearest Maya. I know you are swamped, but still crave the occasional wave of the hand from you.

Fondest love, Decca

To Judith Martin[82]   Oakland
                                                          January 6, 1993

Dear Miss Manners,

Last April you very kindly agreed to be my etiquette consultant.[83]

I need your advice rather urgently. To explain: I've just got a FAX machine, and have been sending out lots of letters on it. One of my sisters in England also has FAX (much to my amazement) so naturally I sent her one straight away. I was surprised that she didn't answer by return—hers came the next day. However, she did say that she was in London when mine arrived, hence delay. Which brings me to the point: What is an answer "by return" in the case of FAX?

For a letter, it's simple; one should answer if possible by return of post. From California, where I live, to England letters take a minimum of 4 days, often much longer, so one is fairly safe in allowing a week or so before answering. One has had it dinned into one since childhood that if you get a letter from somebody, you should answer within a week—or max. two weeks. Anything later requires an apology, or rather an excuse even if untrue ("awfully sorry for late answer—I just got back from Alaska/Timbuctoo/etc," depending on lateness).

With FAX, should one answer within the hour? Or even 15 minutes, given the speediness of transmittal?

---

82. Judith Martin writes a widely syndicated etiquette column under the name Miss Manners. Decca once wrote to Maya Angelou about her correspondence with Miss Manners, saying, "I guess that intellectuals like you don't bother reading Miss Manners, the Comics or the Horrorscopes? Anyway, I rather live for those trivial things."

83. The offer was made in response to a letter Decca had written early in 1992 on behalf of a friend.

Perhaps every new technology requires some re-thinking of the correct response. For example, telegrams (which you are probably too young to remember) almost always had bad news; as they were jolly expensive, the answer was simple, such as "Desperately sorry. Mitford," only 3 words. Or if it was just a broken limb, not a death: "Rotten luck. Mitford." Again, only 3 words; ample, at a shilling a word.

Eagerly awaiting your response. It's now about 1:30 p.m., Wednesday. I'm sitting by my FAX machine.[84]

Yours sincerely, Jessica Mitford

To Maya Angelou   Oakland
                                                               January 21, 1993
Dearest M.,

I was SO distraught at missing yr phone call day before Inaugural. Dink rang, said you'd been trying to reach me—it was the one day in history when the blasted answering machine was on the blink.

Forward to the Main Event. Of course we knew it wld be magnifique—but hadn't realized just HOW marvellous, what a peak experience, it wld be.

We've taped it (natch) & played it over & over; and today the whole poem was in the SF Chronicle.

When you read it over the phone for "shape," sort of in embryo, I cld see that it was going to be YOUR stride, a total Maya production. Absolutely & unequivocally smashing. . . .

Yr loving Decca

To various friends   Oakland
                                                               February 1, 1993
Re: This Side of Glory by David Hilliard[85] & Lewis Cole, Little Brown, 1993. Pages 260–261; fundraiser, featuring Jean Genet, home of Robert Treuhaft & Jessica Mitford.

My recollection of this event is very different from David Hilliard's. As it took place more than 20 years ago, I'm sending my account—and Bob's—to various people who were there. I should much appreciate your comments on what precisely did happen that evening. Just an effort to reconstruct a minuscule slice of history. Here goes with what Bob & I remember:

---

84. Decca's letter was published in Martin's column several months later, but without the sender's name. Miss Manners's published response read in part: "As long as ingenious people keep inventing instant ways of attracting other people's attention, humbler ones, such as your own Miss Manners, will have to keep inventing instant ways of holding them off."

85. Hilliard had been chief of staff of the Black Panther Party.

To start at the beginning, I got a call from David Hilliard on a Friday. He said "we've got this cat Jean Genet here, he's willing to speak for us, we'd like to have a fundraiser at your house on Sunday." I said we'd be pleased & honored to put on a bash for Jean Genet to raise money for the Panthers—who should we invite? All the intellectuals in the Bay Area! said Hilliard, expansively. I said this was a rather tall order to organize in two days, but I'd try. So I started phoning around to say that this cat Jean Genet is coming on Sunday etc. etc. We put on lots of food & half-gallons of wine—turn-out was no problem. At its height, the party was wall-to-wall people throughout the house.

David & a few other Panthers arrived early, and stationed themselves in a row on a large sofa in the sitting-room. Cat Genet came—with Charles Garry, I think, and an interpreter furnished by Ramparts for his speech. I said to him in French, "what do you think of this large crowd, M. Genet? Are you pleased?" To which he replied, "All people are nice—until we start talking politics." Prophetic words, as it turned out.

Genet is a short man, so Bob got a step-ladder for him to stand on so that his speech could be heard and seen to maximum effect through the sitting/dining room part of the house. He spoke eloquently and passionately about racism in the United States and his reason for coming to speak in support of the Panthers, all excellently translated by the Ramparts interpreter. Contrary to David Hilliard's account, Tom Hayden never tried to muscle in.[86] He was sitting listening, like the rest of us. Question period, after Genet's talk. Somebody got up from the floor (actually sitting on the floor, with myriad others) . . . [a] professor or instructor at UC, or SF State?—Anyway, he asked a rather stupid question along the lines of "M. Genet—what do you think we should do?" So Genet, quite rightly in my view, launched into a furious attack against the questioner. "I'm from France, this is YOUR country, and YOU ask ME how to counteract racism in America? Asinine! That's YOUR job . . ." a tirade, well deserved I thought. Tension rose perceptibly.

At this point David Hilliard, in Bob's view not to be outdone in super-militancy, started baiting Tom Hayden. He was saying to Tom (who had been silent up to this point), "Come on, Tom, tell us how you betrayed comrade Bobby Seale when he was handcuffed etc."[87] Tom Hayden said he didn't want to speak. David kept at him. Eventually Tom got up on the stepladder & made a short speech about evils of racism, suggested that the subject shld be taught in teach-ins similar to the anti-Vietnam war [protests].

---

86. In his book, Hilliard wrote that Hayden, although warned beforehand not to "upstage" the Panthers at their own event, "double-crosses us, talks about the moratorium and Vietnam."

87. A reference to the Chicago convention riot conspiracy trial, at which Hayden and Seale were, at first, co-defendants. Seale was shackled in court for disruptively demanding to be represented by the attorney of his choice. After Seale's case was severed, the defendants became known as the Chicago Seven.

Tensions were up many notches. David kept baiting, Tom Hayden was con-ciliatory—situation explosive.

Dan Siegel,[88] who was also sitting on the floor, got up with hands upraised—saying "Cool it" or some such phrase. Or perhaps he didn't say anything. In any case, David Hilliard saw his hand-gesture as a threat. He picked up an empty half-gallon jug & tossed it at Dan—or prepared to toss it. Luckily for all, some-how the weapon slipped out of his hand and fell on the head of Michael McClure's[89] little daughter, who ran shrieking to her daddy. Far from the Hilliard account that the bottle "glances a kid's leg," it hit her square on the forehead, Bob saw the little girl crying & unfortunately told her to shut up—not having seen what actually happened. As M. McClure said afterwards, "It's always the children who get hurt in wars" (my paraphrase as I haven't got a text for this true statement).

Now it was my turn to mount the stepladder to say something along the lines of Thank you all for coming, the party is now over, do come back soon—and similar hostessish sounds. I led them all away, & walked down with J. Genet—who had clearly loved the whole evening, compounded as it was with race & violence, his favorite subjects.

Addendum to the above—Bob's recollection of Tom Hayden's remarks. (Bob was there for all but the bottle-throw, when he'd gone to answer the tele-phone in another room.)

"Tom made a short statement to the effect that he & the other defendants in the Chicago trial had protested the shackling of Seale but no doubt had not done enough. He agreed that it should be treated as a racist issue." . . .

To Donald Graham[90]   Oakland
                                                    March 21, 1993

Dear Don,

I don't know if you'll remember me although we've met glancingly from time to time at your mother's house.

I read yr letter in the NYT Book Review with great interest, & was extremely pleased to see that all those ridic. accusations/distortions were cor-rected by you—yours was, I thought, a classic of restrained and convincing rebuttal. Well done. It was SO good, para by para, sentence by sentence, slicing away at the reviewer's account of Kay's life as portrayed in the Carol Felsenthal effort.[91]

The only reason I'm writing to you is to give a totally different account of your parents when I knew them best, viz. in approx. 1939–40; and what they

---

88. An attorney friend of the Treuhafts.
89. The poet.
90. Katharine Graham's oldest son and successor as publisher of the *Washington Post*.
91. *Power, Privilege and the Post: The Katharine Graham Story* (G. P. Putnam's Sons, 1993).

were really like as a young couple. I haven't read the C. Felsenthal book but I saw an extract in some mag—Vanity Fair? New Yorker? Something like that. Anyway, accdg. to that, and to other accounts that I've read over the years, Kay was a rather pathetic, mousy little creature, dominated by Phil & by her mother.

That's absolutely NOT my recollection. To put you in the picture: my husband Esmond Romilly & I met the Grahams & stayed with them from time to time at blissful Mr. Meyer's house in Westchester. As I think often happens when one is 21 (my age, & Kay's, at the time) we formed a v. fast friendship & the four of us (Kay/Phil/Esmond/me) saw each other a huge lot. So what were they like? For starters, Kay was a funny, sharp, extremely attractive girl; Phil, an adorable fellow, v. comic—all the things we like in people. Kay awfully amusing about her parents, had a direct slant on them. In short, they were marvellous, unforgettable company. Kay—mousy, overshadowed? That's the most ridic. thing I've read about her.

Now, obviously things changed terrifically over the years when Phil got struck by that odious & mysterious disease of manic depression (which I know something about, as it happened to somebody in my own family—total change of personality etc. Well you know all about that). So he wasn't the same person. But Kay was always HER same person, & obviously an extremely strong & capable person at that. What I crave is her own memoirs, so do get her to buck up & write them.

Affectionately, Jessica Mitford

To Constancia Romilly and Benjamin Treuhaft   Oakland
(a jointly written letter)   March 1993
From Bob—typed by Decca

Dearest Dink & Benj,

This is about Nicky.

We seem to avoid talking about him, although I think of him often, as I am sure Decca does.

We had a call a few days ago, out of the blue, from a woman asking if we were Nicky's parents. She was a classmate of his at Washington School, and she too has thought about him a lot over the years.

"We were girl friend-boy friend, and I saw him the day he died. He meant a lot to me."

I invited her for tea last Sunday, and she came in from Hercules (near Pinole) where she now lives with her third husband.

Her name is Cecilia "Kick" Chun,[92] and is, as you might expect, quite pretty.

92. The Treuhafts evidently misheard the name. Her name before she married was Camelia "Cam" Chun.

She works in a hospice and likes the work. She has fond memories of Mrs. King,[93] as who doesn't.

She said Nicky visited her house often. . . . She never visited us because her parents were very strict and wanted her to come home directly from school. Nicky had given her a little heart-shaped locket to wear as a valentine. The poignant, heart-stopping thing is that earlier in the day he was hit by the bus and killed he had been at her house and she had returned it to him.

She explained (to us) that they spent a lot of time together in and around the schoolyard, and the other children teased her cruelly. She felt that it was because she was Chinese.

In giving the locket back she just said "I don't think we can be girl friend-boy friend."

She remembers his face when he left. She learned later that day of the accident and has felt deeply remorseful ever since.

She's a very sweet young woman. . . .

She brought Decca some flowers—Sweet Williams.

Love, Bob

Dink & Benj: P.S. by Decca

I wonder whether it was that abiding memory that made Cecilia choose that particular profession—hospice nurse, a fairly new specialty, looking after people who are dying?

I know it must seem v. odd that in writing A Fine Old Conflict I sort of airbrushed Nicky out of it entirely, not one mention of him—although he was such a star & hugely important factor in our life. Bob Gottlieb (editor of Fine Old C) understood, I think—or anyway, raised no objection—when I explained that to re-live his death (which one has to do, if writing about a person) was a bit more than I cld bear. The only absolutely awful moment of writing about such was about the death of my first baby[94] in Hons/Rebels. Although it was so many years later (the babe died in 1938, book written 1958) it all got refreshed in memory & was the most difficult thing ever written although only a couple of pages. So I didn't do that with Esmond's death—just a footnote saying "killed in action" or some such in Hons/Rebs, again thought puzzling by some readers.

A few memorable Nicky things—I told one to Cecilia when she came over:

He was such an amusing child. The unforgettable Mrs. King was telling his class about her day on Wild Cat's Peak, & she said "It was so windy, my skirt flew up over my head." Nicky: "Did the wild cats peek?"

I can see now in my mind's eye—Nick/Benj tumbling endlessly in play-

---

93. Mrs. King was Camelia and Nicky's teacher, and Chun confirms that both of them were very fond of her. Chun recalled that Mrs. King adored Nicky and cried openly for days in class after his death, as she tried to carry on with her teaching duties.

94. Julia, daughter of Decca and Esmond Romilly.

wrestling on the carpet in sitting-room in 61st St. A moment when Mimi came round—Thanksgiving? Something like that—and I said to the children "That lady almost married Bob. If she had, she'd be your mother." Benj: "Close call!" Nicholas: "You've no right to say close call, you wouldn't have been born at all if somebody hadn't goofed."

Then there was the Nick/Low Priced Al. Low Price Al had a Christmas tree lot, & Nick used to spend endless hours there helping him sell the trees—never got a cent for all that arduous child labor. Pele called him No Price Nick.

Tons more to say, but perhaps you two—Dink/Benj—can write to Bob with your ideas.

Much love, Decca

To the Duchess of Devonshire   Oakland
                                                           May 14, 1993

Dearest Hen,

V.v. glad to have yrs of 8 May. My corrections[95] miniscule . . . Point is, though, that reading the letters memories came flooding back—more like ghosts in fact. Here's the odd thing: I still haven't read the whole lot, am in fact up to page 216, Rue Monsieur & the Colonel. Reason is that although main horror-job (Afterword for me bk) is finished, everything else in life accumulated & now has to be attended to, so NOT being glued every minute to the letters is, Hen, a terrific act of will, or exercise of incredible SELF DISCIPLINE.

Comments on yr comments: Fully agree abt snobbishness already noted by Bob, who'd read the whole thing before yr letter came. I wasn't too surprised, always thought she veered in that direction. But it comes in undistilled double dosage via the letters.

Charlotte's editing: superb. . . . I wrote to C. Mosley saying her job of putting reader in picture via intros. & footnotes FAR superior to most collections of letters I've read. I rather hope to meet her one day—years ago I met Alexander,[96] thought him by far the best of a bad bunch. . . .

A few notes on what I've read so far: 1) H. Acton wouldn't fetch up his Nancy letters. What's that all about? 2) Prod's plan for the Island (get a low val-

---

95. On Charlotte Mosley's forthcoming collection of Nancy Mitford's letters, *Love from Nancy: The Letters of Nancy Mitford* (published in 1993 by Houghton Mifflin in the United States and Stoughton in Britain).

96. Alexander Mosley, Charlotte's husband and Diana's son. When Decca saw him as an adult in 1974, at the Duchess of Devonshire's Irish castle, she wrote, "[W]e hit it off no end—seems his best friends in Chile, where he lived for ages, were all Allende supporters etc, most surprising." Decca had also become friendly with Diana Mosley's son Desmond, from her first marriage, and his wife, Penny. Despite her strong feelings about her sister Diana and Diana's offspring generally, Decca always said there was one good Mosley son (Alexander) and one good Guinness son (Desmond). She also noted after one visit with Desmond and Penny Guinness and their children, "They all loathe Diana, a great bond."

uation & pay me off):[97] oddly, that's rather what happened although with oppo-site effect of the Prod plan, viz. it was valued at (I think) v.v. low price of 7,000 pounds so I was able to buy out the rest of you (Nancy gave me her share, which reduced cost to me) & re-sell later at a profit. Ha ha. I was v. bitter at the way Prod kept intervening—the Ward in Chancery plan,[98] his way of currying favour with the Revereds—and now the Isle plan. Esp. as I was the only one in the family who really liked him in earlier days. That's what I meant by ghosts, actual faces of people flashing through one's head.

I'll be writing again as soon as I've really pondered whole bk. . . . So far I think it's a great antidote to that horrid bk by Lady Selina. . . .

Nancy & money: Did you note how it's a wild see-saw ride, even after she became "so riche" (her to me in the Dior boutique—"poor little Sissie, she's so riche") she's either absolutely awash with dough or again sunk in poverty. Thinking back to childhood, & watching her all through engagement to Hamish & how she loathed Swinbrook & longed to be free of Muv etc.—her fate, to be stuck in that life because she hadn't got any way of escape being without money even after she started writing, was a huge influence on me, then and forever. That is, the rather obvious fact that one can't be indepen-dent of others (whether parents or husbands) unless one can earn one's own living). . . .

Yr loving Henderson

To Constancia Romilly and Benjamin Treuhaft   Oakland
                                                                             May 16, 1993

To Dinky & Benjy.

Dink rang up Bob this a.m. to ask what he & I liked best & least about 50th Wedding Celebrations.

To give my review in a general sort of way before answering specific ques-tion:

In my mind, they merge with memorial services—or memorial meetings, whatever they're called.[99] In each case there are eulogies of the much-loved-by-one-&-all Departed, no longer with us, or the dear old couple still with us, hobbling about (such energetic, wonderfully spry old things!) smugly accepting the tributes showered on them. In each case, dead or alive, the eulogies follow a certain pattern—the main & oft-repeated point being, that he/she/they were such a wonderful ROLE MODEL for younger generations. About now, grand-

---

97. Decca had learned previously of this ploy by her then brother-in-law, Peter Rodd. See letter of July 22, 1964, to Robert Treuhaft.

98. At the time of Decca's elopement with Esmond Romilly.

99. Decca had begun anticipating her golden wedding anniversary celebration years earlier, telling her children, "if Memorial Services shld come first, simply switch the venue."

children can be seen getting restive and/or ostentatiously yawning. By the way there'll also be references made to the fact that the eulogee (if there is such a word) was not entirely without fault, followed by accounts of a few harmless peccadillos. Joke. Laughter.

To get back to Dink's question. Actually, to be truthful, Bob & I have only been to two 50th anniversaries: Jo/Walter Landor, & Barb/Eph Kahn.

Bob said he liked the Landor one best because it was <u>small</u>, very few people outside their families.

I liked the Kahns' best because it was <u>big</u>, & one saw lots of people one hadn't seen for ages.

In general (whether for anniversaries or other semi-public events for lots of people) I far prefer the Benj/Dink scheme of no seated dinner with interminable courses of horrid catered food, but as you've got it Freedom for All, delicious grub <u>au choix</u>. In other words, a grand PARTY with one hopes lots of general chatting. Program shld be short??? Over to you. (But have you ever been trapped in a party where you're having a riveting conversation with somebody—cut short by interminable requisite program???) . . . If I am called upon to speak it will be more or less para 3 of this letter. I'M INCREDIBLY EXCITED FOR THIS ODD MOMENT IN LIFE, & V.V. GRATEFUL TO YOU TWO . . .

     Yr loving Decca

To Eva and Bill Maas[100]   Oakland
                    August 22, 1993

Dearest Eva & Bill,

Thanks SO much for inviting us to yr absolutely spiffing party. It was like being a drowning man, & seeing everyone one's ever known swim before one's eyes. . . .

I must tell a wee vignette before I forget it all. Edith Jenkins[101] arrived same time I did, so we sat together. She started telling me about a big gathering (I forget what for) that she went to a few days ago—her first real social outing since David died, so she was much looking forward to it.

---

100. The former Eva Lapin and her husband.

101. The wife of former San Francisco Communist and waterfront labor leader Dave Jenkins, who had died recently. Until the 1960s, the Jenkinses had been good friends of the Treuhafts, dating back at least to Dave Jenkins's days as head of the California Labor School, where Decca worked. Jenkins's wife, Edith, had been called to testify before the state Un-American Activities Committee at the same time Decca was subpoenaed. Dave Jenkins was later active in Democratic Party politics and became estranged from Decca for decades after he—as she put it many years later—"threw red wine on my best yellow dress for baiting him about his support of Hubert Humphrey—in 1968!" Decca said she "finally decided to bury buried hatchets with him" in a letter she sent him in June 1992.

Person after person came up to her with variations on the theme of "How are you feeling, my dear?" "It must have been a terrible blow." "Are you all right?" "Are you over the worst of it?" and much more along same lines. Edith said that by the end of the evening, she felt as though she'd had open heart surgery—which I thought was rather apt & clever. So the entire time was ruined.

So there are Edith & I sitting together, & just after she'd related this, somebody came up to where we were & said to Edith "How are you feeling? It must have been such a terrible blow. I do hope you are over the worst of it . . ." literally, the exact words of the Edith gathering from several days before. Needless to say I was overcome with giggles & gave E. a sharp pinch in the behind. After that, she stayed by my side upon my promise to protect her from future well-wishers. (I can't remember the first person—nobody I know; but lots more DID come up with similar mournful dirges, but I fended them off with "so sorry, Edith & I were just telling a few jokes.")

The crème de la crème was Barb. Kahn, who came up & said how sorry she was that David died and she had meant to write a letter, but was awfully busy. After she left, Edith said that next time anyone says that she'll say "As you were too busy to write, please shut up!"

However, as E. & I were giggling through it all, it turned out rather well & I think she really did enormously enjoy the party. . . . I'm planning to write to Miss Manners to ask her opinion of correct behaviour on these occasions.

Again—trillion thanks for smashing lunch,

Fondest love, Decca

ps Miss Manners & I are great penpals—at one point, she volunteered to be my official etiquette advisor. . . . So be watching her column, in case she picks up on this.[102]

To Emma (the Good) Tennant   Oakland
October 16, 1993

Darling Emma:

Just arrived last night more dead than a. . . .

Somehow even at Debo's excellent dinner pty . . . & other opportunities I've never really discussed sheep with Toby, esp. the awful thing for them of the sheep dip. I used to go in with Miranda because I feared her eyes wld be damaged by the virulent poisons in the dip, so I'd hold a hanky over her sweet eyes

---

102. A letter from Decca on the incident was finally published more than two years later in Mary Killen's "Dear Mary . . ." advice column in the English publication *The Spectator*. Killen called Decca's joking solution "ideal" and added, "Widows and widowers should seek out jovial minders to accompany them on such early outings following bereavement."

as sheep don't know they shld shut eyes for the purpose. Nanny used to get cross as my bathing suit wld be full of holes & I'd be covered in huge welts. The last time I saw Miranda was in 1939 when Esmond & I were off to America. Without telling Esmond (who would have thought it silly) I got a train to Shipton, went to Miranda's field, called her out of the flock—"Come along, Miranda"—so she hobbled out, <u>huge</u>, a vast plateau of a sheep, all her feet gone with foot rot. I sobbed all the way back to London. I suppose that by now she must be dead? I never tried to reach her again.

One of yr memorable stories was Isabel[103] saying "Mummy I <u>hate</u> my lamb." Different strokes for different blokes. Miranda was the light of my life.

Fondest love to all—DO COME TO CALIF one day. Decca

To Virginia (Tilla) Durr   Oakland
                                                                   October 19, 1993
Darling Tilla,

    . . . I just spoke with Va. . . .

Our conversation got me to pondering my own family difficulties of so long ago; and I thought I'd jot a few ideas about this sort of thing just in case you might find any of this relevant to yr own situation.

Like you, mine started with political disagreements, esp. with my mother but also, of course, Diana & Unity. Relations with my mother were EXTREMELY strained to say the least for <u>many years</u>. However eventually we were reconciled. I'd put this down to two main factors: 1) her unremitting efforts to be friends, 2) the fact that I'd completely established my <u>own</u> independent life, just as you have, in which I was able to respond to her friendship, so that in the end I really rather adored her & came to respect her unwavering loyalty to all her children. . . .

Then I was thinking back to portions of your really 1st rate autobiographical work "The Grievance." (I still wish you'd finish that book, & concentrate on life with yr parents in Denver etc.) . . . [A]gain a parallel: Debo was far prettier than I, far more loved by both parents—but once one is grown-up, surely all that fades into background & one can be terrific friends in spite of early life? These days, Debo & I are v. close, we correspond lots & whenever I'm in England I make a bee-line for her. All hatchets long buried. Put it this way: both Lucy & Debo are stellar quality, whereas you & I plod on doing our respective kinds of work & enjoying life as we live it. Va says that you hate Martha's Vineyard & all it represents—well, I cld say the same about Chatsworth & the ducal life there. But that doesn't stop me from loving Debo's company although our interests are miles apart. . . .

As for political disagreements—including divergent life styles—I'd think that unless they are irreversibly totally incompatible (such as the case with me

---

103. The daughter of Emma and Toby Tennant; granddaughter of the Duchess of Devonshire.

& Diana, whom I've barely glimpsed since I was 18—and then only at Nancy's death bed) one can get on quite well with people with whom one disagrees on most issues. I think that one shouldn't be <u>too</u> inflexible—or take a Holier than Thou posture—which can be a tad confining.

I do hope you won't think this letter intrusive; actually, I rather long for yr views of the above tentative ideas about the similarities in our situations vis a vis family.

Anyway—this brings you tons of love, Decca

To the Duchess of Devonshire   Oakland
November 22, 1993

Dearest Hen,

I rang Rud's hospital early this a.m., got her ward nurse, said I was her cousin ringing up from Calif to find out how she was. Answer: "She's doing poorly," which to me is hospitalese for Dying. (The usual answer being "She's resting comfortably.") I asked for a bit more specific info but the nurse said I should have to come in & speak with the Dr. So I said I couldn't come in, too far.

So a few hours later Id rang to say Rud had died. She, too, had rung hosp. earlier & told that Rud was "failing," so she too was clued in. (That did so remind me of yr t.gram to me from the Isle in 1963 which said "Muv Sailing"—obbido[104] having misspelled Failing. But somehow it did seem so appropriate for Muv in Inch K.)

For so many years, going Rudwards for her smashing Sunday lunches & other treats was one of the main things to look forward to when we came to England. She was such a rare character & her company total joy, to me. . . .

Yr loving Henderson

To Sally Belfrage   Oakland
November 25—"Thanksgiving Day (WHY?)," 1993

Dearest Sally,

I WAS so pleased to get yr FAX of this a.m. . . . much to say. Outline of points: 1) Maya's poem, 2) obits: Jill's[105] in particular, & general thoughts (not forgetting MINE), 3) horridness of Grim Reaper.

I. <u>Maya</u>. To me, of extreme interest.[106] As you prob. know, . . . [her] v. far-right-wing black [friend is] . . . the one who got her to write that ridic.

---

104. Decca's word for an English telephone operator, coined by her son because, she said, "that's how it sounds when [the English] say Operator."

105. Decca's good friend Jill Tweedie had died at age fifty-seven of motor neuron disease. A *Guardian* columnist—writing on feminist issues—and novelist who was a friend as well as colleague of Polly Toynbee, she had become a good friend of Decca's as well. She was a neighbor when Decca stayed in Kentish Town, and Decca on occasion rented her house.

106. Belfrage had sent Decca a clipping from the *Guardian* suggesting similarities between Angelou's inaugural poem and one by Norton F. Tennille Jr. See letter of December 10 to David Pleydell-Bouverie.

endorsement of dread Clarence Thomas in NY Times Op-Ed. I wonder if he fed her the idea of Norton Tennille's poem without revealing the source? I'll be watching closely for U.S. articles about this dicey business. Have chatted to Maya as late as yesterday about many another matter—as of then, perhaps she was unaware of it or not inclined to discuss it??? I, of course, shld never bring it up with her unless/until she does. It's what's known as a breaking story. Time will tell. The thing about Maya is that she's absolutely impervious to criticism of any kind—won't read, or respond to, critical reviews & as I'm sure I told you, our long friendship almost foundered on my disagreement with her article about Judge Thomas. Whatever happens in next few days/weeks, I'll keep you informed.

II. <u>Obits</u>. The first one I got was yours, FAXed to me in darkest Michigan[107] where I felt so lonely & isolated—nobody there, needless to say, had known Jill or even read anything by her. As far as I know her books weren't published in America—I can't think why. Lack of intelligent agent? Who knows. Your obit was superb. . . .

Now, forward to MY obit or rather obits. So far, I think I've got about 3 lined up, as follows: I wrote to you from Michigan asking you to do one for me, as yrs on Jill was so super. So that's for the Indy.[108] Next, Polly wrote: "Oh curious & bitter coincidence, on the morning Jill died there arrived on my desk a very fat folder from the Guardian of cuttings about you, asking me to write your obituary, which made my mouth turn dry and my hands shake with horror." However I bet she will, don't you? Takes care of Guardian. Third, remember how Philip Toynbee was asked to write my obit—see beginning of <u>Faces of Philip</u>. That was for the Times.[109] . . .

It's now 26 November—I'll never get this letter finished at this rate, so will close with MUCH, MUCH love,
Decca

To David Pleydell-Bouverie   Oakland
                                                    December 10, 1993
Dearest Bouv,

Oh dear I'm afraid there has been an <u>appalling</u> misunderstanding. First off, about Maya's Inaug. poem: I agree with all you say—consummate actress—delivered oration so triumphantly which the public cld understand—and the literary snobs who panned it. In fact I'm pretty sure that you/I discussed all

107. Decca was in Ann Arbor for three weeks to teach at the University of Michigan—"rather an awful experience," she wrote, "except I liked the students."
108. *The Independent*.
109. To another correspondent, Decca fretted, "What did that rotter Philip Toynbee actually say???" She tried to enlist her friend to write *The Times* when the obituary ran and to say, "Contrary to PT's biased & untrue obit . . ."

that . . . close to the time when Maya gave that magnificent performance. As I remember, we were totally in accord about the worth, appropriateness of the poem itself and natch the moving way she did it. As you well know, I'm far from an intellectual (more's the pity) and I loved the poem for everything it conveyed.

Secondly, on the plagiarism theme: if you read the Guardian clipping carefully, you'll see that Norton Tennille of Outward Bound & Chronicles (whatever those may be) specifically didn't charge plagiarism.[110] Here's what I did, when a London chum sent me the Guardian clipping: Because of a not-so-lightly veiled threat, I got the clipping to Bob Loomis, Maya's adored editor at Random House, so he/she wld be prepared for an onslaught by the various Maya enemies. In other words, what the politicians call damage control. I was just on phone with B. Loomis. He tells me the following: Norton Tennille is by no means in any way put out with Maya, let alone charging plagiarism. But there are Maya enemies lurking in the wings who'd love to get her squelched by this sort of thing.[111] Like you, B. Loomis points out that "themes" as such (in this case Rock/River/Tree) can't be plagiarized in & of themselves. . . .

The worst—to me, incomprehensible—bit in yr letter was when you taxed me with being irked by Maya's pursuit of the American dream, affluence & acclaim. Honestly, David—how v.v. unfair & untrue. Obviously there are lots of things she's done/written that I disagree with (the awful Clarence Thomas article, and her devotion to a rotter . . .) but I'd always thought of myself as her staunch supporter & admirer for her whole life of effort & totally deserved huge success. (In case you haven't noticed, I'm not a bit averse to collecting lots of dough for various things—such as completely unjustified huge advance for Amer. Way of Birth, & I cld mention lots of others. So I'd hardly be in a position to badmouth someone else for doing ditto.)

So, whilst loving her inaug. poem, I rather disliked her book called <u>Wouldn't Take Nothing for My Journey Now</u>, Random House[112]—that's what I referred to in my letter as being a non-book. I don't know if you've read it, or if so yr opinion of it.

Sorry to be so long-winded, but I was truly wounded by yr letter—beginning with the first sentence, "You are evidently puzzled & critical of Maya's poem," followed by what Howard C. Raether (head of National Assn. of Funeral

---

110. In another letter, Decca wrote that, if read carefully, Tennille's comments were "actually v. conciliatory—he just wants an answer from M. & her publisher. So STUPID not to have replied at once. My guess is that some lawyer . . . advised not to answer. Or possibly . . . just threw his letter away."

111. Decca said she was told by Bob Loomis that "there'd been a vicious attack on Maya in—the New Republic, he thought? saying she gets huge amts of money from Wake Forest for doing nothing plus many other adverse comments about her & her work."

112. This book of essays, published in 1993, has been called a "spiritual classic" by its publisher and others.

Directors) once called "a negative diatribe," my favorite expression because who ever heard of a POSITIVE diatribe? So that's why I wanted to go over yr letter point by point, hoping for a splash of a) understanding, and b) forgiveness for my transgressions if any. . . .

Much love, Decca

To Shana Alexander   Oakland
                                                                                December 12, 1993

Shana—I know you're off 1st thing Monday for conference with editors, but I did want to dash off a line . . .

Book, & editorial advice. In my view, editors exist to help sort out the organization of material—can be super-helpful in that, showing where things shld go etc. But they are NOT to tell a person <u>what</u> to write. . . . [T]he only answer is to follow one's secret heart & write exactly about what YOU want to. The editor, after all, is essentially only a helpmeet, who can be immensely useful if he/she sticks to the job of being an encourager, a goad where needed, and above all an intelligent & sympathetic dispassionate reader who can spot various deficiencies in one's material & see it all with a much needed critical eye. But never, ever, should the editor dictate the subject matter, which is for God's sake absolutely up to the writer. I suppose that being an editor can be, for some, like being a frustrated writer longing to usurp the actual author's job, interjecting his/her ideas of how the book should be written. For myself, I've been jolly lucky in editors: Bob Gottlieb, who was incredibly good at pointing out every sort of shortcoming in my books but never would have dreamed of dictating subject matter; and Billy Abrahams, also smashing at same skillful & sensitive advice & guidance all though, from 1st draft to publication. Sorry to be so longwinded about all this—actually lots more to discuss, one day. . . .

Much love Decca

To Charlotte Mosley   Oakland
                                                                                 January 21, 1994

Dear Charlotte,

. . . Like you I love getting fan letters, and even more so the un-fans. I'd love to see some of yrs from nutters. . . .

About the alleged "Mitford voice"—don't you think that's a pure invention, doesn't exist? I mean take Woman's voice, utterly sui generis, unlike any other voice ever heard; and Nancy's, totally unlike Debo's. Mine, 1/2 American by now.

About the sisterly letters collection.[113] As I said at first, queasy about the

---

113. Charlotte Mosley, following publication of her book of Nancy Mitford's letters the previous year, was contemplating a book of letters among the Mitford sisters. In reply to this letter, she said she didn't think such a book was possible without Decca's letters.

idea. But now I'm even queasier if there is such a word. For reasons a bit complex to explain in a letter, I'd rather bow out. Anyway, you'd have a smashing vol of Debo & Diana letters—and even Woman if she ever penned another like the one you quote in Nancy's about our funny old cousin, turns out to be B. Russell.[114] I was v. pleased to have the copies of mine that you sent me because I'd forgotten so much—such as Muv & the Adept, & her mis-hearing that Dr. Bell (who was about 30) was 65.[115]

I do wish we didn't live 6,000 miles apart, as I shld so love to discuss all this with you. But such is la bloody old vie.

Love & to Alexander, Decca

To Charlotte Mosley   Oakland
                                                 February 8, 1994

Dear Charlotte,

. . . The Nancy/Evelyn exchange does sound like a terrific idea.[116] . . . You say you hope that S. Hastings' forthcoming biog. of E. Waugh doesn't put everyone off the idea forever. Which leads me (gingerly) into the reason for not wanting to be in a Mit. Sis Book of Letters.

Accdg. to Debo, Diana was the one who chose Ly Selina to do authorized biog of Nancy. S. Hastings had never written anything except a rather bad children's bk & some mediocre journalism. . . .

But Diana had what film folk call Creative Control, which I suspect she will have in your Mit. Sis Letters book. Actually, I'd rather not be in the same book with her. I still think that the Diana/Debo letters cld be a v. good effort; just the two of 'em, back & forth, absolutely no need for any of mine. . . .

Love & to Alexander, Decca

To Charlotte Mosley   Oakland
                                                    March 4, 1994

Dear Charlotte,

Thanks awfully for yrs of 29 Feb. Terrific relief that you got the point of mine (not wanting to be in the bk of letters).

A few comments on various things.

Nancy saying that Diana had not really loved Bobo: N. had said much the same to me—probably in conversation not letter. She said that Diana was v.

---

114. Decca once described philosopher Bertrand Russell as "of the Stanleys whence we got all the bad blood."

115. See letter of August 11, 1959, to Robert Treuhaft.

116. Mosley was also considering a book of correspondence between Nancy Mitford and Evelyn Waugh. That book, *The Letters of Nancy Mitford and Evelyn Waugh*, was published in 1996 by Hodder & Stoughton and Houghton Mifflin Company.

jealous of Bobo because the Fuhrer like[d] Bobo best; so for the first time ever, Bobo was the favourite vs. Diana who had always been first in everything, if you see what I mean. Another Nancy comment (might be a letter? or just in conversation? but it stuck in my mind) was that as Debo, going on 16 or so, got prettier & prettier Diana got jealous of her, as 'twere "Mirror, Mirror on the wall, Who is fairest of them all?" Enough of ancient sisterly gossip.

Selina Hastings: you say she <u>proposed</u> herself, not chosen by Diana. So who <u>chose</u> her? Debo says Diana did. Actually there were others vying for the job of Nancy biog—one or two that I know—but Lady Selina (as she signs herself in letters-to-editor) got the go-ahead. . . .

Brian Masters:[117] Even I in my thick-headed way twigged to the fact that the headings & subtitles were not of the makings of B. Masters, but editors. But OH the content of his interview—Diana saying she never was anti-Semitic, never knew Hitler was a cruel monster until after the war!!! Well I never. Enough of all that; I can absolutely see why you are v. fond of her. She was my favourite person in the world when I was a child, our only falling out was over politics, now irrelevant from your point of view as all in the dim past. As for Selina, I don't really know her at all, only from the brief & v. unsatisfactory interviews when she was writing <u>Nancy</u>. . . .

Love from Decca

To Edward Pattillo   Oakland
                                                        March 20 "(or 21)," 1994

Eddie . . .

Va's fantasies about Winston Churchill: no such thing obviously. He never showed up at her house.[118] It was the Secret Service—I was staying with Michael Straight. So when the cops came & said "We've come to take Mrs. Romilly to the church" Va said "WHY I know it would take the police to get Decca into a church!" It was an Historic Occasion, Churchill/FDR at the Arlington church. So when I got back, I rang up Mrs. Roosevelt who arranged for me to come to tea & see Cousin Winston. That's all there was to it, except that Dink aged 8 months or so[119] peed on the White House carpet rather to my discomfort.

That's it for now. . . .

Love, Decca

---

117. Decca is referring here to an article by Masters "In the (hateful) Daily Mail," as she wrote in another letter. She said Masters called himself "a friend of D."

118. Decca was referring to her Christmas 1941 visit with Churchill a few weeks after Esmond Romilly's loss at sea. (See introduction to "America, in Love and War," the second section of this book.) The Secret Service went to the Durrs' house on Christmas Day to invite Decca to accompany them to join the president and the prime minister at an Arlington, Virginia, church.

119. Constancia was actually ten months old at the time, and, as noted previously, the talk with Churchill was far more emotional than Decca acknowledges here.

To Constancia Romilly and Benjamin Treuhaft   Oakland
April 12, 1994

Debo rang up with the sad news that Pam, a.k.a. Woman, died today.

Death totally unexpected. Here are the details, as told to me by Debo:

Woman (aged 86) had as usual driven all by herself to London for a lovely day with her great friend Margaret Budd. They went all over the shops & other London pleasures; that afternoon (I think it was last Thursday or Friday) went for a drink at a friend's house—Woman fell down the steps & broke a leg. Clear through fracture, bone completely severed. So she was rushed to hospital; bone pinned up, and by the next day she was perfectly resting & chatting on phone to Debo etc. Isabel Tennant (Emma's child) went round with her newborn babe, Woman v. pleased to see them—usual chit-chat about what a lovely child etc. Debo was on her way back from Ireland, keeping in touch by telephone; plan was, Debo & Margaret Budd to go see Woman in hospital as [Debo] arrived in London. A message for M. Budd—come immediately, so they did. Debo demanded immediate access to Woman whose bed was enclosed by curtains with some nurses inside the curtains. Nurses said better have a word with the doctor. So they did; he told them to sit down (bad news now obvious) & said Woman had died of a blood clot, I think it's called embolism. He said that often happens when old people have surgery.

So in one way a quick & merciful death. As Debo & I were agreeing, imagine how she of all people wld LOATHE life confined to wheelchair with somebody to look after her and—God forbid—do the cooking. (How I'd hate to be that somebody, come to think of it.) Last time Bob & I saw Woman was last autumn, Chelt. Lit. Festival when she cooked the most delicious 3-course lunch for Bob/me & Liesel Evans, completely single-handed.

So—that's that. Debo's got all the "arrangements" in hand, funeral on Sunday at Swinbrook church. . . . Debo is really devastated as one could tell from her voice.

Much love, Mamma

To the Duchess of Devonshire   Oakland
April 16, 1994

Dearest Hen,

Thanks awfully for yr FAX. . . .

Gloom all round. Dink/Benj awfully sad because although they didn't know her all that well, both remember with such pleasure the times they'd spent with her, & were fully expecting to see her next time in England. Bob's having copies made of some v. good photos taken last yr when we went to lunch there en route to Chelt. Lit. Festival.

Going through all her things must be a truly dread task, although everything is prob. neat as any pin in that house. In fact the thought of it made me feel quite guilty in advance wondering how MY poor survivors will fare when the day comes & they'll find naught but hopeless unsorted piles of things. Almost (but not quite) drove me to do a bit of advance tidying.

How v. excellent that Emma is to have the house & contents. I know she adored Tante Femme[120] as she called Woman. Ages ago, Em told me how at age 14 she was for the 1st time together with all the sisters (except me: Nancy, Pam, Diana & you), & how appalled she was at how all of you teased Woman—worse ragging than any seen since school, she said! So in a way, I think Em saw herself as a Woman champion or protectress. Actually, Woman rather thrived on all that teasing, don't you agree? Anyhow, as I saw it from afar there was a marked change after Nancy died & Woman had been such an utter trouper looking after her. Somehow it looked to me as though she really came into her own re appreciation of her efforts, & rare qualities.

As for me—there was a fairly long estrangement following her missing scrapbook accusation (which you may have forgotten, but I haven't) but of recent yrs we became great friends, Bob & I adored going there, she used to come to parties in London—last one, at S. Belfrage's where she & I sat side by side as a sort of inappropriate Receiving Line. All my friends loved meeting her, & vice versa, I think.

Well Hen I long for all reports of funeral etc.

Much love, Yr Hen

To Clare Samson   Oakland
                                                                                          April 30, 1994
Dearest Clare,

What a SUPER letter—thanks awfully for writing. I immediately rang Id & read it out to her, so for me it was a double bonus as often I can't think of what to chat with her about. . . .

Your letter brought back a never-to-be-forgot moment when Benj was 11 & you were (approx) 14. The background: Idden had been in an X-rated movie, the title of which I've forgotten. You were longing to see it, but she said absolutely not, forbidden to children. Upon which you said, "DECCA would take me." Having heard this from Id, I looked up all the X-rated films on offer & found one called "Les Amants."[121] Id's was long gone by then. So being enor-

---

120. Aunt Woman, in French.

121. Decca appears here to be confusing two separate occasions, judging by her contemporaneous accounts. In one instance, during her 1959 trip to Europe, she and her son went to see *Compulsion* in Paris but wandered into the wrong movie house and instead saw *Les Amants*, which she described as "a long, pointless and *fearfully* improper French movie" that "showed actual sex." (She said she told her son to "shut his eyes, but I don't think he did.") The incident recounted here, in London and also in 1959, apparently involved a different film, which Decca described at the time as "pretty good, we thought." She told the ticket taker her son was American, "thinking they wouldn't care if an American kid saw it."

mously flattered at "Decca would take me," I came round with Benj to fetch you; Id relented. We dressed you up in her high-heeled shoes & other grown-up togs of hers. You, Benj & I got to the cinema—you passed as a grown-up, but not so Benjy. The ticket taker: "Sorry, no children allowed." Me: "He's not a child, he's a dwarf and what's more he's an American. Get on Ben—run inside." Which he did, no more lip out of the ticket taker. The only sad part (for me) was that I thought the film incredibly boring. Do you remember any of that episode? . . .

If we get to England in Sept (which is the present plan), I DO so hope we can meet. I'll be looking out X-rated movies in case there are any.

Much love, Decca

To the Duchess of Devonshire   Oakland
                                                          May 14, 1994

Dearest Hen,

OK, I give in re FAX. But do note that this letter is dated 14 May—being a Saturday, won't go out until Monday 16 May, whereas FAX wld be there <u>this minute</u>. Never mind. I'll FAX no more to thee. (Alt: When I am gone, my Dearest/FAX no sad songs to me.) Postmen this end (in Calif—everywhere in America, I think) are far from orderly. The exciting little pile can arrive anywhere up to 5 p.m., oh <u>Hen</u>, the annoyance of it all.

I WAS glad to get yrs of 11 May—anyway, I thought it was me delinquent re writing as I've been thinking so much about you & longing to be in touch. You/Dink must have same genes or whatever it is that makes you plunge ahead & simply do what must be done, such as arduousness of all the planning of Woman's funeral plus aftermath. Dink was so impressed by yr v. smashing letter to her, which she read out to me by t.phone; and so was I, in view of obviously thousands to answer. (But Hen someone wrote & said you'd forbidden the clergyman to do a sermon—<u>well done</u>, although you must admit it was rather cheeky of you, and SO like Farve with his stopwatch set for 10 mins. for sermons in Swinbrook Church.) . . .

E the G[122] tells me she is indeed writing a memoir of Tante Femme—whether for publication or privately printed, she didn't say.

I do rather hope it's for publication—it cld be a super interesting curiosity of literature. What do you think? Well it'll be up to Emma to decide. I shall urge her to send it out to publishers, such as they are in these forlorn days of publishing. I mean—can't you see it as the sort of thing that wld fascinate people who are all too bored with bios of film stars, rock & roll types, and even the average Mitford sister? Do you remember a thing years ago in Private Eye called "I, Doreen, Memoirs of the Unknown Mitford Sister"?

---

122. Emma the Good, the duchess's daughter.

After Woman died . . . I kept thinking of all the dead people I've known beginning, obviously, with people like Nanny, Muv and my own dead children. Also Hen do you remember as children: "She's dead. She's expired. She's too neriogely put out her tongue, she's (etc). I must make her alive again. How shall I do that? I must prod, I must poke." I don't think I've remembered that for 60 years. But it doesn't work, alas, in real life.

Anyway, for you the loss of Woman must be incredibly awful. For me—obviously far less so, as we so seldom saw each other & also barely wrote letters to & fro. I did get v. fond of her in late years, but absolutely nothing like your v. long-standing & v. close symbiotic relationship—in which she was a familiar in your house & you in hers. . . . I barely knew her as a child, and only fleetingly in the last many decades; but I did (even dimly) note her amazing qualities, which Emma described so vividly.

Yr loving Hen

To the Duchess of Devonshire   Oakland
                                                                  June 24, 1994

Dearest Hen,
    . . . I've wondered about Woman not having any children. Was there any reason that you know of? I suppose she'd have made a super mum, esp. in view of the reviews of Emma & others of that generation, how they adored her when they were little. Conversely, Nancy—although she was said to long for children, I rather pity their fate if she'd had any.

    I do so sympathize with your point—things reminding you of her, & suddenly realizing that there she isn't. The exact same thought kept occurring to me when P. Toynbee died, ditto more recently S. Belfrage.[123] It really takes ages for the fact they are dead to sink in properly.

    Thinking it over, in my case it's the letters that I miss mostly—which, obviously, comes from living so far away from most dead people I really adored. (Oh for the writing on the env!) . . .

Much love,

To Virginia (Tilla) Durr   Oakland
                                                                  August 1, 1994

Dearest Tilla,
    Just back from L.A., & yrs of July 23 to hand. No—I'll never disinter the embalmed hatchet on acct. of calling Va Hell Cat. I think that's perfectly OK (as long as it's out of her hearing! Which shouldn't be hard, as she's getting a bit

---

123. Belfrage had died March 14 of cancer, and Decca went to London within days to say a few words at the funeral.

deaf). We used to call our parents all sorts of cheeky things like TPOF, stood for The Poor Old Female, & for Farve, TPOM. I called him the Old Sub-Human. Anyway there's no comparison, as none of us revered them as you did Cliff—oh, we also called them The Revereds, a splash of irony. . . .

[I am] avid for yr autobiog; it cld be so splendid. Do get at it. Other excellent Red Diaper memoirs are Carl Bernstein's <u>Loyalties</u>, and Mark Lapin's <u>Pledge of Allegiance</u>[124]—if you haven't read these, I URGE you to get them out of the library (may be out of print by now?). Here's an interesting point: the parents of all these, viz. Carl's, Mark's, Sally's,[125] all knew each other—and Va knew all of them, too. Here's another thought: Dink in high school. She changed her spelling to DINKI, craved cashmere sweaters, had ghastly girl friends called Diane & Nancy, although in a v. mixed high school <u>only</u> fraternized with the Diane/Nancy all white kids . . . finally burst out in college. In fact just writing about all this makes me rather long to spin out an essay about you, Dink, Carl, Mark. But you've got to write yours before I can do it properly, so PLEASE get with it. Childhood—teen years—up to about when you were twenty-ish or thereabouts. Just thinking out loud; honestly, the parallels between all of you, children of the 1950's, are striking. . . .

Much love, Decca

To Constancia Romilly   London
                                                    September 18, 1994

Darling Dink & Co.,

. . . This end, shall just try to report on one event, to wit: filming for Channel 4 upcoming documentary on the British Way of Death.[126] The scene, an embalming room in a London mortuary; a fortyish lady embalmer, & me to interview her. She was super good copy, absolutely parroted all the American undertakers' eternal song of the comfort to the bereaved seeing the loved one as they remembered her or him in life. I said that surely people rarely die in full bloom of health? Also, I told her about the Beautiful Memory Picture, a phrase coined in the 1920s by a P.R. man for the funeral industry. She was marvelous—said "That is indeed a lovely thought."

---

124. *Pledge of Allegiance* (Dutton/William Abrahams, 1991). Lapin was the son of the Treuhafts' good friends Adam and Eva Lapin. Decca was a big booster of Mark Lapin's book about growing up in a Communist family in the 1950s. She told one correspondent that Mark Lapin had a lot to "exorcise" because he didn't know his father, the editor of the *Daily Worker* and an underground member of the Party, until he was a teenager, at which point "Mark thought he was an imposter pretending to be his father."

125. The reference is to Sally Belfrage's *Un-American Activities: A Memoir of the Fifties* (Harper-Collins, 1994), which Decca had apparently been discussing in a previous letter to Durr.

126. The documentary, *Over My Dead Body*, focused on the increasing commercialization and Americanization of British funeral practices and featured Decca in a number of scenes.

Her aim is dignity & compassion. I picked up a lethal-looking tool from her table of scissors etc—a trocar, long with pointed tip. "What's this for?" I asked (knowing full well). She explained it's to remove fluids from the cavities. So—said I—you JAB it in the person's stomach like THIS" (doing it). "Is that an example of dignity & compassion???"

Anyway, it was all rather amusing. Lots more along same lines—a casket selection room, all caskets imported from America as there aren't any casket manufacturers in Britain so far.

So that was my 2 days' work, for which thanks to Renee I get 2,500 pounds vs 300 originally offered. She is a miracle worker. . . .

To the Duchess of Devonshire   Oakland
                                                          October 28, 1994

Dearest Hen,

I note that you don't love FAX as I do, so here goes by post, the Long, Slow, Natural Way (advert here for a laxative). To me, bottle with message thrown into the sea wld do as well. Never mind. . . .

Paris. Thanks to Charlotte/Al,[127] we did have a lovely time. First off, they put us into the Hotel Solferino which is smack next door to the Musee d'Orsay. Out of one's window are those beautiful roofs & mysterious windows—perfect spot, with ONE drawback. No bidet, which I was longing for, broken wrist-wise. Instead, a bath, shower, lav in one's quarters, just like any American motel/hotel. Someone told us that nowadays all Fr. hotels are like that. Hen, as a super hotelier or hoteliere yourself, do look into this appalling development.

Charlotte's dinner: There were all sorts of fascinators whose names I didn't get (does that happen to you, Hen? It's so awful, and if I ever set eyes on em again I'd never recognize). After dinner, Cha & I closetted ourselves with her showing me the banned by you bits of Nancy's letters;[128] some v. catty items about me & Bob, many more about the royal family. You shouldn't have done that, Hen. The whole point of letters is to reveal the writer & her various opinions & let the chips fall where they may. Censoring them for fear of offending the subjects is in my view absolutely wrong. . . .

Back to real life: wrist cast off in a wickertoo. . . .
                    Yr loving old Hen

To the Duchess of Devonshire   Oakland
                                                        December 23, 1994

Dearest Hen,

Thanks awfully for yrs of 14 December, about amazing wknd with prince & senator. Isn't Teddy K. a super-pig in all ways, imagine leaving that wretched girl to drown[129]—also he's a disaster as senator, mainly because he doesn't dare open his trap for fear opponents will bring all that up. What's the P. of W.[130] like in real life? Doesn't sound like much of a prize from interminable newspaper accounts. . . .

Enclosed is in lieu of Xmas card (too late anyway). The occasion was part of the S.F. Book Fair at which various writers had to do acts—mine is a Beatles song of yesteryear. . . . Hen—I bet you missed Woman like anything at Xmas. Oh dear I DO wish people wouldn't keep dying. Happens all the time here, too.

Ankle:[131] went to Dr. yesterday; not too encouraging. "Healing nicely" and all that, but he says another month before I can stand on it & a YEAR before I'll be able to walk properly. . . .

A spin off of ankle—this is EYES ONLY, don't tell anyone else. But I thought you might be innarested. . . . As both wrist & ankle[132] were prob. due to being more than tiddly at the time, I've gone on wagon. This has been urged by Drs. for years, on acct. of liver, & they are horrified when I admit to lots of delicious vodka starting in the morning. But not being too interested in liver, I paid no attention. What decided me was the trouble I've caused Dinky and Bob, <u>terribly</u> tiresome for them having to scram about looking after me. So the Dr here urged one of those drying-out places . . . or at the very least, Alcoholics Anonymous or equiv. group. I declined all that as I know I wouldn't be any good at it—all that appalling Frank Talk etc. So I just decided to completely stop, nary a drop of anything, even wine at dinner. Amazingly, it's working perfectly well; I've had naught for 4 weeks & to my surprise, don't even miss it. Known as Cold Turkey. The Dr. feared I'd get delirium tremens, but not a sign of it. Dink was afraid that after all the post-ankle excitement I'd start craving but I don't think I will. I've got all sorts of work coming up, mainly am going to write a long Afterword for American Way of Death, which has been out of print here for about a year; had lunch with Bob Gottlieb (original editor of it) and he was v. enthusiastic about the idea, will bring it out as a paperback. Also, I was spurred on by the incredible amt of research done by the makers of "Over My

---

129. A reference to Senator Kennedy's 1969 car accident on Chappaquiddick Island in Massachusetts that killed Mary Jo Kopechne.

130. Prince Charles, the Prince of Wales, a friend of the duke and duchess.

131. Decca had broken her ankle on the last day of a visit with her daughter and son-in-law in New York. She was hospitalized on her return home, and Constancia Romilly flew to Oakland, spending a week—as Decca later told the duchess—"bossing the hosp. nurses & Drs, absolutely invaluable. Don't you think DAUGHTERS are best asset in the world?" Decca returned to her house in a wheelchair and then walker.

132. The falls that led to the broken bones.

Dead Body," all that about the Service Corp. International which is taking over funeral parlours from Australia to England & already has 9 percent of the U.S. trade. Anyway, that's what I shall be doing beginning mid-Jan, & I've found a v. promising researcher (a young journalist who is v. keen to help; and Bob will also help direct the whole enterprise). . . .

Various treats are coming up, such as Dink/Terry are coming to stay in Feb for her Birthday, 54, hardly credible; and in April, Bob & I will go to Washington with Dink/Terry to have a good close look at the life of Oy #1, now working in the Public Defender's office there.[133] . . .

[W]ill close with much love. Henderson

To the Duchess of Devonshire   Oakland
                                                                    January 12, 1995

Dearest Hen,

It WAS good of you to ring up t'other day, & now yr letter of 2 Jan arrived (yesterday, so took 9 days). Re Topic A (for Alcohol, Abstinence . . . etc): I do know all about Antabuse; but for many reasons, am not sold on it. Mainly, it seems rather pointless; if you KNOW it makes you horribly ill, why bother, if you see what I mean. Oddly, 9:30 a.m. is just when I do rather crave a drink—that is, I used to rely on it for sticky moments when writing, or when having to make a difficult phone call—e.g. to an adversary, such as a funeral director or gov't official in the course of research. But actually I really have stopped craving except for odd moments now & then, when I find that concentrating on something else (such as work one is doing) helps no end. But Hen I'm <u>extremely</u> grateful to ye for bothering about it. You know how it is—only v. few that one is inclined to confide in, such as you, Dink, Bob. The latter have been simply marvellous in all ways re busted ankle (<u>and</u> non-drinking), such as Dink coming out here, & Bob has rigged up an intercom, means I can now summon him from downstairs hosp. bed if needed in the night. . . .

Much Love, Henderson

To Molly Ivins[134]   Oakland
                                                                    January 18, 1995

Dear Molly,

We met ages ago . . . but I feel I know you VERY well as a fervent admirer of yr smashing columns, plus collections of same, which I cherish.

At the moment, I'm embarked on an Afterword for a new edition of <u>The American Way of Death</u>, published in 1963. My effort is to update this now ancient book & describe the many new developments over the past 32 years. . . .

---

133. James Forman had graduated from Yale Law School in 1992. "He'll be needing some grandmotherly advice on how to handle murder cases, parking tickets etc.," Decca wrote another friend.

134. The bitingly funny, progressive syndicated newspaper columnist from Texas.

SCI is easily the juiciest. It first reared its ugly head in the 1970's; today, owns more than 9 percent of all U.S. funeral homes plus scores of cemeteries and—wait for it—flower shops. It is now acquiring hundreds of mortuaries-cemeteries-flower shops in Britain & Australia. The brains behind this malodorous enterprise is one Robert L. Waltrip, chairman of the company, & founder. Needless to say, I yearn to interview him. My hope is to come to Houston with v. excellent research assistant[135] & have a good look at the whole operation. There is also a Funeral Service Museum, a mortuary training center, plus headquarters of SCI, all in one vast complex in Houston. The museum has been written up in the Washington Post & other papers—it opened in October 1992.[136]

Now to the point. I'm wondering if you could put me in touch with some bright journalist, preferably in or near Houston, who might be inclined to a) write an article about SCI, the museum, the whole business. I could supply lots of background info. if you can find a live one to work with; b) furnish me with a bibliography & copies of anything that may have appeared in the Texas press about SCI; c) if/when I do actually visit the SCI h.q., act as what politicians call an Advance Man (or Person?) to line up interviews with Mr. Waltrip and any other likely sources of info, including funeral directors who are part of his scheme and others who have resisted it. This, I know, sounds a bit vague. It should get less so as I get on with research from this end, & have a clearer idea of goals.

I should be most deeply grateful for any ideas you may have.

Longing to hear from you,

Fond regards, Decca (alias Jessica Mitford)

To the Duchess of Devonshire   Oakland
                                                     February 27, 1995
Dearest Hen,

Enclosed a better version of Maxwell's Silver Hammer, PLUS Grace Darling.[137] I expect you'll complain that I sang it out of tune or something? Wish

---

135. Karen Leonard had recently become Decca's research assistant for *American Way of Death Revisited.* She had previously been a consumer advocate on funeral issues and had been widely quoted in the press. Leonard says what really caught Decca's eye was a reference to Leonard in a funeral trade magazine that identified her as the "Jessica Mitford of the Nineties."

136. Decca ultimately went to the museum, accompanied by Ivins and her assistant. As recounted by Karen Leonard, they were treated to a video of *The History of Funeral Service,* one section of which was devoted to "The History of Embalming," including scenes of the monumental funeral tombs of ancient Egypt. At that point, Decca is reported to have leaned over to Ivins and said, "Now THERE is a culture whose funeral directors REALLY got out of hand!" Leonard said they were laughing so hard that she had to usher Ivins from the room until they could collect themselves.

137. Two of Decca's favorite songs that she loved to sing full-throttle at parties and had performed and recorded at the behest of Kathi Kamen Goldmark on Goldmark's boutique label, "Don't Quit Your Day Job" Records. Some of the proceeds from the sale of this first recording, called Decca and the Dectones (a rotating group of pickup kazoo players), went to Benjamin Treuhaft's Send a Piana to Havana campaign. On May 1, 1995, the ragtag group performed at Town Hall in New York.

you'd been here so it cld have been a Honnish Duet. Anyway, do note all the ridic. hoop-la in local papers. . . .

I long for a splash of news. . . .

This end: I'm now almost totally OK. Just in the last 2 or 3 days, I can walk upstairs hence sleep in my own bed and best of all have a bath. Naught but horrid sponge baths for 3 months. Also can walk about a mile or so (with someone), & have been out to dinner/movies. No booze since 22 November, so that's all over for good. . . .

Tomorrow, treat of all time, editor of Mortuary Management is coming here for an interview!! My old prime antagonist, au. of many a livid editorial blasting me & my book. He calls me "Jessica" tout court[138] in his articles, makes me feel FAMOUS like Zsa Zsa or Adlai, no further I.D. needed. . . .

Well Hen do write. H. Birthday 31 March.

Much love, Henderson

To Christopher Cerf[139]   Oakland
                                                                May 3, 1995

Dear Chris,

Thanks a trillion for one of the absolutely best & in all ways most smashing parties of a VERY long life.

The whole thing was thrilling beyond wildest dreams. A wonderful mix of people. . . .

Isn't Kathi Goldmark one of the most remarkable humans ever seen? I still can't figure out how she got all that going—I mean the Decca & Dectones caper.

In the midst of songfest chez vous, Bob Gottlieb in loud stage whisper to Bob Treuhaft "But can't you stop her?" Later, to me: "My dear, in all the years that I've attended every sort of musical event, never, ever have I heard anything quite so a-tonal, so lacking in the rudiments of rhythm, so out of tune as your performance." Good for my character, I guess.

Here's a small token—one of the three surviving copies of Lifeitselfmanship, assembled on our dining-room table in 1956. I still remember the bother of all that stapling. But for 50 cents a copy it was worth it, in those pre-inflation days. We ended up selling about 1,000 of them. . . .

Much love and MANY THANKS, Decca

---

138. *Tout court* means "simply" or "merely" in French.

139. Cerf, son of Bennett Cerf, whose Famous Writers School Decca had helped drive into bankruptcy, had hosted a party at his home on April 27 to celebrate release of the recording of Decca singing, which was billed as "featuring her incomparable rendition of 'Maxwell's Silver Hammer.' " Proceeds from the CD were to benefit the Right to Rock Network and other First Amendment groups. According to Decca, when Goldmark asked Christopher Cerf before the party if he knew about Decca's role in exposing his father's school, he replied, "My father was a wonderful man—but that school was a terrible racket."

To Jane Lawson Bavelas[140]   Oakland
                                                          August 30, 1995

Dear Jane,

Re Barb Kahn, I've been thinking back to our conversation, also had a long chat with Kathy[141] about same. . . .

Kathy says that this depression has been going on as long as she can remember. Not quite my view, I'd have to say for about 20 years, K. thinks it's become such a total way of life that B. wouldn't/couldn't give it up at this late stage. . . .

It's such a shame, as Barb is such a bright, interesting, good companyish type when in a good mood. It's so ghastly to think of how someone so depressed must suffer a good bit of the time.

In a way, I might pinpoint the onset (which was gradual) about the time in the late 1950's-early 60's when people roughly my age, that is between 70 and 80, mostly began thinking of new careers, esp. those who like me & most of my friends had parted company with the Communist Party, which had been until then an all-absorbing interest. I don't know whether you know any of these, but a few examples: Marge Frantz got a PhD and is now a <u>marvellous</u> teacher at U.C. Santa Cruz. Eva Maas (formerly Lapin) became a social worker; is now retired from that, and attends numerous adult education things & has become the world's leading expert on CHARLES DICKENS of all things! Loads more examples, but you get the idea; people on edge of middle-age, 40 to 50, children growing up, went ahead with new interesting projects. Barb didn't. She never got a job, or took up any particular studies; did desultory volunteer work—I simply can't see what they DO at Physicians for Soc. Resp.—and so began to sink into a sort of permanent boredom with life. Do you think that analysis is at all on target? . . .

I do long for YOUR views of all this, and specially any ideas of how one could even begin to discuss it with Barb. . . .

                                   Decca

To the Duchess of Devonshire   Oakland
                                                        September 13, 1995

Dearest Hen,

. . . Thanks awfully for cutting re catacombs, that's REALLY USEFUL so do keep it up. I'm now going page-by-page over old edition of Amer. Way of Death, noting every single line that needs revision—starting with "Acknowledgments." In that, I'd put "My sisters Nancy & Deborah contributed a certain amount of misinformation." Can't remember what yours was. . . . [I]n the updated bk, you'll be in the Acks doubled in spades.

Benj: campaign has been huge success, pianos & money rolling in, & lots

---

140. A friend of Barbara Kahn (then Barbara Allen) since their days together at Vassar College.
141. Barbara Kahn's daughter.

more in the papers about it. He'll be off soon to Cuba with the pianos (in his briefcase? Who knows) and Bob's going along! Date not yet certain, they shld know later this week. Other tuners are longing to go, so I guess it'll be a large party.

Stella:[142] we got a copy of Sept. Harpers Bazaar. . . . First off I thought that S. must have changed her name to Linda Evangelista, the girl whose photo is on the cover, as all those models look SO alike. But then I noted a more Emma-ish look further on, the one with lawyer suit etc., so that must be her? I say—what WOULD Muv think of her great-grandchildren, Flora, Isabel, Oys #1 & #2 & their various lives. . . .

Much love, Henderson

To Edward Pattillo   Oakland
September 20, 1995

Dearest Eddie,

. . . About Nancy's furniture. Ages ago—when Dink was a baby—she'd said she was leaving all her furniture to Constancia. Then some years later, she said she'd heard that furniture got warped in America because of the central heating, so she'd decided <u>not</u> to leave any to Dink.

Amongst [my mother's] belongings were a silver tea service (tray, teapot, hot water jug, sugar bowl, creamer—the works, all sterling silver). Pam took those. She explained: "I know Americans don't go in for tea much, so I thought the teaset wouldn't be much use to you." Also, masses of linen sheets, hand-embroidered coronets and hem-stitching—some even from her trousseau, circa 1903. Nancy took those. She explained: "Ironing linen is <u>such</u> a lot of trouble, and I know you don't have proper servants in America, so I took those." . . .

Enough of this bosh!

Much love, Dec

To Benjamin Treuhaft   Oakland
October 4, 1995

Benj—yr FAX re Nicky[143] was <u>really</u> terrific, we both thought so. One day, shld love to discuss with you. Of course—as years went by, I thought ever so

---

142. The duchess's granddaughter, model Stella Tennant.

143. Benjamin Treuhaft had written his parents after cleaning out his in-box and discovering their March 1993 letter about his brother Nicky. In his belated reply, he told his parents that "finally, two and-a-half years after your letter, I cried over how sad it was for everyone that Nicky died." He told them that, like Nicky's childhood friend, he vaguely recalled fighting with Nicky "as usual" the night before his fatal accident and believed it had something to do with Nicky's paper route (he had been delivering newspapers when struck by a bus). Ben went on to say, "the worst was my feeling, which mildly haunted me for years afterwards, of inability to feel the horror and grief that wracked 574-61st St. I don't know what was wrong with me, I guess I was too scared."

often about what he'd be like aged 20, 30, 40 etc. and now over 50. What he'd have done, all that sort of thing. . . .

More on OJ:[144] Bob & I rather agreed with you, not sure if for exactly same reason—that is, we were pleased with verdict but thought he's prob. guilty.[145] Here's a memory that came back to me: we went down to the Oakland county court house to hear verdict on Oakland 7 case (charged with obstructing the draft office, or conspiracy to do so). Not guilty. So, restlessly not wanting to go straight home, we went to the Cafe Mediterraneum on Tel. Ave—and announced verdict to the people in there. One boy leapt in the air. "And the beauty part is, they're GUILTY!" Not quite an analogy, but made me think back to those days.

Let us know how things go Cubawise. . . .

Love, Mamma

To Frederick Hill[146]

Oakland
October 6, 1995

Dear Fred,

Here goes with a quick run-down of Les Evènements of Oct. 2–3, the Funeral Service Seminar in Tiburon, Calif. to which I was invited as featured speaker by Ron Hast, editor of <u>Mortuary Management</u>. Someone said—like Ralph Nader being asked to address General Motors! Not far off, considering that <u>The American Way of Death</u> is absolutely chockablock with Wise Sayings lifted from said mag.

Needless to say I was absolutely astonished at being invited. Visualize the emotions of a five-year-old being told he's going on a trip to Disneyland, or a teenager given a role in a Hollywood movie; that's how I felt in anticipation of this incredible treat—hobnobbing, or networking to use a more modern expression, with undertakers, casket manufacturers, vault men for two whole days.

My horoscope for the first day of the seminar couldn't have been more propitious. If you think I'm making this up, check Jeane Dixon in the SF Chronicle for Monday, October 2:

> <u>Virgo:</u> (Aug. 23–Sept. 22): Your progressive ideas could upset someone whose beliefs are very different. Hang in there! Keep searching for lost items.

---

144. Former football star and celebrity O. J. Simpson had been found not guilty the previous day of murdering his former wife, Nicole Brown Simpson, and her friend, Ronald Goldman.

145. In another letter, Decca wrote that she and her husband "agreed that a) he's guilty, b) we welcomed the verdict as Benj did, serves the cops right. A thought: sort of an Affirmative Action type of vote? Redressing centuries of injustice in our law courts?"

146. Decca's literary agent at the time. In a letter to a friend, Decca referred to this letter saying, "it's what's called in the trade a 'query letter,' hoping he can flog the idea to some mag. for an article."

Having found my always mislaid specs, I repaired to Tiburon Lodge in Marin County, venue of the seminar, and hung in like mad.

Aside from being one of the most affluent counties in the nation, Marin also has a cremation rate of about three times that of the national average—and thereby hangs most of this tale.

As background: one of the main themes of AWOD was to plug cremation vs ground burial—far cheaper, ecologically sound, etc.

After publication of AWOD cremation rates zoomed from fewer than 4% of American dead in early 1960's to 23% today.

Initial public reaction of the funeral directors and their diverse publications was resistance all the way. Try to talk the funeral buying family out of this disgraceful procedure—what will the neighbors think? Have you no respect for the dead, etc.? And the trump card, to forego the "traditional" funeral with all the trimmings, embalmed and beautified corpse in suitably costly casket, will bring grief—guilt feelings, and other dire mental health consequences to the survivors.

As cremation rates began first to inch up, then to zoom, the industry made a U-turn. The emphasis now is on "serving the family as they wish to be served"—and in the course of it, to upsell cremation. The key word is "Memorialization," which preserves the essential ingredients of the "trad" funeral, embalming and all the trimmings, and "ritual," another buzz word.

While the seminar topics could have fit handily into any trade meeting agenda—"Maintaining an Effective Workforce," "Responding to Community Trends," "Better Public Relations," etc.—the subtext of every speech was how to extract the maximum from the cremation customer.

As to attendance at the seminar—there were 93 registered, some from as far away as New York; a mix of funeral supply men, morticians, plus PR men and Mortuary Management writers. A few women, wives of the foregoing, and no blacks.

There was lots of folksy banter and down-home humor. John Baker, the spry youngish speaker on employee relations leads off by asking the audience "Who is minding the store while you're away?" Someone answers, "My wife." "Can you trust her?" Gales of laughter. And: "Be sure to chit-chat with your customers." "But our customers don't talk!" quipped a casket manufacturer to a roar of hilarity.

The best bits were the exhortations to sell, sell, sell. Alan Severson, editor of Funeral Monitor: "Keep an eye on what you're selling. The consumer needs to know about grief therapy. There's inherent tension between our role as grief counselors and the need for profit" (you can say that again). Enoch Glacock, owner/manager of Abbot & Hast mortuary in L.A.: "We only had two urns, tucked away on a shelf. I built an urn display—they sold like hot cakes!" His speech was smashing, all about how one must spend time with the cremation-minded family, tell them such things as "I feel your pain." Another speaker,

Ron Hast, suggests buying cases of apples which only cost 39 cents a pound, give bags of these to employees of police departments, nurses in hospitals, etc. with a card "We appreciate your good service." Name recognition! The officer on the beat will remember your name next time there's a fatal accident. Tons of good copy here.

As for my part—I was the last speaker, billed as "sharing her insights about funeral service." Ron Hast, host of the gathering, glumly mentioned in his introduction that there had been plenty of protest about my presence at the seminar, and threats from a trade organization to have members cancel their subscriptions to his mag.

Undeterred, I shared my insights, much to the displeasure of my listeners. After my talk, the first question set the tone: "How much money did you make from The American Way of Death?" "Absolute tons," I answered. "So much I can't even count it—it made me fortune." Audible groans from the crowd. "Next question?"

Luckily someone taped the Q & A, some of which is fairly comic. Aside from the meetings, my research assistant Karen Leonard and I roved about the motel, went to the cocktail parties and generally mixed. We have notes of many a deathless exchange.

                    Best regards, Decca

ps I'll be phoning Ron Hast soon, hoping he will share HIS insights into how my talk was received, any cancellation of subs, etc.

To Jeff Elliott[147]   Oakland
                                                              October 6, 1995
Dear Jeff: The speediness of you—unbelievable, I'm SO jealous; but there you are. I'm terrifically grateful for the Q & A transcription, I'd already forgotten almost all of it.

Now, as to the questions you ask. . . .

• If Diana & Bobo did influence Hitler, it wld have been simply to make him underestimate Brit. opposition to fascism. It's all total speculation. But I suppose that people tend to believe what they want, rather than what's actually the fact. Did we go on arguing, if so how etc: actually we didn't see all that much of each other. I went to Paris with Idden, Bobo was in Germany lots of the time. I think I've told all I really remember in Hons/Rebels. I wrote that in 1958–60, about 30 yrs after it happened when memory was slightly fresher—it's now more like SIXTY yrs after the event. No one tried to pressure me to go to Germany.

• Nancy: did I tell in either of my books about when she wrote Wigs on the

---

147. Elliott, editor of the *Albion Monitor* online newspaper, had interviewed Decca extensively for a 33,000-word profile of her that is still available at http://www.albionmonitor.com/decca.

Green, all about Bobo—I'm sure I did. She almost broke with Diana/Bobo over that. She was always anti-fascist, sort of Labour Party supporter. . . .

• Yes I think Esmond did know I wanted to go to Spain.[148] Giles or Peter Nevile wld have told him. . . .

• Stalin: Esmond & I were <u>for</u> him. Mainly for pragmatic reason that his lot won, Trots lost. I think Trotsky wld have been more to our liking philosophically.

• Buddy & I didn't pause to chat with racists or with cops![149] I was the only white at that time, but later lots of whites—mainly from the I.L.W.U., Harry Bridges' union—went & slept in the Gary house for protection. . . .

• Yes, still consider myself a Communist! (So do the undertakers, I'm sure.) . . .

• As I remember, Harry[150] took an elder/censorious view of students—what right had THEY to do all that protesting, not even part of the labor movement? But it's all a bit hazy in my memory. . . .

• I don't know about FTC not going after black morticians. In our case, it was a v. deliberate decision. Clearly, poor blacks were victimized worse if possible than whites by the funeral directors at the time we were writing AWOD. We talked about this a lot. Here are the considerations that made us decide not to go into this at all: 1) Undertaking, insurance, dentistry to some extent—these were about the only trades in which blacks could rise to middle class. Some blacks got really rich out of these trades, esp. undertaking & insurance (see, e.g., Frazier, <u>The Black Bourgeoisie</u>,[151] published I think in the 40's or 50's). But at the same time, the black undertakers were a terrific asset to the civil rights movement. When CRC (remember it was prominently on the Atty Gen's list of subversive orgs) was embattled everywhere, the local black funeral dirs were amongst our best contributors. There was a mag called "The Negro Funeral Director." Its whole tone was totally unlike that of mags like Mort. Management etc. It had lots in it about the emerging civil rights movement in

148. The question Decca was answering here concerned Esmond Romilly's knowledge about Decca's interest in him before their first meeting at a country-house weekend, in the course of which they hatched the plan for Decca to run away to Spain with Romilly.

149. Elliott had asked about the racist riot in progress when Decca and Walter (Buddy) Green arrived at the besieged Wilbur Gary house in the Rollingwood development in San Pablo, California, in 1952. Among other things, Elliott wanted to know if Decca had stopped or argued with the mob before heading into the house to offer assistance. He also asked if Decca had been the only white in the house.

150. In the 1960s, the Treuhafts had hosted a dinner to introduce Harry Bridges and University of California Free Speech Movement leader Mario Savio. They had hoped to link the Old Left with the New, but the two guests of honor were said to have taken an instant dislike to each other, souring an event the Treuhafts had anticipated with excitement. Elliott, in his list of questions, had asked Decca to elaborate on the nature of Bridges's objections to Savio and the student protesters.

151. E. Franklin Frazier's 1957 book <i>Black Bourgeoisie: The Rise of a New Middle Class in the United States</i> has been reissued over the years, most recently in 1997 by the Free Press, a division of Simon & Schuster.

the South. When SNCC people were jailed in Atlanta, a black millionaire mortician bailed them out to the tune of THOUSANDS of dollars. Hence we
decided that the black situation was too complicated, would require a whole
chapter just to explain all that, not really relevant to what we were about, which
was to describe the absurdity of the American way.

****

I hope the above helps. I may get in touch later re yr absolutely invaluable
transcription of the rest of it—longing for the next installment. . . .

Much love, Decca

To Doris Brin Walker   Oakland
                                                        October 20, 1995

Dearest Dob,

Here's a bit from a poem by Blake: "I was angry with my friend; I told my
wrath, my wrath did end. I was angry with my foe; I told it not, my wrath did
grow."

So now, this is the point. When I said that one day I'd explain why I bowed
out of being a reference for your new career,[152] you said no explanation was
necessary; but actually it is necessary, on acct. of message of above poem.

It's all to do with what you said about wanting me to endorse because of
"name recognition." Actually, I was steaming with anger about this. First off,
nobody wants to be listed because of so-called "name recognition" rather than
something one can actually contribute (that's why I invariably decline being on
"advisory boards," "editorial boards" etc., even if the cause is a v. good one,
unless I'm going to be meeting with the board & doing something to help
whatever it is).

Second, far more important—and the main reason I was cross—is the idea
that Bob hasn't got NAME RECOGNITION! How ridic. If you think back,
the local lawyers whom you knew, & some of whom you may have worked with
in some capacity over the years, with super name rec. would be Vince Hallinan
& Charles Garry, both now unavailable. I'd say that in that league, & a close
third so far as being known, loved & admired throughout the Bay Area and by
all generations, would be Bob. Just to mention a few points: his HUAC appearance in 1953, headlines in Trib EASTBAY LAWYER CAUSES DISTUR-
BANCE AT HEARING. The time he kicked in the door at the D.A.'s
office—more Trib. headlines. His secretary told me that many blacks had
phoned along the lines of "Is this the lawyer who caused a row at the HUAC
hearing?" or "Is this the lawyer who kicked in the door at City Hall?" And then

---

152. Walker had asked Decca if she could list her as a reference among "others who are personally familiar with my legal experience and editing skill," saying that she was faxing her instead of
telephoning "to enable you to decline without embarrassment."

said, "He's the one I want to represent my son in a personal injury case." Then: representing the FSM students, & being the first arrested. Also: his epic race for DA against Coakley, in tandem with Bob Scheer for Congress. Those are just some name rec. examples of a v. high order.

Now, Dobby, in yr letter you promise to furnish your lawyer-clients whose work you'll be editing with the inestimably valuable qualities of "tact, discretion, and human understanding." Are you sure that it was tactful, discreet & humanly understanding of you to tell me that Bob doesn't have name recognition?

There! I've done what Blake suggested, because I've always thought of you (and shall always continue to think of you) as one of my very best friends ever, anywhere.

> Much love, Decca

To Dugald Stermer[153]   Oakland
                                                        November 9, 1995

Dearest Dugald,

Thanks SO much for that absolutely smashing dirty book.[154] A thing of great beauty (like all yr bks) and of v.v. much interest to the prurient mind.

I dashed for the picture of Galapagos giant tortoises. Like all English children, we used to keep tortoises—the kind you can buy (or used to be able to) at Woolworth's for 6d., & we used to wonder like mad HOW THEY DID IT. Finally, many years later—more like two generations, actually—my sis. Nancy had tortoises in her garden at Versailles, and we found out their secret. One thing you didn't mention is that there is tremendous banging connected with the act; they make a huge noise banging shell on shell. Once my other sister Pam came dashing into Nancy's drawing room, saying "Those tortoises are hand in glove," rather graphic, don't you think? After that, Bob & I were at a rather grand dinner party in an English country house. Debo was there, & we were telling the other guests about the phenomenon of the tortoises. We offered to show. At our direction, the hostess fetched two lids of rubbish bins (garbage cans, in America) and we got down on the floor & did a rather good imitation—esp. of the expressions on the face of a tortoise, quite grim and unchanged, as in your exquisite drawing.

> Much love & best wishes for success of this marvelous book,
> Decca

---

153. Stermer had been a close friend of Decca since her *Ramparts* days. He is a San Francisco illustrator who decades earlier had designed and written the *Ramparts* magazine back-page ads for Inch Kenneth, an ad campaign dreamed up by their mutual friend Howard Gossage. In addition to four books that he wrote and illustrated, Stermer's work has included the design for the 1984 Olympic medals, campaigns for Levi's, Nike, Jaguar, and the San Diego Zoo, and illustrations for many top American newspapers and magazines.

154. Stermer's new book was *Birds & Bees: A Sexual Study* (HarperSanFrancisco, 1995).

To Virginia (Tilla) Durr   Oakland
                                                     December 6, 1995

Dearest Tilla,

Merry Xmas! Here are two books WELL WORTH your attention. Perhaps you've already got the Strunk & White? It's got excellent advice on commas. I may have put you wrong re commas, never my strong point. . . . I think commas are often (but NOT always) a matter of personal preference; Nancy hardly ever used them, and E. Waugh used to put them in for her.

The Zinsser[155] is delightful, fun to read. . . . Re the chapter on Usage (p. 36), I'm also on the style panel for The American Heritage Dictionary. I remember one comment—we were asked about the word "escapee" to describe one who escapes from jail. I said that I thought the GUARD was the escapee, not the prisoner. . . . Also, when Jamie (Oy #1) was clerk to Sup. Ct. Justice O'Connor, there was an annual tradition in which the four clerks of one justice had lunch with one of the other justices, so that in the course of the year in which they served they got to have private lunches, just the four of them, with each of the nine. It was Scalia's[156] turn. Because he's v. precise about usage, someone asked him what dictionary he uses. Webster, he said. Jamie spoke up to say "Why not American Heritage? My grandmother is on the style panel." "And who is your grandmother?" "Jessica Mitford," said Jamie, upon which Scalia almost fell out of his chair.

I do hope you'll find these books useful; I know I do. By the way, one of my problems is the diff. bet. Brit and U.S. punctuation—e.g., Brits put the comma outside the quotes except where it's inside in the original; here, we usually put the comma inside. U.S.: "Let's go," he said. Brit: "Let's go", he said. . . .

[W]e're off to Maya's for Xmas. . . . Then, in Jan, Debo looms in NY to give a lecture on the Treasures of Chatsworth at the Met!! So I'm going to be on hand to heckle. . . .

                         Much love, Dec

To Virginia (Tilla) Durr   Oakland
                                                     December 18, 1995

Dearest Tilla,

. . . Here's a funny story about MONEY (at least it gave *me* a giggle at the time). When my mother was getting v. ancient, her mind was much on her will. One day she told me about a conversation she'd had with a contemp. of hers, Cousin Maddy. She told me that Maddy had said, "Sydney, as all your daughters except for Decca are rich, why don't you just leave her everything?" "I

---

155. *On Writing Well* by William Knowlton Zinsser (Harper & Row, 1976, and republished in a number of new editions over the years).

156. Conservative Supreme Court Justice Antonin Scalia.

thought about it, Little D.," my mother said. "But then I thought that the rich always like a little bit more, so I decided to leave it equally to all of you." (Don't you rather love "the rich always like a little bit more"? A timeless comment, <u>too</u> true.) At the time my mother related this conversation, Bob & I were actually fairly poor; lots of lawyers in his position had been driven into bankruptcy in the McCarthy years. He was lucky in that respect, & kept his law practice going. But I was contributing almost nothing to the family budget, because CRC didn't have enough money to pay wages, and my one effort to earn—SF Chronicle advertising job—foundered, as described in <u>A Fine Old Conflict</u>.[157]

That's why I didn't understand how/why money became a bone of contention between you & sisters. I mean, why do you care if they're rich & you're not? Last night we went to see Sense & Sensibility—it's THE most smashing movie of all time, you MUST see it. That, of course, is all about money and position, as is everything Jane Austen wrote, which is lovely as a period piece but not really applicable to life today, surely? . . .

LOTS OF LOVE, Merry Xmas, H. New year. Decca

To Dolly McPherson   Oakland
                                                   January 8, 1996

Dearest Dolly,

. . . I've been collecting lots of things—books, reviews, articles—on topics like Million Man March, O.J. Verdict etc. Here's what I'd like to do AFTER the new edition of Amer. Way of Death is finished (which is, alas, many months off at the slow rate I'm going): As background, in the late 40's & fifties the CP had a campaign named (in the ponderous jargon we liked to use) "The Struggle against White Chauvinism."[158] This, to me, was about the most useful & best thing ever about belonging to the CP. It really was immensely instructive. . . .

(Parenthetically, I'm surprised that writers like Cornel West & Henry Louis Gates don't mention the CP—or at least not in what I've read of these authors so far). . . .

Anyway, here's what I have in mind for far-off future: get . . . survivors (lots are dead, alas) of those days, & have some recorded discussions of those days AND obviously the main thing, which is what now? This sounds v. vague—which it is, because it's on back burner at the moment (I'm horribly behind with my work on AWOD). . . .

Much love, Decca

---

157. Decca was referring to the visit by two FBI agents to inform her department head that she was "under surveillance as a suspected Communist."

158. For more background on this program that made an indelible impression on Decca, see the letter of May 1, 1980, to Maya Angelou.

To Thomas R. McDade[159]   Oakland
                                                                            January 27, 1996

Dear Mr. McDade,

Thanks for your FAX of 25 January. Actually the work I'm doing at the moment isn't a sequel to The American Way of Death; it's more of an effort to revise, or update, that book, which was first published in 1963.

As I'm sure you know, there have been many changes in the funeral business over the years, and of course one of the most important is the emergence of SCI as an industry leader. So naturally I'm extremely anxious to get the facts straight about SCI: its history, its goals, its philosophy. I wish to avoid using "baseless gossip and rumors"[160] in my book, and should certainly appreciate it very much if you would point out the "wholly unsubstantiated innuendo and, in some case[s], outright falsehoods" that you refer to, so that these may be corrected in the finished book.

I think that it would be of great value if I could sit down with a representative of SCI to get the true story. In fact, last autumn I made every effort to secure an appointment with Mr. Waltrip for that purpose; but after I had been assured by telephone that he would meet with me in Houston, Mr. Barrett[161] wrote to say "I regret to report that Mr. Waltrip's travel and business commitments over the next couple of months are going to make it impossible to schedule time to visit with you." I then tried to get an appointment with Mr. Barrett—he agreed to see me in Houston, but just when I thought it was all arranged I had a FAX from Connie Smith of Corporate Communications who simply wrote: "This is to advise you that Messrs Boetticher[162] and Barrett will not be available to meet with you on Thursday, May 25th." After that, I sadly gave up trying.[163]

                                    Yours sincerely, Jessica Mitford

---

159. An attorney with McDade & Fogler in Houston, which represented Service Corporation International. Decca was responding to a fax from McDade in which he said he had heard from people who attended Decca's presentation at the Mortuary Management Seminar in October 1995 that she had made "some rather disparaging remarks about SCI and its Chairman, Robert L. Waltrip." Without "suggesting that we are going to sue you or any such thing," McDade noted that "we have had considerable experience with libel and slander cases." He noted that her seminar comments "appear to evidence an intentional pattern to cast SCI in a bad light clothed in wit and humor" and instructed: "You cannot be mean or cute; you only need to tell the truth. We know you can do it."

160. A quotation, of course, from McDade's letter, as is the next quoted comment in her letter.

161. Bill Barrett, SCI Management's director of corporate communications.

162. Bob Boetticher of SCI would later gain some measure of renown when, as director of special projects for SCI, he handled funeral arrangements for President Ronald Reagan.

163. In *The American Way of Death Revisited*, Decca recounted the canceling of her scheduled interview with Waltrip in the spring of 1995. She quoted from an in-house SCI publication sent her by a "disaffected former SCI employee." The article said: "An interview with the media is serious business. The image and reputation of your business is at stake. If the preparation leads you to conclude it is not in your best interest to do the interview, don't."

ps: Incidentally, my name is Mitford, not Midford as you have it; and my husband's name is Treuhaft, not Truehaft.[164]

To Chaka Forman — Oakland
February 3, 1996

Dearest Oy #2,

HAPPY BIRTHDAY!

However, I do wish you'd shape up & try to behave better in future.

First you go & murder a gay priest in the park—honestly, why do you have to go & do things like that? PLUS being HIV positive?

Next thing I know, you are gratuitously getting a poor innocent bloke in trouble by falsely swearing you saw him at the crime scene.[165]

Now, if you'll promise not to do things like this any more, I'll send you more money on your NEXT birthday.

NAUGHTY BOY,

From your loving Grandec and Grandbob

To Terry Weber — Oakland
February 10, 1996

Terbaby—I note that Dink's on for religion in yr school.[166] Plse remind her of the following:

When we lived in Jean Street, she was about 7 & got v. involved with some people down the hill who were evangelists (I guess; never met them, only go by what she told).

There was a song: "I will make you fishers of men," so she fished poor Benj aged one, dragged him down the hill to the meetings. I think one got a prize, or reward, for being a fisher of men? She might remember what it was.

Anyway, so she kept on at me about not believing in God. "Who made man, if God didn't exist?" So I patiently & laboriously explained Evolution (as I understood it, which was perhaps not too well). Life began with cells in the ocean. These developed into fish, which eventually evolved into birds, thence to animals, thence to early man etc.

"All right, Dec. You go on believing that fish turned into birds and animals, and I'll go on believing in God."

---

164. McDade's letter had noted that Decca's husband was "a former labor union attorney, Robert Truehaft."

165. Chaka Forman explains his behavior: "The letter references my roles on 'NYPD Blue' and the ABC miniseries 'Innocent Victims.' Grandec was always a big supporter of my acting career."

166. Terry Weber was teaching at New York's Urban Academy Laboratory High School. As part of a special, schoolwide project on "what's good for kids," one subgroup was looking at whether religion was good for kids. Constancia Romilly had been invited to speak with those students about growing up as, and being, an atheist.

I hadn't much to say at that point. Did she STOP believing in God? If so, when & why? RSVP

Much love, Dec

To various friends   Oakland

February 20, 1996

I am bid to a luncheon on 28 Feb at the Hamlin School, San Francisco, by Tina Brown.[167] (The invitation came in one of those New Yorker cards with a cartoon by Booth on the front showing fighting cats/dogs & a couple, woman yelling: "I feel aggressive today. Not sexy—just aggresive." Do you detect a printer's errer as the late Philip Toynbee spelt it? What happened to renowned New Yorker checkers?)

Inside, the invite reads: "Tina Brown invites you to join in a lunchtime conversation on the occasion of a special issue about American women."

Caroline Graham, West Coast editor of the New Yorker, told me that all the women who are invited will be sent an advance copy of the special issue, edited by Roseanne.[168] She also said that SIXTY were expected to attend, so it won't be exactly an <u>intime</u> chat with the editor. I don't know who the others are; shall contrive to find out next week.

Meanwhile, I'd love to have your views of the new New Yorker. We subscribe, but sad to say I seldom read right through any given issue, so I haven't really got an informed opinion of the virtues/shortcomings of the Tina Brown watch.

But I <u>am</u> aware that there are immensely strong feelings amongst the inner circle types. Some of this can be gleaned from newspapers/gossip columns. . . .

Main complaints: firing of Jamaica Kincaid; general "trendiness"; idea of having Roseanne edit an issue . . .

I'm awfully keen to garner a few other views of the Tina Brown stewardship of the mag, so please write or FAX me. . . .

I forgot to say that also I don't know anything about Roseanne, except for skimming headlines about her. I must be one of the v.v. few who haven't even seen her on telly. I thought she sounded pretty awful—esp as choice as editor of an issue; but then someone said she's v. amusing, has a working-class outlook, sharp, clever etc.

To James Forman Jr.   Oakland

April 1996

Dearest Oy #1,

I was deeply moved by your letter of April 7. Aside from the v. great interest in your upcoming cases, both of which look like cliff-hangers, I was particularly struck with the supreme importance of HOW YOU LOOK.

---

167. At the time, the editor of *The New Yorker.*
168. Comedian, actress, and general-purpose celebrity entertainer Roseanne Barr.

So—as you can imagine, I've been awake nights picturing the horror of you losing the cases because the jurors can <u>see</u> that your careless grandparents have let you go to court in some perfectly DREADFUL looking togs. I mean—there they are, in the jury room. All the evidence is in; you've made what would normally be thought of as one of the most brilliant summations ever heard in the District of Columbia. But did they pay any attention? Not a bit of it.

The foreman has now been picked. He suggests as a first move, taking a straw vote, and to that end he calls upon each juror. Juror #1: "Well—I must say I didn't like the looks of counsel's suit. Did you notice how frayed the cuffs were?" Juror #2: "I was struck by his necktie. Was that an egg stain?" Juror #3: "I don't think so; I understand that Mr. Forman doesn't eat eggs. But he's crazy about bacon. I studied that stain, and to me it looked very much like bacon drippings." And so it goes. The verdict is now a foregone conclusion. GUILTY. . . .

So, what is to be done? Grandbob and I have discussed this at length. For a bit of background: last week we were invited to Herb Caen's 80th birthday—a hugely grand affair held in tents at the Museum of the Legion of Honor, 400 people, all of SF high society. The invitation said "Black Tie." Grandbob got out his ancient tuxedo, last worn about 40 yrs ago; the jacket fit fine, but alas, not the trousers. What to do? A new one would likely cost $500; to rent one is not easy. He went to the Goodwill, and there got <u>the</u> most marvellous trousers for $5.95. So we thought you should do the same. I was just about to write a check for $5.95 when Bob pointed out that you'd need a jacket, which would likely be another $5. So here's the price of an excellent suit, a check for $10.95.

> With fondest best wishes for a Happy
> Birthday & successful trial,
> Grandec and Grandbob

To Mary Clemmey   Oakland
                                                    April 24, 1996

Dearest Clème,

It's been AGES since we heard from you, & we long for news. . . .

I've been in touch with various ones about the sp. New Yorker women's issue—I think I told you a bit about it. Did you read the issue? Some good, some awful. One of the worst was by someone called Daphne Merkin, v. long & all about how she craves to be whipped (she's a masochist) with nary a joke in it. Marina looked up "Merkin" in the OED—says it means "a pubic wig." I looked it up in mine, says "counterfeit hair for women's privy parts," same thing I guess. So she thinks the whole article was just a huge put-on. There've been TWO meetings, 60 woman lunch for Tina Brown, and about 20 at dinner in a tycooness's house. I went to both; not too enlightening. "We women need to talk to each other more," that sort of bosh. Nobody really criticized the issue (although the society writer in Chron. wrote that "Jessica Mitford charmingly bit the hand that fed her and trashed the issue . . .").

Book's chugging towards the end. My dream is to have it all finished by end June or mid-July, then we'll go to Cape Cod where Dink & family, the Snows, Helena & Iain[169] all gather every summer. <u>DO</u> come, you know how you're always on hol, might as well?

I've had a job offer! It's teaching a course at San Francisco State univ., similar to the one I did aeons ago at San Jose. Marvellous high pay, so I'll definitely do it IF the grant they're seeking comes through. . . .

Also, I've got a lawsuit against the Funeral Directors of New Jersey. See attached letter to them from Don Jelinek, who is handling it for me.[170] So I shld be RICH in the near future if all this comes off.

I wish I knew more about English politics. What about Tony Blair?[171] He sounds ghastly from the v. little we read about him. And what about Peter Mandelson?[172] He was staying with the Snows last year in Cape Cod, so we met him briefly. Somehow the matter of GATT and NAFTA came up; he asked me what I thought of them, I said awful; so he accused me of being an Isolationist. We didn't hit it off much.

I've got a smashing new researcher for England—that naughty James Forrester was hopeless; he got engaged & for some silly reason was FAR more interested in his fiancée than in funerals, can't think why. The new one, Sophy Roberts, came out of the blue—she wrote asking to interview me for a paper she's writing (thesis) on Brit. funeral industry; so I smartly turned the tables & asked her if SHE would work for ME. She said snap. She's really good at it. End of paper, end of letter, fondest love from me & Bob—and PLEASE WRITE. . . .

   Decca

---

169. Helena Kennedy and her husband, Dr. Iain Hutchison. Kennedy, the British left-wing lawyer (now Baroness Kennedy and a Labour member of the House of Lords), was a good friend of the Treuhafts. She is the author of *Eve Was Framed: Women and British Justice* (Chatto & Windus, 1995) and *Just Law: The Changing Face of Justice—and Why It Matters to Us All* (Chatto & Windus, 2004).

170. Jelinek, a Berkeley attorney and progressive politician and, for a time, Robert Treuhaft's law partner. He had written a demand letter to the New Jersey State Funeral Directors Association, Inc., informing the organization that he was representing Decca in the matter. The charge was that the association had reneged on a written contract for an appearance by Decca at its convention, for $4,000 plus specified expenses. Jelinek claimed that the invitation was revoked "apparently after your Executive Director told Ms. Mitford that he 'hadn't realized how controversial you are, even 30 years since the *American Way of Death* came out; that I must seek a center path for the organization.' "

171. The prime minister.

172. A combative British Member of Parliament who was at one time a key ally of Tony Blair and is credited with "modernizing" the British Labour Party.

To the Duchess of Devonshire   Oakland
                                                                    April 29, 1996

Hen—I was away (lecherous lecture, San Diego) when yr FAX came—thanks awfully for offering to help funeral-wise.[173] Here's in general the form:

1) Style of funerals—I imagine unchanged forever? When Muv died, you & Nancy both wrote accounts of it; it was in fact same year that <u>American Way of Death</u> was published. Nancy told how a carpenter came to the Isle with planks & tools, measured her, then set about constructing a coffin. I think it was you who told how it was a lovely calm evening (after awful storms) and neighbouring boats followed Muv's boat to Mull, where the coffin was kept overnight, then by motor hearse to Swinbrook, and the whole thing cost 30 quid. So that's the sort of thing I'm interested in. Do they still measure for coffin size? Or are the coffins manufactured elsewhere? Can one have an American casket (in Bakewell, or Brayfield etc)—if so, how many of those do local undertakers sell on average? Maybe Naught is the likely answer. How long does the service last? Where is the coffin during the service? Any sign of "open casket" services?

2) Cost. A trifle embarrassing to ask the survivors; but maybe you cld phone a clergyman or two? They'd likely be au fait of the whole thing. They, also, might be the ones to detect any American influence in general conduct of funeral.

Hen it wld be MOST good of you if you cld even get a fraction of above answered.

> Much love, Henderson

ps Cost is awfully important, to be compared with London prices, also U.S. There used to be a Gov't set price for lowest, I think it was 33 quid? But that was ages ago, part of welfare State; I've no idea if it still obtains. I think clergy would be best source. How about C of E,[174] any different Nonconformist? I suppose there are skeke any RC[175] or Jewish funerals in the country?

To Shana Alexander   Oakland
                                                                       May 22, 1996

Dearest Shana,

   . . . [P]oor Bob is in v.v. bad shape. When I got home last night, there was a note from Benj who had come round to see how he was—saying Bob v.v. strange acting, not at all himself. So today's been all-Medical, beginning with a

---

173. In another letter, Decca commented, "From her letters, I gather that [my Hen is] constantly off to funerals, her main form of social life these days, so she's in prime position to do a spot of research."

174. Church of England.

175. Roman Catholic.

blood test this a.m. and just ending now (approx. 9 p.m.) with a neurologist coming round to see him. Tomorrow looks like approx. the same. It may be result of some pain pills he's been taking. Anyway, I assume they'll find out tomorrow & also find out cure. . . .

Much love, Dec

To various friends   Oakland
                                                                    May 28, 1996

Report on Bob

He's a tad better today—talking ordinary, noting when one tells him things in the paper such as super report on the Nation in the Liz Smith gossip column. Pleased to hear when people have rung up to inquire.

Best of all is what Benj calls my "support group." This consists of regulars—Katie, 3 mornings a week, and Inese[176] who's taken to popping in EVERY day.

Mainly, super-saint Lisa Pollard,[177] a musician by nature, who has deserted her saxophone to come & help—she slept here last night, is terrific at getting him to sit up & drink water. Also she got him a baby cup, all decorated—the point being that one can drink out of it by sucking & it doesn't spill. (Handy idea for future—if anybody we know needs such!)

As he wasn't eating <u>anything</u> for a few days, Benj said he should announce he's on hunger strike in symp. with Pastors for Peace (on hunger strike for 3 months to force gov't to let them take computers to Cuba. As of Sunday's paper, they'd won their point and the Govt had caved in—so they've stopped hunger-striking. Of course it was purely Bob's support that turned the tide, don't you think?)

That's about it for now. Oral surgeon coming round at 5 p.m. today.[178] All Drs. now eating out of hand thanks to brilliant Don Jelinek, who when talking to them on the phone said "Of course Bob Treuhaft is in his 80s, hence rather frail—but he does go to court every day, he's still a practicing lawyer." I've embroidered that to have Don saying "He's just won a very important medical malpractice case—award in the millions. . . ."

End of report. Much love, Dec

---

176. Inese Civkulis had succeeded the Treuhafts' longtime housekeeper, Rita Wiggins, and become equally indispensable. She also catered their parties and helped to care for each of them when they became ill and infirm.

177. Professional musician Lisa Pollard was first recommended by Decca's physical therapist as a walking companion when Decca was under orders to walk more in the recovery from her broken ankle. Pollard became a caretaker and friend in Decca's declining months and on through her husband's final years.

178. The next day, May 29, Robert Treuhaft had a large oral abscess removed, but in the course of the day his condition deteriorated markedly. His thinking and conversation became increasingly confused. Treuhaft was admitted to a local hospital, where doctors speculated he had an infection caused by his surgery.

To various friends   Oakland
                                                             June 1, 1996

Latest on Bob. Dink has now confronted all Drs., viz Dr. Cohn (general—internist), Bloom, tooth surgeon, Herrick, neurologist, plus an infection specialist at hosp & an ear specialist, ditto.

All say that the combination of very bad infection plus huge doses of antibiotics are the cause of him going odd—not talking ordinary, but saying unresponsive things when asked questions.

However, quite a lot of times he seems perfectly O.K., answers things properly. Swelling on jaw very much better.

All Drs. think that he'll have to stay in hosp. a week or more to recover totally. . . .

To Dr. Arlan Cohn   Oakland
                                                             June 21, 1996

Dear Arlan,

Report from the front lines:

Bob Miraculous recovery—he seems utterly OK, going to office etc., & driving his car. Last antibiotics given Wednesday—no more needed, right? He has an appt. to see Dr. McKinley on 2 July re knee.

Decca Not so good. Went with saintly Lisa Pollard to Dr. Hlavac (podiatrist) last Tuesday, 18 June. He says muscle in ankle no good; will be trying a special brace which he's having made, ready in 2 weeks. But thinks it likely that I might have to have fusion op. after all—agreed no rush, maybe Oct–November if brace doesn't work.

Here's another annoying thing: when I clear my throat or cough slightly, phlegm is v.v. dark red, color of very dark raw liver if you see what I mean. Am hoping this will go away, but thought I shld mention it. (I didn't tell Bob or Dinky, but am sending copy of this FAX to Lisa, foremost ally in health matters.)

Also, Lisa's got an excellent acupuncturist who she thinks cld help a lot with extremely tiresome pain in right hip—caused, Dr. Hlavac says, by hopeless ankle. Am using Bob's walker which is a big help. Question: does Medicare or Blue X pay for acupuncture? I'll give you the bloke's name, or rather ask Lisa to do so.

        All the best, Decca

▪▪

> *Within days, Decca was suddenly taken ill. Her daughter, Constancia Romilly, flew out from New York on July 3 after receiving a report from Robert Treuhaft that a needle biopsy had found cancer in her lungs, with other tests showing it had metastasized to the*

adrenals and liver. That same day a bone scan was performed, and cancer was also found in the brain. She underwent immediate radiation to protect her brain function for as long as possible.

■■

To the Duchess of Devonshire Oakland
July 6, 1996

Hen—you are a marvel & thanks SO, SO much.

Here's what's happening this end: we're definitely off to Cape Cod from 7 to 14 August (will send address etc later). Extraorder character Lisa, a musician by nature (saxophonist) has taken a shine to us & has been amazing throughout, beginning with Bob's illness which now seems like ancient history & she takes me to the hosp for everything. Anyway she's coming to Cape Cod with wheelchair so all shld be v. serene. Oys will be there plus Snos, Helena & families; maybe Benj will loom at some pt.

Boring medical news just to keep you in the picture. Turns out cancer is also in bones (bad hip) as well as brain, so it's radiation in all those places daily until 24 July. Doesn't hurt at all plus I get marvellous pain pills <u>and</u> blue cheerup pills—Dink's in charge. So I'm feeling v. well at the moment.

My local researcher Karen Leonard is MOVING IN TO STAY here after Dink leaves next Tuesday 9 July. Idea is that she'll sort out the whole rest of the book & be on phone with Bob Gottlieb & me as needed. Gottlieb plans to spend full time on book after 18 July. Karen will stay here whilst we are at C. Cod. Bob (T) will work on funerals in England until we leave, hence vastly looking forward to Helen[179] FAX next week, so useful. Do thank her no end.

FUTURE PLANS: Am much hoping to get to England, possibly late autumn or even Xmas so don't come here. But DO come to me funeral, about 9 months or a year off accdg to the Dr. I thought I'd make SCI give a free one with all the best? I'll let you know as plans progress.

That's about it for now. Point of brain radiation is to spruce it up a bit so one can get on with the book etc. Time will tell. All hair will fall out I'm told, so various ones are making wigs.

Yr loving and GRATEFUL old Hen

To Robert Treuhaft Oakland
July 10, 1996

3 a.m.—couldn't sleep, having slept all day yesterday.

Bob—it's so ODD to be dying, so I must just jot a few thoughts—starting with fact that I've SO enjoyed life with you in all ways. Isn't it rather amazing

---

179. The duchess's assistant, Helen Marchant.

how we ever met in 1st place—and thinking back to absolutely everything beginning with the A. Hopkins/Abe etc & you being Bob Trueapple. But did you note a common link such as all that about the Census Bldg seat-switch, the soul-mate (Anne's) bedbug switch, the you/Abe poems like Drink a Drink to Dauntless Decca etc? Mainly, of course, you've been incredibly GOOD to me all through life and have TAUGHT me more than I can say, not to mention being incredibly kind & forgiving of faults such as Impatience.

I must say I'm glad it's me first as I v. much doubt I'd bother to go on much if it was you. Also there really is a small bonus—I wonder if you agree? In knowing ahead of time so one can think things out a bit (not just finish book—you know what I mean).

Back to us meeting in Washington. What on earth would have become of ME if we hadn't. There I was surrounded by the Embassy crowd, the importunate Kay Graham rich cousins and even Mike Straight (Va always thought he was about to chuck silly little Binnie for me, but she would think that sort of thing) and YOU loomed. And the Wasserman test[180] in Russian river—"Here's to socialized medicine," remember? And wonderful Nicky (actually I do think of him most days, now aged 52) when Mrs. King told the children her skirt had blown up at Wild Cat's Peak & Nick saying "Did the wild cats peek?" You & Dink, whole relationship over the aeons—goodness what a lucky thing you liked each other almost from word Go. Not quite; I think she rather looked away from you at the very beginning, to my worry. But that soon stopped, & I can skeke imagine a better friendship than you/her. As for Benj—hasn't he turned out amazingly well lately?

So now, about <u>you</u>. You've got the children & Oys all of whom adore you, but you'll need someone—I mean you've got all those household skills, cooking etc., pity to waste don't you agree? Be thinking of someone agreeable. You won't have to as they'll come flocking I bet. I do have some ideas but fear to mention for fear of annoying or being intrusive, none of my business you'll say.

On separate page, am putting down <u>about money.</u>
<u>Yr loving Wief</u>

By the way—do go to that film this evening [and] dinner. . . . I long to hear all about it. . . . Should be v. innaresting

To the Duchess of Devonshire   Oakland
                                                                                              July 11, 1996
Dearest Hen,
I note you are in London but this will doubtless catch up. Thanks awfully for the Jon Sno Cape Coddery. That's where we'll be with them 7 to 14 Aug. The

---

180. An early syphilis test that used to be required before marriage.

packer sent such a funny FAX (selon[181] yr notification, thanks for that) saying he'd never heard a duchess say "Bugger" so much. Well I wonder if he knows all that many duchesses come to think of it?

So what happened—as you have it, pretty much. Coughing blood Xray—first no cancer cells—other procedures—cancer of lung & other places incl. thigh. I asked how long the cancer had been there—can't say for sure, about a year they thought.

Not only no malaise whatsoever, no headache which one wld be absolutely expecting don't you agree with c. of the <u>brain</u>, hardly any pain except in thigh & that's under control with marvellous medicine for same. Daily radiation at hosp. But here's the point Hen: SO much better than just being hit by a car or in plane wreck. At least one can plan a few things—also feeling absolutely OK, life is v.v. pleasurable with people coming to chat plus work on bk. It all really is quite extraorder, do admit. . . .

Needless to say I'm taking <u>full</u> advantage, everyone's bringing meels on wheels, delicious things for me & all marvellous helpers who are absolutely smoothing every path here, so it's sort of a nonstop party, all my favourite people flocking by. So why worry? Also doing all sorts of things such as helping Benj with his Cuba pianos, everyone now in mood to give him dough for same because of their affection for his old Mum. Did I tell that when I went to register at hosp name of Jessica Treuhaft the social worker said "Are you by any chance related to the piano tuner?" Oh I was pleased. Dink's coming to live here with us after C. Cod, isn't she a trouper.

<u>July 12, about 5 a.m. in Calif</u> Yrs[182] of 9:54 from Chatsworth just rec'd, so I've answered most of it. Are you getting envious of my extremely comfortable situation? One day I'll describe the helpers, but will get this off now. Did I tell you about deadline (mot juste) first they said (Drs) about 6 to 9 months but for some reason have upped it to more like 3 months which is rather a drag as was hoping to get to London. Meeting with them in a few days—it's so almost unbellevable, and I suppose they might be all wrong—in which case helpers etc might get livid, boy who cried wolf. By the way Dink thinks v.v. highly of the whole cancer team—she's in constant touch with them FAX/t.phone.

Yr loving Henderson

To the Duchess of Devonshire   Oakland
                                                                        July 13, 1996

Hen . . .

Of course I'd adore to see you, but when, how? Aunt Weenie, "Geoff, George is dead and now Sydney's gone, don't you think we shld meet?" Uncle Geoff—long pause: "But we <u>have</u> met."

---

181. "According to," in French.
182. A fax from the duchess.

It's the when-where, so let's be thinking. My hope was to come to London in autumn but the Drs are so vague about deadlines, first they said 6–9 months then 3 then maybe a year, & you said about the 6 yr lade by which time people will get awfully bored with it all. Any chance you might skip to Cape Cod for a hot moment? It's 3 hrs drive from Boston Airport, our dates 7 to 14 Aug. Whole Dink mob plus Jon Sno etc; Maya Angelou is taking a house there so 'twill be a nonstop party. The packer can tell you how to get there if inclined— oh, DO, Hen.

If you do, that wld just be extra bonus as I do so hope to come for proper visit to England for a proper Honnish chat. Be thinking on't.

This end, am working on funerals in England which Bob is helping with; my smashing researcher Karen Leonard plugging away with editor (Bob Gottlieb) on general rewrite/update, so I'm sure it will get finished.

Am also taking FULL ADVANTAGE of condition to press all sorts of things (lawsuits etc of no interest to you) on ground that you can't refuse a dying person's request. Benj is madly working on his piana/Havana project— see attached, so I'm helping with that too. Having lots of cheering drugs (still no drinks) they may even be giving me street drugs like Speed. Dink is in full control. The Drs this end all say she's more of a colleague, another Dr rather than just a nurse. Bob's being marvellous makes proper boiled eggs for breakker etc., I got a lovely letter from e. the good so thank her, with good joke by Toby's uncle. I do wish that you/Packer or someone cld get the Benj effort into the English papers—Polly Toynbee might help? She was pleased with me FAX to horrible Mail. She's off to Italy in August, said she might come here in Sept.

Yr loving Hen

■■

Decca died ten days later, on July 23, 1996.

THE LAST WORD

Lisa Pollard directed the Green Street Mortuary Band as friends and
relatives gathered for Decca's memorial in San Francisco. On display
in the horse-drawn hearse were memorabilia of Decca's life.

Within hours of her death, the phone calls began: funeral directors from around the country competing for the right to "do Decca." Anticipating public interest in her funeral arrangements, Decca had requested direct cremation, the simplest process, and interviewed a man her research assistant, Karen Leonard, describes as "the funeral director most hated by the industry." Decca expressed herself pleased with his arrangements. (His final bill was $475.)

Decca had always shown a keen interest in her own funeral—"goodness I wish I cld. be there," she once wrote—so she naturally had a few other last wishes. In her final weeks, she called a number of former students and other friends to ask them to act as "bouncers" at the funeral, giving "the bum's rush" to anyone who praised her then added a "but"—a technique she had dreamed up years earlier, after Sonia Orwell's funeral.*

One speaker at Decca's memorial intentionally sprinkled a few "howevers" and "buts" into his tribute. "What would a memorial to Decca be like if we all followed the rules?" he said later. "It felt right to raise a ruckus." Beginning with a tentative objection from a friend in the audience who had not been certain if Decca was truly serious in her confidential request, a rising chorus of protests, hoots, and catcalls greeted each subsequent "but" in the tribute. It was a scene that doubtless had had the honoree chortling when she plotted it, pre-mortem.

Decca's friends arranged a final joke at her expense. Their inspiration was the following passage from her obituary in the *New York Times:*

> Late in life, she was asked what sort of funeral she wanted. An elaborate one, she replied, with "six black horses with plumes and one of those marvelous jobs of embalming that take 20 years off." She added that she wanted "streets to be blocked off, dignitaries to declaim sobbingly over the flower-smothered bier, proclamations to be issued—that sort of thing."

Decca's flip description of her dream funeral had been reported in funeral journals and elsewhere. It was reprinted with such seriousness that she once

---

* See May 26, 1981, letter to Robert Gottlieb.

said it was the one joke she regretted, but the friends planning her funeral—unbeknownst to her family—played out the joke to the hilt, arranging to have six black, plumed horses pull a glass-enclosed antique hearse through the waterfront streets near downtown San Francisco. The twelve-piece Green Street Mortuary Band, led by Decca's saxophonist friend Lisa Pollard, followed the cortege, blaring out such rousing favorites as "When the Saints Come Marching In."

The cost of this pomp was not announced, but Decca—in a decision telegraphed weeks earlier to the Duchess of Devonshire*—requested reimbursement for her cremation from what she considered a fitting source. Her final letter, composed by her assistant, was written at Decca's direction and mailed the day after her death.

■■

To Mr. Robert Waltrip, SCI Corporation

July 24, 1996

Dear sir,

I am the research assistant for Jessica Mitford's revision of The American Way of Death. Although Jessica would have loved to have met you, and had gone to great lengths to do so last year, destiny took you and your entire staff away on business that day. Alas, we landed high and dry in Houston without even a chance to say howdy. Although we got a free tour of your funeral museum, it just wasn't the same.

As you have probably read in The New York Times today, Ms. Mitford has "passed away." Prior to her death, she and I discussed her final arrangements. I think you would be delighted to know that you were in her thoughts.

Ms. Mitford was not a big fan of prepaying, or "preneed" as it is termed in the industry jargon. But the bill did seem to be of concern to her. She made a final request of me that brings me to the purpose of this letter.

Ms. Mitford feels that you should pay the bill. In her own words "after all, look at all the fame I've brought them!"

Enclosed you will find the statement of funeral goods and services selected. I'm sure you will appreciate her frugality. I think you will particularly like the price of $15.45 for the cremation container. While looking through SCI's price lists while we were in Texas, we couldn't find a cremation container for under a couple of hundred! Think of what it would have cost you if she had dropped in Houston!

My Condolences, Karen J. Leonard

---

* See July 6, 1996, letter to the Duchess of Devonshire.

CORRESPONDENTS

Virginia Durr

Doris Brin "Dobby" Walker

Polly Toynbee

Philip Toynbee

Kay Boyle

Pele de Lappe

Ephraim and Barbara Kahn

Robert Gottlieb

Marge Frantz

Katharine Graham

Acknowledgments

Decca's husband, the late Bob Treuhaft, inspired this book and offered me the opportunity to edit it. I'm very grateful to him for that and for his unstinting patience with my barrage of e-mails and phone calls seeking dates, relationships, explanations, context, and the myriad other details that go into making personal correspondence accessible to the public. Bob also deserves my unending gratitude for encouraging me to follow my own editorial instincts, no matter how intrusive they might seem to be. I'm sorry he didn't live to see in print the book he helped launch.

Decca and Bob's children, Dinky Romilly and Ben Treuhaft, and son-in-law, Terry Weber, were similarly helpful and patient as I badgered them mercilessly for background information. All the family, including Decca's beloved "oys" James and Chaka Forman and "step-oy" Ben Weber, were unfailingly tolerant as I tramped around in their family history. It's not easy to countenance a third party's candid portrayal of one's personal relationships, and the courage of Decca's family in doing so awes me.

Many of Decca's letters are maintained in "max. arch. cond." (maximum archival conditions), as Decca liked to joke, by her sister Deborah Devonshire, now the dowager Duchess of Devonshire. Not only did the duchess put at my disposal the incomparable collection of papers at her Chatsworth archive, but she was most hospitable and attentive to my needs and questions during the time I worked there (and throughout this project). She made certain that her entire staff—especially the super-efficient Helen Marchant—furnished me with every conceivable aid; they are a truly dedicated group of people.

Two other libraries have major collections of Decca's papers. The largest is in the Rare Books and Manuscripts archive at Ohio State University, whose staff went well beyond what any researcher has a right to expect. Geoffrey Smith and Elva Griffith were uncommonly responsive, generous, and helpful. Above all, Michael Waite, who catalogued the collection for the archive and later became my on-the-scene personal research assistant, was simply indispensable. His e-mail inbox overflowed with my inquiries, and he fielded them all expertly and thoroughly.

Some of Decca's papers are also housed at the Harry Ransom Humanities

Research Center at the University of Texas in Austin, where Cliff Farrington also doubled as a library employee and my personal assistant. I'm grateful to him and, later, to Victoria Gold for their assistance at the archive. Various staff members, including Tara Wenger, were also helpful.

The towering achievements of people like Decca are not possible without the assistance of a few thoroughly knowledgeable and superbly organized assistants who can never receive sufficient recognition for their work. I received invaluable help and insight from Decca's longtime aide Catherine Edwards, whom Decca aptly called "my smashing assistant Katie." Ev Small, caretaker of Katharine Graham's papers, is another such treasure, and she generously helped me to document and understand the decades-long correspondence between Graham and Decca.

Providing expert research on issues that needed further investigation in England were Mary Crisp and Steve Hopkins.

So many of Decca's friends and correspondents ransacked their attics and basements for Decca's letters and assisted me in other ways that it's not possible to list them all. Among the most helpful of this battalion of supportive friends and relatives were her four longtime local chums, Marge Frantz, Doris Brin Walker, Pele de Lappe, and the late Barbara Kahn. I pestered them often for background information, which they patiently supplied, along with the memories and anecdotes that fleshed out my understanding. Others who generously fielded multiple inquiries were Kathy Kahn, Mary Clemmey, and Karen Leonard.

I'm also indebted for their time and memories to Leah and Jerry Garchik, Michael Barnes and Clare Douglas, Bettina Aptheker, Barbara Quick, Charles Darden, Kathi Kamen Goldmark, Patrick Allitt, Helen Benedict, Michael Tigar, Robert Byrne, Michael Ferber, James Dean Walker, the late Shana Alexander, Eleanor Furman, Dorothy Bryant, Barbara Blakemore, Wendy Cadden, Joan Cadden, Inese Civkulis, Linda Donovan, Kim Jungmin, Jared Dreyfus, Joan Mellen, Camelia Chun Martin, Monique Mendelson, Lisa Pollard, Bill Powell, Di Trevis, Rosemarie Scherman, Douglas Foster, Anne Weills, Dugald Stermer, Bob Stein, Doug Smith, Anthea Fursland, Ann Lyon, Virginia (Tilla) Durr, Peter Stansky, Eve Pell, Kevin Ingram, Erna Smith, Corinne Rafferty, Margot Smith, John Hopkins, Peggy Stinnett, Linda Chase Broda, Sir Martin Gilbert, Christopher Hitchens, Palash Dave, Stephen Crosher, Mark Gravil, John Irwin, Polly Toynbee, Steve Elias, and Cheryl Chapman. I talked and corresponded with numerous other Decca friends and acquaintances in what was, in a sense, a collaborative project. Many of their specific contributions ended up on the cutting-room floor as this book was trimmed to more manageable size, but their assistance was invaluable nevertheless in helping me to understand and convey the nuances of Decca's life and work. My thanks to them all.

Patricia Sullivan, editor of *Freedom Writer*, a splendid book of the civil-rights-era letters of Decca's dear friend Virginia Durr, was a very helpful long-distance colleague, and her book provided important background material. I have also benefited from trading perceptions with another thoughtful writer, Leslie Brody, who is preparing an interpretive book on Decca.

Mary Lovell, author of *The Sisters*, the collective biography of the Mitfords, was most helpful in sharing insights and information and was also hospitable during a research trip to England. I relied on her book for some of the background details that appear in footnotes and help clarify the letters. I also relied heavily for background material on biographies and memoirs by Kevin Ingram, Virginia Durr, Katharine Graham, David Pryce-Jones, and Philip Toynbee. Trusted deskside references included Charlotte Mosley's *Love from Nancy: The Letters of Nancy Mitford* and, of course, Decca's own fine memoirs. Despite the (to me) distasteful political and racial slants that color its commentary, I got several useful biographical details from *The House of Mitford*, written by Decca's nephew Jonathan Guinness and his daughter Catherine Guinness.

Two television documentaries on Decca's life, both of them made decades ago, have been important sources of biographical details and observations from their interviewees, many of whom are no longer living. I was fortunate enough to have access to—and I have quoted from—tapes of unaired interviews for *Portrait of a Muckraker*, made by University of California journalism students Stephen Evans, Ida Landauer, and James Morgan and aired on the Public Broadcasting System in 1987. I also found useful *The Honourable Rebel*, which was produced for the BBC in 1977 by Michael Barnes and subsequently figured in Decca's disputes with her sisters.

Still another helpful biographical resource was Jeff Elliott, a colleague of Decca's who maintains valuable reference materials at the website of his online newspaper, the *Albion Monitor.*

I relied on scores of other institutions and individuals for explanations of obscure references in letters. Institutional assistance came from the dedicated people at a number of archives and reference libraries, including the general and children's reference desks at the Berkeley, California, Public Library, the ILWU library in San Francisco, the National Funeral Directors Association's Howard C. Raether Library, the Tamiment Institute Library at New York University, the Oakland Public Library History Room, the Moorland-Spingarn Research Center at Howard University, the California State Archives, the Churchill Archives Centre at Churchill College (Cambridge University), the San Francisco History Center at the San Francisco Public Library, the *San Francisco Chronicle, Montgomery Advertiser,* and *Marin Independent Journal* libraries, the American Heritage Center at the University of Wyoming, the Special Collections section of the University of Delaware Library, the Special Collections branch of the Southern Illinois University Library, and the Worcester, Massachusetts, Public Library. These institutions and the people who staff them could never get the thanks they deserve. I couldn't close such a list these days without acknowledging my debt for research assistance to Google, on whose Web site I spent many hours tracking down background information that might otherwise not have been available.

The word "patient" comes up a lot in acknowledging those who supported a project as complex and prolonged as this one. No one was more patient than my editor, Bob Gottlieb. His support made this book possible, and after working with him, I fully appreciate Decca's frequent praise for his judgment and sensitivity, which were all the more difficult to maintain in editing a book whose subject was his longtime friend and colleague. His assistant, Diana Tejerina, was my expert and unfailingly good-humored guide through the publishing process. Her successor, Alena Graedon, responded with similar good humor to the many bumps on the road to publication.

Also giving me more than my share of patience were my wife, Pat; my mother, Ann Rosenberg; my daughters, Deborah, Katherine, and Stephanie; my sons-in-law and grandchildren (most of whom are young enough that patience and competition for Daddo's attention do not come easily), and my many tolerant friends. I thank them all for walking down this long road with me.

I'm also grateful to my agent, Fred Hill, who was Bob Treuhaft's co conspirator in placing this wonderful project in my lap.

Finally, of course, I will be forever indebted to Decca herself, not only for providing such wonderful material for this book but for her always stimulating friendship and the generous encouragement she gave me and countless other younger people over the years. Her published works are an inadequate measure of her accomplishments. As testimony from even the most peripheral of her circle attests, Decca helped to further the careers and worthy projects of many other people. As I sought letters and background information from her friends and acquaintances, they often told me gratefully of her long-ago favors and solicitude; there was usually a chuckle in their voices as they recounted these old stories. I was the beneficiary of the debt of gratitude they, too, owe Decca.

Index

Page numbers in *italics* refer to illustrations.
Page numbers in **boldface** refer to letters to the person named.
Page numbers followed by *n* refer to footnotes.

A Note on the Type

This book was set in Janson, a typeface long thought to have been made by the Dutchman Anton Janson, who was a practicing type-founder in Leipzig during the years 1668–1687. However, it has been conclusively demonstrated that these types are actually the work of Nicholas Kis (1650–1702), a Hungarian, who most probably learned his trade from the master Dutch typefounder Dirk Voskens. The type is an excellent example of the influential and sturdy Dutch types that prevailed in England up to the time William Caslon (1692–1766) developed his own incomparable designs from them.

Composed by North Market Street Graphics,
Lancaster, Pennsylvania
Printed and bound by Berryville Graphics,
Berryville, Virginia
Designed by Anthea Lingeman